The Complete Works of Nietzsche

GRAPEVINE INDIA

Published by

GRAPEVINE INDIA PUBLISHERS PVT LTD

www.grapeveineindia.com
Delhi | Mumbai
email: grapevineindiapublishers@gmail.com

Ordering Information:
Quantity sales: Special discounts are available on quantity purchases by corporations, associations, and others. For details, reach out to the publisher.

First published by Grapevine India 2022
Copyright © Grapevine 2022
All rights reserved

CONTENTS

1. Thus Spoke Zarathustra: A Book for Everyone and No One
2. Beyond Good and Evil: Prelude to a Philosophy of the Future
3. On the Genealogy of Morals
4. The Anti-Christ: A Criticism of Christianity
5. The Gay Science: With a Prelude in Rhymes and an Appendix of Songs
6. Ecce Homo: How One Becomes What One Is

Preface

Friedrich Nietzsche may well be the most misunderstood philosopher of all time. Apologists for Nazi doctrines are only the most obvious case among those who have wrongly appropriated him for their own. "No, no," we can almost hear him complaining, "I didn't mean that at all!" And yet, honest attempts to systematize his thought, to get it just right, haven't done much better, so that the ordinary reader can't be sure what he was really getting at. Bits and pieces of his ruined edifice lie all around us, and they don't always fit together. And then there is the problem of translation.

A considerable part and parcel of Nietzsche's genius is his ability to make his language dance, and this is what becomes extraordinarily difficult to translate.

Some have failed in the attempt while others have hardly tried. Our present translator, Thomas Wayne, is himself an aphorist of palpable genius if not yet repute, with several collections to his credit which I have been privileged to edit.

He knows that wordplay is the thing wherein he'll catch the conscience of the reader. I have seen him wrestle with a particularly intractable word or phrase of Nietzsche's masterwork and snatch an exasperated success from the jaws of failure.

While the great tendency among earlier translators has been to smooth out the rough edges, cut corners and sometimes omit troublesome passages outright, this one honors and respects the original as no other.

He has gone into the thicket of Nietzsche's offering with all its nettles and thorns and pestiferous stinging insects to pluck those deliciously tart red and purple berries which are practically the whole reason for such an exercise. Every now and then he comes into a clearing where blinding sun or a blast of fresh wind will clear it all away, making the air pure and all the more worth breathing for the difficulty of attainment. Such is Nietzsche's own embattled and tortured spirit breaking free, and our translator's desire to render it in its ultimate exultation and exaltation in utter spite of whatever would hold it back: Nietzsche not only with every wart and thwart but in full forte.

If Nietzsche's German in its coruscating brilliance, its disorienting jumble and tumble of styles from the highest to the lowest (or vice versa!) doesn't read consistently either like everyday German or its higher expressions in imagistic poetry or polished expository prose, why should Mr. Wayne's altogether admirable attempt to match him in English read like that? Perhaps most in evidence here, he has retained Nietzsche's seemingly inordinate use of italics and even his strange-looking punctuation, regarding these as dynamics in the musical sense.

For our author himself was extraordinarily sensitive to music and allowed his spirit to be ruled by it.

Wayne's close reading of the original text has exposed the deficiencies of earlier translations, preeminent among them that of the highly esteemed Walter Kaufmann. A few cases in point: Kaufmann has arbitrarily grouped Nietzsche's very short, often single-sentence paragraphs (which effectively imitate Biblical verses) into larger paragraphs; conversely, he sometimes breaks up his longer paragraphs for the sake of a "nicer-looking" English text. Not consistent in honoring his italics, let alone his punctuation, Kaufmann and others are guilty of the deplorable tendency to "improve" on the original in their use of a more academic style, smoothing over, toning down, and sometimes omitting its rough vernacularities (especially the adjectives, when they are doubled and tripled to good effect). Much is lost here, to say nothing of the interior rhythms, the grace notes, the not always graceful but omnipresent and striking puns and wordplays.

I note many specific cases in which Mr. Wayne's rendering cuts closer to the bone than Kaufmann's, more sharply and cleanly, and above all more in keeping with the original. Here are just a few. Where K has: "Is not your soul poverty and filth and wretched contentment?", W has: "dirt and dearth and a wretched comfort." K: "I love him who makes virtue his addiction and his catastrophe"; W:"I love him who makes out of his virtue his fancy and his fate." K: "Their devils draw them down"; W: "Their demons demean them." K: "Back to the body, back to life"; W: "Back to life and limb." K: "tomb-tears comfort"; W: "graves' tearcheer." K: "musty mystifiers and hearth-squatters"; W: "muddlers, mumblers and mama's boys." K: "gourmets and gourmands" (how many readers would know or remember the fine distinction here without consulting their dictionary?); W: "lip-lickers and lip-smackers." In these cases and many more, Mr. Wayne has achieved a simplicity as well as alliteration and wordplay that are more in line with Nietzsche's literary genius.

And there are not a few instances in which he improves on Kaufmann's use of English or otherwise clarifies what Nietzsche is really saying. K: "If you believed more in life you would fling yourself less to (wrong preposition) the moment. But you do not have contents enough in yourselves (awkward) for waiting — and not even for idleness"; W: "If you believed more in life you would throw yourselves less into the moment. But you do not have enough in you of what it takes to wait — not even to vegetate." K: "Let man fear woman when she hates; for deep down in his soul man is merely evil, while woman is bad"; W: "For at the bottom of his soul man is merely angry; woman, however, is downright mean."

Let's open the book and see for ourselves which of these is true of Friedrich Nietzsche.

Roger W. Phillips, PhD

Vancouver, Washington

April, 2003

Part One
Zarathustra's Prologue
1

When Zarathustra was thirty years old, he left his home and the lake by his home and went into the mountains. Here he enjoyed his spirit and his solitude, and did not tire of this for ten years. Finally, however, he had a change of heart — and one morning, rising with the dawn, he stood before the sun and spoke to it thus:

"You great star! What would your happiness be if you had not those for whom you shine!

For ten years you have come up here to my cave: you would already have been weary of your light and this journey were it not for me, my eagle, and my serpent.

But we waited for you each morning, relieved you of your overflow, and blessed you for it.

Behold! I am weary of my wisdom; like the bee that has gathered too much honey, I need the hands that stretch out for it.

I want to dispense and distribute, until the wise once more enjoy their folly and the poor once more enjoy their riches.

That is why I must descend to the deep, as you do in the evening when you pass beyond the sea and bring light even to the underworld, you over-rich star!

Like you I must go down, as people say; I want to go down to them.

So bless me then, you tranquil eye, that can look without envy upon even an all-too-great happiness!

Bless the cup which wants to overflow, so that the water flows golden out of it, carrying in every direction the reflection of your delight!

Behold! This cup wants to become empty again and Zarathustra wants to become a man again."

— Thus began Zarathustra's downgoing.

2

Zarathustra climbed down the mountain alone and he came across no one.

But when he came to the forest, an old man stood before him, one who had left his holy hut to search for roots in the forest. And thus spake the old man to Zarathustra:

"This wanderer is no stranger to me: many years ago he passed by here. Zarathustra he was called; but he has changed.

At that time you carried your ashes to the mountain: would you now carry your fire into the valleys? Do you not fear the arsonist's penalty?

Yes, I recognize Zarathustra. Pure is his eye, and no loathing lurks about his mouth. Does he not move along like a dancer?

Changed is Zarathustra, become a child is Zarathustra, an awakened one is Zarathustra: what do you want now with those who sleep?

As though in a sea you have lived in your solitude, and the sea has borne you up. Alas, you want to go ashore? Alas, you want to drag your body around again, yourself?

Zarathustra answered: "I love mankind."

"Why," said the holy man, "do you think I went into the forest and into solitude?

Was it not because I loved man all too much?

Now I love God: man, I do not love. Man is too imperfect a thing for me.

The love of mankind would kill me."

Zarathustra answered: "Did I speak of love? I am bringing mankind a gift."

"Give them nothing," said the holy man. "Take something from them rather and carry it with you — that would suit them best: if only it suits you!

And if you want to give them something, give no more than an alms, and let them beg for that!"

"No," answered Zarathustra, "I give no alms. I am not poor enough for that!"

The holy man laughed at Zarathustra and spoke thus: "Well, see to it that they accept your treasures! They are mistrustful of hermits and do not believe that we come in order to give.

Our steps ring too lonely through the streets. And what if at night in their beds they should hear a man walking, long before the sun comes up, then they probably ask themselves: where is that thief going?

Remain in the forest and do not go to man. Go rather to the animals, even!

Why not be like me — a bear among bears, a bird among birds?"

"And what does the holy man do in the forest?" asked Zarathustra.

The holy man answered: "I make songs and sing them, and when I make songs I laugh, cry, and hum: thus I praise God.

With singing, crying, laughing, and humming I praise the God that is my God. But what do you bring us as a gift?"

When Zarathustra heard these words, he saluted the holy man and said:

"What would I have to give you? But let me hurry away quickly, lest I take something instead!"— And so they parted from each other, the old man and Zarathustra, laughing like two boys.

But when Zarathustra was alone, he spoke thus to his heart: "Could it be possible, then? This old saint in his forest has heard nothing yet about God being dead."

3

When Zarathustra came to the next town which lay by the forest, he found many people gathered in the marketplace there: for it had been promised that a tightrope walker would be seen. And thus spake

Zarathustra to the people:

"I teach you the Superman. Man is something that must be overcome. What have you done to overcome him?

All beings hitherto have created something beyond themselves. And you would be the ebb of this great flood, to return even to the beast rather than overcome the man?

What is the ape to man? A laughingstock or an object of shame. And that is just what man shall be for the Superman: a laughingstock or an object of shame.

You have made your way from worm to man, and much in you is still worm.

Once you were apes, and even now man is still more of an ape than any ape.

But he who is wisest among you is likewise only a hotbed and hybrid of plant and phantom. But do I command you to become plants or phantoms?

Behold, I teach you the Superman!

The Superman is the meaning of the earth. Let your will say: the Superman shall be the meaning of the earth!

I entreat you, my brothers, remain true to the earth and do not believe those who hold out supernatural hopes for you. They are poisoners, whether they know it or not.

They are despisers of life, dying ones and poisoned themselves; the earth is sick of them — let them leave it, then!

Once the sin against God was the greatest sin; but God died, and with that these sinners died, too. Now the worst sin is the sin against the earth, to regard the innards of the inscrutable more highly than the meaning of the earth.

Once the soul looked upon the body with contempt: and at that time this contempt was the highest thing: the soul wanted the body scrawny, scary, starved. Thus the soul thought to escape the body and the earth.

Oh, this soul was itself still scrawny, scary, and starved; and cruelty was the delight of this soul!

But you as well, my brothers, tell me: what does your body proclaim about your soul? Is your soul not dearth and dirt and a wretched comfort?

Verily, man is a filthy stream. One must be a veritable sea in order to absorb such a filthy stream and not become unclean.

Behold, I teach you the Superman: he is that sea, in him your great contempt can be submerged.

What is the greatest thing you can experience? It is the hour of great contempt, when even your happiness turns to disgust, and your reason and virtue too.

The hour when you say: 'What does my happiness matter? It is dearth and dirt and a wretched comfort. But my happiness should justify being itself!'

The hour when you say: 'What does my reason matter: Does it not crave knowledge the same way a lion craves food? It is dearth and dirt and a wretched comfort!'

The hour when you say: 'What does my virtue matter? It has not yet made me mad. How weary I am of my good and evil! That is all dearth and dirt and a wretched comfort!'

The hour when you say: 'What does my justice matter? I do not see that I am fire and coal. But the just are fire and coal.'

The hour when you say: 'What does my pity matter: Is pity not the cross upon which he who loves mankind is nailed? But my pity is no crucifixion.'

Have you ever spoken thus? Have you ever cried thus? Alas, if only I had ever heard you cry thus!

Not your sin but your complacency cries out against heaven, the very stinginess of your sin cries out against heaven!

Where is the lighting which licks you with its tongue? Where is the madness with which you should be injected?

Behold, I teach you the Superman: he is that lightning, he is that madness!"—

When Zarathustra had spoken thus, someone from the crowd cried out:

"We have heard enough from the tightrope walker; now let us see him, too!" And all the people laughed at Zarathustra. The tightrope walker, however, who thought these words applied to him, set about his task.

4

But Zarathustra looked at the people and wondered. Then he spoke thus:

"Man is a rope suspended between animal and Superman — a rope over an abyss.

A dangerous going-over, a dangerous on-the-way, a dangerous lookingback, a dangerous shuddering and standing still.

What is great about man is that he is a bridge, not an end: what can be loved about man is that he is a going-over and a going-under.

I love those who do not know how to live except as downgoers, for they are going over.

I love the great despisers, for they are the great reverers and arrows of longing for the opposite shore.

I love those who do not first seek a reason beyond the stars for going under and sacrificing themselves: but they sacrifice themselves for the earth, that the earth may one day be the Superman's.

I love him who lives in order to know and wants to know in order that the Superman may live. And thus he wills his own downgoing.

I love him who works and invents in order to build the Superman's house and to prepare plant, animal, and earth for him: for thus he wills his own downgoing.

I love him who retains not one drop of spirit for himself but wants it all to be virtue's spirit: thus he strides as spirit across the bridge.

I love him who makes out of his virtue his fancy and his fate: thus for the sake of his virtue he wants to live and no longer live.

I love him who does not want too many virtues. One virtue is more virtue than two, because it is more of a hook to hang ones' fate on.

I love him whose soul squanders itself, who wants no thanks and gives none in return: for he always bestows and wants no part of preserving himself.

I love him who feels ashamed when the dice turn up in his favor, and who then asks: "Am I a false player?" — for he wants to go under.

I love him whose golden words are cast before his deeds, and who does even more than he promises: for he wants his downgoing.

I love him who justifies the future and redeems the past: for he wants to perish in the present.

I love him who castigates his God because he loves Him: for by the wrath of his God he must perish.

I love him whose soul is deep even in the wounding, and whom a little thing can ruin: thus he gladly goes across the bridge.

I love him whose soul is overfull, so that he forgets himself, and in whom all things exist: thus all things become his downgoing.

I love him who is of a free spirit and a free heart: thus his head is only the innards of his heart; his heart, however, drives him to his downgoing.

I love all those who are like heavy raindrops falling individually from the dark cloud that hangs over man: they herald the coming of the lightning and perish as heralds.

Behold, I am a herald of the lightning and a heavy raindrop from the cloud: this lightning, however, is called the Superman." ——

5

When Zarathustra had spoken these words, he looked at the people again and became silent. "There they stand," he said to his heart, "there they laugh: they do not understand me, I am not the mouth for these ears.

Must one first batter their ears so they learn to hear with their eyes? Must one rattle like drums and penitential preachers? Or do they only believe stammerers?

They have something which they are proud of. But what do they call that which they are proud of? They call it culture; it distinguishes them from the goatherds.

That is why they are unwilling to hear the word 'contempt' applied to themselves. So I will appeal to their pride instead.

So I will speak to them of what is most contemptible: that, however, is the last man."

And thus spake Zarathustra to the people:

"It is time for man to set himself a goal. It is time for him to plant the seed of his highest hope.

His soul is still rich enough for that. But one day this soul will be poor and tame, and no higher tree will be able to grow on it anymore.

Alas! The day is coming when man will no longer loose the arrow of his longing beyond man, and the string of his bow will have forgotten how to sing.

I tell you: a man must still have chaos within himself in order to give birth to a dancing star. I tell you: you still have chaos within yourselves.

Alas! The day is coming when man will no longer give birth to a star. Alas! The day of the most despicable man is coming, of him who can no longer despise himself.

Behold! I present to you the last man.

'What is love? What is creation? What is longing? What is a star?' — thus asks the last man, and blinks.

The earth is then grown small, and on it hops the last man, who makes everything small. Like the flea, his kind cannot be exterminated; the last man lives the longest.

'We have discovered happiness' — the last men say, and blink.

They have left the regions where living was hard: for warmth is needed.

They still love their neighbor and rub up against him: for warmth is needed.

Becoming sick and harboring mistrust they consider sinful: one proceeds with caution. He is a fool who still stumbles over stones or men!

A little poison now and then: that makes for pleasant dreams. And a lot of poison in the end for a pleasant death.

One still works, for work is a form of entertainment. But one takes care not to get too caught up in it.

No one is rich or poor anymore: both are too much trouble. Who still wants to rule? Who still wants to obey? Both are too much trouble.

No shepherd and one herd! Everyone wants the same, everyone is the same: he who feels otherwise goes freely to the madhouse.

'Formerly, all the world was mad' — the finest ones say, and blink.

They are clever and know all there is to know: so there is endless mockery.

They still quarrel, but they are soon reconciled — otherwise they might spoil their appetite.

They have their little pleasures for the day and their little pleasures for the night: but they revere their health.

'We have discovered happiness' — the last men say, and blink."

And here ended the first speech of Zarathustra, also known as "The Prologue":

for at this point the cries and mirth of the crowd interrupted him. "Give us this last man, O Zarathustra," — thus they cried — "make us into these last men! Then we will present you with the Superman!" And all the people rejoiced and clucked their tongues. Zarathustra, however, was sad and said to his heart:

"They do not understand me: I am not the mouth for these ears.

No doubt I have lived too long in the mountains; I have listened too much to the trees and the brooks: now I speak to them as though to goatherds.

Unmoved is my soul and clear, like the mountains in the morning. But they think me cold and a scoffer with awful jokes.

And now they look at me and laugh: and while they laugh, they hate me still. There is ice in their laughter."

6

Then something happened, however, that silenced every tongue and entranced every eye. For in the meantime the tightrope walker had begun his 13 performance: he had come out of a small door and was walking along the rope, which was stretched between two towers so that it hung over the people and the marketplace. When he was just halfway across, the small door opened once again, and out jumped a colorful, buffoonish fellow who quickly followed after him.

"Move it, lamefoot," he cried in a terrible voice, "get going, lazybones, chiseler, whey-face! So I don't tickle your heel with my foot! What do you think you're doing here between these towers? Back in the tower is where you belong, behind bars, you who bar the way of one who is your better!" — And with every word he came closer and closer to the tightrope walker: but when he was only one step behind him, that terrible thing happened which silenced every tongue and entranced every eye: — he yelled like the devil and sprang over the one who was in his way. This one, however, seeing his rival thus victorious, lost both his head and his toehold; he cast his pole away and shot quicker than it itself into the depths, a descending whirl of arms and legs. The marketplace and the people were like the sea when a storm comes on: they all flew apart from each other and on top of each other, especially where the body was about to fall.

Zarathustra remained standing there, however, and the body landed right next to him, badly bruised and battered but not yet dead. After a while, the shattered man regained consciousness and saw Zarathustra kneeling beside him.

"What are you doing here?" he said at last. "For a long time I knew that the devil would trip me up. Now he's about to drag me off to hell: do you want to prevent him?"

"On my honor, friend," answered Zarathustra, "all that of which you speak does not exist. There is no devil and there is no hell. Your soul will be dead even sooner than your body: fear nothing henceforth!"

The man looked up mistrustfully. "If you speak the truth," he said, "then I lose nothing when I lose my life. I am not much more than an animal, taught to dance by means of blows and meager fare."

"Not at all," said Zarathustra. "You have made danger your calling; there is nothing to be despised in that. Now, your calling calls you away for good: therefore, I will bury you with my own hands.

After Zarathustra had said this, the dying man answered no more; but he moved his hand as if to seek Zarathustra's hand in gratitude. —

7

Evening came on meanwhile, and the marketplace concealed itself in darkness:

then the crowd dispersed, for even curiosity and terror get tired. Zarathustra, however, remained sitting next to the dead man on the ground, engrossed in thought, oblivious of the time. Finally, though, it became night, and a cold wind blew over the solitary one. Then Zarathustra arose and said to his heart:

"Verily, a fine catch Zarathustra has made today! No men he caught but a corpse instead.

Uncanny is man's being and still without meaning: a buffoon can spell his doom.

I want to teach man the meaning of his being, which is the Superman, that lightning from the dark cloud of man.

But I am still far away from them, and my sense does not speak to their senses. To men I am still something midway between a fool and a corpse.

Dark is the night, and dark are the ways of Zarathustra. Come, you cold and stiff companion! I will carry you to where I can bury you with my own hands."

8

After Zarathustra had said this to his heart, he loaded the corpse on his back and proceeded on his way. And he had not gone a hundred paces when a man snuck up to him and whispered in his ear — and behold! It was the buffoon from the tower! "Go away from this town, O Zarathustra," he said. "Too many hate you here. The good and the just hate you and call you their enemy and despiser; the believers in the true belief hate you and call you a danger to the multitude. You were lucky they laughed at you; and truly, you spoke like a buffoon. You were lucky to have sided with that dead dog; when you degraded yourself that way, you saved yourself for the day. But go away from this town — or tomorrow I will jump over you, a living man over a dead one." And when he had said this, the man disappeared; Zarathustra, however, continued on down the dark streets.

At the town gate he met the gravediggers: they shone a torch in his face, recognized Zarathustra, and mocked him exceedingly. "Zarathustra's carrying the dead dog away: good thing he's become a gravedigger, because our hands are too clean for this mess. Perhaps Zarathustra wants to steal a morsel from the devil? Well then! Good luck at mealtime, too! If only the devil's not a better thief 15 than Zarathustra! — he'll steal both of them, he'll gobble both of them up!" And they laughed with each other and stuck their heads together.

Zarathustra said not a word to that and went on his way. After traveling a couple of hours, past forests and marshes, he heard too much of the hungry howling of wolves, and he himself felt hungry. So he stopped at a lonely house, in which a solitary light was burning.

"Hunger has ambushed me," said Zarathustra, "like a robber. In forests and marshes hunger has ambushed me, and in the deep of night.

My hunger has strange moods. Often it comes to me only after mealtimes, and today it didn't come all day: where could it have tarried?"

And with that Zarathustra knocked at the gate of the house. An old man appeared; he carried the light and asked: "Who comes to me and my bad sleep?"

"A living man and a dead one," said Zarathustra. "Give me something to eat and drink, I forgot it today. He who feeds the hungry refreshes his own soul: thus speaks wisdom."

The old man went away but came right back, offering Zarathustra bread and wine. "This is a bad area for those who hunger," he said; "therefore I live here.

Man and beast come to me, the hermit. But bid your companion eat and drink too; he is wearier than you." Zarathustra answered: "My companion is dead; I could hardly persuade him to join in."

"That doesn't concern me," said the old man morosely; "he who knocks on my door must also take what I offer him. Eat and fare thee well!"

After that Zarathustra went on again for two hours, trusting to the way and the light of the stars: for he was accustomed to night walking and loved to look into the face of all that was at rest.

But when the morning dawned, Zarathustra found himself in a deep wood, and no path showed itself to him anymore. Then he laid the dead man in a hollow tree at his head — for he wanted to protect him from the wolves — and laid himself down on the moss and earth. And immediately he fell asleep, fatigued in body but with an unmoved soul.

9

Zarathustra slept a long time, and not only the rosy dawn but also the morning passed over his face. At last, however, he opened his eyes: astonished, Zarathustra looked into the forest and the stillness; astonished, he looked into himself. Then he rose up quickly, like a sailor who has just spotted land, and shouted for joy: for he had perceived a new truth. And he spoke to his heart thus:

"A light has dawned upon me: I need companions, and live ones — not dead companions and corpses I can carry with me wheresoever I will.

But I need live companions, who follow me because they themselves want to — and there, wheresoever I will.

A light has dawned upon me: not to the people shall Zarathustra speak, but to companions! No shepherd of the herd and herd dog shall Zarathustra be!

To lure many away from the herd — that is why I have come. People and herd shall be angry with me: the shepherds shall call me a robber.

Shepherds I say, but they call themselves the good and the just. Shepherds I say: but they call themselves the believers in the true belief.

Behold the good and the just! Whom do they hate the most? The one who breaks their tables of values, the breaker, the lawbreaker: — that, however, is the creator.

Companions the creator seeks, and not corpses, and not herds and believers, either. Co-creators the creator seeks, those who write new values on new tables.

Companions the creator seeks, and co-harvesters: for to him all things stand ripe for the harvest. But he lacks the hundred sickles: so he plucks the ears of corn and is irritable.

Companions the creator seeks, and those who know how to whet their sickles. Annihilators they will be called, and despisers of good and evil. But they are harvesters and celebrators.

Co-creators Zarathustra seeks, co-harvesters and co-celebrators Zarathustra seeks: what does he have to do with herds and shepherds and corpses?

And you, my first companion, fare thee well! Well I buried you in your hollow tree, well I hid you from the wolves.

But now I part from you, the time is up. Between one dawn and the next a new truth has come to me.

Not a shepherd shall I be, not a gravedigger. Never again will I talk with the people: I have spoken to the dead for the last time.

I will join with the creators, the harvesters, the celebrators: I will show them the rainbow and all the steps to the Superman.

I will sing my song to the lonesome and the twosome; and to him who still has ears for the unheard-of, I will make his heart heavy with my happiness.

To my goal will I go, I will go it my way; over the dawdlers and delayers will I jump. Thus may my going be their downgoing!"

10

Zarathustra had said this to his heart as the sun stood at noontide: then he looked inquiringly on high — for he heard above him the sharp cry of a bird. And behold! An eagle described wide circles through the air, and on him there hung a serpent, not like its prey but like a lady-love: for it had curled itself around the eagle's neck.

"They are my animals!" said Zarathustra, and rejoiced in his heart.

"The proudest animal under the sun and the wisest animal under the sun — they have gone out scouting.

They want to find out whether Zarathustra still lives. Indeed, do I still live?

More dangerous have I found it among man than among beasts;

dangerous ways goes Zarathustra. May my animals lead me!"

After Zarathustra had said this, he reflected on the words of the holy man in the forest, sighed, and spoke to his heart thus:

"Would that I were wiser! Would that I were wise through and through, like my serpent!

But that is asking the impossible: therefore I ask that my pride always accompany my wisdom!

And if one day my wisdom should leave me: alas, she loves to fly away! —

may my pride then fly off — with my folly!" —

— Thus began Zarathustra's downgoing.

Zarathustra's Speeches
On The Three Metamorphoses

I speak to you of three metamorphoses of the spirit: how the spirit becomes a camel, the camel a lion, and finally, the lion a child.

There are many hard things for the spirit, the strong load-bearing spirit in which reverence dwells: in its strength it longs for the hard and the hardest.

What is hard? Thus asks the load-bearing spirit; thus it kneels down like a camel and wants to be well-laden.

What is the hardest thing, you heroes? Thus asks the load-bearing spirit, that I may take it upon myself and rejoice in my strength.

Is it not this: to abase yourself in order to hurt your pride? To let your folly shine in order to mock your wisdom?

Or is it this: to part from your cause when it celebrates its victory? To climb high mountains in order to tempt the tempter?

Or is it this: to nourish your knowledge on acorns and grass, and to suffer the hunger of the soul for the sake of truth?

Or is it this: to be sick and send the consolers home, and to make friends with the deaf, who never hear what you want them to?

Or is it this: to wade in dirty water, when it is the water of truth, and not reject cold frogs and hot toads?

Or is it this: to love those who despise us, and to reach out our hand to the ghost that wants to frighten us?

All these hardest things the load-bearing spirit takes upon itself: like the well-laden camel that hurries into the desert; so the spirit hurries into its desert.

But in the loneliest desert the second metamorphosis takes place: here the spirit becomes a lion; freedom it wants to take as its prey, and to be master of its own desert.

Its last master it seeks here: to him and to its last god it wants to be an enemy; it wants to wrestle for victory with the great dragon.

What is the great dragon which the spirit no longer wants to call God and master? "Thou shalt," the great dragon is called. But the spirit of the lion says, "I will."

"Thou shalt" lies in wait for him, sparkling gold, a scaly beast upon whose every scale a golden "Thou shalt" shines.

Thousand-year-old values shine on these scales, and thus speaks the mightiest of all dragons: "All the values of things — they shine on me.

All value has already been created, and all created value — that is me. Verily, 'I will' shall not be anymore!" Thus speaks the dragon.

My brothers, why is the lion required in the spirit? Why is the resigned and reverent beast of burden not enough?

To create new values — that, even the lion cannot yet do. But to create for itself the freedom for new creation — that the lion's might might do.

To create freedom for itself and a holy 'Nay' even before duty: for that, my brothers, the lion is required.

To assume the right to new values — that is the most terrifying assumption for a load-bearing and reverent spirit. Verily, to it it is preying and the act of a beast of prey.

"Thou shalt" it once loved as its holiest thing: now it must find delusion and despotism in even the holiest thing, to take freedom from its love as its prey: for this preying, the lion is required.

But tell me, my brothers, what can the child do that even the lion could not do? Why must the preying lion yet become a child?

The child is innocence and forgetting, a new beginning, a game, a self-rolling wheel, a first movement, a holy Yea-saying.

Yes, for the game of creation, my brothers, a holy Yea-saying is required: the spirit now wills its will, he who has lost the world gains his world.

I have spoken to you of three metamorphoses of the spirit: how the spirit becomes a camel, the camel a lion and finally, the lion a child. —

Thus spake Zarathustra. And at that time he resided in the town which is called: The Dappled Cow.

On The Academic Chairs Of Virtue

People praised a certain wise man to Zarathustra, one who knew how to speak well about sleep and virtue: he was greatly revered and rewarded for this, and all the youth would sit before his academic chair. Zarathustra went to him, and with all the youth he sat before his academic chair. And thus spake the wise man:

"Honor and modesty before sleep! That is the first thing! And avoid all who sleep badly and stay awake nightly!

Even the thief is modest before sleep: he always steals silently through the night. But the night watchman is shameless; shamelessly he carries his horn.

Sleeping is no mean feat: indeed, it takes staying awake the whole day.

Ten times a day you must overcome yourself: that makes for a good weariness and is opium for the soul.

Ten times a day you must be reconciled with yourself again; for overcoming is a bitterness, and he who is unreconciled sleeps badly.

Ten truths a day you must find; otherwise you will still seek truth at night, and your soul will remain hungry.

Ten times a day you must laugh and be cheerful; otherwise your stomach, that father of affliction, will disturb you in the night.

Few know this: but one must have all the virtues in order to sleep well.

Shall I bear false witness? Shall I commit adultery?

Shall I covet my neighbor's handmaid? All that would go badly with good sleep.

And even if one has all the virtues, one must still understand one thing: how to send the virtues themselves to sleep at the right time.

So they don't quarrel amongst themselves, the nice little ladies! Or over you, you unfortunate soul!

Peace with God and with your neighbor: good sleep demands it so. And peace with your neighbor's devil as well! Or else he will haunt you at night.

Reverence and obedience for authority, even crooked authority! Good sleep demands it so. Can I help it that power likes to walk on crooked legs?

He who leads his sheep to the greenest pastures shall always be called the best shepherd: that goes well with good sleep.

I do not want many honors, nor great treasures: they inflame the spleen.

But one sleeps badly without a good name and a little treasure.

Small company is more welcome to me than bad: but they must come and go at the right time. That goes well with good sleep.

The poor in spirit please me very much, also: they promote sleep. Blessed are they, especially if you always give them their way.

Thus the day passes for the virtuous one. When night comes, then I take good care not to summon sleep! He, sleep, the lord of all the virtues, does not like to be summoned!

Instead I think about what I did and thought that day. Ruminating thus, I ask myself patiently, like a cow: All right, what were your ten overcomings?

And what were the ten reconciliations and the ten truths and the ten laughs with which your heart enjoyed itself?

Weighed and swayed this way by forty thoughts, sleep, the unsummoned one, the lord of all the virtues, steals upon me suddenly.

Sleep taps at my eyes: they grow heavy. Sleep touches my mouth: it stays open.

Verily, on soft soles he comes to me, this dearest of thieves, and steals from me my thoughts: dumb I stand there, like this academic chair.

But not for long do I stand there: soon, I lie there."

When Zarathustra heard the wise man speak thus, he laughed in his heart:

for with that a light had dawned upon him. And thus he spoke to his heart:

"To me this wise man here with his forty thoughts is a fool: but I believe he is well-versed in sleeping.

Happy indeed is he who lives nearby this wise man! Such sleep is contagious; even through a thick wall it is contagious.

A magic dwells in his very academic chair. And not in vain do the youth sit before this preacher of virtue.

His wisdom is: be awake in order to sleep well. And verily, if life had no sense and I had to choose nonsense, then for me too this would be the most choosable nonsense.

Now I clearly understand what was once sought above all when teachers of virtue were sought. Good sleep was being sought, and poppy-flower virtues along with it!

To all these celebrated wise men in their academic chairs, wisdom was sleep without dreams: they knew no better meaning of life.

Even today, to be sure, there are some like this preacher of virtue, and not always so honorable: but their time is up. And they will not be standing much longer: soon they will be lying.

Blessed are the sleepy: for they shall soon nod off.—

Thus spake Zarathustra.

On The Afterworlders

Once Zarathustra too cast his fancy beyond man, like all afterworlders. The work of a suffering and tormented God the world then seemed to me.

A dream the world then seemed to me, the fiction of a God, colored smoke before the eyes of a discontented deity.

Good and evil and joy and sorrow and I and you — colored smoke before creative eyes it seemed to me. The creator wanted to look away from himself, — so he created the world.

Drunken joy it is for the sufferer to look away from his suffering and lose himself. Drunken joy and losing-of-oneself the world once seemed to me.

This world, eternally imperfect, the image of an eternal contradiction and an imperfect image thereof — the drunken joy of an imperfect creator: — thus the world once seemed to me.

Thus I too once cast my fancy beyond man, like all afterworlders. But was it in fact beyond man?

Alas, brothers, this God I created was of man's making and madness, like all gods!

Man he was, and only a poor fragment of man and ego: out of my own ashes and embers he came to me, this phantom, and verily, he did not come to me from beyond!

What happened, my brothers? I overcame myself, the sufferer; I carried my own ashes to the mountain, I devised a brighter flame for myself. And behold!

The phantom retreated from me!

Now, it would be suffering for me and torment for one in recovery to believe in such phantoms: now it would be suffering for me and humiliation.

Thus I speak to afterworlders.

Suffering and impotence it was — that created all afterworlders; and that brief madness of happiness which only the greatest sufferer experiences.

Weariness, which wants the ultimate in one leap, one death leap. A poor ignorant weariness not even willing to will anymore: that created all gods and afterworlds.

Believe me, my brothers! It was the body that despaired of the body, — it groped with the fingers of the deluded spirit upon the ultimate walls.

Believe me, my brothers! It was the body that despaired of the earth, — it heard the belly of being speak to it.

And then it wanted to get through the ultimate walls with its head, and not only with its head, — across to the "other world."

But that "other world" is well-hidden from man, that inhuman, unhuman world which is a heavenly nothing; and the belly of being does not speak at all to man except as man.

Verily, all being is hard to prove and hard to move to speech. Tell me, you brothers, is not the strangest of all things still the best proved?

Yes, this ego and this ego's contradiction and confusion still speak most honestly about its being, this creating, willing, valuing ego, which is the measure and value of things.

And this most honest being, the ego — it speaks of the body and still wants the body, even when it poeticizes and romanticizes and flutters about with broken wings.

More and more honestly it learns to speak, this ego: and the more it learns, the more words and honors it finds for the body and the earth.

A new pride my ego taught me, which I now teach to man: no longer to hide his head in the sand of heavenly things, but to carry it freely, an earthly head that creates meaning for the earth.

A new will, I teach man: to want to follow the path that man has blindly followed and call it good and no longer slink aside from it, as the sick and the dying do!

It was the sick and the dying who despised the body and the earth and devised the heavenly and the redeeming blood-drops: but even these sweet and gloomy poisons they took from the body and the earth!

They wanted to escape their misery, and the stars were too far for them.

Then they sighed: "Oh that there were heavenly paths to sneak into another existence and into happiness!" Then they devised their bypaths and their bloody little draughts!

They fancied themselves transported from their bodies and this earth, these ingrates. But whom can they thank for the convulsions and delight of their transport? Their bodies and this earth.

Zarathustra is gentle with the sick. Verily, he is not angry at their kind of consolation and ingratitude. May they become convalescents and overcomers and create a higher body for themselves!

Nor is Zarathustra angry with the convalescent who looks tenderly upon his illusion and sneaks around the grave of his God in the middle of the night:

but to me his tears still speak of sickness and a sick body.

There have always been many sick people among those who write verse and "converse" with the Lord; furiously they hate those in the know and that youngest of virtues known as honesty.

They always look backward toward dark ages; then indeed delusion and belief were a different thing; reason's fury was likeness with God, and doubt was sin.

All too well I know these godlike ones: they insist upon being believed in and that doubt is sin. All too well I also know what they themselves believe in most.

Verily, it is not in afterworlds and redeeming blood-drops that they most believe: they also believe most in the body, and to them their own body is the thing-in-itself.

But to them it is a sickly thing, and they would gladly slough their skin.

Therefore they hearken to the preachers of death and preach afterworlds themselves.

Hearken rather, my brothers, to the voice of the healthy body: it is a purer and more honest voice.

The healthy body, perfect and foursquare, speaks more purely and honestly:

and it speaks of the meaning of the earth. —

Thus spake Zarathustra.

On The Despisers Of The Body

I want to say a word to the despisers of the body. Not that they should teach and learn differently, but only bid farewell to their own bodies — and thus become silent.

"Body am I and soul" — so speaks the child. And why should we not speak like children?

But the awakened one, the knowing one says: Body am I completely and nothing else; and soul is only a word for something in the body.

The body is a great reason, a multiplicity with one meaning, a war and a peace, a herd and a shepherd.

Your little reason, my brother, which you call "spirit," is also a tool of your body, a little tool and toy of your big reason.

"I," you say, and are proud of this word. But the greater thing — which you do not want to believe in — is your body and its big reason: it does not say "I," it does "I."

What sense feels, what spirit knows, these never are an end in themselves.

But sense and spirit want to persuade you that they are the end of all things: so vain are they.

Sense and spirit are tools and toys: behind them still lies the self. Even with the eyes of the senses the self seeks, even with the ears of the spirit it listens.

Continually the self listens and seeks: it compares, compels, conquers, destroys. It rules and is also the ego's ruler.

Behind your thoughts and feelings, my brother, there stands a mighty commander, an unknown wise man — he is called self. He lives in your body, he is your body.

There is more reason in your body than in your best wisdom. And who knows precisely what your body needs your best wisdom for?

Your self laughs at your ego and its proud leaps. "What are these leaps and flights of fancy to me?" it says to itself. "A detour to my end. I am the ego's leading strings and the prompter of its ideas."

The self says to the ego, "Feel pain here!" And the ego suffers and thinks on how it may suffer no more — and that is just how it should think.

The self says to the ego, "Feel pleasure here!" Then the ego rejoices and thinks on how often it may yet rejoice — and that is just how it should think.

I want to say a word to the despisers of the body. Their contempt makes for their respect. What is it that created respect and contempt and worth and will?

The creative self created for itself respect and contempt, it created for itself joy and sorrow. The creative self created spirit for itself as the hand of its will.

Even in your folly and contempt, you despisers of the body, you serve your self. I tell you: your self itself wants to die and turns away from life.

No longer can it do what it most wants to do: — create beyond itself. This is what it most wants, this is its entire burning desire.

But now it has become too late for that: — so your self wants to go under, you despisers of the body.

Your self wants to go under, and therefore you have become despisers of the body! For you can no longer create beyond yourselves.

And therefore you are angry now with life and with the earth. An unconscious envy is in the squint-eyed look of your contempt.

I do not go your way, you despisers of the body! You are no bridges to the Superman for me! —

Thus spake Zarathustra.

On Joys And Passions

My brother, if you have a virtue and it is your own virtue, then you have it in common with no one else.

Of course, you want to call it by name and caress it; you want to pull its ears and have some fun with it.

And behold! Now you have its name in common with the people and have become people and herd with your virtue.

You would have done better to say: "Inexpressible and nameless is this which is sweetness and agony to my soul and also the hunger of my innards."

Let your virtue be too lofty for the familiarity of names. And if you must speak of it, do not be ashamed to stammer.

Speak and stammer in this manner: "This is my good, this I love, thus it pleases me entirely, thus alone I want the good.

Not as a law of God do I want it, not as a human law and necessity do I want it: no signpost is it for me to super-earths and Edens.

It is an earthly virtue that I love: there is little cleverness in it, and reason least of all.

But this bird has built its nest by me: therefore I love it and embrace it, —now it sits by me on its golden eggs."

In this manner you should stammer and praise your virtue.

Once you had passions and called them evil. But now you have only your virtues: they grew out of your passions.

You placed your highest goal in the heart of these passions: then they grew into your virtues and joys.

And whether you came from the race of the irascible or the sensual or the fanatical or the vengeful:

In the end all your passions became virtues and all your devils angels.

Once you had wild dogs in your cellar: but in the end they changed into birds and lovely songstresses.

Out of your poisons you brewed your balsam; your cow, affliction, you milked, — now you drink the sweet milk of her udder.

And nothing evil grows out of you anymore, unless it be the evil that grows out of the conflict of your virtues.

My brother, if you are lucky, then you have one virtue and no more: so you go more easily over the bridge.

Outstanding it is, to have a lot of virtues, but it is a hard lot; and many a man has gone into the desert and killed himself because he was weary of being the battle and battlefield of virtues.

My brother, is war and battle evil? But this evil is necessary: necessary is the envy and mistrust and backbiting amongst your virtues.

See how each of your virtues covets the highest place: it wants your whole spirit to be its herald, it wants your whole strength in wrath, love, and hate.

Each virtue is jealous of the other, and jealousy is a terrible thing. Even virtues can perish on account of jealousy.

He who is surrounded by the flame of jealousy turns at last, like the scorpion, the poisoned stinger against himself.

Alas, my brother, have you never seen a virtue slander and stab itself?

Man is something that must be overcome: and therefore you are to love your virtues —: for you will perish on account of them.—

Thus spake Zarathustra.

On The Pale Criminal

You are unwilling to kill, you judges and sacrificers, until the animal has nodded his head. Behold, the pale criminal has nodded his head: out of his eye speaks the great contempt.

"My ego is something that should be overcome: my ego is to me the great contempt of man." — Thus out of this eye it speaks.

That he judged himself, that was his highest moment: do not let the sublime one return again to his baseness!

There is no salvation for him who suffers from himself this way, unless it be a speedy death.

Your killing, you judges, should be an act of compassion, not of revenge.

And while you are killing, see to it that you yourselves justify life!

It is not enough that you make your peace with the man you kill. Let your sorrow be love for the Superman: so you justify your living — still!

"Enemy" you should say, but not "villain"; "invalid" you should say, but not "cad"; "fool" you should say, but not "sinner."

And you, red judge, were you to say aloud all you have already done in thought: then everyone would cry: "Away with this filth and poisonous worm!"

But the thought is one thing, the deed another, and the image of the deed yet another still. The wheel of causality rolls not between them.

An image made this pale man pale. He was equal to his deed when he did it, but after the deed was done he could not endure its image.

Then he saw himself ever after as the doer of one deed. Madness I call this:

the exception changed into the rule for him.

The chalk streak charms the hen; the stroke he struck charmed his poor reason — madness after the deed I call this.

Listen, you judges! There is yet another madness: it is that before the deed.

Alas, you have not crept deeply enough into this soul!

Thus speaks the red judge: "Why did this criminal commit murder? He wanted to rob." But I say to you: his soul wanted blood, not loot: he thirsted for the happiness of the knife.

But his poor reason did not grasp this madness and persuaded him: "What does blood matter! it said; "Don't you at least want to make some loot besides?

Take some revenge?

And he listened to his poor reason: like lead its words lay upon him, — so he robbed when he murdered. He did not want to be ashamed of his madness.

And now the lead of his guilt lies upon him again, and once again his poor reason is so stiff, so crippled, so heavy.

If only he could shake his head, then off would roll his burden: but who can shake this head?

What is this man? A heap of diseases which reach out into the world through the spirit: there they want to take their prey.

What is this man? A ball of wild snakes which seldom have peace together, — so they go forth alone and seek prey in the world.

Look at this poor body! What it suffered and longed for it interpreted for itself, — it interpreted it as blood lust and craving for the happiness of the knife.

Upon him who falls ill now falls that evil which is evil now: he wants to cause pain with that which causes him pain. But there have been other times and another evil and good.

Once doubt was evil and the will to self. At that time the sick became heretics and witches: as heretics and witches they suffered and wanted to cause suffering.

But your ears do not want to hear this: it hurts good people, you tell me.

What do I care about your good people!

Much about your good people disgusts me, and verily, it is not their evil.

Oh, how I wish they had a madness in which to perish like this pale criminal!

Verily, I wish their madness had the name of truth or faithfulness or justice:

but they have their virtue in order to live long and in wretched comfort.

I am a railing by the raging stream: clutch me if you can! Your crutch, however, I am not. —

Thus spake Zarathustra.

On Reading And Writing

Of all that is written I love only what a person has written with his blood.

Write with blood: and you will come to find that blood is spirit.

It does not come easy, making out alien blood; I hate the reading idlers.

He who knows the reader does nothing more for the reader. Another century of readers — and the spirit itself will stink.

That everyone is allowed to learn to read spoils in the long run not only writing but also thinking.

Once the spirit was God, then it became man, now it has even become riffraff.

He who writes in blood and aphorisms does not want to be read but to be learned by heart.

In the mountains the shortest path is from peak to peak: but for that you have to have long legs. Aphorisms should be peaks: and those to whom they speak, tall and lofty.

The air thin and pure, with danger near, and the spirit full of joyful malice:

that makes for a good match.

I want to have kobolds around me, for I am bold. Boldness, which scares ghosts away, creates kobolds for itself, — boldness wants to laugh.

I no longer feel as you do: this cloud I see beneath me, this blackness and heaviness over which I laugh, — precisely this is your thundercloud.

You look up when you crave elevation. And I look down because I am elevated.

Who among you can laugh and be elevated at the same time?

He who climbs the highest mountains laughs at all tragic plays and tragic realities.

Valiant, unconcerned, mocking, violent — thus wisdom wants us. She is a woman and always loves only a warrior.

You tell me: "Life is hard to bear." But why would you have your pride in the morning and your resignation in the evening?

Life is hard to bear: but do not pretend to be so tender! We are altogether fine load bearing asses and she-asses.

What do we have in common with the rosebud, which trembles because a drop of dew lies upon its body?

It is true: we love life not because we are used to living but because we are used to loving.

There is always some madness in love. But there is also always some reason in madness.

And even to me, well-disposed to life as I am, the butterflies and soap-bubbles and those of their kind among mankind seem to know the most about happiness.

To see these light, foolish, delicate, movable little souls flutter — that seduces Zarathustra to tears and song.

I would only believe in a God who knew how to dance.

And when I saw my devil, I found him serious, thorough, profound, solemn: he was the spirit of gravity, — through him all things fall.

Not through wrath but through laughter does one kill. Come, let us kill the spirit of gravity!

I have learned to walk: since then I have let myself run. I have learned to fly: since then I don't want a push first in order to get going.

Now I am light, now I fly, now I see myself under me, now a God dances through me.

Thus spake Zarathustra.

On The Tree On The Mountainside

Zarathustra's eye had perceived that a certain youth avoided him. And one evening as he walked alone through the mountains surrounding the town which is called "The Dappled Cow", behold: in his walking there he found the youth, who sat leaning on a tree, casting weary looks into the valley. Zarathustra took hold of the tree by which the youth was sitting and spoke thus:

"If I wanted to shake this tree here with my hands, I would be unable to do so.

But the wind, which we do not see, bends and torments it howsoever it will. We are bent and tormented the worst by invisible hands."

The youth arose dismayed and said: "I hear Zarathustra and I was just now thinking of him." Zarathustra replied:

"Why are you alarmed at that? — But it is the same with man as it is with the tree.

The more it wants to be up in the height and the light, the stronger its roots strive earthward, downward, into the dark, the deep, — into evil."

"Yes, into evil!" cried the youth. "How is it possible that you have discovered my soul?"

Zarathustra smiled and said: "Many a soul will never be discovered unless it is first invented."

"Yes, into evil!" cried the youth once more.

"You have told the truth, Zarathustra. I no longer trust myself ever since I wanted to be up high, and no one trusts me any longer, — how does that happen?

I am changing too fast: my today refutes my yesterday. I often skip steps when I climb, — no step forgives me for that.

When I am up high I always find myself alone. No one speaks to me, the frost of solitude makes me shiver. What do I want up high?

My contempt and my longing increase together; the higher I climb, the more I despise the one who climbs. What does he want up high?

How ashamed I am of my climbing and stumbling! How I hate the fleeing one! How weary I am, up high!"

At this point the youth fell silent. And Zarathustra contemplated the tree beside which they stood and spoke thus:

"This tree stands lonely here in the mountains; high above man and beast it has grown.

And if it wanted to speak, it would have no one who could understand it: so high has it grown.

Now it waits and waits, — but what is it waiting for? It dwells too near the seat of the clouds: perhaps it waits for the first lightning?"

When Zarathustra had said this, the youth cried, with furious gestures, "Yes, Zarathustra, you speak the truth. I longed for my downgoing when I wanted the height, and you are the lightning I have been waiting for! Behold, what is left of me since you came among us? It is envy of you which has destroyed me!" — Thus spoke the youth and wept bitterly. But Zarathustra put his arm around him and led the lad away with him.

And when they had walked together for a while, Zarathustra began to speak thus:

"It breaks my heart. Better than your words can say, your eyes tell me of all your danger. You are not yet free, you are still in quest of freedom. Under-rested your quest has made you, and overwakeful.

You want to be at a free height, your soul thirsts for the stars. But your bad instincts also thirst for freedom.

Your wild dogs want to be at liberty; they bark with pleasure in their cellar when your spirit strives to unmake all prisons.

To me you are still a prisoner who imagines freedom: alas, clever become the souls of such prisoners, but also cunning and wicked.

Even the one who is liberated in spirit must purify himself. Much prison and putrefaction still remains in him: his eye must still become pure.

Yes, I know your danger. But by my love and hope I implore you: do not throw your love and hope away!

You still feel noble, and the others also still feel you are noble, though they hold a grudge against you and give you dirty looks. Know that the noble man stands in everyone's way.

The noble man also stands in the way of the good: and even when they call him good, they do so in order to do him in.

The new the noble man wants to create, and a new virtue. The old the good man wants, and that the old be preserved.

But that is not the danger of the noble man, that he will become one of the good, but that he will become a smart-aleck, a cynic, an annihilator.

Alas, I have known noble men who lost their highest hope. And then they slandered all high hopes.

Then they passed their lives shamelessly, engaged in brief pleasures, barely setting their goals beyond the day.

"Spirit is also sensuality" — so they said. Then the wings of their spirit broke in pieces: now it crawls around and soils what it gnaws on.

Once they thought of becoming heroes: now they are lechers. The hero is a horror and a source of remorse to them.

But by my love and hope I implore you: do not throw away the hero in your soul! Keep holy your highest hope! —

Thus spake Zarathustra.

On The Preachers Of Death

There are preachers of death: and the earth is full of those to whom turning away from life must be preached.

The earth is full of the superfluous, life is spoiled by the many-too-many. May they be enticed by "eternal life" out of this life!

"Yellow ones": so the preachers of death are called, or "black ones." But I want to show them to you in still other colors.

There are the terrible ones who carry the beast of prey around in themselves and have no choice except lust or self-laceration. And even their lust is still self-laceration.

They have not yet become men, these terrible ones: may they preach turning away from life and pass away themselves!

There are the consumptives of the soul: hardly are they born and already they begin to die, longing for the teachings of weariness and resignation.

They would gladly be dead, and we should approve their wish! Let us beware of waking the dead and damaging these living coffins!

They meet a sick man or an old man or a corpse; and right away they say:

"Life is refuted!"

But only they are refuted, and their eye, which sees only this one facet of existence.

Wrapped in thick melancholy and eager for the little accidents that bring death: thus they wait and clench their teeth.

Or else: they reach for sweets and mock their childishness the while; they cling to their shoestring existence, and mock their still living on a shoestring.

Their wisdom runs: "A fool is he who stays alive, but such fools are we, and how! And this is surely the most foolish thing about life!" —

"Life is only suffering" — so others say, and they do not lie. So see to it that you cease! So see to it that the life which is only suffering ceases!

And let the teaching of your virtue run thus: "Thou shalt do away with thyself!

Thou shalt steal away from thyself!" —

"Sensuality is sin," — so say the ones who preach death, — "let us go aside and beget no more children!"

"Giving birth is laborsome," — say the others — "why still give birth? Only unfortunates are born!" And these, too, are preachers of death.

"Pity is necessary," — so says a third group. "Take what I have! Take what I am! Life will bind me that much less!" —

If they were truly full of compassion, they would destroy their neighbor's passion for life. To be evil — that would be their true goodness.

But they want to be released from life: what is it to them if with their chains and gifts they bind others ever more tightly! —

And you too, to whom life is fierce labor and unrest: are you not very weary of life? Are you not very ripe for the preaching of death?

All you to whom fierce labor is dear, and the fast, the new, the unfamiliar, — you are poor at enduring yourselves, your industriousness is a flight and a will to forget yourselves.

If you believed more in life, you would throw yourselves less into the moment. But in you you do not have enough of what it takes to wait — not even to vegetate!

Everywhere resounds the voice of those who preach death: and the earth is full of those to whom death must be preached.

Or "eternal life": it's all the same to me, — if only they pass away quickly!

Thus spake Zarathustra.

On War And Warlike People

We do not wish to be spared by our enemies, nor by those whom we love from the heart. So let me tell you the truth, then!

My brothers in war! I love you from the heart; I am and have been your like.

And I am also your best enemy. So let me tell you the truth, then!

I know the hatred and envy of your hearts. You are not great enough not to know hatred and envy. So be great enough then not to be ashamed of them!

And if you cannot be saints of knowledge, then at least be its warriors.

They are the companions and forerunners of such sanctity.

I see many soldiers: would that I saw many warriors! "Uniform" one calls what they wear: would that it were not uniform what they hide thereby!

You should be one of those whose eye always seeks an enemy — your enemy. And with some of you it is hate at first sight.

Your enemy you shall seek, your war you shall wage, and for your thoughts!

And if your thought should be defeated, then your honesty shall still cry victory meanwhile!

You shall love peace as a means to new wars. And the short peace more than the long.

You I advise not to work but to fight. You I advise not to peace but to victory.

May your work be a fight, may your peace be a victory!

One can only be quiet and sit still when one has bow and arrow: otherwise one squawks and squabbles. May your peace be a victory!

You say it is the good cause that hallows even war? I say to you: it is the good war that hallows every cause.

War and courage have done more great things than love of your neighbor. Not your pity but your bravery has saved the unfortunate thus far.

"What is good?" you ask. To be brave is good. Let the little girls say: "Good is what is pretty and at the same time touching."

They call you heartless: but your heart is true, and I love the modesty of your cordiality. You are ashamed of your flow, and others are ashamed of their ebb.

You are ugly? Well then, my brothers! Put on the sublime, the mantle of the ugly!

And when your soul becomes large, it becomes high-spirited, and in your sublimity there is malice. I know you.

In malice the princeling and the weakling meet. But they misunderstand each other. I know you.

You may only have enemies to hate, not enemies to despise. You must be proud of your enemy: then your enemy's successes will also be your successes.

Rebellion — that is the distinction of a slave. May your distinction be obedience! May your commanding itself be an obeying!

"Thou shalt" sounds sweeter to a good soldier than "I will." And all that is dear to you shall be that which has first been commanded to you.

May your love of life be love for your highest hope: and may your highest hope be the highest thought of life!

Your highest thought, however, shall be commanded to you by me — and it runs: man is something that shall be overcome.

So live your life of obedience and war! Who cares about long life! What warrior wants to be spared! I do not spare you, I love you from the heart, my brothers in war! —

Thus spake Zarathustra.

On The New Idol

Somewhere there are still peoples and herds, but not by us: here there are states.

State? What is that? Well then! Open your ears, for now I will say a word to you about the death of peoples.

State is the name of the coldest of all cold monsters. It lies coldly, too; and this lie crawls out of its mouth: "I, the state, am the people."

It is a lie! It was creators who created peoples and hung a belief and a love above them: thus they served life.

It is destroyers who set up pitfalls for many people and call them "state":

they hang a sword and a hundred inordinate desires above them.

Where there is still a people, they do not know the state, and they hate it as the evil eye and a sin against customs and rights.

This sign I give to you: each people speaks its own tongue of good and evil; its neighbor does not understand it. Its language it has devised for itself in customs and rights.

But the state lies in all tongues of good and evil; and whatever it says, it lies — and whatever it has, it has stolen.

Everything about it is false; with stolen teeth it bites, the snaphappy one.

Even its innards are false.

Speech confusion of good and evil: this sign I give to you as a sign of the state. Verily, the will to death this sign signifies! Verily, it beckons the preachers of death!

Many-too-many are born: the state was devised for the superfluous ones!

Just look how it entices them, the many-too-many! How it gobbles and chews and re-chews them!

"There is nothing greater on earth than I: I am the regulating finger of God"

— thus the monster roars. And not only the long-eared and the short-sighted sink to their knees!

Alas, to you as well, you great souls, it whispers its gloomy lies! Alas, it divines the rich hearts which gladly squander themselves.

Yes, you too it divines, you conquerors of the old God! You have become weary of battle, and now even your weariness serves the new idol!

Heroes and men of honor it wants to set up around itself, the new idol!

Gladly it basks in the sunshine of good consciences, — this cold monster!

It will give you all when you worship it, the new idol: thus it buys the glimmer of your virtue and the glance of your proud eye.

By using you it wants to entice the many-too-many! Yes, a hellish piece of art has been devised here, a horse of death jingling in the trappings of divine honors.

Yes, a dying for many has been devised here which praises itself as life: verily, a heartsend to all preachers of death!

State I call it, where all are poison drinkers, good and bad: state, where all lose themselves, good and bad: state, where the slow suicide of all — is called "life."

Just look at these superfluous ones! They steal for themselves the works of inventors and the treasures of the wise — education they call their theft — and all becomes sickness and distress to them!

Just look at these superfluous ones! They are always sick; they vomit their gall and call it a newspaper. They devour each other and cannot even stomach themselves.

Just look at these superfluous ones! They acquire riches, by the which they become poorer. Power they desire, and first of all that lever of power, lots of money, — these impotent ones!

See them clamber, these quick monkeys! They clamber away, one atop the other, and so drag themselves into the mud and the abyss.

There to the throne they all want to go: it is their madness — as if happiness sat on the throne! Mud often sits on the throne — and oftentimes, too, the throne on mud.

Madmen they are all to me and clambering monkeys and overheated ones.

Their idol, the cold monster, smells evil to me: all together they smell evil to me, these idolaters.

My brother, would you smother in the fumes of their maws and lawless desires? Better to smash the window and jump outside.

Get away from the bad smell! Go away from the idolatry of the superfluous!

Get away from the bad smell! Go away from these human sacrifices!

The earth is still open for great souls. Many seats still stand empty for the lonesome and the twosome, around whom the smell of silent seas blows.

A free life still stands open for great souls. Verily, he who possesses little is so much the less possessed: praised be the little poverty!

There, where the state ends, only there begins the man who is not superfluous:

there begins the song of the necessary one, the unique and irreplaceable melody.

There, where the state ends, just look there my brothers! Do you not see it, the rainbow and the bridges of the Superman? —

Thus spake Zarathustra.

On The Flies Of The Marketplace

Flee, my friend, into your solitude! I see you deafened by the noise of the great men and stung all over by the stings of the little men.

Wood and rock know how to keep a worthy silence with you. Be again like the tree you love, the broad-branching one: silent and attentive it hangs over the sea.

Where solitude ends, there the marketplace begins; and where the marketplace begins, there begins also the noise of the great actors and the buzzing of the poisonous flies.

The best things in the world still amount to nothing without the one who first shows them: great men the people call these showmen.

The people have little grasp of greatness, that is: creativeness. But they have a taste for all showers and actors of great things.

Around the inventors of new values the world revolves — invisibly it revolves. But around the actors the people and the glory revolve: that is how "the world turns."

Spirit the actor has, but little conscience of the spirit. He always believes in that with which he makes the strongest belief, — the belief in himself!

Tomorrow he has a new belief, and the day after tomorrow a newer one.

Quick senses he has, like the people, and fickle moods.

To overthrow — to him that means: to prove. To drive crazy — to him that means: to convince. And blood strikes him as the best of all arguments.

A truth which slips only into fine ears he calls a lie and a nothing. Verily, he only believes in gods that make a great noise in the world!

The marketplace is full of solemn buffoons — and people boast of their great men: to them they are the men of the hour.

But the hour presses them: so they press you. And they also want from you a Yes or a No. Woe, would you set your chair between For and Against?

Do not be jealous on account of these pushy and absolute ones, you lover of the truth! Never yet has truth clung to the arm of an absolutist.

Return to your safety on account of these hasty ones: only in the marketplace is one assaulted with Yes? or No?

Slow is the experience of all deep wells: long must they wait before knowing what fell into their depths.

Apart from fame and marketplace all great things take place: apart from fame and marketplace the inventors of new values have always kept a place.

Flee, my friend, into your solitude: I see you stung all over by poisonous flies. Flee there, to where a rough, strong breeze blows!

Flee into your solitude! You have dwelt too near the small and the pitiful.

Flee from their invisible vengeance! Towards you they have nothing but vengeance.

Raise not a hand against them any longer! Countless are they, and it is not your lot to be a flyswatter.

Countless are these small and pitiful ones; and many a proud building has already been brought down by raindrops and weeds.

You are no stone, but already you have become hollow from many drops. From many drops you will yet break and burst asunder.

I see you worn out by poisonous flies, I see you scratched bloody in a hundred places, and your pride refuses to get angry even once.

Blood they want from you in all innocence, blood their bloodless souls crave — and so they go on stinging in all innocence.

But you, deep one, you suffer too deeply even from small wounds; and before you have even healed, the same poison worm crawls over your hand.

You are too proud to kill these sweet-tooths. Beware, however, lest it become your fate to bear all their poisonous injustice!

They buzz around you with their praise, too: their praise is pushiness. They want to be close to your skin and blood.

They fawn upon you as upon a god or devil: they whine before you as before a god or devil. So what! Fawners and whiners they are and nothing more.

They often try as well to pass themselves off to you as charming. But that was ever the cleverness of the cowardly. Yes, the cowardly are clever!

They think about you a lot with their narrow souls, — you are always unthinkable to them! Whatever is thought about a lot becomes unthinkable.

They punish you for all your virtues. Deep down they only forgive you —your mistakes.

Because you are gentle and fair-minded you say: "Guiltless are they in their small existence." But narrow souls think: "Guilt makes up all great existence."

Even when you are gentle to them, they still feel despised by you; and your good deed they repay with hidden bad deeds.

Your wordless pride always goes against their taste; they rejoice if for once you are modest enough to be vain.

That which we recognize in a man we also inflame in him. So beware of the small people!

Before you they feel small, and their lowness glimmers and glows in invisible vengeance toward you.

Have you not noticed how often they became silent when you walked up to them, and how their strength deserted them like smoke from a dying fire?

Yes, my friend, you are the bad conscience of your neighbors; for they are unworthy of you. Therefore they hate you and would gladly love to suck your blood.

Your neighbors will always be poisonous flies; that which is great in you, — that very thing must make them more poisonous and ever more fly-like.

Flee, my friend, into your solitude and to there where a rough, strong breeze blows! It is not your lot to be a fly-swatter. —

Thus spake Zarathustra.

On Chastity

I love the forest. In the cities it is bad to live; there are too many in heat there.

Is it not better to fall into the hands of a murderer than into the dreams of a woman in heat?

And just look at these men: their eyes say it — they know nothing better on earth than to lie with a woman.

Slime is at the bottom of their souls; and woe if on top of it this slime has spirit!

Would that you were as perfect as animals at least! But to animals belongs innocence.

Do I advise you to kill your senses? I advise you to have innocence of the senses.

Do I advise you to chastity? Chastity is a virtue with some, but with many it is nearly a vice.

They may well abstain: but the bitch Sensuality looks enviously out of all that they do.

Even unto the heights of their virtue and right into the cold spirit this creature and her discord follow them.

And how politely the bitch Sensuality knows how to beg for a piece of spirit when a piece of meat is denied her.

You love tragedies and everything that breaks your heart to smithereens?

But I am suspicious of your bitch.

Your eyes are too cruel for me and you look lustfully for sufferers. Has not your lechery merely disguised and described itself as pity?

And this parable too I offer you: Not a few who wanted to cast out their devils entered themselves into the swine thereby.

Chastity is not to be advised for those who find it hard, lest it become the way to hell — that is to slime and soul-lust.

Do I speak of filthy things? That is not the worst thing.

Not when the truth is filthy, but when it is shallow: that is when the knowing one is reluctant to go into its waters.

Verily, there are thoroughly chaste ones: they are gentler of heart; they laugh more readily and richly than you.

They laugh at chastity too and ask: "What is chastity?"

"Is chastity not folly? But this folly came to us, not we to it.

We offered this guest harbor and heart: now he dwells with us — let him stay as long as he wants!"

Thus spake Zarathustra.

On The Friend

"One is always too many around me" — so thinks the hermit. "Always one times one — in the long run that makes two!"

I and me are always too wrapped up in conversation: how could that be endured unless there were a friend?

For the hermit the friend is always the third person: the third person is the cork that prevents the conversation of the other two from sinking into the depths.

Alas, there are too many depths for all hermits. Therefore they long so for a friend and his height.

Our faith in others betrays wherein we would dearly love to have faith in ourselves. Our longing for a friend is our betrayer.

And often with our love we only want to overleap envy. And often we attack and make an enemy only in order to hide our vulnerability.

"At least be my enemy!" — thus speaks true reverence, which dares not ask for friendship.

If one wants to have a friend, then one must also be willing to wage war for him: and in order to wage war, one must be capable of being an enemy.

One should still honor the enemy in one's friend. Can you go near your friend without going over to him?

In his friend one should have his best enemy. You should be closest to him in your heart when you resist him.

You want to wear no clothes before your friend? It should be an honor to your friend that you show yourself to him as you are? But he wishes you to the devil for it!

He who makes no secret of himself makes others see red: all the more reason to fear nakedness! Of course, if you were gods, then you could be ashamed of your clothes!

You cannot dress finely enough for your friend: for you are to be an arrow and a longing for the Superman to him.

Have you ever seen your friend asleep, — to find out how he looked? What else is your friend's face, though? It is your own face in a rough and imperfect mirror.

Have you ever seen your friend asleep? Were you not frightened that your friend looked like that? Oh, my friend, man is something that must be overcome.

In divining and keeping silent the friend should be a master: you must not want to see all. Your dream should reveal to you what your friend does when he is awake.

Let your pitying be a divining: that you may first see whether your friend wants pity. Perhaps he loves in you the unbroken eye and the look of eternity. Pity for a friend should hide itself under a hard shell: you should break a tooth biting on it. Thus it will have fineness and sweetness.

Are you pure air and solitude and bread and medicine for your friend? Many a man cannot loosen his own chains, and yet he is a savior to his friend. Are you a slave? Then you cannot be a friend. Are you a tyrant? Then you cannot have friends.

All-too-long have a slave and a tyrant been concealed in woman. Therefore woman is not yet capable of friendship: she only knows love. In woman's love there is injustice and blindness towards all that she does not love. And even in the knowing love of woman there is still sneak attack and lightning and night alongside the light.

Woman is not yet capable of friendship: women are still cats and birds. Or at best, cows.

Woman is not yet capable of friendship. But tell me, you men, who among you is capable of friendship?

O your poverty, you men, and your avarice of soul! As much as you give your friend I will yet give my foe, and I will be none the poorer for it also.

There is comradeship: may there be friendship!

Thus spake Zarathustra.

On The Thousand And One Goals

Many lands did Zarathustra see, and many peoples: thus he discovered the good and evil of many peoples. No greater power on earth did Zarathustra find than good and evil.

No people could live without first valuing; if they want to keep their standing, however, they must not value as their neighbor values.

Much that was good to this people was a mockery and a disgrace to another: thus did I find. Much did I find called evil here and adorned with purple honors there.

Never did one neighbor understand the other: ever did his soul marvel at his neighbor's madness and malice.

A table of the good hangs over every people. Behold, it is the table of their overcomings; behold, it is the voice of their will to power.

Whatever is hard they call praiseworthy; whatever is hard and indispensable is called good; and whatever relieves in even the direst need, the rare, the hardest,— that they praise as holy.

Whatever makes them rule and conquer and shine to the horror and envy of their neighbor: that they consider the height, the foremost, the measure, the meaning of all things.

Verily, my brother, if you only knew a people's need and land and sky and neighbor, then you could surely divine the law of their overcomings and why they climb this ladder to their hope.

"You shall always be first and stand apart from the others: your jealous soul shall love none other than a friend" — that made the soul of a Greek tremble: with that he traveled the path of his greatness.

"To speak the truth and do well with bow and arrow" — that seemed both dear and hard to the people from whom my name comes — the name which is both dear and hard to me.

"To honor mother and father and do their will to the very roots of your soul" — this table of overcoming another people hung over themselves and grew powerful and eternal thereby.

"To practice loyalty, and for the sake of loyalty to risk honor and blood, even on evil and dangerous things": teaching themselves thus, another people mastered themselves, and thus mastering themselves, they became pregnant and heavy with great hopes.

Verily, men have given themselves all their good and evil. Verily, they did not take it, they did not find it, it did not come to them as a voice from heaven.

Man first implanted values in things in order to maintain his standing, —he first created meaning in things, a human meaning! That is why he calls himself "Man," that is: the evaluator.

Valuing is creating: hear this, you creators! Valuing itself is of all valued things the treasure and jewel.

Only through valuing is there value: and without valuing the nut of existence would be hollow. Hear this, you creators!

A change in values, — that is a change in creators. He who must be a creator is always destroying.

Creators were peoples first, and only later, individuals; verily, the individual himself is but the latest creation.

Once peoples hung a table of values over themselves. A love which wants to rule and a love which wants to obey have together created for themselves such tables.

The pleasure in the herd is older than the pleasure in the I: and as long as the good conscience is called herd, the bad conscience only says: I.

Verily, the sly I, the loveless one that seeks its advantage in the advantage of many: that is not the beginning of the herd but its downgoing.

It was ever lovers and creators that created good and evil. The fire of love glows in all the names of the virtues, and the fire of anger.

Many lands did Zarathustra see, and many peoples: no greater power on earth did Zarathustra find than the works of the lovers: their names are "good" and "evil."

Verily, the power of this praising and blaming is a monster. Tell me brothers, who will subdue it for me? Tell me, who will throw a chain over the thousand necks of this beast?

Thus far there have been a thousand goals, for there have been a thousand peoples. Only the chain for these thousand necks is still lacking, the one goal is lacking. Mankind still has no goal.

But tell me though, my brothers: if the goal of mankind is still lacking, is not also — mankind itself still lacking? —

Thus spake Zarathustra.

On Neighborly Love

You crowd around your neighbor and have fine words for it. But I tell you: your neighborly love is your bad love of yourselves.

You flee from yourselves to your neighbor and would like to make a virtue of it: but I see through your "selflessness."

The "you" is older than the "I"; the "you" has been canonized, but not yet the "I"; thus man crowds towards his neighbor.

Do I advise you to neighborly love? Rather I advise you to neighborly flight and love for the furthest!

Higher than love for the nearest is love for the furthest and future one; higher still than the love of man I consider the love of things and phantoms.

This phantom which runs here before you, my brother, is fairer than you; why not give him your flesh and bones? But you are afraid and go running off to your neighbor.

You cannot stand to be alone with yourselves and do not love yourselves enough: now you want to mislead your neighbor into love and gild yourselves with his mistake.

I wish that you could not stand any kind of nearest ones and their neighbors; then out of yourselves you would have to create your friend and his overflowing heart.

You call in a witness when you want to speak well of yourselves; and when you have misled him into thinking well of you, he himself thinks well of you.

Not only does he lie who speaks contrary to what he does know, but all the more so he who speaks contrary to what he does not know. And so you speak of yourselves in your dealings and deceive your neighbor with yourselves.

Thus speaks the fool: "Contact with men ruins character, especially if one has none."

The one goes to his neighbor because he seeks himself and the other because he wants to lose himself. Your bad love of yourselves makes solitude a prison for you.

It is those further away who must pay for your love of neighbor; and as soon as there are five of you together, a sixth one must always die.

I do not love your feast-days either: too many actors I found there, and often the spectators acted like actors, too.

Not the neighbor do I teach you, but the friend. May the friend be the feast of the earth for you and an anticipation of the Superman.

I teach you the friend and his overfull heart. But one must be a sponge if one would be loved by hearts that are overfull.

I teach you the friend, in whom the world stands complete, a bowl of the good, — the creative friend, who always has a complete world to bestow.

47 And as the world once rolled apart for him, so it rolls back together again for him in circles, like the development of good through evil, like the development of purpose from chance.

May the future and the furthest be the reason for your today: in your friend you shall love the Superman as your reason.

My brothers, I do not advise you to neighborly love: I advise you to love for the furthest.

Thus spake Zarathustra.

On The Way Of The Creator

Would you go into isolation, my brother? Would you seek the way to yourself?

Stay yet a while and hear me.

"He who seeks easily gets lost himself. All isolation is guilt": thus speaks the herd. And you have long belonged to the herd.

The voice of the herd will still resound in you, too. And when you say: "You and I are no longer of one conscience," it will be a pain and a plaint.

Behold, this pain itself is still brought forth by the one conscience: and the last glimmer of that conscience still gleams on your misery.

But would you go the way of your misery, which is the way to yourself?

Then show me your right and might to it!

Are you a new might and a new right? A first movement? A self-rolling wheel? Can you force even the stars to revolve around you?

Alas, there is so much lustfulness for the heights! There are so many convulsions of the ambitious! Show me that you are not one of the lustful and the ambitious!

Alas, there are so many great thoughts that do no more than a bellows: they inflate and make emptier.

You call yourselves free? Your ruling thought I want to hear and not that you have escaped from a yoke.

Are you one of those allowed to escape from a yoke? There are many who threw away their last value when they threw away their servitude.

Free from what? What is that to Zarathustra? But your eye should clearly announce to me: free for what?

Can you provide yourself with your own good and evil and hang your will up over yourself like a law? Can you be the judge of yourself and the avenger of your own law?

It is terrible being alone with the judge and avenger of your own law. Thus a star is thrown into empty space and into the icy breath of aloneness.

Today you still suffer from the many, you lone one: today you still have all your courage and your hopes.

But one day loneliness will make you weary, one day your pride will cringe and your courage will gnash its teeth. One day you will cry "I am alone!"

One day you will see your high no more and your low all too near; your very loftiness will frighten you like a ghost. One day you will cry: "All is false!"

There are feelings that would kill the loner; should they not succeed, well then, they themselves must die! But are you capable of being a murderer?

My brother, do you know the word "contempt" yet? And the agony of your justice, being just to those who despise you?

You force many to learn anew about you; they charge you harshly for that.

You went near them and passed right over them: that they will never forgive you.

You go above and beyond them: but the higher you climb, the smaller the eye of envy perceives you. The flier, however, is hated most of all.

"How could you be just to me!" — you must say — "I chose your injustice as my allotted part."

Injustice and filth they throw at the loner: but, my brother, if you would be a star, then you must shine for them none the less!

And beware of the good and the just! They like to crucify those who invent their own virtue — they hate the loners.

Beware also of holy simplicity! Everything that is not simple is unholy to them; they also like to play with fire — the stake.

And beware, too, of the attacks of your love! Too quickly the loner extends his hand toward anyone he happens to meet.

To many a man you may not give a hand, only a paw: and I want your paw to have claws, too.

But the worst enemy you can meet will always be yourself; you lie in wait for yourself in caves and forests.

Loner, you go the way to yourself! And your way leads past you yourself and your seven devils!

Heretic you will be to yourself and skeptic and witch and soothsayer and fool and sinner and scoundrel.

You must be willing to burn in your own flame: how could you become new unless you had first become ashes?

Loner, you go the way of the lover: you love yourself and therefore you despise yourself, as only lovers despise.

The lover wants to create because he despises! What does he know of love who has not had to despise precisely that which he loved?

With your love and with your creation go into your isolation, my brother, and only later will justice limp after you.

With my tears go into your isolation, my brother. I love him who wants to create beyond himself and thus go to ruin.—

Thus spake Zarathustra.

On Little Old And Young Ladies

"Why do you steal so shyly through the twilight, Zarathustra? And what do you hide so carefully under your mantle?

Is it a treasure that was given to you? Or a child that was born to you? Or are you yourself now going the way of thieves, you friend of the wicked?" —

Verily, my brother, said Zarathustra, it is a treasure that was given to me: it is a little truth that I carry.

But it is unruly like a young child, and if I do not hold its mouth it will cry too loudly.

As I went my way alone today, at the hour when the sun is sinking, a little old lady met me and spoke to my soul thus:

"Many things has Zarathustra also said to us women, but never has he spoken to us about woman."

And I replied to her: "About woman one should speak only to men."

"Speak also to me about woman," she said; "I am old enough to forget it immediately again."

And I complied with the little old lady and spoke to her thus:

"Everything about woman is a riddle, and everything about woman has one solution: it is called pregnancy.

Man is for woman a means: the end is always the child. But what is woman for man?

Two different things the true man wants: danger and play. Therefore he wants woman as the most dangerous plaything.

Man should be trained for war and women for the recreation of the warrior: all else is folly.

All-too-sweet fruits — these the warrior dislikes. Therefore he likes woman; even the sweetest woman is bitter.

Woman understands children better than man, but man is more childlike than woman.

In the true man a child is hidden: it wants to play. Come on, you women, discover the child in man!

Let women be a plaything, pure and fine, like a precious stone illuminated by the virtues of a world yet to come.

Let the radiance of a star sparkle in your love! Let your hope be: "May I give birth to the Superman!"

Let there be bravery in your love! With your love you should head for him who fills you with dread.

Let your honor be in your love! Woman understands little else of honor. But let this be your honor: always to love more than you are loved, and never to be second.

Let man fear woman when she loves: then she makes any sacrifice, and everything else she considers worthless.

Let man fear woman when she hates: for at the bottom of his soul man is merely angry; woman, however, is downright mean.

Whom does woman hate the most? — Thus said the iron to the magnet: "I hate you the most, because you attract me but are not strong enough to draw me to you."

The happiness of man is: I will. The happiness of woman is: he wills.

"Behold, just now the world has become perfect!" — thus thinks every woman when she obeys out of complete love.

And woman must obey and find a depth for her surface. Surface is woman's nature, a mobile, stormy film on shallow water.

Man's nature, however, is deep: his torrent roars in subterranean caves; woman senses his strength but can make no sense of it. —

Then the little old lady replied to me: "Many charming things Zarathustra has said, especially for those who are young enough for them.

It is strange: Zarathustra knows little about women, and yet he is right about them! Is that because nothing is impossible with woman?

And now accept a little truth by way of thanks! I am old enough for it, anyway!

Bundle it up and keep its mouth shut: otherwise it will cry loudly, this little truth."

"Give me, woman, your little truth!" I said. And thus spake the little old lady:

"You go to women? Do not forget the whip!"—

Thus spake Zarathustra.

On The Adder's Bite

One day, because of the heat, Zarathustra had fallen asleep under a fig tree and had placed his arms across his face. Then an adder came and bit him on the neck, so that he cried out in pain. When he had taken an arm from his face, he took a look at the snake: it recognized Zarathustra by his eyes, wriggled awkwardly, and wanted to get away. "Not so fast," said Zarathustra, "you have not yet accepted my thanks! You have awakened me in time, my way is yet long."

"Your way is yet short," said the adder sadly; "my poison kills." Zarathustra smiled: "When did a dragon ever die from the poison of a snake?" — he said. "But take your poison back! You are not rich enough to give it to me." Then the adder fell upon his neck again and licked his wound.

As Zarathustra related this once to his disciples, they asked him: "And what, O Zarathustra, is the moral of your story?" Then Zarathustra answered them thus:

"The annihilator of morals the good and the just call me: my story is immoral.

But if you have an enemy, do not requite him good for evil: for that would put him to shame. Prove rather that he did you some good.

And better to be angry than to put to shame! And when you are cursed, it pleases me not that you then want to bless. Rather curse a little in return!

And if a great wrong has been done you, then quickly do five small ones in addition! Horrible to behold is he who alone a wrong oppresses.

Were you aware of this already? A shared wrong is half right. And only he who can take it should take a wrong upon himself!

A little revenge is more human than no revenge at all. And if the punishment is not also a right and an honor for the transgressor, I do not care for your punishments either.

It is nobler to admit being wrong than to insist on being right, especially if one is in the right. Only one must be rich enough for that.

I do not care for your cold justice; and out of the eye of your judges there always gazes the executioner and his cold steel.

Tell me, where is the justice which is love with seeing eyes to be found?

So devise for me the love which bears not only all punishment but also all guilt!

So devise for me the justice which acquits everyone except the one who judges!

Would you hear this, too? With him who would be thoroughly just, even the lie becomes mankindliness.

But how could I be thoroughly just? How can I give each his own? Let this be enough for me: I give each my own.

Finally, my brothers, beware of doing the hermit any harm! How could a hermit forget? How could he requite?

A hermit is like a deep well. It is easy to throw a stone in; but once it has sunk to the bottom, tell me, who will bring it out again?

Beware of offending the hermit! But if you have done so, well then, do him in as well!

Thus spake Zarathustra.

On The Child And Marriage

I have a question for you alone, my brother: like a plumb line I cast this question into your soul to see how deep it is.

You are young and wish for a child and marriage. But I ask you: are you a man who is allowed to wish for a child?

Are you the triumphant one, the self-conqueror, the master of the senses, the lord of your virtues? Thus I ask you.

Or does the beast and the utmost necessity speak out of your wish? Or isolation?

Or unrest within yourself?

I wish that your triumph and freedom would yearn for a child. Living monuments you should build to your victory and delivery.

Out beyond yourselves you should build. But first you yourself must be built, foursquare in body and soul.

Not only onward shall your seed be planted but upward! May the garden of marriage help you with that!

A higher body you should create, a first movement, a self-rolling wheel, — a creator you should create.

Marriage: thus I call the will of two to create the one who is more than those who created it. I call marriage the reverence for each other of those who will with such a will.

Let this be the meaning and truth of your marriage. But that which the many-too-many call marriage, these superfluous ones, — alas, what shall I call that?

Alas, this poverty of the soul in twos! Alas, this filth of the soul in twos!

Alas, this wretched comfort in twos!

All this they call marriage; and they say that marriages are made in heaven.

Well, I don't like it, this heaven of the superfluous! No, I don't like it, these animals entangled in the heavenly net!

And may the God who limps this way to bless what he has never joined together stay far away from me!

Do not laugh at such marriages! What child has not had reason to weep over his parents?

Worthy this man seemed to me and ripe for the meaning of the earth: but when I saw his wife, the earth seemed to me a house for the inane.

Yes, I wish that the earth would shake with convulsions when a saint mates with a goose.

This one set out like a hero in quest of truths, and at last he captured a little dressed-up lie. His marriage, he calls it.

That one was reserved in conversation and chose choosily. But in no time he spoiled his company for all time: his marriage, he calls it.

Another one sought a maid with the virtues of an angel. But in no time he became the maid of a woman, and now he even needs to be an angel, too.

Cautious have I now found all buyers, and they all have crafty eyes. But even the craftiest still buys his wife in a poke.

Many short follies — that is called love, by you. And your marriage makes an end of many short follies with one long stupidity.

Your love of woman and woman's love of man: ah, would that it were a fellow- suffering with suffering and veiled deities! But generally two animals hit upon each other.

But even your best love is only an ecstatic allegory and a painful flame. It is a torch to light you to higher ways.

Beyond yourselves you shall love one day! So first learn to love! And you must have had to drink the bitter cup of your love for that.

Bitterness is in the cup of even the best love: thus it produces longing for the Superman, thus it produces thirst in you, the creator.

Thirst in the creator, an arrow and longing for the Superman: speak, my brother, is this your will to marriage?

Holy I call such a will and such a marriage.—

Thus spake Zarathustra.

On Free Death

Many die too late, and some die too early. The teaching still sounds strange: "Die at the right time"

Die at the right time; thus Zarathustra teaches.

Of course, how could he who never lived at the right time ever die at the right time? Would that he had never been born! — Thus I advise the superfluous.

But even the superfluous still make a big to-do about their dying, and even the hollowest nut still wants cracking.

All take dying to be important: but death is not yet a feast. The finest feasts men have not yet learned to consecrate.

The consummating death I present to you, one which proves to be a prick and a promise to the living.

The consummator dies his death triumphantly, ringed round by hoping and promising ones.

Thus one should learn to die; and there should be no feast at which such a dying one does not consecrate the oaths of the living!

To die thus is best; second best, however, is: to die in battle and squander a great soul.

But equally hated by the fighter and the victor is your grinning death, which creeps up like a thief — and yet comes as master.

My death I commend to you, the free death which comes to me because I want it.

And when will I want it? — He who has a goal and a heir wants death at the right time for his goal and his heir.

And out of reverence for his goal and his heir he will hang up no more withered wreaths in the sanctuary of life.

Verily, I will not do as the rope-twisters do: they spin out their thread and as a result continually walk backwards.

Many a one becomes too old for his truths and triumphs, too; a toothless mouth no longer has the right to every truth.

And everyone who desires fame must take leave of honor in good time and practice the difficult art of — leaving at the right time.

When he tastes the sweetest, a person must stop letting himself be eaten:

this is known by those who want to be long-loved.

There are sour apples, of course, whose fate demands that they wait until the last day of fall: and they become ripe, yellow, and wrinkled all at the same time.

With some the heart ages first, and with others, the spirit. And some are old in youth: but late youth preserves long youth.

For many a man life is a failure: a poison maggot eats away at his heart. So let him see to it that his death is that much more of a success.

Many a man never becomes sweet; already in summer he rots. It is cowardice that keeps him attached to his branch.

Many-too-many live and much too long they hang on their branches.

Would that a storm came to shake all this rottenness and worm-eaten mess from the tree!

Would that there came preachers of speedy death! They would be the right storms and shakers of the trees of life! But I hear only the slow death preached and patience with all things "earthly."

Alas, you preach patience with earthly things? It is these earthly things which have too much patience with you, you blasphemers!

Verily, too early died that Hebrew whom the preachers of death honor: and it has been the doom of many ever since that he died too early.

As yet he had known only tears and the melancholy of the Hebrew, along with the hatred of the good and the just, — the Hebrew Jesus: then the longing for death came over him.

If only he had stayed in the desert and far away from the good and the just!

Perhaps he would have learned to live and learned to love the earth — and laughter as well.

Believe me, my brothers! He died too early: he himself would have recanted his teaching had he reached my age! He was noble enough to recant!

But he was still immature. Immaturely the youth loves, and immaturely he hates man and earth. Bound and heavy yet are his temperament and the wings of his spirit.

In the man, however, there is more child than in the youth, and less melancholy:

he has a better grasp of life and death.

Free for death and free in death, a holy naysayer when it is no longer time for yea: thus he grasps life and death.

That your dying be no blasphemy against man and earth: this I ask of the honey of your soul.

In your dying your spirit and your virtue should still glow, like a sunset sky over the earth: otherwise your dying has turned out badly.

So will I myself die, that you friends may love the earth more for my sake; and to the earth will I return, that I may rest in her who bore me.

Verily, Zarathustra had a goal; he threw his ball: now you, my friends, are the heirs of my goal; to you I throw my golden ball.

More than anything else I love to see you throw the golden ball, my friends!

And so I tarry a little longer on earth: forgive me for that!

Thus spake Zarathustra.

On The Bestowing Virtue
1

When Zarathustra had taken leave of the town to which his heart was attached and whose name is "The Dappled Cow," many followed him who called themselves his disciples and gave him escort. Thus they came to a crossroads:

then Zarathustra told them that from thenceforth he wanted to go it alone: for he was a friend of going it alone. But in parting, his disciples gave him a staff, upon whose golden handle a serpent had coiled itself around the sun. Zarathustra was pleased with the staff and leaned upon it; then he spoke thus to his disciples:

Tell me now: how did gold come to have the highest value? Because it is uncommon and useless and luminous and gentle in its brilliance; it always bestows itself.

Only as an image of the highest virtue did gold come to have the highest value. Gold-like gleams the glance of the bestower. Golden brilliance makes peace between moon and sun.

Uncommon is the highest virtue and useless, luminous it is and gentle in its brilliance: a bestowing virtue is the highest virtue.

Verily, I divine you well, my disciples; you strive, like I do, for the bestowing virtue. What would you have in common with cats and wolves?

This is your thirst, to become gifts and offerings yourselves: and therefore you have a thirst to heap up all riches in your soul.

Insatiably your soul strives for treasures and jewels, because your virtue is insatiable in its desire to bestow.

You force all things to you and into you, so that they flow back out of your fountain as gifts of your love.

Verily, a robber of all values such bestowing love must become; but whole and holy I call this selfishness. —

There is another selfishness, an all-too-poor, hungry kind that always wants to steal, — that selfishness of the sick, the sick selfishness.

With the eyes of a thief it looks upon all things brilliant; with hunger's greed it measures him who has plenty to eat; and always it crawls around the table of those who bestow.

Sickness speaks out of such craving, and invisible degeneracy; out of a sick body the thievish greed of this selfishness speaks.

Tell me, my brothers: what do we regard as a bad thing and the worst thing? Is it not degeneracy? — And we always suspect degeneracy when the bestowing soul is lacking.

Our way goes upward, from species to super-species. But we dread the degenerate sense which says: "Everything for me."

Our sense flies upward: thus it is a parable of our body, a parable of enhancement. Such parables of enhancement go by the names of the virtues.

Thus the body goes through history, a becomer and a battler. And the spirit — what is that to the body? The herald of its battles and victories, its comrade and echo.

All the names of good and evil are parables: they do not speak out, they only wink. A fool is he who seeks knowledge from them.

Heed every hour, my brothers, in which your spirit seeks to speak in parables: there is the source of your virtue.

There your body is raised and resurrected; with its delight it enchants the spirit, so that it becomes the creator and evaluator and lover and benefactor of all things.

When your heart flows broad and full like a river, a blessing and a danger to those who border it: there is the source of your virtue.

When you are above praise and blame, and your will wants to command all things, as a lover's will: there is the source of your virtue.

When you despise the pleasant, and the soft bed, and you cannot bed down far enough away from the soft ones: there is the source of your virtue.

When you willers are of one will, and this turnaround in need you treat as necessity: there is the source of your virtue.

Verily, a new good and evil it is! Verily, a new deep roaring and the voice of a new wellspring!

Power it is, this new virtue; a commanding thought it is, and around it, a wise soul: a golden sun, and around it, the serpent of knowledge.

2

Here Zarathustra paused for a while and looked lovingly upon his disciples.

Then he continued to speak thus — and his voice had changed.

Remain true to the earth, my brothers, with the power of your virtue! Let your bestowing love and your knowledge serve the meaning of the earth! Thus I beg and beseech you.

Do not let them fly away from earthly things and beat against eternal walls with their wings! Alas, there has always been so much flown-away virtue!

Lead the flown-away virtue back to earth, as I do — yes, back to life and limb: that it may give the earth its meaning, a human meaning!

A hundred times hitherto has spirit as well as virtue flown away and blundered.

Alas, all this false thinking and blundering dwells in our body to this day:

body and will it has become there.

A hundred times hitherto has spirit as well as virtue tried and erred. Yes, man has been an experiment. Alas, much ignorance and error has become flesh in us!

Not only the reason of millennia — the madness as well breaks out in us.

Dangerous it is to be an heir.

Still we fight step by step with the giant Chance; and nonsense, no-sense, has ruled over the whole of mankind even to this day.

Let your spirit and your virtue serve the meaning of the earth, my brothers:

and let the value of all things be set anew by you! Therefore you shall be fighters!

Therefore you shall be creators!

Through knowing, the body purifies itself; by experimenting with knowledge, the body elevates itself; to those who are in the know all drives sanctify themselves; to those who are elevated the soul becomes elated.

Physician, heal thyself: thus you help your patient, too. Let this be his best help, to see with his own eyes the one who heals himself.

There are a thousand paths that have never yet been trodden, a thousand kinds of health and secret islands of life. Man and man's world is still unexhausted and undiscovered.

Wake up and listen, you loners! From the future come wings with secret wing-beats; and good tidings are proclaimed to fine ears.

You loners of today, you separatists, you shall one day be a people: out of you who have chosen yourselves, a chosen people shall arise: — and out of them, the Superman.

Verily, the earth shall yet come to be a place of recovery! And already there is a new odor around it, one bringing health, — and a new hope!

3

When Zarathustra had said these words, he paused, like one who has not said his last word; for a long while he weighed the staff doubtfully in his hand. At last he spoke thus: and his voice had changed.

Now I go alone, my disciples! You too go away now, and alone! So I will it.

Verily, I advise you: go away from me and protect yourselves against Zarathustra.

And better yet: be ashamed of him! Perhaps he has deceived you.

The man of knowledge must not only love his enemies, he must also be able to hate his friends.

One repays a teacher badly if one always remains only a pupil. And why do you refuse to pluck at my wreath?

You revere me; but what if one day your reverence comes tumbling down?

Beware lest a statue slay you!

You say you believe in Zarathustra? But what does Zarathustra matter?

You are my believers: but what do all believers matter?

You had not yet sought yourselves: then you found me. Thus do all believers; therefore all belief means so little.

Now I bid you lose me and find yourselves; and only when you have all denied me will I return to you.

Verily, with different eyes, my brothers, will I then seek my lost ones; with a different love will I then love you.

And once again you shall be my friends and the children of one hope: then for the third time will I be with you, to celebrate the noontide with you.

And that is the great noontide when man stands in the middle of his path between animal and Superman and celebrates his passage to evening as his highest hope: for it is the way to a new morning.

That is when the one going under will bless himself for being one who is going across; and the sun of his knowledge will stand at noontide.

"Dead are all gods: now we want the Superman to live" — let this be our last will and testament one day, at the great noontide! —

Thus spake Zarathustra.

Part Two

"— and only when you have all denied me will I return to you.

Verily, with different eyes, my brothers, will I then seek my lost ones; with a different love will I then love you."

Zarathustra, On The Bestowing Virtue (Part One)

The Child With The Mirror

Then Zarathustra went back again into the mountains and to the solitude of his cave and avoided men, waiting like a sower who has sown his seed. But his soul became full of impatience and desire for those whom he loved: for he still had much to give them. This, you know, is the hardest thing: to close the open hand out of love, and to preserve one's modesty as a giver.

Thus months and years passed for the solitary one; his wisdom grew, however, and through its plenty caused him pain.

But one morning he awoke even before the rosy dawn, reflected long upon his bed, and said at last to his heart:

"But what frightened me so in my dream that I awoke? Did not a child appear before me, carrying a mirror?

'O Zarathustra' — the child said to me — 'look at yourself in the mirror!'

But when I looked in the mirror, I screamed and my heart was shaken: for I did not see myself there, but a devil's grimace and scornful laughter.

Verily, all too well I understand the dream's sign and warning: my teaching is in danger, tares want to be called wheat!

My enemies have become powerful and have distorted the image of my teaching, so that my dearest ones must blush for shame at the gifts

I have given them.

My friends have been lost to me; the hour has come for me to seek my lost ones!" —

With these words Zarathustra sprang up, not like an anguished man seeking air, but rather like a seer and singer whom the spirit moves. His eagle and his serpent looked upon him in astonishment: for like the rosy dawn an approaching happiness had spread over his countenance.

But what has happened to me, my animals? — said Zarathustra. Am I not transformed? Has blissfulness not come to me like a storm wind?

Foolish is my happiness, and foolishness will it speak: it is still too young — so have patience with it!

I am wounded by my happiness: all who suffer shall be my physicians!

To my friends I can go down again, and to my enemies too! Zarathustra can speak and bestow again, and show love to the dearest again!

My impatient love overflows in torrents, downwards, towards the rising and setting sun. From silent mountains and thunderstorms of pain my soul rushes into the valleys.

Too long have I longed and looked into the distance. Too long have I belonged to solitude: so I have unlearned silence.

Out-and-out mouth have I become, and the surging of a brook out of high rocks: down into the valleys will I plunge my speech.

And may my stream of love plunge into the impassable! How could a stream not find its way to the sea eventually?

Surely there is a lake in me, a solitary, self-contained one; but my stream of love carries it down with it — to the sea!

New ways I go, a new speech comes to me; weary have I become, like all creators, of the old tongues. No longer will my spirit wander on worn-out soles.

Too slowly runs all speech for me: — storm, into your chariot I leap! And even you will I whip with my malice!

Like a cry and a shout for joy will I cross over wide seas, until I find The Blessed Isles, where my friends reside: —

And my enemies among them! How I now love anyone to whom I may simply speak! Even my enemies belong to my blissfulness.

And when I want to mount my wildest horse, it is always my spear that helps me up best: it is my foot's ever-ready servant: —

The spear which I hurl against my enemies! How thankful I am to my enemies for letting me hurl it at last!

The tension of my cloud has been too great: between the lightning's laughter I want to hurl hail showers into the deep.

Violently my breast will heave then, violently will it sound its fury over the mountains: so will its relief come.

Verily, like a storm my happiness comes, and my freedom! But my enemies shall believe that the foul fiend rages over their heads.

Yes, you too will be frightened, my friends, by my wild wisdom; and perhaps you will flee from it, together with my enemies.

Ah, if only I knew how to entice you back with pipes of Pan! Ah, if only my lioness Wisdom would learn to roar tenderly! And many things we have already learned together!

My wild Wisdom became pregnant on lonely mountains; on rough rock she brought forth her young, her youngest.

Now she runs foolishly through the harsh desert and searches and searches for soft turf — my old wild Wisdom!

On your hearts' soft turf, my friends! — on your love she would love to make her beloved's bed! —

Thus spake Zarathustra.

On The Blessed Isles

The figs fall from the trees, they are ripe and sweet; and as they fall their red skin splits open. A north wind am I to ripe figs.

Thus like figs, my friends, these teachings fall to you: now drink in their juice and their sweet flesh! Fall is all around and clear skies and afternoon.

Behold, what fullness is around us! And from out of plenty it is lovely to look out upon distant seas.

Once people said God, when they looked upon distant seas; now, however, I have taught you to say: Superman.

God is a conjecture; but I want your conjectures to reach no further than your creative will.

Could you create a God? — So be quiet then about all gods! But I daresay you could create the Superman.

Perhaps not you yourselves, my brothers! But into fathers and forefathers of the Superman you could re-create yourselves: and may this be your best creation!—

God is a conjecture: but I want your conjectures to be confined to the conceivable.

Could you conceive a God? — But this the will to truth should mean to you, that all things will be transformed into the humanly conceivable, the humanly perceivable, and the humanly perceptible! Your own senses you shall consider to that end!

And that which you have called world shall be re-created by you alone:

your reason, your image, your will, your love it shall itself become! And verily, for your bliss, you knowing ones!

And how would you endure life without this hope, you knowing ones? Neither into the unconceivable nor into the unreasonable could you have been born.

But that I may open my heart entirely to you, my friends: if there were gods, how could I endure it, not to be a god! Therefore there are no Gods.

Well did I draw the conclusion; but now it draws me. —

God is a conjecture: but who could drink in all the agony of this conjecture without dying? Should belief be taken from the creator and soaring at eagle-distances from the eagle?

God is a thought that makes everything straight crooked and everything that stands whirl. What? Should time be gone and all things transitory be but a lie?

To think this is giddiness and dizziness for human limbs, as well as an upchuck for the stomach: verily, the giddy sickness I call it, to conjecture like this.

Evil I call it and misanthropic: all this teaching about the one and the complete and the unmoved and the sufficient and the intransitory!

All the intransitory — that is only a parable! And the poets lie too much! —

But of time and becoming the best parables should speak: they should be a praise and a justification of all transitoriness!

Creation — that is the great salvation from suffering and the lightener of life. But that the creator may come to life, suffering itself is required, and much transformation.

Yes, much bitter dying must be in you life, you creators! Thus you are advocates and justifiers of all transitoriness.

For the creator himself to be the new-born child, he must also be willing to be the mother and the mother's pain.

Verily, through a hundred souls I have gone my way, and through a hundred cradles and birth pangs. Many a farewell I have already taken; I know the heartbreaking last hours.

But my creative will, my fate, wills it so. Or, to say it to you more frankly: just such a fate — my will wills.

All feeling in me suffers and is in prison: but my willing always comes to me as my emancipator and messenger of joy.

Willing sets free: that is the true teaching of will and freedom — thus Zarathustra teaches it to you.

No more willing and no more valuing and no more creating! Oh, may that great weariness always remain far away from me!

In knowing as well I feel only my will's pleasure in begetting and becoming; and if there is innocence in my knowledge, then it is because the will to beget is in it.

Away from God and gods this will has enticed me; what would there be to create then, if gods — were there?

But always it drives me back again to men, my fervent creative will; thus the hammer is driven to the stone.

Alas, you men, an image sleeps in the stone for me, the image of my image!

Alas, that it must sleep in the hardest, homeliest stone!

Now my hammer rages cruelly against its prison. From the stone pieces scatter; what does that matter to me?

I want to complete it; for a shadow came to me — the stillest and lightest of all things once came to me!

The beauty of the Superman came to me as a shadow. Alas, my brothers! Of what regard to me now are — the gods? —

Thus spake Zarathustra.

On The Pitying Ones

My friends, a sarcastic remark has reached your friend: "Just look at Zarathustra!

Does he not wander among us as if among animals?"

But it is better said this way: "The knowing one wanders among men as among animals."

To the knowing one, though, man himself is: the animal that has red cheeks.

How did that happen to man? Is it not because he has had to be ashamed of himself too often?

O my friends! Thus speaks the knowing one: shame, shame, shame — that is the history of man!

And that is why the noble-minded man commands himself not to put to shame: shame he demands of himself before all who suffer.

Verily, I care not for the merciful, who are blessed in their pitying: they are too lacking in shame.

If I must be filled with pity, then I do not want to be called pity-full; and if I am filled with pity it is preferably at a distance.

Preferably too I cover my head and run away before I am recognized: and so I bid you do, my friends!

May my fate always lead those untouched by suffering, like you, across my path, and those with whom I may have hope and meal and honey in common.

Verily, I may have done this and that for those who suffer; but I always seemed to do better when I learned to enjoy myself better.

As long as there have been men, man has enjoyed himself too little: that alone, my brothers, is our original sin!

And when we learn to enjoy ourselves better, then we unlearn best how to cause others pain and contrive pain.

Therefore I wash the hand that has helped the sufferer; therefore I wipe clean my soul, also.

For to have seen the sufferer suffering made me ashamed on account of his shame; and when I helped him, I came down hard on his pride.

Great obligations do not make us grateful but vengeful; and if a small favor is not forgotten it gets to be a gnawing worm.

"Be reserved in accepting! Distinguish by accepting!" — Thus I advise those who have nothing to give away.

I, however, am a giver: gladly I give, as a friend to friends. Strangers and paupers, however, may pluck the fruit themselves from my tree: there is less shame that way.

But beggars should be abolished entirely! Verily, it is annoying to give to them and annoying not to give to them.

And the same goes for sinners and bad consciences! Believe me, my friends: the bite of conscience teaches biting.

Small thoughts, however, are the worst thing. Verily, better even to have wrought evil than to have thought small!

True you say: "The delight in little acts of spite spares us from many a big bad deed." But here one should not want to be spared.

Like a boil is the evil deed: it itches and scratches and breaks out, — it speaks honestly.

"Behold, I am sickness" — thus speaks the evil deed; that is its honesty.

But the small thought is like a fungus: it crawls and cowers and wants to be nowhere at all — until the whole body is rotten and withered with little fungi.

But to him who is possessed by a devil, I whisper this word in his ear: "Better for you still to rear your devil! Even for you there is still a way to greatness!"—

Alas, my brothers! One knows a little too much about everyone! And many a man becomes transparent to us, but we are still far from being able to penetrate him through and through.

It is hard to live with men because keeping silent is so hard. And not towards him who is contrary to us are we most unjust, but towards him who means nothing at all to us.

But if you have a suffering friend, then be a resting place for his suffering, but a hard bed as it were, a field bed: thus you will serve him best.

And if a friend does you ill, then say: "I forgive you for what you did to me; but that you did it to yourself, — how could I forgive that?"

Thus speaks all great love: it overcomes even forgiveness and pity. A person should hold fast to his heart; for once he lets it go, how soon he loses his head!

Alas, where in the world have there been greater follies than among the pitying ones? And what in the world has caused more suffering than the follies of the pitying ones?

Woe unto all lovers who do not yet have a height that is above their pity!

Thus spoke the devil to me once: "Even God has his hell: it is his love for man."

And lately I heard him say this word: "God is dead; God has died of his pity for man." —

So be warned against pity: from there a heavy cloud shall yet come to man!

Verily, I understand weather signs.

But mark this word as well: all great love is above pity, for the beloved it still wants to — create!

"Myself I offer up to my love, and my neighbor as myself" — the speech of all creators runs thus.

All creators, however, are hard. —

Thus spake Zarathustra.

On Priests

And one day Zarathustra gave his disciples a sign and said these words to them: "Here are priests: and although they are my enemies, pass by them quietly and with sleeping swords!

Even among them there are heroes; many of them have suffered too much: so they want to make others suffer.

They are bad enemies: nothing is more vengeful than their humility. And he who touches them is easily defiled.

But my blood is related to theirs: and I want to know that my blood is honored even in theirs." —

And when they had passed by, Zarathustra was seized with pain; and not long had he wrestled with his pain when he began to speak thus:

I pity these priests. They offend my taste, too; but that is the least thing to me, since I am among men.

But I suffer and have suffered with them; to me they are prisoners and marked men. He whom they call Savior has put them in fetters. —

In fetters of false values and fanciful words! Ah, if only someone could save them from their Savior!

Once as the sea tossed them about they thought they had landed on an island; but behold, it was a sleeping monster!

False values and fanciful words: they are the worst monsters for mortals, —fate sleeps long in them and waits.

But at last it comes and watches and gulps and engulfs what has built huts upon it.

O, just look at the huts these priests have built! Churches they call their sweetly-scented dens!

O, that falsified light, that mustified air! Here, where up to its height the soul — cannot fly!

But thus their belief commands: "Up the stairs on your knees, ye sinners!"

Verily, even the shameless I would rather see than the distorted eyes of their shame and devotion!

Who created for themselves such dens and penitence-stairs? Was it not those who wanted to hide themselves and were ashamed before the clear sky?

And only when the clear sky looks again through shattered roofs and down again upon grass and red poppies by shattered walls, — will I again turn my heart toward the dwellings of this God.

That which contradicted them and caused them pain they called God: and verily, there was much heroic character in their worship!

And they knew no other way to love their God than to nail men to the cross!

As corpses they thought to live, in black they draped their corpses; even in their speech I still smell the foul odor of burial chambers.

And he who lives near them lives near black pools out of which the toad, that prophet of evil, sings his song of sweet melancholy.

Better songs they would have to sing for me to learn to believe in their Redeemer: more redeemed his disciples would have to look for me!

Naked I would like to see them: for beauty alone should preach penitence.

But whom could this muffled misery persuade?

Verily, their redeemers themselves did not come from freedom and freedom's seventh heaven! Verily, they themselves never trod upon the carpets of knowledge!

The spirit of these redeemers consisted of gaps; but into each gap they had placed their false idea, their stopgap, which they called God.

Their spirit was drowned in their pity, and when they were swollen and over-swollen with pity, a great folly always swam on top.

Eagerly and with great noise they drove their herd over their footbridge; as if there were but one footbridge to the future! Verily, these shepherds themselves still belonged to the sheep!

Small spirits and spacious souls these shepherds had: but, my brothers, what small countries even the most spacious souls have been so far!

Signs of blood they wrote on the path they took, and their folly taught that truth is proved by blood.

But blood is the worst witness of truth; blood poisons even the purest teaching and turns it into delusion and hatred of the heart.

And if someone goes through fire for his teaching, — what does that prove?

Verily, it means more when out of your own fire your own teaching comes!

Sultry heart and cold head: where these two meet there arises the hothead, the "Savior."

Greater ones there have been, verily, and higher-born ones, than those whom the people call Saviors, those enchanted hotheads!

And by ones greater yet than all Saviors have been must you, my brothers, be saved, if you would find the way to freedom!

Never yet has there been a Superman. Naked have I seen them both, the greatest and the smallest man:

They are still all-too-similar to each other. Verily, even the greatest man I found — all-too-human! —

Thus spake Zarathustra.

On The Virtuous

With thunder and heavenly fireworks must one speak to slack and sleeping senses.

But the voice of beauty speaks softly: it steals only into the most awakened souls.

Softly my shield trembled and laughed today; that is the holy laughter and trembling of beauty.

At you, you virtuous ones, my beauty laughed today. And her voice came to me in this way: "They want as well — to be paid!"

You want to be paid as well, you virtuous ones! You want a reward for virtue and heaven for earth and evermore for your today?

And now you are angry with me because I teach that there is no rewarder and paymaster? And verily, I do not even teach that virtue is its own reward.

Alas, that is my sorrow: reward and penalty have been laid into the ground of things — and now even into the ground of your souls, you virtuous ones!

But like a boar's snout my word shall tear up the ground of your soul; a plowshare I shall be called by you.

All the secrets of your soil shall come to light; and when you lie uprooted and split asunder in the sun, your falsehood will be separated from your truth.

For this is your truth: you are too pure for the filth of the words: revenge, penalty, reward, recompense.

You love your virtue as a mother does her child; but when have you ever heard of a mother who wanted to be paid for her love?

It is the dearest thing itself to you, your virtue. The thirst of the ring is in you: to attain itself again, that is why every ring struggles and gyrates.

And like the dying star is every work of your virtue: its light is still ever on the way and traveling — and when will it no longer be on the way?

Thus the light of your virtue is still on the way, even when the work is done. Though it now be dead and forgotten: its ray of light still lives and travels.

That your virtue is your very self and not a foreign thing, a skin, a covering: that is the truth from the bottom of your souls, you virtuous ones! —

But certainly there are those to whom virtue is the spasm under the lash: and you have hearkened too much to their cries!

And there are others who call virtue the idle-izing of their vices; and if for once their hatred and jealousy stretch out their limbs for a rest, their "justice" becomes lively and rubs its sleepy eyes.

And there are others who are drawn downwards: their demons draw them down. But the more they sink, the more glowingly gleams their eye and the desire for their God.

Alas, their cries have pierced your ears, too, you virtuous ones: "That which is not me, that to me is God and virtue!"

And there are others who come along, heavy and creaking, like carts carrying rocks downhill: they speak much of dignity and virtue, — their brakeshoe they call virtue!

And there are others who are like workaday clocks that have been wound up; they tick and they tock and want their ticktock to be called — virtue!

Verily, with these I have my fun: whenever I find such clocks, I wind them up with my mockery; and thereby they must purr for me!

And others are proud of their handful of justice and desecrate all things for its sake: thus the world is drowned in their injustice.

Alas, how amiss the word "virtue" issues from their mouths! And when they say: "I am just," it always sounds like: "I am just — revenged!"

With their virtue they want to scratch out the eyes of their enemies;

and they elevate themselves only in order to denigrate others.

And again there are those who sit in their swamp and speak out from among the reeds: "Virtue — that is sitting still in the swamp.

We bite no one and avoid him who wants to bite; and in all things we have the opinion that is given us."

And again there are those who love gestures and think: virtue is a sort of gesture.

Their knees perpetually adore and their hands are eulogies to virtue, but their hearts know nothing about it.

And again there are those who hold it a virtue to say: "Virtue is necessary"; but deep down they only believe that the police are necessary.

And many a man who cannot see the sublime in man calls it virtue to see his baseness all-too-closely: thus he calls his evil eye virtue.

And some want to be built up and straightened up and call it virtue; and others want to be thrown down — and that too they call virtue.

And so nearly everyone believes he has his share of virtue; and at the very least each one expects to be an expert on good and evil.

But Zarathustra did not come to say all these liars and fools: "What do you know of virtue? What could you know of virtue?" —

But that you, my friends, might become weary of the old words you have learned from the fools and the liars:

Become weary of the words "reward," "recompense," "penalty," "just revenge" —

Become weary of saying: "That an action is good is because it is selfless."

Alas, my friends! That your self may be in your action, as the mother is in the child: let that be your word of virtue!

Verily, I daresay I have taken away from you a hundred sayings and your virtues' dearest playthings; and now you are angry with me, the way children get angry.

They were playing by the sea, — then a wave came and swept their playthings into the deep: now they weep.

But the same wave shall bring them new playthings and pour out new colorful shells before them!

So they will be consoled; and like them, my friends, you too shall have your consolation — and new colorful shells! —

Thus spake Zarathustra.

On The Rabble

Life is a fountain of delight, but where the rabble also drinks all wells are poisoned.

To all things clean I am well-disposed; but I do not care to see the grinning mouths and the thirst of the unclean.

They cast their eye down into the well: now their nasty smile gleams out of the well upon me.

They have poisoned the holy water with their lechery; and when they called their filthy dreams pleasure, they also poisoned the words.

The flame is put off when they put their damp hearts to the fire; the spirit itself seethes and smokes when the rabble approaches the fire.

Sickly sweet and overmellow the fruit grows in their hand: their glance makes the fruit tree withered at the top and about to topple in the wind.

And many a man who turned away from life only turned way from the rabble: he refused to share fruit and flame and fountain with the rabble.

And many a man who went into the desert and suffered thirst with beasts of prey only refused to sit around the cistern with filthy camel drivers.

And many a man who came along like an annihilator and like a hailstorm to all fruited plains wanted plain and simple to jam his foot down the rabble's throat and stuff its mouth.

And that is not the mouthful which stuck in my throat the most, to know that life itself requires enmity and dying and torture-crosses: —

But I once asked and almost choked on the question: what? does life also find rabble necessary?

Are poisoned wells necessary and stinking fires and sullied dreams and maggots in the bread of life?

Not my hatred but my nausea gnawed hungrily at my life! Alas, I grew weary in spirit when I found even the rabble spirited!

And I turned my back on the ruling class when I saw what they call ruling:

bartering and bargaining for power — with the rabble!

Among men of a foreign tongue I lived, with stopped-up ears: that their bartering tongue might remain foreign to me and their bargaining for power.

And holding my nose, I walked morosely through all yesterday and today: verily, all yesterday and today reeks from the writing rabble!

Like a cripple who has gone deaf and dumb and blind: thus I lived a long time, so as not to live with power- and pleasure- and writing rabble.

Laboriously my spirit climbed the stairs, and warily; alms of delight were its refreshment; life crawled along on a walking stick for the blind.

But what happened to me? How did I free myself from nausea? Who rejuvenated my sight? How did I fly to the height where rabble no longer sit at the well? Did my nausea itself create wings for me and spring-divining powers? Verily, to the summit I had to fly to find again the fountain of delight!

Oh, I found it, my brothers! Here at the summit the fountain of delight gushes forth for me! And it is a life in which no rabble can join in and drink!

Almost too furiously you flow for me, spring of delight! And often in wanting to fill it you empty the cup again!

And I must still learn to approach you more demurely: all-too-furiously my heart still flows toward you: —

My heart, upon which my summer burns, short, hot, melancholy, overhappy: how my summer heart yearns for your coolness!

Gone; the lingering misery of my spring! Gone, the malice of my snowflakes in June! Summer have I become entirely, and summer-noon!

A summer at the summit with cold springs and blissful stillness: O come, my friends, that the stillness may be more blissful still!

For this is our height and our home: here we live too high and steep for the unclean and their thirst!

You friends, just cast your pure eyes into the fountain of my delight! How could it be troubled over that? It shall laugh back at you with its purity.

On the tree Future we build our nest; eagles shall bring us loners food in their beaks!

Verily, no food which the unclean could join in and eat! They would think they were feeding on fire and would burn their mouths!

Verily, no homesteads do we keep ready here for the unclean! An ice-lair our happiness would be to their bodies and to their spirits!

And like strong winds we want to live above them, neighbors to eagles, neighbors to snow, neighbors to the sun: thus do strong winds live.

And like a wind I will one day yet blow among them and take away the breath of their spirit with my spirit: thus my future wills it.

Verily, a strong wind is Zarathustra to all the lower ranks; and with such counsel he counsels his foes and all those who spit and spew: "Beware of spitting against the wind!" —

Thus spake Zarathustra.

On The Tarantulas

Behold, it is the tarantula hole! Do you want to see the tarantula itself? Here hangs its web: touch it, so that it begins to tremble.

Here it comes willingly: welcome, tarantula! Black on your back sits your triangle and token; and I know also what sits in your soul.

Vengeance sits in your soul: wherever you bite, a black scab grows; your venom makes the soul giddy with vengeance!

Thus I speak to you in parable, you who make souls giddy, you preachers of equality! Tarantulas you are to me and hidden seekers of vengeance!

But I will yet bring your hideaways to light: that is why I laugh my laughter of the heights in your face.

That is why I tear at your web, that your fury may lure you out of your hole of lies and your vengeance may jump out from behind your word "justice."

For that man be redeemed from revenge: that to me is the bridge to the highest hope and a rainbow after long storms.

But the tarantulas would have it otherwise, of course. "Precisely this we call justice, that the world be fraught with the storms of our vengeance" — thus they speak to one another.

"Vengeance and insult we shall wreak on all who are not our equals" —thus the tarantula-hearts pledge to themselves.

"And 'will to equality' — henceforth that itself shall be the name for virtue; and against all things with power we will set up a howl!"

You preachers of equality, the tyrant-frenzy of impotence cries out of you thus for "equality": your most secret tyrant-desires disguise themselves thus in words of virtue!

Careworn arrogance, pent-up envy — your father's arrogance and envy perhaps:

that breaks out in you as the flame and frenzy of revenge.

What was mute in the father comes to speech in the son; and often I found the son to be the father's secret laid bare.

Inspired ones they resemble: and yet it is not the heart which inspires them, — but revenge. And when they become subtle and cold, it is not spirit but envy which makes them subtle and cold.

Their envy leads them also down the thinker's path; and this is the mark of their envy — they always go too far: so that at last their weariness has to lay down to sleep on the snow.

Vengeance sounds in their every complaint, there is painmaking in all their praisemaking; and to be judge they judge to be bliss.

But thus I advise you, my friends: mistrust all in whom the impulse to punish is powerful!

They are people of poor kind and breed; out of their faces peer the hangman and the bloodhound.

Mistrust all those who talk much of their justice! Verily, their souls lack not only honey.

And when they call themselves "the good and the just," do not forget that for them to be Pharisees nothing is lacking except — power!

My friends, I will not be confounded and confused with anyone else.

There are those who preach my doctrine: and at the same time they are preachers of equality and tarantulas.

That they speak in favor of life, although they sit in their holes turned away from life, these venomous spiders: this is because they want to cause pain.

They want to cause pain to those now in power: for it is with these that the preaching of death is still most at home.

If it were otherwise, the tarantulas would teach otherwise; and precisely they were formerly the best world-slanderers and heretic-burners.

With these preachers of equality I will not be confounded and confused.

For thus justice speaks to me: "Men are not equal."

And they shall not become so either! What would my love for the Superman be if I spoke otherwise?

On a thousand bridges and foot-paths they shall push towards the future, and more and more war and inequality shall be set amongst them: thus my great love makes me speak!

In their hostilities they shall become inventors of figures and phantoms, and with their figures and phantoms they shall yet fight the highest fight against each other!

Good and evil and rich and poor and high and low and all the names of values:

arms they shall be, and clashing signs, that life must overcome itself time after time!

Upward it wants to build itself with pillars and stairs, this very life: into vast distances it wants to look and out toward blissful areas of beauty, — that is why it requires height!

And because it requires height, it requires stairs and variance amongst climbers and stairs! Life wants to climb and in climbing to overcome itself!

And just look, my friends! Here where the tarantula's hole is, the ruins of an old temple rise upward, — just look with enlightened eyes!

Verily, like the wisest of men, he who once piled his thoughts upward in stone here knew the secret of all life.

That in beauty too there is struggle and inequality, and a war for power and superiority: that he teaches us here in the clearest allegory.

How divinely vault and arch are refracted here in a wrestling match: how with light and shade they strive against each other, the strivers divine —

Let us also be enemies so sure and fine, my friends! Divinely we will strive against each other! —

Woe! Then my old enemy, the tarantula, bit me! Divinely sure and fine it bit me on the finger!

"Punishment and justice there must be" — thus it thinks: "not for nothing shall he sing songs here in honor of hostility!"

Indeed, it has revenged itself! And woe! now it will make my soul giddy with vengeance also!

But so I do not whirl, my friends, bind me fast here to this pillar! I would still rather be a pillar-saint than a whirl of vengefulness!

Verily, no twirl- and whirlwind is Zarathustra; and if he is a dancer, certainly never a tarantella dancer! —

Thus spake Zarathustra.

On The Famous Wise Men

The people you have served and the people's superstition, all you famous wise men! — and not the truth! And that is precisely why they paid you reverence.

And that is also why they put up with your impiety, because to the people it was a joke and a by-way. Thus the master indulges his slaves and even takes delight in their high jinks.

But he who is hated by the people is as a wolf to the dogs: that is the free spirit, the foe of fetters, the non-adorer, the forest dweller.

To chase him from his lair — the people always called that "a sense of propriety": against him they always set their sharpest-toothed dogs.

For "the truth is there: so there the people are! Woe, woe to those who seek!": thus it has resounded down the ages. You wanted to do right by the people in their veneration: you called that: "Will to truth," you famous wise men!

And your heart always said to itself: "I have come from the people: from there as well the voice of God has come to me."

Stiff-necked and clever, like the ass, were you ever as the people's advocate.

And many a mighty one who wanted to fare well with the people also harnessed in front of his charger — a little ass, a famous wise man.

And now I wish that you, you famous wise men, would finally throw off entirely your lion's skin!

The skin of the beast of prey, the mottled one, and the shaggy locks of the searching, researching, conquering one!

Alas, for me to learn to believe in your "truthfulness" you would first have to shatter your revering will.

Truthful — thus I call him who goes into godless deserts and has his revering heart shattered.

In the yellow sands and burned by the sun, he squints thirstily indeed for spring-abounding islands, where living things rest under dark trees.

But his thirst does not persuade him to become like these which are at ease; for where there are oases, there are also idols.

Hungry, violent, solitary, godless: thus the lion-will wills itself.

Free from the happiness of slaves, freed from gods and adoration, fearless and fearsome, great and solitary: such is the will of the truthful.

From time immemorial the truthful, the free spirits, have dwelt in the desert, as lords of the desert; in the cities, however, dwell the well-fed famous wise men, — the draft animals.

For they always draw, as asses — the people's cart!

Not that I am angry with them over that: but to me they remain in service and in harness, even when they glitter with golden trappings.

And they have often been good servants and praiseworthy. For thus speaks virtue: "If you must be a servant, then seek him whom your service best serves!

The spirit and the virtue of your master shall grow by virtue of your being his servant: so you yourself shall grow with his spirit and virtue!"

And verily, you famous wise men, you servants of the people! You yourselves have grown with the people's spirit and virtue — and the people through you! In your honor I say that!

But people you remain to me, even in your virtues, people with feeble eyes, — people who cannot shake a spear at spirit!

Spirit is the life which itself cuts into life: with its own agony it increases its own knowledge, — did you know that already?

And the spirit's happiness is this: to be anointed and consecrated with tears as a sacrificial animal, — did you know that already?

And the blind man's blindness and his searching and groping shall yet testify to the power of the sun into which he has looked, — did you know that already?

And with mountains the knowing one shall learn to build! That the spirit moves mountains means little, — did you know that already?

You know only the spirit's sparks: but you do not see the anvil that it is and the cruelty of its hammer!

Verily, you know not the pride of the spirit! But still less could you endure the modesty of the spirit if ever it wanted to speak!

And never yet have you dared to cast your spirit into a pit of snow: you are not hot enough for that! So you also do not know the delights of its cold.

But in all things you are too familiar with the spirit; and you have often made a poorhouse and a hospital for bad poets out of wisdom.

You are not eagles: so you have also never experienced the happiness of the terror of the spirit. And he who is not a bird should not nest above abysses.

Lukewarm ones you seem to me: but all deep knowledge flows cold. Icecold are the innermost springs of the spirit: a refreshment for hot hands and handlers.

Stiff and honorable you stand there, and with backs straight, you famous wise men! — no strong wind and will drives you.

Have you never seen a sail going across the sea, rounded and distended and trembling from the violence of the wind?

Like a sail, trembling from the violence of the wind, my Wisdom goes across the sea — my wild Wisdom!

But you servants of the people, you famous wise men, — how could you go with me? —

Thus spake Zarathustra.

The Night Song

It is night: now all gushing fountains speak louder. And my soul too is a gushing fountain.

It is night: only now do all lovers' songs awake. And my soul too is the song of a lover.

Something unappeased, unappeasable is within me; it wants to be heard. A craving for love is within me which itself speaks the language of love.

Light am I: ah, to be night! But this is my loneliness, to be girded with light.

Ah, to be dark and nightly! How I would suck on the breasts of the light!

And even you would I bless, you twinkling little stars and glowworms up above! — and be blessed by your gifts of light.

But I live in my own light, I take back into me the flames that break out of me.

I know not the happiness of the receiver; and often have I dreamed that stealing must be even more blessed than receiving.

This is my poverty, that my hand never rests from giving; this is my envy, that I see waiting eyes and the illuminated nights of longing.

O, the unhappiness of all givers! O, eclipse of my sun! O, craving to crave! O, ravenous appetite in satiety!

They take from me: but do I ever touch their souls? There is a cleft between giving and receiving; and the smallest cleft is the last to be spanned.

A hunger grows out of my beauty: I would like to hurt those for whom I shine, I would like to rob those whose gifts were mine: thus I hunger after malice.

Drawing back the hand when a hand is already stretched out for it; hesitating like the waterfall, which hesitates even in its sudden plunge: thus I hunger after malice.

Such vengeance my abundance thinks up: such maliciousness wells up out of my loneliness. My happiness in giving died in giving, my virtue grew weary of itself by virtue of its excess!

The danger for him who always gives is that he will lose his shame; the hand and heart of him who always dispenses has calluses from nothing but dispensing.

My eye no longer overflows over the shame of the supplicant; my hand has grown too hard for the trembling of filled hands.

Where have the tears in my eyes gone, and the bloom in my heart? O, the loneliness of all givers! O, the quietness of all light-givers!

Many suns revolve in desolate space: to all that is dark they speak with their light, — to me they are silent.

O, this is the light's enmity toward the giver of light: mercilessly it travels its course. Unjust toward the giver of light in its heart of hearts, cold toward other suns — thus every sun travels.

Like a storm the suns fly along their course, that is their travel. Their inexorable will they follow, that is their coldness.

Oh, it is only you, you dark ones, you nocturnal ones, who create your warmth from the giver of light! Oh, only you drink milk and comfort from the udders of the light!

Alas, ice is around me, my hand burns itself on the icy! Alas, a thirst is in me that yearns for your thirst!

It is night: alas that I must be light! And have a thirst for the nightly! And loneliness!

It is night: now my longing bursts out of me like a fountain, — for speech I long. It is night: now all gushing fountains speak louder. And my soul too is a gushing fountain.

It is night: only now do all lovers' songs awake. And my soul too is the song of a lover. —

Thus sang Zarathustra.

The Dance Song

One evening Zarathustra went with his disciples through the forest; and as he searched for a well, behold, he came upon a green meadow, quietly surrounded by trees and herbs: upon it maidens were dancing with each other. As soon as the maidens recognized Zarathustra, they stopped dancing; but Zarathustra stepped up to them with a friendly air and said these words:

"Don't stop dancing, you lovely maidens! No killjoy has come to give you the evil eye, no maiden-foe.

God's advocate am I before the devil; he, however, is the spirit of gravity.

How could I, you light things, be a foe of divine dancing? Or of maiden feet with beautiful ankles?

To be sure I am a forest and a night of dark trees: but he who is not afraid of my darkness will also find slopes of roses under my cypresses.

And he will also probably find the little god who is dearest to the maidens: near the spring he lies, quietly, with closed eyes.

Verily, in broad daylight he fell asleep, the lazybones! Maybe he chased too long after butterflies?

Do not be angry with me, you beautiful dancers, if I scold the little god a little!

He will cry out, no doubt, and weep, — but he is a scream even when he weeps!

And with tears in his eyes he shall ask you for a dance; and I myself will sing a song to accompany his dance:

A dancing and mocking song on the spirit of gravity, my all-supreme most high and mighty devil, who is said to be "the master of the world." – And this is the song that Zarathustra sang when Cupid and the maidens danced together:

Into your eyes I looked lately, O Life! And into the unfathomable I then seemed to sink.

But you pulled me out with a golden fishing rod; scornfully you laughed when I called you unfathomable.

"Such is the speech of all fish," you said; "what they cannot fathom is unfathomable.

But I am only fickle and wild and in all things a woman, and not a virtuous one either:

Although you men call me 'the deep one' or 'the true one,' 'the eternal one,' 'the mysterious one'!

But you men always present us with your own virtues — ah, you virtuous men!"

Thus she laughed, the unbelievable one; but I never believe her and her laughter when she speaks ill of herself.

And as I talked confidentially with my wild Wisdom, she said to me angrily: "You want, you crave, you love, that alone is why you praise Life!"

Then I almost answered maliciously and told the angry one the truth; and you cannot answer more maliciously than to "tell the truth" to your Wisdom.

So that is how it stands amongst the three of us. Deep down I love only Life — and most of all, verily, when I hate her!

But that I am well-disposed towards Wisdom and often too well: that is because she reminds me so very much of Life!

She has her eyes, her laugh, and her little golden fishing rod: what can I do if they are both so alike?

And when Life asked me once: "Who then is this Wisdom?" — I said warmly, "Ah, yes! Wisdom!

One thirsts for her and is never satisfied, one looks through veils, one snatches through nets.

Is she beautiful? How should I know? But the oldest carp are still lured by her.

Fickle is she and defiant; often have I seen her bite her lip and comb her hair against the grain.

Perhaps she is wicked and false and in all things a female; but when she speaks badly of herself, precisely then she is most alluring."

When I said this to Life, she laughed spitefully and closed her eyes. "Of whom do you speak?" she said, "Of me, I presume?

And granted that you were right, — to say it to my face like that! But now at least speak of your Wisdom too!"

Ah, and now you have opened your eyes again, O beloved Life! And into the unfathomable have I again seemed to sink. – Thus sang Zarathustra. But when the dance was over and the maidens had gone away, he became sad.

"The sun has long since set," he said at last. "The meadow is damp, a coolness comes this way from the woods.

An unknown presence is around me and looks on pensively. What! You still live, Zarathustra?

Why? Wherefore? Whereby? Whereto? Where? How?

Is it not folly to still live?

Alas, my friends, it is the evening which inquires of me so. Forgive me my sadness!

Evening has come: forgive me that evening has come!"

Thus spake Zarathustra.

The Grave Song

"There is the grave-isle, the silent isle; there too are the graves of my youth.

I will carry an evergreen wreath of life there."

Resolving thus in my heart, I sailed across the sea. —

O, you sights and visions of my youth! O, all you glimpses of love, you divine moments! How did you die so quickly on me? I think of you today as my dead.

From you, my dearest departed, a sweet scent comes to me, heart-loosening and tear-inducing. Verily, it shakes and loosens the heart of the lonely seafarer.

Still I am the one who is richest and most to be envied — I the loneliest one!

For I have had you and you still have me: tell me, to whom, like me, have such rose-apples fallen from the tree?

I am still the earth and heir of your love, flourishing in your memory with many-hued, wild-growing virtues, O you most-beloved ones!

O, we were made to remain close to each other, you sweet strange wonders; and not like shy birds did you come to me and my desire — no, as trusting ones to the trusting one!

Yes, made for fidelity, like me, and for tender eternities: now I must call you out on your infidelity, your divine winks and blinks: no other names have I learned yet.

Verily, too quickly you died on me, you refugees. But you did not flee from me, nor did I flee from you: innocent are we in our infidelity to each other.

To kill me they strangled you, you songbirds of my hopes! Yes, at you, you dearest ones, malice has always shot its arrows — to hit my heart!

And they hit home! But you were always dearest to me, my possession and my being-possessed: therefore you had to die young and all-too-early!

They shot their shafts at the most vulnerable spot I had: that was you, whose skin is like down and even more like the smile that perishes at a glance!

But this word I want to say to my enemies: what is all manslaughtering compared with what you did to me?

What you did to me is worse than all manslaughter; the irretrievable you took from me: — thus I speak to you, my enemies!

Why, you slew the sights and dearest wonders of my youth! My playmates you took from me, the blessed spirits! In their memory I lay down this wreath and this curse.

This curse upon you, my enemies! For surely you cut short my eternity, like a sound that breaks off on a cold night! It hardly came to me, like the blink of a divine eye, — like a wink!

Once upon a pleasant hour my purity spoke thus: "All living things shall be divine to me."

Then you attacked me with filthy phantoms; alas, where has that pleasant hour now flown?

"All days shall be holy to me " — thus the wisdom of my youth spoke once upon a time: verily, a speech of joyful wisdom!

But then you enemies stole my nights from me and sold them into sleepless agony: alas, where has that joyful wisdom now flown?

Once I longed for happy bird-signs; then you led an owl-monster across my path, an adverse sign. Alas, where did my tender longing fly then?

Once I vowed to renounce all disgust: then you changed my near and nearest into abscessed pus. Alas, where did my noblest vow fly then?

As a blind man I once walked blessed paths: then you threw filth on the blind man's path: and now the old blind-footpath disgusts him.

And when I did the hardest thing and celebrated the victory of my overcomings:

then you made those who loved me cry that I had caused them the most woe.

Verily, that was always your doing: you embittered for me my best honey and the industry of my best bees. To my generosity you always sent the freshest beggars; around my pity you always pressed the incurably shameless. Thus you wounded my virtue in its faith.

And when I laid down even my holiest of offerings: at once your "piety" placed its fatter gifts beside it: so that in the fumes of your fat even my holiest offering suffocated.

And once I wanted to dance as I had never yet danced; way up above all the heavens I wanted to dance. Then you won over my favorite minstrel.

And then he struck up a dreadful, dull tune; alas, like a gloomy horn he tooted in my ears.

Murderous minstrel, instrument of malice, most innocent man! There I stood, ready for the best dance: then you murdered my rapture with your rat-atat- tat!

Only in the dance do I know how to speak the parable of the highest things:— and now my highest parable has remained unspoken in my limbs!

My highest hope has remained unspoken and unredeemed! And it has killed for me all the visions and consolations of my youth!

But just how did I endure it? How did I recover from and overcome such wounds? How did my soul rise again from these graves?

Well, an invulnerable, unburiable thing is in me, a rockblaster: it is called my will. Silently it strides and unaltered through the years.

Its walk it wants to walk, upon my feet, my old will; hard of heart its mentality is and invulnerable.

Invulnerable am I only in the heel. Ever have you dwelt there, the same as ever, most patient one! Ever have you broken through all graves!

In you still dwells the unredeemed what-not of my youth; and as life and youth you sit here hoping on yellow grave-ruins.

Yes, to me you are still the one who lays all graves to ruin: Hail to you, my will! And only where there are graves are there resurrections. —

Thus sang Zarathustra.

On Self-Overcoming

"Will to truth" you call it, you wisest ones, that which drives you and makes you feel alive?

Will to the conceivability of all beings: thus I call your will!

All being you want to first make conceivable: for you doubt with a healthy mistrust whether it is even conceivable.

But it shall bow and bend itself to you! Thus your will wills it. Smooth it shall become and subject to the spirit as its mirror and reflection.

That is your whole will, you wisest ones, as a will to power; and likewise when you speak of good and evil and evaluations.

You still want to create a world before which you can kneel: thus it is your ultimate hope and intoxication.

The unwise, I admit, the people, — they are like a river upon which a boat floats along: and on the boat sit the evaluations, solemn and disguised.

Your will and your values you have placed on the river of becoming; to me it betrays an ancient will to power which was believed by the people to be good and evil.

It was you, you wisest ones, who placed such guests on this boat and lent them pomp and proud names, — you and your ruling will!

Further the river now carries your boat; it must carry it. It matters little whether the broken wave foams and angrily opposes the keel!

The river is not your danger nor the end of your good and evil, you wisest ones: but that will itself, the will to power, — the unexhausted, teeming lifewill.

But in order that you may understand my word about good and evil, I also want to say a word about life and the nature of all things living.

After the living thing I went, down the greatest and the least of paths I went in order to discern its nature.

With a hundredfold mirror I even caught its glance when its mouth was closed: that its eye might speak to me. And its eye spoke to me.

But wherever I found living things, there I also heard the speech on obedience.

Every living thing is obedient.

And this is the second thing: whatever cannot obey itself will be commanded.

Such is the nature of living things.

But this is the third thing I heard: that commanding is harder than obeying.

And not only because whatever commands bears the burden of all that obeys and that this burden can easily crush it: —

Trial and risk there seemed to me to be in all commanding; and whenever it commands, the living thing runs a risk.

Yes, even when it commands itself: even then it must make amends for its commands. Judge and avenger and victim of its own law it must become.

But how does this come to pass? — thus I asked myself. What persuades the living thing to obey and command and even in commanding to practice obedience?

Now hear my word, you wisest ones! Test seriously whether I have stolen into the heart of life itself and right down to the roots of its heart!

Wherever I found a living thing, there I found the will to power; and even in the will of the servant I found the will to be master.

Persuaded by his will that the weaker should serve the stronger, he wants to be master over those weaker still; this pleasure alone he will not forego.

And as the lesser surrenders itself to the greater, to have pleasure and power over the least: so too the greatest surrenders itself and for the sake of power stakes — life thereon.

This is the surrender of the greatest, to be risk and danger and a roll of the dice with regard to death.

And where sacrifice and service and amorous looks exist: there too the will to be master exists. On secret paths the weaker steals into the stronghold of the stronger and right into the heart of the more powerful — and there steals power.

And this secret life itself told me: "Behold," it said, "I am that which must always overcome itself.

Of course you call it will to procreation or impetus toward a goal, toward the higher, the further, the more manifold: but all that is one and one secret.

I would rather go to my downfall than to renounce this one thing; and verily, where there is downfall and leaves falling down, behold, there life sacrifices itself — for power!

That I must be struggle and becoming and goal and going against goals: alas, whoever divines my will can also divine well on what crooked paths it must travel.

Whatever I create and however I love it, — soon I must be an adversary to it and to my love: thus my will wills it.

And even you, knowing one, are only a path and footstep of my will: verily, my will to power wanders even on the feet of your will to truth!

He certainly did not hit the truth, he who shot at it with the term "will to existence": that will — does not exist!

For what does not exist cannot will; what is in existence, however, how could that still have a will into existence?

Only where there is life is there also will: not will to life, however; but — so I teach you — will to power!

Many things are valued more highly by the living than life itself; out of the valuing itself, however, speaks — the will to power!"

Thus life taught me once: and out of this I shall yet solve the riddle of your hearts, you wisest ones.

Verily, I say unto you: a good and evil that would be everlasting — that does not exist! Of itself it must overcome itself again and again.

With your values and words of good and evil you exercise your power, you evaluators; and this is your secret love and the glistening, trembling, and overflowing of your souls.

But a stronger power springs up out of your values, and a new overcoming: egg and eggshell is shattered on it.

And he who must be a creator in good and evil: verily, he must first be a destroyer and shatter values.

Thus the highest evil belongs to the highest good: that, however, is the creative.—

Let's just talk about this, you wisest ones, although it is bad. Silence is worse; all suppressed truths become poisonous.

And may all be shattered by our truths which — can be! There is still many a house to build!

Thus spake Zarathustra.

On The Sublime Ones

Calm is the bottom of my sea: who would ever guess that it holds droll monsters?

Immovable is my depth: but it sparkles with swimming riddles and laughter.

A sublime one I saw today, a solemn one, a penitent of the spirit: O, how my soul laughed at his ugliness!

With upraised breast and like those who suck in their breath: thus he stood there, and silent, the sublime one:

Draped with ugly truths, the spoils of his chase, and rich in torn raiment; many thorns adorned him as well — but no rose as yet did I see.

Not yet has he learned laughter and beauty. Gloomy has this hunter returned from the forest of knowledge.

He returned home from the struggle with wild beasts; but out of his seriousness a wild beast still peers — an unvanquished one!

Like a tiger he still stands there, ready to spring; but I do not care for these high-strung souls; to all who are drawn back taut my taste is ill-disposed.

And you say to me, friends, that there is no disputing taste and tasting? But all life is a dispute over taste and tasting!

Taste: that is weight and scale and weigher at the same time; and woe to all the living that would live without dispute and weight and scale and weighers!

If he would grow weary of his sublimity, this sublime one: only then would his beauty begin, — and only then will I taste him and find him tasty.

And only when he turns away from himself will he leap over his own shadow — and verily! into his sun.

All-too-long he sat in the shade, the cheeks of this penitent of the spirit turned pale; he almost starved on his expectations.

Contempt is still in his eye; and disgust lurks in his mouth. It is true that he rests now, but his rest has not yet lain out in the sun.

He should be like a bull; and his happiness should smell of the earth and not of contempt for the earth.

Like a white bull I want to see him, walking before the plowshare, snorting and bellowing; and his bellowing too should praise all things earthly!

His visage is still dark; the shadow of a hand plays upon it. His sense of vision is still overshadowed.

His deed itself is the shadow that is still upon him: the hand darkens the handler. He still has not overcome his deed.

Indeed I love the bull's neck on him: but now I still want to see the eyes of an angel.

He must still as well forget his heroic will: a lifted one he shall be, and not just a lofty one: — the ether itself shall lift him up, the will-forsaken one!

He vanquished monsters, he solved riddles; but still he should redeem his monsters and riddles, still he should change them into heavenly children.

Not yet has his knowledge learned to smile and to exist without jealousy; not yet has his streaming passion grown calm in beauty!

Verily, not in satiety shall his longing plunge and become silent, but in beauty! Grace belongs to the greatness of mind of the high-minded!

With his arm laid across his head: so the hero should rest, so he should also overcome his rest.

But precisely for the hero the beautiful is the hardest thing of all. The beautiful is unattainable by all violent wills.

A little more, a little less: that precisely is much here, that is the most here.

To stand with relaxed muscles and unharnessed will: that is the hardest thing for all of you, you sublime ones!

When power becomes gracious and descends to the visible: such descent I call beauty.

And from no one do I want beauty so precisely as I do from you, you man of power: may your goodness be your final self-conquest.

I believe you capable of any evil: therefore I demand goodness from you.

Verily, I have laughed often at the weaklings who believe themselves good because they have lame paws!

You should strive for the virtue of the pillar: the higher it rises, the ever finer and fairer, but internally harder and sturdier it becomes.

Yes, you sublime one, one day yet you shall be beautiful and hold your own beauty up to the mirror.

Then your soul will shudder with godly desires; and there will be worship even in your vanity!

For this is the secret of the soul: only when the hero has forsaken it is it approached in a dream, — by the superhero. —

Thus spake Zarathustra.

On The Land Of Culture

I flew too far into the future: horror seized me.

And when I looked around me, behold! time was my sole contemporary.

Then I flew backwards, homewards — and ever more hurriedly: thus I came to you, you present-day men, and into the land of culture.

For once I came with an eye for you and a goodly desire: verily, with longing in my heart I came.

But what happened to me? Even though I was so afraid, — I had to laugh!

Never had my eye beheld anything so mottled.

I laughed and laughed, while my foot still trembled and my heart as well:

"Here is certainly the home of all paintpots!" — I said.

With fifty blotches painted on your face and limbs: thus you sat there to my astonishment, you present-day men!

And with fifty mirrors around you which flattered and imitated the play of your colors!

Verily, there is absolutely no better mask you could wear, you present-day men, than your own faces! Who could — recognize you?

Written all over with the characters of the past, and these characters painted over with new characters as well: thus you have hidden yourselves well from all character interpreters.

And even if one were a tester of the reins: who would ever believe you had reins? Out of hues you seem to be baked and out of glued pieces of paper.

All ages and peoples look motley on account of your veils; all customs and beliefs speak motley on account of your gestures.

He who stripped you of veils and wrappings and hues and gestures: he would have just enough left over to scare the birds with.

Verily, I myself am the scared bird who once saw you naked and unpainted; and I flew away when the skeleton beckoned to me lovingly.

Rather would I be a day-laborer in Hades and among the shades of old!

Even the shades of Hades are fatter and fuller than you!

This indeed, is bitterness to my bowels, that neither naked nor clothed can I stand you, you present-day men!

Everything sinister in the future and whatever makes stray birds shudder is truly still more comfy and cosy than your "reality."

For so you speak: "Real are we completely, without beliefs and superstitions": thus you plume yourselves — ah, still without plumes!

Indeed, how could you know how to believe, you mottled ones! — you who are walking refutations of belief itself and a discombobulation of all thought.

Unworthy of belief: that is what I call you, you real-ists!

All ages prate against each other in your spirits: and the dreams and pratings of all ages were still more real than your waking state is!

Unfruitful you are: therefore you lack belief. But he who must create has also always had his vatic dreams and astral signs — and has believed in belief!

Half-open gates you are, at which gravediggers wait. And this is your reality:

"Everything deserves to perish."

Alas, how you stand there before me, you unfruitful ones, how lean in the ribs! And many of you have undoubtedly made allowances for this.

And you have said: "No doubt a god stole something from me on the sly while I was sleeping. Enough, verily, to form himself a little female out of it!

"Marvelous is the poverty of my ribs!" — thus many of you present-day men have already said.

Yes, you make me laugh, you present-day men! And especially when you marvel over yourselves!

And woe unto me if I could not laugh at your marvelling and had to drink down everything adverse in your cups!

So I will make lighter of you, since I have something heavy to carry; and what is it to me if beetles and winged mites also alight on my bundle!

Verily, it shall not be heavier on me! And not from you, you present-day men, shall the great weariness come upon me. —

Alas, where shall I climb now with my longing? From every mountain I look out for father- and mother-lands.

But nowhere have I found a home; restless I feel in every city and ready to leave by every gate.

Alien to me and a mockery are the present-day men, to whom my heart was recently impelled; and expelled am I from father- and mother-lands.

So now I love only my children's land, the undiscovered land, in the most distant sea: towards it I command my sails to seek and seek.

In my children will I make amends for having been the child of my fathers: and in all the future — for this present! —

Thus spake Zarathustra.

On Immaculate Perception

Yesterday as the moon arose, I fancied she was ready to give birth to a sun: so broad and pregnant she lay on the horizon.

But she was a liar to me with her pregnancy; and I would sooner believe in the man in the moon than in the woman.

Certainly, he is not much of a man either, this timid night-wanderer. Verily, with a bad conscience he wanders over roofs.

For he is covetous and envious, the monk in the moon, covetous of the earth and of all lovers' delights.

No, I do not like him, this tomcat on the roofs! All who creep around halfclosed windows are loathsome to me!

Piously and quietly he wanders along on starry carpets:— but I dislike all lightly-treading men's feet upon which not even a spur jingles.

The step of everything honest speaks; but the cat sneaks away along the ground. Behold, along comes the moon, catlike and dishonest. —

This parable I offer to you sentimental dissemblers, you "pure perceivers"!

You I call — lechers!

You too love the earth and the earthly: I divine you well! — but there is shame in your love, as well as a bad conscience, — you resemble the moon!

To contempt for the earthly your spirit has been persuaded but not your innards: these, however, are the strongest thing about you!

And now your spirit is ashamed that it has given in to your innards, and in its shame it pursues crooked and lying ways.

"That would be the utmost thing for me" — thus your lying spirit tells itself: to look upon life without longing, and not like a dog with its tongue hanging out:

To be happy in looking on with a deadened will, without the grip and greed of self-seeking — cold and ashen all over but with drunken moon-eyes!

"That would be the dearest thing for me," — thus the seducee seduces himself — "to love the earth as the moon loves her and to touch her beauty with the eye alone.

And that is what I call the immaculate perception of all things, to want nothing from things: other than being allowed to lie before them like a mirror with a hundred eyes." —

O, you sentimental dissemblers, you lechers! You lack innocence in your desire: and so now you slander desire!

Verily, not as creators, procreators, and would-be merrymakers do you love the earth!

Where is innocence? Where the will to procreate is. And he who wants to create beyond himself has the purest will.

Where is beauty? Where I must will with all my will; where I want to cherish and perish, that an image may remain not only an image.

Cherishing and perishing: these have rhymed together for eternities. Will to love: that is also to be willing to die. Thus I talk to you cowards!

But now your emasculated leering wants to be called "contemplation"! And whatever is groped by cowardly eyes is to be baptized as "beautiful"! O, you besmirchers of noble names!

But this shall be your curse, you immaculate ones, you pure-perceivers, that you shall never give birth: even if you lie broad and pregnant on the horizon!

Verily, you stuff your mouths full with noble words: and we are to believe that your hearts runneth over, you liars?

But my words are low, despised, crooked words: I gladly pick up what falls under the table at your meals.

With them I can still — tell dissemblers the truth! Yes, my fishbones, mussel shells, and prickly leaves shall — tickle the noses of dissemblers!

Bad air is always around you and your meals: your lewd thoughts, lies, and secrecies are certain to be in the air!

First try believing in yourselves — in yourselves and your innards! He who does not believe in himself always lies.

A god's mask you hung up in front of yourselves, you "pure ones": into a god's mask your awful ringed-worm crawled.

Verily, you deceive, you "contemplative ones"! Zarathustra too was once the dupe of your godly exterior; he did not divine the serpents' coils with which it was stuffed.

Once I fancied I saw a god's soul at play in your play, you pure-perceivers!

Once I fancied no better art than your arts!

Snake-filth and foul odor the distance concealed from me: and that a lizard's cunning was crawling around lasciviously here.

But I came near to you: then day came to me — and now it comes to you, —the moon's love affair has come to an end!

Just look there! Unprepared and pale he stands there — before the rosy dawn!

For here she comes already, the glowing one, — her love for the earth is coming! All solar love is innocence and creative desire!

Just look there, how impatiently she comes over the sea! Do you not feel the thirst and the hot breath of her love?

She wants to suck at the sea and drink its depth up to her height: now the sea's desire rises with a thousand breasts.

Kissed and sucked by the sun's thirst it would be; air it would be and height and a footpath of light and light itself!

Verily, like the sun I love life and all deep seas.

And this is what perception means to me: all things deep shall come up —to my height! —

Thus spake Zarathustra.

On The Scholars

While I lay asleep, a sheep ate at the ivy-wreath upon my head, — ate it and said: "Zarathustra is no longer a scholar."

Said it and walked away awkwardly and proudly. A child told it to me.

I like to lie here where the children play, by the broken wall, amid thistles and red poppies.

To the children I am still a scholar, and to the thistles and red poppies too.

Innocent are they, even in their malice.

But to the sheep I am not anymore: thus my lot wills it — may it be blest!

For this is the truth: I have quit the house of the scholars and even slammed the door behind me.

Too long my soul sat hungry at their table; not, like them, am I trained in knowing as though it were nutcracking.

Freedom I love and the air over fresh earth; rather would I sleep on ox-hides than on their honors and respectability.

I am too hot and burned by my own thoughts: often they are ready to take my breath away. Then I must get out in the open and away from all dustencrusted rooms.

But they sit cool in the cool shade: in everything they just want to be spectators and to take care not to sit where the sun burns on the stairs.

Like those who stand on the street and gape at the people who pass by: so too they wait and gape at thoughts that others have thought.

If you grasp them with your hands, then they raise a cloud of dust around themselves like sacks of flour, and involuntarily; but who would ever guess that their dust came from grain and from the yellow delight of summer fields?

When they pretend to be wise, their small sayings and truths make my flesh creep: often there is an odor about their wisdom, as if it came from the swamp: and verily, I have even heard the frog croaking out of it!

Adept are they, they have clever fingers: what can my simplicity do next to their multiplicity? All threading and knitting and weaving their fingers understand: thus they weave the stockings of the spirit!

Good clockworks are they: just be careful to wind them up properly! Then they indicate the hour without fail and make a modest noise besides.

Like millworks they work and like stampers: just throw them your seedcorn!— they know indeed how to grind grain small and make white dust out of it.

They keep a strict eye on each other and do not trust themselves very well. Inventive in sly little tricks, they wait for those whose knowledge goes on lame feet — like spiders they wait. I always saw them prepare their poison with caution: and they always wore glass gloves on their fingers the while.

They also know how to play with loaded dice; and I have found them to play so eagerly that they sweat thereby. We are alien to each other, and their virtues are even more opposed to my taste than their falsehoods and their loaded dice.

And when I lived with them I lived above them. They were livid with me over that.

They wanted to hear nothing about someone wandering over their heads; and so they placed wood and earth and filth between me and their heads. Thus they muffled the sound of my step: and thus far I have been worst heard by the most learned.

All men's faults and weaknesses they placed between themselves and me:— "false ceiling" they call it in their houses.

But in spite of that I wander over their heads with my thoughts; and even if I should wander on my own errors, I would still be over them and their heads. For men are not equal: thus speaks justice. And what I will they would not dare to will!

On The Poets

"Since I have come to know the body better," — said Zarathustra to one of his disciples — "the spirit is but quasi-spirit to me; and all the 'imperishable' is but a parable as well."

"So I heard you say once before," answered the disciple; "and at that time you added: 'But the poets lie too much.' But why did you say that the poets lie too much?"

"Why?" said Zarathustra. "I am not one of those whose why one may inquire about.

Is my experience but of yesterday? It was long ago that I experienced the reasons for my opinions.

Would I not have to be a tun of memory if I wanted to have my reasons with me as well?

It is already too much for me, keeping my opinions themselves; and many a bird keeps flying away.

And at times too I find a creature that has flown to my dovecot, an unknown one, and it trembles when I lay my hand upon it.

But what was it that Zarathustra once said to you? That the poets lie too much? — But Zarathustra too is a poet.

Do you now believe that he spoke the truth here? Why do you believe this?

The disciple replied: "I believe in Zarathustra." But Zarathustra shook his head and smiled.

Belief does not make me blessed, he said, especially not belief in me.

But assuming someone said in all seriousness that the poets lie too much: he would be right, — we do lie too much.

We also know too little and are poor learners: so naturally we have to lie.

And who among us poets has not doctored his wine? Many a poisonous mish-mash has been brewed in our cellars, many an indescribable thing has happened there.

And because we know so little, we are heartily pleased with the poor in spirit, especially if they are little young ladies.

And we have a craving even for the things that the little old ladies tell each other in the evening. We call that the eternal-feminine in ourselves.

And as if there were a special secret passageway to knowledge, covered over for those who learn something: thus we believe in the folk and their "wisdom."

This, however, all poets believe: that whoever pricks up his ears while lying in the grass or upon lonely slopes learns something of the things which lie between heaven and earth.

And should tender emotions come to them, then the poets always fancy that Nature herself has taken a fancy to them:

And that she sneaks up to their ear to whisper secrets therein and amorous flatteries: of this they boast and brag before all mortals!

Alas, there are so many things between heaven and earth of which only the poets have let themselves dream!

And especially above the heavens: for all gods are poetic symbol, poetic swindle!

Verily, we are always drawn up there — namely, to the realm of the clouds:

on these we place our colorful manikins and call them gods and Supermen: —

Are they not just light enough for these chairs after all! — all these gods and Supermen.

Alas, how weary I am of all the inadequate absolutely destined to become event! Alas, how weary I am of the poets!

When Zarathustra spoke thus, his disciple became angry with him but remained silent. And Zarathustra too remained silent; and his eye had turned inward, as if it were looking into far distances. At last he sighed and took a breath. —

I am of today and days past, he said then; but there is something in me that is of tomorrow and the day after and thereafter.

I have grown weary of the poets, the old and the new; superficial they all seem to me and shallow seas.

They have not thought with enough depth: therefore their feeling has not sunk to the bottom.

Some lust and some boredom: that has heretofore been their best reflection.

All their harp jingle-jangle passes for a whiff and whisk of ghost with me; what have they thus far known of the fervor of tones? —

They are also not clean enough for me; they all muddy their water to make it seem deep.

And with that they gladly pass themselves off as mediators; but to me they remain meddlers and middlemen and half-and-halves and ones unclean! —

Alas, well did I cast my net into their seas and wanted to catch good fish; but always I pulled up an old godhead.

Thus the sea gave the hungry one a stone. And they themselves may well have come from the sea.

Surely one finds pearls in them: all the more similar are they themselves to hard shellfish. And instead of a soul I often found salt slime in them.

Even their vanity they learned from the sea: is not the sea the peacock of peacocks?

Even before the ugliest of buffaloes it twirls its tail, never does it grow weary of its lacy fan of silk and silver.

Defiantly the buffalo looks at it, his soul close to the sand, closer still to the thicket, but closest of all to the swamp.

What is beauty and sea and peacock-finery to him? This parable I speak to the poets.

Verily, their spirit itself is the peacock of peacocks and a sea of vanity!

Spectators the spirit of the poet requites — even if they should be buffaloes!

But of this spirit I have grown weary: and I foresee this spirit growing weary of itself.

Transformed already I have seen the poets, and their sights were set against themselves.

Penitents of the spirit I saw coming: they grew out of the poets. —

Thus spake Zarathustra.

On Great Events

There is an island in the sea — not far from Zarathustra's Blessed Isles —

upon which a volcano smokes constantly; of it people say, and especially the little old ladies among the people say, that it is like a boulder placed before the gate to the underworld: and downward through the volcano itself leads the narrow path which guides the way to this gate to the underworld.

Now about the time that Zarathustra took his rest on the Isles of the Blest, it happened that a ship cast anchor on the island where the volcano stands; and her crew went ashore to shoot rabbits. Near the midday hour, however, when the captain and his men were back together again, they suddenly saw a man coming towards them through the air, and a voice distinctly said: "It is time! It is high time!" But when the figure was nearest to them — it flew by quickly, however, like a shadow, in the direction of the volcano — then with great dismay they recognized that it was Zarathustra; then except for the captain himself they had all seen him before, and they loved him as the people love: so that love and awe are together in equal parts.

"Look at that!" said the old helmsman, "there goes Zarathustra into hell!" —

Around the same time that these sailors landed on the fire-island, a rumor was afloat that Zarathustra had disappeared; and when his friends were asked, they reported that he had embarked at night without saying where he intended to travel.

Thus unrest arose; after three days, however, the sailors' story added to this unrest — and then all the people said that the devil had taken Zarathustra. His disciples laughed of course at this talk; and one of them even said: "I would sooner believe that Zarathustra has taken the devil." But in the depths of their souls they were all full of misgiving and longing; and so their joy was great when on the fifth day Zarathustra appeared among them.

And this is the account of Zarathustra's conversation with the firehound:

The earth, he said, has a skin; and this skin has diseases. One of these diseases, for example, is called "man."

And another of these diseases is called "firehound": about him men have told themselves and let themselves be told a whole pack of lies.

To fathom this mystery I went across the sea: and I have seen the truth naked, verily! from the neck down.

Now I know how it is with the firehound; and also with all the eruptionand upheaval-devils, of whom not only the little old ladies are afraid.

"Out with you, firehound, out of your depth!" I cried, "and confess how deep this depth is! Where does what you huff and puff up here come from?

Richly you drink from the sea: your oversalted eloquence proclaims that.

Truly, for a hound from the deep you take too much of your nourishment from the surface!

At best I take you for the earth's ventriloquist: and whenever I have heard eruption- and upheaval- devils speak, I found them like you: salted, false, and shallow.

You know how to bellow and blacken with ashes! You are the best blowhards and are sufficiently learned in the art of making mud boiling hot.

Wherever you are, mud must be nearby, and much that is spongy, hollow, compressed: it wants to go free.

'Freedom' you all love to bellow most of all: but I forget my belief in 'great events' as soon as there is a lot of bellowing and smoke around them.

And believe me, friend Pandemonium! The greatest events — they are not our loudest but our stillest hours.

Not around the inventors of new noise: around the inventors of new values the world revolves; inaudibly it revolves.

And just admit it! Once your noise and smoke have passed away, but little has ever come to pass. What does it matter that a city has become a mummy and a statue lies in the mud?

And this word yet I say to the overthrowers of statues. That is indeed the greatest folly, throwing salt into the sea and statues into the mud.

In the mud of your contempt the statue lay: but that is precisely its statute, that out of contempt its life and living beauty may rise again.

With diviner features it stands now and sufferingly seductive; and verily! it will thank you yet for overthrowing it, you overthrowers!

And with this counsel I counsel kings and churches and all that are weak with age and weak in virtue — just let yourselves be overthrown! That you may come back to life, and that back to you may come — virtue! — " Thus I talked before the firehound; then he interrupted me sullenly and asked: "Church? What is that?"

"Church?" I answered, "that is a kind of state, and what is more, the lyingest kind. But be quiet, you hypocritical hound! No doubt you know your own kind best!

Like you yourself the state is a hypocritical hound; like you it likes to speak with smoke and bellowing, — to make believe, like you, that it speaks from the belly of things.

For by all means it means to be the most important creature on earth, the state; and it is believed to be, too." —

When I said this, the firehound acted as if insane with envy. "What?" he cried, "the most important creature on earth? And it is believed to be, too?" And so much gas and ghastly voices escaped from his throat that I thought he would choke with indignation and envy.

At last he calmed down and his panting subsided; as soon as he was quiet, however, I said laughingly:

"You are offended, firehound: thus I am right about you! And that I may still be right in the end, hear then of a different firehound: he really speaks from the heart of the earth.

Gold his breath exhales and golden rain: his heart wills it so. What are ashes and smoke and even hot slime to him?

Laughter flutters out of him like a colorful cluster of clouds, averse is he to the gurgling and spewing and griping of your bowels!

The gold, however, and the laughter — that he takes from the heart of the earth: for just so you know, — the heart of the earth is of gold."

When the firehound heard this, he could not stand to listen to me any longer. Ashamed, he tucked in his tail, said bow-wow in a mealy-mouthed manner, and crawled down into his hole.

Thus recounted Zarathustra. His disciples, however, hardly listened to him: so great was their desire to tell him of the sailors, the rabbits, and the flying man.

"What should I make of it?" said Zarathustra. "Am I then a ghost?

But it must have been my shadow. Most certainly you have heard something of the wanderer and his shadow?

This, however, is for certain: I must keep a tighter rein on him, — otherwise he will spoil my reputation yet."

And once again Zarathustra shook his head and wondered. "What should I make of it?" he said once again.

"Why did the ghost cry: 'It is time! It is high time!'

For what then is it — high time?" —

Thus spake Zarathustra.

The Soothsayer

—and I saw a great sadness come over mankind. The best grew weary of their works.

A doctrine came out, a belief ran alongside it: 'All is empty, all is the same, all has been!'

And from all the hills it rang out again: 'All is empty, all is the same, all has been!'

Well have we reaped: but for what reason has all our fruit turned rotten and brown? What fell down from the evil moon last night?

All work has been in vain, into poison our wine has been changed, an evil eye has singed our fields and hearts yellow.

Dry we have all become; and if fire lights on us, then like ashes we raise dust: yes, the fire itself we have made tired.

All our wells have run dry, even the sea has receded. All the ground wants to split, but the abyss will not swallow it!

'Alas, where is there still a sea in which we could drown': thus our lament sounds — over shallow swamps.

Verily, we have become too weary even for dying; now we lie awake and go on living — in burial chambers!"

Thus Zarathustra heard a soothsayer speak; and his prophecy touched him to the core and transformed him. Sad and weary he went around; and he became like those of whom the soothsayer had spoken.

"Verily," so he said to his disciples, "a little while then comes this long twilight.

Alas, how shall I bring my light safely through?

Would that it not be snuffed out in this sadness! To remoter worlds it shall surely be a light, and even to remotest nights!"

Thus Zarathustra went around sick at heart; and for three days he took neither food nor drink, had no rest, and lost all speech. At last it happened that he fell into a deep sleep. His disciples, however, sat up in long night-vigils around him and waited anxiously to see whether he would wake and speak again and get over his affliction.

And this is the speech that Zarathustra spoke when he awoke; his voice, however, came to his disciples as though from a great distance:

Hear then the dream I dreamed, you friends, and help me divine its meaning!

It is still a riddle to me, this dream; its meaning is hidden in it and imprisoned and does not yet fly over it with wings free.

All life I had renounced, so I dreamed. Night- and grave-watchman I had become, there, in the lonely mountain-fortress of Death.

I guarded his coffins up there: the damp vaults stood full of such trophies.

Out of glass coffins vanquished life looked at me.

I inhaled the odor of dusty eternities: sultry and dusty lay my soul. And who could ever air out his soul there?

The brightness of midnight was ever around me, loneliness cowered beside her; and thirdly, death-rattling stillness, the worst of my girlfriends.

Keys I carried, the rustiest of all keys; and I knew how to open the creakiest of all gates with them.

Like a most angry croaking the sound ran down the long corridors when the wings of the gate rose: unkindly cried this bird, unwillingly was it awoken.

But it was more frightening yet and more heart-wringing when it became quiet again and still all around, and I sat alone in this malicious silence.

So it went for me, and time crawled along, if there was still time: what do I know about it? But at last that which awoke me came to pass.

Three times blows beat on the gate, three times the vaults resounded and howled: then I went up to the gate.

Alpa! I cried, who carries his ashes up the mountain? Alpa! Alpa! Who carries his ashes up the mountain?

And I pressed in the key and heaved and strained at the gate. But not even a finger's breadth did it stand open:

Then a raging wind tore the wings apart: whistling, screeching, and penetrating, it threw a black coffin at me:

And in the raging and whistling and screeching the coffin burst open and spat out thousand-fold laughter.

And out of a thousand wry faces of children, angels, owls, fools, and childsized butterflies, it laughed and roared and jeered at me.

I was terribly frightened by it: it cast me down. And I screamed with terror like I have never screamed.

But my own scream awoke me: — and I became myself again. —

Thus Zarathustra related his dream and then fell silent: for he did not yet know the meaning of his dream. But the disciple whom he loved the most arose quickly, seized Zarathustra's hand and said:

"Your life itself explains this dream to us, O Zarathustra!

Are you not yourself the wind which with shrill whistling tears open the gates to the fortress of Death?

Are you not yourself the coffin full of colorful acts of malice and life's angelic masks?

Verily, like the thousand-fold laughter of a child Zarathustra enters all death chambers, laughing over these night- and grave-watchmen, and whomever else comes rattling along with gloomy keys.

You will frighten and upset them with your laughter; their swooning and coming-to will prove your power over them.

And even when the long twilight comes and the deadly weariness, you will not set in our sky, you advocate of life!

105 New stars you have let us see and new nightly splendors; verily, laughter itself you have stretched like a many-colored canopy over us.

Now the laughter of children will well up ever after out of coffins; now a strong wind will come triumphantly ever after to all deadly weariness: of this you yourself are our surety and soothsayer.

Verily, they themselves you dreamed, your enemies: that was your worst dream!

But as you awoke from them and became yourself again, so they shall wake up from themselves — and come to you!" —

So spoke the disciple; and now all the others crowded around Zarathustra and seized him by the hand and wanted to talk him into leaving his bed and his sadness and returning to them. But Zarathustra sat upright on his bed, and with a look not his own. Like one who returns home after a long time abroad, he looked upon his disciples and examined their faces; and still he did not recognize them. But when they raised him and set him on his feet, behold, suddenly his eye changed; he grasped everything that had happened, stroked his beard and said in a strong voice:

"Well then! This now has its day; but see to it, my disciples, that we prepare a good meal and without delay! Thus I intend to do penance for bad dreams!

The soothsayer, though, shall eat and drink at my side; and verily, I will yet show him a sea in which he can drown!"

Thus spake Zarathustra. But then he looked long and hard into the face of his disciple, the one who had served as his dream-interpreter, and shook his head. —

On Redemption

One day when Zarathustra crossed over the great bridge, he was beset on all sides by the cripples and beggars, and a hunchback talked to him thus:

"Behold Zarathustra! The people also learn from you and acquire belief in your teaching: but for them to believe entirely in you one more thing is required — you must first still convince us cripples! Here you now have a fine selection and truly, an opportunity with more than one knock! You can heal the blind and make the lame walk; and from him who has too much behind him you can also perhaps take a little away: — that, I think, would be the right way to make the cripples believe in Zarathustra!"

But to him who spoke here Zarathustra replied thus: "When you take away the hump from the hunchback, you take away his spirit — thus the people teach.

And when you give the blind man his sight, then he sees too many bad things on earth: so that he curses the person who healed him. But he who makes the lame man walk does him the greatest harm; for no sooner can he walk than his vices run away with him — thus the people teach with regard to cripples. And why should Zarathustra not also learn from the people when the people learn from Zarathustra?

This is the least thing to me, however, since I have been among men, to see that: 'This one lacks an eye and that one an ear and a third one a leg, and that there are others who have lost their tongue or their nose or their head.'

I see and have seen worse things and all sorts of things so loathsome that of each one I would not speak and of some I would not once keep silent: namely, men who lack everything save for one thing, of which they have too much —men who are nothing more than a huge eye or a huge belly or something else huge, — inverted cripples I call such men.

And when I came out of my solitude and crossed over this bridge for the first time: then I could not believe my eyes and looked and looked again and finally said: 'That is an ear! An ear as big as a man! I took an even closer look: and, actually, under the ear something else was stirring, something pitifully small and poor and slight. And, upon my honor, the monstrous ear sat upon a small thin stalk, — the stalk, however, was a man! Whoever put a magnifying glass up to his eye could probably even make out a small envious face; also, that a bloated little soul was dangling from the stalk. The people, however, told me that the huge ear was not only a man, but a great man, a genius. But I never believed the people when they spoke of great men — and have maintained my belief that it was an inverted cripple who had too little of everything and too much of one thing."

When Zarathustra had spoken thus to the hunchback and to those who had the hunchback as their mouthpiece and advocate, he turned to his disciples with profound discontent and said:

"Verily, my friends, I walk among men as among the fragments and limbs of men! This is the frightful thing to my eye, that I find men shattered and scattered as over a battle- and butcher-field.

And if my eye flees from the now to the formerly, it always finds the same thing: fragments and limbs and terrible accidents — but no men!

The now and the formerly on earth — alas! my friends — that is my most unbearable thing; and I would not know how to live if I were not yet a seer of what is to come.

A seer, a willer, a creator, a future itself and a bridge to the future — and alas, still as it were a cripple on this bridge: all this Zarathustra is.

And you too have often asked yourselves: "Who is Zarathustra to us? What shall we call him? And like I myself you gave yourselves questions as answers.

Is he a promiser? Or a fulfiller? A conqueror? Or an inheritor? A harvest? Or a plowshare? A healer? Or one restored to health?

Is he a poet? Or one who is truthful? A liberator? Or a subjugator? A good guy? Or a bad guy?

I walk among men as among the fragments of the future: that future into which I look.

And this is my every thought, to compose and collect into one what is fragment and riddle and terrible accident.

And how could I stand being a man if man were not also the composer, riddle- reader, and redeemer of chance?

To redeem what is past and remold every 'It was' into 'I willed it so!' — only that would I call redemption!

Will — that is what the liberator and bringer of joy is called: thus I taught you, my friends! But now learn this in addition: the will itself is still a prisoner.

Willing liberates: but what is the name of that which puts even the liberator in chains?

'It was': that is what the will's gnashing of teeth and loneliest tribulation is called. Helpless against what has been done — of all things past it is an angry witness.

Backwards the will cannot will: that it cannot break time and time's inordinate desire, — that is the will's loneliest tribulation.

Willing liberates: what does willing devise for itself to be free of its tribulation and jeer at its jail?

Alas, every prisoner becomes a fool! Foolishly as well the imprisoned will rescues itself.

That time does not run backwards, this is its anger; 'That Which Was' this is what the stone it cannot roll is called.

And so it rolls stones out of anger and discontent and takes revenge on that which does not feel anger and discontent as it does.

Thus the will, the liberator, has become a perpetrator of pain; and on all that is capable of suffering it takes revenge because it cannot go backwards.

This, yes this alone is revenge itself: the will's ill-will toward time and its 'It was.'

Verily, a great folly dwells in our will; and it has turned out to be a curse on all things human that this folly learned spirit!

The spirit of revenge: my friends, this has been man's best reflection hitherto; and where there was suffering there always had to be punishment.

'Punishment,' the name, namely, that revenge has taken for itself: with a lying word it simulates a good conscience.

And because in the willer himself there is the pain of not being able to will backwards, — therefore willing itself and all life — must be punishment!

And then cloud after cloud rolled over the spirit: until at last madness preached: 'Everything passes away; therefore, everything deserves to pass away!'

'And this is justice itself, that law of time that she must devour her own children': thus madness preached.

'Things are morally ordered according to justice and punishment. O, where is the redemption from the flux of things and the punishment called "being"?

Thus madness preached.

'Can there be redemption when there is eternal law? Alas, unrollable is the stone "It was": all punishment must be eternal too!' Thus madness preached.

'No deed can be annulled: how could it be undone through punishment?

This, this is what is eternal in the punishment called "being," that this being must also be deed and debt again, eternally!'

'Unless the will finally redeems itself and willing becomes non-willing—': but you know, my brothers, this fabulous song of madness!

I led you away from these fabulous songs when I taught you: 'The will is a creator.'

All 'it was' is a fragment, a riddle, a terrible accident — until the creative will says to it: 'But thus I willed it!'

— Until the creative will says to it: 'But thus I will it! Thus I will will it!'

But has it already spoken thus? And when did this happen? Has the will already been unharnessed from its own folly?

Has the will already become its own redeemer and bringer of joy? Has it unlearned the spirit of revenge and all gnashing of teeth?

And who has taught it reconciliation with time, and that which is higher than all reconciliation?

That which is higher than all reconciliation must the will which is the will to power will: but how does this happen? Who taught it to will backwards as well?"

— But at this point in his speech it happened that Zarathustra stopped suddenly and looked exactly like someone who was extremely frightened. With terrified eyes he looked at his disciples; his eyes pierced as with arrows their thoughts and hinter-thoughts. But after a little while he laughed again and said, appeased:

"It is hard to live with men because it is so hard to keep silent. Especially for a talkaholic."

— Thus spake Zarathustra. The hunchback, however, had listened to the conversation and covered his face the while; when he heard Zarathustra laugh, however, he looked up curiously and said slowly:

"But why does Zarathustra speak differently to us than he does to his disciples?"

Zarathustra answered: "What is remarkable about that? With hunchbacks one may well speak hunchbacked!"

"Very well," said the hunchback; "and with pupils one may well tell tales out of school.

But why does Zarathustra speak differently to his pupils than he does — to himself?" —

On Man-Craft

Not the height: the descent is what is terrible!

The descent, where the glance plunges down and the hand grasps up. There the heart grows dizzy because of its double will.

Alas, friends, do you guess as well my heart's double will?

This, this is my descent and my danger, that my glance plunges to the height and my hand wants to stick to and stay at — the depth!

My will clings to man, with chains I bind myself to man, because it draws me up to the Superman: for there my other will has a mind to be.

And therefore I live blindly among men: precisely as if I knew them not: lest my hand lose its faith entirely in a sure thing.

I do not know you men: this darkness and consolation is often spread out around me.

I sit at the gateway for the sake of every knave and ask: "Who wants to cheat me?"

This is my first piece of man-craft, to let myself be cheated so as to be off my guard with cheaters.

Alas, if I had to be on my guard with men: how could man be an anchor for my hot-air balloon? Too easily would it sweep me up and away!

This providence lies over my destiny, that I must be without precaution.

And he who would not die of thirst among men must learn to drink from all glasses; and he who would remain clean among men must know how to wash himself even with dirty water.

And thus I often consoled myself: "Well then! Cheer up, old heart! A mishap failed you: enjoy this as your — happiness!"

This, however, is my next piece of man-craft: I spare the vain more than the proud.

Is not wounded vanity the mother of all tragedies? Where pride is wounded, however, there something better than pride may yet grow.

That life may look good, its play must be well-played: but for that, good actors are required.

All the vain I found to be good actors: they act and want to be looked upon with pleasure, — all their spirit is in this will.

They represent themselves, they invent themselves; in their presence I love to look upon life, — it cures melancholy.

Therefore I spare the vain, because they are the physicians to my melancholy and keep me attached to man as to a spectacle.

And then: who has fathomed the full depth of the vain man's modesty? I side and sympathize with him on account of his modesty.

From you he wants to acquire his belief in himself; he lives on your looks, he gobbles up praise from your hands.

He even believes your lies when you lie well about him: for deep down his heart sighs: "What am I!"

And if true virtue be that virtue which has no knowledge of itself: well, then the vain man has no knowledge of his modesty! —

This, however, is my third piece of man-craft, that I do not let your timidity spoil my view of the wicked.

I am happy to see the wonders which the hot sun hatches: tigers and palm trees and rattlesnakes.

Among men too there is a hot sun's handsome brood and many things wonder- worthy with regard to the wicked.

It is true, like your wisest men who did not appear all that wise to me: so too I found man's wickedness to be less than its reputation.

And often I asked with a shake of the head: "Why do you still rattle, you rattlesnakes?"

Verily, there is still a future even for evil! And the hottest south is still undiscovered by man!

How many things now called the most wanton wickedness indeed are but only twelve feet wide and three months long! Someday, however, greater dragons will come into the world.

For that the Superman may not lack his dragon, the superdragon, of which he is worthy: for that much hot sun must still glow on moist primeval forest!

Out of your wildcats tigers must first arise, and out of your poisonous toads, crocodiles: for the good hunter shall have good hunting!

And verily, you good and just ones! In you there is much that is laughable, and above all your fear of that which has hitherto been called "devil"!

Such a stranger you are in your souls to what is great, that to you the Superman would be frightful in his goodness!

And you wise and knowing ones, you would run away from wisdom's broiling sun, in which the Superman bathes his nakedness with pleasure!

You highest of men my eye has met! this is what I doubt in you and secretly laugh about: I suspect that you would call my Superman — devil!

Alas, I grew weary of these highest and best ones: from their "height" I longed to be out, up, out, and away to the Superman!

A shudder came over me when I saw these best ones naked: then I grew myself wings to soar off into distant futures.

Into futures more distant, into souths more southerly than any artist has ever dreamed: there, where gods are ashamed of all clothing!

But disguised I want to see you, you neighbors and fellow men, welladorned and vain and dignified in the role of "the good and the just."

And disguised will I myself sit among you, — in order to mistake myself and you: this, you see, is my last piece of man-craft. —

Thus spake Zarathustra.

The Stillest Hour

What happened to me, my friends? You see me confused, driven away, reluctant-compliant, ready to go — alas, to go away from you!

Yes, once more must Zarathustra go into his solitude: but this time the bear goes back into his den morosely!

What happened to me? Who ordered this? — Alas, my angry mistress wishes it so, she spoke to me; have I never told you her name before?

Yesterday toward evening my stillest hour spoke to me: this is the name of my terrible mistress.

And so it happened — for I must tell you everything, lest your hearts harden toward the suddenly departing one!

Do you know the terror of the one who is falling asleep? —

Down to his very toes he is terrified, because the ground seems to give way beneath him and the dream begins.

I tell you this in the form of a parable. Yesterday, at the stillest hour, the ground gave way: the dream began.

The hour-hand moved, the clock of my life took a breath — never have I heard such stillness around me: so that my heart was terror-struck.

Then it spoke without a voice to me: "You know it, Zarathustra?" —

And I cried out with terror at this whispering, and the blood left my face: but I was silent.

Then it spoke again without a voice to me: "You know it Zarathustra, but you do not say it!"

And at last I answered, like one who was defiant: "Yes, I know it, but I will not say it!"

Then it spoke again without a voice to me: "You will not, Zarathustra? Is that really true? Do not hide in your defiance!" —

And I wept and trembled like a child and said: "Alas, I would indeed but how can I? Let me off this once! It is beyond me!"

Then it spoke again without a voice to me: "What do you matter, Zarathustra!

Speak your word and shatter!" —

And I answered: "Alas, is it my word? Who am I? I await the worthier one; I am unworthy even to shatter upon him."

Then it spoke again without a voice to me. "What do you matter? You are not yet humble enough for me. Humility has the toughest skin." —

And I answered: "What has the skin of my humility not already endured?

At the foot of my height I dwell: how high are my peaks? No one has yet told me.

But I know my valleys well."

Then it spoke again without a voice to me: "O Zarathustra, he who has mountains to move moves valleys and lowlands as well." —

And I answered: "My word has moved no mountains yet, and what I have said has not yet reached men. Yes, I went to men, but I have not yet arrived at them."

Then it spoke again without a voice to me: "What do you know of that? The dew falls on the grass when the night is most reticent." —

And I answered: "They mocked me when I found and made my own way; and my feet were truly trembling in those days.

And so they said to me: 'You forgot the way, now you have also forgotten the way of going!'"

Then it spoke again without a voice to me: "What does their mockery matter?

You are one who has forgotten how to obey: now you shall command!

Do you not know who is most needed by all? He who commands great things.

To complete great things is hard: but what is harder is to command great things.

That is what is most inexcusable in you: you have the power, and you refuse to rule." —

And I answered: "I lack the lion's voice for commanding."

Then it spoke again as if in a whisper to me: "It is the stillest words which bring on the storm. Thoughts that come on dove's feet rule the world.

O Zarathustra, you shall go as a shadow of that which is to come: thus you will command and in commanding go before." —

And I answered: "I am ashamed."

Then it spoke again without a voice to me: "You must still become a child and be without shame.

The pride of youth is still upon you, lately you have become young: but he who would become a child must still overcome his youth." —

And I reflected a long time and trembled. But at last I said what I had had said at first: "I will not."

Then there was laughter around me. Woe, how this laughter tore apart my innards and slit open my heart!

And it spoke for the last time to me: "O Zarathustra, your fruits are ripe, but you are not ripe for your fruits!

So you must go again into your solitude: for you have yet to become mellow."—

And it laughed again and fled: then it grew still around me, as if with a twofold stillness. But I lay on the ground and the sweat poured from my body.

— Now you have heard everything and why I have to go back into my solitude.

Nothing have I held back from you, my friends.

But this too you have heard from me, who of all men is still the most reticent — and wants to be!

I still had something to say to you, I still had something to give to you! Why did I not give it? Am I stingy then? —

But when Zarathustra had spoken these words, he was overcome by the violence of his pain and the imminence of his departure from his friends, so that he wept openly; and no one knew how to console him. In the night, however, he went away alone and left his friends.

Part Three

"You look up when you crave elevation. And I look down because I am elevated.

Who among you can laugh and be elevated at the same time?

Whoever climbs the highest mountains laughs at all tragic plays and tragic realities."

Zarathustra, On Reading And Writing (Part One)

The Wanderer

It was around midnight when Zarathustra made his way across the ridge of the island in order to make the opposite shore by early morning: for he meant to embark there. There was a good roadstead there, you see, where even foreign ships liked to anchor; they took with them many from the Blessed Isles who wanted to cross the sea. So as Zarathustra climbed the mountain now, he thought on the way of the many solitary wanderings he had made since his youth and of how many mountains and ridges and peaks he had already climbed.

"I am a wanderer and a mountain climber," he said to his heart, "the plains I do not love, and it seems I cannot sit still for long.

And as for what may yet come to me in the way of fate and experience, — a wandering will be in it and a mountain climbing: in the end one still only experiences oneself.

The time is past when accidents might still happen to me: and what could still befall me now that is not already my own!

It only comes back, it comes home to me at last — my own self and that part of it which has long been in foreign parts and scattered amongst all things and happenings.

And yet one thing I know: I now stand before my last peak and before that which has been saved up longest for me. Alas, I have to go up my hardest path!

Alas, I have begun my loneliest wandering!

But he who is of my kind does not shun such an hour: the hour which says to him: 'Only now you make your way to greatness! Peak and abyss — this is now resolved into one!

You make your way to greatness: what was hitherto your ultimate danger has now become your ultimate refuge!

You make your way to greatness: your best courage must now consist in this, that behind you no way exists anymore!

You make your way to greatness: no one shall sneak after you here! Your foot itself has erased the path behind you, and above it is written: Impossibility.

And if henceforth all ladders are lacking, then you must still know how to climb upon your own head: how else would you climb upwards?

Upon your own head and above and beyond your own heart! Now must the mildest in you become the harshest.

He who has always been very sparing of himself sickens at last from his very sparingness. Praised be that which hardens! I praise not the land where butter and honey — flow!

Learning to look away from oneself is necessary in order to see much: — this harshness is necessary for every mountain climber.

But he who is too forward with his eyes, like the knowing one, how could he see more than the foreground of anything?

You, however, O Zarathustra, would look at the ground and background of all things: so already you must climb over yourself, — onward, upward, until even your stars are beneath you!

Yes! To look down upon myself and even upon my stars: this would I first call my peak, this would be left behind as my last peak! —

Thus spake Zarathustra to himself while climbing, comforting his heart with hard aphorisms: for he was sore at heart like never before. And when he reached the top of the mountain ridge, behold, there lay the other sea spread out 117 before him: and he stood still and silent a long while. But the night was cold at this height and clear and starry-bright.

"I know my lot," he said at last with sadness. "Well then! I am ready! My last solitude has just begun.

Alas, this black sad sea beneath me! Alas, this pregnant, nightly spleen!

Alas, destiny and sea! To you I must now climb down!

Before my highest mountain I stand and before my longest wandering: therefore I must first descend deeper than I ever have:

— deeper down into pain than I have ever descended, down into its blackest flood! So my destiny wills it: Well then! I am ready.

"Whence come the highest mountains?" So I asked once. Then I learned that they come from the sea.

This testimony is written in their stone and in the walls of their peaks.

From the deepest place must the highest come to its height. —

Thus spake Zarathustra at the summit of the mountain, where it was cold:

but when he came near to the sea and stood at last alone under the cliffs, then he had become weary on the way and was more full of longing than ever before.

"Everything still sleeps," he said; "even the sea sleeps. Sleepy and strange looks its eye casts at me.

But it breathes warmly, I feel it. And I also feel that it dreams. It tosses and turns, dreaming upon hard pillows.

Hark! Hark! How it groans with wicked recollections! Or wicked expectations?

Alas, I am sad with you, you dark monster, and even mad at myself for your sake.

Alas, that my hand has not strength enough! Gladly indeed, would I deliver you from bad dreams! — "

And as Zarathustra spoke thus, he laughed with melancholy and bitterness over himself. "What, Zarathustra!" he said; "would you sing solace even to the sea?

Alas, you love-rich fool Zarathustra, you over-trustful, over-joyful one! But thus were you always: trustful you always came to all that was frightful.

Every monster you wanted to caress. A whiff of warm breath, a little soft tuft of fur on its paw — and immediately you were ready to love it and lure it.

Love is the danger of the loneliest one, love of anything, as long as it lives!

Truly laughable is my folly and my modesty in love! — "

Thus spake Zarathustra and laughed a second time: but then he thought of his abandoned friends — and as if had sinned against them in his thoughts, he became angry with himself at the thought of his thoughts. And thereupon it came to pass that the laughing one wept:— with ire and desire Zarathustra wept bitterly.

On The Vision And The Riddle
1

When it became known among the sailors that Zarathustra was on board the ship — for there was a man from the Blessed Isles who had gone on board with him — there arose a great curiosity and expectation. But Zarathustra kept silent for two days and was cold and deaf with sadness, so that he answered neither looks nor questions. On the evening of the second day, however, he opened his ears again, though he still remained silent: for there were many strange and dangerous things to have an ear to on this ship, which came from afar and would travel even farther. But Zarathustra was a friend to all those who make long journeys and take a dislike to living without danger. And behold! at last in listening his own tongue was loosened, and the ice of his heart broke:— then he began to speak thus:

To you, the daring searchers, researchers, and whoever has set sail with subtle sails on frightful seas, —

To you, the riddle-intoxicated, the twilight-delighted, whose souls are lured by flutes to every mis-abyss:

— For you refuse to grope along a thread with a cowardly hand; and where you can divine you hate to deduce —

To you alone I relate the riddle that I saw, — the vision of the loneliest one.

Gloomy I walked lately through the corpse-hued gloaming, — gloomy and hard, with lips compressed. Not only one sun had set for me.

A path that climbed defiantly through rubble, a spiteful, lonely one to which neither herb nor shrub spoke any longer: a mountain path crunched under the defiance of my foot.

Striding silently over the scornful clatter of pebbles, trampling underfoot the stone that let it slide: thus my foot forced itself upwards.

Upwards: — although he sat on me, half-dwarf, half-mole; lame, laming; dripping lead into my ear, leaden-drop thoughts into my brain.

"O Zarathustra," he whispered tauntingly, syllable by syllable, "you stone of wisdom! You threw yourself high, but every stone that is thrown — must fall!

O Zarathustra, you stone of wisdom, you slingstone, you star-destroyer!

You threw yourself so high, — but every stone that is thrown — must fall!

Sentenced to you yourself and your own stoning: O Zarathustra, you sure threw the stone far, — but it will fall back on you!"

Then the dwarf was silent; and that lasted a long time. His silence oppressed me, however: such a pairing truly makes one lonelier than being alone!

I climbed, I climbed, I dreamed, I thought, — but everything oppressed me.

I was like a sick man whose bad torment makes him weary and whose worse dream wakes him up again from his falling asleep. —

But there is something in me that I call courage: all ill humor it has killed for me hitherto. This courage at last bade me stand still and say:

"Dwarf! You! Or I!" —

Because courage is the best killer, — courage which attacks; for in every attack there is music playing.

Man, however, is the most courageous animal: with that he has overcome every animal. With music playing he even overcame every pain; but human pain is the deepest pain.

Courage also kills giddiness at abysses: and where does man not stand at abysses? Is seeing not itself — seeing abysses?

Courage is the best killer; courage also kills pity. But pity is the deepest abyss: however deeply man looks into life, so deeply too he looks into suffering.

But courage is the best killer, courage which attacks: it even kills death dead, for it says: "Was that life? Well then! Once more!"

In such a saying, however, there is much music playing. He that has ears to hear, let him hear. —

2

"Halt! Dwarf" I said. " I! or you! I, however, am the stronger of us two: you are unaware of my abysmal thought! That — you could not bear!" —

Then happened that which made me lighter: for the dwarf sprang from my shoulder, the snoop! And he squatted on a stone in front of me. But just at the place where we halted there was a gateway.

"See this gateway! Dwarf!" I continued: "it has two faces. Two paths come together here: no one has yet gone to the end of them.

This long lane back here: it lasts an eternity. And that long lane out there, — that is another eternity.

They oppose each other, these paths; they bang their very heads: — and here at this gateway is where they come together. The name of the gateway stands written above: 'Moment.'

But he who went further down one of them — ever further and ever farther:

do you think, dwarf, that these paths would eternally oppose each other?" —

"Everything straight lies," the dwarf muttered contemptuously. "All truth is crooked, time itself is a circle."

"You spirit of gravity!" I said angrily, "don't take the easy way out! Or I will let you crouch where you crouch, lamefoot, and I have carried you high!

"Behold," I went on, "this moment! From this gateway Moment a long eternal lane runs backwards: behind us lies an eternity.

All things that can run, must they not have run along this lane once before?

All things that can happen, must they not have happened, been done, and been over and done with once before?

And if everything has existed before: what do you make of this moment, dwarf? Must not this gateway too — have existed before?

And are not all things knotted firmly together in such a way that this moment draws all things to come after it? Consequently — — itself too?

Then of all things that can run: even in that long lane out there — they must run once more! —

And this slow spider that crawls in the moonlight itself, and you and I in the gateway whispering together, whispering of eternal things — must we not have existed before?

— and must we not return and run in that lane out there before us, in that long eerie lane — must we not return eternally? —"

Thus I talked, and ever more softly: for I was afraid of my own thoughts and hinter-thoughts. Then suddenly I heard a dog howling nearby.

Had I ever heard a dog howl like this? My thoughts ran back. Yes! When I was a child, in my most distant childhood:

— then I had heard a dog growl like this. And saw him too, hair bristling, head up, trembling, in the stillest midnight, when even dogs believe in ghosts:

— so that it moved me to pity. For just then the full moon passed quietly as death over the house, just then it stood still, a round glow, perfectly still on the flat roof, exactly as if on foreign property: — on account of that the dog had been horror-stricken then: for dogs believe in thieves and ghosts. And when I again heard such howling, it moved me to pity once more.

Where had the dwarf gone to now? And the gateway? And the spider? And all the whispering? Was I dreaming then? Had I awoke? Amidst wild cliffs I stood all of a sudden, alone, desolate, in the most desolate moonlight.

But there lay a man! And there! The dog, jumping, bristling, whining, — now he saw me coming — then he howled again, then he yelped: — had I ever heard a dog yelp so for help?

And verily, what I saw, the like of it I had never seen. I saw a young shepherd, writhing, retching, twitching, face contorted, with a heavy black snake hanging out of his mouth.

Had I ever seen so much loathing and pale horror on one face? He had fallen asleep, perhaps? Then the snake had crawled down his throat — there it had bitten itself fast.

My hand yanked at the snake and yanked: — in vain! I could not yank the lizard from his gizzard. Then out of me it cried: "Bite! Bite!

The head off! Bite!" — thus it cried out of me, my horror, my hatred, my loathing, my pity, all my good and bad cried with one cry out of me. —

You daring ones around me! You searchers, researchers, and whoever has set sail with subtle sails on unexplored seas! You riddle-happy ones!

Go ahead, solve for me the riddle I beheld then, interpret for me the vision of the loneliest one!

For it was a vision and a foreseeing: — what did I see then in an allegory?

And who is it that is yet to come one day?

Who is the shepherd into whose throat the snake crawled thus? Who is the man into whose throat all the heaviest, blackest things will crawl thus?

— But the shepherd bit, as my cry advised; he bit off a good mouthful! Far away he spewed the head of the snake —: and sprang up. —

— No longer shepherd, no longer man — a transfigured, light-bathed being that laughed! Never yet on earth has a man laughed as he laughed!

O my brothers, I heard a laughter that was no human laughter, — — and now a thirst eats at me, a longing that never ceases.

My longing for this laughter eats at me: O, how can I stand to live! And how could I stand to die now! —

Thus spake Zarathustra.

On Involuntary Bliss

With such riddles and bitterness in his heart Zarathustra sailed across the sea. But when he was four days' journey from the Blessed Isles and from his friends, then he had overcome all his pain: — triumphant and with firm feet he stood upon his fate once again. And then Zarathustra spoke thus to his jubilant conscience:

I am alone again and want to be, alone with the pure sky and the open sea; and it is afternoon again around me.

It was afternoon one day when I found my friends for the first time, afternoon as well the second time: — at the hour when all light becomes stiller.

For whatever happiness is still on the way between heaven and earth now seeks a bright soul for shelter: through happiness all light has now become stiller.

O afternoon of my life! One day my happiness also descended to the valley to seek shelter; there it found these open, hospitable souls.

O afternoon of my life! What did I not give up in order to have one thing: this live planting of my thoughts and this morning light of my highest hope!

Companions the creator once sought, and children of his hope; and behold, it was found he could not find them unless he first created them himself.

Thus am I in the midst of my work, going to my children and returning from them: for the sake of his children must Zarathustra perfect himself.

For deep down we love only our child and work; and where there is great love for oneself, it is a sign of pregnancy: thus I found it.

My children are still green in their first spring, standing next to each other and jointly jostled by the winds, the trees of my garden and best soil.

And verily! Where such trees stand next to each other, there blessed islands are!

But one day I want to dig them up and place each one alone by itself: that it may learn solitude and defiance and foresight.

Gnarled and crooked and with supple hardness shall it then stand by the sea, a living lighthouse of invincible life.

There, where the storms rush down into the sea and the mountain's snout drinks water, there each one shall one day have his day- and night- watches, for his trial and sentencing.

Tried and sentenced he shall be, to see whether he is of my kin and kind, —

whether he is master of a lofty will, taciturn, even when he does speak, and giving in so much that in giving he takes: —

— that one day he may be my companion and Zarathustra's co-creator and co-celebrator —: one that writes my will on my tablets: to the fuller perfection of all things.

And for his sake and his like I must perfect myself: therefore I turn aside from my good fortune now and offer myself to all misfortune — for my last trial and sentencing.

And verily, it was time for me to be on my way; and the wanderer's shadow and the longest while and the stillest hour — all said to me: "It is high time!"

The wind blew through the keyhole at me and said "Come!" The door flew open cunningly for me and said "Go!"

But I lay enchained by the love for my children: desire set this snare for me, the desire for love, to be my children's prey and lose myself in them.

Desire — to me this only means: having lost myself. I have you, my children! In this having, everything shall be surety and nothing desire.

But the sun of my love lay brooding over me, in his own juices Zarathustra was stewing — then shadows and doubt flew past me.

After frost and winter I even lusted: "O that frost and winter would make me crackle and crunch again!" I sighed: — then icy mists arose out of me.

My past burst its graves, many a buried-alive pain awoke; it had only enjoyed a good night's sleep, tucked away in a winding sheet.

Thus everything called out to me in signs: "It is time!" But I — heard it not: until finally my abyss stirred and my thought bit me.

Alas, abysmal thought that is my thought! When will I find the strength to hear you burrowing and no longer be trembling?

Right up to the throat my heart throbs when I hear you burrowing! Your silence as well wants to throttle me, you abysmally silent one!

Never yet have I dared to summon you up here: quite enough to have carried you around with me! Not yet have I been strong enough for my final lion-wantonness and willfulness.

Your weight was always terrible enough for me; but one day yet I shall find the strength and the lion's voice to summon you up here!

Only when I have overcome myself in that will I then also be ready to overcome myself in that which is greater; and the seal of my perfection shall be a victory!

Meanwhile I still drift upon uncertain seas; Chance, the smooth-tongued one, flatters me; forwards and backwards I look —, still no end do I see.

The hour of my final struggle has not yet come to me, — or has it come to me even now? Verily, with mischievous beauty sea and life look all around at me!

O afternoon of my life! O happiness before night! O haven on higher seas! O peace in uncertainty! How I mistrust you all!

Verily, I am mistrustful of your mischievous beauty! I am like the lover who mistrusts the all-too-velvety smile.

Just as he nudges his beloved before him, tender even in his hardness, the jealous one, — so I nudge this blissful hour before me.

Hence, you blissful hour! With you an involuntary bliss came to me!

Here I stand ready for my deepest pain: untimely you came.

Hence, you blissful hour! Better to take shelter there — with my children!

Hurry! And bless them before evening with my happiness!

There evening draws near even now: the sun is sinking. There goes — my happiness! —

Thus spake Zarathustra. And he waited for his unhappiness all night: but he waited in vain. The night remained bright and still, and happiness itself drew nearer and nearer to him. Towards morning, however, Zarathustra laughed in his heart and said mockingly: "Happiness runs after me. That comes from my not running after women. Happiness, however, is a woman."

Before Sunrise

O heaven above me, you pure one! deep one! You light-abyss! Seeing you I shudder with godly desires!

To project myself to your height — that is my depth! To protect myself in your purity — that is my innocence!

The deity shrouds his beauty: so you conceal your stars. You do not speak: so you reveal your wisdom to me.

Mute over the raging sea you rose for me today, your love and your modesty speaking revelation to my raging soul.

That you came to me beautifully, shrouded in your beauty, that you speak to me mutely, manifest in your wisdom.

O how could I not divine all the modesty of your soul! Before the sun you came to me, the loneliest one!

We have been friends from the very beginning: dread and grief and ground we have in common: even the sun we have in common.

We do not speak to each other because we know too much — : we are silent towards each other, we smile our knowledge towards each other.

Are you not the light to my fire? Do you not have the sister-soul to my insight?

Together we learned to fly; together we learned to rise above ourselves to our very selves and to smile without a cloud: —

— to smile down without a cloud out of lucid eyes and from a distance of miles, while under us aim and blame and constraint dampen like rain.

And when I wandered alone: for whom did my soul hunger in the night and on errant paths? And when I climbed mountains, whom did I seek on the mountains every time if not you?

And all my wandering and mountain climbing: it was only a necessity and a helping hand for the heavy-handed: — my whole will wants only to fly, to fly up into you!

And whom did I hate more than passing clouds and whatever defiles you?

And even my own hate I hated because it defiled you!

I am angry at the passing clouds, these prowling cats of prey: they take from you and me what is ours in common, — the vast, boundless Yea- and Amensaying.

We are angry at these meddlers and mediators, the passing clouds: these half-and-halves that have learned neither to curse nor to bless thoroughly.

Rather would I sit in a Diogenes tub under a closed heaven, rather sit in the abyss with no heaven, than see you, light-heaven, defiled by passing clouds!

And often I have longed to wire them fast with the jagged golden wires of lightning, so that I, like the thunder, could beat the kettledrum on their kettlebellies:—

— an angry kettledrummer, because they rob me of your Yea! and Amen!, you heaven above me, you pure one! light one! You light-abyss! — because they rob you of my Yea! and Amen!

For rather would I have clamor and thunder and weather-curses than this careful, doubtful cat-calm: and among men too I hate most all pussyfooters and half-and-halves and doubting, dawdling passing-clouds.

And "he who cannot learn to bless shall learn to curse!" — this bright teaching fell to me from the bright sky, this star stands in my sky even on black nights.

But I am a blesser and a yea-sayer, if only you are around me, you pure one! light one! You light-abyss! — even into all abysses I then carry my blessing yeasaying.

A blesser I have become and a yea-sayer: I wrestled long for that and was a wrestler so that one day I might free my hands for blessing.

This, however, is my blessing: to stand above everything as its own heaven, its round roof, its azure bell and eternal surety: and blessed is he who blesses thus!

For all things are baptized at the font of eternity and beyond good and evil; good and evil, however, are themselves only shadowy go-betweens and damp calamities and passing clouds. Verily, a blessing it is and no blasphemy when I teach: "Above all things stand the heaven of Chance, the heaven of Innocence, the heaven of Coincidence, the heaven of Exuberance."

"Von Chance" — this is the oldest nobility in the world, this I gave back to all things; I released them from their captivity under Purpose.

This freedom and heaven-serenity I placed like an azure bell over all things when I taught that above them and through them no "eternal will" — wills.

This exuberance and this folly I placed in place of that will when I taught: "In all things one thing is impossible — Reason!"

A little reason to be sure, a seed of wisdom strewn from star to star, — this leaven is mixed in with all things: for the sake of folly wisdom is mixed in with all things!

A little wisdom is quite possible; but this blessed surety I found in all things: that on the feet of Chance they would still rather — dance.

O heaven above me, you pure one, lofty one! This is now your purity for me, that there is no eternal reason-spider and spider web: — that to me you are a dance floor for divine chance, that to me you are a table of the gods for divine dice and dice players!

But you are blushing? Did I speak the unspeakable? Did I blaspheme while meaning to bless you?

Or is it the modesty of being two that makes you blush? — Do you bid me go and be silent because now — day comes? The world is deep — : and deeper than the day has ever conceived. Not everything can be uttered in the presence of day. But day comes: so let us now part!

O heaven above me, you modest one! glowing one! O you, my happiness before sunrise! Day comes: so let us now part! —

Thus spake Zarathustra.

On The Bedwarfing Virtue

1

When Zarathustra was back on solid ground again, he did not set off directly for his mountains and his cave, but took up many paths and questions, inquiring after this and that, so that he said of himself in jest: "Behold a river that in many twists and turns returns to its source!" For he wanted to learn what had happened to man in the meantime: whether he had grown larger or smaller. And one day he saw a row of new houses; then he was amazed and said:

"What do these houses mean? Verily, no great soul placed them here in his own image!

Perhaps a dimwitted child took them out of his toy box? Would that another child might put them back in the box again!

And these rooms and chambers: can men go in and out here? They strike me as being made for silk dolls or sweet-tooths, who are quite sweet on letting themselves be nibbled, too."

And Zarathustra stood still and mused. Finally he said, saddened: "Everything has grown smaller!"

Everywhere I see lower gateways: he who is of my kind still finds a way through, but — he must stoop!

O when will I return to my homeland, where I will not have to stoop anymore — not have to stoop anymore before the small ones!" — And Zarathustra sighed and looked off into the distance. —

That same day, however, he made his speech on the bedwarfing virtue.

2

I pass through this people and keep my eyes open: they do not forgive me for not being envious of their virtues.

They snap at me because I say to them: for small people small virtues are necessary — and because it is hard for me to accept that small people are necessary!

Here I am still like the cock in a strange farmyard whom even the hens peck at; but I take no offense at the hens for that.

I am polite towards them, as towards all small offenses; to be prickly towards what is small strikes me as wisdom for hedgehogs.

They all speak of me when they sit around the fire at night, — they speak of me, but no one thinks — of me!

This is the new stillness I have learned: their clamor around me spreads a mantle over my thoughts.

They clamor amongst each other: "What does this dark cloud want with us? Let us see to it that it brings no plague upon us!"

And the other day a woman pulled her child back to her when it wanted to come to me: "Take the children away!" she cried; "such eyes singe children's souls."

They cough when I speak: they think coughing to be an objection to strong winds, — they guess nothing of the blustering of my happiness!

"We have no time yet for Zarathustra" — thus they object; but who cares about a time that "has no time" for Zarathustra?

And if they praise me at all: how could I possibly go to sleep on their praise?

Their praise is a belt of thorns to me; it scratches me even when I undo it.

And this too I learned among them: the one who praises acts as if he were giving back, but in fact he wants to be given more.

Ask my foot whether it likes their lauding and luring strains! Verily, to such tick-tock time it wants neither to dance nor to stand still.

To a small virtue they want to laud and lure me; to the tick-tock of a small happiness they want to persuade my foot.

I pass through this people and keep my eyes open; they have grown smaller and are growing ever smaller: — that, however, is due to their teaching on happiness and virtue.

Namely, they are modest also in their virtue — for they want comfort.

With comfort, however, only a modest virtue sits well.

I suppose in their way too they learn to step and to step forward: I call that their hobbling —. With that they become a hindrance to anyone who is in a hurry.

And many of them go forward and look backward at the same time, with stiffened necks: I like to smash into them.

Foot and eye shall not lie, nor give each other the lie. But there is much lying by the small people.

Some of them will, but most of them are only willed. Some of them are genuine, but most of them are bad actors.

There are unwitting actors among them and unwilling actors —, the genuine ones are always rare, especially the genuine actors.

Of man there is little here: therefore their women act mannish. For only he who is man enough will redeem the woman in woman.

And this hypocrisy I found to be the worst among them: That even those who are in command feign the virtues of those who serve.

"I serve, you serve, we serve" — thus even the ruling hypocrisy prays here; and woe if the first master is but the first servant!

Alas, I guess the curiosity of my eye flew too far into their hypocrisies too; and well I guessed all their fly-happiness and their buzzing around sunny windowpanes.

So much kindness, so much weakness I see. So much justice and pity, so much weakness.

Round, kind, and goodly they are with each other, just as grains of sand are round, kind, and goodly with each other.

To embrace modestly a small happiness — this they call "resignation"! and at the same time they are already modestly eyeing a new small happiness.

At bottom they simply want one thing most of all: that no one do them ill.

So they get the jump on everyone and do them well.

But this is cowardice, even though it be called virtue.

And if for once they speak harshly, these small people : I hear only their hoarseness in it, — for every draught of air makes them hoarse.

Clever they are, their virtues have clever fingers. But they lack fists, their fingers do not know how to huddle behind fists.

To them virtue is that which makes modest and tame: with that they have made the wolf into a dog and man himself into man's best domestic animal.

"We place our chair in the middle" — this their smirking says to me — "and just as far away from dying gladiators as from satisfied pigs."

But this is — mediocrity: even though it be called moderation. —

3

I pass through this people and let fall many a word: but they know neither how to take it nor how to retain it.

They marvel that I came not to rail against lusts and vice; and verily, I came not to warn against pickpockets either!

They marvel that I am not ready yet to whet and abet their wit: as if they did not already have enough smart-alecks whose voices grate on me like slate pencils!

And when I cry: "A curse on all the cowardly devils in you that like to whine and fold their hands and adore": then they cry: "Zarathustra is godless."

And especially their teachers of resignation cry this —; but precisely into their ears I love to shout: Yes, I am Zarathustra the godless!

These teachers of resignation! Anywhere there is something small and sick and scabby, there they crawl, like lice: and only my nausea prevents me from squashing them.

Well then! This is my sermon for their ears: I am Zarathustra the godless who says here "Who is more godless than I that I may rejoice in his instruction?"

I am Zarathustra the godless: where am I to find my equal? And all those are my equals who give themselves their own wills and give up all resignation.

I am Zarathustra the godless: I cook every chance in my pot regardless. And only when it is fully cooked do I welcome it as my food.

And verily, many a chance came arrogantly to me: but more arrogantly still my will spoke to it, — then it lay there just begging on its knees — begging to find hearth and heart with me, and egging me on fawningly:

"Just look, O Zarathustra, how only a friend comes to a friend!" —

But why do I speak when no one has my ears? And so I will shout it out to all the winds:

You are growing ever smaller, you small people! You are crumbling, you comfort-creatures! You will yet come to ruin —

— by your many small virtues, by your many small omissions, by your many small submissions!

Too tender, too yielding: such is your soil! But for a tree to become great, it must take hard root around hard rock!

Even what you fail to do is woven into the web of all human future; even your naught is a spider web which feeds on the blood of the future.

And when you take, then it is like stealing, you small-virtued ones; but even among thieves honor speaks: "Thou shalt only steal where thou canst not rob."

"It will pass" — that too is a teaching of resignation. But I tell you, you comfort-creatures: it will take a pass at you and take more and more from you!

Alas, if only you would renounce all half-willing and become resolved in idleness as well as in action.

Alas, if only you would understand my word: "Always do what you will, —but first be those who can will!"

"Always love your neighbor as yourself, — but first be those who love themselves — loving with a great love, loving with a great contempt!" Thus speaks Zarathustra the godless. —

But why do I speak when no one has my ears? It is still too early an hour for me here.

My own precursor am I among these people, my own cock-crow down dark lanes.

But their hour is coming! And mine is coming too! Hourly they become smaller, poorer, more unfruitful, — poor plant! poor soil!

And soon they shall stand there for me like dry grass and prairie, and verily!

weary of themselves — and thirsting, more for fire than for water!

O blessed hour of lightning! O mystery before noontide! —

One day yet I will make running fires out of them and heralds with tongues of flame: —

— one day yet they shall herald it with tongues of flame: It is coming, it is nigh, the great noontide!

Thus spake Zarathustra.

On The Mount Of Olives

Winter, a bad guest, sits by me at home; my hands are blue from the handshake of his friendship.

I honor him, this bad guest, but gladly let him sit alone. Gladly I run away from him; and if one runs well, one can escape him!

With warm feet and warm thoughts I run there, where the wind stands still, to the sunny hideout of my mount of olives.

There I laugh at my severe guest and even think well of him for removing flies from my place and silencing many small noises.

For he will not suffer it if a gnat wants to sing, or perhaps two; even the lane he makes lonely, so that the moonlight is frightened there at night.

A hard guest is he, — but I honor him and do not pray, like the weaklings do, to the potbellied fire-idol.

Even a little teeth-chattering rather than idol-worshipping! — thus my kind wills it. And I am especially hostile towards all fervent, stuffy, steamy fireidols.

Him whom I love I love better in winter than in summer; better do I mock my enemies and more valiantly, now that winter sits in my home.

Valiant indeed, even when I crawl into bed —: there my holed-up happiness laughs and even raises holy hell, there even my lie of a dream laughs.

Me — a crawler? Not once in my life have I crawled before the mighty; and if ever I lied, then I lied out of love. That is why I am happy even in a winter bed.

A humble bed warms me more than a rich one, for I am jealous of my poverty.

And in winter she is most faithful to me.

I begin each day with an act of malice; I mock winter with a cold bath: my severe friend of the family grumbles at that.

I also tickle him gladly with a little wax candle: that he may finally let the sky out of its ashy-gray twilight.

For I am especially malicious in the morning: at that early hour when the pail rattles at the well and the horses neigh warmly down gray lanes: —

Impatiently I wait then for the bright sun to finally rise, the snow-bearded winter sky, the ancient wight and white-head, — the winter sky, the quiet one who often keeps even his sun quietly in hiding!

Could it be that I learned the long bright silence from him? Or did he learn it from me? Or did each of us invent it himself?

The source of all good things is thousand-fold, — all good high-spirited things spring to life out of joy: how could they ever do that — only once?

The long silence is also a good high-spirited thing, and like the winter sky, to look out from a bright, round-eyed countenance: —

— like him, to hide his sun and his inflexible solar will, verily, this art and these winter high spirits I have learned well!

My favorite art and act of malice it is, that my silence has learned not to betray itself through silence.

With chit-chat and rattling dice I outwit the solemn ones-in-waiting; my will and purpose shall give all these strict watchdogs the slip.

That no one may see down to my foundation and final will, — that is why I invented the long bright silence.

Many a shrewd man I found: he veiled his face and roiled his water so that no one could see down and through him.

Precisely to him, however, came the shrewder mistrusters and nutcrackers: precisely his most-hidden fish they fished out!

But the clear, the valiant, the transparent — to me these are the shrewdest of the silent: their foundation is so deep that not even the clearest water — reveals it. —

You snow-bearded silent winter sky, you round-eyed whitehead above me!

O you heavenly likeness of my soul and its high spirits! And must I not hide myself like one who has swallowed gold, — lest they slit open my soul?

Must I not walk on stilts, that they may overlook my long legs, — all these envy-imps and injury-pimps around me?

These smoky, room-warm, worn-out, withered, woebegone souls — how could their envy endure my happiness?

So I show them only the ice and winter on my peaks — and not that my mountain winds all the solar zones around itself besides!

They hear only my winter storms whistling: and not that I also travel over warm seas, like longing, heavy, hot, south winds.

They still feel pity at my haps and mishaps: — but my word is: "Let haphazard come to me: it is innocent, like a little child!"

How could they endure my happiness unless I set mishaps and polar bear caps and winter hardships and snowy heavens' coverings around my happiness?— unless I myself sighed before them and chattered with cold and patiently let them swathe me in their pity!

This is the wise high-spiritedness and kind-spiritedness of my soul, that it hides not its winter and its ice storms; it hides not its chilblains either. To one person solitude is the flight of the sick; to another solitude is the flight from the sick.

Let them hear me sighing and chattering from the winter cold, all these poor jealous jokers around me! With such sighing and chattering I still flee their heated rooms.

Let them sigh and sympathize with me over my chilblains: "From the ice of knowledge he will yet freeze to death!" — thus they lament.

In the meantime I run with warm feet here, there, and everywhere on my mount of olives: in the sunny hideout of my mount of olives I sing and mock all pity. —

Thus sang Zarathustra.

On Passing By

Thus, proceeding slowly through many a people and many kinds of towns, Zarathustra returned by roundabout ways to his mountains and his cave. And behold, he thereby came unawares even unto the gate of the great city: here, however, a foaming fool ran up towards him with outstretched hands and stood in his way. This, however, was the same fool that the people called "Zarathustra's ape": for by observing, he had learned something of the phrasing and cadence of his speech and had also borrowed quite readily from the storehouse of his wisdom.

The fool, however, spoke thus to Zarathustra:

"O Zarathustra, here is the great city: here you have nothing to seek and everything to lose.

Why would you wade through this mire? Have some pity on your feet! Better to spit on the city gate and — turn back!

Here it is hell for hermit's thoughts: here great thoughts are boiled alive and cooked bite-size.

Here all great feelings rot away: here only little rattleboned feelings are allowed to rattle!

Don't you already smell the slaughter-houses and soup kitchens of the spirit? Doesn't this city reek from the fumes of slaughtered spirit?

Don't you see the souls hanging there like limp, filthy rags? — And they even make newspapers out of these souls!

Don't you hear here how the spirit has become pun? Ill-willed word-swill it pukes up! — And they even make newspapers out of this word-swill.

They chase each other and know not, whither? They inflame each other and know not, why? They jingle with their tin, they jangle with their gold.

They are cold and seek warmth with distilled spirits; they are hot and seek coolness with frozen spirits; they are all sick and addicted to public opinion.

All lusts and vices are at home here; but there are virtuous ones here too, there is much deftly-placed virtue: —

Much deft virtue with writing-fingers and hard sitting- and waiting-flesh, blessed with little breast-stars and padded, rumpless daughters.

Here there is also much piety and much devout spittle-lickery, wheedlebakery before the God of Hosts.

"From on high," yes, the star and the gracious spittle trickle on down; every starless breast longs to be up there.

The moon has its court, and the court has its mooncalves: to all that comes from the court, however, the beggar-folk and all beggar-virtue pray.

"I serve, you serve, we serve" — thus all deft virtue prays up to the prince:

that the deserved star may be pinned at last upon the narrow breast!

But the moon still revolves around all things earthly: so too the prince still revolves around the most earthly thing of all: — but that is the shopkeeper's gold.

The God of Hosts is no God of gold bars: the prince proposes, but the shopkeeper — disposes!

By all that is bright and strong and good in you, O Zarathustra! Spit on this city of the shopkeepers and turn back!

Here all blood flows foamy and tepid and putrid through all veins: spit on the great city, which is the great dump where all the scum gets in a lather together!

Spit on the city of the flattened souls and the narrow breasts, the sticking eyes, the sticky fingers —

— on the city of the pushy, the brazen, the scribe-babies and crybabies, the perspiringly aspiring: —

— where everything tainted, ill-painted, lewd, sad-hued, overmellow, ulcer-yellow, conspiracy-fellowed comes to a head together:

— spit on the great city and turn back!"— —

Here however, Zarathustra interrupted the foaming fool and shut his mouth.

"Stop at last!" cried Zarathustra, "for a long time now your speech and your kind have disgusted me!

Why did you live so long by the swamp that you yourself had to turn into a frog and a toad?

Does not foamy, putrid swamp blood flow through your own veins now that you have learned to croak and slander so?

Why do you not go into the forest? Or till the soil? Is the sea not full of green isles?

I have contempt for your contempt; and if you warned me, — why did you not warn yourself?

Out of love alone shall my contempt and my bird of warning take wing: but not out of the swamp! —

They call you my ape, you foaming fool: but I call you my grunting swine, — by your grunting you even spoil for me my praise of folly.

What was it then that first made you grunt? Because no one flattered you enough: — that is why you sat yourself down by this filth, that you might have grounds for much grunting, —

— that you might have grounds for much vengeance! For all your foaming, you vain fool, is vengeance: I have divined you well!

But your fools' word does me harm, even if you are right! And even if Zarathustra's word were right a hundred times, you would do wrong with my word every time!"

Thus spake Zarathustra; and he looked out on the great city, sighed and was silent a long time. At last he spoke thus:

I also loathe this great city, and not only this fool. Here and there, there is nothing to make better, nothing to make worse.

Woe on this great city! — And I wish I could already see the pillar of fire in which it will be consumed! For such pillars of fire must precede the great noontide.

But this will have its day and its own fate! —

This lesson, however, I impart to you, you fool, in parting: where one can no longer love, there one should— pass by!

Thus spake Zarathustra, and passed by the fool and the great city.

On The Apostates
1

Alas, already all lies withered and gray which but lately stood green and gay in this meadow! And how much honey of hope I carried from here to my beehives!

All these young hearts have already become old, — and not even old! only weary, vulgar, comfortable: — as they put it, "We have become pious again."

Just recently I saw them run out in the morning on brave feet: but their feet of knowledge grew weary, and now they even slander their morning bravery.

Verily, many of them once lifted their legs like dancers, the laughter in my wisdom winked at them: — then they thought better of it. Just now I saw one of them bent over — crawling to the cross.

Around light and freedom they once fluttered like gnats and young poets. A little older, a little colder: and already they are muddlers, mumblers, and mama's boys.

Did their hearts perhaps despair because solitude had swallowed me up like a whale? Did their ears perhaps hark longingly-long but in vain for me and my trumpet- and herald-calls?

— Alas! there are always but few whose hearts are long on spirit and high spirits; and among these the spirit remains patient, too. The rest, however, are cowards.

The rest: that is always the most, the commonplace, the superfluous, the many-too-many — all these are cowardly! —

He who is of my kind will also run across the experiences of my kind along the way: so that his first companions must be corpses and buffoons.

But his second companions — they will call themselves his believers: a lively bunch, with much love, much folly, much beardless veneration.

On these believers he shall not set his heart, he who is of my kind among mankind; in these springtimes and gay meadows he shall not believe, he who knows flighty-faint human nature!

If they could do otherwise, then they would will otherwise, too. Half-and halves spoil everything whole. That leaves become withered, — what is there to cry about in that?

Let them go ahead and fall, O Zarathustra, and do not cry about it!

Better yet, blow with a rustling wind amongst them, —

— blow amongst these leaves, O Zarathustra: that everything withered may scurry away from you even faster! —

2

"We have become pious again" — so these apostates confess; and many of them are even too cowardly to confess thus.

I look them in the eye, — I say it to their faces and to the redness of their cheeks: you are those who pray again!

But it is a disgrace to pray! Not for everyone, but for you and me and whoever has a conscience in his head! For you it is a disgrace to pray!

You know it well: the cowardly devil in you who is fond of hand-folding and placing-hands-in-lap and wants to have it easier: — this cowardly devil exhorts you: "There is a God!"

But with that you belong to the light-shunning class, those whom the light never leaves in peace; now every day you must stick you head deeper into darkness and dampness!

And verily, you have chosen the hour well: for even now the night birds are flying out again. The hour has come for all the light-shunning folk, the eveningand leisure hour, when they are not — "at leisure."

I hear and smell it: their hour for hunting and ranging, not for a wild hunt of course, but for a tame, lame, prying, soft sashayers'- and prayers'-hunt —

— for a hunt after soulful sneaks: all the hearts' mousetraps have been set once again! And wherever I lift up a curtain, a little night-moth comes rushing out.

Did it perhaps cower there together with another little night-moth? For everywhere I smell little hidden communities; and wherever there are little chambers, there are new devotees within and a devotees' haze.

They spend long evenings sitting together and talking: "Let us become like little children again and say 'Dear God!'" — ruined in mouth and stomach by the pious confectioners.

Or they spend long evening watching a cunning, watchful cross-spider that preaches prudence to the other spiders and teaches thus: "Under crosses there is good spinning!"

Or they spend the day sitting by swamps with fishing rods, thereby thinking themselves profound; but he who fishes where there are no fish I do not even call superficial!

Or they learn to play the harp in a godly-gay way from a poet of song who would love to harp his way into the young girls' hearts: for he has grown weary of the old ladies and their praises.

Or they learn to shudder from a learned half-wit who waits in dark chambers for the spirit to come to him — and the spirit completely deserts him!

Or they listen to an old hobo moan- and groan-whistler who has picked up the sadness of tones from the sad winds; now he whistles like the wind and preaches sadness in sad tones.

And some of them have even become night watchmen: now they know how to blow into horns and go about at night and wake up old things that have long since gone to sleep.

Five remarks about old things I heard last night by the garden wall: they came from such old, sad, dried-up night watchmen as these.

"For a father he doesn't care enough about his children: human fathers do this better!"

"He's too old! In fact, he doesn't care about his children at all anymore" —

thus answered the other night watchman.

"Has he any children then? No one can prove it unless he proves it himself! I have long wanted him to thoroughly prove it for once."

"Prove? As if he had ever proven anything! He finds proving difficult; he thinks the world of people believing in him."

"Yes! Yes! Belief saves him, belief in him. That's just the way of old people!

And that goes for us, too!"—

— Thus the two old night watchmen and light-frightmen spoke to each other and tooted sadly on their horns: so it was last night by the garden wall.

My heart, however, squirmed with laughter and was about to shatter and knew not, whither? and sank into my midriff.

Verily, it will be the death of me yet, to choke with laughter when I see drunken asses and hear night watchmen doubting God thus.

Is not the time long since past for even having such doubts? Who can still awaken such old, sleeping, light-shunning things?

With the old gods after all, the end has long since come to pass: and verily, a gay, goodly, godly ending they had!

They did not "twilight" themselves to death, — that is surely a lie! On the contrary: one day they laughed themselves to death!

That happened when a god himself came out with the ungodliest saying, —

the saying: "There is one God! Thou shalt have no other gods before me!" —

— an old grimbeard of a god, a jealous one, forgot himself this way: —

And then all the gods laughed and rocked back in their chairs and cried out:

"Is this not honest-to-Godliness, that there are gods but no God!"

He that has ears to hear, let him hear. —

Thus talked Zarathustra in the town which he loved and which is also surnamed "The Dappled Cow." For from here he had only two days journey back to his cave and his animals; his soul rejoiced continually, however, at the imminence of his return home. —

The Return Home

O Solitude! My homeland, Solitude! Too long have I lived abroad, savagely in savage remoteness, not to return to you with tears!

Now just threaten me with your finger, the way mothers threaten, now smile at me, the way mothers smile, now just say: "And who was it that once stormed away from me like a stormwind? —

— who cried out in parting: I have sat too long with Solitude, I have unlearned silence! That — you have learned now, I presume?

O Zarathustra, I know everything: and that you were more forsaken among the many, you lone one, than you ever were by me!

Forsakenness is one thing, loneliness another: That — you have learned now! And that among men you will always be savage and strange:

— savage and strange even when they love you: for before anything else they want to be spared!

Here, however, you are at house and home with yourself; here you can speak out about anything and pour out all the reasons, here nothing is ashamed of hidden, hardened feelings.

Here all things come caressingly to your speech and flatter you: for they want to ride upon your back. Here on every simile you ride to every truth.

Upright and uprightly you can speak to all things here: and verily, it sounds like praise to their ears, for someone to speak to all things — straightforwardly!

But being forsaken is another thing. Then, do you remember, O Zarathustra?

When your bird shrieked overhead, when you stood in the forest perplexed, not knowing which way?, next to a corpse: —

— when you said: May my animals lead me! More dangerous have I found it among men than among beasts: — That was forsakenness!

And do you remember, O Zarathustra? When you sat on your island, a well of wine among empty buckets, giving and giving out, bestowing and bestowing out among the thirsty:

— until at last you alone sat thirsty among the drunken ones and complained nightly 'Is taking not more blessed than giving? And stealing not more blessed yet than taking?' — That was forsakenness!

And do you remember, O Zarathustra? When your stillest hour came and drove you away from yourself, when it spoke to you in a wicked whisper: 'Chatter and shatter!'—

— when it made you regret all your waiting and silence and discouraged your humble courage: That was forsakenness!" —

O Solitude! My homeland, Solitude! How blessed and tender your voice speaks to me!

We do not question each other, we do not complain to each other, we go openly together through open doors.

For it is open by you and bright; and here the hours pass by on lighter feet, too. For in the darkness time weighs more heavily on us than in the light.

Here the words and word-coffers of all being spring open for me: here all being wants to become word, here all becoming wants to learn speech from me.

But down there — there all speech is in vain! There forgetting and passingby is the best wisdom: That — I have learned now!

He who would get a grasp on all things human must grasp all things human. But my hands are too clean for that.

Even their breath I do not care to breathe; alas, to have lived so long amidst their clamor and bad breath!

O blessed stillness around me! O pure scents around me! O how from a deep breast this stillness draws pure breath! O how it listens, this blessed stillness!

But down there — there everything speaks, there everything is misheard.

One may ring in one's wisdom with bells: the traders in the marketplace will outjingle it with pennies!

Everything speaks by them, now one knows how to understand any more.

Everything falls to the ground, nothing falls into deep wells any more.

Everything speaks by them, nothing prospers and comes to a proper end.

Everyone cackles, but who wants to sit still on the nest and hatch the eggs?

Everything speaks by them, everything gets talked to death. And that which yesterday was still too hard for time itself and its tooth: today it hangs, gnawed and pawed away, from the mouths of the men of today.

Everything speaks by them, everything is revealed. And what was once called the secret and the secrecy of profound souls now belongs to the streettrumpeters and other butterflies.

O human nature, you curious thing! You noise on dark streets! Now you lie behind me again: my greatest danger lies behind me!

In sparing and pitying my greatest danger always lay; and all human nature wants to be spared and suffered.

With pent-up truths, with a fool's hand and a smitten heart, and rich in pity's little lies: — thus have I always lived among men.

Disguised I sat among them, ready to mistake myself in order to endure them, and readily telling myself: "You fool, you do not understand man!"

One unlearns man when one lives among men: there is too much foreground in all men — what can far-seeing, far-seeking eyes do there?

And when they mistook me: I, fool, spared them more than myself on that account: accustomed as I am to hardness towards myself, and often even taking vengeance on myself for this forbearance.

Stung all over by poisonous flies and hollowed out like a stone by the many drops of spite — thus I sat among them and still tried to persuade myself:

"Everything small is innocent of its smallness!"

Especially those who call themselves "the good" I found to be the most poisonous flies: they sting in all innocence, they lie in all innocence; towards me how could they be — just?

He who lives among the good — pity teaches him to lie. Pity makes the air stuffy for all free souls. For the stupidity of the good is unfathomable.

To conceal myself and my riches — that I learned down there: for I found everyone still poor in spirit. This was the lie of my pity that I knew in everyone.

— that I saw and smelled in everyone what was just enough spirit for them and what was already too much spirit for them!

Their strait-laced sages: I called them sagacious, not strait-laced, — thus I learned to slur words. Their gravediggers: I called them researchers and testers, — thus I learned to change words.

The gravediggers dig themselves sick. Bad fumes rest under old rubbish.

One should not stir up the morass. One should live upon mountains.

With blissful nostrils I breathe mountain freedom again! My nose is freed at last from the smell of all things human in nature!

Tickled by the keen air as if by a sparkling wine, my soul sneezes — sneezes and rejoices to itself: Gesundheit!

Thus spake Zarathustra.

On The Three Evils

1

In a dream, in my last dream of the morning, I stood today on a promontory, — beyond the world: held a pair of scales and weighed the world.

Alas that the rosy dawn came too early to me: she glowed me awake, the jealous one! She is always jealous of the glow of my morning dream.

Measurable by him who has the time, weighable by a good weigher, wingable by means of strong wings, crackable by divine nutcrackers: thus did my dream find the world: —

My dream, a bold sailor, half-ship, half-gale, silent as a butterfly, impatient as a falcon: but how did it have the patience and leisure for world-weighing today!

Did my wisdom secretly speak to it perhaps, my laughing, waking day-wisdom which scoffs at all "infinite worlds"? For it says: "Where there is force, there number will also be mistress: it has more force."

How securely my dream looked upon this finite world, not curiously, not spuriously, not knock-kneed, not pleading:

— as if a full apple offered itself to my hand, a ripe golden apple with coolsmooth, velvety skin: thus the world offered itself to me: —

— as if a tree beckoned to me, a broad-branched and strong-willed one, curved into an armrest and even a footrest for the way-weary: thus stood the world on my promontory:

— as if delicate hands carried a shrine towards me, — a shrine open for the delight of modest, adoring eyes: thus the world offered itself to me today: —

— not riddle enough to scare human love away, not solution enough to lull human wisdom to sleep: — a humanly good thing the world was for me today, of which people have such bad things to say!

How I thank my morning dream for allowing me thus to weigh the world early this morning! As a humanly good thing it came to me, this dream and heartcomforter!

And that I may do the like by day and learn by and after observing its best: I will now place the three worst things on the scale and weigh them in a humanly good way. —

He who taught to bless also taught to curse: what are the three best-cursed things in the world? These I will place on the scale.

Sensuality, lust for power, selfishness: these three have hitherto been the best cursed, worst slanted and slandered, — these three I will weigh in a humanly good way.

Well then! Here is my promontory and there the sea; it rolls itself hither to me, shaggily, fawningly, the faithful old hundred-headed dog-monster that I love.

Well then! Here will I hold the scales over the rolling sea: and a witness too I will choose, to oversee, — you, you recluse-tree, you strongly-scented, broadlyarched one which I love! —

By what bridge does the Now pass to the Hereafter? By what force does the high force its way to the low? And what bids even the highest thing to everupwards grow?

Now the scales are balanced and still; three heavy questions I throw in, three heavy answers the other scale holds.

2

Sensuality: to all hair-shirted despisers of the body, their thorn and stake, and cursed as "the world" by all afterworlders: for it mocks and dupes all confusion- and delusion-teachers.

Sensuality: to the rabble, the slow fire on which they are burned; to all worm-eaten wood, to all stinking rags, the ready lust- and must-oven.

Sensuality: for the free hearts, innocent and free, an earthly garden of delight, all the future's excess thanks to the present.

Sensuality: only for the wilted a sweet poison; for the lion-willed, however, the great cordial and reverently-considered wine of wines.

Sensuality: the great metaphorical happiness for a higher happiness and the highest hope. For to many is marriage promised, and more than marriage, —

— to many that are stranger to each other than man and woman: and who has fully grasped how strange man and woman are to each other?

Sensuality: but I want hedges around my thoughts and even around my words, lest swine and swooners break into my garden!

Lust for power: the red-hot scourge of the hardest of the hard-hearted; the gruesome torture reserved for the cruelest ones themselves; the gloomy flame of living funeral pyres.

Lust for power: the wicked gadfly which is set upon the vainest people; the scorner of all uncertain virtue; it rides on every horse and every sort of pride.

Lust for power: the earthquake that breaks and breaks open everything rotten and hollow; the rumbling, grumbling shatterer of whited sepulchres; the flashing question mark next to premature answers.

Lust for power: before whose glance man creeps and stoops and drudges and becomes lower than serpent and swine: until finally the great contempt cries out of him —, Lust for power: the terrible schoolmistress of the great contempt that preaches in the face of cities and kingdoms "Away with you!" — until out of themselves there cries out "Away with me!"

Lust for power: which, however, also rises alluringly to the pure and solitary ones and up to self-sufficient heights, glowing like a love which paints crimson joys alluringly on earthy skies.

Lust for power: but who would call it lustmania when the high lusts downward for power! Verily, there is nothing sick or manic in such lusting and descending! That the lonely height may not be eternally alone and self-sufficing; that the mountain may come to the valley and the winds of the height to the plains: —

O who could find the right baptismal and moral name for such longing!

"Bestowing virtue" — thus Zarathustra once named the unnameable.

And at that time it also happened — and verily, it happened for the first time! — that his word glorified selfishness, the sound, healthy selfishness which wells up out of a mighty soul: —

— out of a mighty soul, to which the lofty body belongs, the handsome, triumphant, uplifting body around which every thing becomes a mirror:

— the supple, persuasive body, the dancer whose likeness and epitome the self-delighting soul is. The self-delight of such bodies and souls calls itself: "virtue."

With its words about good and bad such self-delight shelters itself as if with sacred groves; with the names of its happiness it banishes everything contemptible from itself.

It banishes everything cowardly from itself; it says: "Bad — that is cowardly!"

It thinks contemptible the ever-sighing, the ever-crying, the worry-warts, and whoever gleans the least little advantage.

It despises as well all woe-happy wisdom: for verily, there is also a wisdom which blooms in the dark, a nightshade wisdom which always says "All is vain!"

Shy mistrust it thinks little of, and anyone who demands oaths instead of looks and hands: also all the all-too-mistrustful wisdom, for such is the nature of cowardly souls.

It thinks even less of the quick-to-please, the doglike, who lie on their backs immediately, the submissive; and there is also a wisdom which is submissive and doglike and pious and quick to please.

Utterly hateful and distasteful to it is he who will never defend himself, he who swallows down poisonous spittle and evil glances, the all-too-patient, allsuffering, all-satisfied one: for that is slavish in nature.

Whether one be slavish before gods and godly kicks, or before humans and stupid human opinions: all slavish nature it spits on, this blessed selfishness!

Bad: so it calls all that is crest-fallen and slavish-knavish, unfree blinkereyes, depressed hearts, and that falsely compliant nature which kisses with thick lily-livered lips.

And mock-wisdom: so it calls all the wit which slaves, grayheads, and weary-warts affect; and especially the whole sick, sophomoric, sophistical priestly-foolishness.

The would-be-wise, however, all the priests, the world-weary, and those whose souls are slavish and womanish in nature, — O how all along their game has been to play a nasty game on selfishness!

And precisely this was meant to pass for virtue and to be virtue, that one play a nasty game on selfishness! And "selfless" — thus with good reason all these world-weary cowards and cross-spiders wished this term upon themselves!

But for all of them the day is now at hand, the transformation, the executioner's sword, the great noontide: many things shall then come to light.

And he who pronounces the "I" wholesome and holy and selfishness blessed, verily, he, a foreteller, tells likewise what he knows: "Behold, it is coming, it is nigh, the great noontide!"

Thus spake Zarathustra.

On The Spirit Of Gravity

1

My glib tongue — is of the people: too coarsely and cordially do I speak for the Angora rabbits. And my word sounds even stranger to all ink-fishes and quill-foxes.

My hand — is a fool's hand: woe to all tables and walls and whatever has room for fool's scrolling, fool's scrawling!

My foot — is a horse's foot; with it I trot and trample over hill and dale, criss-crossing the fields, devilishly pleased with all fast running.

My stomach — is an eagle's stomach, perhaps? For it loves lamb's flesh the best. Certainly, however, it is a bird's stomach.

Nourished on innocent things and on hardly anything, ready and impatient to fly, to fly away — this is now my nature: how could there not be something of a bird-nature therein!

And chiefly, that I may be an enemy to the spirit of gravity — this is birdnature:

and indeed, a sworn enemy, an arch-enemy, the original enemy! O where has my enmity not yet flown and misflown!

Of that I could well sing a song — — and will sing it: even though I am alone in an empty house and must sing it to my own ears.

There are other singers, of course, for whom only a full house can make their throats soft, their hands talkative, their eyes expressive, their hearts awake:— I am not like them. —

2

He who one day teaches men to fly will have removed all boundary stones; all boundary stones will themselves fly in the air for him, the earth he will baptize anew — as "The Light One."

The ostrich runs faster than the fastest horse, but he still sticks his head heavily into the heavy earth: so it is with the man who cannot yet fly.

Earth and life are heavy for him; and thus the spirit of gravity wills it! But he who would be light and a bird must love himself: thus I teach.

Of course not with the love of the sick and the diseased: for with these even self-love stinks!

One must learn to love oneself — thus I teach — with a wholesome and healthy love: to stand by oneself and not go roaming around.

Such roaming around dubs itself "neighborly love": the best lying and dissembling yet has been with these words, and especially by those whom all the world has found to be burdensome.

And verily, it is no commandment for today and tomorrow, to learn to love oneself. On the contrary, of all the arts this is the subtlest, slipperiest, latest, and most patient.

Because for its owner all that is his own is well-hidden; and of all treasure troves our own is the last to be unearthed — thus the spirit of gravity manages it.

Almost as early as the cradle we are showered with grave words and values:

"good" and "evil" — thus this dowry calls itself. For its sake we are forgiven for living.

And therefore one suffers the little children to come unto one, in order to prevent them betimes from loving themselves: thus the spirit of gravity manages it.

And we — we faithfully carry the dowry we are given, on hard shoulders and over rugged mountains! And if we sweat, they say to us: "Yes, life is hard to bear!"

But man is only hard for himself to bear! That comes from carrying too many strange things on his shoulders. Like a camel he kneels down and allows himself to be well-laden.

Especially the strong, load-bearing man in which reverence dwells: too many strange, heavy words and values he loads upon himself, —

then life seems to him a desert!

And verily! Many a thing that is our very own is also hard to bear! And much that is inside man is like an oyster, namely, loathsome and slippery and hard to grasp —, — so that a noble shell with noble embellishment must plead on its behalf.

But this art too one must learn: to have a shell and a fine shine and a prudent blindness!

Many things about man deceive repeatedly, because many a shell is low and sad and too much shell. Much hidden goodness and strength is never divined; the tastiest dainties find no tasters!

Women know that, the daintiest ones do: a little fatter, a little thinner — O how much destiny lies in so little!

Man is hard to discover, and hardest of all for himself; the spirit often lies about the soul. Thus the spirit of gravity manages it.

But he has discovered himself who says: This is my good and evil: with this he has silenced the mole and dwarf which says: "Good for all, evil for all."

Verily, I also do not care for those who call every thing good and this the best of all possible worlds. Those I call the all-satisfied.

Pan-satisfaction, which knows how to taste everything: that is not the best taste! I honor the unruly choosy tongues and stomachs which have learned to say "I" and "Yes" and "No."

But to chew and digest everything — that is truly swinish in nature!

Always to say Ye-haw (Yes and Hee-haw) — only the ass has learned that, and those of his frame of mind! —

Deep yellow and hot red: thus my taste wills it, — it mixes blood with all colors. But he who whitewashes his house betrays a whitewashed soul to me.

Some in love with mummies, the others with ghosts, and both alike foes to all that is flesh and blood — O how they both run contrary to my taste! For I love blood.

And I refuse to reside and abide where everyone spits and spews: that is now my taste, — rather would I live among perjurers and thieves. No one carries gold in his mouth.

Even more repulsive to me, however, are all lickspittles; and the most repulsive human animal I found I christened parasite: it would not love and yet wanted to live on love.

Unhappy I call all those who have but one choice: to become evil beasts or evil tamers of beasts: among such men I would build no tabernacles. Unhappy I also call all those who must always wait, — that runs contrary to my taste: all the publicans and tradesmen and kings and other land- and storekeepers.

Verily, I also learned waiting, and thoroughly so, — but only waiting for myself. And above all else I learned standing and walking and running and jumping and dancing and climbing.

My teaching, however, is this: he who would one day learn to fly must first learn standing and walking and running and jumping and dancing and climbing: you do not fly into flying!

With rope ladders I learned to climb up to many a window, with nimble legs I clambered up high masts: and to sit atop high masts of perception seemed to me no mean bliss, —

— like a small flame flickering atop high masts: a small light, of course, but a great consolation to sailors driven off-course and castaways! —

By many means and methods I came to my truth: not by one ladder did I climb to the height where my eye roams about in my distance.

And only reluctantly did I ever ask about the way, — that always went against my taste! Rather I asked and assayed the ways themselves!

All my going has been a testing and a questioning: and verily, one must also learn to answer such questioning! That, however — is my taste:— not good, not bad, but my taste, for which I no longer make a secret nor feel any shame.

"This — is now my way, — where is yours?" thus I answered those who asked me "the way." For the way — it does not exist!

Thus spake Zarathustra.

On Old And New Tables

1

Here I sit and wait, old broken tables around me and also new half-written tables. When will my hour come?

— the hour of my going down, my downgoing: for yet once more will I go unto men.

For that I now wait: for first the signs must come to me that this is my hour, — namely, the laughing lion with the flight of doves.

In the meantime I talk to myself as one who has the time. No one tells me anything new: so I tell myself to myself. —

2

When I came to men, I found them sitting on an old conceit: they all thought that for a long time now they have known what is good and evil for man.

All talk of virtue they thought to be an old played-out thing; and he who wanted to sleep well always talked about "good" and "evil" before going to sleep!

I disturbed this slumber when I taught: no one yet knows what good and evil is: — unless he be the creator!

— That, however, is he who creates man's goal and gives to the earth its meaning and its future: he first makes something be good or evil.

And I told them to overturn their old academic chairs and wherever that old conceit was seated; I told them to laugh at their virtue-masters and saints and poets and world-saviors.

At their gloomy wise men I told them to laugh, and at whomever was seated in warning like a black scarecrow on the tree of life.

On the great grave-highway I sat down, and even among carrion and vultures — and I laughed at all their days of yore and their rotten decaying splendor.

Verily, like penitential preachers and fools I cried out in rage and shame at all their things great and small, — that their best is so very small! That their worst is so very small! — thus I laughed.

My wise longing, begotten in the mountains, laughed and cried out of me thus, a wild wisdom indeed! — my great wing-tingling longing.

And often it carried me off and up and away and in the midst of laughter: then I flew shuddering, an arrow, through sun-drunken raptures:— out into distant futures which no dream had yet seen, into souths hotter than any artist ever dreamed: there, where dancing gods are ashamed of all clothing:— because I speak in parables and halt and stammer like the poets: and verily, I am ashamed that I must still be a poet! —

Where all becoming seemed to me gods' dancing and gods' exuberancing, and the world was let out and let loose and fleeing back to itself: —

— as an eternal self-fleeing and self-seeking-again of many gods, as the blessed gainsaying, again- hearing, again-adhering to each other of many gods: —

Where all time seemed to me a blessed mockery of moments, where necessity was freedom itself playing happily with the thorn of freedom: —

Where I also found again my old devil and arch-enemy, the spirit of gravity, and all that he has created: constraint, statute, need and result and purpose and will and good and evil: —

For must there not be that which is danced over, danced across? Must there not for the sake of the light, of the lightest — be moles and heavy dwarves?" —

3

It was there also, by the way, where I picked up the word "Superman," and that man is something that must be overcome.

— that man is a bridge and not a goal: counting himself blessed on account of his noontide and evening as the way to new rosy dawns:

— the Zarathustra-word on the great noontide and whatever else I hung above man like another purple sunset sky.

Verily, new stars likewise I let them see, together with new nights; and above the clouds and day and night I even spread laughter like a gay canopy.

I taught them all my aims and schemes: to collect and condense into one what is fragment in man and riddle and terrible chance, — as the composer, riddle-reader, and redeemer of chance I taught them to work on the future and creatively redeem —, all that has been.

To redeem the past in man and re-create every "It was," until the will says:

"But so I willed it! So I will will it —"

— this I called their redemption, this alone I taught them to call redemption.

Now I await my redemption —, that I may go to them for the last time.

For once more will I go to men: to my ruin will I go in going down to them, in dying will I give them my richest gift!

This I learned from the sun when it goes down, aboundingly rich: from inexhaustible riches it showers gold into the sea, —

— so that even the poorest fisherman rows with golden oars! For this did I once see and in the watching did not weary of my tears. — —

Like the sun Zarathustra too wants to go down: now he sits here and waits, old broken tables around him, and also new tables, — half-written.

4

Behold, here is a new table: but where are my brothers who will carry it with me down to the valley and into hearts of flesh?

My great love for the furthest ones demands it thus: do not spare your neighbor!

Man is something that must be overcome.

There are many means and methods of overcoming: watch what you do! But only a buffoon thinks: "Man can also be passed over."

Overcome yourself even in your neighbor: and a right you can seize for yourself you should not allow to be given to you!

What you do, no one can do to you in return. Behold, there is no retribution.

He who cannot command himself shall obey. And many a man can command himself, but much is still lacking before he can also obey himself!

5

Thus the nature of noble soul wills it: they want nothing for free, least of all life.

He who is of the masses wants to live for free; but we others, to whom life has given itself, we are always thinking about what we can best give in return!

And verily, that is a grand speech which says: "What life promises us, that promise we shall keep — to life!"

One should not wish to enjoy where one does not give enjoyment. And —

one should not wish to enjoy!

For enjoyment and innocence are the most modest things: neither would be sought after. One should have them — , but one should rather seek even guilt and pain! —

6

O my brothers, he who is a firstling is always sacrificed. Now, however, we are firstlings.

We all bleed on secret, sacrificial altars, we all burn and broil in honor of ancient idols.

The best in us is still young; that excites old palates. Our flesh is tender, our skin is only a lambskin: — how could we not excite old idol-priests!

In our very selves he still dwells, the old idol-priest who broils our best for his feast. Alas, my brothers, how could firstlings not be sacrifices!

But thus our nature wills it; and I love those who will not preserve themselves.

The downgoers I love with all my love: for they go across. —

7

To be true — few can do that! And those who can do not even want to! The good can do it least of all, however.

O these good men! Good men never tell the truth; for the spirit to be good in such a way is a sickness.

They give way, these good men, they give up; their heart mimics, their foundation obeys: but he who obeys turns a deaf ear to hearing himself!

All that the good call evil must come together in order for one truth to be born: O my brothers, are you also evil enough for this truth?

The bold venture, the long mistrust, the cruel Nay, the disgust, the cut to the quick — how seldom these come together! From such a seed, however —truth is begotten!

All knowledge hitherto has grown up next to a bad conscience! Break, break for me, you knowing ones, the old tables!

8

When the water has been planked over, when walkways and railings leap over the river: verily, he is not believed who then says: "All is in flux."

But even the blockheads contradict him. "What?" the blockheads say, "All in flux? Surely there are walkways and railings over the river?"

"Over the river all is stable, all the values of things, the bridges, the ideas, all the 'good' and 'evil': all that is stable!" —

But comes the hard winter, the river's animal trainer: then even the wittiest learn mistrust; and verily, not only the blockheads then say, "Do not all things —stand still?"

"Basically all things stand still" — , that is a true winter teaching, a good thing for an unfruitful time, a good consolation for hibernators and homebodies.

"Basically all things stand still" —; against that, however, the thawing wind preaches!

The thawing wind, a bull which is no plow-bull, — a raging bull, a destroyer that breaks the ice with angry horns! Ice, however — — breaks walkways!

O my brothers, is not all now in flux? Have not all walkways and railings fallen into the water? Who would still hold onto "good" and "evil"?

"Woe to us! Hail to us! The thawing wind blows!" — Preach thus, my brothers, through all the streets!

9

There is an old delusion called good and evil. Around soothsayers and astrologers the wheel of this delusion has hitherto revolved.

Once upon a time people believed in soothsayers and astrologers: and therefore they believed "Fate is everything: you shall, for you must!"

Then again, they mistrusted all soothsayers and astrologers: and therefore they believed "Freedom is everything: you are able, for you are willing!"

O my brothers, with regard to the stars and the future there has hitherto only been delusion, not knowledge: and therefore with regard to good and evil there has hitherto only been delusion, not knowledge.

10

"Thou shalt not steal! Thou shalt not kill!" — such words were once called holy; before them knees and heads were bent and shoes removed.

But I ask you: where have there ever been better robbers and killers in the world than these holy words?

Is there not in all life itself — robbing and killing? And that such words were called holy, was not truth itself — killed therewith?

Or was it a sermon of death that was called holy, that denies and advises against life? O my brothers, break, break for me the old tables!

11

My pity for all that is past is this, that I see: it is abandoned, —

— abandoned to the mercy, the mind, the madness of every generation that comes along and re-interprets all that has been as its bridge!

A great tyrant might arise, a clever monster who by his favor and disfavor could force and enforce all the past: until it became for him a bridge and a herald and an omen and a cockcrow.

This, however, is the other danger and my other source of pity: whoever is of the masses, his thoughts go back to the grandfather, — with the grandfather, however, time comes to an end.

Thus is all the past abandoned: for it may come that one day the masses become master and drown all time in shallow waters.

Therefore, O my brothers, a new nobility is required, as an adversary to all the rabble and all that is tyrannical and to write anew on new tables the word "noble."

For many noble sorts are required, and many sorts of nobles, for there to be nobility! Or, as I once said in a parable: "Is this not honest-to-Godliness, that there are gods but no God?"

12

O my brothers, I hallow you and show you the way to a new nobility; you shall be breeders and begetters and sowers of the future, —

— verily, not to a nobility you can buy like the shopkeepers do, and with shopkeeper's gold: for whatever has its price has little value.

Not where you come from but where you are going to, make this your honor from now on! Your will and your foot, which has a will to go beyond you yourself, — make this your new honor!

Verily, not that you have served a prince — what do princes matter? — or that you have become a bulwark for whatever stands, so that it stands more solidly!

Not that your kind have become courtly at court and you have learned to stand colorfully, like a flamingo, for long hours in shallow ponds: — for standing ability stands the courtier in good stead; and all courtiers believe that among the blessings after death belongs — permission to sit! —

And not that a spirit which they call holy led your forefathers into promised lands, which I promise not to praise: for where the worst of all trees grew, the crucifix — in that land there is nothing to praise! - — and verily, wherever this "Holy Spirit" led his knights, always in these expeditions there went foremost — goats and geese and geeks and Jesus freaks! —

O my brothers, not backward shall your nobility look, but onward! Exiles you shall be from all father and forefather lands!

Your children's land you shall love: let this love be your new nobility, — the undiscovered land, in the remotest seas! For that I bid your sails seek and seek!

In your children you shall make amends for being your fathers' children; thus shall you redeem all the past! This new table I place over you!

13

"Why live? All is vain! Living — that is threshing straw; living — that is burning oneself and still not getting warm." —

Such antiquated babble still passes for "wisdom"; but because it is old and smells musty it therefore acquires more honor. Even mold ennobles. —

Children might speak thus: they shy away from the fire because it has burned them! There is much childishness in the old books of wisdom!

And he who always "threshes straw," why should he be allowed to slander threshing? Such fools must certainly be muzzled!

They sit down at the table and bring nothing with them, not even a good appetite — and then they backbite "All is vain!"

But to eat and drink well, O my brothers, is certainly no vain art! Break, break for me the tables of the never-happy!

14

"Unto the pure all things are pure" — so speak the people. But I say to you:

Unto the swine all things become swinish!

That is why the dreamers and head-droopers, whose hearts also droop, preach: "The world itself is a filthy monster."

For all these are unclean spirits; but especially those who enjoy neither rest nor repose unless they view the world from the backside, — the afterworlders!

I say it to their faces, though it may not sound nice: The world is like man in that it has a backside — so much is true!

In the world there is much filth: so much is true! But the world itself is not therefore a filthy monster!

In this there is wisdom, that many things in the world smell bad: loathing itself creates wings and spring-divining powers!

In the best there is still something loathsome; and the best is still something that must be overcome. —

O my brothers, in this there is much wisdom, that in the world there is much filth! —

15

Such sayings I heard pious afterworlders saying to their conscience, and verily, without wickedness or falsehood — although there is nothing more false in the world or more wicked.

"Just let the world be! Raise not even one finger against it! They will yet learn to renounce the world for that reason."

"And your own reason — you should stifle and strangle it yourself; for it is a reason of this world, — for that reason you yourself shall learn to renounce the world." —

— Break, break to pieces, O my brothers, these old tables of the pious.

Chatter to pieces the sayings of the world-slanderers!

16

"He who learns much unlearns all violent desire" — this is whispered in all the dark alleys today.

"Wisdom makes weary, it is worth — nothing; thou shalt not desire!" —this new table I found hanging even in open marketplaces.

Break for me, O my brothers, break for me as well this new table! The worldweary hung it up there, and the preachers of death, and the jailors too; for lo, it is also a sermon to servitude: —

Because they learned badly and not the best things, and everything too early and everything too quickly: because they ate badly — for that reason they all got an upset stomach, — for their spirit is an upset stomach: it recommends death! Then verily, my brothers, the spirit is a stomach!

Life is a fountain of delight: but all wells are poisoned for him out of whom an upset stomach, the father of affliction, speaks.

To know: that is delight to the lion-willed! But he who has grown weary is himself only "willed"; every wave plays with him.

And thus is it ever with the weaker sort of men: they lose themselves along the way. And at last their weariness simply asks: "Why did we ever go any way at all? It is all the same!"

It is music to their ears to hear this preached: "Nothing is worthwhile! Thou shalt not will" But this is a sermon to servitude.

O my brothers, like a fresh bluster-wind comes Zarathustra to all the wayweary; many noses will he yet get to sneeze!

Even through walls my free breath blows, and into prisons and imprisoned spirits!

Willing sets free: for willing is creating: thus I teach. And you shall learn only for the sake of creating!

And the learning as well you shall only learn from me, the learning-well! He that has ears to hear, let him hear!

17

There stands the boat, — over there it goes, perhaps into the great nothingness.

— But who is willing to go aboard this "perhaps"?

Not one of you is willing to go aboard the boat of death! Why should you be world-weary then?

World-weary! And not once yet have you been earth-removed! Ever lusting for the earth have I found you, ever in love with your own earth-weariness!

Not in vain does your lip hang down: — a little earth-wish still sits upon it!

And in your eye — does not a little cloud of unforgettable bliss still float there?

There are many good inventions on earth, some of them useful, others pleasant: on their account the earth is to be loved.

And so many kinds of well-invented things are there that it is like a woman's breast: useful and pleasant at the same time.

But you world-weary ones! You earth-lazy ones! You should be stroked with switches! With switch strokes your legs should be made lively again.

For: if you are not invalids and worn-out wretches of which the world is weary, then you are sly sluggards and sweet-toothed huggermuggered pleasurecats.

And if you will not run merrily again, then you shall pass away!

To the incurable one should not wish to be a physician: thus Zarathustra teaches: — then you shall pass away!

But it takes more courage to make an end than to make a new verse: all physicians and poets know this. —

18

O my brothers, there are tables which weariness has created and tables which laziness, the rotten-tasting, has created: although they speak alike, they must be heard quite differently. —

See this one languishing here! An inch short of his goal is he, but out of weariness he has lain down defiantly in the dust here: this brave soul!

Now the sun glows on him and the dogs lick his sweat: but he lies here in his defiance and would rather languish:

— languish an inch short of his goal! Verily, you will yet have to drag him by the hair into his heaven, — this hero!

Better yet, let him lie where he has lain and let sleep, the comforter, come to him with cooling, pouring rain:

Let him lie until he wakes up on his own, — until on his own he renounces all weariness and what weariness has instilled in him.

If only, my brothers, you would scare the dogs away from him, the rotten sneaks, and all the swarming vermin: — all the swarming vermin of the "cultured," that upon the sweat of every hero — make themselves fat! —

19

I form circles around me and holy boundaries; ever fewer climb with me on ever higher mountains: I build a mountain range out of ever holier mountains. —

But to wheresoever you care to climb with me, O my brothers: see to it that a parasite does not climb with you!

Parasite: that is a creeping, cringing creature that wants to grow fat in your sick, sore corners.

And that is its art, to divine in climbing souls where they are weary: in your sorrow and discontent, in your tender modesty, it builds its disgusting nest.

Where the strong are weak, where the noble are all too gentle, — in there it builds its disgusting nest; the parasite lives where the great have little sore spots.

What is the highest species of all being and the lowest? The parasite is the lowest species; but he that is of the highest species feeds the most parasites.

That soul, namely, which has the longest ladder and can go down the deepest: how could it not have the most parasites sitting on it? — the most extensive soul, which can run and ramble and roam the furthest within itself; the most essential soul, which hurls itself with pleasure into chance: —

— the being soul which plunges into becoming, the having soul which insists upon willing and longing: —

— the self-fleeing soul, which catches up with itself in the widest sphere; the wisest soul, which folly sweet-talks the most: - — the most self-loving soul, in which all things have their current and counter-current and ebb and flow: — O how could the highest soul not have the worst parasites?

20

O my brothers, am I cruel then? But I say: what is falling, we should still push!

Everything today — it is falling, it is falling apart: who would hold it up?

but I — I would still push it!

Do you know the delight which rolls stones into steep depths? — These men of today: just look how they roll into my depths!

A preceding act am I to better players, O my brothers! A precedent! Act on my precedent!

And those you do not teach to fly, teach them — to fall faster! —

21

I love the brave; but it is not enough to wield a broadsword, — one must also know whom to hew!

And often there is more bravery in restraining yourself and passing by: thereby you preserve yourself for a worthier enemy.

You should only have enemies you may hate, not enemies you may despise: you must be proud of your enemy: thus I taught once before.

For the worthier enemy, O my friends, you should preserve yourselves: therefore there is much you must pass by, —especially much riff-raff, which noises in your ears about people and peoples.

Keep your eye clear of their For and Against! There is much right, much wrong there: he who looks on flies into a passion.

Viewing thereinto, hewing thereinto — they are one there: therefore go away into the forest and lay your sword to rest!

Go your ways! And let people and peoples go theirs! — dark ways, verily, upon which not even one hope flashes like lightning any longer!

Let the shopkeepers rule there, where all that still glitters is — shopkeeper's gold! It is no longer the time of kings: that which calls itself the people today deserves no kings.

Just look how these peoples themselves now act like the shopkeepers: they glean the least little advantage from every piece of garbage!

They lie in wait for each other, they lie waiting for something from each other, — they call this "good neighborliness." O blessed distant time when a people said to itself: "Over peoples I want to be—master!"

For, my brothers: the best should rule, the best also want to rule! And where the rule is otherwise, there — the best is lacking.

22

If they should — have bread for free, oh my! For what would they cry! Their worktime — that is their true pastime; and they should have it hard!

They are beasts of prey: in their "working" there is still robbing, in their "earning" there is still overreaching! Therefore they should have it hard!

Thus they shall become better beasts of prey, subtler, shrewder, more manlike: for man is the best beast of prey.

Man has already robbed all the animals of their virtues: that is because of all the animals man has had it the hardest.

Only the birds are above him. And if man learned to fly, oh my! to what height — would his rapacity fly!

23

Thus would I have man and woman: the one fit for war, the other fit for childbirth, but both fit for dancing with head and legs.

And lost be that day to us in which there has not been one bit of dancing!

And false be every truth to us in which there has not been one bit of laughter!

24

Your contracting of marriage: see to it that it is not a bad contract! You contracted too quickly: thus what follows — marriage-breaking!

And better yet marriage-breaking than marriage-bending, marriage-lying!

— Thus spoke a woman to me: "Indeed I broke the marriage, but first the marriage broke — me!"

The badly-paired I always found to be the worst revenge seekers: they make the whole world pay because they can no longer run singly.

That is the reason why I want the honest ones to say to each other: "We love each other: let us see to it that we keep each other beloved! Or shall our promise promise to be a mistake?"

— "Give us a trial period and a little marriage, to see whether we are fit for a big marriage! It is a big thing, always to be two!"

Thus I advise all the honest ones: and what would my love for the Superman be, and for all that is to come, if I advised and spoke otherwise!

Not only to bring something forth, but to bring something up — to that, O my brothers, may the garden of marriage help you!

25

He who has become wise to old sources, behold, at last he will search for wellsprings of the future and new sources. —

O my brothers, it will not be long before new peoples spring up and new wellsprings rush down into new depths.

For the earthquake — it fills in many wells, it makes many languish: it also brings to light inner strengths and secrets.

The earthquake reveals new wellsprings. In the earthquake of old peoples new wellsprings burst forth.

And he who cries out: "Behold, here is a well for many who thirst, one heart for many who yearn, one will for many an instrument": — around him gathers a people, that is: many venturers.

Who can command, who must obey — that is ventured here! Alas, with what long searching and guessing and coming-up-wrong and learning and venturing anew!

Human society: it is a venture, thus I teach, — a long search: it searches, however, for the commander! — a venture, O my brothers! And not a covenant! Break, break for me that word of the soft-hearted and half-and-halves!

26

O my brothers! With whom does the greatest danger to all of man's future lie? Is it not with the good and the just? — with those who speak and feel in their hearts: "We already know what is good and just, we possess it, too; woe to those who still seek here!"

And whatever harm the wicked may do: the harm the good do is the most harmful harm!

And whatever harm the world-slanderers may do: the harm the good do is the most harmful harm.

O my brothers, there was once one who looked into the hearts of the good and the just and said: "These are the Pharisees." But he was not understood.

The good and the just themselves were not permitted to understand him:

their spirit was imprisoned by their good conscience. The stupidity of the good is unfathomably shrewd.

The truth, however, is this: the good must be Pharisees, — they have no choice!

The good must crucify the one who invents his own virtue! That is the truth!

The second one, however, he who discovered their land, the land, heart, and soil of the good and the just: it was he who asked: "Whom do they hate the most?"

The creator they hate the most: he who breaks tables and old values, the breaker, — they call him lawbreaker.

For the good — they cannot create: they are always the beginning of the end: they crucify the one who writes new values on new tables, they sacrifice the future to themselves, — they crucify all man's future!

The good — they have always been the beginning of the end. —

27

O my brothers, have you also understood this word? And what I once said about the "last man"? — —

With whom does the greatest danger to all man's future lie? Is it not with the good and the just?

Break, break for me the good and the just! — O my brothers, have you also understood this word?

28

You flee from me? You are terrified? You tremble at this word?

O my brothers, when I bade you break the good and the tables of the good:

only then did I ship man out on his high sea.

And only now does the great terror come to him, the great looking-around, the great sickness, the great nausea, the great seasickness.

False shores and false assurances the good have taught you; you have been born and harbored in the falsehoods of the good. Everything has been thoroughly hooked and crooked by the good.

But he who has discovered the country "Man" has also discovered the country "Man's Future." Now you shall be my seafarers, valiant, patient!

Walk upright betimes, O my brothers, learn to walk upright! The sea rages:

many want to right themselves again on you.

The sea rages: everything is in the sea. Well then! Come on! You old tarhearts!

Fatherland — what of it! There our helm wants to go, where our children's land is! Out there, more raging than the sea, rages our great longing! —

29

"Why so hard!" — the kitchen coal once said to the diamond: "Are we not then close kin?" —

Why so soft? O my brothers, thus I ask you: are you not then — my brothers?

Why so soft, so pliant and compliant? Why so much denial, self-denial, in your hearts? So little destiny in your glances?

And if you would not be destinies and inexorable ones with me: how can you one day — conquer with me?

And if your hardness would not flash and cut and cut to pieces with me:how can you one day — create with me?

For creators are hard. And blessedness must it seem to you, to press your hand upon millennia as upon wax, — blessedness, to write upon the will of millennia as upon bronze, —

harder than bronze, nobler than bronze. Only the noblest is entirely hard.

This new table, O my brothers, I place over you: become hard! —

30

O thou my will! Thou turnaround of all need, my necessity! Preserve me from all small victories!

Thou sending out of my soul which I call fate! Thou In-me! Over-me! Preserve and reserve me for one great fate!

And thy last greatness, my will, reserve it for last, — that thou may be inexorable in thy victory! Alas, who has not been overcome by his victory!

Alas, whose eye would not grow dim in this drunken twilight! Alas, whose foot would not stumble and forget in victory how — to stand!

— That I may one day be ready and ripe at the great noontide: ready and ripe like glowing bronze, lightning-gravid clouds, and swelling milk-udders: ready for my self and my most hidden will: a bow on fire for its arrow, an arrow on fire for its star — a star, ready and ripe at its noontide, glowing, transfixed, transported by annihilating sun-arrows:— a sun itself and an inexorable solar will, ready to annihilate in victory!

O will, turnaround of all need, thou my necessity! Preserve me for one great victory! — —

Thus spake Zarathustra.

The Convalescent
1

One morning, not long after the return to his cave, Zarathustra sprang up from his bed like a madman, cried in a terrible voice, and acted as if someone unwilling to get up still lay on the bed; and so resounded Zarathustra's voice that has animals came to him terrified, and from all the lairs and hiding-places neighboring Zarathustra's cave all the creatures slipped away, — flying, fluttering, creeping, leaping, each according to just the kind of foot or wing it was given. Zarathustra, however, said these words:

Up, abysmal thought, out of my depth! I am your cock and break of day, sleepy worm: up! up! My voice shall cock-a-doodle you awake yet!

Unbind the fetters of your ears: listen! For I want to hear you! up! up! Here is thunder enough to make even the graves sit up and listen!

And wipe the sleep and all that is blind and asinine out of your eyes! Hear me likewise with your eyes; my voice is a cure for those born blind.

And once you are awake, you shall remain eternally awake. It is not my custom to wake great-grandmothers from their sleep in order to bid them — go on sleeping!

You are stirring, stretching, retching? Up! Up! Do not retch — reach me with your speech! Zarathustra summons you, Zarathustra the godless!

I, Zarathustra, the advocate of life, the advocate of suffering, the advocate of the circle — I summon you, my most abysmal thought!

Hail to me! You are coming, — I hear you! My abyss speaks, my lowest depth I have turned up to the light!

Hail to me! Come here! Give me your hand — — ah! Let go! Aah! — —horror, horror, horror — — — woe is me!

2

Hardly had Zarathustra spoken these words, however, when he fell down like a dead man and long remained like a dead man. But when he came to his senses again, he was pale and shaking and remained lying there, desiring neither food nor drink. This condition lasted seven days; his animals, however, did not abandon him day or night, except that the eagle flew off to fetch food. And what he fetched and snatched as plunder he laid upon Zarathustra's bed: so that at last Zarathustra lay amidst yellow and red berries, grapes, rose apples, sweetlyscented herbs, and pine cones. At his feet, however, two lambs were spread out, which the eagle had snatched away with difficulty form their shepherds.

At last, after seven days, Zarathustra rose up from his bed, took a rose apple in his hand, smelled it, and found its odor pleasing. Then his animals thought the time had come to speak with him.

"O Zarathustra," they said, "seven days now you have lain thus with heavy eyes: will you not get back on your feet again at last?

Step out of your cave: the world awaits you like a garden. The wind plays with strong fragrances willing to go your way; and all the brooks look to run after you.

All things long for you because for seven days you have remained alone, —step out of your cave! All things are willing to be your physicians!

Perhaps a new perception has come to you, a sour, serious one? Like leavened dough you lay; your soul rose and swelled over all its borders. —"

— "O my animals," replied Zarathustra, "keep chattering thus and let me listen! It refreshes me so to hear you chatter: where there is chatter the world is indeed as a garden to me.

How pleasing it is that there are words and tones: are not words and tones rainbows and seeming bridges between the eternally separated?

To every soul belongs another world; for every soul every other soul is an afterworld.

Precisely between the most similar things semblance lies most beautifully; for the smallest gap is the hardest to bridge.

As for me — how could there be an outside-me? There is no outside! But with all the tones we forget this; how pleasing it is that we forget!

Are things not given names and tones so that man can refresh himself with them? It is a beautiful tomfoolery, speaking; with it man dances over all things.

How pleasing is all speech and all the deceit of tones! With tones our love dances on multi-colored rainbows." —

"O Zarathustra," the animals then said, "to those who think as we do all things dance of themselves: they come and offer their hand and laugh and flee —and come back.

Everything goes, everything comes back; eternally rolls the wheel of being.

Everything dies, everything blooms again; eternally runs the year of being.

Everything breaks, everything is joined anew; eternally the same house of being builds itself. Everything parts, everything greets each other again; eternally the ring of being remains true to itself.

In every instant begins being; round every 'here' rolls the ball 'there'. The center is everywhere. Curved is the path of eternity." —

— "O you buffoons and hurdy-gurdies," answered Zarathustra and smiled once more; "How well you know what had to be fulfilled in seven days: —

— and how that monster crawled down my throat and choked me! But I bit the head off and spewed it away from me.

And you, — you have already made a lyre lay out of it? Now, however, I lie here, still weary from this biting and spewing, still ill from my own redemption.

And you watched it all? O my animals, are you also cruel? Did you want to watch my great pain, as men do? For man is the cruelest animal.

At tragedies, bullfights, and crucifixions he has hitherto been happiest on earth; and when he invented hell, behold, that was his heaven on earth.

When the great man cries—: at once the small man comes running; and his tongue hangs out of his mouth lasciviously. But he calls it his "pity."

The small man, especially the poet — how eagerly he accuses life in words!

Hear him, but do not fail to hear the delight that is in all accusation!

These accusers of life: life conquers them with the blink of an eye. "Do you love me?" the impudent one says, "wait a little, I do not have time for you yet."

Man is the cruelest animal towards himself; and with all those who call themselves "sinners" and "cross-bearers" and "penitents," do not fail to hear the sensual delight that is in their lamentations and accusations!

And I myself — would I be man's accuser in this? Alas, my animals, this alone have I learned hitherto, that man's worst is necessary for his best, —

— that all the worst is his best strength and the hardest stone for the highest creator; and that man must become better and badder: —

Not on this cross was I nailed, that I know: man is evil, — but I cried as no one yet has cried:

"Alas, that his worst is so very small! Alas, that his best is so very small!"

The great disgust with man, — this had crawled into my throat and choked me: and what the soothsayer had soothsaid: "All is the same, nothing is worthwhile, knowledge strangles."

A long twilight limped along before me, a dead tired, dead drunk sadness that talked with a yawning mouth.

"Eternally he returns, the man you are weary of, the small man" — thus my sadness yawned and dragged its feet and could not fall asleep.

Man's earth became a hollow to me, her breast sank in, all living things became human mold and bones and decomposed past to me.

My sighing sat on all human graves and could no longer rise; my sighing and inquiring croaked and choked and wore away and wailed away day and night:

— "Alas, man returns eternally! The small man returns eternally!"

Naked had I once seen them both, the greatest man and the smallest man:

all-too-similar to each other, — all-too-human still, even the greatest!

All-too-small, the greatest! — this was my disgust with man! And the eternal return of even the smallest! — this was my disgust with all existence!

Ah, horror! Horror! Horror! — — Thus spake Zarathustra and sighed and shuddered; for he was reminded of his sickness. Then, however, his animals let him speak no further.

"Speak no further, you convalescent!" — thus his animals answered him, "but go out where the world awaits you like a garden.

Go out to the roses and the bees and the flights of doves! But especially to the songbirds: that you may learn singing from them!

Because singing is for convalescents; the healthy can speak. And when the healthy man wants songs, he certainly wants songs different from those of the convalescent."

— "O you buffoons and hurdy-gurdies, do be quiet then!" — replied Zarathustra and smiled at his animals. "How well you know what solace I devised for myself in seven days!

That I had to sing again, — this solace I devised for myself and this convalescence:

and right away you are ready to make a lyre lay out of it?"

— "Speak no further, " his animals answered once again; "better yet, you convalescent, first make ready for yourself a lyre, a new lyre!

For behold, O Zarathustra! New lays require new lyres!

Sing and bubble over, O Zarathustra, heal your soul with new songs: that you may bear your great fate, which has been no man's fate yet.

For your animals know it well, O Zarathustra, who you are and must become: behold, you are the teacher of the eternal return — , that is now your fate!

That you as the first must teach this teaching, — how could this great fate not also be your greatest danger and disease!

Behold, we know what you teach: that all things return eternally, and we ourselves along with them; and that we have already existed countless times, and all things with us.

You teach that there is a great year of becoming, a monster of a great year: it must turn itself over and over again, like an hourglass, so that it can run down and run out again: —

— so that all these years are like themselves in the greatest as well as in the least thing, so that we ourselves in every great year are like ourselves, in the greatest as well as in the least thing.

And if you should want to die now, O Zarathustra: behold, we know too how you would speak to yourself: but your animals beseech you not to die yet!

You would speak and without trembling, breathing, on the contrary, a sigh of bliss: for a great heaviness and uneasiness would be taken from you, you most patient one! —

'Now I die and fade away,' you would say, 'and in an instant I am nothing.

Souls are as mortal as bodies.

But the knot of causes in which I am entangled returns, — it will create me again! I myself belong to the causes of the eternal return.

I come again, with this sun, with this earth, with this eagle, with this serpent — not to a new life or a better life or a similar life:

— I come again eternally to this same and selfsame life, in the greatest as well as in the least thing, to teach again the eternal return of all things, —

— to speak again the word on the great earthly and manly noontide, to proclaim again to man the Superman.

I spake my word, I break on my word: my eternal lot wills it so —, as proclaimer I go under!

The hour has now come for the downgoer to bless himself. Thus — ends Zarathustra's downgoing.'" — —

When the animals had spoken these words, they became silent and waited for Zarathustra to say something to them: but Zarathustra did not hear that they were silent. He lay still, rather, with his eyes closed, like one sleeping, although he did not sleep: for just then he was conferring with his soul. The serpent, however, and the eagle, when they found him thus silent, honored the great stillness around him and prudently withdrew.

On The Great Longing

O my soul, I taught you to say "today" as "one day" and "in days of yore" and to dance your roundelay away over all Here and There and Yonder.

O my soul, I rescued you from all corners, I brushed dust, spiders, and twilight away from you.

O my soul, I washed the petty shame and the shady virtue away from you and persuaded you to stand naked before the eyes of the sun.

With the storm called "spirit" I blew over your surging sea; all the clouds I blew away, I even strangled the strangleress called "sin."

O my soul, I gave you the right to say Nay, like the storm, and Yea, like the open sky says Yea: calm as light you stay and make your way now through negating storms.

O my soul, I gave you back the freedom over the created and the uncreated: and who knows as you know the sensuality of the future?

O my soul, I taught you the contempt that comes not as worm-eatenness, the great, the loving contempt that loves the most where it despises the most.

O my soul, I taught you to persuade so that even the grounds are swayed: like the sun which persuades even the sea to its height.

O my soul, I freed you from all obeying, knee-bending, and lord-saying; I even gave you the names "Turnaround In Need" and "Fate."

O my soul, I gave you new names and colorful playthings, I called you "Fate" and "Extent of Extensiveness" and Umbilical Cord Of Time" and "Azure Bell."

O my soul, I gave your soil all wisdom to drink, all new wines and also all immemorially old strong wines of wisdom.

O my soul, every sun I poured forth on you and every night and every silence and every longing: then you shot up like a vine for me.

O my soul, superrich and heavy you stand there now, a vine with swelling udders and crowded brown gold-clusters of grapes: — crowded and clouded by your happiness, waiting with plenty and yet modest on account of your waiting.

O my soul, there is now nowhere a soul that would be more loving and encompassing and far-reaching! Where would future and past be closer together than with you?

O my soul, I gave you all and you have left me all empty-handed: Now you say to me, smiling and full of melancholy: "Which of us has to give thanks? —

— should the giver not give thanks that the receiver has received? Is giving not a necessity? Is receiving not — showing mercy?" —

O my soul, I understand the smile of your melancholy: your superrichness itself now stretches out longing hands!

Your fullness looks out over raging seas and searches and waits; the longing of super-fullness looks out from your smiling eye-skies!

And verily, O my soul! Who could see your smile and not melt into tears?

The angels themselves burst into tears at the super-goodness of your smile.

It is your goodness and super-goodness which refuses to wail and weep: and yet, O my soul, your smile longs for tears and your trembling mouth for sobs.

"Is not all weeping a complaint? And is all complaining not an accusing?"

Thus you talk to yourself and on that account you would rather smile, O my soul, than pour out your sorrow — pour out in trembling tears all your sorrow at your fullness and at all the vine's urgency for the vintager and the vine-knife!

But if you will not weep, will not weep out your purple melancholy, then you will have to sing, O my soul! — Behold, I myself smile, I who prophesy such a thing to you:

— sing, with boisterous song, until all the seas become still, to hearken to your longing, —

— until over still, longing seas the boat glides, the golden wonder around whose gold all good, bad, wondrous things gambol: —

— many creatures great and small also, and all that have light, wondrous feet, so they can run on violet-blue paths, —

— toward the golden wonder, the voluntary ferry-boat and its master: that however, is the vintager, who waits with the adamantine vine-knife, — your great savior, O my soul, the nameless one — for whom only future songs will find names! And verily, already your breath exudes the fragrance of future songs, —

— already you glow and dream, already you drink thirstily at all deep resounding comfort-wells, already your melancholy rests in the bliss of future songs! — —

O my soul, now I have given you all and also my last thing, and you have left me all empty-handed: — that I told you to sing, behold, that was my last thing!

That I told you to sing, speak now, speak: which of us now has to — give thanks? — But better yet: sing to me, sing, O my soul! And let me give thanks! —

Thus spake Zarathustra.

The Other Dance Song
1

Into your eyes I looked lately, O Life: gold I saw glittering in your night-eye, — my heart stood still on account of this delight:— a golden boat I saw glittering on gloomy waters, a sinking, drinking, rewinking golden seesaw-boat!

At my foot, my dance-mad foot, you cast a glance, a smiling inquiring, melting, seesaw glance:

Twice only you stirred your rattle with your little hands — already my foot seesawed with dance-madness. —

My heels pranced, my toes lent an ear in order to understand you: the dancer, you know, has his ear — in his toes!

I sprang toward you: from my spring you hastily withdrew; and your fleeing, flying hair-tongue darted its tongue in and out at me!

Away from you I sprang and from your serpents: there you stood already, half-turned, your eye full of longing.

With crooked looks — you teach me crooked ways; on crooked ways my foot learns — arch tricks!

I fear you near, I love you far; your fleeing calls me, your seeking stalls me:— I suffer, but what would I gladly not suffer for you!

You whose coldness kindles, whose hatred seduces, whose flight binds, whose mockery — induces:— who would not hate you, you great binder, entwiner, seducer, seeker, finder! Who would not love you, you impatient, wind-hastened, guileless childeyed sinner!

Where are you dragging me off to now, you prodigy and problem child?

And now you are fleeing me again, you sweet wildcat and ingrate!

I dance after you, I follow your least little clue. Where are you? Give me your hand! Or just a finger will do!

Here are hollows and thickets: we shall go astray! — Halt! Stand still! Do you not hear owls and bats whistling this way?

You owl! You bat! Are you trying to make a monkey out of me? Where are we? From the dogs you have learned this howling and yelping.

You bare delightfully your little white teeth at me, your wicked eyes leap out at me from beneath a curly little mane.

This is a dance over hill and dale, — would you be my hound or my chamois female?

At my side now! And quickly, you wicked springstress! Up now and over!

— Alas! In springing thereafter I fell headlong!

O see me lying here, pleading for mercy, you haughty lass! Gladly would I go with you — down lovelier paths!

— down paths of love through hushed, varied brush! Or there along the lake: where goldfish swim and dance!

You are weary now? Over there are sheep and sunset skies: is it not nice to sleep when shepherds play their pipes?

You are so very weary? I will carry you there, just let your arms sink! And if you get thirsty, — have I got something, but your mouth would not have it to drink! —

— O this cursed nimble supple serpent and slick witch! Where have you gone? But from your hand on my face I feel two spots and red blotches!

I am truly weary of being your sheepish shepherd all the time! You witch, if until now I have sung for you, now for me you shall — cry!

To the rhythm of my whip you shall cry and dance! Surely I did not forget the whip? — No chance!"

2

Then Life answered me thus and covered her dainty ears the while:

"O Zarathustra! Do not crack your whip so terribly! You know indeed:

noise murders thought, — and just now such tender thoughts come to me.

We are both two true ne'er-do-wells and ne'er-do-ills. Beyond good and evil we found our island and our green meadow — we two alone! Therefore we must indeed suit each other!

And even if we do not love each other thoroughly — , must we then hold a grudge for not being thoroughly loved?

And that I am well-disposed toward you and often too well, that you know:

and the reason is that I am jealous of your wisdom. Ah, that mad old fool of a woman wisdom!

And if your wisdom should ever run away from you, alas! then my love would also run away from you quickly." —

Then Life looked reflectively behind her and around her and softly said: "O Zarathustra, you are not faithful enough to me!

You love me not nearly so much as you say; I know you are thinking of leaving me soon.

There is an old heavy, heavy booming-bell: it booms its way nightly up to your cave: —

— when you hear this bell toll at the midnight hour, then between one and twelve you think of it —

— you think, O Zarathustra, I know it, of leaving me soon!"

"Yes," I answered hesitantly, "but you also know — " And I said something in her ear, right in the midst of her tangled, yellow, silly, shaggy locks.

"You know that, O Zarathustra? No one knows that. —"

And we looked at each other and upon the green meadow over which the cool evening was just coming and we wept together. — Then, however, Life was dearer to me than all my wisdom ever was. —

3

One!

O man! Take heed!

Two!

What words repeat deep midnight's creed?

Three!

"I sleep, I sleep —, Four!

"From deep dream I woke and perceived: —

Five!

"The world is deep, Six!

"And deeper than the day conceived Seven!

"Deep is her woe —, Eight!

"Joy — deeper still than calamity:

Nine!

"Woe bids it: Go!

Ten!

"But all joy wants eternity — , Eleven "— Wants the deep, deep eternity!"

Twelve!

The Seven Seals
(Or: The Yea And Amen Lay)

1

If I be a soothsayer and full of that soothsaying spirit which wanders on a high ridge between two seas, —

wanders like a heavy cloud between past and future, — enemy to sultry lowlands and all that is weary and can neither live nor die:

ready for lightning in its dark breast and for the redeeming flash of light, pregnant with lightning bolts which say yea! laugh yea!, ready for soothsaying thunderbolts:

— blessed however is he who is thus pregnant! And verily, he who shall one day kindle the light of the future must hang a long while, like heavy weather on the mountains! —

O how could I not be fervent for eternity and for the bridal ring of rings, —the ring of return?

Never yet have I found the woman from whom I wanted children, unless it be this woman whom I love: for I love you, O Eternity!

For I love you, Eternity!

2

If ever my wrath broke up graves, moved boundary stones, and rolled old broken tables into steep depths: if ever my scorn blew away decayed words, and like a broom I came to cross-spiders and as a sweeping wind to old musty burial chambers: if ever I sat rejoicing where old gods lie buried, world-blessing, world-loving next to the monuments of old world-slanderers: — for even churches and gods' graves I love, if only heaven's pure eye looks through their broken roofs; gladly I sit like grass and red poppies on broken churches —

O how could I not be fervent for eternity and for the bridal ring of rings, —the ring of return?

Never yet have I found the woman from whom I wanted children, unless it be this woman whom I love: for I love you, O Eternity!

For I love you, O Eternity!

3

If ever a breath of creative breath came to me, and of that heavenly necessity which forces even chance events to dance star-dances in the round:

If ever I laughed with the laughter of creative lightning, which the long thunder of the deed follows after rumblingly but obediently:

If ever I played dice with gods at the table of the gods, the earth, so that the earth did quake and break apart and snort up streams of fire:—

— for the earth is a table of the gods, and trembling with creative new words and divine dice-throws: —

O how could I not be fervent for eternity and for the bridal ring of rings, —

the ring of return?

Never yet have I found the woman from whom I wanted children, unless it be this woman whom I love: for I love you, O Eternity!

For I love you, O Eternity!

4

If ever I drank deep from that foaming spice- and mixing bowl in which all things are well-mixed:

if ever my hand poured the furthest with the nearest and fire with spirit and joy with sorrow and the worst with the kindest:

if I myself be a grain of that redeeming salt which makes all things mix well in the mixing bowl: —

— for there is a salt which binds good with evil; and even the most evil thing is worthy of seasoning and of the last foaming-over: —

O how could I not be fervent for eternity and for the bridal ring of rings, —

the ring of return?

Never yet have I found the woman from whom I wanted children, unless it be this woman whom I love: for I love you, O Eternity!

For I love you, O Eternity!

5

If I be fond of the sea and all that is of the nature of the sea, and even most fond when it angrily opposes me:

if that joy in seeking be in me which drives the sails toward the undiscovered, if a seafarer's joy be in my joy:

if ever my rejoicing cried: "The coast has vanished — now the last chain has fallen from me —

— the unbounded roars around me, far out there time and space gleam for me, well them! come one! old heart!" —

O how could I not be fervent for eternity and for the bridal ring of rings, —

the ring of return?

Never yet have I found the woman from whom I wanted children, unless it be this woman whom I love: for I love you, O Eternity!

For I love you, O Eternity!

6

If my virtue be a dancer's virtue, and if often I have leaped with both feet into golden-emerald ecstasy: if my malice be a laughing malice, at home among rosebeds and lily hedges:

— for in laughter all things evil are together, absolved and resolved as holy, however, by their own bliss: —

and if my alpha and omega be this, that all things heavy shall become light, all bodies dancers, all spirits birds: and verily, this is my alpha and omega! —

O how could I not be fervent for eternity and for the bridal ring of rings, —the ring of return?

Never yet have I found the woman from whom I wanted children, unless it be this woman whom I love: for I love you, O Eternity!

For I love you, O Eternity!

7

If ever I spread a calm heaven above me and with my own wings flew up to my own heaven: if I swam playfully in deep light-distances and my freedom's bird-wisdom came: —

— thus, however, speaks bird-wisdom: "Behold, there is no above, no below! Fling yourself all around, out, back, you light one, Sing! speak no more!

— are all words not made for those who are heavy? Do all words not lie for those who are light? Sing! speak no more!" —

O how could I not be fervent for eternity and for the bridal ring of rings, —the ring of return?

Never yet have I found the woman from whom I wanted children, unless it be this woman whom I love: for I love you, O Eternity!

For I love you, O Eternity!

Fourth and Last Part

Alas, where in the world have greater follies taken place than amongst the pitying ones? And what in the world has caused more suffering than the follies of the pitying ones:

Woe to all lovers who do not yet have a height that is above their pity!

Thus spake the devil to me once: "Even God has his hell: it is his love for man."

And the other day this word I heard him say: "God is dead; God has died of his pity for man."

Thus Spake Zarathustra, Part Two

The Honey Offering

— And again months and years passed over Zarathustra's soul, and he heeded them not; his hair, however, turned white. One day as he sat on a stone in front of his cave and calmly looked out — and one looks out here upon the sea and out across tortuous abysses —, then his animals walked pensively around him and settled themselves at last in front of him.

"O Zarathustra," they said, "perhaps you are looking out for your happiness?"

— "What does happiness matter?" he answered, "I have long ceased to strive for happiness; I strive for my work." — "O Zarathustra," the animals said once more, "you say that like one who has too much of a good thing. Do you not lie in a sky-blue sea of happiness?" — "You buffoons," answered Zarathustra and smiled; "how well you chose your metaphor! But you also know my happiness is heavy and not like a fluid wave: it presses me and refuses to leave me and behaves like molten pitch." —

Then the animals walked pensively around him again and settled themselves once more in front of him. "O Zarathustra," they said,

"So is that why you grow ever yellower and darker although your hair looks white and flaxen? But look, you are sitting in your own sticky mess!" — "What is that you say, my animals?"

Zarathustra said and laughed, "verily, I blasphemed when I spoke of pitch. As it is with me, so it is with all fruits that grow ripe. It is the honey in my veins that makes my blood thicker and also my soul stiller." — "Thus will it be, O Zarathustra," answered the animals and pressed themselves up against him; "but do you not want to climb a high mountain today? The air is pure and one sees more of the world today than ever before." — "Yes, my animals," he answered, "you counsel admirably and after my own heart: I shall climb a high mountain today! But make sure honey is at hand there for me, yellow, white, good, icy-cool, golden honeycomb. For know that on high I will make the honey-sacrifice." —

When Zarathustra was on high, however, he sent those animals home that had accompanied him and found that he was alone: — then he laughed wholeheartedly, looked around himself, and spoke thus:

That I spoke of sacrifices and honey-sacrifices was only a trick of speech and, verily, a useful piece of folly. Up here I can surely speak more freely than before hermits' caves and hermits' domestic animals.

What sacrifice! I squander what is given me, I , a squanderer with a thousand hands: how could I ever call that sacrificing?

And when I craved honey I only craved bait and sweet goo and goop which even grumbling bears and strange, sullen, wicked birds lick up with their tongues:

— the best bait, as hunters and fisherman require. For if the world be like a dark forest of beasts and a garden of delight for all wild hunters, then it strikes me even more so as and I prefer it to be an unfathomably rich sea, — a sea full of colorful fish and crabs which even gods might lust after, in which they might want to be fishermen and net-casters: so rich is the world in strange things, great and small!

Especially the human world, the human sea: into that I now cast my golden fishing rod and say: "Open up, you human abyss!

Open up and cast me your fish and glistening crabs! With my best bait I shall entice the strangest human fish today!

— my happiness itself I shall cast out into all places and spaces amidst sunrise, noon, and sunset, to see whether many human fish do not learn to yank and crank on my happiness:— until biting on my sharp hidden hooks, they must come up to my height, the most motley of abyss-groundlings to the most malicious of all fishers of men.

For this I am at the very bottom and from the very beginning, drawing, drawing in, drawing up, bringing up, a drawer, upbringer, and disciplinarian who once exhorted himself, not for nothing: 'Become who you are!'

Thus men may now come up to me: for I still await the sign that it is time for my descent; not yet do I myself go down, as I must, among men.

That is why I wait here, cunning and mocking on high mountains, not impatient, not patient, as one rather who has also unlearned patience, —because he no longer 'bears patiently.'

For my fate gives me time: perhaps it has forgotten me? Or does it sit in the shade behind a great stone and catch flies?

And verily, I am much obliged to my fate for not hurrying and harrying me and giving me time for jests and gibes: so that today I have climbed this high mountain to catch fish.

Did a man ever catch fish on high mountains, I wonder? And even if it is folly, what I desire and do up here: better yet this than to become solemn and green and yellow from waiting down below —

— a pompous wrath-snorter from waiting, a holy, howling storm from the mountains, an impatient sort that shouts down into the valleys: 'Listen, or I will lash you with the scourge of God!'

Not that I would hold a grudge against such angry ones: they serve well enough for my laughter! They must be quite impatient, these big clamor-drums which get a chance to speak now or never!

I, however, and my destiny — we do not speak to the Now, we also do not speak to the Never: we have patience and time and overtime for speaking, after all. For one day it must surely come and may not pass by.

What must one day come and may not pass by? Our great Hazar, that is, our great faraway human kingdom, the Zarathustra kingdom of a thousand years — —

How faraway may such a "faraway" be? What is that to me? But as far as that stands, this is no less certain to me — with both feet I stand securely on this ground, —

— on eternal ground, on hard, primeval rock, on this highest, hardest primeval mountain range to which all winds come as to a weather divide, asking Where and Whence? and Whither?

Laugh here, laugh, my hearty, healthy malice! From high mountains cast down your glittering, mocking laughter! Lure for me with your glittering the finest human fish!

And whatever belongs to me in all the seas, my in-and-for-me in all things — fish that out for me, bring that up to me: for that I wait, I, the most malicious of all fishermen.

Out, out, my fish hook! In there, down there, bait of my happiness! Drip down your sweetest dew, my heart's honey! Bite, my fishing hook, all black affliction in the belly!

Out there, out there, my eye! O how many seas around me, what dawning human futures! And above me — what rosy-red stillness! What cloudless silence!

The Cry Of Distress

The next day Zarathustra again sat on the stone in front of his cave, while his animals roamed about in the world outside in order to bring home new food — new honey, too: for Zarathustra had lavishly spent and squandered the old honey down to the last drop. But as he sat there thus, with a stick in his hand, tracing the shadow of his figure upon the earth, reflecting, and verily! not upon himself and his shadow — all at once he was startled and started with fright: for next to his shadow he saw yet another shadow. And as he looked quickly around himself and stood up, behold, there stood next to him the soothsayer, the same one he had once given food and drink at his table, the herald of the great weariness who taught: "All is the same, nothing is worthwhile, the world is without meaning, knowledge strangles." But his face had changed meanwhile; and when Zarathustra looked him in the eye, his heart was startled again: so many bad tidings and ashy-gray bolts of lightning ran across that face.

The soothsayer, who realized what had taken place in Zarathustra's soul, wiped his hand over his face, as if he wanted to wipe it away; Zarathustra did the same, too. And when both of them had silently composed and strengthened themselves thus, they shook hands as a sign that they wanted to recognize each other again.

"Welcome," said Zarathustra, "you soothsayer of the great weariness, not in vain shall you once have been my guest and table mate. Eat and drink today also with me, and forgive a merry old man for sitting at the dinner table with you!" —

"A merry old man?" answered the soothsayer, shaking his head, "but whoever you are or want to be, O Zarathustra, you will not be it up here much longer, —in a little while your boat shall no longer be sitting high and dry!" "Am I sitting high and dry then?" — asked Zarathustra, laughing. — "The waves around your mountain," answered the soothsayer, "are rising and rising, the waves of great distress and tribulation: and soon they will raise your boat and carry you away."

— Zarathustra was silent at this and marvelled. — "Do you hear nothing yet?"

continued the soothsayer: "is it not rushing and roaring up from the deep?" —

Zarathustra was silent once again and listened: then he heard a long, long cry which the abysses called out and passed back and forth to one another, for none would have it: so evil did it sound.

"You ill herald," Zarathustra said at last, "that is a cry of distress and the cry of a man; it may well come from a black sea. But what is human distress to me!

The last sin which has been reserved for me, — do you know what it is called?"

— "Pity!" answered the soothsayer from an overflowing heart and raised both hands on high — O Zarathustra, I come to seduce you to your last sin!" —

And hardly had these words been spoken when the cry rang out again, and longer and more anxiously than before, no doubt much closer, too. "Do you hear?

Do you hear, O Zarathustra?" cried the soothsayer, "the cry is aimed at you, it calls out to you: come, come, come, it is time, it is high time!" —

Zarathustra was silent at this, confused and convulsed; at last he asked, like one who hesitates with himself: "And who is it that calls to me there?"

"But surely you know," replied the soothsayer furiously, "why do you hide yourself? It is the higher man that cries out for you!"

"The higher man?" cried Zarathustra, seized with horror: what does he want? What does he want? The higher man? What does he want here?" — and his skin was covered with sweat.

The soothsayer, however, offered no answer to Zarathustra's anxiety but listened and listened to the depth. Yet when it remained silent there for a long time, he looked back and saw Zarathustra standing and trembling.

"O Zarathustra," he began in a sad voice, "you do not stand there as one made giddy by his happiness: you had better dance so you do not fall down!

But even if you wanted to dance before me and leap all your side-leaps: still nobody could say to me: 'Look, here dances the last happy man!'

Anyone who searched for him here, at this height, would have come in vain: caves he would find, possibly, and caves behind caves, hideaways for sly knaves, but no mines of happiness and treasure chambers and new golden lodes of happiness.

Happiness — how could happiness possibly be found with such recluses and solitaries? Must I still seek ultimate happiness on blessed isles and faraway amongst forgotten seas?

But all is the same, nothing is worthwhile, searching does no good, and there are no longer any Blessed Isles!"—

Thus sighed the soothsayer; but with his last sigh Zarathustra became bright and sure again, like one who comes out of a deep gorge into the light. "No!

No! Three times No!" he cried out in a loud voice and stroked his beard — "I know better than that! There are still Blessed Isles! Be silent about that, you sighing sad sack!

Stop splattering about that, you raincloud in the morning! Do I not already stand here wet from your distress and drenched like a dog?

Now I shake myself and run away from you in order to get dry again: you need not be surprised at that! Do I seem discourteous to you? But here is my court.

And as for your higher man: well then! I shall seek him at once in those woods: thence came his cry. Perhaps a wicked beast harasses him there.

He is in my domain: therein he shall not come to harm! And verily, there are many wicked beasts near me."

With these words Zarathustra turned to go. Then the soothsayer said: "O Zarathustra, you are a rogue!

I know it already: you want to get rid of me! You would rather run in the woods and set snares for wicked beasts!

But what good will it do you? — In the evening you will have me again all the same; I will be sitting there in your own cave, patient and heavy like a block of wood — and waiting for you!"

"So be it!" Zarathustra called back as he walked away: "and what is mine in my cave is yours too, my guest!

And if you should find some honey in there, well then! just lick it up, you grumbling bear, and sweeten your soul! For in the evening we both want to be in good spirits, — in good spirits and glad that this day has come to an end! And you yourself shall dance to my songs as my dancing bear.

You do not believe it? You shake your head? Well then! Well then! Old bear!

But I too — am a soothsayer."

Thus spake Zarathustra.

Conversation With The Kings
1

Zarathustra was not yet an hour underway in his mountains and woods when all at once he came upon a strange procession. Right on the path he wanted to go down, along came two kings on foot, adorned with crowns and purple girdles and colorful as flamingoes: they drove a laden ass before them.

"What do these kings want in my kingdom?" Zarathustra said in astonishment to his heart and hid himself quickly behind a bush. But as the kings came up to him, he said in an undertone, like one speaking to himself alone: "Strange!

Strange! What kind of arrangement is this? Two kings I see — and only one ass!"

Then the two kings stopped, smiled, and looked toward the spot where the voice had come from, after which they looked each other in the face. "Such things are also thought amongst ourselves no doubt," said the king on the right, "but one does not speak out about them."

The king on the left, however, shrugged his shoulders and answered: "That may well be a goatherd. Or a hermit who has dwelt too long among rocks and trees. For no society at all also spoils good manners."

"Good manners?" The other king retorted, indignantly and bitterly: "what is it then we are trying to get away from? Is it not 'good manners'? Our 'good society'?

Better, verily, to live among goatherds and hermits than with our gilded, false, over-rouged riffraff, — although they call themselves 'good society', — although they call themselves 'nobility.' But all is false and foul there, first of all the blood, thanks to old bad diseases and worse quack-healers.

The best and dearest to me even today is a healthy peasant, crude, shrewd, stiff-necked, enduring: that is the foremost type today.

The best at present is the peasant; and the peasant type should be master!

But it is the kingdom of the riffraff, — I let nothing fool me. Riffraff, however, that means: mishmash.

Riffraff-mishmash: everything is mixed up with everything else in that, saint and skunk and Junker and Jew and every animal from Noah's ark!

Good manners! All is false and foul with us. No one knows how to show respect any more: precisely that is what we are running away from. They are fulsome, meddlesome dogs, they gild palm leaves.

This loathing chokes me, that even we kings have become fakes, draped and disguised in old yellowed grandfather-splendor, showpieces for the dumbest and the smartest and all those who horse-trade for power today!

We are not the first — and yet must stand for them: of this fraud we finally have become sick and tired.

We have gone out of our way to get away from the rabble, all these crybabies and scribe-blowflies, the shopkeeper stench, the go-getter squirming, the gutter breath —: phooey on living among the rabble, — phooey on standing first among the rabble! Oh, horror! Horror! Horror!

What do we kings matter now!" —

"Your old sickness assails you," the king on the left then said, "nausea assails you, my poor brother. But surely you know that someone is listening to us."

Zarathustra, who had opened wide his eyes and ears at this speech, immediately arose from his hiding place, approached the kings and began:

"He who listens to you, he who gladly listens to you, you kings, he is called Zarathustra.

I am Zarathustra, who once said: 'What do kings matter now!' Forgive me, I was pleased when you said to each other: 'What do we kings matter!'

Here, however, is my kingdom and my domain: what might you possibly be seeking in my kingdom? But perhaps along the way you have found what I am seeking: namely, the higher man."

When the kings heard this, they beat their breasts and said with one voice:

"We are recognized!

With the sword of this word you have hewn through out heart's thickest darkness. You have discovered our distress, for behold! we are on our way to find the higher man — the man that is higher than us: although we are kings. We are leading this ass to him. For the highest man should also be the highest master on earth.

There is no harsher misfortune in all human destiny than when the mighty of the earth are not also the first men. Then everything becomes false and distorted and monstrous.

And when they are the very last and more beast than man: then the riffraff rises and rises in price and at last even riffraff-virtue speaks: 'Behold, I alone am virtue!' " —

'What did I just hear?' answered Zarathustra; 'what wisdom from kings! I am thrilled and verily quite filled with the desire to make a rhyme upon it: —

— even if it may be a rhyme not fit for everyone's ears. I have long since forgotten consideration for long ears. Well then! Come on! (But here it happened that the ass also got a word in: he said quite distinctly and with bad intent, Ye-haw.) Once — in the year of our Lord one, no less —

Drunk without wine the Sibyl did confess:

"All's wrong now, woe!

Ruin! Ruin! World's never sunk so low!

Rome's descended to whoredom and whorish stew, Rome's Caesar sunk to brute, God Himself — turned Jew!"

2

In these rhymes of Zarathustra the kings reveled; the king on the right even said: "O Zarathustra, how well we did in setting out to see you!

For your foes showed us your image in their mirror: there you looked with a devil's wry face and sneered: so that we were afraid of you.

But what was the use! Again and again you pierced our ears and hearts with your sayings. So at last we said: what does it matter how he looks!

We must hear him, the one who teaches: 'You shall love peace as a means to new wars, and the short peace more than the long!'

No one ever spoke such warlike words: 'What is good? To be brave is good.

It is the good war that hallows every cause!

O Zarathustra, our fathers' blood stirred in our veins at such words: it was as the speech of spring to old wine-casks.

When the swords flew every which way, like red-flecked snakes, then our fathers knew that life was good; the sun of all peace seemed weak and lukewarm to them; the long peace, however, made for shame.

How they sighed, our fathers, when they saw sparkling bright, dried-up swords on the wall! Like them they thirsted for war. For a sword wants blood to drink and sparkles with desire." ——

— As the kings talked and chattered with such zeal of the happiness of their fathers, Zarathustra was seized by no small desire to mock their zeal: for it was evident that these were very peaceful kings whom he saw before him, men with old and refined faces. But he restrained himself. "Well then!" he said, "Thither the way leads, there lies Zarathustra's cave; and this day shall have a long evening! Now, however, a cry of distress calls me hastily away from you.

It does my cave honor when kings are willing to sit and wait in it: but you will certainly have to wait a long time!

Well then! So what! Where does one today learn better to wait than at court? And all that remains of the virtue of kings, — is it not today called "waiting- ability?"

Thus spake Zarathustra.

The Leech

And Zarathustra walked pensively, farther and deeper through forests and past marshy grounds; but as it happens with everyone who ponders serious matters, he managed to tread unawares upon a man. And behold, all at once a woeful cry and a pair of curses and twenty bad curse words squirted him in the face: so that in his alarm he raised his staff and even struck the downtrodden one. Immediately thereafter, however, he came to his senses; and his heart laughed at the folly he had just committed.

"Forgive me," he said to the downtrodden one, who had risen up furiously and sat back down, "forgive me and hear first of all a parable.

As a wanderer who dreams of distant things stumbles unawares upon a sleeping dog on a lonely street, a dog that lies in the sun:

— as both of them fly up, let fly at each other like deadly enemies, these two who are scared to death: thus it fared with us.

And yet! And yet — how little was lacking for them to be caressing each other instead, this dog and this lonely one! After all, they are both — lonely!"

— "Whoever you may be," said the downtrodden one, still furious, "you also tread too near me with your parable, and not only with your foot!

What, am I a dog then?" — and with that the sitter arose and pulled his naked arm out of the swamp. For at first he had lain stretched out on the ground, concealed and camouflaged like those who lie in wait for swamp game.

"But what are you doing here!" a startled Zarathustra cried out, for he saw a great deal of blood flowing down the naked arm, — "what has happened to you?

Did a bad animal bite you, you unhappy wretch?"

The bleeding man laughed, still angry. "What is it to you?" he said and wanted to move on. "Here I am at home in my domain. Let him who will ask me: but I will hardly answer a yokel."

"You are mistaken," said Zarathustra with compassion and held him fast, "you are mistaken: here you are not in your domain but in mine, and no one shall come to harm here.

But call me what you will, — I am who I must be. I call myself Zarathustra.

Well then! Thither the way leads to Zarathustra's cave: it is not far, — will you not tend your wounds at my place?

It has gone badly for you in this life, you unhappy wretch: first an animal bit you, and then — a man trampled you!" —

But when the downtrodden one heard the name Zarathustra, he was transformed:

"But what is happening to me! he cried out, "who still matters to me then in this life other than this man, namely Zarathustra, and that one animal that lives on blood, the leech?

On account of the leech I lay here like a fisherman, and my outstretched arm had already been bitten ten times when a still finer leech made a bite for my blood, Zarathustra himself!

O happiness! O miracle! Praised be this day which has allured me into this swamp! Praised be the best, the liveliest cupping glass alive today, praised be the great conscience-leech Zarathustra!" —

Thus spake the downtrodden one; and Zarathustra rejoiced at his words and their fine, reverent manner. "Who are you?" he asked and extended him his hand, "between us much remains to be cleared up and cheered up: but already, it seems to me, a clear, bright day is dawning."

"I am the conscientious one in spirit," the questioned one answered, "and in things of the spirit it is not easy to find one stricter, harder, and harsher than I, save him from whom I learned them, Zarathustra himself.

Better to know nothing than to half-know many things! Better to be a fool on your own account than a wise man in someone else's eyes! I — get down to the ground:— what does it matter whether it is large or small? Whether it is called swamp or sky? A hand's-breadth of ground is enough for me: provided it is genuine ground and grounding!

— a hand's-breadth of ground: upon that a man can stand. In the true science of conscience there is nothing large and nothing small."

"Then perhaps you are an authority on the leech?" asked Zarathustra; "and you trace the leech down to its ultimate roots, you conscientious one?"

"O Zarathustra, how could I presume to undertake that?

I am a master and authority, however, on the leech's brain: — that is my world!

And it is indeed a world! But forgive me that here my pride speaks, for here I have no equal. That is why I said, 'Here I am at home.'

How long have I traced this one thing, the leech's brain, so that here the slippery truth may no longer slip away from me! Here is my domain!

— on account of this I have thrown everything else away, on account of this everything else has become the same to me; and right beside my knowledge my black ignorance lies down.

My conscience of the spirit demands it thus from me, that I know one thing and nothing else: all the half-in-spirit disgust me, all the hazy, hovering, fanciful ones.

Where my honesty ceases I am blind and also want to be blind. But where I want to know I also want to be honest, namely hard, strict, narrow, cruel, and inexorable.

That you once said, O Zarathustra: 'Spirit is the life which itself cuts into life,' that induced and seduced me to your teaching. And verily, with my own blood I have increased my own knowledge!"

— "As the evidence shows," Zarathustra cut in; for blood was still flowing down the conscientious one's naked arm. The fact was that ten leeches had sunk their teeth into it.

"O you odd fellow, how much this evidence here shows me, namely you yourself! And perhaps I should not pour all of it into your austere ears!

Well then! Thus we part here! But I would be glad to stumble upon you again. Up there the way leads to my cave: this night you shall be my dear guest there!

I would also gladly make amends to your body that Zarathustra stepped on you with his feet: I shall reflect on that. Now, however, a cry of distress calls me hastily away from you."

Thus Spake Zarathustra.

The Sorcerer

1

But when Zarathustra took a turn around a rock, he saw not far below him on the same path a man who threw his limbs about like a raving lunatic and thudded to earth at last and lay flat on his belly.

"Halt!" Zarathustra then said to his heart, "that must surely be the higher man; from him there came that sore cry of distress,— I shall see if I can be of help." But when he ran to the spot where the man lay on the ground, he found a trembling old man with staring eyes; and no matter how hard Zarathustra tried to set him upright and back on his feet again, it was in vain. The unfortunate man did not even seem to notice that anyone was around him: on the contrary, he constantly looked around with pathetic gestures, like one desolated and isolated from all the world. Finally, however, after much trembling, twitching, twisting and turning, he began to yammer thus:

Who warms me, who loves me still?

Give hot hands!

Give heart-braziers!

Laid low, shuddering, Like a half-dead man whose feet someone warms —

Shaken, alas! by unknown fevers, Shivering from sharp, icy-frost arrows, Chased by you, Thought!

Ineffable one! Veiled one! Terrible one!

You hunter behind the clouds!

Struck down by you like a flash of lightning, You scornful eye, that eyes me from the dark:

— thus I lie, Bending myself, contorting myself, tortured By all eternal torment, Thunderstruck By you, cruelest hunter, You unknown-God!

Strike deeper!

Strike yet again!

Puncture, shatter this heart!

Why this torture With dull-toothed arrows?

Why do you look again, Not weary of human agony, With mischief-loving divine-lightning-eyes?

You do not want to kill, Only torture, torture?

Why — torture me, You mischief-loving unknown God? —

Aha! You steal near?

At such a midnight hour What do you want? Speak!

You push me, press me —

Ah! already much too close!

Away! Away!

You hear me breathing, You overhear my heart, You jealous one —

but jealous of what?

Away! Away! Why the ladder?

Do you want to get in, Into my heart, To step into, get into My most secret thoughts?

Shameless one! Unknown one — thief!

What do you mean by stealing?

What do you mean by eavesdropping?

What do you mean by torturing?

You torturer!

You — hangman-God!

Or shall I, like a dog, Roll over for you?

Devoted, enthused-outside-myself, Tailwagging my love to you?

In vain! Stick further, Cruelest thorn! No, No dog — only your game am I, Cruelest hunter!

Your proudest captive, You robber behind the clouds!

Speak at last!

What do you want from me, you waylayer?

You lightning-veiled one! Unknown one! Speak, What do you want, unknown — God?

What? Ransom?

Why do you want ransom?

Demand much — that my pride advises!

And be brief — that my other pride advises!

Aha!

You want — me? Me?

Me — entirely? ...

Aha!

And you torture me, fool that you are, Torture my pride to death?

Give me love — who warms me still?

Who loves me still? — give hot hands, Give heart-braziers, Give me, the loneliest one, Whom ice, alas, sevenfold ice Teaches to yearn for enemies, Even for enemies Give, yes, give over, Cruelest enemy, To me — yourself! ——

Away!

There he himself has flown, My last, only companion, My great enemy, My unknown one, My hangman-God! —

— No! Come back, With all your torture!

To the last of all the lonely ones O come back All the little streams of my tears Run their course to you!

And the final flame of my heart —

It flares up for you!

O come back, My unknown God! My pain! My final—happiness!

2

— But here Zarathustra could restrain himself no longer; he took his staff and began hitting the yammerer with all his might. "Stop it!" he yelled at him with fierce laughter, "stop it, you actor! You counterfeiter! You liar through and through! I know you well!

I will certainly make your legs warm, you wicked sorcerer, I understand well how to heat things up for such as you!"

— "Leave off," said the old man and sprang up from the ground, "do not hit me any more, O Zarathustra! I was only playing a game!

Such things belong to my art; you yourself I wanted to put to the test when I gave you this test performance! And verily, you have seen through me well!

But you too gave me no small test of your own: you are hard, you wise Zarathustra!

You strike hard with your 'truths'; your stick forces from me — this truth!"

— "Do not flatter," answered Zarathustra, still enraged and scowling, "you actor through and through! You are false: why do you talk — of truth?

You peacock of peacocks, you sea of vanity, what did you perform before me, you wicked sorcerer? In whom was I to believe when you yammered in such a manner?"

"The penitent of the spirit," said the old man, him — I played: you yourself once coined this term —

— the poet and sorcerer who turns his spirit against himself in the end, the transformed one who freezes to death on account of his bad science and conscience.

And just confess it: it took you a long time, O Zarathustra, to get past my scam and sham! You believed in my distress when you held my head in both your hands, — I heard you yammer, 'We have loved him too little, loved him too little!'

That I deceived you to such a degree, my malice rejoiced inwardly at that."

"You may have deceived subtler ones than I," said Zarathustra harshly. "I am not on the lookout for deceivers, I must be without precaution: thus my lot wills it.

But you — must deceive: to that degree I know you! You must always be double-, triple-, quadruple-, quintuple-dealing! And what you now confessed was not nearly true or false enough for me!

You wicked counterfeiter, how could you do otherwise! Even your sickness would be wearing make-up were you to show yourself to your doctor naked!

Just as even now you 'made-up' your lie before me when you said: 'I was only playing a game! There was seriousness in it, too; you are somewhat of a penitent of the spirit!

I divine you well: you have become the enchanter of all, but you have no lie or ruse left to use against yourself — you are disenchanted with yourself!

You have reaped loathing as your one truth. Not a word of yours is genuine anymore except your mouth: namely, the loathing that clings to your mouth." —

— "But who are you?" the old sorcerer cried here in a defiant voice, "who dares speak to me thus, the greatest man alive today?" — and a green lightning bolt shot from his eye at Zarathustra. But directly thereafter he changed and said sorrowfully:

"O Zarathustra, I am weary of it, my arts are loathsome to me; I am not great, why do I dissimulate? But you know it well — I was seeking greatness!

I wanted to pose as a great man, and persuaded many: but this lie has been too much for me. I am going to pieces over it.

O Zarathustra, everything about me is a lie; but that I am going to pieces —this, my going to pieces, is no lie!" —

"It does you honor," said Zarathustra gloomily, looking downward with a sidelong glance, "it does you honor that you sought greatness, but it also betrays you. You are not great.

You wicked old sorcerer, this is what is best and most honest in you and what I honor in you, that you grew weary of yourself and expressed it: 'I am not great.'

In this I honor you as a penitent of the spirit: and even if it was only a whiff and a whisk, in that one moment you were — genuine.

But speak up, what do you seek here in my woods and rocks? And when you put yourself in my way, to what test did you want to put me? — in what way were you testing me?" —

Thus spake Zarathustra, and his eyes gleamed. The old sorcerer was silent for a while, then he said: "Did I test you? I — only quest.

O Zarathustra, I seek a true, genuine, artless, unambiguous one, a man of all honesty, a vessel of wisdom, a saint of knowledge, a great man!

Do you not know it then, O Zarathustra? I seek Zarathustra."

— And here a long silence ensued between the two; Zarathustra, however, had become so deeply absorbed in thought that he closed his eyes. But then, returning to his interlocutor, he grasped the sorcerer's hand and said, full of politeness and policy:

"Well then! Up there the way leads, there lies Zarathustra's cave. In it you may seek him whom you wish to find.

And ask my animals for advice, my eagle and my serpent: they shall help you seek. My cave is large, however.

I myself, of course — I have never yet seen a great man. Towards what is great the finest eye today is coarse. It is the kingdom of the riffraff.

Many a one have I found indeed that stretched and swelled himself up and the people cried: 'Behold, a great man! But what good are all bellows! In the end the wind comes out.

In the end the frog bursts that has blown itself up too long: then the wind comes out. To prick a swelled-up one in the belly, I call that a fine pastime. Hear that, boys!

This is the day of the riffraff: who even knows what is great, what is small?

Who could have success seeking greatness there? Only a fool: fools succeed.

You seek greatness, you strange fool? Who taught you that? Is today the time for that? O you wicked seeker, why do you seek — to test me?" — —

Thus spake Zarathustra, confident of heart, and went laughingly on his way.

Out Of Service

Not long, however, after Zarathustra had rid himself of the sorcerer, he again saw someone sitting alongside the path he was taking, namely a tall man in black with a pale, haggard face: he vexed him exceedingly. "Woe," he said to his heart, "there sits masked misery, from the species of priests, it seems to me: what do they want in my kingdom?

What! I have hardly escaped that sorcerer: must another necromancer cross my path again, — some wizard with his laying on of hands, some dark miracle-worker by the grace of God, an anointed world-slanderer whom the devil may take!

But the devil is never at the place he should be: he always comes too late, that damned dwarf and clubfoot!"

Thus Zarathustra cursed impatiently in his heart and thought how with an averted glance he might slip past the man in black: but behold, it turned out otherwise.

For at just that moment the sitter had already sighted him; and not unlike one who has met with unexpected good fortune, he sprang up and made straight for Zarathustra.

"Whoever you are, you wayfarer," he said, "help one who has lost his way, a seeker, an old man who could easily come to harm here!

This world here is strange and remote to me, I have even heard wild beasts howling; and he who could have offered me shelter is himself no more.

I was in search of the last pious man, a saint and hermit who, alone in his forest, had not yet heard what all the world knows today."

"What does all the world know today?" asked Zarathustra. "Perhaps this, that the old God is no longer alive, the one in whom all the world once believed?"

"Thou hast said," answered the old man sadly. And I served that old God until his last hours.

But now I am out of service, without a master and yet not free, without a merry hour anymore either, except in remembrances.

Which is why I have climbed in these mountains, to finally have a feast day for myself again, as befits an old pope and church father: for know this, I am the last pope! — a feast day of pious remembrances and divine services.

But now he himself is dead, the most pious man, that saint in the forest who perpetually praised his God with humming and singing.

He himself I found no more when I found his hut, — but there were two wolves within who howled at his death — for all the animals loved him. At that I ran away.

So had I come in vain to these woods and mountains? Then my heart resolved to seek another, the most pious of all those who do not believe in God —, to seek Zarathustra!"

Thus spake the graybeard and peered with a sharp eye at the one who stood before him; Zarathustra, however, seized the hand of the old pope and contemplated it a long while with admiration.

"Behold, you venerable one," he then said, "what a long and handsome hand!

That is the hand of one who has always dispensed blessings. But now it holds fast on him whom you seek, me, Zarathustra.

It is I, the godless Zarathustra, who speaks here: who is more godless than I, that I may rejoice in his teaching?" —

Thus spake Zarathustra and penetrated with his looks the thoughts and hinter-thoughts of the old pope. At last the latter began:

"He who loved and possessed him the most has now also lost him the most —: behold, perhaps I myself am now the more godless of us two? But who could rejoice at that!" —

"You served him to the end?" Zarathustra asked thoughtfully, after a profound silence, "you know how he died? Is it true what they say, that pity choked him, — that he saw how man hung on the cross and could not stand it, that the love of man became his hell and in the end his death?" —

The old pope, however, gave no answer but looked aside shyly and with a painful and gloomy expression.

"Let him go," said Zarathustra after long reflection, in which he still looked the old man straight in the eye.

"Let him go, he is gone. And though it does you honor that you speak only good things of this dead one, you know as well as I do who he was; and that he had strange ways."

"Speaking eye to eyes," said the old pope cheerfully (for he was blind in one eye), in divine matters I am more enlightened than Zarathustra himself — and have the right to be.

My love served him many years, my will followed his will in all things. But a good servant knows everything, and also quite a few things that his master hides from himself.

He was a hidden God, full of secrecy. Verily, even a son he came to have by none other than underhanded means. At the door of his faith stands adultery.

Whoever glorifies him as a God of love does not think highly enough of love itself. Did not this God also want to be judge? But the lover loves beyond reward and recompense.

When he was young, this God out of the Orient, he was harsh and vengeful and built himself a hell for the amusement of his favorites.

In the end, however, he became old and soft and mellow and pitying, more like a grandfather than a father, but most of all like a tottering old grandmother.

There he sat, withered, in his corner by the stove, worrying over his weak legs, world-weary, will-weary, and one day he choked to death on his all-toogreat pity." —

"You old pope," Zarathustra interrupted here, "did you see that with your own two eyes? It could have possibly come off that way: that way and also otherwise.

When gods die, they always die many kinds of death.

But well then! This way or that, this way and that — he is gone! He ran counter to the taste of my eyes and ears, worse I would not say behind his back.

I love all that looks bright and speaks honestly. But he — you know it indeed, you old priest, he had something of your nature about him, of the priestly nature — he was ambiguous.

He was also indistinct. How angry he got with us, this wrath-snorter, for understanding him poorly! But why did he not speak more clearly?

And if the fault lay in our ears, why did he give us ears that heard him poorly? If there was mud in our ears, well then! who put it there?

Too many things he botched, this potter who never finished his apprenticeship.

But that he revenged himself on his earthen and earthly vessels because they turned out badly — that was a sin against good taste.

In piety too there is good taste: it says at last: "Away with such a God! Better to have no God, better to make your own destiny, better to be a fool, better to be a God yourself!"

— "What do I hear!" the old pope said here with pricked-up ears; "O Zarathustra, with such unbelief you are more pious than you know! Some god in you has converted you to your godlessness.

Is it not your piety itself which no longer allows you to believe in a God?

And your overly great honesty will carry you away yet, beyond good and evil!

Behold, what has been reserved for you? You have eyes and hand and mouth predestined for blessing from eternity. One does not bless with the hand alone.

In your presence, although you want to be the godless one, I sense the sacred and pleasant aroma of long blessings: I feel pleased and pained by it.

Let me be your guest, O Zarathustra, for a single night! Nowhere on earth shall I now feel better than with you!" —

"Amen! So be it!" said Zarathustra in great amazement, "up there the way leads, there lies Zarathustra's cave.

Gladly indeed would I see you up there myself, you venerable one, for I love all pious men. But now a cry of distress calls me hastily away from you.

In my domain no one shall come to harm; my cave is a good haven. And I would like best of all to put everyone who is in the doldrums back on firm land and firm legs.

But who could take your melancholy from your shoulders? For that I am too weak. Long, verily, we should have to wait until someone re-awakens your God for you.

For this old God lives no more: he is as dead as a doornail." —

Thus spake Zarathustra.

The Ugliest Man

— And again Zarathustra's feet ran through mountains and forests, and his eyes searched and searched, but he whom they wanted to see was nowhere to be seen, the great crier and sufferer of distress. The entire way, however, he rejoiced in his heart and was thankful. "What good things," he said, "this day has granted me as compensation for having started out badly! What strange partners in conversation I have found!

On their words I shall now chew long as upon good grains; my teeth shall mash and smash them small until they flow like milk into my soul!"- But as the path curved around a rock again, the landscape changed all at once, and Zarathustra entered a kingdom of death. Here black and red cliffs rose up: no grass, no tree, no bird's melody. For it was a valley that all the animals avoided; except that a species of ugly, thick, green snake, when it grew old, came here to die. That is why the shepherds called this valley: Snakes-Death.

Zarathustra, however, was sunk in a black recollection, for to him it seemed as if he had stood in this valley once before. And many weighty things lay heavy on his mind: so that he walked slowly and ever more slowly and at last stood still. But when he opened his eyes he saw, sitting by the path, something shaped like a man, yet hardly like a man, something unspeakable. And all at once a great shame came over Zarathustra at having set eyes on something like that: blushing up to his white hair, he averted his glance and raised his foot to leave this bad place. But then the dead wasteland became noisy: for from the ground it welled up, gurgling and rattling, as water gurgles and rattles at night in cloggedup waterpipes; until at last it became a human voice and human speech: — it sounded thus:

"Zarathustra! Zarathustra! solve my riddle! Speak! Speak! What is the revenge on the witness?

I entice you back, here is slippery ice! Beware, beware that your pride does not break its legs here!

You think yourself wise, you proud Zarathustra! So solve the riddle then, you hard nutcracker, — the riddle that I am! So speak then: who am I?"

— but when Zarathustra had heard these words, — what do you think happened in his soul at that moment? Pity laid him low; and all at once he sank down, like an oak tree that has long withstood many woodcutters,— heavily, suddenly, to the dismay of even those who wanted to fell it. But in no time he got up from the ground again and his face grew hard.

"I know you well," he said in a bronze-like voice: "You are the murderer of God!

Let me go.

You could not stand him who saw you, — who saw you always and through and through, you ugliest man! You took revenge on this witness!"

Thus spake Zarathustra and wanted to be off; but the unspeakable one seized the end of his garment and began to gurgle and search for words again.

"Stay!" he said at last—

—"Stay! Do not pass by! I have divined which ax felled you to the ground: hail to you, O Zarathustra, that you stand again!

You have divined, I know it well, how he who slew him feels, — the murderer of God! Stay! Sit down here by me, it will not be in vain.

To whom should I go, if not to you? Stay, sit down! But do not look at me!

Honor thus — my ugliness!

They persecute me: now you are my last refuge. Not with their hatred, not with their bailiffs: — O, at such persecution I would jeer and cheer and take pride in!

Has not all success hitherto been with the well-persecuted? And he who persecutes well easily learns to follow — after all, all he ever does is — come after!

But it is their pity —

— it is their pity from which I flee and flee to you. O Zarathustra, protect me, you, my last refuge, you, the only one who has divined me:

— you have divined how he who slew him feels. Stay! And should you want to go, you impatient one: go not the way by which I came. That way is bad.

Are you angry with me for gibber-jabbering too long already? But know that it is I, the ugliest man, — who also has the largest, heaviest feet. Where I have gone, the way is bad. I tread all paths to death and ruin.

But that you passed me by in silence: that you blushed, I saw it well: thereby I knew you to be Zarathustra.

Anyone else would have thrown his alms my way, his pity in word and glance. But for that — I am not beggar enough, that you divined for that I am too rich, rich in the great, the terrible, the ugliest, the most unspeakable. Your shame, O Zarathustra, honored me!

With difficulty I escaped the crush of the pity-pushers, — that I might find the only one today who teaches 'Pity is obtrusive' — you, O Zarathustra!

— whether it be the pity of a God or the pity of man: pity goes against modesty.

And not-wanting-to-help can be nobler than that virtue which rushes to help.

Pity, however, this is called virtue itself by all the small people: — they have no respect for great misfortune, for great ugliness, for great failure.

Over them all I look away, as a dog looks away over the backs of swarming herds of sheep. They are small, gray, good-wooled, good-willed people.

As a heron looks away contemptuously over shallow pools, with a laidback head: so I look away over the swarm of gray small waves and wills and souls.

Too long have we given them out to be right, these small people: so that in the end we have given them power as well — now they teach:

'Good is only what small people call good.'

And 'truth' today is what the preacher said who arose himself from them, that odd saint and advocate of the small people who testified of himself: ' I — am the truth.'

For a long time now this immodest one has greatly swelled the small peoples' heads — he who taught no small error when he taught: 'I — am the truth.'

Was an immodest one ever answered more politely? — You, however, O Zarathustra, passed him by and said: 'No! No! Three times no!'

You warned against his error, you first warned against pity — not to all, not to none, but to you and your kind.

You are ashamed at the shame of the great sufferer; and verily, when you say, 'From pity there comes a heavy cloud this way, take heed, you men!'

— when you teach 'All creators are hard, all great love is above pity': O Zarathustra, how well-schooled you seem to be in weather signs!

You yourself, however — warn yourself as well against your pity! For many are on their way to you, many suffering, doubting, desponding, drowning, freezing ones —

I warn you as well against myself. You have divined my best, my worst riddle, me myself and what I did. I know the ax which fells you.

But he — he had to die: he saw with eyes that saw everything, — he saw man's depths and reasons, all his hidden indignity and ugliness.

His pity knew no shame: he crawled into my filthiest corners. This mostinquisitive, over-obtrusive, over-pitying one had to die.

He saw me always: on such a witness I would have revenge — or not live myself.

The God who saw everything, even man: this God had to die! Man could not stand to have such a witness live."

Thus spake the ugliest man. Zarathustra arose, however, and prepared to take his leave: for he felt frozen down to his innards.

"You unspeakable one," he said, "you have warned me against your way. By way of thanks I shall praise mine to you. Behold, up there lies the cave of Zarathustra.

My cave is large and deep and has many nooks and crannies; the most-hidden one finds his hiding place there.

And close by it there are a hundred by-ways and hideaways for creeping, leaping, and fluttering creatures.

You outcast who has cast himself out, you refuse to live among men and men's pity? Well then, do as I do! Thus you shall also learn from me; only the doer learns.

And speak first and next to my animals! The proudest animal and the wisest animal — they could well be the right counselors for both of us!"

Thus spake Zarathustra and went his way, even more reflectively and slowly than before: for he asked himself many things and hardly knew how to answer himself.

"How poor is man though!" he thought in his heart, "how ugly, how throatrattling, how full of hidden shame!

They tell me that man loves himself: alas, how great this self-love must be!

How much contempt it has going against it!

This one here also loved himself when he despised himself, — a great lover he seems to me, and a great despiser.

None yet have I found who despised himself more profoundly: that too is loftiness. Alas, was he perhaps the higher man whose cry I heard?

I love the great despisers. Man, however, is something that must be overcome."

The Voluntary Beggar

When Zarathustra had left the ugliest man, he was frozen and he felt lonely: for much coldness and loneliness had passed through his mind, so that his limbs also became colder. But as he climbed on and on, up, down, sometimes past green meadows, other times over wild stony beds where an impatient brook had possibly lain down to rest in former days: then suddenly he felt warmer again and heartier in spirit.

"But what has happened to me?" he asked himself, "something warm and living quickens me, it must be in my vicinity.

Already I am less alone; unknown companions and brothers roam around me, their warm breath stirs my soul."

But when he explored around himself and searched for the consolers of his loneliness: behold, they were cows standing next to each other on a knoll; their nearness and odor had warmed his heart. These cows, however, seemed to be eagerly listening to a speaker and paid no heed to the one who approached them.

But as Zarathustra drew quite near them, he distinctly heard a man's voice speaking from out of the midst of the cows; and evidently they had turned their heads all together toward the speaker.

Then Zarathustra sprang forth eagerly and pushed the animals apart, for he feared that someone had suffered injury here, which the cows' pity could hardly remedy. But in this he was mistaken; for behold, there sat a man on the ground, and he seemed to be exhorting the animals to have no fear of him, a peaceable man and preacher-on-the-mount out of whose eyes goodness itself preached.

"What do you seek here?" Zarathustra cried out with wonder.

"What do I seek here?" he answered: "the same thing that you seek, you disturber of the peace! namely, happiness on earth.

That, however, I want to learn from these cows. For, do you know, I have already spent half the morning talking to them and just now they were about to tell me. Why do you disturb them?

Except we turn back and become like cows, we shall not enter the kingdom of heaven. One thing namely we should learn from them: chewing the cud.

And verily, what would it profit a man to gain the whole world and not learn this one thing, chewing the cud! He would not be free of his misery.

— his great misery: but today that is called loathing. Who does not have a heart, mouth, and eyes full of loathing today? Even you! Even you! But just look at these cows!"—

Thus spake the preacher-on-the-mount and then turned his own gaze upon Zarathustra — for until then it had rested lovingly upon the cows —: but now he was transformed. "Who is this with whom I speak?" he cried out in alarm and sprang up from the ground.

"This is the man without loathing, this is Zarathustra himself, the conqueror of the great loathing, this is the eye, this is the mouth, this is the heart of Zarathustra himself."

And while he was speaking thus, he kissed, with overflowing eyes, the hands of him with whom he spoke and acted exactly like one to whom a precious gift and gem has unexpectedly fallen from heaven. The cows, however, watched all this and marvelled.

"Speak not of me, you strange one! Delightful one!" said Zarathustra and restrained his tenderness, "speak first to me of yourself! Are you not the voluntary beggar who once threw great riches away, who was ashamed of his riches and of the rich and fled to the poorest to give them his plenty and his heart? But they did not accept him."

"But they did not accept me," said the voluntary beggar, "you know it indeed. So in the end I went to the animals and to these cows."

"There you learned," Zarathustra interrupted the speaker, "how proper giving is harder than proper receiving, and that good gift-giving is an art and the last, craftiest master-art of kindliness."

"Especially nowadays," answered the voluntary beggar, "today, namely, when everything low has become rebellious and skittish and insolent in its own way: namely in the rabble way.

For the hour has come, you know it indeed, for the big, bad, long, slow slave-and-rabble rebellion: it grows and grows!

Now the lower ranks are enraged by every good action and small giveaway; and the over-rich must be on their guard!

Those today who trickle out in drops, like bulging bottles with all-too-small necks — such bottles people are fond of breaking the necks of today.

Lascivious greed, bilious envy, grief-stricken vengefulness, rabble pride: all this exploded in my face. It is no longer true that the poor are blessed. The kingdom of heaven, however, is with the cows.

"And why is it not with the rich?" asked Zarathustra temptingly, while he restrained the cows which snorted familiarly upon the peaceable one.

"Why do you tempt me?" he replied. "You know it even better than I. What drove me to the poorest after all? Was it not loathing for our richest?

— for the convicts of riches, who glean their advantage from every piece of trash, with cold eyes, obscene thoughts, for this riff-raff that stinks to high heaven, — for this gilded, falsified rabble, whose fathers were carrion birds or ragpickers or pickpockets, with wives obliging, lustful, forgetful: — all of them not far from being whores, namely —

Rabble above, rabble below! What do 'poor' and 'rich' even mean today? I forgot the difference — so I fled, further, ever further, until I came to these cows."

Thus spake the peaceable one, and even snorted and sweated during his speech: so that the cows marvelled once more. Zarathustra, however, kept looking at him with a smiling face, silently shaking his head as the other talked so harshly.

"You do violence to yourself, you preacher-on-the-mount, when you use such harsh words. Neither your mouth nor your eye was made for such harshness.

Nor, it seems to me, your very stomach either: such anger and hatred and frothing-over makes it queasy. Your stomach requires softer things: you are no butcher.

A planter and root-gatherer rather you seem to me. Perhaps you grind up grain. Surely, however, you are averse to fleshly joys and love honey."

"You have divined me well," replied the voluntary beggar with a relieved heart. "I love honey, I also grind up grain, for I have sought that which tastes lovely and makes for sweet breath.

— also what takes a long time, a day's and mouth's work for gentle dawdlers and idlers. These cows are surely the most proficient at this: they invented for themselves chewing the cud and lying in the sun. They also abstain from all heavy thoughts, which swell the heart."

— "Well then!" said Zarathustra, "you should also see my animals, my eagle and my serpent — of their like there are none on earth today.

Behold, there leads the way to my cave: be its guest this night. And talk to my animals of the happiness of animals, until I come home myself. For now a cry of distress calls me hastily away from you. New honey too you shall find at my place, icy-fresh golden honeycomb: eat that!

But quickly take leave of your cows now, you strange one! Delightful one!

Even though it may be hard for you. For they are your warmest friends and instructors!"

" — Except for one of whom I am even fonder," answered the voluntary beggar. "You yourself are good and even better than a cow, O Zarathustra!"

"Away, away with you! you wicked flatterer!" Zarathustra cried maliciously, "why do you spoil me with such praise and honey-flattery?"

"Away, away from me!" he cried once more and brandished his stick at the tender beggar: he, however, ran swiftly away.

The Shadow

But no sooner had the voluntary beggar run away than Zarathustra, alone with himself again, heard a new voice behind him: it called out: "Halt! Zarathustra!

So wait then! It is I indeed, O Zarathustra, I, your shadow!" But Zarathustra did not wait, for a sudden annoyance came over him at the great rush and crush in his mountains. "Where has my solitude gone?" he said.

"It is truly becoming too much for me; this mountain range is swarming, my kingdom is no longer of this world, I need new mountains.

My shadow calls me? What does my shadow matter? Let him run after me!

I — shall run away from him."

Thus spake Zarathustra to his heart and ran away. But he who was behind him followed after him: so that presently there were three runners, one after the other, first the voluntary beggar, then Zarathustra, and third and last, his shadow. Not long were they running thus when Zarathustra came to his senses over his folly and with one sudden jerk shook all displeasure and disgust from himself.

"What!" he said, "do not the most ridiculous things always happen to us old hermits and holy men?

Verily, my folly has grown tall in the mountains! Now I hear six old fools' legs clattering, one after the other!

But does Zarathustra really need to be afraid of a shadow? And after all I think he has longer legs than me."

Thus spake Zarathustra, laughing with his eyes and insides, then stopped and quickly turned around — and behold, he almost threw his follower and shadow to the ground: so closely indeed had this shadow followed at his heels, and so weak was he likewise. For when Zarathustra scrutinized him with his eyes, he was terrified as if by a sudden apparition: so thin, dark, hollow, and deathly-weary did this follower appear.

"Who are you?" asked Zarathustra furiously, "what are you doing here?

And why do you call yourself my shadow? I do not like you."

"Forgive me," answered the shadow, "that it is I; and if I do not please you, well then, O Zarathustra! in that I praise you and your good taste.

I am a wanderer who has already walked a great deal at your heals: always on the way but without a goal, without a home, also: so that truly I am little short of being the Eternal Wandering Jew except that I am not eternal and also not a Jew.

What? Must I always be on the way? Whirled about by every wind, restless, driven onward? O earth, you have grown too round for me!

On every surface I have already sat, like weary dust I have fallen asleep on mirrors and windowpanes: everything takes from me, nothing gives, I grow thin — almost like a shadow.

But after you, O Zarathustra, I have chased and paced the longest, and though I hid myself from you, I was definitely your best shadow: wherever you sat there I sat, too.

With you I haunted the coldest, remotest worlds, like a ghost which freely goes over winter roofs and snow.

With you I strove in everything that is forbidden, worst, remotest: and if anything in me be a virtue, then it is that I had no fear of being forbidden.

With you I shattered whatever my heart revered, I overturned all boundary stones and images, I pursued the most dangerous desires — verily, over every crime I have passed at one time.

With you I unlearned the belief in words and values and great names.

When the devil sheds his skin, does not his name fall off as well? For that is also skin. The devil himself is perhaps — skin.

'Nothing is true, everything is permitted': thus I exhorted myself.

With head and heart I plunged myself into the coldest wasters. Alas, how often I stood there naked like a crab after that!

Alas, where have all the good things gone for me, and all shame, and all belief in the good! Alas, where is that innocence I once possessed, the innocence of the good and their noble lies!

Too often, verily, I followed hard on the heels of truth: then she kicked me in the head. Sometimes I meant to lie and behold! only then did I find — the truth.

Too much became clear to me: now it means nothing to me anymore. Nothing that I love lives anymore, — how could I still love myself?

'To live as I please or not to live at all': thus I will it, thus the holiest wills it as well. But alas! how can I even be — pleased?

Do I even have — a goal? A harbor toward which my sail is set?

A fair wind? Alas, only he who knows where he is sailing also knows which wind is good and is his fair wind.

What remains now for me? A heart weary and shameless; a restless will; flutter-wings, a broken backbone.

This quest for my home: O Zarathustra, do you know, this quest has been my inquest; it is eating me up.

'Where is — my home?' I ask and seek and have sought after it, but I have not found it. O eternal everywhere, O eternal nowhere, O eternal — In-vain!"

Thus spake the shadow, and Zarathustra's face grew longer at his words.

"You are my shadow!" he said at last, with sadness.

"Your danger is no small one, you free spirit and wanderer! You have had a bad day: see to it that an even worse evening does not come to you!

To restless ones such as you even prison seems blessed in the end. Have you ever seen how imprisoned criminals sleep? They sleep peacefully, they enjoy their new security.

Beware that in the end a narrow belief does not imprison you, a harsh, stern delusion! For everything narrow and firm induces and seduces you now.

You have lost your goal: alas, how will you while away and smile away this loss? With this loss — you have also lost your way!

You poor rover, roamer, you weary butterfly! Would you like repose and a home tonight? Then go up to my cave!

Over there the way leads to my cave! And now I will quickly run away from you again. Already it is as if a shadow were lying over me.

I want to run alone that it may be bright around me again. For that I must be merry on my legs a long while yet. But this evening with me there will be —dancing!" — —

Thus spake Zarathustra.

At Noontime

— And Zarathustra ran and ran and found no one anymore and was alone and found himself over and over again and enjoyed and savored his solitude and thought of good things, — for hours. Around the noontime hour, however, when the sun stood directly above Zarathustra's head, he came upon an old crooked and gnarled tree which was embraced by the rich love of a grapevine and hidden from itself: from it hung yellow grapes in abundance, confronting the wanderer.

Then he felt a longing to slake a slight thirst and break off a cluster of grapes; but even as he stretched out his arm to do that, he felt an even greater longing: namely, to lie down beside the tree at the perfect noon hour and to sleep.

This Zarathustra did; and as soon as he lay on the ground in the stillness and secrecy of the brightly-colored grass, he had already forgotten his slight thirst and fallen asleep. For as Zarathustra's proverb says: One thing is more necessary than another. Only that his eyes remained open: — for they did not grow weary of seeing and praising the tree and the love of the vine. In falling asleep, however, Zarathustra spoke thus to his heart:

"Hush! Hush! Has not the world just now become perfect? But what is happening to me?

As a delicate wind dances, unseen, upon an inlaid sea, light, featherlight: so — sleep dances upon me.

My eye it closes not, my soul it leaves awake. Light it is, verily! featherlight!

It persuades me, I know not how?, it touches me inwardly with a caressing hand, it forces my hand. Yes, it forces me, so that my soul stretches out: how long and weary she grows, my strange soul! Has a seventh-day evening come to her precisely at noon? Has she already wandered happily among good and ripe things too long?

She stretches herself out long, long — longer! She lies still, my strange soul.

Too many good things has she tasted already; this golden sadness oppresses her, she makes a wry mouth.

— As a ship that comes into its calm cove: — now it leans against the earth, weary from the long voyages and the uncertain seas. Is the earth not truer?

As such a ship rests and nestles itself against the land — then it suffices that a spider spin its thread from the land to it. No stronger ropes are required.

As such a weary ship in the calmest cove: so I too rest near the earth now, true, trusting, waiting, tethered to it with the lightest of threads.

O happiness! O happiness! So, would you sing, O my soul? You lie in the grass. But this is the secret solemn hour when no shepherd plays his flute.

Stay! Hot noontide sleeps upon the meadows. Do not sing! Hush! The world is perfect.

Do not sing, you grass-gosling, O my soul! Do not even whisper! Just look — hush! The old noontide sleeps, he moves his mouth: does he not even now drink a drop of happiness — an old brown drop of golden happiness, of golden wine? It skims over him, his happiness laughs. Thus — laughs a god. Hush! —

— 'For happiness, how little indeed suffices for happiness!' Thus I said once and thought myself clever. but it was blasphemy: that I have learned now.

Clever fools speak better.

Precisely the least thing, the slightest, lightest thing, a lizard's rustling, a whiff, a whisk, an eye-glance — little constitutes the nature of the best happiness.

Hush!

— What has happened to me? Listen! Has time perhaps flown away? Am I not falling? Have I not fallen — listen! into the fountain of eternity?

— What is happening to me? Hush! It pierces me — woe — to the heart?

To the heart! O shatter, shatter, heart, after such happiness, after such piercing!

— What? Has not the world just now become perfect? Round and ripe? O the golden round ring — where does it fly, I wonder? I will run after it! Quickly!

Hush — — "(and here Zarathustra stretched himself and felt that he slept.) "Up," he said to himself, "you sleeper! You noonday sleeper! Well then, come on, old legs! It is time and more than time, many a good stretch of the way still remains for you —

Now you have had a good long rest, how long then? Half an eternity! Well, up now, my old heart! Only after such a sleep, how long may it take you — to wake it off?"

(But then he proceeded to fall asleep again, and his soul spoke against him and defended itself and settled down once again) — "Let me be! Hush! Has not the world just now become perfect? O the golden round ball!" —

"Stand up," said Zarathustra, "you little thief, you lazy day-thief! What!

Still stretching, yawning, sighing, tumbling down into deep fountains?

Who are you though? O my soul!" (and here he was startled, for a sunbeam from heaven fell down upon his face.) "O heaven above me," he said, sighing, and sat upright, "you are looking down at me? You are listening to my strange soul?

When will you drink this drop of dew which has fallen upon all earthly things, — when will you drink this strange soul —

— when, fountain of eternity! you cheerful-frightful noontime-abyss! when will you drink my soul back into yourself?"

Thus spake Zarathustra and arose from his resting place by the tree as if from a strange drunkenness: and behold, the sun still stood straight above his head. But one might rightly gather from this that Zarathustra had not slept long.

The Greeting

It was only late in the afternoon that Zarathustra, after long fruitless searching and wandering around, returned home to his cave. But when he stood opposite it, not more than twenty paces away, what he least expected to happen happened: once again he heard the great cry of distress. And, amazingly! this time it came from his own cave. It was a long, varied, peculiar cry, however, and Zarathustra clearly discerned that it was composed of many voices: heard from afar, though, it might sound like the cry from a single mouth.

Then Zarathustra sprang up towards his cave, and behold! what an eyeful awaited him right after this earful! For they sat all together, those he had passed by during the day: the king on the right and the king on the left, the old sorcerer, the pope, the voluntary beggar, the shadow, the conscientious one in spirit, the sad soothsayer, and the ass; the ugliest man, however, had placed a crown on his head and wound two purple girdles round himself, — for, like all the ugly, he loved to disguise himself and play the dandy. But in the midst of this sad company stood Zarathustra's eagle, ruffled and restless, for he had to answer to too much for which his pride had no answer; the wise serpent hung around his neck, however.

Zarathustra beheld all this with great amazement: then, however, he examined every single one of his guests with genial curiosity, read their souls, and marvelled again. In the meantime the assembled had risen from their seats and waited with reverence for Zarathustra to speak. But Zarathustra spake thus:

"You despairing ones! You strange ones! So I heard your cry of distress? And now, where to seek him whom I sought in vain today: the higher man — : in my own cave he sits, the higher man! But why do I marvel at that?

Have I not lured him to myself with honey offerings and cunning bird calls of my happiness?

But methinks you are poor company for each other, you make each other's hearts surly when you sit together, you criers of distress! First there must come one, — one to make you laugh again, a good joyful tomfool, a dancer and wind and wild child, some old buffoon; — what do you think?

But forgive me, you despairing ones, that I speak to you with such petty words, unworthy, verily, of such guests! But you do not guess what makes my heart courageous :—you yourselves do, and the sight of you, forgive me! For everyone who looks upon one in despair becomes brave. To encourage one in despair — everyone thinks himself strong enough for that.

To me myself you have given this strength — a good gift, my lofty guests!

An honest-to-goodness guest-gift! Well then, do not be angry now if I offer you something of my own as well.

This is my kingdom here and my dominion: what is mine, however, shall this evening and this night be yours. My animals shall serve you: let my cave be your resting place!

In my house and home no one shall despair, in my preserve I shelter each one from his wild beasts. And that is the first thing I offer you: security!

•

The second thing, however, is: my little finger. And once you have that, then go ahead, take the whole hand! and the heart with it! Welcome here, welcome, my guests!"

Thus spake Zarathustra and laughed with love and malice. After this greeting his guests bowed once again and were reverentially silent; the king on the right, however, answered him in their name.

"By the way in which, O Zarathustra, you offered us your hand and your greeting, we recognize you as Zarathustra. You humbled yourself before us; you almost offended our reverence —:but who could humble himself with such pride as you? We ourselves that raises up, it is refreshment for our eyes and hearts.

To view this alone we would gladly climb mountains higher than this one.

For as curiosity seekers we came, we wanted to see what makes dim eyes bright.

And behold, all our cries of distress are over now. Now our hearts and minds are open and overjoyed. Little is lacking: and our spirits will become highspirited.

Nothing more delightful grows on earth, O Zarathustra, than a lofty, strong will: it is the earth's finest growth. An entire landscape refreshes itself on one such tree.

He who grows up like you, O Zarathustra, I liken to the pine: tall, silent, hard, alone, of the best, most pliant wood, magnificent, in the end, however, reaching out for its domain, with strong green branches, asking strong questions of wind and weather and whatever is at home in high places, — answering more strongly, a commander, a conqueror: O who would not climb high mountains to behold such growth?

Here at your tree, O Zarathustra, the gloomy, the failures also refresh themselves; at the sight of you even the restless become secure and cure their hearts.

And verily, many eyes are turned toward your mountains and tree today; a great longing has arisen and many have learned to ask: who is Zarathustra?

And if ever you dripped your song and your honey into their ears: all the hidden, the lonesome, the twosome said all at once to their hearts: 'Does Zarathustra still live? It no longer pays to live, all is the same, all is in vain: or — we must live with Zarathustra!'

'Why does he not come, he who has announced himself for so long?' thus many ask; 'did solitude swallow him up? Or should we perhaps come to him?'

Now it comes about that solitude itself becomes brittle and breaks apart, like a grave that breaks apart and can no longer hold its dead. Everywhere one sees the resurrected.

Now the waves rise and rise around your mountain, O Zarathustra. And however high your height might be, many must go up to you: your boat shall not be high and dry much longer.

And that we despairing ones came to your cave and already despair no more: it is but a sign and symbol that better ones are on their way to you, — for they themselves are on their way to you, the last remnant of God among men, that is: all the men of great longing, great loathing, great disgust, all those who do not want to live unless they learn to hope again — unless they learn from you, O Zarathustra, the great hope!"

Thus spake the king on the right and seized the hand of Zarathustra in order to kiss it; but Zarathustra checked his reverence and stepped back alarmed, as if silently and suddenly fleeing into far distances. After a little while, however, he was already back with his guests, looked at them with bright, searching eyes, and said:

"My guests, you higher men, I will speak plainly and in plain German with you. Not for you have I waited here in these mountains."

("Plainly and in plain German? God help us!" the king on the left said here, in an aside; "you can see he doesn't know our dear Germans, this wise man from the East!"

"But he means 'bluntly and in plain German' — well then! That is not the worst taste nowadays!") "You may truly be higher men all in all," continued Zarathustra, "but for me — you are not high and strong enough.

For me, that is: for the inexorable in me which is silent but will not always be silent. And if you should belong to me, it is surely not as my right arm.

For whoever stands on sickly and frail legs, as you do, wants above all, whether he knows it or hides it from himself: to be spared.

My arms and legs, however, I do not spare; I do not spare my warriors: how could you serve in my war?

With you all my victories would be spoiled. And many of you would fall down if you but heard the loud sound of my drums.

You are not handsome and wellborn enough for me either: I need clean, smooth mirrors for my teaching; on your surface even my own likeness is distorted.

Your shoulders are weighted down by many a burden, many a memory; many a bad dwarf crouches in your corners. There is also hidden rabble in you.

And even though you are high and of a higher kind: much in you is crooked and deformed. There is no blacksmith in the world who could hammer you straight and into shape.

You are only bridges: may higher ones stride across on you! You signify steps: so do not be angry with him who climbs over you to his height!

From your seed a true son and perfect heir may yet grow for me one day: but that is far off. You yourselves are not those to whom my heritage and name belong.

Not for you do I wait here in these mountains, not with you may I descend for the last time. Only as omens have you come to me, that higher ones are already on the way, not the men of great longing, great loathing, great disgust, and that which you have called the last remnant of God, — No! No! Three times no! For others I wait here in these mountains and will not lift my foot from here without them, — for higher, stronger, more victorious, more joyous ones, ones who are built foursquare in body and soul: laughing lions must come!

Oh, my guests, you oddballs, — have you heard nothing yet of my children?

And that they are on their way to me?

But speak to me of my gardens, of my blessed isles, of my new beautiful kind, — why do you not speak to me of that?

This guest-gift I ask of you from your love, that you speak to me of my children.

With this I am rich, with this I became poor: what did I not give, — what would I not give, to have one thing: these children, this live planting, these life-trees of my will and my highest hope!"

Thus spake Zarathustra and stopped suddenly in his speech: for his longing overcame him and he closed his eyes and mouth at the movement of his heart.

And all his guests were also silent and stood still and dismayed: except that the old soothsayer made signs and gestures with his hands.

The Last Supper

For at this point the soothsayer interrupted the greeting of Zarathustra and his guests: he pressed forward, like one who has no time to lose, grabbed Zarathustra's hand and cried: "But Zarathustra!

One thing is more necessary than another, so you yourself said: well then, one thing is more necessary to me now than anything else.

A word at the right time: did you not invite me to a meal? And here there are many who have come a long way. You do not intend to feed us with speeches, do you?

And, to me, all of you have thought far too much about freezing, drowning, suffocating, and other bodily crises: but nobody has thought about my crisis, namely, dying of hunger —"

(Thus spake the soothsayer; but when Zarathustra's animals heard these words, they ran away in terror. For they saw that whatever they had brought home during the day would not be enough to fill up this one soothsayer.) "With dying of thirst thrown in," the soothsayer went on to say. "And although here I hear water splashing like words of wisdom, that is, copiously and tirelessly: I — want wine!

Not everyone is a born water drinker like Zarathustra. Nor does water do for the weary and the withered: wine is our due, — that alone provides sudden recovery and spur-of-the-moment health!"

On this occasion when the soothsayer longed for wine, it chanced that the king on the left, the quiet one, even got a word in for once. "As for wine," he said, "we have seen to it, I, together with my brother, the king on the right, that we have wine enough, — a whole ass-load. So nothing is lacking but bread."

"Bread?" replied Zarathustra and laughed. "But bread is just what hermits do not have. Man, however, does not live by bread alone, but also by the flesh of good lambs, of which I have two: they shall quickly be slaughtered and dressed fragrantly with sage: I love them that way. And there is no lack of roots and fruits either, good enough even for lip-lickers and lip-smackers; in addition, nuts and other riddles for cracking.

Thus we shall have a good meal shortly. But he who wants to eat with us must also be willing to lend a hand, even the kings. For with Zarathustra even a king may be cook."

This proposal appealed to the hearts of all; except that the voluntary beggar objected to the flesh and wine and spices.

"Now just listen to this glutton Zarathustra," he said jokingly: "does one go into caves and high mountains in order to have such meals?

Now I truly understand what he once taught us: 'Praised be the small poverty!" and why he wants to do away with beggars."

"Be of good cheer," Zarathustra answered him, " as I am. Keep to your custom, you splendid one, grind your grain, drink your water, praise your fare: if only it makes you happy!

I am a law only for my kind, I am not a law for all. But he who belongs to me must be strong of bone as well as light of foot, merry for wars and feasts, no prophet of gloom, no John-a-dreams, ready for the hardest thing as if for his feast, hale and whole.

The best belongs to me and mine; and if it is not given us, then we take it: the best food, the purest sky, the strongest thoughts, the finest women!" —

Thus spake Zarathustra; the king on the right, however, replied: "Strange!

Have you ever heard such intelligent things out of the mouth of a wise man?

And verily, it is the strangest thing if a wise man, despite all that, is still intelligent and not an ass."

Thus spake the king on the right and marvelled: the ass, however, said with bad intent "Ye-haw" to his speech. But this was the beginning of that long meal which in the history books is called "The Last Supper." At this same event, however, nothing was spoken of other than the higher man.

The Higher Man

1

When I first came to men, I committed the hermit's folly, the great folly: I stood in the marketplace.

And when I talked to all I talked to none. In the evening, however, tightrope walkers were my companions, and corpses; and I myself nearly a corpse.

But with the new morn a new truth came to me: there I learned to say:

"What do I care about marketplace and rabble and rabble-racket and long rabble ears!"

You higher men, learn this from me: in the marketplace no one believes in higher men. And if you want to speak there, well all right! But the rabble blinks:

"We are all equal."

"You higher men," — thus blinks the rabble — "there are no higher men, we are all equal, man is man, before God — we are all equal!"

Before God! — But now this God has died. And before the rabble we do not want to be equal. You higher men, go away from the marketplace!

2

Before God! — But now this God has died. You higher men, this God was your greatest danger.

Only since he has lain in the grave are you risen again. Only now comes the great noontide, only now the higher man becomes — master!

Have you understood this word, O my brothers? You are alarmed: do your hearts become giddy? Does the abyss now yawn before you? Does the hellhound now yelp at you?

Well then! Come on! You higher men! Only now the mountain of man's future is in labor. God has died: now we want, — the Superman to live.

3

The most concerned ask today: "How is man to be preserved?" But Zarathustra is the one and only one to ask: "How is man to be overcome?"

The Superman is dear to my heart, he is my one and only one, — and not man: not the nearest, not the poorest, not the most suffering, not the best. —

O my brothers, what I can love about man is this, that he is a crossing-over and a going-under. And in you too there is much that makes me love and hope.

That you showed contempt, you higher men, that made me hope. For the great despisers are the great venerators.

That you despaired, in that there is much to honor. For you did not learn how to submit, you did not learn petty acts of prudence.

For today the small people have become master: they all preach prudence and deference and diligence and diffidence and submission and the long-and-soon of petty virtues.

Whatever is womanish in nature, whatever stems from a slavish nature and especially the rabble-mishmash: that now wants to be the master of all human destiny — O horror! Horror! Horror!

That asks and asks and never grows weary of asking: "How is man to be best, longest, most agreeably preserved? With this — they are the masters of today.

Conquer these masters of today, O my brothers, — these small people: they are the Superman's greatest danger!

Conquer, you higher men, the petty virtues, the petty prudence, the grainof- sand deference, the ants' hodge-podge, the wretched comfort, the "happiness of the greatest number" — !

And rather despair than submit. And verily, I love you for not knowing how to live today, you higher men! So it is you live — best!

4

Have you courage, O my brothers? Are you stout-hearted? Not courage before witnesses, but hermit- and eagle-courage, which no God even watches anymore.

Cold souls, mules, the blind, the intoxicated I do not call stout-hearted. He has heart who knows fear but vanquishes fear; he who sees the abyss, but with pride.

He who sees the abyss, but with eagles' eyes, — he who seizes the abyss with eagles' claws: he has courage. — —

5

"Man is evil" — so said all the wisest ones to console me. Alas, if only it were still true today! For evil is man's best strength.

"Man must become better and badder" — thus I teach. The baddest is necessary for the Superman's best.

It may have been good for that preacher of the small people that he suffered and bore the sins of man. But I take pleasure in great sin as my great consolation.

Such a thing, however, is not said for asses' ears. Nor does every word belong in every mouth. These are fine, faraway things: sheeps' hooves should not paw at them!

6

You higher, men do you think I am here to make well what you have made ill?

Or that I wanted to bed you sufferers more comfortably from now on? Or to show new, easier footpaths to you who are unsteady, who have wandered astray, who have climbed astray?

No! No! Three times no! Ever more, ever better ones of your kind shall perish, — for you shall have it ever worse and harder. In this way alone in this way alone man grows tall, to where the lightning strikes and shivers him: high enough for the lightning!

My feeling and longing goes out to the few, the long, the faraway: what is your much, short, small misery to me!

You do not suffer enough yet for me, you have not yet suffered from man.

You would be lying if you said otherwise! None of you suffers what I have suffered.

7

It is not enough for me that the lightning cause no harm any longer. I do not want to divert it: for me it shall learn — to work. —

My wisdom has long since gathered itself like a cloud; it grows stiller and darker. So does any wisdom which shall one day bring forth lightning. —

To these men of today I will not be a light, not be called a light. Them — I will blind: lightning of my wisdom! poke out their eyes!

8

Will nothing beyond your ability: there is a wicked falsehood in those who will beyond their ability.

Especially when they will great things! For they arouse mistrust toward great things, these fine counterfeiters and play-actors: —

— until finally they are false toward themselves, squinty-eyed, whited worm-rot, covered over with strong words, with showpiece virtues, with glittering false works.

Take good care there, you higher men! For nothing is more precious to me and rarer today than honesty.

Is this not the day of the rabble? But the rabble does not know what is large, what is small, what is straight and honest: it is innocently crooked, it lies continually.

9

Have a healthy mistrust today, you higher men, you brave-hearted ones!

You open-hearted ones! And keep your reasons secret! For this is the day of the rabble.

What the rabble once learned to believe without reasons, who could overturn that — with reasons?

And in the marketplace one convinces with gestures. But reasons make the rabble mistrustful.

And if truth triumphed for once, then ask yourself with a healthy mistrust:

"What strong error fought for it?"

Beware of the scholars also! They hate you: for they are unfruitful! They have cold, dried-up eyes; before them every bird lies unplumed.

They plume themselves on the fact that they do not lie: but inability to lie is still a far cry from love of the truth. Beware!

Freedom from fever is still a far cry from insight. Chilled-out spirits I do not believe. He who cannot lie does not know what truth is.

10

If you want to get up high, then use your own legs! Do not let yourselves be carried up, do not set yourselves on foreign backs and heads!

But you are mounted on horseback? You are riding swiftly up to your goal?

All right, my friend! but your lame foot is also on horseback with you!

When you are at your goal, when you leap from your horse: on your very height, you higher man, — you will stumble!

11

You creators, you higher men! One is only pregnant for one's own child.

Let nothing take you in, take you for a ride! Who then is your neighbor? And even if you act "for your neighbor," you certainly do not create for him!

Forget this "for" for me, you creators: your very virtue demands that you have nothing to do with "for" and "to" and "because." You should stop up your ears against these false little words.

This "for your neighbor" is only the virtue of the small people: there it is called "birds of a feather" and "One hand washes the other.": — they have neither the right nor the strength for your self-interest!

In your self-interest, you creators, is the prudence and providence of the pregnant! What no one has yet seen with his eyes, the fruit: this your whole love preserves and protects and nourishes.

Where your whole love is, with your child, there your whole virtue is too!

Your work, your will is your neighbor: do not be taken in be any false values!

12

You creators, you higher men! He who has to give birth is sick; but he who has given birth is unclean. Ask women: they do not give birth for the fun of it.

Pain makes hens and poets cackle.

You creators, much in you is unclean. That is because you have had to be mothers.

A new child: O how much new filth has also come into the world! Go apart!

And he who has given birth should wash his soul clean!

13

Do not be virtuous beyond your powers! And demand nothing from yourselves that goes against probability!

Follow in the footsteps where your father's virtue has already gone! How will you climb high unless your father's will climbs with you?

But he who would be a firstling, see to it that he does not also become a lastling! and where your father's vices are, there you should not mean to imply a saint!

Those whose fathers associated with women and wine and wild swine:

how would it be if they demanded chastity of themselves? It would be folly!

Much, verily, it seems to me, if such a one should be the husband of one or two or three women.

And if he founded monasteries and wrote above the door: "The way to sainthood," I would yet say: Why! It is a new piece of folly.

He founded a refuge and reformatory for himself: much good may it do him!

But I do not believe in it.

Whatever a person brings into solitude grows, including the inner beast.

Thus solitude is inadvisable for many.

Has there ever been anything filthier on earth than the saints of the desert?

Around them not only the devil was loose, — but also the swine.

14

Shy, ashamed, awkward, like a tiger whose leap has failed: thus I often saw you slink aside, you higher men. A throw failed you.

But you dice-throwers, what does it matter? You have not learned to make and mock the game as one must make and mock it. Are we not always sitting at a great game-making and game-mocking table?

And if something great has failed you, are you yourself therefore — a failure?

And if you yourself have failed, is man therefore — a failure? But if man has failed: well then! come on!

15

The higher its kind, the more rarely a thing succeeds. You higher men here, are you not all — failures?

Cheer up, what does it matter! How much is still possible! Learn to laugh at yourselves as one must laugh!

Why even wonder at your failing and half-nailing, you half-broken ones! Is it not pressing and pushing in you — man's future?

Man's farthest, deepest, star-highest, his tremendous strength: is not all this frothing against each other in your pot?

Why wonder that many a pot breaks! Learn to laugh at yourselves as one must laugh! You higher men, O how much is still possible!

And verily, how much has already succeeded! How rich this earth is in small good perfect things, in what has turned out well!

Put small good perfect things around you, you higher men! Their golden ripeness heals the heart. What is perfect teaches hope.

16

What has hitherto been the greatest sin on earth? Was it not the word of him who said: "Woe unto those who laugh here!"

Did he himself find no reasons on earth to laugh? Then he only searched badly. Even a child can find reasons here.

He — did not love enough; otherwise he would have loved us, too, the ones who laugh! But he hated and hooted us; wailing and gnashing of teeth he promised us.

Must one curse right away when one does not love? That — strikes me as bad taste. But thus he did, this absolute one. He came from rabble.

And he himself simply did not love enough: Otherwise he would have been less angry that we did not love him. All great love does not want love: — it wants more.

Avoid all such absolute ones! They are a poor, sick breed, a rabble-breed: they look poorly upon this life, they give this earth the evil eye.

Avoid all such absolute ones! They have heavy feet and sultry hearts: they do not know how to dance. How could the earth possibly be light for such as these!

17

All good things approach their goal crookedly. Like cats they arch their backs, they purr inwardly at their approaching happiness, — all good things laugh.

The stride betrays whether a person already strides on his path: so watch me go! But he who approaches his goal dances.

And, verily, I have not turned into a statue, not yet do I stand here stiff, dull, stony, a pillar; I love running swiftly.

And though there is moor and thick misery on earth: he who has light feet runs away over even the mire and dances as if on cleanly-swept ice.

Lift up your hearts, my brothers, high! higher! And do not forget your legs either! Lift up your legs, too, you good dancers, and better yet: stand on your heads!

18

This crown of the one who laughs, this rose-garland crown: I myself have put on this crown, I myself have pronounced my laughter holy. None other have I found strong enough for it today.

Zarathustra the dancer, Zarathustra the light one, who winks with his wings, ready for flight, winking at all the birds, ready and ripe, a blissful-blithesome one: —

Zarathustra the soothsayer, Zarathustra the soothlaugher, no impatient one, no absolute one, one who loves leaps and side-leaps; I myself have put on this crown!

19

Lift up your hearts, my brothers, high! higher! And do not forget your legs either! Lift up your legs, too, you good dancers, and better yet: stand on your heads!

In happiness too there are heavy animals, there are clodhoppers from the beginning. Strangely they strain themselves, like an elephant straining to stand on its head.

But still it is better to be foolish with happiness than foolish with unhappiness, better to dance like a clod than walk like a cripple. So learn from my wisdom then: even the worst thing has two good reverse sides even the worst thing has good dancing legs: so learn from me yourselves, you higher men, and put yourselves on a proper footing!

So forget for me the sounds of sorrow and all rabble sadness! O how sad even the rabble's clowns seem to me today! But this is the day of the rabble!

20 Be like the wind when it rushes out of its mountain caves: it wants to dance to its own tune, the seas tremble and leap under its footsteps.

That which gives asses wings, which milks lionesses, praised be this good unruly spirit which comes like a stormwind to all present-day and all rabble, foe to all thistle-heads and fiddle-heads and all withered leaves and weeds: praised be this wild, good, free storm-spirit, which dances upon moors and miseries as if upon meadows!

Which hates the rabble-swindbags and all the failed, gloomy brood:

praised be this spirit of all free spirits, the laughing storm which blows dust in the eyes of all black-seeing, abscess-seeking ones!

You higher men, the worst thing about you is: you have all not learned to dance as one must learn to dance — above and beyond yourselves! What does it matter that you have failed!

How much is still possible! So learn to laugh above and beyond yourselves!

Lift up your hearts, you good dancers, high! higher! And do not forget the good laughter either!

This crown of the one who laughs, this rose-garland crown: to you, my brothers, I throw this crown! Laughter I pronounce holy; you higher men, learn — to laugh.

The Song Of Melancholy

1

When Zarathustra gave this speech, he stood near the entrance to his cave; with these last words, however, he slipped away from his guests and fled outside for a little while.

"O pure smells around me," he cried out, "O blissful stillness around me!

But where are my animals? Come here, come here, my eagle and my serpent!

Tell me then, my animals: these higher men all together — perhaps they do not smell so good? O pure smells around me! Only now do I know and feel how I love you, my animals."

— And Zarathustra said once more: "I love you, my animals." The eagle and the serpent, however, nuzzled up and looked up to him when he said these words. Thus they were in a silent threesome together and sniffed and sipped the good air with one another. For the air outside here was better than by the higher men.

2

Hardly had Zarathustra left his cave, however, when the old sorcerer arose, looked cunningly around and said: "He is out!

And already, you higher men — to tickle you with that name of praise and flattery, as he himself does — already my bad spirit of deceit and magic assails me, my melancholy devil, — who is an adversary through and through to this Zarathustra: forgive him! Now he wants to cast a spell before you, it is his hour right now; in vain I struggle with this evil spirit.

To all of you, whatever honors you may grant yourselves with words, whether you call yourselves 'the free spirits' or 'the truthful ones' or 'the penitents of the spirit' or 'the unfettered ones' or 'the ones of great longing' to all of you who suffer, as I do, from the great loathing, for whom the old God has died and no new God as yet is lying in cradle and swaddling clothes, —

to all of you my evil spirit and magic spell-devil is well-disposed.

I know you, you higher men, I know him; I also know this fiend whom I love against my will, this Zarathustra: he himself strikes me more often as like a beautiful saint's mask, — like a new, strange masquerade in which my evil spirit, the melancholy devil, takes pleasure: — I love Zarathustra, so it often strikes me, for the sake of my evil spirit. —

But already he assails me and compels me, this spirit of melancholy, this dusk-devil: and verily, you higher men, he desires —

— do but open your eyes! — he desires to come naked, whether male or female I do not know yet: but he comes, he compels me, woe! open your minds!

Day is dying, evening is now coming to all things, even the best things; hear now and see, you higher men, which devil, whether male or female, this spirit of evening-melancholy shall be!"

Thus spake the old sorcerer, looked cunningly around and then seized his harp.

3

In lightlorn air.

When the dew's comfort already Flows down to earth, Lost to view, unheard too —

Then tender footwear wears The comforter dew, like all the comfort-gentle —:

Do you remember then, do you remember, hot heart, How once you thirsted, For heavenly tears and dew drops, Scorched and weary you thirsted, While on yellow grasspaths Malicious evening sun glances Ran around you through black trees, Blinding, sun-glowing glances, gloating?

"The wooer of truth? You?" — so they sneered —

"No! Only a poet!

A beast, cunning, plundering, prowling, That must lie, That must wittingly, willingly lie:

Lusting after booty, Colorfully masked, Himself a mask, Himself booty —

This — the wooer of truth?

No! Only a fool! Only a poet!

Only speaking colorfully, Only screaming colorfully out of fools' masks, Climbing around on lying word-bridges, On colorful rainbows, Between false heaven And false earths, Roving around, hovering around, —

Only a fool! Only a poet!

This — the wooer of truth?

Not still, stiff, smooth, cold, Turned into a picture, A pillar of God, Not placed before temples, A God's doorkeeper:

No! hostile to such statues of truth, More at home in any wilderness than before temples, Full of cats' mischief, Springing through every window, Just like that, into every chance, Sniffing every primeval forest, Sickeningly-longingly sniffing, That you may run in primeval forests Among variegated beasts of prey Sinfully healthy and colorful and beautiful, With lustful lips, Blissfully scornful, blissfully hellish, blissfully bloodthirsty, Running around peeping, prowling, plundering: —

Or like the eagle that looks long, Long, fixedly, into abysses, Into his abysses: — —

O how his looks spiral downward, Down, in, Into ever deeper depths!

Then, Suddenly, straight sight, Straight flight, Swooping down upon lambs, With ill will towards all lamb souls, Rage-filled ill will towards all that look Sheepish, lamb-eyed, curly-wooled, Gray, with lamb's-sheep's-wellwishing!

Thus Eagle-like, panther-like Are the poets longings, Are your longings beneath a thousand masks, You fool! You poet!

You who have looked at man As God and as sheep —:

Tearing up the God in man As well as the sheep in man, And in tearing, laughing —

This, this is your bliss!

A panther's and eagle's bliss!

A poet's and fool's bliss!" — —

In lightlorn air, When already the crescent moon, Green among crimson reds, And creeping along enviously:

— enemy to the day, With every step secretly Reaping rose-hammocks with a sickle, Till they sink, Nightly down, faintly sinking down: —

Thus I myself sank once Out of my truth-frenzy, Out of my day longings, Weary of the day, sick of the light, — sank downward, eveningward, shadowward:

From one truth Burned and thirsty:

— do you remember yet, do you remember, hot heart, How you thirsted then? —

That I am banished From all truth, Only a fool!

Only a poet!

On Science

Thus sang the sorcerer; and all that were together there went like birds unawares into the net of his cunning and melancholy sensuality. Only the conscientious one in spirit was not caught: he quickly snatched the harp away from the sorcerer and cried: "Air! Let good air in! Let Zarathustra in! You make this cave sultry and poisonous, you wicked old sorcerer!

You seduce, you false one, you subtle one, to unknown wilds and desires.

And woe if such as you speak to and make much ado about the truth!

Woe unto all free spirits that do not beware of such sorcerers! It is all over with their freedom: you lecture and lure them back into prisons, you old melancholy devil, from your lament a bird call sounds, you are like those who with their praise of chastity secretly invite fleshly delights!"

Thus spake the conscientious one; the old sorcerer, however, looked around, enjoyed his victory, and in so doing swallowed the chagrin the conscientious one had caused him. "Be still!" he said in a modest voice, "good songs want to reverberate well; after good songs one should be silent long.

Thus do all these, the higher men. But perhaps you have understood little of my song? In you there is little of the magic spirit."

"You praise me," replied the conscientious one, "by separating me from you, so there! But you others, what do I see? You all still sit there with lustful eyes —:

You free souls, where has your freedom gone? You are almost, methinks, like those who have long watched wicked naked dancing girls: your very souls are dancing!

In you, you higher men, there must be more of what the sorcerer calls his evil spirit of deceit and magic: — we must surely be different.

And verily, we talked and thought enough before Zarathustra came home to his cave, as if I did not know: we are different.

We also seek different things up here, you and I. For I seek more security, therefore I came to Zarathustra. For he is still the sturdiest tower and will — today, when everything totters, when all the earth quakes. You, however, when I see the eyes you make, I almost think you seek more insecurity, — more terror, more danger, more earthquakes.

You lust for, thus I almost conceive it, forgive me my conceit, you higher men, you lust for the worst, most dangerous life, that which terrifies me the most, for the life of wild animals, for forests, caves, steep mountains, and blind abysses.

And not those leaders who lead you out of harm's way please you the most, but those who lead you away from all ways, the misleaders. But even if such lusts in you are real, they still seem impossible to me.

For fear — this is man's primary and primordial feeling; fear explains everything, original sin and original virtue. Out of fear grew even my virtue, which is called: science.

The fear namely before a wild animal — this fear has been bred the longest in man, including the animal he hides inside himself and fears: — Zarathustra calls it 'the inner beast.'

Such long ancient fear, at last grown refined, spiritualized, intellectualized — today, methinks, it goes by the name of: science."

Thus spake the conscientious one; but Zarathustra, who had just returned to his cave and had heard and surmised this last speech, threw a handful of roses at the conscientious one and laughed at his "truths." "What!" he cried, "What did I hear just now? Verily, methinks you are a fool or I myself am one: and your 'truth' I turn lickety-split on its head.

For fear — is the exception with us. Courage, however, and joy and adventure in the uncertain, in the unventured — courage seems to me man's whole prehistory.

The wildest, bravest animals he envied and robbed of all their virtues: only thus did he become — man.

This courage, at last grown refined, spiritualized, intellectualized, this human courage with eagle's wings and serpent's wisdom: today, methinks, it goes by the name of — " "Zarathustra!" all those who sat together cried as one and had a big laugh besides; it arose from them, however, like a heavy cloud. Even the sorcerer laughed and said with wisdom: "Well then! He is gone, my evil spirit!"

"And did I not warn you of him myself when I said he was a cheat, a spirit of falsehood and deceit?

Especially, of course, when he shows himself naked. But what can I do about his mischievous ways! Did I create him and the world?

Well then! Let us make up again and be of good cheer! And although Zarathustra is giving me a dirty look — just look at him! he is angry with me —:

— before the night comes he will learn to love and laud me again, he cannot go long without committing such follies.

He — loves his enemies: of all those I have seen he understands this art the best. But in return he takes revenge — upon his friends!"

Thus spake the old sorcerer, and the higher men applauded him: so that Zarathustra went around and with malice and love shook his friends' hands, —

like one, as it were, who has to make amends and apologize for something to all.

But when he came close by the door to his cave, behold, he lusted once more for the good air outside and for his animals — and he wanted to slip out.

Among Daughters Of The Desert
1

"Do not go away!" said the wanderer then, the one who called himself Zarathustra's shadow, "stay with us, — or else the old gloomy affliction may assail us again.

Already that old sorcerer has treated us with his worst, and just look, there the good pious pope has tears in his eyes and has entirely re-embarked on the sea of melancholy.

These kings here may still put on a brave face before us, I daresay: for of all of us today they have learned that best! But if they had no witnesses, I bet the bad business would also begin again for them —

— the bad business of passing clouds, damp melancholy, overcast skies, stolen suns, howling autumn winds, — the bad business of our howling and distress-crying: stay with us, O Zarathustra! Here there is much hidden misery that wants to speak, much evening, much cloud, much damp air!

You have nourished us with strong manly fare and pithy sayings: do not let the weak womanly spirits assail us again at dessert!

You alone make the air around you strong and clear. Have I ever found on earth such air as with you in your cave?

Many lands have I seen indeed, my nose has learned to examine and appraise many kinds of air: but with you my nostrils taste their greatest delight!

Unless it be, — unless it be —, O forgive me an old recollection! Forgive me an old after-dinner song which I once composed among daughters of the desert: for with them there was the same good, clear, Oriental air; there I was furthest away from cloudy, clammy, melancholy Old Europe!

At that time I loved a certain kind of Oriental maiden and another blue kingdom of heaven, over which no clouds or thoughts hang.

You would not believe how nicely they sat there when they did not dance, profound but without thoughts, like little secrets, like beribboned riddles, like after-dinner nuts —

Many-hued and truly strange, but without clouds: riddles that let themselves be read: for the pleasure of such maidens I then made up an after-dinner psalm."

Thus spake the wanderer and shadow; and before anyone answered him he had already seized the harp of the old sorcerer, crossed his legs, and looked calmly and sagely around him: — with his nostrils, however, he inhaled the air slowly and questioningly, like one who in new lands tastes of new foreign air.

After that he began to sing with a kind of roaring.

2

The desert grows: woe to him who hides deserts!

— Ha! Solemn!

Solemn indeed!

A worthy beginning!

African solemn!

Worthy of a lion Or a moral howling monkey —

— but nothing for you, You dearest lady-loves, At whose feet I For the first time, A European under palm trees, Am allowed to sit. Selah.

Wonderful truly!

Here I sit now, Near the desert, and already So far again from the desert, Even in nothingness still ravaged, Swallowed down, namely, By this smallest of oases: it just opened, yawning, Its lovely mouth, The most fragrant of all little mouths:

Then I fell in, Down, through — in among you, You dearest lady-loves! Selah.

Hail, hail to that whale, If he allowed his guest To have it so well! — do you understand My learned allusion?

Hail to his belly If he had an oasis-belly As lovely as this:

Which I doubt however, — because I come from Europe, Which is more doubt-addicted than any Elderly married woman.

May God make it better!

Amen!

Here I sit now, In this smallest of oases, Like a date, Brown, thoroughly sweet, oozing gold, lusting For a maid's round mouth, But even more for maidenly Icy-cold, snow-white, cutting Incisors: for them, namely, The hearts of all hot dates thirst. Selah.

Similar, all-too-similar To so-called southern fruits I lie here, Sniffed around and played around, By little flying insects, Likewise by still smaller More foolish, more sinful Wishes and whims, —

Encompassed by you, —

You speechless, you ominous Girl-cats, Dudu and Suleika, — ensphinxed, to stuff into one word Many feelings:

(Forgive me God This sin of speech!) — here I sit, sniffing the best air, Edenic air, verily, Bright, light air, golden-striped, As good an air as ever Fell down from the moon —

Was it by chance, Or did it happen through exuberance, As the old poets relate?

But I the doubter doubt it, No doubt because I come From Europe, Which is more doubt-addicted than any Elderly married woman.

May God make it better!

Amen!

Drinking this finest air, With nostrils swollen like goblets Without future, without remembrances, Thus I sit here, you Dearest lady-loves, And look upon the palm tree, How like a dancing girl It bows and kowtows and sways its hips, — one joins along if one watches it long!

Like a dancing girl who, as it would seem to me, Has already stood too long, dangerously long, Always, always on one leg only?

— having forgotten thereon, as it would seem to me, The other leg?

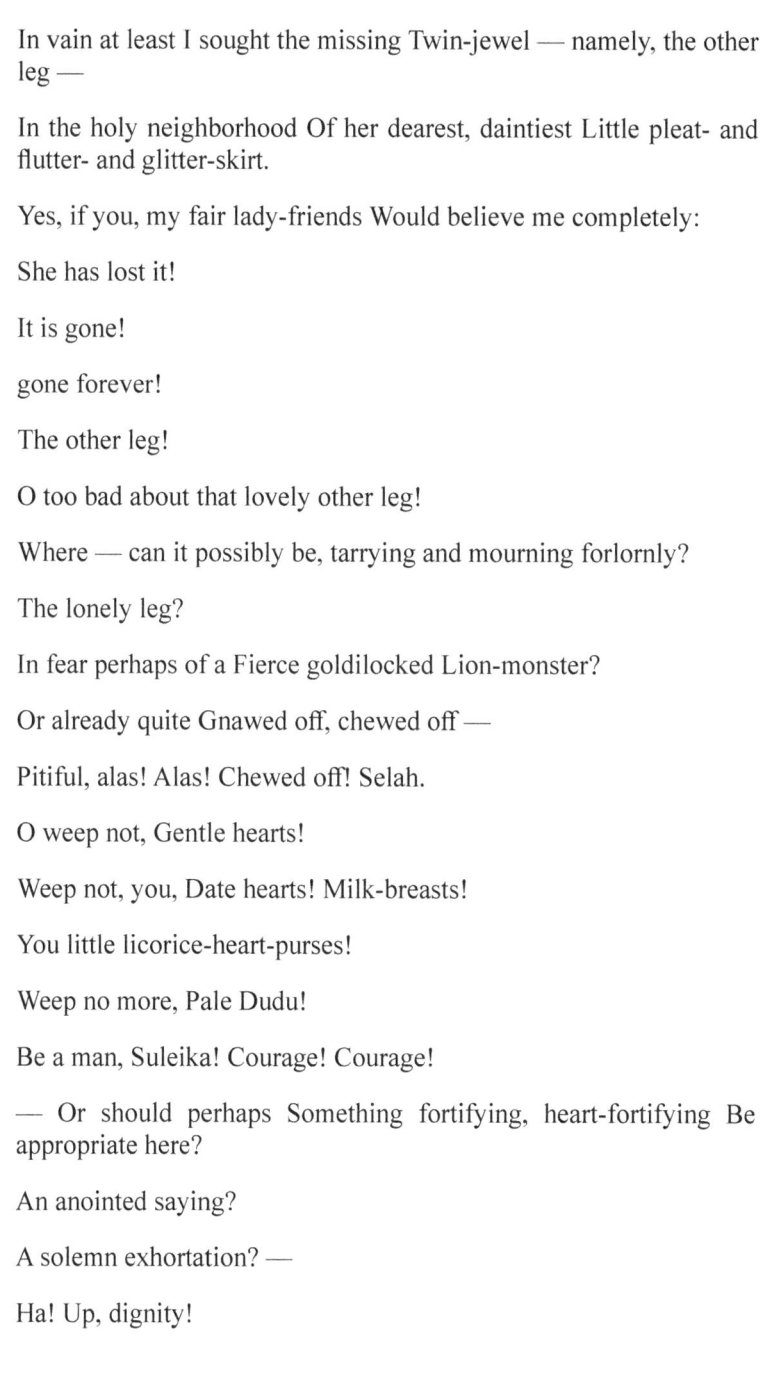

In vain at least I sought the missing Twin-jewel — namely, the other leg —

In the holy neighborhood Of her dearest, daintiest Little pleat- and flutter- and glitter-skirt.

Yes, if you, my fair lady-friends Would believe me completely:

She has lost it!

It is gone!

gone forever!

The other leg!

O too bad about that lovely other leg!

Where — can it possibly be, tarrying and mourning forlornly?

The lonely leg?

In fear perhaps of a Fierce goldilocked Lion-monster?

Or already quite Gnawed off, chewed off —

Pitiful, alas! Alas! Chewed off! Selah.

O weep not, Gentle hearts!

Weep not, you, Date hearts! Milk-breasts!

You little licorice-heart-purses!

Weep no more, Pale Dudu!

Be a man, Suleika! Courage! Courage!

— Or should perhaps Something fortifying, heart-fortifying Be appropriate here?

An anointed saying?

A solemn exhortation? —

Ha! Up, dignity!

Virtuous dignity! European dignity!

Blow, Blow anew, Bellows of virtue!

Ha!

Roar once more, Roar morally!

As a moral lion Roar before the daughters of the desert!

— For virtuous howling, You dearest maidens, Is more than anything else European ardor, European hot-hunger!

And here I stand now, As a European, I can do no other, God help me!

Amen!

The desert grows: woe to him who hides deserts!

The Awakening

1

After the song of the wanderer and shadow, the cave suddenly became full of clamor and laughter: and since all the assembled guests were talking at the same time, and even the ass, with such encouragement, no longer remained silent, a slight antipathy and scorn for his visitors came over Zarathustra: even though he rejoiced at their gladness. For it seemed to him a sign of convalescence.

So he slipped outside and spoke to his animals.

"Where is their distress now?" he said and breathed a sigh of relief himself from his slight disgust, — "with me it seems they have unlearned their distresscrying!

— though unfortunately not yet their crying." And Zarathustra covered his ears, for just then the asses' Ye-haw mingled strangely with the joyful noise of these higher men.

"They are merry," he began again, "and who knows? perhaps at their host's expense; and if they learned to laugh from me, then it is certainly not my laughter that they learned.

But what does it matter! They are old people: they convalesce in their way, they laugh in their way; my ears have surely endured worse and not become surly.

This day is a victory: he yields already, he flees, the spirit of gravity, my old archenemy! How well this day will end, which began so badly and roughly!

And it will end. Already evening is coming: from across the sea he rides here, the good rider! How he sways in his purple saddle, the blessed, homecoming one!

With that the sky looks clear, the world lies deep: O all you oddballs who came to me, it is well worth your while to abide with me!"

Thus spake Zarathustra. And again from the cave came the clamor and laughter of the higher men: then he began once again.

"They are biting, my bait is working, their enemy, the spirit of gravity, is also retreating. Already they are learning to laugh at themselves: do I hear right?

My manly fare is working, my vim- and vigor-aphorisms: and verily, I did not feed them with flatulent vegetables! But with warrior's food, conqueror's food: new appetites I have awakened.

New hopes are in their arms and legs, their hearts are expanding. They are finding new words, soon their spirits will breathe mischief.

Such fare may indeed not be for children, nor for wistful little old and young ladies either. One wins over their innards differently; I am not their physician and teacher.

Loathing is leaving these higher men: well then! — this is my victory. In my kingdom they become secure, all foolish shame runs away, they pour themselves out.

They pour out their hearts, good times return to them, they celebrate and ruminate again, — they become grateful.

This I take to be the best sign. Not long now and they will set up festivals and put up memorials to their old joys.

They are convalescents!" Thus spake Zarathustra joyfully to his heart and gazed out; his animals, however, pressed up against him and honored his happiness and his silence.

2

But suddenly Zarathustra's ear was startled: for the cave, which until then had been full of clamor and laughter, became deathly still all at once; his nose however, smelled a sweetly-smelling dense smoke and incense, as though from burning pine cones.

"What is happening? What are they doing?" he asked himself and stole up to the entrance so he could watch his guests unobserved. But wonder upon wonder!

What was he obliged to see with his own eyes there?

"They have all become pious again, they are praying, they are crazy!" he said, and marvelled beyond measure. And forsooth! all these higher men, the two kings, the retired pope, the wicked sorcerer, the voluntary beggar, the wanderer and shadow, the old soothsayer, the conscientious one in spirit, and the ugliest man: they were all on their knees like children and devout little old ladies and were worshipping the ass. And just then the ugliest man began to gurgle and snortle, as if something inexpressible wanted to come out of him; but when it actually came to be brought forth in words, behold, it was a pious, curious litany in praise of the adored and lightly censed ass. The litany, however, sounded like this:

Amen! And praise and honor and wisdom and glory and strength be to our God, forever and ever!

— The ass, however, cried Ye-haw to that.

He bears our burden, he has assumed the form of a servant, he is patient of heart and never says nay; and he who loves his God chastises him.

— The ass, however, cried Ye-haw to that.

He does not speak: except ever to say yea to the world which he created: thus he praises his world. His slyness it is, not to speak: thus he is seldom found to be wrong.

— The ass, however, cried Ye-haw to that.

Unshowingly he goes through the world: gray is the body color in which he wraps his virtue. If he has spirit, then he hides it; but everyone believes in his long ears.

— The ass, however, cried Ye-haw to that.

What hidden wisdom is this, to have long ears and say only yea and never nay! Has he not created the world in his own image, namely, as stupid as possible?

— The ass, however, cried Ye-haw to that.

You go straight and crooked ways; you care little about what seems straight or crooked to us men. Beyond good and evil is your kingdom. It is your innocence not to know what innocence is.

— The ass, however, cried Ye-haw to that.

Just look how you turn no one away from you, neither beggars nor kings.

You suffer the little children to come unto you, and when the bad boys entice you, you simply say Ye-haw.

— The ass, however, cried Ye-haw to that.

You love she-asses and fresh figs, you eat anything and everything. A thistle tickles your heart when you feel hungry. Therein lies a God's wisdom.

— The ass, however, cried Ye-haw to that.

The Ass Feast

1

At this point in the litany, however, Zarathustra could no longer control himself; he cried out Ye-haw himself and sprang into the midst of his maddened guests. "But what are you doing here, you dear fellows?" he exclaimed, as he pulled those in prayer up from the ground. "Woe, if someone other than Zarathustra had looked upon you:

Everyone would judge you to be with your new belief either the worst of blasphemers or the silliest of all little old ladies!

And even you, you old pope, how is it in keeping with you yourself to worship an ass as God in this manner here?" —

"O Zarathustra," answered the pope, "forgive me, but in divine matters I am even more enlightened than you. And so it stands to reason.

Better to worship God thus, in this form, than in no form at all! Ponder this saying, my noble friend: you will quickly find that there is wisdom in such a saying.

He who said 'God is a spirit' — he took the greatest step and leap to unbelief yet on earth: such a word is not easily amended again on earth!

My old heart skips and leaps that there is still something on earth to worship.

O Zarathustra, forgive an old pious pope's heart! —"

— "And you," said Zarathustra to the wanderer and shadow, "you call and think yourself a free spirit? And you practice such idolatry and hierolatry here?

Upon my word, you do even worse here than with your bad brown maidens, you bad new believer!"

"Bad enough," answered the wanderer and shadow, "you are right: but what can I do about it! The old God lives again, O Zarathustra, you may say what you will.

It is all the fault of the ugliest man: he has awakened him again. And if he should say that he once killed him: with gods death is always just a prejudice."

— "And you," said Zarathustra, "you wicked old sorcerer, what were you up to? Who in this liberated age could go on believing in you when you believe in such divine asininity?

It was stupidity, what you did; how could you, you clever one, do such a stupid thing?"

"O Zarathustra," answered the clever sorcerer, "you are right, it was a stupid thing, — it has also been hard enough on me."

— "And you too," said Zarathustra to the conscientious one in spirit, "just put your finger up to your nose and think it over! Is there nothing here then that goes against your conscience? Is your spirit not too clean for this praying and this devotees' haze?"

"There is something to this," replied the conscientious one and put his finger up to his nose, "there is something to this spectacle that does even my conscience good.

Perhaps I may not believe in God: certainly, however, it strikes me that God is still most worthy of belief in this form.

God is said to be eternal, according to the testimony of the most pious; he who has that much time takes his time. As slowly and as stupidly as possible:

thereby such a one can still go far in the world.

And he who has too much spirit might very well himself become infatuated with stupidity and folly. Ponder this yourself, O Zarathustra!

You yourself — verily! out of super-abundance and wisdom you too could very well turn into an ass.

Does not the consummate wise man gladly walk the crookedest paths?

Self-evidence teaches this, O Zarathustra, — your self-evidence!"

— "And you at last," said Zarathustra and turned toward the ugliest man, who still lay on the ground, raising up his arm to the ass (for he was giving him wine to drink). "Speak, you unspeakable one, what have you done?

You seem transformed to me, your eye is aglow, the mantle of the sublime covers your ugliness: what have you done?

Is it true what they say, that you awakened him again? And why? Was he not with good reason done in and done away with?

You yourself seem awakened to me: what did you do? Why did you revert?

Why did you become converted? Speak, you unspeakable one!

"O Zarathustra," answered the ugliest man, "you are a knave!

Whether he still lives or lives again or is thoroughly dead, — which of us two knows this best? I ask you.

But one thing I know, — from you yourself I learned it once, O Zarathustra:

he who wants to kill most thoroughly, laughs.

'Not by wrath, but by laughter does one kill' — thus you said once. O Zarathustra, you cryptopath, you annihilator without wrath, you dangerous saint, — you are a knave!"

2

Then it happened, however, that Zarathustra, amazed at such pure and simply knavish answers, sprang back to the door of his cave and, turning toward all his guests, cried out in a strong voice:

"O you jesters all of you, you buffoons! Why do you dissemble and disguise yourselves before me?

How the hearts of each of you squirmed with delight and spite that at last you had once again become like little children, namely, pious, —

— that at last you had done as children do, namely, prayed, folded your hands, and said 'Dear God'!"

But leave this nursery now, my own cave, where all childishness is at home today.

Cool your hot child's horseplay and heart's uproar out here!

To be sure: except ye become as little children, ye shall not enter into that kingdom of heaven. (And Zarathustra pointed upward with his hands.) But we have no desire whatsoever for the kingdom of heaven: we have become men, — so we want the kingdom of the earth."

3

And once again Zarathustra began to speak. "O my new friends," he said —"you oddballs, you higher men, how well you please me now, —

— since you have become joyful again! You have all truly blossomed: it seems to me that for such flowers as you new feasts are necessary, — a little brave nonsense, some divine service and ass-feast, some old joyful Zarathustra-fool, a bluster-blast of wind that blows your souls bright.

Forget not this night and this ass-feast, you higher men! You invented this by me, I take that to be a good sign — only convalescents invent such things!

And should you celebrate it again, this ass-feast, do it for the love of yourselves, and do it also for the love of me! And in remembrance of me!"

Thus spake Zarathustra.

The Drunken Song
1

Meanwhile, however, one after the other had stepped outside and into the cool, thoughtful night; Zarathustra himself, however, led the ugliest man by the hand, that he might show him his night world and the big round moon and the silvery waterfalls near his cave. There they stood at last silently next to each other, all of them old people, but with comforted brave hearts and amazed at themselves for having it so good on earth; the secrecy of the night, however, came nearer and nearer their hearts. And once again Zarathustra thought to himself:

"O how well they please me now, these higher men!" — but he did not say it aloud, for he honored their happiness and their silence. —

And then happened that which on this long astonishing day was most astonishing: the ugliest man began one more time and for the last time to gurgle and snortle, and when he brought it forth into words, behold, a question popped out of his mouth round and clean, a good deep, clear question which moved the hearts of all who listened to him.

"My friends, all of you," said the ugliest man, "what do you think? For the sake of this day — I am satisfied for the first time to have lived my entire life.

And that I testify to so much is still not enough for me. It is worth while to live on earth: one day, one feast day with Zarathustra has taught me to love the earth.

'Was that — life?' I will say to death. 'Well then! Once more!'

My friends, what do you think? Will you not, as I do, say to death: 'Was that — life? Well then, for Zarathustra's sake! Once more!'"

Thus spake the ugliest man; but it was not long before midnight. And what do you think happened then? As soon as the higher men heard his question, they suddenly became aware of their transformation and recuperation and who had given it to them: then they ran up to Zarathustra, thanking, revering, caressing, kissing his hands, each in his own curious manner: so that some laughed, some wept. The old soothsayer, however, danced with delight; and even if he was, as some story-tellers say, full of sweet wine at the time, he was certainly fuller still of sweet life and had renounced all weariness. There are even those who report that the ass danced at that time; not for nothing, namely, had the ugliest man given him wine to drink beforehand. Now that may have been so or else otherwise; and if in truth the ass did not dance that evening, then greater and stranger marvels than the dancing of an ass did take place at that time. In short, as Zarathustra's adage has it: "What does it matter!"

2

But Zarathustra, when this took place with the ugliest man, stood there as if drunk: his glance grew dim, his tongue stammered, his feet staggered. And who could even guess what thoughts passed through Zarathustra's soul then?

Evidently, however, his spirit withdrew and flew on ahead and was in faraway places and, as it were, "on a high mountain ridge," as is written, "between two seas, — between past and future, wandering as a heavy cloud." Gradually, however, while the higher men held him in their arms, he returned to himself somewhat and restrained with his hands the press of reverent and concerned ones; nevertheless, he did not speak. Suddenly, however, he turned his head quickly, for he seemed to hear something: then he put his finger up to his mouth and said:

"Come!"

And immediately it became still and mysterious all around; slowly up from the deep, however, came the sound of a bell. Zarathustra hearkened to it, as did the higher men; but then he put his finger up to his mouth a second time and said again: "Come! Come! Midnight is approaching!" — and his voice had changed. But still he did not stir from the spot: then it became even more still and mysterious, and everything hearkened, even the ass and Zarathustra's honorary animals, the eagle and the serpent, as well as Zarathustra's cave and the big cool moon and the night itself. Zarathustra, however, put his hand up to his mouth for a third time and said:

"Come! Come! Come! Let us wander now! It is the hour! Let us wander into the night!"

3

You higher men, midnight is approaching: then I will whisper something in your ear, as that old bell whispers it in my ear, —

— as secretly, as horribly, as heartily as that midnight bell which has seen more than any man tells it to me:

— which has already counted your fathers' heart-smart-beats — alas! alas!

how it sighs! how in a dream it laughs! the old deep, deep midnight!

Hush! Hush! Here is many a thing heard that may not be heard by day; now, however, in the cool air, when all your hearts' uproar has also become still, —

— now it speaks, now it is heard, now it steals into nocturnal, overwakeful souls: alas! alas! how it sighs! how in a dream it laughs!

— do you not hear it, how secretly, horribly, heartily it speaks to you, the old deep, deep midnight?

O man, take heed!

4

Woe is me! Where has the time gone? Have I not sunk into deep wells? The world sleeps —

Alas! Alas! The dog howls, the moon shines. Rather would I die, die, than tell you what my midnight heart thinks.

Now I have already died. It is over. Spider, why do you spin around me? Do you want blood? Alas! Alas! The dew is falling, the hour is coming —

— the hour when I shiver and freeze, the hour which asks and asks and asks: "Who has the heart enough for it?

— who shall be lord of the earth? Who will say: 'thus shall you flow, you great and small streams!'"

— the hour draws near: O man, you higher man, take heed! this speech is for fine ears, for thine ears — what words repeat deep midnight's creed?

5

I am borne away, my soul dances. Day's work! Day's work! Who shall be lord of the earth?

The moon is cool, the wind is silent. Alas! Alas! Did you fly high enough yet?

You have been dancing: but a leg is by no means a wing.

You good dancers, now all joy is over: wine has turned to lees, every cup has become brittle, the graves stammer.

You did not fly high enough: now the graves stammer: "Free the dead! Why is night so long? Does not the moon make us drunk?"

You higher men, free the graves, wake up the corpses! Why does the worm still burrow? It draws near, the hour draws near, —

— the bell booms, the heart still rattles, the bore-worm, the heart-worm still burrows. Alas! Alas! The world is deep!

6

Sweet lyre! Sweet lyre! I love your tone, your drunken croaking tone! —

how long, from how far your tone comes to me, from afar, from the ponds of love!

You old bell, you sweet lyre! Every pain has rent your heart, father-pain, fathers' pain, forefathers' pain; your speech has become ripe, —

— ripe like golden autumn and afternoon, like my hermit-heart — now you speak: the world itself has become ripe, the grape turns brown, — now it wants to die, to die of happiness. You higher men, do you not smell it?

A smell is secretly welling up, — a scent and smell of eternity, a rosy-blessed, brown gold-wine-smell of old happiness, — of drunken midnight-death-happiness, which sings: the world is deep, and deeper than the day conceived!

7

Let me be! Let me be! I am too pure for thee. Touch me not! Has not my world just now become perfect?

My skin is too pure for your hands. Let me be, you dumb, doltish, dull day!

Is midnight not brighter?

The purest should be lords of the earth, the least known, the strongest, the midnight souls that are brighter and deeper than any day.

O day, you grope for me? You grope for my happiness? To you I am rich, solitary, a treasure mine, a chamber of gold?

O world, you want me? Do I seem worldly to you? Do I seem spiritual to you? Do I seem godly to you? But day and world, you are too clumsy —

— have cleverer hands, reach for deeper happiness, for deeper unhappiness, reach for some God, do not reach for me:

— my unhappiness, my happiness is deep, you strange day, but yet I am no God, no God's hell: deep is its woe.

8

God's woe is deeper, you strange world! Reach for God's woe, not for me!

What am I? A drunken sweet lyre, — a midnight-lyre, a bell-frog that no one understands but which must speak before the deaf, you higher men! For you do not understand me!

Gone! Gone! O youth! O noon! O afternoon! Now evening and night and midnight have come, — the dog howls, the wind:

— is the wind not a dog? It whines, it yelps, it howls, Alas! Alas! how it sighs! how it laughs, how it wheezes and gasps, the midnight!

How prosaically she speaks just now, this drunken poetess! she has overdrunk her drunkenness perhaps? she has become overawake? she ruminates?

— upon her woe she ruminates, in a dream, the old deep midnight, and even more, upon her joy. For joy, though woe is deep: joy is deeper still than calamity.

9

You vine! Why do you praise me? I have cut you after all! I am cruel, you bleed—: what means your praise of my drunken cruelty?

"Whatever has become perfect, everything ripe — wants to die!" so you say.

Blessed, blessed be the vine-dresser's knife! But everything unripe wants to live: woe!

Woe says: "Go! Away, you woe!" But everything that suffers wants to live, that it may become ripe and full of joy and longing, — longing for the further, the higher, the brighter. "I want heirs," thus says everything that suffers, "I want children, I do not want myself," —

But joy wants neither heirs nor children, — joy wants itself, wants eternity, wants recurrence, wants everything-like-itself eternally.

Woe says: "Break, bleed, heart! Walk, leg! Wing, fly! Get on! Get up! Pain!"

Well then! Come on! O my old heart: Woe bids it: "Go!"

10

You higher men, what think you? Am I a soothsayer? A dreamer? A drunkard?

A dream-interpreter? A midnight-bell?

A drop of dew? A fume and perfume of eternity? Do you not hear it? Do you not smell it? Just now my world has become perfect, midnight is also midday, —

Pain is also a joy, a curse is also a blessing, night is also a sun, — go away or you will learn: a wise man is also a fool.

Have you ever said yes to one joy? O, my friends, then you also said yes to all woe. All things are linked together, threaded together, head-over-heels together, —

— have you ever wanted once twice, have you ever said "You please me, happiness! Hush! Moment!" then you wanted it all back!

— all anew, all eternal, all linked together, threaded together, head-overheels together, O then you so loved the world, —

— you eternal ones, love it eternally and for all time: and to woe as well you say: Go, but come back! For all joy wants — eternity!

11

All joy wants the eternity of all things, wants honey, wants lees, wants drunken midnight, wants graves, wants graves' tear-cheer, wants gilded sunset sky —

— what does joy not want! it is thirstier, heartier, hungrier, more horrible, more stealthy than all woe, it wants itself, it bites into itself, the will of the ring strives within it, —

— it wants love, it wants hate, it is overrich, bestows, throws away, begs that someone take it, thanks the taker, it would dearly love to be hated, — so rich is joy that it thirsts for woe, for hell, for shame, for the lame, for the world, — for this world, O you know it for sure!

You higher men, for you it longs, joy, the unruly, happy one — for your woe, you failures! All eternal joy longs for the failures.

For all joy wants itself, therefore it also wants calamity! O happiness, O pain! O break, heart! You higher men, do learn this, joy wants eternity, — joy wants the eternity of all things, wants the deep, deep eternity!

12

Have you learned my song now? Have you guessed what it means? Well then! Come on! You higher men, then sing me now my roundelay!

Sing me yourselves now the song whose name is "Once more," whose sense is "Unto all eternity!" — sing, you higher men, Zarathustra's roundelay!

O man! Take heed!

What words repeat deep midnight's creed?

"I sleep, I sleep —, "From deep dream I woke and perceived: —

"The world is deep, "And deeper than the day conceived.

"Deep is her woe—, "Joy — deeper still than calamity:

"Woe bids it: Go!

"But all joy wants eternity —, "— Wants the deep, deep eternity!"

The Sign

The morning after this night, however, Zarathustra sprang up from his bed, girded his loins, and came out of his cave, glowing and strong, like a morning sun that comes out of dark mountains.

"You great star," he said, as he had said once before, "you deep eye of happiness, what would all your happiness be if you had not those for whom you shine?

And if they remained in their chambers while you were already awake and coming and dispensing and distributing: how angry your proud shame would be over that!

Well then! They still sleep, these higher men, while I am awake: these are not my proper companions! Not for them do I wait here in my mountains.

To my work I want to get, to my day: but they do not get what the signs of my morning are, my step — is no wake-up call for them.

They still sleep in my cave, their dream still drinks on my drunken songs.

But the ear that is all ears for me, — the obedient ear is lacking in their limbs."

— This Zarathustra had said to his heart as the sun arose: then he looked up inquiringly, for he heard the sharp cry of his eagle above him. "Well then!" he shouted on high, "thus is it pleasing and fitting to me. My animals are awake, for I am awake. My eagle is awake and like me honors the sun. With eagles' talons he grasps for the new light. You are my proper animals; I love you.

But I still lack my proper men!" —

Thus spake Zarathustra; but then it happened that he suddenly heard himself swarmed around and fluttered around, as if by a myriad of birds, — the whirring of so many wings, however, and the crowding around his head was so great that he closed his eyes. And verily, like a cloud it fell upon him, like a cloud of arrows showering itself upon a new foe. But behold, here it was a cloud of love, and upon a new friend.

"What is happening to me?" thought Zarathustra in his astonished heart and sat down slowly on the large stone which lay next to the exit to his cave.

But as he reached around him and above him and below him with his hands and warded off the tender birds, behold, then something even stranger happened to him: for hereby he reached unawares into a thick warm clump of hair; at the same time, however, a roar rang out before him, — a gentle, long lion's roar.

"The sign is at hand," said Zarathustra, and he had a change of heart. And in truth, when it grew clear before him, a yellow, powerful animal lay there at his feet and nestled its head on his knee and would not leave him for love, behaving like a dog that has found his master again. The doves, however, were no less zealous with their love than the lion; and whenever a dove flitted across the lion's nose, the lion shook his head and marveled and laughed about it.

To all this Zarathustra said but a word: "My children are near, my children" —, then he became quite mute. His heart, however, was loosed, and tears dropped down from his eyes and fell upon his hands. And he heeded nothing anymore and sat there motionless, without defending himself against the animals anymore either. Then the doves flew here and there and perched on his shoulder and caressed his white hair and did not grow weary of tenderness and rejoicing. The strong lion, however, continually licked the tears which fell down upon Zarathustra's hands and roared and growled shyly. Thus these animals carried on.

All this lasted a long time, or a short time: for, properly speaking, there is no time on earth for such things —. Meanwhile, however, the higher men in Zarathustra's cave had awakened and arranged themselves in a train in order to go and meet Zarathustra and bid him good morning: for they had found when they awoke that already he no longer tarried among them. But when they reached the door of the cave and the sound of their footsteps had run on ahead of them, then the lion was mightily startled, turned suddenly away from Zarathustra and sprang toward the cave, roaring wildly: the higher men, however, when they heard him roar, all cried out, as if with one voice, fled back, and vanished in a trice.

Zarathustra himself, however, dazed and estranged, arose from his seat, stood there amazed, questioned his heart, deliberated and was alone. "What did I hear, though?" he said at last slowly. "What just happened to me?"

And then the recollection came to him and at one glance he grasped all that had taken place between yesterday and today. "Here is indeed the stone," he said and stroked his beard, "upon which I sat yesterday morning; and here the soothsayer came to me, and here I first heard the cry of distress.

O you higher men, yes, it was of your distress that this soothsayer soothsaid to me yesterday morning, to your distress he wanted to induce and seduce me: 'O Zarathustra,' he said to me, 'I come to seduce you to your last sin.'

"To my last sin?" cried Zarathustra and laughed angrily at his own words:

"but what has been reserved for me as my last sin?"

— And once again Zarathustra sank into himself and sat down on the large stone and pondered. Suddenly he sprang up, —

"Pity! Pity for the higher man!" he cried out, and his countenance turned to bronze. "Well then! That — has had its time!

My suffering and my pity — what does that matter!

Do I strive for happiness? I strive for my work!

Well then! The lion has come, my children are near, Zarathustra has become ripe, my hour is come: —

This is my morning, my day is begun: up now, up, you great noontide!" — —

Thus spake Zarathustra and left his cave, glowing and strong, like a morning sun that comes out of dark mountains.

Beyond Good and Evil: Prelude to a Philosophy of the Future

PREFACE

SUPPOSING that Truth is a woman—what then? Is there not ground for suspecting that all philosophers, in so far as they have been dogmatists, have failed to understand women—that the terrible seriousness and clumsy importunity with which they have usually paid their addresses to Truth, have been unskilled and unseemly methods for winning a woman? Certainly she has never allowed herself to be won; and at present every kind of dogma stands with sad and discouraged mien—IF, indeed, it stands at all! For there are scoffers who maintain that it has fallen, that all dogma lies on the ground—nay more, that it is at its last gasp. But to speak seriously, there are good grounds for hoping that all dogmatizing in philosophy, whatever solemn, whatever conclusive and decided airs it has assumed, may have been only a noble puerilism and tyronism; and probably the time is at hand when it will be once and again understood WHAT has actually sufficed for the basis of such imposing and absolute philosophical edifices as the dogmatists have hitherto reared: perhaps some popular superstition of immemorial time (such as the soul-superstition, which, in the form of subject- and ego-superstition, has not yet ceased doing mischief): perhaps some play upon words, a deception on the part of grammar, or an audacious generalization of very restricted, very personal, very human—all-too-human facts. The philosophy of the dogmatists, it is to be hoped, was only a promise for thousands of years afterwards, as was astrology in still earlier times, in the service of which probably more labour, gold, acuteness, and patience have been spent than on any actual science hitherto: we owe to it, and to its "super-terrestrial" pretensions in Asia and Egypt, the grand style of architecture. It seems that in order to inscribe themselves upon the heart of humanity with everlasting claims, all great things have first to wander about the earth as enormous and awe-inspiring caricatures: dogmatic philosophy has been a caricature of this kind—for instance, the Vedanta doctrine in Asia, and Platonism in Europe. Let us not be ungrateful to it, although it must certainly be confessed that the worst, the most tiresome, and the most dangerous of errors hitherto has been a dogmatist error—namely, Plato's invention of Pure Spirit and the Good in Itself. But now when it has been surmounted, when Europe, rid of this nightmare, can again draw breath freely and at least enjoy a healthier—sleep, we, WHOSE DUTY IS WAKEFULNESS ITSELF, are the heirs of all the strength which the struggle against this error has fostered. It amounted to the very inversion of truth, and the denial of the PERSPECTIVE—the fundamental condition—of life, to speak of Spirit and the Good as Plato spoke of them; indeed one might ask, as a physician: "How did such a malady attack that finest product of antiquity, Plato?

Had the wicked Socrates really corrupted him? Was Socrates after all a corrupter of youths, and deserved his hemlock?" But the struggle against Plato, or—to speak plainer, and for the "people"—the struggle against the ecclesiastical oppression of millenniums of Christianity (FOR CHRISTIANITY IS PLATONISM FOR THE "PEOPLE"), produced in Europe a magnificent tension of soul, such as had not existed anywhere previously; with such a tensely strained bow one can now aim at the furthest goals. As a matter of fact, the European feels this tension as a state of distress, and twice attempts have been made in grand style to unbend the bow: once by means of Jesuitism, and the second time by means of democratic enlightenment—which, with the aid of liberty of the press and newspaper-reading, might, in fact, bring it about that the spirit would not so easily find itself in "distress"! (The Germans invented gunpowder—all credit to them! but they again made things square—they invented printing.) But we, who are neither Jesuits, nor democrats, nor even sufficiently Germans, we GOOD EUROPEANS, and free, VERY free spirits—we have it still, all the distress of spirit and all the tension of its bow! And perhaps also the arrow, the duty, and, who knows? THE GOAL TO AIM AT....

Sils Maria Upper Engadine, JUNE, 1885.

CHAPTER I. PREJUDICES OF PHILOSOPHERS

1. The Will to Truth, which is to tempt us to many a hazardous enterprise, the famous Truthfulness of which all philosophers have hitherto spoken with respect, what questions has this Will to Truth not laid before us! What strange, perplexing, questionable questions! It is already a long story; yet it seems as if it were hardly commenced. Is it any wonder if we at last grow distrustful, lose patience, and turn impatiently away? That this Sphinx teaches us at last to ask questions ourselves? WHO is it really that puts questions to us here? WHAT really is this "Will to Truth" in us? In fact we made a long halt at the question as to the origin of this Will—until at last we came to an absolute standstill before a yet more fundamental question. We inquired about the VALUE of this Will. Granted that we want the truth: WHY NOT RATHER untruth? And uncertainty? Even ignorance? The problem of the value of truth presented itself before us—or was it we who presented ourselves before the problem? Which of us is the Oedipus here? Which the Sphinx? It would seem to be a rendezvous of questions and notes of interrogation. And could it be believed that it at last seems to us as if the problem had never been propounded before, as if we were the first to discern it, get a sight of it, and RISK RAISING it? For there is risk in raising it, perhaps there is no greater risk.

2. "HOW COULD anything originate out of its opposite? For example, truth out of error? or the Will to Truth out of the will to deception? or the generous deed out of selfishness? or the pure sun-bright vision of the wise man out of covetousness? Such genesis is impossible; whoever dreams of it is a fool, nay, worse than a fool; things of the highest value must have a different origin, an origin of THEIR own— in this transitory, seductive, illusory, paltry world, in this turmoil of delusion and cupidity, they cannot have their source. But rather in the lap of Being, in the intransitory, in the concealed God, in the 'Thing-in-itself—THERE must be their source, and nowhere else!"— This mode of reasoning discloses the typical prejudice by which metaphysicians of all times can be recognized, this mode of valuation is at the back of all their logical procedure; through this "belief" of

theirs, they exert themselves for their "knowledge," for something that is in the end solemnly christened "the Truth." The fundamental belief of metaphysicians is THE BELIEF IN ANTITHESES OF VALUES. It never occurred even to the wariest of them to doubt here on the very threshold (where doubt, however, was most necessary); though they had made a solemn vow, "DE OMNIBUS DUBITANDUM." For it may be doubted, firstly, whether antitheses exist at all; and secondly, whether the popular valuations and antitheses of value upon which metaphysicians have set their seal, are not perhaps merely superficial estimates, merely provisional perspectives, besides being probably made from some corner, perhaps from below—"frog perspectives," as it were, to borrow an expression current among painters. In spite of all the value which may belong to the true, the positive, and the unselfish, it might be possible that a higher and more fundamental value for life generally should be assigned to pretence, to the will to delusion, to selfishness, and cupidity. It might even be possible that WHAT constitutes the value of those good and respected things, consists precisely in their being insidiously related, knotted, and crocheted to these evil and apparently opposed things—perhaps even in being essentially identical with them. Perhaps! But who wishes to concern himself with such dangerous "Perhapses"! For that investigation one must await the advent of a new order of philosophers, such as will have other tastes and inclinations, the reverse of those hitherto prevalent—philosophers of the dangerous "Perhaps" in every sense of the term. And to speak in all seriousness, I see such new philosophers beginning to appear.

3. Having kept a sharp eye on philosophers, and having read between their lines long enough, I now say to myself that the greater part of conscious thinking must be counted among the instinctive functions, and it is so even in the case of philosophical thinking; one has here to learn anew, as one learned anew about heredity and "innateness." As little as the act of birth comes into consideration in the whole process and procedure of heredity, just as little is "being-conscious" OPPOSED to the instinctive in any decisive sense; the greater part of the conscious thinking of a philosopher is secretly influenced by his instincts, and forced into definite channels. And behind all logic and its seeming sovereignty of movement, there are valuations, or to speak more plainly, physiological demands, for the maintenance of a definite mode of life For example, that the certain is worth more than

the uncertain, that illusion is less valuable than "truth" such valuations, in spite of their regulative importance for US, might notwithstanding be only superficial valuations, special kinds of niaiserie, such as may be necessary for the maintenance of beings such as ourselves. Supposing, in effect, that man is not just the "measure of things."

4. The falseness of an opinion is not for us any objection to it: it is here, perhaps, that our new language sounds most strangely. The question is, how far an opinion is life-furthering, life-preserving, species-preserving, perhaps species-rearing, and we are fundamentally inclined to maintain that the falsest opinions (to which the synthetic judgments a priori belong), are the most indispensable to us, that without a recognition of logical fictions, without a comparison of reality with the purely IMAGINED world of the absolute and immutable, without a constant counterfeiting of the world by means of numbers, man could not live—that the renunciation of false opinions would be a renunciation of life, a negation of life. TO RECOGNISE UNTRUTH AS A CONDITION OF LIFE; that is certainly to impugn the traditional ideas of value in a dangerous manner, and a philosophy which ventures to do so, has thereby alone placed itself beyond good and evil.

5. That which causes philosophers to be regarded half-distrustfully and half-mockingly, is not the oft-repeated discovery how innocent they are—how often and easily they make mistakes and lose their way, in short, how childish and childlike they are,—but that there is not enough honest dealing with them, whereas they all raise a loud and virtuous outcry when the problem of truthfulness is even hinted at in the remotest manner. They all pose as though their real opinions had been discovered and attained through the self-evolving of a cold, pure, divinely indifferent dialectic (in contrast to all sorts of mystics, who, fairer and foolisher, talk of "inspiration"), whereas, in fact, a prejudiced proposition, idea, or "suggestion," which is generally their heart's desire abstracted and refined, is defended by them with arguments sought out after the event. They are all advocates who do not wish to be regarded as such, generally astute defenders, also, of their prejudices, which they dub "truths,"—and VERY far from having the conscience which bravely admits this to itself, very far from having the good taste of the courage which goes so far as to let this be

understood, perhaps to warn friend or foe, or in cheerful confidence and self-ridicule. The spectacle of the Tartuffery of old Kant, equally stiff and decent, with which he entices us into the dialectic by-ways that lead (more correctly mislead) to his "categorical imperative"—makes us fastidious ones smile, we who find no small amusement in spying out the subtle tricks of old moralists and ethical preachers. Or, still more so, the hocus-pocus in mathematical form, by means of which Spinoza has, as it were, clad his philosophy in mail and mask—in fact, the "love of HIS wisdom," to translate the term fairly and squarely—in order thereby to strike terror at once into the heart of the assailant who should dare to cast a glance on that invincible maiden, that Pallas Athene:—how much of personal timidity and vulnerability does this masquerade of a sickly recluse betray!

6. It has gradually become clear to me what every great philosophy up till now has consisted of—namely, the confession of its originator, and a species of involuntary and unconscious auto-biography; and moreover that the moral (or immoral) purpose in every philosophy has constituted the true vital germ out of which the entire plant has always grown. Indeed, to understand how the abstrusest metaphysical assertions of a philosopher have been arrived at, it is always well (and wise) to first ask oneself: "What morality do they (or does he) aim at?" Accordingly, I do not believe that an "impulse to knowledge" is the father of philosophy; but that another impulse, here as elsewhere, has only made use of knowledge (and mistaken knowledge!) as an instrument. But whoever considers the fundamental impulses of man with a view to determining how far they may have here acted as INSPIRING GENII (or as demons and cobolds), will find that they have all practiced philosophy at one time or another, and that each one of them would have been only too glad to look upon itself as the ultimate end of existence and the legitimate LORD over all the other impulses. For every impulse is imperious, and as SUCH, attempts to philosophize. To be sure, in the case of scholars, in the case of really scientific men, it may be otherwise—"better," if you will; there there may really be such a thing as an "impulse to knowledge," some kind of small, independent clock-work, which, when well wound up, works away industriously to that end, WITHOUT the rest of the scholarly impulses taking any material part therein. The actual "interests" of the scholar, therefore, are generally in quite another direction—in the family, perhaps, or in money-making, or in politics;

it is, in fact, almost indifferent at what point of research his little machine is placed, and whether the hopeful young worker becomes a good philologist, a mushroom specialist, or a chemist; he is not CHARACTERISED by becoming this or that. In the philosopher, on the contrary, there is absolutely nothing impersonal; and above all, his morality furnishes a decided and decisive testimony as to WHO HE IS,—that is to say, in what order the deepest impulses of his nature stand to each other.

7. How malicious philosophers can be! I know of nothing more stinging than the joke Epicurus took the liberty of making on Plato and the Platonists; he called them Dionysiokolakes. In its original sense, and on the face of it, the word signifies "Flatterers of Dionysius"—consequently, tyrants' accessories and lick-spittles; besides this, however, it is as much as to say, "They are all ACTORS, there is nothing genuine about them" (for Dionysiokolax was a popular name for an actor). And the latter is really the malignant reproach that Epicurus cast upon Plato: he was annoyed by the grandiose manner, the mise en scene style of which Plato and his scholars were masters—of which Epicurus was not a master! He, the old schoolteacher of Samos, who sat concealed in his little garden at Athens, and wrote three hundred books, perhaps out of rage and ambitious envy of Plato, who knows! Greece took a hundred years to find out who the garden-god Epicurus really was. Did she ever find out?

8. There is a point in every philosophy at which the "conviction" of the philosopher appears on the scene; or, to put it in the words of an ancient mystery:

Adventavit asinus, Pulcher et fortissimus.

9. You desire to LIVE "according to Nature"? Oh, you noble Stoics, what fraud of words! Imagine to yourselves a being like Nature, boundlessly extravagant, boundlessly indifferent, without purpose or consideration, without pity or justice, at once fruitful and barren and uncertain: imagine to yourselves INDIFFERENCE as a power—how COULD you live in accordance with such indifference? To live—is not that just endeavouring to be otherwise than this Nature? Is not

living valuing, preferring, being unjust, being limited, endeavouring to be different? And granted that your imperative, "living according to Nature," means actually the same as "living according to life"—how could you do DIFFERENTLY? Why should you make a principle out of what you yourselves are, and must be? In reality, however, it is quite otherwise with you: while you pretend to read with rapture the canon of your law in Nature, you want something quite the contrary, you extraordinary stage-players and self-deluders! In your pride you wish to dictate your morals and ideals to Nature, to Nature herself, and to incorporate them therein; you insist that it shall be Nature "according to the Stoa," and would like everything to be made after your own image, as a vast, eternal glorification and generalism of Stoicism! With all your love for truth, you have forced yourselves so long, so persistently, and with such hypnotic rigidity to see Nature FALSELY, that is to say, Stoically, that you are no longer able to see it otherwise—and to crown all, some unfathomable superciliousness gives you the Bedlamite hope that BECAUSE you are able to tyrannize over yourselves—Stoicism is self-tyranny—Nature will also allow herself to be tyrannized over: is not the Stoic a PART of Nature?... But this is an old and everlasting story: what happened in old times with the Stoics still happens today, as soon as ever a philosophy begins to believe in itself. It always creates the world in its own image; it cannot do otherwise; philosophy is this tyrannical impulse itself, the most spiritual Will to Power, the will to "creation of the world," the will to the causa prima.

10. The eagerness and subtlety, I should even say craftiness, with which the problem of "the real and the apparent world" is dealt with at present throughout Europe, furnishes food for thought and attention; and he who hears only a "Will to Truth" in the background, and nothing else, cannot certainly boast of the sharpest ears. In rare and isolated cases, it may really have happened that such a Will to Truth—a certain extravagant and adventurous pluck, a metaphysician's ambition of the forlorn hope—has participated therein: that which in the end always prefers a handful of "certainty" to a whole cartload of beautiful possibilities; there may even be puritanical fanatics of conscience, who prefer to put their last trust in a sure nothing, rather than in an uncertain something. But that is Nihilism, and the sign of a despairing, mortally wearied soul, notwithstanding the courageous bearing such a virtue may display. It seems, however, to be otherwise

with stronger and livelier thinkers who are still eager for life. In that they side AGAINST appearance, and speak superciliously of "perspective," in that they rank the credibility of their own bodies about as low as the credibility of the ocular evidence that "the earth stands still," and thus, apparently, allowing with complacency their securest possession to escape (for what does one at present believe in more firmly than in one's body?),—who knows if they are not really trying to win back something which was formerly an even securer possession, something of the old domain of the faith of former times, perhaps the "immortal soul," perhaps "the old God," in short, ideas by which they could live better, that is to say, more vigorously and more joyously, than by "modern ideas"? There is DISTRUST of these modern ideas in this mode of looking at things, a disbelief in all that has been constructed yesterday and today; there is perhaps some slight admixture of satiety and scorn, which can no longer endure the BRIC-A-BRAC of ideas of the most varied origin, such as so-called Positivism at present throws on the market; a disgust of the more refined taste at the village-fair motleyness and patchiness of all these reality-philosophasters, in whom there is nothing either new or true, except this motleyness. Therein it seems to me that we should agree with those skeptical anti-realists and knowledge-microscopists of the present day; their instinct, which repels them from MODERN reality, is unrefuted... what do their retrograde by-paths concern us! The main thing about them is NOT that they wish to go "back," but that they wish to get AWAY therefrom. A little MORE strength, swing, courage, and artistic power, and they would be OFF—and not back!

11. It seems to me that there is everywhere an attempt at present to divert attention from the actual influence which Kant exercised on German philosophy, and especially to ignore prudently the value which he set upon himself. Kant was first and foremost proud of his Table of Categories; with it in his hand he said: "This is the most difficult thing that could ever be undertaken on behalf of metaphysics." Let us only understand this "could be"! He was proud of having DISCOVERED a new faculty in man, the faculty of synthetic judgment a priori. Granting that he deceived himself in this matter; the development and rapid flourishing of German philosophy depended nevertheless on his pride, and on the eager rivalry of the younger generation to discover if possible something—at all events "new faculties"—of which to be still prouder!—But let us reflect for a moment—it is high

time to do so. "How are synthetic judgments a priori POSSIBLE?" Kant asks himself—and what is really his answer? "BY MEANS OF A MEANS (faculty)"—but unfortunately not in five words, but so circumstantially, imposingly, and with such display of German profundity and verbal flourishes, that one altogether loses sight of the comical niaiserie allemande involved in such an answer. People were beside themselves with delight over this new faculty, and the jubilation reached its climax when Kant further discovered a moral faculty in man—for at that time Germans were still moral, not yet dabbling in the "Politics of hard fact." Then came the honeymoon of German philosophy. All the young theologians of the Tubingen institution went immediately into the groves—all seeking for "faculties." And what did they not find—in that innocent, rich, and still youthful period of the German spirit, to which Romanticism, the malicious fairy, piped and sang, when one could not yet distinguish between "finding" and "inventing"! Above all a faculty for the "transcendental"; Schelling christened it, intellectual intuition, and thereby gratified the most earnest longings of the naturally pious-inclined Germans. One can do no greater wrong to the whole of this exuberant and eccentric movement (which was really youthfulness, notwithstanding that it disguised itself so boldly, in hoary and senile conceptions), than to take it seriously, or even treat it with moral indignation. Enough, however—the world grew older, and the dream vanished. A time came when people rubbed their foreheads, and they still rub them today. People had been dreaming, and first and foremost—old Kant. "By means of a means (faculty)"—he had said, or at least meant to say. But, is that—an answer? An explanation? Or is it not rather merely a repetition of the question? How does opium induce sleep? "By means of a means (faculty)," namely the virtus dormitiva, replies the doctor in Moliere,

Quia est in eo virtus dormitiva,

Cujus est natura sensus assoupire.

But such replies belong to the realm of comedy, and it is high time to replace the Kantian question, "How are synthetic judgments a PRIORI possible?" by another question, "Why is belief in such judgments necessary?"—in effect, it is high time that we should understand that such judgments must be believed to be true, for the sake of the preservation of creatures like ourselves; though they still might naturally be false judgments! Or, more plainly spoken, and roughly and readily—synthetic judgments a priori should not "be possible" at all; we have no right to them; in our mouths they are nothing but false judgments. Only, of course, the belief in their truth is necessary, as plausible belief and ocular evidence belonging to the perspective view of life. And finally, to call to mind the enormous influence which "German philosophy"—I hope you understand its right to inverted commas (goosefeet)?—has exercised throughout the whole of Europe, there is no doubt that a certain VIRTUS DORMITIVA had a share in it; thanks to German philosophy, it was a delight to the noble idlers, the virtuous, the mystics, the artiste, the three-fourths Christians, and the political obscurantists of all nations, to find an antidote to the still overwhelming sensualism which overflowed from the last century into this, in short—"sensus assoupire."...

12. As regards materialistic atomism, it is one of the best-refuted theories that have been advanced, and in Europe there is now perhaps no one in the learned world so unscholarly as to attach serious signification to it, except for convenient everyday use (as an abbreviation of the means of expression)—thanks chiefly to the Pole Boscovich: he and the Pole Copernicus have hitherto been the greatest and most successful opponents of ocular evidence. For while Copernicus has persuaded us to believe, contrary to all the senses, that the earth does NOT stand fast, Boscovich has taught us to abjure the belief in the last thing that "stood fast" of the earth—the belief in "substance," in "matter," in the earth-residuum, and particle-atom: it is the greatest triumph over the senses that has hitherto been gained on earth. One must, however, go still further, and also declare war, relentless war to the knife, against the "atomistic requirements" which still lead a dangerous after-life in places where no one suspects them, like the more celebrated "metaphysical requirements": one must also above all give the finishing stroke to that other and more portentous atomism which Christianity has taught best and longest, the SOUL-ATOMISM. Let it be permitted to designate by this expression the belief which regards the soul as something indestructible, eternal, indivisible, as a monad, as an atomon: this belief ought to be expelled from science! Between ourselves, it is not at all necessary to get rid of "the soul" thereby, and thus renounce one of the oldest and most venerated hypotheses—as happens frequently to the clumsiness of naturalists, who can hardly touch on the soul without immediately

losing it. But the way is open for new acceptations and refinements of the soul-hypothesis; and such conceptions as "mortal soul," and "soul of subjective multiplicity," and "soul as social structure of the instincts and passions," want henceforth to have legitimate rights in science. In that the NEW psychologist is about to put an end to the superstitions which have hitherto flourished with almost tropical luxuriance around the idea of the soul, he is really, as it were, thrusting himself into a new desert and a new distrust—it is possible that the older psychologists had a merrier and more comfortable time of it; eventually, however, he finds that precisely thereby he is also condemned to INVENT—and, who knows? perhaps to DISCOVER the new.

13. Psychologists should bethink themselves before putting down the instinct of self-preservation as the cardinal instinct of an organic being. A living thing seeks above all to DISCHARGE its strength—life itself is WILL TO POWER; self-preservation is only one of the indirect and most frequent RESULTS thereof. In short, here, as everywhere else, let us beware of SUPERFLUOUS teleological principles!—one of which is the instinct of self-preservation (we owe it to Spinoza's inconsistency). It is thus, in effect, that method ordains, which must be essentially economy of principles.

14. It is perhaps just dawning on five or six minds that natural philosophy is only a world-exposition and world-arrangement (according to us, if I may say so!) and NOT a world-explanation; but in so far as it is based on belief in the senses, it is regarded as more, and for a long time to come must be regarded as more—namely, as an explanation. It has eyes and fingers of its own, it has ocular evidence and palpableness of its own: this operates fascinatingly, persuasively, and CONVINCINGLY upon an age with fundamentally plebeian tastes—in fact, it follows instinctively the canon of truth of eternal popular sensualism. What is clear, what is "explained"? Only that which can be seen and felt—one must pursue every problem thus far. Obversely, however, the charm of the Platonic mode of thought, which was an ARISTOCRATIC mode, consisted precisely in RESISTANCE to obvious sense-evidence—perhaps among men who enjoyed even stronger and more fastidious senses than our contemporaries, but who knew how to find a higher triumph in

remaining masters of them: and this by means of pale, cold, grey conceptional networks which they threw over the motley whirl of the senses—the mob of the senses, as Plato said. In this overcoming of the world, and interpreting of the world in the manner of Plato, there was an ENJOYMENT different from that which the physicists of today offer us—and likewise the Darwinists and anti-teleologists among the physiological workers, with their principle of the "smallest possible effort," and the greatest possible blunder. "Where there is nothing more to see or to grasp, there is also nothing more for men to do"—that is certainly an imperative different from the Platonic one, but it may notwithstanding be the right imperative for a hardy, laborious race of machinists and bridge-builders of the future, who have nothing but ROUGH work to perform.

15. To study physiology with a clear conscience, one must insist on the fact that the sense-organs are not phenomena in the sense of the idealistic philosophy; as such they certainly could not be causes! Sensualism, therefore, at least as regulative hypothesis, if not as heuristic principle. What? And others say even that the external world is the work of our organs? But then our body, as a part of this external world, would be the work of our organs! But then our organs themselves would be the work of our organs! It seems to me that this is a complete REDUCTIO AD ABSURDUM, if the conception CAUSA SUI is something fundamentally absurd. Consequently, the external world is NOT the work of our organs—?

16. There are still harmless self-observers who believe that there are "immediate certainties"; for instance, "I think," or as the superstition of Schopenhauer puts it, "I will"; as though cognition here got hold of its object purely and simply as "the thing in itself," without any falsification taking place either on the part of the subject or the object. I would repeat it, however, a hundred times, that "immediate certainty," as well as "absolute knowledge" and the "thing in itself," involve a CONTRADICTIO IN ADJECTO; we really ought to free ourselves from the misleading significance of words! The people on their part may think that cognition is knowing all about things, but the philosopher must say to himself: "When I analyze the process that is expressed in the sentence, 'I think,' I find a whole series of daring assertions, the argumentative proof of which would be difficult,

perhaps impossible: for instance, that it is I who think, that there must necessarily be something that thinks, that thinking is an activity and operation on the part of a being who is thought of as a cause, that there is an 'ego,' and finally, that it is already determined what is to be designated by thinking—that I KNOW what thinking is. For if I had not already decided within myself what it is, by what standard could I determine whether that which is just happening is not perhaps 'willing' or 'feeling'? In short, the assertion 'I think,' assumes that I COMPARE my state at the present moment with other states of myself which I know, in order to determine what it is; on account of this retrospective connection with further 'knowledge,' it has, at any rate, no immediate certainty for me."—In place of the "immediate certainty" in which the people may believe in the special case, the philosopher thus finds a series of metaphysical questions presented to him, veritable conscience questions of the intellect, to wit: "Whence did I get the notion of 'thinking'? Why do I believe in cause and effect? What gives me the right to speak of an 'ego,' and even of an 'ego' as cause, and finally of an 'ego' as cause of thought?" He who ventures to answer these metaphysical questions at once by an appeal to a sort of INTUITIVE perception, like the person who says, "I think, and know that this, at least, is true, actual, and certain"—will encounter a smile and two notes of interrogation in a philosopher nowadays. "Sir," the philosopher will perhaps give him to understand, "it is improbable that you are not mistaken, but why should it be the truth?"

17. With regard to the superstitions of logicians, I shall never tire of emphasizing a small, terse fact, which is unwillingly recognized by these credulous minds—namely, that a thought comes when "it" wishes, and not when "I" wish; so that it is a PERVERSION of the facts of the case to say that the subject "I" is the condition of the predicate "think." ONE thinks; but that this "one" is precisely the famous old "ego," is, to put it mildly, only a supposition, an assertion, and assuredly not an "immediate certainty." After all, one has even gone too far with this "one thinks"—even the "one" contains an INTERPRETATION of the process, and does not belong to the process itself. One infers here according to the usual grammatical formula—"To think is an activity; every activity requires an agency that is active; consequently"... It was pretty much on the same lines that the older atomism sought, besides the operating "power," the material particle wherein it resides and out of which it operates—

the atom. More rigorous minds, however, learnt at last to get along without this "earth-residuum," and perhaps some day we shall accustom ourselves, even from the logician's point of view, to get along without the little "one" (to which the worthy old "ego" has refined itself).

18. It is certainly not the least charm of a theory that it is refutable; it is precisely thereby that it attracts the more subtle minds. It seems that the hundred-times-refuted theory of the "free will" owes its persistence to this charm alone; some one is always appearing who feels himself strong enough to refute it.

19. Philosophers are accustomed to speak of the will as though it were the best-known thing in the world; indeed, Schopenhauer has given us to understand that the will alone is really known to us, absolutely and completely known, without deduction or addition. But it again and again seems to me that in this case Schopenhauer also only did what philosophers are in the habit of doing—he seems to have adopted a POPULAR PREJUDICE and exaggerated it. Willing seems to me to be above all something COMPLICATED, something that is a unity only in name—and it is precisely in a name that popular prejudice lurks, which has got the mastery over the inadequate precautions of philosophers in all ages. So let us for once be more cautious, let us be "unphilosophical": let us say that in all willing there is firstly a plurality of sensations, namely, the sensation of the condition "AWAY FROM WHICH we go," the sensation of the condition "TOWARDS WHICH we go," the sensation of this "FROM" and "TOWARDS" itself, and then besides, an accompanying muscular sensation, which, even without our putting in motion "arms and legs," commences its action by force of habit, directly we "will" anything. Therefore, just as sensations (and indeed many kinds of sensations) are to be recognized as ingredients of the will, so, in the second place, thinking is also to be recognized; in every act of the will there is a ruling thought;—and let us not imagine it possible to sever this thought from the "willing," as if the will would then remain over! In the third place, the will is not only a complex of sensation and thinking, but it is above all an EMOTION, and in fact the emotion of the command. That which is termed "freedom of the will" is essentially the emotion of supremacy in respect to him who must obey: "I am free, 'he' must

obey"—this consciousness is inherent in every will; and equally so the straining of the attention, the straight look which fixes itself exclusively on one thing, the unconditional judgment that "this and nothing else is necessary now," the inward certainty that obedience will be rendered—and whatever else pertains to the position of the commander. A man who WILLS commands something within himself which renders obedience, or which he believes renders obedience. But now let us notice what is the strangest thing about the will,—this affair so extremely complex, for which the people have only one name. Inasmuch as in the given circumstances we are at the same time the commanding AND the obeying parties, and as the obeying party we know the sensations of constraint, impulsion, pressure, resistance, and motion, which usually commence immediately after the act of will; inasmuch as, on the other hand, we are accustomed to disregard this duality, and to deceive ourselves about it by means of the synthetic term "I": a whole series of erroneous conclusions, and consequently of false judgments about the will itself, has become attached to the act of willing—to such a degree that he who wills believes firmly that willing SUFFICES for action. Since in the majority of cases there has only been exercise of will when the effect of the command—consequently obedience, and therefore action—was to be EXPECTED, the APPEARANCE has translated itself into the sentiment, as if there were a NECESSITY OF EFFECT; in a word, he who wills believes with a fair amount of certainty that will and action are somehow one; he ascribes the success, the carrying out of the willing, to the will itself, and thereby enjoys an increase of the sensation of power which accompanies all success. "Freedom of Will"—that is the expression for the complex state of delight of the person exercising volition, who commands and at the same time identifies himself with the executor of the order—who, as such, enjoys also the triumph over obstacles, but thinks within himself that it was really his own will that overcame them. In this way the person exercising volition adds the feelings of delight of his successful executive instruments, the useful "underwills" or under-souls—indeed, our body is but a social structure composed of many souls—to his feelings of delight as commander. L'EFFET C'EST MOI. what happens here is what happens in every well-constructed and happy commonwealth, namely, that the governing class identifies itself with the successes of the commonwealth. In all willing it is absolutely a question of commanding and obeying, on the basis, as already said, of a social structure composed of many "souls", on which account a philosopher should claim the right to include willing-as-such within the sphere of morals—regarded as the doctrine of the relations of supremacy under which the phenomenon of "life" manifests itself.

20. That the separate philosophical ideas are not anything optional or autonomously evolving, but grow up in connection and relationship with each other, that, however suddenly and arbitrarily they seem to appear in the history of thought, they nevertheless belong just as much to a system as the collective members of the fauna of a Continent—is betrayed in the end by the circumstance: how unfailingly the most diverse philosophers always fill in again a definite fundamental scheme of POSSIBLE philosophies. Under an invisible spell, they always revolve once more in the same orbit, however independent of each other they may feel themselves with their critical or systematic wills, something within them leads them, something impels them in definite order the one after the other—to wit, the innate methodology and relationship of their ideas. Their thinking is, in fact, far less a discovery than a re-recognizing, a remembering, a return and a home-coming to a far-off, ancient common-household of the soul, out of which those ideas formerly grew: philosophizing is so far a kind of atavism of the highest order. The wonderful family resemblance of all Indian, Greek, and German philosophizing is easily enough explained. In fact, where there is affinity of language, owing to the common philosophy of grammar—I mean owing to the unconscious domination and guidance of similar grammatical functions—it cannot but be that everything is prepared at the outset for a similar development and succession of philosophical systems, just as the way seems barred against certain other possibilities of world-interpretation. It is highly probable that philosophers within the domain of the Ural-Altaic languages (where the conception of the subject is least developed) look otherwise "into the world," and will be found on paths of thought different from those of the Indo-Germans and Mussulmans, the spell of certain grammatical functions is ultimately also the spell of PHYSIOLOGICAL valuations and racial conditions.—So much by way of rejecting Locke's superficiality with regard to the origin of ideas.

21. The CAUSA SUI is the best self-contradiction that has yet been conceived, it is a sort of logical violation and unnaturalness; but the extravagant pride of man has managed to entangle itself profoundly

and frightfully with this very folly. The desire for "freedom of will" in the superlative, metaphysical sense, such as still holds sway, unfortunately, in the minds of the half-educated, the desire to bear the entire and ultimate responsibility for one's actions oneself, and to absolve God, the world, ancestors, chance, and society therefrom, involves nothing less than to be precisely this CAUSA SUI, and, with more than Munchausen daring, to pull oneself up into existence by the hair, out of the slough of nothingness. If any one should find out in this manner the crass stupidity of the celebrated conception of "free will" and put it out of his head altogether, I beg of him to carry his "enlightenment" a step further, and also put out of his head the contrary of this monstrous conception of "free will": I mean "non-free will," which is tantamount to a misuse of cause and effect. One should not wrongly MATERIALISE "cause" and "effect," as the natural philosophers do (and whoever like them naturalize in thinking at present), according to the prevailing mechanical doltishness which makes the cause press and push until it "effects" its end; one should use "cause" and "effect" only as pure CONCEPTIONS, that is to say, as conventional fictions for the purpose of designation and mutual understanding,—NOT for explanation. In "being-in-itself" there is nothing of "casual-connection," of "necessity," or of "psychological non-freedom"; there the effect does NOT follow the cause, there "law" does not obtain. It is WE alone who have devised cause, sequence, reciprocity, relativity, constraint, number, law, freedom, motive, and purpose; and when we interpret and intermix this symbol-world, as "being-in-itself," with things, we act once more as we have always acted—MYTHOLOGICALLY. The "non-free will" is mythology; in real life it is only a question of STRONG and WEAK wills.—It is almost always a symptom of what is lacking in himself, when a thinker, in every "causal-connection" and "psychological necessity," manifests something of compulsion, indigence, obsequiousness, oppression, and non-freedom; it is suspicious to have such feelings—the person betrays himself. And in general, if I have observed correctly, the "non-freedom of the will" is regarded as a problem from two entirely opposite standpoints, but always in a profoundly PERSONAL manner: some will not give up their "responsibility," their belief in THEMSELVES, the personal right to THEIR merits, at any price (the vain races belong to this class); others on the contrary, do not wish to be answerable for anything, or blamed for anything, and owing to an inward self-contempt, seek to GET OUT OF THE BUSINESS, no matter how. The latter, when they write books, are in the habit at present of taking the side of criminals; a sort of socialistic sympathy is their favourite disguise. And as a matter of fact, the fatalism of the weak-willed embellishes itself surprisingly when it can pose as "la religion de la souffrance humaine"; that is ITS "good taste."

22. Let me be pardoned, as an old philologist who cannot desist from the mischief of putting his finger on bad modes of interpretation, but "Nature's conformity to law," of which you physicists talk so proudly, as though—why, it exists only owing to your interpretation and bad "philology." It is no matter of fact, no "text," but rather just a naively humanitarian adjustment and perversion of meaning, with which you make abundant concessions to the democratic instincts of the modern soul! "Everywhere equality before the law—Nature is not different in that respect, nor better than we": a fine instance of secret motive, in which the vulgar antagonism to everything privileged and autocratic—likewise a second and more refined atheism—is once more disguised. "Ni dieu, ni maitre"—that, also, is what you want; and therefore "Cheers for natural law!"—is it not so? But, as has been said, that is interpretation, not text; and somebody might come along, who, with opposite intentions and modes of interpretation, could read out of the same "Nature," and with regard to the same phenomena, just the tyrannically inconsiderate and relentless enforcement of the claims of power—an interpreter who should so place the unexceptionalness and unconditionalness of all "Will to Power" before your eyes, that almost every word, and the word "tyranny" itself, would eventually seem unsuitable, or like a weakening and softening metaphor—as being too human; and who should, nevertheless, end by asserting the same about this world as you do, namely, that it has a "necessary" and "calculable" course, NOT, however, because laws obtain in it, but because they are absolutely LACKING, and every power effects its ultimate consequences every moment. Granted that this also is only interpretation—and you will be eager enough to make this objection?—well, so much the better.

23. All psychology hitherto has run aground on moral prejudices and timidities, it has not dared to launch out into the depths. In so far as it is allowable to recognize in that which has hitherto been written, evidence of that which has hitherto been kept silent, it seems as if nobody had yet harboured the notion of psychology as the Morphology

and DEVELOPMENT-DOCTRINE OF THE WILL TO POWER, as I conceive of it. The power of moral prejudices has penetrated deeply into the most intellectual world, the world apparently most indifferent and unprejudiced, and has obviously operated in an injurious, obstructive, blinding, and distorting manner. A proper physio-psychology has to contend with unconscious antagonism in the heart of the investigator, it has "the heart" against it even a doctrine of the reciprocal conditionalness of the "good" and the "bad" impulses, causes (as refined immorality) distress and aversion in a still strong and manly conscience—still more so, a doctrine of the derivation of all good impulses from bad ones. If, however, a person should regard even the emotions of hatred, envy, covetousness, and imperiousness as life-conditioning emotions, as factors which must be present, fundamentally and essentially, in the general economy of life (which must, therefore, be further developed if life is to be further developed), he will suffer from such a view of things as from sea-sickness. And yet this hypothesis is far from being the strangest and most painful in this immense and almost new domain of dangerous knowledge, and there are in fact a hundred good reasons why every one should keep away from it who CAN do so! On the other hand, if one has once drifted hither with one's bark, well! very good! now let us set our teeth firmly! let us open our eyes and keep our hand fast on the helm! We sail away right OVER morality, we crush out, we destroy perhaps the remains of our own morality by daring to make our voyage thither—but what do WE matter. Never yet did a PROFOUNDER world of insight reveal itself to daring travelers and adventurers, and the psychologist who thus "makes a sacrifice"— it is not the sacrifizio dell' intelletto, on the contrary!—will at least be entitled to demand in return that psychology shall once more be recognized as the queen of the sciences, for whose service and equipment the other sciences exist. For psychology is once more the path to the fundamental problems.

CHAPTER II. THE FREE SPIRIT

24. O sancta simplicitas! In what strange simplification and falsification man lives! One can never cease wondering when once one has got eyes for beholding this marvel! How we have made everything around us clear and free and easy and simple! how we have been able to give our senses a passport to everything superficial, our thoughts a godlike desire for wanton pranks and wrong inferences!—how from the beginning, we have contrived to retain our ignorance in order to enjoy an almost inconceivable freedom, thoughtlessness, imprudence, heartiness, and gaiety—in order to enjoy life! And only on this solidified, granite-like foundation of ignorance could knowledge rear itself hitherto, the will to knowledge on the foundation of a far more powerful will, the will to ignorance, to the uncertain, to the untrue! Not as its opposite, but—as its refinement! It is to be hoped, indeed, that LANGUAGE, here as elsewhere, will not get over its awkwardness, and that it will continue to talk of opposites where there are only degrees and many refinements of gradation; it is equally to be hoped that the incarnated Tartuffery of morals, which now belongs to our unconquerable "flesh and blood," will turn the words round in the mouths of us discerning ones. Here and there we understand it, and laugh at the way in which precisely the best knowledge seeks most to retain us in this SIMPLIFIED, thoroughly artificial, suitably imagined, and suitably falsified world: at the way in which, whether it will or not, it loves error, because, as living itself, it loves life!

25. After such a cheerful commencement, a serious word would fain be heard; it appeals to the most serious minds. Take care, ye philosophers and friends of knowledge, and beware of martyrdom! Of suffering "for the truth's sake"! even in your own defense! It spoils all the innocence and fine neutrality of your conscience; it makes you headstrong against objections and red rags; it stupefies, animalizes, and brutalizes, when in the struggle with danger, slander, suspicion, expulsion, and even worse consequences of enmity, ye have at last to play your last card as protectors of truth upon earth—as though "the Truth" were such an innocent and incompetent creature as to require protectors! and you of all people, ye knights of the sorrowful

countenance, Messrs Loafers and Cobweb-spinners of the spirit! Finally, ye know sufficiently well that it cannot be of any consequence if YE just carry your point; ye know that hitherto no philosopher has carried his point, and that there might be a more laudable truthfulness in every little interrogative mark which you place after your special words and favourite doctrines (and occasionally after yourselves) than in all the solemn pantomime and trumping games before accusers and law-courts! Rather go out of the way! Flee into concealment! And have your masks and your ruses, that ye may be mistaken for what you are, or somewhat feared! And pray, don't forget the garden, the garden with golden trellis-work! And have people around you who are as a garden—or as music on the waters at eventide, when already the day becomes a memory. Choose the GOOD solitude, the free, wanton, lightsome solitude, which also gives you the right still to remain good in any sense whatsoever! How poisonous, how crafty, how bad, does every long war make one, which cannot be waged openly by means of force! How PERSONAL does a long fear make one, a long watching of enemies, of possible enemies! These pariahs of society, these long-pursued, badly-persecuted ones—also the compulsory recluses, the Spinozas or Giordano Brunos—always become in the end, even under the most intellectual masquerade, and perhaps without being themselves aware of it, refined vengeance-seekers and poison-Brewers (just lay bare the foundation of Spinoza's ethics and theology!), not to speak of the stupidity of moral indignation, which is the unfailing sign in a philosopher that the sense of philosophical humour has left him. The martyrdom of the philosopher, his "sacrifice for the sake of truth," forces into the light whatever of the agitator and actor lurks in him; and if one has hitherto contemplated him only with artistic curiosity, with regard to many a philosopher it is easy to understand the dangerous desire to see him also in his deterioration (deteriorated into a "martyr," into a stage-and-tribune-bawler). Only, that it is necessary with such a desire to be clear WHAT spectacle one will see in any case—merely a satyric play, merely an epilogue farce, merely the continued proof that the long, real tragedy IS AT AN END, supposing that every philosophy has been a long tragedy in its origin.

26. Every select man strives instinctively for a citadel and a privacy, where he is FREE from the crowd, the many, the majority—where he may forget "men who are the rule," as their exception;—exclusive

only of the case in which he is pushed straight to such men by a still stronger instinct, as a discerner in the great and exceptional sense. Whoever, in intercourse with men, does not occasionally glisten in all the green and grey colours of distress, owing to disgust, satiety, sympathy, gloominess, and solitariness, is assuredly not a man of elevated tastes; supposing, however, that he does not voluntarily take all this burden and disgust upon himself, that he persistently avoids it, and remains, as I said, quietly and proudly hidden in his citadel, one thing is then certain: he was not made, he was not predestined for knowledge. For as such, he would one day have to say to himself: "The devil take my good taste! but 'the rule' is more interesting than the exception—than myself, the exception!" And he would go DOWN, and above all, he would go "inside." The long and serious study of the AVERAGE man—and consequently much disguise, self-overcoming, familiarity, and bad intercourse (all intercourse is bad intercourse except with one's equals):—that constitutes a necessary part of the life-history of every philosopher; perhaps the most disagreeable, odious, and disappointing part. If he is fortunate, however, as a favourite child of knowledge should be, he will meet with suitable auxiliaries who will shorten and lighten his task; I mean so-called cynics, those who simply recognize the animal, the commonplace and "the rule" in themselves, and at the same time have so much spirituality and ticklishness as to make them talk of themselves and their like BEFORE WITNESSES—sometimes they wallow, even in books, as on their own dung-hill. Cynicism is the only form in which base souls approach what is called honesty; and the higher man must open his ears to all the coarser or finer cynicism, and congratulate himself when the clown becomes shameless right before him, or the scientific satyr speaks out. There are even cases where enchantment mixes with the disgust—namely, where by a freak of nature, genius is bound to some such indiscreet billy-goat and ape, as in the case of the Abbe Galiani, the profoundest, acutest, and perhaps also filthiest man of his century—he was far profounder than Voltaire, and consequently also, a good deal more silent. It happens more frequently, as has been hinted, that a scientific head is placed on an ape's body, a fine exceptional understanding in a base soul, an occurrence by no means rare, especially among doctors and moral physiologists. And whenever anyone speaks without bitterness, or rather quite innocently, of man as a belly with two requirements, and a head with one; whenever any one sees, seeks, and WANTS to see only hunger, sexual instinct, and vanity as the real and only motives of human actions; in short, when any one speaks "badly"—and not even "ill"—of man, then ought the lover of knowledge to hearken attentively and diligently; he ought, in general, to have an open ear wherever there is talk without indignation. For the indignant man, and he who perpetually tears and lacerates himself with his own teeth (or, in place of himself, the world, God, or society), may indeed, morally speaking, stand higher than the laughing and self-satisfied satyr, but in every other sense he is the more ordinary, more indifferent, and less instructive case. And no one is such a LIAR as the indignant man.

27. It is difficult to be understood, especially when one thinks and lives gangasrotogati [Footnote: Like the river Ganges: presto.] among those only who think and live otherwise—namely, kurmagati [Footnote: Like the tortoise: lento.], or at best "froglike," mandeikagati [Footnote: Like the frog: staccato.] (I do everything to be "difficultly understood" myself!)—and one should be heartily grateful for the good will to some refinement of interpretation. As regards "the good friends," however, who are always too easy-going, and think that as friends they have a right to ease, one does well at the very first to grant them a play-ground and romping-place for misunderstanding—one can thus laugh still; or get rid of them altogether, these good friends—and laugh then also!

28. What is most difficult to render from one language into another is the TEMPO of its style, which has its basis in the character of the race, or to speak more physiologically, in the average TEMPO of the assimilation of its nutriment. There are honestly meant translations, which, as involuntary vulgarizations, are almost falsifications of the original, merely because its lively and merry TEMPO (which overleaps and obviates all dangers in word and expression) could not also be rendered. A German is almost incapacitated for PRESTO in his language; consequently also, as may be reasonably inferred, for many of the most delightful and daring NUANCES of free, free-spirited thought. And just as the buffoon and satyr are foreign to him in body and conscience, so Aristophanes and Petronius are untranslatable for him. Everything ponderous, viscous, and pompously clumsy, all long-winded and wearying species of style, are developed in profuse variety among Germans—pardon me for stating the fact that even Goethe's prose, in its mixture of stiffness

and elegance, is no exception, as a reflection of the "good old time" to which it belongs, and as an expression of German taste at a time when there was still a "German taste," which was a rococo-taste in moribus et artibus. Lessing is an exception, owing to his histrionic nature, which understood much, and was versed in many things; he who was not the translator of Bayle to no purpose, who took refuge willingly in the shadow of Diderot and Voltaire, and still more willingly among the Roman comedy-writers—Lessing loved also free-spiritism in the TEMPO, and flight out of Germany. But how could the German language, even in the prose of Lessing, imitate the TEMPO of Machiavelli, who in his "Principe" makes us breathe the dry, fine air of Florence, and cannot help presenting the most serious events in a boisterous allegrissimo, perhaps not without a malicious artistic sense of the contrast he ventures to present—long, heavy, difficult, dangerous thoughts, and a TEMPO of the gallop, and of the best, wantonest humour? Finally, who would venture on a German translation of Petronius, who, more than any great musician hitherto, was a master of PRESTO in invention, ideas, and words? What matter in the end about the swamps of the sick, evil world, or of the "ancient world," when like him, one has the feet of a wind, the rush, the breath, the emancipating scorn of a wind, which makes everything healthy, by making everything RUN! And with regard to Aristophanes—that transfiguring, complementary genius, for whose sake one PARDONS all Hellenism for having existed, provided one has understood in its full profundity ALL that there requires pardon and transfiguration; there is nothing that has caused me to meditate more on PLATO'S secrecy and sphinx-like nature, than the happily preserved petit fait that under the pillow of his death-bed there was found no "Bible," nor anything Egyptian, Pythagorean, or Platonic—but a book of Aristophanes. How could even Plato have endured life—a Greek life which he repudiated—without an Aristophanes!

29. It is the business of the very few to be independent; it is a privilege of the strong. And whoever attempts it, even with the best right, but without being OBLIGED to do so, proves that he is probably not only strong, but also daring beyond measure. He enters into a labyrinth, he multiplies a thousandfold the dangers which life in itself already brings with it; not the least of which is that no one can see how and where he loses his way, becomes isolated, and is torn piecemeal by some minotaur of conscience. Supposing such a one comes to grief,

it is so far from the comprehension of men that they neither feel it, nor sympathize with it. And he cannot any longer go back! He cannot even go back again to the sympathy of men!

30. Our deepest insights must—and should—appear as follies, and under certain circumstances as crimes, when they come unauthorizedly to the ears of those who are not disposed and predestined for them. The exoteric and the esoteric, as they were formerly distinguished by philosophers—among the Indians, as among the Greeks, Persians, and Mussulmans, in short, wherever people believed in gradations of rank and NOT in equality and equal rights—are not so much in contradistinction to one another in respect to the exoteric class, standing without, and viewing, estimating, measuring, and judging from the outside, and not from the inside; the more essential distinction is that the class in question views things from below upwards—while the esoteric class views things FROM ABOVE DOWNWARDS. There are heights of the soul from which tragedy itself no longer appears to operate tragically; and if all the woe in the world were taken together, who would dare to decide whether the sight of it would NECESSARILY seduce and constrain to sympathy, and thus to a doubling of the woe?... That which serves the higher class of men for nourishment or refreshment, must be almost poison to an entirely different and lower order of human beings. The virtues of the common man would perhaps mean vice and weakness in a philosopher; it might be possible for a highly developed man, supposing him to degenerate and go to ruin, to acquire qualities thereby alone, for the sake of which he would have to be honoured as a saint in the lower world into which he had sunk. There are books which have an inverse value for the soul and the health according as the inferior soul and the lower vitality, or the higher and more powerful, make use of them. In the former case they are dangerous, disturbing, unsettling books, in the latter case they are herald-calls which summon the bravest to THEIR bravery. Books for the general reader are always ill-smelling books, the odour of paltry people clings to them. Where the populace eat and drink, and even where they reverence, it is accustomed to stink. One should not go into churches if one wishes to breathe PURE air.

31. In our youthful years we still venerate and despise without the art

of NUANCE, which is the best gain of life, and we have rightly to do hard penance for having fallen upon men and things with Yea and Nay. Everything is so arranged that the worst of all tastes, THE TASTE FOR THE UNCONDITIONAL, is cruelly befooled and abused, until a man learns to introduce a little art into his sentiments, and prefers to try conclusions with the artificial, as do the real artists of life. The angry and reverent spirit peculiar to youth appears to allow itself no peace, until it has suitably falsified men and things, to be able to vent its passion upon them: youth in itself even, is something falsifying and deceptive. Later on, when the young soul, tortured by continual disillusions, finally turns suspiciously against itself—still ardent and savage even in its suspicion and remorse of conscience: how it upbraids itself, how impatiently it tears itself, how it revenges itself for its long self-blinding, as though it had been a voluntary blindness! In this transition one punishes oneself by distrust of one's sentiments; one tortures one's enthusiasm with doubt, one feels even the good conscience to be a danger, as if it were the self-concealment and lassitude of a more refined uprightness; and above all, one espouses upon principle the cause AGAINST "youth."—A decade later, and one comprehends that all this was also still—youth!

32. Throughout the longest period of human history—one calls it the prehistoric period—the value or non-value of an action was inferred from its CONSEQUENCES; the action in itself was not taken into consideration, any more than its origin; but pretty much as in China at present, where the distinction or disgrace of a child redounds to its parents, the retro-operating power of success or failure was what induced men to think well or ill of an action. Let us call this period the PRE-MORAL period of mankind; the imperative, "Know thyself!" was then still unknown.—In the last ten thousand years, on the other hand, on certain large portions of the earth, one has gradually got so far, that one no longer lets the consequences of an action, but its origin, decide with regard to its worth: a great achievement as a whole, an important refinement of vision and of criterion, the unconscious effect of the supremacy of aristocratic values and of the belief in "origin," the mark of a period which may be designated in the narrower sense as the MORAL one: the first attempt at self-knowledge is thereby made. Instead of the consequences, the origin—what an inversion of perspective! And assuredly an inversion effected only after long struggle and wavering! To be sure, an ominous new superstition, a

peculiar narrowness of interpretation, attained supremacy precisely thereby: the origin of an action was interpreted in the most definite sense possible, as origin out of an INTENTION; people were agreed in the belief that the value of an action lay in the value of its intention. The intention as the sole origin and antecedent history of an action: under the influence of this prejudice moral praise and blame have been bestowed, and men have judged and even philosophized almost up to the present day.—Is it not possible, however, that the necessity may now have arisen of again making up our minds with regard to the reversing and fundamental shifting of values, owing to a new self-consciousness and acuteness in man—is it not possible that we may be standing on the threshold of a period which to begin with, would be distinguished negatively as ULTRA-MORAL: nowadays when, at least among us immoralists, the suspicion arises that the decisive value of an action lies precisely in that which is NOT INTENTIONAL, and that all its intentionalness, all that is seen, sensible, or "sensed" in it, belongs to its surface or skin—which, like every skin, betrays something, but CONCEALS still more? In short, we believe that the intention is only a sign or symptom, which first requires an explanation—a sign, moreover, which has too many interpretations, and consequently hardly any meaning in itself alone: that morality, in the sense in which it has been understood hitherto, as intention-morality, has been a prejudice, perhaps a prematureness or preliminariness, probably something of the same rank as astrology and alchemy, but in any case something which must be surmounted. The surmounting of morality, in a certain sense even the self-mounting of morality—let that be the name for the long-secret labour which has been reserved for the most refined, the most upright, and also the most wicked consciences of today, as the living touchstones of the soul.

33. It cannot be helped: the sentiment of surrender, of sacrifice for one's neighbour, and all self-renunciation-morality, must be mercilessly called to account, and brought to judgment; just as the aesthetics of "disinterested contemplation," under which the emasculation of art nowadays seeks insidiously enough to create itself a good conscience. There is far too much witchery and sugar in the sentiments "for others" and "NOT for myself," for one not needing to be doubly distrustful here, and for one asking promptly: "Are they not perhaps—DECEPTIONS?"—That they PLEASE—him who has

them, and him who enjoys their fruit, and also the mere spectator—that is still no argument in their FAVOUR, but just calls for caution. Let us therefore be cautious!

34. At whatever standpoint of philosophy one may place oneself nowadays, seen from every position, the ERRONEOUSNESS of the world in which we think we live is the surest and most certain thing our eyes can light upon: we find proof after proof thereof, which would fain allure us into surmises concerning a deceptive principle in the "nature of things." He, however, who makes thinking itself, and consequently "the spirit," responsible for the falseness of the world—an honourable exit, which every conscious or unconscious advocatus dei avails himself of—he who regards this world, including space, time, form, and movement, as falsely DEDUCED, would have at least good reason in the end to become distrustful also of all thinking; has it not hitherto been playing upon us the worst of scurvy tricks? and what guarantee would it give that it would not continue to do what it has always been doing? In all seriousness, the innocence of thinkers has something touching and respect-inspiring in it, which even nowadays permits them to wait upon consciousness with the request that it will give them HONEST answers: for example, whether it be "real" or not, and why it keeps the outer world so resolutely at a distance, and other questions of the same description. The belief in "immediate certainties" is a MORAL NAIVETE which does honour to us philosophers; but—we have now to cease being "MERELY moral" men! Apart from morality, such belief is a folly which does little honour to us! If in middle-class life an ever-ready distrust is regarded as the sign of a "bad character," and consequently as an imprudence, here among us, beyond the middle-class world and its Yeas and Nays, what should prevent our being imprudent and saying: the philosopher has at length a RIGHT to "bad character," as the being who has hitherto been most befooled on earth—he is now under OBLIGATION to distrustfulness, to the wickedest squinting out of every abyss of suspicion.—Forgive me the joke of this gloomy grimace and turn of expression; for I myself have long ago learned to think and estimate differently with regard to deceiving and being deceived, and I keep at least a couple of pokes in the ribs ready for the blind rage with which philosophers struggle against being deceived. Why NOT? It is nothing more than a moral prejudice that truth is worth more than semblance; it is, in fact, the worst proved

supposition in the world. So much must be conceded: there could have been no life at all except upon the basis of perspective estimates and semblances; and if, with the virtuous enthusiasm and stupidity of many philosophers, one wished to do away altogether with the "seeming world"—well, granted that YOU could do that,—at least nothing of your "truth" would thereby remain! Indeed, what is it that forces us in general to the supposition that there is an essential opposition of "true" and "false"? Is it not enough to suppose degrees of seemingness, and as it were lighter and darker shades and tones of semblance—different valeurs, as the painters say? Why might not the world WHICH CONCERNS US—be a fiction? And to any one who suggested: "But to a fiction belongs an originator?"—might it not be bluntly replied: WHY? May not this "belong" also belong to the fiction? Is it not at length permitted to be a little ironical towards the subject, just as towards the predicate and object? Might not the philosopher elevate himself above faith in grammar? All respect to governesses, but is it not time that philosophy should renounce governess-faith?

35. O Voltaire! O humanity! O idiocy! There is something ticklish in "the truth," and in the SEARCH for the truth; and if man goes about it too humanely—"il ne cherche le vrai que pour faire le bien"—I wager he finds nothing!

36. Supposing that nothing else is "given" as real but our world of desires and passions, that we cannot sink or rise to any other "reality" but just that of our impulses—for thinking is only a relation of these impulses to one another:—are we not permitted to make the attempt and to ask the question whether this which is "given" does not SUFFICE, by means of our counterparts, for the understanding even of the so-called mechanical (or "material") world? I do not mean as an illusion, a "semblance," a "representation" (in the Berkeleyan and Schopenhauerian sense), but as possessing the same degree of reality as our emotions themselves—as a more primitive form of the world of emotions, in which everything still lies locked in a mighty unity, which afterwards branches off and develops itself in organic processes (naturally also, refines and debilitates)—as a kind of instinctive life in which all organic functions, including self-regulation, assimilation, nutrition, secretion, and change of matter, are still synthetically united

with one another—as a PRIMARY FORM of life?—In the end, it is not only permitted to make this attempt, it is commanded by the conscience of LOGICAL METHOD. Not to assume several kinds of causality, so long as the attempt to get along with a single one has not been pushed to its furthest extent (to absurdity, if I may be allowed to say so): that is a morality of method which one may not repudiate nowadays—it follows "from its definition," as mathematicians say. The question is ultimately whether we really recognize the will as OPERATING, whether we believe in the causality of the will; if we do so—and fundamentally our belief IN THIS is just our belief in causality itself—we MUST make the attempt to posit hypothetically the causality of the will as the only causality. "Will" can naturally only operate on "will"—and not on "matter" (not on "nerves," for instance): in short, the hypothesis must be hazarded, whether will does not operate on will wherever "effects" are recognized—and whether all mechanical action, inasmuch as a power operates therein, is not just the power of will, the effect of will. Granted, finally, that we succeeded in explaining our entire instinctive life as the development and ramification of one fundamental form of will—namely, the Will to Power, as my thesis puts it; granted that all organic functions could be traced back to this Will to Power, and that the solution of the problem of generation and nutrition—it is one problem—could also be found therein: one would thus have acquired the right to define ALL active force unequivocally as WILL TO POWER. The world seen from within, the world defined and designated according to its "intelligible character"—it would simply be "Will to Power," and nothing else.

37. "What? Does not that mean in popular language: God is disproved, but not the devil?"—On the contrary! On the contrary, my friends! And who the devil also compels you to speak popularly!

38. As happened finally in all the enlightenment of modern times with the French Revolution (that terrible farce, quite superfluous when judged close at hand, into which, however, the noble and visionary spectators of all Europe have interpreted from a distance their own indignation and enthusiasm so long and passionately, UNTIL THE TEXT HAS DISAPPEARED UNDER THE INTERPRETATION), so a noble posterity might once more misunderstand the whole of

the past, and perhaps only thereby make ITS aspect endurable.—Or rather, has not this already happened? Have not we ourselves been—that "noble posterity"? And, in so far as we now comprehend this, is it not—thereby already past?

39. Nobody will very readily regard a doctrine as true merely because it makes people happy or virtuous—excepting, perhaps, the amiable "Idealists," who are enthusiastic about the good, true, and beautiful, and let all kinds of motley, coarse, and good-natured desirabilities swim about promiscuously in their pond. Happiness and virtue are no arguments. It is willingly forgotten, however, even on the part of thoughtful minds, that to make unhappy and to make bad are just as little counter-arguments. A thing could be TRUE, although it were in the highest degree injurious and dangerous; indeed, the fundamental constitution of existence might be such that one succumbed by a full knowledge of it—so that the strength of a mind might be measured by the amount of "truth" it could endure—or to speak more plainly, by the extent to which it REQUIRED truth attenuated, veiled, sweetened, damped, and falsified. But there is no doubt that for the discovery of certain PORTIONS of truth the wicked and unfortunate are more favourably situated and have a greater likelihood of success; not to speak of the wicked who are happy—a species about whom moralists are silent. Perhaps severity and craft are more favourable conditions for the development of strong, independent spirits and philosophers than the gentle, refined, yielding good-nature, and habit of taking things easily, which are prized, and rightly prized in a learned man. Presupposing always, to begin with, that the term "philosopher" be not confined to the philosopher who writes books, or even introduces HIS philosophy into books!—Stendhal furnishes a last feature of the portrait of the free-spirited philosopher, which for the sake of German taste I will not omit to underline—for it is OPPOSED to German taste. "Pour etre bon philosophe," says this last great psychologist, "il faut etre sec, clair, sans illusion. Un banquier, qui a fait fortune, a une partie du caractere requis pour faire des decouvertes en philosophie, c'est-a-dire pour voir clair dans ce qui est."

40. Everything that is profound loves the mask: the profoundest things have a hatred even of figure and likeness. Should not the CONTRARY only be the right disguise for the shame of a God to

go about in? A question worth asking!—it would be strange if some mystic has not already ventured on the same kind of thing. There are proceedings of such a delicate nature that it is well to overwhelm them with coarseness and make them unrecognizable; there are actions of love and of an extravagant magnanimity after which nothing can be wiser than to take a stick and thrash the witness soundly: one thereby obscures his recollection. Many a one is able to obscure and abuse his own memory, in order at least to have vengeance on this sole party in the secret: shame is inventive. They are not the worst things of which one is most ashamed: there is not only deceit behind a mask—there is so much goodness in craft. I could imagine that a man with something costly and fragile to conceal, would roll through life clumsily and rotundly like an old, green, heavily-hooped wine-cask: the refinement of his shame requiring it to be so. A man who has depths in his shame meets his destiny and his delicate decisions upon paths which few ever reach, and with regard to the existence of which his nearest and most intimate friends may be ignorant; his mortal danger conceals itself from their eyes, and equally so his regained security. Such a hidden nature, which instinctively employs speech for silence and concealment, and is inexhaustible in evasion of communication, DESIRES and insists that a mask of himself shall occupy his place in the hearts and heads of his friends; and supposing he does not desire it, his eyes will some day be opened to the fact that there is nevertheless a mask of him there—and that it is well to be so. Every profound spirit needs a mask; nay, more, around every profound spirit there continually grows a mask, owing to the constantly false, that is to say, SUPERFICIAL interpretation of every word he utters, every step he takes, every sign of life he manifests.

41. One must subject oneself to one's own tests that one is destined for independence and command, and do so at the right time. One must not avoid one's tests, although they constitute perhaps the most dangerous game one can play, and are in the end tests made only before ourselves and before no other judge. Not to cleave to any person, be it even the dearest—every person is a prison and also a recess. Not to cleave to a fatherland, be it even the most suffering and necessitous—it is even less difficult to detach one's heart from a victorious fatherland. Not to cleave to a sympathy, be it even for higher men, into whose peculiar torture and helplessness chance has given us an insight. Not to cleave to a science, though it tempt one

with the most valuable discoveries, apparently specially reserved for us. Not to cleave to one's own liberation, to the voluptuous distance and remoteness of the bird, which always flies further aloft in order always to see more under it—the danger of the flier. Not to cleave to our own virtues, nor become as a whole a victim to any of our specialties, to our "hospitality" for instance, which is the danger of dangers for highly developed and wealthy souls, who deal prodigally, almost indifferently with themselves, and push the virtue of liberality so far that it becomes a vice. One must know how TO CONSERVE ONESELF—the best test of independence.

42. A new order of philosophers is appearing; I shall venture to baptize them by a name not without danger. As far as I understand them, as far as they allow themselves to be understood—for it is their nature to WISH to remain something of a puzzle—these philosophers of the future might rightly, perhaps also wrongly, claim to be designated as "tempters." This name itself is after all only an attempt, or, if it be preferred, a temptation.

43. Will they be new friends of "truth," these coming philosophers? Very probably, for all philosophers hitherto have loved their truths. But assuredly they will not be dogmatists. It must be contrary to their pride, and also contrary to their taste, that their truth should still be truth for every one—that which has hitherto been the secret wish and ultimate purpose of all dogmatic efforts. "My opinion is MY opinion: another person has not easily a right to it"—such a philosopher of the future will say, perhaps. One must renounce the bad taste of wishing to agree with many people. "Good" is no longer good when one's neighbour takes it into his mouth. And how could there be a "common good"! The expression contradicts itself; that which can be common is always of small value. In the end things must be as they are and have always been—the great things remain for the great, the abysses for the profound, the delicacies and thrills for the refined, and, to sum up shortly, everything rare for the rare.

44. Need I say expressly after all this that they will be free, VERY free spirits, these philosophers of the future—as certainly also they will

not be merely free spirits, but something more, higher, greater, and fundamentally different, which does not wish to be misunderstood and mistaken? But while I say this, I feel under OBLIGATION almost as much to them as to ourselves (we free spirits who are their heralds and forerunners), to sweep away from ourselves altogether a stupid old prejudice and misunderstanding, which, like a fog, has too long made the conception of "free spirit" obscure. In every country of Europe, and the same in America, there is at present something which makes an abuse of this name a very narrow, prepossessed, enchained class of spirits, who desire almost the opposite of what our intentions and instincts prompt—not to mention that in respect to the NEW philosophers who are appearing, they must still more be closed windows and bolted doors. Briefly and regrettably, they belong to the LEVELLERS, these wrongly named "free spirits"— as glib-tongued and scribe-fingered slaves of the democratic taste and its "modern ideas" all of them men without solitude, without personal solitude, blunt honest fellows to whom neither courage nor honourable conduct ought to be denied, only, they are not free, and are ludicrously superficial, especially in their innate partiality for seeing the cause of almost ALL human misery and failure in the old forms in which society has hitherto existed—a notion which happily inverts the truth entirely! What they would fain attain with all their strength, is the universal, green-meadow happiness of the herd, together with security, safety, comfort, and alleviation of life for every one, their two most frequently chanted songs and doctrines are called "Equality of Rights" and "Sympathy with All Sufferers"— and suffering itself is looked upon by them as something which must be DONE AWAY WITH. We opposite ones, however, who have opened our eye and conscience to the question how and where the plant "man" has hitherto grown most vigorously, believe that this has always taken place under the opposite conditions, that for this end the dangerousness of his situation had to be increased enormously, his inventive faculty and dissembling power (his "spirit") had to develop into subtlety and daring under long oppression and compulsion, and his Will to Life had to be increased to the unconditioned Will to Power—we believe that severity, violence, slavery, danger in the street and in the heart, secrecy, stoicism, tempter's art and devilry of every kind,—that everything wicked, terrible, tyrannical, predatory, and serpentine in man, serves as well for the elevation of the human species as its opposite—we do not even say enough when we only say THIS MUCH, and in any case we find ourselves here, both with our speech and our silence, at the OTHER extreme of all modern ideology and gregarious desirability, as their antipodes perhaps? What wonder that we "free spirits" are not exactly the most communicative spirits? that we do not wish to betray in every respect WHAT a spirit can free itself from, and WHERE perhaps it will then be driven? And as to the import of the dangerous formula, "Beyond Good and Evil," with which we at least avoid confusion, we ARE something else than "libres-penseurs," "liben pensatori" "free-thinkers," and whatever these honest advocates of "modern ideas" like to call themselves. Having been at home, or at least guests, in many realms of the spirit, having escaped again and again from the gloomy, agreeable nooks in which preferences and prejudices, youth, origin, the accident of men and books, or even the weariness of travel seemed to confine us, full of malice against the seductions of dependency which he concealed in honours, money, positions, or exaltation of the senses, grateful even for distress and the vicissitudes of illness, because they always free us from some rule, and its "prejudice," grateful to the God, devil, sheep, and worm in us, inquisitive to a fault, investigators to the point of cruelty, with unhesitating fingers for the intangible, with teeth and stomachs for the most indigestible, ready for any business that requires sagacity and acute senses, ready for every adventure, owing to an excess of "free will", with anterior and posterior souls, into the ultimate intentions of which it is difficult to pry, with foregrounds and backgrounds to the end of which no foot may run, hidden ones under the mantles of light, appropriators, although we resemble heirs and spendthrifts, arrangers and collectors from morning till night, misers of our wealth and our full-crammed drawers, economical in learning and forgetting, inventive in scheming, sometimes proud of tables of categories, sometimes pedants, sometimes night-owls of work even in full day, yea, if necessary, even scarecrows—and it is necessary nowadays, that is to say, inasmuch as we are the born, sworn, jealous friends of SOLITUDE, of our own profoundest midnight and midday solitude—such kind of men are we, we free spirits! And perhaps ye are also something of the same kind, ye coming ones? ye NEW philosophers?

CHAPTER III. THE RELIGIOUS MOOD

45. The human soul and its limits, the range of man's inner experiences hitherto attained, the heights, depths, and distances of these experiences, the entire history of the soul UP TO THE PRESENT TIME, and its still unexhausted possibilities: this is the preordained hunting-domain for a born psychologist and lover of a "big hunt". But how often must he say despairingly to himself: "A single individual! alas, only a single individual! and this great forest, this virgin forest!" So he would like to have some hundreds of hunting assistants, and fine trained hounds, that he could send into the history of the human soul, to drive HIS game together. In vain: again and again he experiences, profoundly and bitterly, how difficult it is to find assistants and dogs for all the things that directly excite his curiosity. The evil of sending scholars into new and dangerous hunting-domains, where courage, sagacity, and subtlety in every sense are required, is that they are no longer serviceable just when the "BIG hunt," and also the great danger commences,—it is precisely then that they lose their keen eye and nose. In order, for instance, to divine and determine what sort of history the problem of KNOWLEDGE AND CONSCIENCE has hitherto had in the souls of homines religiosi, a person would perhaps himself have to possess as profound, as bruised, as immense an experience as the intellectual conscience of Pascal; and then he would still require that wide-spread heaven of clear, wicked spirituality, which, from above, would be able to oversee, arrange, and effectively formulate this mass of dangerous and painful experiences.—But who could do me this service! And who would have time to wait for such servants!—they evidently appear too rarely, they are so improbable at all times! Eventually one must do everything ONESELF in order to know something; which means that one has MUCH to do!—But a curiosity like mine is once for all the most agreeable of vices— pardon me! I mean to say that the love of truth has its reward in heaven, and already upon earth.

46. Faith, such as early Christianity desired, and not infrequently achieved in the midst of a skeptical and southernly free-spirited world, which had centuries of struggle between philosophical schools behind it and in it, counting besides the education in tolerance which

the Imperium Romanum gave—this faith is NOT that sincere, austere slave-faith by which perhaps a Luther or a Cromwell, or some other northern barbarian of the spirit remained attached to his God and Christianity, it is much rather the faith of Pascal, which resembles in a terrible manner a continuous suicide of reason—a tough, long-lived, worm-like reason, which is not to be slain at once and with a single blow. The Christian faith from the beginning, is sacrifice the sacrifice of all freedom, all pride, all self-confidence of spirit, it is at the same time subjection, self-derision, and self-mutilation. There is cruelty and religious Phoenicianism in this faith, which is adapted to a tender, many-sided, and very fastidious conscience, it takes for granted that the subjection of the spirit is indescribably PAINFUL, that all the past and all the habits of such a spirit resist the absurdissimum, in the form of which "faith" comes to it. Modern men, with their obtuseness as regards all Christian nomenclature, have no longer the sense for the terribly superlative conception which was implied to an antique taste by the paradox of the formula, "God on the Cross". Hitherto there had never and nowhere been such boldness in inversion, nor anything at once so dreadful, questioning, and questionable as this formula: it promised a transvaluation of all ancient values—It was the Orient, the PROFOUND Orient, it was the Oriental slave who thus took revenge on Rome and its noble, light-minded toleration, on the Roman "Catholicism" of non-faith, and it was always not the faith, but the freedom from the faith, the half-stoical and smiling indifference to the seriousness of the faith, which made the slaves indignant at their masters and revolt against them. "Enlightenment" causes revolt, for the slave desires the unconditioned, he understands nothing but the tyrannous, even in morals, he loves as he hates, without NUANCE, to the very depths, to the point of pain, to the point of sickness—his many HIDDEN sufferings make him revolt against the noble taste which seems to DENY suffering. The skepticism with regard to suffering, fundamentally only an attitude of aristocratic morality, was not the least of the causes, also, of the last great slave-insurrection which began with the French Revolution.

47. Wherever the religious neurosis has appeared on the earth so far, we find it connected with three dangerous prescriptions as to regimen: solitude, fasting, and sexual abstinence—but without its being possible to determine with certainty which is cause and which is effect, or IF any relation at all of cause and effect exists there.

This latter doubt is justified by the fact that one of the most regular symptoms among savage as well as among civilized peoples is the most sudden and excessive sensuality, which then with equal suddenness transforms into penitential paroxysms, world-renunciation, and will-renunciation, both symptoms perhaps explainable as disguised epilepsy? But nowhere is it MORE obligatory to put aside explanations around no other type has there grown such a mass of absurdity and superstition, no other type seems to have been more interesting to men and even to philosophers—perhaps it is time to become just a little indifferent here, to learn caution, or, better still, to look AWAY, TO GO AWAY—Yet in the background of the most recent philosophy, that of Schopenhauer, we find almost as the problem in itself, this terrible note of interrogation of the religious crisis and awakening. How is the negation of will POSSIBLE? how is the saint possible?—that seems to have been the very question with which Schopenhauer made a start and became a philosopher. And thus it was a genuine Schopenhauerian consequence, that his most convinced adherent (perhaps also his last, as far as Germany is concerned), namely, Richard Wagner, should bring his own life-work to an end just here, and should finally put that terrible and eternal type upon the stage as Kundry, type vecu, and as it loved and lived, at the very time that the mad-doctors in almost all European countries had an opportunity to study the type close at hand, wherever the religious neurosis—or as I call it, "the religious mood"—made its latest epidemical outbreak and display as the "Salvation Army"—If it be a question, however, as to what has been so extremely interesting to men of all sorts in all ages, and even to philosophers, in the whole phenomenon of the saint, it is undoubtedly the appearance of the miraculous therein—namely, the immediate SUCCESSION OF OPPOSITES, of states of the soul regarded as morally antithetical: it was believed here to be self-evident that a "bad man" was all at once turned into a "saint," a good man. The hitherto existing psychology was wrecked at this point, is it not possible it may have happened principally because psychology had placed itself under the dominion of morals, because it BELIEVED in oppositions of moral values, and saw, read, and INTERPRETED these oppositions into the text and facts of the case? What? "Miracle" only an error of interpretation? A lack of philology?

48. It seems that the Latin races are far more deeply attached to their Catholicism than we Northerners are to Christianity generally, and

that consequently unbelief in Catholic countries means something quite different from what it does among Protestants—namely, a sort of revolt against the spirit of the race, while with us it is rather a return to the spirit (or non-spirit) of the race.

We Northerners undoubtedly derive our origin from barbarous races, even as regards our talents for religion—we have POOR talents for it. One may make an exception in the case of the Celts, who have theretofore furnished also the best soil for Christian infection in the North: the Christian ideal blossomed forth in France as much as ever the pale sun of the north would allow it. How strangely pious for our taste are still these later French skeptics, whenever there is any Celtic blood in their origin! How Catholic, how un-German does Auguste Comte's Sociology seem to us, with the Roman logic of its instincts! How Jesuitical, that amiable and shrewd cicerone of Port Royal, Sainte-Beuve, in spite of all his hostility to Jesuits! And even Ernest Renan: how inaccessible to us Northerners does the language of such a Renan appear, in whom every instant the merest touch of religious thrill throws his refined voluptuous and comfortably couching soul off its balance! Let us repeat after him these fine sentences—and what wickedness and haughtiness is immediately aroused by way of answer in our probably less beautiful but harder souls, that is to say, in our more German souls!—"DISONS DONC HARDIMENT QUE LA RELIGION EST UN PRODUIT DE L'HOMME NORMAL, QUE L'HOMME EST LE PLUS DANS LE VRAI QUANT IL EST LE PLUS RELIGIEUX ET LE PLUS ASSURE D'UNE DESTINEE INFINIE.... C'EST QUAND IL EST BON QU'IL VEUT QUE LA VIRTU CORRESPONDE A UN ORDER ETERNAL, C'EST QUAND IL CONTEMPLE LES CHOSES D'UNE MANIERE DESINTERESSEE QU'IL TROUVE LA MORT REVOLTANTE ET ABSURDE. COMMENT NE PAS SUPPOSER QUE C'EST DANS CES MOMENTS-LA, QUE L'HOMME VOIT LE MIEUX?"... These sentences are so extremely ANTIPODAL to my ears and habits of thought, that in my first impulse of rage on finding them, I wrote on the margin, "LA NIAISERIE RELIGIEUSE PAR EXCELLENCE!"—until in my later rage I even took a fancy to them, these sentences with their truth absolutely inverted! It is so nice and such a distinction to have one's own antipodes!

49. That which is so astonishing in the religious life of the ancient Greeks is the irrestrainable stream of GRATITUDE which it pours

forth—it is a very superior kind of man who takes SUCH an attitude towards nature and life.—Later on, when the populace got the upper hand in Greece, FEAR became rampant also in religion; and Christianity was preparing itself.

50. The passion for God: there are churlish, honest-hearted, and importunate kinds of it, like that of Luther—the whole of Protestantism lacks the southern DELICATEZZA. There is an Oriental exaltation of the mind in it, like that of an undeservedly favoured or elevated slave, as in the case of St. Augustine, for instance, who lacks in an offensive manner, all nobility in bearing and desires. There is a feminine tenderness and sensuality in it, which modestly and unconsciously longs for a UNIO MYSTICA ET PHYSICA, as in the case of Madame de Guyon. In many cases it appears, curiously enough, as the disguise of a girl's or youth's puberty; here and there even as the hysteria of an old maid, also as her last ambition. The Church has frequently canonized the woman in such a case.

51. The mightiest men have hitherto always bowed reverently before the saint, as the enigma of self-subjugation and utter voluntary privation—why did they thus bow? They divined in him—and as it were behind the questionableness of his frail and wretched appearance—the superior force which wished to test itself by such a subjugation; the strength of will, in which they recognized their own strength and love of power, and knew how to honour it: they honoured something in themselves when they honoured the saint. In addition to this, the contemplation of the saint suggested to them a suspicion: such an enormity of self-negation and anti-naturalness will not have been coveted for nothing—they have said, inquiringly. There is perhaps a reason for it, some very great danger, about which the ascetic might wish to be more accurately informed through his secret interlocutors and visitors? In a word, the mighty ones of the world learned to have a new fear before him, they divined a new power, a strange, still unconquered enemy:—it was the "Will to Power" which obliged them to halt before the saint. They had to question him.

52. In the Jewish "Old Testament," the book of divine justice, there are men, things, and sayings on such an immense scale, that Greek and Indian literature has nothing to compare with it. One stands with fear and reverence before those stupendous remains of what man was formerly, and one has sad thoughts about old Asia and its little out-pushed peninsula Europe, which would like, by all means, to figure before Asia as the "Progress of Mankind." To be sure, he who is himself only a slender, tame house-animal, and knows only the wants of a house-animal (like our cultured people of today, including the Christians of "cultured" Christianity), need neither be amazed nor even sad amid those ruins—the taste for the Old Testament is a touchstone with respect to "great" and "small": perhaps he will find that the New Testament, the book of grace, still appeals more to his heart (there is much of the odour of the genuine, tender, stupid beadsman and petty soul in it). To have bound up this New Testament (a kind of ROCOCO of taste in every respect) along with the Old Testament into one book, as the "Bible," as "The Book in Itself," is perhaps the greatest audacity and "sin against the Spirit" which literary Europe has upon its conscience.

53. Why Atheism nowadays? "The father" in God is thoroughly refuted; equally so "the judge," "the rewarder." Also his "free will": he does not hear—and even if he did, he would not know how to help. The worst is that he seems incapable of communicating himself clearly; is he uncertain?—This is what I have made out (by questioning and listening at a variety of conversations) to be the cause of the decline of European theism; it appears to me that though the religious instinct is in vigorous growth,—it rejects the theistic satisfaction with profound distrust.

54. What does all modern philosophy mainly do? Since Descartes—and indeed more in defiance of him than on the basis of his procedure—an ATTENTAT has been made on the part of all philosophers on the old conception of the soul, under the guise of a criticism of the subject and predicate conception—that is to say, an ATTENTAT on the fundamental presupposition of Christian doctrine. Modern philosophy, as epistemological skepticism, is secretly or openly ANTI-CHRISTIAN, although (for keener ears, be it said) by no means anti-religious. Formerly, in effect, one believed in "the soul"

as one believed in grammar and the grammatical subject: one said, "I" is the condition, "think" is the predicate and is conditioned—to think is an activity for which one MUST suppose a subject as cause. The attempt was then made, with marvelous tenacity and subtlety, to see if one could not get out of this net,—to see if the opposite was not perhaps true: "think" the condition, and "I" the conditioned; "I," therefore, only a synthesis which has been MADE by thinking itself. KANT really wished to prove that, starting from the subject, the subject could not be proved—nor the object either: the possibility of an APPARENT EXISTENCE of the subject, and therefore of "the soul," may not always have been strange to him,—the thought which once had an immense power on earth as the Vedanta philosophy.

55. There is a great ladder of religious cruelty, with many rounds; but three of these are the most important. Once on a time men sacrificed human beings to their God, and perhaps just those they loved the best—to this category belong the firstling sacrifices of all primitive religions, and also the sacrifice of the Emperor Tiberius in the Mithra-Grotto on the Island of Capri, that most terrible of all Roman anachronisms. Then, during the moral epoch of mankind, they sacrificed to their God the strongest instincts they possessed, their "nature"; THIS festal joy shines in the cruel glances of ascetics and "anti-natural" fanatics. Finally, what still remained to be sacrificed? Was it not necessary in the end for men to sacrifice everything comforting, holy, healing, all hope, all faith in hidden harmonies, in future blessedness and justice? Was it not necessary to sacrifice God himself, and out of cruelty to themselves to worship stone, stupidity, gravity, fate, nothingness? To sacrifice God for nothingness—this paradoxical mystery of the ultimate cruelty has been reserved for the rising generation; we all know something thereof already.

56. Whoever, like myself, prompted by some enigmatical desire, has long endeavoured to go to the bottom of the question of pessimism and free it from the half-Christian, half-German narrowness and stupidity in which it has finally presented itself to this century, namely, in the form of Schopenhauer's philosophy; whoever, with an Asiatic and super-Asiatic eye, has actually looked inside, and into the most world-renouncing of all possible modes of thought— beyond good and evil, and no longer like Buddha and Schopenhauer,

under the dominion and delusion of morality,—whoever has done this, has perhaps just thereby, without really desiring it, opened his eyes to behold the opposite ideal: the ideal of the most world-approving, exuberant, and vivacious man, who has not only learnt to compromise and arrange with that which was and is, but wishes to have it again AS IT WAS AND IS, for all eternity, insatiably calling out da capo, not only to himself, but to the whole piece and play; and not only the play, but actually to him who requires the play—and makes it necessary; because he always requires himself anew—and makes himself necessary.—What? And this would not be—circulus vitiosus deus?

57. The distance, and as it were the space around man, grows with the strength of his intellectual vision and insight: his world becomes profounder; new stars, new enigmas, and notions are ever coming into view. Perhaps everything on which the intellectual eye has exercised its acuteness and profundity has just been an occasion for its exercise, something of a game, something for children and childish minds. Perhaps the most solemn conceptions that have caused the most fighting and suffering, the conceptions "God" and "sin," will one day seem to us of no more importance than a child's plaything or a child's pain seems to an old man;—and perhaps another plaything and another pain will then be necessary once more for "the old man"—always childish enough, an eternal child!

58. Has it been observed to what extent outward idleness, or semi-idleness, is necessary to a real religious life (alike for its favourite microscopic labour of self-examination, and for its soft placidity called "prayer," the state of perpetual readiness for the "coming of God"), I mean the idleness with a good conscience, the idleness of olden times and of blood, to which the aristocratic sentiment that work is DISHONOURING—that it vulgarizes body and soul—is not quite unfamiliar? And that consequently the modern, noisy, time-engrossing, conceited, foolishly proud laboriousness educates and prepares for "unbelief" more than anything else? Among these, for instance, who are at present living apart from religion in Germany, I find "free-thinkers" of diversified species and origin, but above all a majority of those in whom laboriousness from generation to generation has dissolved the religious instincts; so that they no longer

know what purpose religions serve, and only note their existence in the world with a kind of dull astonishment. They feel themselves already fully occupied, these good people, be it by their business or by their pleasures, not to mention the "Fatherland," and the newspapers, and their "family duties"; it seems that they have no time whatever left for religion; and above all, it is not obvious to them whether it is a question of a new business or a new pleasure—for it is impossible, they say to themselves, that people should go to church merely to spoil their tempers. They are by no means enemies of religious customs; should certain circumstances, State affairs perhaps, require their participation in such customs, they do what is required, as so many things are done—with a patient and unassuming seriousness, and without much curiosity or discomfort;—they live too much apart and outside to feel even the necessity for a FOR or AGAINST in such matters. Among those indifferent persons may be reckoned nowadays the majority of German Protestants of the middle classes, especially in the great laborious centres of trade and commerce; also the majority of laborious scholars, and the entire University personnel (with the exception of the theologians, whose existence and possibility there always gives psychologists new and more subtle puzzles to solve). On the part of pious, or merely church-going people, there is seldom any idea of HOW MUCH good-will, one might say arbitrary will, is now necessary for a German scholar to take the problem of religion seriously; his whole profession (and as I have said, his whole workmanlike laboriousness, to which he is compelled by his modern conscience) inclines him to a lofty and almost charitable serenity as regards religion, with which is occasionally mingled a slight disdain for the "uncleanliness" of spirit which he takes for granted wherever any one still professes to belong to the Church. It is only with the help of history (NOT through his own personal experience, therefore) that the scholar succeeds in bringing himself to a respectful seriousness, and to a certain timid deference in presence of religions; but even when his sentiments have reached the stage of gratitude towards them, he has not personally advanced one step nearer to that which still maintains itself as Church or as piety; perhaps even the contrary. The practical indifference to religious matters in the midst of which he has been born and brought up, usually sublimates itself in his case into circumspection and cleanliness, which shuns contact with religious men and things; and it may be just the depth of his tolerance and humanity which prompts him to avoid the delicate trouble which tolerance itself brings with it.—Every age has its own divine type of naivete, for the discovery of which other ages may envy it: and how much naivete—adorable, childlike, and boundlessly foolish naivete is involved in this belief of the scholar in his superiority, in the good conscience of his tolerance, in the unsuspecting, simple certainty with which his instinct treats the religious man as a lower and less valuable type, beyond, before, and ABOVE which he himself has developed—he, the little arrogant dwarf and mob-man, the sedulously alert, head-and-hand drudge of "ideas," of "modern ideas"!

59. Whoever has seen deeply into the world has doubtless divined what wisdom there is in the fact that men are superficial. It is their preservative instinct which teaches them to be flighty, lightsome, and false. Here and there one finds a passionate and exaggerated adoration of "pure forms" in philosophers as well as in artists: it is not to be doubted that whoever has NEED of the cult of the superficial to that extent, has at one time or another made an unlucky dive BENEATH it. Perhaps there is even an order of rank with respect to those burnt children, the born artists who find the enjoyment of life only in trying to FALSIFY its image (as if taking wearisome revenge on it), one might guess to what degree life has disgusted them, by the extent to which they wish to see its image falsified, attenuated, ultrified, and deified,—one might reckon the homines religiosi among the artists, as their HIGHEST rank. It is the profound, suspicious fear of an incurable pessimism which compels whole centuries to fasten their teeth into a religious interpretation of existence: the fear of the instinct which divines that truth might be attained TOO soon, before man has become strong enough, hard enough, artist enough.... Piety, the "Life in God," regarded in this light, would appear as the most elaborate and ultimate product of the FEAR of truth, as artist-adoration and artist-intoxication in presence of the most logical of all falsifications, as the will to the inversion of truth, to untruth at any price. Perhaps there has hitherto been no more effective means of beautifying man than piety, by means of it man can become so artful, so superficial, so iridescent, and so good, that his appearance no longer offends.

60. To love mankind FOR GOD'S SAKE—this has so far been the noblest and remotest sentiment to which mankind has attained. That love to mankind, without any redeeming intention in the background, is only an ADDITIONAL folly and brutishness, that the inclination to this love has first to get its proportion, its delicacy, its gram of

salt and sprinkling of ambergris from a higher inclination—whoever first perceived and "experienced" this, however his tongue may have stammered as it attempted to express such a delicate matter, let him for all time be holy and respected, as the man who has so far flown highest and gone astray in the finest fashion!

61. The philosopher, as WE free spirits understand him—as the man of the greatest responsibility, who has the conscience for the general development of mankind,—will use religion for his disciplining and educating work, just as he will use the contemporary political and economic conditions. The selecting and disciplining influence— destructive, as well as creative and fashioning—which can be exercised by means of religion is manifold and varied, according to the sort of people placed under its spell and protection. For those who are strong and independent, destined and trained to command, in whom the judgment and skill of a ruling race is incorporated, religion is an additional means for overcoming resistance in the exercise of authority—as a bond which binds rulers and subjects in common, betraying and surrendering to the former the conscience of the latter, their inmost heart, which would fain escape obedience. And in the case of the unique natures of noble origin, if by virtue of superior spirituality they should incline to a more retired and contemplative life, reserving to themselves only the more refined forms of government (over chosen disciples or members of an order), religion itself may be used as a means for obtaining peace from the noise and trouble of managing GROSSER affairs, and for securing immunity from the UNAVOIDABLE filth of all political agitation. The Brahmins, for instance, understood this fact. With the help of a religious organization, they secured to themselves the power of nominating kings for the people, while their sentiments prompted them to keep apart and outside, as men with a higher and super-regal mission. At the same time religion gives inducement and opportunity to some of the subjects to qualify themselves for future ruling and commanding the slowly ascending ranks and classes, in which, through fortunate marriage customs, volitional power and delight in self-control are on the increase. To them religion offers sufficient incentives and temptations to aspire to higher intellectuality, and to experience the sentiments of authoritative self-control, of silence, and of solitude. Asceticism and Puritanism are almost indispensable means of educating and ennobling a race which seeks to rise above

its hereditary baseness and work itself upwards to future supremacy. And finally, to ordinary men, to the majority of the people, who exist for service and general utility, and are only so far entitled to exist, religion gives invaluable contentedness with their lot and condition, peace of heart, ennoblement of obedience, additional social happiness and sympathy, with something of transfiguration and embellishment, something of justification of all the commonplaceness, all the meanness, all the semi-animal poverty of their souls. Religion, together with the religious significance of life, sheds sunshine over such perpetually harassed men, and makes even their own aspect endurable to them, it operates upon them as the Epicurean philosophy usually operates upon sufferers of a higher order, in a refreshing and refining manner, almost TURNING suffering TO ACCOUNT, and in the end even hallowing and vindicating it. There is perhaps nothing so admirable in Christianity and Buddhism as their art of teaching even the lowest to elevate themselves by piety to a seemingly higher order of things, and thereby to retain their satisfaction with the actual world in which they find it difficult enough to live—this very difficulty being necessary.

62. To be sure—to make also the bad counter-reckoning against such religions, and to bring to light their secret dangers—the cost is always excessive and terrible when religions do NOT operate as an educational and disciplinary medium in the hands of the philosopher, but rule voluntarily and PARAMOUNTLY, when they wish to be the final end, and not a means along with other means. Among men, as among all other animals, there is a surplus of defective, diseased, degenerating, infirm, and necessarily suffering individuals; the successful cases, among men also, are always the exception; and in view of the fact that man is THE ANIMAL NOT YET PROPERLY ADAPTED TO HIS ENVIRONMENT, the rare exception. But worse still. The higher the type a man represents, the greater is the improbability that he will SUCCEED; the accidental, the law of irrationality in the general constitution of mankind, manifests itself most terribly in its destructive effect on the higher orders of men, the conditions of whose lives are delicate, diverse, and difficult to determine. What, then, is the attitude of the two greatest religions above-mentioned to the SURPLUS of failures in life? They endeavour to preserve and keep alive whatever can be preserved; in fact, as the religions FOR SUFFERERS, they take the part of these upon

principle; they are always in favour of those who suffer from life as from a disease, and they would fain treat every other experience of life as false and impossible. However highly we may esteem this indulgent and preservative care (inasmuch as in applying to others, it has applied, and applies also to the highest and usually the most suffering type of man), the hitherto PARAMOUNT religions—to give a general appreciation of them—are among the principal causes which have kept the type of "man" upon a lower level—they have preserved too much THAT WHICH SHOULD HAVE PERISHED. One has to thank them for invaluable services; and who is sufficiently rich in gratitude not to feel poor at the contemplation of all that the "spiritual men" of Christianity have done for Europe hitherto! But when they had given comfort to the sufferers, courage to the oppressed and despairing, a staff and support to the helpless, and when they had allured from society into convents and spiritual penitentiaries the broken-hearted and distracted: what else had they to do in order to work systematically in that fashion, and with a good conscience, for the preservation of all the sick and suffering, which means, in deed and in truth, to work for the DETERIORATION OF THE EUROPEAN RACE? To REVERSE all estimates of value—THAT is what they had to do! And to shatter the strong, to spoil great hopes, to cast suspicion on the delight in beauty, to break down everything autonomous, manly, conquering, and imperious—all instincts which are natural to the highest and most successful type of "man"—into uncertainty, distress of conscience, and self-destruction; forsooth, to invert all love of the earthly and of supremacy over the earth, into hatred of the earth and earthly things—THAT is the task the Church imposed on itself, and was obliged to impose, until, according to its standard of value, "unworldliness," "unsensuousness," and "higher man" fused into one sentiment. If one could observe the strangely painful, equally coarse and refined comedy of European Christianity with the derisive and impartial eye of an Epicurean god, I should think one would never cease marvelling and laughing; does it not actually seem that some single will has ruled over Europe for eighteen centuries in order to make a SUBLIME ABORTION of man? He, however, who, with opposite requirements (no longer Epicurean) and with some divine hammer in his hand, could approach this almost voluntary degeneration and stunting of mankind, as exemplified in the European Christian (Pascal, for instance), would he not have to cry aloud with rage, pity, and horror: "Oh, you bunglers, presumptuous pitiful bunglers, what have you done! Was that a work for your hands? How you have hacked and botched my finest stone! What have you presumed to do!"—I should say that Christianity has hitherto been the most portentous of presumptions. Men, not great enough, nor hard enough, to be entitled as artists to take part in fashioning MAN; men, not sufficiently strong and far-sighted to ALLOW, with sublime self-constraint, the obvious law of the thousandfold failures and perishings to prevail; men, not sufficiently noble to see the radically different grades of rank and intervals of rank that separate man from man:—SUCH men, with their "equality before God," have hitherto swayed the destiny of Europe; until at last a dwarfed, almost ludicrous species has been produced, a gregarious animal, something obliging, sickly, mediocre, the European of the present day.

CHAPTER IV. APOPHTHEGMS AND INTERLUDES

63. He who is a thorough teacher takes things seriously—and even himself—only in relation to his pupils.

64. "Knowledge for its own sake"—that is the last snare laid by morality: we are thereby completely entangled in morals once more.

65. The charm of knowledge would be small, were it not so much shame has to be overcome on the way to it.

65A. We are most dishonourable towards our God: he is not PERMITTED to sin.

66. The tendency of a person to allow himself to be degraded, robbed, deceived, and exploited might be the diffidence of a God among men.

67. Love to one only is a barbarity, for it is exercised at the expense of all others. Love to God also!

68. "I did that," says my memory. "I could not have done that," says my pride, and remains inexorable. Eventually—the memory yields.

69. One has regarded life carelessly, if one has failed to see the hand that—kills with leniency.

70. If a man has character, he has also his typical experience, which always recurs.

71. THE SAGE AS ASTRONOMER.—So long as thou feelest the stars as an "above thee," thou lackest the eye of the discerning one.

72. It is not the strength, but the duration of great sentiments that makes great men.

73. He who attains his ideal, precisely thereby surpasses it.

73A. Many a peacock hides his tail from every eye—and calls it his pride.

74. A man of genius is unbearable, unless he possess at least two

things besides: gratitude and purity.

75. The degree and nature of a man's sensuality extends to the highest altitudes of his spirit.

76. Under peaceful conditions the militant man attacks himself.

77. With his principles a man seeks either to dominate, or justify, or honour, or reproach, or conceal his habits: two men with the same principles probably seek fundamentally different ends therewith.

78. He who despises himself, nevertheless esteems himself thereby, as a despiser.

79. A soul which knows that it is loved, but does not itself love, betrays its sediment: its dregs come up.

80. A thing that is explained ceases to concern us—What did the God mean who gave the advice, "Know thyself!" Did it perhaps imply "Cease to be concerned about thyself! become objective!"—And Socrates?—And the "scientific man"?

81. It is terrible to die of thirst at sea. Is it necessary that you should so salt your truth that it will no longer—quench thirst?

82. "Sympathy for all"—would be harshness and tyranny for THEE, my good neighbour.

83. INSTINCT—When the house is on fire one forgets even the dinner—Yes, but one recovers it from among the ashes.

84. Woman learns how to hate in proportion as she—forgets how to charm.

85. The same emotions are in man and woman, but in different TEMPO, on that account man and woman never cease to misunderstand each other.

86. In the background of all their personal vanity, women themselves have still their impersonal scorn—for "woman".

87. FETTERED HEART, FREE SPIRIT—When one firmly fetters one's heart and keeps it prisoner, one can allow one's spirit many liberties: I said this once before But people do not believe it when I say so, unless they know it already.

88. One begins to distrust very clever persons when they become embarrassed.

89. Dreadful experiences raise the question whether he who experiences them is not something dreadful also.

90. Heavy, melancholy men turn lighter, and come temporarily to their surface, precisely by that which makes others heavy—by hatred and love.

91. So cold, so icy, that one burns one's finger at the touch of him! Every hand that lays hold of him shrinks back!—And for that very reason many think him red-hot.

92. Who has not, at one time or another—sacrificed himself for the sake of his good name?

93. In affability there is no hatred of men, but precisely on that account a great deal too much contempt of men.

94. The maturity of man—that means, to have reacquired the seriousness that one had as a child at play.

95. To be ashamed of one's immorality is a step on the ladder at the end of which one is ashamed also of one's morality.

96. One should part from life as Ulysses parted from Nausicaa—blessing it rather than in love with it.

97. What? A great man? I always see merely the play-actor of his own ideal.

98. When one trains one's conscience, it kisses one while it bites.

99. THE DISAPPOINTED ONE SPEAKS—"I listened for the echo and I heard only praise."

100. We all feign to ourselves that we are simpler than we are, we thus relax ourselves away from our fellows.

101. A discerning one might easily regard himself at present as the animalization of God.

102. Discovering reciprocal love should really disenchant the lover with regard to the beloved. "What! She is modest enough to love even you? Or stupid enough? Or—or—-"

103. THE DANGER IN HAPPINESS.—"Everything now turns out best for me, I now love every fate:—who would like to be my fate?"

104. Not their love of humanity, but the impotence of their love, prevents the Christians of today—burning us.

105. The pia fraus is still more repugnant to the taste (the "piety") of the free spirit (the "pious man of knowledge") than the impia fraus. Hence the profound lack of judgment, in comparison with the Church, characteristic of the type "free spirit"—as ITS non-freedom.

106. By means of music the very passions enjoy themselves.

107. A sign of strong character, when once the resolution has been taken, to shut the ear even to the best counter-arguments. Occasionally, therefore, a will to stupidity.

108. There is no such thing as moral phenomena, but only a moral interpretation of phenomena.

109. The criminal is often enough not equal to his deed: he extenuates and maligns it.

110. The advocates of a criminal are seldom artists enough to turn the beautiful terribleness of the deed to the advantage of the doer.

111. Our vanity is most difficult to wound just when our pride has been wounded.

112. To him who feels himself preordained to contemplation and not to belief, all believers are too noisy and obtrusive; he guards against them.

113. "You want to prepossess him in your favour? Then you must be embarrassed before him."

114. The immense expectation with regard to sexual love, and the coyness in this expectation, spoils all the perspectives of women at the outset.

115. Where there is neither love nor hatred in the game, woman's play is mediocre.

116. The great epochs of our life are at the points when we gain courage to rebaptize our badness as the best in us.

117. The will to overcome an emotion, is ultimately only the will of another, or of several other, emotions.

118. There is an innocence of admiration: it is possessed by him to whom it has not yet occurred that he himself may be admired some day.

119. Our loathing of dirt may be so great as to prevent our cleaning ourselves—"justifying" ourselves.

120. Sensuality often forces the growth of love too much, so that its root remains weak, and is easily torn up.

121. It is a curious thing that God learned Greek when he wished to turn author—and that he did not learn it better.

122. To rejoice on account of praise is in many cases merely politeness of heart—and the very opposite of vanity of spirit.

123. Even concubinage has been corrupted—by marriage.

124. He who exults at the stake, does not triumph over pain, but because of the fact that he does not feel pain where he expected it. A parable.

125. When we have to change an opinion about any one, we charge heavily to his account the inconvenience he thereby causes us.

126. A nation is a detour of nature to arrive at six or seven great men.—Yes, and then to get round them.

127. In the eyes of all true women science is hostile to the sense of shame. They feel as if one wished to peep under their skin with it—or worse still! under their dress and finery.

128. The more abstract the truth you wish to teach, the more must you allure the senses to it.

129. The devil has the most extensive perspectives for God; on that account he keeps so far away from him:—the devil, in effect, as the oldest friend of knowledge.

130. What a person IS begins to betray itself when his talent decreases,—when he ceases to show what he CAN do. Talent is also an adornment; an adornment is also a concealment.

131. The sexes deceive themselves about each other: the reason is that in reality they honour and love only themselves (or their own ideal, to express it more agreeably). Thus man wishes woman to be peaceable: but in fact woman is ESSENTIALLY unpeaceable, like the cat, however well she may have assumed the peaceable demeanour.

132. One is punished best for one's virtues.

133. He who cannot find the way to HIS ideal, lives more frivolously and shamelessly than the man without an ideal.

134. From the senses originate all trustworthiness, all good conscience, all evidence of truth.

135. Pharisaism is not a deterioration of the good man; a considerable part of it is rather an essential condition of being good.

136. The one seeks an accoucheur for his thoughts, the other seeks some one whom he can assist: a good conversation thus originates.

137. In intercourse with scholars and artists one readily makes mistakes of opposite kinds: in a remarkable scholar one not infrequently finds a mediocre man; and often, even in a mediocre artist, one finds a very remarkable man.

138. We do the same when awake as when dreaming: we only invent and imagine him with whom we have intercourse—and forget it immediately.

139. In revenge and in love woman is more barbarous than man.

140. ADVICE AS A RIDDLE.—"If the band is not to break, bite it first—secure to make!"

141. The belly is the reason why man does not so readily take himself for a God.

142. The chastest utterance I ever heard: "Dans le veritable amour c'est l'ame qui enveloppe le corps."

143. Our vanity would like what we do best to pass precisely for what is most difficult to us.—Concerning the origin of many systems of morals.

144. When a woman has scholarly inclinations there is generally

something wrong with her sexual nature. Barrenness itself conduces to a certain virility of taste; man, indeed, if I may say so, is "the barren animal."

145. Comparing man and woman generally, one may say that woman would not have the genius for adornment, if she had not the instinct for the SECONDARY role.

146. He who fights with monsters should be careful lest he thereby become a monster. And if thou gaze long into an abyss, the abyss will also gaze into thee.

147. From old Florentine novels—moreover, from life: Buona femmina e mala femmina vuol bastone.—Sacchetti, Nov. 86.

148. To seduce their neighbour to a favourable opinion, and afterwards to believe implicitly in this opinion of their neighbour—who can do this conjuring trick so well as women?

149. That which an age considers evil is usually an unseasonable echo of what was formerly considered good—the atavism of an old ideal.

150. Around the hero everything becomes a tragedy; around the demigod everything becomes a satyr-play; and around God everything becomes—what? perhaps a "world"?

151. It is not enough to possess a talent: one must also have your permission to possess it;—eh, my friends?

152. "Where there is the tree of knowledge, there is always Paradise": so say the most ancient and the most modern serpents.

153. What is done out of love always takes place beyond good and evil.

154. Objection, evasion, joyous distrust, and love of irony are signs of health; everything absolute belongs to pathology.

155. The sense of the tragic increases and declines with sensuousness.

156. Insanity in individuals is something rare—but in groups, parties, nations, and epochs it is the rule.

157. The thought of suicide is a great consolation: by means of it one gets successfully through many a bad night.

158. Not only our reason, but also our conscience, truckles to our strongest impulse—the tyrant in us.

159. One MUST repay good and ill; but why just to the person who did us good or ill?

160. One no longer loves one's knowledge sufficiently after one has communicated it.

161. Poets act shamelessly towards their experiences: they exploit them.

162. "Our fellow-creature is not our neighbour, but our neighbour's neighbour":—so thinks every nation.

163. Love brings to light the noble and hidden qualities of a lover—his rare and exceptional traits: it is thus liable to be deceptive as to his normal character.

164. Jesus said to his Jews: "The law was for servants;—love God as I love him, as his Son! What have we Sons of God to do with morals!"

165. IN SIGHT OF EVERY PARTY.—A shepherd has always need of a bell-wether—or he has himself to be a wether occasionally.

166. One may indeed lie with the mouth; but with the accompanying grimace one nevertheless tells the truth.

167. To vigorous men intimacy is a matter of shame—and something precious.

168. Christianity gave Eros poison to drink; he did not die of it, certainly, but degenerated to Vice.

169. To talk much about oneself may also be a means of concealing oneself.

170. In praise there is more obtrusiveness than in blame.

171. Pity has an almost ludicrous effect on a man of knowledge, like tender hands on a Cyclops.

172. One occasionally embraces some one or other, out of love to mankind (because one cannot embrace all); but this is what one must

never confess to the individual.

173. One does not hate as long as one disesteems, but only when one esteems equal or superior.

174. Ye Utilitarians—ye, too, love the UTILE only as a VEHICLE for your inclinations,—ye, too, really find the noise of its wheels insupportable!

175. One loves ultimately one's desires, not the thing desired.

176. The vanity of others is only counter to our taste when it is counter to our vanity.

177. With regard to what "truthfulness" is, perhaps nobody has ever been sufficiently truthful.

178. One does not believe in the follies of clever men: what a forfeiture of the rights of man!

179. The consequences of our actions seize us by the forelock, very indifferent to the fact that we have meanwhile "reformed."

180. There is an innocence in lying which is the sign of good faith in a cause.

181. It is inhuman to bless when one is being cursed.

182. The familiarity of superiors embitters one, because it may not be returned.

183. "I am affected, not because you have deceived me, but because I can no longer believe in you."

184. There is a haughtiness of kindness which has the appearance of wickedness.

185. "I dislike him."—Why?—"I am not a match for him."—Did any one ever answer so?

CHAPTER V. THE NATURAL HISTORY OF MORALS

186. The moral sentiment in Europe at present is perhaps as subtle, belated, diverse, sensitive, and refined, as the "Science of Morals" belonging thereto is recent, initial, awkward, and coarse-fingered:—an interesting contrast, which sometimes becomes incarnate and obvious in the very person of a moralist. Indeed, the expression, "Science of Morals" is, in respect to what is designated thereby, far too presumptuous and counter to GOOD taste,—which is always a foretaste of more modest expressions. One ought to avow with the utmost fairness WHAT is still necessary here for a long time, WHAT is alone proper for the present: namely, the collection of material, the comprehensive survey and classification of an immense domain of delicate sentiments of worth, and distinctions of worth, which live, grow, propagate, and perish—and perhaps attempts to give a clear idea of the recurring and more common forms of these living crystallizations—as preparation for a THEORY OF TYPES of morality. To be sure, people have not hitherto been so modest. All the philosophers, with a pedantic and ridiculous seriousness, demanded of themselves something very much higher, more pretentious, and ceremonious, when they concerned themselves with morality as a science: they wanted to GIVE A BASIC to morality—and every philosopher hitherto has believed that he has given it a basis; morality itself, however, has been regarded as something "given." How far from their awkward pride was the seemingly insignificant problem—left in dust and decay—of a description of forms of morality, notwithstanding that the finest hands and senses could hardly be fine enough for it! It was precisely owing to moral philosophers' knowing the moral facts imperfectly, in an arbitrary epitome, or an accidental abridgement—perhaps as the morality of their environment, their position, their church, their Zeitgeist, their climate and zone—it was precisely because they were badly instructed with regard to nations, eras, and past ages, and were by no means eager to know about these matters, that they did not even come in sight of the real problems of morals—problems which only disclose themselves by a comparison of MANY kinds of morality. In every "Science of Morals" hitherto, strange as it may sound, the problem of morality itself has been OMITTED: there has been no suspicion that there

was anything problematic there! That which philosophers called "giving a basis to morality," and endeavoured to realize, has, when seen in a right light, proved merely a learned form of good FAITH in prevailing morality, a new means of its EXPRESSION, consequently just a matter-of-fact within the sphere of a definite morality, yea, in its ultimate motive, a sort of denial that it is LAWFUL for this morality to be called in question—and in any case the reverse of the testing, analyzing, doubting, and vivisecting of this very faith. Hear, for instance, with what innocence—almost worthy of honour— Schopenhauer represents his own task, and draw your conclusions concerning the scientificness of a "Science" whose latest master still talks in the strain of children and old wives: "The principle," he says (page 136 of the Grundprobleme der Ethik), [Footnote: Pages 54-55 of Schopenhauer's Basis of Morality, translated by Arthur B. Bullock, M.A. (1903).] "the axiom about the purport of which all moralists are PRACTICALLY agreed: neminem laede, immo omnes quantum potes juva—is REALLY the proposition which all moral teachers strive to establish, ... the REAL basis of ethics which has been sought, like the philosopher's stone, for centuries."—The difficulty of establishing the proposition referred to may indeed be great—it is well known that Schopenhauer also was unsuccessful in his efforts; and whoever has thoroughly realized how absurdly false and sentimental this proposition is, in a world whose essence is Will to Power, may be reminded that Schopenhauer, although a pessimist, ACTUALLY—played the flute... daily after dinner: one may read about the matter in his biography. A question by the way: a pessimist, a repudiator of God and of the world, who MAKES A HALT at morality—who assents to morality, and plays the flute to laede-neminem morals, what? Is that really—a pessimist?

187. Apart from the value of such assertions as "there is a categorical imperative in us," one can always ask: What does such an assertion indicate about him who makes it? There are systems of morals which are meant to justify their author in the eyes of other people; other systems of morals are meant to tranquilize him, and make him self-satisfied; with other systems he wants to crucify and humble himself, with others he wishes to take revenge, with others to conceal himself, with others to glorify himself and gave superiority and distinction,— this system of morals helps its author to forget, that system makes him, or something of him, forgotten, many a moralist would like

to exercise power and creative arbitrariness over mankind, many another, perhaps, Kant especially, gives us to understand by his morals that "what is estimable in me, is that I know how to obey—and with you it SHALL not be otherwise than with me!" In short, systems of morals are only a SIGN-LANGUAGE OF THE EMOTIONS.

188. In contrast to laisser-aller, every system of morals is a sort of tyranny against "nature" and also against "reason", that is, however, no objection, unless one should again decree by some system of morals, that all kinds of tyranny and unreasonableness are unlawful What is essential and invaluable in every system of morals, is that it is a long constraint. In order to understand Stoicism, or Port Royal, or Puritanism, one should remember the constraint under which every language has attained to strength and freedom—the metrical constraint, the tyranny of rhyme and rhythm. How much trouble have the poets and orators of every nation given themselves!—not excepting some of the prose writers of today, in whose ear dwells an inexorable conscientiousness—"for the sake of a folly," as utilitarian bunglers say, and thereby deem themselves wise—"from submission to arbitrary laws," as the anarchists say, and thereby fancy themselves "free," even free-spirited. The singular fact remains, however, that everything of the nature of freedom, elegance, boldness, dance, and masterly certainty, which exists or has existed, whether it be in thought itself, or in administration, or in speaking and persuading, in art just as in conduct, has only developed by means of the tyranny of such arbitrary law, and in all seriousness, it is not at all improbable that precisely this is "nature" and "natural"—and not laisser-aller! Every artist knows how different from the state of letting himself go, is his "most natural" condition, the free arranging, locating, disposing, and constructing in the moments of "inspiration"—and how strictly and delicately he then obeys a thousand laws, which, by their very rigidness and precision, defy all formulation by means of ideas (even the most stable idea has, in comparison therewith, something floating, manifold, and ambiguous in it). The essential thing "in heaven and in earth" is, apparently (to repeat it once more), that there should be long OBEDIENCE in the same direction, there thereby results, and has always resulted in the long run, something which has made life worth living; for instance, virtue, art, music, dancing, reason, spirituality—anything whatever that is transfiguring, refined, foolish, or divine. The long bondage of the spirit, the distrustful constraint in the

communicability of ideas, the discipline which the thinker imposed on himself to think in accordance with the rules of a church or a court, or conformable to Aristotelian premises, the persistent spiritual will to interpret everything that happened according to a Christian scheme, and in every occurrence to rediscover and justify the Christian God:—all this violence, arbitrariness, severity, dreadfulness, and unreasonableness, has proved itself the disciplinary means whereby the European spirit has attained its strength, its remorseless curiosity and subtle mobility; granted also that much irrecoverable strength and spirit had to be stifled, suffocated, and spoilt in the process (for here, as everywhere, "nature" shows herself as she is, in all her extravagant and INDIFFERENT magnificence, which is shocking, but nevertheless noble). That for centuries European thinkers only thought in order to prove something—nowadays, on the contrary, we are suspicious of every thinker who "wishes to prove something"— that it was always settled beforehand what WAS TO BE the result of their strictest thinking, as it was perhaps in the Asiatic astrology of former times, or as it is still at the present day in the innocent, Christian-moral explanation of immediate personal events "for the glory of God," or "for the good of the soul":—this tyranny, this arbitrariness, this severe and magnificent stupidity, has EDUCATED the spirit; slavery, both in the coarser and the finer sense, is apparently an indispensable means even of spiritual education and discipline. One may look at every system of morals in this light: it is "nature" therein which teaches to hate the laisser-aller, the too great freedom, and implants the need for limited horizons, for immediate duties— it teaches the NARROWING OF PERSPECTIVES, and thus, in a certain sense, that stupidity is a condition of life and development. "Thou must obey some one, and for a long time; OTHERWISE thou wilt come to grief, and lose all respect for thyself"—this seems to me to be the moral imperative of nature, which is certainly neither "categorical," as old Kant wished (consequently the "otherwise"), nor does it address itself to the individual (what does nature care for the individual!), but to nations, races, ages, and ranks; above all, however, to the animal "man" generally, to MANKIND.

189. Industrious races find it a great hardship to be idle: it was a master stroke of ENGLISH instinct to hallow and begloom Sunday to such an extent that the Englishman unconsciously hankers for his week—and work-day again:—as a kind of cleverly devised,

cleverly intercalated FAST, such as is also frequently found in the ancient world (although, as is appropriate in southern nations, not precisely with respect to work). Many kinds of fasts are necessary; and wherever powerful influences and habits prevail, legislators have to see that intercalary days are appointed, on which such impulses are fettered, and learn to hunger anew. Viewed from a higher standpoint, whole generations and epochs, when they show themselves infected with any moral fanaticism, seem like those intercalated periods of restraint and fasting, during which an impulse learns to humble and submit itself—at the same time also to PURIFY and SHARPEN itself; certain philosophical sects likewise admit of a similar interpretation (for instance, the Stoa, in the midst of Hellenic culture, with the atmosphere rank and overcharged with Aphrodisiacal odours).—Here also is a hint for the explanation of the paradox, why it was precisely in the most Christian period of European history, and in general only under the pressure of Christian sentiments, that the sexual impulse sublimated into love (amour-passion).

190. There is something in the morality of Plato which does not really belong to Plato, but which only appears in his philosophy, one might say, in spite of him: namely, Socratism, for which he himself was too noble. "No one desires to injure himself, hence all evil is done unwittingly. The evil man inflicts injury on himself; he would not do so, however, if he knew that evil is evil. The evil man, therefore, is only evil through error; if one free him from error one will necessarily make him—good."—This mode of reasoning savours of the POPULACE, who perceive only the unpleasant consequences of evil-doing, and practically judge that "it is STUPID to do wrong"; while they accept "good" as identical with "useful and pleasant," without further thought. As regards every system of utilitarianism, one may at once assume that it has the same origin, and follow the scent: one will seldom err.—Plato did all he could to interpret something refined and noble into the tenets of his teacher, and above all to interpret himself into them—he, the most daring of all interpreters, who lifted the entire Socrates out of the street, as a popular theme and song, to exhibit him in endless and impossible modifications—namely, in all his own disguises and multiplicities. In jest, and in Homeric language as well, what is the Platonic Socrates, if not—[Greek words inserted here.]

191. The old theological problem of "Faith" and "Knowledge," or more plainly, of instinct and reason—the question whether, in respect to the valuation of things, instinct deserves more authority than rationality, which wants to appreciate and act according to motives, according to a "Why," that is to say, in conformity to purpose and utility—it is always the old moral problem that first appeared in the person of Socrates, and had divided men's minds long before Christianity. Socrates himself, following, of course, the taste of his talent—that of a surpassing dialectician—took first the side of reason; and, in fact, what did he do all his life but laugh at the awkward incapacity of the noble Athenians, who were men of instinct, like all noble men, and could never give satisfactory answers concerning the motives of their actions? In the end, however, though silently and secretly, he laughed also at himself: with his finer conscience and introspection, he found in himself the same difficulty and incapacity. "But why"—he said to himself—"should one on that account separate oneself from the instincts! One must set them right, and the reason ALSO—one must follow the instincts, but at the same time persuade the reason to support them with good arguments." This was the real FALSENESS of that great and mysterious ironist; he brought his conscience up to the point that he was satisfied with a kind of self-outwitting: in fact, he perceived the irrationality in the moral judgment.—Plato, more innocent in such matters, and without the craftiness of the plebeian, wished to prove to himself, at the expenditure of all his strength—the greatest strength a philosopher had ever expended—that reason and instinct lead spontaneously to one goal, to the good, to "God"; and since Plato, all theologians and philosophers have followed the same path—which means that in matters of morality, instinct (or as Christians call it, "Faith," or as I call it, "the herd") has hitherto triumphed. Unless one should make an exception in the case of Descartes, the father of rationalism (and consequently the grandfather of the Revolution), who recognized only the authority of reason: but reason is only a tool, and Descartes was superficial.

192. Whoever has followed the history of a single science, finds in its development a clue to the understanding of the oldest and commonest processes of all "knowledge and cognizance": there, as here, the premature hypotheses, the fictions, the good stupid will to "belief," and the lack of distrust and patience are first developed—our senses learn late, and never learn completely, to be subtle,

reliable, and cautious organs of knowledge. Our eyes find it easier on a given occasion to produce a picture already often produced, than to seize upon the divergence and novelty of an impression: the latter requires more force, more "morality." It is difficult and painful for the ear to listen to anything new; we hear strange music badly. When we hear another language spoken, we involuntarily attempt to form the sounds into words with which we are more familiar and conversant—it was thus, for example, that the Germans modified the spoken word ARCUBALISTA into ARMBRUST (cross-bow). Our senses are also hostile and averse to the new; and generally, even in the "simplest" processes of sensation, the emotions DOMINATE—such as fear, love, hatred, and the passive emotion of indolence.—As little as a reader nowadays reads all the single words (not to speak of syllables) of a page—he rather takes about five out of every twenty words at random, and "guesses" the probably appropriate sense to them—just as little do we see a tree correctly and completely in respect to its leaves, branches, colour, and shape; we find it so much easier to fancy the chance of a tree. Even in the midst of the most remarkable experiences, we still do just the same; we fabricate the greater part of the experience, and can hardly be made to contemplate any event, EXCEPT as "inventors" thereof. All this goes to prove that from our fundamental nature and from remote ages we have been—ACCUSTOMED TO LYING. Or, to express it more politely and hypocritically, in short, more pleasantly—one is much more of an artist than one is aware of.—In an animated conversation, I often see the face of the person with whom I am speaking so clearly and sharply defined before me, according to the thought he expresses, or which I believe to be evoked in his mind, that the degree of distinctness far exceeds the STRENGTH of my visual faculty—the delicacy of the play of the muscles and of the expression of the eyes MUST therefore be imagined by me. Probably the person put on quite a different expression, or none at all.

193. Quidquid luce fuit, tenebris agit: but also contrariwise. What we experience in dreams, provided we experience it often, pertains at last just as much to the general belongings of our soul as anything "actually" experienced; by virtue thereof we are richer or poorer, we have a requirement more or less, and finally, in broad daylight, and even in the brightest moments of our waking life, we are ruled to some extent by the nature of our dreams. Supposing that someone

has often flown in his dreams, and that at last, as soon as he dreams, he is conscious of the power and art of flying as his privilege and his peculiarly enviable happiness; such a person, who believes that on the slightest impulse, he can actualize all sorts of curves and angles, who knows the sensation of a certain divine levity, an "upwards" without effort or constraint, a "downwards" without descending or lowering—without TROUBLE!—how could the man with such dream-experiences and dream-habits fail to find "happiness" differently coloured and defined, even in his waking hours! How could he fail—to long DIFFERENTLY for happiness? "Flight," such as is described by poets, must, when compared with his own "flying," be far too earthly, muscular, violent, far too "troublesome" for him.

194. The difference among men does not manifest itself only in the difference of their lists of desirable things—in their regarding different good things as worth striving for, and being disagreed as to the greater or less value, the order of rank, of the commonly recognized desirable things:—it manifests itself much more in what they regard as actually HAVING and POSSESSING a desirable thing. As regards a woman, for instance, the control over her body and her sexual gratification serves as an amply sufficient sign of ownership and possession to the more modest man; another with a more suspicious and ambitious thirst for possession, sees the "questionableness," the mere apparentness of such ownership, and wishes to have finer tests in order to know especially whether the woman not only gives herself to him, but also gives up for his sake what she has or would like to have—only THEN does he look upon her as "possessed." A third, however, has not even here got to the limit of his distrust and his desire for possession: he asks himself whether the woman, when she gives up everything for him, does not perhaps do so for a phantom of him; he wishes first to be thoroughly, indeed, profoundly well known; in order to be loved at all he ventures to let himself be found out. Only then does he feel the beloved one fully in his possession, when she no longer deceives herself about him, when she loves him just as much for the sake of his devilry and concealed insatiability, as for his goodness, patience, and spirituality. One man would like to possess a nation, and he finds all the higher arts of Cagliostro and Catalina suitable for his purpose. Another, with a more refined thirst for possession, says to himself: "One may not deceive where one desires to possess"—he is irritated and impatient at the idea that a

mask of him should rule in the hearts of the people: "I must, therefore, MAKE myself known, and first of all learn to know myself!" Among helpful and charitable people, one almost always finds the awkward craftiness which first gets up suitably him who has to be helped, as though, for instance, he should "merit" help, seek just THEIR help, and would show himself deeply grateful, attached, and subservient to them for all help. With these conceits, they take control of the needy as a property, just as in general they are charitable and helpful out of a desire for property. One finds them jealous when they are crossed or forestalled in their charity. Parents involuntarily make something like themselves out of their children—they call that "education"; no mother doubts at the bottom of her heart that the child she has borne is thereby her property, no father hesitates about his right to HIS OWN ideas and notions of worth. Indeed, in former times fathers deemed it right to use their discretion concerning the life or death of the newly born (as among the ancient Germans). And like the father, so also do the teacher, the class, the priest, and the prince still see in every new individual an unobjectionable opportunity for a new possession. The consequence is...

195. The Jews—a people "born for slavery," as Tacitus and the whole ancient world say of them; "the chosen people among the nations," as they themselves say and believe—the Jews performed the miracle of the inversion of valuations, by means of which life on earth obtained a new and dangerous charm for a couple of millenniums. Their prophets fused into one the expressions "rich," "godless," "wicked," "violent," "sensual," and for the first time coined the word "world" as a term of reproach. In this inversion of valuations (in which is also included the use of the word "poor" as synonymous with "saint" and "friend") the significance of the Jewish people is to be found; it is with THEM that the SLAVE-INSURRECTION IN MORALS commences.

196. It is to be INFERRED that there are countless dark bodies near the sun—such as we shall never see. Among ourselves, this is an allegory; and the psychologist of morals reads the whole star-writing merely as an allegorical and symbolic language in which much may be unexpressed.

197. The beast of prey and the man of prey (for instance, Caesar Borgia) are fundamentally misunderstood, "nature" is misunderstood, so long as one seeks a "morbidness" in the constitution of these healthiest of all tropical monsters and growths, or even an innate "hell" in them—as almost all moralists have done hitherto. Does it not seem that there is a hatred of the virgin forest and of the tropics among moralists? And that the "tropical man" must be discredited at all costs, whether as disease and deterioration of mankind, or as his own hell and self-torture? And why? In favour of the "temperate zones"? In favour of the temperate men? The "moral"? The mediocre?—This for the chapter: "Morals as Timidity."

198. All the systems of morals which address themselves with a view to their "happiness," as it is called—what else are they but suggestions for behaviour adapted to the degree of DANGER from themselves in which the individuals live; recipes for their passions, their good and bad propensities, insofar as such have the Will to Power and would like to play the master; small and great expediencies and elaborations, permeated with the musty odour of old family medicines and old-wife wisdom; all of them grotesque and absurd in their form—because they address themselves to "all," because they generalize where generalization is not authorized; all of them speaking unconditionally, and taking themselves unconditionally; all of them flavoured not merely with one grain of salt, but rather endurable only, and sometimes even seductive, when they are over-spiced and begin to smell dangerously, especially of "the other world." That is all of little value when estimated intellectually, and is far from being "science," much less "wisdom"; but, repeated once more, and three times repeated, it is expediency, expediency, expediency, mixed with stupidity, stupidity, stupidity—whether it be the indifference and statuesque coldness towards the heated folly of the emotions, which the Stoics advised and fostered; or the no-more-laughing and no-more-weeping of Spinoza, the destruction of the emotions by their analysis and vivisection, which he recommended so naively; or the lowering of the emotions to an innocent mean at which they may be satisfied, the Aristotelianism of morals; or even morality as the enjoyment of the emotions in a voluntary attenuation and spiritualization by the symbolism of art, perhaps as music, or as love of God, and of mankind for God's sake—for in religion the

passions are once more enfranchised, provided that...; or, finally, even the complaisant and wanton surrender to the emotions, as has been taught by Hafis and Goethe, the bold letting-go of the reins, the spiritual and corporeal licentia morum in the exceptional cases of wise old codgers and drunkards, with whom it "no longer has much danger."—This also for the chapter: "Morals as Timidity."

199. Inasmuch as in all ages, as long as mankind has existed, there have also been human herds (family alliances, communities, tribes, peoples, states, churches), and always a great number who obey in proportion to the small number who command—in view, therefore, of the fact that obedience has been most practiced and fostered among mankind hitherto, one may reasonably suppose that, generally speaking, the need thereof is now innate in every one, as a kind of FORMAL CONSCIENCE which gives the command "Thou shalt unconditionally do something, unconditionally refrain from something", in short, "Thou shalt". This need tries to satisfy itself and to fill its form with a content, according to its strength, impatience, and eagerness, it at once seizes as an omnivorous appetite with little selection, and accepts whatever is shouted into its ear by all sorts of commanders—parents, teachers, laws, class prejudices, or public opinion. The extraordinary limitation of human development, the hesitation, protractedness, frequent retrogression, and turning thereof, is attributable to the fact that the herd-instinct of obedience is transmitted best, and at the cost of the art of command. If one imagine this instinct increasing to its greatest extent, commanders and independent individuals will finally be lacking altogether, or they will suffer inwardly from a bad conscience, and will have to impose a deception on themselves in the first place in order to be able to command just as if they also were only obeying. This condition of things actually exists in Europe at present—I call it the moral hypocrisy of the commanding class. They know no other way of protecting themselves from their bad conscience than by playing the role of executors of older and higher orders (of predecessors, of the constitution, of justice, of the law, or of God himself), or they even justify themselves by maxims from the current opinions of the herd, as "first servants of their people," or "instruments of the public weal". On the other hand, the gregarious European man nowadays assumes an air as if he were the only kind of man that is allowable, he glorifies his qualities, such as public spirit, kindness, deference, industry,

temperance, modesty, indulgence, sympathy, by virtue of which he is gentle, endurable, and useful to the herd, as the peculiarly human virtues. In cases, however, where it is believed that the leader and bell-wether cannot be dispensed with, attempt after attempt is made nowadays to replace commanders by the summing together of clever gregarious men all representative constitutions, for example, are of this origin. In spite of all, what a blessing, what a deliverance from a weight becoming unendurable, is the appearance of an absolute ruler for these gregarious Europeans—of this fact the effect of the appearance of Napoleon was the last great proof the history of the influence of Napoleon is almost the history of the higher happiness to which the entire century has attained in its worthiest individuals and periods.

200. The man of an age of dissolution which mixes the races with one another, who has the inheritance of a diversified descent in his body—that is to say, contrary, and often not only contrary, instincts and standards of value, which struggle with one another and are seldom at peace—such a man of late culture and broken lights, will, on an average, be a weak man. His fundamental desire is that the war which is IN HIM should come to an end; happiness appears to him in the character of a soothing medicine and mode of thought (for instance, Epicurean or Christian); it is above all things the happiness of repose, of undisturbedness, of repletion, of final unity—it is the "Sabbath of Sabbaths," to use the expression of the holy rhetorician, St. Augustine, who was himself such a man.—Should, however, the contrariety and conflict in such natures operate as an ADDITIONAL incentive and stimulus to life—and if, on the other hand, in addition to their powerful and irreconcilable instincts, they have also inherited and indoctrinated into them a proper mastery and subtlety for carrying on the conflict with themselves (that is to say, the faculty of self-control and self-deception), there then arise those marvelously incomprehensible and inexplicable beings, those enigmatical men, predestined for conquering and circumventing others, the finest examples of which are Alcibiades and Caesar (with whom I should like to associate the FIRST of Europeans according to my taste, the Hohenstaufen, Frederick the Second), and among artists, perhaps Leonardo da Vinci. They appear precisely in the same periods when that weaker type, with its longing for repose, comes to the front; the two types are complementary to each other, and spring from the same

causes.

201. As long as the utility which determines moral estimates is only gregarious utility, as long as the preservation of the community is only kept in view, and the immoral is sought precisely and exclusively in what seems dangerous to the maintenance of the community, there can be no "morality of love to one's neighbour." Granted even that there is already a little constant exercise of consideration, sympathy, fairness, gentleness, and mutual assistance, granted that even in this condition of society all those instincts are already active which are latterly distinguished by honourable names as "virtues," and eventually almost coincide with the conception "morality": in that period they do not as yet belong to the domain of moral valuations—they are still ULTRA-MORAL. A sympathetic action, for instance, is neither called good nor bad, moral nor immoral, in the best period of the Romans; and should it be praised, a sort of resentful disdain is compatible with this praise, even at the best, directly the sympathetic action is compared with one which contributes to the welfare of the whole, to the RES PUBLICA. After all, "love to our neighbour" is always a secondary matter, partly conventional and arbitrarily manifested in relation to our FEAR OF OUR NEIGHBOUR. After the fabric of society seems on the whole established and secured against external dangers, it is this fear of our neighbour which again creates new perspectives of moral valuation. Certain strong and dangerous instincts, such as the love of enterprise, foolhardiness, revengefulness, astuteness, rapacity, and love of power, which up till then had not only to be honoured from the point of view of general utility—under other names, of course, than those here given—but had to be fostered and cultivated (because they were perpetually required in the common danger against the common enemies), are now felt in their dangerousness to be doubly strong—when the outlets for them are lacking—and are gradually branded as immoral and given over to calumny. The contrary instincts and inclinations now attain to moral honour, the gregarious instinct gradually draws its conclusions. How much or how little dangerousness to the community or to equality is contained in an opinion, a condition, an emotion, a disposition, or an endowment—that is now the moral perspective, here again fear is the mother of morals. It is by the loftiest and strongest instincts, when they break out passionately and carry the individual far above and beyond the average, and the low level of the gregarious conscience,

that the self-reliance of the community is destroyed, its belief in itself, its backbone, as it were, breaks, consequently these very instincts will be most branded and defamed. The lofty independent spirituality, the will to stand alone, and even the cogent reason, are felt to be dangers, everything that elevates the individual above the herd, and is a source of fear to the neighbour, is henceforth called EVIL, the tolerant, unassuming, self-adapting, self-equalizing disposition, the MEDIOCRITY of desires, attains to moral distinction and honour. Finally, under very peaceful circumstances, there is always less opportunity and necessity for training the feelings to severity and rigour, and now every form of severity, even in justice, begins to disturb the conscience, a lofty and rigorous nobleness and self-responsibility almost offends, and awakens distrust, "the lamb," and still more "the sheep," wins respect. There is a point of diseased mellowness and effeminacy in the history of society, at which society itself takes the part of him who injures it, the part of the CRIMINAL, and does so, in fact, seriously and honestly. To punish, appears to it to be somehow unfair—it is certain that the idea of "punishment" and "the obligation to punish" are then painful and alarming to people. "Is it not sufficient if the criminal be rendered HARMLESS? Why should we still punish? Punishment itself is terrible!"—with these questions gregarious morality, the morality of fear, draws its ultimate conclusion. If one could at all do away with danger, the cause of fear, one would have done away with this morality at the same time, it would no longer be necessary, it WOULD NOT CONSIDER ITSELF any longer necessary!—Whoever examines the conscience of the present-day European, will always elicit the same imperative from its thousand moral folds and hidden recesses, the imperative of the timidity of the herd "we wish that some time or other there may be NOTHING MORE TO FEAR!" Some time or other—the will and the way THERETO is nowadays called "progress" all over Europe.

202. Let us at once say again what we have already said a hundred times, for people's ears nowadays are unwilling to hear such truths—OUR truths. We know well enough how offensive it sounds when any one plainly, and without metaphor, counts man among the animals, but it will be accounted to us almost a CRIME, that it is precisely in respect to men of "modern ideas" that we have constantly applied the terms "herd," "herd-instincts," and such like expressions. What avail is it? We cannot do otherwise, for it is precisely here that our new

insight is. We have found that in all the principal moral judgments, Europe has become unanimous, including likewise the countries where European influence prevails in Europe people evidently KNOW what Socrates thought he did not know, and what the famous serpent of old once promised to teach—they "know" today what is good and evil. It must then sound hard and be distasteful to the ear, when we always insist that that which here thinks it knows, that which here glorifies itself with praise and blame, and calls itself good, is the instinct of the herding human animal, the instinct which has come and is ever coming more and more to the front, to preponderance and supremacy over other instincts, according to the increasing physiological approximation and resemblance of which it is the symptom. MORALITY IN EUROPE AT PRESENT IS HERDING-ANIMAL MORALITY, and therefore, as we understand the matter, only one kind of human morality, beside which, before which, and after which many other moralities, and above all HIGHER moralities, are or should be possible. Against such a "possibility," against such a "should be," however, this morality defends itself with all its strength, it says obstinately and inexorably "I am morality itself and nothing else is morality!" Indeed, with the help of a religion which has humoured and flattered the sublimest desires of the herding-animal, things have reached such a point that we always find a more visible expression of this morality even in political and social arrangements: the DEMOCRATIC movement is the inheritance of the Christian movement. That its TEMPO, however, is much too slow and sleepy for the more impatient ones, for those who are sick and distracted by the herding-instinct, is indicated by the increasingly furious howling, and always less disguised teeth-gnashing of the anarchist dogs, who are now roving through the highways of European culture. Apparently in opposition to the peacefully industrious democrats and Revolution-ideologues, and still more so to the awkward philosophasters and fraternity-visionaries who call themselves Socialists and want a "free society," those are really at one with them all in their thorough and instinctive hostility to every form of society other than that of the AUTONOMOUS herd (to the extent even of repudiating the notions "master" and "servant"—ni dieu ni maitre, says a socialist formula); at one in their tenacious opposition to every special claim, every special right and privilege (this means ultimately opposition to EVERY right, for when all are equal, no one needs "rights" any longer); at one in their distrust of punitive justice (as though it were a violation of the weak, unfair to the NECESSARY consequences of all former society); but equally at one in their religion of sympathy, in their compassion for all that feels, lives, and suffers (down to the very animals, up even to "God"—the extravagance of "sympathy for God" belongs to a democratic age); altogether at one in the cry and impatience of their sympathy, in their deadly hatred of suffering generally, in their almost feminine incapacity for witnessing it or ALLOWING it; at one in their involuntary beglooming and heart-softening, under the spell of which Europe seems to be threatened with a new Buddhism; at one in their belief in the morality of MUTUAL sympathy, as though it were morality in itself, the climax, the ATTAINED climax of mankind, the sole hope of the future, the consolation of the present, the great discharge from all the obligations of the past; altogether at one in their belief in the community as the DELIVERER, in the herd, and therefore in "themselves."

203. We, who hold a different belief—we, who regard the democratic movement, not only as a degenerating form of political organization, but as equivalent to a degenerating, a waning type of man, as involving his mediocrising and depreciation: where have WE to fix our hopes? In NEW PHILOSOPHERS—there is no other alternative: in minds strong and original enough to initiate opposite estimates of value, to transvalue and invert "eternal valuations"; in forerunners, in men of the future, who in the present shall fix the constraints and fasten the knots which will compel millenniums to take NEW paths. To teach man the future of humanity as his WILL, as depending on human will, and to make preparation for vast hazardous enterprises and collective attempts in rearing and educating, in order thereby to put an end to the frightful rule of folly and chance which has hitherto gone by the name of "history" (the folly of the "greatest number" is only its last form)—for that purpose a new type of philosopher and commander will some time or other be needed, at the very idea of which everything that has existed in the way of occult, terrible, and benevolent beings might look pale and dwarfed. The image of such leaders hovers before OUR eyes:—is it lawful for me to say it aloud, ye free spirits? The conditions which one would partly have to create and partly utilize for their genesis; the presumptive methods and tests by virtue of which a soul should grow up to such an elevation and power as to feel a CONSTRAINT to these tasks; a transvaluation of values, under the new pressure and hammer of which a conscience should be steeled and a heart transformed into brass, so as to bear the weight of such responsibility; and on the other hand the necessity

for such leaders, the dreadful danger that they might be lacking, or miscarry and degenerate:—these are OUR real anxieties and glooms, ye know it well, ye free spirits! these are the heavy distant thoughts and storms which sweep across the heaven of OUR life. There are few pains so grievous as to have seen, divined, or experienced how an exceptional man has missed his way and deteriorated; but he who has the rare eye for the universal danger of "man" himself DETERIORATING, he who like us has recognized the extraordinary fortuitousness which has hitherto played its game in respect to the future of mankind—a game in which neither the hand, nor even a "finger of God" has participated!—he who divines the fate that is hidden under the idiotic unwariness and blind confidence of "modern ideas," and still more under the whole of Christo-European morality—suffers from an anguish with which no other is to be compared. He sees at a glance all that could still BE MADE OUT OF MAN through a favourable accumulation and augmentation of human powers and arrangements; he knows with all the knowledge of his conviction how unexhausted man still is for the greatest possibilities, and how often in the past the type man has stood in presence of mysterious decisions and new paths:—he knows still better from his painfulest recollections on what wretched obstacles promising developments of the highest rank have hitherto usually gone to pieces, broken down, sunk, and become contemptible. The UNIVERSAL DEGENERACY OF MANKIND to the level of the "man of the future"—as idealized by the socialistic fools and shallow-pates—this degeneracy and dwarfing of man to an absolutely gregarious animal (or as they call it, to a man of "free society"), this brutalizing of man into a pigmy with equal rights and claims, is undoubtedly POSSIBLE! He who has thought out this possibility to its ultimate conclusion knows ANOTHER loathing unknown to the rest of mankind—and perhaps also a new MISSION!

CHAPTER VI. WE SCHOLARS

204. At the risk that moralizing may also reveal itself here as that which it has always been—namely, resolutely MONTRER SES PLAIES, according to Balzac—I would venture to protest against an improper and injurious alteration of rank, which quite unnoticed, and as if with the best conscience, threatens nowadays to establish itself in the relations of science and philosophy. I mean to say that one must have the right out of one's own EXPERIENCE—experience, as it seems to me, always implies unfortunate experience?—to treat of such an important question of rank, so as not to speak of colour like the blind, or AGAINST science like women and artists ("Ah! this dreadful science!" sigh their instinct and their shame, "it always FINDS THINGS OUT!"). The declaration of independence of the scientific man, his emancipation from philosophy, is one of the subtler after-effects of democratic organization and disorganization: the self-glorification and self-conceitedness of the learned man is now everywhere in full bloom, and in its best springtime—which does not mean to imply that in this case self-praise smells sweet. Here also the instinct of the populace cries, "Freedom from all masters!" and after science has, with the happiest results, resisted theology, whose "hand-maid" it had been too long, it now proposes in its wantonness and indiscretion to lay down laws for philosophy, and in its turn to play the "master"—what am I saying! to play the PHILOSOPHER on its own account. My memory—the memory of a scientific man, if you please!—teems with the naivetes of insolence which I have heard about philosophy and philosophers from young naturalists and old physicians (not to mention the most cultured and most conceited of all learned men, the philologists and schoolmasters, who are both the one and the other by profession). On one occasion it was the specialist and the Jack Horner who instinctively stood on the defensive against all synthetic tasks and capabilities; at another time it was the industrious worker who had got a scent of OTIUM and refined luxuriousness in the internal economy of the philosopher, and felt himself aggrieved and belittled thereby. On another occasion it was the colour-blindness of the utilitarian, who sees nothing in philosophy but a series of REFUTED systems, and an extravagant expenditure which "does nobody any good". At another time the fear of disguised mysticism and of the boundary-adjustment of knowledge became conspicuous,

at another time the disregard of individual philosophers, which had involuntarily extended to disregard of philosophy generally. In fine, I found most frequently, behind the proud disdain of philosophy in young scholars, the evil after-effect of some particular philosopher, to whom on the whole obedience had been foresworn, without, however, the spell of his scornful estimates of other philosophers having been got rid of—the result being a general ill-will to all philosophy. (Such seems to me, for instance, the after-effect of Schopenhauer on the most modern Germany: by his unintelligent rage against Hegel, he has succeeded in severing the whole of the last generation of Germans from its connection with German culture, which culture, all things considered, has been an elevation and a divining refinement of the HISTORICAL SENSE, but precisely at this point Schopenhauer himself was poor, irreceptive, and un-German to the extent of ingeniousness.) On the whole, speaking generally, it may just have been the humanness, all-too-humanness of the modern philosophers themselves, in short, their contemptibleness, which has injured most radically the reverence for philosophy and opened the doors to the instinct of the populace. Let it but be acknowledged to what an extent our modern world diverges from the whole style of the world of Heraclitus, Plato, Empedocles, and whatever else all the royal and magnificent anchorites of the spirit were called, and with what justice an honest man of science MAY feel himself of a better family and origin, in view of such representatives of philosophy, who, owing to the fashion of the present day, are just as much aloft as they are down below—in Germany, for instance, the two lions of Berlin, the anarchist Eugen Duhring and the amalgamist Eduard von Hartmann. It is especially the sight of those hotch-potch philosophers, who call themselves "realists," or "positivists," which is calculated to implant a dangerous distrust in the soul of a young and ambitious scholar those philosophers, at the best, are themselves but scholars and specialists, that is very evident! All of them are persons who have been vanquished and BROUGHT BACK AGAIN under the dominion of science, who at one time or another claimed more from themselves, without having a right to the "more" and its responsibility—and who now, creditably, rancorously, and vindictively, represent in word and deed, DISBELIEF in the master-task and supremacy of philosophy After all, how could it be otherwise? Science flourishes nowadays and has the good conscience clearly visible on its countenance, while that to which the entire modern philosophy has gradually sunk, the remnant of philosophy of the present day, excites distrust and displeasure, if not scorn and pity Philosophy reduced to a "theory of knowledge," no more in fact than a diffident science of epochs and doctrine of forbearance a philosophy that never even gets beyond the threshold, and rigorously DENIES itself the right to enter—that is philosophy in its last throes, an end, an agony, something that awakens pity. How could such a philosophy—RULE!

205. The dangers that beset the evolution of the philosopher are, in fact, so manifold nowadays, that one might doubt whether this fruit could still come to maturity. The extent and towering structure of the sciences have increased enormously, and therewith also the probability that the philosopher will grow tired even as a learner, or will attach himself somewhere and "specialize" so that he will no longer attain to his elevation, that is to say, to his superspection, his circumspection, and his DESPECTION. Or he gets aloft too late, when the best of his maturity and strength is past, or when he is impaired, coarsened, and deteriorated, so that his view, his general estimate of things, is no longer of much importance. It is perhaps just the refinement of his intellectual conscience that makes him hesitate and linger on the way, he dreads the temptation to become a dilettante, a millepede, a milleantenna, he knows too well that as a discerner, one who has lost his self-respect no longer commands, no longer LEADS, unless he should aspire to become a great play-actor, a philosophical Cagliostro and spiritual rat-catcher—in short, a misleader. This is in the last instance a question of taste, if it has not really been a question of conscience. To double once more the philosopher's difficulties, there is also the fact that he demands from himself a verdict, a Yea or Nay, not concerning science, but concerning life and the worth of life—he learns unwillingly to believe that it is his right and even his duty to obtain this verdict, and he has to seek his way to the right and the belief only through the most extensive (perhaps disturbing and destroying) experiences, often hesitating, doubting, and dumbfounded. In fact, the philosopher has long been mistaken and confused by the multitude, either with the scientific man and ideal scholar, or with the religiously elevated, desensualized, desecularized visionary and God-intoxicated man; and even yet when one hears anybody praised, because he lives "wisely," or "as a philosopher," it hardly means anything more than "prudently and apart." Wisdom: that seems to the populace to be a kind of flight, a means and artifice for withdrawing successfully from a bad game; but the GENUINE philosopher—does it not seem so to US,

my friends?—lives "unphilosophically" and "unwisely," above all, IMPRUDENTLY, and feels the obligation and burden of a hundred attempts and temptations of life—he risks HIMSELF constantly, he plays THIS bad game.

206. In relation to the genius, that is to say, a being who either ENGENDERS or PRODUCES—both words understood in their fullest sense—the man of learning, the scientific average man, has always something of the old maid about him; for, like her, he is not conversant with the two principal functions of man. To both, of course, to the scholar and to the old maid, one concedes respectability, as if by way of indemnification—in these cases one emphasizes the respectability—and yet, in the compulsion of this concession, one has the same admixture of vexation. Let us examine more closely: what is the scientific man? Firstly, a commonplace type of man, with commonplace virtues: that is to say, a non-ruling, non-authoritative, and non-self-sufficient type of man; he possesses industry, patient adaptableness to rank and file, equability and moderation in capacity and requirement; he has the instinct for people like himself, and for that which they require—for instance: the portion of independence and green meadow without which there is no rest from labour, the claim to honour and consideration (which first and foremost presupposes recognition and recognisability), the sunshine of a good name, the perpetual ratification of his value and usefulness, with which the inward DISTRUST which lies at the bottom of the heart of all dependent men and gregarious animals, has again and again to be overcome. The learned man, as is appropriate, has also maladies and faults of an ignoble kind: he is full of petty envy, and has a lynx-eye for the weak points in those natures to whose elevations he cannot attain. He is confiding, yet only as one who lets himself go, but does not FLOW; and precisely before the man of the great current he stands all the colder and more reserved—his eye is then like a smooth and irresponsive lake, which is no longer moved by rapture or sympathy. The worst and most dangerous thing of which a scholar is capable results from the instinct of mediocrity of his type, from the Jesuitism of mediocrity, which labours instinctively for the destruction of the exceptional man, and endeavours to break—or still better, to relax—every bent bow To relax, of course, with consideration, and naturally with an indulgent hand—to RELAX with confiding sympathy that is the real art of Jesuitism, which has always understood how to

introduce itself as the religion of sympathy.

207. However gratefully one may welcome the OBJECTIVE spirit—and who has not been sick to death of all subjectivity and its confounded IPSISIMOSITY!—in the end, however, one must learn caution even with regard to one's gratitude, and put a stop to the exaggeration with which the unselfing and depersonalizing of the spirit has recently been celebrated, as if it were the goal in itself, as if it were salvation and glorification—as is especially accustomed to happen in the pessimist school, which has also in its turn good reasons for paying the highest honours to "disinterested knowledge" The objective man, who no longer curses and scolds like the pessimist, the IDEAL man of learning in whom the scientific instinct blossoms forth fully after a thousand complete and partial failures, is assuredly one of the most costly instruments that exist, but his place is in the hand of one who is more powerful He is only an instrument, we may say, he is a MIRROR—he is no "purpose in himself" The objective man is in truth a mirror accustomed to prostration before everything that wants to be known, with such desires only as knowing or "reflecting" implies—he waits until something comes, and then expands himself sensitively, so that even the light footsteps and gliding-past of spiritual beings may not be lost on his surface and film Whatever "personality" he still possesses seems to him accidental, arbitrary, or still oftener, disturbing, so much has he come to regard himself as the passage and reflection of outside forms and events He calls up the recollection of "himself" with an effort, and not infrequently wrongly, he readily confounds himself with other persons, he makes mistakes with regard to his own needs, and here only is he unrefined and negligent Perhaps he is troubled about the health, or the pettiness and confined atmosphere of wife and friend, or the lack of companions and society—indeed, he sets himself to reflect on his suffering, but in vain! His thoughts already rove away to the MORE GENERAL case, and tomorrow he knows as little as he knew yesterday how to help himself He does not now take himself seriously and devote time to himself he is serene, NOT from lack of trouble, but from lack of capacity for grasping and dealing with HIS trouble The habitual complaisance with respect to all objects and experiences, the radiant and impartial hospitality with which he receives everything that comes his way, his habit of inconsiderate good-nature, of dangerous indifference as to Yea and Nay: alas! there

are enough of cases in which he has to atone for these virtues of his!—and as man generally, he becomes far too easily the CAPUT MORTUUM of such virtues. Should one wish love or hatred from him—I mean love and hatred as God, woman, and animal understand them—he will do what he can, and furnish what he can. But one must not be surprised if it should not be much—if he should show himself just at this point to be false, fragile, questionable, and deteriorated. His love is constrained, his hatred is artificial, and rather UN TOUR DE FORCE, a slight ostentation and exaggeration. He is only genuine so far as he can be objective; only in his serene totality is he still "nature" and "natural." His mirroring and eternally self-polishing soul no longer knows how to affirm, no longer how to deny; he does not command; neither does he destroy. "JE NE MEPRISE PRESQUE RIEN"—he says, with Leibniz: let us not overlook nor undervalue the PRESQUE! Neither is he a model man; he does not go in advance of any one, nor after, either; he places himself generally too far off to have any reason for espousing the cause of either good or evil. If he has been so long confounded with the PHILOSOPHER, with the Caesarian trainer and dictator of civilization, he has had far too much honour, and what is more essential in him has been overlooked—he is an instrument, something of a slave, though certainly the sublimest sort of slave, but nothing in himself—PRESQUE RIEN! The objective man is an instrument, a costly, easily injured, easily tarnished measuring instrument and mirroring apparatus, which is to be taken care of and respected; but he is no goal, not outgoing nor upgoing, no complementary man in whom the REST of existence justifies itself, no termination—and still less a commencement, an engendering, or primary cause, nothing hardy, powerful, self-centred, that wants to be master; but rather only a soft, inflated, delicate, movable potter's-form, that must wait for some kind of content and frame to "shape" itself thereto—for the most part a man without frame and content, a "selfless" man. Consequently, also, nothing for women, IN PARENTHESI.

208. When a philosopher nowadays makes known that he is not a skeptic—I hope that has been gathered from the foregoing description of the objective spirit?—people all hear it impatiently; they regard him on that account with some apprehension, they would like to ask so many, many questions... indeed among timid hearers, of whom there are now so many, he is henceforth said to be

dangerous. With his repudiation of skepticism, it seems to them as if they heard some evil-threatening sound in the distance, as if a new kind of explosive were being tried somewhere, a dynamite of the spirit, perhaps a newly discovered Russian NIHILINE, a pessimism BONAE VOLUNTATIS, that not only denies, means denial, but—dreadful thought! PRACTISES denial. Against this kind of "goodwill"—a will to the veritable, actual negation of life—there is, as is generally acknowledged nowadays, no better soporific and sedative than skepticism, the mild, pleasing, lulling poppy of skepticism; and Hamlet himself is now prescribed by the doctors of the day as an antidote to the "spirit," and its underground noises. "Are not our ears already full of bad sounds?" say the skeptics, as lovers of repose, and almost as a kind of safety police; "this subterranean Nay is terrible! Be still, ye pessimistic moles!" The skeptic, in effect, that delicate creature, is far too easily frightened; his conscience is schooled so as to start at every Nay, and even at that sharp, decided Yea, and feels something like a bite thereby. Yea! and Nay!—they seem to him opposed to morality; he loves, on the contrary, to make a festival to his virtue by a noble aloofness, while perhaps he says with Montaigne: "What do I know?" Or with Socrates: "I know that I know nothing." Or: "Here I do not trust myself, no door is open to me." Or: "Even if the door were open, why should I enter immediately?" Or: "What is the use of any hasty hypotheses? It might quite well be in good taste to make no hypotheses at all. Are you absolutely obliged to straighten at once what is crooked? to stuff every hole with some kind of oakum? Is there not time enough for that? Has not the time leisure? Oh, ye demons, can ye not at all WAIT? The uncertain also has its charms, the Sphinx, too, is a Circe, and Circe, too, was a philosopher."—Thus does a skeptic console himself; and in truth he needs some consolation. For skepticism is the most spiritual expression of a certain many-sided physiological temperament, which in ordinary language is called nervous debility and sickliness; it arises whenever races or classes which have been long separated, decisively and suddenly blend with one another. In the new generation, which has inherited as it were different standards and valuations in its blood, everything is disquiet, derangement, doubt, and tentativeness; the best powers operate restrictively, the very virtues prevent each other growing and becoming strong, equilibrium, ballast, and perpendicular stability are lacking in body and soul. That, however, which is most diseased and degenerated in such nondescripts is the WILL; they are no longer familiar with independence of decision, or the courageous feeling of pleasure in willing—they are doubtful of the "freedom of the will" even in their dreams Our present-day Europe, the scene of a senseless, precipitate attempt at a radical blending of classes, and CONSEQUENTLY of races, is therefore skeptical in all its heights and depths, sometimes exhibiting the mobile skepticism which springs impatiently and wantonly from branch to branch, sometimes with gloomy aspect, like a cloud over-charged with interrogative signs—and often sick unto death of its will! Paralysis of will, where do we not find this cripple sitting nowadays! And yet how bedecked oftentimes' How seductively ornamented! There are the finest gala dresses and disguises for this disease, and that, for instance, most of what places itself nowadays in the show-cases as "objectiveness," "the scientific spirit," "L'ART POUR L'ART," and "pure voluntary knowledge," is only decked-out skepticism and paralysis of will—I am ready to answer for this diagnosis of the European disease—The disease of the will is diffused unequally over Europe, it is worst and most varied where civilization has longest prevailed, it decreases according as "the barbarian" still—or again—asserts his claims under the loose drapery of Western culture It is therefore in the France of today, as can be readily disclosed and comprehended, that the will is most infirm, and France, which has always had a masterly aptitude for converting even the portentous crises of its spirit into something charming and seductive, now manifests emphatically its intellectual ascendancy over Europe, by being the school and exhibition of all the charms of skepticism The power to will and to persist, moreover, in a resolution, is already somewhat stronger in Germany, and again in the North of Germany it is stronger than in Central Germany, it is considerably stronger in England, Spain, and Corsica, associated with phlegm in the former and with hard skulls in the latter—not to mention Italy, which is too young yet to know what it wants, and must first show whether it can exercise will, but it is strongest and most surprising of all in that immense middle empire where Europe as it were flows back to Asia—namely, in Russia There the power to will has been long stored up and accumulated, there the will—uncertain whether to be negative or affirmative—waits threateningly to be discharged (to borrow their pet phrase from our physicists) Perhaps not only Indian wars and complications in Asia would be necessary to free Europe from its greatest danger, but also internal subversion, the shattering of the empire into small states, and above all the introduction of parliamentary imbecility, together with the obligation of every one to read his newspaper at breakfast I do not say this as one who desires it, in my heart I should rather prefer the contrary—I mean such an increase in the threatening attitude of Russia, that Europe would have to make up its mind to become equally threatening—namely, TO ACQUIRE ONE WILL, by means of a new caste to rule over the Continent, a persistent, dreadful will of its own, that can set its aims thousands of years ahead; so that the long spun-out comedy of its petty-statism, and its dynastic as well as its democratic many-willed-ness, might finally be brought to a close. The time for petty politics is past; the next century will bring the struggle for the dominion of the world—the COMPULSION to great politics.

209. As to how far the new warlike age on which we Europeans have evidently entered may perhaps favour the growth of another and stronger kind of skepticism, I should like to express myself preliminarily merely by a parable, which the lovers of German history will already understand. That unscrupulous enthusiast for big, handsome grenadiers (who, as King of Prussia, brought into being a military and skeptical genius—and therewith, in reality, the new and now triumphantly emerged type of German), the problematic, crazy father of Frederick the Great, had on one point the very knack and lucky grasp of the genius: he knew what was then lacking in Germany, the want of which was a hundred times more alarming and serious than any lack of culture and social form—his ill-will to the young Frederick resulted from the anxiety of a profound instinct. MEN WERE LACKING; and he suspected, to his bitterest regret, that his own son was not man enough. There, however, he deceived himself; but who would not have deceived himself in his place? He saw his son lapsed to atheism, to the ESPRIT, to the pleasant frivolity of clever Frenchmen—he saw in the background the great bloodsucker, the spider skepticism; he suspected the incurable wretchedness of a heart no longer hard enough either for evil or good, and of a broken will that no longer commands, is no longer ABLE to command. Meanwhile, however, there grew up in his son that new kind of harder and more dangerous skepticism—who knows TO WHAT EXTENT it was encouraged just by his father's hatred and the icy melancholy of a will condemned to solitude?—the skepticism of daring manliness, which is closely related to the genius for war and conquest, and made its first entrance into Germany in the person of the great Frederick. This skepticism despises and nevertheless grasps; it undermines and takes possession; it does not believe, but it does not thereby lose itself; it gives the spirit a dangerous liberty, but it keeps

strict guard over the heart. It is the GERMAN form of skepticism, which, as a continued Fredericianism, risen to the highest spirituality, has kept Europe for a considerable time under the dominion of the German spirit and its critical and historical distrust Owing to the insuperably strong and tough masculine character of the great German philologists and historical critics (who, rightly estimated, were also all of them artists of destruction and dissolution), a NEW conception of the German spirit gradually established itself—in spite of all Romanticism in music and philosophy—in which the leaning towards masculine skepticism was decidedly prominent whether, for instance, as fearlessness of gaze, as courage and sternness of the dissecting hand, or as resolute will to dangerous voyages of discovery, to spiritualized North Pole expeditions under barren and dangerous skies. There may be good grounds for it when warm-blooded and superficial humanitarians cross themselves before this spirit, CET ESPRIT FATALISTE, IRONIQUE, MEPHISTOPHELIQUE, as Michelet calls it, not without a shudder. But if one would realize how characteristic is this fear of the "man" in the German spirit which awakened Europe out of its "dogmatic slumber," let us call to mind the former conception which had to be overcome by this new one—and that it is not so very long ago that a masculinized woman could dare, with unbridled presumption, to recommend the Germans to the interest of Europe as gentle, good-hearted, weak-willed, and poetical fools. Finally, let us only understand profoundly enough Napoleon's astonishment when he saw Goethe it reveals what had been regarded for centuries as the "German spirit" "VOILA UN HOMME!"—that was as much as to say "But this is a MAN! And I only expected to see a German!"

210. Supposing, then, that in the picture of the philosophers of the future, some trait suggests the question whether they must not perhaps be skeptics in the last-mentioned sense, something in them would only be designated thereby—and not they themselves. With equal right they might call themselves critics, and assuredly they will be men of experiments. By the name with which I ventured to baptize them, I have already expressly emphasized their attempting and their love of attempting is this because, as critics in body and soul, they will love to make use of experiments in a new, and perhaps wider and more dangerous sense? In their passion for knowledge, will they have to go further in daring and painful attempts than the sensitive

and pampered taste of a democratic century can approve of?—There is no doubt these coming ones will be least able to dispense with the serious and not unscrupulous qualities which distinguish the critic from the skeptic I mean the certainty as to standards of worth, the conscious employment of a unity of method, the wary courage, the standing-alone, and the capacity for self-responsibility, indeed, they will avow among themselves a DELIGHT in denial and dissection, and a certain considerate cruelty, which knows how to handle the knife surely and deftly, even when the heart bleeds They will be STERNER (and perhaps not always towards themselves only) than humane people may desire, they will not deal with the "truth" in order that it may "please" them, or "elevate" and "inspire" them—they will rather have little faith in "TRUTH" bringing with it such revels for the feelings. They will smile, those rigorous spirits, when any one says in their presence "That thought elevates me, why should it not be true?" or "That work enchants me, why should it not be beautiful?" or "That artist enlarges me, why should he not be great?" Perhaps they will not only have a smile, but a genuine disgust for all that is thus rapturous, idealistic, feminine, and hermaphroditic, and if any one could look into their inmost hearts, he would not easily find therein the intention to reconcile "Christian sentiments" with "antique taste," or even with "modern parliamentarism" (the kind of reconciliation necessarily found even among philosophers in our very uncertain and consequently very conciliatory century). Critical discipline, and every habit that conduces to purity and rigour in intellectual matters, will not only be demanded from themselves by these philosophers of the future, they may even make a display thereof as their special adornment—nevertheless they will not want to be called critics on that account. It will seem to them no small indignity to philosophy to have it decreed, as is so welcome nowadays, that "philosophy itself is criticism and critical science—and nothing else whatever!" Though this estimate of philosophy may enjoy the approval of all the Positivists of France and Germany (and possibly it even flattered the heart and taste of KANT: let us call to mind the titles of his principal works), our new philosophers will say, notwithstanding, that critics are instruments of the philosopher, and just on that account, as instruments, they are far from being philosophers themselves! Even the great Chinaman of Konigsberg was only a great critic.

211. I insist upon it that people finally cease confounding philosophical

workers, and in general scientific men, with philosophers—that precisely here one should strictly give "each his own," and not give those far too much, these far too little. It may be necessary for the education of the real philosopher that he himself should have once stood upon all those steps upon which his servants, the scientific workers of philosophy, remain standing, and MUST remain standing he himself must perhaps have been critic, and dogmatist, and historian, and besides, poet, and collector, and traveler, and riddle-reader, and moralist, and seer, and "free spirit," and almost everything, in order to traverse the whole range of human values and estimations, and that he may BE ABLE with a variety of eyes and consciences to look from a height to any distance, from a depth up to any height, from a nook into any expanse. But all these are only preliminary conditions for his task; this task itself demands something else—it requires him TO CREATE VALUES. The philosophical workers, after the excellent pattern of Kant and Hegel, have to fix and formalize some great existing body of valuations—that is to say, former DETERMINATIONS OF VALUE, creations of value, which have become prevalent, and are for a time called "truths"—whether in the domain of the LOGICAL, the POLITICAL (moral), or the ARTISTIC. It is for these investigators to make whatever has happened and been esteemed hitherto, conspicuous, conceivable, intelligible, and manageable, to shorten everything long, even "time" itself, and to SUBJUGATE the entire past: an immense and wonderful task, in the carrying out of which all refined pride, all tenacious will, can surely find satisfaction. THE REAL PHILOSOPHERS, HOWEVER, ARE COMMANDERS AND LAW-GIVERS; they say: "Thus SHALL it be!" They determine first the Whither and the Why of mankind, and thereby set aside the previous labour of all philosophical workers, and all subjugators of the past—they grasp at the future with a creative hand, and whatever is and was, becomes for them thereby a means, an instrument, and a hammer. Their "knowing" is CREATING, their creating is a law-giving, their will to truth is—WILL TO POWER.— Are there at present such philosophers? Have there ever been such philosophers? MUST there not be such philosophers some day? ...

212. It is always more obvious to me that the philosopher, as a man INDISPENSABLE for the morrow and the day after the morrow, has ever found himself, and HAS BEEN OBLIGED to find himself, in contradiction to the day in which he lives; his enemy has always

been the ideal of his day. Hitherto all those extraordinary furtherers of humanity whom one calls philosophers—who rarely regarded themselves as lovers of wisdom, but rather as disagreeable fools and dangerous interrogators—have found their mission, their hard, involuntary, imperative mission (in the end, however, the greatness of their mission), in being the bad conscience of their age. In putting the vivisector's knife to the breast of the very VIRTUES OF THEIR AGE, they have betrayed their own secret; it has been for the sake of a NEW greatness of man, a new untrodden path to his aggrandizement. They have always disclosed how much hypocrisy, indolence, self-indulgence, and self-neglect, how much falsehood was concealed under the most venerated types of contemporary morality, how much virtue was OUTLIVED, they have always said "We must remove hence to where YOU are least at home" In the face of a world of "modern ideas," which would like to confine every one in a corner, in a "specialty," a philosopher, if there could be philosophers nowadays, would be compelled to place the greatness of man, the conception of "greatness," precisely in his comprehensiveness and multifariousness, in his all-roundness, he would even determine worth and rank according to the amount and variety of that which a man could bear and take upon himself, according to the EXTENT to which a man could stretch his responsibility Nowadays the taste and virtue of the age weaken and attenuate the will, nothing is so adapted to the spirit of the age as weakness of will consequently, in the ideal of the philosopher, strength of will, sternness, and capacity for prolonged resolution, must specially be included in the conception of "greatness", with as good a right as the opposite doctrine, with its ideal of a silly, renouncing, humble, selfless humanity, was suited to an opposite age—such as the sixteenth century, which suffered from its accumulated energy of will, and from the wildest torrents and floods of selfishness In the time of Socrates, among men only of worn-out instincts, old conservative Athenians who let themselves go—"for the sake of happiness," as they said, for the sake of pleasure, as their conduct indicated—and who had continually on their lips the old pompous words to which they had long forfeited the right by the life they led, IRONY was perhaps necessary for greatness of soul, the wicked Socratic assurance of the old physician and plebeian, who cut ruthlessly into his own flesh, as into the flesh and heart of the "noble," with a look that said plainly enough "Do not dissemble before me! here—we are equal!" At present, on the contrary, when throughout Europe the herding-animal alone attains to honours, and dispenses honours, when "equality of right" can too readily be transformed into equality in wrong—I mean to say into general war against everything rare, strange, and privileged, against the higher man, the higher soul, the higher duty, the higher responsibility, the creative plenipotence and lordliness—at present it belongs to the conception of "greatness" to be noble, to wish to be apart, to be capable of being different, to stand alone, to have to live by personal initiative, and the philosopher will betray something of his own ideal when he asserts "He shall be the greatest who can be the most solitary, the most concealed, the most divergent, the man beyond good and evil, the master of his virtues, and of super-abundance of will; precisely this shall be called GREATNESS: as diversified as can be entire, as ample as can be full." And to ask once more the question: Is greatness POSSIBLE—nowadays?

213. It is difficult to learn what a philosopher is, because it cannot be taught: one must "know" it by experience—or one should have the pride NOT to know it. The fact that at present people all talk of things of which they CANNOT have any experience, is true more especially and unfortunately as concerns the philosopher and philosophical matters:—the very few know them, are permitted to know them, and all popular ideas about them are false. Thus, for instance, the truly philosophical combination of a bold, exuberant spirituality which runs at presto pace, and a dialectic rigour and necessity which makes no false step, is unknown to most thinkers and scholars from their own experience, and therefore, should any one speak of it in their presence, it is incredible to them. They conceive of every necessity as troublesome, as a painful compulsory obedience and state of constraint; thinking itself is regarded by them as something slow and hesitating, almost as a trouble, and often enough as "worthy of the SWEAT of the noble"—but not at all as something easy and divine, closely related to dancing and exuberance! "To think" and to take a matter "seriously," "arduously"—that is one and the same thing to them; such only has been their "experience."—Artists have here perhaps a finer intuition; they who know only too well that precisely when they no longer do anything "arbitrarily," and everything of necessity, their feeling of freedom, of subtlety, of power, of creatively fixing, disposing, and shaping, reaches its climax—in short, that necessity and "freedom of will" are then the same thing with them. There is, in fine, a gradation of rank in psychical states, to which the gradation of rank in the problems corresponds; and the highest

problems repel ruthlessly every one who ventures too near them, without being predestined for their solution by the loftiness and power of his spirituality. Of what use is it for nimble, everyday intellects, or clumsy, honest mechanics and empiricists to press, in their plebeian ambition, close to such problems, and as it were into this "holy of holies"—as so often happens nowadays! But coarse feet must never tread upon such carpets: this is provided for in the primary law of things; the doors remain closed to those intruders, though they may dash and break their heads thereon. People have always to be born to a high station, or, more definitely, they have to be BRED for it: a person has only a right to philosophy—taking the word in its higher significance—in virtue of his descent; the ancestors, the "blood," decide here also. Many generations must have prepared the way for the coming of the philosopher; each of his virtues must have been separately acquired, nurtured, transmitted, and embodied; not only the bold, easy, delicate course and current of his thoughts, but above all the readiness for great responsibilities, the majesty of ruling glance and contemning look, the feeling of separation from the multitude with their duties and virtues, the kindly patronage and defense of whatever is misunderstood and calumniated, be it God or devil, the delight and practice of supreme justice, the art of commanding, the amplitude of will, the lingering eye which rarely admires, rarely looks up, rarely loves....

CHAPTER VII. OUR VIRTUES

214. OUR Virtues?—It is probable that we, too, have still our virtues, although naturally they are not those sincere and massive virtues on account of which we hold our grandfathers in esteem and also at a little distance from us. We Europeans of the day after tomorrow, we firstlings of the twentieth century—with all our dangerous curiosity, our multifariousness and art of disguising, our mellow and seemingly sweetened cruelty in sense and spirit—we shall presumably, IF we must have virtues, have those only which have come to agreement with our most secret and heartfelt inclinations, with our most ardent requirements: well, then, let us look for them in our labyrinths!—where, as we know, so many things lose themselves, so many things get quite lost! And is there anything finer than to SEARCH for one's own virtues? Is it not almost to BELIEVE in one's own virtues? But this "believing in one's own virtues"—is it not practically the same as what was formerly called one's "good conscience," that long, respectable pigtail of an idea, which our grandfathers used to hang behind their heads, and often enough also behind their understandings? It seems, therefore, that however little we may imagine ourselves to be old-fashioned and grandfatherly respectable in other respects, in one thing we are nevertheless the worthy grandchildren of our grandfathers, we last Europeans with good consciences: we also still wear their pigtail.—Ah! if you only knew how soon, so very soon—it will be different!

215. As in the stellar firmament there are sometimes two suns which determine the path of one planet, and in certain cases suns of different colours shine around a single planet, now with red light, now with green, and then simultaneously illumine and flood it with motley colours: so we modern men, owing to the complicated mechanism of our "firmament," are determined by DIFFERENT moralities; our actions shine alternately in different colours, and are seldom unequivocal—and there are often cases, also, in which our actions are MOTLEY-COLOURED.

216. To love one's enemies? I think that has been well learnt: it takes place thousands of times at present on a large and small scale; indeed, at times the higher and sublimer thing takes place:—we learn to DESPISE when we love, and precisely when we love best; all of it, however, unconsciously, without noise, without ostentation, with the shame and secrecy of goodness, which forbids the utterance of the pompous word and the formula of virtue. Morality as attitude—is opposed to our taste nowadays. This is ALSO an advance, as it was an advance in our fathers that religion as an attitude finally became opposed to their taste, including the enmity and Voltairean bitterness against religion (and all that formerly belonged to freethinker-pantomime). It is the music in our conscience, the dance in our spirit, to which Puritan litanies, moral sermons, and goody-goodness won't chime.

217. Let us be careful in dealing with those who attach great importance to being credited with moral tact and subtlety in moral discernment! They never forgive us if they have once made a mistake BEFORE us (or even with REGARD to us)—they inevitably become our instinctive calumniators and detractors, even when they still remain our "friends."—Blessed are the forgetful: for they "get the better" even of their blunders.

218. The psychologists of France—and where else are there still psychologists nowadays?—have never yet exhausted their bitter and manifold enjoyment of the betise bourgeoise, just as though... in short, they betray something thereby. Flaubert, for instance, the honest citizen of Rouen, neither saw, heard, nor tasted anything else in the end; it was his mode of self-torment and refined cruelty. As this is growing wearisome, I would now recommend for a change something else for a pleasure—namely, the unconscious astuteness with which good, fat, honest mediocrity always behaves towards loftier spirits and the tasks they have to perform, the subtle, barbed, Jesuitical astuteness, which is a thousand times subtler than the taste and understanding of the middle-class in its best moments—subtler even than the understanding of its victims:—a repeated proof that "instinct" is the most intelligent of all kinds of intelligence which have hitherto been discovered. In short, you psychologists, study the philosophy of the "rule" in its struggle with the "exception":

there you have a spectacle fit for Gods and godlike malignity! Or, in plainer words, practise vivisection on "good people," on the "homo bonae voluntatis," ON YOURSELVES!

219. The practice of judging and condemning morally, is the favourite revenge of the intellectually shallow on those who are less so, it is also a kind of indemnity for their being badly endowed by nature, and finally, it is an opportunity for acquiring spirit and BECOMING subtle—malice spiritualises. They are glad in their inmost heart that there is a standard according to which those who are over-endowed with intellectual goods and privileges, are equal to them, they contend for the "equality of all before God," and almost NEED the belief in God for this purpose. It is among them that the most powerful antagonists of atheism are found. If any one were to say to them "A lofty spirituality is beyond all comparison with the honesty and respectability of a merely moral man"—it would make them furious, I shall take care not to say so. I would rather flatter them with my theory that lofty spirituality itself exists only as the ultimate product of moral qualities, that it is a synthesis of all qualities attributed to the "merely moral" man, after they have been acquired singly through long training and practice, perhaps during a whole series of generations, that lofty spirituality is precisely the spiritualising of justice, and the beneficent severity which knows that it is authorized to maintain GRADATIONS OF RANK in the world, even among things—and not only among men.

220. Now that the praise of the "disinterested person" is so popular one must—probably not without some danger—get an idea of WHAT people actually take an interest in, and what are the things generally which fundamentally and profoundly concern ordinary men—including the cultured, even the learned, and perhaps philosophers also, if appearances do not deceive. The fact thereby becomes obvious that the greater part of what interests and charms higher natures, and more refined and fastidious tastes, seems absolutely "uninteresting" to the average man—if, notwithstanding, he perceive devotion to these interests, he calls it desinteresse, and wonders how it is possible to act "disinterestedly." There have been philosophers who could give this popular astonishment a seductive and mystical, other-worldly expression (perhaps because they did not know the higher nature by

experience?), instead of stating the naked and candidly reasonable truth that "disinterested" action is very interesting and "interested" action, provided that... "And love?"—What! Even an action for love's sake shall be "unegoistic"? But you fools—! "And the praise of the self-sacrificer?"—But whoever has really offered sacrifice knows that he wanted and obtained something for it—perhaps something from himself for something from himself; that he relinquished here in order to have more there, perhaps in general to be more, or even feel himself "more." But this is a realm of questions and answers in which a more fastidious spirit does not like to stay: for here truth has to stifle her yawns so much when she is obliged to answer. And after all, truth is a woman; one must not use force with her.

221. "It sometimes happens," said a moralistic pedant and trifle-retailer, "that I honour and respect an unselfish man: not, however, because he is unselfish, but because I think he has a right to be useful to another man at his own expense. In short, the question is always who HE is, and who THE OTHER is. For instance, in a person created and destined for command, self-denial and modest retirement, instead of being virtues, would be the waste of virtues: so it seems to me. Every system of unegoistic morality which takes itself unconditionally and appeals to every one, not only sins against good taste, but is also an incentive to sins of omission, an ADDITIONAL seduction under the mask of philanthropy—and precisely a seduction and injury to the higher, rarer, and more privileged types of men. Moral systems must be compelled first of all to bow before the GRADATIONS OF RANK; their presumption must be driven home to their conscience—until they thoroughly understand at last that it is IMMORAL to say that 'what is right for one is proper for another.'"—So said my moralistic pedant and bonhomme. Did he perhaps deserve to be laughed at when he thus exhorted systems of morals to practise morality? But one should not be too much in the right if one wishes to have the laughers on ONE'S OWN side; a grain of wrong pertains even to good taste.

222. Wherever sympathy (fellow-suffering) is preached nowadays—and, if I gather rightly, no other religion is any longer preached—let the psychologist have his ears open through all the vanity, through all the noise which is natural to these preachers (as to all preachers), he

will hear a hoarse, groaning, genuine note of SELF-CONTEMPT. It belongs to the overshadowing and uglifying of Europe, which has been on the increase for a century (the first symptoms of which are already specified documentarily in a thoughtful letter of Galiani to Madame d'Epinay)—IF IT IS NOT REALLY THE CAUSE THEREOF! The man of "modern ideas," the conceited ape, is excessively dissatisfied with himself—this is perfectly certain. He suffers, and his vanity wants him only "to suffer with his fellows."

223. The hybrid European—a tolerably ugly plebeian, taken all in all—absolutely requires a costume: he needs history as a storeroom of costumes. To be sure, he notices that none of the costumes fit him properly—he changes and changes. Let us look at the nineteenth century with respect to these hasty preferences and changes in its masquerades of style, and also with respect to its moments of desperation on account of "nothing suiting" us. It is in vain to get ourselves up as romantic, or classical, or Christian, or Florentine, or barocco, or "national," in moribus et artibus: it does not "clothe us"! But the "spirit," especially the "historical spirit," profits even by this desperation: once and again a new sample of the past or of the foreign is tested, put on, taken off, packed up, and above all studied—we are the first studious age in puncto of "costumes," I mean as concerns morals, articles of belief, artistic tastes, and religions; we are prepared as no other age has ever been for a carnival in the grand style, for the most spiritual festival—laughter and arrogance, for the transcendental height of supreme folly and Aristophanic ridicule of the world. Perhaps we are still discovering the domain of our invention just here, the domain where even we can still be original, probably as parodists of the world's history and as God's Merry-Andrews,—perhaps, though nothing else of the present have a future, our laughter itself may have a future!

224. The historical sense (or the capacity for divining quickly the order of rank of the valuations according to which a people, a community, or an individual has lived, the "divining instinct" for the relationships of these valuations, for the relation of the authority of the valuations to the authority of the operating forces),—this historical sense, which we Europeans claim as our specialty, has come to us in the train of the enchanting and mad semi-barbarity into which Europe has been

plunged by the democratic mingling of classes and races—it is only the nineteenth century that has recognized this faculty as its sixth sense. Owing to this mingling, the past of every form and mode of life, and of cultures which were formerly closely contiguous and superimposed on one another, flows forth into us "modern souls"; our instincts now run back in all directions, we ourselves are a kind of chaos: in the end, as we have said, the spirit perceives its advantage therein. By means of our semi-barbarity in body and in desire, we have secret access everywhere, such as a noble age never had; we have access above all to the labyrinth of imperfect civilizations, and to every form of semi-barbarity that has at any time existed on earth; and in so far as the most considerable part of human civilization hitherto has just been semi-barbarity, the "historical sense" implies almost the sense and instinct for everything, the taste and tongue for everything: whereby it immediately proves itself to be an IGNOBLE sense. For instance, we enjoy Homer once more: it is perhaps our happiest acquisition that we know how to appreciate Homer, whom men of distinguished culture (as the French of the seventeenth century, like Saint-Evremond, who reproached him for his ESPRIT VASTE, and even Voltaire, the last echo of the century) cannot and could not so easily appropriate—whom they scarcely permitted themselves to enjoy. The very decided Yea and Nay of their palate, their promptly ready disgust, their hesitating reluctance with regard to everything strange, their horror of the bad taste even of lively curiosity, and in general the averseness of every distinguished and self-sufficing culture to avow a new desire, a dissatisfaction with its own condition, or an admiration of what is strange: all this determines and disposes them unfavourably even towards the best things of the world which are not their property or could not become their prey—and no faculty is more unintelligible to such men than just this historical sense, with its truckling, plebeian curiosity. The case is not different with Shakespeare, that marvelous Spanish-Moorish-Saxon synthesis of taste, over whom an ancient Athenian of the circle of AEschylus would have half-killed himself with laughter or irritation: but we—accept precisely this wild motleyness, this medley of the most delicate, the most coarse, and the most artificial, with a secret confidence and cordiality; we enjoy it as a refinement of art reserved expressly for us, and allow ourselves to be as little disturbed by the repulsive fumes and the proximity of the English populace in which Shakespeare's art and taste lives, as perhaps on the Chiaja of Naples, where, with all our senses awake, we go our way, enchanted and voluntarily, in spite of the drain-odour of the lower quarters of the town. That as men of the "historical sense" we have our virtues, is not to be disputed:—we are unpretentious, unselfish, modest, brave, habituated to self-control and self-renunciation, very grateful, very patient, very complaisant—but with all this we are perhaps not very "tasteful." Let us finally confess it, that what is most difficult for us men of the "historical sense" to grasp, feel, taste, and love, what finds us fundamentally prejudiced and almost hostile, is precisely the perfection and ultimate maturity in every culture and art, the essentially noble in works and men, their moment of smooth sea and halcyon self-sufficiency, the goldenness and coldness which all things show that have perfected themselves. Perhaps our great virtue of the historical sense is in necessary contrast to GOOD taste, at least to the very bad taste; and we can only evoke in ourselves imperfectly, hesitatingly, and with compulsion the small, short, and happy godsends and glorifications of human life as they shine here and there: those moments and marvelous experiences when a great power has voluntarily come to a halt before the boundless and infinite,— when a super-abundance of refined delight has been enjoyed by a sudden checking and petrifying, by standing firmly and planting oneself fixedly on still trembling ground. PROPORTIONATENESS is strange to us, let us confess it to ourselves; our itching is really the itching for the infinite, the immeasurable. Like the rider on his forward panting horse, we let the reins fall before the infinite, we modern men, we semi-barbarians—and are only in OUR highest bliss when we—ARE IN MOST DANGER.

225. Whether it be hedonism, pessimism, utilitarianism, or eudaemonism, all those modes of thinking which measure the worth of things according to PLEASURE and PAIN, that is, according to accompanying circumstances and secondary considerations, are plausible modes of thought and naivetes, which every one conscious of CREATIVE powers and an artist's conscience will look down upon with scorn, though not without sympathy. Sympathy for you!—to be sure, that is not sympathy as you understand it: it is not sympathy for social "distress," for "society" with its sick and misfortuned, for the hereditarily vicious and defective who lie on the ground around us; still less is it sympathy for the grumbling, vexed, revolutionary slave-classes who strive after power—they call it "freedom." OUR sympathy is a loftier and further-sighted sympathy:—we see how MAN dwarfs himself, how YOU dwarf him! and there are moments

when we view YOUR sympathy with an indescribable anguish, when we resist it,—when we regard your seriousness as more dangerous than any kind of levity. You want, if possible—and there is not a more foolish "if possible"—TO DO AWAY WITH SUFFERING; and we?—it really seems that WE would rather have it increased and made worse than it has ever been! Well-being, as you understand it—is certainly not a goal; it seems to us an END; a condition which at once renders man ludicrous and contemptible—and makes his destruction DESIRABLE! The discipline of suffering, of GREAT suffering—know ye not that it is only THIS discipline that has produced all the elevations of humanity hitherto? The tension of soul in misfortune which communicates to it its energy, its shuddering in view of rack and ruin, its inventiveness and bravery in undergoing, enduring, interpreting, and exploiting misfortune, and whatever depth, mystery, disguise, spirit, artifice, or greatness has been bestowed upon the soul—has it not been bestowed through suffering, through the discipline of great suffering? In man CREATURE and CREATOR are united: in man there is not only matter, shred, excess, clay, mire, folly, chaos; but there is also the creator, the sculptor, the hardness of the hammer, the divinity of the spectator, and the seventh day—do ye understand this contrast? And that YOUR sympathy for the "creature in man" applies to that which has to be fashioned, bruised, forged, stretched, roasted, annealed, refined—to that which must necessarily SUFFER, and IS MEANT to suffer? And our sympathy—do ye not understand what our REVERSE sympathy applies to, when it resists your sympathy as the worst of all pampering and enervation?—So it is sympathy AGAINST sympathy!—But to repeat it once more, there are higher problems than the problems of pleasure and pain and sympathy; and all systems of philosophy which deal only with these are naivetes.

226. WE IMMORALISTS.—This world with which WE are concerned, in which we have to fear and love, this almost invisible, inaudible world of delicate command and delicate obedience, a world of "almost" in every respect, captious, insidious, sharp, and tender—yes, it is well protected from clumsy spectators and familiar curiosity! We are woven into a strong net and garment of duties, and CANNOT disengage ourselves—precisely here, we are "men of duty," even we! Occasionally, it is true, we dance in our "chains" and betwixt our "swords"; it is none the less true that more often we gnash our teeth

under the circumstances, and are impatient at the secret hardship of our lot. But do what we will, fools and appearances say of us: "These are men WITHOUT duty,"—we have always fools and appearances against us!

227. Honesty, granting that it is the virtue of which we cannot rid ourselves, we free spirits—well, we will labour at it with all our perversity and love, and not tire of "perfecting" ourselves in OUR virtue, which alone remains: may its glance some day overspread like a gilded, blue, mocking twilight this aging civilization with its dull gloomy seriousness! And if, nevertheless, our honesty should one day grow weary, and sigh, and stretch its limbs, and find us too hard, and would fain have it pleasanter, easier, and gentler, like an agreeable vice, let us remain HARD, we latest Stoics, and let us send to its help whatever devilry we have in us:—our disgust at the clumsy and undefined, our "NITIMUR IN VETITUM," our love of adventure, our sharpened and fastidious curiosity, our most subtle, disguised, intellectual Will to Power and universal conquest, which rambles and roves avidiously around all the realms of the future—let us go with all our "devils" to the help of our "God"! It is probable that people will misunderstand and mistake us on that account: what does it matter! They will say: "Their 'honesty'—that is their devilry, and nothing else!" What does it matter! And even if they were right—have not all Gods hitherto been such sanctified, re-baptized devils? And after all, what do we know of ourselves? And what the spirit that leads us wants TO BE CALLED? (It is a question of names.) And how many spirits we harbour? Our honesty, we free spirits—let us be careful lest it become our vanity, our ornament and ostentation, our limitation, our stupidity! Every virtue inclines to stupidity, every stupidity to virtue; "stupid to the point of sanctity," they say in Russia,—let us be careful lest out of pure honesty we eventually become saints and bores! Is not life a hundred times too short for us—to bore ourselves? One would have to believe in eternal life in order to...

228. I hope to be forgiven for discovering that all moral philosophy hitherto has been tedious and has belonged to the soporific appliances—and that "virtue," in my opinion, has been MORE injured by the TEDIOUSNESS of its advocates than by anything else; at the same time, however, I would not wish to overlook their general

usefulness. It is desirable that as few people as possible should reflect upon morals, and consequently it is very desirable that morals should not some day become interesting! But let us not be afraid! Things still remain today as they have always been: I see no one in Europe who has (or DISCLOSES) an idea of the fact that philosophizing concerning morals might be conducted in a dangerous, captious, and ensnaring manner—that CALAMITY might be involved therein. Observe, for example, the indefatigable, inevitable English utilitarians: how ponderously and respectably they stalk on, stalk along (a Homeric metaphor expresses it better) in the footsteps of Bentham, just as he had already stalked in the footsteps of the respectable Helvetius! (no, he was not a dangerous man, Helvetius, CE SENATEUR POCOCURANTE, to use an expression of Galiani). No new thought, nothing of the nature of a finer turning or better expression of an old thought, not even a proper history of what has been previously thought on the subject: an IMPOSSIBLE literature, taking it all in all, unless one knows how to leaven it with some mischief. In effect, the old English vice called CANT, which is MORAL TARTUFFISM, has insinuated itself also into these moralists (whom one must certainly read with an eye to their motives if one MUST read them), concealed this time under the new form of the scientific spirit; moreover, there is not absent from them a secret struggle with the pangs of conscience, from which a race of former Puritans must naturally suffer, in all their scientific tinkering with morals. (Is not a moralist the opposite of a Puritan? That is to say, as a thinker who regards morality as questionable, as worthy of interrogation, in short, as a problem? Is moralizing not-immoral?) In the end, they all want English morality to be recognized as authoritative, inasmuch as mankind, or the "general utility," or "the happiness of the greatest number,"—no! the happiness of ENGLAND, will be best served thereby. They would like, by all means, to convince themselves that the striving after English happiness, I mean after COMFORT and FASHION (and in the highest instance, a seat in Parliament), is at the same time the true path of virtue; in fact, that in so far as there has been virtue in the world hitherto, it has just consisted in such striving. Not one of those ponderous, conscience-stricken herding-animals (who undertake to advocate the cause of egoism as conducive to the general welfare) wants to have any knowledge or inkling of the facts that the "general welfare" is no ideal, no goal, no notion that can be at all grasped, but is only a nostrum,—that what is fair to one MAY NOT at all be fair to another, that the requirement of one morality for all is really a detriment to higher men, in short, that there is a DISTINCTION OF

RANK between man and man, and consequently between morality and morality. They are an unassuming and fundamentally mediocre species of men, these utilitarian Englishmen, and, as already remarked, in so far as they are tedious, one cannot think highly enough of their utility. One ought even to ENCOURAGE them, as has been partially attempted in the following rhymes:—

Hail, ye worthies, barrow-wheeling,

"Longer—better," aye revealing,

Stiffer aye in head and knee;

Unenraptured, never jesting,

Mediocre everlasting,

SANS GENIE ET SANS ESPRIT!

229. In these later ages, which may be proud of their humanity, there still remains so much fear, so much SUPERSTITION of the fear, of the "cruel wild beast," the mastering of which constitutes the very pride of these humaner ages—that even obvious truths, as if by the agreement of centuries, have long remained unuttered, because they have the appearance of helping the finally slain wild beast back to life again. I perhaps risk something when I allow such a truth to escape; let others capture it again and give it so much "milk of pious sentiment" [FOOTNOTE: An expression from Schiller's William Tell, Act IV, Scene 3.] to drink, that it will lie down quiet and forgotten, in its old corner.—One ought to learn anew about cruelty, and open one's eyes; one ought at last to learn impatience, in order that such immodest gross errors—as, for instance, have been fostered by ancient and modern philosophers with regard to tragedy—may no longer wander about virtuously and boldly. Almost everything that we call "higher culture" is based upon the spiritualising and intensifying of CRUELTY—this is my thesis; the "wild beast" has not been slain at all, it lives, it flourishes, it has only been—transfigured. That which constitutes the painful delight of tragedy is cruelty; that which

operates agreeably in so-called tragic sympathy, and at the basis even of everything sublime, up to the highest and most delicate thrills of metaphysics, obtains its sweetness solely from the intermingled ingredient of cruelty. What the Roman enjoys in the arena, the Christian in the ecstasies of the cross, the Spaniard at the sight of the faggot and stake, or of the bull-fight, the present-day Japanese who presses his way to the tragedy, the workman of the Parisian suburbs who has a homesickness for bloody revolutions, the Wagnerienne who, with unhinged will, "undergoes" the performance of "Tristan and Isolde"—what all these enjoy, and strive with mysterious ardour to drink in, is the philtre of the great Circe "cruelty." Here, to be sure, we must put aside entirely the blundering psychology of former times, which could only teach with regard to cruelty that it originated at the sight of the suffering of OTHERS: there is an abundant, super-abundant enjoyment even in one's own suffering, in causing one's own suffering—and wherever man has allowed himself to be persuaded to self-denial in the RELIGIOUS sense, or to self-mutilation, as among the Phoenicians and ascetics, or in general, to desensualisation, decarnalisation, and contrition, to Puritanical repentance-spasms, to vivisection of conscience and to Pascal-like SACRIFIZIA DELL' INTELLETO, he is secretly allured and impelled forwards by his cruelty, by the dangerous thrill of cruelty TOWARDS HIMSELF.— Finally, let us consider that even the seeker of knowledge operates as an artist and glorifier of cruelty, in that he compels his spirit to perceive AGAINST its own inclination, and often enough against the wishes of his heart:—he forces it to say Nay, where he would like to affirm, love, and adore; indeed, every instance of taking a thing profoundly and fundamentally, is a violation, an intentional injuring of the fundamental will of the spirit, which instinctively aims at appearance and superficiality,—even in every desire for knowledge there is a drop of cruelty.

230. Perhaps what I have said here about a "fundamental will of the spirit" may not be understood without further details; I may be allowed a word of explanation.—That imperious something which is popularly called "the spirit," wishes to be master internally and externally, and to feel itself master; it has the will of a multiplicity for a simplicity, a binding, taming, imperious, and essentially ruling will. Its requirements and capacities here, are the same as those assigned by physiologists to everything that lives, grows, and

multiplies. The power of the spirit to appropriate foreign elements reveals itself in a strong tendency to assimilate the new to the old, to simplify the manifold, to overlook or repudiate the absolutely contradictory; just as it arbitrarily re-underlines, makes prominent, and falsifies for itself certain traits and lines in the foreign elements, in every portion of the "outside world." Its object thereby is the incorporation of new "experiences," the assortment of new things in the old arrangements—in short, growth; or more properly, the FEELING of growth, the feeling of increased power—is its object. This same will has at its service an apparently opposed impulse of the spirit, a suddenly adopted preference of ignorance, of arbitrary shutting out, a closing of windows, an inner denial of this or that, a prohibition to approach, a sort of defensive attitude against much that is knowable, a contentment with obscurity, with the shutting-in horizon, an acceptance and approval of ignorance: as that which is all necessary according to the degree of its appropriating power, its "digestive power," to speak figuratively (and in fact "the spirit" resembles a stomach more than anything else). Here also belong an occasional propensity of the spirit to let itself be deceived (perhaps with a waggish suspicion that it is NOT so and so, but is only allowed to pass as such), a delight in uncertainty and ambiguity, an exulting enjoyment of arbitrary, out-of-the-way narrowness and mystery, of the too-near, of the foreground, of the magnified, the diminished, the misshapen, the beautified—an enjoyment of the arbitrariness of all these manifestations of power. Finally, in this connection, there is the not unscrupulous readiness of the spirit to deceive other spirits and dissemble before them—the constant pressing and straining of a creating, shaping, changeable power: the spirit enjoys therein its craftiness and its variety of disguises, it enjoys also its feeling of security therein—it is precisely by its Protean arts that it is best protected and concealed!—COUNTER TO this propensity for appearance, for simplification, for a disguise, for a cloak, in short, for an outside—for every outside is a cloak—there operates the sublime tendency of the man of knowledge, which takes, and INSISTS on taking things profoundly, variously, and thoroughly; as a kind of cruelty of the intellectual conscience and taste, which every courageous thinker will acknowledge in himself, provided, as it ought to be, that he has sharpened and hardened his eye sufficiently long for introspection, and is accustomed to severe discipline and even severe words. He will say: "There is something cruel in the tendency of my spirit": let the virtuous and amiable try to convince him that it is not so! In fact, it would sound nicer, if, instead of our cruelty, perhaps our "extravagant honesty" were talked about, whispered about, and glorified—we free, VERY free spirits—and some day perhaps SUCH will actually be our—posthumous glory! Meanwhile—for there is plenty of time until then—we should be least inclined to deck ourselves out in such florid and fringed moral verbiage; our whole former work has just made us sick of this taste and its sprightly exuberance. They are beautiful, glistening, jingling, festive words: honesty, love of truth, love of wisdom, sacrifice for knowledge, heroism of the truthful—there is something in them that makes one's heart swell with pride. But we anchorites and marmots have long ago persuaded ourselves in all the secrecy of an anchorite's conscience, that this worthy parade of verbiage also belongs to the old false adornment, frippery, and gold-dust of unconscious human vanity, and that even under such flattering colour and repainting, the terrible original text HOMO NATURA must again be recognized. In effect, to translate man back again into nature; to master the many vain and visionary interpretations and subordinate meanings which have hitherto been scratched and daubed over the eternal original text, HOMO NATURA; to bring it about that man shall henceforth stand before man as he now, hardened by the discipline of science, stands before the OTHER forms of nature, with fearless Oedipus-eyes, and stopped Ulysses-ears, deaf to the enticements of old metaphysical bird-catchers, who have piped to him far too long: "Thou art more! thou art higher! thou hast a different origin!"—this may be a strange and foolish task, but that it is a TASK, who can deny! Why did we choose it, this foolish task? Or, to put the question differently: "Why knowledge at all?" Every one will ask us about this. And thus pressed, we, who have asked ourselves the question a hundred times, have not found and cannot find any better answer....

231. Learning alters us, it does what all nourishment does that does not merely "conserve"—as the physiologist knows. But at the bottom of our souls, quite "down below," there is certainly something unteachable, a granite of spiritual fate, of predetermined decision and answer to predetermined, chosen questions. In each cardinal problem there speaks an unchangeable "I am this"; a thinker cannot learn anew about man and woman, for instance, but can only learn fully—he can only follow to the end what is "fixed" about them in himself. Occasionally we find certain solutions of problems which make strong beliefs for us; perhaps they are henceforth called

"convictions." Later on—one sees in them only footsteps to self-knowledge, guide-posts to the problem which we ourselves ARE—or more correctly to the great stupidity which we embody, our spiritual fate, the UNTEACHABLE in us, quite "down below."—In view of this liberal compliment which I have just paid myself, permission will perhaps be more readily allowed me to utter some truths about "woman as she is," provided that it is known at the outset how literally they are merely—MY truths.

232. Woman wishes to be independent, and therefore she begins to enlighten men about "woman as she is"—THIS is one of the worst developments of the general UGLIFYING of Europe. For what must these clumsy attempts of feminine scientificality and self-exposure bring to light! Woman has so much cause for shame; in woman there is so much pedantry, superficiality, schoolmasterliness, petty presumption, unbridledness, and indiscretion concealed—study only woman's behaviour towards children!—which has really been best restrained and dominated hitherto by the FEAR of man. Alas, if ever the "eternally tedious in woman"—she has plenty of it!—is allowed to venture forth! if she begins radically and on principle to unlearn her wisdom and art-of charming, of playing, of frightening away sorrow, of alleviating and taking easily; if she forgets her delicate aptitude for agreeable desires! Female voices are already raised, which, by Saint Aristophanes! make one afraid:—with medical explicitness it is stated in a threatening manner what woman first and last REQUIRES from man. Is it not in the very worst taste that woman thus sets herself up to be scientific? Enlightenment hitherto has fortunately been men's affair, men's gift—we remained therewith "among ourselves"; and in the end, in view of all that women write about "woman," we may well have considerable doubt as to whether woman really DESIRES enlightenment about herself—and CAN desire it. If woman does not thereby seek a new ORNAMENT for herself—I believe ornamentation belongs to the eternally feminine?—why, then, she wishes to make herself feared: perhaps she thereby wishes to get the mastery. But she does not want truth—what does woman care for truth? From the very first, nothing is more foreign, more repugnant, or more hostile to woman than truth—her great art is falsehood, her chief concern is appearance and beauty. Let us confess it, we men: we honour and love this very art and this very instinct in woman: we who have the hard task, and for our recreation gladly

seek the company of beings under whose hands, glances, and delicate follies, our seriousness, our gravity, and profundity appear almost like follies to us. Finally, I ask the question: Did a woman herself ever acknowledge profundity in a woman's mind, or justice in a woman's heart? And is it not true that on the whole "woman" has hitherto been most despised by woman herself, and not at all by us?—We men desire that woman should not continue to compromise herself by enlightening us; just as it was man's care and the consideration for woman, when the church decreed: mulier taceat in ecclesia. It was to the benefit of woman when Napoleon gave the too eloquent Madame de Stael to understand: mulier taceat in politicis!—and in my opinion, he is a true friend of woman who calls out to women today: mulier taceat de mulierel.

233. It betrays corruption of the instincts—apart from the fact that it betrays bad taste—when a woman refers to Madame Roland, or Madame de Stael, or Monsieur George Sand, as though something were proved thereby in favour of "woman as she is." Among men, these are the three comical women as they are—nothing more!—and just the best involuntary counter-arguments against feminine emancipation and autonomy.

234. Stupidity in the kitchen; woman as cook; the terrible thoughtlessness with which the feeding of the family and the master of the house is managed! Woman does not understand what food means, and she insists on being cook! If woman had been a thinking creature, she should certainly, as cook for thousands of years, have discovered the most important physiological facts, and should likewise have got possession of the healing art! Through bad female cooks—through the entire lack of reason in the kitchen—the development of mankind has been longest retarded and most interfered with: even today matters are very little better. A word to High School girls.

235. There are turns and casts of fancy, there are sentences, little handfuls of words, in which a whole culture, a whole society suddenly crystallises itself. Among these is the incidental remark of Madame de Lambert to her son: "MON AMI, NE VOUS PERMETTEZ JAMAIS

QUE DES FOLIES, QUI VOUS FERONT GRAND PLAISIR"—the motherliest and wisest remark, by the way, that was ever addressed to a son.

236. I have no doubt that every noble woman will oppose what Dante and Goethe believed about woman—the former when he sang, "ELLA GUARDAVA SUSO, ED IO IN LEI," and the latter when he interpreted it, "the eternally feminine draws us ALOFT"; for THIS is just what she believes of the eternally masculine.

237. SEVEN APOPHTHEGMS FOR WOMEN

How the longest ennui flees, When a man comes to our knees!

Age, alas! and science staid, Furnish even weak virtue aid.

Sombre garb and silence meet: Dress for every dame—discreet.

Whom I thank when in my bliss? God!—and my good tailoress!

Young, a flower-decked cavern home; Old, a dragon thence doth roam.

Noble title, leg that's fine, Man as well: Oh, were HE mine!

Speech in brief and sense in mass—Slippery for the jenny-ass!

237A. Woman has hitherto been treated by men like birds, which, losing their way, have come down among them from an elevation: as something delicate, fragile, wild, strange, sweet, and animating—but as something also which must be cooped up to prevent it flying away.

238. To be mistaken in the fundamental problem of "man and woman," to deny here the profoundest antagonism and the necessity for an eternally hostile tension, to dream here perhaps of equal rights, equal training, equal claims and obligations: that is a TYPICAL sign of shallow-mindedness; and a thinker who has proved himself shallow at this dangerous spot—shallow in instinct!—may generally be regarded as suspicious, nay more, as betrayed, as discovered; he

will probably prove too "short" for all fundamental questions of life, future as well as present, and will be unable to descend into ANY of the depths. On the other hand, a man who has depth of spirit as well as of desires, and has also the depth of benevolence which is capable of severity and harshness, and easily confounded with them, can only think of woman as ORIENTALS do: he must conceive of her as a possession, as confinable property, as a being predestined for service and accomplishing her mission therein—he must take his stand in this matter upon the immense rationality of Asia, upon the superiority of the instinct of Asia, as the Greeks did formerly; those best heirs and scholars of Asia—who, as is well known, with their INCREASING culture and amplitude of power, from Homer to the time of Pericles, became gradually STRICTER towards woman, in short, more Oriental. HOW necessary, HOW logical, even HOW humanely desirable this was, let us consider for ourselves!

239. The weaker sex has in no previous age been treated with so much respect by men as at present—this belongs to the tendency and fundamental taste of democracy, in the same way as disrespectfulness to old age—what wonder is it that abuse should be immediately made of this respect? They want more, they learn to make claims, the tribute of respect is at last felt to be well-nigh galling; rivalry for rights, indeed actual strife itself, would be preferred: in a word, woman is losing modesty. And let us immediately add that she is also losing taste. She is unlearning to FEAR man: but the woman who "unlearns to fear" sacrifices her most womanly instincts. That woman should venture forward when the fear-inspiring quality in man—or more definitely, the MAN in man—is no longer either desired or fully developed, is reasonable enough and also intelligible enough; what is more difficult to understand is that precisely thereby—woman deteriorates. This is what is happening nowadays: let us not deceive ourselves about it! Wherever the industrial spirit has triumphed over the military and aristocratic spirit, woman strives for the economic and legal independence of a clerk: "woman as clerkess" is inscribed on the portal of the modern society which is in course of formation. While she thus appropriates new rights, aspires to be "master," and inscribes "progress" of woman on her flags and banners, the very opposite realises itself with terrible obviousness: WOMAN RETROGRADES. Since the French Revolution the influence of woman in Europe has DECLINED in proportion as she has increased

her rights and claims; and the "emancipation of woman," insofar as it is desired and demanded by women themselves (and not only by masculine shallow-pates), thus proves to be a remarkable symptom of the increased weakening and deadening of the most womanly instincts. There is STUPIDITY in this movement, an almost masculine stupidity, of which a well-reared woman—who is always a sensible woman—might be heartily ashamed. To lose the intuition as to the ground upon which she can most surely achieve victory; to neglect exercise in the use of her proper weapons; to let-herself-go before man, perhaps even "to the book," where formerly she kept herself in control and in refined, artful humility; to neutralize with her virtuous audacity man's faith in a VEILED, fundamentally different ideal in woman, something eternally, necessarily feminine; to emphatically and loquaciously dissuade man from the idea that woman must be preserved, cared for, protected, and indulged, like some delicate, strangely wild, and often pleasant domestic animal; the clumsy and indignant collection of everything of the nature of servitude and bondage which the position of woman in the hitherto existing order of society has entailed and still entails (as though slavery were a counter-argument, and not rather a condition of every higher culture, of every elevation of culture):—what does all this betoken, if not a disintegration of womanly instincts, a defeminising? Certainly, there are enough of idiotic friends and corrupters of woman among the learned asses of the masculine sex, who advise woman to defeminize herself in this manner, and to imitate all the stupidities from which "man" in Europe, European "manliness," suffers,—who would like to lower woman to "general culture," indeed even to newspaper reading and meddling with politics. Here and there they wish even to make women into free spirits and literary workers: as though a woman without piety would not be something perfectly obnoxious or ludicrous to a profound and godless man;—almost everywhere her nerves are being ruined by the most morbid and dangerous kind of music (our latest German music), and she is daily being made more hysterical and more incapable of fulfilling her first and last function, that of bearing robust children. They wish to "cultivate" her in general still more, and intend, as they say, to make the "weaker sex" STRONG by culture: as if history did not teach in the most emphatic manner that the "cultivating" of mankind and his weakening—that is to say, the weakening, dissipating, and languishing of his FORCE OF WILL—have always kept pace with one another, and that the most powerful and influential women in the world (and lastly, the mother of Napoleon) had just to thank their force of will—and not their schoolmasters—for their power and ascendancy over men. That which inspires respect in woman, and often enough fear also, is her NATURE, which is more "natural" than that of man, her genuine, carnivora-like, cunning flexibility, her tiger-claws beneath the glove, her NAIVETE in egoism, her untrainableness and innate wildness, the incomprehensibleness, extent, and deviation of her desires and virtues. That which, in spite of fear, excites one's sympathy for the dangerous and beautiful cat, "woman," is that she seems more afflicted, more vulnerable, more necessitous of love, and more condemned to disillusionment than any other creature. Fear and sympathy it is with these feelings that man has hitherto stood in the presence of woman, always with one foot already in tragedy, which rends while it delights—What? And all that is now to be at an end? And the DISENCHANTMENT of woman is in progress? The tediousness of woman is slowly evolving? Oh Europe! Europe! We know the horned animal which was always most attractive to thee, from which danger is ever again threatening thee! Thy old fable might once more become "history"—an immense stupidity might once again overmaster thee and carry thee away! And no God concealed beneath it—no! only an "idea," a "modern idea"!

CHAPTER VIII. PEOPLES AND COUNTRIES

240. I HEARD, once again for the first time, Richard Wagner's overture to the Mastersinger: it is a piece of magnificent, gorgeous, heavy, latter-day art, which has the pride to presuppose two centuries of music as still living, in order that it may be understood:—it is an honour to Germans that such a pride did not miscalculate! What flavours and forces, what seasons and climes do we not find mingled in it! It impresses us at one time as ancient, at another time as foreign, bitter, and too modern, it is as arbitrary as it is pompously traditional, it is not infrequently roguish, still oftener rough and coarse—it has fire and courage, and at the same time the loose, dun-coloured skin of fruits which ripen too late. It flows broad and full: and suddenly there is a moment of inexplicable hesitation, like a gap that opens between cause and effect, an oppression that makes us dream, almost a nightmare; but already it broadens and widens anew, the old stream of delight—the most manifold delight,—of old and new happiness; including ESPECIALLY the joy of the artist in himself, which he refuses to conceal, his astonished, happy cognizance of his mastery of the expedients here employed, the new, newly acquired, imperfectly tested expedients of art which he apparently betrays to us. All in all, however, no beauty, no South, nothing of the delicate southern clearness of the sky, nothing of grace, no dance, hardly a will to logic; a certain clumsiness even, which is also emphasized, as though the artist wished to say to us: "It is part of my intention"; a cumbersome drapery, something arbitrarily barbaric and ceremonious, a flirring of learned and venerable conceits and witticisms; something German in the best and worst sense of the word, something in the German style, manifold, formless, and inexhaustible; a certain German potency and super-plenitude of soul, which is not afraid to hide itself under the RAFFINEMENTS of decadence—which, perhaps, feels itself most at ease there; a real, genuine token of the German soul, which is at the same time young and aged, too ripe and yet still too rich in futurity. This kind of music expresses best what I think of the Germans: they belong to the day before yesterday and the day after tomorrow—THEY HAVE AS YET NO TODAY.

241. We "good Europeans," we also have hours when we allow

ourselves a warm-hearted patriotism, a plunge and relapse into old loves and narrow views—I have just given an example of it—hours of national excitement, of patriotic anguish, and all other sorts of old-fashioned floods of sentiment. Duller spirits may perhaps only get done with what confines its operations in us to hours and plays itself out in hours—in a considerable time: some in half a year, others in half a lifetime, according to the speed and strength with which they digest and "change their material." Indeed, I could think of sluggish, hesitating races, which even in our rapidly moving Europe, would require half a century ere they could surmount such atavistic attacks of patriotism and soil-attachment, and return once more to reason, that is to say, to "good Europeanism." And while digressing on this possibility, I happen to become an ear-witness of a conversation between two old patriots—they were evidently both hard of hearing and consequently spoke all the louder. "HE has as much, and knows as much, philosophy as a peasant or a corps-student," said the one—"he is still innocent. But what does that matter nowadays! It is the age of the masses: they lie on their belly before everything that is massive. And so also in politicis. A statesman who rears up for them a new Tower of Babel, some monstrosity of empire and power, they call 'great'—what does it matter that we more prudent and conservative ones do not meanwhile give up the old belief that it is only the great thought that gives greatness to an action or affair. Supposing a statesman were to bring his people into the position of being obliged henceforth to practise 'high politics,' for which they were by nature badly endowed and prepared, so that they would have to sacrifice their old and reliable virtues, out of love to a new and doubtful mediocrity;—supposing a statesman were to condemn his people generally to 'practise politics,' when they have hitherto had something better to do and think about, and when in the depths of their souls they have been unable to free themselves from a prudent loathing of the restlessness, emptiness, and noisy wranglings of the essentially politics-practising nations;—supposing such a statesman were to stimulate the slumbering passions and avidities of his people, were to make a stigma out of their former diffidence and delight in aloofness, an offence out of their exoticism and hidden permanency, were to depreciate their most radical proclivities, subvert their consciences, make their minds narrow, and their tastes 'national'—what! a statesman who should do all this, which his people would have to do penance for throughout their whole future, if they had a future, such a statesman would be GREAT, would he?"—"Undoubtedly!" replied the other old patriot vehemently, "otherwise he COULD NOT have done it! It was mad perhaps to wish such a thing! But perhaps everything great has been just as mad at its commencement!"—"Misuse of words!" cried his interlocutor, contradictorily—"strong! strong! Strong and mad! NOT great!"—The old men had obviously become heated as they thus shouted their "truths" in each other's faces, but I, in my happiness and apartness, considered how soon a stronger one may become master of the strong, and also that there is a compensation for the intellectual superficialising of a nation—namely, in the deepening of another.

242. Whether we call it "civilization," or "humanising," or "progress," which now distinguishes the European, whether we call it simply, without praise or blame, by the political formula the DEMOCRATIC movement in Europe—behind all the moral and political foregrounds pointed to by such formulas, an immense PHYSIOLOGICAL PROCESS goes on, which is ever extending the process of the assimilation of Europeans, their increasing detachment from the conditions under which, climatically and hereditarily, united races originate, their increasing independence of every definite milieu, that for centuries would fain inscribe itself with equal demands on soul and body,—that is to say, the slow emergence of an essentially SUPER-NATIONAL and nomadic species of man, who possesses, physiologically speaking, a maximum of the art and power of adaptation as his typical distinction. This process of the EVOLVING EUROPEAN, which can be retarded in its TEMPO by great relapses, but will perhaps just gain and grow thereby in vehemence and depth—the still-raging storm and stress of "national sentiment" pertains to it, and also the anarchism which is appearing at present—this process will probably arrive at results on which its naive propagators and panegyrists, the apostles of "modern ideas," would least care to reckon. The same new conditions under which on an average a levelling and mediocrising of man will take place—a useful, industrious, variously serviceable, and clever gregarious man—are in the highest degree suitable to give rise to exceptional men of the most dangerous and attractive qualities. For, while the capacity for adaptation, which is every day trying changing conditions, and begins a new work with every generation, almost with every decade, makes the POWERFULNESS of the type impossible; while the collective impression of such future Europeans will probably be that of numerous, talkative, weak-willed, and very handy workmen

who REQUIRE a master, a commander, as they require their daily bread; while, therefore, the democratising of Europe will tend to the production of a type prepared for SLAVERY in the most subtle sense of the term: the STRONG man will necessarily in individual and exceptional cases, become stronger and richer than he has perhaps ever been before—owing to the unprejudicedness of his schooling, owing to the immense variety of practice, art, and disguise. I meant to say that the democratising of Europe is at the same time an involuntary arrangement for the rearing of TYRANTS—taking the word in all its meanings, even in its most spiritual sense.

243. I hear with pleasure that our sun is moving rapidly towards the constellation Hercules: and I hope that the men on this earth will do like the sun. And we foremost, we good Europeans!

244. There was a time when it was customary to call Germans "deep" by way of distinction; but now that the most successful type of new Germanism is covetous of quite other honours, and perhaps misses "smartness" in all that has depth, it is almost opportune and patriotic to doubt whether we did not formerly deceive ourselves with that commendation: in short, whether German depth is not at bottom something different and worse—and something from which, thank God, we are on the point of successfully ridding ourselves. Let us try, then, to relearn with regard to German depth; the only thing necessary for the purpose is a little vivisection of the German soul.—The German soul is above all manifold, varied in its source, aggregated and super-imposed, rather than actually built: this is owing to its origin. A German who would embolden himself to assert: "Two souls, alas, dwell in my breast," would make a bad guess at the truth, or, more correctly, he would come far short of the truth about the number of souls. As a people made up of the most extraordinary mixing and mingling of races, perhaps even with a preponderance of the pre-Aryan element as the "people of the centre" in every sense of the term, the Germans are more intangible, more ample, more contradictory, more unknown, more incalculable, more surprising, and even more terrifying than other peoples are to themselves:— they escape DEFINITION, and are thereby alone the despair of the French. It IS characteristic of the Germans that the question: "What is German?" never dies out among them. Kotzebue certainly knew

his Germans well enough: "We are known," they cried jubilantly to him—but Sand also thought he knew them. Jean Paul knew what he was doing when he declared himself incensed at Fichte's lying but patriotic flatteries and exaggerations,—but it is probable that Goethe thought differently about Germans from Jean Paul, even though he acknowledged him to be right with regard to Fichte. It is a question what Goethe really thought about the Germans?—But about many things around him he never spoke explicitly, and all his life he knew how to keep an astute silence—probably he had good reason for it. It is certain that it was not the "Wars of Independence" that made him look up more joyfully, any more than it was the French Revolution,— the event on account of which he RECONSTRUCTED his "Faust," and indeed the whole problem of "man," was the appearance of Napoleon. There are words of Goethe in which he condemns with impatient severity, as from a foreign land, that which Germans take a pride in, he once defined the famous German turn of mind as "Indulgence towards its own and others' weaknesses." Was he wrong? it is characteristic of Germans that one is seldom entirely wrong about them. The German soul has passages and galleries in it, there are caves, hiding-places, and dungeons therein, its disorder has much of the charm of the mysterious, the German is well acquainted with the bypaths to chaos. And as everything loves its symbol, so the German loves the clouds and all that is obscure, evolving, crepuscular, damp, and shrouded, it seems to him that everything uncertain, undeveloped, self-displacing, and growing is "deep". The German himself does not EXIST, he is BECOMING, he is "developing himself". "Development" is therefore the essentially German discovery and hit in the great domain of philosophical formulas,—a ruling idea, which, together with German beer and German music, is labouring to Germanise all Europe. Foreigners are astonished and attracted by the riddles which the conflicting nature at the basis of the German soul propounds to them (riddles which Hegel systematised and Richard Wagner has in the end set to music). "Good-natured and spiteful"— such a juxtaposition, preposterous in the case of every other people, is unfortunately only too often justified in Germany one has only to live for a while among Swabians to know this! The clumsiness of the German scholar and his social distastefulness agree alarmingly well with his physical rope-dancing and nimble boldness, of which all the Gods have learnt to be afraid. If any one wishes to see the "German soul" demonstrated ad oculos, let him only look at German taste, at German arts and manners what boorish indifference to "taste"! How the noblest and the commonest stand there in juxtaposition! How disorderly and how rich is the whole constitution of this soul! The German DRAGS at his soul, he drags at everything he experiences. He digests his events badly; he never gets "done" with them; and German depth is often only a difficult, hesitating "digestion." And just as all chronic invalids, all dyspeptics like what is convenient, so the German loves "frankness" and "honesty"; it is so CONVENIENT to be frank and honest!—This confidingness, this complaisance, this showing-the-cards of German HONESTY, is probably the most dangerous and most successful disguise which the German is up to nowadays: it is his proper Mephistophelean art; with this he can "still achieve much"! The German lets himself go, and thereby gazes with faithful, blue, empty German eyes—and other countries immediately confound him with his dressing-gown!—I meant to say that, let "German depth" be what it will—among ourselves alone we perhaps take the liberty to laugh at it—we shall do well to continue henceforth to honour its appearance and good name, and not barter away too cheaply our old reputation as a people of depth for Prussian "smartness," and Berlin wit and sand. It is wise for a people to pose, and LET itself be regarded, as profound, clumsy, good-natured, honest, and foolish: it might even be—profound to do so! Finally, we should do honour to our name—we are not called the "TIUSCHE VOLK" (deceptive people) for nothing....

245. The "good old" time is past, it sang itself out in Mozart—how happy are WE that his ROCOCO still speaks to us, that his "good company," his tender enthusiasm, his childish delight in the Chinese and its flourishes, his courtesy of heart, his longing for the elegant, the amorous, the tripping, the tearful, and his belief in the South, can still appeal to SOMETHING LEFT in us! Ah, some time or other it will be over with it!—but who can doubt that it will be over still sooner with the intelligence and taste for Beethoven! For he was only the last echo of a break and transition in style, and NOT, like Mozart, the last echo of a great European taste which had existed for centuries. Beethoven is the intermediate event between an old mellow soul that is constantly breaking down, and a future over-young soul that is always COMING; there is spread over his music the twilight of eternal loss and eternal extravagant hope,—the same light in which Europe was bathed when it dreamed with Rousseau, when it danced round the Tree of Liberty of the Revolution, and finally almost fell down in adoration before Napoleon. But how rapidly does

THIS very sentiment now pale, how difficult nowadays is even the APPREHENSION of this sentiment, how strangely does the language of Rousseau, Schiller, Shelley, and Byron sound to our ear, in whom COLLECTIVELY the same fate of Europe was able to SPEAK, which knew how to SING in Beethoven!—Whatever German music came afterwards, belongs to Romanticism, that is to say, to a movement which, historically considered, was still shorter, more fleeting, and more superficial than that great interlude, the transition of Europe from Rousseau to Napoleon, and to the rise of democracy. Weber—but what do WE care nowadays for "Freischutz" and "Oberon"! Or Marschner's "Hans Heiling" and "Vampyre"! Or even Wagner's "Tannhauser"! That is extinct, although not yet forgotten music. This whole music of Romanticism, besides, was not noble enough, was not musical enough, to maintain its position anywhere but in the theatre and before the masses; from the beginning it was second-rate music, which was little thought of by genuine musicians. It was different with Felix Mendelssohn, that halcyon master, who, on account of his lighter, purer, happier soul, quickly acquired admiration, and was equally quickly forgotten: as the beautiful EPISODE of German music. But with regard to Robert Schumann, who took things seriously, and has been taken seriously from the first—he was the last that founded a school,—do we not now regard it as a satisfaction, a relief, a deliverance, that this very Romanticism of Schumann's has been surmounted? Schumann, fleeing into the "Saxon Switzerland" of his soul, with a half Werther-like, half Jean-Paul-like nature (assuredly not like Beethoven! assuredly not like Byron!)—his MANFRED music is a mistake and a misunderstanding to the extent of injustice; Schumann, with his taste, which was fundamentally a PETTY taste (that is to say, a dangerous propensity—doubly dangerous among Germans—for quiet lyricism and intoxication of the feelings), going constantly apart, timidly withdrawing and retiring, a noble weakling who revelled in nothing but anonymous joy and sorrow, from the beginning a sort of girl and NOLI ME TANGERE—this Schumann was already merely a GERMAN event in music, and no longer a European event, as Beethoven had been, as in a still greater degree Mozart had been; with Schumann German music was threatened with its greatest danger, that of LOSING THE VOICE FOR THE SOUL OF EUROPE and sinking into a merely national affair.

246. What a torture are books written in German to a reader who has

a THIRD ear! How indignantly he stands beside the slowly turning swamp of sounds without tune and rhythms without dance, which Germans call a "book"! And even the German who READS books! How lazily, how reluctantly, how badly he reads! How many Germans know, and consider it obligatory to know, that there is ART in every good sentence—art which must be divined, if the sentence is to be understood! If there is a misunderstanding about its TEMPO, for instance, the sentence itself is misunderstood! That one must not be doubtful about the rhythm-determining syllables, that one should feel the breaking of the too-rigid symmetry as intentional and as a charm, that one should lend a fine and patient ear to every STACCATO and every RUBATO, that one should divine the sense in the sequence of the vowels and diphthongs, and how delicately and richly they can be tinted and retinted in the order of their arrangement—who among book-reading Germans is complaisant enough to recognize such duties and requirements, and to listen to so much art and intention in language? After all, one just "has no ear for it"; and so the most marked contrasts of style are not heard, and the most delicate artistry is as it were SQUANDERED on the deaf.—These were my thoughts when I noticed how clumsily and unintuitively two masters in the art of prose-writing have been confounded: one, whose words drop down hesitatingly and coldly, as from the roof of a damp cave—he counts on their dull sound and echo; and another who manipulates his language like a flexible sword, and from his arm down into his toes feels the dangerous bliss of the quivering, over-sharp blade, which wishes to bite, hiss, and cut.

247. How little the German style has to do with harmony and with the ear, is shown by the fact that precisely our good musicians themselves write badly. The German does not read aloud, he does not read for the ear, but only with his eyes; he has put his ears away in the drawer for the time. In antiquity when a man read—which was seldom enough—he read something to himself, and in a loud voice; they were surprised when any one read silently, and sought secretly the reason of it. In a loud voice: that is to say, with all the swellings, inflections, and variations of key and changes of TEMPO, in which the ancient PUBLIC world took delight. The laws of the written style were then the same as those of the spoken style; and these laws depended partly on the surprising development and refined requirements of the ear and larynx; partly on the strength, endurance,

and power of the ancient lungs. In the ancient sense, a period is above all a physiological whole, inasmuch as it is comprised in one breath. Such periods as occur in Demosthenes and Cicero, swelling twice and sinking twice, and all in one breath, were pleasures to the men of ANTIQUITY, who knew by their own schooling how to appreciate the virtue therein, the rareness and the difficulty in the deliverance of such a period;—WE have really no right to the BIG period, we modern men, who are short of breath in every sense! Those ancients, indeed, were all of them dilettanti in speaking, consequently connoisseurs, consequently critics—they thus brought their orators to the highest pitch; in the same manner as in the last century, when all Italian ladies and gentlemen knew how to sing, the virtuosoship of song (and with it also the art of melody) reached its elevation. In Germany, however (until quite recently when a kind of platform eloquence began shyly and awkwardly enough to flutter its young wings), there was properly speaking only one kind of public and APPROXIMATELY artistical discourse—that delivered from the pulpit. The preacher was the only one in Germany who knew the weight of a syllable or a word, in what manner a sentence strikes, springs, rushes, flows, and comes to a close; he alone had a conscience in his ears, often enough a bad conscience: for reasons are not lacking why proficiency in oratory should be especially seldom attained by a German, or almost always too late. The masterpiece of German prose is therefore with good reason the masterpiece of its greatest preacher: the BIBLE has hitherto been the best German book. Compared with Luther's Bible, almost everything else is merely "literature"—something which has not grown in Germany, and therefore has not taken and does not take root in German hearts, as the Bible has done.

248. There are two kinds of geniuses: one which above all engenders and seeks to engender, and another which willingly lets itself be fructified and brings forth. And similarly, among the gifted nations, there are those on whom the woman's problem of pregnancy has devolved, and the secret task of forming, maturing, and perfecting— the Greeks, for instance, were a nation of this kind, and so are the French; and others which have to fructify and become the cause of new modes of life—like the Jews, the Romans, and, in all modesty be it asked: like the Germans?—nations tortured and enraptured by unknown fevers and irresistibly forced out of themselves, amorous and longing for foreign races (for such as "let themselves

be fructified"), and withal imperious, like everything conscious of being full of generative force, and consequently empowered "by the grace of God." These two kinds of geniuses seek each other like man and woman; but they also misunderstand each other—like man and woman.

249. Every nation has its own "Tartuffery," and calls that its virtue.—One does not know—cannot know, the best that is in one.

250. What Europe owes to the Jews?—Many things, good and bad, and above all one thing of the nature both of the best and the worst: the grand style in morality, the fearfulness and majesty of infinite demands, of infinite significations, the whole Romanticism and sublimity of moral questionableness—and consequently just the most attractive, ensnaring, and exquisite element in those iridescences and allurements to life, in the aftersheen of which the sky of our European culture, its evening sky, now glows—perhaps glows out. For this, we artists among the spectators and philosophers, are—grateful to the Jews.

251. It must be taken into the bargain, if various clouds and disturbances—in short, slight attacks of stupidity—pass over the spirit of a people that suffers and WANTS to suffer from national nervous fever and political ambition: for instance, among present-day Germans there is alternately the anti-French folly, the anti-Semitic folly, the anti-Polish folly, the Christian-romantic folly, the Wagnerian folly, the Teutonic folly, the Prussian folly (just look at those poor historians, the Sybels and Treitschkes, and their closely bandaged heads), and whatever else these little obscurations of the German spirit and conscience may be called. May it be forgiven me that I, too, when on a short daring sojourn on very infected ground, did not remain wholly exempt from the disease, but like every one else, began to entertain thoughts about matters which did not concern me—the first symptom of political infection. About the Jews, for instance, listen to the following:—I have never yet met a German who was favourably inclined to the Jews; and however decided the repudiation of actual anti-Semitism may be on the part of all

prudent and political men, this prudence and policy is not perhaps directed against the nature of the sentiment itself, but only against its dangerous excess, and especially against the distasteful and infamous expression of this excess of sentiment;—on this point we must not deceive ourselves. That Germany has amply SUFFICIENT Jews, that the German stomach, the German blood, has difficulty (and will long have difficulty) in disposing only of this quantity of "Jew"—as the Italian, the Frenchman, and the Englishman have done by means of a stronger digestion:—that is the unmistakable declaration and language of a general instinct, to which one must listen and according to which one must act. "Let no more Jews come in! And shut the doors, especially towards the East (also towards Austria)!"—thus commands the instinct of a people whose nature is still feeble and uncertain, so that it could be easily wiped out, easily extinguished, by a stronger race. The Jews, however, are beyond all doubt the strongest, toughest, and purest race at present living in Europe, they know how to succeed even under the worst conditions (in fact better than under favourable ones), by means of virtues of some sort, which one would like nowadays to label as vices—owing above all to a resolute faith which does not need to be ashamed before "modern ideas", they alter only, WHEN they do alter, in the same way that the Russian Empire makes its conquest—as an empire that has plenty of time and is not of yesterday—namely, according to the principle, "as slowly as possible"! A thinker who has the future of Europe at heart, will, in all his perspectives concerning the future, calculate upon the Jews, as he will calculate upon the Russians, as above all the surest and likeliest factors in the great play and battle of forces. That which is at present called a "nation" in Europe, and is really rather a RES FACTA than NATA (indeed, sometimes confusingly similar to a RES FICTA ET PICTA), is in every case something evolving, young, easily displaced, and not yet a race, much less such a race AERE PERENNUS, as the Jews are such "nations" should most carefully avoid all hot-headed rivalry and hostility! It is certain that the Jews, if they desired—or if they were driven to it, as the anti-Semites seem to wish—COULD now have the ascendancy, nay, literally the supremacy, over Europe, that they are NOT working and planning for that end is equally certain. Meanwhile, they rather wish and desire, even somewhat importunely, to be insorbed and absorbed by Europe, they long to be finally settled, authorized, and respected somewhere, and wish to put an end to the nomadic life, to the "wandering Jew",— and one should certainly take account of this impulse and tendency, and MAKE ADVANCES to it (it possibly betokens a mitigation of the Jewish instincts) for which purpose it would perhaps be useful and fair to banish the anti-Semitic bawlers out of the country. One should make advances with all prudence, and with selection, pretty much as the English nobility do It stands to reason that the more powerful and strongly marked types of new Germanism could enter into relation with the Jews with the least hesitation, for instance, the nobleman officer from the Prussian border it would be interesting in many ways to see whether the genius for money and patience (and especially some intellect and intellectuality—sadly lacking in the place referred to) could not in addition be annexed and trained to the hereditary art of commanding and obeying—for both of which the country in question has now a classic reputation But here it is expedient to break off my festal discourse and my sprightly Teutonomania for I have already reached my SERIOUS TOPIC, the "European problem," as I understand it, the rearing of a new ruling caste for Europe.

252. They are not a philosophical race—the English: Bacon represents an ATTACK on the philosophical spirit generally, Hobbes, Hume, and Locke, an abasement, and a depreciation of the idea of a "philosopher" for more than a century. It was AGAINST Hume that Kant uprose and raised himself; it was Locke of whom Schelling RIGHTLY said, "JE MEPRISE LOCKE"; in the struggle against the English mechanical stultification of the world, Hegel and Schopenhauer (along with Goethe) were of one accord; the two hostile brother-geniuses in philosophy, who pushed in different directions towards the opposite poles of German thought, and thereby wronged each other as only brothers will do.—What is lacking in England, and has always been lacking, that half-actor and rhetorician knew well enough, the absurd muddle-head, Carlyle, who sought to conceal under passionate grimaces what he knew about himself: namely, what was LACKING in Carlyle—real POWER of intellect, real DEPTH of intellectual perception, in short, philosophy. It is characteristic of such an unphilosophical race to hold on firmly to Christianity—they NEED its discipline for "moralizing" and humanizing. The Englishman, more gloomy, sensual, headstrong, and brutal than the German—is for that very reason, as the baser of the two, also the most pious: he has all the MORE NEED of Christianity. To finer nostrils, this English Christianity itself has still a characteristic English taint of spleen and alcoholic excess, for which, owing to good reasons, it is used as an antidote—the finer poison to neutralize the coarser: a finer

form of poisoning is in fact a step in advance with coarse-mannered people, a step towards spiritualization. The English coarseness and rustic demureness is still most satisfactorily disguised by Christian pantomime, and by praying and psalm-singing (or, more correctly, it is thereby explained and differently expressed); and for the herd of drunkards and rakes who formerly learned moral grunting under the influence of Methodism (and more recently as the "Salvation Army"), a penitential fit may really be the relatively highest manifestation of "humanity" to which they can be elevated: so much may reasonably be admitted. That, however, which offends even in the humanest Englishman is his lack of music, to speak figuratively (and also literally): he has neither rhythm nor dance in the movements of his soul and body; indeed, not even the desire for rhythm and dance, for "music." Listen to him speaking; look at the most beautiful Englishwoman WALKING—in no country on earth are there more beautiful doves and swans; finally, listen to them singing! But I ask too much...

253. There are truths which are best recognized by mediocre minds, because they are best adapted for them, there are truths which only possess charms and seductive power for mediocre spirits:—one is pushed to this probably unpleasant conclusion, now that the influence of respectable but mediocre Englishmen—I may mention Darwin, John Stuart Mill, and Herbert Spencer—begins to gain the ascendancy in the middle-class region of European taste. Indeed, who could doubt that it is a useful thing for SUCH minds to have the ascendancy for a time? It would be an error to consider the highly developed and independently soaring minds as specially qualified for determining and collecting many little common facts, and deducing conclusions from them; as exceptions, they are rather from the first in no very favourable position towards those who are "the rules." After all, they have more to do than merely to perceive:—in effect, they have to BE something new, they have to SIGNIFY something new, they have to REPRESENT new values! The gulf between knowledge and capacity is perhaps greater, and also more mysterious, than one thinks: the capable man in the grand style, the creator, will possibly have to be an ignorant person;—while on the other hand, for scientific discoveries like those of Darwin, a certain narrowness, aridity, and industrious carefulness (in short, something English) may not be unfavourable for arriving at them.—Finally, let it not be forgotten that the English,

with their profound mediocrity, brought about once before a general depression of European intelligence.

What is called "modern ideas," or "the ideas of the eighteenth century," or "French ideas"—that, consequently, against which the GERMAN mind rose up with profound disgust—is of English origin, there is no doubt about it. The French were only the apes and actors of these ideas, their best soldiers, and likewise, alas! their first and profoundest VICTIMS; for owing to the diabolical Anglomania of "modern ideas," the AME FRANCAIS has in the end become so thin and emaciated, that at present one recalls its sixteenth and seventeenth centuries, its profound, passionate strength, its inventive excellency, almost with disbelief. One must, however, maintain this verdict of historical justice in a determined manner, and defend it against present prejudices and appearances: the European NOBLESSE—of sentiment, taste, and manners, taking the word in every high sense—is the work and invention of FRANCE; the European ignobleness, the plebeianism of modern ideas—is ENGLAND'S work and invention.

254. Even at present France is still the seat of the most intellectual and refined culture of Europe, it is still the high school of taste; but one must know how to find this "France of taste." He who belongs to it keeps himself well concealed:—they may be a small number in whom it lives and is embodied, besides perhaps being men who do not stand upon the strongest legs, in part fatalists, hypochondriacs, invalids, in part persons over-indulged, over-refined, such as have the AMBITION to conceal themselves.

They have all something in common: they keep their ears closed in presence of the delirious folly and noisy spouting of the democratic BOURGEOIS. In fact, a besotted and brutalized France at present sprawls in the foreground—it recently celebrated a veritable orgy of bad taste, and at the same time of self-admiration, at the funeral of Victor Hugo. There is also something else common to them: a predilection to resist intellectual Germanizing—and a still greater inability to do so! In this France of intellect, which is also a France of pessimism, Schopenhauer has perhaps become more at home, and more indigenous than he has ever been in Germany; not to speak of Heinrich Heine, who has long ago been re-incarnated in the more refined and fastidious lyrists of Paris; or of Hegel, who at present, in the form of Taine—the FIRST of living historians—exercises an almost tyrannical influence. As regards Richard Wagner, however, the more French music learns to adapt itself to the actual needs of the AME MODERNE, the more will it "Wagnerite"; one can safely predict that beforehand,—it is already taking place sufficiently! There are, however, three things which the French can still boast of with pride as their heritage and possession, and as indelible tokens of their ancient intellectual superiority in Europe, in spite of all voluntary or involuntary Germanizing and vulgarizing of taste. FIRSTLY, the capacity for artistic emotion, for devotion to "form," for which the expression, L'ART POUR L'ART, along with numerous others, has been invented:—such capacity has not been lacking in France for three centuries; and owing to its reverence for the "small number," it has again and again made a sort of chamber music of literature possible, which is sought for in vain elsewhere in Europe.—The SECOND thing whereby the French can lay claim to a superiority over Europe is their ancient, many-sided, MORALISTIC culture, owing to which one finds on an average, even in the petty ROMANCIERS of the newspapers and chance BOULEVARDIERS DE PARIS, a psychological sensitiveness and curiosity, of which, for example, one has no conception (to say nothing of the thing itself!) in Germany. The Germans lack a couple of centuries of the moralistic work requisite thereto, which, as we have said, France has not grudged: those who call the Germans "naive" on that account give them commendation for a defect. (As the opposite of the German inexperience and innocence IN VOLUPTATE PSYCHOLOGICA, which is not too remotely associated with the tediousness of German intercourse,— and as the most successful expression of genuine French curiosity and inventive talent in this domain of delicate thrills, Henri Beyle may be noted; that remarkable anticipatory and forerunning man, who, with a Napoleonic TEMPO, traversed HIS Europe, in fact, several centuries of the European soul, as a surveyor and discoverer thereof:—it has required two generations to OVERTAKE him one way or other, to divine long afterwards some of the riddles that perplexed and enraptured him—this strange Epicurean and man of interrogation, the last great psychologist of France).—There is yet a THIRD claim to superiority: in the French character there is a successful half-way synthesis of the North and South, which makes them comprehend many things, and enjoins upon them other things, which an Englishman can never comprehend. Their temperament, turned alternately to and from the South, in which from time to time the Provencal and Ligurian blood froths over, preserves them from the dreadful, northern grey-in-grey, from sunless conceptual-spectrism and from poverty of blood—our GERMAN infirmity of taste, for the excessive prevalence of which at the present moment, blood and iron, that is to say "high politics," has with great resolution been prescribed (according to a dangerous healing art, which bids me wait and wait, but not yet hope).—There is also still in France a pre-understanding and ready welcome for those rarer and rarely gratified men, who are too comprehensive to find satisfaction in any kind of fatherlandism, and know how to love the South when in the North and the North when in the South—the born Midlanders, the "good Europeans." For them BIZET has made music, this latest genius, who has seen a new beauty and seduction,—who has discovered a piece of the SOUTH IN MUSIC.

255. I hold that many precautions should be taken against German music. Suppose a person loves the South as I love it—as a great school of recovery for the most spiritual and the most sensuous ills, as a boundless solar profusion and effulgence which o'erspreads a sovereign existence believing in itself—well, such a person will learn to be somewhat on his guard against German music, because, in injuring his taste anew, it will also injure his health anew. Such a Southerner, a Southerner not by origin but by BELIEF, if he should dream of the future of music, must also dream of it being freed from the influence of the North; and must have in his ears the prelude to a deeper, mightier, and perhaps more perverse and mysterious music, a super-German music, which does not fade, pale, and die away, as all German music does, at the sight of the blue, wanton sea and the Mediterranean clearness of sky—a super-European music, which holds its own even in presence of the brown sunsets of the desert, whose soul is akin to the palm-tree, and can be at home and can roam with big, beautiful, lonely beasts of prey... I could imagine a music of which the rarest charm would be that it knew nothing more of good and evil; only that here and there perhaps some sailor's home-sickness, some golden shadows and tender weaknesses might sweep lightly over it; an art which, from the far distance, would see the colours of a sinking and almost incomprehensible MORAL world fleeing towards it, and would be hospitable enough and profound

enough to receive such belated fugitives.

256. Owing to the morbid estrangement which the nationality-craze has induced and still induces among the nations of Europe, owing also to the short-sighted and hasty-handed politicians, who with the help of this craze, are at present in power, and do not suspect to what extent the disintegrating policy they pursue must necessarily be only an interlude policy—owing to all this and much else that is altogether unmentionable at present, the most unmistakable signs that EUROPE WISHES TO BE ONE, are now overlooked, or arbitrarily and falsely misinterpreted. With all the more profound and large-minded men of this century, the real general tendency of the mysterious labour of their souls was to prepare the way for that new SYNTHESIS, and tentatively to anticipate the European of the future; only in their simulations, or in their weaker moments, in old age perhaps, did they belong to the "fatherlands"—they only rested from themselves when they became "patriots." I think of such men as Napoleon, Goethe, Beethoven, Stendhal, Heinrich Heine, Schopenhauer: it must not be taken amiss if I also count Richard Wagner among them, about whom one must not let oneself be deceived by his own misunderstandings (geniuses like him have seldom the right to understand themselves), still less, of course, by the unseemly noise with which he is now resisted and opposed in France: the fact remains, nevertheless, that Richard Wagner and the LATER FRENCH ROMANTICISM of the forties, are most closely and intimately related to one another. They are akin, fundamentally akin, in all the heights and depths of their requirements; it is Europe, the ONE Europe, whose soul presses urgently and longingly, outwards and upwards, in their multifarious and boisterous art—whither? into a new light? towards a new sun? But who would attempt to express accurately what all these masters of new modes of speech could not express distinctly? It is certain that the same storm and stress tormented them, that they SOUGHT in the same manner, these last great seekers! All of them steeped in literature to their eyes and ears—the first artists of universal literary culture—for the most part even themselves writers, poets, intermediaries and blenders of the arts and the senses (Wagner, as musician is reckoned among painters, as poet among musicians, as artist generally among actors); all of them fanatics for EXPRESSION "at any cost"—I specially mention Delacroix, the nearest related to Wagner; all of them great discoverers in the realm of the sublime,

also of the loathsome and dreadful, still greater discoverers in effect, in display, in the art of the show-shop; all of them talented far beyond their genius, out and out VIRTUOSI, with mysterious accesses to all that seduces, allures, constrains, and upsets; born enemies of logic and of the straight line, hankering after the strange, the exotic, the monstrous, the crooked, and the self-contradictory; as men, Tantaluses of the will, plebeian parvenus, who knew themselves to be incapable of a noble TEMPO or of a LENTO in life and action—think of Balzac, for instance,—unrestrained workers, almost destroying themselves by work; antinomians and rebels in manners, ambitious and insatiable, without equilibrium and enjoyment; all of them finally shattering and sinking down at the Christian cross (and with right and reason, for who of them would have been sufficiently profound and sufficiently original for an ANTI-CHRISTIAN philosophy?);— on the whole, a boldly daring, splendidly overbearing, high-flying, and aloft-up-dragging class of higher men, who had first to teach their century—and it is the century of the MASSES—the conception "higher man."... Let the German friends of Richard Wagner advise together as to whether there is anything purely German in the Wagnerian art, or whether its distinction does not consist precisely in coming from SUPER-GERMAN sources and impulses: in which connection it may not be underrated how indispensable Paris was to the development of his type, which the strength of his instincts made him long to visit at the most decisive time—and how the whole style of his proceedings, of his self-apostolate, could only perfect itself in sight of the French socialistic original. On a more subtle comparison it will perhaps be found, to the honour of Richard Wagner's German nature, that he has acted in everything with more strength, daring, severity, and elevation than a nineteenth-century Frenchman could have done—owing to the circumstance that we Germans are as yet nearer to barbarism than the French;—perhaps even the most remarkable creation of Richard Wagner is not only at present, but for ever inaccessible, incomprehensible, and inimitable to the whole latter-day Latin race: the figure of Siegfried, that VERY FREE man, who is probably far too free, too hard, too cheerful, too healthy, too ANTI-CATHOLIC for the taste of old and mellow civilized nations. He may even have been a sin against Romanticism, this anti-Latin Siegfried: well, Wagner atoned amply for this sin in his old sad days, when—anticipating a taste which has meanwhile passed into politics—he began, with the religious vehemence peculiar to him, to preach, at least, THE WAY TO ROME, if not to walk therein.—That these last words may not be misunderstood, I will call to my aid a few powerful rhymes, which will even betray to less delicate ears what I mean—what I mean COUNTER TO the "last Wagner" and his Parsifal music:—

—Is this our mode?—From German heart came this vexed ululating? From German body, this self-lacerating? Is ours this priestly hand-dilation, This incense-fuming exaltation? Is ours this faltering, falling, shambling, This quite uncertain ding-dong-dangling? This sly nun-ogling, Ave-hour-bell ringing, This wholly false enraptured heaven-o'erspringing?—Is this our mode?—Think well!—ye still wait for admission—For what ye hear is ROME—ROME'S FAITH BY INTUITION!

CHAPTER IX. WHAT IS NOBLE?

257. EVERY elevation of the type "man," has hitherto been the work of an aristocratic society and so it will always be—a society believing in a long scale of gradations of rank and differences of worth among human beings, and requiring slavery in some form or other. Without the PATHOS OF DISTANCE, such as grows out of the incarnated difference of classes, out of the constant out-looking and down-looking of the ruling caste on subordinates and instruments, and out of their equally constant practice of obeying and commanding, of keeping down and keeping at a distance—that other more mysterious pathos could never have arisen, the longing for an ever new widening of distance within the soul itself, the formation of ever higher, rarer, further, more extended, more comprehensive states, in short, just the elevation of the type "man," the continued "self-surmounting of man," to use a moral formula in a supermoral sense. To be sure, one must not resign oneself to any humanitarian illusions about the history of the origin of an aristocratic society (that is to say, of the preliminary condition for the elevation of the type "man"): the truth is hard. Let us acknowledge unprejudicedly how every higher civilization hitherto has ORIGINATED! Men with a still natural nature, barbarians in every terrible sense of the word, men of prey, still in possession of unbroken strength of will and desire for power, threw themselves upon weaker, more moral, more peaceful races (perhaps trading or cattle-rearing communities), or upon old mellow civilizations in which the final vital force was flickering out in brilliant fireworks of wit and depravity. At the commencement, the noble caste was always the barbarian caste: their superiority did not consist first of all in their physical, but in their psychical power—they were more COMPLETE men (which at every point also implies the same as "more complete beasts").

258. Corruption—as the indication that anarchy threatens to break out among the instincts, and that the foundation of the emotions, called "life," is convulsed—is something radically different according to the organization in which it manifests itself. When, for instance, an aristocracy like that of France at the beginning of the Revolution, flung away its privileges with sublime disgust and sacrificed itself to an excess of its moral sentiments, it was corruption:—it was really

only the closing act of the corruption which had existed for centuries, by virtue of which that aristocracy had abdicated step by step its lordly prerogatives and lowered itself to a FUNCTION of royalty (in the end even to its decoration and parade-dress). The essential thing, however, in a good and healthy aristocracy is that it should not regard itself as a function either of the kingship or the commonwealth, but as the SIGNIFICANCE and highest justification thereof—that it should therefore accept with a good conscience the sacrifice of a legion of individuals, who, FOR ITS SAKE, must be suppressed and reduced to imperfect men, to slaves and instruments. Its fundamental belief must be precisely that society is NOT allowed to exist for its own sake, but only as a foundation and scaffolding, by means of which a select class of beings may be able to elevate themselves to their higher duties, and in general to a higher EXISTENCE: like those sun-seeking climbing plants in Java—they are called Sipo Matador,—which encircle an oak so long and so often with their arms, until at last, high above it, but supported by it, they can unfold their tops in the open light, and exhibit their happiness.

259. To refrain mutually from injury, from violence, from exploitation, and put one's will on a par with that of others: this may result in a certain rough sense in good conduct among individuals when the necessary conditions are given (namely, the actual similarity of the individuals in amount of force and degree of worth, and their co-relation within one organization). As soon, however, as one wished to take this principle more generally, and if possible even as the FUNDAMENTAL PRINCIPLE OF SOCIETY, it would immediately disclose what it really is—namely, a Will to the DENIAL of life, a principle of dissolution and decay. Here one must think profoundly to the very basis and resist all sentimental weakness: life itself is ESSENTIALLY appropriation, injury, conquest of the strange and weak, suppression, severity, obtrusion of peculiar forms, incorporation, and at the least, putting it mildest, exploitation;—but why should one for ever use precisely these words on which for ages a disparaging purpose has been stamped? Even the organization within which, as was previously supposed, the individuals treat each other as equal—it takes place in every healthy aristocracy—must itself, if it be a living and not a dying organization, do all that towards other bodies, which the individuals within it refrain from doing to each other it will have to be the incarnated Will to Power, it will endeavour

to grow, to gain ground, attract to itself and acquire ascendancy—not owing to any morality or immorality, but because it LIVES, and because life IS precisely Will to Power. On no point, however, is the ordinary consciousness of Europeans more unwilling to be corrected than on this matter, people now rave everywhere, even under the guise of science, about coming conditions of society in which "the exploiting character" is to be absent—that sounds to my ears as if they promised to invent a mode of life which should refrain from all organic functions. "Exploitation" does not belong to a depraved, or imperfect and primitive society it belongs to the nature of the living being as a primary organic function, it is a consequence of the intrinsic Will to Power, which is precisely the Will to Life—Granting that as a theory this is a novelty—as a reality it is the FUNDAMENTAL FACT of all history let us be so far honest towards ourselves!

260. In a tour through the many finer and coarser moralities which have hitherto prevailed or still prevail on the earth, I found certain traits recurring regularly together, and connected with one another, until finally two primary types revealed themselves to me, and a radical distinction was brought to light. There is MASTER-MORALITY and SLAVE-MORALITY,—I would at once add, however, that in all higher and mixed civilizations, there are also attempts at the reconciliation of the two moralities, but one finds still oftener the confusion and mutual misunderstanding of them, indeed sometimes their close juxtaposition—even in the same man, within one soul. The distinctions of moral values have either originated in a ruling caste, pleasantly conscious of being different from the ruled—or among the ruled class, the slaves and dependents of all sorts. In the first case, when it is the rulers who determine the conception "good," it is the exalted, proud disposition which is regarded as the distinguishing feature, and that which determines the order of rank. The noble type of man separates from himself the beings in whom the opposite of this exalted, proud disposition displays itself he despises them. Let it at once be noted that in this first kind of morality the antithesis "good" and "bad" means practically the same as "noble" and "despicable",—the antithesis "good" and "EVIL" is of a different origin. The cowardly, the timid, the insignificant, and those thinking merely of narrow utility are despised; moreover, also, the distrustful, with their constrained glances, the self-abasing, the dog-like kind of men who let themselves be abused, the mendicant flatterers, and

above all the liars:—it is a fundamental belief of all aristocrats that the common people are untruthful. "We truthful ones"—the nobility in ancient Greece called themselves. It is obvious that everywhere the designations of moral value were at first applied to MEN; and were only derivatively and at a later period applied to ACTIONS; it is a gross mistake, therefore, when historians of morals start with questions like, "Why have sympathetic actions been praised?" The noble type of man regards HIMSELF as a determiner of values; he does not require to be approved of; he passes the judgment: "What is injurious to me is injurious in itself;" he knows that it is he himself only who confers honour on things; he is a CREATOR OF VALUES. He honours whatever he recognizes in himself: such morality equals self-glorification. In the foreground there is the feeling of plenitude, of power, which seeks to overflow, the happiness of high tension, the consciousness of a wealth which would fain give and bestow:—the noble man also helps the unfortunate, but not—or scarcely—out of pity, but rather from an impulse generated by the super-abundance of power. The noble man honours in himself the powerful one, him also who has power over himself, who knows how to speak and how to keep silence, who takes pleasure in subjecting himself to severity and hardness, and has reverence for all that is severe and hard. "Wotan placed a hard heart in my breast," says an old Scandinavian Saga: it is thus rightly expressed from the soul of a proud Viking. Such a type of man is even proud of not being made for sympathy; the hero of the Saga therefore adds warningly: "He who has not a hard heart when young, will never have one." The noble and brave who think thus are the furthest removed from the morality which sees precisely in sympathy, or in acting for the good of others, or in DESINTERESSEMENT, the characteristic of the moral; faith in oneself, pride in oneself, a radical enmity and irony towards "selflessness," belong as definitely to noble morality, as do a careless scorn and precaution in presence of sympathy and the "warm heart."—It is the powerful who KNOW how to honour, it is their art, their domain for invention. The profound reverence for age and for tradition—all law rests on this double reverence,—the belief and prejudice in favour of ancestors and unfavourable to newcomers, is typical in the morality of the powerful; and if, reversely, men of "modern ideas" believe almost instinctively in "progress" and the "future," and are more and more lacking in respect for old age, the ignoble origin of these "ideas" has complacently betrayed itself thereby. A morality of the ruling class, however, is more especially foreign and irritating to present-day taste in the sternness of its principle that one has duties only to one's equals; that one may act towards beings of a lower rank, towards all that is foreign, just as seems good to one, or "as the heart desires," and in any case "beyond good and evil": it is here that sympathy and similar sentiments can have a place. The ability and obligation to exercise prolonged gratitude and prolonged revenge—both only within the circle of equals,—artfulness in retaliation, RAFFINEMENT of the idea in friendship, a certain necessity to have enemies (as outlets for the emotions of envy, quarrelsomeness, arrogance—in fact, in order to be a good FRIEND): all these are typical characteristics of the noble morality, which, as has been pointed out, is not the morality of "modern ideas," and is therefore at present difficult to realize, and also to unearth and disclose.—It is otherwise with the second type of morality, SLAVE-MORALITY. Supposing that the abused, the oppressed, the suffering, the unemancipated, the weary, and those uncertain of themselves should moralize, what will be the common element in their moral estimates? Probably a pessimistic suspicion with regard to the entire situation of man will find expression, perhaps a condemnation of man, together with his situation. The slave has an unfavourable eye for the virtues of the powerful; he has a skepticism and distrust, a REFINEMENT of distrust of everything "good" that is there honoured—he would fain persuade himself that the very happiness there is not genuine. On the other hand, THOSE qualities which serve to alleviate the existence of sufferers are brought into prominence and flooded with light; it is here that sympathy, the kind, helping hand, the warm heart, patience, diligence, humility, and friendliness attain to honour; for here these are the most useful qualities, and almost the only means of supporting the burden of existence. Slave-morality is essentially the morality of utility. Here is the seat of the origin of the famous antithesis "good" and "evil":—power and dangerousness are assumed to reside in the evil, a certain dreadfulness, subtlety, and strength, which do not admit of being despised. According to slave-morality, therefore, the "evil" man arouses fear; according to master-morality, it is precisely the "good" man who arouses fear and seeks to arouse it, while the bad man is regarded as the despicable being. The contrast attains its maximum when, in accordance with the logical consequences of slave-morality, a shade of depreciation—it may be slight and well-intentioned—at last attaches itself to the "good" man of this morality; because, according to the servile mode of thought, the good man must in any case be the SAFE man: he is good-natured, easily deceived, perhaps a little stupid, un bonhomme. Everywhere that slave-morality gains the ascendancy, language shows a tendency to approximate the significations of the words "good" and "stupid."—A last fundamental difference: the desire for FREEDOM, the instinct for happiness and the refinements of the feeling of liberty belong as necessarily to slave-morals and morality, as artifice and enthusiasm in reverence and devotion are the regular symptoms of an aristocratic mode of thinking and estimating.—Hence we can understand without further detail why love AS A PASSION—it is our European specialty—must absolutely be of noble origin; as is well known, its invention is due to the Provencal poet-cavaliers, those brilliant, ingenious men of the "gai saber," to whom Europe owes so much, and almost owes itself.

261. Vanity is one of the things which are perhaps most difficult for a noble man to understand: he will be tempted to deny it, where another kind of man thinks he sees it self-evidently. The problem for him is to represent to his mind beings who seek to arouse a good opinion of themselves which they themselves do not possess—and consequently also do not "deserve,"—and who yet BELIEVE in this good opinion afterwards. This seems to him on the one hand such bad taste and so self-disrespectful, and on the other hand so grotesquely unreasonable, that he would like to consider vanity an exception, and is doubtful about it in most cases when it is spoken of. He will say, for instance: "I may be mistaken about my value, and on the other hand may nevertheless demand that my value should be acknowledged by others precisely as I rate it:—that, however, is not vanity (but self-conceit, or, in most cases, that which is called 'humility,' and also 'modesty')." Or he will even say: "For many reasons I can delight in the good opinion of others, perhaps because I love and honour them, and rejoice in all their joys, perhaps also because their good opinion endorses and strengthens my belief in my own good opinion, perhaps because the good opinion of others, even in cases where I do not share it, is useful to me, or gives promise of usefulness:—all this, however, is not vanity." The man of noble character must first bring it home forcibly to his mind, especially with the aid of history, that, from time immemorial, in all social strata in any way dependent, the ordinary man WAS only that which he PASSED FOR:—not being at all accustomed to fix values, he did not assign even to himself any other value than that which his master assigned to him (it is the peculiar RIGHT OF MASTERS to create values). It may be looked upon as the result of an extraordinary atavism, that the ordinary man,

even at present, is still always WAITING for an opinion about himself, and then instinctively submitting himself to it; yet by no means only to a "good" opinion, but also to a bad and unjust one (think, for instance, of the greater part of the self-appreciations and self-depreciations which believing women learn from their confessors, and which in general the believing Christian learns from his Church). In fact, conformably to the slow rise of the democratic social order (and its cause, the blending of the blood of masters and slaves), the originally noble and rare impulse of the masters to assign a value to themselves and to "think well" of themselves, will now be more and more encouraged and extended; but it has at all times an older, ampler, and more radically ingrained propensity opposed to it—and in the phenomenon of "vanity" this older propensity overmasters the younger. The vain person rejoices over EVERY good opinion which he hears about himself (quite apart from the point of view of its usefulness, and equally regardless of its truth or falsehood), just as he suffers from every bad opinion: for he subjects himself to both, he feels himself subjected to both, by that oldest instinct of subjection which breaks forth in him.—It is "the slave" in the vain man's blood, the remains of the slave's craftiness—and how much of the "slave" is still left in woman, for instance!—which seeks to SEDUCE to good opinions of itself; it is the slave, too, who immediately afterwards falls prostrate himself before these opinions, as though he had not called them forth.—And to repeat it again: vanity is an atavism.

262. A SPECIES originates, and a type becomes established and strong in the long struggle with essentially constant UNFAVOURABLE conditions. On the other hand, it is known by the experience of breeders that species which receive super-abundant nourishment, and in general a surplus of protection and care, immediately tend in the most marked way to develop variations, and are fertile in prodigies and monstrosities (also in monstrous vices). Now look at an aristocratic commonwealth, say an ancient Greek polis, or Venice, as a voluntary or involuntary contrivance for the purpose of REARING human beings; there are there men beside one another, thrown upon their own resources, who want to make their species prevail, chiefly because they MUST prevail, or else run the terrible danger of being exterminated. The favour, the super-abundance, the protection are there lacking under which variations are fostered; the species needs itself as species, as something which, precisely by virtue of its hardness,

its uniformity, and simplicity of structure, can in general prevail and make itself permanent in constant struggle with its neighbours, or with rebellious or rebellion-threatening vassals. The most varied experience teaches it what are the qualities to which it principally owes the fact that it still exists, in spite of all Gods and men, and has hitherto been victorious: these qualities it calls virtues, and these virtues alone it develops to maturity. It does so with severity, indeed it desires severity; every aristocratic morality is intolerant in the education of youth, in the control of women, in the marriage customs, in the relations of old and young, in the penal laws (which have an eye only for the degenerating): it counts intolerance itself among the virtues, under the name of "justice." A type with few, but very marked features, a species of severe, warlike, wisely silent, reserved, and reticent men (and as such, with the most delicate sensibility for the charm and nuances of society) is thus established, unaffected by the vicissitudes of generations; the constant struggle with uniform UNFAVOURABLE conditions is, as already remarked, the cause of a type becoming stable and hard. Finally, however, a happy state of things results, the enormous tension is relaxed; there are perhaps no more enemies among the neighbouring peoples, and the means of life, even of the enjoyment of life, are present in superabundance. With one stroke the bond and constraint of the old discipline severs: it is no longer regarded as necessary, as a condition of existence—if it would continue, it can only do so as a form of LUXURY, as an archaizing TASTE. Variations, whether they be deviations (into the higher, finer, and rarer), or deteriorations and monstrosities, appear suddenly on the scene in the greatest exuberance and splendour; the individual dares to be individual and detach himself. At this turning-point of history there manifest themselves, side by side, and often mixed and entangled together, a magnificent, manifold, virgin-forest-like up-growth and up-striving, a kind of TROPICAL TEMPO in the rivalry of growth, and an extraordinary decay and self-destruction, owing to the savagely opposing and seemingly exploding egoisms, which strive with one another "for sun and light," and can no longer assign any limit, restraint, or forbearance for themselves by means of the hitherto existing morality. It was this morality itself which piled up the strength so enormously, which bent the bow in so threatening a manner:—it is now "out of date," it is getting "out of date." The dangerous and disquieting point has been reached when the greater, more manifold, more comprehensive life IS LIVED BEYOND the old morality; the "individual" stands out, and is obliged to have recourse to his own law-giving, his own arts and artifices for self-preservation, self-elevation, and self-deliverance. Nothing but new "Whys," nothing but new "Hows," no common formulas any longer, misunderstanding and disregard in league with each other, decay, deterioration, and the loftiest desires frightfully entangled, the genius of the race overflowing from all the cornucopias of good and bad, a portentous simultaneousness of Spring and Autumn, full of new charms and mysteries peculiar to the fresh, still inexhausted, still unwearied corruption. Danger is again present, the mother of morality, great danger; this time shifted into the individual, into the neighbour and friend, into the street, into their own child, into their own heart, into all the most personal and secret recesses of their desires and volitions. What will the moral philosophers who appear at this time have to preach? They discover, these sharp onlookers and loafers, that the end is quickly approaching, that everything around them decays and produces decay, that nothing will endure until the day after tomorrow, except one species of man, the incurably MEDIOCRE. The mediocre alone have a prospect of continuing and propagating themselves—they will be the men of the future, the sole survivors; "be like them! become mediocre!" is now the only morality which has still a significance, which still obtains a hearing.—But it is difficult to preach this morality of mediocrity! it can never avow what it is and what it desires! it has to talk of moderation and dignity and duty and brotherly love—it will have difficulty IN CONCEALING ITS IRONY!

263. There is an INSTINCT FOR RANK, which more than anything else is already the sign of a HIGH rank; there is a DELIGHT in the NUANCES of reverence which leads one to infer noble origin and habits. The refinement, goodness, and loftiness of a soul are put to a perilous test when something passes by that is of the highest rank, but is not yet protected by the awe of authority from obtrusive touches and incivilities: something that goes its way like a living touchstone, undistinguished, undiscovered, and tentative, perhaps voluntarily veiled and disguised. He whose task and practice it is to investigate souls, will avail himself of many varieties of this very art to determine the ultimate value of a soul, the unalterable, innate order of rank to which it belongs: he will test it by its INSTINCT FOR REVERENCE. DIFFERENCE ENGENDRE HAINE: the vulgarity of many a nature spurts up suddenly like dirty water, when any holy vessel, any jewel from closed shrines, any book bearing the marks of great destiny, is

brought before it; while on the other hand, there is an involuntary silence, a hesitation of the eye, a cessation of all gestures, by which it is indicated that a soul FEELS the nearness of what is worthiest of respect. The way in which, on the whole, the reverence for the BIBLE has hitherto been maintained in Europe, is perhaps the best example of discipline and refinement of manners which Europe owes to Christianity: books of such profoundness and supreme significance require for their protection an external tyranny of authority, in order to acquire the PERIOD of thousands of years which is necessary to exhaust and unriddle them. Much has been achieved when the sentiment has been at last instilled into the masses (the shallow-pates and the boobies of every kind) that they are not allowed to touch everything, that there are holy experiences before which they must take off their shoes and keep away the unclean hand—it is almost their highest advance towards humanity. On the contrary, in the so-called cultured classes, the believers in "modern ideas," nothing is perhaps so repulsive as their lack of shame, the easy insolence of eye and hand with which they touch, taste, and finger everything; and it is possible that even yet there is more RELATIVE nobility of taste, and more tact for reverence among the people, among the lower classes of the people, especially among peasants, than among the newspaper-reading DEMIMONDE of intellect, the cultured class.

264. It cannot be effaced from a man's soul what his ancestors have preferably and most constantly done: whether they were perhaps diligent economizers attached to a desk and a cash-box, modest and citizen-like in their desires, modest also in their virtues; or whether they were accustomed to commanding from morning till night, fond of rude pleasures and probably of still ruder duties and responsibilities; or whether, finally, at one time or another, they have sacrificed old privileges of birth and possession, in order to live wholly for their faith—for their "God,"—as men of an inexorable and sensitive conscience, which blushes at every compromise. It is quite impossible for a man NOT to have the qualities and predilections of his parents and ancestors in his constitution, whatever appearances may suggest to the contrary. This is the problem of race. Granted that one knows something of the parents, it is admissible to draw a conclusion about the child: any kind of offensive incontinence, any kind of sordid envy, or of clumsy self-vaunting—the three things which together have constituted the genuine plebeian type in all

times—such must pass over to the child, as surely as bad blood; and with the help of the best education and culture one will only succeed in DECEIVING with regard to such heredity.—And what else does education and culture try to do nowadays! In our very democratic, or rather, very plebeian age, "education" and "culture" MUST be essentially the art of deceiving—deceiving with regard to origin, with regard to the inherited plebeianism in body and soul. An educator who nowadays preached truthfulness above everything else, and called out constantly to his pupils: "Be true! Be natural! Show yourselves as you are!"—even such a virtuous and sincere ass would learn in a short time to have recourse to the FURCA of Horace, NATURAM EXPELLERE: with what results? "Plebeianism" USQUE RECURRET. [FOOTNOTE: Horace's "Epistles," I. x. 24.]

265. At the risk of displeasing innocent ears, I submit that egoism belongs to the essence of a noble soul, I mean the unalterable belief that to a being such as "we," other beings must naturally be in subjection, and have to sacrifice themselves. The noble soul accepts the fact of his egoism without question, and also without consciousness of harshness, constraint, or arbitrariness therein, but rather as something that may have its basis in the primary law of things:—if he sought a designation for it he would say: "It is justice itself." He acknowledges under certain circumstances, which made him hesitate at first, that there are other equally privileged ones; as soon as he has settled this question of rank, he moves among those equals and equally privileged ones with the same assurance, as regards modesty and delicate respect, which he enjoys in intercourse with himself—in accordance with an innate heavenly mechanism which all the stars understand. It is an ADDITIONAL instance of his egoism, this artfulness and self-limitation in intercourse with his equals—every star is a similar egoist; he honours HIMSELF in them, and in the rights which he concedes to them, he has no doubt that the exchange of honours and rights, as the ESSENCE of all intercourse, belongs also to the natural condition of things. The noble soul gives as he takes, prompted by the passionate and sensitive instinct of requital, which is at the root of his nature. The notion of "favour" has, INTER PARES, neither significance nor good repute; there may be a sublime way of letting gifts as it were light upon one from above, and of drinking them thirstily like dew-drops; but for those arts and displays the noble soul has no aptitude. His egoism hinders him here:

in general, he looks "aloft" unwillingly—he looks either FORWARD, horizontally and deliberately, or downwards—HE KNOWS THAT HE IS ON A HEIGHT.

266. "One can only truly esteem him who does not LOOK OUT FOR himself."—Goethe to Rath Schlosser.

267. The Chinese have a proverb which mothers even teach their children: "SIAO-SIN" ("MAKE THY HEART SMALL"). This is the essentially fundamental tendency in latter-day civilizations. I have no doubt that an ancient Greek, also, would first of all remark the self-dwarfing in us Europeans of today—in this respect alone we should immediately be "distasteful" to him.

268. What, after all, is ignobleness?—Words are vocal symbols for ideas; ideas, however, are more or less definite mental symbols for frequently returning and concurring sensations, for groups of sensations. It is not sufficient to use the same words in order to understand one another: we must also employ the same words for the same kind of internal experiences, we must in the end have experiences IN COMMON. On this account the people of one nation understand one another better than those belonging to different nations, even when they use the same language; or rather, when people have lived long together under similar conditions (of climate, soil, danger, requirement, toil) there ORIGINATES therefrom an entity that "understands itself"—namely, a nation. In all souls a like number of frequently recurring experiences have gained the upper hand over those occurring more rarely: about these matters people understand one another rapidly and always more rapidly—the history of language is the history of a process of abbreviation; on the basis of this quick comprehension people always unite closer and closer. The greater the danger, the greater is the need of agreeing quickly and readily about what is necessary; not to misunderstand one another in danger—that is what cannot at all be dispensed with in intercourse. Also in all loves and friendships one has the experience that nothing of the kind continues when the discovery has been made that in using the same words, one of the two parties has feelings,

thoughts, intuitions, wishes, or fears different from those of the other. (The fear of the "eternal misunderstanding": that is the good genius which so often keeps persons of different sexes from too hasty attachments, to which sense and heart prompt them—and NOT some Schopenhauerian "genius of the species"!) Whichever groups of sensations within a soul awaken most readily, begin to speak, and give the word of command—these decide as to the general order of rank of its values, and determine ultimately its list of desirable things. A man's estimates of value betray something of the STRUCTURE of his soul, and wherein it sees its conditions of life, its intrinsic needs. Supposing now that necessity has from all time drawn together only such men as could express similar requirements and similar experiences by similar symbols, it results on the whole that the easy COMMUNICABILITY of need, which implies ultimately the undergoing only of average and COMMON experiences, must have been the most potent of all the forces which have hitherto operated upon mankind. The more similar, the more ordinary people, have always had and are still having the advantage; the more select, more refined, more unique, and difficultly comprehensible, are liable to stand alone; they succumb to accidents in their isolation, and seldom propagate themselves. One must appeal to immense opposing forces, in order to thwart this natural, all-too-natural PROGRESSUS IN SIMILE, the evolution of man to the similar, the ordinary, the average, the gregarious—to the IGNOBLE—!

269. The more a psychologist—a born, an unavoidable psychologist and soul-diviner—turns his attention to the more select cases and individuals, the greater is his danger of being suffocated by sympathy: he NEEDS sternness and cheerfulness more than any other man. For the corruption, the ruination of higher men, of the more unusually constituted souls, is in fact, the rule: it is dreadful to have such a rule always before one's eyes. The manifold torment of the psychologist who has discovered this ruination, who discovers once, and then discovers ALMOST repeatedly throughout all history, this universal inner "desperateness" of higher men, this eternal "too late!" in every sense—may perhaps one day be the cause of his turning with bitterness against his own lot, and of his making an attempt at self-destruction—of his "going to ruin" himself. One may perceive in almost every psychologist a tell-tale inclination for delightful intercourse with commonplace and well-ordered men; the fact is thereby disclosed

that he always requires healing, that he needs a sort of flight and forgetfulness, away from what his insight and incisiveness—from what his "business"—has laid upon his conscience. The fear of his memory is peculiar to him. He is easily silenced by the judgment of others; he hears with unmoved countenance how people honour, admire, love, and glorify, where he has PERCEIVED—or he even conceals his silence by expressly assenting to some plausible opinion. Perhaps the paradox of his situation becomes so dreadful that, precisely where he has learnt GREAT SYMPATHY, together with great CONTEMPT, the multitude, the educated, and the visionaries, have on their part learnt great reverence—reverence for "great men" and marvelous animals, for the sake of whom one blesses and honours the fatherland, the earth, the dignity of mankind, and one's own self, to whom one points the young, and in view of whom one educates them. And who knows but in all great instances hitherto just the same happened: that the multitude worshipped a God, and that the "God" was only a poor sacrificial animal! SUCCESS has always been the greatest liar—and the "work" itself is a success; the great statesman, the conqueror, the discoverer, are disguised in their creations until they are unrecognizable; the "work" of the artist, of the philosopher, only invents him who has created it, is REPUTED to have created it; the "great men," as they are revered, are poor little fictions composed afterwards; in the world of historical values spurious coinage PREVAILS. Those great poets, for example, such as Byron, Musset, Poe, Leopardi, Kleist, Gogol (I do not venture to mention much greater names, but I have them in my mind), as they now appear, and were perhaps obliged to be: men of the moment, enthusiastic, sensuous, and childish, light-minded and impulsive in their trust and distrust; with souls in which usually some flaw has to be concealed; often taking revenge with their works for an internal defilement, often seeking forgetfulness in their soaring from a too true memory, often lost in the mud and almost in love with it, until they become like the Will-o'-the-Wisps around the swamps, and PRETEND TO BE stars—the people then call them idealists,—often struggling with protracted disgust, with an ever-reappearing phantom of disbelief, which makes them cold, and obliges them to languish for GLORIA and devour "faith as it is" out of the hands of intoxicated adulators:—what a TORMENT these great artists are and the so-called higher men in general, to him who has once found them out! It is thus conceivable that it is just from woman—who is clairvoyant in the world of suffering, and also unfortunately eager to help and save to an extent far beyond her powers—that THEY have learnt so readily those outbreaks of boundless devoted SYMPATHY, which the multitude, above all the reverent multitude, do not understand, and overwhelm with prying and self-gratifying interpretations. This sympathizing invariably deceives itself as to its power; woman would like to believe that love can do EVERYTHING—it is the SUPERSTITION peculiar to her. Alas, he who knows the heart finds out how poor, helpless, pretentious, and blundering even the best and deepest love is—he finds that it rather DESTROYS than saves!—It is possible that under the holy fable and travesty of the life of Jesus there is hidden one of the most painful cases of the martyrdom of KNOWLEDGE ABOUT LOVE: the martyrdom of the most innocent and most craving heart, that never had enough of any human love, that DEMANDED love, that demanded inexorably and frantically to be loved and nothing else, with terrible outbursts against those who refused him their love; the story of a poor soul insatiated and insatiable in love, that had to invent hell to send thither those who WOULD NOT love him—and that at last, enlightened about human love, had to invent a God who is entire love, entire CAPACITY for love—who takes pity on human love, because it is so paltry, so ignorant! He who has such sentiments, he who has such KNOWLEDGE about love—SEEKS for death!—But why should one deal with such painful matters? Provided, of course, that one is not obliged to do so.

270. The intellectual haughtiness and loathing of every man who has suffered deeply—it almost determines the order of rank HOW deeply men can suffer—the chilling certainty, with which he is thoroughly imbued and coloured, that by virtue of his suffering he KNOWS MORE than the shrewdest and wisest can ever know, that he has been familiar with, and "at home" in, many distant, dreadful worlds of which "YOU know nothing"!—this silent intellectual haughtiness of the sufferer, this pride of the elect of knowledge, of the "initiated," of the almost sacrificed, finds all forms of disguise necessary to protect itself from contact with officious and sympathizing hands, and in general from all that is not its equal in suffering. Profound suffering makes noble: it separates.—One of the most refined forms of disguise is Epicurism, along with a certain ostentatious boldness of taste, which takes suffering lightly, and puts itself on the defensive against all that is sorrowful and profound. They are "gay men" who make use of gaiety, because they are misunderstood on account of it—they WISH to be misunderstood. There are "scientific minds"

who make use of science, because it gives a gay appearance, and because scientificness leads to the conclusion that a person is superficial—they WISH to mislead to a false conclusion. There are free insolent minds which would fain conceal and deny that they are broken, proud, incurable hearts (the cynicism of Hamlet—the case of Galiani); and occasionally folly itself is the mask of an unfortunate OVER-ASSURED knowledge.—From which it follows that it is the part of a more refined humanity to have reverence "for the mask," and not to make use of psychology and curiosity in the wrong place.

271. That which separates two men most profoundly is a different sense and grade of purity. What does it matter about all their honesty and reciprocal usefulness, what does it matter about all their mutual good-will: the fact still remains—they "cannot smell each other!" The highest instinct for purity places him who is affected with it in the most extraordinary and dangerous isolation, as a saint: for it is just holiness—the highest spiritualization of the instinct in question. Any kind of cognizance of an indescribable excess in the joy of the bath, any kind of ardour or thirst which perpetually impels the soul out of night into the morning, and out of gloom, out of "affliction" into clearness, brightness, depth, and refinement:—just as much as such a tendency DISTINGUISHES—it is a noble tendency—it also SEPARATES.—The pity of the saint is pity for the FILTH of the human, all-too-human. And there are grades and heights where pity itself is regarded by him as impurity, as filth.

272. Signs of nobility: never to think of lowering our duties to the rank of duties for everybody; to be unwilling to renounce or to share our responsibilities; to count our prerogatives, and the exercise of them, among our DUTIES.

273. A man who strives after great things, looks upon every one whom he encounters on his way either as a means of advance, or a delay and hindrance—or as a temporary resting-place. His peculiar lofty BOUNTY to his fellow-men is only possible when he attains his elevation and dominates. Impatience, and the consciousness of being always condemned to comedy up to that time—for even strife

is a comedy, and conceals the end, as every means does—spoil all intercourse for him; this kind of man is acquainted with solitude, and what is most poisonous in it.

274. THE PROBLEM OF THOSE WHO WAIT.—Happy chances are necessary, and many incalculable elements, in order that a higher man in whom the solution of a problem is dormant, may yet take action, or "break forth," as one might say—at the right moment. On an average it DOES NOT happen; and in all corners of the earth there are waiting ones sitting who hardly know to what extent they are waiting, and still less that they wait in vain. Occasionally, too, the waking call comes too late—the chance which gives "permission" to take action—when their best youth, and strength for action have been used up in sitting still; and how many a one, just as he "sprang up," has found with horror that his limbs are benumbed and his spirits are now too heavy! "It is too late," he has said to himself—and has become self-distrustful and henceforth for ever useless.—In the domain of genius, may not the "Raphael without hands" (taking the expression in its widest sense) perhaps not be the exception, but the rule?—Perhaps genius is by no means so rare: but rather the five hundred HANDS which it requires in order to tyrannize over the [GREEK INSERTED HERE], "the right time"—in order to take chance by the forelock!

275. He who does not WISH to see the height of a man, looks all the more sharply at what is low in him, and in the foreground—and thereby betrays himself.

276. In all kinds of injury and loss the lower and coarser soul is better off than the nobler soul: the dangers of the latter must be greater, the probability that it will come to grief and perish is in fact immense, considering the multiplicity of the conditions of its existence.—In a lizard a finger grows again which has been lost; not so in man.—

277. It is too bad! Always the old story! When a man has finished building his house, he finds that he has learnt unawares something

which he OUGHT absolutely to have known before he—began to build. The eternal, fatal "Too late!" The melancholia of everything COMPLETED—!

278.—Wanderer, who art thou? I see thee follow thy path without scorn, without love, with unfathomable eyes, wet and sad as a plummet which has returned to the light insatiated out of every depth—what did it seek down there?—with a bosom that never sighs, with lips that conceal their loathing, with a hand which only slowly grasps: who art thou? what hast thou done? Rest thee here: this place has hospitality for every one—refresh thyself! And whoever thou art, what is it that now pleases thee? What will serve to refresh thee? Only name it, whatever I have I offer thee! "To refresh me? To refresh me? Oh, thou prying one, what sayest thou! But give me, I pray thee—-" What? what? Speak out! "Another mask! A second mask!"

279. Men of profound sadness betray themselves when they are happy: they have a mode of seizing upon happiness as though they would choke and strangle it, out of jealousy—ah, they know only too well that it will flee from them!

280. "Bad! Bad! What? Does he not—go back?" Yes! But you misunderstand him when you complain about it. He goes back like every one who is about to make a great spring.

281.—"Will people believe it of me? But I insist that they believe it of me: I have always thought very unsatisfactorily of myself and about myself, only in very rare cases, only compulsorily, always without delight in 'the subject,' ready to digress from 'myself,' and always without faith in the result, owing to an unconquerable distrust of the POSSIBILITY of self-knowledge, which has led me so far as to feel a CONTRADICTIO IN ADJECTO even in the idea of 'direct knowledge' which theorists allow themselves:—this matter of fact is almost the most certain thing I know about myself. There must be a sort of repugnance in me to BELIEVE anything definite about myself.—Is there perhaps some enigma therein? Probably; but fortunately nothing for my own teeth.—Perhaps it betrays the species to which I belong?—but not to myself, as is sufficiently agreeable to me."

282.—"But what has happened to you?"—"I do not know," he said, hesitatingly; "perhaps the Harpies have flown over my table."—It sometimes happens nowadays that a gentle, sober, retiring man becomes suddenly mad, breaks the plates, upsets the table, shrieks, raves, and shocks everybody—and finally withdraws, ashamed, and raging at himself—whither? for what purpose? To famish apart? To suffocate with his memories?—To him who has the desires of a lofty and dainty soul, and only seldom finds his table laid and his food prepared, the danger will always be great—nowadays, however, it is extraordinarily so. Thrown into the midst of a noisy and plebeian age, with which he does not like to eat out of the same dish, he may readily perish of hunger and thirst—or, should he nevertheless finally "fall to," of sudden nausea.—We have probably all sat at tables to which we did not belong; and precisely the most spiritual of us, who are most difficult to nourish, know the dangerous DYSPEPSIA which originates from a sudden insight and disillusionment about our food and our messmates—the AFTER-DINNER NAUSEA.

283. If one wishes to praise at all, it is a delicate and at the same time a noble self-control, to praise only where one DOES NOT agree—otherwise in fact one would praise oneself, which is contrary to good taste:—a self-control, to be sure, which offers excellent opportunity and provocation to constant MISUNDERSTANDING. To be able to allow oneself this veritable luxury of taste and morality, one must not live among intellectual imbeciles, but rather among men whose misunderstandings and mistakes amuse by their refinement—or one will have to pay dearly for it!—"He praises me, THEREFORE he acknowledges me to be right"—this asinine method of inference spoils half of the life of us recluses, for it brings the asses into our neighbourhood and friendship.

284. To live in a vast and proud tranquility; always beyond... To have, or not to have, one's emotions, one's For and Against, according to

choice; to lower oneself to them for hours; to SEAT oneself on them as upon horses, and often as upon asses:—for one must know how to make use of their stupidity as well as of their fire. To conserve one's three hundred foregrounds; also one's black spectacles: for there are circumstances when nobody must look into our eyes, still less into our "motives." And to choose for company that roguish and cheerful vice, politeness. And to remain master of one's four virtues, courage, insight, sympathy, and solitude. For solitude is a virtue with us, as a sublime bent and bias to purity, which divines that in the contact of man and man—"in society"—it must be unavoidably impure. All society makes one somehow, somewhere, or sometime—"commonplace."

285. The greatest events and thoughts—the greatest thoughts, however, are the greatest events—are longest in being comprehended: the generations which are contemporary with them do not EXPERIENCE such events—they live past them. Something happens there as in the realm of stars. The light of the furthest stars is longest in reaching man; and before it has arrived man DENIES—that there are stars there. "How many centuries does a mind require to be understood?"—that is also a standard, one also makes a gradation of rank and an etiquette therewith, such as is necessary for mind and for star.

286. "Here is the prospect free, the mind exalted." [FOOTNOTE: Goethe's "Faust," Part II, Act V. The words of Dr. Marianus.]—But there is a reverse kind of man, who is also upon a height, and has also a free prospect—but looks DOWNWARDS.

287. What is noble? What does the word "noble" still mean for us nowadays? How does the noble man betray himself, how is he recognized under this heavy overcast sky of the commencing plebeianism, by which everything is rendered opaque and leaden?—It is not his actions which establish his claim—actions are always ambiguous, always inscrutable; neither is it his "works." One finds nowadays among artists and scholars plenty of those who betray by their works that a profound longing for nobleness impels them; but this very NEED of nobleness is radically different from the needs

of the noble soul itself, and is in fact the eloquent and dangerous sign of the lack thereof. It is not the works, but the BELIEF which is here decisive and determines the order of rank—to employ once more an old religious formula with a new and deeper meaning—it is some fundamental certainty which a noble soul has about itself, something which is not to be sought, is not to be found, and perhaps, also, is not to be lost.—THE NOBLE SOUL HAS REVERENCE FOR ITSELF.—

288. There are men who are unavoidably intellectual, let them turn and twist themselves as they will, and hold their hands before their treacherous eyes—as though the hand were not a betrayer; it always comes out at last that they have something which they hide—namely, intellect. One of the subtlest means of deceiving, at least as long as possible, and of successfully representing oneself to be stupider than one really is—which in everyday life is often as desirable as an umbrella,—is called ENTHUSIASM, including what belongs to it, for instance, virtue. For as Galiani said, who was obliged to know it: VERTU EST ENTHOUSIASME.

289. In the writings of a recluse one always hears something of the echo of the wilderness, something of the murmuring tones and timid vigilance of solitude; in his strongest words, even in his cry itself, there sounds a new and more dangerous kind of silence, of concealment. He who has sat day and night, from year's end to year's end, alone with his soul in familiar discord and discourse, he who has become a cave-bear, or a treasure-seeker, or a treasure-guardian and dragon in his cave—it may be a labyrinth, but can also be a gold-mine—his ideas themselves eventually acquire a twilight-colour of their own, and an odour, as much of the depth as of the mould, something uncommunicative and repulsive, which blows chilly upon every passer-by. The recluse does not believe that a philosopher—supposing that a philosopher has always in the first place been a recluse—ever expressed his actual and ultimate opinions in books: are not books written precisely to hide what is in us?—indeed, he will doubt whether a philosopher CAN have "ultimate and actual" opinions at all; whether behind every cave in him there is not, and must necessarily be, a still deeper cave: an ampler, stranger, richer world beyond the surface, an abyss behind every bottom, beneath

every "foundation." Every philosophy is a foreground philosophy—this is a recluse's verdict: "There is something arbitrary in the fact that the PHILOSOPHER came to a stand here, took a retrospect, and looked around; that he HERE laid his spade aside and did not dig any deeper—there is also something suspicious in it." Every philosophy also CONCEALS a philosophy; every opinion is also a LURKING-PLACE, every word is also a MASK.

290. Every deep thinker is more afraid of being understood than of being misunderstood. The latter perhaps wounds his vanity; but the former wounds his heart, his sympathy, which always says: "Ah, why would you also have as hard a time of it as I have?"

291. Man, a COMPLEX, mendacious, artful, and inscrutable animal, uncanny to the other animals by his artifice and sagacity, rather than by his strength, has invented the good conscience in order finally to enjoy his soul as something SIMPLE; and the whole of morality is a long, audacious falsification, by virtue of which generally enjoyment at the sight of the soul becomes possible. From this point of view there is perhaps much more in the conception of "art" than is generally believed.

292. A philosopher: that is a man who constantly experiences, sees, hears, suspects, hopes, and dreams extraordinary things; who is struck by his own thoughts as if they came from the outside, from above and below, as a species of events and lightning-flashes PECULIAR TO HIM; who is perhaps himself a storm pregnant with new lightnings; a portentous man, around whom there is always rumbling and mumbling and gaping and something uncanny going on. A philosopher: alas, a being who often runs away from himself, is often afraid of himself—but whose curiosity always makes him "come to himself" again.

293. A man who says: "I like that, I take it for my own, and mean to guard and protect it from every one"; a man who can conduct a case, carry out a resolution, remain true to an opinion, keep hold

of a woman, punish and overthrow insolence; a man who has his indignation and his sword, and to whom the weak, the suffering, the oppressed, and even the animals willingly submit and naturally belong; in short, a man who is a MASTER by nature—when such a man has sympathy, well! THAT sympathy has value! But of what account is the sympathy of those who suffer! Or of those even who preach sympathy! There is nowadays, throughout almost the whole of Europe, a sickly irritability and sensitiveness towards pain, and also a repulsive irrestrainableness in complaining, an effeminizing, which, with the aid of religion and philosophical nonsense, seeks to deck itself out as something superior—there is a regular cult of suffering. The UNMANLINESS of that which is called "sympathy" by such groups of visionaries, is always, I believe, the first thing that strikes the eye.—One must resolutely and radically taboo this latest form of bad taste; and finally I wish people to put the good amulet, "GAI SABER" ("gay science," in ordinary language), on heart and neck, as a protection against it.

294. THE OLYMPIAN VICE.—Despite the philosopher who, as a genuine Englishman, tried to bring laughter into bad repute in all thinking minds—"Laughing is a bad infirmity of human nature, which every thinking mind will strive to overcome" (Hobbes),—I would even allow myself to rank philosophers according to the quality of their laughing—up to those who are capable of GOLDEN laughter. And supposing that Gods also philosophize, which I am strongly inclined to believe, owing to many reasons—I have no doubt that they also know how to laugh thereby in an overman-like and new fashion—and at the expense of all serious things! Gods are fond of ridicule: it seems that they cannot refrain from laughter even in holy matters.

295. The genius of the heart, as that great mysterious one possesses it, the tempter-god and born rat-catcher of consciences, whose voice can descend into the nether-world of every soul, who neither speaks a word nor casts a glance in which there may not be some motive or touch of allurement, to whose perfection it pertains that he knows how to appear,—not as he is, but in a guise which acts as an ADDITIONAL constraint on his followers to press ever closer to him, to follow him more cordially and thoroughly;—the genius of

the heart, which imposes silence and attention on everything loud and self-conceited, which smoothes rough souls and makes them taste a new longing—to lie placid as a mirror, that the deep heavens may be reflected in them;—the genius of the heart, which teaches the clumsy and too hasty hand to hesitate, and to grasp more delicately; which scents the hidden and forgotten treasure, the drop of goodness and sweet spirituality under thick dark ice, and is a divining-rod for every grain of gold, long buried and imprisoned in mud and sand; the genius of the heart, from contact with which every one goes away richer; not favoured or surprised, not as though gratified and oppressed by the good things of others; but richer in himself, newer than before, broken up, blown upon, and sounded by a thawing wind; more uncertain, perhaps, more delicate, more fragile, more bruised, but full of hopes which as yet lack names, full of a new will and current, full of a new ill-will and counter-current... but what am I doing, my friends? Of whom am I talking to you? Have I forgotten myself so far that I have not even told you his name? Unless it be that you have already divined of your own accord who this questionable God and spirit is, that wishes to be PRAISED in such a manner? For, as it happens to every one who from childhood onward has always been on his legs, and in foreign lands, I have also encountered on my path many strange and dangerous spirits; above all, however, and again and again, the one of whom I have just spoken: in fact, no less a personage than the God DIONYSUS, the great equivocator and tempter, to whom, as you know, I once offered in all secrecy and reverence my first-fruits—the last, as it seems to me, who has offered a SACRIFICE to him, for I have found no one who could understand what I was then doing. In the meantime, however, I have learned much, far too much, about the philosophy of this God, and, as I said, from mouth to mouth—I, the last disciple and initiate of the God Dionysus: and perhaps I might at last begin to give you, my friends, as far as I am allowed, a little taste of this philosophy? In a hushed voice, as is but seemly: for it has to do with much that is secret, new, strange, wonderful, and uncanny. The very fact that Dionysus is a philosopher, and that therefore Gods also philosophize, seems to me a novelty which is not unensnaring, and might perhaps arouse suspicion precisely among philosophers;—among you, my friends, there is less to be said against it, except that it comes too late and not at the right time; for, as it has been disclosed to me, you are loth nowadays to believe in God and gods. It may happen, too, that in the frankness of my story I must go further than is agreeable to the strict usages of your ears? Certainly the God in question went further, very much further, in such dialogues, and was always many paces ahead of me... Indeed, if it were allowed, I should have to give him, according to human usage, fine ceremonious tides of lustre and merit, I should have to extol his courage as investigator and discoverer, his fearless honesty, truthfulness, and love of wisdom. But such a God does not know what to do with all that respectable trumpery and pomp. "Keep that," he would say, "for thyself and those like thee, and whoever else require it! I—have no reason to cover my nakedness!" One suspects that this kind of divinity and philosopher perhaps lacks shame?—He once said: "Under certain circumstances I love mankind"—and referred thereby to Ariadne, who was present; "in my opinion man is an agreeable, brave, inventive animal, that has not his equal upon earth, he makes his way even through all labyrinths. I like man, and often think how I can still further advance him, and make him stronger, more evil, and more profound."—"Stronger, more evil, and more profound?" I asked in horror. "Yes," he said again, "stronger, more evil, and more profound; also more beautiful"—and thereby the tempter-god smiled with his halcyon smile, as though he had just paid some charming compliment. One here sees at once that it is not only shame that this divinity lacks;—and in general there are good grounds for supposing that in some things the Gods could all of them come to us men for instruction. We men are—more human.—

296. Alas! what are you, after all, my written and painted thoughts! Not long ago you were so variegated, young and malicious, so full of thorns and secret spices, that you made me sneeze and laugh—and now? You have already doffed your novelty, and some of you, I fear, are ready to become truths, so immortal do they look, so pathetically honest, so tedious! And was it ever otherwise? What then do we write and paint, we mandarins with Chinese brush, we immortalisers of things which LEND themselves to writing, what are we alone capable of painting? Alas, only that which is just about to fade and begins to lose its odour! Alas, only exhausted and departing storms and belated yellow sentiments! Alas, only birds strayed and fatigued by flight, which now let themselves be captured with the hand—with OUR hand! We immortalize what cannot live and fly much longer, things only which are exhausted and mellow! And it is only for your AFTERNOON, you, my written and painted thoughts, for which alone I have colours, many colours, perhaps, many variegated softenings, and fifty yellows and browns and greens and reds;—but nobody will

divine thereby how ye looked in your morning, you sudden sparks and marvels of my solitude, you, my old, beloved—EVIL thoughts!

THE GENEALOGY OF MORALS

FIRST ESSAY.
"GOOD AND EVIL," "GOOD AND BAD."
1.

Those English psychologists, who up to the present are the only philosophers who are to be thanked for any endeavour to get as far as a history of the origin of morality—these men, I say, offer us in their own personalities no paltry problem;—they even have, if I am to be quite frank about it, in their capacity of living riddles, an advantage over their books—they themselves are interesting! These English psychologists—what do they really mean? We always find them voluntarily or involuntarily at the same task of pushing to the front the partie honteuse of our inner world, and looking for the efficient, governing, and decisive principle in that precise quarter where the intellectual self-respect of the race would be the most reluctant to find it (for example, in the vis inertiæ of habit, or in forgetfulness, or in a blind and fortuitous mechanism and association of ideas, or in some factor that is purely passive, reflex, molecular, or fundamentally stupid)—what is the real motive power which always impels these psychologists in precisely this direction? Is it an instinct for human disparagement somewhat sinister, vulgar, and malignant, or perhaps incomprehensible even to itself? or perhaps a touch of pessimistic jealousy, the mistrust of disillusioned idealists who have become gloomy,[Pg 18] poisoned, and bitter? or a petty subconscious enmity and rancour against Christianity (and Plato), that has conceivably never crossed the threshold of consciousness? or just a vicious taste for those elements of life which are bizarre, painfully paradoxical, mystical, and illogical? or, as a final alternative, a dash of each of these motives—a little vulgarity, a little gloominess, a little anti-Christianity, a little craving for the necessary piquancy?

But I am told that it is simply a case of old frigid and tedious frogs crawling and hopping around men and inside men, as if they were as thoroughly at home there, as they would be in a swamp.

I am opposed to this statement, nay, I do not believe it; and if, in the impossibility of knowledge, one is permitted to wish, so do I wish from my heart that just the converse metaphor should apply, and that these analysts with their psychological microscopes should be, at bottom, brave, proud, and magnanimous animals who know how to bridle both their hearts and their smarts, and have specifically trained themselves to sacrifice what is desirable to what is true, any truth in fact, even the simple, bitter, ugly, repulsive, unchristian, and immoral truths—for there are truths of that description.

2.

All honour, then, to the noble spirits who would fain dominate these historians of morality. But it is certainly a pity that they lack the historical[Pg 19] sense itself, that they themselves are quite deserted by all the beneficent spirits of history. The whole train of their thought runs, as was always the way of old-fashioned philosophers, on thoroughly unhistorical lines: there is no doubt on this point. The crass ineptitude of their genealogy of morals is immediately apparent when the question arises of ascertaining the origin of the idea and judgment of "good." "Man had originally," so speaks their decree, "praised and called 'good' altruistic acts from the standpoint of those on whom they were conferred, that is, those to whom they were useful; subsequently the origin of this praise was forgotten, and altruistic acts, simply because, as a sheer matter of habit, they were praised as good, came also to be felt as good—as though they contained in themselves some intrinsic goodness." The thing is obvious:—this initial derivation contains already all the typical and idiosyncratic traits of the English psychologists—we have "utility," "forgetting," "habit," and finally "error," the whole assemblage forming the basis of a system of values, on which the higher man has up to the present prided himself as though it were a kind of privilege of man in general. This pride must be brought low, this system of values must lose its values: is that attained?

Now the first argument that comes ready to my hand is that the real homestead of the concept "good" is sought and located in the wrong place: the judgment "good" did not originate among those to whom goodness was shown. Much[Pg 20] rather has it been the good themselves, that is, the aristocratic, the powerful, the high-stationed, the high-minded, who have felt that they themselves were good, and that their actions were good, that is to say of the first order, in contradistinction to all the low, the low-minded, the vulgar, and the plebeian. It was out of this pathos of distance that they first arrogated the right to create values for their own profit, and to coin the names of such values: what had they to do with utility? The standpoint of utility is as alien and as inapplicable as it could possibly be, when we have to deal with so volcanic an effervescence of supreme values, creating and demarcating as they do a hierarchy within themselves: it is at this juncture that one arrives at an appreciation of the contrast to that tepid temperature, which is the presupposition on which every combination of worldly wisdom and every calculation of practical expediency is always based—and not for one occasional, not for one exceptional instance, but chronically. The pathos of nobility and distance, as I have said, the chronic and despotic esprit de corps and fundamental instinct of a higher dominant race coming into association with a meaner race, an "under race," this is the origin of the antithesis of good and bad.

(The masters' right of giving names goes so far that it is permissible to look upon language itself as the expression of the power of the masters: they say "this is that, and that," they seal finally every object and every event with a[Pg 21] sound, and thereby at the same time take possession of it.) It is because of this origin that the word "good" is far from having any necessary connection with altruistic acts, in accordance with the superstitious belief of these moral philosophers. On the contrary, it is on the occasion of the decay of aristocratic values, that the antitheses between "egoistic" and "altruistic" presses more and more heavily on the human conscience—it is, to use my own language, the herd instinct which finds in this antithesis an expression in many ways. And even then it takes a considerable time for this instinct to become sufficiently dominant, for the valuation to be inextricably dependent on this antithesis (as is the case in contemporary Europe); for to-day that prejudice is predominant, which, acting even now with all the intensity of an obsession and brain disease, holds that "moral," "altruistic," and "désintéressé" are concepts of equal value.

3.

In the second place, quite apart from the fact that this hypothesis as to the genesis of the value "good" cannot be historically upheld, it suffers from an inherent psychological contradiction. The utility of altruistic conduct has presumably been the origin of its being praised, and this origin has become forgotten:—But in what conceivable way is this forgetting possible! Has perchance the utility of such conduct ceased at some given moment? The contrary is the case. This utility has rather been experienced every day[Pg 22] at all times, and is consequently a feature that obtains a new and regular emphasis with every fresh day; it follows that, so far from vanishing from the consciousness, so far indeed from being forgotten, it must necessarily become impressed on the consciousness with ever-increasing distinctness. How much more logical is that contrary theory (it is not the truer for that) which is represented, for instance, by Herbert Spencer, who places the concept "good" as essentially similar to the concept "useful," "purposive," so that in the judgments "good" and "bad" mankind is simply summarising and investing with a sanction its unforgotten and unforgettable experiences concerning the "useful-purposive" and the "mischievous-non-purposive." According to this theory, "good" is the attribute of that which has previously shown itself useful; and so is able to claim to be considered "valuable in the highest degree," "valuable in itself." This method of explanation is also, as I have said, wrong, but at any rate the explanation itself is coherent, and psychologically tenable.

4.

The guide-post which first put me on the right track was this question—what is the true etymological significance of the various symbols for the idea "good" which have been coined in the various languages? I then found that they all led back to the same evolution of the same idea—that everywhere "aristocrat," "noble" (in the social sense), is the root idea, out of which have necessarily developed[Pg 23] "good" in the sense of "with aristocratic soul," "noble," in the sense of "with a soul of high calibre," "with a privileged soul"—a development which invariably runs parallel with that other evolution by which "vulgar," "plebeian," "low," are made to change finally into "bad." The most eloquent proof of this last contention is the German word "schlecht" itself: this word is identical with "schlicht"— (compare "schlechtweg" and "schlechterdings")—which, originally and as yet without any sinister innuendo, simply denoted the plebeian man in contrast to the aristocratic man. It is at the sufficiently late period of the Thirty Years' War that this sense becomes changed to the sense now current. From the standpoint of the Genealogy of Morals this discovery seems to be substantial: the lateness of it is to be attributed to the retarding influence exercised in the modern world by democratic prejudice in the sphere of all questions of origin. This extends, as will shortly be shown, even to the province of natural science and physiology, which, prima facie is the most objective. The extent of the mischief which is caused by this prejudice (once it is free of all trammels except those of its own malice), particularly to Ethics and History, is shown by the notorious case of Buckle: it was in Buckle that that plebeianism of the modern spirit, which is of English origin, broke out once again from its malignant soil with all the violence of a slimy volcano, and with that salted, rampant, and vulgar eloquence with which up to the present time all volcanoes have spoken.

5.

With regard to our problem, which can justly be called an intimate problem, and which elects to appeal to only a limited number of ears: it is of no small interest to ascertain that in those words and roots which denote "good" we catch glimpses of that arch-trait, on the strength of which the aristocrats feel themselves to be beings of a higher order than their fellows. Indeed, they call themselves in perhaps the most frequent instances simply after their superiority in power (e.g. "the powerful," "the lords," "the commanders"), or after the most obvious sign of their superiority, as for example "the rich," "the possessors" (that is the meaning of arya; and the Iranian and Slav languages correspond). But they also call themselves after some characteristic idiosyncrasy; and this is the case which now concerns us. They name themselves, for instance, "the truthful": this is first done by the Greek nobility whose mouthpiece is found in Theognis, the Megarian poet. The word ἐσθλος, which is coined for the purpose, signifies etymologically "one who is," who has reality, who is real, who is true; and then with a subjective twist, the "true," as the "truthful": at this stage in the evolution of the idea, it becomes the motto and party cry of the nobility, and quite completes the transition to the meaning "noble," so as to place outside the pale the lying, vulgar man, as Theognis conceives and portrays him—till finally the word after the decay of the nobility is left to delineate[Pg 25] psychological noblesse, and becomes as it were ripe and mellow. In the word κακός as in δειλός (the plebeian in contrast to the ἀγαθός) the cowardice is emphasised. This affords perhaps an inkling on what lines the etymological origin of the very ambiguous ἀγαθός is to be investigated. In the Latin malus (which I place side by side with μέλας) the vulgar man can be distinguished as the dark-coloured, and above all as the black-haired ("hic niger est"), as the pre-Aryan inhabitants of the Italian soil, whose complexion formed the clearest feature of distinction from the dominant blondes, namely, the Aryan conquering race:—at any rate Gaelic has afforded me the exact analogue—Fin (for instance, in the name Fin-Gal), the distinctive word of the nobility, finally—good, noble, clean, but originally the blonde-haired man in contrast to the dark black-haired aboriginals. The Celts, if I may make a parenthetic statement, were throughout a blonde race; and it is wrong to connect, as Virchow still connects, those traces of an essentially dark-haired population which are to be seen on the more elaborate ethnographical maps of Germany with any Celtic ancestry or with any admixture of Celtic blood: in this context it is rather the pre-Aryan population of Germany which surges up to these districts. (The same is true substantially of the whole of Europe: in point of fact, the subject race has finally again obtained the upper hand, in complexion and the shortness of the skull, and perhaps in the intellectual and social qualities. Who can guarantee that modern democracy, still more[Pg 26] modern anarchy, and indeed that tendency to the "Commune," the most primitive form of society, which is now common to all the Socialists in Europe, does not in its real essence signify a monstrous reversion—and that the conquering and master race—the Aryan race, is not also becoming inferior physiologically?) I believe that I can explain the Latin bonus as the "warrior": my hypothesis is that I am right in deriving bonus from an older duonus (compare bellum = duellum = duen-lum, in which the word duonus appears to me to be contained). Bonus accordingly as the man of discord, of variance, "entzweiung" (duo), as the warrior: one sees what in ancient Rome "the good" meant for a man. Must not our actual German word gut mean "the godlike, the man of godlike race"? and be identical with the national name (originally the nobles' name) of the Goths?

The grounds for this supposition do not appertain to this work.

6.

Above all, there is no exception (though there are opportunities for exceptions) to this rule, that the idea of political superiority always resolves itself into the idea of psychological superiority, in those cases where the highest caste is at the same time the priestly caste, and in accordance with its general characteristics confers on itself the privilege of a title which alludes specifically to its priestly function. It is in these cases, for instance, that "clean" and "unclean" confront[Pg 27] each other for the first time as badges of class distinction; here again there develops a "good" and a "bad," in a sense which has ceased to be merely social. Moreover, care should be taken not to take these ideas of "clean" and "unclean" too seriously, too broadly, or too symbolically: all the ideas of ancient man have, on the contrary, got to be understood in their initial stages, in a sense which is, to an almost inconceivable extent, crude, coarse, physical, and narrow, and above all essentially unsymbolical. The "clean man" is originally only a man who washes himself, who abstains from certain foods which are conducive to skin diseases, who does not sleep with the unclean women of the lower classes, who has a horror of blood—not more, not much more! On the other hand, the very nature of a priestly aristocracy shows the reasons why just at such an early juncture there should ensue a really dangerous sharpening and intensification of opposed values: it is, in fact, through these opposed values that gulfs are cleft in the social plane, which a veritable Achilles of free thought would shudder to cross. There is from the outset a certain diseased taint in such sacerdotal aristocracies, and in the habits which prevail in such societies—habits which, averse as they are to action, constitute a compound of introspection and explosive emotionalism, as a result of which there appears that introspective morbidity and neurasthenia, which adheres almost inevitably to all priests at all times: with regard, however, to the remedy which they themselves have invented[Pg 28] for this disease—the philosopher has no option but to state, that it has proved itself in its effects a hundred times more dangerous than the disease, from which it should have been the deliverer. Humanity itself is still diseased from the effects of the naïvetés of this priestly cure. Take, for instance, certain kinds of diet (abstention from flesh), fasts, sexual continence, flight into the wilderness (a kind of Weir-Mitchell isolation, though of course without that system of excessive feeding and fattening which is the most efficient antidote to all the hysteria of the ascetic ideal); consider too the whole metaphysic of the priests, with its war on the senses, its enervation, its hair-splitting; consider its self-hypnotism on the fakir and Brahman principles (it uses Brahman as a glass disc and obsession), and that climax which we can understand only too well of an unusual satiety with its panacea of nothingness (or God:—the demand for a unio mystica with God is the demand of the Buddhist for nothingness, Nirvana—and nothing else!). In sacerdotal societies every element is on a more dangerous scale, not merely cures and remedies, but also pride, revenge, cunning, exaltation, love, ambition, virtue, morbidity:—further, it can fairly be stated that it is on the soil of this essentially dangerous form of human society, the sacerdotal form, that man really becomes for the first time an interesting animal, that it is in this form that the soul of man has in a higher sense attained depths and become evil—and those are the two fundamental forms of the superiority which up[Pg 29] to the present man has exhibited over every other animal.

7.

The reader will have already surmised with what ease the priestly mode of valuation can branch off from the knightly aristocratic mode, and then develop into the very antithesis of the latter: special impetus is given to this opposition, by every occasion when the castes of the priests and warriors confront each other with mutual jealousy and cannot agree over the prize. The knightly-aristocratic "values" are based on a careful cult of the physical, on a flowering, rich, and even effervescing healthiness, that goes considerably beyond what is necessary for maintaining life, on war, adventure, the chase, the dance, the tourney—on everything, in fact, which is contained in strong, free, and joyous action. The priestly-aristocratic mode of valuation is—we have seen—based on other hypotheses: it is bad enough for this class when it is a question of war! Yet the priests are, as is notorious, the worst enemies—why? Because they are the weakest. Their weakness causes their hate to expand into a monstrous and sinister shape, a shape which is most crafty and most poisonous. The really great haters in the history of the world have always been priests, who are also the cleverest haters—in comparison with the cleverness of priestly revenge, every other piece of cleverness is practically negligible. Human history would be too fatuous for anything were it not for the cleverness imported into it by the[Pg 30] weak—take at once the most important instance. All the world's efforts against the "aristocrats," the "mighty," the "masters," the "holders of power," are negligible by comparison with what has been accomplished against those classes by the Jews—the Jews, that priestly nation which eventually realised that the one method of effecting satisfaction on its enemies and tyrants was by means of a radical transvaluation of values, which was at the same time an act of the cleverest revenge. Yet the method was only appropriate to a nation of priests, to a nation of the most jealously nursed priestly revengefulness. It was the Jews who, in opposition to the aristocratic equation (good = aristocratic = beautiful = happy = loved by the gods), dared with a terrifying logic to suggest the contrary equation, and indeed to maintain with the teeth of the most profound hatred (the hatred of weakness) this contrary equation, namely, "the wretched are alone the good; the poor, the weak, the lowly, are alone the good; the suffering, the needy, the sick, the loathsome, are the only ones who are pious, the only ones who are blessed, for them alone is salvation—but you, on the other hand, you aristocrats, you men of power, you are to all eternity the evil, the horrible, the covetous, the insatiate, the godless; eternally also shall you be the unblessed, the cursed, the damned!" We know who it was who reaped the heritage of this Jewish transvaluation. In the context of the monstrous and inordinately fateful initiative which the Jews have exhibited in connection with[Pg 31] this most fundamental of all declarations of war, I remember the passage which came to my pen on another occasion (Beyond Good and Evil, Aph. 195)—that it was, in fact, with the Jews that the revolt of the slaves begins in the sphere of morals; that revolt which has behind it a history of two millennia, and which at the present day has only moved out of our sight, because it—has achieved victory.

8.

But you understand this not? You have no eyes for a force which has taken two thousand years to achieve victory?—There is nothing wonderful in this: all lengthy processes are hard to see and to realise. But this is what took place: from the trunk of that tree of revenge and hate, Jewish hate,—that most profound and sublime hate, which creates ideals and changes old values to new creations, the like of which has never been on earth,—there grew a phenomenon which was equally incomparable, a new love, the most profound and sublime of all kinds of love;—and from what other trunk could it have grown? But beware of supposing that this love has soared on its upward growth, as in any way a real negation of that thirst for revenge, as an antithesis to the Jewish hate! No, the contrary is the truth! This love grew out of that hate, as its crown, as its triumphant crown, circling wider and wider amid the clarity and fulness of the sun, and pursuing in the very kingdom of light and height its goal of hatred, its victory, its spoil, its strategy,[Pg 32] with the same intensity with which the roots of that tree of hate sank into everything which was deep and evil with increasing stability and increasing desire. This Jesus of Nazareth, the incarnate gospel of love, this "Redeemer" bringing salvation and victory to the poor, the sick, the sinful—was he not really temptation in its most sinister and irresistible form, temptation to take the tortuous path to those very Jewish values and those very Jewish ideals? Has not Israel really obtained the final goal of its sublime revenge, by the tortuous paths of this "Redeemer," for all that he might pose as Israel's adversary and Israel's destroyer? Is it not due to the black magic of a really great policy of revenge, of a far-seeing, burrowing revenge, both acting and calculating with slowness, that Israel himself must repudiate before all the world the actual instrument of his own revenge and nail it to the cross, so that all the world—that is, all the enemies of Israel—could nibble without suspicion at this very bait? Could, moreover, any human mind with all its elaborate ingenuity invent a bait that was more truly dangerous? Anything that was even equivalent in the power of its seductive, intoxicating, defiling, and corrupting influence to that symbol of the holy cross, to that awful paradox of a "god on the cross," to that mystery of the unthinkable, supreme, and utter horror of the self-crucifixion of a god for the salvation of man? It is at least certain that sub hoc signo Israel, with its revenge and transvaluation of all values, has up to the present always triumphed again over[Pg 33] all other ideals, over all more aristocratic ideals.

9.

"But why do you talk of nobler ideals? Let us submit to the facts; that the people have triumphed—or the slaves, or the populace, or the herd, or whatever name you care to give them—if this has happened through the Jews, so be it! In that case no nation ever had a greater mission in the world's history. The 'masters' have been done away with; the morality of the vulgar man has triumphed. This triumph may also be called a blood-poisoning (it has mutually fused the races)—I do not dispute it; but there is no doubt but that this intoxication has succeeded. The 'redemption' of the human race (that is, from the masters) is progressing swimmingly; everything is obviously becoming Judaised, or Christianised, or vulgarised (what is there in the words?). It seems impossible to stop the course of this poisoning through the whole body politic of mankind—but its tempo and pace may from the present time be slower, more delicate, quieter, more discreet—there is time enough. In view of this context has the Church nowadays any necessary purpose? has it, in fact, a right to live? Or could man get on without it? Quæritur. It seems that it fetters and retards this tendency, instead of accelerating it. Well, even that might be its utility. The Church certainly is a crude and boorish institution, that is repugnant to an intelligence with any pretence at delicacy, to a[Pg 34] really modern taste. Should it not at any rate learn to be somewhat more subtle? It alienates nowadays, more than it allures. Which of us would, forsooth, be a freethinker if there were no Church? It is the Church which repels us, not its poison—apart from the Church we like the poison." This is the epilogue of a freethinker to my discourse, of an honourable animal (as he has given abundant proof), and a democrat to boot; he had up to that time listened to me, and could not endure my silence, but for me, indeed, with regard to this topic there is much on which to be silent.

10.

The revolt of the slaves in morals begins in the very principle of resentment becoming creative and giving birth to values—a resentment experienced by creatures who, deprived as they are of the proper outlet of action, are forced to find their compensation in an imaginary revenge. While every aristocratic morality springs from a triumphant affirmation of its own demands, the slave morality says "no" from the very outset to what is "outside itself," "different from itself," and "not itself": and this "no" is its creative deed. This volte-face of the valuing standpoint—this inevitable gravitation to the objective instead of back to the subjective—is typical of "resentment": the slave-morality requires as the condition of its existence an external and objective world, to employ physiological terminology, it requires objective stimuli[Pg 35] to be capable of action at all—its action is fundamentally a reaction. The contrary is the case when we come to the aristocrat's system of values: it acts and grows spontaneously, it merely seeks its antithesis in order to pronounce a more grateful and exultant "yes" to its own self;—its negative conception, "low," "vulgar," "bad," is merely a pale late-born foil in comparison with its positive and fundamental conception (saturated as it is with life and passion), of "we aristocrats, we good ones, we beautiful ones, we happy ones."

When the aristocratic morality goes astray and commits sacrilege on reality, this is limited to that particular sphere with which it is not sufficiently acquainted—a sphere, in fact, from the real knowledge of which it disdainfully defends itself. It misjudges, in some cases, the sphere which it despises, the sphere of the common vulgar man and the low people: on the other hand, due weight should be given to the consideration that in any case the mood of contempt, of disdain, of superciliousness, even on the supposition that it falsely portrays the object of its contempt, will always be far removed from that degree of falsity which will always characterise the attacks—in effigy, of course—of the vindictive hatred and revengefulness of the weak in onslaughts on their enemies. In point of fact, there is in contempt too strong an admixture of nonchalance, of casualness, of boredom, of impatience, even of personal exultation, for it to be capable of distorting its victim into a real caricature or a real monstrosity. Attention again should be paid to the almost benevolent[Pg 36] nuances which, for instance, the Greek nobility imports into all the words by which it distinguishes the common people from itself; note how continuously a kind of pity, care, and consideration imparts its honeyed flavour, until at last almost all the words which are applied to the vulgar man survive finally as expressions for "unhappy," "worthy of pity" (compare δειλο, δείλαιος, πονηρός, μοχθηρός]; the latter two names really denoting the vulgar man as labour-slave and beast of burden)—and how, conversely, "bad," "low," "unhappy" have never ceased to ring in the Greek ear with a tone in which "unhappy" is the predominant note: this is a heritage of the old noble aristocratic morality, which remains true to itself even in contempt (let philologists remember the sense in which ὀιζυρός, ἄνολβος, τλήμων, δυστυχεῖν, ξυμφορά used to be employed). The "well-born" simply felt themselves the "happy"; they did not have to manufacture their happiness artificially through looking at their enemies, or in cases to talk and lie themselves into happiness (as is the custom with all resentful men); and similarly, complete men as they were, exuberant with strength, and consequently necessarily energetic, they were too wise to dissociate happiness from action—activity becomes in their minds necessarily counted as happiness (that is the etymology of εὖ πρᾶττειν)—all in sharp contrast to the "happiness" of the weak and the oppressed, with their festering venom and malignity, among whom happiness appears essentially as a narcotic, a deadening, a quietude, a peace, a[Pg 37] "Sabbath," an enervation of the mind and relaxation of the limbs,—in short, a purely passive phenomenon. While the aristocratic man lived in confidence and openness with himself (γενναῖος, "nobleε-born," emphasises the nuance "sincere," and perhaps also "naïf"), the resentful man, on the other hand, is neither sincere nor naïf, nor honest and candid with himself. His soul squints; his mind loves hidden crannies, tortuous paths and back-doors, everything secret appeals to him as his world, his safety, his balm; he is past master in silence, in not forgetting, in waiting, in provisional self-depreciation and self-abasement. A race of such resentful men will of necessity eventually prove more prudent than any aristocratic race, it will honour prudence on quite a distinct scale, as, in fact, a paramount condition of existence, while prudence among aristocratic men is apt to be tinged with a delicate flavour of luxury and refinement; so among them it plays nothing like so integral a part as that complete certainty of function of the governing unconscious instincts, or as indeed a certain lack of prudence, such as a vehement and valiant charge, whether against danger or the enemy, or as those ecstatic bursts of rage, love, reverence, gratitude, by which at all times noble souls have recognised each other. When the resentment of the aristocratic man manifests itself, it fulfils and exhausts itself in an immediate reaction, and consequently instills no venom: on the other hand, it never manifests itself at all in countless instances, when in the case of the feeble and weak it would be inevitable. An[Pg 38] inability to take seriously for any length of time their enemies, their disasters, their misdeeds—that is the sign of the full strong natures who possess a superfluity of moulding plastic force, that heals completely and produces forgetfulness: a good example of this in the modern world is Mirabeau, who had no memory for any insults and meannesses which were practised on him, and who was only incapable of forgiving because he forgot. Such a man indeed shakes off with a shrug many a worm which would have buried itself in another; it is only in characters like these that we see the possibility (supposing, of course, that there is such a possibility in the world) of the real "love of one's enemies." What respect for his enemies is found, forsooth, in an aristocratic man—and such a reverence is already a bridge to love! He insists on having his enemy to himself as his distinction. He tolerates no other enemy but a man in whose character there is nothing to despise and much to honour! On the other hand, imagine the "enemy" as the resentful man conceives him— and it is here exactly that we see his work, his creativeness; he has conceived "the evil enemy," the "evil one," and indeed that is the root idea from which he now evolves as a contrasting and corresponding figure a "good one," himself—his very self!

11

The method of this man is quite contrary to that of the aristocratic man, who conceives the root idea "good" spontaneously and straight[Pg 39] away, that is to say, out of himself, and from that material then creates for himself a concept of "bad"! This "bad" of aristocratic origin and that "evil" out of the cauldron of unsatisfied hatred—the former an imitation, an "extra," an additional nuance; the latter, on the other hand, the original, the beginning, the essential act in the conception of a slave-morality—these two words "bad" and "evil," how great a difference do they mark, in spite of the fact that they have an identical contrary in the idea "good." But the idea "good" is not the same: much rather let the question be asked, "Who is really evil according to the meaning of the morality of resentment?" In all sternness let it be answered thus:—just the good man of the other morality, just the aristocrat, the powerful one, the one who rules, but who is distorted by the venomous eye of resentfulness, into a new colour, a new signification, a new appearance. This particular point we would be the last to deny: the man who learnt to know those "good" ones only as enemies, learnt at the same time not to know them only as "evil enemies" and the same men who inter pares were kept so rigorously in bounds through convention, respect, custom, and gratitude, though much more through mutual vigilance and jealousy inter pares, these men who in their relations with each other find so many new ways of manifesting consideration, self-control, delicacy, loyalty, pride, and friendship, these men are in reference to what is outside their circle (where the foreign element, a foreign country, begins), not much better than[Pg 40] beasts of prey, which have been let loose. They enjoy there freedom from all social control, they feel that in the wilderness they can give vent with impunity to that tension which is produced by enclosure and imprisonment in the peace of society, they revert to the innocence of the beast-of-prey conscience, like jubilant monsters, who perhaps come from a ghastly bout of murder, arson, rape, and torture, with bravado and a moral equanimity, as though merely some wild student's prank had been played, perfectly convinced that the poets have now an ample theme to sing and celebrate. It is impossible not to recognise at the core of all these aristocratic races the beast of prey; the magnificent blonde brute, avidly rampant for spoil and victory; this hidden core needed an outlet from time to time, the beast must get loose again, must return into the wilderness—the Roman, Arabic, German, and Japanese nobility, the Homeric heroes, the Scandinavian Vikings, are all alike in this need. It is the aristocratic races who have left the idea "Barbarian" on all the tracks in which they have marched; nay, a consciousness of this very barbarianism, and even a pride in it, manifests itself even in their highest civilisation (for example, when Pericles says to his Athenians in that celebrated funeral oration, "Our audacity has forced a way over every land and sea, rearing everywhere imperishable memorials of itself for good and for evil"). This audacity of aristocratic races, mad, absurd, and spasmodic as may be its expression; the incalculable and fantastic nature of their enterprises,[Pg 41]Pericles sets in special relief and glory the ʼραθυμία of the Athenians, their nonchalance and contempt for safety, body, life, and comfort, their awful joy and intense delight in all destruction, in all the ecstasies of victory and cruelty,—all these features become crystallised, for those who suffered thereby in the picture of the "barbarian," of the "evil enemy," perhaps of the "Goth" and of the "Vandal." The profound, icy mistrust which the German provokes, as soon as he arrives at power,—even at the present time,—is always still an aftermath of that inextinguishable horror with which for whole centuries Europe has regarded the wrath of the blonde Teuton beast (although between the old Germans and ourselves there exists scarcely a psychological, let alone a physical, relationship). I have once called attention to the embarrassment of Hesiod, when he conceived the series of social ages, and endeavoured to express them in gold, silver, and bronze. He could only dispose of the contradiction, with which he was confronted, by the Homeric world, an age magnificent indeed, but at the same time so awful and so violent, by making two ages out of one, which he henceforth placed one behind each other—first, the age of the heroes and demigods, as that world had remained in the memories of the aristocratic families, who found therein their own ancestors; secondly, the bronze age, as that corresponding age appeared to the descendants of the oppressed, spoiled, ill-treated, exiled, enslaved; namely, as an age of bronze, as I have said, hard, cold, terrible, without feelings and without conscience, crushing everything,[Pg 42] and bespattering everything with blood. Granted the truth of the theory now believed to be true, that the very essence of all civilisation is to train out of man, the beast of prey, a tame and civilised animal, a domesticated animal, it follows indubitably that we must regard as the real tools of civilisation all those instincts of reaction and resentment, by the help of which the aristocratic races, together with their ideals, were finally degraded and overpowered; though that has not yet come to be synonymous with saying that the bearers of those tools also represented the civilisation. It is rather the contrary that is not only probable—nay, it is palpable to-day; these bearers of vindictive instincts that have to be bottled up, these descendants of all European and non-European slavery, especially of the pre-Aryan population—these people, I say, represent the decline of humanity! These "tools of civilisation" are a disgrace to humanity, and constitute in reality more of an argument against civilisation, more of a reason why civilisation should be suspected. One may be perfectly justified in being always afraid of the blonde beast that lies at the core of all aristocratic races, and in being on one's guard: but who would not a hundred times prefer to be afraid, when one at the same time admires, than to be immune from fear, at the cost of being perpetually obsessed with the loathsome spectacle of the distorted, the dwarfed, the stunted, the envenomed? And is that not our fate? What produces to-day our repulsion towards "man"?—for we suffer from "man," there is no doubt[Pg 43] about it.

It is not fear; it is rather that we have nothing more to fear from men; it is that the worm "man" is in the foreground and pullulates; it is that the "tame man," the wretched mediocre and unedifying creature, has learnt to consider himself a goal and a pinnacle, an inner meaning, an historic principle, a "higher man"; yes, it is that he has a certain right so to consider himself, in so far as he feels that in contrast to that excess of deformity, disease, exhaustion, and effeteness whose odour is beginning to pollute present-day Europe, he at any rate has achieved a relative success, he at any rate still says "yes" to life.

12.

I cannot refrain at this juncture from uttering a sigh and one last hope. What is it precisely which I find intolerable? That which I alone cannot get rid of, which makes me choke and faint? Bad air! bad air! That something misbegotten comes near me; that I must inhale the odour of the entrails of a misbegotten soul!—That excepted, what can one not endure in the way of need, privation, bad weather, sickness, toil, solitude? In point of fact, one manages to get over everything, born as one is to a burrowing and battling existence; one always returns once again to the light, one always lives again one's golden hour of victory—and then one stands as one was born, unbreakable, tense, ready for something more difficult, for something more distant, like a bow stretched but the tauter by every strain.[Pg 44] But from time to time do ye grant me—assuming that "beyond good and evil" there are goddesses who can grant—one glimpse, grant me but one glimpse only, of something perfect, fully realised, happy, mighty, triumphant, of something that still gives cause for fear! A glimpse of a man that justifies the existence of man, a glimpse of an incarnate human happiness that realises and redeems, for the sake of which one may hold fast to the belief in man! For the position is this: in the dwarfing and levelling of the European man lurks our greatest peril, for it is this outlook which fatigues—we see to-day nothing which wishes to be greater, we surmise that the process is always still backwards, still backwards towards something more attenuated, more inoffensive, more cunning, more comfortable, more mediocre, more indifferent, more Chinese, more Christian—man, there is no doubt about it, grows always "better" —the destiny of Europe lies even in this—that in losing the fear of man, we have also lost the hope in man, yea, the will to be man. The sight of man now fatigues.—What is present-day Nihilism if it is not that?—We are tired of man.

13.

But let us come back to it; the problem of another origin of the good—of the good, as the resentful man has thought it out—demands its solution. It is not surprising that the lambs should bear a grudge against the great birds of prey, but that is no reason for blaming the great birds of prey[Pg 45] for taking the little lambs. And when the lambs say among themselves, "These birds of prey are evil, and he who is as far removed from being a bird of prey, who is rather its opposite, a lamb,—is he not good?" then there is nothing to cavil at in the setting up of this ideal, though it may also be that the birds of prey will regard it a little sneeringly, and perchance say to themselves, "We bear no grudge against them, these good lambs, we even like them: nothing is tastier than a tender lamb." To require of strength that it should not express itself as strength, that it should not be a wish to overpower, a wish to overthrow, a wish to become master, a thirst for enemies and antagonisms and triumphs, is just as absurd as to require of weakness that it should express itself as strength. A quantum of force is just such a quantum of movement, will, action—rather it is nothing else than just those very phenomena of moving, willing, acting, and can only appear otherwise in the misleading errors of language (and the fundamental fallacies of reason which have become petrified therein), which understands, and understands wrongly, all working as conditioned by a worker, by a "subject." And just exactly as the people separate the lightning from its flash, and interpret the latter as a thing done, as the working of a subject which is called lightning, so also does the popular morality separate strength from the expression of strength, as though behind the strong man there existed some indifferent neutral substratum, which enjoyed a caprice and option as to whether or not it should[Pg 46] express strength. But there is no such substratum, there is no "being" behind doing, working, becoming; "the doer" is a mere appanage to the action. The action is everything. In point of fact, the people duplicate the doing, when they make the lightning lighten, that is a "doing-doing": they make the same phenomenon first a cause, and then, secondly, the effect of that cause. The scientists fail to improve matters when they say, "Force moves, force causes," and so on. Our whole science is still, in spite of all its coldness, of all its freedom from passion, a dupe of the tricks of language, and has never succeeded in getting rid of that superstitious changeling "the subject" (the atom, to give another instance, is such a changeling, just as the Kantian "Thing-in-itself"). What wonder, if the suppressed and stealthily simmering passions of revenge and hatred exploit for their own advantage this belief, and indeed hold no belief with a more steadfast enthusiasm than this—"that the strong has the option of being weak, and the bird of prey of being a lamb." Thereby do they win for themselves the right of attributing to the birds of prey the responsibility for being birds of prey: when the oppressed, down-trodden, and overpowered say to themselves with the vindictive guile of weakness, "Let us be otherwise than the evil, namely, good! and good is every one who does not oppress, who hurts no one, who does not attack, who does not pay back, who hands over revenge to God, who holds himself, as we do, in hiding; who goes out of the way of evil, and demands, in short, little[Pg 47] from life; like ourselves the patient, the meek, the just,"—yet all this, in its cold and unprejudiced interpretation, means nothing more than "once for all, the weak are weak; it is good to do nothing for which we are not strong enough"; but this dismal state of affairs, this prudence of the lowest order, which even insects possess (which in a great danger are fain to sham death so as to avoid doing "too much"), has, thanks to the counterfeiting and self-deception of weakness, come to masquerade in the pomp of an ascetic, mute, and expectant virtue, just as though the very weakness of the weak— that is, forsooth, its being, its working, its whole unique inevitable inseparable reality—were a voluntary result, something wished, chosen, a deed, an act of merit. This kind of man finds the belief in a neutral, free-choosing "subject" necessary from an instinct of self-preservation, of self-assertion, in which every lie is fain to sanctify itself. The subject (or, to use popular language, the soul) has perhaps proved itself the best dogma in the world simply because it rendered possible to the horde of mortal, weak, and oppressed individuals of every kind, that most sublime specimen of self-deception, the interpretation of weakness as freedom, of being this, or being that, as merit.

14.

Will any one look a little into—right into—the mystery of how ideals are manufactured in this world? Who has the courage to do it? Come!

Here we have a vista opened into these grimy[Pg 48] workshops. Wait just a moment, dear Mr. Inquisitive and Foolhardy; your eye must first grow accustomed to this false changing light—Yes! Enough! Now speak! What is happening below down yonder? Speak out that what you see, man of the most dangerous curiosity—for now I am the listener.

"I see nothing, I hear the more. It is a cautious, spiteful, gentle whispering and muttering together in all the corners and crannies. It seems to me that they are lying; a sugary softness adheres to every sound. Weakness is turned to merit, there is no doubt about it—it is just as you say."

Further!

"And the impotence which requites not, is turned to 'goodness,' craven baseness to meekness, submission to those whom one hates, to obedience (namely, obedience to one of whom they say that he ordered this submission—they call him God). The inoffensive character of the weak, the very cowardice in which he is rich, his standing at the door, his forced necessity of waiting, gain here fine names, such as 'patience,' which is also called 'virtue'; not being able to avenge one's self, is called not wishing to avenge one's self, perhaps even forgiveness (for they know not what they do—we alone know what they do). They also talk of the 'love of their enemies' and sweat thereby."

Further!

"They are miserable, there is no doubt about it, all these whisperers and counterfeiters in the[Pg 49] corners, although they try to get warm by crouching close to each other, but they tell me that their misery is a favour and distinction given to them by God, just as one beats the dogs one likes best; that perhaps this misery is also a preparation, a probation, a training; that perhaps it is still more something which will one day be compensated and paid back with a tremendous interest in gold, nay in happiness. This they call 'Blessedness.'"

Further!

"They are now giving me to understand, that not only are they better men than the mighty, the lords of the earth, whose spittle they have got to lick (not out of fear, not at all out of fear! But because God ordains that one should honour all authority)—not only are they better men, but that they also have a 'better time,' at any rate, will one day have a 'better time.' But enough! Enough! I can endure it no longer. Bad air! Bad air! These workshops where ideals are manufactured—verily they reek with the crassest lies."

Nay. Just one minute! You are saying nothing about the masterpieces of these virtuosos of black magic, who can produce whiteness, milk, and innocence out of any black you like: have you not noticed what a pitch of refinement is attained by their chef d'œuvre, their most audacious, subtle, ingenious, and lying artist-trick? Take care! These cellar-beasts, full of revenge and hate—what do they make, forsooth, out of their revenge and hate? Do you hear these words? Would you suspect, if you trusted only their[Pg 50] words, that you are among men of resentment and nothing else?

"I understand, I prick my ears up again (ah! ah! ah! and I hold my nose). Now do I hear for the first time that which they have said so often: 'We good, we are the righteous'—what they demand they call not revenge but 'the triumph of righteousness'; what they hate is not their enemy, no, they hate 'unrighteousness,' 'godlessness'; what they believe in and hope is not the hope of revenge, the intoxication of sweet revenge (—"sweeter than honey," did Homer call it?), but the victory of God, of the righteous God over the 'godless'; what is left for them to love in this world is not their brothers in hate, but their 'brothers in love,' as they say, all the good and righteous on the earth."

And how do they name that which serves them as a solace against all the troubles of life—their phantasmagoria of their anticipated future blessedness?

"How? Do I hear right? They call it 'the last judgment,' the advent of their kingdom, 'the kingdom of God'—but in the meanwhile they live 'in faith,' 'in love,' 'in hope.'"

Enough! Enough!

15.

In the faith in what? In the love for what? In the hope of what? These weaklings!—they also, forsooth, wish to be the strong some time; there is no doubt about it, some time their kingdom also must come—"the kingdom of God" is their name for it, as has been mentioned:[Pg 51] they are so meek in everything! Yet in order to experience that kingdom it is necessary to live long, to live beyond death,—yes, eternal life is necessary so that one can make up for ever for that earthly life "in faith," "in love," "in hope." Make up for what? Make up by what? Dante, as it seems to me, made a crass mistake when with awe-inspiring ingenuity he placed that inscription over the gate of his hell, "Me too made eternal love": at any rate the following inscription would have a much better right to stand over the gate of the Christian Paradise and its "eternal blessedness"—"Me too made eternal hate"—granted of course that a truth may rightly stand over the gate to a lie! For what is the blessedness of that Paradise? Possibly we could quickly surmise it; but it is better that it should be explicitly attested by an authority who in such matters is not to be disparaged, Thomas of Aquinas, the great teacher and saint. "Beati in regno celesti" says he, as gently as a lamb, "videbunt pœnas damnatorum, ut beatitudo illis magis complaceat." Or if we wish to hear a stronger tone, a word from the mouth of a triumphant father of the Church, who warned his disciples against the cruel ecstasies of the public spectacles—But why? Faith offers us much more,—says he, de Spectac., c. 29 ss.,—something much stronger; thanks to the redemption, joys of quite another kind stand at our disposal; instead of athletes we have our martyrs; we wish for blood, well, we have the blood of Christ—but what then awaits us on the day of his return, of his triumph. And then does he[Pg 52] proceed, does this enraptured visionary: "at enim supersunt alia spectacula, ille ultimas et perpetuus judicii dies, ille nationibus insperatus, ille derisus, cum tanta sæculi vetustas et tot ejus nativitates uno igne haurientur. Quæ tunc spectaculi latitudo! Quid admirer! quid rideam! Ubigaudeam! Ubi exultem, spectans tot et tantos reges, qui in cœlum recepti nuntiabantur, cum ipso Jove et ipsis suis testibus in imis tenebris congemescentes! Item præsides" (the provincial governors) "persecutores dominici nominis sævioribus quam ipsi flammis sævierunt insultantibus contra Christianos liquescentes! Quos præterea sapientes illos philosophos coram discipulis suis una conflagrantibus erubescentes, quibus nihil ad deum pertinere suadebant, quibus animas aut nullas aut non in pristina corpora redituras affirmabant! Etiam poetas non ad Rhadamanti nec ad Minois, sed ad inopinati Christi tribunal palpitantes! Tunc magis tragœdi audiendi, magis scilicet vocales" (with louder tones and more violent shrieks) "in sua propria calamitate; tunc histriones cognoscendi, solutiores multo per ignem; tunc spectandus auriga in flammea rota totus rubens, tunc xystici contemplandi non in gymnasiis, sed in igne jaculati, nisi quod ne tunc quidem illos velim vivos, ut qui malim ad eos potius conspectum insatiabilem conferre, qui in dominum scevierunt. Hic est ille, dicam fabri aut quæstuariæ filius" (as is shown by the whole of the following, and in particular by this well-known description of the mother of Jesus from the Talmud, Tertullian is henceforth referring to the Jews), "sabbati destructor, Samarites et dæmonium habens. Hic[Pg 53] est quem a Juda redemistis, hic est ille arundine et colaphis diverberatus, sputamentis de decoratus, felle et acete potatus. Hic est, quem clam discentes subripuerunt, ut resurrexisse dicatur vel hortulanus detraxit, ne lactucæ suæ frequentia commeantium laderentur. Ut talia species, ut talibus exultes, quis tibi prætor aut consul aut sacerdos de sua liberalitate prastabit? Et tamen hæc jam habemus quodammodo per fidem spiritu imaginante repræsentata. Ceterum qualia illa sunt, quæ nec oculus vidit nec auris audivit nec in cor hominis ascenderunt?" (I Cor. ii. 9.) "Credo circo et utraque cavea" (first and fourth row, or, according to others, the comic and the tragic stage) "et omni studio gratiora." Per fidem: so stands it written.

16.

Let us come to a conclusion. The two opposing values, "good and bad," "good and evil," have fought a dreadful, thousand-year fight in the world, and though indubitably the second value has been for a long time in the preponderance, there are not wanting places where the fortune of the fight is still undecisive. It can almost be said that in the meanwhile the fight reaches a higher and higher level, and that in the meanwhile it has become more and more intense, and always more and more psychological; so that nowadays there is perhaps no more decisive mark of the higher nature, of the more psychological nature, than to be in that sense self-contradictory, and to be actually still a battleground[Pg 54] for those two opposites. The symbol of this fight, written in a writing which has remained worthy of perusal throughout the course of history up to the present time, is called "Rome against Judæa, Judæa against Rome." Hitherto there has been no greater event than that fight, the putting of that question, that deadly antagonism. Rome found in the Jew the incarnation of the unnatural, as though it were its diametrically opposed monstrosity, and in Rome the Jew was held to be convicted of hatred of the whole human race: and rightly so, in so far as it is right to link the well-being and the future of the human race to the unconditional mastery of the aristocratic values, of the Roman values. What, conversely, did the Jews feel against Rome? One can surmise it from a thousand symptoms, but it is sufficient to carry one's mind back to the Johannian Apocalypse, that most obscene of all the written outbursts, which has revenge on its conscience. (One should also appraise at its full value the profound logic of the Christian instinct, when over this very book of hate it wrote the name of the Disciple of Love, that self-same disciple to whom it attributed that impassioned and ecstatic Gospel—

therein lurks a portion of truth, however much literary forging may have been necessary for this purpose.) The Romans were the strong and aristocratic; a nation stronger and more aristocratic has never existed in the world, has never even been dreamed of; every relic of them, every inscription enraptures, granted that one can divine what it is that writes the inscription.[Pg 55] The Jews, conversely, were that priestly nation of resentment par excellence, possessed by a unique genius for popular morals: just compare with the Jews the nations with analogous gifts, such as the Chinese or the Germans, so as to realise afterwards what is first rate, and what is fifth rate.

Which of them has been provisionally victorious, Rome or Judæa? but there is not a shadow of doubt; just consider to whom in Rome itself nowadays you bow down, as though before the quintessence of all the highest values—and not only in Rome, but almost over half the world, everywhere where man has been tamed or is about to be tamed—to three Jews, as we know, and one Jewess (to Jesus of Nazareth, to Peter the fisher, to Paul the tent-maker, and to the mother of the aforesaid Jesus, named Mary). This is very remarkable: Rome is undoubtedly defeated. At any rate there took place in the Renaissance a brilliantly sinister revival of the classical ideal, of the aristocratic valuation of all things: Rome herself, like a man waking up from a trance, stirred beneath the burden of the new Judaised Rome that had been built over her, which presented the appearance of an œcumenical synagogue and was called the "Church": but immediately Judæa triumphed again, thanks to that fundamentally popular (German and English) movement of revenge, which is called the Reformation, and taking also into account its inevitable corollary, the restoration of the Church—the restoration also of the ancient graveyard peace[Pg 56] of classical Rome. Judæa proved yet once more victorious over the classical ideal in the French Revolution, and in a sense which was even more crucial and even more profound: the last political aristocracy that existed in Europe, that of the French seventeenth and eighteenth centuries, broke into pieces beneath the instincts of a resentful populace—never had the world heard a greater jubilation, a more uproarious enthusiasm: indeed, there took place in the midst of it the most monstrous and unexpected phenomenon; the ancient ideal itself swept before the eyes and conscience of humanity with all its life and with unheard-of splendour, and in opposition to resentment's lying war-cry of the prerogative of the most, in opposition to the will to lowliness, abasement, and equalisation, the will to a retrogression and twilight of humanity, there rang out once again, stronger, simpler, more penetrating than ever, the terrible and enchanting counter-warcry of the prerogative of the few! Like a final signpost to other ways, there appeared Napoleon, the most unique and violent anachronism that ever existed, and in him the incarnate problem of the aristocratic ideal in itself—consider well what a problem it is:—Napoleon, that synthesis of Monster and Superman.

17.

Was it therewith over? Was that greatest of all antitheses of ideals thereby relegated ad acta for all time? Or only postponed, postponed for a long[Pg 57] time? May there not take place at some time or other a much more awful, much more carefully prepared flaring up of the old conflagration? Further! Should not one wish that consummation with all one's strength?—will it one's self? demand it one's self? He who at this juncture begins, like my readers, to reflect, to think further, will have difficulty in coming quickly to a conclusion,—ground enough for me to come myself to a conclusion, taking it for granted that for some time past what I mean has been sufficiently clear, what I exactly mean by that dangerous motto which is inscribed on the body of my last book: Beyond Good and Evil—at any rate that is not the same as "Beyond Good and Bad."

Note.—I avail myself of the opportunity offered by this treatise to express, openly and formally, a wish which up to the present has only been expressed in occasional conversations with scholars, namely, that some Faculty of philosophy should, by means of a series of prize essays, gain the glory of having promoted the further study of the history of morals—perhaps this book may serve to give forcible impetus in such a direction. With regard to a possibility of this character, the following question deserves consideration. It merits quite as much the attention of philologists and historians as of actual professional philosophers.

"What indication of the history of the evolution of the moral ideas is afforded by philology, and especially by etymological investigation?"

On the other hand, it is of course equally necessary to induce physiologists and doctors to be interested in these problems (of the value of the valuations which have prevailed up to the present): in this connection the professional philosophers may be trusted to act as the spokesmen and intermediaries in these particular instances, after, of course, they have quite succeeded in transforming the relationship between[Pg 58] philosophy and physiology and medicine, which is originally one of coldness and suspicion, into the most friendly and fruitful reciprocity. In point of fact, all tables of values, all the "thou shalts" known to history and ethnology, need primarily a physiological, at any rate in preference to a psychological, elucidation and interpretation; all equally require a critique from medical science. The question, "What is the value of this or that table of 'values' and morality?" will be asked from the most varied standpoints. For instance, the question of "valuable for what" can never be analysed with sufficient nicety. That, for instance, which would evidently have value with regard to promoting in a race the greatest possible powers of endurance (or with regard to increasing its adaptability to a specific climate, or with regard to the preservation of the greatest number) would have nothing like the same value, if it were a question of evolving a stronger species. In gauging values, the good of the majority and the good of the minority are opposed standpoints: we leave it to the naïveté of English biologists to regard the former standpoint as intrinsically superior. All the sciences have now to pave the way for the future task of the philosopher; this task being understood to mean, that he must solve the problem of value, that he has to fix the hierarchy of values.

SECOND ESSAY.
"GUILT," "BAD CONSCIENCE," AND THE LIKE.

1.

The breeding of an animal that can promise—is not this just that very paradox of a task which nature has set itself in regard to man? Is not this the very problem of man? The fact that this problem has been to a great extent solved, must appear all the more phenomenal to one who can estimate at its full value that force of forgetfulness which works in opposition to it. Forgetfulness is no mere vis inertiæ, as the superficial believe, rather is it a power of obstruction, active and, in the strictest sense of the word, positive—a power responsible for the fact that what we have lived, experienced, taken into ourselves, no more enters into consciousness during the process of digestion (it might be called psychic absorption) than all the whole manifold process by which our physical nutrition, the so-called "incorporation," is carried on. The temporary shutting of the doors and windows of consciousness, the relief from the clamant alarums and excursions, with which our subconscious world of servant organs works in mutual co-operation and antagonism; a little quietude, a little tabula rasa of the consciousness, so as to make room again for the new, and above all for the more noble functions and functionaries, room for government, foresight, predetermination (for our organism is on an oligarchic model)—this[Pg 62] is the utility, as I have said, of the active forgetfulness, which is a very sentinel and nurse of psychic order, repose, etiquette; and this shows at once why it is that there can exist no happiness, no gladness, no hope, no pride, no real present, without forgetfulness. The man in whom this preventative apparatus is damaged and discarded, is to be compared to a dyspeptic, and it is something more than a comparison—he can "get rid of" nothing. But this very animal who finds it necessary to be forgetful, in whom, in fact, forgetfulness represents a force and a form of robust health, has reared for himself an opposition-power, a memory, with whose help forgetfulness is, in certain instances, kept in check—in the cases, namely, where promises have to be made;—so that it is by no means a mere passive inability to get rid of a once indented impression, not merely the indigestion occasioned by a once pledged word, which one cannot dispose of, but an active refusal to get rid of it, a continuing and a wish to continue what has once been willed, an actual memory of the will; so that between the original "I will," "I shall do," and the actual discharge of the will, its act, we can easily interpose a world of new strange phenomena, circumstances, veritable volitions, without the snapping of this long chain of the will. But what is the underlying hypothesis of all this? How thoroughly, in order to be able to regulate the future in this way, must man have first learnt to distinguish between necessitated and accidental phenomena, to think causally, to see the distant as present and to anticipate it, to fix with certainty[Pg 63] what is the end, and what is the means to that end; above all, to reckon, to have power to calculate—how thoroughly must man have first become calculable, disciplined, necessitated even for himself and his own conception of himself, that, like a man entering into a promise, he could guarantee himself as a future.

2.

This is simply the long history of the origin of responsibility. That task of breeding an animal which can make promises, includes, as we have already grasped, as its condition and preliminary, the more immediate task of first making man to a certain extent, necessitated, uniform, like among his like, regular, and consequently calculable. The immense work of what I have called, "morality of custom"[1] (cp. Dawn of Day, Aphs. 9, 14, and 16), the actual work of man on himself during the longest period of the human race, his whole prehistoric work, finds its meaning, its great justification (in spite of all its innate hardness, despotism, stupidity, and idiocy) in this fact: man, with the help of the morality of customs and of social strait-waistcoats, was made genuinely calculable. If, however, we place ourselves at the end of this colossal process, at the point where the tree finally matures its fruits, when society and its morality of custom finally bring to light that to which it was only the means, then do we find as the ripest fruit on its tree the sovereign individual, that resembles only himself, that has got loose from the morality of[Pg 64] custom, the autonomous "super-moral" individual (for "autonomous" and "moral" are mutually-exclusive terms),—in short, the man of the personal, long, and independent will, competent to promise, and we find in him a proud consciousness (vibrating in every fibre), of what has been at last achieved and become vivified in him, a genuine consciousness of power and freedom, a feeling of human perfection in general. And this man who has grown to freedom, who is really competent to promise, this lord of the free will, this sovereign—how is it possible for him not to know how great is his superiority over everything incapable of binding itself by promises, or of being its own security, how great is the trust, the awe, the reverence that he awakes—he "deserves" all three—not to know that with this mastery over himself he is necessarily also given the mastery over circumstances, over nature, over all creatures with shorter wills, less reliable characters? The "free" man, the owner of a long unbreakable will, finds in this possession his standard of value: looking out from himself upon the others, he honours or he despises, and just as necessarily as he honours his peers, the strong and the reliable (those who can bind themselves by promises),—that is, every one who promises like a sovereign, with difficulty, rarely and slowly, who is sparing with his trusts but confers honour by the very fact of trusting, who gives his word as something that can be relied on, because he knows himself strong enough to keep it even in the teeth of disasters, even in the "teeth of fate,"—so with equal necessity will he have the[Pg 65] heel of his foot ready for the lean and empty jackasses, who promise when they have no business to do so, and his rod of chastisement ready for the liar, who already breaks his word at the very minute when it is on his lips. The proud knowledge of the extraordinary privilege of responsibility, the consciousness of this rare freedom, of this power over himself and over fate, has sunk right down to his innermost depths, and has become an instinct, a dominating instinct—what name will he give to it, to this dominating instinct, if he needs to have a word for it? But there is no doubt about it—the sovereign man calls it his conscience.

3.

His conscience?—One apprehends at once that the idea "conscience," which is here seen in its supreme manifestation, supreme in fact to almost the point of strangeness, should already have behind it a long history and evolution. The ability to guarantee one's self with all due pride, and also at the same time to say yes to one's self—that is, as has been said, a ripe fruit, but also a late fruit:—How long must needs this fruit hang sour and bitter on the tree! And for an even longer period there was not a glimpse of such a fruit to to be had— no one had taken it on himself to promise it, although everything on the tree was quite ready for it, and everything was maturing for that very consummation. "How is a memory to be made for the man-animal? How is an impression to be so deeply fixed upon this ephemeral[Pg 66] understanding, half dense, and half silly, upon this incarnate forgetfulness, that it will be permanently present?" As one may imagine, this primeval problem was not solved by exactly gentle answers and gentle means; perhaps there is nothing more awful and more sinister in the early history of man than his system of mnemonics. "Something is burnt in so as to remain in his memory: only that which never stops hurting remains in his memory." This is an axiom of the oldest (unfortunately also the longest) psychology in the world. It might even be said that wherever solemnity, seriousness, mystery, and gloomy colours are now found in the life of the men and of nations of the world, there is some survival of that horror which was once the universal concomitant of all promises, pledges, and obligations. The past, the past with all its length, depth, and hardness, wafts to us its breath, and bubbles up in us again, when we become "serious." When man thinks it necessary to make for himself a memory, he never accomplishes it without blood, tortures, and sacrifice; the most dreadful sacrifices and forfeitures (among them the sacrifice of the first-born), the most loathsome mutilation (for instance, castration), the most cruel rituals of all the religious cults (for all religions are really at bottom systems of cruelty)—all these things originate from that instinct which found in pain its most potent mnemonic. In a certain sense the whole of asceticism is to be ascribed to this: certain ideas have got to be made inextinguishable, omnipresent, "fixed," with the object of hypnotising the whole nervous[Pg 67] and intellectual system through these "fixed ideas"— and the ascetic methods and modes of life are the means of freeing those ideas from the competition of all other ideas so as to make them "unforgettable." The worse memory man had, the ghastlier the signs presented by his customs; the severity of the penal laws affords in particular a gauge of the extent of man's difficulty in conquering forgetfulness, and in keeping a few primal postulates of social intercourse ever present to the minds of those who were the slaves of every momentary emotion and every momentary desire. We Germans do certainly not regard ourselves as an especially cruel and hardhearted nation, still less as an especially casual and happy-go-lucky one; but one has only to look at our old penal ordinances in order to realise what a lot of trouble it takes in the world to evolve a "nation of thinkers" (I mean: the European nation which exhibits at this very day the maximum of reliability, seriousness, bad taste, and positiveness, which has on the strength of these qualities a right to train every kind of European mandarin). These Germans employed terrible means to make for themselves a memory, to enable them to master their rooted plebeian instincts and the brutal crudity of those instincts: think of the old German punishments, for instance, stoning (as far back as the legend, the millstone falls on the head of the guilty man), breaking on the wheel (the most original invention and speciality of the German genius in the sphere of punishment), dart-throwing, tearing, or trampling by horses ("quartering"),[Pg 68] boiling the criminal in oil or wine (still prevalent in the fourteenth and fifteenth centuries), the highly popular flaying ("slicing into strips"), cutting the flesh out of the breast; think also of the evil-doer being besmeared with honey, and then exposed to the flies in a blazing sun. It was by the help of such images and precedents that man eventually kept in his memory five or six "I will nots" with regard to which he had already given his promise, so as to be able to enjoy the advantages of society—and verily with the help of this kind of memory man eventually attained "reason"! Alas! reason, seriousness, mastery over the emotions, all these gloomy, dismal things which are called reflection, all these privileges and pageantries of humanity: how dear is the price that they have exacted! How much blood and cruelty is the foundation of all "good things"!

4.

But how is it that that other melancholy object, the consciousness of sin, the whole "bad conscience," came into the world? And it is here that we turn back to our genealogists of morals. For the second time I say—or have I not said it yet?—that they are worth nothing. Just their own five-spans-long limited modern experience; no knowledge of the past, and no wish to know it; still less a historic instinct, a power of "second sight" (which is what is really required in this case)—and despite this to go in for the history of morals. It stands to reason that this must needs produce results which[Pg 69] are removed from the truth by something more than a respectful distance.

Have these current genealogists of morals ever allowed themselves to have even the vaguest notion, for instance, that the cardinal moral idea of "ought"[2] originates from the very material idea of "owe"? Or that punishment developed as a retaliation absolutely independently of any preliminary hypothesis of the freedom or determination of the will?—And this to such an extent, that a high degree of civilisation was always first necessary for the animal man to begin to make those much more primitive distinctions of "intentional," "negligent," "accidental," "responsible," and their contraries, and apply them in the assessing of punishment. That idea—"the wrong-doer deserves punishment because he might have acted otherwise," in spite of the fact that it is nowadays so cheap, obvious, natural, and inevitable, and that it has had to serve as an illustration of the way in which the sentiment of justice appeared on earth, is in point of fact an exceedingly late, and even refined form of human judgment and inference; the placing of this idea back at the beginning of the world is simply a clumsy violation of the principles of primitive psychology. Throughout the longest period of human history punishment was never based on the responsibility of the evil-doer for his action, and was consequently not based on the hypothesis[Pg 70] that only the guilty should be punished;—on the contrary, punishment was inflicted in those days for the same reason that parents punish their children even nowadays, out of anger at an injury that they have suffered, an anger which vents itself mechanically on the author of the injury—but this anger is kept in bounds and modified through the idea that every injury has somewhere or other its equivalent price, and can really be paid off, even though it be by means of pain to the author. Whence is it that this ancient deep-rooted and now perhaps ineradicable idea has drawn its strength, this idea of an equivalency between injury and pain? I have already revealed its origin, in the contractual relationship between creditor and ower, that is as old as the existence of legal rights at all, and in its turn points back to the primary forms of purchase, sale, barter, and trade.

5.

The realisation of these contractual relations excites, of course (as would be already expected from our previous observations), a great deal of suspicion and opposition towards the primitive society which made or sanctioned them. In this society promises will be made; in this society the object is to provide the promiser with a memory; in this society, so may we suspect, there will be full scope for hardness, cruelty, and pain: the "ower," in order to induce credit in his promise of repayment, in order to give a guarantee of the earnestness and sanctity of his promise, in order[Pg 71] to drill into his own conscience the duty, the solemn duty, of repayment, will, by virtue of a contract with his creditor to meet the contingency of his not paying, pledge something that he still possesses, something that he still has in his power, for instance, his life or his wife, or his freedom or his body (or under certain religious conditions even his salvation, his soul's welfare, even his peace in the grave; so in Egypt, where the corpse of the ower found even in the grave no rest from the creditor—of course, from the Egyptian standpoint, this peace was a matter of particular importance). But especially has the creditor the power of inflicting on the body of the ower all kinds of pain and torture—the power, for instance, of cutting off from it an amount that appeared proportionate to the greatness of the debt;—this point of view resulted in the universal prevalence at an early date of precise schemes of valuation, frequently horrible in the minuteness and meticulosity of their application, legally sanctioned schemes of valuation for individual limbs and parts of the body. I consider it as already a progress, as a proof of a freer, less petty, and more Roman conception of law, when the Roman Code of the Twelve Tables decreed that it was immaterial how much or how little the creditors in such a contingency cut off, "si plus minusve secuerunt, ne fraude esto." Let us make the logic of the whole of this equalisation process clear; it is strange enough. The equivalence consists in this: instead of an advantage directly compensatory of his injury (that is, instead of an equalisation in money,[Pg 72] lands, or some kind of chattel), the creditor is granted by way of repayment and compensation a certain sensation of satisfaction—the satisfaction of being able to vent, without any trouble, his power on one who is powerless, the delight "de faire le mal pour le plaisir de le faire," the joy in sheer violence: and this joy will be relished in proportion to the lowness and humbleness of the creditor in the social scale, and is quite apt to have the effect of the most delicious dainty, and even seem the foretaste of a higher social position. Thanks to the punishment of the "ower," the creditor participates in the rights of the masters. At last he too, for once in a way, attains the edifying consciousness of being able to despise and ill-treat a creature—as an "inferior"—or at any rate of seeing him being despised and ill-treated, in case the actual power of punishment, the administration of punishment, has already become transferred to the "authorities." The compensation consequently consists in a claim on cruelty and a right to draw thereon.

6.

It is then in this sphere of the law of contract that we find the cradle of the whole moral world of the ideas of "guilt," "conscience," "duty," the "sacredness of duty,"—their commencement, like the commencement of all great things in the world, is thoroughly and continuously saturated with blood. And should we not add that this world has never really lost a certain savour of blood and torture (not even in old Kant; the[Pg 73] categorical imperative reeks of cruelty). It was in this sphere likewise that there first became formed that sinister and perhaps now indissoluble association of the ideas of "guilt" and "suffering." To put the question yet again, why can suffering be a compensation for "owing"?—Because the infliction of suffering produces the highest degree of happiness, because the injured party will get in exchange for his loss (including his vexation at his loss) an extraordinary counter-pleasure: the infliction of suffering—a real feast, something that, as I have said, was all the more appreciated the greater the paradox created by the rank and social status of the creditor. These observations are purely conjectural; for, apart from the painful nature of the task, it is hard to plumb such profound depths: the clumsy introduction of the idea of "revenge" as a connecting-link simply hides and obscures the view instead of rendering it clearer (revenge itself simply leads back again to the identical problem—"How can the infliction of suffering be a satisfaction?"). In my opinion it is repugnant to the delicacy, and still more to the hypocrisy of tame domestic animals (that is, modern men; that is, ourselves), to realise with all their energy the extent to which cruelty constituted the great joy and delight of ancient man, was an ingredient which seasoned nearly all his pleasures, and conversely the extent of the naïveté and innocence with which he manifested his need for cruelty, when he actually made as a matter of principle "disinterested malice" (or, to use Spinoza's expression, the sympathia malevolens) into a normal[Pg 74] characteristic of man— as consequently something to which the conscience says a hearty yes. The more profound observer has perhaps already had sufficient opportunity for noticing this most ancient and radical joy and delight of mankind; in Beyond Good and Evil, Aph. 188 (and even earlier, in The Dawn of Day, Aphs. 18, 77, 113), I have cautiously indicated the continually growing spiritualisation and "deification" of cruelty, which pervades the whole history of the higher civilisation (and in the larger sense even constitutes it). At any rate the time is not so long past when it was impossible to conceive of royal weddings and national festivals on a grand scale, without executions, tortures, or perhaps an auto-da-fé", or similarly to conceive of an aristocratic household, without a creature to serve as a butt for the cruel and malicious baiting of the inmates. (The reader will perhaps remember Don Quixote at the court of the Duchess: we read nowadays the whole of Don Quixote with a bitter taste in the mouth, almost with a sensation of torture, a fact which would appear very strange and very incomprehensible to the author and his contemporaries—they read it with the best conscience in the world as the gayest of books; they almost died with laughing at it.) The sight of suffering does one good, the infliction of suffering does one more good—this is a hard maxim, but none the less a fundamental maxim, old, powerful, and "human, all-too-human"; one, moreover, to which perhaps even the apes as well would subscribe: for it is said that in inventing bizarre[Pg 75] cruelties they are giving abundant proof of their future humanity, to which, as it were, they are playing the prelude. Without cruelty, no feast: so teaches the oldest and longest history of man—and in punishment too is there so much of the festive.

7.

Entertaining, as I do, these thoughts, I am, let me say in parenthesis, fundamentally opposed to helping our pessimists to new water for the discordant and groaning mills of their disgust with life; on the contrary, it should be shown specifically that, at the time when mankind was not yet ashamed of its cruelty, life in the world was brighter than it is nowadays when there are pessimists. The darkening of the heavens over man has always increased in proportion to the growth of man's shame before man. The tired pessimistic outlook, the mistrust of the riddle of life, the icy negation of disgusted ennui, all those are not the signs of the most evil age of the human race: much rather do they come first to the light of day, as the swamp-flowers, which they are, when the swamp to which they belong, comes into existence—I mean the diseased refinement and moralisation, thanks to which the "animal man" has at last learnt to be ashamed of all his instincts. On the road to angelhood (not to use in this context a harder word) man has developed that dyspeptic stomach and coated tongue, which have made not only the joy and innocence of the animal repulsive to him, but[Pg 76] also life itself:—so that sometimes he stands with stopped nostrils before his own self, and, like Pope Innocent the Third, makes a black list of his own horrors ("unclean generation, loathsome nutrition when in the maternal body, badness of the matter out of which man develops, awful stench, secretion of saliva, urine, and excrement"). Nowadays, when suffering is always trotted out as the first argument against existence, as its most sinister query, it is well to remember the times when men judged on converse principles because they could not dispense with the infliction of suffering, and saw therein a magic of the first order, a veritable bait of seduction to life.

Perhaps in those days (this is to solace the weaklings) pain did not hurt so much as it does nowadays: any physician who has treated negroes (granted that these are taken as representative of the prehistoric man) suffering from severe internal inflammations which would bring a European, even though he had the soundest constitution, almost to despair, would be in a position to come to this conclusion. Pain has not the same effect with negroes. (The curve of human sensibilities to pain seems indeed to sink in an extraordinary and almost sudden fashion, as soon as one has passed the upper ten thousand or ten millions of over-civilised humanity, and I personally have no doubt that, by comparison with one painful night passed by one single hysterical chit of a cultured woman, the suffering of all the animals taken together who have been put to the question of the knife, so as to give scientific answers, are simply[Pg 77] negligible.) We may perhaps be allowed to admit the possibility of the craving for cruelty not necessarily having become really extinct: it only requires, in view of the fact that pain hurts more nowadays, a certain sublimation and subtilisation, it must especially be translated to the imaginative and psychic plane, and be adorned with such smug euphemisms, that even the most fastidious and hypocritical conscience could never grow suspicious of their real nature ("Tragic pity" is one of these euphemisms: another is "les nostalgies de la croix"). What really raises one's indignation against suffering is not suffering intrinsically, but the senselessness of suffering; such a senselessness, however, existed neither in Christianity, which interpreted suffering into a whole mysterious salvation-apparatus, nor in the beliefs of the naive ancient man, who only knew how to find a meaning in suffering from the standpoint of the spectator, or the inflictor of the suffering. In order to get the secret, undiscovered, and unwitnessed suffering out of the world it was almost compulsory to invent gods and a hierarchy of intermediate beings, in short, something which wanders even among secret places, sees even in the dark, and makes a point of never missing an interesting and painful spectacle. It was with the help of such inventions that life got to learn the tour de force, which has become part of its stock-in-trade, the tour de force of self-justification, of the justification of evil; nowadays this would perhaps require other auxiliary devices (for instance, life as a riddle, life as a problem of[Pg 78] knowledge). "Every evil is justified in the sight of which a god finds edification," so rang the logic of primitive sentiment—and, indeed, was it only of primitive? The gods conceived as friends of spectacles of cruelty—oh how far does this primeval conception extend even nowadays into our European civilisation! One would perhaps like in this context to consult Luther and Calvin. It is at any rate certain that even the Greeks knew no more piquant seasoning for the happiness of their gods than the joys of cruelty. What, do you think, was the mood with which Homer makes his gods look down upon the fates of men? What final meaning have at bottom the Trojan War and similar tragic horrors? It is impossible to entertain any doubt on the point: they were intended as festival games for the gods, and, in so far as the poet is of a more godlike breed than other men, as festival games also for the poets. It was in just this spirit and no other, that at a later date the moral philosophers of Greece conceived the eyes of God as still looking down on the moral struggle, the heroism, and the self-torture of the virtuous; the Heracles of duty was on a stage, and was conscious of the fact; virtue without witnesses was something quite unthinkable for this nation of actors. Must not that philosophic invention, so audacious and so fatal, which was then absolutely new to Europe, the invention of "free will," of the absolute spontaneity of man in good and evil, simply have been made for the specific purpose of justifying the idea, that the interest of[Pg 79] the gods in humanity and human virtue was inexhaustible?

There would never on the stage of this free-will world be a dearth of really new, really novel and exciting situations, plots, catastrophes. A world thought out on completely deterministic lines would be easily guessed by the gods, and would consequently soon bore them—sufficient reason for these friends of the gods, the philosophers, not to ascribe to their gods such a deterministic world. The whole of ancient humanity is full of delicate consideration for the spectator, being as it is a world of thorough publicity and theatricality, which could not conceive of happiness without spectacles and festivals.—And, as has already been said, even in great punishment there is so much which is festive.

8.

The feeling of "ought," of personal obligation (to take up again the train of our inquiry), has had, as we saw, its origin in the oldest and most original personal relationship that there is, the relationship between buyer and seller, creditor and ower: here it was that individual confronted individual, and that individual matched himself against individual. There has not yet been found a grade of civilisation so low, as not to manifest some trace of this relationship. Making prices, assessing values, thinking out equivalents, exchanging—

all this preoccupied the primal thoughts of man to such an extent that in a certain sense[Pg 80] it constituted thinking itself: it was here that was trained the oldest form of sagacity, it was here in this sphere that we can perhaps trace the first commencement of man's pride, of his feeling of superiority over other animals. Perhaps our word "Mensch" (manas) still expresses just something of this self-pride: man denoted himself as the being who measures values, who values and measures, as the "assessing" animal par excellence. Sale and purchase, together with their psychological concomitants, are older than the origins of any form of social organisation and union: it is rather from the most rudimentary form of individual right that the budding consciousness of exchange, commerce, debt, right, obligation, compensation was first transferred to the rudest and most elementary of the social complexes (in their relation to similar complexes), the habit of comparing force with force, together with that of measuring, of calculating. His eye was now focussed to this perspective; and with that ponderous consistency characteristic of ancient thought, which, though set in motion with difficulty, yet proceeds inflexibly along the line on which it has started, man soon arrived at the great generalisation, "everything has its price, all can be paid for," the oldest and most naive moral canon of justice, the beginning of all "kindness," of all "equity," of all "goodwill," of all "objectivity" in the world. Justice in this initial phase is the goodwill among people of about equal power to come to terms with each other, to come to an understanding again by means of a settlement, and with regard to the less[Pg 81] powerful, to compel them to agree among themselves to a settlement.

9.

Measured always by the standard of antiquity (this antiquity, moreover, is present or again possible at all periods), the community stands to its members in that important and radical relationship of creditor to his "owers." Man lives in a community, man enjoys the advantages of a community (and what advantages! we occasionally underestimate them nowadays), man lives protected, spared, in peace and trust, secure from certain injuries and enmities, to which the man outside the community, the "peaceless" man, is exposed,—a German understands the original meaning of "Elend" (êlend),—secure because he has entered into pledges and obligations to the community in respect of these very injuries and enmities. What happens when this is not the case? The community, the defrauded creditor, will get itself paid, as well as it can, one can reckon on that. In this case the question of the direct damage done by the offender is quite subsidiary: quite apart from this the criminal[3] is above all a breaker, a breaker of word and covenant to the whole, as regards all the advantages and amenities of the communal life in which up to that time he had participated. The criminal is an "ower" who not only fails to repay the advances and advantages that have been given to him, but even sets out to attack his creditor:[Pg 82] consequently he is in the future not only, as is fair, deprived of all these advantages and amenities—he is in addition reminded of the importance of those advantages. The wrath of the injured creditor, of the community, puts him back in the wild and outlawed status from which he was previously protected: the community repudiates him— and now every kind of enmity can vent itself on him. Punishment is in this stage of civilisation simply the copy, the mimic, of the normal treatment of the hated, disdained, and conquered enemy, who is not only deprived of every right and protection but of every mercy; so we have the martial law and triumphant festival of the væ victis! in all its mercilessness and cruelty. This shows why war itself (counting the sacrificial cult of war) has produced all the forms under which punishment has manifested itself in history.

10.

As it grows more powerful, the community tends to take the offences of the individual less seriously, because they are now regarded as being much less revolutionary and dangerous to the corporate existence: the evil-doer is no more outlawed and put outside the pale, the common wrath can no longer vent itself upon him with its old licence,—on the contrary, from this very time it is against this wrath, and particularly against the wrath of those directly injured, that the evil-doer is carefully shielded and protected by the community. As, in fact, the penal law[Pg 83] develops, the following characteristics become more and more clearly marked: compromise with the wrath of those directly affected by the misdeed; a consequent endeavour to localise the matter and to prevent a further, or indeed a general spread of the disturbance; attempts to find equivalents and to settle the whole matter (compositio); above all, the will, which manifests itself with increasing definiteness, to treat every offence as in a certain degree capable of being paid off, and consequently, at any rate up to a certain point, to isolate the offender from his act. As the power and the self-consciousness of a community increases, so proportionately does the penal law become mitigated; conversely every weakening and jeopardising of the community revives the harshest forms of that law. The creditor has always grown more humane proportionately as he has grown more rich; finally the amount of injury he can endure without really suffering becomes the criterion of his wealth. It is possible to conceive of a society blessed with so great a consciousness of its own power as to indulge in the most aristocratic luxury of letting its wrong-doers go scot-free.—"What do my parasites matter to me?" might society say. "Let them live and flourish! I am strong enough for it."—The justice which began with the maxim, "Everything can be paid off, everything must be paid off," ends with connivance at the escape of those who cannot pay to escape—it ends, like every good thing on earth, by destroying itself.—The self-destruction of Justice! we know[Pg 84] the pretty name it calls itself—Grace! it remains, as is obvious, the privilege of the strongest, better still, their super-law.

11.

A deprecatory word here against the attempts, that have lately been made, to find the origin of justice on quite another basis—namely, on that of resentment. Let me whisper a word in the ear of the psychologists, if they would fain study revenge itself at close quarters: this plant blooms its prettiest at present among Anarchists and anti-Semites, a hidden flower, as it has ever been, like the violet, though, forsooth, with another perfume. And as like must necessarily emanate from like, it will not be a matter for surprise that it is just in such circles that we see the birth of endeavours (it is their old birthplace—compare above, First Essay, paragraph 14), to sanctify revenge under the name of justice (as though Justice were at bottom merely a development of the consciousness of injury), and thus with the rehabilitation of revenge to reinstate generally and collectively all the reactive emotions. I object to this last point least of all. It even seems meritorious when regarded from the standpoint of the whole problem of biology (from which standpoint the value of these emotions has up to the present been underestimated). And that to which I alone call attention, is the circumstance that it is the spirit of revenge itself, from which develops this new nuance of scientific equity (for the benefit of hate, envy, mistrust,[Pg 85] jealousy, suspicion, rancour, revenge). This scientific "equity" stops immediately and makes way for the accents of deadly enmity and prejudice, so soon as another group of emotions comes on the scene, which in my opinion are of a much higher biological value than these reactions, and consequently have a paramount claim to the valuation and appreciation of science: I mean the really active emotions, such as personal and material ambition, and so forth. (E. Dühring, Value of Life; Course of Philosophy, and passim.) So much against this tendency in general: but as for the particular maxim of Dühring's, that the home of Justice is to be found in the sphere of the reactive feelings, our love of truth compels us drastically to invert his own proposition and to oppose to him this other maxim: the last sphere conquered by the spirit of justice is the sphere of the feeling of reaction! When it really comes about that the just man remains just even as regards his injurer (and not merely cold, moderate, reserved, indifferent: being just is always a positive state); when, in spite of the strong provocation of personal insult, contempt, and calumny, the lofty and clear objectivity of the just and judging eye (whose glance is as profound as it is gentle) is untroubled, why then we have a piece of perfection, a past master of the world—something, in fact, which it would not be wise to expect, and which should not at any rate be too easily believed. Speaking generally, there is no doubt but that even the justest individual only requires a little dose of[Pg 86] hostility, malice, or innuendo to drive the blood into his brain and the fairness from it. The active man, the attacking, aggressive man is always a hundred degrees nearer to justice than the man who merely reacts; he certainly has no need to adopt the tactics, necessary in the case of the reacting man, of making false and biassed valuations of his object. It is, in point of fact, for this reason that the aggressive man has at all times enjoyed the stronger, bolder, more aristocratic, and also freer outlook, the better conscience. On the other hand, we already surmise who it really is that has on his conscience the invention of the "bad conscience,"—the resentful man! Finally, let man look at himself in history. In what sphere up to the present has the whole administration of law, the actual need of law, found its earthly home? Perchance in the sphere of the reacting man? Not for a minute: rather in that of the active, strong, spontaneous, aggressive man? I deliberately defy the above-mentioned agitator (who himself makes this self-confession, "the creed of revenge has run through all my works and endeavours like the red thread of Justice"), and say, that judged historically law in the world represents the very war against the reactive feelings, the very war waged on those feelings by the powers of activity and aggression, which devote some of their strength to damming and keeping within bounds this effervescence of hysterical reactivity, and to forcing it to some compromise. Everywhere where justice is practised and justice is maintained, it is to be observed that the[Pg

87] stronger power, when confronted with the weaker powers which are inferior to it (whether they be groups, or individuals), searches for weapons to put an end to the senseless fury of resentment, while it carries on its object, partly by taking the victim of resentment out of the clutches of revenge, partly by substituting for revenge a campaign of its own against the enemies of peace and order, partly by finding, suggesting, and occasionally enforcing settlements, partly by standardising certain equivalents for injuries, to which equivalents the element of resentment is henceforth finally referred. The most drastic measure, however, taken and effectuated by the supreme power, to combat the preponderance of the feelings of spite and vindictiveness—it takes this measure as soon as it is at all strong enough to do so—is the foundation of law, the imperative declaration of what in its eyes is to be regarded as just and lawful, and what unjust and unlawful: and while, after the foundation of law, the supreme power treats the aggressive and arbitrary acts of individuals, or of whole groups, as a violation of law, and a revolt against itself, it distracts the feelings of its subjects from the immediate injury inflicted by such a violation, and thus eventually attains the very opposite result to that always desired by revenge, which sees and recognises nothing but the standpoint of the injured party. From henceforth the eye becomes trained to a more and more impersonal valuation of the deed, even the eye of the injured party himself (though this is in the final stage of all, as has been[Pg 88] previously remarked)— on this principle "right" and "wrong" first manifest themselves after the foundation of law (and not, as Dühring maintains, only after the act of violation). To talk of intrinsic right and intrinsic wrong is absolutely non-sensical; intrinsically, an injury, an oppression, an exploitation, an annihilation can be nothing wrong, inasmuch as life is essentially (that is, in its cardinal functions) something which functions by injuring, oppressing, exploiting, and annihilating, and is absolutely inconceivable without such a character. It is necessary to make an even more serious confession:—viewed from the most advanced biological standpoint, conditions of legality can be only exceptional conditions, in that they are partial restrictions of the real life-will, which makes for power, and in that they are subordinated to the life-will's general end as particular means, that is, as means to create larger units of strength. A legal organisation, conceived of as sovereign and universal, not as a weapon in a fight of complexes of power, but as a weapon against fighting, generally something after the style of Dühring's communistic model of treating every will as equal with every other will, would be a principle hostile to life, a destroyer and dissolver of man, an outrage on the future of man, a symptom of fatigue, a secret cut to Nothingness.—

12.

A word more on the origin and end of punishment—two problems which are or ought to be kept distinct, but which unfortunately are usually lumped into one. And what tactics have our moral genealogists employed up to the present in these cases? Their inveterate naïveté. They find out some "end" in the punishment, for instance, revenge and deterrence, and then in all their innocence set this end at the beginning, as the causa fiendi of the punishment, and—they have done the trick. But the patching up of a history of the origin of law is the last use to which the "End in Law"[4] ought to be put. Perhaps there is no more pregnant principle for any kind of history than the following, which, difficult though it is to master, should none the less be mastered in every detail.—The origin of the existence of a thing and its final utility, its practical application and incorporation in a system of ends, are toto cœlo opposed to each other—everything, anything, which exists and which prevails anywhere, will always be put to new purposes by a force superior to itself, will be commandeered afresh, will be turned and transformed to new uses; all "happening" in the organic world consists of overpowering and dominating, and again all overpowering and domination is a new interpretation and adjustment, which must necessarily obscure or absolutely extinguish the subsisting "meaning" and "end." The most perfect comprehension of the utility of any physiological organ (or also of a legal institution, social custom, political habit, form in art or in religious worship) does not for a minute imply any simultaneous comprehension of its origin: this may seem uncomfortable and unpalatable to the older men,—for it has been the immemorial belief that understanding the final cause or the utility of a thing, a form, an institution, means also understanding the reason for its origin: to give an example of this logic, the eye was made to see, the hand was made to grasp. So even punishment was conceived as invented with a view to punishing. But all ends and all utilities are only signs that a Will to Power has mastered a less powerful force, has impressed thereon out of its own self the meaning of a function; and the whole history of a "Thing," an organ, a custom, can on the same principle be regarded as a continuous "sign-chain" of perpetually new interpretations and adjustments, whose causes, so far from needing to have even a mutual connection, sometimes follow and alternate with each other absolutely haphazard. Similarly, the evolution of a "thing," of a custom, is anything but its progressus to an end, still less a logical and direct progressus attained with the minimum expenditure of energy and cost: it is rather the succession of processes of subjugation, more or less profound, more or less mutually independent, which operate on the thing itself; it is, further, the resistance which in each case invariably displayed this subjugation, the Protean wriggles by way of defence and reaction, and, further, the results of successful counter-efforts. The form is fluid, but the[Pg 91] meaning is even more so— even inside every individual organism the case is the same: with every genuine growth of the whole, the "function" of the individual organs becomes shifted,—in certain cases a partial perishing of these organs, a diminution of their numbers (for instance, through annihilation of the connecting members), can be a symptom of growing strength and perfection. What I mean is this: even partial loss of utility, decay, and degeneration, loss of function and purpose, in a word, death, appertain to the conditions of the genuine progressus; which always appears in the shape of a will and way to greater power, and is always realised at the expense of innumerable smaller powers. The magnitude of a "progress" is gauged by the greatness of the sacrifice that it requires: humanity as a mass sacrificed to the prosperity of the one stronger species of Man—that would be a progress. I emphasise all the more this cardinal characteristic of the historic method, for the reason that in its essence it runs counter to predominant instincts and prevailing taste, which much prefer to put up with absolute casualness, even with the mechanical senselessness of all phenomena, than with the theory of a power-will, in exhaustive play throughout all phenomena. The democratic idiosyncrasy against everything which rules and wishes to rule, the modern misarchism (to coin a bad word for a bad thing), has gradually but so thoroughly transformed itself into the guise of intellectualism, the most abstract intellectualism, that even nowadays it penetrates and has the right to penetrate step[Pg 92] by step into the most exact and apparently the most objective sciences: this tendency has, in fact, in my view already dominated the whole of physiology and biology, and to their detriment, as is obvious, in so far as it has spirited away a radical idea, the idea of true activity. The tyranny of this idiosyncrasy, however, results in the theory of "adaptation" being pushed forward into the van of the argument, exploited; adaptation—that means to say, a second-class activity, a mere capacity for "reacting"; in fact, life itself has been defined (by Herbert Spencer) as an increasingly effective internal adaptation to external circumstances. This definition, however, fails to realise the real essence of life, its will to power. It fails to appreciate the paramount superiority enjoyed by those plastic forces of spontaneity, aggression, and encroachment with their new interpretations and tendencies, to the operation of which adaptation is only a natural corollary: consequently the sovereign office of the highest functionaries in the organism itself (among which the life-will appears as an active and formative principle) is repudiated. One remembers Huxley's reproach to Spencer of his "administrative Nihilism": but it is a case of something much more than "administration."

13.

To return to our subject, namely punishment, we must make consequently a double distinction: first, the relatively permanent element, the custom,[Pg 93] the act, the "drama," a certain rigid sequence of methods of procedure; on the other hand, the fluid element, the meaning, the end, the expectation which is attached to the operation of such procedure. At this point we immediately assume, per analogiam (in accordance with the theory of the historic method, which we have elaborated above), that the procedure itself is something older and earlier than its utilisation in punishment, that this utilisation was introduced and interpreted into the procedure (which had existed for a long time, but whose employment had another meaning), in short, that the case is different from that hitherto supposed by our naïf genealogists of morals and of law, who thought that the procedure was invented for the purpose of punishment, in the same way that the hand had been previously thought to have been invented for the purpose of grasping. With regard to the other element in punishment, its fluid element, its meaning, the idea of punishment in a very late stage of civilisation (for instance, contemporary Europe) is not content with manifesting merely one meaning, but manifests a whole synthesis "of meanings." The past general history of punishment, the history of its employment for the most diverse ends, crystallises eventually into a kind of unity, which is difficult to analyse into its parts, and which, it is necessary to emphasise, absolutely defies definition. (It is nowadays impossible to say definitely the precise reason for punishment: all ideas, in which a whole process is promiscuously comprehended, elude definition; it is only that which[Pg 94] has no history, which can be defined.) At an earlier stage, on the contrary, that synthesis of meanings appears much less rigid and much more elastic; we can realise how in each individual case the elements of the synthesis change their value and their position, so that now one element and now another stands out and predominates over the others, nay, in certain cases one element (perhaps the end of deterrence) seems to eliminate all the rest. At any rate, so as to give some idea of the uncertain, supplementary, and accidental nature of the meaning of punishment and of the manner in which one identical procedure can be employed and adapted for the most diametrically opposed objects, I will at this point give a scheme that has suggested itself to me, a scheme itself based on comparatively small and accidental material.—Punishment, as rendering the criminal harmless and incapable of further injury.—Punishment, as compensation for the injury sustained by the injured party, in any form whatsoever (including the form of sentimental compensation).—Punishment, as an isolation of that which disturbs the equilibrium, so as to prevent the further spreading of the disturbance.—Punishment as a means of inspiring fear of those who determine and execute the punishment.—Punishment as a kind of compensation for advantages which the wrong-doer has up to that time enjoyed (for example, when he is utilised as a slave in the mines).—Punishment, as the elimination of an element of decay (sometimes of a whole branch, as according to the Chinese laws, consequently as a means to the purification[Pg 95] of the race, or the preservation of a social type).—-Punishment as a festival, as the violent oppression and humiliation of an enemy that has at last been subdued.—Punishment as a mnemonic, whether for him who suffers the punishment—the so-called "correction," or for the witnesses of its administration. Punishment, as the payment of a fee stipulated for by the power which protects the evil-doer from the excesses of revenge.—Punishment, as a compromise with the natural phenomenon of revenge, in so far as revenge is still maintained and claimed as a privilege by the stronger races.—Punishment as a declaration and measure of war against an enemy of peace, of law, of order, of authority, who is fought by society with the weapons which war provides, as a spirit dangerous to the community, as a breaker of the contract on which the community is based, as a rebel, a traitor, and a breaker of the peace.

14.

This list is certainly not complete; it is obvious that punishment is overloaded with utilities of all kinds. This makes it all the more permissible to eliminate one supposed utility, which passes, at any rate in the popular mind, for its most essential utility, and which is just what even now provides the strongest support for that faith in punishment which is nowadays for many reasons tottering. Punishment is supposed to have the value of exciting in the guilty the consciousness of guilt; in punishment is sought the proper instrumentum of that psychic reaction which becomes known as a "bad conscience," "remorse." But this theory is even, from the point of view of the present, a violation of reality and psychology: and how much more so is the case when we have to deal with the longest period of man's history, his primitive history! Genuine remorse is certainly extremely rare among wrong-doers and the victims of punishment; prisons and houses of correction are not the soil on which this worm of remorse pullulates for choice—this is the unanimous opinion of all conscientious observers, who in many cases arrive at such a judgment with enough reluctance and against their own personal wishes. Speaking generally, punishment hardens and numbs, it produces concentration, it sharpens the consciousness of alienation, it strengthens the power of resistance. When it happens that it breaks the man's energy and brings about a piteous prostration and abjectness, such a result is certainly even less salutary than the average effect of punishment, which is characterised by a harsh and sinister doggedness. The thought of those prehistoric millennia brings us to the unhesitating conclusion, that it was simply through punishment that the evolution of the consciousness of guilt was most forcibly retarded—at any rate in the victims of the punishing power. In particular, let us not underestimate the extent to which, by the very sight of the judicial and executive procedure, the wrong-doer is himself prevented from feeling that his deed, the character of his act, is intrinsically reprehensible: for he sees clearly the same kind of acts practised in the service of justice, and then called good, and practised with a good conscience; acts such as espionage, trickery, bribery, trapping, the whole intriguing and insidious art of the policeman and the informer—the whole system, in fact, manifested in the different kinds of punishment (a system not excused by passion, but based on principle), of robbing, oppressing, insulting, imprisoning, racking, murdering.—All this he sees treated by his judges, not as acts meriting censure and condemnation in themselves, but only in a particular context and application. It was not on this soil that grew the "bad conscience," that most sinister and interesting plant of our earthly vegetation— in point of fact, throughout a most lengthy period, no suggestion of having to do with a "guilty man" manifested itself in the consciousness of the man who judged and punished. One had merely to deal with an author of an injury, an irresponsible piece of fate. And the man himself, on whom the punishment subsequently fell like a piece of fate, was occasioned no more of an "inner pain" than would be occasioned by the sudden approach of some uncalculated event, some terrible natural catastrophe, a rushing, crushing avalanche against which there is no resistance.

15.

This truth came insidiously enough to the consciousness of Spinoza (to the disgust of his commentators, who (like Kuno Fischer, for instance) give themselves no end of trouble to misunderstand him on this point), when one afternoon (as he sat raking up who knows what memory) he indulged in the question of what was really left for him personally of the celebrated morsus conscientiæ— Spinoza, who had relegated "good and evil" to the sphere of human imagination, and indignantly defended the honour of his "free" God against those blasphemers who affirmed that God did everything sub ratione boni ("but this was tantamount to subordinating God to fate, and would really be the greatest of all absurdities"). For Spinoza the world had returned again to that innocence in which it lay before the discovery of the bad conscience: what, then, had happened to the morsus conscientiæ? "The antithesis of gaudium," said he at last to himself,—"A sadness accompanied by the recollection of a past event which has turned out contrary to all expectation" (Eth. III., Propos. XVIII. Schol. i. ii.). Evil-doers have throughout thousands of years felt when overtaken by punishment exactly like Spinoza, on the subject of their "offence": "here is something which went wrong contrary to my anticipation," not "I ought not to have done this."— They submitted themselves to punishment, just as one submits one's self to a disease, to a misfortune, or to death, with that stubborn and resigned fatalism which gives the Russians, for instance, even nowadays, the advantage over us Westerners, in the handling of life. If at that period there was a critique of action, the criterion was prudence: the real effect of punishment is unquestionably chiefly to be found in a sharpening of the sense of prudence, in a lengthening of the memory, in a will to adopt more of a policy of caution, suspicion, and secrecy; in the recognition that there are many things which are unquestionably beyond one's capacity; in a kind of improvement in self-criticism. The broad effects which can be obtained by punishment in man and beast, are the increase of fear, the sharpening of the sense of cunning, the mastery of the desires: so it is that punishment tames man, but does not make him "better"—it would be more correct even to go so far as to assert the contrary ("Injury makes a man cunning," says a popular proverb: so far as it makes him cunning, it makes him also bad. Fortunately, it often enough makes him stupid).

16.

At this juncture I cannot avoid trying to give a tentative and provisional expression to my own hypothesis concerning the origin of the bad conscience: it is difficult to make it fully appreciated, and it requires continuous meditation, attention, and digestion. I regard the bad conscience as the serious illness which man was bound to contract under the stress of the most radical change which he has ever experienced—that change, when he found himself finally imprisoned within the pale of society and of peace.

Just like the plight of the water-animals, when they were compelled either to become land-animals or to perish, so was the plight of these[Pg 100] half-animals, perfectly adapted as they were to the savage life of war, prowling, and adventure—suddenly all their instincts were rendered worthless and "switched off." Henceforward they had to walk on their feet—"carry themselves," whereas heretofore they had been carried by the water: a terrible heaviness oppressed them. They found themselves clumsy in obeying the simplest directions, confronted with this new and unknown world they had no longer their old guides—the regulative instincts that had led them unconsciously to safety—they were reduced, were those unhappy creatures, to thinking, inferring, calculating, putting together causes and results, reduced to that poorest and most erratic organ of theirs, their "consciousness." I do not believe there was ever in the world such a feeling of misery, such a leaden discomfort—further, those old instincts had not immediately ceased their demands! Only it was difficult and rarely possible to gratify them: speaking broadly, they were compelled to satisfy themselves by new and, as it were, hole-and-corner methods. All instincts which do not find a vent without, turn inwards—this is what I mean by the growing "internalisation" of man: consequently we have the first growth in man, of what subsequently was called his soul. The whole inner world, originally as thin as if it had been stretched between two layers of skin, burst apart and expanded proportionately, and obtained depth, breadth, and height, when man's external outlet became obstructed. These terrible bulwarks,[Pg 101] with which the social organisation protected itself against the old instincts of freedom (punishments belong pre-eminently to these bulwarks), brought it about that all those instincts of wild, free, prowling man became turned backwards against man himself. Enmity, cruelty, the delight in persecution, in surprises, change, destruction—the turning all these instincts against their own possessors: this is the origin of the "bad conscience." It was man, who, lacking external enemies and obstacles, and imprisoned as he was in the oppressive narrowness and monotony of custom, in his own impatience lacerated, persecuted, gnawed, frightened, and ill-treated himself; it was this animal in the hands of the tamer, which beat itself against the bars of its cage; it was this being who, pining and yearning for that desert home of which it had been deprived, was compelled to create out of its own self, an adventure, a torture-chamber, a hazardous and perilous desert—it was this fool, this homesick and desperate prisoner—who invented the "bad conscience." But thereby he introduced that most grave and sinister illness, from which mankind has not yet recovered, the suffering of man from the disease called man, as the result of a violent breaking from his animal past, the result, as it were, of a spasmodic plunge into a new environment and new conditions of existence, the result of a declaration of war against the old instincts, which up to that time had been the staple of his power, his joy, his formidableness. Let us immediately add that this fact of an animal ego turning against itself,[Pg 102] taking part against itself, produced in the world so novel, profound, unheard-of, problematic, inconsistent, and pregnant a phenomenon, that the aspect of the world was radically altered thereby. In sooth, only divine spectators could have appreciated the drama that then began, and whose end baffles conjecture as yet—a drama too subtle, too wonderful, too paradoxical to warrant its undergoing a non-sensical and unheeded performance on some random grotesque planet! Henceforth man is to be counted as one of the most unexpected and sensational lucky shots in the game of the "big baby" of Heracleitus, whether he be called Zeus or Chance—he awakens on his behalf the interest, excitement, hope, almost the confidence, of his being the harbinger and forerunner of something, of man being no end, but only a stage, an interlude, a bridge, a great promise.

17.

It is primarily involved in this hypothesis of the origin of the bad conscience, that that alteration was no gradual and no voluntary alteration, and that it did not manifest itself as an organic adaptation to new conditions, but as a break, a jump, a necessity, an inevitable fate, against which there was no resistance and never a spark of resentment. And secondarily, that the fitting of a hitherto unchecked and amorphous population into a fixed form, starting as it had done in an act of violence, could only be accomplished by acts of violence and nothing else—that the oldest[Pg 103] "State" appeared consequently as a ghastly tyranny, a grinding ruthless piece of machinery, which went on working, till this raw material of a semi-animal populace was not only thoroughly kneaded and elastic, but also moulded. I used the word "State": my meaning is self-evident, namely, a herd of blonde beasts of prey, a race of conquerors and masters, which with all its warlike organisation and all its organising power pounces with its terrible claws on a population, in numbers possibly tremendously superior, but as yet formless, as yet nomad. Such is the origin of the "State." That fantastic theory that makes it begin with a contract is, I think, disposed of. He who can command, he who is a master by "nature," he who comes on the scene forceful in deed and gesture—what has he to do with contracts? Such beings defy calculation, they come like fate, without cause, reason, notice, excuse, they are there like the lightning is there, too terrible, too sudden, too convincing, too "different," to be personally even hated. Their work is an instinctive creating and impressing of forms, they are the most involuntary, unconscious artists that there are:—their appearance produces instantaneously a scheme of sovereignty which is live, in which the functions are partitioned and apportioned, in which above all no part is received or finds a place, until pregnant with a "meaning" in regard to the whole. They are ignorant of the meaning of guilt, responsibility, consideration, are these born organisers; in them predominates that terrible artist-egoism, that[Pg 104] gleams like brass, and that knows itself justified to all eternity, in its work, even as a mother in her child. It is not in them that there grew the bad conscience, that is elementary—but it would not have grown without them, repulsive growth as it was, it would be missing, had not a tremendous quantity of freedom been expelled from the world by the stress of their hammer-strokes, their artist violence, or been at any rate made invisible and, as it were, latent. This instinct of freedom forced into being latent—it is already clear—this instinct of freedom forced back, trodden back, imprisoned within itself, and finally only able to find vent and relief in itself; this, only this, is the beginning of the "bad conscience."

18.

Beware of thinking lightly of this phenomenon, by reason of its initial painful ugliness. At bottom it is the same active force which is at work on a more grandiose scale in those potent artists and organisers, and builds states, which here, internally, on a smaller and pettier scale and with a retrogressive tendency, makes itself a bad science in the "labyrinth of the breast," to use Goethe's phrase, and which builds negative ideals; it is, I repeat, that identical instinct of freedom (to use my own language, the will to power): only the material, on which this force with all its constructive and tyrannous nature is let loose, is here man himself, his whole old animal self—and not as in the case of that more grandiose and sensational[Pg 105] phenomenon, the other man, other men. This secret self-tyranny, this cruelty of the artist, this delight in giving a form to one's self as a piece of difficult, refractory, and suffering material, in burning in a will, a critique, a contradiction, a contempt, a negation; this sinister and ghastly labour of love on the part of a soul, whose will is cloven in two within itself, which makes itself suffer from delight in the infliction of suffering; this wholly active bad conscience has finally (as one already anticipates)—true fountainhead as it is of idealism and imagination—produced an abundance of novel and amazing beauty and affirmation, and perhaps has really been the first to give birth to beauty at all. What would beauty be, forsooth, if its contradiction had not first been presented to consciousness, if the ugly had not first said to itself, "I am ugly"? At any rate, after this hint the problem of how far idealism and beauty can be traced in such opposite ideas as "selflessness," self-denial, self-sacrifice, becomes less problematical; and indubitably in future we shall certainly know the real and original character of the delight experienced by the self-less, the self-denying, the self-sacrificing: this delight is a phase of cruelty.—So much provisionally for the origin of "altruism" as a moral value, and the marking out the ground from which this value has grown: it is only the bad conscience, only the will for self-abuse, that provides the necessary conditions for the existence of altruism as a value.

19.

Undoubtedly the bad conscience is an illness, but an illness like pregnancy is an illness. If we search out the conditions under which this illness reaches its most terrible and sublime zenith, we shall see what really first brought about its entry into the world. But to do this we must take a long breath, and we must first of all go back once again to an earlier point of view. The relation at civil law of the ower to his creditor (which has already been discussed in detail), has been interpreted once again (and indeed in a manner which historically is exceedingly remarkable and suspicious) into a relationship, which is perhaps more incomprehensible to us moderns than to any other era; that is, into the relationship of the existing generation to its ancestors. Within the original tribal association—we are talking of primitive times—each living generation recognises a legal obligation towards the earlier generation, and particularly towards the earliest, which founded the family (and this is something much more than a mere sentimental obligation, the existence of which, during the longest period of man's history, is by no means indisputable). There prevails in them the conviction that it is only thanks to sacrifices and efforts of their ancestors, that the race persists at all—and that this has to be paid back to them by sacrifices and services. Thus is recognised the owing of a debt, which accumulates continually by reason of these ancestors never[Pg 107] ceasing in their subsequent life as potent spirits to secure by their power new privileges and advantages to the race. Gratis, perchance? But there is no gratis for that raw and "mean-souled" age. What return can be made?—Sacrifice (at first, nourishment, in its crudest sense), festivals, temples, tributes of veneration, above all, obedience—since all customs are, quâ works of the ancestors, equally their precepts and commands—are the ancestors ever given enough? This suspicion remains and grows: from time to time it extorts a great wholesale ransom, something monstrous in the way of repayment of the creditor (the notorious sacrifice of the first-born, for example, blood, human blood in any case). The fear of ancestors and their power, the consciousness of owing debts to them, necessarily increases, according to this kind of logic, in the exact proportion that the race itself increases, that the race itself becomes more victorious, more independent, more honoured, more feared. This, and not the contrary, is the fact. Each step towards race decay, all disastrous events, all symptoms of degeneration, of approaching disintegration, always diminish the fear of the founders' spirit, and whittle away the idea of his sagacity, providence, and potent presence. Conceive this crude kind of logic carried to its climax: it follows that the ancestors of the most powerful races must, through the growing fear that they exercise on the imaginations, grow themselves into monstrous dimensions, and become relegated to the gloom of a divine mystery that transcends imagination—the ancestor becomes at[Pg 108] last necessarily transfigured into a god. Perhaps this is the very origin of the gods, that is, an origin from fear! And those who feel bound to add, "but from piety also," will have difficulty in maintaining this theory, with regard to the primeval and longest period of the human race. And of course this is even more the case as regards the middle period, the formative period of the aristocratic races—the aristocratic races which have given back with interest to their founders, the ancestors (heroes, gods), all those qualities which in the meanwhile have appeared in themselves, that is, the aristocratic qualities. We will later on glance again at the ennobling and promotion of the gods (which of course is totally distinct from their "sanctification"): let us now provisionally follow to its end the course of the whole of this development of the consciousness of "owing."

20.

According to the teaching of history, the consciousness of owing debts to the deity by no means came to an end with the decay of the clan organisation of society; just as mankind has inherited the ideas of "good" and "bad" from the race-nobility (together with its fundamental tendency towards establishing social distinctions), so with the heritage of the racial and tribal gods it has also inherited the incubus of debts as yet unpaid and the desire to discharge them. The transition is effected by those large populations of slaves and bondsmen, who, whether through[Pg 109] compulsion or through submission and "mimicry," have accommodated themselves to the religion of their masters; through this channel these inherited tendencies inundate the world. The feeling of owing a debt to the deity has grown continuously for several centuries, always in the same proportion in which the idea of God and the consciousness of God have grown and become exalted among mankind. (The whole history of ethnic fights, victories, reconciliations, amalgamations, everything, in fact, which precedes the eventual classing of all the social elements in each great race-synthesis, are mirrored in the hotch-potch genealogy of their gods, in the legends of their fights, victories, and reconciliations. Progress towards universal empires invariably means progress towards universal deities; despotism, with its subjugation of the independent nobility, always paves the way for some system or other of monotheism.) The appearance of the Christian god, as the record god up to this time, has for that very reason brought equally into the world the record amount of guilt consciousness. Granted that we have gradually started on the reverse movement, there is no little probability in the deduction, based on the continuous decay in the belief in the Christian god, to the effect that there also already exists a considerable decay in the human consciousness of owing (ought); in fact, we cannot shut our eyes to the prospect of the complete and eventual triumph of atheism freeing mankind from all this feeling of obligation to their origin, their causa prima. Atheism and a kind of second[Pg 110] innocence complement and supplement each other.

21.

So much for my rough and preliminary sketch of the interrelation of the ideas "ought" (owe) and "duty" with the postulates of religion. I have intentionally shelved up to the present the actual moralisation of these ideas (their being pushed back into the conscience, or more precisely the interweaving of the bad conscience with the idea of God), and at the end of the last paragraph used language to the effect that this moralisation did not exist, and that consequently these ideas had necessarily come to an end, by reason of what had happened to their hypothesis, the credence in our "creditor," in God. The actual facts differ terribly from this theory. It is with the moralisation of the ideas "ought" and "duty," and with their being pushed back into the bad conscience, that comes the first actual attempt to reverse the direction of the development we have just described, or at any rate to arrest its evolution; it is just at this juncture that the very hope of an eventual redemption has to put itself once for all into the prison of pessimism, it is at this juncture that the eye has to recoil and rebound in despair from off an adamantine impossibility, it is at this juncture that the ideas "guilt" and "duty" have to turn backwards— turn backwards against whom? There is no doubt about it; primarily against the "ower," in whom the bad conscience now establishes itself, eats, extends, and grows[Pg 111] like a polypus throughout its length and breadth, all with such virulence, that at last, with the impossibility of paying the debt, there becomes conceived the idea of the impossibility of paying the penalty, the thought of its inexpiability (the idea of "eternal punishment")—finally, too, it turns against the "creditor," whether found in the causa prima of man, the origin of the human race, its sire, who henceforth becomes burdened with a curse ("Adam," "original sin," "determination of the will"), or in Nature from whose womb man springs, and on whom the responsibility for the principle of evil is now cast ("Diabolisation of Nature"), or in existence generally, on this logic an absolute white elephant, with which mankind is landed (the Nihilistic flight from life, the demand for Nothingness, or for the opposite of existence, for some other existence, Buddhism and the like)—till suddenly we stand before that paradoxical and awful expedient, through which a tortured humanity has found a temporary alleviation, that stroke of genius called Christianity:—God personally immolating himself for the debt of man, God paying himself personally out of a pound of his own flesh, God as the one being who can deliver man from what man had become unable to deliver himself—the creditor playing scapegoat for his debtor, from love (can you believe it?), from love of his debtor!...

22.

The reader will already have conjectured what took place on the stage and behind the scenes of[Pg 112] this drama. That will for self-torture, that inverted cruelty of the animal man, who, turned subjective and scared into introspection (encaged as he was in "the State," as part of his taming process), invented the bad conscience so as to hurt himself, after the natural outlet for this will to hurt, became blocked—in other words, this man of the bad conscience exploited the religious hypothesis so as to carry his martyrdom to the ghastliest pitch of agonised intensity. Owing something to God: this thought becomes his instrument of torture. He apprehends in God the most extreme antitheses that he can find to his own characteristic and ineradicable animal instincts, he himself gives a new interpretation to these animal instincts as being against what he "owes" to God (as enmity, rebellion, and revolt against the "Lord," the "Father," the "Sire," the "Beginning of the world"), he places himself between the horns of the dilemma, "God" and "Devil." Every negation which he is inclined to utter to himself, to the nature, naturalness, and reality of his being, he whips into an ejaculation of "yes," uttering it as something existing, living, efficient, as being God, as the holiness of God, the judgment of God, as the hangmanship of God, as transcendence, as eternity, as unending torment, as hell, as infinity of punishment and guilt. This is a kind of madness of the will in the sphere of psychological cruelty which is absolutely unparalleled:—

man's will to find himself guilty and blameworthy to the point of inexpiability, his will to think of himself as punished, without the punishment ever being[Pg 113] able to balance the guilt, his will to infect and to poison the fundamental basis of the universe with the problem of punishment and guilt, in order to cut off once and for all any escape out of this labyrinth of "fixed ideas," his will for rearing an ideal—that of the "holy God"—face to face with which he can have tangible proof of his own un-worthiness. Alas for this mad melancholy beast man! What phantasies invade it, what paroxysms of perversity, hysterical senselessness, and mental bestiality break out immediately, at the very slightest check on its being the beast of action. All this is excessively interesting, but at the same time tainted with a black, gloomy, enervating melancholy, so that a forcible veto must be invoked against looking too long into these abysses. Here is disease, undubitably, the most ghastly disease that has as yet played havoc among men: and he who can still hear (but man turns now deaf ears to such sounds), how in this night of torment and nonsense there has rung out the cry of love, the cry of the most passionate ecstasy, of redemption in love, he turns away gripped by an invincible horror—in man there is so much that is ghastly—too long has the world been a mad-house.

23.

Let this suffice once for all concerning the origin of the "holy God." The fact that in itself the conception of gods is not bound to lead necessarily to this degradation of the imagination (a temporary representation of whose vagaries we felt bound[Pg 114] give), the fact that there exist nobler methods of utilising the invention of gods than in this self-crucifixion and self-degradation of man, in which the last two thousand years of Europe have been past masters—these facts can fortunately be still perceived from every glance that we cast at the Grecian gods, these mirrors of noble and grandiose men, in which the animal in man felt itself deified, and did not devour itself in subjective frenzy. These Greeks long utilised their gods as simple buffers against the "bad conscience"—so that they could continue to enjoy their freedom of soul: this, of course, is diametrically opposed to Christianity's theory of its god. They went very far on this principle, did these splendid and lion-hearted children; and there is no lesser authority than that of the Homeric Zeus for making them realise occasionally that they are taking life too casually. "Wonderful," says he on one occasion—it has to do with the case of Ægistheus, a very bad case indeed—

"Wonderful how they grumble, the mortals against the immortals,

Only from us, they presume, comes evil, but in their folly,

Fashion they, spite of fate, the doom of their own disaster."

Yet the reader will note and observe that this Olympian spectator and judge is far from being angry with them and thinking evil of them on this score. "How foolish they are," so thinks he[Pg 115] of the misdeeds of mortals—and "folly," "imprudence," "a little brain disturbance," and nothing more, are what the Greeks, even of the strongest, bravest period, have admitted to be the ground of much that is evil and fatal.—Folly, not sin, do you understand?... But even this brain disturbance was a problem—"Come, how is it even possible? How could it have really got in brains like ours, the brains of men of aristocratic ancestry, of men of fortune, of men of good natural endowments, of men of the best society, of men of nobility and virtue?" This was the question that for century on century the aristocratic Greek put to himself when confronted with every (to him incomprehensible) outrage and sacrilege with which one of his peers had polluted himself. "It must be that a god had infatuated him," he would say at last, nodding his head.—This solution is typical of the Greeks, ... accordingly the gods in those times subserved the functions of justifying man to a certain extent even in evil—in those days they took upon themselves not the punishment, but, what is more noble, the guilt.

24.

I conclude with three queries, as you will see. "Is an ideal actually set up here, or is one pulled down?" I am perhaps asked.... But have ye sufficiently asked yourselves how dear a payment has the setting up of every ideal in the world exacted? To achieve that consummation how much truth must always be traduced and misunderstood, how many lies must be sanctified,[Pg 116] how much conscience has got to be disturbed, how many pounds of "God" have got to be sacrificed every time? To enable a sanctuary to be set up a sanctuary has got to be destroyed: that is a law—show me an instance where it has not been fulfilled!... We modern men, we inherit the immemorial tradition of vivisecting the conscience, and practising cruelty to our animal selves. That is the sphere of our most protracted training, perhaps of our artistic prowess, at any rate of our dilettantism and our perverted taste. Man has for too long regarded his natural proclivities with an "evil eye," so that eventually they have become in his system affiliated to a bad conscience. A converse endeavour would be intrinsically feasible—but who is strong enough to attempt it?—namely, to affiliate to the "bad conscience" all those unnatural proclivities, all those transcendental aspirations, contrary to sense, instinct, nature, and animalism—in short, all past and present ideals, which are all ideals opposed to life, and traducing the world. To whom is one to turn nowadays with such hopes and pretensions?—It is just the good men that we should thus bring about our ears; and in addition, as stands to reason, the indolent, the hedgers, the vain, the hysterical, the tired.... What is more offensive or more thoroughly calculated to alienate, than giving any hint of the exalted severity with which we treat ourselves? And again how conciliatory, how full of love does all the world show itself towards us so soon as we do as all the world docs, and "let ourselves go" like all the world. For such a[Pg 117] consummation we need spirits of different calibre than seems really feasible in this age; spirits rendered potent through wars and victories, to whom conquest, adventure, danger, even pain, have become a need; for such a consummation we need habituation to sharp, rare air, to winter wanderings, to literal and metaphorical ice and mountains; we even need a kind of sublime malice, a supreme and most self-conscious insolence of knowledge, which is the appanage of great health; we need (to summarise the awful truth) just this great health!

Is this even feasible to-day?... But some day, in a stronger age than this rotting and introspective present, must he in sooth come to us, even the redeemer of great love and scorn, the creative spirit, rebounding by the impetus of his own force back again away from every transcendental plane and dimension, he whose solitude is misunderstood (sic) of the people, as though it were a flight from reality;—while actually it is only his diving, burrowing, and penetrating into reality, so that when he comes again to the light he can at once bring about by these means the redemption of this reality; its redemption from the curse which the old ideal has laid upon it. This man of the future, who in this wise will redeem us from the old ideal, as he will from that ideal's necessary corollary of great nausea, will to nothingness, and Nihilism; this tocsin of noon and of the great verdict, which renders the will again free, who gives back to the world its goal and to man his hope, this Antichrist and Antinihilist, this conqueror of God and of Nothingness—he must one day come.

25.

But what am I talking of? Enough! Enough? At this juncture I have only one proper course, silence: otherwise tresspass on a domain open alone to one who is younger than I, one stronger, more "future" than I—open alone to Zarathustra, Zarathustra the godless.

[1]The German is: "Sittlichkeit der Sitte." H. B. S.

[2]The German world "schuld" means both debt and guilt. Cp. the English "owe" and "ought," by which I occasionally render the double meaning.—H. B. S.

[3]German: "Verbrecher."—H.B.S.

[4]An allusion to Der Zweck im Recht, by the great German jurist, Professor Ihering.

THIRD ESSAY.
WHAT IS THE MEANING OF ASCETIC IDEALS?

"Careless, mocking, forceful—so does wisdom wish us: she is a woman, and never loves any one but a warrior."

Thus Spake Zarathustra.

1.

What is the meaning of ascetic ideals? In artists, nothing, or too much; in philosophers and scholars, a kind of "flair" and instinct for the conditions most favourable to advanced intellectualism; in women, at best an additional seductive fascination, a little morbidezza on a fine piece of flesh, the angelhood of a fat, pretty animal; in physiological failures and whiners (in the majority of mortals), an attempt to pose as "too good" for this world, a holy form of debauchery, their chief weapon in the battle with lingering pain and ennui; in priests, the actual priestly faith, their best engine of power, and also the supreme authority for power; in saints, finally a pretext for hibernation, their novissima gloriæ cupido, their peace in nothingness ("God"), their form of madness.

But in the very fact that the ascetic ideal has meant so much to man, lies expressed the fundamental feature of man's will, his horror vacui: he needs a goal—and he will sooner will nothingness than not will at all.—Am I not understood?—Have I not been understood?—"Certainly not, sir?"—Well, let us begin at the beginning.

2.

What is the meaning of ascetic ideals? Or, to take an individual case in regard to which I have[Pg 122] often been consulted, what is the meaning, for example, of an artist like Richard Wagner paying homage to chastity in his old age? He had always done so, of course, in a certain sense, but it was not till quite the end, that he did so in an ascetic sense. What is the meaning of this "change of attitude," this radical revolution in his attitude—for that was what it was? Wagner veered thereby straight round into his own opposite. What is the meaning of an artist veering round into his own opposite? At this point (granted that we do not mind stopping a little over this question), we immediately call to mind the best, strongest, gayest, and boldest period, that there perhaps ever was in Wagner's life: that was the period, when he was genuinely and deeply occupied with the idea of "Luther's Wedding." Who knows what chance is responsible for our now having the Meistersingers instead of this wedding music? And how much in the latter is perhaps just an echo of the former? But there is no doubt but that the theme would have dealt with the praise of chastity. And certainly it would also have dealt with the praise of sensuality, and even so, it would seem quite in order, and even so, it would have been equally Wagnerian. For there is no necessary antithesis between chastity and sensuality: every good marriage, every authentic heart-felt love transcends this antithesis. Wagner would, it seems to me, have done well to have brought this pleasing reality home once again to his Germans, by means of a bold and graceful "Luther Comedy," for there[Pg 123] were and are among the Germans many revilers of sensuality; and perhaps Luther's greatest merit lies just in the fact of his having had the courage of his sensuality (it used to be called, prettily enough, "evangelistic freedom "). But even in those cases where that antithesis between chastity and sensuality does exist, there has fortunately been for some time no necessity for it to be in any way a tragic antithesis. This should, at any rate, be the case with all beings who are sound in mind and body, who are far from reckoning their delicate balance between "animal" and "angel," as being on the face of it one of the principles opposed to existence—the most subtle and brilliant spirits, such as Goethe, such as Hafiz, have even seen in this a further charm of life. Such "conflicts" actually allure one to life. On the other hand, it is only too clear that when once these ruined swine are reduced to worshipping chastity—and there are such swine—they only see and worship in it the antithesis to themselves, the antithesis to ruined swine. Oh what a tragic grunting and eagerness! You can just think of it—they worship that painful and superfluous contrast, which Richard Wagner in his latter days undoubtedly wished to set to music, and to place on the stage! "For what purpose, forsooth?" as we may reasonably ask. What did the swine matter to him; what do they matter to us?

3.

At this point it is impossible to beg the further question of what he really had to do with[Pg 124] that manly (ah, so unmanly) country bumpkin, that poor devil and natural, Parsifal, whom he eventually made a Catholic by such fraudulent devices. What? Was this Parsifal really meant seriously? One might be tempted to suppose the contrary, even to wish it—that the Wagnerian Parsifal was meant joyously, like a concluding play of a trilogy or satyric drama, in which Wagner the tragedian wished to take farewell of us, of himself, above all of tragedy, and to do so in a manner that should be quite fitting and worthy, that is, with an excess of the most extreme and flippant parody of the tragic itself, of the ghastly earthly seriousness and earthly woe of old—a parody of that most crude phase in the unnaturalness of the ascetic ideal, that had at length been overcome. That, as I have said, would have been quite worthy of a great tragedian; who like every artist first attains the supreme pinnacle of his greatness when he can look down into himself and his art, when he can laugh at himself. Is Wagner's Parsifal his secret laugh of superiority over himself, the triumph of that supreme artistic freedom and artistic transcendency which he has at length attained. We might, I repeat, wish it were so, for what can Parsifal, taken seriously, amount to? Is it really necessary to see in it (according to an expression once used against me) the product of an insane hate of knowledge, mind, and flesh? A curse on flesh and spirit in one breath of hate? An apostasy and reversion to the morbid Christian and obscurantist ideals? And finally a self-negation and self-elimination on the[Pg 125] part of an artist, who till then had devoted all the strength of his will to the contrary, namely, the highest artistic expression of soul and body. And not only of his art; of his life as well. Just remember with what enthusiasm Wagner followed in the footsteps of Feuerbach. Feuerbach's motto of "healthy sensuality" rang in the ears of Wagner during the thirties and forties of the century, as it did in the ears of many Germans (they dubbed themselves "Young Germans"), like the word of redemption. Did he eventually change his mind on the subject? For it seems at any rate that he eventually wished to change his teaching on that subject ... and not only is that the case with the Parsifal trumpets on the stage: in the melancholy, cramped, and embarrassed lucubrations of his later years, there are a hundred places in which there are manifestations of a secret wish and will, a despondent, uncertain, unavowed will to preach actual retrogression, conversion, Christianity, mediævalism, and to say to his disciples, "All is vanity! Seek salvation elsewhere!" Even the "blood of the Redeemer" is once invoked.

4.

Let me speak out my mind in a case like this, which has many painful elements—and it is a typical case: it is certainly best to separate an artist from his work so completely that he cannot be taken as seriously as his work. He is after all merely the presupposition of his work,[Pg 126] the womb, the soil, in certain cases the dung and manure, on which and out of which it grows—and consequently, in most cases, something that must be forgotten if the work itself is to be enjoyed. The insight into the origin of a work is a matter for psychologists and vivisectors, but never either in the present or the future for the æsthetes, the artists. The author and creator of Parsifal was as little spared the necessity of sinking and living himself into the terrible depths and foundations of mediæval soul-contrasts, the necessity of a malignant abstraction from all intellectual elevation, severity, and discipline, the necessity of a kind of mental perversity (if the reader will pardon me such a word), as little as a pregnant woman is spared the horrors and marvels of pregnancy, which, as I have said, must be forgotten if the child is to be enjoyed. We must guard ourselves against the confusion, into which an artist himself would fall only too easily (to employ the English terminology) out of psychological "contiguity"; as though the artist himself actually were the object which he is able to represent, imagine, and express. In point of fact, the position is that even if he conceived he were such an object, he would certainly not represent, conceive, express it. Homer would not have created an Achilles, nor Goethe a Faust, if Homer had been an Achilles or if Goethe had been a Faust. A complete and perfect artist is to all eternity separated from the "real," from the actual; on the other hand, it will be appreciated that he can at times get tired to the point of despair of this[Pg 127] eternal "unreality" and falseness of his innermost being—and that he then sometimes attempts to trespass on to the most forbidden ground, on reality, and attempts to have real existence. With what success? The success will be guessed—it is the typical velleity of the artist; the same velleity to which Wagner fell a victim in his old age, and for which he had to pay so dearly and so fatally (he lost thereby his most valuable friends). But after all, quite apart from this velleity, who would not wish emphatically for Wagner's own sake that he had taken farewell of us and of his art in a different manner, not with a Parsifal, but in more victorious, more self-confident, more Wagnerian style—a style less misleading, a style less ambiguous with regard to his whole meaning, less Schopenhauerian, less Nihilistic?...

5.

What, then, is the meaning of ascetic ideals? In the case of an artist we are getting to understand their meaning: Nothing at all ... or so much that it is as good as nothing at all. Indeed, what is the use of them? Our artists have for a long time past not taken up a sufficiently independent attitude, either in the world or against it, to warrant their valuations and the changes in these valuations exciting interest. At all times they have played the valet of some morality, philosophy, or religion, quite apart from the fact that unfortunately they have often enough been the inordinately supple courtiers of their clients[Pg 128] and patrons, and the inquisitive toadies of the powers that are existing, or even of the new powers to come. To put it at the lowest, they always need a rampart, a support, an already constituted authority: artists never stand by themselves, standing alone is opposed to their deepest instincts. So, for example, did Richard Wagner take, "when the time had come," the philosopher Schopenhauer for his covering man in front, for his rampart. Who would consider it even thinkable, that he would have had the courage for an ascetic ideal, without the support afforded him by the philosophy of Schopenhauer, without the authority of Schopenhauer, which dominated Europe in the seventies? (This is without consideration of the question whether an artist without the milk[1] of an orthodoxy would have been possible at all.) This brings us to the more serious question: What is the meaning of a real philosopher paying homage to the ascetic ideal, a really self-dependent intellect like Schopenhauer, a man and knight with a glance of bronze, who has the courage to be himself, who knows how to stand alone without first waiting for men who cover him in front, and the nods of his superiors? Let us now consider at once the remarkable attitude of Schopenhauer towards art, an attitude which has even a fascination for certain types. For that is obviously the reason why Richard Wagner all at once went over to[Pg 129] Schopenhauer (persuaded thereto, as one knows, by a poet, Herwegh), went over so completely that there ensued the cleavage of a complete theoretic contradiction between his earlier and his later æsthetic faiths—the earlier, for example, being expressed in Opera and Drama, the later in the writings which he published from 1870 onwards. In particular,

Wagner from that time onwards (and this is the volte-face which alienates us the most) had no scruples about changing his judgment concerning the value and position of music itself. What did he care if up to that time he had made of music a means, a medium, a "woman," that in order to thrive needed an end, a man—that is, the drama? He suddenly realised that more could be effected by the novelty of the Schopenhauerian theory in majorem musicæ gloriam—that is to say, by means of the sovereignty of music, as Schopenhauer understood it; music abstracted from and opposed to all the other arts, music as the independent art-in-itself, not like the other arts, affording reflections of the phenomenal world, but rather the language of the will itself, speaking straight out of the "abyss" as its most personal, original, and direct manifestation. This extraordinary rise in the value of music (a rise which seemed to grow out of the Schopenhauerian philosophy) was at once accompanied by an unprecedented rise in the estimation in which the musician himself was held: he became now an oracle, a priest, nay, more than a priest, a kind of mouthpiece for the "intrinsic essence of things," a telephone from the other world—from[Pg 130] henceforward he talked not only music, did this ventriloquist of God, he talked metaphysic; what wonder that one day he eventually talked ascetic ideals.

6.

Schopenhauer has made use of the Kantian treatment of the æsthetic problem—though he certainly did not regard it with the Kantian eyes. Kant thought that he showed honour to art when he favoured and placed in the foreground those of the predicates of the beautiful, which constitute the honour of knowledge: impersonality and universality. This is not the place to discuss whether this was not a complete mistake; all that I wish to emphasise is that Kant, just like other philosophers, instead of envisaging the æsthetic problem from the standpoint of the experiences of the artist (the creator), has only considered art and beauty from the standpoint of the spectator, and has thereby imperceptibly imported the spectator himself into the idea of the "beautiful"! But if only the philosophers of the beautiful had sufficient knowledge of this "spectator"!—Knowledge of him as a great fact of personality, as a great experience, as a wealth of strong and most individual events, desires, surprises, and raptures in the sphere of beauty! But, as I feared, the contrary was always the case. And so we get from our philosophers, from the very beginning, definitions on which the lack of a subtler personal experience squats like a fat worm of crass error, as it does on Kant's famous definition of the[Pg 131] beautiful. "That is beautiful," says Kant, "which pleases without interesting." Without interesting! Compare this definition with this other one, made by a real "spectator" and "artist"—by Stendhal, who once called the beautiful une promesse de bonheur. Here, at any rate, the one point which Kant makes prominent in the æsthetic position is repudiated and eliminated—le désintéressement. Who is right, Kant or Stendhal? When, forsooth, our æsthetes never get tired of throwing into the scales in Kant's favour the fact that under the magic of beauty men can look at even naked female statues "without interest," we can certainly laugh a little at their expense:—in regard to this ticklish point the experiences of artists are more "interesting," and at any rate Pygmalion was not necessarily an "unæsthetic man." Let us think all the better of the innocence of our æsthetes, reflected as it is in such arguments; let us, for instance, count to Kant's honour the country-parson naïveté of his doctrine concerning the peculiar character of the sense of touch! And here we come back to Schopenhauer, who stood in much closer neighbourhood to the arts than did Kant, and yet never escaped outside the pale of the Kantian definition; how was that? The circumstance is marvellous enough: he interprets the expression, "without interest," in the most personal fashion, out of an experience which must in his case have been part and parcel of his regular routine. On few subjects does Schopenhauer speak with such certainty as on the working of æsthetic contemplation: he says of it that[Pg 132] it simply counteracts sexual interest, like lupulin and camphor; he never gets tired of glorifying this escape from the "Life-will" as the great advantage and utility of the æsthetic state. In fact, one is tempted to ask if his fundamental conception of Will and Idea, the thought that there can only exist freedom from the "will" by means of "idea," did not originate in a generalisation from this sexual experience. (In all questions concerning the Schopenhauerian philosophy, one should, by the bye, never lose sight of the consideration that it is the conception of a youth of twenty-six, so that it participates not only in what is peculiar to Schopenhauer's life, but in what is peculiar to that special period of his life.) Let us listen, for instance, to one of the most expressive among the countless passages which he has written in honour of the æsthetic state (World as Will and Idea, i. 231); let us listen to the tone, the suffering, the happiness, the gratitude, with which such words are uttered: "This is the painless state which Epicurus praised as the highest good and as the state of the gods; we are during that moment freed from the vile pressure of the will, we celebrate the Sabbath of the will's hard labour, the wheel of Ixion stands still." What vehemence of language! What images of anguish and protracted revulsion! How almost pathological is that temporal antithesis between "that moment" and everything else, the "wheel of Ixion," "the hard labour of the will," "the vile pressure of the will." But granted that Schopenhauer was a hundred times right for himself[Pg 133] personally, how does that help our insight into the nature of the beautiful? Schopenhauer has described one effect of the beautiful,—the calming of the will,—but is this effect really normal? As has been mentioned, Stendhal, an equally sensual but more happily constituted nature than Schopenhauer, gives prominence to another effect of the "beautiful." "The beautiful promises happiness." To him it is just the excitement of the "will" (the "interest") by the beauty that seems the essential fact. And does not Schopenhauer ultimately lay himself open to the objection, that he is quite wrong in regarding himself as a Kantian on this point, that he has absolutely failed to understand in a Kantian sense the Kantian definition of the beautiful—;that the beautiful pleased him as well by means of an interest, by means, in fact, of the strongest and most personal interest of all, that: of the victim of torture who escapes from his torture?— And to come back again to our first question, "What is the meaning of a philosopher paying homage to ascetic ideals?" We get now, at any rate, a first hint; he wishes to escape from a torture.

7.

Let us beware of making dismal faces at the word "torture"—there is certainly in this case enough to deduct, enough to discount—there is even something to laugh at. For we must certainly not underestimate the fact that Schopenhauer, who in practice treated sexuality as a[Pg 134] personal enemy (including its tool, woman, that "instrumentum diaboli"), needed enemies to keep him in a good humour; that he loved grim, bitter, blackish-green words; that he raged for the sake of raging, out of passion; that he would have grown ill, would have become a pessimist (for he was not a pessimist, however much he wished to be), without his enemies, without Hegel, woman, sensuality, and the whole "will for existence" "keeping on." Without them Schopenhauer would not have "kept on," that is a safe wager; he would have run away: but his enemies held him fast, his enemies always enticed him back again to existence, his wrath was just as theirs' was to the ancient Cynics, his balm, his recreation, his recompense, his remedium against disgust, his happiness. So much with regard to what is most personal in the case of Schopenhauer; on the other hand, there is still much which is typical in him—and only now we come back to our problem. It is an accepted and indisputable fact, so long as there are philosophers in the world and wherever philosophers have existed (from India to England, to take the opposite poles of philosophic ability), that there exists a real irritation and rancour on the part of philosophers towards sensuality. Schopenhauer is merely the most eloquent, and if one has the ear for it, also the most fascinating and enchanting outburst. There similarly exists a real philosophic bias and affection for the whole ascetic ideal; there should be no illusions on this score. Both these feelings, as has been said, belong to the type; if a philosopher[Pg 135] lacks both of them, then he is—you may be certain of it—never anything but a "pseudo." What does this mean? For this state of affairs must first be, interpreted: in itself it stands there stupid, to all eternity, like any "Thing-in-itself." Every animal, including la bête philosophe, strives instinctively after an optimum of favourable conditions, under which he can let his whole strength have play, and achieves his maximum consciousness of power; with equal instinctiveness, and with a fine perceptive flair which is superior to any reason, every animal shudders mortally at every kind of disturbance and hindrance which obstructs or could obstruct his way to that optimum (it is not his way to happiness of which I am talking, but his way to power, to action, the most powerful action, and in point of fact in many cases his way to unhappiness). Similarly, the philosopher shudders mortally at marriage, together with all that could persuade him to it—marriage as a fatal hindrance on the way to the optimum. Up to the present what great philosophers have been married? Heracleitus, Plato, Descartes, Spinoza, Leibnitz, Kant, Schopenhauer—they were not married, and, further, one cannot imagine them as married. A married philosopher belongs to comedy, that is my rule; as for that exception of a Socrates—the malicious Socrates married himself, it seems, ironice, just to prove this very rule. Every philosopher would say, as Buddha said, when the birth of a son was announced to him: "Râhoula has been born to me, a fetter has been forged for me" (Râhoula means here[Pg 136] "a little demon"); there must come an hour of reflection to every "free spirit" (granted that he has had previously an hour of thoughtlessness), just as one came once to the same Buddha: "Narrowly cramped," he reflected, "is life in the house; it is a place of uncleanness; freedom is found in leaving the house." Because he thought like this, he left the house. So many bridges to independence are shown in the ascetic idea], that the philosopher cannot refrain from exultation and clapping of hands when he hears the history of all those resolute ones, who on one day uttered a nay to all servitude and went into some desert; even granting that they were only strong asses, and the absolute opposite of strong minds. What, then, does the ascetic ideal mean in a philosopher? This is my answer—it will have been guessed long ago: when he sees this ideal the philosopher smiles because he sees therein an optimum of the conditions of the highest and boldest intellectuality; he does not thereby deny "existence," he rather affirms thereby his existence and only his existence, and this perhaps to the point of not being far off the blasphemous wish, pereat mundus, fiat philosophia, fiat philosophus, fiam!

8.

These philosophers, you see, are by no means uncorrupted witnesses and judges of the value of the ascetic ideal. They think of themselves —what is the "saint" to them? They think of that which to them personally is most indispensable; of[Pg 137] freedom from compulsion, disturbance, noise: freedom from business, duties, cares; of clear head; of the dance, spring, and flight of thoughts; of good air—rare, clear, free, dry, as is the air on the heights, in which every animal creature becomes more intellectual and gains wings; they think of peace in every cellar; all the hounds neatly chained; no baying of enmity and uncouth rancour; no remorse of wounded ambition; quiet and submissive internal organs, busy as mills, but unnoticed; the heart alien, transcendent, future, posthumous—to summarise, they mean by the ascetic ideal the joyous asceticism of a deified and newly fledged animal, sweeping over life rather than resting. We know what are the three great catch-words of the ascetic ideal: poverty, humility, chastity; and now just look closely at the life of all the great fruitful inventive spirits—you will always find again and again these three qualities up to a certain extent. Not for a minute, as is self-evident, as though, perchance, they were part of their virtues—what has this type of man to do with virtues?—but as the most essential and natural conditions of their best existence, their finest fruitfulness. In this connection it is quite possible that their predominant intellectualism had first to curb an unruly and irritable pride, or an insolent sensualism, or that it had all its work cut out to maintain its wish for the "desert" against perhaps an inclination to luxury and dilettantism, or similarly against an extravagant liberality of heart and hand. But their intellect did effect all this, simply because it was the dominant instinct, which carried through its orders in the case[Pg 138] of all the other instincts. It effects it still; if it ceased to do so, it would simply not be dominant. But there is not one iota of "virtue" in all this. Further, the desert, of which I just spoke, in which the strong, independent, and well-equipped spirits retreat into their hermitage—oh, how different is it from the cultured classes' dream of a desert! In certain cases, in fact, the cultured classes themselves are the desert. And it is certain that all the actors of the intellect would not endure this desert for a minute. It is nothing like romantic and Syrian enough for them, nothing like enough of a stage desert! Here as well there are plenty of asses, but at this point the resemblance ceases. But a desert nowadays is something like this—perhaps a deliberate obscurity; a getting-out-of the way of one's self; a fear of noise, admiration, papers, influence; a little office, a daily task, something that hides rather than brings to light; sometimes associating with harmless, cheerful beasts and fowls, the sight of which refreshes; a mountain for company, but not a dead one, one with eyes (that is, with lakes); in certain cases even a room in a crowded hotel where one can reckon on not being recognised, and on being able to talk with impunity to every one: here is the desert—oh, it is lonely enough, believe me! I grant that when Heracleitus retreated to the courts and cloisters of the colossal temple of Artemis, that "wilderness" was worthier; why do we lack such temples? (perchance we do not lack them: I just think of my splendid study in the Piazza di San Marco, in spring, of course, and in the morning, between ten and twelve). But that which Heracleitus[Pg 139] shunned is still just what we too avoid nowadays: the noise and democratic babble of the Ephesians, their politics, their news from the "empire" (I mean, of course, Persia), their market-trade in "the things of to-day "—for there is one thing from which we philosophers especially need a rest—from the things of "to-day." We honour the silent, the cold, the noble, the far, the past, everything, in fact, at the sight of which the soul is not bound to brace itself up and defend itself—something with which one can speak without speaking aloud. Just listen now to the tone a spirit has when it speaks; every spirit has its own tone and loves its own tone. That thing yonder, for instance, is bound to be an agitator, that is, a hollow head, a hollow mug: whatever may go into him, everything comes back from him dull and thick, heavy with the echo of the great void. That spirit yonder nearly always speaks hoarse: has he, perchance, thought himself hoarse? It may be so—ask the physiologists—but he who thinks in words, thinks as a speaker and not as a thinker (it shows that he does not think of objects or think objectively, but only of his relations with objects—that, in point of fact, he only thinks of himself and his audience). This third one speaks aggressively, he comes too near our body, his breath blows on us—we shut our mouth involuntarily, although he speaks to us through a book: the tone of his style supplies the reason—he has no time, he has small faith in himself, he finds expression now or never. But a spirit who is sure of himself speaks softly; he seeks secrecy, he lets himself be awaited, A philosopher is recognised by the [Pg 140] fact that he shuns three brilliant and noisy things—fame, princes, and women: which is not to say that they do not come to him. He shuns every glaring light: therefore he shuns his time and its "daylight." Therein he is as a shadow; the deeper sinks the sun, the greater grows the shadow. As for his humility, he endures, as he endures darkness, a certain dependence and obscurity: further, he is afraid of the shock of lightning, he shudders at the insecurity of a tree which is too isolated and too exposed, on which every storm vents its temper, every temper its storm. His "maternal" instinct, his secret love for that which grows in him, guides him into states where he is relieved from the necessity of taking care of himself, in the same way in which the "mother" instinct in woman has thoroughly maintained up to the present woman's dependent position. After all, they demand little enough, do these philosophers, their favourite motto is, "He who possesses is possessed." All this is not, as I must say again and again, to be attributed to a virtue, to a meritorious wish for moderation and simplicity; but because their supreme lord so demands of them, demands wisely and inexorably; their lord who is eager only for one thing, for which alone he musters, and for which alone he hoards everything—time, strength, love, interest. This kind of man likes not to be disturbed by enmity, he likes not to be disturbed by friendship, it is a type which forgets or despises easily. It strikes him as bad form to play the martyr, "to suffer for truth"—he leaves all that to the ambitious and to the stage-heroes of the intellect, and to all those, in fact, who have time[Pg 141] enough for such luxuries (they themselves, the philosophers, have something to do for truth). They make a sparing use of big words; they are said to be adverse to the word "truth" itself: it has a "high falutin'" ring. Finally, as far as the chastity of philosophers is concerned, the fruitfulness of this type of mind is manifestly in another sphere than that of children; perchance in some other sphere, too, they have the survival of their name, their little immortality (philosophers in ancient India would express themselves with still greater boldness: "Of what use is posterity to him whose soul is the world?"). In this attitude there is not a trace of chastity, by reason of any ascetic scruple or hatred of the flesh, any more than it is chastity for an athlete or a jockey to abstain from women; it is rather the will of the dominant instinct, at any rate, during the period of their advanced philosophic pregnancy. Every artist knows the harm done by sexual intercourse on occasions of great mental strain and preparation; as far as the strongest artists and those with the surest instincts are concerned, this is not necessarily a case of experience—hard experience—but it is simply their "maternal" instinct which, in order to benefit the growing work, disposes recklessly (beyond all its normal stocks and supplies) of the vigour of its animal life; the greater power then absorbs the lesser. Let us now apply this interpretation to gauge correctly the case of Schopenhauer, which we have already mentioned: in his case, the sight of the beautiful acted manifestly like a resolving irritant on the chief power of his nature (the power of contemplation and of intense[Pg 142] penetration); so that this strength exploded and became suddenly master of his consciousness. But this by no means excludes the possibility of that particular sweetness and fulness, which is peculiar to the æsthetic state, springing directly from the ingredient of sensuality (just as that "idealism" which is peculiar to girls at puberty originates in the same source)—it may be, consequently, that sensuality is not removed by the approach of the æsthetic state, as Schopenhauer believed, but merely becomes transfigured, and ceases to enter into the consciousness as sexual excitement. (I shall return once again to this point in connection with the more delicate problems of the physiology of the æsthetic, a subject which up to the present has been singularly untouched and unelucidated.)

9.

A certain asceticism, a grimly gay whole-hearted renunciation, is, as we have seen, one of the most favourable conditions for the highest intellectualism, and, consequently, for the most natural corollaries of such intellectualism: we shall therefore be proof against any surprise at the philosophers in particular always treating the ascetic ideal with a certain amount of predilection. A serious historical investigation shows the bond between the ascetic ideal and philosophy to be still much tighter and still much stronger. It may be said that it was only in the leading strings of this ideal that philosophy really learnt to make its first steps and baby paces—alas how clumsily, alas how crossly, alas[Pg 143] how ready to tumble down and lie on its stomach was this shy little darling of a brat with its bandy legs! The early history of philosophy is like that of all good things;—for a long time they had not the courage to be themselves, they kept always looking round to see if no one would come to their help; further, they were afraid of all who looked at them. Just enumerate in order the particular tendencies and virtues of the philosopher—his tendency to doubt, his tendency to deny, his tendency to wait (to be "ephectic"), his tendency to analyse, search, explore, dare, his tendency to compare and to equalise, his will to be neutral and objective, his will for everything which is "sine ira et studio":—has it yet been realised that for quite a lengthy period these tendencies went counter to the first claims of morality and conscience? (To say nothing at all of Reason, which even Luther chose to call Frau Klüglin,[2] the sly whore.) Has it been yet appreciated that a philosopher, in the event of his arriving at self-consciousness, must needs feel himself an incarnate "nitimur in vetitum"—and consequently guard himself against "his own sensations," against self-consciousness? It is, I repeat, just the same with all good things, on which we now pride ourselves; even judged by the standard of the ancient Greeks, our whole modern life, in so far as it is not weakness, but power and the consciousness of power, appears pure "Hybris" and godlessness: for the things which are the very reverse of those which[Pg 144] we honour to-day, have had for a long time conscience on their side, and God as their guardian. "Hybris" is our whole attitude to nature nowadays, our violation of nature with the help of machinery, and all the unscrupulous ingenuity of our scientists and engineers. "Hybris" is our attitude to God, that is, to some alleged teleological and ethical spider behind the meshes of the great trap of the causal web. Like Charles the Bold in his war with Louis the Eleventh, we may say, "je combats l'universelle araignée"; "Hybris" is our attitude to ourselves—for we experiment with ourselves in a way that we would not allow with any animal, and with pleasure and curiosity open our soul in our living body: what matters now to us the "salvation" of the soul? We heal ourselves afterwards: being ill is instructive, we doubt it not, even more instructive than being well—inoculators of disease seem to us to-day even more necessary than any medicine-men and "saviours." There is no doubt we do violence to ourselves nowadays, we crackers of the soul's kernel, we incarnate riddles, who are ever asking riddles, as though life were naught else than the cracking of a nut; and even thereby must we necessarily become day by day more and more worthy to be asked questions and worthy to ask them, even thereby do we perchance also become worthier to—live?

... All good things were once bad things; from every original sin has grown an original virtue. Marriage, for example, seemed for a long time a sin against the rights of the community; a man formerly paid a fine for the insolence of [Pg 145] claiming one woman to himself (to this phase belongs, for instance, the jus primæ noctis, to-day still in Cambodia the privilege of the priest, that guardian of the "good old customs").

The soft, benevolent, yielding, sympathetic feelings—eventually valued so highly that they almost became "intrinsic values," were for a very long time actually despised by their possessors: gentleness was then a subject for shame, just as hardness is now (compare Beyond Good and Evil, Aph. 260). The submission to law: oh, with what qualms of conscience was it that the noble races throughout the world renounced the vendetta and gave the law power over themselves! Law was long a vetitum, a blasphemy, an innovation; it was introduced with force, like a force, to which men only submitted with a sense of personal shame. Every tiny step forward in the world was formerly made at the cost of mental and physical torture. Nowadays the whole of this point of view—"that not only stepping forward, nay, stepping at all, movement, change, all needed their countless martyrs," rings in our ears quite strangely. I have put it forward in the Dawn of Day, Aph. 18. "Nothing is purchased more dearly," says the same book a little later, "than the modicum of human reason and freedom which is now our pride. But that pride is the reason why it is now almost impossible for us to feel in sympathy with those immense periods of the 'Morality of Custom,' which lie at the beginning of the 'world's history,' constituting as they do the real decisive historical principle which has[Pg 146] fixed the character of humanity; those periods, I repeat, when throughout the world suffering passed for virtue, cruelty for virtue, deceit for virtue, revenge for virtue, repudiation of the reason for virtue; and when, conversely, well-being passed current for danger, the desire for knowledge for danger, pity for danger, peace for danger, being pitied for shame, work for shame, madness for divinity, and change for immorality and incarnate corruption!"

10.

There is in the same book, Aph. 12, an explanation of the burden of unpopularity under which the earliest race of contemplative men had to live—despised almost as widely as they were first feared! Contemplation first appeared on earth in a disguised shape, in an ambiguous form, with an evil heart and often with an uneasy head: there is no doubt about it. The inactive, brooding, unwarlike element in the instincts of contemplative men long invested them with a cloud of suspicion: the only way to combat this was to excite a definite fear. And the old Brahmans, for example, knew to a nicety how to do this! The oldest philosophers were well versed in giving to their very existence and appearance, meaning, firmness, background, by reason whereof men learnt to fear them; considered more precisely, they did this from an even more fundamental need, the need of inspiring in themselves fear and self-reverence. For they found even in their own souls all the valuations turned against themselves; they had to[Pg 147] fight down every kind of suspicion and antagonism against "the philosophic element in themselves." Being men of a terrible age, they did this with terrible means: cruelty to themselves, ingenious self-mortification—this was the chief method of these ambitious hermits and intellectual revolutionaries, who were obliged to force down the gods and the traditions of their own soul, so as to enable themselves to believe in their own revolution. I remember the famous story of the King Vicvamitra, who, as the result of a thousand years of self-martyrdom, reached such a consciousness of power and such a confidence in himself that he undertook to build a new heaven: the sinister symbol of the oldest and newest history of philosophy in the whole world. Every one who has ever built anywhere a "new heaven" first found the power thereto in his own hell.... Let us compress the facts into a short formula. The philosophic spirit had, in order to be possible to any extent at all, to masquerade and disguise itself as one of the previously fixed types of the contemplative man, to disguise itself as priest, wizard, soothsayer, as a religious man generally: the ascetic ideal has for a long time served the philosopher as a superficial form, as a condition which enabled him to exist.... To be able to be a philosopher he had to exemplify the ideal; to exemplify it, he was bound to believe in it. The peculiarly etherealised abstraction of philosophers, with their negation of the world, their enmity to life, their disbelief in the senses, which has been maintained up to the most recent time, and has almost thereby come to be[Pg 148] accepted as the ideal philosophic attitude—this abstraction is the result of those enforced conditions under which philosophy came into existence, and continued to exist; inasmuch as for quite a very long time philosophy would have been absolutely impossible in the world without an ascetic cloak and dress, without an ascetic self-misunderstanding. Expressed plainly and palpably, the ascetic priest has taken the repulsive and sinister form of the caterpillar, beneath which and behind which alone philosophy could live and slink about....

Has all that really changed? Has that flamboyant and dangerous winged creature, that "spirit" which that caterpillar concealed within itself, has it, I say, thanks to a sunnier, warmer, lighter world, really and finally flung off its hood and escaped into the light? Can we to-day point to enough pride, enough daring, enough courage, enough self-confidence, enough mental will, enough will for responsibility, enough freedom of the will, to enable the philosopher to be now in the world really—possible?

11.

And now, after we have caught sight of the ascetic priest, let us tackle our problem. What is the meaning of the ascetic ideal? It now first becomes serious—vitally serious. We are now confronted with the real representatives of the serious. "What is the meaning of all seriousness?" This even more radical question is perchance already on the tip of our tongue: a question, fairly, for physiologists, but which we for the time[Pg 149] being skip. In that ideal the ascetic priest finds not only his faith, but also his will, his power, his interest. His right to existence stands and falls with that ideal. What wonder that we here run up against a terrible opponent (on the supposition, of course, that we are the opponents of that ideal), an opponent fighting for his life against those who repudiate that ideal!. .. On the other hand, it is from the outset improbable that such a biased attitude towards our problem will do him any particular good; the ascetic priest himself will scarcely prove the happiest champion of his own ideal (on the same principle on which a woman usually fails when she wishes to champion "woman")—let alone proving the most objective critic and judge of the controversy now raised. We shall therefore—so much is already obvious—rather have actually to help him to defend himself properly against ourselves, than we shall have to fear being too well beaten by him. The idea, which is the subject of this dispute, is the value of our life from the standpoint of the ascetic priests: this life, then (together with the whole of which it is a part, "Nature," "the world," the whole sphere of becoming and passing away), is placed by them in relation to an existence of quite another character, which it excludes and to which it is opposed, unless it deny its own self: in this case, the case of an ascetic life, life is taken as a bridge to another existence. The ascetic treats life as a maze, in which one must walk backwards till one comes to the place where it starts; or he treats it as an error which one may,[Pg 150] nay must, refute by action: for he demands that he should be followed; he enforces, where he can, his valuation of existence. What does this mean? Such a monstrous valuation is not an exceptional case, or a curiosity recorded in human history: it is one of the most general and persistent facts that there are. The reading from the vantage of a distant star of the capital letters of our earthly life, would perchance lead to the conclusion that the earth was the especially ascetic planet, a den of discontented, arrogant, and repulsive creatures, who never got rid of a deep disgust of themselves, of the world, of all life, and did themselves as much hurt as possible out of pleasure in hurting—presumably their one and only pleasure. Let us consider how regularly, how universally, how practically at every single period the ascetic priest puts in his appearance: he belongs to no particular race; he thrives everywhere; he grows out of all classes. Not that he perhaps bred this valuation by heredity and propagated it—the contrary is the case. It must be a necessity of the first order which makes this species, hostile, as it is, to life, always grow again and always thrive again.—Life itself must certainly have an interest in the continuance of such a type of self-contradiction. For an ascetic life is a self-contradiction: here rules resentment without parallel, the resentment of an insatiate instinct and ambition, that would be master, not over some element in life, but over life itself, over life's deepest, strongest, innermost conditions; here is an attempt made to utilise power to dam the sources of power; here does[Pg 151] the green eye of jealousy turn even against physiological well-being, especially against the expression of such well-being, beauty, joy; while a sense of pleasure is experienced and sought in abortion, in decay, in pain, in misfortune, in ugliness, in voluntary punishment, in the exercising, flagellation, and sacrifice of the self. All this is in the highest degree paradoxical: we are here confronted with a rift that wills itself to be a rift, which enjoys itself in this very suffering, and even becomes more and more certain of itself, more and more triumphant, in proportion as its own presupposition, physiological vitality, decreases. "The triumph just in the supreme agony:" under this extravagant emblem did the ascetic ideal fight from of old; in this mystery of seduction, in this picture of rapture and torture, it recognised its brightest light, its salvation, its final victory. Crux, nux, lux—it has all these three in one.

12.

Granted that such an incarnate will for contradiction and unnaturalness is induced to philosophise; on what will it vent its pet caprice? On that which has been felt with the greatest certainty to be true, to be real; it will look for error in those very places where the life instinct fixes truth with the greatest positiveness. It will, for instance, after the example of the ascetics of the Vedanta Philosophy, reduce matter to an illusion, and similarly treat pain, multiplicity, the whole logical contrast of "Subject" and "Object"—errors, nothing[Pg 152] but errors! To renounce the belief in one's own ego, to deny to one's self one's own "reality"—what a triumph! and here already we have a much higher kind of triumph, which is not merely a triumph over the senses, over the palpable, but an infliction of violence and cruelty on reason; and this ecstasy culminates in the ascetic self-contempt, the ascetic scorn of one's own reason making this decree: there is a domain of truth and of life, but reason is specially excluded therefrom.. ... By the bye, even in the Kantian idea of "the intellegible character of things" there remains a trace of that schism, so dear to the heart of the ascetic, that schism which likes to turn reason against reason; in fact, "intelligible character" means in Kant a kind of quality in things of which the intellect comprehends this much, that for it, the intellect, it is absolutely incomprehensible. After all, let us, in our character of knowers, not be ungrateful towards such determined reversals of the ordinary perspectives and values, with which the mind had for too long raged against itself with an apparently futile sacrilege! In the same way the very seeing of another vista, the very wishing to see another vista, is no little training and preparation of the intellect for its eternal "Objectivity"—objectivity being understood not as "contemplation without interest" (for that is inconceivable and nonsensical), but as the ability to have the pros and cons in one's power and to switch them on and off, so as to get to know how to utilise, for the advancement of knowledge, the difference in the perspective and in the emotional[Pg 153] interpretations. But let us, forsooth, my philosophic colleagues, henceforward guard ourselves more carefully against this mythology of dangerous ancient ideas, which has set up a "pure, will-less, painless, timeless subject of knowledge"; let us guard ourselves from the tentacles of such contradictory ideas as "pure reason," "absolute spirituality," "knowledge-in-itself":—in these theories an eye that cannot be thought of is required to think, an eye which ex hypothesi has no direction at all, an eye in which the active and interpreting functions are cramped, are absent; those functions, I say, by means of which "abstract" seeing first became seeing something; in these theories consequently the absurd and the non-sensical is always demanded of the eye. There is only a seeing from a perspective, only a "knowing" from a perspective, and the more emotions we express over a thing, the more eyes, different eyes, we train on the same thing, the more complete will be our "idea" of that thing, our "objectivity." But the elimination of the will altogether, the switching off of the emotions all and sundry, granted that we could do so, what! would not that be called intellectual castration?

13.

But let us turn back. Such a self-contradiction, as apparently manifests itself among the ascetics, "Life turned against Life," is— this much is absolutely obvious—from the physiological and not now from the psychological standpoint, simply[Pg 154] nonsense. It can only be an apparent contradiction; it must be a kind of provisional expression, an explanation, a formula, an adjustment, a psychological misunderstanding of something, whose real nature could not be understood for a long time, and whose real essence could not be described; a mere word jammed into an old gap of human knowledge. To put briefly the facts against its being real: the ascetic ideal springs from the prophylactic and self-preservative instincts which mark a decadent life, which seeks by every means in its power to maintain its position and fight for its existence; it points to a partial physiological depression and exhaustion, against which the most profound and intact life-instincts fight ceaselessly with new weapons and discoveries. The ascetic ideal is such a weapon: its position is consequently exactly the reverse of that which the worshippers of the ideal imagine—life struggles in it and through it with death and against death; the ascetic ideal is a dodge for the preservation of life. An important fact is brought out in the extent to which, as history teaches, this ideal could rule and exercise power over man, especially in all those places where the civilisation and taming of man was completed: that fact is, the diseased state of man up to the present, at any rate, of the man who has been tamed, the physiological struggle of man with death (more precisely, with the disgust with life, with exhaustion, with the wish for the "end"). The ascetic priest is the incarnate wish for an existence of another kind,[Pg 155] an existence on another plane,—he is, in fact, the highest point of this wish, its official ecstasy and passion: but it is the very power of this wish which is the fetter that binds him here; it is just that which makes him into a tool that must labour to create more favourable conditions for earthly existence, for existence on the human plane—it is with this very power that he keeps the whole herd of failures, distortions, abortions, unfortunates, sufferers from themselves of every kind, fast to existence, while he as the herdsman goes instinctively on in front. You understand me already: this ascetic priest, this apparent enemy of life, this denier—he actually belongs to the really great conservative and affirmative forces of life.... What does it come from, this diseased state? For man is more diseased, more uncertain, more changeable, more unstable than any other animal, there is no doubt of it—he is the diseased animal: what does it spring from? Certainly he has also dared, innovated, braved more, challenged fate more than all the other animals put together; he, the great experimenter with himself, the unsatisfied, the insatiate, who struggles for the supreme mastery with beast, Nature, and gods, he, the as yet ever uncompelled, the ever future, who finds no more any rest from his own aggressive strength, goaded inexorably on by the spur of the future dug into the flesh of the present:—how should not so brave and rich an animal also be the most endangered, the animal with the longest and deepest sickness among all sick animals?... Man is sick of it, oft[Pg 156] enough there are whole epidemics of this satiety (as about 1348, the time of the Dance of Death): but even this very nausea, this tiredness, this disgust with himself, all this is discharged from him with such force that it is immediately made into a new fetter. His "nay," which he utters to life, brings to light as though by magic an abundance of graceful "yeas"; even when he wounds himself, this master of destruction, of self-destruction, it is subsequently the wound itself that forces him to live.

14.

The more normal is this sickliness in man—and we cannot dispute this normality—the higher honour should be paid to the rare cases of psychical and physical powerfulness, the windfalls of humanity, and the more strictly should the sound be guarded from that worst of air, the air of the sick-room. Is that done? The sick are the greatest danger for the healthy; it is not from the strongest that harm comes to the strong, but from the weakest. Is that known? Broadly considered, it is not for a minute the fear of man, whose diminution should be wished for; for this fear forces the strong to be strong, to be at times terrible—it preserves in its integrity the sound type of man. What is to be feared, what does work with a fatality found in no other fate, is not the great fear of, but the great nausea with, man; and equally so the great pity for man. Supposing that both these things were one day to[Pg 157] espouse each other, then inevitably the maximum of monstrousness would immediately come into the world—the "last will" of man, his will for nothingness, Nihilism. And, in sooth, the way is well paved thereto. He who not only has his nose to smell with, but also has eyes and ears, he sniffs almost wherever he goes today an air something like that of a mad-house, the air of a hospital—I am speaking, as stands to reason, of the cultured areas of mankind, of every kind of "Europe" that there is in fact in the world. The sick are the great danger of man, not the evil, not the "beasts of prey." They who are from the outset botched, oppressed, broken, those are they, the weakest are they, who most undermine the life beneath the feet of man, who instil the most dangerous venom and scepticism into our trust in life, in man, in ourselves. Where shall we escape from it, from that covert look (from which we carry away a deep sadness), from that averted look of him who is misborn from the beginning, that look which betrays what such a man says to himself—that look which is a groan?" Would that I were something else," so groans this look, "but there is no hope. I am what I am: how could I get away from myself? And, verily—I am sick of myself!" On such a soil of self-contempt, a veritable swamp soil, grows that weed, that poisonous growth, and all so tiny, so hidden, so ignoble, so sugary. Here teem the worms of revenge and vindictiveness; here the air reeks of things secret and unmentionable; here is ever[Pg 158] spun the net of the most malignant conspiracy—the conspiracy of the sufferers against the sound and the victorious; here is the sight of the victorious hated. And what lying so as not to acknowledge this hate as hate! What a show of big words and attitudes, what an art of "righteous" calumniation! These abortions! what a noble eloquence gushes from their lips! What an amount of sugary, slimy, humble submission oozes in their eyes! What do they really want? At any rate to represent righteousness ness, love, wisdom, superiority, that is the ambition of these "lowest ones," these sick ones! And how clever does such an ambition make them! You cannot, in fact, but admire the counterfeiter dexterity with which the stamp of virtue, even the ring, the golden ring of virtue, is here imitated. They have taken a lease of virtue absolutely for themselves, have these weaklings and wretched invalids, there is no doubt of it; "We alone are the good, the righteous," so do they speak, "we alone are the homines bonæ voluntatis." They stalk about in our midst as living reproaches, as warnings to us—as though health, fitness, strength, pride, the sensation of power, were really vicious things in themselves, for which one would have some day to do penance, bitter penance. Oh, how they themselves are ready in their hearts to exact penance, how they thirst after being hangmen!

Among them is an abundance of revengeful ones disguised as judges, who ever mouth the word righteousness like a venomous spittle—with[Pg 159] mouth, I say, always pursed, always ready to spit at everything, which does not wear a discontented look, but is of good cheer as it goes on its way. Among them, again, is that most loathsome species of the vain, the lying abortions, who make a point of representing "beautiful souls," and perchance of bringing to the market as "purity of heart" their distorted sensualism swathed in verses and other bandages; the species of "self-comforters" and masturbators of their own souls. The sick man's will to represent some form or other of superiority, his instinct for crooked paths, which lead to a tyranny over the healthy—where can it not be found, this will to power of the very weakest? The sick woman especially: no one surpasses her in refinements for ruling, oppressing, tyrannising. The sick woman, moreover, spares nothing living, nothing dead; she grubs up again the most buried things (the Bogos say, "Woman is a hyena"). Look into the background of every family, of every body, of every community: everywhere the fight of the sick against the healthy—a silent fight for the most part with minute poisoned powders, with pin-pricks, with spiteful grimaces of patience, but also at times with that diseased pharisaism of pure pantomime, which plays for choice the rôle of "righteous indignation." Right into the hallowed chambers of knowledge can it make itself heard, can this hoarse yelping of sick hounds, this rabid lying and frenzy of such "noble" Pharisees (I remind readers, who have ears, once more of that Berlin apostle of revenge, Eugen Dühring, who makes the most disreputable and[Pg 160] revolting use in all present-day Germany of moral refuse; Dühring, the paramount moral blusterer that there is to-day, even among his own kidney, the Anti-Semites). They are all men of resentment, are these physiological distortions and worm-riddled objects, a whole quivering kingdom of burrowing revenge, indefatigable and insatiable in its outbursts against the happy, and equally so in disguises for revenge, in pretexts for revenge: when will they really reach their final, fondest, most sublime triumph of revenge? At that time, doubtless, when they succeed in pushing their own misery, in fact, all misery, into the consciousness of the happy; so that the latter begin one day to be ashamed of their happiness, and perchance say to themselves when they meet, "It is a shame to be happy! there is too much misery!" ... But there could not possibly be a greater and more fatal misunderstanding than that of the happy, the fit, the strong in body and soul, beginning in this way to doubt their right to happiness. Away with this "perverse world"! Away with this shameful soddenness of sentiment! Preventing the sick making the healthy sick—for that is what such a soddenness comes to—this ought to be our supreme object in the world—but for this it is above all essential that the healthy should remain separated from the sick, that they should even guard themselves from the look of the sick, that they should not even associate with the sick. Or may it, perchance, be their mission to be nurses or doctors? But they could not mistake and disown their mission more grossly—the higher must not[Pg 161] degrade itself to be the tool of the lower, the pathos of distance must to all eternity keep their missions also separate. The right of the happy to existence, the right of bells with a full tone over the discordant cracked bells, is verily a thousand times greater: they alone are the sureties of the future, they alone are bound to man's future. What they can, what they must do, that can the sick never do, should never do! but if they are to be enabled to do what only they must do, how can they possibly be free to play the doctor, the comforter, the "Saviour" of the sick?... And therefore good air! good air! and away, at any rate, from the neighbourhood of all the madhouses and hospitals of civilisation! And therefore good company, our own company, or solitude, if it must be so! but away, at any rate, from the evil fumes of internal corruption and the secret worm-eaten state of the sick! that, forsooth, my friends, we may defend ourselves, at any rate for still a time, against the two worst plagues that could have been reserved for us—against the great nausea with man! against the great pity for man!

15.

If you have understood in all their depths—and I demand that you should grasp them profoundly and understand them profoundly—the reasons for the impossibility of its being the business of the healthy to nurse the sick, to make the sick healthy, it follows that you have grasped this further necessity—the necessity of doctors and nurses[Pg 162] who themselves are sick. And now we have and hold with both our hands the essence of the ascetic priest. The ascetic priest must be accepted by us as the predestined saviour, herdsman, and champion of the sick herd: thereby do we first understand his awful historic mission. The lordship over sufferers is his kingdom, to that points his instinct, in that he finds his own special art, his master-skill, his kind of happiness. He must himself be sick, he must be kith and kin to the sick and the abortions so as to understand them, so as to arrive at an understanding with them; but he must also be strong, even more master of himself than of others, impregnable, forsooth, in his will for power, so as to acquire the trust and the awe of the weak, so that he can be their hold, bulwark, prop, compulsion, overseer, tyrant, god. He has to protect them, protect his herds—against whom? Against the healthy, doubtless also against the envy towards the healthy. He must be the natural adversary and scorner of every rough, stormy, reinless, hard, violently-predatory health and power. The priest is the first form of the more delicate animal that scorns more easily than it hates. He will not be spared the waging of war with the beasts of prey, a war of guile (of "spirit") rather than of force, as is self-evident—he will in certain cases find it necessary to conjure up out of himself, or at any rate to represent practically a new type of the beast of prey—a new animal monstrosity in which the polar bear, the supple, cold, crouching panther, and, not least important, the fox, are joined together in a trinity as fascinating[Pg 163] as it is fearsome. If necessity exacts it, then will he come on the scene with bearish seriousness, venerable, wise, cold, full of treacherous superiority, as the herald and mouthpiece of mysterious powers, sometimes going among even the other kind of beasts of prey, determined as he is to sow on their soil, wherever he can, suffering, discord, self-contradiction, and only too sure of his art, always to be lord of sufferers at all times. He brings with him, doubtless, salve and balsam; but before he can play the physician he must first wound; so, while he soothes the pain which the wound makes, he at the same time poisons the wound. Well versed is he in this above all things, is this wizard and wild beast tamer, in whose vicinity everything healthy must needs become ill, and everything ill must needs become tame. He protects, in sooth, his sick herd well enough, does this strange herdsman; he protects them also against themselves, against the sparks (even in the centre of the herd) of wickedness, knavery, malice, and all the other ills that the plaguey and the sick are heir to; he fights with cunning, hardness, and stealth against anarchy and against the ever imminent break-up inside the herd, where resentment, that most dangerous blasting-stuff and explosive, ever accumulates and accumulates. Getting rid of this blasting-stuff in such a way that it does not blow up the herd and the herdsman, that is his real feat, his supreme utility; if you wish to comprise in the shortest formula the value of the priestly life, it would be correct to say the priest is the diverter of the course of resentment. Every sufferer, in fact, searches[Pg 164] instinctively for a cause of his suffering; to put it more exactly, a doer,—to put it still more precisely, a sentient responsible doer,—in brief, something living, on which, either actually or in effigie, he can on any pretext vent his emotions. For the venting of emotions is the sufferer's greatest attempt at alleviation, that is to say, stupefaction, his mechanically desired narcotic against pain of any kind. It is in this phenomenon alone that is found, according to my judgment, the real physiological cause of resentment, revenge, and their family is to be found—that is, in a demand for the deadening of pain through emotion: this cause is generally, but in my view very erroneously, looked for in the defensive parry of a bare protective principle of reaction, of a "reflex movement" in the case of any sudden hurt and danger, after the manner that a decapitated frog still moves in order to get away from a corrosive acid. But the difference is fundamental. In one case the object is to prevent being hurt any more; in the other case the object is to deaden a racking, insidious, nearly unbearable pain by a more violent emotion of any kind whatsoever, and at any rate for the time being to drive it out of the consciousness—for this purpose an emotion is needed, as wild an emotion as possible, and to excite that emotion some excuse or other is needed. "It must be somebody's fault that I feel bad"—this kind of reasoning is peculiar to all invalids, and is but the more pronounced, the more ignorant they remain of the real cause of their feeling bad, the physiological cause (the cause may lie in a[Pg 165] disease of the nervus sympathicus, or in an excessive secretion of bile, or in a want of sulphate and phosphate of potash in the blood, or in pressure in the bowels which stops the circulation of the blood, or in degeneration of the ovaries, and so forth). Ail sufferers have an awful resourcefulness and ingenuity in finding excuses for painful emotions; they even enjoy their jealousy, their broodings over base actions and apparent injuries, they burrow through the intestines of their past and present in their search for obscure mysteries, wherein they will be at liberty to wallow in a torturing suspicion and get drunk on the venom of their own malice—they tear open the oldest wounds, they make themselves bleed from the scars which have long been healed, they make evil-doers out of friends, wife, child, and everything which is nearest to them. "I suffer: it must be somebody's fault"—so thinks every sick sheep. But his herdsman, the ascetic priest, says to him, "Quite so, my sheep, it must be the fault of some one; but thou thyself art that some one, it is all the fault of thyself alone—it is the fault of thyself alone against thyself": that is bold enough, false enough, but one thing is at least attained; thereby, as I have said, the course of resentment is—diverted.

16.

You can see now what the remedial instinct of life has at least tried to effect, according to my conception, through the ascetic priest, and the[Pg 166] purpose for which he had to employ a temporary tyranny of such paradoxical and anomalous ideas as "guilt," "sin," "sinfulness," "corruption," "damnation." What was done was to make the sick harmless up to a certain point, to destroy the incurable by means of themselves, to turn the milder cases severely on to themselves, to give their resentment a backward direction ("man needs but one thing"), and to exploit similarly the bad instincts of all sufferers with a view to self-discipline, self-surveillance, self-mastery. It is obvious that there can be no question at all in the case of a "medication" of this kind, a mere emotional medication, of any real healing of the sick in the physiological sense; it cannot even for a moment be asserted that in this connection the instinct of life has taken healing as its goal and purpose. On the one hand, a kind of congestion and organisation of the sick (the word "Church" is the most popular name for it): on the other, a kind of provisional safeguarding of the comparatively healthy, the more perfect specimens, the cleavage of a rift between healthy and sick—for a long time that was all! and it was much! it was very much!

I am proceeding, as you see, in this essay, from an hypothesis which, as far as such readers as I want are concerned, does not require to be proved; the hypothesis that "sinfulness" in man is not an actual fact, but rather merely the interpretation of a fact, of a physiological discomfort,—a discomfort seen through a moral religious perspective which is no longer binding upon us.[Pg 167] The fact, therefore, that any one feels "guilty," "sinful," is certainly not yet any proof that he is right in feeling so, any more than any one is healthy simply because he feels healthy. Remember the celebrated witch-ordeals: in those days the most acute and humane judges had no doubt but that in these cases they were confronted with guilt,—the "witches" themselves had no doubt on the point,—and yet the guilt was lacking. Let me elaborate this hypothesis: I do not for a minute accept the very "pain in the soul" as a real fact, but only as an explanation (a casual explanation) of facts that could not hitherto be precisely formulated; I regard it therefore as something as yet absolutely in the air and devoid of scientific cogency—just a nice fat word in the place of a lean note of interrogation. When any one fails to get rid of his "pain in the soul," the cause is, speaking crudely, to be found not in his "soul" but more probably in his stomach (speaking crudely, I repeat, but by no means wishing thereby that you should listen to me or understand me in a crude spirit). A strong and well-constituted man digests his experiences (deeds and misdeeds all included) just as he digests his meats, even when he has some tough morsels to swallow. If he fails to "relieve himself" of an experience, this kind of indigestion is quite as much physiological as the other indigestion—and indeed, in more ways than one, simply one of the results of the other. You can adopt such a theory, and yet entre nous be nevertheless the strongest opponent of all materialism.

17.

But is he really a physician, this ascetic priest? We already understand why we are scarcely allowed to call him a physician, however much he likes to feel a "saviour" and let himself be worshipped as a saviour. [3] It is only the actual suffering, the discomfort of the sufferer, which he combats, not its cause, not the actual state of sickness—this needs must constitute our most radical objection to priestly medication. But just once put yourself into that point of view, of which the priests have a monopoly, you will find it hard to exhaust your amazement, at what from that standpoint he has completely seen, sought, and found. The mitigation of suffering, every kind of "consoling"—all this manifests itself as his very genius: with what ingenuity has he interpreted his mission of consoler, with what aplomb and audacity has he chosen weapons necessary for the part. Christianity in particular should be dubbed a great treasure-chamber of ingenious consolations,—such a store of refreshing, soothing, deadening drugs has it accumulated within itself; so many of the most dangerous and daring expedients has it hazarded; with such subtlety, refinement, Oriental refinement, has it divined what emotional stimulants can conquer, at any rate for a time, the deep depression, the leaden fatigue, the black melancholy of physiological cripples—for, speaking[Pg 169] generally, all religions are mainly concerned with fighting a certain fatigue and heaviness that has infected everything. You can regard it as prima facie probable that in certain places in the world there was almost bound to prevail from time to time among large masses of the population a sense of physiological depression, which, however, owing to their lack of physiological knowledge, did not appear to their consciousness as such, so that consequently its "cause" and its cure can only be sought and essayed in the science of moral psychology (this, in fact, is my most general formula for what is generally called a "religion"). Such a feeling of depression can have the most diverse origins; it may be the result of the crossing of too heterogeneous races (or of classes—genealogical and racial differences are also brought out in the classes: the European "Weltschmerz," the "Pessimism" of the nineteenth century, is really the result of an absurd and sudden class-mixture); it may be brought about by a mistaken emigration—a race falling into a climate for which its power of adaptation is insufficient (the case of the Indians in India); it may be the effect of old age and fatigue (the Parisian pessimism from 1850 onwards); it may be a wrong diet (the alcoholism of the Middle Ages, the nonsense of vegetarianism—which, however, have in their favour the authority of Sir Christopher in Shakespeare); it may be blood-deterioration, malaria, syphilis, and the like (German depression after the Thirty Years' War, which infected half Germany with evil diseases,[Pg 170] and thereby paved the way for German servility, for German pusillanimity). In such a case there is invariably recourse to a war on a grand scale with the feeling of depression; let us inform ourselves briefly on its most important practices and phases (I leave on one side, as stands to reason, the actual philosophic war against the feeling of depression which is usually simultaneous—it is interesting enough, but too absurd, too practically negligible, too full of cobwebs, too much of a hole-and-corner affair, especially when pain is proved to be a mistake, on the naïf hypothesis that pain must needs vanish when the mistake underlying it is recognised—but behold! it does anything but vanish ...). That dominant depression is primarily fought by weapons which reduce the consciousness of life itself to the lowest degree. Wherever possible, no more wishes, no more wants; shun everything which produces emotion, which produces "blood" (eating no salt, the fakir hygiene); no love; no hate; equanimity; no revenge; no getting rich; no work; begging; as far as possible, no woman, or as little woman as possible; as far as the intellect is concerned, Pascal's principle, "il faut s'abêtir." To put the result in ethical and psychological language, "self-annihilation," "sanctification"; to put it in physiological language, "hypnotism"—the attempt to find some approximate human equivalent for what hibernation is for certain animals, for what æstivation is for many tropical plants, a minimum of assimilation and metabolism in which life just manages to subsist without really coming into the[Pg 171] consciousness. An amazing amount of human energy has been devoted to this object—

perhaps uselessly? There cannot be the slightest doubt but that such sportsmen of "saintliness," in whom at times nearly every nation has abounded, have really found a genuine relief from that which they have combated with such a rigorous training—in countless cases they really escaped by the help of their system of hypnotism away from deep physiological depression; their method is consequently counted among the most universal ethnological facts. Similarly it is improper to consider such a plan for starving the physical element and the desires, as in itself a symptom of insanity (as a clumsy species of roast-beef-eating "freethinkers" and Sir Christophers are fain to do); all the more certain is it that their method can and does pave the way to all kinds of mental disturbances, for instance, "inner lights" (as far as the case of the Hesychasts of Mount Athos), auditory and visual hallucinations, voluptuous ecstasies and effervescences of sensualism (the history of St. Theresa). The explanation of such events given by the victims is always the acme of fanatical falsehood; this is self-evident. Note well, however, the tone of implicit gratitude that rings in the very will for an explanation of such a character. The supreme state, salvation itself, that final goal of universal hypnosis and peace, is always regarded by them as the mystery of mysteries, which even the most supreme symbols are inadequate to express; it is regarded as an entry and homecoming to the essence of things, as a liberation from all[Pg 172] illusions, as "knowledge," as "truth," as "being" as an escape from every end, every wish, every action, as something even beyond Good and Evil.

"Good and Evil," quoth the Buddhists, "both are fetters. The perfect man is master of them both."

"The done and the undone," quoth the disciple of the Vedânta, "do him no hurt; the good and the evil he shakes from off him, sage that he is; his kingdom suffers no more from any act; good and evil, he goes beyond them both."—An absolutely Indian conception, as much Brahmanist as Buddhist. Neither in the Indian nor in the Christian doctrine is this "Redemption" regarded as attainable by means of virtue and moral improvement, however high they may place the value of the hypnotic efficiency of virtue: keep clear on this point—indeed it simply corresponds with the facts. The fact that they remained true on this point is perhaps to be regarded as the best specimen of realism in the three great religions, absolutely soaked as they are with morality, with this one exception. "For those who know, there is no duty." "Redemption is not attained by the acquisition of virtues; for redemption consists in being one with Brahman, who is incapable of acquiring any perfection; and equally little does it consist in the giving up of faults, for the Brahman, unity with whom is what constitutes redemption, is eternally pure" (these passages are from the Commentaries of the Cankara, quoted from the first real European expert of the Indian philosophy, my friend Paul Deussen). We wish, therefore, to pay honour to the idea of "redemption"[Pg 173] in the great religions, but it is somewhat hard to remain serious in view of the appreciation meted out to the deep sleep by these exhausted pessimists who are too tired even to dream—to the deep sleep considered, that is, as already a fusing into Brahman, as the attainment of the unio mystica with God. "When he has completely gone to sleep," says on this point the oldest and most venerable "script," "and come to perfect rest, so that he sees no more any vision, then, oh dear one, is he united with Being, he has entered into his own self—encircled by the Self with its absolute knowledge, he has no more any consciousness of that which is without or of that which is within. Day and night cross not these bridges, nor age, nor death, nor suffering, nor good deeds, nor evil deeds." "In deep sleep," say similarly the believers in this deepest of the three great religions, "does the soul lift itself from out this body of ours, enters the supreme light and stands out therein in its true shape: therein is it the supreme spirit itself, which travels about, while it jests and plays and enjoys itself, whether with women, or chariots, or friends; there do its thoughts turn no more back to this appanage of a body, to which the 'prana' (the vital breath) is harnessed like a beast of burden to the cart." None the less we will take care to realise (as we did when discussing "redemption") that in spite of all its pomps of Oriental extravagance this simply expresses the same criticism on life as did the clear, cold, Greekly cold, but yet suffering Epicurus. The hypnotic sensation of nothingness, the peace[Pg 174] of deepest sleep, anæsthesia in short—that is what passes with the sufferers and the absolutely depressed for, forsooth, their supreme good, their value of values; that is what must be treasured by them as something positive, be felt by them as the essence of the Positive (according to the same logic of the feelings, nothingness is in all pessimistic religions called God).

18.

Such a hypnotic deadening of sensibility and susceptibility to pain, which presupposes somewhat rare powers, especially courage, contempt of opinion, intellectual stoicism, is less frequent than another and certainly easier training which is tried against states of depression. I mean mechanical activity. It is indisputable that a suffering existence can be thereby considerably alleviated. This fact is called to-day by the somewhat ignoble title of the "Blessing of work." The alleviation consists in the attention of the sufferer being absolutely diverted from suffering, in the incessant monopoly of the consciousness by action, so that consequently there is little room left for suffering—for narrow is it, this chamber of human consciousness! Mechanical activity and its corollaries, such as absolute regularity, punctilious unreasoning obedience, the chronic routine of life, the complete occupation of time, a certain liberty to be impersonal, nay, a training in "impersonality," self-forgetfulness, "incuria sui"—with what thoroughness and expert subtlety have all[Pg 175] these methods been exploited by the ascetic priest in his war with pain!

When he has to tackle sufferers of the lower orders, slaves, or prisoners (or women, who for the most part are a compound of labour-slave and prisoner), all he has to do is to juggle a little with the names, and to rechristen, so as to make them see henceforth a benefit, a comparative happiness, in objects which they hated—the slave's discontent with his lot was at any rate not invented by the priests. An even more popular means of fighting depression is the ordaining of a little joy, which is easily accessible and can be made into a rule; this medication is frequently used in conjunction with the former ones. The most frequent form in which joy is prescribed as a cure is the joy in producing joy (such as doing good, giving presents, alleviating, helping, exhorting, comforting, praising, treating with distinction); together with the prescription of "love your neighbour." The ascetic priest prescribes, though in the most cautious doses, what is practically a stimulation of the strongest and most life-assertive impulse—the Will for Power. The happiness involved in the "smallest superiority" which is the concomitant of all benefiting, helping, extolling, making one's self useful, is the most ample consolation, of which, if they are well-advised, physiological distortions avail themselves: in other cases they hurt each other, and naturally in obedience to the same radical instinct. An investigation of the origin of Christianity in the

Roman world shows that co-operative unions for poverty,[Pg 176] sickness, and burial sprang up in the lowest stratum of contemporary society, amid which the chief antidote against depression, the little joy experienced in mutual benefits, was deliberately fostered. Perchance this was then a novelty, a real discovery? This conjuring up of the will for co-operation, for family organisation, for communal life, for "Cœnacula" necessarily brought the Will for Power, which had been already infinitesimally stimulated, to a new and much fuller manifestation. The herd organisation is a genuine advance and triumph in the fight with depression. With the growth of the community there matures even to individuals a new interest, which often enough takes him out of the more personal element in his discontent, his aversion to himself, the "despectus sui" of Geulincx. All sick and diseased people strive instinctively after a herd-organisation, out of a desire to shake off their sense of oppressive discomfort and weakness; the ascetic priest divines this instinct and promotes it; wherever a herd exists it is the instinct of weakness which has wished for the herd, and the cleverness of the priests which has organised it, for, mark this: by an equally natural necessity the strong strive as much for isolation as the weak for union: when the former bind themselves it is only with a view to an aggressive joint action and joint satisfaction of their Will for Power, much against the wishes of their individual consciences; the latter, on the contrary, range themselves together with positive delight in such a muster—their instincts are as much gratified thereby as the instincts of the[Pg 177] "born master" (that is, the solitary beast-of-prey species of man) are disturbed and wounded to the quick by organisation. There is always lurking beneath every oligarchy—such is the universal lesson of history—the desire for tyranny. Every oligarchy is continually quivering with the tension of the effort required by each individual to keep mastering this desire. (Such, e.g., was the Greek; Plato shows it in a hundred places, Plato, who knew his contemporaries—and himself.)

19.

The methods employed by the ascetic priest, which we have already learnt to know—stifling of all vitality, mechanical energy, the little joy, and especially the method of "love your neighbour" herd-organisation, the awaking of the communal consciousness of power, to such a pitch that the individual's disgust with himself becomes eclipsed by his delight in the thriving of the community—these are, according to modern standards, the "innocent" methods employed in the fight with depression; let us turn now to the more interesting topic of the "guilty" methods. The guilty methods spell one thing: to produce emotional excess—which is used as the most efficacious anæsthetic against their depressing state of protracted pain; this is why priestly ingenuity has proved quite inexhaustible in thinking out this one question: "By what means can you produce an emotional excess?" This sounds harsh: it is manifest that it would sound[Pg 178] nicer and would grate on one's ears less, if I were to say, forsooth: "The ascetic priest made use at all times of the enthusiasm contained in all strong emotions." But what is the good of still soothing the delicate ears of our modern effeminates? What is the good on our side of budging one single inch before their verbal Pecksniffianism. For us psychologists to do that would be at once practical Pecksniffianism, apart from the fact of its nauseating us. The good taste (others might say, the righteousness) of a psychologist nowadays consists, if at all, in combating the shamefully moralised language with which all modern judgments on men and things are smeared. For, do not deceive yourself: what constitutes the chief characteristic of modern souls and of modern books is not the lying, but the innocence which is part and parcel of their intellectual dishonesty. The inevitable running up against this "innocence" everywhere constitutes the most distasteful feature of the somewhat dangerous business which a modern psychologist has to undertake: it is a part of our great danger—it is a road which perhaps leads us straight to the great nausea—I know quite well the purpose which all modern books will and can serve (granted that they last, which I am not afraid of, and granted equally that there is to be at some future day a generation with a more rigid, more severe, and healthier taste)—the function which all modernity generally will serve with posterity: that of an emetic,— and this by reason of its moral sugariness and falsity, its[Pg 179] ingrained feminism, which it is pleased to call "Idealism," and at any rate believes to be idealism. Our cultured men of to-day, our "good" men, do not lie—that is true; but it does not redound to their honour! The real lie, the genuine, determined, "honest" lie (on whose value you can listen to Plato) would prove too tough and strong an article for them by a long way; it would be asking them to do what people have been forbidden to ask them to do, to open their eyes to their own selves, and to learn to distinguish between "true" and "false" in their own selves. The dishonest lie alone suits them: everything which feels a good man is perfectly incapable of any other attitude to anything than that of a dishonourable liar, an absolute liar, but none the less an innocent liar, a blue-eyed liar, a virtuous liar. These "good men," they are all now tainted with morality through and through, and as far as honour is concerned they are disgraced and corrupted for all eternity. Which of them could stand a further truth "about man"? or, put more tangibly, which of them could put up with a true biography? One or two instances: Lord Byron composed a most personal autobiography, but Thomas Moore was "too good" for it; he burnt his friend's papers. Dr. Gwinner, Schopenhauer's executor, is said to have done the same; for Schopenhauer as well wrote much about himself, and perhaps also against himself: (εἰς ἑαυτόν). The virtuous American Thayer, Beethoven's biographer, suddenly stopped his work: he had come to a certain[Pg 180] point in that honourable and simple life, and could stand it no longer. Moral: What sensible man nowadays writes one honest word about himself? He must already belong to the Order of Holy Foolhardiness. We are promised an autobiography of Richard Wagner; who doubts but that it would be a clever autobiography? Think, forsooth, of the grotesque horror which the Catholic priest Janssen aroused in Germany with his inconceivably square and harmless pictures of the German Reformation; what wouldn't people do if some real psychologist were to tell us about a genuine Luther, tell us, not with the moralist simplicity of a country priest or the sweet and cautious modesty of a Protestant historian, but say with the fearlessness of a Taine, that springs from force of character and not from a prudent toleration of force. (The Germans, by the bye, have already produced the classic specimen of this toleration—they may well be allowed to reckon him as one of their own, in Leopold Ranke, that born classical advocate of every causa fortior, that cleverest of all the clever opportunists.)

20.

But you will soon understand me.—Putting it shortly, there is reason enough, is there not, for us psychologists nowadays never getting from a certain mistrust of out own selves? Probably even we ourselves are still "too good" for our work, probably, whatever contempt we[Pg 181] feel for this popular craze for morality, we ourselves are perhaps none the less its victims, prey, and slaves; probably it infects even us. Of what was that diplomat warning us, when he said to his colleagues: "Let us especially mistrust our first impulses, gentlemen! they are almost always good"? So should nowadays every psychologist talk to his colleagues. And thus we get back to our problem, which in point of fact does require from us a certain severity, a certain mistrust especially against "first impulses." The ascetic ideal in the service of projected emotional excess:—he who remembers the previous essay will already partially anticipate the essential meaning compressed into these above ten words. The thorough unswitching of the human soul, the plunging of it into terror, frost, ardour, rapture, so as to free it, as through some lightning shock, from all the smallness and pettiness of unhappiness, depression, and discomfort: what ways lead to this goal? And which of these ways does so most safely?... At bottom all great emotions have this power, provided that they find a sudden outlet—emotions such as rage, fear, lust, revenge, hope, triumph, despair, cruelty; and, in sooth, the ascetic priest has had no scruples in taking into his service the whole pack of hounds that rage in the human kennel, unleashing now these and now those, with the same constant object of waking man out of his protracted melancholy, of chasing away, at any rate for a time, his dull pain, his shrinking misery, but always under the sanction of a religious interpretation and justification.[Pg 182] This emotional excess has subsequently to be paid for, this is self-evident—it makes the ill more ill—and therefore this kind of remedy for pain is according to modern standards a "guilty" kind.

The dictates of fairness, however, require that we should all the more emphasise the fact that this remedy is applied with a good conscience, that the ascetic priest has prescribed it in the most implicit belief in its utility and indispensability;—often enough almost collapsing in the presence of the pain which he created;—that we should similarly emphasise the fact that the violent physiological revenges of such excesses, even perhaps the mental disturbances, are not absolutely inconsistent with the general tenor of this kind of remedy; this remedy, which, as we have shown previously, is not for the purpose of healing diseases, but of fighting the unhappiness of that depression, the alleviation and deadening of which was its object. The object was consequently achieved. The keynote by which the ascetic priest was enabled to get every kind of agonising and ecstatic music to play on the fibres of the human soul—was, as every one knows, the exploitation of the feeling of "guilt." I have already indicated in the previous essay the origin of this feeling—as a piece of animal psychology and nothing else: we were thus confronted with the feeling of "guilt," in its crude state, as it were. It was first in the hands of the priest, real artist that he was in the feeling of guilt, that it took shape—oh, what a shape![Pg 183] "Sin"—for that is the name of the new priestly version of the animal "bad-conscience" (the inverted cruelty)—has up to the present been the greatest event in the history of the diseased soul: in "sin" we find the most perilous and fatal masterpiece of religious interpretation. Imagine man, suffering from himself, some way or other but at any rate physiologically, perhaps like an animal shut up in a cage, not clear as to the why and the wherefore! imagine him in his desire for reasons—reasons bring relief—in his desire again for remedies, narcotics at last, consulting one, who knows even the occult—and see, lo and behold, he gets a hint from his wizard, the ascetic priest, his first hint on the "cause" of his trouble: he must search for it in himself, in his guiltiness, in a piece of the past, he must understand his very suffering as a state of punishment. He has heard, he has understood, has the unfortunate: he is now in the plight of a hen round which a line has been drawn. He never gets out of the circle of lines. The sick man has been turned into "the sinner"—and now for a few thousand years we never get away from the sight of this new invalid, of "a sinner"—shall we ever get away from it?—wherever we just look, everywhere the hypnotic gaze of the sinner always moving in one direction (in the direction of guilt, the only cause of suffering); everywhere the evil conscience, this "greuliche thier,"[4] to use Luther's language; everywhere rumination over the past, a distorted view of action, the gaze of the "green-eyed[Pg 184] monster" turned on all action; everywhere the wilful misunderstanding of suffering, its transvaluation into feelings of guilt, fear of retribution; everywhere the scourge, the hairy shirt, the starving body, contrition; everywhere the sinner breaking himself on the ghastly wheel of a restless and morbidly eager conscience; everywhere mute pain, extreme fear, the agony of a tortured heart, the spasms of an unknown happiness, the shriek for "redemption." In point of fact, thanks to this system of procedure, the old depression, dullness, and fatigue were absolutely conquered, life itself became very interesting again, awake, eternally awake, sleepless, glowing, burnt away, exhausted and yet not tired—such was the figure cut by man, "the sinner," who was initiated into these mysteries. This grand old wizard of an ascetic priest fighting with depression—he had clearly triumphed, his kingdom had come: men no longer grumbled at pain, men panted after pain: "More pain! More pain!" So for centuries on end shrieked the demand of his acolytes and initiates. Every emotional excess which hurt; everything which broke, overthrew, crushed, transported, ravished; the mystery of torture-chambers, the ingenuity of hell itself—all this was now discovered, divined, exploited, all this was at the service of the wizard, all this served to promote the triumph of his ideal, the ascetic ideal. "My kingdom is not of this world," quoth he, both at the beginning and at the end: had he still the right to talk like that?—Goethe has maintained that there are only thirty-six tragic situations: we would infer from that, did we not know otherwise,[Pg 185] that Goethe was no ascetic priest. He—knows more.

21.

So far as all this kind of priestly medicine-mongering, the "guilty" kind, is concerned, every word of criticism is superfluous. As for the suggestion that emotional excess of the type, which in these cases the ascetic priest is fain to order to his sick patients (under the most sacred euphemism, as is obvious, and equally impregnated with the sanctity of his purpose), has ever really been of use to any sick man, who, forsooth, would feel inclined to maintain a proposition of that character? At any rate, some understanding should be come to as to the expression "be of use." If you only wish to express that such a system of treatment has reformed man, I do not gainsay it: I merely add that "reformed" conveys to my mind as much as "tamed," "weakened," "discouraged," "refined," "daintified," "emasculated" (and thus it means almost as much as injured). But when you have to deal principally with sick, depressed, and oppressed creatures, such a system, even granted that it makes the ill "better," under any circumstances also makes them more ill: ask the mad-doctors the invariable result of a methodical application of penance-torture, contrition, and salvation ecstasies. Similarly ask history. In every body politic where the ascetic priest has established this treatment of the sick, disease has on every occasion spread with sinister speed throughout[Pg 186] its length and breadth. What was always the "result"? A shattered nervous system, in addition to the existing malady, and this in the greatest as in the smallest, in the individuals as in masses. We find, in consequence of the penance and redemption-training, awful epileptic epidemics, the greatest known to history, such as the St. Vitus and St. John dances of the Middle Ages; we find, as another phase of its after-effect, frightful mutilations and chronic depressions, by means of which the temperament of a nation or a city (Geneva, Bale) is turned once for all into its opposite;—this training, again, is responsible for the witch-hysteria, a phenomenon analogous to somnambulism (eight great epidemic outbursts of this only between 1564 and 1605);—we find similarly in its train those delirious death-cravings of large masses, whose awful "shriek," "evviva la morte!" was heard over the whole of Europe, now interrupted by voluptuous variations and anon by a rage for destruction, just as the same emotional sequence with the same intermittencies and sudden changes is now universally observed in every case where the ascetic doctrine of sin scores once more a great success (religious neurosis appears as a manifestation of the devil, there is no doubt of it. What is it? Quæritur). Speaking generally, the ascetic ideal and its sublime-moral cult, this most ingenious, reckless, and perilous systematisation of all methods of emotional excess, is writ large in a dreadful and unforgettable fashion on the whole history of man, and unfortunately not only on history. I was scarcely able to put forward any other element which attacked the[Pg 187] health and race efficiency of Europeans with more destructive power than did this ideal; it can be dubbed, without exaggeration, the real fatality in the history of the health of the European man. At the most you can merely draw a comparison with the specifically German influence: I mean the alcohol poisoning of Europe, which up to the present has kept pace exactly with the political and racial pre–dominance of the Germans (where they inoculated their blood, there too did they inoculate their vice). Third in the series comes syphilis—magno sed proximo intervallo.

22.

The ascetic priest has, wherever he has obtained the mastery, corrupted the health of the soul, he has consequently also corrupted taste in artibus et litteris—he corrupts it still. "Consequently?" I hope I shall be granted this "consequently"; at any rate, I am not going to prove it first. One solitary indication, it concerns the arch-book of Christian literature, their real model, their "book-in-itself." In the very midst of the Græco-Roman splendour, which was also a splendour of books, face to face with an ancient world of writings which had not yet fallen into decay and ruin, at a time when certain books were still to be read, to possess which we would give nowadays half our literature in exchange, at that time the simplicity and vanity of Christian agitators (they are generally called Fathers of the Church) dared to declare: "We too have our classical literature, we do not need that of the Greeks"—and meanwhile they[Pg 188] proudly pointed to their books of legends, their letters of apostles, and their apologetic tractlets, just in the same way that to-day the English "Salvation Army" wages its fight against Shakespeare and other "heathens" with an analogous literature. You already guess it, I do not like the "New Testament"; it almost upsets me that I stand so isolated in my taste so far as concerns this valued, this over-valued

Scripture; the taste of two thousand years is against me; but what boots it! "Here I stand! I cannot help myself"[5]—I have the courage of my bad taste. The Old Testament—yes, that is something quite different, all honour to the Old Testament! I find therein great men, an heroic landscape, and one of the rarest phenomena in the world, the incomparable naïveté of the strong heart; further still, I find a people. In the New, on the contrary, just a hostel of petty sects, pure rococo of the soul, twisting angles and fancy touches, nothing but conventicle air, not to forget an occasional whiff of bucolic sweetness which appertains to the epoch (and the Roman province) and is less Jewish than Hellenistic. Meekness and braggadocio cheek by jowl; an emotional garrulousness that almost deafens; passionate hysteria, but no passion; painful pantomime; here manifestly every one lacked good breeding. How dare any one make so much fuss about their little failings as do these pious little fellows! No one cares a straw about it—let[Pg 189] alone God. Finally they actually wish to have "the crown of eternal life," do all these little provincials! In return for what, in sooth? For what end? It is impossible to carry insolence any further. An immortal Peter! who could stand him! They have an ambition which makes one laugh: the thing dishes up cut and dried his most personal life, his melancholies, and common-or-garden troubles, as though the Universe itself were under an obligation to bother itself about them, for it never gets tired of wrapping up God Himself in the petty misery in which its troubles are involved. And how about the atrocious form of this chronic hobnobbing with God? This Jewish, and not merely Jewish, slobbering and clawing importunacy towards God!—There exist little despised "heathen nations" in East Asia, from whom these first Christians could have learnt something worth learning, a little tact in worshiping; these nations do not allow themselves to say aloud the name of their God. This seems to me delicate enough, it is certain that it is too delicate, and not only for primitive Christians; to take a contrast, just recollect Luther, the most "eloquent" and insolent peasant whom Germany has had, think of the Lutherian tone, in which he felt quite the most in his element during his tête-à-têtes with God. Luther's opposition to the mediæval saints of the Church (in particular, against "that devil's hog, the Pope"), was, there is no doubt, at bottom the opposition of a boor, who was offended at the good etiquette of the Church, that worship-etiquette of the sacerdotal code, which only admits[Pg 190] to the holy of holies the initiated and the silent, and shuts the door against the boors. These definitely were not to be allowed a hearing in this planet—but Luther the peasant simply wished it otherwise;

as it was, it was not German enough for him. He personally wished himself to talk direct, to talk personally, to talk "straight from the shoulder" with his God. Well, he's done it. The ascetic ideal, you will guess, was at no time and in no place, a school of good taste, still less of good manners—at the best it was a school for sacerdotal manners: that is, it contains in itself something which was a deadly enemy to all good manners. Lack of measure, opposition to measure, it is itself a "non plus ultra."

23.

The ascetic ideal has corrupted not only health and taste, there are also third, fourth, fifth, and sixth things which it has corrupted—I shall take care not to go through the catalogue (when should I get to the end?). I have here to expose not what this ideal effected; but rather only what it means, on what it is based, what lies lurking behind it and under it, that of which it is the provisional expression, an obscure expression bristling with queries and misunderstandings. And with this object only in view I presumed "not to spare" my readers a glance at the awfulness of its results, a glance at its fatal results; I did this to prepare them for the final and most awful aspect presented to me by the question of the significance of that[Pg 191] ideal. What is the significance of the power of that ideal, the monstrousness of its power? Why is it given such an amount of scope? Why is not a better resistance offered against it? The ascetic ideal expresses one will: where is the opposition will, in which an opposition ideal expresses itself? The ascetic ideal has an aim— this goal is, putting it generally, that all the other interests of human life should, measured by its standard, appear petty and narrow; it explains epochs, nations, men, in reference to this one end; it forbids any other interpretation, any other end; it repudiates, denies, affirms, confirms, only in the sense of its own interpretation (and was there ever a more thoroughly elaborated system of interpretation?); it subjects itself to no power, rather does it believe in its own precedence over every power—it believes that nothing powerful exists in the world that has not first got to receive from "it" a meaning, a right to exist, a value, as being an instrument in its work, a way and means to its end, to one end. Where is the counterpart of this complete system of will, end, and interpretation? Why is the counterpart lacking? Where is the other "one aim"? But I am told it is not lacking, that not only has it fought a long and fortunate fight with that ideal, but that further it has already won the mastery over that ideal in all essentials: let our whole modern science attest this—that modern science, which, like the genuine reality-philosophy which it is, manifestly believes in itself alone, manifestly has the courage to be itself, the will to be itself, and has got on well[Pg 192] enough without God, another world, and negative virtues.

With all their noisy agitator-babble, however, they effect nothing with me; these trumpeters of reality are bad musicians, their voices do not come from the deeps with sufficient audibility, they are not the mouthpiece for the abyss of scientific knowledge—for to-day scientific knowledge is an abyss—the word "science," in such trumpeter-mouths, is a prostitution, an abuse, an impertinence. The truth is just the opposite from what is maintained in the ascetic theory. Science has to-day absolutely no belief in itself, let alone in an ideal superior to itself, and wherever science still consists of passion, love, ardour, suffering, it is not the opposition to that ascetic ideal, but rather the incarnation of its latest and noblest form. Does that ring strange? There are enough brave and decent working people, even among the learned men of to-day, who like their little corner, and who, just because they are pleased so to do, become at times indecently loud with their demand, that people to-day should be quite content, especially in science—for in science there is so much useful work to do. I do not deny it—there is nothing I should like less than to spoil the delight of these honest workers in their handiwork; for I rejoice in their work. But the fact of science requiring hard work, the fact of its having contented workers, is absolutely no proof of science as a whole having to-day one end, one will, one ideal, one passion for a great faith; the contrary, as I have said, is the case. When science is not the latest manifestation of the ascetic ideal—but these[Pg 193] are cases of such rarity, selectness, and exquisiteness, as to preclude the general judgment being affected thereby—science is a hiding-place for every kind of cowardice, disbelief, remorse, despectio sui, bad conscience—it is the very anxiety that springs from having no ideal, the suffering from the lack of a great love, the discontent with an enforced moderation. Oh, what does all science not cover to-day? How much, at any rate, does it not try to cover? The diligence of our best scholars, their senseless industry, their burning the candle of their brain at both ends—their very mastery in their handiwork—how often is the real meaning of all that to prevent themselves continuing to see a certain thing? Science as a self-anæsthetic: do you know that? You wound them—every one who consorts with scholars experiences this—you wound them sometimes to the quick through just a harmless word; when you think you are paying them a compliment you embitter them beyond all bounds, simply because you didn't have the finesse to infer the real kind of customers you had to tackle, the sufferer kind (who won't own up even to themselves what they really are), the dazed and unconscious kind who have only one fear—coming to consciousness.

24.

And now look at the other side, at those rare cases, of which I spoke, the most supreme idealists to be found nowadays among philosophers and scholars. Have we, perchance, found in them the sought-for opponents of the ascetic ideal, its[Pg 194] anti-idealists? In fact, they believe themselves to be such, these "unbelievers" (for they are all of them that): it seems that this idea is their last remnant of faith, the idea of being opponents of this ideal, so earnest are they on this subject, so passionate in word and gesture;—but does it follow that what they believe must necessarily be true? We "knowers" have grown by degrees suspicious of all kinds of believers, our suspicion has step by step habituated us to draw just the opposite conclusions to what people have drawn before; that is to say, wherever the strength of a belief is particularly prominent to draw the conclusion of the difficulty of proving what is believed, the conclusion of its actual improbability. We do not again deny that "faith produces salvation": for that very reason we do deny that faith proves anything,—a strong faith, which produces happiness, causes suspicion of the object of that faith, it does not establish its "truth," it does establish a certain probability of—illusion. What is now the position in these cases? These solitaries and deniers of to-day; these fanatics in one thing, in their claim to intellectual cleanness; these hard, stern, continent, heroic spirits, who constitute the glory of our time; all these pale atheists, anti-Christians, immoralists, Nihilists; these sceptics, "ephectics," and "hectics" of the intellect (in a certain sense they are the latter, both collectively and individually); these supreme idealists of knowledge, in whom alone nowadays the intellectual conscience dwells and is alive—in point of fact they believe themselves as far away as possible from the ascetic[Pg 195] ideal, do these "free, very free spirits": and yet, if I may reveal what they themselves cannot see—for they stand too near themselves: this ideal is simply their ideal, they represent it nowadays and perhaps no one else, they themselves are its most spiritualised product, its most advanced picket of skirmishers and scouts, its most insidious delicate and elusive form of seduction.—If I am in any way a reader of riddles, then I will be one with this sentence: for some time past there have been no free spirits; for they still believe in truth. When the Christian Crusaders in the East came into collision with that invincible order of assassins, that order of free spirits par excellence, whose lowest grade lives in a state of discipline such as no order of monks has ever attained, then in some way or other they managed to get an inkling of that symbol and tally-word, that was reserved for the highest grade alone as their secretum, "Nothing is true, everything is allowed,"—in sooth, that was freedom of thought, thereby was taking leave of the very belief in truth. Has indeed any European, any Christian freethinker, ever yet wandered into this proposition and its labyrinthine consequences? Does he know from experience the Minotauros of this den.—I doubt it—nay, I know otherwise. Nothing is more really alien to these "mono-fanatics," these so-called "free spirits," than freedom and unfettering in that sense; in no respect are they more closely tied, the absolute fanaticism of their belief in truth is unparalleled. I know all this perhaps too much from experience at close quarters—that dignified philosophic abstinence to which[Pg 196] a belief like that binds its adherents, that stoicism of the intellect, which eventually vetoes negation as rigidly as it does affirmation, that wish for standing still in front of the actual, the factum brutum, that fatalism in "petits faits" (ce petit faitalism, as I call it), in which French Science now attempts a kind of moral superiority over German, this renunciation of interpretation generally (that is, of forcing, doctoring, abridging, omitting, suppressing, inventing, falsifying, and all the other essential attributes of interpretation)—all this, considered broadly, expresses the asceticism of virtue, quite as efficiently as does any repudiation of the senses (it is at bottom only a modus of that repudiation.) But what forces it into that unqualified will for truth is the faith in the ascetic ideal itself, even though it take the form of its unconscious imperatives,—make no mistake about it, it is the faith, I repeat, in a metaphysical value, an intrinsic value of truth, of a character which is only warranted and guaranteed in this ideal (it stands and falls with that ideal). Judged strictly, there does not exist a science without its "hypotheses," the thought of such a science is inconceivable, illogical: a philosophy, a faith, must always exist first to enable science to gain thereby a direction, a meaning, a limit and method, a right to existence. (He who holds a contrary opinion on the subject—he, for example, who takes it upon himself to establish philosophy "upon a strictly scientific basis"—has first got to "turn up-side-down" not only philosophy but also truth itself—the gravest insult which could possibly be offered to two such respectable[Pg

197] females!) Yes, there is no doubt about it—and here I quote my Joyful Wisdom, cp. Book V. Aph. 344: "The man who is truthful in that daring and extreme fashion, which is the presupposition of the faith in science, asserts thereby a different world from that of life, nature, and history; and in so far as he asserts the existence of that different world, come, must he not similarly repudiate its counterpart, this world, our world? The belief on which our faith in science is based has remained to this day a metaphysical belief—even we knowers of to-day, we godless foes of metaphysics, we too take our fire from that conflagration which was kindled by a thousand-year-old faith, from that Christian belief, which was also Plato's belief, the belief that God is truth, that truth is divine.... But what if this belief becomes more and more incredible, what if nothing proves itself to be divine, unless it be error, blindness, lies—what if God, Himself proved Himself to be our oldest lie?"—It is necessary to stop at this point and to consider the situation carefully. Science itself now needs a justification (which is not for a minute to say that there is such a justification). Turn in this context to the most ancient and the most modern philosophers: they all fail to realise the extent of the need of a justification on the part of the Will for Truth—here is a gap in every philosophy—what is it caused by? Because up to the present the ascetic ideal dominated all philosophy, because Truth was fixed as Being, as God, as the Supreme Court of Appeal, because Truth was not allowed to be a problem. Do you understand this[Pg 198] "allowed"? From the minute that the belief in the God of the ascetic ideal is repudiated, there exists a new problem: the problem of the value of truth. The Will for Truth needed a critique—let us define by these words our own task—-the value of truth is tentatively to be called in question.... (If this seems too laconically expressed, I recommend the reader to peruse again that passage from the Joyful Wisdom which bears the title, "How far we also are still pious," Aph. 344, and best of all the whole fifth book of that work, as well as the Preface to The Dawn of Day.)

25.

No! You can't get round me with science, when I search for the natural antagonists of the ascetic ideal, when I put the question: "Where is the opposed will in which the opponent ideal expresses itself?" Science is not, by a long way, independent enough to fulfil this function; in every department science needs an ideal value, a power which creates values, and in whose service it can believe in itself —science itself never creates values. Its relation to the ascetic ideal is not in itself antagonistic; speaking roughly, it rather represents the progressive force in the inner evolution of that ideal. Tested more exactly, its opposition and antagonism are concerned not with the ideal itself, but only with that ideal's outworks, its outer garb, its masquerade, with its temporary hardening, stiffening, and dogmatising—it makes the life in the ideal free once more, while it repudiates its superficial[Pg 199] elements. These two phenomena, science and the ascetic ideal, both rest on the same basis—I have already made this clear—the basis, I say, oft the same over-appreciation of truth (more accurately the same belief in the impossibility of valuing and of criticising truth), and consequently they are necessarily allies, so that, in the event of their being attacked, they must always be attacked and called into question together. A valuation of the ascetic ideal inevitably entails a valuation of science as well; lose no time in seeing this clearly, and be sharp to catch it! (Art, I am speaking provisionally, for I will treat it on some other occasion in greater detail,—art, I repeat, in which lying is sanctified and the will for deception has good conscience on its side, is much more fundamentally opposed to the ascetic ideal than is science: Plato's instinct felt this—Plato, the greatest enemy of art which Europe has produced up to the present. Plato versus Homer, that is the complete, the true antagonism—on the one side, the whole-hearted "transcendental," the great defamer of life; on the other, its involuntary panegyrist, the golden nature. An artistic subservience to the service of the ascetic ideal is consequently the most absolute artistic corruption that there can be, though unfortunately it is one of the most frequent phases, for nothing is more corruptible than an artist.) Considered physiologically, moreover, science rests on the same, basis as does the ascetic ideal: a certain impoverishment of life is the presupposition of the latter as of the former—add, frigidity of the emotions, slackening of the tempo, the substitution of dialectic for[Pg 200] instinct, seriousness impressed on mien and gesture (seriousness, that most unmistakable sign of strenuous metabolism, of struggling, toiling life). Consider the periods in a nation in which the learned man comes into prominence; they are the periods of exhaustion, often of sunset, of decay—the effervescing strength, the confidence in life, the confidence in the future are no more. The preponderance of the mandarins never signifies any good, any more than does the advent of democracy, or arbitration instead of war, equal rights for women, the religion of pity, and all the other symptoms of declining life. (Science handled as a problem! what is the meaning of science?—upon this point the Preface to the Birth of Tragedy.) No! this "modern science"—mark you this well—is at times the best ally for the ascetic ideal, and for the very reason that it is the ally which is most unconscious, most automatic, most secret, and most subterranean! They have been playing into each other's hands up to the present, have these "poor in spirit" and the scientific opponents of that ideal (take care, by the bye, not to think that these opponents are the antithesis of this ideal, that they are the rich in spirit—that they are not; I have called them the hectic in spirit). As for these celebrated victories of science; there is no doubt that they are victories—but victories over what? There was not for a single minute any victory among their list over the ascetic ideal, rather was it made stronger, that is to say, more elusive, more abstract, more insidious, from the fact that a wall, an outwork, that had got[Pg 201] built on to the main fortress and disfigured its appearance, should from time to time be ruthlessly destroyed and broken down by science. Does any one seriously suggest that the downfall of the theological astronomy signified the downfall of that ideal?—Has, perchance, man grown less in need of a transcendental solution of his riddle of existence, because since that time this existence has become more random, casual, and superfluous in the visible order of the universe? Has there not been since the time of Copernicus an unbroken progress in the self-belittling of man and his will for belittling himself? Alas, his belief in his dignity, his uniquenesses irreplaceableness in the scheme of existence, is gone—he has become animal, literal, unqualified, and unmitigated animal, he who in his earlier belief was almost God ("child of God," "demi-God"). Since Copernicus man seems to have fallen on to a steep plane—he rolls faster and faster away from the centre—whither? into nothingness? into the "thrilling sensation of his own nothingness"—Well! this would be the straight way—to the old ideal?—All science (and by no means only astronomy, with regard to the humiliating and deteriorating effect of which Kant has made a remarkable confession, "it annihilates my own importance"), all science, natural as much as unnatural—by unnatural I mean the self-critique of reason—nowadays sets out to talk man out of his present opinion of himself, as though that opinion had been nothing but a bizarre piece of conceit; you might go so far as to say that science finds its peculiar pride, its peculiar bitter form of stoical ataraxia, in preserving man's contempt of himself[Pg 202], that state which it took so much trouble to bring about, as man's final and most serious claim to self-appreciation (rightly so, in point of fact, for he who despises is always "one who has not forgotten how to appreciate"). But does all this involve any real effort to counteract the ascetic ideal? Is it really seriously suggested that Kant's victory over the theological dogmatism about "God," "Soul," "Freedom," "Immortality," has damaged that ideal in any way (as the theologians have imagined to be the case for a long time past)?— And in this connection it does not concern us for a single minute, if Kant himself intended any such consummation. It is certain that from the time of Kant every type of transcendentalist is playing a winning game—they are emancipated from the theologians; what luck!—he has revealed to them that secret art, by which they can now pursue their "heart's desire" on their own responsibility, and with all the respectability of science. Similarly, who can grumble at the agnostics, reverers, as they are, of the unknown and the absolute mystery, if they now worship their very query as God? (Xaver Doudan talks somewhere of the ravages which l'habitude d'admirer l'inintelligible au lieu de rester tout simplement dans l'inconnu has produced—the ancients, he thinks, must have been exempt from those ravages.) Supposing that everything, "known" to man, fails to satisfy his desires, and on the contrary contradicts and horrifies them, what a divine way out of all this to be able to look for the responsibility, not in the "desiring" but in "knowing"!—"There[Pg 203] is no knowledge. Consequently— there is a God"; what a novel elegantia syllogismi! what a triumph for the ascetic ideal!

26.

Or, perchance, does the whole of modern history show in its demeanour greater confidence in life, greater confidence in its ideals? Its loftiest pretension is now to be a mirror; it repudiates all teleology; it will have no more "proving"; it disdains to play the judge, and thereby shows its good taste—it asserts as little as it denies, it fixes, it "describes." All this is to a high degree ascetic, but at the same time it is to a much greater degree nihilistic; make no mistake about this! You see in the historian a gloomy, hard, but determined gaze,— an eye that looks out as an isolated North Pole explorer looks out (perhaps so as not to look within, so as not to look back?)—there is snow—here is life silenced, the last crows which caw here are called "whither?" "Vanity," "Nada"—here nothing more flourishes and grows, at the most the metapolitics of St. Petersburg and the "pity" of Tolstoi. But as for that other school of historians, a perhaps still more "modern" school, a voluptuous and lascivious school which ogles life and the ascetic ideal with equal fervour, which uses the word "artist" as a glove, and has nowadays established a "corner" for itself, in all the praise given to contemplation; oh, what a thirst do these sweet intellectuals excite even for[Pg 204] ascetics and winter landscapes! Nay! The devil take these "contemplative" folk! How much liefer would I wander with those historical Nihilists through the gloomiest, grey, cold mist!—nay, I shall not mind listening (supposing I have to choose) to one who is completely unhistorical and anti-historical (a man, like Dühring for instance, over whose periods a hitherto shy and unavowed species of "beautiful souls" has grown intoxicated in contemporary Germany, the species anarchistica within the educated proletariate). The "contemplative" are a hundred times worse—I never knew anything which produced such intense nausea as one of those "objective" chairs,[6] one of those scented mannikins-about-town of history, a thing half-priest, half-satyr (Renan parfum), which betrays by the high, shrill falsetto of his applause what he lacks and where he lacks it, who betrays where in this case the Fates have plied their ghastly shears, alas! in too surgeon-like a fashion! This is distasteful to me, and irritates my patience; let him keep patient at such sights who has nothing to lose thereby,—such a sight enrages me, such spectators embitter me against the "play," even more than does the play itself (history itself, you understand); Anacreontic moods imperceptibly come over me. This Nature, who gave to the steer its horn, to the lion its χάσμ' ὀδόντων, for what purpose did Nature give me my foot?—To kick, by St. Anacreon, and not merely to run away! To trample on all the[Pg 205] worm-eaten "chairs," the cowardly contemplators, the lascivious eunuchs of history, the flirters with ascetic ideals, the righteous hypocrites of impotence! All reverence on my part to the ascetic ideal, in so far as it is honourable! So long as it believes in itself and plays no pranks on us! But I like not all these coquettish bugs who have an insatiate ambition to smell of the infinite, until eventually the infinite smells of bugs; I like not the whited sepulchres with their stagey reproduction of life; I like not the tired and the used up who wrap themselves in wisdom and look "objective"; I like not the agitators dressed up as heroes, who hide their dummy-heads behind the stalking-horse of an ideal; I like not the ambitious artists who would fain play the ascetic and the priest, and are at bottom nothing but tragic clowns; I like not, again, these newest speculators in idealism, the Anti-Semites, who nowadays roll their eyes in the patent Christian-Aryan-man-of-honour fashion, and by an abuse of moralist attitudes and agitation dodges, so cheap as to exhaust any patience, strive to excite all the blockhead elements in the populace (the invariable success of every kind of intellectual charlatanism in present-day Germany hangs together with the almost indisputable and already quite palpable desolation of the German mind, whose cause I look for in a too exclusive diet, of papers, politics, beer, and Wagnerian music, not forgetting the condition precedent of this diet, the national exclusiveness and vanity, the strong but narrow principle, "Germany, Germany above everything,"[7][Pg 206] and finally the paralysis agitans of "modern ideas"). Europe nowadays is, above all, wealthy and ingenious in means of excitement; it apparently has no more crying necessity than stimulantia and alcohol. Hence the enormous counterfeiting of ideals, those most fiery spirits of the mind; hence too the repulsive, evil-smelling, perjured, pseudo-alcoholic air everywhere. I should like to know how many cargoes of imitation idealism, of hero-costumes and high falutin' clap-trap, how many casks of sweetened pity liqueur (Firm: la religion de la souffrance), how many crutches of righteous indignation for the help of these flat-footed intellects, how many comedians of the Christian moral ideal would need to-day to be exported from Europe, to enable its air to smell pure again. It is obvious that, in regard to this over-production, a new trade possibility lies open; it is obvious that there is a new business to be done in little ideal idols and obedient "idealists"—don't pass over this tip! Who has sufficient courage? We have in our hands the possibility of idealising the whole earth. But what am I talking about courage? we only need one thing here—a hand, a free, a very free hand.

27.

Enough! enough! let us leave these curiosities and complexities of the modern spirit, which excite as much laughter as disgust. Our problem can[Pg 207] certainly do without them, the problem of meaning of the ascetic ideal—what has it got to do with yesterday or to-day? those things shall be handled by me more thoroughly and severely in another connection (under the title "A Contribution to the History of European Nihilism," I refer for this to a work which I am preparing: The Will to Power, an Attempt at a Transvaluation of All Values). The only reason why I come to allude to it here is this: the ascetic ideal has at times, even in the most intellectual sphere, only one real kind of enemies and damagers: these are the comedians of this ideal—for they awake mistrust. Everywhere otherwise, where the mind is at work seriously, powerfully, and without counterfeiting, it dispenses altogether now with an ideal (the popular expression for this abstinence is "Atheism")—with the exception of the will for truth. But this will, this remnant of an ideal, is, if you will believe me, that ideal itself in its severest and cleverest formulation, esoteric through and through, stripped of all outworks, and consequently not so much its remnant as its kernel. Unqualified honest atheism (and its air only do we breathe, we, the most intellectual men of this age) is not opposed to that ideal, to the extent that it appears to be; it is rather one of the final phases of its evolution, one of its syllogisms and pieces of inherent logic—it is the awe-inspiring catastrophe of a two-thousand-year training in truth, which finally forbids itself the lie of the belief in God. (The same course of development in India—quite independently, and consequently[Pg 208] of some demonstrative value—the same ideal driving to the same conclusion the decisive point reached five hundred years before the European era, or more precisely at the time of Buddha—it started in the Sankhyam philosophy, and then this was popularised through Buddha, and made into a religion.)

What, I put the question with all strictness, has really triumphed over the Christian God? The answer stands in my Joyful Wisdom, Aph. 357: "the Christian morality itself, the idea of truth, taken as it was with increasing seriousness, the confessor-subtlety of the Christian conscience translated and sublimated into the scientific conscience into intellectual cleanness at any price. Regarding Nature as though it were a proof of the goodness and guardianship of God; interpreting history in honour of a divine reason, as a constant proof of a moral order of the world and a moral teleology; explaining our own personal experiences, as pious men have for long enough explained them, as though every arrangement, every nod, every single thing were invented and sent out of love for the salvation of the soul; all this is now done away with, all this has the conscience against it, and is regarded by every subtler conscience as disreputable, dishonourable, as lying, feminism, weakness, cowardice—by means of this severity, if by means of anything at all, are we, in sooth, good Europeans and heirs of Europe's longest and bravest self-mastery."... All great things go to ruin by reason of themselves, by reason of an act of self-dissolution: so wills the law of life,[Pg 209] the law of necessary "self-mastery" even in the essence of life—ever is the law-giver finally exposed to the cry, "patere legem quam ipse tulisti"; in thus wise did Christianity go to ruin as a dogma, through its own morality; in thus wise must Christianity go again to ruin to-day as a morality—we are standing on the threshold of this event. After Christian truthfulness has drawn one conclusion after the other, it finally draws its strongest conclusion, its conclusion against itself; this, however, happens, when it puts the question, "what is the meaning of every will for truth?" And here again do I touch on my problem, on our problem, my unknown friends (for as yet I know of no friends): what sense has our whole being, if it does not mean that in our own selves that will for truth has come to its own consciousness as a problem?--By reason of this attainment of self-consciousness on the part of the will for truth, morality from henceforward—there is no doubt about it—goes to pieces: this is that great hundred-act play that is reserved for the next two centuries of Europe, the most terrible, the most mysterious, and perhaps also the most hopeful of all plays.

28.

If you except the ascetic ideal, man, the animal man had no meaning. His existence on earth contained no end; "What is the purpose of man at all?" was a question without an answer; the will for man and the world was lacking; behind every great human destiny rang as a refrain a still[Pg 210] greater "Vanity!" The ascetic ideal simply means this: that something was lacking, that a tremendous void encircled man—he did not know how to justify himself, to explain himself, to affirm himself, he suffered from the problem of his own meaning. He suffered also in other ways, he was in the main a diseased animal; but his problem was not suffering itself, but the lack of an answer to that crying question, "To what purpose do we suffer?" Man, the bravest animal and the one most inured to suffering, does not repudiate suffering in itself: he wills it, he even seeks it out, provided that he is shown a meaning for it, a purpose of suffering. Not suffering, but the senselessness of suffering was the curse which till then lay spread over humanity—and the ascetic ideal gave it a meaning! It was up till then the only meaning; but any meaning is better than no meaning; the ascetic ideal was in that connection the "faute de mieux" par excellence that existed at that time. In that ideal suffering found an explanation; the tremendous gap seemed filled; the door to all suicidal Nihilism was closed. The explanation—there is no doubt about it—brought in its train new suffering, deeper, more penetrating, more venomous, gnawing more brutally into life: it brought all suffering under the perspective of guilt; but in spite of all that—man was saved thereby, he had a meaning, and from henceforth was no more like a leaf in the wind, a shuttle-cock of chance, of nonsense, he could now "will" something—absolutely immaterial to what end, to what purpose, with what means he wished:[Pg 211] the will itself was saved. It is absolutely impossible to disguise what in point of fact is made clear by every complete will that has taken its direction from the ascetic ideal: this hate of the human, and even more of the animal, and more still of the material, this horror of the senses, of reason itself, this fear of happiness and beauty, this desire to get right away from all illusion, change, growth, death, wishing and even desiring—all this means—let us have the courage to grasp it—a will for Nothingness, a will opposed to life, a repudiation of the most fundamental conditions of life, but it is and remains a will!—and to say at the end that which I said at the beginning—man will wish Nothingness rather than not wish at all.

[1]An allusion to the celebrated monologue in William Tell.

[2]Mistress Sly.—Tr.

[3]In the German text "Heiland." This has the double meaning of "healer" and "saviour."—H. B. S.

[4]"Horrible beast."

[5]"Here I stand! I cannot help myself. God help me! Amen"—were Luther's words before the Reichstag at Worms.—H. B. S.

[6]E.g. Lectureships.

[7]An allusion to the well-known patriotic song.—H. B. S.

PEOPLES AND COUNTRIES.
Translated by J. M. KENNEDY.

[The following twenty-seven fragments were intended by Nietzsche to form a supplement to Chapter VIII. of Beyond Good and Evil, dealing with Peoples and Countries.]

1.

The Europeans now imagine themselves as representing, in the main, the highest types of men on earth.

2.

A characteristic of Europeans: inconsistency between word and deed; the Oriental is true to himself in daily life. How the European has established colonies is explained by his nature, which resembles that of a beast of prey.

This inconsistency is explained by the fact that Christianity has abandoned the class from which it sprang.

This is the difference between us and the Hellenes: their morals grew up among the governing castes. Thucydides' morals are the same as those that exploded everywhere with Plato.

Attempts towards honesty at the Renaissance, for example: always for the benefit of the arts. Michael Angelo's conception of God as the "Tyrant of the World" was an honest one.

3.

I rate Michael Angelo higher than Raphael, because, through all the Christian clouds and prejudices of his time, he saw the ideal of a culture nobler than the Christo-Raphaelian: whilst Raphael truly and modestly glorified only the values handed down to him, and did not carry within himself any inquiring, yearning instincts. Michael Angelo, on the other hand, saw and felt the problem of the law-giver of new values: the problem of the conqueror made perfect, who first had to subdue the "hero within himself," the man exalted to his highest pedestal, master even of his pity, who mercilessly shatters and annihilates everything that does not bear his own stamp, shining in Olympian divinity. Michael Angelo was naturally only at certain moments so high and so far beyond his age and Christian Europe: for the most part he adopted a condescending attitude towards the eternal feminine in Christianity; it would seem, indeed, that in the end he broke down before her, and gave up the ideal of his most inspired hours. It was an ideal which only a man in the strongest and highest vigour of life could bear; but not a man advanced in years! Indeed, he would have had to demolish Christianity with his ideal! But he was not thinker and philosopher enough for that Perhaps Leonardo da Vinci alone of those artists had a really super-Christian outlook. He knows the East, the "land of dawn," within himself as well as without himself. There is something super-European[Pg 217] and silent in him: a characteristic of every one who has seen too wide a circle of things good and bad.

4.

How much we have learnt and learnt anew in fifty years! The whole Romantic School with its belief in "the people" is refuted! No Homeric poetry as "popular" poetry! No deification of the great powers of Nature! No deduction from language-relationship to race-relationship! No "intellectual contemplations" of the supernatural! No truth enshrouded in religion!

The problem of truthfulness is quite a new one. I am astonished. From this standpoint we regard such natures as Bismarck as culpable out of carelessness, such as Richard Wagner out of want of modesty; we would condemn Plato for his pia fraus, Kant for the derivation of his Categorical Imperative, his own belief certainly not having come to him from this source.

Finally, even doubt turns against itself: doubt in doubt. And the question as to the value of truthfulness and its extent lies there.

5.

What I observe with pleasure in the German is his Mephistophelian nature; but, to tell the truth, one must have a higher conception of Mephistopheles than Goethe had, who found it necessary to diminish his Mephistopheles in order to magnify his "inner Faust." The true German Mephistopheles[Pg 218] is much more dangerous, bold, wicked, and cunning, and consequently more open-hearted: remember the nature of Frederick the Great, or of that much greater

Frederick, the Hohenstaufen, Frederick II.

The real German Mephistopheles crosses the Alps, and believes that everything there belongs to him. Then he recovers himself, like Winckelmann, like Mozart. He looks upon Faust and Hamlet as caricatures, invented to be laughed at, and upon Luther also. Goethe had his good German moments, when he laughed inwardly at all these things. But then he fell back again into his cloudy moods.

6.

Perhaps the Germans have only grown up in a wrong climate! There is something in them that might be Hellenic!—something that is awakened when they are brought into touch with the South—Winckelmann, Goethe, Mozart. We should not forget, however, that we are still young. Luther is still our last event; our last book is still the Bible. The Germans have never yet "moralised." Also, the very food of the Germans was their doom: its consequence, Philistinism.

7.

The Germans are a dangerous people: they are experts at inventing intoxicants. Gothic, rococo (according to Semper), the historical sense and exoticism, Hegel, Richard Wagner—Leibniz,[Pg 219] too (dangerous at the present day)—(they even idealised the serving soul as the virtue of scholars and soldiers, also as the simple mind). The Germans may well be the most composite people on earth.

"The people of the Middle," the inventors of porcelain, and of a kind of Chinese breed of Privy Councillor.

8.

The smallness and baseness of the German soul were not and are not consequences of the system of small states; for it is well known that the inhabitants of much smaller states were proud and independent: and it is not a large state per se that makes souls freer and more manly. The man whose soul obeys the slavish command: "Thou shalt and must kneel!" in whose body there is an involuntary bowing and scraping to titles, orders, gracious glances from above—well, such a man in an "Empire" will only bow all the more deeply and lick the dust more fervently in the presence of the greater sovereign than in the presence of the lesser: this cannot be doubted. We can still see in the lower classes of Italians that aristocratic self-sufficiency; manly discipline and self-confidence still form a part of the long history of their country: these are virtues which once manifested themselves before their eyes. A poor Venetian gondolier makes a far better figure than a Privy Councillor from Berlin, and is even a better man in the end—any one can see this. Just ask the women.

9.

Most artists, even some of the greatest (including the historians) have up to the present belonged to the serving classes (whether they serve people of high position or princes or women or "the masses"), not to speak of their dependence upon the Church and upon moral law. Thus Rubens portrayed the nobility of his age; but only according to their vague conception of taste, not according to his own measure of beauty on the whole, therefore, against his own taste. Van Dyck was nobler in this respect: who in all those whom he painted added a certain amount of what he himself most highly valued: he did not descend from himself, but rather lifted up others to himself when he "rendered."

The slavish humility of the artist to his public (as Sebastian Bach has testified in undying and outrageous words in the dedication of his High Mass) is perhaps more difficult to perceive in music; but it is all the more deeply engrained. A hearing would be refused me if I endeavoured to impart my views on this subject. Chopin possesses distinction, like Van Dyck. The disposition of Beethoven is that of a proud peasant; of Haydn, that of a proud servant. Mendelssohn, too, possesses distinction—like Goethe, in the most natural way in the world.

10.

We could at any time have counted on the fingers of one hand those German learned men[Pg 221] who possessed wit: the remainder have understanding, and a few of them, happily, that famous "childlike character" which divines.... It is our privilege: with this "divination" German science has discovered some things which we can hardly conceive of, and which, after all, do not exist, perhaps. It is only the Jews among the Germans who do not "divine" like them.

11.

As Frenchmen reflect the politeness and esprit of French society, so do Germans reflect something of the deep, pensive earnestness of their mystics and musicians, and also of their silly childishness. The Italian exhibits a great deal of republican distinction and art, and can show himself to be noble and proud without vanity.

12.

A larger number of the higher and better-endowed men will, I hope, have in the end so much self-restraint as to be able to get rid of their bad taste for affectation and sentimental darkness, and to turn against Richard Wagner as much as against Schopenhauer. These two Germans are leading us to ruin; they flatter our dangerous qualities. A stronger future is prepared for us in Goethe, Beethoven, and Bismarck than in these racial aberrations. We have had no philosophers yet.

13.

The peasant is the commonest type of noblesse, for he is dependent upon himself most of all. Peasant blood is still the best blood in Germany —for example, Luther, Niebuhr, Bismarck.

Bismarck a Slav. Let any one look upon the face of Germans. Everything that had manly, exuberant blood in it went abroad. Over the smug populace remaining, the slave-souled people, there came an improvement from abroad, especially by a mixture of Slavonic blood.

The Brandenburg nobility and the Prussian nobility in general (and the peasant of certain North German districts), comprise at present the most manly natures in Germany.

That the manliest men shall rule: this is only the natural order of things.

14.

The future of German culture rests with the sons of the Prussian officers.

15.

There has always been a want of wit in Germany, and mediocre heads attain there to the highest honours, because even they are rare. What is most highly prized is diligence and perseverance and a certain cold-blooded, critical outlook, and, for the sake of such qualities, German scholarship and the German military system have become paramount in Europe.

16.

Parliaments may be very useful to a strong and versatile statesman: he has something there to rely upon (every such thing must, however, be able to resist!)—upon which he can throw a great deal of responsibility. On the whole, however, I could wish that the counting mania and the superstitious belief in majorities were not established in Germany, as with the Latin races, and that one could finally invent something new even in politics! It is senseless and dangerous to let the custom of universal suffrage—which is still but a short time under cultivation, and could easily be uprooted—take a deeper root: whilst, of course, its introduction was merely an expedient to steer clear of temporary difficulties.

17.

Can any one interest himself in this German Empire? Where is the new thought? Is it only a new combination of power? All the worse, if it does not know its own mind. Peace and laisser aller are not types of politics for which I have any respect. Ruling, and helping the highest thoughts to victory—the only things that can make me interested in Germany. England's small-mindedness is the great danger now on earth. I observe more inclination towards greatness in the feelings of the Russian Nihilists than in those of the English Utilitarians. We require an intergrowth of the German and Slav races, and [Pg 224] we require, too, the cleverest financiers, the Jews, for us to become masters of the world.

(a) The sense of reality.

(b) A giving-up of the English principle of the people's right of representation. We require the representation of the great interests.

(c) We require an unconditional union with Russia, together with a mutual plan of action which shall not permit any English schemata to obtain the mastery in Russia. No American future!

(d) A national system of politics is untenable, and embarrassment by Christian views is a very great evil. In Europe all sensible people are sceptics, whether they say so or not.

18.

I see over and beyond all these national wars, new "empires," and whatever else lies in the foreground. What I am concerned with—for I see it preparing itself slowly and hesitatingly—is the United Europe. It was the only real work, the one impulse in the souls, of all the broad-minded and deep-thinking men of this century—this preparation of a new synthesis, and the tentative effort to anticipate the future of "the European." Only in their weaker moments, or when they grew old, did they fall back again into the national narrowness of the "Fatherlanders"—then they were once more "patriots." I am thinking of men like Napoleon, Heinrich Heine, Goethe, Beethoven, Stendhal, Schopenhauer. Perhaps[Pg 225] Richard Wagner likewise belongs to their number, concerning whom, as a successful type of German obscurity, nothing can be said without some such "perhaps."

But to the help of such minds as feel the need of a new unity there comes a great explanatory economic fact: the small States of Europe—I refer to all our present kingdoms and "empires"—will in a short time become economically untenable, owing to the mad, uncontrolled struggle for the possession of local and international trade. Money is even now compelling European nations to amalgamate into one Power. In order, however, that Europe may enter into the battle for the mastery of the world with good prospects of victory (it is easy to perceive against whom this battle will be waged), she must probably "come to an understanding" with England. The English colonies are needed for this struggle, just as much as modern Germany, to play her new rôle of broker and middleman, requires the colonial possessions of Holland. For no one any longer believes that England alone is strong enough to continue to act her old part for fifty years more; the impossibility of shutting out homines novi from the government will ruin her, and her continual change of political parties is a fatal obstacle to the carrying out of any tasks which require to be spread out over a long period of time. A man must to-day be a soldier first and foremost that he may not afterwards lose his credit as a merchant. Enough; here, as in other matters, the coming century will be found following in the footsteps of[Pg 226] Napoleon—the first man, and the man of greatest initiative and advanced views, of modern times. For the tasks of the next century, the methods of popular representation and parliaments are the most inappropriate imaginable.

19.

The condition of Europe in the next century will once again lead to the breeding of manly virtues, because men will live in continual danger. Universal military service is already the curious antidote which we possess for the effeminacy of democratic ideas, and it has grown up out of the struggle of the nations. (Nation—men who speak one language and read the same newspapers. These men now call themselves "nations," and would far too readily trace their descent from the same source and through the same history; which, however, even with the assistance of the most malignant lying in the past, they have not succeeded in doing.)

20.

What quagmires and mendacity must there be about if it is possible, in the modern European hotch-potch, to raise questions of "race"! (It being premised that the origin of such writers is not in Horneo and Borneo.)

21.

Maxim: To associate with no man who takes any part in the mendacious race swindle.

22.

With the freedom of travel now existing, groups of men of the same kindred can join together and establish communal habits and customs. The overcoming of "nations."

23.

To make Europe a centre of culture, national stupidities should not make us blind to the fact that in the higher regions there is already a continuous reciprocal dependence. France and German philosophy. Richard Wagner and Paris (1830-50). Goethe and Greece. All things are impelled towards, a synthesis of the European past in the highest types of mind.

24.

Mankind has still much before it—how, generally speaking, could the ideal be taken from the past? Perhaps merely in relation to the present, which latter is possibly a lower region.

25.

This is our distrust, which recurs again and again; our care, which never lets us sleep; our question, which no one listens to or wishes to listen to; our Sphinx, near which there is more than one precipice: we believe that the men of present-day Europe are deceived in regard to the things which we love best, and a pitiless demon[Pg 228] (no, not pitiless, only indifferent and puerile)—plays with our hearts and their enthusiasm, as it may perhaps have already played with everything that lived and loved; I believe that everything which we Europeans of to-day are in the habit of admiring as the values of all these respected things called "humanity," "mankind," "sympathy," "pity," may be of some value as the debilitation and moderating of certain powerful and dangerous primitive impulses. Nevertheless, in the long run all these things are nothing else than the belittlement of the entire type "man," his mediocrisation, if in such a desperate situation I may make use of such a desperate expression. I think that the commedia umana for an epicurean spectator-god must consist in this: that the Europeans, by virtue of their growing morality, believe in all their innocence and vanity that they are rising higher and higher, whereas the truth is that they are sinking lower and lower—i.e. through the cultivation of all the virtues which are useful to a herd, and through the repression of the other and contrary virtues which give rise to a new, higher, stronger, masterful race of men—the first-named virtues merely develop the herd-animal in man and stabilitate the animal "man," for until now man has been "the animal as yet unstabilitated."

26.

Genius and Epoch.—Heroism is no form of selfishness, for one is shipwrecked by it.... The[Pg 229] direction of power is often conditioned by the state of the period in which the great man happens to be born; and this fact brings about the superstition that he is the expression of his time. But this same power could be applied in several different ways; and between him and his time there is always this difference: that public opinion always worships the herd instinct,—i.e. the instinct of the weak,—while he, the strong man, rights for strong ideals.

27.

The fate now overhanging Europe is simply this: that it is exactly her strongest sons that come rarely and late to the spring-time of their existence; that, as a rule, when they are already in their early youth they perish, saddened, disgusted, darkened in mind, just because they have already, with the entire passion of their strength, drained to the dregs the cup of disillusionment, which in our days means the cup of knowledge, and they would not have been the strongest had they not also been the most disillusionised. For that is the test of their power—they must first of all rise out of the illness of their epoch to reach their own health. A late spring-time is their mark of distinction; also, let us add, late merriment, late folly, the late exuberance of joy! For this is the danger of to-day: everything that we loved when we were young has betrayed us. Our last love—the love which makes us acknowledge her, our love for Truth—let us take care that she, too, does not betray us!

The Anti-Christ: A Criticism of Christianity
INTRODUCTION

Save for his raucous, rhapsodical autobiography, "Ecce Homo," "The Antichrist" is the last thing that Nietzsche ever wrote, and so it may be accepted as a statement of some of his most salient ideas in their final form. Notes for it had been accumulating for years and it was to have constituted the first volume of his long-projected magnum opus, "The Will to Power." His full plan for this work, as originally drawn up, was as follows:

Vol. I. The Antichrist: an Attempt at a Criticism of Christianity.

Vol. II. The Free Spirit: a Criticism of Philosophy as a Nihilistic Movement.

Vol. III. The Immoralist: a Criticism of Morality, the Most Fatal Form of Ignorance.

Vol. IV. Dionysus: the Philosophy of Eternal Recurrence.

The first sketches for "The Will to Power" were made in 1884, soon after the publication of the first three parts of "Thus Spake Zarathustra," and thereafter, for four years, Nietzsche piled up notes. They were written at all the places he visited on his endless travels in search of health—at Nice, at Venice, at Sils-Maria in the Engadine (for long his favourite resort), at Cannobio, at Zürich, at Genoa, at Chur, at Leipzig. Several times his work was interrupted by other books, first by "Beyond Good and Evil," then by "The Genealogy of Morals" (written in twenty days), then by his Wagner pamphlets. Almost as often he changed his plan. Once he decided to expand "The Will to Power" to ten volumes, with "An Attempt at a New Interpretation of the World" as a general sub-title. Again he adopted the sub-title of "An Interpretation of All That Happens." Finally, he hit upon "An Attempt at a Transvaluation of All Values," and went back to four volumes, though with a number of changes in their arrangement. In September, 1888, he began actual work upon the first volume, and before the end of the month it was completed. The Summer had been one of almost hysterical creative activity. Since the middle of June he had written two other small books, "The Case of Wagner" and "The Twilight of the Idols," and before the end of the year he was destined to write "Ecce Homo." Some time during December his health began to fail rapidly, and soon after the New Year he was helpless. Thereafter he wrote no more.

The Wagner diatribe and "The Twilight of the Idols" were published immediately, but "The Antichrist" did not get into type until 1895. I suspect that the delay was due to the influence of the philosopher's sister, Elisabeth Förster-Nietzsche, an intelligent and ardent but by no means uniformly judicious propagandist of his ideas. During his dark days of neglect and misunderstanding, when even family and friends kept aloof, Frau Förster-Nietzsche went with him farther than any other, but there were bounds beyond which she, also, hesitated to go, and those bounds were marked by crosses. One notes, in her biography of him—a useful but not always accurate work—an evident desire to purge him of the accusation of mocking at sacred things. He had, she says, great admiration for "the elevating effect of Christianity ... upon the weak and ailing," and "a real liking for sincere, pious Christians," and "a tender love for the Founder of Christianity." All his wrath, she continues, was reserved for "St. Paul and his like," who perverted the Beatitudes, which Christ intended for the lowly only, into a universal religion which made war upon aristocratic values. Here, obviously, one is addressed by an interpreter who cannot forget that she is the daughter of a Lutheran pastor and the grand-daughter of two others; a touch of conscience gets into her reading of "The Antichrist." She even hints that the text may have been garbled, after the author's collapse, by some more sinister heretic. There is not the slightest reason to believe that any such garbling ever took place, nor is there any evidence that their common heritage of piety rested upon the brother as heavily as it rested upon the sister. On the contrary, it must be manifest that Nietzsche, in this book, intended to attack Christianity headlong and with all arms, that for all his rapid writing he put the utmost care into it, and that he wanted it to be printed exactly as it stands. The ideas in it were anything but new to him when he set them down. He had been developing them since the days of his beginning. You will find some of them, clearly recognizable, in the first book he ever wrote, "The Birth of Tragedy." You will find the most important of all of them—the conception of Christianity as ressentiment—set forth at length in the first part of "The Genealogy of Morals," published under his own supervision in 1887. And the rest are scattered through the whole vast mass of his notes, sometimes as mere questionings but often worked out very carefully. Moreover, let it not be forgotten that it was Wagner's yielding to Christian sentimentality in "Parsifal" that transformed Nietzsche from the first among his literary advocates into the most bitter of his opponents. He could forgive every other sort of mountebankery, but not that. "In me," he once said, "the Christianity of my forbears reaches its logical conclusion. In me the stern intellectual conscience that Christianity fosters and makes paramount turns against Christianity. In me Christianity ... devours itself."

In truth, the present philippic is as necessary to the completeness of the whole of Nietzsche's system as the keystone is to the arch. All the curves of his speculation lead up to it. What he flung himself against, from beginning to end of his days of writing, was always, in the last analysis, Christianity in some form or other—Christianity as a system of practical ethics, Christianity as a political code, Christianity as meta physics, Christianity as a gauge of the truth. It would be difficult to think of any intellectual enterprise on his long list that did not, more or less directly and clearly, relate itself to this master enterprise of them all. It was as if his apostasy from the faith of his fathers, filling him with the fiery zeal of the convert, and particularly of the convert to heresy, had blinded him to every other element in the gigantic self-delusion of civilized man. The will to power was his answer to Christianity's affectation of humility and self-sacrifice; eternal recurrence was his mocking criticism of Christian optimism and millennialism; the superman was his candidate for the place of the Christian ideal of the "good" man, prudently abased before the throne of God. The things he chiefly argued for were anti-Christian things— the abandonment of the purely moral view of life, the rehabilitation of instinct, the dethronement of weakness and timidity as ideals, the renunciation of the whole hocus-pocus of dogmatic religion, the extermination of false aristocracies (of the priest, of the politician, of the plutocrat), the revival of the healthy, lordly "innocence" that was Greek. If he was anything in a word, Nietzsche was a Greek born two thousand years too late. His dreams were thoroughly Hellenic; his whole manner of thinking was Hellenic; his peculiar errors were Hellenic no less. But his Hellenism, I need not add, was anything but the pale neo-Platonism that has run like a thread through the thinking of the Western world since the days of the Christian Fathers.

From Plato, to be sure, he got what all of us must get, but his real forefather was Heraclitus. It is in Heraclitus that one finds the germ of his primary view of the universe—a view, to wit, that sees it, not as moral phenomenon, but as mere aesthetic representation. The God that Nietzsche imagined, in the end, was not far from the God that such an artist as Joseph Conrad imagines—a supreme craftsman, ever experimenting, ever coming closer to an ideal balancing of lines and forces, and yet always failing to work out the final harmony.

The late war, awakening all the primitive racial fury of the Western nations, and therewith all their ancient enthusiasm for religious taboos and sanctions, naturally focused attention upon Nietzsche, as upon the most daring and provocative of recent amateur theologians. The Germans, with their characteristic tendency to ex plain their every act in terms as realistic and unpleasant as possible, appear to have mauled him in a belated and unexpected embrace, to the horror, I daresay, of the Kaiser, and perhaps to the even greater horror of Nietzsche's own ghost. The folks of Anglo-Saxondom, with their equally characteristic tendency to explain all their enterprises romantically, simultaneously set him up as the Antichrist he no doubt secretly longed to be. The result was a great deal of misrepresentation and misunderstanding of him. From the pulpits of the allied countries, and particularly from those of England and the United States, a horde of patriotic ecclesiastics denounced him in extravagant terms as the author of all the horrors of the time, and in the newspapers, until the Kaiser was elected sole bugaboo, he shared the honors of that office with von Hindenburg, the Crown Prince, Capt. Boy-Ed, von Bernstorff and von Tirpitz. Most of this denunciation, of course, was frankly idiotic—the naïve pishposh of suburban Methodists, notoriety-seeking college professors, almost illiterate editorial writers, and other such numskulls. In much of it, including not a few official hymns of hate, Nietzsche was gravely discovered to be the teacher of such spokesmen of the extremest sort of German nationalism as von Bernhardi and von Treitschke—which was just as intelligent as making George Bernard Shaw the mentor of Lloyd-George. In other solemn pronunciamentoes he was credited with being philosophically responsible for various imaginary crimes of the enemy—the wholesale slaughter or mutilation of prisoners of war, the deliberate burning down of Red Cross hospitals, the utilization of the corpses of the slain for soap-making. I amused myself, in those gaudy days, by collecting newspaper clippings to this general effect, and later on I shall probably publish a digest of them, as a contribution to the study of war hysteria. The thing went to unbelievable lengths. On the strength of the fact that I had published a book on Nietzsche in 1906, six years after his death, I was called upon by agents of the Department of Justice, elaborately outfitted with badges, to meet the charge that I was an intimate associate and agent of "the German monster, Nietzsky." I quote the official procès verbal, an indignant but often misspelled document. Alas, poor Nietzsche! After all his laborious efforts to prove that he was not a German, but a Pole—even after his heroic readiness, via anti-anti-Semitism, to meet the deduction that, if a Pole, then probably also a Jew!

But under all this alarmed and preposterous tosh there was at least a sound instinct, and that was the instinct which recognized Nietzsche as the most eloquent, pertinacious and effective of all the critics of the philosophy to which the Allies against Germany stood committed, and on the strength of which, at all events in theory, the United States had engaged itself in the war. He was not, in point of fact, involved with the visible enemy, save in remote and transient ways; the German, officially, remained the most ardent of Christians during the war and became a democrat at its close. But he was plainly a foe of democracy in all its forms, political, religious and epistemological, and what is worse, his opposition was set forth in terms that were not only extraordinarily penetrating and devastating, but also uncommonly offensive. It was thus quite natural that he should have aroused a degree of indignation verging upon the pathological in the two countries that had planted themselves upon the democratic platform most boldly, and that felt it most shaky, one may add, under their feet. I daresay that Nietzsche, had he been alive, would have got a lot of satisfaction out of the execration thus heaped upon him, not only because, being a vain fellow, he enjoyed execration as a tribute to his general singularity, and hence to his superiority, but also and more importantly because, being no mean psychologist, he would have recognized the disconcerting doubts underlying it. If Nietzsche's criticism of democracy were as ignorant and empty, say, as the average evangelical clergyman's criticism of Darwin's hypothesis of natural selection, then the advocates of democracy could afford to dismiss it as loftily as the Darwinians dismiss the blather of the holy clerks. And if his attack upon Christianity were mere sound and fury, signifying nothing, then there would be no call for anathemas from the sacred desk. But these onslaughts, in point of fact, have behind them a tremendous learning and a great deal of point and plausibility—there are, in brief, bullets in the gun, teeth in the tiger,—and so it is no wonder that they excite the ire of men who hold, as a primary article of belief, that their acceptance would destroy civilization, darken the sun, and bring Jahveh to sobs upon His Throne.

But in all this justifiable fear, of course, there remains a false assumption, and that is the assumption that Nietzsche proposed to destroy Christianity altogether, and so rob the plain people of the world of their virtue, their spiritual consolations, and their hope of heaven. Nothing could be more untrue. The fact is that Nietzsche had no interest whatever in the delusions of the plain people— that is, intrinsically. It seemed to him of small moment what they believed, so long as it was safely imbecile. What he stood against was not their beliefs, but the elevation of those beliefs, by any sort of democratic process, to the dignity of a state philosophy—what he feared most was the pollution and crippling of the superior minority by intellectual disease from below. His plain aim in "The Antichrist" was to combat that menace by completing the work begun, on the one hand, by Darwin and the other evolutionist philosophers, and, on the other hand, by German historians and philologians. The net effect of this earlier attack, in the eighties, had been the collapse of Christian theology as a serious concern of educated men. The mob, it must be obvious, was very little shaken; even to this day it has not put off its belief in the essential Christian doctrines. But the intelligentsia, by 1885, had been pretty well convinced. No man of sound information, at the time Nietzsche planned "The Antichrist," actually believed that the world was created in seven days, or that its fauna was once overwhelmed by a flood as a penalty for the sins of man, or that Noah saved the boa constrictor, the prairie dog and the pediculus capitis by taking a pair of each into the ark, or that Lot's wife was turned into a pillar of salt, or that a fragment of the True Cross could cure hydrophobia. Such notions, still almost universally prevalent in Christendom a century before, were now confined to the great body of ignorant and credulous men—that is, to ninety-five or ninety-six percent. of the race. For a man of the superior minority to subscribe to one of them publicly was already sufficient to set him off as one in imminent need of psychiatrical attention. Belief in them had become a mark of inferiority, like the allied belief in madstones, magic and apparitions.

But though the theology of Christianity had thus sunk to the lowly estate of a mere delusion of the rabble, propagated on that level by the ancient caste of sacerdotal parasites, the ethics of Christianity continued to enjoy the utmost acceptance, and perhaps even more acceptance than ever before. It seemed to be generally felt, in fact, that they simply must be saved from the wreck—that the world would vanish into chaos if they went the way of the revelations supporting them. In this fear a great many judicious men joined, and so there arose what was, in essence, an absolutely new Christian cult—a cult, to wit, purged of all the supernaturalism superimposed upon the older cult by generations of theologians, and harking back to what was conceived to be the pure ethical doctrine of Jesus. This cult still flourishes; Protestantism tends to become identical with it; it invades Catholicism as Modernism; it is supported by great numbers of men whose intelligence is manifest and whose sincerity is not open to question. Even Nietzsche himself yielded to it in weak moments, as you will discover on examining his somewhat laborious effort to make Paul the villain of Christian theology, and Jesus no more than an innocent bystander. But this sentimental yielding never went far enough to distract his attention for long from his main idea, which was this: that Christian ethics were quite as dubious, at bottom, as Christian theology—that they were founded, just as surely as such childish fables as the story of Jonah and the whale, upon the peculiar prejudices and credulities, the special desires and appetites, of inferior men—that they warred upon the best interests of men of a better sort quite as unmistakably as the most extravagant of objective superstitions. In brief, what he saw in Christian ethics, under all the poetry and all the fine show of altruism and all the theoretical benefits therein, was a democratic effort to curb the egoism of the strong—a conspiracy of the chandala against the free functioning of their superiors, nay, against the free progress of mankind. This theory is the thing he exposes in "The Antichrist," bringing to the business his amazingly chromatic and exigent eloquence at its finest flower. This is the "conspiracy" he sets forth in all the panoply of his characteristic italics, dashes, sforzando interjections and exclamation points.

Well, an idea is an idea. The present one may be right and it may be wrong. One thing is quite certain: that no progress will be made against it by denouncing it as merely immoral. If it is ever laid at all, it must be laid evidenti ally, logically. The notion to the contrary is thoroughly democratic; the mob is the most ruthless of tyrants; it is always in a democratic society that heresy and felony tend to be most constantly confused. One hears without surprise of a Bismarck philosophizing placidly (at least in his old age) upon the delusion of Socialism and of a Frederick the Great playing the hose of his cynicism upon the absolutism that was almost identical with his own person, but men in the mass never brook the destructive discussion of their fundamental beliefs, and that impatience is naturally most evident in those societies in which men in the mass are most influential. Democracy and free speech are not facets of one gem; democracy and free speech are eternal enemies. But in any battle between an institution and an idea, the idea, in the long run, has the better of it. Here I do not venture into the absurdity of arguing that, as the world wags on, the truth always survives. I believe nothing of the sort. As a matter of fact, it seems to me that an idea that happens to be true—or, more exactly, as near to truth as any human idea can be, and yet remain generally intelligible—it seems to me that such an idea carries a special and often fatal handi cap. The majority of men prefer delusion to truth. It soothes. It is easy to grasp. Above all, it fits more snugly than the truth into a universe of false appearances—of complex and irrational phenomena, defectively grasped. But though an idea that is true is thus not likely to prevail, an idea that is attacked enjoys a great advantage. The evidence behind it is now supported by sympathy, the sporting instinct, sentimentality—and sentimentality is as powerful as an army with banners. One never hears of a martyr in history whose notions are seriously disputed today. The forgotten ideas are those of the men who put them forward soberly and quietly, hoping fatuously that they would conquer by the force of their truth; these are the ideas that we now struggle to rediscover. Had Nietzsche lived to be burned at the stake by outraged Mississippi Methodists, it would have been a glorious day for his doctrines. As it is, they are helped on their way every time they are denounced as immoral and against God. The war brought down upon them the maledictions of vast herds of right-thinking men. And now "The Antichrist," after fifteen years of neglect, is being reprinted....

One imagines the author, a sardonic wraith, snickering somewhat sadly over the fact. His shade, wherever it suffers, is favoured in these days by many such consolations, some of them of much greater horsepower. Think of the facts and arguments, even the underlying theories and attitudes, that have been borrowed from him, consciously and unconsciously, by the foes of Bolshevism during these last thrilling years! The face of democracy, suddenly seen hideously close, has scared the guardians of the reigning plutocracy half to death, and they have gone to the devil himself for aid. Southern Senators, almost illiterate men, have mixed his acids with well water and spouted them like affrighted geysers, not knowing what they did.

Nor are they the first to borrow from him. Years ago I called attention to the debt incurred with characteristic forgetfulness of obligation by the late Theodore Roosevelt, in "The Strenuous Life" and elsewhere. Roosevelt, a typical apologist for the existing order, adeptly dragging a herring across the trail whenever it was menaced, yet managed to delude the native boobery, at least until toward the end, into accepting him as a fiery exponent of pure democracy. Perhaps he even fooled himself; charlatans usually do so soon or late. A study of Nietzsche reveals the sources of much that was honest in him, and exposes the hollowness of much that was sham. Nietzsche, an infinitely harder and more courageous intellect, was incapable of any such confusion of ideas; he seldom allowed sentimentality to turn him from the glaring fact. What is called Bolshevism today he saw clearly a generation ago and described for what it was and is—democracy in another aspect, the old ressentiment of the lower orders in free function once more. Socialism, Puritanism, Philistinism, Christianity—he saw them all as allotropic forms of democracy, as variations upon the endless struggle of quantity against quality, of the weak and timorous against the strong and enterprising, of the botched against the fit. The world needed a staggering exaggeration to make it see even half of the truth. It trembles today as it trembled during the French Revolution. Perhaps it would tremble less if it could combat the monster with a clearer conscience and less burden of compromising theory—if it could launch its forces frankly at the fundamental doctrine, and not merely employ them to police the transient orgy.

Nietzsche, in the long run, may help it toward that greater honesty. His notions, propagated by cuttings from cuttings from cuttings, may conceivably prepare the way for a sounder, more healthful theory of society and of the state, and so free human progress from the stupidities which now hamper it, and men of true vision from the despairs which now sicken them. I say it is conceivable, but I doubt that it is probable. The soul and the belly of mankind are too evenly balanced; it is not likely that the belly will ever put away its hunger or forget its power. Here, perhaps, there is an example of the eternal recurrence that Nietzsche was fond of mulling over in his blacker moods. We are in the midst of one of the perennial risings of the lower orders. It got under way long before any of the current Bolshevist demons was born; it was given its long, secure start by the intolerable tyranny of the plutocracy—the end product of the Eighteenth Century revolt against the old aristocracy. It found resistance suddenly slackened by civil war within the plutocracy itself—one gang of traders falling upon another gang, to the tune of vast hymn-singing and yells to God. Perhaps it has already passed its apogee; the plutocracy, chastened, shows signs of a new solidarity; the wheel continues to swing 'round. But this combat between proletariat and plutocracy is, after all, itself a civil war. Two inferiorities struggle for the privilege of polluting the world. What actual difference does it make to a civilized man, when there is a steel strike, whether the workmen win or the mill-owners win? The conflict can interest him only as spectacle, as the conflict between Bonaparte and the old order in Europe interested Goethe and Beethoven. The victory, whichever way it goes, will simply bring chaos nearer, and so set the stage for a genuine revolution later on, with (let us hope) a new feudalism or something better coming out of it, and a new Thirteenth Century at dawn. This seems to be the slow, costly way of the worst of habitable worlds.

In the present case my money is laid upon the plutocracy. It will win because it will be able, in the long run, to enlist the finer intelligences. The mob and its maudlin causes attract only sentimentalists and scoundrels, chiefly the latter. Politics, under a democracy, reduces itself to a mere struggle for office by flatterers of the proletariat; even when a superior man prevails at that disgusting game he must prevail at the cost of his self-respect. Not many superior men make the attempt. The average great captain of the rabble, when he is not simply a weeper over irremediable wrongs, is a hypocrite so far gone that he is unconscious of his own hypocrisy—a slimy fellow, offensive to the nose. The plutocracy can recruit measurably more respectable janissaries, if only because it can make self-interest less obviously costly to amour propre. Its defect and its weakness lie in the fact that it is still too young to have acquired dignity. But lately sprung from the mob it now preys upon, it yet shows some of the habits of mind of that mob: it is blatant, stupid, ignorant, lacking in all delicate instinct and governmental finesse. Above all, it remains somewhat heavily moral. One seldom finds it undertaking one of its characteristic imbecilities without offering a sonorous moral reason; it spends almost as much to support the Y. M. C. A., vice-crusading, Prohibition and other such puerilities as it spends upon Congressmen, strike-breakers, gun-men, kept patriots and newspapers. In England the case is even worse. It is almost impossible to find a wealthy industrial over there who is not also an eminent non-conformist layman, and even among financiers there are praying brothers. On the Continent, the day is saved by the fact that the plutocracy tends to become more and more Jewish. Here the intellectual cynicism of the Jew almost counterbalances his social unpleasantness. If he is destined to lead the plutocracy of the world out of Little Bethel he will fail, of course, to turn it into an aristocracy—i. e., a caste of gentlemen—, but he will at least make it clever, and hence worthy of consideration. The case against the Jews is long and damning; it would justify ten thousand times as many pogroms as now go on in the world. But whenever you find a Davidsbündlerschaft making practise against the Philistines, there you will find a Jew laying on. Maybe it was this fact that caused Nietzsche to speak up for the children of Israel quite as often as he spoke against them. He was not blind to their faults, but when he set them beside Christians he could not deny their general superiority. Perhaps in America and England, as on the Continent, the increasing Jewishness of the plutocracy, while cutting it off from all chance of ever developing into an aristocracy, will yet lift it to such a dignity that it will at least deserve a certain grudging respect.

But even so, it will remain in a sort of half-world, midway between the gutter and the stars. Above it will still stand the small group of men that constitutes the permanent aristocracy of the race—the men of imagination and high purpose, the makers of genuine progress, the brave and ardent spirits, above all petty fears and discontents and above all petty hopes and ideals no less. There were heroes before Agamemnon; there will be Bachs after Johann Sebastian. And beneath the Judaized plutocracy, the sublimated bourgeoisie, there the immemorial proletariat, I venture to guess, will roar on, endlessly tortured by its vain hatreds and envies, stampeded and made to tremble by its ancient superstitions, prodded and made miserable by its sordid and degrading hopes. It seems to me very likely that, in this proletariat, Christianity will continue to survive. It is nonsense, true enough, but it is sweet. Nietzsche, denouncing its dangers as a poison, almost falls into the error of denying it its undoubtedly sugary smack. Of all the religions ever devised by the great practical jokers of the race, this is the one that offers most for the least money, so to speak, to the inferior man. It starts out by denying his inferiority in plain terms: all men are equal in the sight of God. It ends by erecting that inferiority into a sort of actual superiority: it is a merit to be stupid, and miserable, and sorely put upon—of such are the celestial elect. Not all the eloquence of a million Nietzsches, nor all the painful marshalling of evidence of a million Darwins and Harnacks, will ever empty that great consolation of its allure. The most they can ever accomplish is to make the superior orders of men acutely conscious of the exact nature of it, and so give them armament against the contagion. This is going on; this is being done. I think that "The Antichrist" has a useful place in that enterprise. It is strident, it is often extravagant, it is, to many sensitive men, in the worst of possible taste, but at bottom it is enormously apt and effective—and on the surface it is undoubtedly a good show. One somehow enjoys, with the malice that is native to man, the spectacle of anathemas batted back; it is refreshing to see the pitchfork employed against gentlemen who have doomed such innumerable caravans to hell. In Nietzsche they found, after many long years, a foeman worthy of them—not a mere fancy swordsman like Voltaire, or a mob orator like Tom Paine, or a pedant like the heretics of exegesis, but a gladiator armed with steel and armoured with steel, and showing all the ferocious gusto of a mediaeval bishop. It is a pity that Holy Church has no process for the elevation of demons, like its process for the canonization of saints. There must be a long roll of black miracles to the discredit of the Accursed Friedrich—sinners purged of conscience and made happy in their sinning, clerics shaken in their theology by visions of a new and better holy city, the strong made to exult, the weak robbed of their old sad romance. It would be a pleasure to see the Advocatus Diaboli turn from the table of the prosecution to the table of the defence, and move in solemn form for the damnation of the Naumburg hobgoblin....

Of all Nietzsche's books, "The Antichrist" comes nearest to conventionality in form. It presents a connected argument with very few interludes, and has a beginning, a middle and an end. Most of his works are in the form of col lections of apothegms, and sometimes the subject changes on every second page. This fact constitutes one of the counts in the orthodox indictment of him: it is cited as proof that his capacity for consecutive thought was limited, and that he was thus deficient mentally, and perhaps a downright moron. The argument, it must be obvious, is fundamentally nonsensical. What deceives the professors is the traditional prolixity of philosophers. Because the average philosophical writer, when he essays to expose his ideas, makes such inordinate drafts upon the parts of speech that the dictionary is almost emptied these defective observers jump to the conclusion that his intrinsic notions are of corresponding weight. This is not unseldom quite untrue. What makes philosophy so garrulous is not the profundity of philosophers, but their lack of art; they are like physicians who sought to cure a slight hyperacidity by giving the patient a carload of burned oyster-shells to eat. There is, too, the endless poll-parrotting that goes on: each new philosopher must prove his learning by laboriously rehearsing the ideas of all previous philosophers.... Nietzsche avoided both faults. He always assumed that his readers knew the books, and that it was thus unnecessary to rewrite them. And, having an idea that seemed to him to be novel and original, he stated it in as few words as possible, and then shut down. Sometimes he got it into a hundred words; sometimes it took a thousand; now and then, as in the present case, he developed a series of related ideas into a connected book. But he never wrote a word too many. He never pumped up an idea to make it appear bigger than it actually was. The pedagogues, alas, are not accustomed to that sort of writing in serious fields. They resent it, and sometimes they even try to improve it. There exists, in fact, a huge and solemn tome on Nietzsche by a learned man of America in which all of his brilliancy is painfully translated into the windy phrases of the seminaries. The tome is satisfactorily ponderous, but the meat of the cocoanut is left out: there is actually no discussion of the Nietzschean view of Christianity!... Always Nietzsche daunts the pedants. He employed too few words for them—and he had too many ideas.

The present translation of "The Antichrist" is published by agreement with Dr. Oscar Levy, editor of the English edition of Nietzsche. There are two earlier translations, one by Thomas Common and the other by Anthony M. Ludovici. That of Mr. Common follows the text very closely, and thus occasionally shows some essentially German turns of phrase; that of Mr. Ludovici is more fluent but rather less exact. I do not offer my own version on the plea that either of these is useless; on the contrary, I cheerfully acknowledge that they have much merit, and that they helped me at almost every line. I began this new Englishing of the book, not in any hope of supplanting them, and surely not with any notion of meeting a great public need, but simply as a private amusement in troubled days. But as I got on with it I began to see ways of putting some flavour of Nietzsche's peculiar style into the English, and so amusement turned into a more or less serious labour. The result, of course, is far from satisfactory, but it at least represents a very diligent attempt. Nietzsche, always under the influence of French models, wrote a German that differs materially from any other German that I know. It is more nervous, more varied, more rapid in tempo; it runs to more effective climaxes; it is never stodgy. His marks begin to show upon the writing of the younger Germans of today. They are getting away from the old thunderous manner, with its long sentences and its tedious grammatical complexities. In the course of time, I daresay, they will develop a German almost as clear as French and almost as colourful and resilient as English.

I owe thanks to Dr. Levy for his imprimatur, to Mr. Theodor Hemberger for criticism, and to Messrs. Common and Ludovici for showing me the way around many a difficulty.

H. L. Mencken.

PREFACE

This book belongs to the most rare of men. Perhaps not one of them is yet alive. It is possible that they may be among those who understand my "Zarathustra": how could I confound myself with those who are now sprouting ears?—First the day after tomorrow must come for me. Some men are born posthumously.

The conditions under which any one understands me, and necessarily understands me—I know them only too well. Even to endure my seriousness, my passion, he must carry intellectual integrity to the verge of hardness. He must be accustomed to living on mountain tops—and to looking upon the wretched gabble of politics and nationalism as beneath him. He must have become indifferent; he must never ask of the truth whether it brings profit to him or a fatality to him.... He must have an inclination, born of strength, for questions that no one has the courage for; the courage for the forbidden; predestination for the labyrinth. The experience of seven solitudes. New ears for new music. New eyes for what is most distant. A new conscience for truths that have hitherto remained unheard. And the will to economize in the grand manner—to hold together his strength, his enthusiasm.... Reverence for self; love of self; absolute freedom of self....

Very well, then! of that sort only are my readers, my true readers, my readers foreordained: of what account are the rest?—The rest are merely humanity.—One must make one's self superior to humanity, in power, in loftiness of soul,—in contempt.

Friedrich W. Nietzsche.

THE ANTICHRIST
1.

—Let us look each other in the face. We are Hyperboreans—we know well enough how remote our place is. "Neither by land nor by water will you find the road to the Hyperboreans": even Pindar,[1] in his day, knew that much about us. Beyond the North, beyond the ice, beyond death—our life, our happiness.... We have discovered that happiness; we know the way; we got our knowledge of it from thousands of years in the labyrinth. Who else has found it?—The man of today?—"I don't know either the way out or the way in; I am whatever doesn't know either the way out or the way in"—so sighs the man of today.... This is the sort of modernity that made us ill,—we sickened on lazy peace, cowardly compro mise, the whole virtuous dirtiness of the modern Yea and Nay. This tolerance and largeur of the heart that "forgives" everything because it "understands" everything is a sirocco to us. Rather live amid the ice than among modern virtues and other such south-winds!... We were brave enough; we spared neither ourselves nor others; but we were a long time finding out where to direct our courage. We grew dismal; they called us fatalists. Our fate—it was the fulness, the tension, the storing up of powers. We thirsted for the lightnings and great deeds; we kept as far as possible from the happiness of the weakling, from "resignation"... There was thunder in our air; nature, as we embodied it, became overcast—for we had not yet found the way. The formula of our happiness: a Yea, a Nay, a straight line, a goal....

[1]Cf. the tenth Pythian ode. See also the fourth book of Herodotus. The Hyperboreans were a mythical people beyond the Rhipaean mountains, in the far North. They enjoyed unbroken happiness and perpetual youth.

2.

What is good?—Whatever augments the feeling of power, the will to power, power itself, in man.

What is evil?—Whatever springs from weakness.

What is happiness?—The feeling that power increases—that

resistance is overcome.

Not contentment, but more power; not peace at any price, but war; not virtue, but efficiency (virtue in the Renaissance sense, virtu, virtue free of moral acid).

The weak and the botched shall perish: first principle of our charity. And one should help them to it.

What is more harmful than any vice?—Practical sympathy for the botched and the weak—Christianity....

3.

The problem that I set here is not what shall replace mankind in the order of living creatures (—man is an end—): but what type of man must be bred, must be willed, as being the most valuable, the most worthy of life, the most secure guarantee of the future.

This more valuable type has appeared often enough in the past: but always as a happy accident, as an exception, never as deliberately willed. Very often it has been precisely the most feared; hitherto it has been almost the terror of terrors;—and out of that terror the contrary type has been willed, cultivated and attained: the domestic animal, the herd animal, the sick brute-man—the Christian....

4.

Mankind surely does not represent an evolution toward a better or stronger or higher level, as progress is now understood. This "progress" is merely a modern idea, which is to say, a false idea. The European of today, in his essential worth, falls far below the European of the Renaissance; the process of evolution does not necessarily mean elevation, enhancement, strengthening.

True enough, it succeeds in isolated and individual cases in various parts of the earth and under the most widely different cultures, and in these cases a higher type certainly manifests itself; something which, compared to mankind in the mass, appears as a sort of superman. Such happy strokes of high success have always been possible, and will remain possible, perhaps, for all time to come. Even whole races, tribes and nations may occasionally represent such lucky accidents.

5.

We should not deck out and embellish Christianity: it has waged a war to the death against this higher type of man, it has put all the deepest instincts of this type under its ban, it has developed its concept of evil, of the Evil One himself, out of these instincts—the strong man as the typical reprobate, the "outcast among men." Christianity has taken the part of all the weak, the low, the botched; it has made an ideal out of antagonism to all the self-preservative instincts of sound life; it has corrupted even the faculties of those natures that are intellectually most vigorous, by representing the highest intellectual values as sinful, as misleading, as full of temptation. The most lamentable example: the corruption of Pascal, who believed that his intellect had been destroyed by original sin, whereas it was actually destroyed by Christianity!—

6.

It is a painful and tragic spectacle that rises before me: I have drawn back the curtain from the rottenness of man. This word, in my mouth, is at least free from one suspicion: that it involves a moral accusation against humanity. It is used—and I wish to emphasize the fact again—without any moral significance: and this is so far true that the rottenness I speak of is most apparent to me precisely in those quarters where there has been most aspiration, hitherto, toward "virtue" and "godliness." As you probably surmise, I understand rottenness in the sense of décadence: my argument is that all the values on which mankind now fixes its highest aspirations are décadence-values.

I call an animal, a species, an individual corrupt, when it loses its instincts, when it chooses, when it prefers, what is injurious to it. A history of the "higher feelings," the "ideals of humanity"—and it is possible that I'll have to write it—would almost explain why man is so degenerate. Life itself appears to me as an instinct for growth, for survival, for the accumulation of forces, for power: whenever the will to power fails there is disaster. My contention is that all the highest values of humanity have been emptied of this will—that the values of décadence, of nihilism, now prevail under the holiest names.

7.

Christianity is called the religion of pity.—Pity stands in opposition to all the tonic passions that augment the energy of the feeling of aliveness: it is a depressant. A man loses power when he pities. Through pity that drain upon strength which suffering works is multiplied a thousandfold. Suffering is made contagious by pity; under certain circumstances it may lead to a total sacrifice of life and living energy—a loss out of all proportion to the magnitude of the cause (—the case of the death of the Nazarene). This is the first view of it; there is, however, a still more important one. If one measures the effects of pity by the gravity of the reactions it sets up, its character as a menace to life appears in a much clearer light. Pity thwarts the whole law of evolution, which is the law of natural selection. It preserves whatever is ripe for destruction; it fights on the side of those disinherited and condemned by life; by maintaining life in so many of the botched of all kinds, it gives life itself a gloomy and dubious aspect. Mankind has ventured to call pity a virtue (—in every superior moral system it appears as a weakness—); going still further, it has been called the virtue, the source and foundation of all other virtues—but let us always bear in mind that this was from the standpoint of a philosophy that was nihilistic, and upon whose shield the denial of life was inscribed. Schopenhauer was right in this: that by means of pity life is denied, and made worthy of denial— pity is the technic of nihilism. Let me repeat: this depressing and contagious instinct stands against all those instincts which work for the preservation and enhancement of life: in the rôle of protector of the miserable, it is a prime agent in the promotion of décadence—pity persuades to extinction.... Of course, one doesn't say "extinction": one says "the other world," or "God," or "the true life," or Nirvana, salvation, blessedness.... This innocent rhetoric, from the realm of religious-ethical balderdash, appears a good deal less innocent when one reflects upon the tendency that it conceals beneath sublime words: the tendency to destroy life. Schopenhauer was hostile to life: that is why pity appeared to him as a virtue.... Aristotle, as every one knows, saw in pity a sickly and dangerous state of mind, the remedy for which was an occasional purgative: he regarded tragedy as that purgative. The instinct of life should prompt us to seek some means of puncturing any such pathological and dangerous accumulation of pity as that appearing in Schopenhauer's case (and also, alack, in that of our whole literary décadence, from St. Petersburg to Paris, from Tolstoi to Wagner), that it may burst and be discharged.... Nothing is more unhealthy, amid all our unhealthy modernism, than Christian pity. To be the doctors here, to be unmerciful here, to wield the knife here—all this is our business, all this is our sort of humanity, by this sign we are philosophers, we Hyperboreans!—

8.

It is necessary to say just whom we regard as our antagonists: theologians and all who have any theological blood in their veins—this is our whole philosophy.... One must have faced that menace at close hand, better still, one must have had experience of it directly and almost succumbed to it, to realize that it is not to be taken lightly (—the alleged free-thinking of our naturalists and physiologists seems to me to be a joke—they have no passion about such things; they have not suffered—). This poisoning goes a great deal further than most people think: I find the arrogant habit of the theologian among all who regard themselves as "idealists"—among all who, by virtue of a higher point of departure, claim a right to rise above reality, and to look upon it with suspicion.... The idealist, like the ecclesiastic, carries all sorts of lofty concepts in his hand (—and not only in his hand!); he launches them with benevolent contempt against "understanding," "the senses," "honor," "good living," "science"; he sees such things as beneath him, as pernicious and seductive forces, on which "the soul" soars as a pure thing-in-itself—as if humility, chastity, poverty, in a word, holiness, had not already done much more damage to life than all imaginable horrors and vices.... The pure soul is a pure lie.... So long as the priest, that professional denier, calumniator and poisoner of life, is accepted as a higher variety of man, there can be no answer to the question, What is truth? Truth has already been stood on its head when the obvious attorney of mere emptiness is mistaken for its representative....

9.

Upon this theological instinct I make war: I find the tracks of it everywhere. Whoever has theological blood in his veins is shifty and dishonourable in all things. The pathetic thing that grows out of this condition is called faith: in other words, closing one's eyes upon one's self once for all, to avoid suffering the sight of incurable falsehood. People erect a concept of morality, of virtue, of holiness upon this false view of all things; they ground good conscience upon faulty vision; they argue that no other sort of vision has value any more, once they have made theirs sacrosanct with the names of "God," "salvation" and "eternity." I unearth this theological instinct in all directions: it is the most widespread and the most subterranean form of falsehood to be found on earth. Whatever a theologian regards as true must be false: there you have almost a criterion of truth. His profound instinct of self-preservation stands against truth ever coming into honour in any way, or even getting stated. Wherever the influence of theologians is felt there is a transvaluation of values, and the concepts "true" and "false" are forced to change places: whatever is most damaging to life is there called "true," and whatever exalts it, intensifies it, approves it, justifies it and makes it triumphant is there called "false."... When theologians, working through the "consciences" of princes (or of peoples—), stretch out their hands for power, there is never any doubt as to the fundamental issue: the will to make an end, the nihilistic will exerts that power....

10.

Among Germans I am immediately understood when I say that theological blood is the ruin of philosophy. The Protestant pastor is the grandfather of German philosophy; Protestantism itself is its peccatum originale. Definition of Protestantism: hemiplegic paralysis of Christianity—and of reason.... One need only utter the words "Tübingen School" to get an understanding of what German philosophy is at bottom—a very artful form of theology.... The Suabians are the best liars in Germany; they lie innocently.... Why all the rejoicing over the appearance of Kant that went through the learned world of Germany, three-fourths of which is made up of the sons of preachers and teachers—why the German conviction still echoing, that with Kant came a change for the better? The theological instinct of German scholars made them see clearly just what had become possible again.... A backstairs leading to the old ideal stood open; the concept of the "true world," the concept of morality as the essence of the world (—the two most vicious errors that ever existed!), were once more, thanks to a subtle and wily scepticism, if not actually demonstrable, then at least no longer refutable.... Reason, the prerogative of reason, does not go so far.... Out of reality there had been made "appearance"; an absolutely false world, that of being, had been turned into reality.... The success of Kant is merely a theological success; he was, like Luther and Leibnitz, but one more impediment to German integrity, already far from steady.—

11.

A word now against Kant as a moralist. A virtue must be our invention; it must spring out of our personal need and defence. In every other case it is a source of danger. That which does not belong to our life menaces it; a virtue which has its roots in mere respect for the concept of "virtue," as Kant would have it, is pernicious.

"Virtue," "duty," "good for its own sake," goodness grounded upon impersonality or a notion of universal validity—these are all chimeras, and in them one finds only an expression of the decay, the last collapse of life, the Chinese spirit of Königsberg. Quite the contrary is demanded by the most profound laws of self-preservation and of growth: to wit, that every man find his own virtue, his own categorical imperative. A nation goes to pieces when it confounds its duty with the general concept of duty. Nothing works a more complete and penetrating disaster than every "impersonal" duty, every sacrifice before the Moloch of abstraction.—To think that no one has thought of Kant's categorical imperative as dangerous to life!... The theological instinct alone took it under protection!—An action prompted by the life-instinct proves that it is a right action by the amount of pleasure that goes with it: and yet that Nihilist, with his bowels of Christian dogmatism, regarded pleasure as an objection.... What destroys a man more quickly than to work, think and feel without inner necessity, without any deep personal desire, without pleasure—as a mere automaton of duty? That is the recipe for décadence, and no less for idiocy.... Kant became an idiot.—And such a man was the contemporary of Goethe! This calamitous spinner of cobwebs passed for the German philosopher—still passes today!... I forbid myself to say what I think of the Germans.... Didn't Kant see in the French Revolution the transformation of the state from the inorganic form to the organic? Didn't he ask himself if there was a single event that could be explained save on the assumption of a moral faculty in man, so that on the basis of it, "the tendency of mankind toward the good" could be explained, once and for all time? Kant's answer: "That is revolution." Instinct at fault in everything and anything, instinct as a revolt against nature, German décadence as a philosophy—that is Kant! —

12.

I put aside a few sceptics, the types of decency in the history of philosophy: the rest haven't the slightest conception of intellectual integrity. They behave like women, all these great enthusiasts and prodigies—they regard "beautiful feelings" as arguments, the "heaving breast" as the bellows of divine inspiration, conviction as the criterion of truth. In the end, with "German" innocence, Kant tried to give a scientific flavour to this form of corruption, this dearth of intellectual conscience, by calling it "practical reason." He deliberately invented a variety of reasons for use on occasions when it was desirable not to trouble with reason—that is, when morality, when the sublime command "thou shalt," was heard. When one recalls the fact that, among all peoples, the philosopher is no more than a development from the old type of priest, this inheritance from the priest, this fraud upon self, ceases to be remarkable. When a man feels that he has a divine mission, say to lift up, to save or to liberate mankind—when a man feels the divine spark in his heart and believes that he is the mouthpiece of super natural imperatives—when such a mission inflames him, it is only natural that he should stand beyond all merely reasonable standards of judgment. He feels that he is himself sanctified by this mission, that he is himself a type of a higher order!... What has a priest to do with philosophy! He stands far above it!—And hitherto the priest has ruled!—He has determined the meaning of "true" and "not true"!...

13.

Let us not underestimate this fact: that we ourselves, we free spirits, are already a "transvaluation of all values," a visualized declaration of war and victory against all the old concepts of "true" and "not true." The most valuable intuitions are the last to be attained; the most valuable of all are those which determine methods. All the methods, all the principles of the scientific spirit of today, were the targets for thousands of years of the most profound contempt; if a man inclined to them he was excluded from the society of "decent" people—he passed as "an enemy of God," as a scoffer at the truth, as one "possessed." As a man of science, he belonged to the Chandala[2].... We have had the whole pathetic stupidity of mankind against us—their every notion of what the truth ought to be, of what the service of the truth ought to be—their every "thou shalt" was launched against us.... Our objectives, our methods, our quiet, cautious, distrustful manner—all appeared to them as absolutely discreditable and contemptible.—Looking back, one may almost ask one's self with reason if it was not actually an aesthetic sense that kept men blind so long: what they demanded of the truth was picturesque effectiveness, and of the learned a strong appeal to their senses. It was our modesty that stood out longest against their taste.... How well they guessed that, these turkey-cocks of God!

[2]The lowest of the Hindu castes.

14.

We have unlearned something. We have become more modest in every way. We no longer derive man from the "spirit," from the "godhead"; we have dropped him back among the beasts. We regard him as the strongest of the beasts because he is the craftiest; one of the re sults thereof is his intellectuality. On the other hand, we guard ourselves against a conceit which would assert itself even here: that man is the great second thought in the process of organic evolution. He is, in truth, anything but the crown of creation: beside him stand many other animals, all at similar stages of development.... And even when we say that we say a bit too much, for man, relatively speaking, is the most botched of all the animals and the sickliest, and he has wandered the most dangerously from his instincts—though for all that, to be sure, he remains the most interesting!—As regards the lower animals, it was Descartes who first had the really admirable daring to describe them as machina; the whole of our physiology is directed toward proving the truth of this doctrine. Moreover, it is illogical to set man apart, as Descartes did: what we know of man today is limited precisely by the extent to which we have regarded him, too, as a machine. Formerly we accorded to man, as his inheritance from some higher order of beings, what was called "free will"; now we have taken even this will from him, for the term no longer describes anything that we can understand. The old word "will" now connotes only a sort of result, an individual reaction, that follows inevitably upon a series of partly discordant and partly harmonious stimuli—the will no longer "acts," or "moves."... Formerly it was thought that man's consciousness, his "spirit," offered evidence of his high origin, his divinity. That he might be perfected, he was advised, tortoise-like, to draw his senses in, to have no traffic with earthly things, to shuffle off his mortal coil—then only the important part of him, the "pure spirit," would remain. Here again we have thought out the thing better: to us consciousness, or "the spirit," appears as a symptom of a relative imperfection of the organism, as an experiment, a groping, a misunderstanding, as an affliction which uses up nervous force unnecessarily—we deny that anything can be done perfectly so long as it is done consciously. The "pure spirit" is a piece of pure stupidity: take away the nervous system and the senses, the so-called "mortal shell," and the rest is miscalculation—that is all!...

15.

Under Christianity neither morality nor religion has any point of contact with actuality. It offers purely imaginary causes ("God," "soul," "ego," "spirit," "free will"—or even "unfree"), and purely imaginary effects ("sin," "salvation," "grace," "punishment," "forgiveness of sins"). Intercourse between imaginary beings ("God," "spirits," "souls"); an imaginary natural history (anthropocentric; a total denial of the concept of natural causes); an imaginary psychology (misunderstandings of self, misinterpretations of agreeable or disagreeable general feelings—for example, of the states of the nervus sympathicus with the help of the sign-language of religio-ethical balderdash—, "repentance," "pangs of conscience," "temptation by the devil," "the presence of God"); an imaginary teleology (the "kingdom of God," "the last judgment," "eternal life").—This purely fictitious world, greatly to its disadvantage, is to be differentiated from the world of dreams; the latter at least reflects reality, whereas the former falsifies it, cheapens it and denies it. Once the concept of "nature" had been opposed to the concept of "God," the word "natural" necessarily took on the meaning of "abominable"—the whole of that fictitious world has its sources in hatred of the natural (—the real!—), and is no more than evidence of a profound uneasiness in the presence of reality.... This explains everything. Who alone has any reason for living his way out of reality? The man who suffers under it. But to suffer from reality one must be a botched reality.... The preponderance of pains over pleasures is the cause of this fictitious morality and religion: but such a preponderance also supplies the formula for décadence....

16.

A criticism of the Christian concept of God leads inevitably to the same conclusion.—A nation that still believes in itself holds fast to its own god. In him it does honour to the conditions which enable it to survive, to its virtues—it projects its joy in itself, its feeling of power, into a being to whom one may offer thanks. He who is rich will give of his riches; a proud people need a god to whom they can make sacrifices.... Religion, within these limits, is a form of gratitude. A man is grateful for his own existence: to that end he needs a god.— Such a god must be able to work both benefits and injuries; he must be able to play either friend or foe—he is wondered at for the good he does as well as for the evil he does. But the castration, against all nature, of such a god, making him a god of goodness alone, would be contrary to human inclination. Mankind has just as much need for an evil god as for a good god; it doesn't have to thank mere tolerance and humanitarianism for its own existence.... What would be the value of a god who knew nothing of anger, revenge, envy, scorn, cunning, violence? who had perhaps never experienced the rapturous ardeurs of victory and of destruction? No one would understand such a god: why should any one want him?—True enough, when a nation is on the downward path, when it feels its belief in its own future, its hope of freedom slipping from it, when it begins to see submission as a first necessity and the virtues of submission as measures of self-preservation, then it must overhaul its god. He then becomes a hypocrite, timorous and demure; he counsels "peace of soul," hate-no-more, leniency, "love" of friend and foe. He moralizes endlessly; he creeps into every private virtue; he becomes the god of every man; he becomes a private citizen, a cosmopolitan.... Formerly he represented a people, the strength of a people, everything aggressive and thirsty for power in the soul of a people; now he is simply the good god.... The truth is that there is no other alternative for gods: either they are the will to power—in which case they are national gods—or incapacity for power—in which case they have to be good....

17.

Wherever the will to power begins to decline, in whatever form, there is always an accompanying decline physiologically, a décadence. The divinity of this décadence, shorn of its masculine virtues and passions, is converted perforce into a god of the physiologically degraded, of the weak. Of course, they do not call themselves the weak; they call themselves "the good."... No hint is needed to indicate the moments in history at which the dualistic fiction of a good and an evil god first became possible. The same instinct which prompts the inferior to reduce their own god to "goodness-in-itself" also prompts them to eliminate all good qualities from the god of their superiors; they make revenge on their masters by making a devil of the latter's god.—The good god, and the devil like him—both are abortions of décadence.—How can we be so tolerant of the naïveté of Christian theologians as to join in their doctrine that the evolution of the concept of god from "the god of Israel," the god of a people, to the Christian god, the essence of all goodness, is to be described as progress?— But even Renan does this. As if Renan had a right to be naïve! The contrary actually stares one in the face. When everything necessary to ascending life; when all that is strong, courageous, masterful and proud has been eliminated from the concept of a god; when he has sunk step by step to the level of a staff for the weary, a sheet-anchor for the drowning; when he becomes the poor man's god, the sinner's god, the invalid's god par excellence, and the attribute of "saviour" or "redeemer" remains as the one essential attribute of divinity—just what is the significance of such a metamorphosis? what does such a reduction of the godhead imply?—To be sure, the "kingdom of God" has thus grown larger. Formerly he had only his own people, his "chosen" people. But since then he has gone wandering, like his people themselves, into foreign parts; he has given up settling down quietly anywhere; finally he has come to feel at home everywhere, and is the great cosmopolitan—until now he has the "great majority" on his side, and half the earth. But this god of the "great majority," this democrat among gods, has not become a proud heathen god: on the contrary, he remains a Jew, he remains a god in a corner, a god of all the dark nooks and crevices, of all the noisesome quarters of the world!... His earthly kingdom, now as always, is a kingdom of the underworld, a souterrain kingdom, a ghetto kingdom.... And he himself is so pale, so weak, so décadent.... Even the palest of the pale are able to master him—messieurs the metaphysicians, those albinos of the intellect. They spun their webs around him for so long that finally he was hypnotized, and began to spin himself, and became another metaphysician. Thereafter he resumed once more his old busi ness of spinning the world out of his inmost being sub specie Spinozae; thereafter he became ever thinner and paler—became the "ideal," became "pure spirit," became "the absolute," became "the thing-in-itself."... The collapse of a god: he became a "thing-in-itself."

18.

The Christian concept of a god—the god as the patron of the sick, the god as a spinner of cobwebs, the god as a spirit—is one of the most corrupt concepts that has ever been set up in the world: it probably touches low-water mark in the ebbing evolution of the god-type. God degenerated into the contradiction of life. Instead of being its transfiguration and eternal Yea! In him war is declared on life, on nature, on the will to live! God becomes the formula for every slander upon the "here and now," and for every lie about the "beyond"! In him nothingness is deified, and the will to nothingness is made holy!...

19.

The fact that the strong races of northern Europe did not repudiate this Christian god does little credit to their gift for religion—and not much more to their taste. They ought to have been able to make an end of such a moribund and worn-out product of the décadence. A curse lies upon them because they were not equal to it; they made illness, decrepitude and contradiction a part of their instincts—and since then they have not managed to create any more gods. Two thousand years have come and gone—and not a single new god! Instead, there still exists, and as if by some intrinsic right,—as if he were the ultimatum and maximum of the power to create gods, of the creator spiritus in mankind—this pitiful god of Christian monotono-theism! This hybrid image of decay, conjured up out of emptiness, contradiction and vain imagining, in which all the instincts of décadence, all the cowardices and wearinesses of the soul find their sanction!—

20.

In my condemnation of Christianity I surely hope I do no injustice to a related religion with an even larger number of believers: I allude to Buddhism. Both are to be reckoned among the nihilistic religions— they are both décadence religions—but they are separated from each other in a very remarkable way. For the fact that he is able to compare them at all the critic of Christianity is indebted to the scholars of India.—Buddhism is a hundred times as realistic as Christianity—it is part of its living heritage that it is able to face problems objectively and coolly; it is the product of long centuries of philosophical speculation. The concept, "god," was already disposed of before it appeared. Buddhism is the only genuinely positive religion to be encountered in history, and this applies even to its epistemology (which is a strict phenomenalism). It does not speak of a "struggle with sin," but, yielding to reality, of the "struggle with suffering." Sharply differentiating itself from Christianity, it puts the self-deception that lies in moral concepts behind it; it is, in my phrase, beyond good and evil.—The two physiological facts upon which it grounds itself and upon which it bestows its chief attention are: first, an excessive sensitiveness to sensation, which manifests itself as a refined susceptibility to pain, and secondly, an extraordinary spirituality, a too protracted concern with concepts and logical procedures, under the influence of which the instinct of personality has yielded to a notion of the "impersonal." (—Both of these states will be familiar to a few of my readers, the objectivists, by experience, as they are to me). These physiological states produced a depression, and Buddha tried to combat it by hygienic measures. Against it he prescribed a life in the open, a life of travel; moderation in eating and a careful selection of foods; caution in the use of intoxicants; the same caution in arousing any of the passions that foster a bilious habit and heat the blood; finally, no worry, either on one's own account or on account of others. He encourages ideas that make for either quiet contentment or good cheer—he finds means to combat ideas of other sorts. He understands good, the state of goodness, as something which promotes health. Prayer is not included, and neither is asceticism. There is no categorical imperative nor any disciplines, even within the walls of a monastery (—it is always possible to leave—). These things would have been simply means of increasing the excessive sensitiveness above mentioned. For the same reason he does not advocate any conflict with unbelievers; his teaching is antagonistic to nothing so much as to revenge, aversion, ressentiment (—"enmity never brings an end to enmity": the moving refrain of all Buddhism....) And in all this he was right, for it is precisely these passions which, in view of his main regiminal purpose, are unhealthful. The mental fatigue that he observes, already plainly displayed in too much "objectivity" (that is, in the individual's loss of interest in himself, in loss of balance and of "egoism"), he combats by strong efforts to lead even the spiritual interests back to the ego. In Buddha's teaching egoism is a duty. The "one thing needful," the question "how can you be delivered from suffering," regulates and determines the whole spiritual diet. (—Perhaps one will here recall that Athenian who also declared war upon pure "scientificality," to wit, Socrates, who also elevated egoism to the estate of a morality).

21.

The things necessary to Buddhism are a very mild climate, customs of great gentleness and liberality, and no militarism; moreover, it must get its start among the higher and better edu cated classes. Cheerfulness, quiet and the absence of desire are the chief desiderata, and they are attained. Buddhism is not a religion in which perfection is merely an object of aspiration: perfection is actually normal.—

Under Christianity the instincts of the subjugated and the oppressed come to the fore: it is only those who are at the bottom who seek their salvation in it. Here the prevailing pastime, the favourite remedy for boredom is the discussion of sin, self-criticism, the inquisition of conscience; here the emotion produced by power (called "God") is pumped up (by prayer); here the highest good is regarded as unattainable, as a gift, as "grace." Here, too, open dealing is lacking; concealment and the darkened room are Christian. Here body is despised and hygiene is denounced as sensual; the church even ranges itself against cleanliness (—the first Christian order after the banishment of the Moors closed the public baths, of which there were 270 in Cordova alone). Christian, too, is a certain cruelty toward one's self and toward others; hatred of unbelievers; the will to persecute. Sombre and disquieting ideas are in the foreground; the most esteemed states of mind, bearing the most respectable names, are epileptoid; the diet is so regulated as to engender morbid symptoms and over-stimulate the nerves. Christian, again, is all deadly enmity to the rulers of the earth, to the "aristocratic"—along with a sort of secret rivalry with them (—one resigns one's "body" to them; one wants only one's "soul"...). And Christian is all hatred of the intellect, of pride, of courage, of freedom, of intellectual libertinage; Christian is all hatred of the senses, of joy in the senses, of joy in general....

22.

When Christianity departed from its native soil, that of the lowest orders, the underworld of the ancient world, and began seeking power among barbarian peoples, it no longer had to deal with exhausted men, but with men still inwardly savage and capable of self-torture— in brief, strong men, but bungled men. Here, unlike in the case of the Buddhists, the cause of discontent with self, suffering through self, is not merely a general sensitiveness and susceptibility to pain, but, on the contrary, an inordinate thirst for inflicting pain on others, a tendency to obtain subjective satisfaction in hostile deeds and ideas. Christianity had to embrace barbaric concepts and valuations in order to obtain mastery over barbarians: of such sort, for example, are the sacrifices of the first-born, the drinking of blood as a sacrament, the disdain of the intellect and of culture; torture in all its forms, whether bodily or not; the whole pomp of the cult. Buddhism is a religion for peoples in a further state of development, for races that have become kind, gentle and over-spiritualized (—Europe is not yet ripe for it—): it is a summons that takes them back to peace and cheerfulness, to a careful rationing of the spirit, to a certain hardening of the body. Christianity aims at mastering beasts of prey; its modus operandi is to make them ill—to make feeble is the Christian recipe for taming, for "civilizing." Buddhism is a religion for the closing, over-wearied stages of civilization. Christianity appears before civilization has so much as begun—under certain circumstances it lays the very foundations thereof.

23.

Buddhism, I repeat, is a hundred times more austere, more honest, more objective. It no longer has to justify its pains, its susceptibility to suffering, by interpreting these things in terms of sin—it simply says, as it simply thinks, "I suffer." To the barbarian, however, suffering in itself is scarcely understandable: what he needs, first of all, is an explanation as to why he suffers. (His mere instinct prompts him to deny his suffering altogether, or to endure it in silence.) Here the word "devil" was a blessing: man had to have an omnipotent and terrible enemy—there was no need to be ashamed of suffering at the hands of such an enemy.—

At the bottom of Christianity there are several subtleties that belong to the Orient. In the first place, it knows that it is of very little consequence whether a thing be true or not, so long as it is believed to be true. Truth and faith: here we have two wholly distinct worlds of ideas, almost two diametrically opposite worlds—the road to the one and the road to the other lie miles apart. To understand that fact thoroughly—this is almost enough, in the Orient, to make one a sage. The Brahmins knew it, Plato knew it, every student of the esoteric knows it. When, for example, a man gets any pleasure out of the notion that he has been saved from sin, it is not necessary for him to be actually sinful, but merely to feel sinful. But when faith is thus exalted above everything else, it necessarily follows that reason, knowledge and patient inquiry have to be discredited: the road to the truth becomes a forbidden road.—Hope, in its stronger forms, is a great deal more powerful stimulans to life than any sort of realized joy can ever be. Man must be sustained in suffering by a hope so high that no conflict with actuality can dash it—so high, indeed, that no fulfilment can satisfy it: a hope reaching out beyond this world. (Precisely because of this power that hope has of making the suffering hold out, the Greeks regarded it as the evil of evils, as the most malign of evils; it remained behind at the source of all evil.)[3]—In order that love may be possible, God must become a person; in order that the lower instincts may take a hand in the matter God must be young. To satisfy the ardor of the woman a beautiful saint must appear on the scene, and to satisfy that of the men there must be a virgin. These things are necessary if Christianity is to assume lordship over a soil on which some aphrodisiacal or Adonis cult has already established a notion as to what a cult ought to be. To insist upon chastity greatly strengthens the vehemence and subjectivity of the religious instinct—

it makes the cult warmer, more enthusiastic, more soulful.—Love is the state in which man sees things most decidedly as they are not. The force of illusion reaches its highest here, and so does the capacity for sweetening, for transfiguring. When a man is in love he endures more than at any other time; he submits to anything. The problem was to devise a religion which would allow one to love: by this means the worst that life has to offer is overcome—it is scarcely even noticed.—So much for the three Christian virtues: faith, hope and charity: I call them the three Christian ingenuities.—Buddhism is in too late a stage of development, too full of positivism, to be shrewd in any such way.—

[3]That is, in Pandora's box.

24.

Here I barely touch upon the problem of the origin of Christianity. The first thing necessary to its solution is this: that Christianity is to be understood only by examining the soil from which it sprung—it is not a reaction against Jewish instincts; it is their inevitable product; it is simply one more step in the awe-inspiring logic of the Jews. In the words of the Saviour, "salvation is of the Jews."[4]—The second thing to remember is this: that the psychological type of the Galilean is still to be recognized, but it was only in its most degenerate form (which is at once maimed and overladen with foreign features) that it could serve in the manner in which it has been used: as a type of the Saviour of mankind.—

[4]John iv, 22.

The Jews are the most remarkable people in the history of the world, for when they were confronted with the question, to be or not to be, they chose, with perfectly unearthly deliberation, to be at any price: this price involved a radical falsification of all nature, of all naturalness, of all reality, of the whole inner world, as well as of the outer. They put themselves against all those conditions under which, hitherto, a people had been able to live, or had even been permitted to live; out of themselves they evolved an idea which stood in direct opposition to natural conditions—one by one they distorted religion, civilization, morality, history and psychology until each became a contradiction of its natural significance. We meet with the same phenomenon later on, in an incalculably exaggerated form, but only as a copy: the Christian church, put beside the "people of God," shows a complete lack of any claim to originality. Precisely for this reason the Jews are the most fateful people in the history of the world: their influence has so falsified the reasoning of mankind in this matter that today the Christian can cherish anti-Semitism without realizing that it is no more than the final consequence of Judaism.

In my "Genealogy of Morals" I give the first psychological explanation of the concepts underlying those two antithetical things, a noble morality and a ressentiment morality, the second of which is a mere product of the denial of the former. The Judaeo-Christian moral system belongs to the second division, and in every detail. In order to be able to say Nay to everything representing an ascending evolution of life—that is, to well-being, to power, to beauty, to self-approval—the instincts of ressentiment, here become downright genius, had to invent an other world in which the acceptance of life appeared as the most evil and abominable thing imaginable. Psychologically, the Jews are a people gifted with the very strongest vitality, so much so that when they found themselves facing impossible conditions of life they chose voluntarily, and with a profound talent for self-preservation, the side of all those instincts which make for décadence—not as if mastered by them, but as if detecting in them a power by which "the world" could be defied. The Jews are the very opposite of décadents: they have simply been forced into appearing in that guise, and with a degree of skill approaching the non plus ultra of histrionic genius they have managed to put themselves at the head of all décadent movements (—for example, the Christianity of Paul—), and so make of them something stronger than any party frankly saying Yes to life. To the sort of men who reach out for power under Judaism and Christianity,—that is to say, to the priestly class—décadence is no more than a means to an end. Men of this sort have a vital interest in making mankind sick, and in confusing the values of "good" and "bad," "true" and "false" in a manner that is not only dangerous to life, but also slanders it.

25.

The history of Israel is invaluable as a typical history of an attempt to denaturize all natural values: I point to five facts which bear this out. Originally, and above all in the time of the monarchy, Israel maintained the right attitude of things, which is to say, the natural attitude. Its Jahveh was an expression of its consciousness of power, its joy in itself, its hopes for itself: to him the Jews looked for victory and salvation and through him they expected nature to give them whatever was necessary to their existence—above all, rain. Jahveh is the god of Israel, and consequently the god of justice: this is the logic of every race that has power in its hands and a good conscience in the use of it. In the religious ceremonial of the Jews both aspects of this self-approval stand revealed. The nation is grateful for the high destiny that has enabled it to obtain dominion; it is grateful for the benign procession of the seasons, and for the good fortune attending its herds and its crops.—This view of things remained an ideal for a long while, even after it had been robbed of validity by tragic blows: anarchy within and the Assyrian without. But the people still retained, as a projection of their highest yearnings, that vision of a king who was at once a gallant warrior and an upright judge—a vision best visualized in the typical prophet (i. e., critic and satirist of the moment), Isaiah.—But every hope remained unfulfilled. The old god no longer could do what he used to do. He ought to have been abandoned. But what actually happened? Simply this: the conception of him was changed—the conception of him was denaturized; this was the price that had to be paid for keeping him.—Jahveh, the god of "justice"—he is in accord with Israel no more, he no longer vizualizes the national egoism; he is now a god only conditionally.... The public notion of this god now becomes merely a weapon in the hands of clerical agitators, who interpret all happiness as a reward and all unhappiness as a punishment for obedience or disobedience to him, for "sin": that most fraudulent of all imaginable interpretations, whereby a "moral order of the world" is set up, and the fundamental concepts, "cause" and "effect," are stood on their heads. Once natural causation has been swept out of the world by doctrines of reward and punishment some sort of un-natural causation becomes necessary: and all other varieties of the denial of nature follow it. A god who demands—in place of a god who helps, who gives counsel, who is at bottom merely a name for every happy inspiration of courage and self-reliance.... Morality is no longer a reflection of the conditions which make for the sound life and development of the people; it is no longer the primary life-instinct; instead it has become abstract and in opposition to life—a fundamental perversion of the fancy, an "evil eye" on all things. What is Jewish, what is Christian morality? Chance robbed of its innocence; unhappiness polluted with the idea of "sin"; well-being represented as a danger, as a "temptation"; a physiological disorder produced by the canker worm of conscience....

26.

The concept of god falsified; the concept of morality falsified;—but even here Jewish priest-craft did not stop. The whole history of Israel ceased to be of any value: out with it!—These priests accomplished that miracle of falsification of which a great part of the Bible is the documentary evidence; with a degree of contempt unparalleled, and in the face of all tradition and all historical reality, they translated the past of their people into religious terms, which is to say, they converted it into an idiotic mechanism of salvation, whereby all offences against Jahveh were punished and all devotion to him was rewarded. We would regard this act of historical falsification as something far more shameful if familiarity with the ecclesiastical interpretation of history for thousands of years had not blunted our inclinations for uprightness in historicis. And the philosophers support the church: the lie about a "moral order of the world" runs through the whole of philosophy, even the newest. What is the meaning of a "moral order of the world"? That there is a thing called the will of God which, once and for all time, determines what man ought to do and what he ought not to do; that the worth of a people, or of an individual thereof, is to be measured by the extent to which they or he obey this will of God; that the destinies of a people or of an individual are controlled by this will of God, which rewards or punishes according to the degree of obedience manifested.—In place of all that pitiable lie reality has this to say: the priest, a parasitical variety of man who can exist only at the cost of every sound view of life, takes the name of God in vain: he calls that state of human society in which he himself determines the value of all things "the kingdom of God"; he calls the means whereby that state of affairs is attained "the will of God"; with cold-blooded cynicism he estimates all peoples, all ages and all individuals by the extent of their subservience or opposition to the power of the priestly order. One observes him at work: under the hand of the Jewish priesthood the great age of Israel became an age of decline; the Exile, with its long series of misfortunes, was transformed into a punishment for that great age—during which priests had not yet come into existence. Out of the powerful and wholly free heroes of Israel's history they fashioned, according to their changing needs, either wretched bigots and hypocrites or men entirely "godless." They reduced every great event to the idiotic formula: "obedient or disobedient to God."—They went a step further: the "will of God" (in other words some means necessary for preserving the power of the priests) had to be determined—and to this end they had to have a "revelation." In plain English, a gigantic literary fraud had to be perpetrated, and "holy scriptures" had to be concocted—and so, with the utmost hierarchical pomp, and days of penance and much lamentation over the long days of "sin" now ended, they were duly published. The "will of God," it appears, had long stood like a rock; the trouble was that mankind had neglected the "holy scriptures".... But the "will of God" had already been revealed to Moses.... What happened? Simply this: the priest had formulated, once and for all time and with the strictest meticulousness, what tithes were to be paid to him, from the largest to the smallest (—not forgetting the most appetizing cuts of meat, for the priest is a great consumer of beefsteaks); in brief, he let it be known just what he wanted, what "the will of God" was.... From this time forward things were so arranged that the priest became indispensable everywhere; at all the great natural events of life, at birth, at marriage, in sickness, at death, not to say at the "sacrifice" (that is, at meal-times), the holy parasite put in his appearance, and proceeded to denaturize it—in his own phrase, to "sanctify" it.... For this should be noted: that every natural habit, every natural institution (the state, the administration of justice, marriage, the care of the sick and of the poor), everything demanded by the life-instinct, in short, everything that has any value in itself, is reduced to absolute worthlessness and even made the reverse of valuable by the parasitism of priests (or, if you chose, by the "moral order of the world"). The fact requires a sanction—a power to grant values becomes necessary, and the only way it can create such values is by denying nature.... The priest depreciates and desecrates nature: it is only at this price that he can exist at all.—Disobedience to God, which actually means to the priest, to "the law," now gets the name of "sin"; the means prescribed for "reconciliation with God" are, of course, precisely the means which bring one most effectively under the thumb of the priest; he alone can "save".... Psychologically considered, "sins" are indispensable to every society organized on an ecclesiastical basis; they are the only reliable weapons of power; the priest lives upon sins; it is necessary to him that there be "sinning".... Prime axiom: "God forgiveth him that repenteth"—in plain English, him that submitteth to the priest.

27.

Christianity sprang from a soil so corrupt that on it everything natural, every natural value, every reality was opposed by the deepest instincts of the ruling class—it grew up as a sort of war to the death upon reality, and as such it has never been surpassed. The "holy people," who had adopted priestly values and priestly names for all things, and who, with a terrible logical consistency, had rejected everything of the earth as "unholy," "worldly," "sinful"—this people put its instinct into a final for mula that was logical to the point of self-annihilation: as Christianity it actually denied even the last form of reality, the "holy people," the "chosen people," Jewish reality itself. The phenomenon is of the first order of importance: the small insurrectionary movement which took the name of Jesus of Nazareth is simply the Jewish instinct redivivus—in other words, it is the priestly instinct come to such a pass that it can no longer endure the priest as a fact; it is the discovery of a state of existence even more fantastic than any before it, of a vision of life even more unreal than that necessary to an ecclesiastical organization. Christianity actually denies the church....

I am unable to determine what was the target of the insurrection said to have been led (whether rightly or wrongly) by Jesus, if it was not the Jewish church—"church" being here used in exactly the same sense that the word has today. It was an insurrection against the "good and just," against the "prophets of Israel," against the whole hierarchy of society—not against corruption, but against caste, privilege, order, formalism. It was unbelief in "superior men," a Nay flung at everything that priests and theologians stood for. But the hierarchy that was called into question, if only for an instant, by this movement was the structure of piles which, above everything, was necessary to the safety of the Jewish people in the midst of the "waters"—it represented their last possibility of survival; it was the final residuum of their independent political existence; an attack upon it was an attack upon the most profound national instinct, the most powerful national will to live, that has ever appeared on earth. This saintly anarchist, who aroused the people of the abyss, the outcasts and "sinners," the Chandala of Judaism, to rise in revolt against the established order of things—and in language which, if the Gospels are to be credited, would get him sent to Siberia today—this man was certainly a political criminal, at least in so far as it was possible to be one in so absurdly unpolitical a community. This is what brought him to the cross: the proof thereof is to be found in the inscription that was put upon the cross. He died for his own sins—there is not the slightest ground for believing, no matter how often it is asserted, that he died for the sins of others. —

28.

As to whether he himself was conscious of this contradiction—whether, in fact, this was the only contradiction he was cognizant of—that is quite another question. Here, for the first time, I touch upon the problem of the psychology of the Saviour.—I confess, to begin with, that there are very few books which offer me harder reading than the Gospels. My difficulties are quite different from those which enabled the learned curiosity of the German mind to achieve one of its most unforgettable triumphs. It is a long while since I, like all other young scholars, enjoyed with all the sapient laboriousness of a fastidious philologist the work of the incomparable Strauss.[5] At that time I was twenty years old: now I am too serious for that sort of thing. What do I care for the contradictions of "tradition"? How can any one call pious legends "traditions"? The histories of saints present the most dubious variety of literature in existence; to examine them by the scientific method, in the entire absence of corroborative documents, seems to me to condemn the whole inquiry from the start—it is simply learned idling....

[5]David Friedrich Strauss (1808-74), author of "Das Leben Jesu" (1835-6), a very famous work in its day. Nietzsche here refers to it.

29.

What concerns me is the psychological type of the Saviour. This type might be depicted in the Gospels, in however mutilated a form and however much overladen with extraneous characters—that is, in spite of the Gospels; just as the figure of Francis of Assisi shows itself in his legends in spite of his legends. It is not a question of mere truthful evidence as to what he did, what he said and how he actually died; the question is, whether his type is still conceivable, whether it has been handed down to us.—All the attempts that I know of to read the history of a "soul" in the Gospels seem to me to reveal only a lamentable psychological levity. M. Renan, that mountebank in psychologicus, has contributed the two most unseemly notions to this business of explaining the type of Jesus: the notion of the genius and that of the hero ("héros"). But if there is anything essentially unevangelical, it is surely the concept of the hero. What the Gospels make instinctive is precisely the reverse of all heroic struggle, of all taste for conflict: the very incapacity for resistance is here converted into something moral: ("resist not evil!"—the most profound sentence in the Gospels, perhaps the true key to them), to wit, the blessedness of peace, of gentleness, the inability to be an enemy. What is the meaning of "glad tidings"?—The true life, the life eternal has been found—it is not merely promised, it is here, it is in you; it is the life that lies in love free from all retreats and exclusions, from all keeping of distances. Every one is the child of God—Jesus claims nothing for himself alone—as the child of God each man is the equal of every other man.... Imagine making Jesus a hero!—And what a tremendous misunderstanding appears in the word "genius"! Our whole conception of the "spiritual," the whole conception of our civilization, could have had no meaning in the world that Jesus lived in. In the strict sense of the physiologist, a quite different word ought to be used here.... We all know that there is a morbid sensibility of the tactile nerves which causes those suffering from it to recoil from every touch, and from every effort to grasp a solid object. Brought to its logical conclusion, such a physiological habitus becomes an instinctive hatred of all reality, a flight into the "intangible," into the "incomprehensible"; a distaste for all formulae, for all conceptions of time and space, for everything established—customs, institutions, the church—; a feeling of being at home in a world in which no sort of reality survives, a merely "inner" world, a "true" world, an "eternal" world.... "The Kingdom of God is within you"....

30.

The instinctive hatred of reality: the consequence of an extreme susceptibility to pain and irritation—so great that merely to be "touched" becomes unendurable, for every sensation is too profound.

The instinctive exclusion of all aversion, all hostility, all bounds and distances in feeling: the consequence of an extreme susceptibility to pain and irritation—so great that it senses all resistance, all compulsion to resistance, as unbearable anguish (—that is to say, as harmful, as prohibited by the instinct of self-preservation), and regards blessedness (joy) as possible only when it is no longer necessary to offer resistance to anybody or anything, however evil or dangerous—love, as the only, as the ultimate possibility of life....

These are the two physiological realities upon and out of which the doctrine of salvation has sprung. I call them a sublime super-development of hedonism upon a thoroughly unsalubrious soil. What stands most closely related to them, though with a large admixture of Greek vitality and nerve-force, is epicureanism, the theory of salvation of paganism. Epicurus was a typical décadent: I was the first to recognize him.—The fear of pain, even of infinitely slight pain—the end of this can be nothing save a religion of love....

31.

I have already given my answer to the problem. The prerequisite to it is the assumption that the type of the Saviour has reached us only in a greatly distorted form. This distortion is very probable: there are many reasons why a type of that sort should not be handed down in a pure form, complete and free of additions. The milieu in which this strange figure moved must have left marks upon him, and more must have been imprinted by the history, the destiny, of the early Christian communities; the latter indeed, must have embellished the type retrospectively with characters which can be understood only as serving the purposes of war and of propaganda. That strange and sickly world into which the Gospels lead us—a world apparently out of a Russian novel, in which the scum of society, nervous maladies and "childish" idiocy keep a tryst—must, in any case, have coarsened the type: the first disciples, in particular, must have been forced to translate an existence visible only in symbols and incomprehensibilities into their own crudity, in order to understand it at all—in their sight the type could take on reality only after it had been recast in a familiar mould.... The prophet, the messiah, the future judge, the teacher of morals, the worker of wonders, John the Baptist—all these merely presented chances to misunderstand it.... Finally, let us not underrate the proprium of all great, and especially all sectarian veneration: it tends to erase from the venerated objects all its original traits and idiosyncrasies, often so painfully strange— it does not even see them. It is greatly to be regretted that no Dostoyevsky lived in the neighbourhood of this most interesting décadent—I mean some one who would have felt the poignant charm of such a compound of the sublime, the morbid and the childish. In the last analysis, the type, as a type of the décadence, may actually have been peculiarly complex and contradictory: such a possibility is not to be lost sight of. Nevertheless, the probabilities seem to be against it, for in that case tradition would have been particularly accurate and objective, whereas we have reasons for assuming the contrary. Meanwhile, there is a contradiction between the peaceful preacher of the mount, the sea-shore and the fields, who appears like a new Buddha on a soil very unlike India's, and the aggressive fanatic, the mortal enemy of theologians and ecclesiastics, who stands glorified by Renan's malice as "le grand maître en ironie." I myself haven't any doubt that the greater part of this venom (and no less of esprit) got itself into the concept of the Master only as a result of the excited nature of Christian propaganda: we all know the unscrupulousness of sectarians when they set out to turn their leader into an apologia for themselves. When the early Christians had need of an adroit, contentious, pugnacious and maliciously subtle theologian to tackle other theologians, they created a "god" that met that need, just as they put into his mouth without hesitation certain ideas that were necessary to them but that were utterly at odds with the Gospels—"the second coming," "the last judgment," all sorts of expectations and promises, current at the time.—

32.

I can only repeat that I set myself against all efforts to intrude the fanatic into the figure of the Saviour: the very word impérieux, used by Renan, is alone enough to annul the type. What the "glad tidings" tell us is simply that there are no more contradictions; the kingdom of heaven belongs to children; the faith that is voiced here is no more an embattled faith—it is at hand, it has been from the beginning, it is a sort of recrudescent childishness of the spirit. The physiologists, at all events, are familiar with such a delayed and incomplete puberty in the living organism, the result of degeneration. A faith of this sort is not furious, it does not de nounce, it does not defend itself: it does not come with "the sword"—it does not realize how it will one day set man against man. It does not manifest itself either by miracles, or by rewards and promises, or by "scriptures": it is itself, first and last, its own miracle, its own reward, its own promise, its own "kingdom of God." This faith does not formulate itself—it simply lives, and so guards itself against formulae. To be sure, the accident of environment, of educational background gives prominence to concepts of a certain sort: in primitive Christianity one finds only concepts of a Judaeo-Semitic character (—that of eating and drinking at the last supper belongs to this category—an idea which, like everything else Jewish, has been badly mauled by the church). But let us be careful not to see in all this anything more than symbolical language, semantics[6] an opportunity to speak in parables. It is only on the theory that no work is to be taken literally that this anti-realist is able to speak at all. Set down among Hindus he would have made use of the concepts of Sankhya,[7] and among Chinese he would have employed those of Lao-tse[8]—and in neither case would it have made any difference to him.—With a little freedom in the use of words, one might actually call Jesus a "free spirit"[9]—he cares nothing for what is established: the word killeth,[10] whatever is established killeth. The idea of "life" as an experience, as he alone conceives it, stands opposed to his mind to every sort of word, formula, law, belief and dogma. He speaks only of inner things: "life" or "truth" or "light" is his word for the innermost—in his sight everything else, the whole of reality, all nature, even language, has significance only as sign, as allegory.—Here it is of paramount importance to be led into no error by the temptations lying in Christian, or rather ecclesiastical prejudices: such a symbolism par excellence stands outside all religion, all notions of worship, all history, all natural science, all worldly experience, all knowledge, all politics, all psychology, all books, all art—his "wisdom" is precisely a pure ignorance[11] of all such things. He has never heard of culture; he doesn't have to make war on it—he doesn't even deny it.... The same thing may be said of the state, of the whole bourgeoise social order, of labour, of war—he has no ground for denying "the world," for he knows nothing of the ecclesiastical concept of "the world".... Denial is precisely the thing that is impossible to him.—In the same way he lacks argumentative capacity, and has no belief that an article of faith, a "truth," may be established by proofs (—his proofs are inner "lights," subjective sensations of happiness and self-approval, simple "proofs of power"—). Such a doctrine cannot contradict: it doesn't know that other doctrines exist, or can exist, and is wholly incapable of imagining anything opposed to it.... If anything of the sort is ever encountered, it laments the "blindness" with sincere sympathy—for it alone has "light"—but it does not offer objections....

[6]The word Semiotik is in the text, but it is probable that Semantik is what Nietzsche had in mind.

[7]One of the six great systems of Hindu philosophy.

[8]The reputed founder of Taoism.

[9]Nietzsche's name for one accepting his own philosophy.

[10]That is, the strict letter of the law—the chief target of Jesus's early preaching.

[11]A reference to the "pure ignorance" (reine Thorheit) of Parsifal.

33.

In the whole psychology of the "Gospels" the concepts of guilt and punishment are lacking, and so is that of reward. "Sin," which means anything that puts a distance between God and man, is abolished—this is precisely the "glad tidings." Eternal bliss is not merely promised, nor is it bound up with conditions: it is conceived as the only reality—what remains consists merely of signs useful in speaking of it.

The results of such a point of view project themselves into a new way of life, the special evangelical way of life. It is not a "belief" that marks off the Christian; he is distinguished by a different mode of action; he acts differently. He offers no resistance, either by word or in his heart, to those who stand against him. He draws no distinction between strangers and countrymen, Jews and Gentiles ("neighbour," of course, means fellow-believer, Jew). He is angry with no one, and he despises no one. He neither appeals to the courts of justice nor heeds their mandates ("Swear not at all").[12] He never under any circumstances divorces his wife, even when he has proofs of her infidelity.—And under all of this is one principle; all of it arises from one instinct.—

[12]Matthew v, 34.

The life of the Saviour was simply a carrying out of this way of life—and so was his death.... He no longer needed any formula or ritual in his relations with God—not even prayer. He had rejected the whole of the Jewish doctrine of repentance and atonement; he knew that it was only by a way of life that one could feel one's self "divine," "blessed," "evangelical," a "child of God." Not by "repentance," not by "prayer and forgiveness" is the way to God: only the Gospel way leads to God—it is itself "God!"—What the Gospels abolished was the Judaism in the concepts of "sin," "forgiveness of sin," "faith," "salvation through faith"—the whole ecclesiastical dogma of the Jews was denied by the "glad tidings."

The deep instinct which prompts the Christian how to live so that he will feel that he is "in heaven" and is "immortal," despite many reasons for feeling that he is not "in heaven": this is the only psychological reality in "salvation."—A new way of life, not a new faith....

34.

If I understand anything at all about this great symbolist, it is this: that he regarded only subjective realities as realities, as "truths" — that he saw everything else, everything natural, temporal, spatial and historical, merely as signs, as materials for parables. The concept of "the Son of God" does not connote a concrete person in history, an isolated and definite individual, but an "eternal" fact, a psychological symbol set free from the concept of time. The same thing is true, and in the highest sense, of the God of this typical symbolist, of the "kingdom of God," and of the "sonship of God." Nothing could be more un-Christian than the crude ecclesiastical notions of God as a person, of a "kingdom of God" that is to come, of a "kingdom of heaven" beyond, and of a "son of God" as the second person of the Trinity. All this—if I may be forgiven the phrase—is like thrusting one's fist into the eye (and what an eye!) of the Gospels: a disrespect for symbols amounting to world-historical cynicism.... But it is nevertheless obvious enough what is meant by the symbols "Father" and "Son"—not, of course, to every one—: the word "Son" expresses entrance into the feeling that there is a general transformation of all things (beatitude), and "Father" expresses that feeling itself—the sensation of eternity and of perfection.—I am ashamed to remind you of what the church has made of this symbolism: has it not set an Amphitryon story[13] at the threshold of the Christian "faith"? And a dogma of "immaculate conception" for good measure?... And thereby it has robbed conception of its immaculateness—

[13] Amphitryon was the son of Alcaeus, King of Tiryns. His wife was Alcmene. During his absence she was visited by Zeus, and bore Heracles.

The "kingdom of heaven" is a state of the heart—not something to come "beyond the world" or "after death." The whole idea of natural death is absent from the Gospels: death is not a bridge, not a passing; it is absent because it belongs to a quite different, a merely apparent world, useful only as a symbol. The "hour of death" is not a Christian idea—"hours," time, the physical life and its crises have no existence for the bearer of "glad tidings.".... The "kingdom of God" is not something that men wait for: it had no yesterday and no day after tomorrow, it is not going to come at a "millennium"—it is an experience of the heart, it is everywhere and it is nowhere....

35.

This "bearer of glad tidings" died as he lived and taught—not to "save mankind," but to show mankind how to live. It was a way of life that he bequeathed to man: his demeanour before the judges, before the officers, before his accusers—his demeanour on the cross. He does not resist; he does not defend his rights; he makes no effort to ward off the most extreme penalty—more, he invites it.... And he prays, suffers and loves with those, in those, who do him evil.... Not to defend one's self, not to show anger, not to lay blames.... On the contrary, to submit even to the Evil One—to love him....

36.

—We free spirits—we are the first to have the necessary prerequisite to understanding what nineteen centuries have misunderstood—that instinct and passion for integrity which makes war upon the "holy lie" even more than upon all other lies.... Mankind was unspeakably far from our benevolent and cautious neutrality, from that discipline of the spirit which alone makes possible the solution of such strange and subtle things: what men always sought, with shameless egoism, was their own advantage therein; they created the church out of denial of the Gospels....

Whoever sought for signs of an ironical divinity's hand in the great drama of existence would find no small indication thereof in the stupendous question-mark that is called Christianity. That mankind should be on its knees before the very antithesis of what was the origin, the meaning and the law of the Gospels—that in the concept of the "church" the very things should be pronounced holy that the "bearer of glad tidings" regards as beneath him and behind him—it would be impossible to surpass this as a grand example of world-historical irony—

37.

—Our age is proud of its historical sense: how, then, could it delude itself into believing that the crude fable of the wonder-worker and Saviour constituted the beginnings of Christianity—and that everything spiritual and symbolical in it only came later? Quite to the contrary, the whole history of Christianity—from the death on the cross onward—is the history of a progressively clumsier misunderstanding of an original symbolism. With every extension of Christianity among larger and ruder masses, even less capable of grasping the principles that gave birth to it, the need arose to make it more and more vulgar and barbarous—it absorbed the teachings and rites of all the subterranean cults of the imperium Romanum, and the absurdities engendered by all sorts of sickly reasoning. It was the fate of Christianity that its faith had to become as sickly, as low and as vulgar as the needs were sickly, low and vulgar to which it had to administer. A sickly barbarism finally lifts itself to power as the church—the church, that incarnation of deadly hostility to all honesty, to all loftiness of soul, to all discipline of the spirit, to all spontaneous and kindly humanity.—Christian values—noble values: it is only we, we free spirits, who have re-established this greatest of all antitheses in values!...

38.

—I cannot, at this place, avoid a sigh. There are days when I am visited by a feeling blacker than the blackest melancholy—contempt of man. Let me leave no doubt as to what I despise, whom I despise: it is the man of today, the man with whom I am unhappily contemporaneous. The man of today—I am suffocated by his foul breath!... Toward the past, like all who understand, I am full of tolerance, which is to say, generous self-control: with gloomy caution I pass through whole millenniums of this madhouse of a world, call it "Christianity," "Christian faith" or the "Christian church," as you will—I take care not to hold mankind responsible for its lunacies. But my feeling changes and breaks out irresistibly the moment I enter modern times, our times. Our age knows better.... What was formerly merely sickly now becomes indecent—it is indecent to be a Christian today. And here my disgust begins.—I look about me: not a word survives of what was once called "truth"; we can no longer bear to hear a priest pronounce the word. Even a man who makes the most modest pretensions to integrity must know that a theologian, a priest, a pope of today not only errs when he speaks, but actually lies— and that he no longer escapes blame for his lie through "innocence" or "ignorance." The priest knows, as every one knows, that there is no longer any "God," or any "sinner," or any "Saviour"—that "free will" and the "moral order of the world" are lies—: serious reflection, the profound self-conquest of the spirit, allow no man to pretend that he does not know it.... All the ideas of the church are now recognized for what they are—as the worst counterfeits in existence, invented to debase nature and all natural values; the priest himself is seen as he actually is—as the most dangerous form of parasite, as the venomous spider of creation.... We know, our conscience now knows—just what the real value of all those sinister inventions of priest and church has been and what ends they have served, with their debasement of humanity to a state of self-pollution, the very sight of which excites loathing,—the concepts "the other world," "the last judgment," "the immortality of the soul," the "soul" itself: they are all merely so many instruments of torture, systems of cruelty, whereby the priest becomes master and remains master.... Every one knows this, but nevertheless things remain as before. What has become of the last trace of decent feeling, of self-respect, when our statesmen, otherwise an unconventional class of men and thoroughly anti-Christian in their acts, now call themselves Christians and go to the communion-table?... A prince at the head of his armies, magnificent as the expression of the egoism and arrogance of his people—and yet acknowledging, without any shame, that he is a Christian!... Whom, then, does Christianity deny? what does it call "the world"? To be a soldier, to be a judge, to be a patriot; to defend one's self; to be careful of one's honour; to desire one's own advantage; to be proud ... every act of everyday, every instinct, every valuation that shows itself in a deed, is now anti-Christian: what a monster of falsehood the modern man must be to call himself nevertheless, and without shame, a Christian!—

39.

—I shall go back a bit, and tell you the authentic history of Christianity.—The very word "Christianity" is a misunderstanding—at bottom there was only one Christian, and he died on the cross. The "Gospels" died on the cross. What, from that moment onward, was called the "Gospels" was the very reverse of what he had lived: "bad tidings," a Dysangelium.[14] It is an error amounting to nonsensicality to see in "faith," and particularly in faith in salvation through Christ, the distinguishing mark of the Christian: only the Christian way of life, the life lived by him who died on the cross, is Christian.... To this day such a life is still possible, and for certain men even necessary: genuine, primitive Christianity will remain possible in all ages.... Not faith, but acts; above all, an avoidance of acts, a different state of being.... States of consciousness, faith of a sort, the acceptance, for example, of anything as true—as every psychologist knows, the value of these things is perfectly indifferent and fifth-rate compared to that of the instincts: strictly speaking, the whole concept of intellectual causality is false. To reduce being a Christian, the state of Christianity, to an acceptance of truth, to a mere phenomenon of consciousness, is to formulate the negation of Christianity. In fact, there are no Christians. The "Christian"—he who for two thousand years has passed as a Christian—is simply a psycho logical self-delusion. Closely examined, it appears that, despite all his "faith," he has been ruled only by his instincts—and what instincts!—In all ages—for example, in the case of Luther—"faith" has been no more than a cloak, a pretense, a curtain behind which the instincts have played their game—a shrewd blindness to the domination of certain of the instincts.... I have already called "faith" the specially Christian form of shrewdness—people always talk of their "faith" and act according to their instincts.... In the world of ideas of the Christian there is nothing that so much as touches reality: on the contrary, one recognizes an instinctive hatred of reality as the motive power, the only motive power at the bottom of Christianity. What follows therefrom? That even here, in psychologicis, there is a radical error, which is to say one conditioning fundamentals, which is to say, one in substance. Take away one idea and put a genuine reality in its place—and the whole of Christianity crumbles to nothingness!—Viewed calmly, this strangest of all phenomena, a religion not only depending on errors, but inventive and ingenious only in devising injurious errors, poisonous to life and to the heart—this remains a spectacle for the gods—for those gods who are also philosophers, and whom I have encountered, for example, in the celebrated dialogues at Naxos. At the moment when their disgust leaves them (—and us!) they will be thankful for the spectacle afforded by the Christians: perhaps because of this curious exhibition alone the wretched little planet called the earth deserves a glance from omnipotence, a show of divine interest.... Therefore, let us not underestimate the Christians: the Christian, false to the point of innocence, is far above the ape—in its application to the Christians a well-known theory of descent becomes a mere piece of politeness....

[14]So in the text. One of Nietzsche's numerous coinages, obviously suggested by Evangelium, the German for gospel.

40.

—The fate of the Gospels was decided by death—it hung on the "cross."... It was only death, that unexpected and shameful death; it was only the cross, which was usually reserved for the canaille only—it was only this appalling paradox which brought the disciples face to face with the real riddle: "Who was it? what was it?"—The feeling of dismay, of profound affront and injury; the suspicion that such a death might involve a refutation of their cause; the terrible question, "Why just in this way?"—this state of mind is only too easy to understand. Here everything must be accounted for as necessary; everything must have a meaning, a reason, the highest sort of reason; the love of a disciple excludes all chance. Only then did the chasm of doubt yawn: "Who put him to death? who was his natural enemy?"— this question flashed like a lightning-stroke. Answer: dominant Judaism, its ruling class. From that moment, one found one's self in revolt against the established order, and began to understand Jesus as in revolt against the established order. Until then this militant, this nay-saying, nay-doing element in his character had been lacking; what is more, he had appeared to present its opposite. Obviously, the little community had not understood what was precisely the most important thing of all: the example offered by this way of dying, the freedom from and superiority to every feeling of ressentiment—a plain indication of how little he was understood at all! All that Jesus could hope to accomplish by his death, in itself, was to offer the strongest possible proof, or example, of his teachings in the most public manner.... But his disciples were very far from forgiving his death—though to have done so would have accorded with the Gospels in the highest degree; and neither were they prepared to offer themselves, with gentle and serene calmness of heart, for a similar death.... On the contrary, it was precisely the most unevangelical of feelings, revenge, that now possessed them. It seemed impossible that the cause should perish with his death: "recompense" and "judgment" became necessary (—yet what could be less evangelical than "recompense," "punishment," and "sitting in judgment"!). Once more the popular belief in the coming of a messiah appeared in the foreground; attention was rivetted upon an historical moment: the "kingdom of God" is to come, with judgment upon his enemies.... But in all this there was a wholesale misunderstanding: imagine the "kingdom of God" as a last act, as a mere promise! The Gospels had been, in fact, the incarnation, the fulfilment, the realization of this "kingdom of God." It was only now that all the familiar contempt for and bitterness against Pharisees and theologians began to appear in the character of the Master—he was thereby turned into a Pharisee and theologian himself! On the other hand, the savage veneration of these completely unbalanced souls could no longer endure the Gospel doctrine, taught by Jesus, of the equal right of all men to be children of God: their revenge took the form of elevating Jesus in an extravagant fashion, and thus separating him from themselves: just as, in earlier times, the Jews, to revenge themselves upon their enemies, separated themselves from their God, and placed him on a great height. The One God and the Only Son of God: both were products of ressentiment....

41.

—And from that time onward an absurd problem offered itself: "how could God allow it!" To which the deranged reason of the little community formulated an answer that was terrifying in its absurdity: God gave his son as a sacrifice for the forgiveness of sins. At once there was an end of the gospels! Sacrifice for sin, and in its most obnoxious and barbarous form: sacrifice of the innocent for the sins of the guilty! What appalling paganism!—Jesus him self had done away with the very concept of "guilt," he denied that there was any gulf fixed between God and man; he lived this unity between God and man, and that was precisely his "glad tidings".... And not as a mere privilege!—From this time forward the type of the Saviour was corrupted, bit by bit, by the doctrine of judgment and of the second coming, the doctrine of death as a sacrifice, the doctrine of the resurrection, by means of which the entire concept of "blessedness," the whole and only reality of the gospels, is juggled away—in favour of a state of existence after death!... St. Paul, with that rabbinical impudence which shows itself in all his doings, gave a logical quality to that conception, that indecent conception, in this way: "If Christ did not rise from the dead, then all our faith is in vain!"— And at once there sprang from the Gospels the most contemptible of all unfulfillable promises, the shameless doctrine of personal immortality.... Paul even preached it as a reward....

42.

One now begins to see just what it was that came to an end with the death on the cross: a new and thoroughly original effort to found a Buddhistic peace movement, and so establish happiness on earth— real, not merely promised. For this remains—as I have already pointed out—the essential difference between the two religions of décadence: Buddhism promises nothing, but actually fulfils; Christianity promises everything, but fulfils nothing.—Hard upon the heels of the "glad tidings" came the worst imaginable: those of Paul. In Paul is incarnated the very opposite of the "bearer of glad tidings"; he represents the genius for hatred, the vision of hatred, the relentless logic of hatred. What, indeed, has not this dysangelist sacrificed to hatred! Above all, the Saviour: he nailed him to his own cross. The life, the example, the teaching, the death of Christ, the meaning and the law of the whole gospels—nothing was left of all this after that counterfeiter in hatred had reduced it to his uses. Surely not reality; surely not historical truth!... Once more the priestly instinct of the Jew perpetrated the same old master crime against history— he simply struck out the yesterday and the day before yesterday of Christianity, and invented his own history of Christian beginnings. Going further, he treated the history of Israel to another falsification, so that it became a mere prologue to his achievement: all the prophets, it now appeared, had referred to his "Saviour."... Later on the church even falsified the history of man in order to make it a prologue to Christianity.... The figure of the Saviour, his teaching, his way of life, his death, the meaning of his death, even the consequences of his death—nothing remained untouched, nothing remained in even remote contact with reality. Paul simply shifted the centre of gravity of that whole life to a place behind this existence—in the lie of the "risen" Jesus. At bottom, he had no use for the life of the Saviour—what he needed was the death on the cross, and something more. To see anything honest in such a man as Paul, whose home was at the centre of the Stoical enlightenment, when he converts an hallucination into a proof of the resurrection of the Saviour, or even to believe his tale that he suffered from this hallucination himself— this would be a genuine niaiserie in a psychologist. Paul willed the end; therefore he also willed the means.... What he himself didn't believe was swallowed readily enough by the idiots among whom he spread his teaching.—What he wanted was power; in Paul the priest once more reached out for power—he had use only for such concepts, teachings and symbols as served the purpose of tyrannizing over the masses and organizing mobs. What was the only part of Christianity that Mohammed borrowed later on? Paul's invention, his device for establishing priestly tyranny and organizing the mob: the belief in the immortality of the soul—that is to say, the doctrine of "judgment"....

43.

When the centre of gravity of life is placed, not in life itself, but in "the beyond"—in nothingness—then one has taken away its centre of gravity altogether. The vast lie of personal immortality destroys all reason, all natural instinct—henceforth, everything in the instincts that is beneficial, that fosters life and that safeguards the future is a cause of suspicion. So to live that life no longer has any meaning: this is now the "meaning" of life.... Why be public-spirited? Why take any pride in descent and forefathers? Why labour together, trust one another, or concern one's self about the common welfare, and try to serve it?... Merely so many "temptations," so many strayings from the "straight path."—"One thing only is necessary".... That every man, because he has an "immortal soul," is as good as every other man; that in an infinite universe of things the "salvation" of every individual may lay claim to eternal importance; that insignificant bigots and the three-fourths insane may assume that the laws of nature are constantly suspended in their behalf—it is impossible to lavish too much contempt upon such a magnification of every sort of selfishness to infinity, to insolence. And yet Christianity has to thank precisely this miserable flattery of personal vanity for its triumph—it was thus that it lured all the botched, the dissatisfied, the fallen upon evil days, the whole refuse and off-scouring of humanity to its side. The "salvation of the soul"—in plain English: "the world revolves around me.".... The poisonous doctrine, "equal rights for all," has been propagated as a Christian principle: out of the secret nooks and crannies of bad instinct Christianity has waged a deadly war upon all feelings of reverence and distance between man and man, which is to say, upon the first prerequisite to every step upward, to every development of civilization—out of the ressentiment of the masses it has forged its chief weapons against us, against everything noble, joyous and high-spirited on earth, against our happiness on earth.... To allow "immortality" to every Peter and Paul was the greatest, the most vicious outrage upon noble humanity ever perpetrated.—And let us not underestimate the fatal influence that Christianity has had, even upon politics! Nowadays no one has courage any more for special rights, for the right of dominion, for feelings of honourable pride in himself and his equals—for the pathos of distance.... Our politics is sick with this lack of courage!—The aristocratic attitude of mind has been undermined by the lie of the equality of souls; and if belief in the "privileges of the majority" makes and will continue to make revolutions—it is Christianity, let us not doubt, and Christian valuations, which convert every revolution into a carnival of blood and crime! Christianity is a revolt of all creatures that creep on the ground against everything that is lofty: the gospel of the "lowly" lowers....

44.

—The gospels are invaluable as evidence of the corruption that was already persistent within the primitive community. That which Paul, with the cynical logic of a rabbi, later developed to a conclusion was at bottom merely a process of decay that had begun with the death of the Saviour.—These gospels cannot be read too carefully; difficulties lurk behind every word. I confess—I hope it will not be held against me—that it is precisely for this reason that they offer first-rate joy to a psychologist—as the opposite of all merely naïve corruption, as refinement par excellence, as an artistic triumph in psychological corruption. The gospels, in fact, stand alone. The Bible as a whole is not to be compared to them. Here we are among Jews: this is the first thing to be borne in mind if we are not to lose the thread of the matter. This positive genius for conjuring up a delusion of personal "holiness" unmatched anywhere else, either in books or by men; this elevation of fraud in word and attitude to the level of an art—all this is not an accident due to the chance talents of an individual, or to any violation of nature. The thing responsible is race. The whole of Judaism appears in Christianity as the art of concocting holy lies, and there, after many centuries of earnest Jewish training and hard practice of Jewish technic, the business comes to the stage of mastery. The Christian, that ultima ratio of lying, is the Jew all over again—he is threefold the Jew.... The underlying will to make use only of such concepts, symbols and attitudes as fit into priestly practice, the instinctive repudiation of every other mode of thought, and every other method of estimating values and utilities—this is not only tradition, it is inheritance: only as an inheritance is it able to operate with the force of nature. The whole of mankind, even the best minds of the best ages (with one exception, perhaps hardly human—), have permitted themselves to be deceived. The gospels have been read as a book of innocence ... surely no small indication of the high skill with which the trick has been done.—Of course, if we could actually see these astounding bigots and bogus saints, even if only for an instant, the farce would come to an end,—and it is precisely because I cannot read a word of theirs without seeing their attitudinizing that I have made an end of them.... I simply cannot endure the way they have of rolling up their eyes.—For the majority, happily enough, books are mere literature.—Let us not be led astray: they say "judge not," and yet they condemn to hell whoever stands in their way. In letting God sit in judgment they judge themselves; in glorifying God they glorify themselves; in demanding that every one show the virtues which they themselves happen to be capable of—still more, which they must have in order to remain on top—they assume the grand air of men struggling for virtue, of men engaging in a war that virtue may prevail. "We live, we die, we sacrifice ourselves for the good" (—"the truth," "the light," "the kingdom of God"): in point of fact, they simply do what they cannot help doing. Forced, like hypocrites, to be sneaky, to hide in corners, to slink along in the shadows, they convert their necessity into a duty: it is on grounds of duty that they account for their lives of humility, and that humility becomes merely one more proof of their piety.... Ah, that humble, chaste, charitable brand of fraud! "Virtue itself shall bear witness for us.".... One may read the gospels as books of moral seduction: these petty folks fasten themselves to morality—they know the uses of morality! Morality is the best of all devices for leading mankind by the nose!—The fact is that the conscious conceit of the chosen here disguises itself as modesty: it is in this way that they, the "community," the "good and just," range themselves, once and for always, on one side, the side of "the truth"—and the rest of mankind, "the world," on the other.... In that we observe the most fatal sort of megalomania that the earth has ever seen: little abortions of bigots and liars began to claim exclusive rights in the concepts of "God," "the truth," "the light," "the spirit," "love," "wisdom" and "life," as if these things were synonyms of themselves and thereby they sought to fence themselves off from the "world"; little super-Jews, ripe for some sort of madhouse, turned values upside down in order to meet their notions, just as if the Christian were the meaning, the salt, the standard and even the last judgment of all the rest.... The whole disaster was only made possible by the fact that there already existed in the world a similar megalomania, allied to this one in race, to wit, the Jewish: once a chasm began to yawn between Jews and Judaeo-Christians, the latter had no choice but to employ the self-preservative measures that the Jewish instinct had devised, even against the Jews themselves, whereas the Jews had employed them only against non-Jews. The Christian is simply a Jew of the "reformed" confession.—

45.

—I offer a few examples of the sort of thing these petty people have got into their heads—what they have put into the mouth of the Master: the unalloyed creed of "beautiful souls."—

"And whosoever shall not receive you, nor hear you, when ye depart thence, shake off the dust under your feet for a testimony against them. Verily I say unto you, it shall be more tolerable for Sodom and Gomorrha in the day of judgment, than for that city" (Mark vi, 11)—How evangelical!...

"And whosoever shall offend one of these little ones that believe in me, it is better for him that a millstone were hanged about his neck, and he were cast into the sea" (Mark ix, 42).—How evangelical!...

"And if thine eye offend thee, pluck it out: it is better for thee to enter into the kingdom of God with one eye, than having two eyes to be cast into hell fire; Where the worm dieth not, and the fire is not quenched." (Mark ix, 47.[15])—It is not exactly the eye that is meant....

[15]To which, without mentioning it, Nietzsche adds verse 48.

"Verily I say unto you, That there be some of them that stand here, which shall not taste of death, till they have seen the kingdom of God come with power." (Mark ix, 1.)—Well lied, lion![16]....

[16]A paraphrase of Demetrius' "Well roar'd, Lion!" in act v, scene 1 of "A Midsummer Night's Dream." The lion, of course, is the familiar Christian symbol for Mark.

"Whosoever will come after me, let him deny himself, and take up his cross, and follow me. For..." (Note of a psychologist. Christian morality is refuted by its fors: its reasons are against it,—this makes it Christian.) Mark viii, 34.—

"Judge not, that ye be not judged. With what measure ye mete, it shall be measured to you again." (Matthew vii, 1.[17])—What a notion of justice, of a "just" judge!...

[17]Nietzsche also quotes part of verse 2.

"For if ye love them which love you, what reward have ye? do not even the publicans the same? And if ye salute your brethren only, what do ye more than others? do not even the publicans so?" (Matthew v, 46.[18])—Principle of "Christian love": it insists upon being well paid in the end....

[18]The quotation also includes verse 47.

"But if ye forgive not men their trespasses, neither will your Father forgive your trespasses." (Matthew vi, 15.)—Very compromising for the said "father."...

"But seek ye first the kingdom of God, and his righteousness; and all these things shall be added unto you." (Matthew vi, 33.)—All these things: namely, food, clothing, all the necessities of life. An error, to put it mildly.... A bit before this God appears as a tailor, at least in certain cases....

"Rejoice ye in that day, and leap for joy: for, behold, your reward is great in heaven: for in the like manner did their fathers unto the prophets." (Luke vi, 23.)—Impudent rabble! It compares itself to the prophets....

"Know ye not that ye are the temple of God, and that the spirit of God dwelleth in you? If any man defile the temple of God, him shall God destroy; for the temple of God is holy, which temple ye are." (Paul, 1 Corinthians iii, 16.[19])—For that sort of thing one cannot have enough contempt....

[19]And 17.

"Do ye not know that the saints shall judge the world? and if the world shall be judged by you, are ye unworthy to judge the smallest matters?" (Paul, 1 Corinthians vi, 2.)—Unfortunately, not merely the speech of a lunatic.... This frightful impostor then proceeds: "Know ye not that we shall judge angels? how much more things that pertain to this life?"...

"Hath not God made foolish the wisdom of this world? For after that in the wisdom of God the world by wisdom knew not God, it pleased God by the foolishness of preaching to save them that believe.... Not many wise men after the flesh, not men mighty, not many noble are called: But God hath chosen the foolish things of the world to confound the wise; and God hath chosen the weak things of the world to confound the things which are mighty; And base things of the world, and things which are despised, hath God chosen, yea, and things which are not, to bring to nought things that are: That no flesh should glory in his presence." (Paul, 1 Corinthians i, 20ff.[20])—In order to understand this passage, a first-rate example of the psychology underlying every Chandala-morality, one should read the first part of my "Genealogy of Morals": there, for the first time, the antagonism between a noble morality and a morality born of ressentiment and impotent vengefulness is exhibited. Paul was the greatest of all apostles of revenge....

[20]Verses 20, 21, 26, 27, 28, 29.

46.

—What follows, then? That one had better put on gloves before reading the New Testament. The presence of so much filth makes it very advisable. One would as little choose "early Christians" for companions as Polish Jews: not that one need seek out an objection to them.... Neither has a pleasant smell.—I have searched the New Testament in vain for a single sympathetic touch; nothing is there that is free, kindly, open-hearted or upright. In it humanity does not even make the first step upward—the instinct for cleanliness is lacking.... Only evil instincts are there, and there is not even the courage of these evil instincts. It is all coward ice; it is all a shutting of the eyes, a self-deception. Every other book becomes clean, once one has read the New Testament: for example, immediately after reading Paul I took up with delight that most charming and wanton of scoffers, Petronius, of whom one may say what Domenico Boccaccio wrote of Cæsar Borgia to the Duke of Parma: "è tutto festo"—immortally healthy, immortally cheerful and sound.... These petty bigots make a capital miscalculation. They attack, but everything they attack is thereby distinguished. Whoever is attacked by an "early Christian" is surely not befouled.... On the contrary, it is an honour to have an "early Christian" as an opponent. One cannot read the New Testament without acquired admiration for whatever it abuses—not to speak of the "wisdom of this world," which an impudent windbag tries to dispose of "by the foolishness of preaching."... Even the scribes and pharisees are benefitted by such opposition: they must certainly have been worth something to have been hated in such an indecent manner. Hypocrisy—as if this were a charge that the "early Christians" dared to make!—After all, they were the privileged, and that was enough: the hatred of the Chandala needed no other excuse. The "early Christian"—and also, I fear, the "last Christian," whom I may perhaps live to see—is a rebel against all privilege by profound instinct—he lives and makes war for ever for "equal rights."... Strictly speaking, he has no alternative. When a man proposes to represent, in his own person, the "chosen of God"—or to be a "temple of God," or a "judge of the angels"—then every other criterion, whether based upon honesty, upon intellect, upon manliness and pride, or upon beauty and freedom of the heart, becomes simply "worldly"—evil in itself.... Moral: every word that comes from the lips of an "early

Christian" is a lie, and his every act is instinctively dishonest—all his values, all his aims are noxious, but whoever he hates, whatever he hates, has real value.... The Christian, and particularly the Christian priest, is thus a criterion of values.

—Must I add that, in the whole New Testament, there appears but a solitary figure worthy of honour? Pilate, the Roman viceroy. To regard a Jewish imbroglio seriously—that was quite beyond him. One Jew more or less—what did it matter?... The noble scorn of a Roman, before whom the word "truth" was shamelessly mishandled, enriched the New Testament with the only saying that has any value—and that is at once its criticism and its destruction: "What is truth?..."

47.

—The thing that sets us apart is not that we are unable to find God, either in history, or in nature, or behind nature—but that we regard what has been honoured as God, not as "divine," but as pitiable, as absurd, as injurious; not as a mere error, but as a crime against life.... We deny that God is God.... If any one were to show us this Christian God, we'd be still less inclined to believe in him.—In a formula: deus, qualem Paulus creavit, dei negatio.—Such a religion as Christianity, which does not touch reality at a single point and which goes to pieces the moment reality asserts its rights at any point, must be inevitably the deadly enemy of the "wisdom of this world," which is to say, of science—and it will give the name of good to whatever means serve to poison, calumniate and cry down all intellectual discipline, all lucidity and strictness in matters of intellectual conscience, and all noble coolness and freedom of the mind. "Faith," as an imperative, vetoes science—in praxi, lying at any price.... Paul well knew that lying—that "faith"—was necessary; later on the church borrowed the fact from Paul.—The God that Paul invented for himself, a God who "reduced to absurdity" "the wisdom of this world" (especially the two great enemies of superstition, philology and medicine), is in truth only an indication of Paul's resolute determination to accomplish that very thing himself: to give one's own will the name of God, thora— that is essentially Jewish. Paul wants to dispose of the "wisdom of this world": his enemies are the good philologians and physicians of the Alexandrine school—on them he makes his war. As a matter of fact no man can be a philologian or a physician without being also Antichrist. That is to say, as a philologian a man sees behind the "holy books," and as a physician he sees behind the physiological degeneration of the typical Christian. The physician says "incurable";

the philologian says "fraud."...

48.

—Has any one ever clearly understood the celebrated story at the beginning of the Bible—of God's mortal terror of science?... No one, in fact, has understood it. This priest-book par excellence opens, as is fitting, with the great inner difficulty of the priest: he faces only one great danger; ergo, "God" faces only one great danger.—

The old God, wholly "spirit," wholly the high-priest, wholly perfect, is promenading his garden: he is bored and trying to kill time. Against boredom even gods struggle in vain.[21] What does he do? He creates man—man is entertaining.... But then he notices that man is also bored. God's pity for the only form of distress that invades all paradises knows no bounds: so he forthwith creates other animals. God's first mistake: to man these other animals were not entertaining—he sought dominion over them; he did not want to be an "animal" himself.—So God created woman. In the act he brought boredom to an end—and also many other things! Woman was the second mistake of God.—"Woman, at bottom, is a serpent, Heva"— every priest knows that; "from woman comes every evil in the world"—every priest knows that, too. Ergo, she is also to blame for science.... It was through woman that man learned to taste of the tree of knowledge.—What happened? The old God was seized by mortal terror. Man himself had been his greatest blunder; he had created a rival to himself; science makes men godlike—it is all up with priests and gods when man becomes scientific!—Moral: science is the forbidden per se; it alone is forbidden. Science is the first of sins, the germ of all sins, the original sin. This is all there is of morality.— "Thou shall not know":—the rest follows from that.—God's mortal terror, however, did not hinder him from being shrewd. How is one to protect one's self against science? For a long while this was the capital problem. Answer: Out of paradise with man! Happiness, leisure, foster thought—and all thoughts are bad thoughts!—Man must not think.—And so the priest invents distress, death, the mortal dangers of childbirth, all sorts of misery, old age, decrepitude, above all, sickness—nothing but devices for making war on science! The troubles of man don't allow him to think.... Nevertheless—how terrible!—, the edifice of knowledge begins to tower aloft, invading heaven, shadowing the gods—what is to be done?—The old God invents war; he separates the peoples; he makes men destroy one another (—the priests have always had need of war....). War—among other things, a great disturber of science!—Incredible! Knowledge, deliverance from the priests, prospers in spite of war.—So the old God comes to his final resolution: "Man has become scientific—there is no help for it: he must be drowned!"...

[21]A paraphrase of Schiller's "Against stupidity even gods struggle in vain."

49.

—I have been understood. At the opening of the Bible there is the whole psychology of the priest.—The priest knows of only one great danger: that is science—the sound comprehension of cause and effect. But science flourishes, on the whole, only under favourable conditions—a man must have time, he must have an overflowing intellect, in order to "know."... "Therefore, man must be made unhappy,"—this has been, in all ages, the logic of the priest.—It is easy to see just what, by this logic, was the first thing to come into the world:—"sin."... The concept of guilt and punishment, the whole "moral order of the world," was set up against science—against the deliverance of man from priests.... Man must not look outward; he must look inward. He must not look at things shrewdly and cautiously, to learn about them; he must not look at all; he must suffer.... And he must suffer so much that he is always in need of the priest.—Away with physicians! What is needed is a Saviour.—The concept of guilt and punishment, including the doctrines of "grace," of "salvation," of "forgiveness"—lies through and through, and absolutely without psychological reality—were devised to destroy man's sense of causality: they are an attack upon the concept of cause and effect!—And not an attack with the fist, with the knife, with honesty in hate and love! On the contrary, one inspired by the most cowardly, the most crafty, the most ignoble of instincts! An attack of priests! An attack of parasites! The vampirism of pale, subterranean leeches!... When the natural consequences of an act are no longer "natural," but are regarded as produced by the ghostly creations of superstition—by "God," by "spirits," by "souls"—and reckoned as merely "moral" consequences, as rewards, as punishments, as hints, as lessons, then the whole ground-work of knowledge is destroyed—then the greatest of crimes against humanity has been perpetrated.—I repeat that sin, man's self-desecration par excellence, was invented in order to make science, culture, and every elevation and ennobling of man impossible; the priest rules through the invention of sin.—

50.

—In this place I can't permit myself to omit a psychology of "belief," of the "believer," for the special benefit of "believers." If there remain any today who do not yet know how indecent it is to be "believing"—or how much a sign of décadence, of a broken will to live—then they will know it well enough tomorrow. My voice reaches even the deaf.—It appears, unless I have been incorrectly informed, that there prevails among Christians a sort of criterion of truth that is called "proof by power." "Faith makes blessed: therefore it is true."—It might be objected right here that blessedness is not dem onstrated, it is merely promised: it hangs upon "faith" as a condition—one shall be blessed because one believes.... But what of the thing that the priest promises to the believer, the wholly transcendental "beyond"—how is that to be demonstrated?—The "proof by power," thus assumed, is actually no more at bottom than a belief that the effects which faith promises will not fail to appear. In a formula: "I believe that faith makes for blessedness—therefore, it is true."... But this is as far as we may go. This "therefore" would be absurdum itself as a criterion of truth.—But let us admit, for the sake of politeness, that blessedness by faith may be demonstrated (—not merely hoped for, and not merely promised by the suspicious lips of a priest): even so, could blessedness—in a technical term, pleasure—ever be a proof of truth? So little is this true that it is almost a proof against truth when sensations of pleasure influence the answer to the question "What is true?" or, at all events, it is enough to make that "truth" highly suspicious. The proof by "pleasure" is a proof of "pleasure"—nothing more; why in the world should it be assumed that true judgments give more pleasure than false ones, and that, in conformity to some pre-established harmony, they necessarily bring agreeable feelings in their train?—The experience of all disciplined and profound minds teaches the contrary. Man has had to fight for every atom of the truth, and has had to pay for it almost everything that the heart, that human love, that human trust cling to. Greatness of soul is needed for this business: the service of truth is the hardest of all services.—What, then, is the meaning of integrity in things intellectual? It means that a man must be severe with his own heart, that he must scorn "beautiful feelings," and that he makes every Yea and Nay a matter of conscience!—Faith makes blessed: therefore, it lies....

51.

The fact that faith, under certain circumstances, may work for blessedness, but that this blessedness produced by an idée fixe by no means makes the idea itself true, and the fact that faith actually moves no mountains, but instead raises them up where there were none before: all this is made sufficiently clear by a walk through a lunatic asylum. Not, of course, to a priest: for his instincts prompt him to the lie that sickness is not sickness and lunatic asylums not lunatic asylums. Christianity finds sickness necessary, just as the Greek spirit had need of a superabundance of health—the actual ulterior purpose of the whole system of salvation of the church is to make people ill. And the church itself—doesn't it set up a Catholic lunatic asylum as the ultimate ideal?—The whole earth as a madhouse?— The sort of religious man that the church wants is a typical décadent; the moment at which a religious crisis dominates a people is always marked by epidemics of nervous disorder; the "inner world" of the religious man is so much like the "inner world" of the overstrung and exhausted that it is difficult to distinguish between them; the "highest" states of mind, held up before mankind by Christianity as of supreme worth, are actually epileptoid in form—the church has granted the name of holy only to lunatics or to gigantic frauds in majorem dei honorem.... Once I ventured to designate the whole Christian system of training[22] in penance and salvation (now best studied in England) as a method of producing a folie circulaire upon a soil already prepared for it, which is to say, a soil thoroughly unhealthy. Not every one may be a Christian: one is not "converted" to Christianity—one must first be sick enough for it.... We others, who have the courage for health and likewise for contempt,—we may well despise a religion that teaches misunderstanding of the body! that refuses to rid itself of the superstition about the soul! that makes a "virtue" of insufficient nourishment! that combats health as a sort of enemy, devil, temptation! that persuades itself that it is possible to carry about a "perfect soul" in a cadaver of a body, and that, to this end, had to devise for itself a new concept of "perfection," a pale, sickly, idiotically ecstatic state of existence, so-called "holiness"—a holiness that is itself merely a series of symptoms of an impoverished, enervated and incurably disordered body!... The Christian movement, as a European movement, was from the start no more than a general uprising of all sorts of outcast and refuse elements (—who now, under cover of Christianity, aspire to power). It does not represent the decay of a race; it represents, on the contrary, a conglomeration of décadence products from all directions, crowding together and seeking one another out. It was not, as has been thought, the corruption of antiquity, of noble antiquity, which made Christianity possible; one cannot too sharply challenge the learned imbecility which today maintains that theory. At the time when the sick and rotten Chandala classes in the whole imperium were Christianized, the contrary type, the nobility, reached its finest and ripest development. The majority became master; democracy, with its Christian instincts, triumphed.... Christianity was not "national," it was not based on race—it appealed to all the varieties of men disinherited by life, it had its allies everywhere. Christianity has the rancour of the sick at its very core—the instinct against the healthy, against health. Everything that is well-constituted, proud, gallant and, above all, beautiful gives offence to its ears and eyes. Again I remind you of Paul's priceless saying: "And God hath chosen the weak things of the world, the foolish things of the world, the base things of the world, and things which are despised":[23] this was the formula; in hoc signo the décadence triumphed.—God on the cross—is man always to miss the frightful inner significance of this symbol?—Everything that suffers, everything that hangs on the cross, is divine.... We all hang on the cross, consequently we are divine.... We alone are divine.... Christianity was thus a victory: a nobler attitude of mind was destroyed by it—Christianity remains to this day the greatest misfortune of humanity.—

[22]The word training is in English in the text.

[23]1 Corinthians i, 27, 28.

52.

Christianity also stands in opposition to all intellectual well-being,—sick reasoning is the only sort that it can use as Christian reasoning; it takes the side of everything that is idiotic; it pronounces a curse upon "intellect," upon the superbia of the healthy intellect. Since sickness is inherent in Christianity, it follows that the typically Christian state of "faith" must be a form of sickness too, and that all straight, straightforward and scientific paths to knowledge must be banned by the church as forbidden ways. Doubt is thus a sin from the start.... The complete lack of psychological cleanliness in the priest—revealed by a glance at him—is a phenomenon resulting from décadence,—one may observe in hysterical women and in rachitic children how regularly the falsification of instincts, delight in lying for the mere sake of lying, and incapacity for looking straight and walking straight are symptoms of décadence. "Faith" means the will to avoid knowing what is true. The pietist, the priest of either sex, is a fraud because he is sick: his instinct demands that the truth shall never be allowed its rights on any point. "Whatever makes for illness is good; whatever issues from abundance, from superabundance, from power, is evil": so argues the believer. The impulse to lie—it is by this that I recognize every foreordained theologian.—Another characteristic of the theologian is his unfitness for philology. What I here mean by philology is, in a general sense, the art of reading with profit—the capacity for absorbing facts without interpreting them falsely, and without losing caution, patience and subtlety in the effort to understand them. Philology as ephexis[24] in interpretation: whether one be dealing with books, with newspaper reports, with the most fateful events or with weather statistics—not to mention the "salvation of the soul."... The way in which a theologian, whether in Berlin or in Rome, is ready to explain, say, a "passage of Scripture," or an experience, or a victory by the national army, by turning upon it the high illumination of the Psalms of David, is always so daring that it is enough to make a philologian run up a wall. But what shall he do when pietists and other such cows from Suabia[25] use the "finger of God" to convert their miserably commonplace and huggermugger existence into a miracle of "grace," a "providence" and an "experience of salvation"? The most modest exercise of the intellect, not to say of decency, should certainly be enough to convince these interpreters of the perfect childishness and unworthiness of such a misuse of the divine digital dexterity. However small our piety, if we ever encountered a god who always cured us of a cold in the head at just the right time, or got us into our carriage at the very instant heavy rain began to fall, he would seem so absurd a god that he'd have to be abolished even if he existed. God as a domestic servant, as a letter carrier, as an almanac-man—at bottom, he is a mere name for the stupidest sort of chance.... "Divine Prov idence," which every third man in "educated Germany" still believes in, is so strong an argument against God that it would be impossible to think of a stronger. And in any case it is an argument against Germans!...

[24] That is, to say, scepticism. Among the Greeks scepticism was also occasionally called ephecticism.

[25] A reference to the University of Tübingen and its famous school of Biblical criticism. The leader of this school was F. C. Baur, and one

of the men greatly influenced by it was Nietzsche's pet abomination, David F. Strauss, himself a Suabian. Vide § 10 and § 28.

53.

—It is so little true that martyrs offer any support to the truth of a cause that I am inclined to deny that any martyr has ever had anything to do with the truth at all. In the very tone in which a martyr flings what he fancies to be true at the head of the world there appears so low a grade of intellectual honesty and such insensibility to the problem of "truth," that it is never necessary to refute him. Truth is not something that one man has and another man has not: at best, only peasants, or peasant-apostles like Luther, can think of truth in any such way. One may rest assured that the greater the degree of a man's intellectual conscience the greater will be his modesty, his discretion, on this point. To know in five cases, and to refuse, with delicacy, to know anything further.... "Truth," as the word is understood by every prophet, every sectarian, every free-thinker, every Socialist and every churchman, is simply a complete proof that not even a beginning has been made in the intellectual discipline and self-control that are necessary to the unearthing of even the smallest truth.—The deaths of the martyrs, it may be said in passing, have been misfortunes of history: they have misled.... The conclusion that all idiots, women and plebeians come to, that there must be something in a cause for which any one goes to his death (or which, as under primitive Christianity, sets off epidemics of death-seeking)—this conclusion has been an unspeakable drag upon the testing of facts, upon the whole spirit of inquiry and investigation. The martyrs have damaged the truth.... Even to this day the crude fact of persecution is enough to give an honourable name to the most empty sort of sectarianism.— But why? Is the worth of a cause altered by the fact that some one had laid down his life for it?—An error that becomes honourable is simply an error that has acquired one seductive charm the more: do you suppose, Messrs. Theologians, that we shall give you the chance to be martyred for your lies?—One best disposes of a cause by respectfully putting it on ice—that is also the best way to dispose of theologians.... This was precisely the world-historical stupidity of all the persecutors: that they gave the appearance of honour to the cause they opposed—that they made it a present of the fascination of martyrdom.... Women are still on their knees before an error because they have been told that some one died on the cross for it. Is the cross, then, an argument?—But about all these things there is one, and one only, who has said what has been needed for thousands of years—Zarathustra.

They made signs in blood along the way that they went, and their folly taught them that the truth is proved by blood.

But blood is the worst of all testimonies to the truth; blood poisoneth even the purest teaching and turneth it into madness and hatred in the heart.

And when one goeth through fire for his teaching—what doth that prove? Verily, it is more when one's teaching cometh out of one's own burning![26]

[26]The quotations are from "Also sprach Zarathustra" ii, 24: "Of Priests."

54.

Do not let yourself be deceived: great intellects are sceptical. Zarathustra is a sceptic. The strength, the freedom which proceed from intellectual power, from a superabundance of intellectual power, manifest themselves as scepticism. Men of fixed convictions do not count when it comes to determining what is fundamental in values and lack of values. Men of convictions are prisoners. They do not see far enough, they do not see what is below them: whereas a man who would talk to any purpose about value and non-value must be able to see five hundred convictions beneath him—and behind him.... A mind that aspires to great things, and that wills the means thereto, is necessarily sceptical. Freedom from any sort of conviction belongs to strength, and to an independent point of view.... That grand passion which is at once the foundation and the power of a sceptic's existence, and is both more enlightened and more despotic than he is himself, drafts the whole of his intellect into its service; it makes him unscrupulous; it gives him courage to employ unholy means; under certain circumstances it does not begrudge him even convictions. Conviction as a means: one may achieve a good deal by means of a conviction. A grand passion makes use of and uses up convictions; it does not yield to them—it knows itself to be sovereign.—On the contrary, the need of faith, of something unconditioned by yea or nay, of Carlylism, if I may be allowed the word, is a need of weakness. The man of faith, the "believer" of any sort, is necessarily a dependent man—such a man cannot posit himself as a goal, nor can he find goals within himself. The "believer" does not belong to himself; he can only be a means to an end; he must be used up; he needs some one to use him up. His instinct gives the highest honours to an ethic of self-effacement; he is prompted to embrace it by everything: his prudence, his experience, his vanity. Every sort of faith is in itself an evidence of self-effacement, of self-estrangement.... When one reflects how necessary it is to the great majority that there be regulations to restrain them from without and hold them fast, and to what extent control, or, in a higher sense, slavery, is the one and only condition which makes for the well-being of the weak-willed man, and especially woman, then one at once understands conviction and "faith." To the man with convictions they are his backbone. To avoid seeing many things, to be impartial about nothing, to be a party man through and through, to estimate all values strictly and infallibly—these are conditions necessary to the existence of such a man. But by the same token they are antagonists of the truthful man—of the truth.... The believer is not free to answer the question, "true" or "not true," according to the dictates of his own conscience: integrity on this point would work his instant downfall. The pathological limitations of his vision turn the man of convictions into a fanatic—Savonarola, Luther, Rousseau, Robespierre, Saint-Simon—these types stand in opposition to the strong, emancipated spirit. But the grandiose attitudes of these sick intellects, these intellectual epileptics, are of influence upon the great masses—fanatics are picturesque, and mankind prefers observing poses to listening to reasons....

55.

—One step further in the psychology of conviction, of "faith." It is now a good while since I first proposed for consideration the question whether convictions are not even more dangerous enemies to truth than lies. ("Human, All-Too-Human," I, aphorism 483.)[27] This time I desire to put the question definitely: is there any actual difference between a lie and a conviction?—All the world believes that there is; but what is not believed by all the world!—Every conviction has its history, its primitive forms, its stage of tentativeness and error: it becomes a conviction only after having been, for a long time, not one, and then, for an even longer time, hardly one. What if falsehood be also one of these embryonic forms of conviction?—Sometimes all that is needed is a change in persons: what was a lie in the father becomes a conviction in the son.—I call it lying to refuse to see what one sees, or to refuse to see it as it is: whether the lie be uttered before witnesses or not before witnesses is of no consequence. The most common sort of lie is that by which a man deceives himself: the deception of others is a relatively rare offence.—Now, this will not to see what one sees, this will not to see it as it is, is almost the first requisite for all who belong to a party of whatever sort: the party man becomes inevitably a liar. For example, the German historians are convinced that Rome was synonymous with despotism and that the Germanic peoples brought the spirit of liberty into the world: what is the difference between this conviction and a lie? Is it to be wondered at that all partisans, including the German historians, instinctively roll the fine phrases of morality upon their tongues—that morality almost owes its very survival to the fact that the party man of every sort has need of it every moment?—"This is our conviction: we publish it to the whole world; we live and die for it—let us respect all who have convictions!"—I have actually heard such sentiments from the mouths of anti-Semites. On the contrary, gentlemen! An anti-Semite surely does not become more respectable because he lies on principle.... The priests, who have more finesse in such matters, and who well understand the objection that lies against the notion of a conviction, which is to say, of a falsehood that becomes a matter of principle because it serves a purpose, have borrowed from the Jews the shrewd device of sneaking in the concepts, "God," "the will of God" and "the revelation of God" at this place. Kant, too, with his categorical imperative, was on the same road: this was his practical reason.[28] There are questions regarding the truth or untruth of which it is not for man to decide; all the capital questions, all the capital problems of valuation, are beyond human reason.... To know the limits of reason—that alone is genuine philosophy.... Why did God make a revelation to man? Would God have done anything superfluous? Man could not find out for himself what was good and what was evil, so God taught him His will.... Moral: the priest does not lie—the question, "true" or "untrue," has nothing to do with such things as the priest discusses; it is impossible to lie about these things. In order to lie here it would be necessary to know what is true. But this is more than man can know; therefore, the priest is simply the mouthpiece of God.—Such a priestly syllogism is by no means merely Jewish and Christian; the right to lie and the shrewd dodge of "revelation" belong to the general priestly type—to the priest of the décadence as well as to the priest of pagan times (—Pagans are all those who say yes to life, and to whom "God" is a word signifying acquiescence in all things).—The "law," the "will of God," the "holy book," and "inspiration"—all these things are merely words for the conditions under which the priest comes to power and with which he maintains his power,—these concepts are to be found at the bottom of all priestly organizations, and of all priestly or priestly-philosophical schemes of governments. The "holy lie"—common alike to Confucius, to the Code of Manu, to Mohammed and to the Christian church—is not even wanting in Plato. "Truth is here": this means, no matter where it is heard, the priest lies....

[27]The aphorism, which is headed "The Enemies of Truth," makes the direct statement: "Convictions are more dangerous enemies of truth than lies."

[28]A reference, of course, to Kant's "Kritik der praktischen Vernunft" (Critique of Practical Reason).

56.

—In the last analysis it comes to this: what is the end of lying? The fact that, in Christianity, "holy" ends are not visible is my objection to the means it employs. Only bad ends appear: the poisoning, the calumniation, the denial of life, the despising of the body, the degradation and self-contamination of man by the concept of sin—therefore, its means are also bad.—I have a contrary feeling when I read the Code of Manu, an incomparably more intellectual and superior work, which it would be a sin against the intelligence to so much as name in the same breath with the Bible. It is easy to see why: there is a genuine philosophy behind it, in it, not merely an evil-smelling mess of Jewish rabbinism and superstition,—it gives even the most fastidious psychologist something to sink his teeth into. And, not to forget what is most important, it differs fundamentally from every kind of Bible: by means of it the nobles, the philosophers and the warriors keep the whip-hand over the majority; it is full of noble valuations, it shows a feeling of perfection, an acceptance of life, and triumphant feeling toward self and life—the sun shines upon the whole book.—All the things on which Christianity vents its fathomless vulgarity—for example, procreation, women and marriage—are here handled earnestly, with reverence and with love and confidence. How can any one really put into the hands of children and ladies a book which contains such vile things as this: "to avoid fornication, let every man have his own wife, and let every woman have her own husband; ... it is better to marry than to burn"?[29] And is it possible to be a Christian so long as the origin of man is Christianized, which is to say, befouled, by the doctrine of the immaculata conceptio?... I know of no book in which so many delicate and kindly things are said of women as in the Code of Manu; these old grey-beards and saints have a way of being gallant to women that it would be impossible, perhaps, to surpass. "The mouth of a woman," it says in one place, "the breasts of a maiden, the prayer of a child and the smoke of sacrifice are always pure." In another place: "there is nothing purer than the light of the sun, the shadow cast by a cow, air, water, fire and the breath of a maiden." Finally, in still another place—perhaps this is also a holy lie—: "all the orifices of the body above the navel are pure, and all below are impure. Only in the maiden is the whole body pure."

[29]1 Corinthians vii, 2, 9.

57.

One catches the unholiness of Christian means in flagranti by the simple process of putting the ends sought by Christianity beside the ends sought by the Code of Manu—by putting these enormously antithetical ends under a strong light. The critic of Christianity cannot evade the necessity of making Christianity contemptible.—A book of laws such as the Code of Manu has the same origin as every other good law-book: it epitomizes the experience, the sagacity and the ethical experimentation of long centuries; it brings things to a conclusion; it no longer creates. The prerequisite to a codification of this sort is recognition of the fact that the means which establish the authority of a slowly and painfully attained truth are fundamentally different from those which one would make use of to prove it. A law-book never recites the utility, the grounds, the casuistical antecedents of a law: for if it did so it would lose the imperative tone, the "thou shall," on which obedience is based. The problem lies exactly here.— At a certain point in the evolution of a people, the class within it of the greatest insight, which is to say, the greatest hindsight and foresight, declares that the series of experiences determining how all shall live—or can live—has come to an end. The object now is to reap as rich and as complete a harvest as possible from the days of experiment and hard experience. In consequence, the thing that is to be avoided above everything is further experimentation—the continuation of the state in which values are fluent, and are tested, chosen and criticized ad infinitum. Against this a double wall is set up: on the one hand, revelation, which is the assumption that the reasons lying behind the laws are not of human origin, that they were not sought out and found by a slow process and after many errors, but that they are of divine ancestry, and came into being complete, perfect, without a history, as a free gift, a miracle...; and on the other hand, tradition, which is the assumption that the law has stood unchanged from time immemorial, and that it is impious and a crime against one's forefathers to bring it into question. The authority of the law is thus grounded on the thesis: God gave it, and the fathers lived it.—The higher motive of such procedure lies in the design to distract consciousness, step by step, from its concern with notions of right living (that is to say, those that have been proved to be right by wide and carefully considered experience), so that instinct attains to a perfect automatism—a primary necessity to every sort of mastery, to every sort of perfection in the art of life. To draw up such a law-book as Manu's means to lay before a people the possibility of future mastery, of attainable perfection—it permits them to aspire to the highest reaches of the art of life. To that end the thing must be made unconscious: that is the aim of every holy lie.—The order of castes, the highest, the dominating law, is merely the ratification of an order of nature, of a natural law of the first rank, over which no arbitrary fiat, no "modern idea," can exert any influence. In every healthy society there are three physiological types, gravitating toward differentiation but mutually conditioning one another, and each of these has its own hygiene, its own sphere of work, its own special mastery and feeling of perfection. It is not Manu but nature that sets off in one class those who are chiefly intellectual, in another those who are marked by muscular strength and temperament, and in a third those who are distinguished in neither one way or the other, but show only mediocrity—the last-named represents the great majority, and the first two the select. The superior caste—I call it the fewest— has, as the most perfect, the privileges of the few: it stands for happiness, for beauty, for everything good upon earth. Only the most intellectual of men have any right to beauty, to the beautiful; only in them can goodness escape being weakness. Pulchrum est paucorum hominum:[30] goodness is a privilege. Nothing could be more unbecoming to them than uncouth manners or a pessimistic look, or an eye that sees ugliness—or indignation against the general aspect of things. Indigna tion is the privilege of the Chandala; so is pessimism. "The world is perfect"—so prompts the instinct of the intellectual, the instinct of the man who says yes to life. "Imperfection, whatever is inferior to us, distance, the pathos of distance, even the Chandala themselves are parts of this perfection." The most intelligent men, like the strongest, find their happiness where others would find only disaster: in the labyrinth, in being hard with themselves and with others, in effort; their delight is in self-mastery; in them asceticism becomes second nature, a necessity, an instinct. They regard a difficult task as a privilege; it is to them a recreation to play with burdens that would crush all others.... Knowledge—a form of asceticism.—They are the most honourable kind of men: but that does not prevent them being the most cheerful and most amiable. They rule, not because they want to, but because they are; they are not at liberty to play second.—The second caste: to this belong the guardians of the law, the keepers of order and security, the more noble warriors, above all, the king as the highest form of warrior, judge and preserver of the law. The second in rank constitute the executive arm of the intellectuals, the next to them in rank, taking from them all that is rough in the business of ruling—their followers, their right hand, their most apt disciples.—In all this, I repeat, there is nothing arbitrary, nothing "made up"; whatever is to the contrary is made up—by it nature is brought to shame.... The order of castes, the order of rank, simply formulates the supreme law of life itself; the separation of the three types is necessary to the maintenance of society, and to the evolution of higher types, and the highest types—the inequality of rights is essential to the existence of any rights at all.—A right is a privilege. Every one enjoys the privileges that accord with his state of existence. Let us not underestimate the privileges of the mediocre. Life is always harder as one mounts the heights—the cold increases, responsibility increases. A high civilization is a pyramid: it can stand only on a broad base; its primary prerequisite is a strong and soundly consolidated mediocrity. The handicrafts, commerce, agriculture, science, the greater part of art, in brief, the whole range of occupational activities, are compatible only with mediocre ability and aspiration; such callings would be out of place for exceptional men; the instincts which belong to them stand as much opposed to aristocracy as to anarchism. The fact that a man is publicly useful, that he is a wheel, a function, is evidence of a natural predisposition; it is not society, but the only sort of happiness that the majority are capable of, that makes them intelligent machines. To the mediocre mediocrity is a form of happiness; they have a natural instinct for mastering one thing, for specialization. It would be altogether unworthy of a profound intellect to see anything objectionable in mediocrity in itself. It is, in fact, the first prerequisite to the appearance of the exceptional: it is a necessary condition to a high degree of civilization. When the exceptional man handles the mediocre man with more delicate fingers than he applies to himself or to his equals, this is not merely kindness of heart—it is simply his duty.... Whom do I hate most heartily among the rabbles of today? The rabble of Socialists, the apostles to the Chandala, who undermine the workingman's instincts, his pleasure, his feeling of contentment with his petty existence—who make him envious and teach him revenge.... Wrong never lies in unequal rights; it lies in the assertion of "equal" rights.... What is bad? But I have already answered: all that proceeds from weakness, from envy, from revenge.—The anarchist and the Christian have the same ancestry....

[30] Few men are noble.

58.

In point of fact, the end for which one lies makes a great difference: whether one preserves thereby or destroys. There is a perfect likeness between Christian and anarchist: their object, their instinct, points only toward destruction. One need only turn to history for a proof of this: there it appears with appalling distinctness. We have just studied a code of religious legislation whose object it was to convert the conditions which cause life to flourish into an "eternal" social organization,—Christianity found its mission in putting an end to such an organization, because life flourished under it. There the benefits that reason had produced during long ages of experiment and insecurity were applied to the most remote uses, and an effort was made to bring in a harvest that should be as large, as rich and as complete as possible; here, on the contrary, the harvest is blighted overnight.... That which stood there aere perennis, the imperium Romanum, the most magnificent form of organization under difficult conditions that has ever been achieved, and compared to which everything before it and after it appears as patchwork, bungling, dilletantism—those holy anarchists made it a matter of "piety" to destroy "the world," which is to say, the imperium Romanum, so that in the end not a stone stood upon another—and even Germans and other such louts were able to become its masters.... The Christian and the anarchist: both are décadents; both are incapable of any act that is not disintegrating, poisonous, degenerating, blood-sucking; both have an instinct of mortal hatred of everything that stands up, and is great, and has durability, and promises life a future.... Christianity was the vampire of the imperium Romanum,—overnight it destroyed the vast achievement of the Romans: the conquest of the soil for a great culture that could await its time. Can it be that this fact is not yet understood? The imperium Romanum that we know, and that the history of the Roman provinces teaches us to know better and better,—this most admirable of all works of art in the grand manner was merely the beginning, and the structure to follow was not to prove its worth for thousands of years. To this day, nothing on a like scale sub specie aeterni has been brought into being, or even dreamed of!—This organization was strong enough to withstand bad emperors: the accident of personality has nothing to do with such things—the first principle of all genuinely great architecture. But it was not strong enough to stand up against the corruptest of all forms of corruption—against Christians.... These stealthy worms, which under the cover of night, mist and duplicity, crept upon every individual, sucking him dry of all earnest interest in real things, of all instinct for reality—this cowardly, effeminate and sugar-coated gang gradually alienated all "souls," step by step, from that colossal edifice, turning against it all the meritorious, manly and noble natures that had found in the cause of Rome their own cause, their own serious purpose, their own pride. The sneakishness of hypocrisy, the secrecy of the conventicle, concepts as black as hell, such as the sacrifice of the innocent, the unio mystica in the drinking of blood, above all, the slowly rekindled fire of revenge, of Chandala revenge—all that sort of thing became master of Rome: the same kind of religion which, in a pre-existent form, Epicurus had combatted. One has but to read Lucretius to know what Epicurus made war upon—not paganism, but "Christianity," which is to say, the corruption of souls by means of the concepts of guilt, punishment and immortality.—He combatted the subterranean cults, the whole of latent Christianity—to deny immortality was already a form of genuine salvation.—Epicurus had triumphed, and every respectable intellect in Rome was Epicurean—when Paul appeared ... Paul, the Chandala hatred of Rome, of "the world," in the flesh and inspired by genius—the Jew, the eternal Jew par excellence.... What he saw was how, with the aid of the small sectarian Christian movement that stood apart from Judaism, a "world conflagration" might be kindled; how, with the symbol of "God on the cross," all secret seditions, all the fruits of anarchistic intrigues in the empire, might be amalgamated into one immense power. "Salvation is of the Jews."—Christianity is the formula for exceeding and summing up the subterranean cults of all varieties, that of Osiris, that of the Great Mother, that of Mithras, for instance: in his discernment of this fact the genius of Paul showed itself. His instinct was here so sure that, with reckless violence to the truth, he put the ideas which lent fascination to every sort of Chandala religion into the mouth of the "Saviour" as his own inventions, and not only into the mouth—he made out of him something that even a priest of Mithras could understand.... This was his revelation at Damascus: he grasped the fact that he needed the belief in immortality in order to rob "the world" of its value, that the concept of "hell" would master Rome—that the notion of a "beyond" is the death of life.... Nihilist and Christian: they rhyme in German, and they do more than rhyme....

59.

The whole labour of the ancient world gone for naught: I have no word to describe the feelings that such an enormity arouses in me.—And, considering the fact that its labour was merely preparatory, that with adamantine self-consciousness it laid only the foundations for a work to go on for thousands of years, the whole meaning of antiquity disappears!... To what end the Greeks? to what end the Romans?—All the prerequisites to a learned culture, all the methods of science, were already there; man had already perfected the great and incomparable art of reading profitably—that first necessity to the tradition of culture, the unity of the sciences; the natural sciences, in alliance with mathematics and mechanics, were on the right road,—the sense of fact, the last and more valuable of all the senses, had its schools, and its traditions were already centuries old! Is all this properly understood? Every essential to the beginning of the work was ready:—and the most essential, it cannot be said too often, are methods, and also the most difficult to develop, and the longest opposed by habit and laziness. What we have today reconquered, with unspeakable self-discipline, for ourselves—for certain bad instincts, certain Christian instincts, still lurk in our bodies—that is to say, the keen eye for reality, the cautious hand, patience and seriousness in the smallest things, the whole integrity of knowledge—all these things were already there, and had been there for two thousand years! More, there was also a refined and excellent tact and taste! Not as mere brain-drilling! Not as "German" culture, with its loutish manners! But as body, as bearing, as instinct—in short, as reality.... All gone for naught! Overnight it became merely a memory!—The Greeks! The Romans! Instinctive nobility, taste, methodical inquiry, genius for organization and administration, faith in and the will to secure the future of man, a great yes to everything entering into the imperium Romanum and palpable to all the senses, a grand style that was beyond mere art, but had become reality, truth, life....—All overwhelmed in a night, but not by a convulsion of nature! Not trampled to death by Teutons and others of heavy hoof! But brought to shame by crafty, sneaking, invisible, anæmic vampires! Not conquered,—only sucked dry!... Hidden vengefulness, petty envy, became master! Everything wretched, intrinsically ailing, and invaded by bad feelings, the whole ghetto-world of the soul, was at once on top!—One needs but read any of the Christian agitators, for example, St. Augustine, in order to realize, in order to smell, what filthy fellows came to the top. It would be an error, however, to assume that there was any lack of understanding in the leaders of the Christian movement:—ah, but they were clever, clever to the point of holiness, these fathers of the church! What they lacked was something quite different. Nature neglected—perhaps forgot—to give them even the most modest endowment of respectable, of upright, of cleanly instincts.... Between ourselves, they are not even men.... If Islam despises Christianity, it has a thousandfold right to do so: Islam at least assumes that it is dealing with men....

60.

Christianity destroyed for us the whole harvest of ancient civilization, and later it also destroyed for us the whole harvest of Mohammedan civilization. The wonderful culture of the Moors in Spain, which was fundamentally nearer to us and appealed more to our senses and tastes than that of Rome and Greece, was trampled down (—I do not say by what sort of feet—) Why? Because it had to thank noble and manly instincts for its origin—because it said yes to life, even to the rare and refined luxuriousness of Moorish life!... The crusaders later made war on something before which it would have been more fitting for them to have grovelled in the dust—a civilization beside which even that of our nineteenth century seems very poor and very "senile."— What they wanted, of course, was booty: the orient was rich.... Let us put aside our prejudices! The crusades were a higher form of piracy, nothing more! The German nobility, which is fundamentally a Viking nobility, was in its element there: the church knew only too well how the German nobility was to be won.... The German noble, always the "Swiss guard" of the church, always in the service of every bad instinct of the church—but well paid.... Consider the fact that it is precisely the aid of German swords and German blood and valour that has enabled the church to carry through its war to the death upon everything noble on earth! At this point a host of painful questions suggest themselves. The German nobility stands outside the history of the higher civilization: the reason is obvious.... Christianity, alcohol— the two great means of corruption.... Intrinsically there should be no more choice between Islam and Christianity than there is between an Arab and a Jew. The decision is already reached; nobody remains at liberty to choose here. Either a man is a Chandala or he is not.... "War to the knife with Rome! Peace and friendship with Islam!": this was the feeling, this was the act, of that great free spirit, that genius among German emperors, Frederick II. What! must a German first be a genius, a free spirit, before he can feel decently? I can't make out how a German could ever feel Christian....

61.

Here it becomes necessary to call up a memory that must be a hundred times more painful to Germans. The Germans have destroyed for Europe the last great harvest of civilization that Europe was ever to reap—the Renaissance. Is it understood at last, will it ever be understood, what the Renaissance was? The transvaluation of Christian values,—an attempt with all available means, all instincts and all the resources of genius to bring about a triumph of the opposite values, the more noble values.... This has been the one great war of the past; there has never been a more critical question than that of the Renaissance—it is my question too—; there has never been a form of attack more fundamental, more direct, or more violently delivered by a whole front upon the center of the enemy! To attack at the critical place, at the very seat of Christianity, and there enthrone the more noble values—that is to say, to insinuate them into the instincts, into the most fundamental needs and appetites of those sitting there.... I see before me the possibility of a perfectly heavenly enchantment and spectacle:—it seems to me to scintillate with all the vibrations of a fine and delicate beauty, and within it there is an art so divine, so infernally divine, that one might search in vain for thousands of years for another such possibility; I see a spectacle so rich in significance and at the same time so wonderfully full of paradox that it should arouse all the gods on Olympus to immortal laughter—Cæsar Borgia as pope!... Am I understood?... Well then, that would have been the sort of triumph that I alone am longing for today—: by it Christianity would have been swept away!—What happened? A German monk, Luther, came to Rome. This monk, with all the vengeful instincts of an unsuccessful priest in him, raised a rebellion against the Renaissance in Rome.... Instead of grasping, with profound thanksgiving, the miracle that had taken place: the conquest of Christianity at its capital—instead of this, his hatred was stimulated by the spectacle. A religious man thinks only of himself.—Luther saw only the depravity of the papacy at the very moment when the opposite was becoming apparent: the old corruption, the peccatum originale, Christianity itself, no longer occupied the papal chair! Instead there was life! Instead there was the triumph of life! Instead there was a great yea to all lofty, beautiful and daring things!... And Luther restored the church: he attacked it.... The Renaissance—an event without meaning, a great futility!—Ah, these Germans, what they have not cost us! Futility—that has always been the work of the Germans.— The Reformation; Leibnitz; Kant and so-called German philosophy; the war of "liberation"; the empire—every time a futile substitute for something that once existed, for something irrecoverable.... These Germans, I confess, are my enemies: I despise all their uncleanliness in concept and valuation, their cowardice before every honest yea and nay. For nearly a thousand years they have tangled and confused everything their fingers have touched; they have on their conscience all the half-way measures, all the three-eighths-way measures, that Europe is sick of,—they also have on their conscience the uncleanest variety of Christianity that exists, and the most incurable and indestructible—Protestantism.... If man kind never manages to get rid of Christianity the Germans will be to blame....

62.

—With this I come to a conclusion and pronounce my judgment. I condemn Christianity; I bring against the Christian church the most terrible of all the accusations that an accuser has ever had in his mouth. It is, to me, the greatest of all imaginable corruptions; it seeks to work the ultimate corruption, the worst possible corruption. The Christian church has left nothing untouched by its depravity; it has turned every value into worthlessness, and every truth into a lie, and every integrity into baseness of soul. Let any one dare to speak to me of its "humanitarian" blessings! Its deepest necessities range it against any effort to abolish distress; it lives by distress; it creates distress to make itself immortal.... For example, the worm of sin: it was the church that first enriched mankind with this misery!—The "equality of souls before God"—this fraud, this pretext for the rancunes of all the base-minded—this explosive concept, ending in revolution, the modern idea, and the notion of overthrowing the whole social order —this is Christian dynamite.... The "humanitarian" blessings of Christianity forsooth! To breed out of humanitas a self-contradiction, an art of self-pollution, a will to lie at any price, an aversion and contempt for all good and honest instincts! All this, to me, is the "humanitarianism" of Christianity!—Parasitism as the only practice of the church; with its anæmic and "holy" ideals, sucking all the blood, all the love, all the hope out of life; the beyond as the will to deny all reality; the cross as the distinguishing mark of the most subterranean conspiracy ever heard of,—against health, beauty, well-being, intellect, kindness of soul—against life itself....

This eternal accusation against Christianity I shall write upon all walls, wherever walls are to be found—I have letters that even the blind will be able to see.... I call Christianity the one great curse, the one great intrinsic depravity, the one great instinct of revenge, for which no means are venomous enough, or secret, subterranean and small enough,—I call it the one immortal blemish upon the human race....

And mankind reckons time from the dies nefastus when this fatality befell—from the first day of Christianity!—Why not rather from its last?—From today?—The transvaluation of all values!...

THE END

The Gay Science: With a Prelude in Rhymes and an Appendix of Songs

EDITORIAL NOTE

"The Joyful Wisdom," written in 1882, just before "Zarathustra," is rightly judged to be one of Nietzsche's best books. Here the essentially grave and masculine face of the poet-philosopher is seen to light up and suddenly break into a delightful smile. The warmth and kindness that beam from his features will astonish those hasty psychologists who have never divined that behind the destroyer is the creator, and behind the blasphemer the lover of life. In the retrospective valuation of his work which appears in "Ecce Homo" the author himself observes with truth that the fourth book, "Sanctus Januarius," deserves especial attention: "The whole book is a gift from the Saint, and the introductory verses express my gratitude for the most wonderful month of January that I have ever spent." Book fifth "We Fearless Ones," the Appendix "Songs of Prince Free-as-a-Bird," and the Preface, were added to the second edition in 1887.

The translation of Nietzsche's poetry has proved viiito be a more embarrassing problem than that of his prose. Not only has there been a difficulty in finding adequate translators—a difficulty overcome, it is hoped, by the choice of Miss Petre and Mr Cohn,—but it cannot be denied that even in the original the poems are of unequal merit. By the side of such masterpieces as "To the Mistral" are several verses of comparatively little value. The Editor, however, did not feel justified in making a selection, as it was intended that the edition should be complete. The heading, "Jest, Ruse and Revenge," of the "Prelude in Rhyme" is borrowed from Goethe.

JEST, RUSE AND REVENGE.
A PRELUDE IN RHYME.

1.

Invitation.
Venture, comrades, I implore you,
On the fare I set before you,
You will like it more to-morrow,
Better still the following day:
If yet more you're then requiring,
Old success I'll find inspiring,
And fresh courage thence will borrow
Novel dainties to display.

2.

My Good Luck.
Weary of Seeking had I grown,
So taught myself the way to Find:
Back by the storm I once was blown,
But follow now, where drives the wind.

3.

Undismayed.
Where you're standing, dig, dig out:
Down below's the Well:
Let them that walk in darkness shout:
"Down below—there's Hell!"

4.

Dialogue.
A. Was I ill? and is it ended?
Pray, by what physician tended?
I recall no pain endured!
B. Now I know your trouble's ended:
He that can forget, is cured.

5.

To the Virtuous.
Let our virtues be easy and nimble-footed in motion,
Like unto Homer's verse ought they to come and to go.

6.

Worldly Wisdom.
Stay not on level plain,
Climb not the mount too high,
But half-way up remain—
The world you'll best descry!

7.

Vademecum—Vadetecum.
Attracted by my style and talk
You'd follow, in my footsteps walk?
Follow yourself unswervingly,
So—careful!—shall you follow me.

8.

The Third Sloughing.
My skin bursts, breaks for fresh rebirth,
And new desires come thronging:
Much I've devoured, yet for more earth
The serpent in me's longing.
'Twixt stone and grass I crawl once more,
Hungry, by crooked ways,
To eat the food I ate before,
Earth-fare all serpents praise!

9.

My Roses.
My luck's good—I'd make yours fairer,
(Good luck ever needs a sharer),
Will you stop and pluck my roses?
Oft mid rocks and thorns you'll linger,
Hide and stoop, suck bleeding finger—
Will you stop and pluck my roses?
For my good luck's a trifle vicious,
Fond of teasing, tricks malicious—
Will you stop and pluck my roses?

10.

The Scorner.
Many drops I waste and spill,
So my scornful mood you curse:
Who to brim his cup doth fill,
Many drops must waste and spill—
Yet he thinks the wine no worse.

11.
The Proverb Speaks.
Harsh and gentle, fine and mean,
Quite rare and common, dirty and clean,
The fools' and the sages' go-between:
All this I will be, this have been,
Dove and serpent and swine, I ween!

12.
To a Lover of Light.
That eye and sense be not fordone
E'en in the shade pursue the sun!

13.
For Dancers.
Smoothest ice,
A paradise
To him who is a dancer nice.

14.
The Brave Man.
A feud that knows not flaw nor break,
Rather then patched-up friendship, take.

15.
Rust.
Rust's needed: keenness will not satisfy!
"He is too young!" the rabble loves to cry.

16.
Excelsior.
"How shall I reach the top?" No time
For thus reflecting! Start to climb!

17.
The Man of Power Speaks.
Ask never! Cease that whining, pray!
Take without asking, take alway!

18.
Narrow Souls.
Narrow souls hate I like the devil,
Souls wherein grows nor good nor evil.

19.

Accidentally a Seducer.[3]
He shot an empty word
Into the empty blue;
But on the way it met
A woman whom it slew.

20.

For Consideration.
A twofold pain is easier far to bear
Than one: so now to suffer wilt thou dare?

21.

Against Pride.
Brother, to puff thyself up ne'er be quick:
For burst thou shalt be by a tiny prick!

22.

Man and Woman.
"The woman seize, who to thy heart appeals!"
Man's motto: woman seizes not, but steals.

23.

Interpretation.
If I explain my wisdom, surely
'Tis but entangled more securely,
I can't expound myself aright:
But he that's boldly up and doing,
His own unaided course pursuing,
Upon my image casts more light!

24.

A Cure for Pessimism.
Those old capricious fancies, friend!
You say your palate naught can please,
I hear you bluster, spit and wheeze,
My love, my patience soon will end!
Pluck up your courage, follow me—
Here's a fat toad! Now then, don't blink,
Swallow it whole, nor pause to think!
From your dyspepsia you'll be free!

25.

A Request.
Many men's minds I know full well,
Yet what mine own is, cannot tell.

I cannot see—my eye's too near—
And falsely to myself appear.
'Twould be to me a benefit
Far from myself if I could sit,
Less distant than my enemy,
19And yet my nearest friend's too nigh—
'Twixt him and me, just in the middle!
What do I ask for? Guess my riddle!

26.

My Cruelty.
I must ascend an hundred stairs,
I must ascend: the herd declares
I'm cruel: "Are we made of stone?"
I must ascend an hundred stairs:
All men the part of stair disown.

27.

The Wanderer.
"No longer path! Abyss and silence chilling!"
Thy fault! To leave the path thou wast too willing!
Now comes the test! Keep cool—eyes bright and clear!
Thou'rt lost for sure, if thou permittest—fear.

28.

Encouragement for Beginners.
See the infant, helpless creeping—
Swine around it grunt swine-talk—
Weeping always, naught but weeping,
Will it ever learn to walk?
Never fear! Just wait, I swear it
Soon to dance will be inclined,
And this babe, when two legs bear it,
Standing on its head you'll find.

29.

Planet Egoism.
Did I not turn, a rolling cask,
Ever about myself, I ask,
How could I without burning run
Close on the track of the hot sun?

30.

The Neighbour.
Too nigh, my friend my joy doth mar,
I'd have him high above and far,

Or how can he become my star?

31.
The Disguised Saint.
Lest we for thy bliss should slay thee,
In devil's wiles thou dost array thee,
Devil's wit and devil's dress.
But in vain! Thy looks betray thee
And proclaim thy holiness.

32.
The Slave.
A. He stands and listens: whence his pain?
What smote his ears? Some far refrain?
Why is his heart with anguish torn?
B. Like all that fetters once have worn,
He always hears the clinking—chain!

33.
The Lone One.
I hate to follow and I hate to lead.
Obedience? no! and ruling? no, indeed!
Wouldst fearful be in others' sight?
Then e'en thyself thou must affright:
The people but the Terror's guidance heed.
I hate to guide myself, I hate the fray.
Like the wild beasts I'll wander far afield.
In Error's pleasing toils I'll roam
Awhile, then lure myself back home,
Back home, and—to my self-seduction yield.

34.
Seneca et hoc Genus omne.
They write and write (quite maddening me)
Their "sapient" twaddle airy,
As if 'twere primum scribere,
Deinde philosophari.

35.
Ice.
Yes! I manufacture ice:
Ice may help you to digest:
If you had much to digest,
How you would enjoy my ice!

36.

Youthful Writings.
My wisdom's A and final O
Was then the sound that smote mine ear.
22Yet now it rings no longer so,
My youth's eternal Ah! and Oh!
Is now the only sound I hear.[4]

37.

Foresight.
In yonder region travelling, take good care!
An hast thou wit, then be thou doubly ware!
They'll smile and lure thee; then thy limbs they'll tear:
Fanatics' country this where wits are rare!

38.

The Pious One Speaks.
God loves us, for he made us, sent us here!—
"Man hath made God!" ye subtle ones reply.
His handiwork he must hold dear,
And what he made shall he deny?
There sounds the devil's halting hoof, I fear.

39.

In Summer.
In sweat of face, so runs the screed,
We e'er must eat our bread,
Yet wise physicians if we heed
"Eat naught in sweat," 'tis said.
The dog-star's blinking: what's his need?
What tells his blazing sign?
In sweat of face (so runs his screed)
We're meant to drink our wine!

40.

Without Envy.
His look bewrays no envy: and ye laud him?
He cares not, asks not if your throng applaud him!
He has the eagle's eye for distance far,
He sees you not, he sees but star on star!

41.

Heraclitism.
Brethren, war's the origin
Of happiness on earth:
Powder-smoke and battle-din

Witness friendship's birth!
Friendship means three things, you know,—
Kinship in luckless plight,
Equality before the foe
Freedom—in death's sight!

42.

Maxim of the Over-refined.
"Rather on your toes stand high
Than crawl upon all fours,
Rather through the keyhole spy
Than through open doors!"

43.

Exhortation.
Renown you're quite resolved to earn?
My thought about it
Is this: you need not fame, must learn
To do without it!

44.

Thorough.
I an Inquirer? No, that's not my calling
Only I weigh a lot—I'm such a lump!—
And through the waters I keep falling, falling,
Till on the ocean's deepest bed I bump.

45.

The Immortals.
"To-day is meet for me, I come to-day,"
Such is the speech of men foredoomed to stay.
"Thou art too soon," they cry, "thou art too late,"
What care the Immortals what the rabble say?

46.

Verdicts of the Weary.
The weary shun the glaring sun, afraid,
And only care for trees to gain the shade.

47.

Descent.
"He sinks, he falls," your scornful looks portend:
The truth is, to your level he'll descend.
His Too Much Joy is turned to weariness,
His Too Much Light will in your darkness end.

48.

Nature Silenced.[5]
Around my neck, on chain of hair,
The timepiece hangs—a sign of care.
For me the starry course is o'er,
No sun and shadow as before,
No cockcrow summons at the door,
For nature tells the time no more!
Too many clocks her voice have drowned,
And droning law has dulled her sound.

49.

The Sage Speaks.
Strange to the crowd, yet useful to the crowd,
I still pursue my path, now sun, now cloud,
But always pass above the crowd!

50.

He lost his Head....
She now has wit—how did it come her way?
A man through her his reason lost, they say.
His head, though wise ere to this pastime lent,
Straight to the devil—no, to woman went!

51.

A Pious Wish.
"Oh, might all keys be lost! 'Twere better so
And in all keyholes might the pick-lock go!"
Who thus reflects ye may as—picklock know.

52.

Foot Writing.
I write not with the hand alone,
My foot would write, my foot that capers,
Firm, free and bold, it's marching on
Now through the fields, now through the papers.

53.

"Human, All-too-Human."...
Shy, gloomy, when your looks are backward thrust,
Trusting the future where yourself you trust,
Are you an eagle, mid the nobler fowl,
Or are you like Minerva's darling owl?

54.
To my Reader.
Good teeth and a digestion good
I wish you—these you need, be sure!
And, certes, if my book you've stood,
Me with good humour you'll endure.

55.
The Realistic Painter.
"To nature true, complete!" so he begins.
Who complete Nature to his canvas wins?
Her tiniest fragment's endless, no constraint
Can know: he paints just what his fancy pins:
What does his fancy pin? What he can paint!

56.
Poets' Vanity.
Glue, only glue to me dispense,
The wood I'll find myself, don't fear!
To give four senseless verses sense—
That's an achievement I revere!

57.
Taste in Choosing.
If to choose my niche precise
Freedom I could win from fate,
I'd be in midst of Paradise—
Or, sooner still—before the gate!

58.
The Crooked Nose.
Wide blow your nostrils, and across
The land your nose holds haughty sway:
So you, unhorned rhinoceros,
Proud mannikin, fall forward aye!
The one trait with the other goes:
A straight pride and a crooked nose.

59.
The Pen is Scratching....
The pen is scratching: hang the pen!
To scratching I'm condemned to sink!
I grasp the inkstand fiercely then
And write in floods of flowing ink.
How broad, how full the stream's career!
What luck my labours doth requite!

'Tis true, the writing's none too clear—
What then? Who reads the stuff I write?

60.

Loftier Spirits.
This man's climbing up—let us praise him—
But that other we love
From aloft doth eternally move,
So above even praise let us raise him,
He comes from above!

61.

The Sceptic Speaks.
Your life is half-way o'er;
The clock-hand moves; your soul is thrilled with fear,
It roamed to distant shore
And sought and found not, yet you—linger here!
Your life is half-way o'er;
That hour by hour was pain and error sheer:
Why stay? What seek you more?
"That's what I'm seeking—reasons why I'm here!"

62.

Ecce Homo.
Yes, I know where I'm related,
Like the flame, unquenched, unsated,
I consume myself and glow:
All's turned to light I lay my hand on,
All to coal that I abandon,
Yes, I am a flame, I know!

63.

Star Morality.[6]
Foredoomed to spaces vast and far,
What matters darkness to the star?
Roll calmly on, let time go by,
Let sorrows pass thee—nations die!
Compassion would but dim the light
That distant worlds will gladly sight.
To thee one law—be pure and bright!

BOOK FIRST
1.

The Teachers of the Object of Existence.—Whether I look with a good or an evil eye upon men, I find them always at one problem, each and all of them: to do that which conduces to the conservation of the human species. And certainly not out of any sentiment of love for this species, but simply because nothing in them is older, stronger, more inexorable, and more unconquerable than that instinct,— because it is precisely the essence of our race and herd. Although we are accustomed readily enough, with our usual short-sightedness, to separate our neighbours precisely into useful and hurtful, into good and evil men, yet when we make a general calculation, and on longer reflection on the whole question, we become distrustful of this defining and separating, and finally leave it alone. Even the most hurtful man is still perhaps, in respect to the conservation of the race, the most useful of all; for he conserves in himself or by his effect on others, impulses without which mankind might long ago have languished or decayed. Hatred, delight in mischief, rapacity and ambition, and whatever else is called evil—belong to the marvellous economy of the conservation of the race; to be sure a costly, lavish, and on the whole very foolish economy:—which has, however, hitherto preserved our race, as is demonstrated to us. I no longer know, my dear fellow-man and neighbour, if thou canst at all live to the disadvantage of the race, and therefore, "unreasonably" and "badly"; that which could have injured the race has perhaps died out many millenniums ago, and now belongs to the things which are no longer possible even to God. Indulge thy best or thy worst desires, and above all, go to wreck!—in either case thou art still probably the furtherer and benefactor of mankind in some way or other, and in that respect thou mayest have thy panegyrists—and similarly thy mockers! But thou wilt never find him who would be quite qualified to mock at thee, the individual, at thy best, who could bring home to thy conscience its limitless, buzzing and croaking wretchedness so as to be in accord with truth! To laugh at oneself as one would have to laugh in order to laugh out of the veriest truth,—to do this the best have not hitherto had enough of the sense of truth, and the most endowed have had far too little genius! There is perhaps still a future even for laughter! When the maxim, "The race is all, the individual is nothing,"—has incorporated itself in humanity, and when access stands open to every one at all times to this ultimate emancipation and irresponsibility.—Perhaps then laughter will have united with wisdom, perhaps then there will be only "joyful wisdom."

Meanwhile, however, it is quite otherwise, meanwhile the comedy of existence has not yet "become conscious" of itself, meanwhile it is still the period of tragedy, the period of morals and religions. What does the ever new appearing of founders of morals and religions, of instigators of struggles for moral valuations, of teachers of remorse of conscience and religious war, imply? What do these heroes on this stage imply? For they have hitherto been the heroes of it, and all else, though solely visible for the time being, and too close to one, has served only as preparation for these heroes, whether as machinery and coulisse, or in the rôle of confidants and valets. (The poets, for example, have always been the valets of some morality or other.)— It is obvious of itself that these tragedians also work in the interest of the race, though they may believe that they work in the interest of God, and as emissaries of God. They also further the life of the species, in that they further the belief in life. "It is worth while to live"—each of them calls out,—"there is something of importance in this life; life has something behind it and under it; take care!" That impulse, which rules equally in the noblest and the ignoblest, the impulse towards the conservation of the species, breaks forth from time to time as reason and passion of spirit; it has then a brilliant train of motives about it, and tries with all its power to make us forget that fundamentally it is just impulse, instinct, folly and baselessness. Life should be loved, for ...! Man should benefit himself and his neighbour, for ...! And whatever all these shoulds and fors imply, and may imply in future! In order that that which necessarily and always happens of itself and without design, may henceforth appear to be done by design, and may appeal to men as reason and ultimate command,—for that purpose the ethiculturist comes forward as the teacher of design in existence; for that purpose he devises a second and different existence, and by means of this new mechanism he lifts the old common existence off its old common hinges. No! he does not at all want us to laugh at existence, nor even at ourselves—nor at himself; to him an individual is always an individual, something first and last and immense, to him there are no species, no sums, no noughts. However foolish and fanatical his inventions and valuations may be, however much he may misunderstand the course of nature and deny its conditions—and all systems of ethics hitherto have been foolish and anti-natural to such a degree that mankind would have been ruined by any one of them had it got the upper hand,—at any rate, every time that "the hero" came upon the stage something new was attained: the frightful counterpart of laughter, the profound convulsion of many individuals at the thought, "Yes, it is worth while to live! yes, I am worthy to live!"—life, and thou, and I, and all of us together became for a while interesting to ourselves once more.— It is not to be denied that hitherto laughter and reason and nature have in the long run got the upper hand of all the great teachers of design: in the end the short tragedy always passed over once more into the eternal comedy of existence; and the "waves of innumerable laughters"—to use the expression of Æschylus—must also in the end beat over the greatest of these tragedies. But with all this corrective laughter, human nature has on the whole been changed by the ever new appearance of those teachers of the design of existence,—human nature has now an additional requirement, the very requirement of the ever new appearance of such teachers and doctrines of "design." Man has gradually become a visionary animal, who has to fulfil one more condition of existence than the other animals: man must from time to time believe that he knows why he exists; his species cannot flourish without periodically confiding in life! Without the belief in reason in life! And always from time to time will the human race decree anew that "there is something which really may not be laughed at." And the most clairvoyant philanthropist will add that "not only laughing and joyful wisdom, but also the tragic, with all its sublime irrationality, counts among the means and necessities for the conservation of the race!"—And consequently! Consequently! Consequently! Do you understand me, oh my brothers? Do you understand this new law of ebb and flow? We also shall have our time!

2.

The Intellectual Conscience.—I have always the same experience over again, and always make a new effort against it; for although it is evident to me I do not want to believe it: in the greater number of men the intellectual conscience is lacking; indeed, it would often seem to me that in demanding such a thing, one is as solitary in the largest cities as in the desert. Everyone looks at you with strange eyes, and continues to make use of his scales, calling this good and that bad; and no one blushes for shame when you remark that these weights are not the full amount,—there is also no indignation against you; perhaps they laugh at your doubt. I mean to say that the greater number of people do not find it contemptible to believe this or that, and live according to it, without having been previously aware of the ultimate and surest reasons for and against it, and without even giving themselves any trouble about such reasons afterwards,—the most gifted men and the noblest women still belong to this "greater number." But what is kind-heartedness, refinement and genius to me, if the man with these virtues harbours indolent sentiments in belief and judgment, if the longing for certainty does not rule in him, as his innermost desire and profoundest need—as that which separates higher from lower men! In certain pious people I have found a hatred of reason, and have been favourably disposed to them for it:

their bad, intellectual conscience still betrayed itself, at least in this manner! But to stand in the midst of this rerum concordia discors and all the marvellous uncertainty and ambiguity of existence, and not to question, not to tremble with desire and delight in questioning, not even to hate the questioner—perhaps even to make merry over him to the extent of weariness—that is what I regard as contemptible, and it is this sentiment which I first of all search for in every one:—some folly or other always persuades me anew that every man has this sentiment, as man. This is my special kind of unrighteousness.

3.

Noble and Ignoble.—To ignoble natures all noble, magnanimous sentiments appear inexpedient, and on that account first and foremost, as incredible: they blink with their eyes when they hear of such matters, and seem inclined to say, "there will, no doubt, be some advantage therefrom, one cannot see through all walls;"—they are jealous of the noble person, as if he sought advantage by back-stair methods. When they are all too plainly convinced of the absence of selfish intentions and emoluments, the noble person is regarded by them as a kind of fool: they despise him in his gladness, and laugh at the lustre of his eye. "How can a person rejoice at being at a disadvantage, how can a person with open eyes want to meet with disadvantage! It must be a disease of the reason with which the noble affection is associated,"—so they think, and they look depreciatingly thereon; just as they depreciate the joy which the lunatic derives from his fixed idea. The ignoble nature is distinguished by the fact that it keeps its advantage steadily in view, and that this thought of the end and advantage is even stronger than its strongest impulse: not to be tempted to inexpedient activities by its impulses—that is its wisdom and inspiration. In comparison with the ignoble nature the higher nature is more irrational:—for the noble, magnanimous, and self-sacrificing person succumbs in fact to his impulses, and in his best moments his reason lapses altogether. An animal, which at the risk of life protects its young, or in the pairing season follows the female where it meets with death, does not think of the risk and the death; its reason pauses likewise, because its delight in its young, or in the female, and the fear of being deprived of this delight, dominate it exclusively; it becomes stupider than at other times, like the noble and magnanimous person. He possesses feelings of pleasure and pain of such intensity that the intellect must either be silent before them, or yield itself to their service: his heart then goes into his head, and one henceforth speaks of "passions." (Here and there to be sure, the antithesis to this, and as it were the "reverse of passion," presents itself; for example in Fontenelle, to whom some one once laid the hand on the heart with the words, "What you have there, my dearest friend, is brain also.") It is the unreason, or perverse reason of passion, which the ignoble man despises in the noble individual, especially when it concentrates upon objects whose value appears to him to be altogether fantastic and arbitrary. He is offended at him who succumbs to the passion of the belly, but he understands the allurement which here plays the tyrant; but he does not understand, for example, how a person out of love of knowledge can stake his health and honour on the game. The taste of the higher nature devotes itself to exceptional matters, to things which usually do not affect people, and seem to have no sweetness; the higher nature has a singular standard of value. Besides, it is mostly of the belief that it has not a singular standard of value in its idiosyncrasies of taste; it rather sets up its values and non-values as the generally valid values and non-values, and thus becomes incomprehensible and impracticable. It is very rarely that a higher nature has so much reason over and above as to understand and deal with everyday men as such; for the most part it believes in its passion as if it were the concealed passion of every one, and precisely in this belief it is full of ardour and eloquence. If then such exceptional men do not perceive themselves as exceptions, how can they ever understand the ignoble natures and estimate average men fairly! Thus it is that they also speak of the folly, inexpediency and fantasy of mankind, full of astonishment at the madness of the world, and that it will not recognise the "one thing needful for it."—This is the eternal unrighteousness of noble natures.

4.

That which Preserves the Species.—The strongest and most evil spirits have hitherto advanced mankind the most: they always rekindled the sleeping passions—all orderly arranged society lulls the passions to sleep; they always reawakened the sense of comparison, of contradiction, of delight in the new, the adventurous, the untried; they compelled men to set opinion against opinion, ideal plan against ideal plan. By means of arms, by upsetting boundary-stones, by violations of piety most of all: but also by new religions and morals! The same kind of "wickedness" is in every teacher and preacher of the new—which makes a conqueror infamous, although it expresses itself more refinedly, and does not immediately set the muscles in motion (and just on that account does not make so infamous!). The new, however, is under all circumstances the evil, as that which wants to conquer, which tries to upset the old boundary-stones and the old piety; only the old is the good! The good men of every age are those who go to the roots of the old thoughts and bear fruit with them, the agriculturists of the spirit. But every soil becomes finally exhausted, and the ploughshare of evil must always come once more.—There is at present a fundamentally erroneous theory of morals which is much celebrated, especially in England: according to it the judgments "good" and "evil" are the accumulation of the experiences of that which is "expedient" and "inexpedient"; according to this theory, that which is called good is conservative of the species, what is called evil, however, is detrimental to it. But in reality the evil impulses are just in as high a degree expedient, indispensable, and conservative of the species as the good:—only, their function is different.

5.

Unconditional Duties.—All men who feel that they need the strongest words and intonations, the most eloquent gestures and attitudes, in order to operate at all—revolutionary politicians, socialists, preachers of repentance with or without Christianity, with all of whom there must be no mere half-success,—all these speak of "duties," and indeed, always of duties, which have the character of being unconditional—without 41such they would have no right to their excessive pathos: they know that right well! They grasp, therefore, at philosophies of morality which preach some kind of categorical imperative, or they assimilate a good lump of religion, as, for example, Mazzini did. Because they want to be trusted unconditionally, it is first of all necessary for them to trust themselves unconditionally, on the basis of some ultimate, undebatable command, sublime in itself, as the ministers and instruments of which, they would fain feel and announce themselves. Here we have the most natural, and for the most part, very influential opponents of moral enlightenment and scepticism: but they are rare. On the other hand, there is always a very numerous class of those opponents wherever interest teaches subjection, while repute and honour seem to forbid it. He who feels himself dishonoured at the thought of being the instrument of a prince, or of a party and sect, or even of wealthy power (for example, as the descendant of a proud, ancient family), but wishes just to be this instrument, or must be so before himself and before the public—such a person has need of pathetic principles which can at all times be appealed to:—principles of an unconditional ought, to which a person can subject himself without shame, and can show himself subjected. All more refined servility holds fast to the categorical imperative, and is the mortal enemy of those who want to take away the unconditional character of duty: propriety demands this from them, and not only propriety.

6.

Loss of Dignity.—Meditation has lost all its dignity of form; the ceremonial and solemn bearing of the meditative person have been made a mockery, and one would no longer endure a wise man of the old style. We think too hastily and on the way and while walking and in the midst of business of all kinds, even when we think on the most serious matters; we require little preparation, even little quiet:—it is as if each of us carried about an unceasingly revolving machine in his head, which still works, even under the most unfavourable circumstances. Formerly it was perceived in a person that on some occasion he wanted to think—it was perhaps the exception!—that he now wanted to become wiser and collected his mind on a thought: he put on a long face for it, as for a prayer, and arrested his step—nay, stood still for hours on the street when the thought "came"—on one or on two legs. It was thus "worthy of the affair"!

7.

Something for the Laborious.—He who at present wants to make moral questions a subject of study has an immense field of labour before him. All kinds of passions must be thought about singly, and followed singly throughout periods, peoples, great and insignificant individuals; all their rationality, all their valuations and elucidations of things, ought to come to light! Hitherto all that has given colour to existence has lacked a history: where would one find a history of love, of avarice, of envy, of conscience, of piety, of cruelty? Even a comparative history of law, as also of punishment, has hitherto been completely lacking. Have the different divisions of the day, the consequences of a regular appointment of the times for labour, feast, and repose, ever been made the object of investigation? Do we know the moral effects of the alimentary substances? Is there a philosophy of nutrition? (The ever-recurring outcry for and against vegetarianism proves that as yet there is no such philosophy!) Have the experiences with regard to communal living, for example, in monasteries, been collected? Has the dialectic of marriage and friendship been set forth? The customs of the learned, of trades-people, of artists, and of mechanics—have they already found their thinkers? There is so much to think of thereon! All that up till now has been considered as the "conditions of existence," of human beings, and all reason, passion and superstition in this consideration—have they been investigated to the end? The observation alone of the different degrees of development which the human impulses have attained, and could yet attain, according to the different moral climates, would furnish too much work for the most laborious; whole generations, and regular co-operating generations of the learned, would be needed in order to exhaust the points of view and the material here furnished. The same is true of the determining of the reasons for the differences of the moral climates ("on what account does this sun of a fundamental moral judgment and standard of highest value shine here—and that sun there?"). And there is again a new labour which points out the erroneousness of all these reasons, and determines the entire essence of the moral judgments hitherto made. Supposing all these labours to be accomplished, the most critical of all questions would then come into the foreground: whether science is in a position to furnish goals for human action, after it has proved that it can take them away and annihilate them—and then would be the time for a process of experimenting in which every kind of heroism could satisfy itself, an experimenting for centuries, which would put into the shade all the great labours and sacrifices of previous history. Science has not hitherto built its Cyclopic structures; for that also the time will come.

8.

Unconscious Virtues.—All qualities in a man of which he is conscious—and especially when he presumes that they are visible and evident to his environment also—are subject to quite other laws of development than those qualities which are unknown to him, or imperfectly known, which by their subtlety can also conceal themselves from the subtlest observer, and hide as it were behind nothing,—as in the case of the delicate sculptures on the scales of reptiles (it would be an error to suppose them an adornment or a defence—for one sees them only with the microscope; consequently, with an eye artificially strengthened to an extent of vision which similar animals, to which they might perhaps have meant adornment or defence, do not possess!) Our visible moral qualities, and especially our moral qualities believed to be visible, follow their own course,—and our invisible qualities of similar name, which in relation to others neither serve for adornment nor defence, also follow their own course: quite a different course probably, and with lines and refinements, and sculptures, which might perhaps give pleasure to a God with a divine microscope. We have, for example, our diligence, our ambition, our acuteness: all the world knows about them,—and besides, we have probably once more our diligence, our ambition, our acuteness; but for these—our reptile scales—the microscope has not yet been invented!—And here the adherents of instinctive morality will say, "Bravo! He at least regards unconscious virtues as possible—that suffices us!"—Oh, ye unexacting creatures!

9.

Our Eruptions.—Numberless things which humanity acquired in its earlier stages, but so weakly and embryonically that it could not be noticed that they were acquired, are thrust suddenly into light long afterwards, perhaps after the lapse of centuries: they have in the interval become strong and mature. In some ages this or that talent, this or that virtue seems to be entirely lacking, as it is in some men; but let us wait only for the grandchildren and grandchildren's children, if we have time to wait,—they bring the interior of their grandfathers into the sun, that interior of which the grandfathers themselves were unconscious. The son, indeed, is often the betrayer of his father; 46the latter understands himself better since he has got his son. We have all hidden gardens and plantations in us; and by another simile, we are all growing volcanoes, which will have their hours of eruption:—how near or how distant this is, nobody of course knows, not even the good God.

10.

A Species of Atavism.—I like best to think of the rare men of an age as suddenly emerging aftershoots of past cultures, and of their persistent strength: like the atavism of a people and its civilisation:—there is thus still something in them to think of! They now seem strange, rare, and extraordinary: and he who feels these forces in himself has to foster them in face of a different, opposing world; he has to defend them, honour them, and rear them to maturity: and he either becomes a great man thereby, or a deranged and eccentric person, unless he should altogether break down betimes. Formerly these rare qualities were usual, and were consequently regarded as common: they did not distinguish people. Perhaps they were demanded and presupposed; it was impossible to become great with them, for indeed there was also no danger of becoming insane and solitary with them.—It is principally in the old-established families and castes of a people that such after-effects of old impulses present themselves, while there is no probability of such atavism where races, habits, and valuations change too rapidly. For the tempo of the evolutional forces in peoples implies just as much as in music; for our case an andante of evolution is absolutely necessary, as the tempo of a passionate and slow spirit:—and the spirit of conserving families is certainly of that sort.

11.

Consciousness.—Consciousness is the last and latest development of the organic, and consequently also the most unfinished and least powerful of these developments. Innumerable mistakes originate out of consciousness, which, "in spite of fate," as Homer says, cause an animal or a man to break down earlier than might be necessary. If the conserving bond of the instincts were not very much more powerful, it would not generally serve as a regulator: by perverse judging and dreaming with open eyes, by superficiality and credulity, in short, just by consciousness, mankind would necessarily have broken down: or rather, without the former there would long ago have been nothing more of the latter! Before a function is fully formed and matured, it is a danger to the organism: all the better if it be then thoroughly tyrannised over! Consciousness is thus thoroughly tyrannised over— and not least by the pride in it! It is thought that here is the quintessence of man; that which is enduring, eternal, ultimate, and most original in him! Consciousness is regarded as a fixed, given magnitude! Its growth and intermittences are denied! It is accepted as the "unity of the organism"!—This ludicrous overvaluation and misconception of consciousness, has as its result the great utility, that a too rapid maturing of it has thereby been hindered. Because men believed that they already possessed consciousness, they gave themselves very little trouble to acquire it—and even now it is not otherwise! It is still an entirely new problem just dawning on the human eye and hardly yet plainly recognisable: to embody knowledge in ourselves and make it instinctive,—a problem which is only seen by those who have grasped the fact that hitherto our errors alone have been embodied in us, and that all our consciousness is relative to errors!

12.

The Goal of Science.—What? The ultimate goal of science is to create the most pleasure possible to man, and the least possible pain? But what if pleasure and pain should be so closely connected that he who wants the greatest possible amount of the one must also have the greatest possible amount of the other,—that he who wants to experience the "heavenly high jubilation,"[7] must also be ready to be "sorrowful unto death"?(ref. same footnote) And it is so, perhaps! The Stoics at least believed it was so, and they were consistent when they wished to have the least possible pleasure, in order to have the least possible pain from life. (When one uses the expression: "The virtuous man is the happiest," it is as much the sign-board of the school for the masses, as a casuistic subtlety for the subtle.) At present also ye have still the choice: either the least possible pain, in short painlessness—and after all, socialists and politicians of all parties could not honourably promise more to their people,—or the greatest possible amount of pain, as the price of the growth of a fullness of refined delights and enjoyments rarely tasted hitherto! If ye decide for the former, if ye therefore want to depress and minimise man's capacity for pain, well, ye must also depress and minimise his capacity for enjoyment. In fact, one can further the one as well as the other goal by science! Perhaps science is as yet best known by its capacity for depriving man of enjoyment, and making him colder, more statuesque, and more Stoical. But it might also turn out to be the great pain-bringer!—And then, perhaps, its counteracting force would be discovered simultaneously, its immense capacity for making new sidereal worlds of enjoyment beam forth!

13.

The Theory of the Sense of Power.—We exercise our power over others by doing them good or by doing them ill—that is all we care for! Doing ill to those on whom we have to make our power felt; for pain is a far more sensitive means for that purpose than pleasure:— pain always asks concerning the cause, while pleasure is inclined to keep within itself and not look backward. Doing good and being kind to those who are in any way already dependent on us (that is, who are accustomed to think of us as their raison d'être); we want to increase their power, because we thus increase our own; or we want to show 50them the advantage there is in being in our power,—they thus become more contented with their position, and more hostile to the enemies of our power and readier to contend with them. If we make sacrifices in doing good or in doing ill, it does not alter the ultimate value of our actions; even if we stake our life in the cause, as martyrs for the sake of our church, it is a sacrifice to our longing for power, or for the purpose of conserving our sense of power. He who under these circumstances feels that he "is in possession of truth," how many possessions does he not let go, in order to preserve this feeling! What does he not throw overboard, in order to keep himself "up,"—that is to say, above the others who lack the "truth"! Certainly the condition we are in when we do ill is seldom so pleasant, so purely pleasant, as that in which we practise kindness,—it is an indication that we still lack power, or it betrays ill-humour at this defect in us; it brings with it new dangers and uncertainties as to the power we already possess, and clouds our horizon by the prospect of revenge, scorn, punishment and failure. Perhaps only those most susceptible to the sense of power, and eager for it, will prefer to impress the seal of power on the resisting individual,—those to whom the sight of the already subjugated person as the object of benevolence is a burden and a tedium. It is a question how a person is accustomed to season his life; it is a matter of taste whether a person would rather have the slow or the sudden, the safe or the dangerous and daring increase of power,—he seeks this or that seasoning always 51according to his temperament. An easy booty is something contemptible to proud natures; they have an agreeable sensation only at the sight of men of unbroken spirit who could be enemies to them, and similarly, also, at the sight of all not easily accessible possession; they are often hard toward the sufferer, for he is not worthy of their effort or their pride,— but they show themselves so much the more courteous towards their equals, with whom strife and struggle would in any case be full of honour, if at any time an occasion for it should present itself. It is under the agreeable feelings of this perspective that the members of the knightly caste have habituated themselves to exquisite courtesy toward one another.—Pity is the most pleasant feeling in those who have not much pride, and have no prospect of great conquests: the easy booty—and that is what every sufferer is—is for them an enchanting thing. Pity is said to be the virtue of the gay lady.

14.

What is called Love.—The lust of property and love: what different associations each of these ideas evoke!—and yet it might be the same impulse twice named: on the one occasion disparaged from the standpoint of those already possessing (in whom the impulse has attained something of repose, and who are now apprehensive for the safety of their "possession"); on the other occasion viewed from the standpoint of the unsatisfied and thirsty, and therefore glorified as "good." Our 52love of our neighbour,—is it not a striving after new property? And similarly our love of knowledge, of truth; and in general all the striving after novelties? We gradually become satiated with the old, the securely possessed, and again stretch out our hands; even the finest landscape in which we live for three months is no longer certain of our love, and any kind of more distant coast excites our covetousness: the possession for the most part becomes smaller through possessing. Our pleasure in ourselves seeks to maintain itself, by always transforming something new into ourselves,—that is just possessing. To become satiated with a possession, that is to become satiated with ourselves. (One can also suffer from excess,—even the desire to cast away, to share out, can assume the honourable name of "love.") When we see any one suffering, we willingly utilise the opportunity then afforded to take possession of him; the beneficent and sympathetic man, for example, does this; he also calls the desire for new possession awakened in him, by the name of "love," and has enjoyment in it, as in a new acquisition suggesting itself to him. The love of the sexes, however, betrays itself most plainly as the striving after possession: the lover wants the unconditioned, sole possession of the person longed for by him; he wants just as absolute power over her soul as over her body; he wants to be loved solely, and to dwell and rule in the other soul as what is highest and most to be desired. When one considers that this means precisely to exclude all the world from a precious possession, a happiness, and an enjoyment; when one considers 53that the lover has in view the impoverishment and privation of all other rivals, and would like to become the dragon of his golden hoard, as the most inconsiderate and selfish of all "conquerors" and exploiters; when one considers finally that to the lover himself, the whole world besides appears indifferent, colourless, and worthless, and that he is ready to make every sacrifice, disturb every arrangement, and put every other interest behind his own,—one is verily surprised that this ferocious lust of property and injustice of sexual love should have been glorified and deified to such an extent at all times; yea, that out of this love the conception of love as the antithesis of egoism should have been derived, when it is perhaps precisely the most unqualified expression of egoism. Here, evidently, the non-possessors and desirers have determined the usage of language,—there were, of course, always too many of them. Those who have been favoured with much possession and satiety, have, to be sure, dropped a word now and then about the "raging demon," as, for instance, the most lovable and most beloved of all the Athenians—Sophocles; but Eros always laughed at such revilers,— they were always his greatest favourites.—There is, of course, here and there on this terrestrial sphere a kind of sequel to love, in which that covetous longing of two persons for one another has yielded to a new desire and covetousness, to a common, higher thirst for a superior ideal standing above them: but who knows this love? Who has experienced it? Its right name is friendship.

15.

Out of the Distance.—This mountain makes the whole district which it dominates charming in every way, and full of significance: after we have said this to ourselves for the hundredth time, we are so irrationally and so gratefully disposed towards it, as the giver of this charm, that we fancy it must itself be the most charming thing in the district—and so we climb it, and are undeceived. All of a sudden, it itself, and the whole landscape around and under us, is as it were disenchanted; we had forgotten that many a greatness, like many a goodness, wants only to be seen at a certain distance, and entirely from below, not from above,—it is thus only that it operates. Perhaps you know men in your neighbourhood who can only look at themselves from a certain distance to find themselves at all endurable, or attractive and enlivening; they are to be dissuaded from self-knowledge.

16.

Across the Plank.—One must be able to dissimulate in intercourse with persons who are ashamed of their feelings; they experience a sudden aversion towards anyone who surprises them in a state of tender, or enthusiastic and high-running feeling, as if he had seen their secrets. If one wants to be kind to them in such moments one should make them laugh, or say some kind of cold, playful wickedness:—their feeling thereby congeals, and they are again self-possessed. But I give the moral before the story.—We were once 55on a time so near one another in the course of our lives, that nothing more seemed to hinder our friendship and fraternity, and there was merely a small plank between us. While you were just about to step on it, I asked you: "Do you want to come across the plank to me?" But then you did not want to come any longer; and when I again entreated, you were silent. Since then mountains and torrents, and whatever separates and alienates, have interposed between us, and even if we wanted to come to one another, we could no longer do so! When, however, you now remember that small plank, you have no longer words,—but merely sobs and amazement.

17.

Motivation of Poverty.—We cannot, to be sure, by any artifice make a rich and richly-flowing virtue out of a poor one, but we can gracefully enough reinterpret its poverty into necessity, so that its aspect no longer gives pain to us, and we do not make any reproachful faces at fate on account of it. It is thus that the wise gardener does, who puts the tiny streamlet of his garden into the arms of a fountain-nymph, and thus motivates the poverty:—and who would not like him need the nymphs!

18.

Ancient Pride.—The ancient savour of nobility is lacking in us, because the ancient slave is lacking in our sentiment. A Greek of noble descent found such immense intermediate stages, and such a distance betwixt his elevation and that ultimate baseness, that he could hardly even see the slave plainly: even Plato no longer saw him entirely. It is otherwise with us, accustomed as we are to the doctrine of the equality of men, although not to the equality itself. A being who has not the free disposal of himself and has not got leisure,—that is not regarded by us as anything contemptible; there is perhaps too much of this kind of slavishness in each of us, in accordance with the conditions of our social order and activity, which are fundamentally different from those of the ancients.—The Greek philosopher went through life with the secret feeling that there were many more slaves than people supposed—that is to say, that every one was a slave who was not a philosopher. His pride was puffed up when he considered that even the mightiest of the earth were thus to be looked upon as slaves. This pride is also unfamiliar to us, and impossible; the word "slave" has not its full force for us even in simile.

19.

Evil.—Test the life of the best and most productive men and nations, and ask yourselves whether a tree which is to grow proudly heavenward can dispense with bad weather and tempests: whether disfavour and opposition from without, whether every kind of hatred, jealousy, stubbornness, distrust, severity, greed, and violence do not belong to the favouring circumstances without which a great growth even in virtue is hardly possible? The poison by which the weaker nature is destroyed is strengthening to the strong individual—and he does not call it poison.

20.

Dignity of Folly.—Several millenniums further on in the path of the last century!—and in everything that man does the highest prudence will be exhibited: but just thereby prudence will have lost all its dignity. It will then, sure enough, be necessary to be prudent, but it will also be so usual and common, that a more fastidious taste will feel this necessity as vulgarity. And just as a tyranny of truth and science would be in a position to raise the value of falsehood, a tyranny of prudence could force into prominence a new species of nobleness. To be noble—that might then mean, perhaps, to be capable of follies.

21.

To the Teachers of Unselfishness.—The virtues of a man are called good, not in respect of the results they have for himself, but in respect of the results which we expect therefrom for ourselves and for society:—we have all along had very little unselfishness, very little "non-egoism" in our praise of the virtues! For otherwise it could not but have been seen that the virtues (such as diligence, obedience, chastity, piety, justice) are mostly injurious to their possessors, as impulses which rule in them too vehemently and ardently, and do not want to be kept in co-ordination with the other impulses by the reason. If you have a virtue, an actual, perfect virtue (and not merely a kind of impulse towards virtue!)—you are its victim! But your neighbour praises your virtue precisely on that account! One praises the diligent man though he injures his sight, or the originality and freshness of his spirit, by his diligence; the youth is honoured and regretted who has "worn himself out by work," because one passes the judgment that "for society as a whole the loss of the best individual is only a small sacrifice! A pity that this sacrifice should be necessary! A much greater pity, it is true, if the individual should think differently, and regard his preservation and development as more important than his work in the service of society!" And so one regrets this youth, not on his own account, but because a devoted instrument, regardless of self—a so-called "good man," has been lost to society by his death. Perhaps one further considers the question, whether it would not have been more advantageous for the interests of society if he had laboured with less disregard of himself, and had preserved himself longer,—indeed, one readily admits an advantage therefrom, but one esteems the other advantage, namely, that a sacrifice has been made, and that the disposition of the sacrificial animal has once more been obviously endorsed—as higher and more enduring. It is accordingly, on the one part, the instrumental character in the virtues which is praised when the virtues are praised, and on the other part, the blind, ruling impulse in every virtue, which refuses to let itself be kept within bounds by the general advantage to the individual; in short, what is praised is the unreason in the virtues, in consequence of which the individual allows himself to be transformed into a function of the whole. The praise of the virtues is the praise of something which is privately injurious to the individual; it is praise of impulses which deprive man of his noblest self-love, and the power to take the best care of himself. To be sure, for the teaching and embodying of virtuous habits a series of effects of virtue are displayed, which make it appear that virtue and private advantage are closely related,— and there is in fact such a relationship! Blindly furious diligence, for example, the typical virtue of an instrument, is represented as the way to riches and honour, and as the most beneficial antidote to tedium and passion: but people are silent concerning its danger, its greatest dangerousness. Education proceeds in this manner throughout: it endeavours, by a series of enticements and advantages, to determine the individual to a certain mode of thinking and acting, which, when it has become habit, impulse and passion, rules in him and over him, in opposition to his ultimate advantage, but "for the general good." How often do I see that blindly furious diligence does indeed create riches and honours, but at the same time deprives the organs of the refinement by virtue of which alone an enjoyment of riches and honours is possible; so that really the main expedient for combating tedium and passion, simultaneously blunts the senses and makes the spirit refractory towards new stimuli! (The busiest of all ages—our age—does not know how to make anything out of its great diligence and wealth, except always more and more wealth, and more and more diligence; there is even more genius needed for laying out wealth than for acquiring it!—Well, we shall have our "grandchildren"!) If the education succeeds, every virtue of the individual is a public utility, and a private disadvantage in respect to the highest private end,—probably some psycho-æsthetic stunting, or even premature dissolution. One should consider successively from the same standpoint the virtues of obedience, chastity, piety, and justice. The praise of the unselfish, self-sacrificing, virtuous person— he, consequently, who does not expend his whole energy and reason for his own conservation, development, elevation, furtherance and augmentation of power, but lives as regards himself unassumingly and thoughtlessly, perhaps even indifferently or ironically,—this praise has in any case not originated out of the spirit of unselfishness!

The "neighbour" praises unselfishness because he profits by it! If the neighbour were "unselfishly" disposed himself, he would reject that destruction of power, that injury for his advantage, he would thwart such inclinations in their origin, and above all he would manifest his unselfishness just by not giving it a good name! The fundamental contradiction in that morality which at present stands in high honour is here indicated: the motives to such a morality are in antithesis to its principle! That with which this morality wishes to prove itself, refutes it out of its criterion of what is moral! The maxim, "Thou shalt renounce thyself and offer thyself as a sacrifice," in order not to be inconsistent with its own morality, could only be decreed by a being who himself renounced his own advantage thereby, and who perhaps in the required self-sacrifice of individuals brought about his own dissolution. As soon, however, as the neighbour (or society) recommended altruism on account of its utility, the precisely antithetical proposition, "Thou shalt seek thy advantage even at the expense of everybody else," was brought into use: accordingly, "thou shalt," and "thou shalt not," are preached in one breath!

22.

L'Ordre du Jour pour le Roi.—The day commences: let us begin to arrange for this day the business and fêtes of our most gracious lord, who at present is still pleased to repose. His Majesty has bad weather to-day: we shall be careful not to call it bad; we shall not speak of the weather,—but we shall go through to-day's business somewhat more ceremoniously and make the fêtes somewhat more festive than would otherwise be necessary. His Majesty may perhaps even be sick: we shall give the last good news of the evening at breakfast, the arrival of M. Montaigne, who knows how to joke so pleasantly about his sickness,—he suffers from stone. We shall receive several persons (persons!—what would that old inflated frog, who will be among them, say, if he heard this word! "I am no person," he would say, "but always the thing itself")—and the reception will last longer than is pleasant to anybody; a sufficient reason for telling about the poet who wrote over his door, "He who enters here will do me an honour; he who does not—a favour."—That is, forsooth, saying a discourteous thing in a courteous manner! And perhaps this poet is quite justified on his part in being discourteous; they say that the rhymes are better than the rhymester. Well, let him still make many of them, and withdraw himself as much as possible from the world: and that is doubtless the significance of his well-bred rudeness! A prince, on the other hand, is always of more value than his "verse," even when—but what are we about? We gossip, and the whole court believes that we have already been at work and racked our brains: there is no light to be seen earlier than that which burns in our window.—Hark! Was that not the bell? The devil! The day and the dance commence, and we do not know our rounds! We must then improvise,—all the world improvises its day. To-day, let us for once do like all the world!—And therewith vanished my wonderful morning dream, probably owing to the violent strokes of the tower-clock, which just then announced the fifth hour with all the importance which is peculiar to it. It seems to me that, on this occasion, the God of dreams wanted to make merry over my habits,—it is my habit to commence the day by arranging it properly, to make it endurable for myself, and it is possible that I may often have done this too formally, and too much like a prince.

23.

The Characteristics of Corruption.—Let us observe the following characteristics in that condition of society from time to time necessary, which is designated by the word "corruption." Immediately upon the appearance of corruption anywhere, a motley superstition gets the upper hand, and the hitherto universal belief of a people becomes colourless and impotent in comparison with it; for superstition is freethinking of the second rank,—he who gives himself over to it selects certain forms and formulæ which appeal to him, and permits himself a right of choice. The superstitious man is always much more of a "person," in comparison with the religious man, and a superstitious society will be one in which there are many individuals, and a delight in individuality. Seen from this standpoint superstition always appears as a progress in comparison with belief, and as a sign that the intellect becomes more independent and claims to have its rights. Those who reverence the old religion and the religious disposition then complain of corruption,—they have hitherto also determined the usage of language, and have given a bad repute to superstition, even among the freest spirits. Let us learn that it is a symptom of enlightenment.—Secondly, a society in which corruption takes a hold is blamed for effeminacy: for the appreciation of war, and the delight in war perceptibly diminish in such a society, and the conveniences of life are now just as eagerly sought after as were military and gymnastic honours formerly. But one is accustomed to overlook the fact that the old national energy and national passion, which acquired a magnificent splendour in war and in the tourney, has now transferred itself into innumerable private passions, and has merely become less visible; indeed in periods of "corruption" the quantity and quality of the expended energy of a people is probably greater than ever, and the individual spends it lavishly, to such an extent as could not be done formerly—he was not then rich enough to do so! And thus it is precisely in times of "effeminacy" that tragedy runs at large in and out of doors, it is then that ardent love and ardent hatred are born, and the flame of knowledge flashes heavenward in full blaze.—Thirdly, as if in amends for the reproach of superstition and effeminacy, it is customary to say of such periods of corruption that they are milder, and that cruelty has then greatly diminished in comparison with the older, more credulous, and stronger period. But to this praise I am just as little able to assent as to that reproach: I only grant so much—namely, that cruelty now becomes more refined, and its older forms are henceforth counter to the taste; but the wounding and torturing by word and look reaches its highest development in times of corruption,—it is now only that wickedness is created, and the delight in wickedness. The men of the period of corruption are witty and calumnious; they know that there are yet other ways of murdering than by the dagger and the ambush—they know also that all that is well said is believed in.—Fourthly, it is when "morals decay" that those beings whom one calls tyrants first make their appearance; they are the forerunners of the individual, and as it were early matured firstlings. Yet a little while, and this fruit of fruits hangs ripe and yellow on the tree of a people,—and only for the sake of such fruit did this tree exist! When the decay has reached its worst, and likewise the conflict of all sorts of tyrants, there always arises the Cæsar, the final tyrant, who puts an end to the exhausted struggle for sovereignty, by making the exhaustedness work for him. In his time the individual is usually most mature, and consequently the "culture" is highest and most fruitful, but not on his account nor through him: although the men of highest culture love to flatter their Cæsar by pretending that they are his creation. The truth, however, is that they need quietness externally, because internally they have disquietude and labour. In these times bribery and treason are at their height: for the love of the ego, then first discovered, is much more powerful than the love of the old, used-up, hackneyed "fatherland"; and the need to be secure in one way or other against the frightful fluctuations of fortune, opens even the nobler hands, as soon as a richer and more powerful person shows himself ready to put gold into them. There is then so little certainty with regard to the future; people live only for the day: a condition of mind which enables every deceiver to play an easy game,—people of course only let themselves be misled and bribed "for the present," and reserve for themselves futurity and virtue. The individuals, as is well known, the men who only live for themselves, provide for the moment more than do their opposites, the gregarious men, because they consider themselves just as incalculable as the future; and similarly they attach themselves willingly to despots, because they believe themselves capable of activities and expedients, which can neither reckon on being understood by the multitude, nor on finding favour with them,—but the tyrant or the Cæsar understands the rights of the Individual even in his excesses, and has an interest in speaking on behalf of a bolder private morality, and even in giving his hand to it. For he thinks of himself, and wishes people to think of him what Napoleon once uttered in his classical style—"I have the right to answer by an eternal 'thus I am' to everything about which complaint is brought against me. I am apart from all the world, I accept conditions from nobody. I wish people also to submit to my fancies, and to take it quite as a simple matter, if I should indulge in this or that diversion." Thus spoke Napoleon once to his wife, when she had reasons for calling in question the fidelity of her husband.—The times of corruption are the seasons when the apples fall from the tree: I mean the individuals, the seed-bearers of the future, the pioneers of the spiritual colonisation and of a new construction of national and social unions. Corruption is only an abusive term for the harvest time of a people.

24.

Different Dissatisfactions.—The feeble and as it were feminine dissatisfied people have ingenuity for beautifying and deepening life; the strong dissatisfied people—the masculine persons among them, to continue the metaphor—have the ingenuity for improving and safeguarding life. The former show their weakness and feminine character by willingly letting themselves be temporarily deceived, and perhaps even by putting up with a little ecstasy and enthusiasm on a time, but on the whole they are never to be satisfied, and suffer from the incurability of their dissatisfaction; moreover they are the patrons of all those who manage to concoct opiate and narcotic comforts, and just on that account averse to those who value the physician higher than the priest,—they thereby encourage the continuance of actual distress! If there had not been a surplus of dissatisfied persons of this kind in Europe since the time of the Middle Ages, the remarkable capacity of Europeans for constant transformation would perhaps not have originated at all; for the claims of the strong dissatisfied persons are too gross, and really too modest to resist being finally quieted down. China is an instance of a country in which dissatisfaction on a grand scale and the capacity for transformation have died out for many centuries; and the Socialists and state-idolaters of Europe could easily bring things to Chinese conditions and to a Chinese "happiness," with their measures for the amelioration and security of life, provided that they could first of all root out the sicklier, tenderer, more feminine dissatisfaction and Romanticism which are still very abundant among us. Europe is an invalid who owes her best thanks to her incurability and the eternal transformations of her sufferings; these constant new situations, these equally constant new dangers, pains, and make-shifts, have at last generated an intellectual sensitiveness which is almost equal to genius, and is in any case the mother of all genius.

25.

Not Pre-ordained to Knowledge.—There is a purblind humility not at all rare, and when a person is afflicted with it, he is once for all unqualified for being a disciple of knowledge. It is this in fact: the moment a man of this kind perceives anything striking, he turns as it were on his heel, and says to himself: "You have deceived yourself! Where have your wits been! This cannot be the truth!"—and then, instead of looking at it and listening to it with more attention, he runs out of the way of the striking object as if intimidated, and seeks to get it out of his head as quickly as possible. For his fundamental rule runs thus: "I want to see nothing that contradicts the usual opinion concerning things! Am I created for the purpose of discovering new truths? There are already too many of the old ones."

26.

What is Living?—Living—that is to continually eliminate from ourselves what is about to die; Living—that is to be cruel and inexorable towards all that becomes weak and old in ourselves, and not only in ourselves. Living—that means, therefore, to be without piety toward the dying, the wretched and the old? To be continually a murderer?—And yet old Moses said: "Thou shalt not kill!"

27.

The Self-Renouncer.—What does the self-renouncer do? He strives after a higher world, he wants to fly longer and further and higher than all men of affirmation—he throws away many things that would burden his flight, and several things among them that are not valueless, that are not unpleasant to him: he sacrifices them to his desire for elevation. Now this sacrificing, this casting away, is the very thing which becomes visible in him: on that account one calls him the self-renouncer, and as such he stands before us, enveloped in his cowl, and as the soul of a hair-shirt. With this effect, however, which he makes upon us he is well content: he wants to keep concealed from us his desire, his pride, his intention of flying above us.—Yes! He is wiser than we thought, and so courteous towards us—this affirmer! For that is what he is, like us, even in his self-renunciation.

28.

Injuring with one's best Qualities.—Our strong points sometimes drive us so far forward that we cannot any longer endure our weaknesses, and we perish by them: we also perhaps see this result beforehand, but nevertheless do not want it to be otherwise. We then become hard towards that which would fain be spared in us, and our pitilessness is also our greatness. Such an experience, which must in the end cost us our life, is a symbol of the collective effect of great men upon others and upon their epoch:—it is just with their best abilities, with that which only they can do, that they destroy much that is weak, uncertain, evolving, and willing, and are thereby injurious. Indeed, the case may happen in which, taken on the whole, they only do injury, because their best is accepted and drunk up as it were solely by those who lose their understanding and their egoism by it, as by too strong a beverage; they become so intoxicated that they go breaking their limbs on all the wrong roads where their drunkenness drives them.

29.

Adventitious Liars.—When people began to combat the unity of Aristotle in France, and consequently also to defend it, there was once more to be seen that which has been seen so often, but seen so unwillingly:—people imposed false reasons on themselves on account of which those laws ought to exist, merely for the sake of not acknowledging to themselves that they had accustomed themselves to the authority of those laws, and did not want any longer to have things otherwise. And people do so in every prevailing morality and religion, and have always done so: the reasons and intentions behind the habit, are only added surreptitiously when people begin to combat the habit, and ask for reasons and intentions. It is here that the great dishonesty of the conservatives of all times hides:—they are adventitious liars.

30.

The Comedy of Celebrated Men.—Celebrated men who need their fame, as, for instance, all politicians, no longer select their associates and friends without after-thoughts: from the one they want a portion of the splendour and reflection of his virtues; from the other they want the fear-inspiring power of certain dubious qualities in him, of which everybody is aware; from another they steal his reputation for idleness and basking in the sun, because it is advantageous for their own ends to be regarded temporarily as heedless and lazy:—it conceals the fact that they lie in ambush; they now use the visionaries, now the experts, now the brooders, now the pedants in their neighbourhood, as their actual selves for the time, but very soon they do not need them any longer! And thus while their environment and outside die off continually, everything seems to crowd into this environment, and wants to become a "character" of it; they are like great cities in this respect. Their repute is continually in process of mutation, like their character, for their changing methods require this change, and they show and exhibit sometimes this and sometimes that actual or fictitious quality on the stage; their friends and associates, as we have said, belong to these stage properties. On the other hand, that which they aim at must remain so much the more steadfast, and burnished and resplendent in the distance,—and this also sometimes needs its comedy and its stage-play.

31.

Commerce and Nobility.—Buying and selling is now regarded as something ordinary, like the art of reading and writing; everyone is now trained to it even when he is not a tradesman, exercising himself daily in the art; precisely as formerly in the period of uncivilised humanity, everyone was a hunter and exercised himself day by day in the art of hunting. Hunting was then something common: but just as this finally became a privilege of the powerful and noble, and thereby lost the character of the commonplace and the ordinary—by ceasing to be necessary and by becoming an affair of fancy and luxury:—so it might become the same some day with buying and selling. Conditions of society are imaginable in which there will be no selling and buying, and in which the necessity for this art will become quite lost; perhaps it may then happen that individuals who are less subjected to the law of the prevailing condition of things will indulge in buying and selling as a luxury of sentiment. It is then only that commerce would acquire nobility, and the noble would then perhaps occupy themselves just as readily with commerce as they have done hitherto with war and politics: while on the other hand the valuation of politics might then have entirely altered. Already even politics ceases to be the business of a gentleman; and it is possible that one day it may be found to be so vulgar as to be brought, like all party literature and daily literature, under the rubric: "Prostitution of the intellect."

32.

Undesirable Disciples.—What shall I do with these two youths! called out a philosopher dejectedly, who "corrupted" youths, as Socrates had once corrupted them,—they are unwelcome disciples to me. One of them cannot say "Nay," and the other says "Half and half" to everything. Provided they grasped my doctrine, the former would suffer too much, for my mode of thinking requires a martial soul, willingness to cause pain, delight in denying, and a hard skin,—he would succumb by open wounds and internal injuries. And the other will choose the mediocre in everything he represents, and thus make a mediocrity of the whole,—I should like my enemy to have such a disciple.

33.

Outside the Lecture-room.—"In order to prove that man after all belongs to the good-natured animals, I would remind you how credulous he has been for so long a time. It is now only, quite late, and after an immense self-conquest, that he has become a distrustful animal,—yes! man is now more wicked than ever."—I do not understand this; why should man now be more distrustful and more wicked?—"Because he now has science,—because he needs to have it!"—

34.

Historia abscondita.—Every great man has a power which operates backward; all history is 74again placed on the scales on his account, and a thousand secrets of the past crawl out of their lurking-places— into his sunlight. There is absolutely no knowing what history may be some day. The past is still perhaps undiscovered in its essence! There are yet so many retroactive powers needed!

35.

Heresy and Witchcraft.—To think otherwise than is customary—that is by no means so much the activity of a better intellect, as the activity of strong, wicked inclinations,—severing, isolating, refractory, mischief-loving, malicious inclinations. Heresy is the counterpart of witchcraft, and is certainly just as little a merely harmless affair, or a thing worthy of honour in itself. Heretics and sorcerers are two kinds of bad men; they have it in common that they also feel themselves wicked; their unconquerable delight is to attack and injure whatever rules,—whether it be men or opinions. The Reformation, a kind of duplication of the spirit of the Middle Ages at a time when it had no longer a good conscience, produced both of these kinds of people in the greatest profusion.

36.

Last Words.—It will be recollected that the Emperor Augustus, that terrible man, who had himself as much in his own power, and who could be silent as well as any wise Socrates, became indiscreet about himself in his last words; for 75the first time he let his mask fall, when he gave to understand that he had carried a mask and played a comedy,—he had played the father of his country and wisdom on the throne well, even to the point of illusion! Plaudite amici, comoedia finita est!—The thought of the dying Nero: qualis artifex pereo! was also the thought of the dying Augustus: histrionic conceit! histrionic loquacity! And the very counterpart to the dying Socrates!—But Tiberius died silently, that most tortured of all self-torturers,—he was genuine and not a stage-player! What may have passed through his head in the end! Perhaps this: "Life—that is a long death. I am a fool, who shortened the lives of so many! Was I created for the purpose of being a benefactor? I should have given them eternal life: and then I could have seen them dying eternally. I had such good eyes for that: qualis spectator pereo!" When he seemed once more to regain his powers after a long death-struggle, it was considered advisable to smother him with pillows,—he died a double death.

37.

Owing to three Errors.—Science has been furthered during recent centuries, partly because it was hoped that God's goodness and wisdom would be best understood therewith and thereby—the principal motive in the soul of great Englishmen (like Newton); partly because the absolute utility of knowledge was believed in, and especially the most intimate connection of morality, knowledge, and happiness—the principal motive in the soul of great Frenchmen (like Voltaire); and partly because it was thought that in science there was something unselfish, harmless, self-sufficing, lovable, and truly innocent to be had, in which the evil human impulses did not at all participate—the principal motive in the soul of Spinoza, who felt himself divine, as a knowing being:—it is consequently owing to three errors that science has been furthered.

38.

Explosive People.—When one considers how ready are the forces of young men for discharge, one does not wonder at seeing them decide so unfastidiously and with so little selection for this or that cause: that which attracts them is the sight of eagerness about any cause, as it were the sight of the burning match—not the cause itself. The more ingenious seducers on that account operate by holding out the prospect of an explosion to such persons, and do not urge their cause by means of reasons; these powder-barrels are not won over by means of reasons!

39.

Altered Taste.—The alteration of the general taste is more important than the alteration of opinions; opinions, with all their proving, refuting, and intellectual masquerade, are merely symptoms of altered taste, and are certainly not what they are still so often claimed to be, the causes of the altered taste. How does the general taste alter? By the fact of individuals, the powerful and influential persons, expressing and tyrannically enforcing without any feeling of shame, their hoc est ridiculum, hoc est absurdum; the decisions, therefore, of their taste and their disrelish:—they thereby lay a constraint upon many people, out of which there gradually grows a habituation for still more, and finally a necessity for all. The fact, however, that these individuals feel and "taste" differently, has usually its origin in a peculiarity of their mode of life, nourishment, or digestion, perhaps in a surplus or deficiency of the inorganic salts in their blood and brain, in short in their physis; they have, however, the courage to avow their physical constitution, and to lend an ear even to the most delicate tones of its requirements: their æsthetic and moral judgments are those "most delicate tones" of their physis.

40.

The Lack of a noble Presence.—Soldiers and their leaders have always a much higher mode of comportment toward one another than workmen and their employers. At present at least, all militarily established civilisation still stands high above all so-called industrial civilisation; the latter, in its present form, is in general the meanest mode of existence that has ever been. It is simply the law of necessity that operates here: people want to live, and have to sell themselves; but they despise him who exploits their necessity, and purchases the workman. It is curious that the subjection to powerful, fear-inspiring, and even dreadful individuals, to tyrants and leaders of armies, is not at all felt so painfully as the subjection to such undistinguished and uninteresting persons as the captains of industry; in the employer the workman usually sees merely a crafty, blood-sucking dog of a man, speculating on every necessity, whose name, form, character, and reputation are altogether indifferent to him. It is probable that the manufacturers and great magnates of commerce have hitherto lacked too much all those forms and attributes of a superior race, which alone make persons interesting; if they had had the nobility of the nobly-born in their looks and bearing, there would perhaps have been no socialism in the masses of the people. For these are really ready for slavery of every kind, provided that the superior class above them constantly shows itself legitimately superior, and born to command—by its noble presence! The commonest man feels that nobility is not to be improvised, and that it is his part to honour it as the fruit of protracted race-culture,—but the absence of superior presence, and the notorious vulgarity of manufacturers with red, fat hands, brings up the thought to him that it is only chance and fortune that has here elevated the one above the other; well then—so he reasons with himself—let us in our turn tempt chance and fortune! Let us in our turn throw the dice!—and socialism commences.

41.

Against Remorse.—The thinker sees in his own actions attempts and questionings to obtain information about something or other; success and failure are answers to him first and foremost. To vex himself, however, because something does not succeed, or to feel remorse at all—he leaves that to those who act because they are commanded to do so, and expect to get a beating when their gracious master is not satisfied with the result.

42.

Work and Ennui.—In respect to seeking work for the sake of the pay, almost all men are alike at present in civilised countries; to all of them work is a means, and not itself the end; on which account they are not very select in the choice of the work, provided it yields an abundant profit. But still there are rarer men who would rather perish than work without delight in their labour: the fastidious people, difficult to satisfy, whose object is not served by an abundant profit, unless the work itself be the reward of all rewards. Artists and contemplative men of all kinds belong to this rare species of human beings; and also the idlers who spend their life in hunting and travelling, or in love affairs and adventures. They all seek toil and trouble in so far as these are associated with pleasure, and they want the severest and hardest labour, if it be necessary. In other respects, however, they have a resolute indolence, even should impoverishment, dishonour, and danger to health and life be associated therewith. They are not so much afraid of ennui as of labour without pleasure; indeed they require much ennui, if their work is to succeed with them. For the thinker and for all inventive spirits ennui is the unpleasant "calm" of the soul which precedes the happy voyage and the dancing breezes; he must endure it, he must await the effect it has on him:—it is precisely this which lesser natures cannot at all experience! It is common to scare away ennui in every way, just as it is common to labour without pleasure. It perhaps distinguishes the Asiatics above the Europeans, that they are capable of a longer and profounder repose; even their narcotics operate slowly and require patience, in contrast to the obnoxious suddenness of the European poison, alcohol.

43.

What the Laws Betray.—One makes a great mistake when one studies the penal laws of a people, as if they were an expression of its character; the laws do not betray what a people is, but what appears to them foreign, strange, monstrous, and outlandish. The laws concern themselves with the exceptions to the morality of custom; and the severest punishments fall on acts which conform to the customs of the neighbouring peoples. Thus among the Wahabites, there are only two mortal sins: having another God than the Wahabite God, and—smoking (it is designated by them as "the disgraceful kind of drinking"). "And how is it with regard to murder and adultery?"—asked the Englishman with astonishment on learning these things. "Well, God is gracious and pitiful!" answered the old chief.—Thus among the ancient Romans there was the idea that a woman could only sin mortally in two ways: by adultery on the one hand, and—by wine-drinking on the other. Old Cato pretended 81that kissing among relatives had only been made a custom in order to keep women in control on this point; a kiss meant: did her breath smell of wine? Wives had actually been punished by death who were surprised taking wine: and certainly not merely because women under the influence of wine sometimes unlearn altogether the art of saying No; the Romans were afraid above all things of the orgiastic and Dionysian spirit with which the women of Southern Europe at that time (when wine was still new in Europe) were sometimes visited, as by a monstrous foreignness which subverted the basis of Roman sentiments; it seemed to them treason against Rome, as the embodiment of foreignness.

44.

The Believed Motive.—However important it may be to know the motives according to which mankind has really acted hitherto, perhaps the belief in this or that motive, and therefore that which mankind has assumed and imagined to be the actual mainspring of its activity hitherto, is something still more essential for the thinker to know. For the internal happiness and misery of men have always come to them through their belief in this or that motive,—not however, through that which was actually the motive! All about the latter has an interest of secondary rank.

45.

Epicurus.—Yes, I am proud of perceiving the character of Epicurus differently from anyone else perhaps, and of enjoying the happiness of the afternoon of antiquity in all that I hear and read of him:—I see his eye gazing out on a broad whitish sea, over the shore-rocks on which the sunshine rests, while great and small creatures play in its light, secure and calm like this light and that eye itself. Such happiness could only have been devised by a chronic sufferer, the happiness of an eye before which the sea of existence has become calm, and which can no longer tire of gazing at the surface and at the variegated, tender, tremulous skin of this sea. Never previously was there such a moderation of voluptuousness.

46.

Our Astonishment.—There is a profound and fundamental satisfaction in the fact that science ascertains things that hold their ground, and again furnish the basis for new researches:—it could certainly be otherwise. Indeed, we are so much convinced of all the uncertainty and caprice of our judgments, and of the everlasting change of all human laws and conceptions, that we are really astonished how persistently the results of science hold their ground! In earlier times people knew nothing of this changeability of all human things; the custom of morality maintained the belief that the whole inner life of man was bound to iron necessity by eternal fetters:—perhaps people then felt a similar voluptuousness of astonishment when they listened to tales and fairy stories. The wonderful did so much good to those men, who might well get tired sometimes of the regular and the eternal. To leave the ground for once! To soar! To stray! To be mad!—that belonged to the paradise and the revelry of earlier times; while our felicity is like that of the shipwrecked man who has gone ashore, and places himself with both feet on the old, firm ground—in astonishment that it does not rock.

47.

The Suppression of the Passions.—When one continually prohibits the expression of the passions as something to be left to the "vulgar," to coarser, bourgeois, and peasant natures—that is, when one does not want to suppress the passions themselves, but only their language and demeanour, one nevertheless realises therewith just what one does not want: the suppression of the passions themselves, or at least their weakening and alteration,—as the court of Louis XIV. (to cite the most instructive instance), and all that was dependent on it, experienced. The generation that followed, trained in suppressing their expression, no longer possessed the passions themselves, but had a pleasant, superficial, playful disposition in their place,—a generation which was so permeated with the incapacity to be ill-mannered, that even an injury was not taken and retaliated, except with courteous words. Perhaps our own time furnishes the most remarkable counterpart to this period: I see everywhere (in life, in the theatre, and not least in all that is written) satisfaction at all the coarser outbursts and gestures of passion; a certain convention of passionateness is now desired,—only not the passion itself! Nevertheless it will thereby be at last reached, and our posterity will have a genuine savagery, and not merely a formal savagery and unmannerliness.

48.

Knowledge of Distress.—Perhaps there is nothing by which men and periods are so much separated from one another, as by the different degrees of knowledge of distress which they possess; distress of the soul as well as of the body. With respect to the latter, owing to lack of sufficient self-experience, we men of the present day (in spite of our deficiencies and infirmities), are perhaps all of us blunderers and visionaries in comparison with the men of the age of fear—the longest of all ages,—when the individual had to protect himself against violence, and for that purpose had to be a man of violence himself. At that time a man went through a long schooling of corporeal tortures and privations, and found even in a certain kind of cruelty toward himself, in a voluntary use of pain, a necessary means for his preservation; at that time a person trained his environment to the endurance of pain; at that time a person willingly inflicted pain, and saw the most frightful things of this kind happen to others, without having any other feeling than for his own security. As regards the distress of the soul, however, I now look at every man with respect to whether he knows it by experience or by description; whether he still regards it as necessary to simulate this knowledge, perhaps as an indication 85of more refined culture; or whether, at the bottom of his heart, he does not at all believe in great sorrows of soul, and at the naming of them has in his mind a similar experience as at the naming of great corporeal sufferings, such as tooth-aches, and stomach-aches. It is thus, however, that it seems to be with most people at present. Owing to the universal inexperience of both kinds of pain, and the comparative rarity of the spectacle of a sufferer, an important consequence results: people now hate pain far more than earlier man did, and calumniate it worse than ever; indeed people nowadays can hardly endure the thought of pain, and make out of it an affair of conscience and a reproach to collective existence. The appearance of pessimistic philosophies is not at all the sign of great and dreadful miseries; for these interrogative marks regarding the worth of life appear in periods when the refinement and alleviation of existence already deem the unavoidable gnat-stings of the soul and body as altogether too bloody and wicked; and in the poverty of actual experiences of pain, would now like to make painful general ideas appear as suffering of the worst kind.—There might indeed be a remedy for pessimistic philosophies and the excessive sensibility which seems to me the real "distress of the present":—but perhaps this remedy already sounds too cruel, and would itself be reckoned among the symptoms owing to which people at present conclude that "existence is something evil." Well! the remedy for "the distress" is distress.

49.

Magnanimity and allied Qualities.—Those paradoxical phenomena, such as the sudden coldness in the demeanour of good-natured men, the humour of the melancholy, and above all magnanimity, as a sudden renunciation of revenge or of the gratification of envy—appear in men in whom there is a powerful inner impulsiveness, in men of sudden satiety and sudden disgust. Their satisfactions are so rapid and violent that satiety, aversion, and flight into the antithetical taste, immediately follow upon them: in this contrast the convulsion of feeling liberates itself, in one person by sudden coldness, in another by laughter, and in a third by tears and self-sacrifice. The magnanimous person appears to me—at least that kind of magnanimous person who has always made most impression—as a man with the strongest thirst for vengeance, to whom a gratification presents itself close at hand, and who already drinks it off in imagination so copiously, thoroughly, and to the last drop, that an excessive, rapid disgust follows this rapid licentiousness;—he now elevates himself "above himself," as one says, and forgives his enemy, yea, blesses and honours him. With this violence done to himself, however, with this mockery of his impulse to revenge, even still so powerful, he merely yields to the new impulse, the disgust which has become powerful, and does this just as impatiently and licentiously, as a short time previously he forestalled, and as it were exhausted, the joy of revenge with his fantasy. In magnanimity 87there is the same amount of egoism as in revenge, but a different quality of egoism.

50.

The Argument of Isolation.—The reproach of conscience, even in the most conscientious, is weak against the feeling: "This and that are contrary to the good morals of your society." A cold glance or a wry mouth, on the part of those among whom and for whom one has been educated, is still feared even by the strongest. What is really feared there? Isolation! as the argument which demolishes even the best arguments for a person or cause!—It is thus that the gregarious instinct speaks in us.

51.

Sense for Truth.—Commend me to all scepticism where I am permitted to answer: "Let us put it to the test!" But I don't wish to hear anything more of things and questions which do not admit of being tested. That is the limit of my "sense for truth": for bravery has there lost its right.

52.

What others Know of us.—That which we know of ourselves and have in our memory is not so decisive for the happiness of our life as is generally believed. One day it flashes upon our mind what others know of us (or think they know)—and then we acknowledge that it is the more powerful. We get on with our bad conscience more easily than with our bad reputation.

53.

Where Goodness Begins.—Where bad eyesight can no longer see the evil impulse as such, on account of its refinement,—there man sets up the kingdom of goodness; and the feeling of having now gone over into the kingdom of goodness brings all those impulses (such as the feelings of security, of comfortableness, of benevolence) into simultaneous activity, which were threatened and confined by the evil impulses. Consequently, the duller the eye so much the further does goodness extend! Hence the eternal cheerfulness of the populace and of children! Hence the gloominess and grief (allied to the bad conscience) of great thinkers.

54.

The Consciousness of Appearance.—How wonderfully and novelly, and at the same time how awfully and ironically, do I feel myself situated with respect to collective existence, with my knowledge! I have discovered for myself that the old humanity and animality, yea, the collective primeval age, and the past of all sentient being, continues to meditate, love, hate, and reason in me,—I have suddenly awoke in the midst of this dream, but merely to the consciousness that I just dream, and that I must dream on in order not to perish; just as the sleep-walker must dream on in order not to tumble down. What is it that is now "appearance" to me! Verily, not the antithesis of any kind of essence,—what knowledge can I assert of any kind of essence whatsoever, except merely the predicates of its appearance! Verily not a dead mask which one could put upon an unknown X, and which to be sure one could also remove! Appearance is for me the operating and living thing itself; which goes so far in its self-mockery as to make me feel that here there is appearance, and Will o' the Wisp, and spirit-dance, and nothing more,—that among all these dreamers, I also, the "thinker," dance my dance, that the thinker is a means of prolonging further the terrestrial dance, and in so far is one of the masters of ceremony of existence, and that the sublime consistency and connectedness of all branches of knowledge is perhaps, and will perhaps, be the best means for maintaining the universality of the dreaming, the complete, mutual understandability of all those dreamers, and thereby the duration of the dream.

55.

The Ultimate Nobility of Character.—What then makes a person "noble"? Certainly not that he makes sacrifices; even the frantic libertine makes sacrifices. Certainly not that he generally follows his passions; there are contemptible passions. Certainly not that he does something for others and without selfishness; perhaps the effect of selfishness is precisely at its greatest in the noblest persons.—But that the passion which seizes the noble man is a peculiarity, without his knowing that it is so: the use of a rare and singular measuring-rod, almost a frenzy: the feeling of heat in things which feel cold to all other persons: a divining of values for which scales have not yet been invented: a sacrificing on altars which are consecrated to an unknown God: a bravery without the desire for honour: a self-sufficiency which has superabundance, and imparts to men and things. Hitherto, therefore, it has been the rare in man, and the unconsciousness of this rareness, that has made men noble. Here, however, let us consider that everything ordinary, immediate, and indispensable, in short, what has been most preservative of the species, and generally the rule in mankind hitherto, has been judged unreasonable and calumniated in its entirety by this standard, in favour of the exceptions. To become the advocate of the rule—that may perhaps be the ultimate form and refinement in which nobility of character will reveal itself on earth.

56.

The Desire for Suffering.—When I think of the desire to do something, how it continually tickles and stimulates millions of young Europeans, who cannot endure themselves and all their ennui,—I conceive that there must be a desire in them to suffer something, in order to derive from their suffering a worthy motive for acting, for doing something. Distress is necessary! Hence the cry of the politicians, hence the many false, trumped-up, exaggerated "states of distress" of all possible kinds, and the blind readiness to believe in them. This young world desires that there should arrive or appear from the outside—not happiness—but misfortune; and their imagination is already busy beforehand to form a monster out of it, so that they may afterwards be able to fight with a monster. If these distress-seekers felt the power to benefit themselves, to do something for themselves from internal sources, they would also understand how to create a distress of their own, specially their own, from internal sources. Their inventions might then be more refined, and their gratifications might sound like good music: while at present they fill the world with their cries of distress, and consequently too often with the feeling of distress in the first place! They do not know what to make of themselves—and so they paint the misfortune of others on the wall; they always need others! And always again other others!—Pardon me, my friends, I have ventured to paint my happiness on the wall.

BOOK SECOND
57.

To the Realists.—Ye sober beings, who feel yourselves armed against passion and fantasy, and would gladly make a pride and an ornament out of your emptiness, ye call yourselves realists and give to understand that the world is actually constituted as it appears to you; before you alone reality stands unveiled, and ye yourselves would perhaps be the best part of it,—oh, ye dear images of Sais! But are not ye also in your unveiled condition still extremely passionate and dusky beings compared with the fish, and still all too like an enamoured artist?[8]—and what is "reality" to an enamoured artist! Ye still carry about with you the valuations of things which had their origin in the passions and infatuations of earlier centuries! There is still a secret and ineffaceable drunkenness embodied in your sobriety! Your love of "reality," for example—oh, that is an old, primitive "love"! In every feeling, in every sense-impression, there is a portion of this old love: and similarly also some kind of fantasy, prejudice, irrationality, ignorance, fear, and whatever else has become mingled and woven into it. There is that mountain! There is that cloud! What is "real" in them? Remove the phantasm and the whole human element therefrom, ye sober ones! Yes, if ye could do that! If ye could forget your origin, your past, your preparatory schooling,—your whole history as man and beast! There is no "reality" for us—nor for you either, ye sober ones,—we are far from being so alien to one another as ye suppose, and perhaps our good-will to get beyond drunkenness is just as respectable as your belief that ye are altogether incapable of drunkenness.

58.

Only as Creators!—It has caused me the greatest trouble, and for ever causes me the greatest trouble, to perceive that unspeakably more depends upon what things are called, than on what they are. The reputation, the name and appearance, the importance, the usual measure and weight of things—each being in origin most frequently an error and arbitrariness thrown over the things like a garment, and quite alien to their essence and even to their exterior—have gradually, by the belief therein and its continuous growth from generation to generation, grown as it were on-and-into things and become their very body; the appearance at the very beginning becomes almost always the essence in the end, and operates as the essence! What a fool he would be who would think it enough to refer here to this origin and this nebulous veil of illusion, in order to annihilate that which virtually passes for the world—namely, so-called "reality"! It is only as creators that we can annihilate!—But let us not forget this: it suffices to create new names and valuations and probabilities, in order in the long run to create new "things."

59.

We Artists!—When we love a woman we have readily a hatred against nature, on recollecting all the disagreeable natural functions to which every woman is subject; we prefer not to think of them at all, but if once our soul touches on these things it twitches impatiently, and glances, as we have said, contemptuously at nature:—we are hurt; nature seems to encroach upon our possessions, and with the profanest hands. We then shut our ears against all physiology, and we decree in secret that "we will hear nothing of the fact that man is something else than soul and form!" "The man under the skin" is an abomination and monstrosity, a blasphemy of God and of love to all lovers.—Well, just as the lover still feels with respect to nature and natural functions, so did every worshipper of God and his "holy omnipotence" formerly feel: in all that was said of nature by astronomers, geologists, physiologists, and physicians, he saw an encroachment on his most precious possession, and consequently an attack,—and moreover also an impertinence of the assailant! The "law of nature" sounded to him as blasphemy against God; in truth he would too willingly have seen the whole of mechanics traced back to moral acts of volition and arbitrariness:—but because nobody could render him this service, he concealed nature and mechanism from himself as best he could, and lived in a dream. Oh, those men of former times understood how to dream, and did not need first to go to sleep!—and we men of the present day also still understand it too well, with all our good-will for wakefulness and daylight! It suffices to love, to hate, to desire, and in general to feel,—immediately the spirit and the power of the dream come over us, and we ascend, with open eyes and indifferent to all danger, the most dangerous paths, to the roofs and towers of fantasy, and without any giddiness, as persons born for climbing—we the night-walkers by day! We artists! We concealers of naturalness! We moon-struck and God-struck ones! We dead-silent, untiring wanderers on heights which we do not see as heights, but as our plains, as our places of safety!

60.

Women and their Effect in the Distance.—Have I still ears? Am I only ear, and nothing else besides? Here I stand in the midst of the surging of the breakers, whose white flames fork up to my feet;—

from all sides there is howling, threatening, crying, and screaming at me, while in the lowest depths the old earth-shaker sings his aria, hollow like a roaring bull; he beats such an earth-shaker's measure thereto, that even the hearts of these weathered rock-monsters tremble at the sound. Then, suddenly, as if born out of nothingness, there appears before the portal of this hellish labyrinth, only a few fathoms distant,—a great sailing-ship gliding silently along like a ghost. Oh, this ghostly beauty! With what enchantment it seizes me! What? Has all the repose and silence in the world embarked here? Does my happiness itself sit in this quiet place, my happier ego, my second immortalised self? Still not dead, yet also no longer living? As a ghost-like, calm, gazing, gliding, sweeping, neutral being? Similar to the ship, which, with its white sails, like an immense butterfly, passes over the dark sea! Yes! Passing over existence! That is it! That would be it!——It seems that the noise here has made me a visionary? All great noise causes one to place happiness in the calm and the distance. When a man is in the midst of his hubbub, in the midst of the breakers of his plots and plans, he there sees perhaps calm, enchanting beings glide past him, for whose happiness and retirement he longs—they are women. He almost thinks that there with the women dwells his better self; that in these calm places even the loudest breakers become still as death, and life itself a dream of life. But still! But still! My noble enthusiast, there is also in the most beautiful sailing-ship so much noise and bustling, and alas, so much petty, pitiable bustling! The enchantment and the most powerful effect of women is, to use the language of philosophers, an effect at a distance, an actio in distans; there belongs thereto, however, primarily and above all,—distance!

61.

In Honour of Friendship.—That the sentiment of friendship was regarded by antiquity as the highest sentiment, higher even than the most vaunted pride of the self-sufficient and wise, yea as it were its sole and still holier brotherhood, is very well expressed by the story of the Macedonian king who made the present of a talent to a cynical Athenian philosopher from whom he received it back again. "What?" said the king, "has he then no friend?" He therewith meant to say, "I honour this pride of the wise and independent man, but I should have honoured his humanity still higher if the friend in him had gained the victory over his pride. The philosopher has lowered himself in my estimation, for he showed that he did not know one of the two highest sentiments—and in fact the higher of them!"

62.
Love.—Love pardons even the passion of the beloved.

63.
Woman in Music.—How does it happen that warm and rainy winds bring the musical mood and the inventive delight in melody with them? Are they not the same winds that fill the churches and give women amorous thoughts?

64.
Sceptics.—I fear women who have become old are more sceptical in the secret recesses of their hearts than any of the men are; they believe in the superficiality of existence as in its essence, and all virtue and profundity is to them only the disguising of this "truth," the very desirable disguising of a pudendum,—an affair, therefore, of decency and of modesty, and nothing more!

65.
Devotedness.—There are noble women with a certain poverty of spirit, who, in order to express their profoundest devotedness, have no other alternative but to offer their virtue and modesty: it is the highest thing they have. And this present is often accepted without putting the recipient under such deep obligation as the giver supposed,—a very melancholy story!

66.
The Strength of the Weak.—Women are all skilful in exaggerating their weaknesses, indeed they are inventive in weaknesses, so as to seem quite fragile ornaments to which even a grain of dust does harm; their existence is meant to bring home to man's mind his coarseness, and to appeal to his conscience. They thus defend themselves against the strong and all "rights of might."

67.
Self-dissembling.—She loves him now and has since been looking forth with as quiet confidence as a cow; but alas! It was precisely his delight that she seemed so fitful and absolutely incomprehensible! He had rather too much steady weather in himself already! Would she not do well to feign her old character? to feign indifference? Does not—love itself advise her to do so? Vivat comœdia!

68.

Will and Willingness.—Some one brought a youth to a wise man and said, "See, this is one who is being corrupted by women!" The wise man shook his head and smiled. "It is men," he called out, "who corrupt women; and everything that women lack should be atoned for and improved in men,—for man creates for himself the ideal of woman, and woman moulds herself according to this ideal."—"You are too tender-hearted towards women," said one of the bystanders, "you do not know them!" The wise man answered: "Man's attribute is will, woman's attribute is willingness,—such is the law of the sexes, verily! a hard law for woman! All human beings are innocent of their existence, women, however, are doubly innocent; who could have enough of salve and gentleness for them!"—"What about salve! What about gentleness!" called out another person in the crowd, "we must educate women better!"—"We must educate men better," said the wise man, and made a sign to the youth to follow him.—The youth, however, did not follow him.

69.

Capacity for Revenge.—That a person cannot and consequently will not defend himself, does not yet cast disgrace upon him in our eyes; but we despise the person who has neither the ability nor the good-will for revenge—whether it be a man or a woman. Would a woman be able to captivate us (or, as people say, to "fetter" us) whom we did not credit with knowing how to employ the dagger (any kind of dagger) skilfully against us under certain circumstances? Or against herself; which in a certain case might be the severest revenge (the Chinese revenge).

70.

The Mistresses of the Masters.—A powerful contralto voice, as we occasionally hear it in the theatre, raises suddenly for us the curtain on possibilities in which we usually do not believe; all at once we are convinced that somewhere in the world there may be women with high, heroic, royal souls, capable and prepared for magnificent remonstrances, resolutions, and self-sacrifices, capable and prepared for domination over men, because in them the best in man, superior to sex, has become a corporeal ideal. To be sure, it is not the intention of the theatre that such voices should give such a conception of women; they are usually intended to represent the ideal male lover, for example, a Romeo; but, to judge by my experience, the theatre regularly miscalculates here, and the musician also, who expects such effects from such a voice. People do not believe in these lovers;

these voices still contain a tinge of the motherly and housewifely character, and most of all when love is in their tone.

71.

On Female Chastity.—There is something quite astonishing and extraordinary in the education of women of the higher class; indeed, there is perhaps nothing more paradoxical. All the world is agreed to educate them with as much ignorance as possible in eroticis, and to inspire their soul with a profound shame of such things, and the extremest impatience and horror at the suggestion of them. It is really here only that all the "honour" of woman is at stake; what would one not forgive them in other respects! But here they are intended to remain ignorant to the very backbone:—they are intended to have neither eyes, ears, words, nor thoughts for this, their "wickedness"; indeed knowledge here is already evil. And then! To be hurled as with an awful thunderbolt into reality and knowledge with marriage—and indeed by him whom they most love and esteem: to have to encounter love and shame in contradiction, yea, to have to feel rapture, abandonment, duty, sympathy, and fright at the unexpected proximity of God and animal, and whatever else besides! all at once!—There, in fact, a psychic entanglement has been effected which is quite unequalled! Even the sympathetic curiosity of the wisest discerner of men does not suffice to divine how this or that woman gets along with the solution of this enigma and the enigma of this solution; what dreadful, far-reaching suspicions must awaken thereby in the poor unhinged soul; and forsooth, how the ultimate philosophy and scepticism of the woman casts anchor at this 105point!—Afterwards the same profound silence as before: and often even a silence to herself, a shutting of her eyes to herself.—Young wives on that account make great efforts to appear superficial and thoughtless; the most ingenious of them simulate a kind of impudence.—Wives easily feel their husbands as a question-mark to their honour, and their children as an apology or atonement,—they require children, and wish for them in quite another spirit than a husband wishes for them.—In short, one cannot be gentle enough towards women!

72.

Mothers.—Animals think differently from men with respect to females; with them the female is regarded as the productive being. There is no paternal love among them, but there is such a thing as love of the children of a beloved, and habituation to them. In the young, the females find gratification for their lust of dominion; the young are a property, an occupation, something quite comprehensible to them, with which they can chatter: all this conjointly is maternal love,—it is to be compared to the love of the artist for his work. Pregnancy has made the females gentler, more expectant, more timid, more submissively inclined; and similarly intellectual pregnancy engenders the character of the contemplative, who are allied to women in character:—they are the masculine mothers.—Among animals the masculine sex is regarded as the beautiful sex.

73.

Saintly Cruelty.—A man holding a newly born child in his hands came to a saint. "What should I do with the child," he asked, "it is wretched, deformed, and has not even enough of life to die." "Kill it," cried the saint with a dreadful voice, "kill it, and then hold it in thy arms for three days and three nights to brand it on thy memory:—thus wilt thou never again beget a child when it is not the time for thee to beget."—When the man had heard this he went away disappointed; and many found fault with the saint because he had advised cruelty, for he had advised to kill the child. "But is it not more cruel to let it live?" asked the saint.

74.

The Unsuccessful.—Those poor women always fail of success who become agitated and uncertain, and talk too much in presence of him whom they love; for men are most successfully seduced by a certain subtle and phlegmatic tenderness.

75.

The Third Sex.—"A small man is a paradox, but still a man,—but the small woman seems to me to be of another sex in comparison with well-grown ones"—said an old dancing-master. A small woman is never beautiful—said old Aristotle.

76.

The greatest Danger.—Had there not at all times been a larger number of men who regarded the cultivation of their mind—their "rationality"—as their pride, their obligation, their virtue, and were injured or shamed by all play of fancy and extravagance of thinking—as lovers of "sound common sense":—mankind would long ago have perished! Incipient insanity has hovered, and hovers continually over mankind as its greatest danger: that is precisely the breaking out of inclination in feeling, seeing, and hearing; the enjoyment of the unruliness of the mind; the delight in human unreason. It is not truth and certainty that is the antithesis of the world of the insane, but the universality and all-obligatoriness of a belief, in short, non-voluntariness in forming opinions. And the greatest labour of human beings hitherto has been to agree with one another regarding a great many things, and to impose upon themselves a law of agreement—indifferent whether these things are true or false. This is the discipline of the mind which has preserved mankind;—but the counter-impulses are still so powerful that one can really speak of the future of mankind with little confidence. The ideas of things still continually shift and move, and will perhaps alter more than ever in the future; it is continually the most select spirits themselves who strive against universal obligatoriness—the investigators of truth above all! The accepted belief, as the belief of all the world, continually engenders a disgust and a new longing in the more ingenious minds; and already the slow tempo which it demands for all intellectual processes (the imitation of the tortoise, which is here recognised as the rule) [108] makes the artists and poets runaways:—it is in these impatient spirits that a downright delight in delirium breaks out, because delirium has such a joyful tempo! Virtuous intellects, therefore, are needed—ah! I want to use the least ambiguous word,—virtuous stupidity is needed, imperturbable conductors of the slow spirits are needed, in order that the faithful of the great collective belief may remain with one another and dance their dance further: it is a necessity of the first importance that here enjoins and demands. We others are the exceptions and the danger,—we eternally need protection!—Well, there can actually be something said in favour of the exceptions provided that they never want to become the rule.

77.

The Animal with good Conscience.—It is not unknown to me that there is vulgarity in everything that pleases Southern Europe—whether it be Italian opera (for example, Rossini's and Bellini's), or the Spanish adventure-romance (most readily accessible to us in the French garb of Gil Blas)—but it does not offend me, any more than the vulgarity which one encounters in a walk through Pompeii, or even in the reading of every ancient book: what is the reason of this? Is it because shame is lacking here, and because the vulgar always comes forward just as sure and certain of itself as anything noble, lovely, and passionate in the same kind of music or romance? "The animal has its rights like man, so let it run about freely; and you, my dear fellow-man, [109] are still this animal, in spite of all!"—that seems to me the moral of the case, and the peculiarity of southern humanity. Bad taste has its rights like good taste, and even a prerogative over the latter when it is the great requisite, the sure satisfaction, and as it were a universal language, an immediately intelligible mask and attitude; the excellent, select taste on the other hand has always something of a seeking, tentative character, not fully certain that it understands,—it is never, and has never been popular! The masque is and remains popular! So let all this masquerade run along in the melodies and cadences, in the leaps and merriment of the rhythm of these operas! Quite the ancient life! What does one understand of it, if one does not understand the delight in the masque, the good conscience of all masquerade! Here is the bath and the refreshment of the ancient spirit:—and perhaps this bath was still more necessary for the rare and sublime natures of the ancient world than for the vulgar.—On the other hand, a vulgar turn in northern works, for example in German music, offends me unutterably. There is shame in it, the artist has lowered himself in his own sight, and could not even avoid blushing: we are ashamed with him, and are so hurt because we surmise that he believed he had to lower himself on our account.

78.

What we should be Grateful for.—It is only the artists, and especially the theatrical artists who have furnished men with eyes and ears to hear and see with some pleasure what everyone is in himself, what he experiences and aims at: it is only they who have taught us how to estimate the hero that is concealed in each of these commonplace men, and the art of looking at ourselves from a distance as heroes, and as it were simplified and transfigured,—the art of "putting ourselves on the stage" before ourselves. It is thus only that we get beyond some of the paltry details in ourselves! Without that art we should be nothing but fore-ground, and would live absolutely under the spell of the perspective which makes the closest and the commonest seem immensely large and like reality in itself.—Perhaps there is merit of a similar kind in the religion which commanded us to look at the sinfulness of every individual man with a magnifying-glass, and to make a great, immortal criminal out of the sinner; in that it put eternal perspectives around man, it taught him to see himself from a distance, and as something past, something entire.

79.

The Charm of Imperfection.—I see here a poet, who, like so many men, exercises a higher charm by his imperfections than by all that is rounded off and takes perfect shape under his hands,—indeed, he derives his advantage and reputation far more from his actual limitations than from his abundant powers. His work never expresses altogether what he would really like to express, what he would like to have seen: he appears to have had the foretaste of a vision and never the vision itself:—but an extraordinary longing for this vision has remained in his soul; and from this he derives his equally extraordinary eloquence of longing and craving. With this he raises those who listen to him above his work and above all "works," and gives them wings to rise higher than hearers have ever risen before, thus making them poets and seers themselves; they then show an admiration for the originator of their happiness, as if he had led them immediately to the vision of his holiest and ultimate verities, as if he had reached his goal, and had actually seen and communicated his vision. It is to the advantage of his reputation that he has not really arrived at his goal.

80.

Art and Nature.—The Greeks (or at least the Athenians) liked to hear good talking: indeed they had an eager inclination for it, which distinguished them more than anything else from non-Greeks. And so they required good talking even from passion on the stage, and submitted to the unnaturalness of dramatic verse with delight:—in nature, forsooth, passion is so sparing of words! so dumb and confused! Or if it finds words, so embarrassed and irrational and a shame to itself! We have now, all of us, thanks to the Greeks, accustomed ourselves to this unnaturalness on the stage, as we endure that other unnaturalness, the singing passion, and willingly endure it, thanks to the Italians.—It has become a necessity to us, which we cannot satisfy out of the resources of actuality, to hear men talk well and in full detail in the most trying situations: it enraptures us at present when the tragic hero still finds words, reasons, eloquent gestures, and on the whole a bright spirituality, where life approaches the abysses, and where the actual man mostly loses his head, and certainly his fine language. This kind of deviation from nature is perhaps the most agreeable repast for man's pride: he loves art generally on account of it, as the expression of high, heroic unnaturalness and convention. One rightly objects to the dramatic poet when he does not transform everything into reason and speech, but always retains a remnant of silence:—just as one is dissatisfied with an operatic musician who cannot find a melody for the highest emotion, but only an emotional, "natural" stammering and crying. Here nature has to be contradicted! Here the common charm of illusion has to give place to a higher charm! The Greeks go far, far in this direction—frightfully far! As they constructed the stage as narrow as possible and dispensed with all the effect of deep backgrounds, as they made pantomime and easy motion impossible to the actor, and transformed him into a solemn, stiff, masked bogey, so they have also deprived passion itself of its deep background, and have dictated to it a law of fine talk; indeed, they have really done everything to counteract the elementary effect of representations that inspire pity and terror: they did not want pity and terror,—with due deference, with the highest deference to Aristotle!

but he certainly did not hit the nail, to say nothing of the head of the nail, when he spoke about the final aim of Greek tragedy! Let us but look at the Grecian tragic poets with respect to what most excited their diligence, their inventiveness, and their emulation,—certainly it was not the intention of subjugating the spectators by emotion! The Athenian went to the theatre to hear fine talking! And fine talking was arrived at by Sophocles!—pardon me this heresy!—It is very different with serious opera: all its masters make it their business to prevent their personages being understood. "An occasional word picked up may come to the assistance of the inattentive listener; but on the whole the situation must be self-explanatory,—the talking is of no account!"—so they all think, and so they have all made fun of the words. Perhaps they have only lacked courage to express fully their extreme contempt for words: a little additional insolence in Rossini, and he would have allowed la-la-la-la to be sung throughout—and it might have been the rational course! The personages of the opera are not meant to be believed "in their words," but in their tones! That is the difference, that is the fine unnaturalness on account of which people go to the opera! Even the recitativo secco is not really intended to be heard as words and text: this kind of half-music is meant rather in the first place to give the musical ear a little repose (the repose from melody, as from the sublimest, and on that account the most straining enjoyment of this art),—but very soon something different results, namely, an increasing impatience, an increasing resistance, a new longing for entire music, for melody.—How is it with the art of Richard Wagner as seen from this standpoint? Is it perhaps the same? Perhaps otherwise? It would often seem to me as if one needed to have learned by heart both the words and the music of his creations before the performances; for without that—so it seemed to me—one may hear neither the words, nor even the music.

81.

Grecian Taste.—"What is beautiful in it?"—asked a certain geometrician, after a performance of the Iphigenia—"there is nothing proved in it!" Could the Greeks have been so far from this taste? In Sophocles at least "everything is proved."

82.

Esprit Un-Grecian.—The Greeks were exceedingly logical and plain in all their thinking; they did not get tired of it, at least during their long flourishing period, as is so often the case with the French; who too willingly made a little excursion into the opposite, and in fact endure the spirit of logic only when it betrays its sociable courtesy, its sociable self-renunciation, by a multitude of such little excursions into its opposite. Logic appears to them as necessary as bread and water, but also like these as a kind of prison-fare, as soon as it is to be taken pure and by itself. In good society one must never want to be in the right absolutely and solely, as all pure logic requires; hence, the little dose of irrationality in all French esprit.—The social sense of the Greeks was far less developed than that of the French in the present and the past; hence, so little esprit in their cleverest men, hence, so little wit, even in their wags, hence—alas! But people will not readily believe these tenets of mine, and how much of the kind I have still on my soul!—Est res magna tacere—says Martial, like all garrulous people.

83.

Translations.—One can estimate the amount of the historical sense which an age possesses by the way in which it makes translations and seeks to embody in itself past periods and literatures. The French of Corneille, and even the French of the Revolution, appropriated Roman antiquity in a manner for which we would no longer have the courage—owing to our superior historical sense. And Roman antiquity itself: how violently, and at the same time how naïvely, did it lay its hand on everything excellent and elevated belonging to the older Grecian antiquity! How they translated these writings into the Roman present! How they wiped away intentionally and unconcernedly the wing-dust of the butterfly moment! It is thus that Horace now and then translated Alcæus or Archilochus, it is thus that Propertius translated Callimachus and Philetas (poets of equal rank with Theocritus, if we be allowed to judge): of what consequence was it to them that the actual creator experienced this and that, and had inscribed the indication thereof in his poem!—as poets they were averse to the antiquarian, inquisitive spirit which precedes the historical sense; as poets they did not respect those essentially personal traits and names, nor anything peculiar to city, coast, or century, such as its costume and mask, but at once put the present and the Roman in its place. They seem to us to ask: "Should we not make the old new for ourselves, and adjust ourselves to it? Should we not be allowed to inspire this dead body with our soul? for it is dead indeed: how loathsome is everything dead!"—They did not know the pleasure of the historical sense; the past and the alien was painful to them, and as Romans it was an incitement to a Roman conquest. In fact, they conquered when they translated,—not only in that they omitted the historical: no, they added also allusions to the present; above all, they struck out the name of the poet and put their own in its place—not with the feeling of theft, but with the very best conscience of the imperium Romanum.

84.

The Origin of Poetry.—The lovers of the fantastic in man, who at the same time represent the doctrine of instinctive morality, draw this conclusion: "Granted that utility has been honoured at all times as the highest divinity, where then in all the world has poetry come from?—this rhythmising of speech which thwarts rather than furthers plainness of communication, and which, nevertheless, has sprung up everywhere on the earth, and still springs up, as a mockery of all useful purpose! The wildly beautiful irrationality of poetry refutes you, ye utilitarians! The wish to get rid of utility in some way—that is precisely what has elevated man, that is what has inspired him to morality and art!" Well, I must here speak for once to please the utilitarians,—they are so seldom in the right that it is pitiful! In the old times which called poetry into being, people had still utility in view with respect to it, and a very important utility—at the time when rhythm was introduced into speech, the force which arranges all the particles of the sentence anew, commands the choosing of the words, recolours the thought, and makes it more obscure, more foreign, and more distant: to be sure a superstitious utility! It was intended that a human entreaty should be more profoundly impressed upon the Gods by virtue of rhythm, after it had been observed that men could remember a verse better than an unmetrical speech. It was likewise thought that people could make themselves audible at greater distances by the rhythmical beat; the rhythmical prayer seemed to come nearer to the ear of the Gods. Above all, however, people wanted to have the advantage of the elementary conquest which man experiences in himself when he hears music: rhythm is a constraint; it produces an unconquerable desire to yield, to join in; not only the step of the foot, but also the soul itself follows the measure,—probably the soul of the Gods also, as people thought! They attempted, therefore, to constrain the Gods by rhythm and to exercise a power over them; they threw poetry around the Gods like a magic noose. There was a still more wonderful idea, and it has perhaps operated most powerfully of all in the originating of poetry. Among the Pythagoreans it made its appearance as a philosophical doctrine and as an artifice of teaching: but long before there were philosophers music was acknowledged to possess the power of unburdening the emotions, of purifying the soul, of soothing the ferocia animi—and this was owing to the rhythmical element in music. When the proper tension and harmony of the soul were lost a person had to dance to the measure of the singer,—that was the recipe of this medical art. By means of it Terpander quieted a tumult, Empedocles calmed a maniac, Damon purged a love-sick youth; by means of it even the maddened, revengeful Gods were treated for the purpose of a cure. First of all, it was by driving the frenzy and wantonness of their emotions to the highest pitch, by making the furious mad, and the revengeful intoxicated with vengeance:—all the orgiastic cults seek to discharge the ferocia of a deity all at once and thus make an orgy, so that the deity may feel freer and quieter afterwards, and leave man in peace. Melos, according to its root, signifies a soothing means, not because the song is gentle itself, but because its after-effect makes gentle.— And not only in the religious song, but also in the secular song of the most ancient times the prerequisite is that the rhythm should exercise a magical influence; for example, in drawing water, or in rowing: the song is for the enchanting of the spirits supposed to be active thereby; it makes them obliging, involuntary, and the instruments of man. And as often as a person acts he has occasion to sing, every action is dependent on the assistance of spirits: 119magic song and incantation appear to be the original form of poetry. When verse also came to be used in oracles—the Greeks said that the hexameter was invented at Delphi,—the rhythm was here also intended to exercise a compulsory influence. To make a prophecy—that means originally (according to what seems to me the probable derivation of the Greek word) to determine something; people thought they could determine the future by winning Apollo over to their side: he who, according to the most ancient idea, is far more than a foreseeing deity.

According as the formula is pronounced with literal and rhythmical correctness, it determines the future: the formula, however, is the invention of Apollo, who as the God of rhythm, can also determine the goddesses of fate.—Looked at and investigated as a whole, was there ever anything more serviceable to the ancient superstitious species of human being than rhythm? People could do everything with it: they could make labour go on magically; they could compel a God to appear, to be near at hand, and listen to them; they could arrange the future for themselves according to their will; they could unburden their own souls of any kind of excess (of anxiety, of mania, of sympathy, of revenge), and not only their own soul, but the souls of the most evil spirits,—without verse a person was nothing, by means of verse a person became almost a God. Such a fundamental feeling no longer allows itself to be fully eradicated,—and even now, after millenniums of long labour in combating such superstition, the very wisest of us occasionally becomes the 120fool of rhythm, be it only that one perceives a thought to be truer when it has a metrical form and approaches with a divine hopping. Is it not a very funny thing that the most serious philosophers, however anxious they are in other respects for strict certainty, still appeal to poetical sayings in order to give their thoughts force and credibility?—and yet it is more dangerous to a truth when the poet assents to it than when he contradicts it! For, as Homer says, "The singers speak much falsehood!"—

85.

The Good and the Beautiful.—Artists glorify continually—they do nothing else,—and indeed they glorify all those conditions and things that have a reputation, so that man may feel himself good or great, or intoxicated, or merry, or pleased and wise by it. Those select things and conditions whose value for human happiness is regarded as secure and determined, are the objects of artists: they are ever lying in wait to discover such things, to transfer them into the domain of art. I mean to say that they are not themselves the valuers of happiness and of the happy ones, but they always press close to these valuers with the greatest curiosity and longing, in order immediately to use their valuations advantageously. As besides their impatience, they have also the big lungs of heralds and the feet of runners, they are likewise always among the first to glorify the new excellency, and often seem to be those who first of all called it good and valued it as good. 121This, however, as we have said, is an error; they are only faster and louder than the actual valuers:—And who then are these?—They are the rich and the leisurely.

86.

The Theatre.—This day has given me once more strong and elevated sentiments, and if I could have music and art in the evening, I know well what music and art I should not like to have; namely, none of that which would fain intoxicate its hearers and excite them to a crisis of strong and high feeling,—those men with commonplace souls, who in the evening are not like victors on triumphal cars, but like tired mules to whom life has rather too often applied the whip. What would those men at all know of "higher moods," unless there were expedients for causing ecstasy and idealistic strokes of the whip!—and thus they have their inspirers as they have their wines. But what is their drink and their drunkenness to me! Does the inspired one need wine? He rather looks with a kind of disgust at the agency and the agent which are here intended to produce an effect without sufficient reason,—an imitation of the high tide of the soul! What? One gives the mole wings and proud fancies—before going to sleep, before he creeps into his hole? One sends him into the theatre and puts great magnifying-glasses to his blind and tired eyes? Men, whose life is not "action" but business, sit in front of the stage and look at strange beings to whom life is more than business? "This is proper," you say, "this 122is entertaining, this is what culture wants!"—Well then! culture is too often lacking in me, for this sight is too often disgusting to me. He who has enough of tragedy and comedy in himself surely prefers to remain away from the theatre; or, as the exception, the whole procedure—theatre and public and poet included—becomes for him a truly tragic and comic play, so that the performed piece counts for little in comparison. He who is something like Faust and Manfred, what does it matter to him about the Fausts and Manfreds of the theatre!—while it certainly gives him something to think about that such figures are brought into the theatre at all. The strongest thoughts and passions before those who are not capable of thought and passion—but of intoxication only! And those as a means to this end! And theatre and music the hashish-smoking and betel-chewing of Europeans! Oh, who will narrate to us the whole history of narcotics!—It is almost the history of "culture," the so-called higher culture!

87.

The Conceit of Artists.—I think artists often do not know what they can do best, because they are too conceited, and have set their minds on something loftier than those little plants appear to be, which can grow up to perfection on their soil, fresh, rare, and beautiful. The final value of their own garden and vineyard is superciliously underestimated by them, and their love and their insight are not of the same quality. Here is a musician, who, more than any one else, has the genius for discovering the tones peculiar to suffering, oppressed, tortured souls, and who can endow even dumb animals with speech. No one equals him in the colours of the late autumn, in the indescribably touching happiness of a last, a final, and all too short enjoyment; he knows a chord for those secret and weird midnights of the soul when cause and effect seem out of joint, and when every instant something may originate "out of nothing." He draws his resources best of all out of the lower depths of human happiness, and so to speak, out of its drained goblet, where the bitterest and most nauseous drops have ultimately, for good or for ill, commingled with the sweetest. He knows the weary shuffling along of the soul which can no longer leap or fly, yea, not even walk; he has the shy glance of concealed pain, of understanding without comfort, of leave-taking without avowal; yea, as the Orpheus of all secret misery, he is greater than anyone; and in fact much has been added to art by him which was hitherto inexpressible and not even thought worthy of art, and which was only to be scared away, by words, and not grasped—many small and quite microscopic features of the soul: yes, he is the master of miniature. But he does not wish to be so! His character is more in love with large walls and daring frescoes! He fails to see that his spirit has a different taste and inclination, and prefers to sit quietly in the corners of ruined houses:—concealed in this way, concealed even from himself, he there paints his proper masterpieces, all of which are very short, often only one bar in length,—there only does he become quite good, great, and perfect, perhaps there only.—But he does not know it! He is too conceited to know it.

88.

Earnestness for the Truth.—Earnest for the truth! What different things men understand by these words! Just the same opinions, and modes of demonstration and testing which a thinker regards as a frivolity in himself, to which he has succumbed with shame at one time or other,—just the same opinions may give to an artist, who comes in contact with them and accepts them temporarily, the consciousness that the profoundest earnestness for the truth has now taken hold of him, and that it is worthy of admiration that, although an artist, he at the same time exhibits the most ardent desire for the antithesis of the apparent. It is thus possible that a person may, just by his pathos of earnestness, betray how superficially and sparingly his intellect has hitherto operated in the domain of knowledge.—And is not everything that we consider important our betrayer? It shows where our motives lie, and where our motives are altogether lacking.

89.

Now and Formerly.—Of what consequence is all our art in artistic products, if that higher art, the art of the festival, be lost by us? Formerly all artistic products were exhibited on the great festive path of humanity, as tokens of remembrance, and monuments of high and happy moments. One now seeks to allure the exhausted and sickly from the great suffering path of humanity for a wanton moment by means of works of art; one furnishes them with a little ecstasy and insanity.

90.

Lights and Shades.—Books and writings are different with different thinkers. One writer has collected together in his book all the rays of light which he could quickly plunder and carry home from an illuminating experience; while another gives only the shadows, and the grey and black replicas of that which on the previous day had towered up in his soul.

91.

Precaution.—Alfieri, as is well known, told a great many falsehoods when he narrated the history of his life to his astonished contemporaries. He told falsehoods owing to the despotism toward himself which he exhibited, for example, in the way in which he created his own language, and tyrannised himself into a poet:—he finally found a rigid form of sublimity into which he forced his life and his memory; he must have suffered much in the process.—I would also give no credit to a history of Plato's life written by himself, as little as to Rousseau's, or to the Vita nuova of Dante.

92.

Prose and Poetry.—Let it be observed that the great masters of prose have almost always been poets as well, whether openly, or only in secret and 126for the "closet"; and in truth one only writes good prose in view of poetry! For prose is an uninterrupted, polite warfare with poetry; all its charm consists in the fact that poetry is constantly avoided, and contradicted; every abstraction wants to have a gibe at poetry, and wishes to be uttered with a mocking voice; all dryness and coolness is meant to bring the amiable goddess into an amiable despair; there are often approximations and reconciliations for the moment, and then a sudden recoil and a burst of laughter; the curtain is often drawn up and dazzling light let in just while the goddess is enjoying her twilights and dull colours; the word is often taken out of her mouth and chanted to a melody while she holds her fine hands before her delicate little ears—and so there are a thousand enjoyments of the warfare, the defeats included, of which the unpoetic, the so-called prose-men know nothing at all:—they consequently write and speak only bad prose! Warfare is the father of all good things, it is also the father of good prose!—There have been four very singular and truly poetical men in this century who have arrived at mastership in prose, for which otherwise this century is not suited, owing to lack of poetry, as we have indicated. Not to take Goethe into account, for he is reasonably claimed by the century that produced him, I look only on Giacomo Leopardi, Prosper Mérimée, Ralph Waldo Emerson, and Walter Savage Landor, the author of Imaginary Conversations, as worthy to be called masters of prose.

93.

But why, then, do you Write?—A: I do not belong to those who think with the wet pen in hand; and still less to those who yield themselves entirely to their passions before the open ink-bottle, sitting on their chair and staring at the paper. I am always vexed and abashed by writing; writing is a necessity for me,—even to speak of it in a simile is disagreeable. B: But why, then, do you write? A: Well, my dear Sir, to tell you in confidence, I have hitherto found no other means of getting rid of my thoughts. B: And why do you wish to get rid of them? A: Why I wish? Do I really wish! I must.—B: Enough!

Enough!

94.

Growth after Death.—Those few daring words about moral matters which Fontenelle threw into his immortal Dialogues of the Dead, were regarded by his age as paradoxes and amusements of a not unscrupulous wit; even the highest judges of taste and intellect saw nothing more in them,—indeed, Fontenelle himself perhaps saw nothing more. Then something incredible takes place: these thoughts become truths! Science proves them! The game becomes serious! And we read those dialogues with a feeling different from that with which Voltaire and Helvetius read them, and we involuntarily raise their originator into another and much higher class of intellects than they did.—Rightly? Wrongly?

95.

Chamfort.—That such a judge of men and of the multitude as Chamfort should side with the multitude, instead of standing apart in philosophical resignation and defence—I am at a loss to explain, except as follows:—There was an instinct in him stronger than his wisdom, and it had never been gratified: the hatred against all noblesse of blood; perhaps his mother's old and only too explicable hatred, which was consecrated in him by love of her,—an instinct of revenge from his boyhood, which waited for the hour to avenge his mother. But then the course of his life, his genius, and alas! most of all, perhaps, the paternal blood in his veins, had seduced him to rank and consider himself equal to the noblesse—for many, many years! In the end, however, he could not endure the sight of himself, the "old man" under the old régime, any longer; he got into a violent, penitential passion, and in this state he put on the raiment of the populace as his special kind of hair-shirt! His bad conscience was the neglect of revenge.—If Chamfort had then been a little more of the philosopher, the Revolution would not have had its tragic wit and its sharpest sting; it would have been regarded as a much more stupid affair, and would have had no such seductive influence on men's minds. But Chamfort's hatred and revenge educated an entire generation; and the most illustrious men passed through his school. Let us but consider that Mirabeau looked up to Chamfort as to his higher and older self, from whom he expected (and endured) impulses, warnings, and condemnations,—Mirabeau, who as a man belongs to an entirely different order of greatness, as the very foremost among the statesman-geniuses of yesterday and to-day.—Strange, that in spite of such a friend and advocate—we possess Mirabeau's letters to Chamfort—this wittiest of all moralists has remained unfamiliar to the French, quite the same as Stendhal, who has perhaps had the most penetrating eyes and ears of any Frenchman of this century. Is it because the latter had really too much of the German and the Englishman in his nature for the Parisians to endure him?—while Chamfort, a man with ample knowledge of the profundities and secret motives of the soul, gloomy, suffering, ardent—a thinker who found laughter necessary as the remedy of life, and who almost gave himself up as lost every day that he had not laughed,—seems much more like an Italian, and related by blood to Dante and Leopardi, than like a Frenchman. One knows Chamfort's last words: "Ah! mon ami," he said to Sieyès, "je m'en vais enfin de ce monde, où il faut que le cœur se brise ou se bronze—." These were certainly not the words of a dying Frenchman.

96.

Two Orators.—Of these two orators the one arrives at a full understanding of his case only when he yields himself to emotion; it is only this that pumps sufficient blood and heat into his brain to compel his high intellectuality to reveal itself. 130The other attempts, indeed, now and then to do the same: to state his case sonorously, vehemently, and spiritedly with the aid of emotion,—but usually with bad success. He then very soon speaks obscurely and confusedly; he exaggerates, makes omissions, and excites suspicion of the justice of his case: indeed, he himself feels this suspicion, and the sudden changes into the coldest and most repulsive tones (which raise a doubt in the hearer as to his passionateness being genuine) are thereby explicable. With him emotion always drowns the spirit; perhaps because it is stronger than in the former. But he is at the height of his power when he resists the impetuous storm of his feeling, and as it were scorns it; it is then only that his spirit emerges fully from its concealment, a spirit logical, mocking, and playful, but nevertheless awe-inspiring.

97.

The Loquacity of Authors.—There is a loquacity of anger—frequent in Luther, also in Schopenhauer. A loquacity which comes from too great a store of conceptual formulæ, as in Kant. A loquacity which comes from delight in ever new modifications of the same idea: one finds it in Montaigne. A loquacity of malicious natures: whoever reads writings of our period will recollect two authors in this connection. A loquacity which comes from delight in fine words and forms of speech: by no means rare in Goethe's prose. A loquacity which comes from pure satisfaction in noise and confusion of feelings: for example in Carlyle.

98.

In Honour of Shakespeare.—The best thing I could say in honour of Shakespeare, the man, is that he believed in Brutus and cast not a shadow of suspicion on the kind of virtue which Brutus represents! It is to him that Shakespeare consecrated his best tragedy—it is at present still called by a wrong name,—to him and to the most terrible essence of lofty morality. Independence of soul!—that is the question at issue! No sacrifice can be too great there: one must be able to sacrifice to it even one's dearest friend, though he be also the grandest of men, the ornament of the world, the genius without peer,—if one really loves freedom as the freedom of great souls, and if this freedom be threatened by him:—it is thus that Shakespeare must have felt! The elevation in which he places Cæsar is the most exquisite honour he could confer upon Brutus; it is thus only that he lifts into vastness the inner problem of his hero, and similarly the strength of soul which could cut this knot!—And was it actually political freedom that impelled the poet to sympathy with Brutus,—and made him the accomplice of Brutus? Or was political freedom merely a symbol for something inexpressible? Do we perhaps stand before some sombre event or adventure of the poet's own soul, which has remained unknown, and of which he only cared to speak symbolically? What is all Hamlet-melancholy in comparison with the melancholy of Brutus!—and perhaps Shakespeare also knew this, as he knew the other, by experience! Perhaps he also had his dark hour and his bad angel, just as Brutus had them!—But whatever similarities and secret relationships of that kind there may have been, Shakespeare cast himself on the ground and felt unworthy and alien in presence of the aspect and virtue of Brutus:—he has inscribed the testimony thereof in the tragedy itself. He has twice brought in a poet in it, and twice heaped upon him such an impatient and extreme contempt, that it sounds like a cry,—like the cry of self-contempt. Brutus, even Brutus loses patience when the poet appears, self-important, pathetic, and obtrusive, as poets usually are,—persons who seem to abound in the possibilities of greatness, even moral greatness, and nevertheless rarely attain even to ordinary uprightness in the philosophy of practice and of life. "He may know the times, but I know his temper,—away with the jigging fool!"—shouts Brutus. We may translate this back into the soul of the poet that composed it.

99.

The Followers of Schopenhauer.—What one sees at the contact of civilized peoples with barbarians,—namely, that the lower civilization regularly accepts in the first place the vices, weaknesses, and excesses of the higher; then, from that point onward, feels the influence of a charm; and finally, by means of the appropriated vices and weaknesses, also allows something of the valuable influence of the higher culture to leaven it:—one can also see this close at hand and without journeys to barbarian peoples, to be sure, somewhat refined and spiritualised, and not so readily palpable. What are the German followers of Schopenhauer still accustomed to receive first of all from their master:—those who, when placed beside his superior culture, must deem themselves sufficiently barbarous to be first of all barbarously fascinated and seduced by him. Is it his hard matter-of-fact sense, his inclination to clearness and rationality, which often makes him appear so English, and so unlike Germans?

Or the strength of his intellectual conscience, which endured a lifelong contradiction of "being" and "willing," and compelled him to contradict himself constantly even in his writings on almost every point? Or his purity in matters relating to the Church and the Christian God?—for here he was pure as no German philosopher had been hitherto, so that he lived and died "as a Voltairian." Or his immortal doctrines of the intellectuality of intuition, the apriority of the law of causality, the instrumental nature of the intellect, and the non-freedom of the will? No, nothing of this enchants, nor is felt as enchanting; but Schopenhauer's mystical embarrassments and shufflings in those passages where the matter-of-fact thinker allowed himself to be seduced and corrupted by the vain impulse to be the unraveller of the world's riddle: his undemonstrable doctrine of one will ("all causes are merely occasional causes of the phenomenon of the will at such a time and at such a place," "the will to live, whole and undivided, is present in every being, even in the smallest, as perfectly as in the sum of all that was, is, and will be"); his denial of the individual ("all lions are really only one lion," "plurality of individuals is an appearance," as also development is only an appearance: he calls the opinion of Lamarck "an ingenious, absurd error"); his fantasy about genius ("in æsthetic contemplation the individual is no longer an individual, but a pure, will-less, painless, timeless subject of knowledge," "the subject, in that it entirely merges in the contemplated object, has become this object itself"); his nonsense about sympathy, and about the outburst of the principium individuationis thus rendered possible, as the source of all morality; including also such assertions as, "dying is really the design of existence," "the possibility should not be absolutely denied that a magical effect could proceed from a person already dead":—these, and similar extravagances and vices of the philosopher, are always first accepted and made articles of faith; for vices and extravagances are always easiest to imitate, and do not require a long preliminary practice.

But let us speak of the most celebrated of the living Schopenhauerians, Richard Wagner.—It has happened to him as it has already happened to many an artist: he made a mistake in the interpretation of the characters he created, and misunderstood the unexpressed philosophy of the art peculiarly his own. Richard Wagner allowed himself to be misled by Hegel's influence till the middle of his life; and he did the same again when later on he read Schopenhauer's doctrine between the lines of his characters, and began to express himself with such terms as 135"will," "genius," and "sympathy." Nevertheless it will remain true that nothing is more counter to Schopenhauer's spirit than the essentially Wagnerian element in Wagner's heroes: I mean the innocence of the supremest selfishness, the belief in strong passion as the good in itself, in a word, the Siegfried trait in the countenances of his heroes.

"All that still smacks more of Spinoza than of me,"—Schopenhauer would probably have said. Whatever good reasons, therefore, Wagner might have had to be on the outlook for other philosophers than Schopenhauer, the enchantment to which he succumbed in respect to this thinker, not only made him blind towards all other philosophers, but even towards science itself; his entire art is more and more inclined to become the counterpart and complement of the Schopenhauerian philosophy, and it always renounces more emphatically the higher ambition to become the counterpart and complement of human knowledge and science. And not only is he allured thereto by the whole mystic pomp of this philosophy (which would also have allured a Cagliostro), the peculiar airs and emotions of the philosopher have all along been seducing him as well! For example, Wagner's indignation about the corruption of the German language is Schopenhauerian; and if one should commend his imitation in this respect, it is nevertheless not to be denied that Wagner's style itself suffers in no small degree from all the tumours and turgidities, the sight of which made Schopenhauer so furious; and that, in respect to the German-writing Wagnerians, Wagneromania 136is beginning to be as dangerous as only some kinds of Hegelomania have been. Schopenhauerian is Wagner's hatred of the Jews, to whom he is unable to do justice, even in their greatest exploit: are not the Jews the inventors of Christianity! The attempt of Wagner to construe Christianity as a seed blown away from Buddhism, and his endeavour to initiate a Buddhistic era in Europe, under a temporary approximation to Catholic-Christian formulas and sentiments, are both Schopenhauerian. Wagner's preaching in favour of pity in dealing with animals is Schopenhauerian; Schopenhauer's predecessor here, as is well known, was Voltaire, who already perhaps, like his successors, knew how to disguise his hatred of certain men and things as pity towards animals. At least Wagner's hatred of science, which manifests itself in his preaching, has certainly not been inspired by the spirit of charitableness and kindness—nor by the spirit at all, as is sufficiently obvious.—Finally, it is of little importance what the philosophy of an artist is, provided it is only a supplementary philosophy, and does not do any injury to his art itself. We cannot be sufficiently on our guard against taking a dislike to an artist on account of an occasional, perhaps very unfortunate and presumptuous masquerade; let us not forget that the dear artists are all of them something of actors—and must be so; it would be difficult for them to hold out in the long run without stage-playing. Let us be loyal to Wagner in that which is true and original in him,—and especially in this point, that we, his disciples, remain loyal to ourselves in that which is true and original in us.

Let us allow him his intellectual humours and spasms, let us in fairness rather consider what strange nutriments and necessaries an art like his is entitled to, in order to be able to live and grow! It is of no account that he is often wrong as a thinker; justice and patience are not his affair. It is sufficient that his life is right in his own eyes, and maintains its right,—the life which calls to each of us: "Be a man, and do not follow me—but thyself! thyself!" Our life, also ought to maintain its right in our own eyes! We also are to grow and blossom out of ourselves, free and fearless, in innocent selfishness! And so, on the contemplation of such a man, these thoughts still ring in my ears to-day, as formerly: "That passion is better than stoicism or hypocrisy; that straightforwardness, even in evil, is better than losing oneself in trying to observe traditional morality; that the free man is just as able to be good as evil, but that the unemancipated man is a disgrace to nature, and has no share in heavenly or earthly bliss; finally, that all who wish to be free must become so through themselves, and that freedom falls to nobody's lot as a gift from Heaven." (Richard Wagner in Bayreuth, Vol. I. of this Translation, pp. 199-200).

100.

Learning to do Homage.—One must learn the art of homage, as well as the art of contempt. Whoever goes in new paths and has led many persons therein, discovers with astonishment how awkward and incompetent all of them are in the expression of their gratitude, and indeed how rarely gratitude is able even to express itself. It is always as if something comes into people's throats when their gratitude wants to speak, so that it only hems and haws, and becomes silent again. The way in which a thinker succeeds in tracing the effect of his thoughts, and their transforming and convulsing power, is almost a comedy: it sometimes seems as if those who have been operated upon felt profoundly injured thereby, and could only assert their independence, which they suspect to be threatened, by all kinds of improprieties. It needs whole generations in order merely to devise a courteous convention of gratefulness; it is only very late that the period arrives when something of spirit and genius enters into gratitude. Then there is usually some one who is the great receiver of thanks, not only for the good he himself has done, but mostly for that which has been gradually accumulated by his predecessors, as a treasure of what is highest and best.

101.

Voltaire.—Wherever there has been a court, it has furnished the standard of good-speaking, and with this also the standard of style for writers. The court language, however, is the language of the courtier who has no profession, and who even in conversations on scientific subjects avoids all convenient, technical expressions, because they smack of the profession; on that account the technical expression, and everything that betrays the specialist, is a blemish of style in countries which have a court culture. At present, when all courts have become caricatures of past and present times, one is astonished to find even Voltaire unspeakably reserved and scrupulous on this point (for example, in his judgments concerning such stylists as Fontenelle and Montesquieu),—we are now, all of us, emancipated from court taste, while Voltaire was its perfecter!

102.

A Word for Philologists.—It is thought that there are books so valuable and royal that whole generations of scholars are well employed when through their efforts these books are kept genuine and intelligible,— to confirm this belief again and again is the purpose of philology. It presupposes that the rare men are not lacking (though they may not be visible), who actually know how to use such valuable books:— those men perhaps who write such books themselves, or could write them. I mean to say that philology presupposes a noble belief,—that for the benefit of some few who are always "to come," and are not there, a very great amount of painful, and even dirty labour has to be done beforehand: it is all labour in usum Delphinorum.

103.

German Music.—German music, more than any other, has now become European music; because the changes which Europe experienced through the Revolution have therein alone found expression: it is only German music that knows how to express the agitation of popular masses, the tremendous artificial uproar, which does not even need to be very noisy,—while Italian opera, for example, knows only the choruses of domestics or soldiers, but not "the people." There is the additional fact that in all German music a profound bourgeois jealousy of the noblesse can be traced, especially a jealousy of esprit and élégance, as the expressions of a courtly, chivalrous, ancient, and self-confident society. It is not music like that of Goethe's musician at the gate, which was pleasing also "in the hall," and to the king as well; it is not here said: "The knights looked on with martial air; with bashful eyes the ladies." Even the Graces are not allowed in German music without a touch of remorse; it is only with Pleasantness, the country sister of the Graces that the German begins to feel morally at ease—and from this point up to his enthusiastic, learned, and often gruff "sublimity" (the Beethoven-like sublimity), he feels more and more so. If we want to imagine the man of this music,—well, let us just imagine Beethoven as he appeared beside Goethe, say, at their meeting at Teplitz: as semi-barbarism beside culture, as the masses beside the nobility, as the good-natured man beside the good and more than "good" man, as the visionary beside the artist, as the man needing comfort beside the comforted, as the man given to exaggeration and distrust beside the man of reason, as the crank and self-tormenter, as the foolish, enraptured, blessedly unfortunate, sincerely immoderate man, as the pretentious and awkward man,—and altogether 141 as the "untamed man": it was thus that Goethe conceived and characterised him, Goethe, the exceptional German, for whom a music of equal rank has not yet been found!—Finally, let us consider whether the present, continually extending contempt of melody and the stunting of the sense for melody among Germans should not be understood as a democratic impropriety and an after-effect of the Revolution? For melody has such an obvious delight in conformity to law, and such an aversion to everything evolving, unformed and arbitrary, that it sounds like a note out of the ancient European regime, and as a seduction and re-duction back to it.

104.

The Tone of the German Language.—We know whence the German originated which for several centuries has been the universal, literary language of Germany. The Germans, with their reverence for everything that came from the court, intentionally took the chancery style as their pattern in all that they had to write, especially in their letters, records, wills, &c. To write in the chancery style, that was to write in court and government style,—that was regarded as something select compared with the language of the city in which a person lived. People gradually drew this inference, and spoke also as they wrote,— they thus became still more select in the forms of their words, in the choice of their terms and modes of expression, and finally also in their tones: they affected a court tone when they spoke, and the affectation at last became natural. Perhaps nothing quite similar has ever happened elsewhere:—the predominance of the literary style over the talk, and the formality and affectation of an entire people, becoming the basis of a common and no longer dialectical language. I believe that the sound of the German language in the Middle Ages, and especially after the Middle Ages, was extremely rustic and vulgar; it has ennobled itself somewhat during the last centuries, principally because it was found necessary to imitate so many French, Italian, and Spanish sounds, and particularly on the part of the German (and Austrian) nobility, who could not at all content themselves with their mother-tongue. But notwithstanding this practice, German must have sounded intolerably vulgar to Montaigne, and even to Racine: even at present, in the mouths of travellers among the Italian populace, it still sounds very coarse, sylvan, and hoarse, as if it had originated in smoky rooms and outlandish districts.—Now I notice that at present a similar striving after selectness of tone is spreading among the former admirers of the chancery style, and that the Germans are beginning to accommodate themselves to a peculiar "witchery of sound," which might in the long run become an actual danger to the German language,—for one may seek in vain for more execrable sounds in Europe. Something mocking, cold, indifferent, and careless in the voice: that is what at present sounds "noble" to the Germans—and I hear the approval of this nobleness in the voices of young officials, teachers, women, and trades-people; indeed, even the little girls already imitate this German of the officers. For the officer, and in fact the Prussian officer is the inventor of these tones: this same officer, who, as soldier and professional man possesses that admirable tact for modesty which the Germans as a whole might well imitate (German professors and musicians included!). But as soon as he speaks and moves he is the most immodest and inelegant figure in old Europe—no doubt unconsciously to himself! And unconsciously also to the good Germans, who gaze at him as the man of the foremost and most select society, and willingly let him "give them his tone." And indeed he gives it to them!—in the first place it is the sergeant-majors and non-commissioned officers that imitate his tone and coarsen it. One should note the roars of command, with which the German cities are absolutely surrounded at present, when there is drilling at all the gates: what presumption, furious imperiousness, and mocking coldness speaks in this uproar! Could the Germans actually be a musical people?—It is certain that the Germans martialise themselves at present in the tone of their language: it is probable that, being exercised to speak martially, they will finally write martially also. For habituation to definite tones extends deeply into the character:—people soon have the words and modes of expression, and finally also the thoughts which just suit these tones! Perhaps they already write in the officers' style; perhaps I only read too little of what is at present written in Germany to know this. But one thing I know all the surer: the German public declarations which also reach places abroad, are not inspired by German music, but just by that new tone of tasteless arrogance. Almost in every speech of the foremost German statesman, and even when he makes himself heard through his imperial mouth-piece, there is an accent which the ear of a foreigner repudiates with aversion: but the Germans endure it,— they endure themselves.

105.

The Germans as Artists.—When once a German actually experiences passion (and not only, as is usual, the mere inclination to it), he then behaves just as he must do in passion, and does not think further of his behaviour. The truth is, however, that he then behaves very awkwardly and uglily, and as if destitute of rhythm and melody; so that onlookers are pained or moved thereby, but nothing more— unless he elevate himself to the sublimity and enrapturedness of which certain passions are capable. Then even the German becomes beautiful. The perception of the height at which beauty begins to shed its charm even over Germans, raises German artists to the height, to the supreme height, and to the extravagances of passion: they have an actual, profound longing, therefore, to get beyond, or at least to look beyond the ugliness and awkwardness—into a better, easier, more southern, more sunny world. And thus their convulsions are often merely indications that they would like to dance: these poor bears in whom hidden nymphs and satyrs, and sometimes still higher divinities, carry on their game!

106.

Music as Advocate.—"I have a longing for a master of the musical art," said an innovator to his disciple, "that he may learn from me my ideas and speak them more widely in his language: I shall thus be better able to reach men's ears and hearts. For by means of tones one can seduce men to every error and every truth: who could refute a tone?"—"You would, therefore, like to be regarded as irrefutable?" said his disciple. The innovator answered: "I should like the germ to become a tree. In order that a doctrine may become a tree, it must be believed in for a considerable period; in order that it may be believed in it must be regarded as irrefutable. Storms and doubts and worms and wickedness are necessary to the tree, that it may manifest its species and the strength of its germ; let it perish if it is not strong enough! But a germ is always merely annihilated,—not refuted!"—When he had said this, his disciple called out impetuously: "But I believe in your cause, and regard it as so strong that I will say everything against it, everything that I still have in my heart."—The innovator laughed to himself and threatened the disciple with his finger. "This kind of discipleship," said he then, "is the best, but it is dangerous, and not every kind of doctrine can stand it."

107.

Our Ultimate Gratitude to Art.—If we had not approved of the Arts and invented this sort of cult 146of the untrue, the insight into the general untruth and falsity of things now given us by science—an insight into delusion and error as conditions of intelligent and sentient existence—would be quite unendurable. Honesty would have disgust and suicide in its train. Now, however, our honesty has a counterpoise which helps us to escape such consequences;—namely, Art, as the good-will to illusion. We do not always restrain our eyes from rounding off and perfecting in imagination: and then it is no longer the eternal imperfection that we carry over the river of Becoming—for we think we carry a goddess, and are proud and artless in rendering this service. As an æsthetic phenomenon existence is still endurable to us; and by Art, eye and hand and above all the good conscience are given to us, to be able to make such a phenomenon out of ourselves. We must rest from ourselves occasionally by contemplating and looking down upon ourselves, and by laughing or weeping over ourselves from an artistic remoteness: we must discover the hero, and likewise the fool, that is hidden in our passion for knowledge; we must now and then be joyful in our folly, that we may continue to be joyful in our wisdom! And just because we are heavy and serious men in our ultimate depth, and are rather weights than men, there is nothing that does us so much good as the fool's cap and bells: we need them in presence of ourselves—we need all arrogant, soaring, dancing, mocking, childish and blessed Art, in order not to lose the free dominion over things which our ideal demands of us. It would be backsliding for us, 147with our susceptible integrity, to lapse entirely into morality, and actually become virtuous monsters and scarecrows, on account of the over-strict requirements which we here lay down for ourselves. We ought also to be able to stand above morality, and not only stand with the painful stiffness of one who every moment fears to slip and fall, but we should also be able to soar and play above it! How could we dispense with Art for that purpose, how could we dispense with the fool?—And as long as you are still ashamed of yourselves in any way, you still do not belong to us!

BOOK THIRD

108.

New Struggles.—After Buddha was dead people showed his shadow for centuries afterwards in a cave,—an immense frightful shadow. God is dead: but as the human race is constituted, there will perhaps be caves for millenniums yet, in which people will show his shadow,— And we—we have still to overcome his shadow!

109.

Let us be on our Guard.—Let us be on our guard against thinking that the world is a living being. Where could it extend itself? What could it nourish itself with? How could it grow and increase? We know tolerably well what the organic is; and we are to reinterpret the emphatically derivative, tardy, rare and accidental, which we only perceive on the crust of the earth, into the essential, universal and eternal, as those do who call the universe an organism? That disgusts me. Let us now be on our guard against believing that the universe is a machine; it is assuredly not constructed with a view to one end; we invest it with far too high an honour with the word "machine." Let us be on our guard against supposing that anything so methodical as the cyclic motions of our neighbouring stars obtains generally and throughout the universe; indeed a glance at the Milky Way induces doubt as to whether there are not many cruder and more contradictory motions there, and even stars with continuous, rectilinearly gravitating orbits, and the like. The astral arrangement in which we live is an exception; this arrangement, and the relatively long durability which is determined by it, has again made possible the exception of exceptions, the formation of organic life. The general character of the world, on the other hand, is to all eternity chaos; not by the absence of necessity, but in the sense of the absence of order, structure, form, beauty, wisdom, and whatever else our æsthetic humanities are called. Judged by our reason, the unlucky casts are far oftenest the rule, the exceptions are not the secret purpose; and the whole musical box repeats eternally its air, which can never be called a melody,—and finally the very expression, "unlucky cast" is already an anthropomorphising which involves blame. But how could we presume to blame or praise the universe! Let us be on our guard against ascribing to it heartlessness and unreason, or their opposites; it is neither perfect, nor beautiful, nor noble; nor does it seek to be anything of the kind, it does not at all attempt to imitate man! It is altogether unaffected by our æsthetic and moral judgments! Neither has it any self-preservative instinct, nor instinct at all; it also knows no law. Let us be on our guard against saying that there are laws in nature. There are only necessities: there is no one who commands, no one who obeys, no one who transgresses. When you know that there is no design, you know also that there is no chance: for it is only where there is a world of design that the word "chance" has a meaning. Let us be on our guard against saying that death is contrary to life. The living being is only a species of dead being, and a very rare species.—Let us be on our guard against thinking that the world eternally creates the new. There are no eternally enduring substances; matter is just another such error as the God of the Eleatics. But when shall we be at an end with our foresight and precaution! When will all these shadows of God cease to obscure us? When shall we have nature entirely undeified! When shall we be permitted to naturalise ourselves by means of the pure, newly discovered, newly redeemed nature?

110.

Origin of Knowledge.—Throughout immense stretches of time the intellect has produced nothing but errors; some of them proved to be useful and preservative of the species: he who fell in with them, or inherited them, waged the battle for himself and his offspring with better success. Those erroneous articles of faith which were successively transmitted by inheritance, and have finally become almost the property and stock of the human species, are, for example, the following:—that there are enduring things, that there are equal things, that there are things, substances, and bodies, that a thing is what it appears, that our will is free, that what is good for me is also good absolutely. It was only very late that the deniers and doubters of such propositions came forward,—it was only very late that truth made its appearance as the most impotent form of knowledge. It seemed as if it were impossible to get along with truth, our organism was adapted for the very opposite; all its higher functions, the perceptions of the senses, and in general every kind of sensation co-operated with those primevally embodied, fundamental errors. Moreover, those propositions became the very standards of knowledge according to which the "true" and the "false" were determined—throughout the whole domain of pure logic. The strength of conceptions does not, therefore, depend on their degree of truth, but on their antiquity, their embodiment, their character as conditions of life. Where life and knowledge seemed to conflict, there has never been serious contention; denial and doubt have there been regarded as madness. The exceptional thinkers like the Eleatics, who, in spite of this, advanced and maintained the antitheses of the natural errors, believed that it was possible also to live these counterparts: it was they who devised the sage as the man of immutability, impersonality and universality of intuition, as one and all at the same time, with a special faculty for that reverse kind of knowledge; they were of the belief that their knowledge was at the same time the principle of life. To be able to affirm all this, however, they had to deceive themselves concerning their own condition: they had to attribute to themselves impersonality and unchanging permanence, they had to mistake the nature of the philosophic individual, deny the force 155of the impulses in cognition, and conceive of reason generally as an entirely free and self-originating activity; they kept their eyes shut to the fact that they also had reached their doctrines in contradiction to valid methods, or through their longing for repose or for exclusive possession or for domination.

The subtler development of sincerity and of scepticism finally made these men impossible; their life also and their judgments turned out to be dependent on the primeval impulses and fundamental errors of all sentient being.—The subtler sincerity and scepticism arose whenever two antithetical maxims appeared to be applicable to life, because both of them were compatible with the fundamental errors; where, therefore, there could be contention concerning a higher or lower degree of utility for life; and likewise where new maxims proved to be, not in fact useful, but at least not injurious, as expressions of an intellectual impulse to play a game that was, like all games, innocent and happy. The human brain was gradually filled with such judgments and convictions; and in this tangled skein there arose ferment, strife and lust for power. Not only utility and delight, but every kind of impulse took part in the struggle for "truths": the intellectual struggle became a business, an attraction, a calling, a duty, an honour—: cognizing and striving for the true finally arranged themselves as needs among other needs. From that moment, not only belief and conviction, but also examination, denial, distrust and contradiction became forces; all "evil" instincts were subordinated to knowledge, were placed in its service, and acquired the 156prestige of the permitted, the honoured, the useful, and finally the appearance and innocence of the good. Knowledge, thus became a portion of life itself, and as life it became a continually growing power: until finally the cognitions and those primeval, fundamental, errors clashed with each other, both as life, both as power, both in the same man. The thinker is now the being in whom the impulse to truth and those life-preserving errors wage their first conflict, now that the impulse to truth has also proved itself to be a life-preserving power. In comparison with the importance of this conflict everything else is indifferent; the final question concerning the conditions of life is here raised, and the first attempt is here made to answer it by experiment.

How far is truth susceptible of embodiment?—that is the question, that is the experiment.

111.

Origin of the Logical.—Where has logic originated in men's heads? Undoubtedly out of the illogical, the domain of which must originally have been immense. But numberless beings who reasoned otherwise than we do at present, perished; albeit that they may have come nearer to truth than we! Whoever, for example, could not discern the "like" often enough with regard to food, and with regard to animals dangerous to him, whoever, therefore, deduced too slowly, or was too circumspect in his deductions, had smaller probability of survival than he who in all similar things immediately divined the equality. The preponderating inclination, however, to deal with the similar as the equal—an illogical inclination, for there is nothing equal in itself—first created the whole basis of logic. It was just so (in order that the conception of substance might originate, this being indispensable to logic, although in the strictest sense nothing actual corresponds to it) that for a long period the changing process in things had to be overlooked, and remain unperceived; the beings not seeing correctly had an advantage over those who saw everything "in flux." In itself every high degree of circumspection in conclusions, every sceptical inclination, is a great danger to life. No living being would have been preserved unless the contrary inclination—to affirm rather than suspend judgment, to mistake and fabricate rather than wait, to assent rather than deny, to decide rather than be in the right—had been cultivated with extraordinary assiduity.—The course of logical thought and reasoning in our modern brain corresponds to a process and struggle of impulses, which singly and in themselves are all very illogical and unjust; we experience usually only the result of the struggle, so rapidly and secretly does this primitive mechanism now operate in us.

112.

Cause and Effect.—We say it is "explanation"; but it is only in "description" that we are in advance of the older stages of knowledge and science. We describe better,—we explain just as little as our predecessors. We have discovered a manifold succession where the naïve man and investigator of older cultures saw only two things, "cause" and "effect," as it was said; we have perfected the conception of becoming, but have not got a knowledge of what is above and behind the conception. The series of "causes" stands before us much more complete in every case; we conclude that this and that must first precede in order that that other may follow—but we have not grasped anything thereby. The peculiarity, for example, in every chemical process seems a "miracle," the same as before, just like all locomotion; nobody has "explained" impulse. How could we ever explain! We operate only with things which do not exist, with lines, surfaces, bodies, atoms, divisible times, divisible spaces—how can explanation ever be possible when we first make everything a conception, our conception! It is sufficient to regard science as the exactest humanising of things that is possible; we always learn to describe ourselves more accurately by describing things and their successions. Cause and effect: there is probably never any such duality; in fact there is a continuum before us, from which we isolate a few portions;—just as we always observe a motion as isolated points, and therefore do not properly see it, but infer it. The abruptness with which many effects take place leads us into error; it is however only an abruptness for us. There is an infinite multitude of processes in that abrupt moment which escape us. An intellect which could see cause and effect as a continuum, which could see the flux of events not according to our mode of perception, as things arbitrarily separated and broken—would throw aside 159the conception of cause and effect, and would deny all conditionality.

113.

The Theory of Poisons.—So many things have to be united in order that scientific thinking may arise, and all the necessary powers must have been devised, exercised, and fostered singly! In their isolation, however, they have very often had quite a different effect than at present, when they are confined within the limits of scientific thinking and kept mutually in check:—they have operated as poisons; for example, the doubting impulse, the denying impulse, the waiting impulse, the collecting impulse, the disintegrating impulse. Many hecatombs of men were sacrificed ere these impulses learned to understand their juxtaposition and regard themselves as functions of one organising force in one man! And how far are we still from the point at which the artistic powers and the practical wisdom of life shall co-operate with scientific thinking, so that a higher organic system may be formed, in relation to which the scholar, the physician, the artist, and the lawgiver, as we know them at present, will seem sorry antiquities!

114.

The Extent of the Moral.—We construct a new picture, which we see immediately with the aid of all the old experiences which we have had, always according to the degree of our honesty and justice. The only events are moral events, even in the domain of sense-perception.

115.

The Four Errors.—Man has been reared by his errors: firstly, he saw himself always imperfect; secondly, he attributed to himself imaginary qualities; thirdly, he felt himself in a false position in relation to the animals and nature; fourthly, he always devised new tables of values, and accepted them for a time as eternal and unconditioned, so that at one time this, and at another time that human impulse or state stood first, and was ennobled in consequence. When one has deducted the effect of these four errors, one has also deducted humanity, humaneness, and "human dignity."

116.

Herd-Instinct.—Wherever we meet with a morality we find a valuation and order of rank of the human impulses and activities. These valuations and orders of rank are always the expression of the needs of a community or herd: that which is in the first place to its advantage—and in the second place and third place—is also the authoritative standard for the worth of every individual. By morality the individual is taught to become a function of the herd, and to ascribe to himself value only as a function. As the conditions for the maintenance of one community have been very different from those of another community, there have been very different moralities; and in respect to the future essential transformations of herds and communities, states and societies, one can prophesy that there will still be very divergent moralities. Morality is the herd-instinct in the individual.

117.

The Herd's Sting of Conscience.—In the longest and remotest ages of the human race there was quite a different sting of conscience from that of the present day. At present one only feels responsible for what one intends and for what one does, and we have our pride in ourselves. All our professors of jurisprudence start with this sentiment of individual independence and pleasure, as if the source of right had taken its rise here from the beginning. But throughout the longest period in the life of mankind there was nothing more terrible to a person than to feel himself independent. To be alone, to feel independent, neither to obey nor to rule, to represent an individual—that was no pleasure to a person then, but a punishment; he was condemned "to be an individual." Freedom of thought was regarded as discomfort personified. While we feel law and regulation as constraint and loss, people formerly regarded egoism as a painful thing, and a veritable evil. For a person to be himself, to value himself according to his own measure and weight—that was then quite distasteful. The inclination to such a thing would have been regarded as madness; for all miseries and terrors were associated with being alone. At that time the "free will" had bad conscience in close proximity to it; and the less independently a person acted, the more the herd-instinct, and not his personal character, expressed itself in his conduct, so much the more moral did he esteem himself. All that did injury to the herd, whether the individual had intended it or not, then caused him a sting of conscience—and his neighbour likewise, indeed the whole herd!—It is in this respect that we have most changed our mode of thinking.

118.

Benevolence.—Is it virtuous when a cell transforms itself into the function of a stronger cell? It must do so. And is it wicked when the stronger one assimilates the other? It must do so likewise: it is necessary, for it has to have abundant indemnity and seeks to regenerate itself. One has therefore to distinguish the instinct of appropriation, and the instinct of submission, in benevolence, according as the stronger or the weaker feels benevolent. Gladness and covetousness are united in the stronger person, who wants to transform something to his function: gladness and desire-to-be-coveted in the weaker person, who would like to become a function.—The former case is essentially pity, a pleasant excitation of the instinct of appropriation at the sight of the weaker: it is to be remembered, however, that "strong" and "weak" are relative conceptions.

119.

No Altruism!—I see in many men an excessive impulse and delight in wanting to be a function; they strive after it, and have the keenest scent for all those positions in which precisely they themselves can be functions. Among such persons are those women who transform themselves into just that function of a man that is but weakly developed in him, and then become his purse, or his politics, or his social intercourse. Such beings maintain themselves best when they insert themselves in an alien organism; if they do not succeed they become vexed, irritated, and eat themselves up.

120.

Health of the Soul.—The favourite medico-moral formula (whose originator was Ariston of Chios), "Virtue is the health of the soul," would, at least in order to be used, have to be altered to this: "Thy virtue is the health of thy soul." For there is no such thing as health in itself, and all attempts to define a thing in that way have lamentably failed. It is necessary to know thy aim, thy horizon, thy powers, thy impulses, thy errors, and especially the ideals and fantasies of thy soul, in order to determine what health implies even for thy body. There are consequently innumerable kinds of physical health; and the more one again permits the unique and unparalleled to raise its head, the more one unlearns the dogma of the "Equality of men," so much the more also must the conception of a normal health, together with a normal diet and a normal course of disease, be abrogated by our physicians. And then only would it be time to turn our thoughts to the health and disease of the soul and make the special virtue of everyone consist in its health; but, to be sure, what appeared as health in one person might appear as the contrary 164of health in another. In the end the great question might still remain open: whether we could do without sickness, even for the development of our virtue, and whether our thirst for knowledge and self-knowledge would not especially need the sickly soul as well as the sound one; in short, whether the mere will to health is not a prejudice, a cowardice, and perhaps an instance of the subtlest barbarism and unprogressiveness.

121.

Life no Argument.—We have arranged for ourselves a world in which we can live—by the postulating of bodies, lines, surfaces, causes and effects, motion and rest, form and content: without these articles of faith no one could manage to live at present! But for all that they are still unproved. Life is no argument; error might be among the conditions of life.

122.

The Element of Moral Scepticism in Christianity.—Christianity also has made a great contribution to enlightenment, and has taught moral scepticism in a very impressive and effective manner—accusing and embittering, but with untiring patience and subtlety; it annihilated in every individual the belief in his virtues: it made the great virtuous ones, of whom antiquity had no lack, vanish for ever from the earth, those popular men, who, in the belief in their perfection, walked about with the dignity of a hero of the bull-fight. When, trained in this Christian school of scepticism, we 165now read the moral books of the ancients, for example those of Seneca and Epictetus, we feel a pleasurable superiority, and are full of secret insight and penetration,—it seems to us as if a child talked before an old man, or a pretty, gushing girl before La Rochefoucauld:—we know better what virtue is! After all, however, we have applied the same scepticism to all religious states and processes, such as sin, repentance, grace, sanctification, &c., and have allowed the worm to burrow so well, that we have now the same feeling of subtle superiority and insight even in reading all Christian books:—we know also the religious feelings better! And it is time to know them well and describe them well, for the pious ones of the old belief die out also; let us save their likeness and type, at least for the sake of knowledge.

123.

Knowledge more than a Means.—Also without this passion—I refer to the passion for knowledge—science would be furthered: science has hitherto increased and grown up without it. The good faith in science, the prejudice in its favour, by which States are at present dominated (it was even the Church formerly), rests fundamentally on the fact that the absolute inclination and impulse has so rarely revealed itself in it, and that science is regarded not as a passion, but as a condition and an "ethos." Indeed, amour-plaisir of knowledge (curiosity) often enough suffices, amour-vanité suffices, and habituation to it, with the afterthought of obtaining honour and bread; it even suffices for many that they do not know what to do with a surplus of leisure, except to continue reading, collecting, arranging, observing and narrating; their "scientific impulse" is their ennui. Pope Leo X. once (in the brief to Beroaldus) sang the praise of science; he designated it as the finest ornament and the greatest pride of our life, a noble employment in happiness and in misfortune; "without it," he says finally, "all human undertakings would be without a firm basis,—even with it they are still sufficiently mutable and insecure!" But this rather sceptical Pope, like all other ecclesiastical panegyrists of science, suppressed his ultimate judgment concerning it. If one may deduce from his words what is remarkable enough for such a lover of art, that he places science above art, it is after all, however, only from politeness that he omits to speak of that which he places high above all science: the "revealed truth," and the "eternal salvation of the soul,"—what are ornament, pride, entertainment and security of life to him, in comparison thereto? "Science is something of secondary rank, nothing ultimate or unconditioned, no object of passion"—this judgment was kept back in Leo's soul: the truly Christian judgment concerning science! In antiquity its dignity and appreciation were lessened by the fact that, even among its most eager disciples, the striving after virtue stood foremost, and that people thought they had given the highest praise to knowledge when they celebrated it as the best means to virtue. It is something new in history that knowledge claims to be more than a means.

124.

In the Horizon of the Infinite.—We have left the land and have gone aboard ship! We have broken down the bridge behind us,—nay, more, the land behind us! Well, little ship! look out! Beside thee is the ocean; it is true it does not always roar, and sometimes it spreads out like silk and gold and a gentle reverie. But times will come when thou wilt feel that it is infinite, and that there is nothing more frightful than infinity. Oh, the poor bird that felt itself free, and now strikes against the walls of this cage! Alas, if homesickness for the land should attack thee, as if there had been more freedom there,—and there is no "land" any longer!

125.

The Madman.—Have you ever heard of the madman who on a bright morning lighted a lantern and ran to the market-place calling out unceasingly: "I seek God! I seek God!"—As there were many people standing about who did not believe in God, he caused a great deal of amusement. Why! is he lost? said one. Has he strayed away like a child? said another. Or does he keep himself hidden? Is he afraid of us? Has he taken a sea-voyage? Has he emigrated?—the people cried out laughingly, all in a hubbub. The insane man jumped into their midst and transfixed them with his glances. "Where is God gone?" he called out. "I mean to tell you! We have killed him,—you and I! We are all his murderers! But how have we done it? How were we able to drink up the 168sea? Who gave us the sponge to wipe away the whole horizon? What did we do when we loosened this earth from its sun? Whither does it now move? Whither do we move? Away from all suns? Do we not dash on unceasingly? Backwards, sideways, forwards, in all directions? Is there still an above and below? Do we not stray, as through infinite nothingness? Does not empty space breathe upon us? Has it not become colder? Does not night come on continually, darker and darker? Shall we not have to light lanterns in the morning? Do we not hear the noise of the grave-diggers who are burying God? Do we not smell the divine putrefaction?—for even Gods putrefy! God is dead! God remains dead! And we have killed him! How shall we console ourselves, the most murderous of all murderers? The holiest and the mightiest that the world has hitherto possessed, has bled to death under our knife,—who will wipe the blood from us? With what water could we cleanse ourselves? What lustrums, what sacred games shall we have to devise? Is not the magnitude of this deed too great for us? Shall we not ourselves have to become Gods, merely to seem worthy of it? There never was a greater event,—and on account of it, all who are born after us belong to a higher history than any history hitherto!"—Here the madman was silent and looked again at his hearers; they also were silent and looked at him in surprise. At last he threw his lantern on the ground, so that it broke in pieces and was extinguished. "I come too early," he then said, "I am not yet at the right time. This prodigious event is still on its way, and is travelling,—it has not yet reached men's ears. Lightning and thunder need time, the light of the stars needs time, deeds need time, even after they are done, to be seen and heard. This deed is as yet further from them than the furthest star,—and yet they have done it!"—It is further stated that the madman made his way into different churches on the same day, and there intoned his Requiem aeternam deo. When led out and called to account, he always gave the reply: "What are these churches now, if they are not the tombs and monuments of God?"—

126.

Mystical Explanations.—Mystical explanations are regarded as profound; the truth is that they do not even go the length of being superficial.

127.

After-Effect of the most Ancient Religiousness.—The thoughtless man thinks that the Will is the only thing that operates, that willing is something simple, manifestly given, underived, and comprehensible in itself. He is convinced that when he does anything, for example, when he delivers a blow, it is he who strikes, and he has struck because he willed to strike. He does not notice anything of a problem therein, but the feeling of willing suffices to him, not only for the acceptance of cause and effect, but also for the belief that he understands their relationship. Of the mechanism of the occurrence and of the manifold subtle operations that must be performed in order that the blow may result, and likewise of the incapacity of the Will in itself to effect even the smallest part of those operations—he knows nothing. The Will is to him a magically operating force; the belief in the Will as the cause of effects is the belief in magically operating forces. In fact, whenever he saw anything happen, man originally believed in a Will as cause, and in personally willing beings operating in the background,—the conception of mechanism was very remote from him. Because, however, man for immense periods of time believed only in persons (and not in matter, forces, things, &c.), the belief in cause and effect has become a fundamental belief with him, which he applies everywhere when anything happens,—and even still uses instinctively as a piece of atavism of remotest origin. The propositions, "No effect without a cause," and "Every effect again implies a cause," appear as generalisations of several less general propositions:—"Where there is operation there has been willing," "Operating is only possible on willing beings." "There is never a pure, resultless experience of activity, but every experience involves stimulation of the Will" (to activity, defence, revenge or retaliation). But in the primitive period of the human race, the latter and the former propositions were identical, the first were not generalisations of the second, but the second were explanations of the first.—Schopenhauer, with his assumption that all that exists is something volitional, has set a primitive mythology on the throne; he seems never to have attempted an analysis of the Will, because he believed like everybody in the simplicity and immediateness of all volition:—while volition is in fact such a cleverly practised mechanical process that it almost escapes the observing eye. I set the following propositions against those of Schopenhauer:—Firstly, in order that Will may arise, an idea of pleasure and pain is necessary. Secondly, that a vigorous excitation may be felt as pleasure or pain, is the affair of the interpreting intellect, which, to be sure, operates thereby for the most part unconsciously to us, and one and the same excitation may be interpreted as pleasure or pain. Thirdly, it is only in an intellectual being that there is pleasure, displeasure and Will; the immense majority of organisms have nothing of the kind.

128.

The Value of Prayer.—Prayer has been devised for such men as have never any thoughts of their own, and to whom an elevation of the soul is unknown, or passes unnoticed; what shall these people do in holy places and in all important situations in life which require repose and some kind of dignity? In order at least that they may not disturb, the wisdom of all the founders of religions, the small as well as the great, has commended to them the formula of prayer, as a long mechanical labour of the lips, united with an effort of the memory, and with a uniform, prescribed attitude of hands and feet— and eyes! They may then, like the Tibetans, chew the cud of their "om mane padme hum," innumerable times, or, as in Benares, count the name of God Ram-Ram-Ram (and so on, with or without grace) on their fingers; or honour Vishnu with his thousand names of invocation, Allah with his ninety-nine; or they may make use of the prayer-wheels and the rosary: the main thing is that they are settled down for a time at this work, and present a tolerable appearance; their mode of prayer is devised for the advantage of the pious who have thought and elevation of their own. But even these have their weary hours when a series of venerable words and sounds and a mechanical, pious ritual does them good. But supposing that these rare men—in every religion the religious man is an exception—know how to help themselves, the poor in spirit do not know, and to forbid them the prayer-babbling would mean to take their religion from them, a fact which Protestantism brings more and more to light. All that religion wants with such persons is that they should keep still with their eyes, hands, legs, and all their organs: they thereby become temporarily beautified and—more human-looking!

129.

The Conditions for God.—"God himself cannot subsist without wise men," said Luther, and with good reason; but "God can still less subsist without unwise men,"—good Luther did not say that!

130.

A Dangerous Resolution.—The Christian resolution to find the world ugly and bad has made the world ugly and bad.

131.

Christianity and Suicide.—Christianity made use of the excessive longing for suicide at the time of its origin as a lever for its power: it left only two forms of suicide, invested them with the highest dignity and the highest hopes, and forbade all others in a dreadful manner. But martyrdom and the slow self-annihilation of the ascetic were permitted.

132.

Against Christianity.—It is now no longer our reason, but our taste that decides against Christianity.

133.

Axioms.—An unavoidable hypothesis on which mankind must always fall back again, is, in the long run, more powerful than the most firmly believed belief in something untrue (like the Christian belief). In the long run: that means a hundred thousand years from now.

134.

Pessimists as Victims.—When a profound dislike of existence gets the upper hand, the after-effect of a great error in diet of which a people has been long guilty comes to light. The spread of Buddhism (not its origin) is thus to a considerable extent dependent on the excessive and almost exclusive rice-fare of the Indians, and on the universal enervation that results therefrom. Perhaps the modern, European discontentedness is to be looked 174upon as caused by the fact that the world of our forefathers, the whole Middle Ages, was given to drink, owing to the influence of German tastes in Europe: the Middle Ages, that means the alcoholic poisoning of Europe.— The German dislike of life (including the influence of the cellar-air and stove-poison in German dwellings), is essentially a cold-weather complaint.

135.

Origin of Sin.—Sin, as it is at present felt wherever Christianity prevails or has prevailed, is a Jewish feeling and a Jewish invention; and in respect to this background of all Christian morality, Christianity has in fact aimed at "Judaising" the whole world. To what an extent this has succeeded in Europe is traced most accurately in the extent of our alienness to Greek antiquity—a world without the feeling of sin—in our sentiments even at present; in spite of all the good will to approximation and assimilation, which whole generations and many distinguished individuals have not failed to display. "Only when thou repentest is God gracious to thee"—that would arouse the laughter or the wrath of a Greek: he would say, "Slaves may have such sentiments." Here a mighty being, an almighty being, and yet a revengeful being, is presupposed; his power is so great that no injury whatever can be done to him, except in the point of honour. Every sin is an infringement of respect, a crimen læsæ majestatis divinæ—and nothing more! Contrition, degradation, rolling-in-the-dust,—these are the first and 175last conditions on which his favour depends: the restoration, therefore, of his divine honour! If injury be caused otherwise by sin, if a profound, spreading evil be propagated by it, an evil which, like a disease, attacks and strangles one man after another—that does not trouble this honour-craving Oriental in heaven; sin is an offence against him, not against mankind!—to him on whom he has bestowed his favour he bestows also this indifference to the natural consequences of sin. God and mankind are here thought of as separated, as so antithetical that sin against the latter cannot be at all possible,—all deeds are to be looked upon solely with respect to their supernatural consequences, and not with respect to their natural results: it is thus that the Jewish feeling, to which all that is natural seems unworthy in itself, would have things. The Greeks, on the other hand, were more familiar with the thought that transgression also may have dignity,—even theft, as in the case of Prometheus, even the slaughtering of cattle as the expression of frantic jealousy, as in the case of Ajax; in their need to attribute dignity to transgression and embody it therein, they invented tragedy,—an art and a delight, which in its profoundest essence has remained alien to the Jew, in spite of all his poetic endowment and taste for the sublime.

136.

The Chosen People.—The Jews, who regard themselves as the chosen people among the nations, and that too because they are the moral genius among the nations (in virtue of their capacity for despising 176the human in themselves more than any other people)—the Jews have a pleasure in their divine monarch and saint similar to that which the French nobility had in Louis XIV. This nobility had allowed its power and autocracy to be taken from it, and had become contemptible: in order not to feel this, in order to be able to forget it, an unequalled royal magnificence, royal authority and plenitude of power was needed, to which there was access only for the nobility. As in accordance with this privilege they raised themselves to the elevation of the court, and from that elevation saw everything under them,—saw everything contemptible,—they got beyond all uneasiness of conscience. They thus elevated intentionally the tower of the royal power more and more into the clouds, and set the final coping-stone of their own power thereon.

137.

Spoken in Parable.—A Jesus Christ was only possible in a Jewish landscape—I mean in one over which the gloomy and sublime thunder-cloud of the angry Jehovah hung continually. Here only was the rare, sudden flashing of a single sunbeam through the dreadful, universal and continuous nocturnal-day regarded as a miracle of "love," as a beam of the most unmerited "grace." Here only could Christ dream of his rainbow and celestial ladder on which God descended to man; everywhere else the clear weather and the sun were considered the rule and the commonplace.

138.

The Error of Christ.—The founder of Christianity thought there was nothing from which men suffered so much as from their sins:—it was his error, the error of him who felt himself without sin, to whom experience was lacking in this respect! It was thus that his soul filled with that marvellous, fantastic pity which had reference to a trouble that even among his own people, the inventors of sin, was rarely a great trouble! But Christians understood subsequently how to do justice to their master, and to sanctify his error into a "truth."

139.
Colour of the Passions.—Natures such as the apostle Paul, have an evil eye for the passions; they learn to know only the filthy, the distorting, and the heart-breaking in them,—their ideal aim, therefore, is the annihilation of the passions; in the divine they see complete purification from passion. The Greeks, quite otherwise than Paul and the Jews, directed their ideal aim precisely to the passions, and loved, elevated, embellished and deified them: in passion they evidently not only felt themselves happier, but also purer and diviner than otherwise.—And now the Christians? Have they wished to become Jews in this respect? Have they perhaps become Jews!

140.
Too Jewish.—If God had wanted to become an object of love, he would first of all have had to 178forgo judging and justice:—a judge, and even a gracious judge, is no object of love. The founder of Christianity showed too little of the finer feelings in this respect—being a Jew.

141.
Too Oriental.—What? A God who loves men, provided that they believe in him, and who hurls frightful glances and threatenings at him who does not believe in this love! What? A conditioned love as the feeling of an almighty God! A love which has not even become master of the sentiment of honour and of the irritable desire for vengeance! How Oriental is all that! "If I love thee, what does it concern thee?"[9] is already a sufficient criticism of the whole of Christianity.

142.
Frankincense.—Buddha says: "Do not flatter thy benefactor!" Let one repeat this saying in a Christian church:—it immediately purifies the air of all Christianity.

143.
The Greatest Utility of Polytheism.—For the individual to set up his own ideal and derive from it his laws, his pleasures and his rights—that has perhaps been hitherto regarded as the most monstrous of all human aberrations, and as idolatry in itself; in fact, the few who have ventured to do this have always needed to apologise to themselves, 179usually in this wise: "Not I! not I! but a God, through my instrumentality!" It was in the marvellous art and capacity for creating Gods—in polytheism—that this impulse was permitted to

discharge itself, it was here that it became purified, perfected, and ennobled; for it was originally a commonplace and unimportant impulse, akin to stubbornness, disobedience and envy. To be hostile to this impulse towards the individual ideal,—that was formerly the law of every morality. There was then only one norm, "the man"—and every people believed that it had this one and ultimate norm. But above himself, and outside of himself, in a distant over-world, a person could see a multitude of norms: the one God was not the denial or blasphemy of the other Gods! It was here that individuals were first permitted, it was here that the right of individuals was first respected. The inventing of Gods, heroes and supermen of all kinds, as well as co-ordinate men and undermen—dwarfs, fairies, centaurs, satyrs, demons, devils—was the inestimable preliminary to the justification of the selfishness and sovereignty of the individual: the freedom which was granted to one God in respect to other Gods, was at last given to the individual himself in respect to laws, customs and neighbours. Monotheism, on the contrary, the rigid consequence of the doctrine of one normal human being—consequently the belief in a normal God, beside whom there are only false, spurious Gods—has perhaps been the greatest danger of mankind in the past: man was then threatened by that premature state of inertia, which, so far as we can see, most of the 180other species of animals reached long ago, as creatures who all believe in one normal animal and ideal in their species, and definitely translated their morality of custom into flesh and blood. In polytheism man's free-thinking and many-sided thinking had a prototype set up: the power to create for himself new and individual eyes, always newer and more individualised: so that it is for man alone, of all the animals, that there are no eternal horizons and perspectives.

144.

Religious Wars.—The greatest advance of the masses hitherto has been religious war, for it proves that the masses have begun to deal reverently with conceptions of things. Religious wars only result, when human reason generally has been refined by the subtle disputes of sects; so that even the populace becomes punctilious and regards trifles as important, actually thinking it possible that the "eternal salvation of the soul" may depend upon minute distinctions of concepts.

145.

Danger of Vegetarians.—The immense prevalence of rice-eating impels to the use of opium and narcotics, in like manner as the immense prevalence of potato-eating impels to the use of brandy:—

it also impels, however, in its more subtle after-effects to modes of thought and feeling which operate narcotically. This is in accord with the fact that those who promote narcotic modes of thought and feeling, like those Indian teachers, 181praise a purely vegetable diet, and would like to make it a law for the masses: they want thereby to call forth and augment the need which they are in a position to satisfy.

146.

German Hopes.—Do not let us forget that the names of peoples are generally names of reproach. The Tartars, for example, according to their name, are "the dogs"; they were so christened by the Chinese. "Deutschen" (Germans) means originally "heathen": it is thus that the Goths after their conversion named the great mass of their unbaptized fellow-tribes, according to the indication in their translation of the Septuagint, in which the heathen are designated by the word which in Greek signifies "the nations." (See Ulfilas.)—It might still be possible for the Germans to make an honourable name ultimately out of their old name of reproach, by becoming the first non-Christian nation of Europe; for which purpose Schopenhauer, to their honour, regarded them as highly qualified. The work of Luther would thus be consummated,—he who taught them to be anti-Roman and to say: "Here I stand! I cannot do otherwise!"—

147.

Question and Answer.—What do savage tribes at present accept first of all from Europeans? Brandy and Christianity, the European narcotics.—And by what means are they fastest ruined?—By the European narcotics.

148.

Where Reformations Originate.—At the time of the great corruption of the church it was least of all corrupt in Germany: it was on that account that the Reformation originated here, as a sign that even the beginnings of corruption were felt to be unendurable. For, comparatively speaking, no people was ever more Christian than the Germans at the time of Luther; their Christian culture was just about to burst into bloom with a hundred-fold splendour,—one night only was still lacking; but that night brought the storm which put an end to all.

149.

The Failure of Reformations.—It testifies to the higher culture of the Greeks, even in rather early ages, that attempts to establish new Grecian religions frequently failed; it testifies that quite early there must have been a multitude of dissimilar individuals in Greece, whose dissimilar troubles were not cured by a single recipe of faith and hope. Pythagoras and Plato, perhaps also Empedocles, and already much earlier the Orphic enthusiasts, aimed at founding new religions; and the two first-named were so endowed with the qualifications for founding religions, that one cannot be sufficiently astonished at their failure: they just reached the point of founding sects. Every time that the Reformation of an entire people fails and only sects raise their heads, one may conclude that the people already contains many types, and has begun to free itself from the gross herding instincts and the morality of custom,—a momentous state of suspense, which one is accustomed to disparage as decay of morals and corruption, while it announces the maturing of the egg and the early rupture of the shell. That Luther's Reformation succeeded in the north, is a sign that the north had remained backward in comparison with the south of Europe, and still had requirements tolerably uniform in colour and kind; and there would have been no Christianising of Europe at all, if the culture of the old world of the south had not been gradually barbarized by an excessive admixture of the blood of German barbarians, and thus lost its ascendency. The more universally and unconditionally an individual, or the thought of an individual, can operate, so much more homogeneous and so much lower must be the mass that is there operated upon; while counter-strivings betray internal counter-requirements, which also want to gratify and realise themselves. Reversely, one may always conclude with regard to an actual elevation of culture, when powerful and ambitious natures only produce a limited and sectarian effect: this is true also for the separate arts, and for the provinces of knowledge. Where there is ruling there are masses: where there are masses there is need of slavery. Where there is slavery the individuals are but few, and have the instincts and conscience of the herd opposed to them.

150.

Criticism of Saints.—Must one then, in order to have a virtue, be desirous of having it precisely in its most brutal form?—as the Christian saints desired and needed;—those who only endured life with the thought that at the sight of their virtue self-contempt might seize every man. A virtue with such an effect I call brutal.

151.

The Origin of Religion.—The metaphysical requirement is not the origin of religions, as Schopenhauer claims, but only a later sprout from them. Under the dominance of religious thoughts we have accustomed ourselves to the idea of "another (back, under, or upper) world," and feel an uncomfortable void and privation through the annihilation of the religious illusion;—and then "another world" grows out of this feeling once more, but now it is only a metaphysical world, and no longer a religious one. That however which in general led to the assumption of "another world" in primitive times, was not an impulse or requirement, but an error in the interpretation of certain natural phenomena, a difficulty of the intellect.

152.

The greatest Change.—The lustre and the hues of all things have changed! We no longer quite understand how earlier men conceived of the most familiar and frequent things,—for example, of the day, and the awakening in the morning: owing to their belief in dreams the waking state seemed to them differently illuminated. And similarly of the whole of life, with its reflection of death and its significance: our "death" is an entirely different 185death. All events were of a different lustre, for a God shone forth in them; and similarly of all resolutions and peeps into the distant future: for people had oracles, and secret hints, and believed in prognostication. "Truth" was conceived in quite a different manner, for the insane could formerly be regarded as its mouthpiece—a thing which makes us shudder, or laugh. Injustice made a different impression on the feelings: for people were afraid of divine retribution, and not only of legal punishment and disgrace. What joy was there in an age when men believed in the devil and tempter! What passion was there when people saw demons lurking close at hand! What philosophy was there when doubt was regarded as sinfulness of the most dangerous kind, and in fact as an outrage on eternal love, as distrust of everything good, high, pure, and compassionate!—We have coloured things anew, we paint them over continually,—but what have we been able to do hitherto in comparison with the splendid colouring of that old master!—I mean ancient humanity.

153.

Homo poeta.—"I myself who have made this tragedy of tragedies altogether independently, in so far as it is completed; I who have first entwined the perplexities of morality about existence, and have tightened them so that only a God could unravel them—so Horace demands!—I have already in the fourth act killed all the Gods—for the sake of morality! What is now to be done about the fifth act? Where shall I get the tragic dénouement! Must I now think about a comic dénouement?"

154.

Differences in the Dangerousness of Life.—You don't know at all what you experience; you run through life as if intoxicated, and now and then fall down a stair. Thanks however to your intoxication you still do not break your limbs: your muscles are too languid and your head too confused to find the stones of the staircase as hard as we others do! For us life is a greater danger: we are made of glass—alas, if we should strike against anything! And all is lost if we should fall!

155.

What we Lack.—We love the grandeur of Nature and have discovered it; that is because human grandeur is lacking in our minds. It was the reverse with the Greeks: their feeling towards Nature was quite different from ours.

156.

The most Influential Person.—The fact that a person resists the whole spirit of his age, stops it at the door, and calls it to account, must exert an influence! It is indifferent whether he wishes to exert an influence; the point is that he can.

157.

Mentiri.—Take care!—he reflects: he will have a lie ready immediately. This is a stage in the civilisation of whole nations. Consider only what the Romans expressed by mentiri!

158.

An Inconvenient Peculiarity.—To find everything deep is an inconvenient peculiarity: it makes one constantly strain one's eyes, so that in the end one always finds more than one wishes.

159.

Every Virtue has its Time.—The honesty of him who is at present inflexible often causes him remorse; for inflexibility is the virtue of a time different from that in which honesty prevails.

160.

In Intercourse with Virtues.—One can also be undignified and flattering towards a virtue.

161.

To the Admirers of the Age.—The runaway priest and the liberated criminal are continually making grimaces; what they want is a look without a past.—But have you ever seen men who know that their looks reflect the future, and who are so courteous to you, the admirers of the "age," that they assume a look without a future.

162.

Egoism.—Egoism is the perspective law of our sentiment, according to which the near appears large and momentous, while in the distance the magnitude and importance of all things diminish.

163.

After a Great Victory.—The best thing in a great victory is that it deprives the conqueror of the fear of defeat. "Why should I not be worsted for once?" he says to himself, "I am now rich enough to stand it."

164.

Those who Seek Repose.—I recognise the minds that seek repose by the many dark objects with which they surround themselves: those who want to sleep darken their chambers, or creep into caverns. A hint to those who do not know what they really seek most, and would like to know!

165.

The Happiness of Renunciation.—He who has absolutely dispensed with something for a long time will almost imagine, when he accidentally meets with it again, that he has discovered it,—and what happiness every discoverer has! Let us be wiser than the serpents that lie too long in the same sunshine.

166.

Always in our own Society.—All that is akin to me in nature and history speaks to me, praises me, urges me forward and comforts me—: other things are unheard by me, or immediately forgotten. We are only in our own society always.

167.

Misanthropy and Philanthropy.—We only speak about being sick of men when we can no longer 189digest them, and yet have the stomach full of them. Misanthropy is the result of a far too eager philanthropy and "cannibalism,"—but who ever bade you swallow men like oysters, my Prince Hamlet!

168.

Concerning an Invalid.—"Things go badly with him!"—What is wrong?—"He suffers from the longing to be praised, and finds no sustenance for it."—Inconceivable! All the world does honour to him, and he is reverenced not only in deed but in word!—"Certainly, but he is dull of hearing for the praise. When a friend praises him it sounds to him as if the friend praised himself; when an enemy praises him, it sounds to him as if the enemy wanted to be praised for it; when, finally, some one else praises him—there are by no means so many of these, he is so famous!—he is offended because they neither want him for a friend nor for an enemy; he is accustomed to say: 'What do I care for those who can still pose as the all-righteous towards me!'"

169.

Avowed Enemies.—Bravery in presence of an enemy is a thing by itself: a person may possess it and still be a coward and an irresolute numskull. That was Napoleon's opinion concerning the "bravest man" he knew, Murat:—whence it follows that avowed enemies are indispensable to some men, if they are to attain to their virtue, to their manliness, to their cheerfulness.

170.

With the Multitude.—He has hitherto gone with the multitude and is its panegyrist; but one day he will be its opponent! For he follows it in the belief that his laziness will find its advantage thereby; he has not yet learned that the multitude is not lazy enough for him! that it always presses forward! that it does not allow any one to stand still!—And he likes so well to stand still!

171.

Fame.—When the gratitude of many to one casts aside all shame, then fame originates.

172.

The Perverter of Taste.—A: "You are a perverter of taste—they say so everywhere!" B: "Certainly! I pervert every one's taste for his party:—no party forgives me for that."

173.

To be Profound and to Appear Profound.—He who knows that he is profound strives for clearness; he who would like to appear profound to the multitude strives for obscurity. The multitude thinks everything profound of which it cannot see the bottom; it is so timid and goes so unwillingly into the water.

174.

Apart.—Parliamentarism, that is to say, the public permission to choose between five main political 191opinions, insinuates itself into the favour of the numerous class who would fain appear independent and individual, and like to fight for their opinions. After all, however, it is a matter of indifference whether one opinion is imposed upon the herd, or five opinions are permitted to it.—He who diverges from the five public opinions and goes apart, has always the whole herd against him.

175.

Concerning Eloquence.—What has hitherto had the most convincing eloquence? The rolling of the drum: and as long as kings have this at their command, they will always be the best orators and popular leaders.

176.

Compassion.—The poor, ruling princes! All their rights now change unexpectedly into claims, and all these claims immediately sound like pretensions! And if they but say "we," or "my people," wicked old Europe begins laughing. Verily, a chief-master-of-ceremonies of the modern world would make little ceremony with them; perhaps he would decree that "les souverains rangent aux parvenus."

177.

On "Educational Matters."—In Germany an important educational means is lacking for higher men; namely, the laughter of higher men; these men do not laugh in Germany.

178.
For Moral Enlightenment.—The Germans must be talked out of their Mephistopheles—and out of their Faust also. These are two moral prejudices against the value of knowledge.

179.
Thoughts.—Thoughts are the shadows of our sentiments—always, however, obscurer, emptier, and simpler.

180.
The Good Time for Free Spirits.—Free Spirits take liberties even with regard to Science—and meanwhile they are allowed to do so,—while the Church still remains!—In so far they have now their good time.

181.
Following and Leading.—A: "Of the two, the one will always follow, the other will always lead, whatever be the course of their destiny. And yet the former is superior to the other in virtue and intellect." B: "And yet? And yet? That is spoken for the others; not for me, not for us!—Fit secundum regulam."

182.
In Solitude.—When one lives alone one does not speak too loudly, and one does not write too loudly either, for one fears the hollow reverberation—the criticism of the nymph Echo.—And all voices sound differently in solitude!

183.
The Music of the Best Future.—The first musician for me would be he who knew only the sorrow of the profoundest happiness, and no other sorrow: there has not hitherto been such a musician.

184.
Justice.—Better allow oneself to be robbed than have scarecrows around one—that is my taste. And under all circumstances it is just a matter of taste—and nothing more!

185.
Poor.—He is now poor, but not because everything has been taken from him, but because he has thrown everything away:—what does he care? He is accustomed to find new things.—It is the poor who

misunderstand his voluntary poverty.

186.

Bad Conscience.—All that he now does is excellent and proper—and yet he has a bad conscience with it all. For the exceptional is his task.

187.

Offensiveness in Expression.—This artist offends me by the way in which he expresses his ideas, his very excellent ideas: so diffusely and forcibly, and with such gross rhetorical artifices, as if he were speaking to the mob. We feel always as if "in bad company" when devoting some time to his art.

188.

Work.—How close work and the workers now stand even to the most leisurely of us! The royal courtesy in the words: "We are all workers," would have been a cynicism and an indecency even under Louis XIV.

189.

The Thinker.—He is a thinker: that is to say, he knows how to take things more simply than they are.

190.

Against Eulogisers.—A: "One is only praised by one's equals!" B: "Yes! And he who praises you says: 'You are my equal!'"

191.

Against many a Vindication.—The most perfidious manner of injuring a cause is to vindicate it intentionally with fallacious arguments.

192.

The Good-natured.—What is it that distinguishes the good-natured, whose countenances beam kindness, from other people? They feel quite at ease in presence of a new person, and are quickly enamoured of him; they therefore wish him well; their first opinion is: "He pleases me." With them there follow in succession the wish to appropriate (they make little scruple about the person's worth), rapid appropriation, joy in the possession, and actions in favour of the person possessed.

193.

Kant's Joke.—Kant tried to prove, in a way that dismayed "everybody," that "everybody" was in the right:—that was his secret joke. He wrote against the learned, in favour of popular prejudice; he wrote, however, for the learned and not for the people.

194.

The "Open-hearted" Man.—That man acts probably always from concealed motives; for he has always communicable motives on his tongue, and almost in his open hand.

195.

Laughable!—See! See! He runs away from men—: they follow him, however, because he runs before them,—they are such a gregarious lot!

196.

The Limits of our Sense of Hearing.—We hear only the questions to which we are capable of finding an answer.

197.

Caution therefore!—There is nothing we are fonder of communicating to others than the seal of secrecy—together with what is under it.

198.

Vexation of the Proud Man.—The proud man is vexed even with those who help him forward: he looks angrily at his carriage-horses!

199.

Liberality.—Liberality is often only a form of timidity in the rich.

200.

Laughing.—To laugh means to love mischief, but with a good conscience.

201.

In Applause.—In applause there is always some kind of noise: even in self-applause.

202.

A Spendthrift.—He has not yet the poverty of the rich man who has counted all his treasure,—he squanders his spirit with the irrationalness of the spendthrift Nature.

203.

Hic niger est.—Usually he has no thoughts,—but in exceptional cases bad thoughts come to him.

204.

Beggars and Courtesy.—"One is not discourteous when one knocks at a door with a stone when the bell-pull is awanting"—so think all beggars and necessitous persons, but no one thinks they are in the right.

205.

Need.—Need is supposed to be the cause of things; but in truth it is often only the effect of the things themselves.

206.

During the Rain.—It rains, and I think of the poor people who now crowd together with their many cares, which they are unaccustomed to conceal; all of them, therefore, ready and anxious to give pain to one another, and thus provide themselves with a pitiable kind of comfort, even in bad weather. This, this only, is the poverty of the poor!

207.

The Envious Man.—That is an envious man—it is not desirable that he should have children; he would be envious of them, because he can no longer be a child.

208.

A Great Man!—Because a person is "a great man," we are not authorised to infer that he is a man. Perhaps he is only a boy, or a chameleon of all ages, or a bewitched girl.

209.

A Mode of Asking for Reasons.—There is a mode of asking for our reasons which not only makes us forget our best reasons, but also arouses in us a spite and repugnance against reason generally:—a very stupefying mode of questioning, and properly an artifice of tyrannical men!

210.

Moderation in Diligence.—One must not be anxious to surpass the diligence of one's father—that would make one ill.

211.

Secret Enemies.—To be able to keep a secret enemy—that is a luxury which the morality even of the highest-minded persons can rarely afford.

212.

Not Letting oneself be Deluded.—His spirit has bad manners, it is hasty and always stutters with impatience; so that one would hardly suspect the deep breathing and the large chest of the soul in which it resides.

213.

The Way to Happiness.—A sage asked of a fool the way to happiness. The fool answered without delay, like one who had been asked the way to the next town: "Admire yourself, and live on the street!" "Hold," cried the sage, "you require too much; it suffices to admire oneself!" The fool replied: "But how can one constantly admire without constantly despising?"

214.

Faith Saves.—Virtue gives happiness and a state of blessedness only to those who have a strong faith in their virtue:—not, however, to the more refined souls whose virtue consists of a profound distrust of themselves and of all virtue. After all, therefore, it is "faith that saves" here also!—and be it well observed, not virtue!

215.

The Ideal and the Material.—You have a noble ideal before your eyes: but are you also such a noble stone that such a divine image could be formed out of you? And without that—is not all your labour barbaric sculpturing? A blasphemy of your ideal!

216.

Danger in the Voice.—With a very loud voice a person is almost incapable of reflecting on subtle matters.

217.
Cause and Effect.—Before the effect one believes in other causes than after the effect.

218.
My Antipathy.—I do not like those people who, in order to produce an effect, have to burst like bombs, and in whose neighbourhood one is always in danger of suddenly losing one's hearing—or even something more.

219.
The Object of Punishment.—The object of punishment is to improve him who punishes,—that is the ultimate appeal of those who justify punishment.

220.
Sacrifice.—The victims think otherwise than the spectators about sacrifice and sacrificing: but they have never been allowed to express their opinion.

221.
Consideration.—Fathers and sons are much more considerate of one another than mothers and daughters.

222.
Poet and Liar.—The poet sees in the liar his foster-brother whose milk he has drunk up; the latter has thus remained wretched, and has not even attained to a good conscience.

223.
Vicariousness of the Senses.—"We have also eyes in order to hear with them,"—said an old confessor who had grown deaf; "and among the blind he that has the longest ears is king."

224.
Animal Criticism.—I fear the animals regard man as a being like themselves, very seriously endangered by a loss of sound animal understanding;—they regard him perhaps as the absurd animal, the laughing animal, the crying animal, the unfortunate animal.

225.
The Natural.—"Evil has always had the great effect! And Nature is evil! Let us therefore be natural!"—so reason secretly the great aspirants after effect, who are too often counted among great men.

226.
The Distrustful and their Style.—We say the strongest things simply, provided people are about us who believe in our strength:—such an environment educates to "simplicity of style." The distrustful, on the other hand, speak emphatically; they make things emphatic.

227.
Fallacy, Fallacy.—He cannot rule himself; therefore that woman concludes that it will be easy to rule him, and throws out her lines to catch him;—the poor creature, who in a short time will be his slave.

228.
Against Mediators.—He who attempts to mediate between two decided thinkers is rightly called mediocre: he has not an eye for seeing the unique; similarising and equalising are signs of weak eyes.

229.
Obstinacy and Loyalty.—Out of obstinacy he holds fast to a cause of which the questionableness has become obvious,—he calls that, however, his "loyalty."

230.
Lack of Reserve.—His whole nature fails to convince—that results from the fact that he has never been reticent about a good action he has performed.

231.
The "Plodders."—Persons slow of apprehension think that slowness forms part of knowledge.

232.
Dreaming.—Either one does not dream at all, or one dreams in an interesting manner. One must learn to be awake in the same fashion:—either not at all, or in an interesting manner.

233.

The most Dangerous Point of View.—What I now do, or neglect to do, is as important for all that is to come, as the greatest event of the past: in this immense perspective of effects all actions are equally great and small.

234.

Consolatory Words of a Musician.—"Your life does not sound into people's ears: for them you live a dumb life, and all refinements of melody, all fond resolutions in following or leading the way, are concealed from them. To be sure you do not parade the thoroughfares with regimental music,—but these good people have no right to say on that account that your life is lacking in music. He that hath ears let him hear."

235.

Spirit and Character.—Many a one attains his full height of character, but his spirit is not adapted to the elevation,—and many a one reversely.

236.

To Move the Multitude.—Is it not necessary for him who wants to move the multitude to give a stage representation of himself? Has he not first to translate himself into the grotesquely obvious, and then set forth his whole personality and cause in that vulgarised and simplified fashion!

237.

The Polite Man.—"He is so polite!"—Yes, he has always a sop for Cerberus with him, and is so timid that he takes everybody for Cerberus, even you and me,—that is his "politeness."

238.

Without Envy.—He is wholly without envy, but there is no merit therein: for he wants to conquer a land which no one has yet possessed and hardly any one has even seen.

239.

The Joyless Person.—A single joyless person is enough to make constant displeasure and a clouded heaven in a household; and it is only by a miracle that such a person is lacking!—Happiness is not nearly such a contagious disease;—how is that!

240.

On the Sea-Shore.—I would not build myself a house (it is an element of my happiness not to be a house-owner!). If I had to do so, however, I should build it, like many of the Romans, right into the sea,—I should like to have some secrets in common with that beautiful monster.

241.

Work and Artist.—This artist is ambitious and nothing more; ultimately, however, his work is only a magnifying glass, which he offers to every one who looks in his direction.

242.

Suum cuique.—However great be my greed of knowledge, I cannot appropriate aught of things but what already belongs to me,—the property of others still remains in the things. How is it possible for a man to be a thief or a robber!

243.

Origin of "Good" and "Bad."—He only will devise an improvement who can feel that "this is not good."

244.

Thoughts and Words.—Even our thoughts we are unable to render completely in words.

245.

Praise in Choice.—The artist chooses his subjects; that is his mode of praising.

246.

Mathematics.—We want to carry the refinement and rigour of mathematics into all the sciences, as far as it is in any way possible, not in the belief that we shall apprehend things in this way, but in order thereby to assert our human relation to things. Mathematics is only a means to general and ultimate human knowledge.

247.

Habits.—All habits make our hand wittier and our wit unhandier.

248.
Books.—Of what account is a book that never carries us away beyond all books!

249.
The Sigh of the Seeker of Knowledge.—"Oh, my covetousness! In this soul there is no disinterestedness—but an all-desiring self, which, by means of many individuals, would fain see as with its own eyes, and grasp as with its own hands—a self bringing back even the entire past, and wanting to lose nothing that could in any way belong to it! Oh, this flame of my covetousness! Oh, that I were reincarnated in a hundred individuals!"—He who does not know this sigh by experience, does not know the passion of the seeker of knowledge either.

250.
Guilt.—Although the most intelligent judges of the witches, and even the witches themselves, were convinced of the guilt of witchcraft, the guilt, nevertheless, was not there. So it is with all guilt.

251.
Misunderstood Sufferers.—Great natures suffer otherwise than their worshippers imagine; they suffer most severely from the ignoble, petty emotions of certain evil moments; in short, from doubt of their own greatness;—not however from the sacrifices and martyrdoms which their tasks require of them. As long as Prometheus sympathises with men and sacrifices himself for them, he is happy and proud in himself; but on becoming envious of Zeus and of the homage which mortals pay him—then Prometheus suffers!

252.
Better to be in Debt.—"Better to remain in debt than to pay with money which does not bear our stamp!"—that is what our sovereignty prefers.

253.
Always at Home.—One day we attain our goal—and then refer with pride to the long journeys we have made to reach it. In truth, we did not notice that we travelled. We got into the habit of thinking that we were at home in every place.

254.

Against Embarrassment.—He who is always thoroughly occupied is rid of all embarrassment.

255.

Imitators.—A: "What? You don't want to have imitators?" B: "I don't want people to do anything after me; I want every one to do something before himself (as a pattern to himself)—just as I do." A: "Consequently—?"

256.

Skinniness.—All profound men have their happiness in imitating the flying-fish for once, and playing on the crests of the waves; they think that what is best of all in things is their surface: their skinniness—sit venia verbo.

257.

From Experience.—A person often does not know how rich he is, until he learns from experience what rich men even play the thief on him.

258.

The Deniers of Chance.—No conqueror believes in chance.

259.

From Paradise.—"Good and Evil are God's prejudices"—said the serpent.

260.

One times One.—One only is always in the wrong, but with two truth begins.—One only cannot prove himself right; but two are already beyond refutation.

261.

Originality.—What is originality? To see something that does not yet bear a name, that cannot yet be named, although it is before everybody's eyes. As people are usually constituted, it is the name that first makes a thing generally visible to them.—Original persons have also for the most part been the namers of things.

262.

Sub specie aeterni.—A: "You withdraw faster and faster from the living; they will soon strike you out of their lists!"—B: "It is the only way to participate in the privilege of the dead." A: "In what privilege?"—B: "No longer having to die."

263.

Without Vanity.—When we love we want our defects to remain concealed,—not out of vanity, but lest the person loved should suffer therefrom. Indeed, the lover would like to appear as a God,—and not out of vanity either.

264.

What we Do.—What we do is never understood, but only praised and blamed.

265.

Ultimate Scepticism.—But what after all are man's truths?—They are his irrefutable errors.

266.

Where Cruelty is Necessary.—He who is great is cruel to his second-rate virtues and judgments.

267.

With a high Aim.—With a high aim a person is superior even to justice, and not only to his deeds and his judges.

268.

What makes Heroic?—To face simultaneously one's greatest suffering and one's highest hope.

269.

What dost thou Believe in?—In this: That the weights of all things must be determined anew.

270.

What Saith thy Conscience?—"Thou shalt become what thou art."

271.

Where are thy Greatest Dangers?—In pity.

272.
What dost thou Love in others?—My hopes.

273.
Whom dost thou call Bad?—Him who always wants to put others to shame.

274.
What dost thou think most humane?—To spare a person shame.

275.
What is the Seal of Liberty Attained?—To be no longer ashamed of oneself.

BOOK FOURTH
SANCTUS JANUARIUS

Thou who with cleaving fiery lances
The stream of my soul from its ice dost free,
Till with a rush and a roar it advances
To enter with glorious hoping the sea:
Brighter to see and purer ever,
Free in the bonds of thy sweet constraint,—
So it praises thy wondrous endeavour,
January, thou beauteous saint!
Genoa, January 1882.

276.

For the New Year.—I still live, I still think; I must still live, for I must still think. Sum, ergo cogito: cogito, ergo sum. To-day everyone takes the liberty of expressing his wish and his favourite thought: well, I also mean to tell what I have wished for myself to-day, and what thought first crossed my mind this year,—a thought which ought to be the basis, the pledge and the sweetening of all my future life! I want more and more to perceive the necessary characters in things as the beautiful:—I shall thus be one of those who beautify things. Amor fati: let that henceforth be my love! I do not want to wage war with the ugly. I do not want to accuse, I do not want even to accuse the accusers. Looking aside, let that be my sole negation! And all in all, to sum up: I wish to be at any time hereafter only a yea-sayer!

277.

Personal Providence.—There is a certain climax in life, at which, notwithstanding all our freedom, and however much we may have denied all directing reason and goodness in the beautiful chaos of existence, we are once more in great danger of intellectual bondage, and have to face our hardest test. For now the thought of a personal Providence first presents itself before us with its most persuasive force, and has the best of advocates, apparentness, in its favour, now when it is obvious that all and everything that happens to us always turns out for the best. The life of every day and of every hour seems to be anxious for nothing else but always to prove this proposition anew; let it be what it will, bad or good weather, the loss of a friend, a sickness, a calumny, the non-receipt of a letter, the spraining of one's foot, a glance into a shop-window, a counter-argument, the opening of a book, a dream, a deception:—it shows itself immediately, or very soon afterwards as something "not permitted to be absent,"—it is full of profound significance and utility precisely for us! Is there a more dangerous temptation to rid ourselves of the belief in the Gods of Epicurus, those careless, unknown Gods, and believe in some anxious and mean Divinity, who knows personally every little hair on our heads, and feels no disgust in rendering the most wretched services? Well—I mean in spite of all this! we want to leave the Gods alone (and the serviceable genii likewise), and wish to content ourselves with the assumption that our own practical and theoretical skilfulness in explaining and suitably arranging events has now reached its highest point. We do not want either to think too highly of this dexterity of our wisdom, when the wonderful harmony which results from playing on our instrument sometimes surprises us too much: a harmony which sounds too well for us to dare to ascribe it to ourselves. In fact, now and then there is one who plays with us—beloved Chance: he leads our hand occasionally, and even the all-wisest Providence could not devise any finer music than that of which our foolish hand is then capable.

278.

The Thought of Death.—It gives me a melancholy happiness to live in the midst of this confusion of streets, of necessities, of voices: how much enjoyment, impatience and desire, how much thirsty life and drunkenness of life comes to light here every moment! And yet it will soon be so still for all these shouting, lively, life-loving people! How everyone's shadow, his gloomy travelling-companion stands behind him! It is always as in the last moment before the departure of an emigrant-ship: people have more than ever to say to one another, the hour presses, the ocean with its lonely silence waits impatiently behind all the noise—so greedy, so certain of its prey! And all, all, suppose that the past has been nothing, or a small matter, that the near future is everything: hence this haste, this crying, this self-deafening and self-overreaching! Everyone wants to be foremost in this future,—and yet death and the stillness of death are the only things certain and common to all in this future! How strange that this sole thing that is certain and common to all, exercises almost no influence on men, and that they are the furthest from regarding themselves as the brotherhood of death! It makes me happy to see that men do not want to think at all of the idea of death! I would fain do something to make the idea of life even a hundred times more worthy of their attention.

279.

Stellar Friendship.—We were friends, and have become strangers to each other. But this is as it ought to be, and we do not want either to conceal or obscure the fact, as if we had to be ashamed of it. We are two ships, each of which has its goal and its course; we may, to be sure, cross one another in our paths, and celebrate a feast together as we did before,—and then the gallant ships lay quietly in one harbour, and in one sunshine, so that it might have been thought they were already at their goal, and that they had had one goal. But then the almighty strength of our tasks forced us apart once more into different seas and into different zones, and perhaps we shall never see one another again,—or perhaps we may see one another, but not know one another again; the different seas and suns have altered us! That we had to become strangers to one another is the law to which we are subject: just by that shall we become more sacred to one another! Just by that shall the thought of our former friendship become holier! There is probably some immense, invisible curve and stellar orbit in which our courses and goals, so widely different, may be comprehended as small stages of the way,—let us raise ourselves to this thought! But our life is too short, and our power of vision too limited for 217us to be more than friends in the sense of that sublime possibility.—And so we will believe in our stellar friendship, though we should have to be terrestrial enemies to one another.

280.

Architecture for Thinkers.—An insight is needed (and that probably very soon) as to what is specially lacking in our great cities— namely, quiet, spacious, and widely extended places for reflection, places with long, lofty colonnades for bad weather, or for too sunny days, where no noise of wagons or of shouters would penetrate, and where a more refined propriety would prohibit loud praying even to the priest: buildings and situations which as a whole would express the sublimity of self-communion and seclusion from the world. The time is past when the Church possessed the monopoly of reflection, when the vita contemplativa had always in the first place to be the vita religiosa: and everything that the Church has built expresses this thought. I know not how we could content ourselves with their structures, even if they should be divested of their ecclesiastical purposes: these structures speak a far too pathetic and too biassed speech, as houses of God and places of splendour for supernatural intercourse, for us godless ones to be able to think our thoughts in them. We want to have ourselves translated into stone and plant, we want to go for a walk in ourselves when we wander in these halls and gardens.

281.

Knowing how to Find the End.—Masters of the first rank are recognised by knowing in a perfect manner how to find the end, in the whole as well as in the part; be it the end of a melody or of a thought, be it the fifth act of a tragedy or of a state affair. The masters of the second degree always become restless towards the end, and seldom dip down into the sea with such proud, quiet equilibrium as, for example, the mountain-ridge at Porto fino—where the Bay of Genoa sings its melody to an end.

282.

The Gait.—There are mannerisms of the intellect by which even great minds betray that they originate from the populace, or from the semi-populace:—it is principally the gait and step of their thoughts which betray them; they cannot walk. It was thus that even Napoleon, to his profound chagrin, could not walk "legitimately" and in princely fashion on occasions when it was necessary to do so properly, as in great coronation processions and on similar occasions: even there he was always just the leader of a column—proud and brusque at the same time, and very self-conscious of it all.—It is something laughable to see those writers who make the folding robes of their periods rustle around them: they want to cover their feet.

283.

Pioneers.—I greet all the signs indicating that a more manly and warlike age is commencing, which will, above all, bring heroism again into honour! 219For it has to prepare the way for a yet higher age, and gather the force which the latter will one day require,—the age which will carry heroism into knowledge, and wage war for the sake of ideas and their consequences. For that end many brave pioneers are now needed, who, however, cannot originate out of nothing,—and just as little out of the sand and slime of present-day civilisation and the culture of great cities: men silent, solitary and resolute, who know how to be content and persistent in invisible activity: men who with innate disposition seek in all things that which is to be overcome in them: men to whom cheerfulness, patience, simplicity, and contempt of the great vanities belong just as much as do magnanimity in victory and indulgence to the trivial vanities of all the vanquished: men with an acute and independent judgment regarding all victors, and concerning the part which chance has played in the winning of victory and fame: men with their own holidays, their own work-days, and their own periods of mourning; accustomed to command with perfect assurance, and equally ready, if need be, to obey, proud in the one case as in the other, equally serving their own interests: men more imperilled, more productive, more happy! For believe me!—the secret of realising the largest productivity and the greatest enjoyment of existence is to live in danger! Build your cities on the slope of Vesuvius! Send your ships into unexplored seas! Live in war with your equals and with yourselves! Be robbers and spoilers, ye knowing ones, as long as ye cannot be rulers and possessor! The time will soon pass when you can be satisfied to live like timorous deer concealed in the forests. Knowledge will finally stretch out her hand for that which belongs to her:—she means to rule and possess, and you with her!

284.

Belief in Oneself.—In general, few men have belief in themselves:—and of those few some are endowed with it as a useful blindness or partial obscuration of intellect (what would they perceive if they could see to the bottom of themselves!). The others must first acquire the belief for themselves: everything good, clever, or great that they do, is first of all an argument against the sceptic that dwells in them: the question is how to convince or persuade this sceptic, and for that purpose genius almost is needed. They are signally dissatisfied with themselves.

285.

Excelsior!—"Thou wilt never more pray, never more worship, never more repose in infinite trust—thou refusest to stand still and dismiss thy thoughts before an ultimate wisdom, an ultimate virtue, an ultimate power,—thou hast no constant guardian and friend in thy seven solitudes—thou livest without the outlook on a mountain that has snow on its head and fire in its heart—there is no longer any requiter for thee, nor any amender with his finishing touch—there is no longer any reason in that which happens, or any love in that which will happen to thee—there is no longer any resting-place for thy weary heart, where it has only to find and no longer to seek, thou art opposed to any kind of ultimate peace, thou desirest the eternal recurrence of war and peace:—man of renunciation, wilt thou renounce in all these things? Who will give thee the strength to do so? No one has yet had this strength!"—There is a lake which one day refused to flow away, and threw up a dam at the place where it had hitherto flowed away: since then this lake has always risen higher and higher. Perhaps the very renunciation will also furnish us with the strength with which the renunciation itself can be borne; perhaps man will ever rise higher and higher from that point onward, when he no longer flows out into a God.

286.

A Digression.—Here are hopes; but what will you see and hear of them, if you have not experienced glance and glow and dawn of day in your own souls? I can only suggest—I cannot do more! To move the stones, to make animals men—would you have me do that? Alas, if you are yet stones and animals, seek first your Orpheus!

287.

Love of Blindness.—"My thoughts," said the wanderer to his shadow, "ought to show me where I stand, but they should not betray to me whither I go. I love ignorance of the future, and do not want to come to grief by impatience and anticipatory tasting of promised things."

288.

Lofty Moods.—It seems to me that most men do not believe in lofty moods, unless it be for the moment, or at the most for a quarter of an hour,—except the few who know by experience a longer duration of high feeling. But to be absolutely a man with a single lofty feeling, the incarnation of a single lofty mood—that has hitherto been only a dream and an enchanting possibility: history does not yet give us any trustworthy example of it. Nevertheless it could some day produce such men also—when a multitude of favourable conditions have been created and established, which at present even the happiest chance is unable to throw together. Perhaps that very state which has hitherto entered into our soul as an exception, felt with horror now and then, may be the usual condition of those future souls: a continuous movement between high and low, and the feeling of high and low, a constant state of mounting as on steps, and at the same time reposing as on clouds.

289.

Aboard Ship!—When one considers how a full philosophical justification of his mode of living and thinking operates upon every individual—namely, as a warming, blessing, and fructifying sun, specially shining on him; how it makes him independent of praise and blame, self-sufficient, rich and generous in the bestowal of happiness and kindness; how it unceasingly transforms the evil to the good, brings all the energies to bloom 223and maturity, and altogether hinders the growth of the greater and lesser weeds of chagrin and discontent:—one at last cries out importunately: Oh, that many such new suns were created! The evil man, also, the unfortunate man, and the exceptional man, shall each have his philosophy, his rights, and his sunshine! It is not sympathy with them that is necessary!—we must unlearn this arrogant fancy, notwithstanding that humanity has so long learned it and used it exclusively—we have not to set up any confessor, exorcist, or pardoner for them! It is a new justice, however, that is necessary! And a new solution! And new philosophers! The moral earth also is round! The moral earth also has its antipodes! The antipodes also have their right to exist! there is still another world to discover—and more than one! Aboard ship! ye philosophers!

290.

One Thing is Needful.—To "give style" to one's character—that is a grand and a rare art! He who surveys all that his nature presents in its strength and in its weakness, and then fashions it into an ingenious plan, until everything appears artistic and rational, and even the weaknesses enchant the eye—exercises that admirable art. Here there has been a great amount of second nature added, there a portion of first nature has been taken away:—in both cases with long exercise and daily labour at the task. Here the ugly, which does not permit of being taken away, has been concealed, there it has been re-interpreted 224into the sublime. Much of the vague, which refuses to take form, has been reserved and utilised for the perspectives:—it is meant to give a hint of the remote and immeasurable. In the end, when the work has been completed, it is revealed how it was the constraint of the same taste that organised and fashioned it in whole or in part: whether the taste was good or bad is of less importance than one thinks,—it is sufficient that it was a taste!—It will be the strong imperious natures which experience their most refined joy in such constraint, in such confinement and perfection under their own law; the passion of their violent volition lessens at the sight of all disciplined nature, all conquered and ministering nature: even when they have palaces to build and gardens to lay out, it is not to their taste to allow nature to be free.—It is the reverse with weak characters who have not power over themselves, and hate the restriction of style: they feel that if this repugnant constraint were laid upon them, they would necessarily become vulgarised under it: they become slaves as soon as they serve, they hate service. Such intellects—they may be intellects of the first rank—are always concerned with fashioning or interpreting themselves and their surroundings as free nature—wild, arbitrary, fantastic, confused and surprising: and it is well for them to do so, because only in this manner can they please themselves! For one thing is needful: namely, that man should attain to satisfaction with himself—be it but through this or that fable and artifice: it is only then that man's aspect is at all 225endurable! He who is dissatisfied with himself is ever ready to avenge himself on that account: we others will be his victims, if only in having always to endure his ugly aspect. For the aspect of the ugly makes one mean and sad.

291.

Genoa.—I have looked upon this city, its villas and pleasure-grounds and the wide circuit of its inhabited heights and slopes, for a considerable time: in the end I must say that I see countenances out of past generations,—this district is strewn with the images of bold and autocratic men. They have lived and have wanted to live on—they say so with their houses, built and decorated for centuries, and not for the passing hour: they were well disposed to life, however ill-disposed they may often have been towards themselves. I always see the builder, how he casts his eye on all that is built around him far and near, and likewise on the city, the sea, and the chain of mountains; how he expresses power and conquest in his gaze: all this he wishes to fit into his plan, and in the end make it his property, by its becoming a portion of the same. The whole district is overgrown with this superb, insatiable egoism of the desire to possess and exploit; and as these men when abroad recognised no frontiers, and in their thirst for the new placed a new world beside the old, so also at home everyone rose up against everyone else, and devised some mode of expressing his superiority, and of placing between himself and his neighbour his personal illimitableness. Everyone 226won for himself his home once more by over-powering it with his architectural thoughts, and by transforming it into a delightful sight for his race. When we consider the mode of building cities in the north, the law and the general delight in legality and obedience, impose upon us: we thereby divine the propensity to equality and submission which must have ruled in those builders. Here, however, on turning every corner you find a man by himself, who knows the sea, knows adventure, and knows the Orient, a man who is averse to law and to neighbour, as if it bored him to have to do with them, a man who scans all that is already old and established, with envious glances: with a wonderful craftiness of fantasy, he would like, at least in thought, to establish all this anew, to lay his hand upon it, and introduce his meaning into it—if only for the passing hour of a sunny afternoon, when for once his insatiable and melancholy soul feels satiety, and when only what is his own, and nothing strange, may show itself to his eye.

292.

To the Preachers of Morality.—I do not mean to moralise, but to those who do, I would give this advice: if you mean ultimately to deprive the best things and the best conditions of all honour and worth, continue to speak of them in the same way as heretofore! Put them at the head of your morality, and speak from morning till night of the happiness of virtue, of repose of soul, of righteousness, and of reward and punishment in the nature of things: according as you go on in this manner, all these good things will finally acquire a popularity and a street-cry for themselves: but then all the gold on them will also be worn off, and more besides: all the gold in them will have changed into lead. Truly, you understand the reverse art of alchemy, the depreciating of the most valuable things! Try, just for once, another recipe, in order not to realise as hitherto the opposite of what you mean to attain: deny those good things, withdraw from them the applause of the populace and discourage the spread of them, make them once more the concealed chastities of solitary souls, say that morality is something forbidden! Perhaps you will thus win over for those things the sort of men who are only of any account, I mean the heroic. But then there must be something formidable in them, and not as hitherto something disgusting! Might one not be inclined to say at present with reference to morality what Master Eckardt says: "I pray God to deliver me from God!"

293.

Our Atmosphere.—We know it well: to him who only casts a glance now and then at science, as in taking a walk (in the manner of women, and alas! also like many artists), the strictness in its service, its inexorability in small matters as well as in great, its rapidity in weighing, judging and condemning, produce something of a feeling of giddiness and fright. It is especially terrifying to him that the hardest is here demanded, that the best is done without the reward of praise or distinction; it is rather as among soldiers—almost nothing but blame and sharp reprimand is heard; for doing well prevails here as the rule, doing ill as the exception; the rule, however, has, here as everywhere, a silent tongue. It is the same with this "severity of science" as with the manners and politeness of the best society: it frightens the uninitiated. He, however, who is accustomed to it, does not like to live anywhere but in this clear, transparent, powerful, and highly electrified atmosphere, this manly atmosphere. Anywhere else it is not pure and airy enough for him: he suspects that there his best art would neither be properly advantageous to anyone else, nor a delight to himself, that through misunderstandings half of his life would slip through his fingers, that much foresight, much concealment, and reticence would constantly be necessary,—nothing but great and useless losses of power! In this keen and clear element, however, he has his entire power: here he can fly! Why should he again go down into those muddy waters where he has to swim and wade and soil his wings!—No! There it is too hard for us to live! we cannot help it that we are born for the atmosphere, the pure atmosphere, we rivals of the ray of light; and that we should like best to ride like it on the atoms of ether, not away from the sun, but towards the sun! That, however, we cannot do:—so we want to do the only thing that is in our power: namely, to bring light to the earth, we want to be "the light of the earth!" And for that purpose we have our wings and our swiftness and our severity, on that account we are manly, and even terrible like the fire. Let those fear us, who do not know how to warm and brighten themselves by our influence!

294.

Against the Disparagers of Nature.—They are disagreeable to me, those men in whom every natural inclination forthwith becomes a disease, something disfiguring, or even disgraceful. They have seduced us to the opinion that the inclinations and impulses of men are evil; they are the cause of our great injustice to our own nature, and to all nature! There are enough of men who may yield to their impulses gracefully and carelessly: but they do not do so, for fear of that imaginary "evil thing" in nature! That is the cause why there is so little nobility to be found among men: the indication of which will always be to have no fear of oneself, to expect nothing disgraceful from oneself, to fly without hesitation whithersoever we are impelled—we free-born birds! Wherever we come, there will always be freedom and sunshine around us.

295.

Short-lived Habits.—I love short-lived habits, and regard them as an invaluable means for getting a knowledge of many things and various conditions, to the very bottom of their sweetness and bitterness; my nature is altogether arranged for short-lived habits, even in the needs of its bodily health, and in general, as far as I can see, from the lowest up to the highest matters. I always think that this will at last satisfy me permanently (the short-lived habit has also that characteristic belief of passion, the belief in everlasting duration; I am to be envied for having found it and recognised it), and then it nourishes me at noon and at eve, and spreads a profound satisfaction around me and in me, so that I have no longing for anything else, not needing to compare, or despise, or hate. But one day the habit has had its time: the good thing separates from me, not as something which then inspires disgust in me—but peaceably and as though satisfied with me, as I am with it; as if we had to be mutually thankful, and thus shook hands for farewell. And already the new habit waits at the door, and similarly also my belief—indestructible fool and sage that I am!—that this new habit will be the right one, the ultimate right one. So it is with me as regards foods, thoughts, men, cities, poems, music, doctrines, arrangements of the day, and modes of life.—On the other hand, I hate permanent habits, and feel as if a tyrant came into my neighbourhood, and as if my life's breath condensed, when events take such a form that permanent habits seem necessarily to grow out of them: for example, through an official position, through constant companionship with the same persons, through a settled abode, or through a uniform state of health. Indeed, from the bottom of my soul I am gratefully disposed to all my misery and sickness, and to whatever is imperfect in me, because such things leave me a hundred back-doors through which I can escape from permanent habits. The most unendurable thing, to be sure, the really terrible thing, would be a life without habits, a life which 231continually required improvisation:—that would be my banishment and my Siberia.

296.

A Fixed Reputation.—A fixed reputation was formerly a matter of the very greatest utility; and wherever society continues to be ruled by the herd-instinct, it is still most suitable for every individual to give to his character and business the appearance of unalterableness,— even when they are not so in reality. "One can rely on him, he remains the same"—that is the praise which has most significance in all dangerous conditions of society. Society feels with satisfaction that it has a reliable tool ready at all times in the virtue of this one, in the ambition of that one, and in the reflection and passion of a third one,—it honours this tool-like nature, this self-constancy, this unchangeableness in opinions, efforts, and even in faults, with the highest honours. Such a valuation, which prevails and has prevailed everywhere simultaneously with the morality of custom, educates "characters," and brings all changing, re-learning, and self-transforming into disrepute. Be the advantage of this mode of thinking ever so great otherwise, it is in any case the mode of judging which is most injurious to knowledge: for precisely the good-will of the knowing one ever to declare himself unhesitatingly as opposed to his former opinions, and in general to be distrustful of all that wants to be fixed in him—is here condemned and brought into disrepute. The disposition of the thinker, as incompatible with 232a "fixed reputation," is regarded as dishonourable, while the petrifaction of opinions has all the honour to itself:—we have at present still to live under the interdict of such rules! How difficult it is to live when one feels that the judgment of many millenniums is around one and against one. It is probable that for many millenniums knowledge was afflicted with a bad conscience, and that there must have been much self-contempt and secret misery in the history of the greatest intellects.

297.

Ability to Contradict.—Everyone knows at present that the ability to endure contradiction is a high indication of culture. Some people even know that the higher man courts opposition, and provokes it, so as to get a cue to his hitherto unknown partiality. But the ability to contradict, the attainment of good conscience in hostility to the accustomed, the traditional and the hallowed,—that is more than both the above-named abilities, and is the really great, new and astonishing thing in our culture, the step of all steps of the emancipated intellect: who knows that?—

298.

A Sigh.—I caught this notion on the way, and rapidly took the readiest, poor words to hold it fast, so that it might not again fly away. And now it has died in these dry words, and hangs and flaps about in them—and I hardly know now, when I look upon it, how I could have had such happiness when I caught this bird.

299.

What one should Learn from Artists.—What means have we for making things beautiful, attractive, and desirable, when they are not so?—and I suppose they are never so in themselves! We have here something to learn from physicians, when, for example, they dilute what is bitter, or put wine and sugar into their mixing-bowl; but we have still more to learn from artists, who in fact, are continually concerned in devising such inventions and artifices. To withdraw from things until one no longer sees much of them, until one has even to see things into them, in order to see them at all—or to view them from the side, and as in a frame—or to place them so that they partly disguise themselves and only permit of perspective views— or to look at them through coloured glasses, or in the light of the sunset—or to furnish them with a surface or skin which is not fully transparent: we should learn all that from artists, and moreover be wiser than they. For this fine power of theirs usually ceases with them where art ceases and life begins; we, however, want to be the poets of our life, and first of all in the smallest and most commonplace matters.

300.

Prelude to Science.—Do you believe then that the sciences would have arisen and grown up if the sorcerers, alchemists, astrologers and witches had not been their forerunners; those who, with their promisings and foreshadowings, had first to create a thirst, a hunger, and a taste for hidden and forbidden powers? Yea, that infinitely more had to be promised than could ever be fulfilled, in order that something might be fulfilled in the domain of knowledge? Perhaps the whole of religion, also, may appear to some distant age as an exercise and a prelude, in like manner as the prelude and preparation of science here exhibit themselves, though not at all practised and regarded as such. Perhaps religion may have been the peculiar means for enabling individual men to enjoy but once the entire self-satisfaction of a God and all his self-redeeming power. Indeed!—one may ask—would man have learned at all to get on the tracks of hunger and thirst for himself, and to extract satiety and fullness out of himself, without that religious schooling and preliminary history? Had Prometheus first to fancy that he had stolen the light, and that he did penance for the theft—in order finally to discover that he had created the light, in that he had longed for the light, and that not only man, but also God had been the work of his hands and the clay in his hands? All mere creations of the creator?—just as the illusion, the theft, the Caucasus, the vulture, and the whole tragic Prometheia of all thinkers!

301.

Illusion of the Contemplative.—Higher men are distinguished from lower, by seeing and hearing immensely more, and in a thoughtful manner—and it is precisely this that distinguishes man from the animal, and the higher animal from the lower. The world always becomes fuller for him who grows up into the full stature of humanity; there are always more interesting fishing-hooks, thrown out to him; the number of his stimuli is continually on the increase, and similarly the varieties of his pleasure and pain,—the higher man becomes always at the same time happier and unhappier. An illusion, however, is his constant accompaniment all along: he thinks he is placed as a spectator and auditor before the great pantomime and concert of life; he calls his nature a contemplative nature, and thereby overlooks the fact that he himself is also a real creator, and continuous poet of life,—that he no doubt differs greatly from the actor in this drama, the so-called practical man, but differs still more from a mere onlooker or spectator before the stage. There is certainly vis contemplativa, and re-examination of his work peculiar to him as poet, but at the same time, and first and foremost, he has the vis creativa, which the practical man or doer lacks, whatever appearance and current belief may say to the contrary. It is we, we who think and feel, that actually and unceasingly make something which does not yet exist: the whole eternally increasing world of valuations, colours, weights, perspectives, gradations, affirmations and negations. This composition of ours is continually learnt, practised, and translated into flesh and actuality, and even into the commonplace, by the so-called practical men (our actors, as we have said). Whatever has value in the present world, has it not in itself, by its nature,—nature is always worthless:—but a value was once given to it, bestowed upon it, 236and it was we who gave and bestowed! We only have created the world which is of any account to man!—But it is precisely this knowledge that we lack, and when we get hold of it for a moment we have forgotten it the next: we misunderstand our highest power, we contemplative men, and estimate ourselves at too low a rate,—we are neither as proud nor as happy as we might be.

302.

The Danger of the Happiest Ones.—To have fine senses and a fine taste; to be accustomed to the select and the intellectually best as our proper and readiest fare; to be blessed with a strong, bold, and daring soul; to go through life with a quiet eye and a firm step, ever ready for the worst as for a festival, and full of longing for undiscovered worlds and seas, men and Gods; to listen to all joyous music, as if there, perhaps, brave men, soldiers and seafarers, took a brief repose and enjoyment, and in the profoundest pleasure of the moment were overcome with tears and the whole purple melancholy of happiness: who would not like all this to be his possession, his condition! It was the happiness of Homer! The condition of him who invented the Gods for the Greeks,—nay, who invented his Gods for himself! But let us not conceal the fact that with this happiness of Homer in one's soul, one is more liable to suffering than any other creature under the sun! And only at this price do we purchase the most precious pearl that the waves of existence have hitherto washed ashore! As its possessor one always becomes more 237sensitive to pain, and at last too sensitive: a little displeasure and loathing sufficed in the end to make Homer disgusted with life. He was unable to solve a foolish little riddle which some young fishers proposed to him! Yes, the little riddles are the dangers of the happiest ones!—

303.

Two Happy Ones.—Certainly this man, notwithstanding his youth, understands the improvisation of life, and astonishes even the acutest observers. For it seems that he never makes a mistake, although he constantly plays the most hazardous games. One is reminded of the improvising masters of the musical art, to whom even the listeners would fain ascribe a divine infallibility of the hand, notwithstanding that they now and then make a mistake, as every mortal is liable to do. But they are skilled and inventive, and always ready in a moment to arrange into the structure of the score the most accidental tone (where the jerk of a finger or a humour brings it about), and to animate the accident with a fine meaning and a soul.—Here is quite a different man: everything that he intends and plans fails with him in the long run. That on which he has now and again set his heart has already brought him several times to the abyss, and to the very verge of ruin; and if he has as yet got out of the scrape, it certainly has not been merely with a "black eye." Do you think he is unhappy over it? He resolved long ago not to regard his own wishes and plans as of so much importance. "If this does not succeed with me,"—he says to himself, "perhaps that will succeed; and on the whole I do not know but that I am under more obligation to thank my failures than any of my successes. Am I made to be headstrong, and to wear the bull's horns? That which constitutes the worth and the sum of life for me, lies somewhere else; I know more of life, because I have been so often on the point of losing it; and just on that account I have more of life than any of you!"

304.

In Doing we Leave Undone.—In the main all those moral systems are distasteful to me which say: "Do not do this! Renounce! Overcome thyself!" On the other hand I am favourable to those moral systems which stimulate me to do something, and to do it again from morning till evening, and dream of it at night, and think of nothing else but to do it well, as well as it is possible for me alone! From him who so lives there fall off one after the other the things that do not pertain to such a life: without hatred or antipathy, he sees this take leave of him to-day, and that to-morrow, like the yellow leaves which every livelier breeze strips from the tree: or he does not see at all that they take leave of him, so firmly is his eye fixed upon his goal, and generally forward, not sideways, backward, nor downward. "Our doing must determine what we leave undone; in that we do, we leave undone"—so it pleases me, so runs my placitum. But I do not mean to strive with open eyes for my impoverishment; I do not like any of the negative virtues whose very essence is negation and self-renunciation.

305.

Self-control.—Those moral teachers who first and foremost order man to get himself into his own power, induce thereby a curious infirmity in him,—namely, a constant sensitiveness with reference to all natural strivings and inclinations, and as it were, a sort of itching. Whatever may henceforth drive him, draw him, allure or impel him, whether internally or externally—it always seems to this sensitive being, as if his self-control were in danger: he is no longer at liberty to trust himself to any instinct, to any free flight, but stands constantly with defensive mien, armed against himself, with sharp distrustful eye, the eternal watcher of his stronghold, to which office he has appointed himself. Yes, he can be great in that position! But how unendurable he has now become to others, how difficult even for himself to bear, how impoverished and cut off from the finest accidents of his soul! Yea, even from all further instruction! For we must be able to lose ourselves at times, if we want to learn something of what we have not in ourselves.

306.

Stoic and Epicurean.—The Epicurean selects the situations, the persons, and even the events which suit his extremely sensitive, intellectual constitution; he renounces the rest—that is to say, by far the greater part of experience—because it would be 240too strong and too heavy fare for him. The Stoic, on the contrary, accustoms himself to swallow stones and vermin, glass-splinters and scorpions, without feeling any disgust: his stomach is meant to become indifferent in the end to all that the accidents of existence cast into it:—he reminds one of the Arabic sect of the Assaua, with which the French became acquainted in Algiers; and like those insensible persons, he also likes well to have an invited public at the exhibition of his insensibility, the very thing the Epicurean willingly dispenses with:—he has of course his "garden"! Stoicism may be quite advisable for men with whom fate improvises, for those who live in violent times and are dependent on abrupt and changeable individuals. He, however, who anticipates that fate will permit him to spin "a long thread," does well to make his arrangements in Epicurean fashion; all men devoted to intellectual labour have done it hitherto! For it would be a supreme loss to them to forfeit their fine sensibility, and acquire the hard, stoical hide with hedgehog prickles in exchange.

307.

In Favour of Criticism.—Something now appears to thee as an error which thou formerly lovedst as a truth, or as a probability: thou pushest it from thee and imaginest that thy reason has there gained a victory. But perhaps that error was then, when thou wast still another person—thou art always another person,—just as necessary to thee as all thy present "truths," like a skin, as it 241were, which concealed and veiled from thee much which thou still mayst not see. Thy new life, and not thy reason, has slain that opinion for thee: thou dost not require it any longer, and now it breaks down of its own accord, and the irrationality crawls out of it as a worm into the light. When we make use of criticism it is not something arbitrary and impersonal,—it is, at least very often, a proof that there are lively, active forces in us, which cast a skin. We deny, and must deny, because something in us wants to live and affirm itself, something which we perhaps do not as yet know, do not as yet see!—So much in favour of criticism.

308.

The History of each Day.—What is it that constitutes the history of each day for thee? Look at thy habits of which it consists: are they the product of numberless little acts of cowardice and laziness, or of thy bravery and inventive reason? Although the two cases are so different, it is possible that men might bestow the same praise upon thee, and that thou mightst also be equally useful to them in the one case as in the other. But praise and utility and respectability may suffice for him whose only desire is to have a good conscience,—not however for thee, the "trier of the reins," who hast a consciousness of the conscience!

309.

Out of the Seventh Solitude.—One day the wanderer shut a door behind him, stood still, and 242wept. Then he said: "Oh, this inclination and impulse towards the true, the real, the non-apparent, the certain! How I detest it! Why does this gloomy and passionate taskmaster follow just me? I should like to rest, but it does not permit me to do so. Are there not a host of things seducing me to tarry! Everywhere there are gardens of Armida for me, and therefore there will always be fresh separations and fresh bitterness of heart! I must set my foot forward, my weary wounded foot: and because I feel I must do this, I often cast grim glances back at the most beautiful things which could not detain me—because they could not detain me!"

310.

Will and Wave.—How eagerly this wave comes hither, as if it were a question of its reaching something! How it creeps with frightful haste into the innermost corners of the rocky cliff! It seems that it wants to forestall some one; it seems that something is concealed there that has value, high value.—And now it retreats somewhat more slowly, still quite white with excitement,—is it disappointed? Has it found what it sought? Does it merely pretend to be disappointed?—But already another wave approaches, still more eager and wild than the first, and its soul also seems to be full of secrets and of longing for treasure-seeking. Thus live the waves,—thus live we who exercise will!—I do not say more.—But what! Ye distrust me? Ye are angry at me, ye beautiful monsters? Do ye fear that I will quite betray your secret? Well! Just be angry with me, raise your green, dangerous bodies as high as ye can, make a wall between me and the sun—as at present! Verily, there is now nothing more left of the world save green twilight and green lightning-flashes. Do as ye will, ye wanton creatures, roar with delight and wickedness—or dive under again, pour your emeralds down into the depths, and cast your endless white tresses of foam and spray over them—it is all the same to me, for all is so well with you, and I am so pleased with you for it all: how could I betray you! For—take this to heart!—I know you and your secret, I know your race! You and I are indeed of one race! You and I have indeed one secret!

311.

Broken Lights.—We are not always brave, and when we are weary, people of our stamp are liable to lament occasionally in this wise:—"It is so hard to cause pain to men—oh, that it should be necessary! What good is it to live concealed, when we do not want to keep to ourselves that which causes vexation? Would it not be more advisable to live in the madding crowd, and compensate individuals for sins that are committed and must be committed against mankind in general? Foolish with fools, vain with the vain, enthusiastic with enthusiasts? Would that not be reasonable when there is such an inordinate amount of divergence in the main? When I hear of the malignity of others against me—is not my first feeling that of satisfaction? It is well that it should be so!—I seem to myself to say to them—I am so little in harmony with you, and have so much truth on my side: see henceforth that ye be merry at my expense as often as ye can! Here are my defects and mistakes, here are my illusions, my bad taste, my confusion, my tears, my vanity, my owlish concealment, my contradictions! Here you have something to laugh at! Laugh then, and enjoy yourselves! I am not averse to the law and nature of things, which is that defects and errors should give pleasure!—To be sure there were once 'more glorious' times, when as soon as any one got an idea, however moderately new it might be, he would think himself so indispensable as to go out into the street with it, and call to everybody: 'Behold! the kingdom of heaven is at hand!'—I should not miss myself, if I were a-wanting. We are none of us indispensable!"—As we have said, however, we do not think thus when we are brave; we do not think about it at all.

312.

My Dog.—I have given a name to my suffering, and call it "dog,"—

it is just as faithful, just as importunate and shameless, just as entertaining, just as wise, as any other dog—and I can domineer over it, and vent my bad humour on it, as others do with their dogs, servants, and wives.

313.

No Picture of a Martyr.—I will take my cue from Raphael, and not paint any more martyr pictures. There are enough of sublime things without its being necessary to seek sublimity where it is linked with cruelty; moreover my ambition would not be gratified in the least if I aspired to be a sublime executioner.

314.

New Domestic Animals.—I want to have my lion and my eagle about me, that I may always have hints and premonitions concerning the amount of my strength or weakness. Must I look down on them to-day, and be afraid of them? And will the hour come once more when they will look up to me, and tremble?—

315.

The Last Hour.—Storms are my danger. Shall I have my storm in which I shall perish, just as Oliver Cromwell perished in his storm? Or shall I go out as a light does, not first blown out by the wind, but grown tired and weary of itself—a burnt-out light? Or finally, shall I blow myself out, so as not to burn out!

316.

Prophetic Men.—Ye cannot divine how sorely prophetic men suffer: ye think only that a fine "gift" has been given to them, and would fain have it yourselves,—but I will express my meaning by a simile. How much may not the animals suffer from the electricity of the atmosphere and the clouds! Some of them, as we see, have a prophetic faculty with regard to the weather, for example, apes (as one can observe very well even in Europe,—and not only in menageries, but at Gibraltar). But it never occurs to us that it is their sufferings—that are their prophets! When strong positive electricity, under the influence of an approaching cloud not at all visible, is suddenly converted into negative electricity, and an alteration of the weather is imminent, these animals then behave as if an enemy were approaching them, and prepare for defence, or flight: they generally hide themselves,—they do not think of the bad weather as weather, but as an enemy whose hand they already feel!

317.

Retrospect.—We seldom become conscious of the real pathos of any period of life as such, as long as we continue in it, but always think it is the only possible and reasonable thing for us henceforth, and that it is altogether ethos and not pathos[10]—to speak and distinguish like the Greeks. A few notes of music to-day recalled a winter and a house, and a life of utter solitude to my mind, and at the same time the sentiments in which I then lived: I thought I should be able to live in such a state always. But now I understand that it was entirely pathos and passion, something comparable to this painfully bold and truly comforting music,—it is not one's lot to have these sensations for years, still less for eternities: otherwise one would become too "ethereal" for this planet.

318.

Wisdom in Pain.—In pain there is as much wisdom as in pleasure: like the latter it is one of the best self-preservatives of a species. Were it not so, pain would long ago have been done away with; that it is hurtful is no argument against it, for to be hurtful is its very essence. In pain I hear the commanding call of the ship's captain: "Take in sail!" "Man," the bold seafarer, must have learned to set his sails in a thousand different ways, otherwise he could not have sailed long, for the ocean would soon have swallowed him up. We must also know how to live with reduced energy: as soon as pain gives its precautionary signal, it is time to reduce the speed—some great danger, some storm, is approaching, and we do well to "catch" as little wind as possible.—It is true that there are men who, on the approach of severe pain, hear the very opposite call of command, and never appear more proud, more martial, or more happy, than when the storm is brewing; indeed, pain itself provides them with their supreme moments! These are the heroic men, the great pain-bringers of mankind: those few and rare ones who need just the same apology as pain generally,—and verily, it should not be denied them! They are forces of the greatest importance for preserving and advancing the species, were it only because they are opposed to smug ease, and do not conceal their disgust at this kind of happiness.

319.

As Interpreters of our Experiences.—One form of honesty has always been lacking among founders of religions and their kin:—they have never made their experiences a matter of the intellectual conscience. "What did I really experience? What then took place in me and around me? Was my understanding clear enough? Was my will directly opposed to all deception of the senses, and courageous in its defence against fantastic notions?"—None of them ever asked these questions, nor to this day do any of the good religious people ask them. They have rather a thirst for things which are contrary to reason, and they don't want to have too much difficulty in satisfying this thirst,—so they experience "miracles" and "regenerations," and hear the voices of angels! But we who are different, who are thirsty for reason, want to look as carefully into our experiences, as in the case of a scientific experiment, hour by hour, day by day! We ourselves want to be our own experiments, and our own subjects of experiment.

320.

On Meeting Again.—A: Do I quite understand you? You are in search of something? Where, in the midst of the present, actual world, is your niche and star? Where can you lay yourself in the sun, so that you also may have a surplus of well-being, that your existence may justify itself? Let everyone do that for himself—you seem to say, —and let him put talk about generalities, concern about others and society, out of his mind!—B: I want more; I am no seeker. I want to create my own sun for myself.

321.

A New Precaution.—Let us no longer think so much about punishing, blaming, and improving! We shall seldom be able to alter an individual, and if we should succeed in doing so, something else may also succeed, perhaps unawares: we may have been altered by him! Let us rather see to it that our own influence on all that is to come outweighs and overweighs his influence! Let us not struggle in direct conflict!—all blaming, punishing, and desire to improve comes under this category. But let us elevate ourselves all the higher! Let us ever give to our pattern more shining colours! Let us obscure the other by our light! No! We do not mean to become darker ourselves on his account, like all that punish and are discontented! Let us rather go aside! Let us look away!

322.

A Simile.—Those thinkers in whom all the stars move in cyclic orbits, are not the most profound. He who looks into himself, as into an immense universe, and carries Milky Ways in himself, knows also how irregular all Milky Ways are; they lead into the very chaos and labyrinth of existence.

323.

Happiness in Destiny.—Destiny confers its greatest distinction upon us when it has made us fight 250for a time on the side of our adversaries. We are thereby predestined to a great victory.

324.

In Media Vita.—No! Life has not deceived me! On the contrary, from year to year I find it richer, more desirable and more mysterious—from the day on which the great liberator broke my fetters, the thought that life may be an experiment of the thinker—and not a duty, not a fatality, not a deceit!—And knowledge itself may be for others something different; for example, a bed of ease, or the path to a bed of ease, or an entertainment, or a course of idling,—for me it is a world of dangers and victories, in which even the heroic sentiments have their arena and dancing-floor. "Life as a means to knowledge"—with this principle in one's heart, one can not only be brave, but can even live joyfully and laugh joyfully! And who could know how to laugh well and live well, who did not first understand the full meaning of war and victory!

325.

What Belongs to Greatness.—Who can attain to anything great if he does not feel the force and will in himself to inflict great pain? The ability to suffer is a small matter: in that line, weak women and even slaves often attain masterliness. But not to perish from internal distress and doubt when one inflicts great anguish and hears the cry of this anguish—that is great, that belongs to greatness.

326.

Physicians of the Soul and Pain.—All preachers of morality, as also all theologians, have a bad habit in common: all of them try to persuade man that he is very ill, and that a severe, final, radical cure is necessary. And because mankind as a whole has for centuries listened too eagerly to those teachers, something of the superstition that the human race is in a very bad way has actually come over men: so that they are now far too ready to sigh; they find nothing more in life and make melancholy faces at each other, as if life were indeed very hard to endure. In truth, they are inordinately assured of their life and in love with it, and full of untold intrigues and subtleties for suppressing everything disagreeable and for extracting the thorn from pain and misfortune. It seems to me that people always speak with exaggeration about pain and misfortune, as if it were a matter of good behaviour to exaggerate here: on the other hand people are intentionally silent in regard to the number of expedients for alleviating pain; as for instance, the deadening of it, or feverish flurry of thought, or a peaceful position, or good and bad reminiscences, intentions, hopes,—also many kinds of pride and fellow-feeling which have almost the effect of anæsthetics: while in the greatest degree of pain fainting takes place of itself. We understand very well how to pour sweetness on our bitterness, especially on the bitterness of our soul; we find a remedy in our bravery and sublimity, as well as in the nobler delirium of submission and resignation. A loss scarcely remains a loss for an hour: in some way or other a gift from heaven has always fallen into our lap at the same moment—a new form of strength, for example: be it but a new opportunity for the exercise of strength! What have the preachers of morality not dreamt concerning the inner "misery" of evil men! What lies have they not told us about the misfortunes of impassioned men! Yes, lying is here the right word: they were only too well aware of the overflowing happiness of this kind of man, but they kept silent as death about it; because it was a refutation of their theory, according to which happiness only originates through the annihilation of the passions and the silencing of the will! And finally, as regards the recipe of all those physicians of the soul and their recommendation of a severe radical cure, we may be allowed to ask: Is our life really painful and burdensome enough for us to exchange it with advantage for a Stoical mode of life, and Stoical petrification? We do not feel sufficiently miserable to have to feel ill in the Stoical fashion!

327.

Taking Things Seriously.—The intellect is with most people an awkward, obscure and creaking machine, which is difficult to set in motion: they call it "taking a thing seriously" when they work with this machine, and want to think well—oh, how burdensome must good thinking be to them! That delightful animal, man, seems to lose his good-humour whenever he thinks well; he becomes "serious"! And "where there is laughing and gaiety, thinking cannot be worth anything:"—so speaks the prejudice of this serious animal against all "Joyful Wisdom."—Well, then! Let us show that it is prejudice!

328.

Doing Harm to Stupidity.—It is certain that the belief in the reprehensibility of egoism, preached with such stubbornness and conviction, has on the whole done harm to egoism (in favour of the herd-instinct, as I shall repeat a hundred times!), especially by depriving it of a good conscience, and bidding us seek in it the true source of all misfortune. "Thy selfishness is the bane of thy life"—so rang the preaching for millenniums: it did harm, as we have said, to selfishness, and deprived it of much spirit, much cheerfulness, much ingenuity, and much beauty; it stultified and deformed and poisoned selfishness!—Philosophical antiquity, on the other hand, taught that there was another principal source of evil: from Socrates downwards, the thinkers were never weary of preaching that "your thoughtlessness and stupidity, your unthinking way of living according to rule, and your subjection to the opinion of your neighbour, are the reasons why you so seldom attain to happiness,—we thinkers are, as thinkers, the happiest of mortals." Let us not decide here whether this preaching against stupidity was more sound than the preaching against selfishness; it is certain, however, that stupidity was thereby deprived of its good conscience:—these philosophers did harm to stupidity.

329.

Leisure and Idleness.—There is an Indian savagery, a savagery peculiar to the Indian blood, in the manner in which the Americans strive after gold: and the breathless hurry of their work—the characteristic vice of the new world—already begins to infect old Europe, and makes it savage also, spreading over it a strange lack of intellectuality. One is now ashamed of repose: even long reflection almost causes remorse of conscience. Thinking is done with a stop-watch, as dining is done with the eyes fixed on the financial newspaper; we live like men who are continually "afraid of letting opportunities slip." "Better do anything whatever, than nothing"—this principle also is a noose with which all culture and all higher taste may be strangled. And just as all form obviously disappears in this hurry of workers, so the sense for form itself, the ear and the eye for the melody of movement, also disappear. The proof of this is the clumsy perspicuity which is now everywhere demanded in all positions where a person would like to be sincere with his fellows, in intercourse with friends, women, relatives, children, teachers, pupils, leaders and princes,—one has no longer either time or energy for ceremonies, for roundabout courtesies, for any esprit in conversation, or for any otium whatever. For life in the hunt for gain continually compels a person to consume his intellect, even to exhaustion, in constant dissimulation, overreaching, or forestalling: the real virtue nowadays is to do something in a 255shorter time than another person. And so there are only rare hours of sincere intercourse permitted: in them, however, people are tired, and would not only like "to let themselves go," but to stretch their legs out wide in awkward style. The way people write their letters nowadays is quite in keeping with the age; their style and spirit will always be the true "sign of the times." If there be still enjoyment in society and in art, it is enjoyment such as over-worked slaves provide for themselves. Oh, this moderation in "joy" of our cultured and uncultured classes! Oh, this increasing suspiciousness of all enjoyment! Work is winning over more and more the good conscience to its side: the desire for enjoyment already calls itself "need of recreation," and even begins to be ashamed of itself. "One owes it to one's health," people say, when they are caught at a picnic. Indeed, it might soon go so far that one could not yield to the desire for the vita contemplativa (that is to say, excursions with thoughts and friends), without self-contempt and a bad conscience.—Well! Formerly it was the very reverse: it was "action" that suffered from a bad conscience. A man of good family concealed his work when need compelled him to labour. The slave laboured under the weight of the feeling that he did something contemptible:—the "doing" itself was something contemptible. "Only in otium and bellum is there nobility and honour:" so rang the voice of ancient prejudice!

330.

Applause.—The thinker does not need applause nor the clapping of hands, provided he be sure of the clapping of his own hands: the latter, however, he cannot do without. Are there men who could also do without this, and in general without any kind of applause? I doubt it: and even as regards the wisest, Tacitus, who is no calumniator of the wise, says: quando etiam sapientibus gloriæ cupido novissima exuitur—that means with him: never.

331.

Better Deaf than Deafened.—Formerly a person wanted to have a calling, but that no longer suffices to-day, for the market has become too large,—there has now to be bawling. The consequence is that even good throats outcry each other, and the best wares are offered for sale with hoarse voices; without market-place bawling and hoarseness there is now no longer any genius.—It is, sure enough, an evil age for the thinker: he has to learn to find his stillness betwixt two noises, and has to pretend to be deaf until he finally becomes so. As long as he has not learned this, he is in danger of perishing from impatience and headaches.

332.

The Evil Hour.—There has perhaps been an evil hour for every philosopher, in which he thought: What do I matter, if people should not believe my poor arguments!—And then some malicious bird has flown past him and twittered: "What do you matter? What do you matter?"

333.

What does Knowing Mean?—Non ridere, non lugere, neque detestari, sed intelligere! says Spinoza, so simply and sublimely, as is his wont. Nevertheless, what else is this intelligere ultimately, but just the form in which the three other things become perceptible to us all at once? A result of the diverging and opposite impulses of desiring to deride, lament and execrate? Before knowledge is possible each of these impulses must first have brought forward its one-sided view of the object or event. The struggle of these one-sided views occurs afterwards, and out of it there occasionally arises a compromise, a pacification, a recognition of rights on all three sides, a sort of justice and agreement: for in virtue of the justice and agreement all those impulses can maintain themselves in existence and retain their mutual rights. We, to whose consciousness only the closing reconciliation scenes and final settling of accounts of these long processes manifest themselves, think on that account that intelligere is something conciliating, just and good, something essentially antithetical to the impulses; whereas it is only a certain relation of the impulses to one another. For a very long time conscious thinking was regarded as thinking proper: it is now only that the truth dawns upon us that the greater part of our intellectual activity goes on unconsciously and unfelt by us; I believe, however, that the impulses which are here in mutual conflict understand right well how to make themselves felt by one another, and how to cause pain:—the violent, sudden exhaustion which overtakes all thinkers, may have its origin here (it is the exhaustion of the battle-field). Aye, perhaps in our struggling interior there is much concealed heroism, but certainly nothing divine, or eternally-reposing-in-itself, as Spinoza supposed. Conscious thinking, and especially that of the philosopher, is the weakest, and on that account also the relatively mildest and quietest mode of thinking: and thus it is precisely the philosopher who is most easily misled concerning the nature of knowledge.

334.

One must Learn to Love.—This is our experience in music: we must first learn in general to hear, to hear fully, and to distinguish a theme or a melody, we have to isolate and limit it as a life by itself; then we need to exercise effort and good-will in order to endure it in spite of its strangeness, we need patience towards its aspect and expression, and indulgence towards what is odd in it:—in the end there comes a moment when we are accustomed to it, when we expect it, when it dawns upon us that we should miss it if it were lacking; and then it goes on to exercise its spell and charm more and more, and does not cease until we have become its humble and enraptured lovers, who want it, and want it again, and ask for nothing better from the world.—It is thus with us, however, not only in music: it is precisely thus that we have learned to love all things that we now love. We are always finally recompensed for our good-will, our patience, reasonableness and gentleness towards what is unfamiliar, by the unfamiliar slowly throwing off its veil and presenting itself to us as a new, ineffable beauty:—that is its thanks for our hospitality. He also who loves himself must have learned it in this way: there is no other way. Love also has to be learned.

335.

Cheers for Physics!—How many men are there who know how to observe? And among the few who do know,—how many observe themselves? "Everyone is furthest from himself"—all the "triers of the reins" know that to their discomfort; and the saying, "Know thyself," in the mouth of a God and spoken to man, is almost a mockery. But that the case of self-observation is so desperate, is attested best of all by the manner in which almost everybody talks of the nature of a moral action, that prompt, willing, convinced, loquacious manner, with its look, its smile, and its pleasing eagerness! Everyone seems inclined to say to you: "Why, my dear Sir, that is precisely my affair! You address yourself with your question to him who is authorised to answer, for I happen to be wiser with regard to this matter than in anything else. Therefore, when a man decides that 'this is right,' when he accordingly concludes that 'it must therefore be done,' and thereupon does what he has thus recognised as right and designated as necessary—then the nature of his action is moral!" But, my friend, you are talking to me about three actions instead of one: your deciding, for instance, that "this is right," is also an action,—could one not judge either morally or immorally? Why do you regard this, and just this, as right?—"Because my conscience tells me so; conscience never speaks immorally, indeed it determines in the first place what shall be moral!"—But why do you listen to the voice of your conscience? And in how far are you justified in regarding such a judgment as true and infallible? This belief—is there no further conscience for it? Do you know nothing of an intellectual conscience? A conscience behind your "conscience"? Your decision, "this is right," has a previous history in your impulses, your likes and dislikes, your experiences and non-experiences; "how has it originated?" you must ask, and afterwards the further question: "what really impels me to give ear to it?" You can listen to its command like a brave soldier who hears the command of his officer. Or like a woman who loves him who commands. Or like a flatterer and coward, afraid of the commander. Or like a blockhead who follows because he has nothing to say to the contrary. In short, you can give ear to your conscience in a hundred different ways. But that you hear this or that judgment as the voice of conscience, consequently, that you feel a thing to be right—may have its cause in the fact that you have never reflected about yourself, and have blindly accepted from your childhood what has been designated to you as right: or in the fact that hitherto bread and honours have fallen to your share with that which you call your duty,—it is "right" to you, because it seems to be your "condition of existence" (that you, however, have a right to existence appears to you as irrefutable!). The persistency of your moral judgment might still be just a proof of personal wretchedness or impersonality; your "moral force" might have its source in your obstinacy—or in your incapacity to perceive new ideals! And to be brief: if you had thought more acutely, observed more accurately, and had learned more, you would no longer under all circumstances call this and that your "duty" and your "conscience": the knowledge how moral judgments have in general always originated, would make you tired of these pathetic words,—as you have already grown tired of other pathetic words, for instance "sin," "salvation," and "redemption."—And now, my friend, do not talk to me about the categorical imperative! That word tickles my ear, and I must laugh in spite of your presence and your seriousness. In this connection I recollect old Kant, who, as a punishment for having gained possession surreptitiously of the "thing in itself"—also a very ludicrous affair!—was imposed upon by the categorical imperative, and with that in his heart strayed back again to "God," the "soul," "freedom," and "immortality," like a fox which strays back into its cage: and it had been his strength and shrewdness which had broken open this cage!—What? You admire the categorical imperative in you? This "persistency" of your so-called moral judgment? This absoluteness of the feeling that "as I think on this matter, so must everyone think"? Admire rather your selfishness therein! And the blindness, paltriness, and modesty of your selfishness! For it is selfishness in a person to regard his judgment as universal law, and a blind, paltry and modest selfishness besides, because it betrays that you have not yet discovered yourself, that you have not yet created for yourself any individual, quite individual ideal:—for this could never be the ideal of another, to say nothing of all, of every one!——He who still thinks that "each would have to act in this manner in this case," has not yet advanced half a dozen paces in self-knowledge: otherwise he would know that there neither are nor can be similar actions,—that every action that has been done, has been done in an entirely unique and inimitable manner, and that it will be the same with regard to all future actions; that all precepts of conduct (and even the most esoteric and subtle precepts of all moralities up to the present), apply only to the coarse exterior,—that by means of them, indeed, a semblance of equality can be attained, but only a semblance,—that in outlook or retrospect, every action is and remains an impenetrable affair,—that our opinions of "good," "noble" and "great" can never be demonstrated by our actions, because no action is cognisable,—that our opinions, estimates, and tables of values are certainly among the most powerful levers in the mechanism of our actions, that in every single case, nevertheless, the law of their mechanism is untraceable. Let us confine ourselves, therefore, to the purification of our opinions and appreciations, and to the construction of new tables of value of our own:—we will, however, brood no longer over the "moral worth of our actions"! Yes, my friends! As regards the whole moral twaddle of people about one another, it is time to be disgusted with it! To sit in judgment morally ought to be opposed to our taste! Let us leave this nonsense and this bad taste to those who have nothing else to do, save to drag the past a little distance further through time, and who are never themselves the present,—consequently to the many, to the majority! We, however, would seek to become what we are,—the new, the unique, the incomparable, making laws for ourselves and creating ourselves! And for this purpose we must become the best students and discoverers of all the laws and necessities in the world. We must be physicists in order to be creators in that sense,—whereas hitherto all appreciations and ideals have been based on ignorance of physics, or in contradiction to it. And therefore, three cheers for physics! And still louder cheers for that which impels us to it—our honesty.

336.

Avarice of Nature.—Why has nature been so niggardly towards humanity that she has not let human beings shine, this man more and that man less, according to their inner abundance of light? Why have not great men such a fine visibility in their rising and setting as the sun? How much less equivocal would life among men then be!

337.

Future "Humanity."—When I look at this age with the eye of a distant future, I find nothing so remarkable in the man of the present day as his peculiar virtue and sickness called "the historical sense." It is a tendency to something quite new and foreign in history: if this embryo were given several centuries and more, there might finally evolve out of it a marvellous plant, with a smell equally marvellous, on account of which our old earth might be more pleasant to live in than it has been hitherto. We moderns are just beginning to form the chain of a very powerful, future sentiment, link by link,—we hardly know what we are doing. It almost seems to us as if it were not the question of a new sentiment, but of the decline of all old sentiments:—the historical sense is still something so poor and cold, and many are attacked by it as by a frost, and are made poorer and colder by it. To others it appears as the indication of stealthily approaching age, and our planet is regarded by them as a melancholy invalid, who, in order to forget his present condition, writes the history of his youth. In fact, this is one aspect of the new sentiment. He who knows how to regard the history of man in its entirety as his own history, feels in the immense generalisation all the grief of the invalid who thinks of health, of the old man who thinks of the dream of his youth, of the lover who is robbed of his beloved, of the martyr whose ideal is destroyed, of the hero on the evening of the indecisive battle which has brought him wounds and the loss of a friend. But to bear this immense sum of grief of all kinds, to be able to bear it, and yet still be the hero who at the commencement of a second day of battle greets the dawn and his happiness, as one who has an horizon of centuries before and behind him, as the heir of all nobility, of all past intellect, and the obligatory heir (as the noblest) of all the old nobles; while at the same time the first of a new nobility, the equal of which has never been seen nor even dreamt of: to take all this upon his soul, the oldest, the newest, the losses, hopes, conquests, and victories of mankind: to have all this at last in one soul, and to comprise it in one feeling:—this would necessarily furnish a happiness which man has not hitherto known,—a God's happiness, full of power and love, full of tears and laughter, a happiness which, like the sun in the evening, continually gives of its inexhaustible riches and empties into the sea,—and like the sun, too, feels itself richest when even the poorest fisherman rows with golden oars! This divine feeling might then be called—humanity!

338.

The Will to Suffering and the Compassionate.—Is it to your advantage to be above all compassionate? And is it to the advantage of the sufferers when you are so? But let us leave the first question for a moment without an answer.—That from which we suffer most profoundly and personally is almost incomprehensible and inaccessible to every one else: in this matter we are hidden from our neighbour even when he eats at the same table with us. Everywhere, however, where we are noticed as sufferers, our suffering is interpreted in a shallow way; it belongs to the nature of the emotion of pity to divest unfamiliar suffering of its properly personal character:—our "benefactors" lower our value and volition more than our enemies. In most benefits which are conferred on the unfortunate there is something shocking in the intellectual levity with which the compassionate person plays the rôle of fate: he knows nothing of all the inner consequences and complications which are called misfortune for me or for you! The entire economy of my soul and its adjustment by "misfortune," the uprising of new sources and needs, the closing up of old wounds, the repudiation of whole periods of the past—none of these things which may be connected with misfortune preoccupy the dear sympathiser. He wishes to succour, and does not reflect that there is a personal necessity for misfortune; that terror, want, impoverishment, midnight watches, adventures, hazards and mistakes are as necessary to me and to you as their opposites, yea, that, to speak mystically, the path to one's own heaven always leads through the voluptuousness of one's own hell. No, he knows nothing thereof. The "religion of compassion" (or "the heart") bids him help, and he thinks he has helped best when he has helped most speedily! If you adherents of this religion actually have the same sentiments towards yourselves which you have towards your fellows, if you are unwilling to endure your own suffering even for an hour, and continually forestall all possible misfortune, if you regard suffering and pain generally as evil, as detestable, as deserving of annihilation, and as blots on existence, well, you have then, besides your religion of compassion, yet another religion in your heart (and this is perhaps the mother of the former)—the religion of smug ease. Ah, how little you know of the happiness of man, you comfortable and good-natured ones!—for happiness and misfortune are brother and sister, and twins, who grow tall together, or, as with you, remain small together!

But now let us return to the first question.—How is it at all possible for a person to keep to his path! Some cry or other is continually calling one aside: our eye then rarely lights on anything without it becoming necessary for us to leave for a moment our own affairs and rush to give assistance. I know there are hundreds of respectable and laudable methods of making me stray from my course, and in truth the most "moral" of methods! Indeed, the opinion of the present-day preachers of the morality of compassion goes so far as to imply that just this, and this alone is moral:—to stray from our course to that extent and to run to the assistance of our neighbour. I am equally certain that I need only give myself over to the sight of one case of actual distress, and I, too, am lost! And if a suffering friend said to me, "See, I shall soon die, only promise to die with me"—I might promise it, just as—to select for once bad examples for good reasons—the sight of a small, mountain people struggling for freedom, would bring me to the point of offering them my hand and my life. Indeed, there is even a secret seduction in all this awakening of compassion, and calling for help: our "own way" is a thing too hard and insistent, and too far removed from the love and gratitude of others,—we escape from it and from our most personal conscience, not at all unwillingly, and, seeking security in the conscience of others, we take refuge in the lovely temple of the "religion of pity." As soon now as any war breaks out, there always breaks out at the same time a certain secret delight precisely in the noblest class of the people: they rush with rapture to meet the new danger of death, because they believe that in the sacrifice for their country they have finally that long-sought-for permission—the permission to shirk their aim:—war is for them a detour to suicide, a detour, however, with a good conscience. And although silent here about some things, I will not, however, be silent about my morality, which says to me: Live in concealment in order that thou mayest live to thyself. Live ignorant of that which seems to thy age to be most important! Put at least the skin of three centuries betwixt thyself and the present day! And the clamour of the present day, the noise of wars and revolutions, ought to be a murmur to thee! Thou wilt also want to help, but only those whose distress thou entirely understandest, because they have one sorrow and one hope in common with thee—thy friends: and only in the way that thou helpest thyself:—I want to make them more courageous, more enduring, more simple, more joyful! I want to teach them that which at present so few understand, and the preachers of fellowship in sorrow least of all:—namely, fellowship in joy!

339.

Vita femina.—To see the ultimate beauties in a work—all knowledge and good-will is not enough; it requires the rarest, good chance for the veil of clouds to move for once from the summits, and for the sun to shine on them. We must not only stand at precisely the right place to see this, our very soul itself must have pulled away the veil from its heights, and must be in need of an external expression and simile, so as to have a support and remain master of itself. All these, however, are so rarely united at the same time that I am inclined to believe that the highest summit of all that is good, be it work, deed, man, or nature, has hitherto remained for most people, and even for the best, as something concealed and shrouded:—that, however, which unveils itself to us, unveils itself to us but once. The Greeks indeed prayed: "Twice and thrice, everything beautiful!" Ah, they had their good reason to call on the Gods, for ungodly actuality does not furnish us with the beautiful at all, or only does so once! I mean to say that the world is overfull of beautiful things, but it is nevertheless poor, very poor, in beautiful moments, and in the unveiling of those beautiful things. But perhaps this is the greatest charm of life: it puts a gold-embroidered veil of lovely potentialities over itself, promising, resisting, modest, mocking, sympathetic, seductive. Yes, life is a woman!

340.

The Dying Socrates.—I admire the courage and wisdom of Socrates in all that he did, said—and did not say. This mocking and amorous demon and rat-catcher of Athens, who made the most insolent youths tremble and sob was not only the wisest babbler that has ever lived, but was just as great in his silence. I would that he had also been silent in the last moment of his life,—perhaps he might then have belonged to a still higher order of intellects. Whether it was death, or the poison, or piety, or wickedness—something or other loosened his tongue at that moment, and he said: "O Crito, I owe a cock to Asclepios." For him who has ears, this ludicrous and terrible "last word" implies: "O Crito, life is a long sickness!" Is it possible! A man like him, who had lived cheerfully and to all appearance as a soldier,—was a pessimist! He had merely put on a good demeanour towards life, and had all along concealed his ultimate judgment, his profoundest sentiment! Socrates, Socrates had suffered from life! And he also took his revenge for it—with that veiled, fearful, pious, and blasphemous phrase! Had even a Socrates to revenge himself? Was there a grain too little of magnanimity in his superabundant virtue? Ah, my friends! We must surpass even the Greeks!

341.

The Heaviest Burden.—What if a demon crept after thee into thy loneliest loneliness some day or night, and said to thee: "This life, as thou livest it at present, and hast lived it, thou must live it once more, and also innumerable times; and there will be nothing new in it, but every pain and every joy and every thought and every sigh, and all the unspeakably small and great in thy life must come to thee again, and all in the same series and sequence—and similarly this spider and this moonlight among the trees, and similarly this moment, and I myself. The eternal sand-glass of existence will ever be turned once more, and thou with it, thou speck of dust!"—Wouldst thou not throw thyself down and gnash thy teeth, and curse the demon that so spake? Or hast thou once experienced a tremendous moment in which thou wouldst answer him: "Thou art a God, and never did I hear aught more divine!" If that thought acquired power over thee, as thou art, it would transform thee, and perhaps crush thee; the question with regard to all and everything: "Dost thou want this once more, and also for innumerable times?" would lie as the heaviest burden upon thy activity! Or, how wouldst thou have to become favourably inclined to thyself and to life, so as to long for nothing more ardently than for this last eternal sanctioning and sealing?—

342.

Incipit Tragœdia.—When Zarathustra was thirty years old, he left his home and the Lake of Urmi, and went into the mountains. There he enjoyed his spirit and his solitude, and for ten years did not weary of it. But at last his heart changed,—and rising one morning with the rosy dawn, he went before the sun and spake thus unto it: "Thou great star! What would be thy happiness if thou hadst not those for whom thou shinest! For ten years hast thou climbed hither unto my cave: thou wouldst have wearied of thy light and of the journey, had it not been for me, mine eagle, and my serpent. But we awaited thee every morning, took 272from thee thine overflow, and blessed thee for it. Lo! I am weary of my wisdom, like the bee that hath gathered too much honey; I need hands outstretched to take it. I would fain bestow and distribute, until the wise have once more become joyous in their folly, and the poor happy in their riches. Therefore must I descend into the deep, as thou doest in the evening, when thou goest behind the sea and givest light also to the nether-world, thou most rich star! Like thee must I go down, as men say, to whom I shall descend. Bless me then, thou tranquil eye, that canst behold even the greatest happiness without envy! Bless the cup that is about to overflow, that the water may flow golden out of it, and carry everywhere the reflection of thy bliss! Lo! This cup is again going to empty itself, and Zarathustra is again going to be a man."—Thus began Zarathustra's down-going.

BOOK FIFTH
WE FEARLESS ONES

"Carcasse, tu trembles? Tu tremblerais bien davantage, si tu savais, où je te mène."—Turenne.

343.

What our Cheerfulness Signifies.—The most important of more recent events—that "God is dead," that the belief in the Christian God has become unworthy of belief—already begins to cast its first shadows over Europe. To the few at least whose eye, whose suspecting glance, is strong enough and subtle enough for this drama, some sun seems to have set, some old, profound confidence seems to have changed into doubt: our old world must seem to them daily more darksome, distrustful, strange and "old." In the main, however, one may say that the event itself is far too great, too remote, too much beyond most people's power of apprehension, for one to suppose that so much as the report of it could have reached them; not to speak of many who already knew what had really taken place, and what must all collapse now that this belief had been undermined,—because so much was built upon it, so much rested on it, and had become one with it: for example, our entire European morality. This lengthy, vast and uninterrupted process of crumbling, destruction, ruin and overthrow which is now imminent: who has realised it sufficiently to-day to have to stand up as the teacher and herald of such a tremendous logic of terror, as the prophet of a period of gloom and eclipse, the like of which has probably never taken place on earth before?...

Even we, the born riddle-readers, who wait as it were on the mountains posted 'twixt to-day and to-morrow, and engirt by their contradiction, we, the firstlings and premature children of the coming century, into whose sight especially the shadows which must forthwith envelop Europe should already have come—how is it that even we, without genuine sympathy for this period of gloom, contemplate its advent without any personal solicitude or fear? Are we still, perhaps, too much under the immediate effects of the event—and are these effects, especially as regards ourselves, perhaps the reverse of what was to be expected—not at all sad and depressing, but rather like a new and indescribable variety of light, happiness, relief, enlivenment, encouragement, and dawning day?... In fact, we philosophers and "free spirits" feel ourselves irradiated as by a new dawn by the report that the "old God is dead"; our hearts overflow with gratitude, astonishment, presentiment and expectation. At last the horizon seems open once more, granting even that it is not bright; our ships can at last put out to sea in face of every danger; every hazard is again permitted to the discerner; the sea, our sea, again lies open before us; perhaps never before did such an "open sea" exist.—

344.

To what Extent even We are still Pious.—It is said with good reason that convictions have no civic rights in the domain of science: it is only when a 277conviction voluntarily condescends to the modesty of an hypothesis, a preliminary standpoint for experiment, or a regulative fiction, that its access to the realm of knowledge, and a certain value therein, can be conceded,—always, however, with the restriction that it must remain under police supervision, under the police of our distrust.—Regarded more accurately, however, does not this imply that only when a conviction ceases to be a conviction can it obtain admission into science? Does not the discipline of the scientific spirit just commence when one no longer harbours any conviction?... It is probably so: only, it remains to be asked whether, in order that this discipline may commence, it is not necessary that there should already be a conviction, and in fact one so imperative and absolute, that it makes a sacrifice of all other convictions. One sees that science also rests on a belief: there is no science at all "without premises." The question whether truth is necessary, must not merely be affirmed beforehand, but must be affirmed to such an extent that the principle, belief, or conviction finds expression, that "there is nothing more necessary than truth, and in comparison with it everything else has only a secondary value."—This absolute will to truth: what is it? Is it the will not to allow ourselves to be deceived? Is it the will not to deceive? For the will to truth could also be interpreted in this fashion, provided one includes under the generalisation, "I will not deceive," the special case, "I will not deceive myself." But why not deceive? Why not allow oneself to be 278deceived?—Let it be noted that the reasons for the former eventuality belong to a category quite different from those for the latter: one does not want to be deceived oneself, under the supposition that it is injurious, dangerous, or fatal to be deceived,—in this sense science would be a prolonged process of caution, foresight and utility; against which, however, one might reasonably make objections. What? is not-wishing-to-be-deceived really less injurious, less dangerous, less fatal? What do you know of the character of existence in all its phases to be able to decide whether the greater advantage is on the side of absolute distrust, or of absolute trustfulness? In case, however, of both being necessary, much trusting and much distrusting, whence then should science derive the absolute belief, the conviction on which it rests, that truth is more important than anything else, even than every other conviction? This conviction could not have arisen if truth and untruth had both continually proved themselves to be useful: as is the case. Thus—the belief in science, which now undeniably exists, cannot have had its origin in such a utilitarian calculation, but rather in spite of the fact of the inutility and dangerousness of the "Will to truth," of "truth at all costs," being continually demonstrated. "At all costs": alas, we understand that sufficiently well, after having sacrificed and slaughtered one belief after another at this altar!—Consequently, "Will to truth" does not imply, "I will not allow myself to be deceived," but—there is no other alternative—"I will not deceive, not even myself": 279and thus we have reached the realm of morality. For, let one just ask oneself fairly: "Why wilt thou not deceive?" especially if it should seem—and it does seem—as if life were laid out with a view to appearance, I mean, with a view to error, deceit, dissimulation, delusion, self-delusion; and when on the other hand it is a matter of fact that the great type of life has always manifested itself on the side of the most unscrupulous πολύτροποι. Such an intention might perhaps, to express it mildly, be a piece of Quixotism, a little enthusiastic craziness; it might also, however, be something worse, namely, a destructive principle, hostile to life.... "Will to Truth,"—that might be a concealed Will to Death.— Thus the question, Why is there science? leads back to the moral problem: What in general is the purpose of morality, if life, nature, and history are "non-moral"? There is no doubt that the conscientious man in the daring and extreme sense in which he is presupposed by the belief in science, affirms thereby a world other than that of life, nature, and history; and in so far as he affirms this "other world," what? must he not just thereby—deny its counterpart, this world, our world?... But what I have in view will now be understood, namely, that it is always a metaphysical belief on which our belief in science rests,—and that even we knowing ones of to-day, the godless and anti-metaphysical, still take our fire from the conflagration kindled by a belief a millennium old, the Christian belief, which was also the belief of Plato, that God is truth, that the truth is divine.... But what if 280this itself always becomes more untrustworthy, what if nothing any longer proves itself divine, except it be error, blindness, and falsehood;—what if God himself turns out to be our most persistent lie?—

345.

Morality as a Problem.—A defect in personality revenges itself everywhere: an enfeebled, lank, obliterated, self-disavowing and disowning personality is no longer fit for anything good—it is least of all fit for philosophy. "Selflessness" has no value either in heaven or on earth; the great problems all demand great love, and it is only the strong, well-rounded, secure spirits, those who have a solid basis, that are qualified for them. It makes the most material difference whether a thinker stands personally related to his problems, having his fate, his need, and even his highest happiness therein; or merely impersonally, that is to say, if he can only feel and grasp them with the tentacles of cold, prying thought. In the latter case I warrant that nothing comes of it: for the great problems, granting that they let themselves be grasped at all, do not let themselves be held by toads and weaklings: that has ever been their taste—a taste also which they share with all high-spirited women.—How is it that I have not yet met with any one, not even in books, who seems to have stood to morality in this position, as one who knew morality as a problem, and this problem as his own personal need, affliction, pleasure and passion? It is obvious that up to the present morality has not been a problem at all; it has rather been the very ground on which people have met, after all distrust, dissension, and contradiction, the hallowed place of peace, where thinkers could obtain rest even from themselves, could recover breath and revive. I see no one who has ventured to criticise the estimates of moral worth. I miss in this connection even the attempts of scientific curiosity, and the fastidious, groping imagination of psychologists and historians, which easily anticipates a problem and catches it on the wing, without rightly knowing what it catches. With difficulty I have discovered some scanty data for the purpose of furnishing a history of the origin of these feelings and estimates of value (which is something different from a criticism of them, and also something different from a history of ethical systems). In an individual case, I have done everything to encourage the inclination and talent for this kind of history—in vain, as it would seem to me at present. There is little to be learned from those historians of morality (especially Englishmen): they themselves are usually, quite unsuspiciously, under the influence of a definite morality, and act unwittingly as its armour-bearers and followers—perhaps still repeating sincerely the popular superstition of Christian Europe, that the characteristic of moral action consists in abnegation, self-denial, self-sacrifice, or in fellow-feeling and fellow-suffering. The usual error in their premises is their insistence on a certain consensus among human beings, at least among civilised human beings, with regard to certain propositions of morality, and from thence they conclude that these propositions are absolutely binding even upon you and me; or reversely, they come to the conclusion that no morality at all is binding, after the truth has dawned upon them that to different peoples moral valuations are necessarily different: both of which conclusions are equally childish follies. The error of the more subtle amongst them is that they discover and criticise the probably foolish opinions of a people about its own morality, or the opinions of mankind about human morality generally; they treat accordingly of its origin, its religious sanctions, the superstition of free will, and such matters; and they think that just by so doing they have criticised the morality itself. But the worth of a precept, "Thou shalt," is still fundamentally different from and independent of such opinions about it, and must be distinguished from the weeds of error with which it has perhaps been overgrown: just as the worth of a medicine to a sick person is altogether independent of the question whether he has a scientific opinion about medicine, or merely thinks about it as an old wife would do. A morality could even have grown out of an error: but with this knowledge the problem of its worth would not even be touched.—Thus, no one has hitherto tested the value of that most celebrated of all medicines, called morality: for which purpose it is first of all necessary for one—to call it in question. Well, that is just our work.—

346.

Our Note of Interrogation.—But you don't understand it? As a matter of fact, an effort will be 283necessary in order to understand us. We seek for words; we seek perhaps also for ears. Who are we after all? If we wanted simply to call ourselves in older phraseology, atheists, unbelievers, or even immoralists, we should still be far from thinking ourselves designated thereby: we are all three in too late a phase for people generally to conceive, for you, my inquisitive friends, to be able to conceive, what is our state of mind under the circumstances. No! we have no longer the bitterness and passion of him who has broken loose, who has to make for himself a belief, a goal, and even a martyrdom out of his unbelief! We have become saturated with the conviction (and have grown cold and hard in it) that things are not at all divinely ordered in this world, nor even according to human standards do they go on rationally, mercifully, or justly: we know the fact that the world in which we live is ungodly, immoral, and "inhuman,"—we have far too long interpreted it to ourselves falsely and mendaciously, according to the wish and will of our veneration, that is to say, according to our need. For man is a venerating animal! But he is also a distrustful animal: and that the world is not worth what we have believed it to be worth is about the surest thing our distrust has at last managed to grasp. So much distrust, so much philosophy! We take good care not to say that the world is of less value: it seems to us at present absolutely ridiculous when man claims to devise values to surpass the values of the actual world,—it is precisely from that point that we have retraced our steps; 284as from an extravagant error of human conceit and irrationality, which for a long period has not been recognised as such. This error had its last expression in modern Pessimism; an older and stronger manifestation in the teaching of Buddha; but Christianity also contains it, more dubiously, to be sure, and more ambiguously, but none the less seductive on that account. The whole attitude of "man versus the world," man as world-denying principle, man as the standard of the value of things, as judge of the world, who in the end puts existence itself on his scales and finds it too light—the monstrous impertinence of this attitude has dawned upon us as such, and has disgusted us,—we now laugh when we find, "Man and World" placed beside one another, separated by the sublime presumption of the little word "and"! But how is it? Have we not in our very laughing just made a further step in despising mankind? And consequently also in Pessimism, in despising the existence cognisable by us? Have we not just thereby become liable to a suspicion of an opposition between the world in which we have hitherto been at home with our venerations—for the sake of which we perhaps endure life—and another world which we ourselves are: an inexorable, radical, most profound suspicion concerning ourselves, which is continually getting us Europeans more annoyingly into its power, and could easily face the coming generation with the terrible alternative: "Either do away with your venerations, or—with yourselves!" The latter would be Nihilism—but would not the former also be Nihilism? This is our note of interrogation.

347.

Believers and their Need of Belief.—How much faith a person requires in order to flourish, how much "fixed opinion" he requires which he does not wish to have shaken, because he holds himself thereby—is a measure of his power (or more plainly speaking, of his weakness). Most people in old Europe, as it seems to me, still need Christianity at present, and on that account it still finds belief. For such is man: a theological dogma might be refuted to him a thousand times,—provided, however, that he had need of it, he would again and again accept it as "true,"—according to the famous "proof of power" of which the Bible speaks. Some have still need of metaphysics; but also the impatient longing for certainty which at present discharges itself in scientific, positivist fashion among large numbers of the people, the longing by all means to get at something stable (while on account of the warmth of the longing the establishing of the certainty is more leisurely and negligently undertaken): even this is still the longing for a hold, a support; in short, the instinct of weakness, which, while not actually creating religions, metaphysics, and convictions of all kinds, nevertheless—preserves them. In fact, around all these positivist systems there fume the vapours of a certain pessimistic gloom, something of weariness, fatalism, disillusionment, and fear of new disillusionment—or else manifest animosity, ill-humour, anarchic exasperation, and whatever there is of symptom or masquerade of the feeling of weakness. Even the readiness with which our cleverest contemporaries get lost in wretched corners and alleys, for example, in Vaterländerei (so I designate Jingoism, called chauvinisme in France, and "deutsch" in Germany), or in petty æsthetic creeds in the manner of Parisian naturalisme (which only brings into prominence and uncovers that aspect of nature which excites simultaneously disgust and astonishment—they like at present to call this aspect la vérité vraie), or in Nihilism in the St Petersburg style (that is to say, in the belief in unbelief, even to martyrdom for it):—this shows always and above all the need of belief, support, backbone, and buttress.... Belief is always most desired, most pressingly needed where there is a lack of will: for the will, as emotion of command, is the distinguishing characteristic of sovereignty and power. That is to say, the less a person knows how to command, the more urgent is his desire for one who commands, who commands sternly,—a God, a prince, a caste, a physician, a confessor, a dogma, a party conscience. From whence perhaps it could be inferred that the two world-religions, Buddhism and Christianity, might well have had the cause of their rise, and especially of their rapid extension, in an extraordinary malady of the will. And in truth it has been so: both religions lighted upon a longing, monstrously exaggerated by malady of the will, for an imperative, a "Thou-shalt," a longing going the length of despair; both religions were teachers of fanaticism in times of slackness of will-power, and thereby offered to innumerable persons a support, a new possibility of exercising will, an enjoyment in willing. For in fact fanaticism is the sole "volitional strength" to which the weak and irresolute can be excited, as a sort of hypnotising of the entire sensory-intellectual system, in favour of the over-abundant nutrition (hypertrophy) of a particular point of view and a particular sentiment, which then dominates—the Christian calls it his faith. When a man arrives at the fundamental conviction that he requires to be commanded, he becomes "a believer." Reversely, one could imagine a delight and a power of self-determining, and a freedom of will whereby a spirit could bid farewell to every belief, to every wish for certainty, accustomed as it would be to support itself on slender cords and possibilities, and to dance even on the verge of abysses. Such a spirit would be the free spirit par excellence.

348.

The Origin of the Learned.—The learned man in Europe grows out of all the different ranks and social conditions, like a plant requiring no specific soil: on that account he belongs essentially and involuntarily to the partisans of democratic thought. But this origin betrays itself.

If one has trained one's glance to some extent to recognise in a learned book or scientific treatise the intellectual idiosyncrasy of the learned man—all of them have such idiosyncrasy,—and if we take it by surprise, we shall almost always get a glimpse behind it of the "antecedent history" of the 288learned man and his family, especially of the nature of their callings and occupations. Where the feeling finds expression, "That is at last proved, I am now done with it," it is commonly the ancestor in the blood and instincts of the learned man that approves of the "accomplished work" in the nook from which he sees things;—the belief in the proof is only an indication of what has been looked upon for ages by a laborious family as "good work." Take an example: the sons of registrars and office-clerks of every kind, whose main task has always been to arrange a variety of material, distribute it in drawers, and systematise it generally, evince, when they become learned men, an inclination to regard a problem as almost solved when they have systematised it.

There are philosophers who are at bottom nothing but systematising brains—the formal part of the paternal occupation has become its essence to them. The talent for classifications, for tables of categories, betrays something; it is not for nothing that a person is the child of his parents. The son of an advocate will also have to be an advocate as investigator: he seeks as a first consideration, to carry the point in his case, as a second consideration, he perhaps seeks to be in the right. One recognises the sons of Protestant clergymen and schoolmasters by the naïve assurance with which as learned men they already assume their case to be proved, when it has but been presented by them staunchly and warmly: they are thoroughly accustomed to people believing in them,—it belonged to their fathers' "trade"! 289A Jew, contrariwise, in accordance with his business surroundings and the past of his race, is least of all accustomed—to people believing him. Observe Jewish scholars with regard to this matter,—they all lay great stress on logic, that is to say, on compelling assent by means of reasons; they know that they must conquer thereby, even when race and class antipathy is against them, even where people are unwilling to believe them. For in fact, nothing is more democratic than logic: it knows no respect of persons, and takes even the crooked nose as straight. (In passing we may remark that in respect to logical thinking, in respect to cleaner intellectual habits, Europe is not a little indebted to the Jews; above all the Germans, as being a lamentably déraisonnable race, who, even at the present day, must always have their "heads washed"[11] in the first place. Wherever the Jews have attained to influence, they have taught to analyse more subtly, to argue more acutely, to write more clearly and purely: it has always been their problem to bring a people "to raison.")

349.

The Origin of the Learned once more.—To seek self-preservation merely, is the expression of a state of distress, or of limitation of the true, fundamental instinct of life, which aims at the extension of power, and with this in view often enough calls in question self-preservation and sacrifices it. It should be taken as symptomatic when individual philosophers, as for example, the consumptive Spinoza, have seen and have been obliged to see the principal feature of life precisely in the so-called self-preservative instinct:—they have just been men in states of distress. That our modern natural sciences have entangled themselves so much with Spinoza's dogma (finally and most grossly in Darwinism, with its inconceivably one-sided doctrine of the "struggle for existence"—), is probably owing to the origin of most of the inquirers into nature: they belong in this respect to the people, their forefathers have been poor and humble persons, who knew too well by immediate experience the difficulty of making a living. Over the whole of English Darwinism there hovers something of the suffocating air of over-crowded England, something of the odour of humble people in need and in straits. But as an investigator of nature, a person ought to emerge from his paltry human nook: and in nature the state of distress does not prevail, but superfluity, even prodigality to the extent of folly. The struggle for existence is only an exception, a temporary restriction of the will to live; the struggle, be it great or small, turns everywhere on predominance, on increase and expansion, on power, in conformity to the will to power, which is just the will to live.

350.

In Honour of Homines Religiosi.—The struggle against the church is most certainly (among other things—for it has a manifold significance) the struggle of the more ordinary, cheerful, confiding, superficial natures against the rule of the graver, profounder, more contemplative natures, that is to say, the more malign and suspicious men, who with long continued distrust in the worth of life, brood also over their own worth:—the ordinary instinct of the people, its sensual gaiety, its "good heart," revolts against them. The entire Roman Church rests on a Southern suspicion of the nature of man (always misunderstood in the North), a suspicion whereby the European South has succeeded to the inheritance of the profound Orient—the mysterious, venerable Asia—and its contemplative spirit. Protestantism was a popular insurrection in favour of the simple, the respectable, the superficial (the North has always been more good-natured and more shallow than the South), but it was the French Revolution that first gave the sceptre wholly and solemnly into the hands of the "good man" (the sheep, the ass, the goose, and everything incurably shallow, bawling, and fit for the Bedlam of "modern ideas").

351.

In Honour of Priestly Natures.—I think that philosophers have always felt themselves furthest removed from that which the people (in all classes of society nowadays) take for wisdom: the prudent, bovine placidity, piety, and country-parson meekness, which lies in the meadow and gazes at life seriously and ruminatingly:—this is probably because philosophers have not had sufficiently the taste of the "people," or of the country-parson for that kind of wisdom. Philosophers will also perhaps be the latest to acknowledge that the people should understand something of that which lies furthest from them, something of the great passion of the thinker, who lives and must live continually in the storm-cloud of the highest problems and the heaviest responsibilities (consequently, not gazing at all, to say nothing of doing so indifferently, securely, objectively). The people venerate an entirely different type of man when on their part they form the ideal of a "sage," and they are a thousand times justified in rendering homage with the highest eulogies and honours to precisely that type of men—namely, the gentle, serious, simple, chaste, priestly natures and those related to them,—it is to them that the praise falls due in the popular veneration of wisdom. And to whom should the people ever have more reason to be grateful than to these men who pertain to its class and rise from its ranks, but are persons consecrated, chosen, and sacrificed for its good—they themselves believe themselves sacrificed to God,—before whom the people can pour forth its heart with impunity, by whom it can get rid of its secrets, cares, and worse things (for the man who "communicates himself" gets rid of himself, and he who has "confessed" forgets). Here there exists a great need: for sewers and pure cleansing waters are required also for spiritual filth, and rapid currents of love are needed, and strong, lowly, pure hearts, who qualify and sacrifice themselves for such service of the non-public health department— for it is a sacrificing, the priest is, and continues to be, a human sacrifice.... The people regard such sacrificed, silent, serious men of "faith" as "wise," that is to say, as men who have become sages, as "reliable" in relation to their own unreliability. Who would desire to deprive the people of that expression and that veneration?—But as is fair on the other side, among philosophers the priest also is still held to belong to the "people," and is not regarded as a sage, because, above all, they themselves do not believe in "sages," and they already scent "the people" in this very belief and superstition. It was modesty which invented in Greece the word "philosopher," and left to the play-actors of the spirit the superb arrogance of assuming the name "wise"—the modesty of such monsters of pride and self-glorification as Pythagoras and Plato.—

352.

Why we can hardly Dispense with Morality.—The naked man is generally an ignominious spectacle—I speak of us European males (and by no means of European females!). If the most joyous company at table suddenly found themselves stripped and divested of their garments through the trick of an enchanter, I believe that not only would the joyousness be gone and the strongest appetite lost;—it seems that we Europeans cannot at all dispense with the masquerade that is called clothing. But should not the disguise of "moral men," the screening under moral formulæ and notions of decency, the whole kindly concealment of our conduct under conceptions of duty, virtue, public sentiment, honourableness, and disinterestedness, have just as good reasons in support of it? Not that I mean hereby that human wickedness and baseness, in short, the evil wild beast in us, should be disguised; on the contrary, my idea is that it is precisely as tame animals that we are an ignominious spectacle and require moral disguising,—that the "inner man" in Europe is far from having enough of intrinsic evil "to let himself be seen" with it (to be beautiful with it). The European disguises himself in morality because he has become a sick, sickly, crippled animal, who has good reasons for being "tame," because he is almost an abortion, an imperfect, weak and clumsy thing.... It is not the fierceness of the beast of prey that finds moral disguise necessary, but the gregarious animal, with its profound mediocrity, anxiety and ennui. Morality dresses up the European—let us acknowledge it!—in more distinguished, more important, more conspicuous guise—in "divine" guise—

353.

The Origin of Religions.—The real inventions of founders of religions are, on the one hand, to establish a definite mode of life and everyday custom, which operates as disciplina voluntatis, and at the same time does away with ennui; and on the other hand, to give to that very mode of life an interpretation, by virtue of which it appears illumined with the highest value; so that it henceforth becomes a good for which people struggle, and under certain circumstances lay down their lives. In truth, the second of these inventions is the more essential: the first, the mode of life, has usually been there already, side by side, however, with other modes of life, and still unconscious of the value which it embodies. The import, the originality of the founder of a religion, discloses itself usually in the fact that he sees the mode of life, selects it, and divines for the first time the purpose for which it can be used, how it can be interpreted. Jesus (or Paul), for example, found around him the life of the common people in the Roman province, a modest, virtuous, oppressed life: he interpreted it, he put the highest significance and value into it—and thereby the courage to despise every other mode of life, the calm fanaticism of the Moravians, the secret, subterranean self-confidence which goes on increasing, and is at last ready "to overcome the world" (that is to say, Rome, and the upper classes throughout the empire). Buddha, in like manner, found the same type of man,—he found it in fact dispersed among all the classes and social ranks of a people who were good and kind (and above all inoffensive), owing to indolence, and who likewise owing to indolence, lived abstemiously, almost without requirements. He understood that such a type of man, with all its vis inertiae, had inevitably to glide into a belief which promises to avoid the return of earthly ill (that is to say, labour and activity generally),—this "understanding" was his genius. The founder of a religion possesses psychological infallibility in the knowledge of a definite, average type of souls, who have not yet recognised themselves as akin. It is he who brings them together: the founding of a religion, therefore, always becomes a long ceremony of recognition.—

354.

The "Genius of the Species."—The problem of consciousness (or more correctly: of becoming conscious of oneself) meets us only when we begin to perceive in what measure we could dispense with it: and it is at the beginning of this perception that we are now placed by physiology and zoology (which have thus required two centuries to overtake the hint thrown out in advance by Leibnitz). For we could in fact think, feel, will, and recollect, we could likewise "act" in every sense of the term, and nevertheless nothing of it all would require to "come into consciousness" (as one says metaphorically). The whole of life would be possible without its seeing itself as it were in a mirror: as in fact even at present the far greater part of our life still goes on without this mirroring,—and even our thinking, feeling, volitional life as well, however painful this statement may sound to an older philosopher. What then is the purpose of consciousness generally, when it is in the main superfluous?—Now it seems to me, if you will hear my answer and its perhaps extravagant supposition, that the subtlety and strength of consciousness are always in proportion to the capacity for communication of a man (or an animal), the capacity for communication in its turn being in proportion to the necessity for communication: the latter not to be understood as if precisely the individual himself who is master in the art of communicating and making known his necessities would at the same time have to be most dependent upon others for his necessities. It seems to me, however, to be so in relation to whole races and successions of generations: where necessity and need have long compelled men to communicate with their fellows and understand one another rapidly and subtly, a surplus of the power and art of communication is at last acquired, as if it were a fortune which had gradually accumulated, and now waited for an heir to squander it prodigally (the so-called artists are these heirs, in like manner the orators, preachers, and authors: all of them men who come at the end of a long succession, "late-born" always, in the best sense of the word, and as has been said, squanderers by their very nature). Granted that this observation is correct, I may proceed further to the conjecture that consciousness generally has only been developed under the pressure of the necessity for communication,—that from the first it has been necessary and useful only between man and man (especially between those commanding and those obeying), and has only developed in proportion to its utility.

Consciousness is properly only a connecting network between man and man,—it is only as such that it has had to develop; the recluse and wild-beast species of men would not have needed it. The very fact that our actions, thoughts, feelings and motions come within the range of our consciousness—at least a part of them—is the result of a terrible, prolonged "must" ruling man's destiny: as the most endangered animal he needed help and protection; he needed his fellows, he was obliged to express his distress, he had to know how to make himself understood—and for all this he needed "consciousness" first of all, consequently, to "know" himself what he lacked, to "know" how he felt and to "know" what he thought. For, to repeat it once more, man, like every living creature, thinks unceasingly, but does not know it; the thinking which is becoming conscious of itself is only the smallest part thereof, we may say, the most superficial part, the worst part:—for this conscious thinking alone is done in words, that is to say, in the symbols for communication, by means of which the origin of consciousness is revealed. In short, the development of speech and the development of consciousness (not of reason, but of reason becoming self-conscious) go hand in hand. Let it be further accepted that it is not only speech that serves as a bridge between man and man, but also the looks, the pressure and the gestures; our becoming conscious of our sense impressions, our power of being able to fix them, and as it were to locate them outside of ourselves, has increased in proportion as the necessity has increased for communicating them to others by means of signs. The sign-inventing man is at the same time the man who is always more acutely self-conscious; it is only as a social animal that man has learned to become conscious of himself,—he is doing so still, and doing so more and more.—As is obvious, my idea is that consciousness does not properly belong to the individual existence of man, but rather to the social and gregarious nature in him; that, as follows therefrom, it is only in relation to communal and gregarious utility that it is finely developed; and that consequently each of us, in spite of the best intention of understanding himself as individually as possible, and of "knowing himself," will always just call into consciousness the non-individual in him, namely, his "averageness";—that our thought itself is continuously as it were outvoted by the character of consciousness—by the imperious "genius of the species" therein—and is translated back into the perspective of the herd. Fundamentally our actions are in an incomparable manner altogether personal, unique and absolutely individual—there is no doubt about it; but as soon as we translate them into consciousness, they do not appear so any longer.... This is the proper phenomenalism and perspectivism as I understand it: the nature of animal consciousness involves the notion that the world of which we can become conscious is only a superficial and symbolic world, a generalised and vulgarised world;—that everything which becomes conscious becomes just thereby shallow, meagre, relatively stupid,—a generalisation, a symbol, a characteristic of the herd; that with the evolving of consciousness there is always combined a great, radical perversion, falsification, superficialisation, and generalisation. Finally, the growing consciousness is a danger, and whoever lives among the most conscious Europeans knows even that it is a disease. As may be conjectured, it is not the antithesis of subject and object with which I am here concerned: I leave that distinction to the epistemologists who have remained entangled in the toils of grammar (popular metaphysics). It is still less the antithesis of "thing in itself" and phenomenon, for we do not "know" enough to be entitled even to make such a distinction. Indeed, we have not any organ at all for knowing or for "truth"; we "know" (or believe, or fancy) just as much as may be of use in the interest of the human herd, the species; and even what is here called "usefulness" is ultimately only a belief, a fancy, and perhaps precisely the most fatal stupidity by which we shall one day be ruined.

355.

The Origin of our Conception of "Knowledge."—I take this explanation from the street. I heard one of the people saying that "he knew me," so I asked myself: What do the people really understand by knowledge? What do they want when they seek "knowledge"? Nothing more than that what is strange is to be traced back to something known. And we philosophers—have we really understood anything more by knowledge? The known, that is to say, what we are accustomed to, so that we no longer marvel at it, the commonplace, any kind of rule to which we are habituated, all and everything in which we know ourselves to be at home:—what? is our need of knowing not just this need of the known? the will to discover in everything strange, unusual, or questionable, something which no longer disquiets us? Is it not possible that it should be the instinct of fear which enjoins upon us to know? Is it not possible that the rejoicing of the discerner should be just his 301rejoicing in the regained feeling of security?... One philosopher imagined the world "known" when he had traced it back to the "idea": alas, was it not because the idea was so known, so familiar to him? because he had so much less fear of the "idea"—Oh, this moderation of the discerners! let us but look at their principles, and at their solutions of the riddle of the world in this connection! When they again find aught in things, among things, or behind things, that is unfortunately very well known to us, for example, our multiplication table, or our logic, or our willing and desiring, how happy they immediately are! For "what is known is understood": they are unanimous as to that. Even the most circumspect among them think that the known is at least more easily understood than the strange; that for example, it is methodically ordered to proceed outward from the "inner world," from "the facts of consciousness," because it is the world which is better known to us! Error of errors! The known is the accustomed, and the accustomed is the most difficult of all to "understand," that is to say, to perceive as a problem, to perceive as strange, distant, "outside of us."... The great certainty of the natural sciences in comparison with psychology and the criticism of the elements of consciousness—unnatural sciences as one might almost be entitled to call them—rests precisely on the fact that they take what is strange as their object: while it is almost like something contradictory and absurd to wish to take generally what is not strange as an object....

356.

In what Manner Europe will always become "more Artistic."— Providing a living still enforces even in the present day (in our transition period when so much ceases to enforce) a definite rôle on almost all male Europeans, their so-called callings; some have the liberty, an apparent liberty, to choose this rôle themselves, but most have it chosen for them. The result is strange enough. Almost all Europeans confound themselves with their rôle when they advance in age; they themselves are the victims of their "good acting," they have forgotten how much chance, whim and arbitrariness swayed them when their "calling" was decided—and how many other rôles they could perhaps have played: for it is now too late! Looked at more closely, we see that their characters have actually evolved out of their rôle, nature out of art. There were ages in which people believed with unshaken confidence, yea, with piety, in their predestination for this very business, for that very mode of livelihood, and would not at all acknowledge chance, or the fortuitous rôle, or arbitrariness therein. Ranks, guilds, and hereditary trade privileges succeeded, with the help of this belief, in rearing those extraordinary broad towers of society which distinguished the Middle Ages, and of which at all events one thing remains to their credit: capacity for duration (and duration is a value of the first rank on earth!). But there are ages entirely the reverse, the properly democratic ages, in which people tend to become more and more oblivious of this conviction, and a sort of impudent conviction and quite contrary mode of viewing things comes to the front, the Athenian conviction which is first observed in the epoch of Pericles, the American conviction of the present day, which wants also more and more to become an European conviction, whereby the individual is convinced that he can do almost anything, that he can play almost any rôle, whereby everyone makes experiments with himself, improvises, tries anew, tries with delight, whereby all nature ceases and becomes art.... The Greeks, having adopted this rôle-creed—an artist creed, if you will—underwent step by step, as is well known, a curious transformation, not in every respect worthy of imitation: they became actual stage-players; and as such they enchanted, they conquered all the world, and at last even the conqueror of the world, (for the Graeculus histrio conquered Rome, and not Greek culture, as the naïve are accustomed to say....) What I fear, however, and what is at present obvious, if we desire to perceive it, is that we modern men are quite on the same road already; and whenever man begins to discover in what respect he plays a rôle, and to what extent he can be a stage-player, he becomes a stage-player.... A new flora and fauna of men thereupon springs up, which cannot grow in more stable, more restricted eras—or is left "at the bottom," under the ban and suspicion of infamy—, thereupon the most interesting and insane periods of history always make their appearance, in which "stage-players," all kinds of stage-players, are the real masters. Precisely thereby another species of man is always more and more injured, and in the end made impossible: above all the great "architects"; the building power is now being paralysed; the courage that makes plans for the distant future is disheartened; there begins to be a lack of organising geniuses. Who is there who would now venture to undertake works for the completion of which millenniums would have to be reckoned upon? The fundamental belief is dying out, on the basis of which one could calculate, promise and anticipate the future in one's plan, and offer it as a sacrifice thereto, that in fact man has only value and significance in so far as he is a stone in a great building; for which purpose he has first of all to be solid, he has to be a "stone."... Above all, not a—stage-player! In short—alas! this fact will be hushed up for some considerable time to come!—that which from henceforth will no longer be built, and can no longer be built, is—a society in the old sense of the term;

to build this structure everything is lacking, above all, the material. None of us are any longer material for a society: that is a truth which is seasonable at present! It seems to me a matter of indifference that meanwhile the most short-sighted, perhaps the most honest, and at any rate the noisiest species of men of the present day, our friends the Socialists, believe, hope, dream, and above all scream and scribble almost the opposite; in fact one already reads their watchword of the future: "free society," on all tables and walls. Free society? Indeed! Indeed! But you know, gentlemen, sure enough whereof one builds it? Out of wooden iron! Out of the famous wooden iron! And not even out of wooden....

357.

The old Problem: "What is German?"—Let us count up apart the real acquisitions of philosophical thought for which we have to thank German intellects: are they in any allowable sense to be counted also to the credit of the whole race? Can we say that they are at the same time the work of the "German soul," or at least a symptom of it, in the sense in which we are accustomed to think, for example, of Plato's ideomania, his almost religious madness for form, as an event and an evidence of the "Greek soul"? Or would the reverse perhaps be true? Were they so individual, so much an exception to the spirit of the race, as was, for example, Goethe's Paganism with a good conscience? Or as Bismarck's Macchiavelism was with a good conscience, his so-called "practical politics" in Germany? Did our philosophers perhaps even go counter to the need of the "German soul"? In short, were the German philosophers really philosophical Germans?—I call to mind three cases. Firstly, Leibnitz's incomparable insight—with which he obtained the advantage not only over Descartes, but over all who had philosophised up to his time,—that consciousness is only an accident of mental representation, and not its necessary and essential attribute; that consequently what we call consciousness only constitutes a state of our spiritual and psychical world (perhaps a morbid state), and is far from being that world itself:—is there anything German in this thought, the profundity of which has not as yet been exhausted? Is there reason to think that a person of the Latin race would not readily have stumbled on this reversal of the apparent?—for it is a reversal. Let us call to mind secondly, the immense note of interrogation which Kant wrote after the notion of causality. Not that he at all doubted its legitimacy, like Hume: on the contrary, he began cautiously to define the domain within which this notion has significance generally (we have not even yet got finished with the marking out of these limits). Let us take thirdly, the astonishing hit of Hegel, who stuck at no logical usage or fastidiousness when he ventured to teach that the conceptions of kinds develop out of one another: with which theory the thinkers in Europe were prepared for the last great scientific movement, for Darwinism—for without Hegel there would have been no Darwin. Is there anything German in this Hegelian innovation which first introduced the decisive conception of evolution into science? Yes, without doubt we feel that there is something of ourselves "discovered" and divined in all three cases; we are thankful for it, and at the same time surprised; each of these three principles is a thoughtful piece of German self-confession, self-understanding, and self-knowledge. We feel with Leibnitz that "our inner world is far richer, ampler, and more concealed"; as Germans we are doubtful, like Kant, about the ultimate validity of scientific knowledge of nature, and in general about whatever can be known causaliter: the knowable as such now appears to us of less worth. We Germans should still have been Hegelians, even though there had never been a Hegel, inasmuch as we (in contradistinction to all Latin peoples) instinctively attribute to becoming, to evolution, a profounder significance and higher value than to that which "is"—we hardly believe at all in the validity of the concept "being." This is all the more the case because we are not inclined to concede to our human logic that it is logic in itself, that it is the only kind of logic (we should rather like, on the contrary, to convince ourselves that it is only a special case, and perhaps one of the strangest and most stupid).

A fourth question would be whether also Schopenhauer with his Pessimism, that is to say the problem of the worth of existence, had to be a German. I think not. The event after which this problem was to be expected with certainty, so that an astronomer of the soul could have calculated the day and the hour for it—namely, the decay of the belief in the Christian God, the victory of scientific atheism,—is a universal European event, in which all races are to have their share of service and honour. On the contrary, it has to be ascribed precisely to the Germans—those with whom Schopenhauer was contemporary,— that they delayed this victory of atheism longest, and endangered it most. Hegel especially was its retarder par excellence, in virtue of the grandiose attempt which he made to persuade us of the divinity of existence, with the help at the very last of our sixth sense, "the historical sense." As philosopher, Schopenhauer was the first avowed and inflexible atheist we Germans have had: his hostility to Hegel had here its background. The non-divinity of existence was regarded by him as something understood, palpable, indisputable; he always lost his philosophical composure and got into a passion when he saw anyone hesitate and beat about the bush here. It is at this point that his thorough uprightness of character comes in: unconditional, honest atheism is precisely the preliminary condition for his raising the problem, as a final and hardwon victory of the European conscience, as the most prolific act of two thousand years' discipline to truth, which in the end no longer tolerates the lie of the belief in a God.... One sees what has really gained the victory over the Christian God—, Christian morality itself, the conception of veracity, taken ever more strictly, the confessional subtlety of the Christian conscience, translated and sublimated to the scientific conscience, to intellectual purity at any price. To look upon nature as if it were a proof of the goodness and care of a God; to interpret history in honour of a divine reason, as a constant testimony to a moral order in the world and a moral final purpose; to explain personal experiences as pious men have long enough explained them, as if everything were a dispensation or intimation of Providence, something planned and sent on behalf of the salvation of the soul: all that is now past, it has conscience against it, it is regarded by all the more acute consciences as disreputable and dishonourable, as mendaciousness, feminism, weakness, and cowardice,—by virtue of this severity, if by anything, we are good Europeans, the heirs of Europe's longest and bravest self-conquest. When we thus 309reject the Christian interpretation, and condemn its "significance" as a forgery, we are immediately confronted in a striking manner with the Schopenhauerian question: Has existence then a significance at all?—the question which will require a couple of centuries even to be completely heard in all its profundity.

Schopenhauer's own answer to this question was—if I may be forgiven for saying so—a premature, juvenile reply, a mere compromise, a stoppage and sticking in the very same Christian-ascetic, moral perspectives, the belief in which had got notice to quit along with the belief in God.... But he raised the question—as a good European, as we have said, and not as a German.—Or did the Germans prove at least by the way in which they seized on the Schopenhauerian question, their inner connection and relationship to him, their preparation for his problem, and their need of it? That there has been thinking and printing even in Germany since Schopenhauer's time on the problem raised by him,—it was late enough!—does not at all suffice to enable us to decide in favour of this closer relationship; one could, on the contrary, lay great stress on the peculiar awkwardness of this post-Schopenhauerian Pessimism—Germans evidently do not behave themselves there as in their element. I do not at all allude here to Eduard von Hartmann; on the contrary, my old suspicion is not vanished even at present that he is too clever for us; I mean to say that as arrant rogue from the very first, he did not perhaps make merry solely over German Pessimism—and that in the end he might probably "bequeathe" 310to them the truth as to how far a person could bamboozle the Germans themselves in the age of bubble companies. But further, are we perhaps to reckon to the honour of Germans, the old humming-top, Bahnsen, who all his life spun about with the greatest pleasure around his realistically dialectic misery and "personal ill-luck,"—was that German? (In passing I recommend his writings for the purpose for which I myself have used them, as anti-pessimistic fare, especially on account of his elegantia psychologica, which, it seems to me, could alleviate even the most constipated body and soul). Or would it be proper to count such dilettanti and old maids as the mawkish apostle of virginity, Mainländer, among the genuine Germans? After all he was probably a Jew (all Jews become mawkish when they moralise). Neither Bahnsen, nor Mainländer, nor even Eduard von Hartmann, give us a reliable grasp of the question whether the pessimism of Schopenhauer (his frightened glance into an undeified world, which has become stupid, blind, deranged and problematic, his honourable fright) was not only an exceptional case among Germans, but a German event: while everything else which stands in the foreground, like our valiant politics and our joyful Jingoism (which decidedly enough regards everything with reference to a principle sufficiently unphilosophical: "Deutschland, Deutschland, über Alles,"[12] consequently sub specie speciei, namely, the German species), testifies very plainly to the contrary. No! 311The Germans of to-day are not pessimists! And Schopenhauer was a pessimist, I repeat it once more, as a good European, and not as a German.

358.

The Peasant Revolt of the Spirit.—We Europeans find ourselves in view of an immense world of ruins, where some things still tower aloft, while other objects stand mouldering and dismal, where most things however already lie on the ground, picturesque enough—where were there ever finer ruins?—overgrown with weeds, large and small. It is the Church which is this city of decay: we see the religious organisation of Christianity shaken to its deepest foundations. The belief in God is overthrown, the belief in the Christian ascetic ideal is now fighting its last fight. Such a long and solidly built work as Christianity—it was the last construction of the Romans!—could not of course be demolished all at once; every sort of earthquake had to shake it, every sort of spirit which perforates, digs, gnaws and moulders had to assist in the work of destruction. But that which is strangest is that those who have exerted themselves most to retain and preserve Christianity, have been precisely those who did most to destroy it,—the Germans. It seems that the Germans do not understand the essence of a Church. Are they not spiritual enough, or not distrustful enough to do so? In any case the structure of the Church rests on a southern freedom and liberality of spirit, and similarly on a southern suspicion of nature, man, and spirit,—it rests on a knowledge of man, 312an experience of man, entirely different from what the north has had. The Lutheran Reformation in all its length and breadth was the indignation of the simple against something "complicated." To speak cautiously, it was a coarse, honest misunderstanding, in which much is to be forgiven,—people did not understand the mode of expression of a victorious Church, and only saw corruption; they misunderstood the noble scepticism, the luxury of scepticism and toleration which every victorious, self-confident power permits.... One overlooks the fact readily enough at present that as regards all cardinal questions concerning power Luther was badly endowed; he was fatally short-sighted, superficial and imprudent— and above all, as a man sprung from the people, he lacked all the hereditary qualities of a ruling caste, and all the instincts for power; so that his work, his intention to restore the work of the Romans, merely became involuntarily and unconsciously the commencement of a work of destruction. He unravelled, he tore asunder with honest rage, where the old spider had woven longest and most carefully. He gave the sacred books into the hands of everyone,—they thereby got at last into the hands of the philologists, that is to say, the annihilators of every belief based upon books. He demolished the conception of "the Church" in that he repudiated the belief in the inspiration of the Councils: for only under the supposition that the inspiring spirit which had founded the Church still lives in it, still builds it, still goes on building its house, does the conception of "the Church" retain its power. He gave back 313to the priest sexual intercourse: but three-fourths of the reverence of which the people (and above all the women of the people) are capable, rests on the belief that an exceptional man in this respect will also be an exceptional man in other respects. It is precisely here that the popular belief in something superhuman in man, in a miracle, in the saving God in man, has its most subtle and insidious advocate. After Luther had given a wife to the priest, he had to take from him auricular confession; that was psychologically right: but thereby he practically did away with the Christian priest himself, whose profoundest utility has ever consisted in his being a sacred ear, a silent well, and a grave for secrets. "Every man his own priest"—behind such formulæ and their bucolic slyness, there was concealed in Luther the profoundest hatred of "higher men" and the rule of "higher men," as the Church had conceived them. Luther disowned an ideal which he did not know how to attain, while he seemed to combat and detest the degeneration thereof. As a matter of fact, he, the impossible monk, repudiated the rule of the homines religiosi; he consequently brought about precisely the same thing within the ecclesiastical social order that he combated so impatiently in the civic order,—namely a "peasant insurrection."—As to all that grew out of his Reformation afterwards, good and bad, which can at present be almost counted up,—who would be naïve enough to praise or blame Luther simply on account of these results? He is innocent of all; he knew not what he did. The art of making the European spirit shallower, especially in the north, or more good-natured, if people would rather hear it designated by a moral expression, undoubtedly took a clever step in advance in the Lutheran Reformation; and similarly there grew out of it the mobility and disquietude of the spirit, its thirst for independence, its belief in the right to freedom, and its "naturalness." If people wish to ascribe to the Reformation in the last instance the merit of having prepared and favoured that which we at present honour as "modern science," they must of course add that it is also accessory to bringing about the degeneration of the modern scholar with his lack of reverence, of shame and of profundity; and that it is also responsible for all naïve candour and plain-dealing in matters of knowledge, in short for the plebeianism of the spirit which is peculiar to the last two centuries, and from which even pessimism hitherto, has not in any way delivered us. "Modern ideas" also belong to this peasant insurrection of the north against the colder, more ambiguous, more suspicious spirit of the south, which has built itself its greatest monument in the Christian Church. Let us not forget in the end what a Church is, and especially, in contrast to every "State": a Church is above all an authoritative organisation which secures to the most spiritual men the highest rank, and believes in the power of spirituality so far as to forbid all grosser appliances of authority. Through this alone the Church is under all circumstances a nobler institution than the State.—

359.

Vengeance on Intellect and other Backgrounds of Morality.— Morality—where do you think it has its most dangerous and rancorous advocates?—There, for example, is an ill-constituted man, who does not possess enough of intellect to be able to take pleasure in it, and just enough of culture to be aware of the fact; bored, satiated, and a self-despiser; besides being cheated unfortunately by some hereditary property out of the last consolation, the "blessing of labour," the self-forgetfulness in the "day's work"; one who is thoroughly ashamed of his existence—perhaps also harbouring some vices,—and who on the other hand (by means of books to which he has no right, or more intellectual society than he can digest), cannot help vitiating himself more and more, and making himself vain and irritable: such a thoroughly poisoned man—for intellect becomes poison, culture becomes poison, possession becomes poison, solitude becomes poison, to such ill-constituted beings—gets at last into a habitual state of vengeance and inclination to vengeance.... What do you think he finds necessary, absolutely necessary in order to give himself the appearance in his own eyes of superiority over more intellectual men, so as to give himself the delight of perfect revenge, at least in imagination? It is always morality that he requires, one may wager on it; always the big moral words, always the high-sounding words: justice, wisdom, holiness, virtue; always the stoicism of gestures (how well stoicism hides what one does not 316possess!); always the mantle of wise silence, of affability, of gentleness, and whatever else the idealist-mantle is called in which the incurable self-despisers and also the incurably conceited walk about. Let me not be misunderstood: out of such born enemies of the spirit there arises now and then that rare specimen of humanity who is honoured by the people under the name of saint or sage: it is out of such men that there arise those prodigies of morality that make a noise, that make history,—St Augustine was one of these men. Fear of the intellect, vengeance on the intellect—Oh! how often have these powerfully impelling vices become the root of virtues! Yea, virtue itself!—And asking the question among ourselves, even the philosopher's pretension to wisdom, which has occasionally been made here and there on the earth, the maddest and most immodest of all pretensions,—has it not always been, in India as well as in Greece, above all a means of concealment? Sometimes, perhaps, from the point of view of education which hallows so many lies, it has been a tender regard for growing and evolving persons, for disciples who have often to be guarded against themselves by means of the belief in a person (by means of an error). In most cases, however, it is a means of concealment for a philosopher, behind which he seeks protection, owing to exhaustion, age, chilliness, or hardening; as a feeling of the approaching end, as the sagacity of the instinct which animals have before their death,—they go apart, remain at rest, choose solitude, creep into caves, become wise.... What? Wisdom a means of concealment of the philosopher from—intellect?—

360.

Two Kinds of Causes which are Confounded.—It seems to me one of my most essential steps and advances that I have learned to distinguish the cause of the action generally from the cause of action in a particular manner, say, in this direction, with this aim. The first kind of cause is a quantum of stored-up force, which waits to be used in some manner, for some purpose; the second kind of cause, on the contrary, is something quite unimportant in comparison with the first, an insignificant hazard for the most part, in conformity with which the quantum of force in question "discharges" itself in some unique and definite manner: the lucifer-match in relation to the barrel of gunpowder. Among those insignificant hazards and lucifer-matches I count all the so-called "aims," and similarly the still more so-called "occupations" of people: they are relatively optional, arbitrary, and almost indifferent in relation to the immense quantum of force which presses on, as we have said, to be used up in any way whatever. One generally looks at the matter in a different manner: one is accustomed to see the impelling force precisely in the aim (object, calling, &c.), according to a primeval error,—but it is only the directing force; the steersman and the steam have thereby been confounded. And yet it is not even always the steersman, the directing force.... Is the "aim," the "purpose," not often enough only an extenuating pretext, an additional self-blinding of conceit, which does not wish it to be said that the ship follows the stream into which it has accidentally run? That it "wishes" to go that way, because it must go that way? That it has a direction, sure enough, but—not a steersman? We still require a criticism of the conception of "purpose."

361.

The Problem of the Actor.—The problem of the actor has disquieted me the longest; I was uncertain (and am sometimes so still) whether one could not get at the dangerous conception of "artist"—a conception hitherto treated with unpardonable leniency—from this point of view. Falsity with a good conscience; delight in dissimulation breaking forth as power, pushing aside, overflowing, and sometimes extinguishing the so-called "character"; the inner longing to play a rôle, to assume a mask, to put on an appearance; a surplus of capacity for adaptations of every kind, which can no longer gratify themselves in the service of the nearest and narrowest utility: all that perhaps does not pertain solely to the actor in himself?... Such an instinct would develop most readily in families of the lower class of the people, who have had to pass their lives in absolute dependence, under shifting pressure and constraint, who (to accommodate themselves to their conditions, to adapt themselves always to new circumstances) had again and again to pass themselves off and represent themselves as different persons,—thus having gradually qualified themselves to adjust the mantle to every wind, thereby almost becoming the mantle itself, as masters of the embodied and incarnated art of eternally playing the game of hide and seek, which one calls mimicry among the animals:—until at last this ability, stored up from generation to generation, has become domineering, irrational and intractable, till as instinct it begins to command the other instincts, and begets the actor, the "artist" (the buffoon, the pantaloon, the Jack-Pudding, the fool, and the clown in the first place, also the classical type of servant, Gil Blas: for in such types one has the precursors of the artist, and often enough even of the "genius"). Also under higher social conditions there grows under similar pressure a similar species of men. Only the histrionic instinct is there for the most part held strictly in check by another instinct, for example, among "diplomatists";—for the rest, I should think that it would always be open to a good diplomatist to become a good actor on the stage, provided his dignity "allowed" it. As regards the Jews, however, the adaptable people par excellence, we should, in conformity to this line of thought, expect to see among them a world-historical institution from the very beginning, for the rearing of actors, a genuine breeding-place for actors; and in fact the question is very pertinent just now: what good actor at present is not—a Jew? The Jew also, as a born literary man, as the actual ruler of the European press, exercises this power on the basis of his histrionic capacity: for the literary man is essentially an actor,—he plays the part of "expert," of "specialist."—Finally women. If we consider the whole history of women, are they not obliged first of all, and above all to be actresses? If we listen to doctors who have hypnotised women, or, finally, if we love them—and let ourselves be "hypnotised" by them,—what is always divulged thereby? That they "give themselves airs," even when they—"give themselves."... Woman is so artistic....

362.

My Belief in the Virilising of Europe.—We owe it to Napoleon (and not at all to the French Revolution, which had in view the "fraternity" of the nations, and the florid interchange of good graces among people generally) that several warlike centuries, which have not had their like in past history, may now follow one another—in short, that we have entered upon the classical age of war, war at the same time scientific and popular, on the grandest scale (as regards means, talents and discipline), to which all coming millenniums will look back with envy and awe as a work of perfection:—for the national movement out of which this martial glory springs, is only the counter-choc against Napoleon, and would not have existed without him. To him, consequently, one will one day be able to attribute the fact that man in Europe has again got the upper hand of the merchant and the Philistine; perhaps even of "woman" also, who has become pampered owing to Christianity and the extravagant spirit of the eighteenth century, and still more owing to "modern ideas." Napoleon, who saw in modern ideas, and accordingly in civilisation, something like a personal enemy, has by this hostility proved himself one of the greatest continuators of the Renaissance: he has brought to the surface a whole block of the ancient character, the decisive block perhaps, the block of granite. And who knows but that this block of ancient character will in the end get the upper hand of the national movement, and will have to make itself in a positive sense the heir and continuator of Napoleon:—who, as one knows, wanted one Europe, which was to be mistress of the world.—

363.

How each Sex has its Prejudice about Love.—Notwithstanding all the concessions which I am inclined to make to the monogamic prejudice, I will never admit that we should speak of equal rights in the love of man and woman: there are no such equal rights. The reason is that man and woman understand something different by the term love,—and it belongs to the conditions of love in both sexes that the one sex does not presuppose the same feeling, the same conception of "love," in the other sex. What woman understands by love is clear enough: complete surrender (not merely devotion) of soul and body, without any motive, without any reservation, rather with shame and terror at the thought of a devotion restricted by clauses or associated with conditions. In this absence of conditions her love is precisely a faith: woman has no other.—Man, when he loves a woman, wants precisely this love from her; he is consequently, as regards himself, furthest removed from the prerequisites of feminine love; granted, however, that there should also be men to whom on their side the demand for complete devotion is not unfamiliar,—well, they are really—not men. A man who loves like a woman becomes thereby a slave; a woman, however, who loves like a woman becomes thereby a more perfect woman.... The passion of woman in its unconditional renunciation of its own rights presupposes in fact that there does not exist on the other side an equal pathos, an equal desire for renunciation: for if both renounced themselves out of love, there would result— well, I don't know what, perhaps a horror vacui? Woman wants to be taken and accepted as a possession, she wishes to be merged in the conceptions of "possession" and "possessed"; consequently she wants one who takes, who does not offer and give himself away, but who reversely is rather to be made richer in "himself"—by the increase of power, happiness and faith which the woman herself gives to him. Woman gives herself, man takes her.—I do not think one will get over this natural contrast by any social contract, or with the very best will to do justice, however desirable it may be to avoid bringing the severe, frightful, enigmatical, and unmoral elements of this antagonism constantly before our eyes. For love, regarded as complete, great, and full, is nature, and as nature, is to all eternity something "unmoral."—Fidelity is accordingly included in woman's love, it follows from the definition thereof; with man fidelity may readily result in consequence of his love, perhaps as gratitude or idiosyncrasy of taste, and so-called elective affinity, but it does not belong to the essence of his love—and indeed so little, that one might almost be entitled to speak of a natural opposition between love and fidelity in man, whose love is just a desire to possess, and

[870] FRIEDRICH NIETZSCHE

not a renunciation and giving away; the desire to possess, however, comes to an end every time with the possession.... As a matter of fact it is the more subtle and jealous thirst for possession in the man (who is rarely and tardily convinced of having this "possession"), which makes his love continue; in that case it is even possible that the love may increase after the surrender,—he does not readily own that a woman has nothing more to "surrender" to him.—

364.

The Anchorite Speaks.—The art of associating with men rests essentially on one's skilfulness (which presupposes long exercise) in accepting a repast, in taking a repast in the cuisine of which one has no confidence. Provided one comes to the table with the hunger of a wolf everything is easy ("the worst society gives thee experience"—as Mephistopheles says); but one has not got this wolf's-hunger when one needs it! Alas! how difficult are our fellow-men to digest! First principle: to stake one's courage as in a misfortune, to seize boldly, to admire oneself at the same time, to take one's repugnance between one's teeth, to cram down one's disgust. Second principle: to "improve" one's fellow-man, by praise for example, so that he may begin to sweat out his self-complacency; or to seize a tuft of his good or "interesting" qualities, and pull at it till one gets his whole virtue out, and can 324put him under the folds of it. Third principle: self-hypnotism. To fix one's eye on the object of one's intercourse, as on a glass knob, until, ceasing to feel pleasure or pain thereat, one falls asleep unobserved, becomes rigid, and acquires a fixed pose: a household recipe used in married life and in friendship, well tested and prized as indispensable, but not yet scientifically formulated. Its proper name is—patience.—

365.

The Anchorite Speaks once more.—We also have intercourse with "men," we also modestly put on the clothes in which people know us (as such), respect us and seek us; and we thereby mingle in society, that is to say, among the disguised who do not wish to be so called; we also do like all prudent masqueraders, and courteously dismiss all curiosity which has not reference merely to our "clothes." There are however other modes and artifices for "going about" among men and associating with them: for example, as a ghost,—which is very advisable when one wants to scare them, and get rid of them easily. An example: a person grasps at us, and is unable to seize us. That frightens him. Or we enter by a closed door. Or when the lights are extinguished. Or after we are dead. The latter is the artifice of posthumous men par excellence. ("What?" said such a one once impatiently, "do you think we should delight in enduring this strangeness, coldness, death-stillness about us, all this subterranean, hidden, dim, undiscovered solitude, which is called life with us, and might just as well be called death, if we were not conscious of what will arise out of us,—and that only after our death shall we attain to our life and become living, ah! very living! we posthumous men!"—)

366.

At the Sight of a Learned Book.—We do not belong to those who only get their thoughts from books, or at the prompting of books,—it is our custom to think in the open air, walking, leaping, climbing, or dancing on lonesome mountains by preference, or close to the sea, where even the paths become thoughtful. Our first question concerning the value of a book, a man, or a piece of music is: Can it walk? or still better: Can it dance?... We seldom read; we do not read the worse for that—oh, how quickly do we divine how a person has arrived at his thoughts:— whether sitting before an ink-bottle with compressed belly and head bent over the paper: oh, how quickly we are then done with his book! The constipated bowels betray themselves, one may wager on it, just as the atmosphere of the room, the ceiling of the room, the smallness of the room, betray themselves.—These were my feelings as I was closing a straightforward, learned book, thankful, very thankful, but also relieved.... In the book of a learned man there is almost always something oppressive and oppressed: the "specialist" comes to light somewhere, his ardour, his seriousness, his wrath, his over-estimation of the nook in which he sits and spins, his hump—every specialist has his hump. A learned book also always mirrors a distorted soul: every trade distorts. Look at our friends again with whom we have spent our youth, after they have taken possession of their science: alas! how the reverse has always taken place! Alas! how they themselves are now for ever occupied and possessed by their science! Grown into their nook, crumpled into unrecognisability, constrained, deprived of their equilibrium, emaciated and angular everywhere, perfectly round only in one place,—we are moved and silent when we find them so. Every handicraft, granting even that it has a golden floor,[13] has also a leaden ceiling above it, which presses and presses on the soul, till it is pressed into a strange and distorted shape. There is nothing to alter here. We need not think that it is at all possible to obviate this disfigurement by any educational artifice whatever. Every kind of perfection is purchased at a high price on earth, where everything is perhaps purchased too dear; one is an expert in one's department at the price of being also a victim of one's department. But you want to have it otherwise—"more reasonable," above all more convenient— is it not so, my dear contemporaries? Very well! But then you will also immediately get something different: that is to say, instead of the craftsman and expert, the literary man, the versatile, "many-sided" littérateur, who to be sure lacks the hump—not taking account of the hump or bow which he makes before you as the shopman of the intellect and the "porter" of culture—, the littérateur, who is really nothing, but "represents" almost everything: he plays and "represents" the expert, he also takes it upon himself in all modesty to see that he is paid, honoured and celebrated in this position.—No, my learned friends! I bless you even on account of your humps! And also because like me you despise the littérateurs and parasites of culture! And because you do not know how to make merchandise of your intellect! And have so many opinions which cannot be expressed in money value! And because you do not represent anything which you are not! Because your sole desire is to become masters of your craft; because you reverence every kind of mastership and ability, and repudiate with the most relentless scorn everything of a make-believe, half-genuine, dressed-up, virtuoso, demagogic, histrionic nature in litteris et artibus—all that which does not convince you by its absolute genuineness of discipline and preparatory training, or cannot stand your test! (Even genius does not help a person to get over such a defect, however well it may be able to deceive with regard to it: one understands this if one has once looked closely at our most gifted painters and musicians,—who almost without exception, can artificially and supplementarily appropriate to themselves (by means of artful inventions of style, make-shifts, and even principles), the appearance of that genuineness, that solidity of training and culture; to be sure, without thereby deceiving themselves, without thereby imposing perpetual silence on their bad consciences. For you know well enough that all great modern artists suffer from bad consciences?...)

367.

How one has to Distinguish first of all in Works of Art.—Everything that is thought, versified, painted and composed, yea, even built and moulded, belongs either to monologic art, or to art before witnesses. Under the latter there is also to be included the apparently monologic art which involves the belief in God, the whole lyric of prayer; because for a pious man there is no solitude,—we, the godless, have been the first to devise this invention. I know of no profounder distinction in all the perspective of the artist than this: Whether he looks at his growing work of art (at "himself—") with the eye of the witness; or whether he "has forgotten the world," as is the essential thing in all monologic art,——it rests on forgetting, it is the music of forgetting.

368.

The Cynic Speaks.—My objections to Wagner's music are physiological objections. Why should I therefore begin by disguising them under æsthetic formulæ? My "point" is that I can no longer breathe freely when this music begins to operate on me; my foot immediately becomes indignant at it and rebels: for what it needs is time, dance and march; it demands first of all from music the ecstasies which are in good walking, striding, leaping and dancing. But do not my stomach, my heart, my blood and my bowels also protest? Do I not become hoarse unawares under its influence? And then I ask myself what it is really that my body wants from music generally. 329I believe it wants to have relief: so that all animal functions should be accelerated by means of light, bold, unfettered, self-assured rhythms; so that brazen, leaden life should be gilded by means of golden, good, tender harmonies. My melancholy would fain rest its head in the hiding-places and abysses of perfection: for this reason I need music. What do I care for the drama! What do I care for the spasms of its moral ecstasies, in which the "people" have their satisfaction! What do I care for the whole pantomimic hocus-pocus of the actor!... It will now be divined that I am essentially anti-theatrical at heart,— but Wagner on the contrary, was essentially a man of the stage and an actor, the most enthusiastic mummer-worshipper that has ever existed, even among musicians!... And let it be said in passing that if Wagner's theory was that "drama is the object, and music is only the means to it,"—his practice on the contrary from beginning to end has been to the effect that "attitude is the object, drama and even music can never be anything else but means to that." Music as a means of elucidating, strengthening and intensifying dramatic poses and the actor's appeal to the senses, and Wagnerian drama only an opportunity for a number of dramatic attitudes! Wagner possessed, along with all other instincts, the dictatorial instinct of a great actor in all and everything, and as has been said, also as a musician.—I once made this clear with some trouble to a thorough-going Wagnerian, and I had reasons for adding:—"Do be a little more honest with yourself: we are not now in the theatre. In the theatre we are only 330honest in the mass; as individuals we lie, we belie even ourselves. We leave ourselves at home when we go to the theatre; we there renounce the right to our own tongue and choice, to our taste, and even to our courage as we possess it and practise it within our own four walls in relation to God and man. No one takes his finest taste in art into the theatre with him, not even the artist who works for the theatre: there one is people, public, herd, woman, Pharisee, voting animal, democrat, neighbour, and fellow-creature; there even the most personal conscience succumbs to the levelling charm of the 'great multitude'; there stupidity operates as wantonness and contagion; there the neighbour rules, there one becomes a neighbour...." (I have forgotten to mention what my enlightened Wagnerian answered to my physiological objections: "So the fact is that you are really not healthy enough for our music?"—)

369.

Juxtapositions in us.—Must we not acknowledge to ourselves, we artists, that there is a strange discrepancy in us; that on the one hand our taste, and on the other hand our creative power, keep apart in an extraordinary manner, continue apart, and have a separate growth;—I mean to say that they have entirely different gradations and tempi of age, youth, maturity, mellowness and rottenness? So that, for example, a musician could all his life create things which contradict all that his ear and heart, spoilt as they are for listening, prize, relish and prefer:—he would not even require 331to be aware of the contradiction! As an almost painfully regular experience shows, a person's taste can easily outgrow the taste of his power, even without the latter being thereby paralysed or checked in its productivity. The reverse, however, can also to some extent take place,—and it is to this especially that I should like to direct the attention of artists. A constant producer, a man who is a "mother" in the grand sense of the term, one who no longer knows or hears of anything except pregnancies and child-beds of his spirit, who has no time at all to reflect and make comparisons with regard to himself and his work, who is also no longer inclined to exercise his taste, but simply forgets it, letting it take its chance of standing, lying or falling,—perhaps such a man at last produces works on which he is then not at all fit to pass a judgment: so that he speaks and thinks foolishly about them and about himself. This seems to me almost the normal condition with fruitful artists,—nobody knows a child worse than its parents—and the rule applies even (to take an immense example) to the entire Greek world of poetry and art, which was never "conscious" of what it had done....

370.

What is Romanticism?—It will be remembered perhaps, at least among my friends, that at first I assailed the modern world with some gross errors and exaggerations, but at any rate with hope in my heart. I recognised—who knows from what personal experiences?—the philosophical pessimism 332of the nineteenth century as the symptom of a higher power of thought, a more daring courage and a more triumphant plenitude of life than had been characteristic of the eighteenth century, the age of Hume, Kant, Condillac, and the sensualists: so that the tragic view of things seemed to me the peculiar luxury of our culture, its most precious, noble, and dangerous mode of prodigality; but nevertheless, in view of its overflowing wealth, a justifiable luxury. In the same way I interpreted for myself German music as the expression of a Dionysian power in the German soul: I thought I heard in it the earthquake by means of which a primeval force that had been imprisoned for ages was finally finding vent—indifferent as to whether all that usually calls itself culture was thereby made to totter. It is obvious that I then misunderstood what constitutes the veritable character both of philosophical pessimism and of German music,—namely, their Romanticism. What is Romanticism? Every art and every philosophy may be regarded as a healing and helping appliance in the service of growing, struggling life: they always presuppose suffering and sufferers. But there are two kinds of sufferers: on the one hand those that suffer from overflowing vitality, who need Dionysian art, and require a tragic view and insight into life; and on the other hand those who suffer from reduced vitality, who seek repose, quietness, calm seas, and deliverance from themselves through art or knowledge, or else intoxication, spasm, bewilderment and madness. All Romanticism in art and knowledge responds to the twofold 333craving of the latter; to them Schopenhauer as well as Wagner responded (and responds),—to name those most celebrated and decided romanticists who were then misunderstood by me (not however to their disadvantage, as may be reasonably conceded to me). The being richest in overflowing vitality, the Dionysian God and man, may not only allow himself the spectacle of the horrible and questionable, but even the fearful deed itself, and all the luxury of destruction, disorganisation and negation. With him evil, senselessness and ugliness seem as it were licensed, in consequence of the overflowing plenitude of procreative, fructifying power, which can convert every desert into a luxuriant orchard. Conversely, the greatest sufferer, the man poorest in vitality, would have most need of mildness, peace and kindliness in thought and action: he would need, if possible, a God who is specially the God of the sick, a "Saviour"; similarly he would have need of logic, the abstract intelligibility of existence—for logic soothes and gives confidence;—in short he would need a certain warm, fear-dispelling narrowness and imprisonment within optimistic horizons. In this manner I gradually began to understand Epicurus, the opposite of a Dionysian pessimist;—in a similar manner also the "Christian," who in fact is only a type of Epicurean, and like him essentially a romanticist:—and my vision has always become keener in tracing that most difficult and insidious of all forms of retrospective inference, which most mistakes have been made—the inference from the work to its author, from the deed to its doer, from the ideal to him who 334needs it, from every mode of thinking and valuing to the imperative want behind it.—In regard to all æsthetic values I now avail myself of this radical distinction: I ask in every single case, "Has hunger or superfluity become creative here?" At the outset another distinction might seem to recommend itself more—it is far more conspicuous,—namely, to have in view whether the desire for rigidity, for perpetuation, for being is the cause of the creating, or the desire for destruction, for change, for the new, for the future—for becoming. But when looked at more carefully, both these kinds of desire prove themselves ambiguous, and are explicable precisely according to the before-mentioned and, as it seems to me, rightly preferred scheme. The desire for destruction, change and becoming, may be the expression of overflowing power, pregnant with futurity (my terminus for this is of course the word "Dionysian"); but it may also be the hatred of the ill-constituted, destitute and unfortunate, which destroys, and must destroy, because the enduring, yea, all that endures, in fact all being, excites and provokes it. To understand this emotion we have but to look closely at our anarchists. The will to perpetuation requires equally a double interpretation. It may on the one hand proceed from gratitude and love:—art of this origin will always be an art of apotheosis, perhaps dithyrambic, as with Rubens, mocking divinely, as with Hafiz, or clear and kind-hearted as with Goethe, and spreading a Homeric brightness and glory over everything (in this case I speak of Apollonian art). It may also, however, be the tyrannical will of a 335sorely-suffering, struggling or tortured being, who would like to stamp his most personal, individual and narrow characteristics, the very idiosyncrasy of his suffering, as an obligatory law and constraint on others; who, as it were, takes revenge on all things, in that he imprints, enforces and brands his image, the image of his torture, upon them. The latter is romantic pessimism in its most extreme form, whether it be as Schopenhauerian will-philosophy, or as Wagnerian music:—romantic pessimism, the last great event in the destiny of our civilisation. (That there may be quite a different kind of pessimism, a classical pessimism—this presentiment and vision belongs to me, as something inseparable from me, as my proprium and ipsissimum; only that the word "classical" is repugnant to my ears, it has become far too worn; too indefinite and indistinguishable. I call that pessimism of the future,—for it is coming! I see it coming!—Dionysian pessimism.)

371.

We Unintelligible Ones.—Have we ever complained among ourselves of being misunderstood, misjudged, and confounded with others; of being calumniated, misheard, and not heard? That is just our lot—alas, for a long time yet! say, to be modest, until 1901—, it is also our distinction; we should not have sufficient respect for ourselves if we wished it otherwise. People confound us with others—the reason of it is that we ourselves grow, we change continually, we cast off old bark, we still slough every spring, we always become younger, higher, stronger, as men of the future, we thrust our roots always more powerfully into the deep—into evil—, while at the same time we embrace the heavens ever more lovingly, more extensively, and suck in their light ever more eagerly with all our branches and leaves. We grow like trees—that is difficult to understand, like all life!—not in one place, but everywhere, not in one direction only, but upwards and outwards, as well as inwards and downwards. At the same time our force shoots forth in stem, branches, and roots; we are really no longer free to do anything separately, or to be anything separately.... Such is our lot, as we have said: we grow in height; and even should it be our calamity—for we dwell ever closer to the lightning!—well, we honour it none the less on that account; it is that which we do not wish to share with others, which we do not wish to bestow upon others, the fate of all elevation, our fate....

372.

Why we are not Idealists.—Formerly philosophers were afraid of the senses: have we, perhaps, been far too forgetful of this fear? We are at present all of us sensualists, we representatives of the present and of the future in philosophy,—not according to theory, however, but in praxis, in practice.... Those former philosophers, on the contrary, thought that the senses lured them out of their world, the cold realm of "ideas," to a dangerous southern island, where they were afraid that their philosopher-virtues would melt away like snow in the sun. "Wax in the ears," was then almost a condition of philosophising; a genuine philosopher no longer listened to life, in so far as life is music, he denied the music of life—it is an old philosophical superstition that all music is Sirens' music.—Now we should be inclined at the present day to judge precisely in the opposite manner (which in itself might be just as false), and to regard ideas, with their cold, anæmic appearance, and not even in spite of this appearance, as worse seducers than the senses. They have always lived on the "blood" of the philosopher, they always consumed his senses, and indeed, if you will believe me, his "heart" as well. Those old philosophers were heartless: philosophising was always a species of vampirism. At the sight of such figures even as Spinoza, do you not feel a profoundly enigmatical and disquieting sort of impression? Do you not see the drama which is here performed, the constantly increasing pallor—, the spiritualisation always more ideally displayed? Do you not imagine some long-concealed blood-sucker in the background, which makes its beginning with the senses, and in the end retains or leaves behind nothing but bones and their rattling?—I mean categories, formulæ, and words (for you will pardon me in saying that what remains of Spinoza, amor intellectualis dei, is rattling and nothing more! What is amor, what is deus, when they have lost every drop of blood?...) In summa: all philosophical idealism has hitherto been something like a disease, where it has not been, as in the case of Plato, the prudence of superabundant and dangerous healthfulness, the fear of overpowering senses, and the wisdom of a wise Socratic.—Perhaps, is it the case that we moderns are merely not sufficiently sound to require Plato's idealism? And we do not fear the senses because——.

373.

"Science" as Prejudice.—It follows from the laws of class distinction that the learned, in so far as they belong to the intellectual middle-class, are debarred from getting even a sight of the really great problems and notes of interrogation. Besides, their courage, and similarly their outlook, does not reach so far,—and above all, their need, which makes them investigators, their innate anticipation and desire that things should be constituted in such and such a way, their fears and hopes are too soon quieted and set at rest. For example, that which makes the pedantic Englishman, Herbert Spencer, so enthusiastic in his way, and impels him to draw a line of hope, a horizon of desirability, the final reconciliation of "egoism and altruism" of which he dreams,—that almost causes nausea to people like us:—a humanity with such Spencerian perspectives as ultimate perspectives would seem to us deserving of contempt, of extermination! But the fact that something has to be taken by him as his highest hope, which is regarded, and may well be regarded, by others merely as a distasteful possibility, is a note of interrogation which Spencer could not have foreseen.... It is just the same with the belief with which at present so many materialistic natural-scientists are content, the belief in a world which is supposed to have its equivalent and measure in human thinking and human valuations, a "world of truth" at which we might be able ultimately to arrive with the help of our insignificant, four-cornered human reason! What? do we actually wish to have existence debased in that fashion to a ready-reckoner exercise and calculation for stay-at-home mathematicians? We should not, above all, seek to divest existence of its ambiguous character: good taste forbids it, gentlemen, the taste of reverence for everything that goes beyond your horizon! That a world-interpretation is alone right by which you maintain your position, by which investigation and work can go on scientifically in your sense (you really mean mechanically?), an interpretation which acknowledges numbering, calculating, weighing, seeing and handling, and nothing more—such an idea is a piece of grossness and naïvety, provided it is not lunacy and idiocy.

Would the reverse not be quite probable, that the most superficial and external characters of existence—its most apparent quality, its outside, its embodiment—should let themselves be apprehended first? perhaps alone allow themselves to be apprehended? A "scientific" interpretation of the world as you understand it might consequently still be one of the stupidest that is to say, the most destitute of significance, of all possible world-interpretations:—I say this in confidence to my friends the Mechanicians, who to-day like to hobnob with philosophers, and absolutely believe that mechanics is the teaching of the first and last laws upon which, as upon a ground-floor, all existence must be built. But an essentially mechanical world would be an essentially meaningless world! Supposing we valued the worth of a music with reference to how much it could be counted, calculated, or formulated—how absurd such a "scientific" estimate of music would be! What would one have apprehended, understood, or discerned in it! Nothing, absolutely nothing of what is really "music" in it!...

374.

Our new "Infinite."—How far the perspective character of existence extends, or whether it have any other character at all, whether an existence without explanation, without "sense" does not just become "nonsense," whether, on the other hand, all existence is not essentially an explaining existence—these questions, as is right and proper, cannot be determined even by the most diligent and severely conscientious analysis and self-examination of the intellect, because in this analysis the human intellect cannot avoid seeing itself in its perspective forms, and only in them. We cannot see round our corner: it is hopeless curiosity to want to know what other modes of intellect and perspective there might be: for example, whether any kind of being could perceive time backwards, or alternately forwards and backwards (by which another direction of life and another conception of cause and effect would be given). But I think that we are to-day at least far from the ludicrous immodesty of decreeing from our nook that there can only be legitimate perspectives from that nook. The world, on the contrary, has once more become "infinite" to us: in so far we cannot dismiss the possibility that it contains infinite interpretations. Once more the great horror seizes us—but who would desire forthwith to deify once more this monster of an unknown world in the old fashion? And perhaps worship the unknown thing as the "unknown person" in future? Ah! there are too many ungodly possibilities of interpretation comprised in this unknown, too much devilment, stupidity and folly of interpretation.—also our own human, all too human interpretation itself, which we know....

375.

Why we Seem to be Epicureans.—We are cautious, we modern men, with regard to final convictions, our distrust lies in wait for the enchantments and tricks of conscience involved in every strong belief, in every absolute Yea and Nay: how is this explained? Perhaps one may see in it a good deal of the caution of the "burnt child," of the disillusioned idealist; but one may also see in it another and better element, the joyful curiosity of a former lingerer in the corner, who has been brought to despair by his nook, and now luxuriates and revels in its antithesis, in the unbounded, in the "open air in itself." Thus there is developed an almost Epicurean inclination for knowledge, which does not readily lose sight of the questionable character of things; likewise also a repugnance to pompous moral phrases and attitudes, a taste that repudiates all coarse, square contrasts, and is proudly conscious of its habitual reserve. For this too constitutes our pride, this easy tightening of the reins in our headlong impulse after certainty, this self-control of the rider in his most furious riding: for now, as of old we have mad, fiery steeds under us, and if we delay, it is certainly least of all the danger which causes us to delay....

376.

Our Slow Periods.—It is thus that artists feel, and all men of "works," the maternal species of men: they always believe at every chapter of their life—a work always makes a chapter—that they have already reached the goal itself; they would always patiently accept death with the feeling: "we are ripe for it." This is not the expression of exhaustion,—but rather that of a certain autumnal sunniness and mildness, which the work itself, the maturing of the work, always leaves behind in its originator. Then the tempo of life slows down—turns thick and flows with honey—into long pauses, into the belief in the long pause....

377.

We Homeless Ones.—Among the Europeans of to-day there are not lacking those who may call themselves homeless ones in a way which is at once a distinction and an honour; it is by them that my secret wisdom and gaya scienza is expressly to be laid to heart. For their lot is hard, their hope uncertain; it is a clever feat to devise consolation for them. But what good does it do! We children of the future, how could we be at home in the present? We are unfavourable to all ideals which could make us feel at home in this frail, broken-down, transition period; and as regards the "realities" thereof, we do not believe in their endurance. The ice which still carries us has become very thin: the thawing wind blows; we ourselves, the homeless ones, are an influence that breaks the ice, and the other all too thin "realities."... We "preserve" nothing, nor would we return to any past age; we are not at all "liberal," we do not labour for "progress," we do not need first to stop our ears to the song of the market-place and the sirens of the future—their song of "equal rights," "free society," "no longer either lords or slaves," does not allure us! We do not by any means think it desirable that the kingdom of righteousness and peace should be established on earth (because under any circumstances it would be the kingdom of the profoundest mediocrity and Chinaism); we rejoice in all men, who, like ourselves, love danger, war and adventure, who do not make compromises, nor let themselves be captured, conciliated and stunted; we count ourselves among the conquerors; we ponder over the need of a new order of things, even of a new slavery—for every strengthening and elevation of the type "man" also involves a new form of slavery. Is it not obvious that with all this we must feel ill at ease in an age which claims the honour of being the most humane, gentle and just that the sun has ever seen? What a pity that at the mere mention of these fine words, the thoughts at the back of our minds are all the more unpleasant, that we see therein only the expression—or the masquerade—of profound weakening, exhaustion, age, and declining power! What can it matter to us with what kind of tinsel an invalid decks out his weakness? He may parade it as his virtue; there is no doubt whatever that weakness makes people gentle, alas, so gentle, so just, so inoffensive, so "humane"!—The "religion of pity," to which people would like to persuade us—yes, we know sufficiently well the hysterical little men and women who need this religion at present as a cloak and adornment! We are no humanitarians; we should not dare to speak of our "love of mankind"; for that, a person of our stamp is not enough of an actor! Or not sufficiently Saint-Simonist, not sufficiently French. A person must have been affected with a Gallic excess of erotic susceptibility and amorous impatience even to approach mankind honourably with his lewdness.... Mankind! Was there ever a more hideous old woman among all old women (unless perhaps it were "the Truth": a question for philosophers)? No, we do not love Mankind! On the other hand, however, we are not nearly "German" enough (in the sense in which the word "German" is current at present) to advocate nationalism and race-hatred, or take delight in the national heart-itch and blood-poisoning, on account of which the nations of Europe are at present bounded off and secluded from one another as if by quarantines. We are too unprejudiced for that, too perverse, too fastidious; also too well-informed, and too much "travelled." We prefer much rather to live on mountains, apart and "out of season," in past or coming centuries, in order merely to spare ourselves the silent rage to which we know we should be condemned as witnesses of a system of politics which makes the German nation barren by making it vain, and which is a petty system besides:—will it not be necessary for this system to plant itself between two mortal hatreds, lest its own creation should immediately collapse? Will it not be obliged to desire the perpetuation of the petty-state system of Europe?... We homeless ones are too diverse and mixed in race and descent as "modern men," and are consequently little tempted to participate in the falsified racial self-admiration and lewdness which at present display themselves in Germany, as signs of German sentiment, and which strike one as doubly false and unbecoming in the people with the "historical sense." We are, in a word—and it shall be our word of honour!—good Europeans, the heirs of Europe, the rich, over-wealthy heirs, also the too deeply pledged heirs of millenniums of European thought. As such, we have also outgrown Christianity, and are disinclined to it— and just because we have grown out of it, because our forefathers were Christians uncompromising in their Christian integrity, who willingly sacrificed possessions and positions, blood and country, for the sake of their belief. We—do the same. For what, then? For our unbelief? For all sorts of unbelief? Nay, you know better than that, my friends! The hidden Yea in you is stronger than all the Nays and Perhapses, of which you and your age are sick; 346and when you are obliged to put out to sea, you emigrants, it is—once more a faith which urges you thereto!...

378.

"And once more Grow Clear."—We, the generous and rich in spirit, who stand at the sides of the streets like open fountains and would hinder no one from drinking from us: we do not know, alas! how to defend ourselves when we should like to do so; we have no means of preventing ourselves being made turbid and dark,—we have no means of preventing the age in which we live casting its "up-to-date rubbish" into us, nor of hindering filthy birds throwing their excrement, the boys their trash, and fatigued resting travellers their misery, great and small, into us. But we do as we have always done: we take whatever is cast into us down into our depths—for we are deep, we do not forget—and once more grow clear....

379.

The Fool's Interruption.—It is not a misanthrope who has written this book: the hatred of men costs too dear to-day. To hate as they formerly hated man, in the fashion of Timon, completely, without qualification, with all the heart, from the pure love of hatred—for that purpose one would have to renounce contempt:—and how much refined pleasure, how much patience, how much benevolence even, do we owe to contempt! Moreover we are thereby the "elect of

God": refined contempt is our taste and privilege, our art, our virtue perhaps, we, the most modern amongst the moderns!... Hatred, on the contrary, makes equal, it puts men face to face, in hatred there is honour; finally, in hatred there is fear, quite a large amount of fear. We fearless ones, however, we, the most intellectual men of the period, know our advantage well enough to live without fear as the most intellectual persons of this age. People will not easily behead us, shut us up, or banish us; they will not even ban or burn our books. The age loves intellect, it loves us, and needs us, even when we have to give it to understand that we are artists in despising; that all intercourse with men is something of a horror to us; that with all our gentleness, patience, humanity and courteousness, we cannot persuade our nose to abandon its prejudice against the proximity of man; that we love nature the more, the less humanly things are done by her, and that we love art when it is the flight of the artist from man, or the raillery of the artist at man, or the raillery of the artist at himself....

380.

"The Wanderer" Speaks.—In order for once to get a glimpse of our European morality from a distance, in order to compare it with other earlier or future moralities, one must do as the traveller who wants to know the height of the towers of a city: for that purpose he leaves the city. "Thoughts concerning moral prejudices," if they are not to be prejudices concerning prejudices, presuppose a position outside of morality, some sort of world beyond good and evil, to which one must ascend, climb, or fly—and in the given case at any rate, a position beyond our good and evil, an emancipation from all "Europe," understood as a sum of inviolable valuations which have become part and parcel of our flesh and blood. That one wants in fact to get outside, or aloft, is perhaps a sort of madness, a peculiarly unreasonable "thou must"—for even we thinkers have our idiosyncrasies of "unfree will"—: the question is whether one can really get there. That may depend on manifold conditions: in the main it is a question of how light or how heavy we are, the problem of our "specific gravity." One must be very light in order to impel one's will to knowledge to such a distance, and as it were beyond one's age, in order to create eyes for oneself for the survey of millenniums, and a pure heaven in these eyes besides! One must have freed oneself from many things by which we Europeans of to-day are oppressed, hindered, held down, and made heavy. The man of such a "Beyond," who wants to get even in sight of the highest standards of worth of his age, must first of all "surmount" this age in himself—it is the test of his power—and consequently not only his age, but also his past aversion and opposition to his age, his suffering caused by his age, his unseasonableness, his Romanticism....

381.

The Question of Intelligibility.—One not only wants to be understood when one writes, but also—quite as certainly—not to be understood. It is by no means an objection to a book when someone finds it unintelligible: perhaps this might just have been the intention of its author,—perhaps he did not want to be understood by "anyone." A distinguished intellect and taste, when it wants to communicate its thoughts, always selects its hearers; by selecting them, it at the same time closes its barriers against "the others." It is there that all the more refined laws of style have their origin: they at the same time keep off, they create distance, they prevent "access" (intelligibility, as we have said,)—while they open the ears of those who are acoustically related to them. And to say it between ourselves and with reference to my own case,—I do not desire that either my ignorance, or the vivacity of my temperament, should prevent me being understood by you, my friends: I certainly do not desire that my vivacity should have that effect, however much it may impel me to arrive quickly at an object, in order to arrive at it at all. For I think it is best to do with profound problems as with a cold bath—quickly in, quickly out. That one does not thereby get into the depths, that one does not get deep enough down—is a superstition of the hydrophobic, the enemies of cold water; they speak without experience. Oh! the great cold makes one quick!—And let me ask by the way: Is it a fact that a thing has been misunderstood and unrecognised when it has only been touched upon in passing, glanced at, flashed at? Must one absolutely sit upon it in the first place? Must one have brooded on it as on an egg? Diu noctuque incubando, as Newton said of himself? At least there are truths of a peculiar shyness and ticklishness which one can only get hold of suddenly, and in no other way,—which one must either take by surprise, or leave alone.... Finally, my brevity has still another value: on those questions which pre-occupy me, I must say a great deal briefly, in order that it may be heard yet more briefly. For as immoralist, one has to take care lest one ruins innocence, I mean the asses and old maids of both sexes, who get nothing from life but their innocence; moreover my writings are meant to fill them with enthusiasm, to elevate them, to encourage them in virtue. I should be at a loss to know of anything more amusing than to see enthusiastic old asses and maids moved by the sweet feelings of virtue: and "that have I seen"—spake Zarathustra. So much with respect to brevity; the matter stands worse as regards my ignorance, of which I make no secret to myself. There are hours in which I am ashamed of it; to be sure there are likewise hours in which I am ashamed of this shame. Perhaps we philosophers, all of us, are badly placed at present with regard to knowledge: science is growing, the most learned of us are on the point of discovering that we know too little. But it would be worse still if it were otherwise,—if we knew too much; our duty is and remains, first of all, not to get into confusion about ourselves. We are different from the learned; although it cannot be denied that amongst other things we are also learned. We have different needs, a different growth, a different digestion: we need more, we need also less. There is no formula 351as to how much an intellect needs for its nourishment; if, however, its taste be in the direction of independence, rapid coming and going, travelling, and perhaps adventure for which only the swiftest are qualified, it prefers rather to live free on poor fare, than to be unfree and plethoric. Not fat, but the greatest suppleness and power is what a good dancer wishes from his nourishment,—and I know not what the spirit of a philosopher would like better than to be a good dancer. For the dance is his ideal, and also his art, in the end likewise his sole piety, his "divine service."...

382.

Great Healthiness.—We, the new, the nameless, the hard-to-understand, we firstlings of a yet untried future—we require for a new end also a new means, namely, a new healthiness, stronger, sharper, tougher, bolder and merrier than any healthiness hitherto. He whose soul longs to experience the whole range of hitherto recognised values and desirabilities, and to circumnavigate all the coasts of this ideal "Mediterranean Sea," who, from the adventures of his most personal experience, wants to know how it feels to be a conqueror, and discoverer of the ideal—as likewise how it is with the artist, the saint, the legislator, the sage, the scholar, the devotee, the prophet, and the godly Nonconformist of the old style:—requires one thing above all for that purpose, great healthiness—such healthiness as one not only possesses, but also constantly acquires and must acquire, because one continually sacrifices it again, and must sacrifice 352it!—And now, after having been long on the way in this fashion, we Argonauts of the ideal, who are more courageous perhaps than prudent, and often enough shipwrecked and brought to grief, nevertheless, as said above, healthier than people would like to admit, dangerously healthy, always healthy again,—it would seem, as if in recompense for it all, that we have a still undiscovered country before us, the boundaries of which no one has yet seen, a beyond to all countries and corners of the ideal known hitherto, a world so over-rich in the beautiful, the strange, the questionable, the frightful, and the divine, that our curiosity as well as our thirst for possession thereof, have got out of hand—alas! that nothing will now any longer satisfy us! How could we still be content with the man of the present day after such peeps, and with such a craving in our conscience and consciousness? What a pity; but it is unavoidable that we should look on the worthiest aims and hopes of the man of the present day with ill-concealed amusement, and perhaps should no longer look at them. Another ideal runs on before us, a strange, tempting ideal, full of danger, to which we should not like to persuade any one, because we do not so readily acknowledge any one's right thereto: the ideal of a spirit who plays naïvely (that is to say involuntarily and from overflowing abundance and power) with everything that has hitherto been called holy, good, inviolable, divine; to whom the loftiest conception which the people have reasonably made their measure of value, would already imply danger, ruin, abasement, or at least relaxation, 353blindness, or temporary self-forgetfulness; the ideal of a humanly superhuman welfare and benevolence, which may often enough appear inhuman, for example, when put by the side of all past seriousness on earth, and in comparison with all past solemnities in bearing, word, tone, look, morality and pursuit, as their truest involuntary parody,— but with which, nevertheless, perhaps the great seriousness only commences, the proper interrogation mark is set up, the fate of the soul changes, the hour-hand moves, and tragedy begins....

383.

Epilogue.—But while I slowly, slowly finish the painting of this sombre interrogation-mark, and am still inclined to remind my readers of the virtues of right reading—oh, what forgotten and unknown virtues—it comes to pass that the wickedest, merriest, gnome-like laughter resounds around me: the spirits of my book themselves pounce upon me, pull me by the ears, and call me to order. "We cannot endure it any longer," they shout to me, "away, away with this raven-black music. Is it not clear morning round about us? And green, soft ground and turf, the domain of the dance? Was there ever a better hour in which to be joyful? Who will sing us a song, a morning song, so sunny, so light and so fledged that it will not scare the tantrums,—but will rather invite them to take part in the singing and dancing. And better a simple rustic bagpipe than such weird sounds, such toad-croakings, grave-voices and marmot-pipings, with which you have hitherto regaled us in your wilderness, 354Mr Anchorite and Musician of the Future! No! Not such tones! But let us strike up something more agreeable and more joyful!"— You would like to have it so, my impatient friends? Well! Who would not willingly accord with your wishes? My bagpipe is waiting, and my voice also—it may sound a little hoarse; take it as it is! don't forget we are in the mountains! But what you will hear is at least new; and if you do not understand it, if you misunderstand the singer, what does it matter! That—has always been "The Singer's Curse."[14] So much the more distinctly can you hear his music and melody, so much the better also can you—dance to his piping. Would you like to do that?...

Ecce Homo: How One Becomes What One Is
PREFACE

1

As it is my intention within a very short time to confront my fellow-men with the very greatest demand that has ever yet been made upon them, it seems to me above all necessary to declare here who and what I am. As a matter of fact, this ought to be pretty well known already, for I have not "held my tongue" about myself. But the disparity which obtains between the greatness of my task and the smallness of my contemporaries, is revealed by the fact that people have neither heard me nor yet seen me. I live on my own self-made credit, and it is probably only a prejudice to suppose that I am alive at all. I do but require to speak to any one of the scholars who come to the Ober-Engadine in the summer in order to convince myself that I am not alive.... Under these circumstances, it is a duty—and one against which my customary reserve, and to a still greater degree the pride of my instincts, rebel—to say: Listen! for I am such and such a person. For Heaven's sake do not confound me with any one else!

2

I am, for instance, in no wise a bogey man, or moral monster. On the contrary, I am the very[Pg 2] opposite in nature to the kind of man that has been honoured hitherto as virtuous. Between ourselves, it seems to me that this is precisely a matter on which I may feel proud. I am a disciple of the philosopher Dionysus, and I would prefer to be even a satyr than a saint. But just read this book! Maybe I have here succeeded in expressing this contrast in a cheerful and at the same time sympathetic manner—maybe this is the only purpose of the present work.

The very last thing I should promise to accomplish would be to "improve" mankind. I do not set up any new idols; may old idols only learn what it costs to have legs of clay. To overthrow idols (idols is the name I give to all ideals) is much more like my business. In proportion as an ideal world has been falsely assumed, reality has been robbed of its value, its meaning, and its truthfulness.... The "true world" and the "apparent world"—in plain English, the fictitious world and reality.... Hitherto the lie of the ideal has been the curse of reality; by means of it the very source of mankind's instincts has become mendacious and false; so much so that those values have come to be worshipped which are the exact opposite of the ones which would ensure man's prosperity, his future, and his great right to a future.

3

He who knows how to breathe in the air of my writings is conscious that it is the air of the heights, that it is bracing. A man must be built[Pg 3] for it, otherwise the chances are that it will chill him. The ice is near, the loneliness is terrible—but how serenely everything lies in the sunshine! how freely one can breathe! how much, one feels, lies beneath one! Philosophy, as I have understood it hitherto, is a voluntary retirement into regions of ice and mountain-peaks—the seeking—out of everything strange and questionable in existence, everything upon which, hitherto, morality has set its ban. Through long experience, derived from such wanderings in forbidden country, I acquired an opinion very different from that which may seem generally desirable, of the causes which hitherto have led to men's moralising and idealising. The secret history of philosophers, the psychology of their great names, was revealed to me. How much truth can a certain mind endure; how much truth can it dare?—these questions became for me ever more and more the actual test of values. Error (the belief in the ideal) is not blindness; error is cowardice.... Every conquest, every step forward in knowledge, is the outcome of courage, of hardness towards one's self, of cleanliness towards one's self. I do not refute ideals; all I do is to draw on my gloves in their presence.... Nitimur in vetitum; with this device my philosophy will one day be victorious; for that which has hitherto been most stringently forbidden is, without exception, Truth.

4

In my lifework, my Zarathustra holds a place apart. With it, I gave my fellow-men the greatest[Pg 4] gift that has ever been bestowed upon them. This book, the voice of which speaks out across the ages, is not only the loftiest book on earth, literally the book of mountain air,—the whole phenomenon, mankind, lies at an incalculable distance beneath it,—but it is also the deepest book, born of the inmost abundance of truth; an inexhaustible well, into which no pitcher can be lowered without coming up again laden with gold and with goodness. Here it is not a "prophet" who speaks, one of those gruesome hybrids of sickness and Will to Power, whom men call founders of religions. If a man would not do a sad wrong to his wisdom, he must, above all give proper heed to the tones—the halcyonic tones—that fall from the lips of Zarathustra:—

"The most silent words are harbingers of the storm; thoughts that come on dove's feet lead the world.

"The figs fall from the trees; they are good and sweet, and, when they fall, their red skins are rent.

"A north wind am I unto ripe figs.

"Thus, like figs, do these precepts drop down to you, my friends; now drink their juice and their sweet pulp.

"It is autumn all around, and clear sky, and afternoon."

No fanatic speaks to you here; this is not a "sermon"; no faith is demanded in these pages. From out an infinite treasure of light and well of joy, drop by drop, my words fall out—a slow and gentle gait is the cadence of these discourses. Such things can reach only the most elect; it is[Pg 5] a rare privilege to be a listener here; not every? one who likes can have ears to hear Zarathustra. I Is not Zarathustra, because of these things, a seducer? ... But what, indeed, does he himself say, when for the first time he goes back to his solitude? Just the reverse of that which any "Sage," "Saint," "Saviour of the world," and other decadent would say.... Not only his words, but he himself is other than they.

"Alone do I now go, my disciples! Get ye also hence, and alone!

Thus would I have it.

"Verily, I beseech you: take your leave of me and arm yourselves against Zarathustra! And better still, be ashamed of him! Maybe he hath deceived you.

"The knight of knowledge must be able not only to love his enemies, but also to hate his friends.

"The man who remaineth a pupil requiteth his teacher but ill. And why would ye not pluck at my wreath?

"Ye honour me; but what if your reverence should one day break down? Take heed, lest a statue crush you.

"Ye say ye believe in Zarathustra? But of; what account is Zarathustra? Ye are my believers: but of what account are all believers?

"Ye had not yet sought yourselves when ye found me. Thus do all believers; therefore is all believing worth so little.

"Now I bid you lose me and find yourselves; and only when ye have all denied me will I come back unto you."

FRIEDRICH NIETZSCHE.

On this perfect day, when everything is ripening, and not only the grapes are getting brown, a ray of sunshine has fallen on my life: I looked behind me, I looked before me, and never have I seen so many good things all at once. Not in vain have I buried my four-and-fortieth year to-day; I had the right to bury it—that in it which still had life, has been saved and is immortal. The first book of the Transvaluation of all Values, The Songs of Zarathustra, The Twilight of the Idols, my attempt, to philosophise with the hammer—all these things are the gift of this year, and even of its last quarter. How could I help being thankful to the whole of my life?That is why I am now going to tell myself the story of my life.

WHY I AM SO WISE
1

The happiness of my existence, its unique character perhaps, consists in its fatefulness: to speak in a riddle, as my own father I am already dead, as my own mother I still live and grow old. This double origin, taken as it were from the highest and lowest rungs of the ladder of life, at once a decadent and a beginning, this, if anything, explains that neutrality, that freedom from partisanship in regard to the general problem of existence, which perhaps distinguishes me. To the first indications of ascending or of descending life my nostrils are more sensitive than those of any man that has yet lived. In this domain I am a master to my backbone—I know both sides, for I am both sides. My father died in his six-and-thirtieth year: he was delicate, lovable, and morbid, like one who is preordained to pay simply a flying visit—a gracious reminder of life rather than life itself. In the same year that his life declined mine also declined: in my six-and-thirtieth year I reached the lowest point in my vitality,—I still lived, but[Pg 10] my eyes could distinguish nothing that lay three paces away from me. At that time—it was the year 1879—I resigned my professorship at Bâle, lived through the summer like a shadow in St. Moritz, and spent the following winter, the most sunless of my life, like a shadow in Naumburg. This was my lowest ebb. During this period I wrote The Wanderer and His Shadow. Without a doubt I was conversant with shadows then. The winter that followed, my first winter in Genoa, brought forth that sweetness and spirituality which is almost inseparable from extreme poverty of blood and muscle, in the shape of The Dawn of Day. The perfect lucidity and cheerfulness, the intellectual exuberance even, that this work reflects, coincides, in my case, not only with the most profound physiological weakness, but also with an excess of suffering. In the midst of the agony of a headache which lasted three days, accompanied by violent nausea, I was possessed of most singular dialectical clearness, and in absolutely cold blood I then thought out things, for which, in my more healthy moments, I am not enough of a climber, not sufficiently subtle, not sufficiently cold. My readers perhaps know to what extent I consider dialectic a symptom of decadence, as, for instance, in the most famous of all cases—the case of Socrates. All the morbid disturbances of the intellect, even that semi-stupor which accompanies fever, have, unto this day, remained completely unknown to me; and for my first information concerning their nature and frequency, I was obliged to have recourse to the learned works which have been compiled on the[Pg 11] subject. My circulation is slow. No one has ever been able to detect fever in me. A doctor who treated me for some time as a nerve patient finally declared: "No! there is nothing wrong with your nerves, it is simply I who am nervous." It has been absolutely impossible to ascertain any local degeneration in me, nor any organic stomach trouble, however much I may have suffered from profound weakness of the gastric system as the result of general exhaustion. Even my eye trouble, which sometimes approached so parlously near to blindness, was only an effect and not a cause; for, whenever my general vital condition improved, my power of vision also increased. Having admitted all this, do I need to say that I am experienced in questions of decadence? I know them inside and out. Even that filigree art of prehension and comprehension in general, that feeling for delicate shades of difference, that psychology of "seeing through brick walls," and whatever else I may be able to do, was first learnt then, and is the specific gift of that period during which everything in me was subtilised,—observation itself, together with all the organs of observation. To look upon healthier concepts and values from the standpoint of the sick, and conversely to look down upon the secret work of the instincts of decadence from the standpoint of him who is laden and self-reliant with the richness of life—this has been my longest exercise, my principal experience. If in anything at all, it was in this that I became a master. To-day my hand knows the trick, I now have the knack of reversing perspectives: the first reason perhaps why a[Pg 12] Transvaluation of all Values has been possible to me alone.

2

For, apart from the fact that I am a decadent, I am also the reverse of such a creature. Among other things my proof of this is, that I always instinctively select the proper remedy when my spiritual or bodily health is low; whereas the decadent, as such, invariably chooses those remedies which are bad for him. As a whole I was sound, but in certain details I was a decadent. That energy with which I sentenced myself to absolute solitude, and to a severance from all those conditions in life to which I had grown accustomed; my discipline of myself, and my refusal to allow myself to be pampered, to be tended hand and foot, and to be doctored—all this betrays the absolute certainty of my instincts respecting what at that time was most needful to me. I placed myself in my own hands, I restored myself to health: the first condition of success in such an undertaking, as every physiologist will admit, is that at bottom a man should be sound. An intrinsically morbid nature cannot become healthy. On the other hand, to an intrinsically sound nature, illness may even constitute a powerful stimulus to life, to a surplus of life. It is in this light that I now regard the long period of illness that I endured: it seemed as if I had discovered life afresh, my own self included. I tasted all good things and even trifles in a way in which it was not easy for others to taste them—out of my Will to Health and to Life I made my[Pg 13] philosophy.... For this should be thoroughly understood; it was during those years in which my vitality reached its lowest point that I ceased from being a pessimist: the instinct of self-recovery forbade my holding to a philosophy of poverty and desperation. Now, by what signs are Nature's lucky strokes recognised among men? They are recognised by the fact that any such lucky stroke gladdens our senses; that he is carved from one integral block, which is hard, sweet, and fragrant as well. He enjoys that only which is good for him; his pleasure, his desire, ceases when the limits of that which is good for him are overstepped. He divines remedies for injuries; he knows how to turn serious accidents to his own advantage; that which does not kill him makes him stronger. He instinctively gathers his material from all he sees, hears, and experiences. He is a selective principle; he rejects much. He is always in his own company, whether his intercourse be with books, with men, or with natural scenery; he honours the things he chooses, the things he acknowledges, the things he trusts. He reacts slowly to all kinds of stimuli, with that tardiness which long caution and deliberate pride have bred in him—he tests the approaching stimulus; he would not dream of meeting it half-way. He believes neither in "ill-luck" nor "guilt"; he can digest himself and others; he knows how to forget—he is strong enough to make everything turn to his own advantage.

Lo then! I am the very reverse of a decadent, for he whom I have just described is none other than myself.

3

This double thread of experiences, this means of access to two worlds that seem so far asunder, finds in every detail its counterpart in my own nature—I am my own complement: I have a "second" sight, as well as a first. And perhaps I also have a third sight. By the very nature of my origin I was allowed an outlook beyond all merely local, merely national and limited horizons; it required no effort on my part to be a "good European." On the other hand, I am perhaps more German than modern Germans—mere Imperial Germans—can hope to be,—I, the last anti-political German. Be this as it may, my ancestors were Polish noblemen: it is owing to them that I have so much race instinct in my blood—who knows? perhaps even the liberum veto[1] When I think of the number of times in my travels that I have been accosted as a Pole, even by Poles themselves, and how seldom I have been taken for a German, it seems to me as if I belonged to those only who have a sprinkling of German in them. But my mother, Franziska Oehler, is at any rate something very German; as is also my paternal grandmother, Erdmuthe Krause. The latter spent the whole of her youth in good old Weimar, not without coming into contact with Goethe's circle. Her brother, Krause, the Professor of Theology in[Pg 15] Königsberg, was called to the post of General Superintendent at Weimar after Herder's death. It is not unlikely that her mother, my great grandmother, is mentioned in young Goethe's diary under the name of "Muthgen." She married twice, and her second husband was Superintendent Nietzsche of Eilenburg. In 1813, the year of the great war, when Napoleon with his general staff entered Eilenburg on the 10th of October, she gave birth to a son. As a daughter of Saxony she was a great admirer of Napoleon, and maybe I am so still. My father, born in 1813, died in 1849. Previous to taking over the pastorship of the parish of Röcken, not far from Lützen, he lived for some years at the Castle of Altenburg, where he had charge of the education of the four princesses. His pupils are the Queen of Hanover, the Grand-Duchess Constantine, the Grand-Duchess of Oldenburg, and the Princess Theresa of Saxe-Altenburg. He was full of loyal respect for the Prussian King, Frederick William the Fourth, from whom he obtained his living at Röcken; the events of 1848 saddened him extremely. As I was born on the 15 th of October, the birthday of the king above mentioned, I naturally received the Hohenzollern names of Frederick William. There was at all events one advantage in the choice of this day: my birthday throughout the whole of my childhood was a day of public rejoicing. I regard it as a great privilege to have had such a father: it even seems to me that this embraces all that I can claim in the matter of privileges—life, the great yea to life, excepted. What I owe to him above all is this, that I do not need any special intention, but[Pg 16] merely a little patience, in order involuntarily to enter a world of higher and more delicate things. There I am at home, there alone does my inmost passion become free. The fact that I had to pay for this privilege almost with my life, certainly does not make it a bad bargain. In order to understand even a little of my Zarathustra, perhaps a man must be situated and constituted very much as I am myself—with one foot beyond the realm of the living.

4

I have never understood the art of arousing ill-feeling against myself,—this is also something for which I have to thank my incomparable father,—even when it seemed to me highly desirable to do so. However un-Christian it may seem, I do not even bear any ill-feeling towards myself. Turn my life about as you may, you will find but seldom—perhaps indeed only once—any trace of some one's having shown me ill-will. You might perhaps discover, however, too many traces of goodwill.... My experiences even with those on whom every other man has burnt his fingers, speak without exception in their favour; I tame every bear, I can make even clowns behave decently. During the seven years in which I taught Greek to the sixth form of the College at Bâle, I never had occasion to administer a punishment; the laziest youths were diligent in my class. The unexpected has always found me equal to it; I must be unprepared in order to keep my self-command. Whatever the instrument was, even if it were as out of tune as the instrument[Pg 17] "man" can possibly be,—it was only when I was ill that I could not succeed in making it express something that was worth hearing. And how often have I not been told by the "instruments" themselves, that they had never before heard their voices express such beautiful things.... This was said to me most delightfully perhaps by that young fellow Heinrich von Stein, who died at such an unpardonably early age, and who, after having considerately asked leave to do so, once appeared in Sils-Maria for a three days' sojourn, telling everybody there that it was not for the Engadine that he had come. This excellent person, who with all the impetuous simplicity of a young Prussian nobleman, had waded deep into the swamp of Wagnerism (and into that of Dübringism[2] into the bargain!), seemed almost transformed during these three days by a hurricane of freedom, like one who has been suddenly raised to his full height and given wings. Again and again I said to him that this was all owing to the splendid air; everybody felt the same,—one could not stand 6000 feet above Bayreuth for nothing,—but he would not believe me.... Be this as it may, if I have been the victim of many a small or even great offence, it was not "will," and least of all ill-will that actuated the offenders; but rather, as I have already suggested, it was goodwill, the cause of no small amount of mischief in f my life, about which I had to complain. My experience gave me a right to feel suspicious in regard[Pg 18] to all so-called "unselfish" instincts, in regard to the whole of "neighbourly love" which is ever ready and waiting with deeds or with advice. To me it seems that these instincts are a sign of weakness, they are an example of the inability to withstand a stimulus—it is only among decadents that this pity is called a virtue. What I reproach the pitiful with is, that they are too ready to forget shame, reverence, and the delicacy of feeling which knows how to keep at a distance; they do not remember that this gushing pity stinks of the mob, and that it is next of kin to bad manners—that pitiful hands may be thrust with results fatally destructive into a great destiny, into a lonely and wounded retirement, and into the privileges with which great guilt endows one. The overcoming of pity I reckon among the noble virtues; In the "Temptation of Zarathustra" I have imagined a case, in which a great cry of distress reaches his ears, in which pity swoops down upon him like a last sin, and would make him break faith with himself. To remain one's own master in such circumstances, to keep the sublimity of one's mission pure in such cases,—pure from the many ignoble and more short-sighted impulses which come into play in so-called unselfish actions,—this is the rub, the last test perhaps which a Zarathustra has to undergo—the actual proof of his power.

5

In yet another respect I am no more than my father over again, and as it were the continuation of his life after an all-too-early death. Like every[Pg 19] man who has never been able to meet his equal, and unto whom the concept "retaliation" is just as incomprehensible as the notion of "equal rights," I have forbidden myself the use of any sort of measure of security or protection— and also, of course, of defence and "justification"—in all cases in which I have been made the victim either of trifling or even very great foolishness. My form of retaliation consists in this: as soon as possible to set a piece of cleverness at the heels of an act of stupidity; by this means perhaps it may still be possible to overtake it. To speak in a parable: I dispatch a pot of jam in order to get rid of a bitter experience.... Let anybody only give me offence, I shall "retaliate," he can be quite sure of that: before long I discover an opportunity of expressing my thanks to the "offender" (among other things even for the offence)—or of asking him for something, which can be more courteous even than giving. It also seems to me that the rudest word, the rudest letter, is more good-natured, more straightforward, than silence. Those—who keep silent are almost always lacking in subtlety and refinement of heart; silence is an objection, to swallow a grievance must necessarily produce a bad temper—it even upsets the stomach. All silent people are dyspeptic. You perceive that I should not like to see rudeness undervalued; it is by far the most humane form of contradiction, and, in the midst of modern effeminacy, it is one of our first virtues; If one is sufficiently rich for it, it may even be a joy to be wrong. If a god were to descend to this earth, he would have to[Pg 20] do nothing but wrong—to take guilt not punishment, on one's shoulders, is the first proof of divinity.

6

Freedom from resentment and the understanding of the nature of resentment—who knows how very much after all I am indebted to my long illness for these two things? The problem is not exactly simple: a man must have experienced both through his strength and through his weakness, If illness and weakness are to be charged with anything at all, it is with the fact that when they prevail, the very instinct of recovery, which is the instinct of defence and of war in man, becomes decayed. He knows not how to get rid of anything, how to come to terms with anything, and how to cast anything behind him. Everything wounds him. People and things draw importunately near, all experiences strike deep, memory is a gathering wound. To be ill is a sort of resentment in itself. Against this resentment the invalid has only one great remedy—I call it Russian fatalism, that fatalism which is free from revolt, and with which the Russian soldier, to whom a campaign proves unbearable, ultimately lays himself down in the snow. To accept nothing more, to undertake nothing more, to absorb nothing more—to cease entirely from reacting.... The tremendous sagacity of this fatalism, which does not always imply merely the courage for death, but which in the most dangerous cases may actually constitute a self-preservative measure, amounts to a reduction of activity in the vital[Pg 21] functions, the slackening down of which is like a sort of will to hibernate. A few steps farther in this direction we find the fakir, who will sleep for weeks in a tomb.... Owing to the fact that one would be used up too quickly if one reacted, one no longer reacts at all: this is the principle. And nothing on earth consumes a man more quickly than the passion of resentment. Mortification, morbid susceptibility, the inability to wreak revenge, the desire and thirst for revenge, the concoction of every sort of poison—this is surely the most injurious manner of reacting which could possibly be conceived by exhausted men. It involves a rapid wasting away of nervous energy, an abnormal increase of detrimental secretions, as, for instance, that of bile into the stomach. To the sick man resentment ought to be more strictly forbidden than anything else—it is his special danger: unfortunately, however, it is also his most natural propensity. This was fully grasped by that profound physiologist Buddha. His "religion," which it would be better to call a system of hygiene, in order to avoid confounding it with a creed so wretched as Christianity, depended for its effect upon the triumph over resentment: to make the soul free therefrom was considered the first step towards recovery. "Not through hostility is hostility put to flight; through friendship does hostility end": this stands at the beginning of Buddha's teaching—this is not a precept of morality, but of physiology. Resentment born of weakness is not more deleterious to anybody than it is to the weak man himself[Pg 22]— conversely, in the case of that man whose nature is fundamentally a rich one, resentment is a superfluous feeling, a feeling to remain master of which is almost a proof of riches. Those of my readers who know the earnestness-with which my philosophy wages war against the feelings of revenge and rancour, even to the extent of attacking the doctrine of "free will" (my conflict with Christianity is only a particular instance of it), will understand why I wish to focus attention upon my own personal attitude and the certainty of my practical instincts precisely in this matter. In my moments of decadence I forbade myself the indulgence of the above feelings, because they were harmful; as soon as my life recovered enough riches and pride, however, I regarded them again as forbidden, but this time because they were beneath me. That "Russian fatalism" of which I have spoken manifested itself in me in such a way that for years I held tenaciously to almost insufferable conditions, places, habitations, and companions, once chance had placed them on my path—it was better than changing them, than feeling that they could be changed, than revolting against them.... He who stirred me from this fatalism, he who violently tried to shake me into consciousness, seemed to me then a mortal enemy—in point of fact, there was danger of death each time this was done. To regard one's self as a destiny, not to wish one's self "different"—this, in such circumstances, is sagacity, itself.

7

War, on the other hand, is something different. At heart I am a warrior. Attacking belongs to my instincts. To be able to be an enemy, to be an enemy—maybe these things presuppose a strong nature; in any case all strong natures involve these things. Such natures need resistance, consequently they go in search of obstacles: the pathos of aggression belongs of necessity to strength as much as the feelings of revenge and of rancour belong to weakness. Woman, for instance, is revengeful; her weakness involves this passion, just as it involves her susceptibility in the presence of other people's suffering. The strength of the aggressor can be measured by the opposition which he needs; every increase of growth betrays itself by a seeking out of more formidable opponents—or problems: for a philosopher who is combative challenges even problems to a duel. The task is not to overcome opponents in general, but only those opponents against whom one has to summon all one's strength, one's skill, and one's swordsmanship—in fact, opponents who are one's equals.... To be one's enemy's equal—this is the first condition of an honourable duel. Where one despises, one cannot wage war. Where one commands, where one sees something beneath one, one ought not to wage war. My war tactics can be reduced to four principles A First, I attack only things that are triumphant—if necessary I wait until they become triumphant. Secondly, I attack only those things against which I find no[Pg 24] allies, against which I stand alone—against which I compromise nobody but myself.... I have not yet taken one single step before the public eye, which did not compromise me: that is my criterion of a proper mode of action. Thirdly, I never make personal attacks—I use a personality merely as a magnifying-glass, by means of which I render a general, but elusive and scarcely noticeable evil, more apparent. In this way I attacked David Strauss, or rather the success given to a senile book by the cultured classes of Germany—by this means I caught German culture red-handed. In this way I attacked Wagner, or rather the falsity or mongrel instincts of our "culture" which confounds the super-refined with the strong, and the effete with the great. Fourthly, I attack only those things from which all personal differences are excluded, in which any such thing as a background of disagreeable experiences is lacking. On the contrary, attacking is to me a proof of goodwill and, in certain circumstances, of gratitude. By means of it, I do honour to a thing, I distinguish a thing; whether I associate my name with that of an institution or a person, by being against or for either, is all the same to me. If I wage war against Christianity, I feel justified in doing so, because in that quarter I have met with no fatal experiences and difficulties—the most earnest Christians have always been kindly disposed to me. I, personally, the most essential opponent of Christianity, am far from holding the individual responsible for what is the fatality of long ages.

May I be allowed to hazard a suggestion concerning one last trait in my character, which in my intercourse with other men has led me into some difficulties? I am gifted with a sense of cleanliness the keenness of which is phenomenal; so much so, that I can ascertain physiologically—that is to say, smell—the proximity, nay, the inmost core, the "entrails" of every human soul.... This sensitiveness of mine is furnished with psychological antennæ, wherewith I feel and grasp every secret: the quality of concealed filth lying at the base of many a human character which may be the inevitable outcome of base blood, and which education may have veneered, is revealed to me at the first glance. If my observation has been correct, such people, whom my sense of cleanliness rejects, also become conscious, on their part, of the cautiousness to which my loathing prompts me: and this does not make them any more fragrant.... In keeping with a custom which I have long observed,—pure habits and honesty towards myself are among the first conditions of my existence, I would die in unclean surroundings,—I swim, bathe, and splash about, as it were, incessantly in water, in any kind of perfectly transparent and shining element. That is why my relations with my fellows try my patience to no small extent; my humanity does not consist in the fact that I understand the feelings of my fellows, but that I can endure to understand.... My humanity is a perpetual process of self-mastery. But I need solitude—that is to say, recovery,[Pg 26] return to myself, the breathing of free, crisp, bracing air.... The whole of my Zarathustra is a dithyramb in honour of solitude, or, if I have been understood, in honour of purity. Thank Heaven, it is not in honour of "pure foolery"![3] He who has an eye for colour will call him a diamond. The loathing of mankind, of the rabble, was always my greatest danger.... Would you hearken to the words spoken by Zarathustra concerning deliverance from loathing?

"What forsooth hath come unto me? How did I deliver myself from loathing? Who hath made mine eye younger? How did I soar to the height, where there are no more rabble sitting about the well?

"Did my very loathing forge me wings and the strength to scent fountains afar off? Verily to the loftiest heights did I need to fly, to find once more the spring of joyfulness.

"Oh, I found it, my brethren! Up here, on the loftiest height, the spring of joyfulness gusheth forth for me. And there is a life at the well of which no rabble can drink with you.

"Almost too fiercely dost thou rush, for me, thou spring of joyfulness! And ofttimes dost thou empty the pitcher again in trying to fill it.

"And yet must I learn to draw near thee more humbly. Far too eagerly doth my heart jump to meet thee.

"My heart, whereon my summer burneth, my short, hot, melancholy, over-blessed summer: how my summer heart yearneth for thy coolness!

"Farewell, the lingering affliction of my spring! Past is the wickedness of my snowflakes in June! Summer have I become entirely, and summer noontide!

"A summer in the loftiest heights, with cold springs and blessed stillness: oh come, my friends, that the stillness may wax even more blessed!

"For this is our height and our home: too high and steep is our dwelling for all the unclean and their appetites.

"Do but cast your pure eyes into the well of my joyfulness, my friends! How could it thus become muddy! It will laugh back at you with its purity.

"On the tree called Future do we build our nest: eagles shall bring food in their beaks unto us lonely ones!

"Verily not the food whereof the unclean might partake. They would think they ate fire and would burn their mouths!

"Verily, no abodes for the unclean do we here hold in readiness! To their bodies our happiness would seem an ice-cavern, and to their spirits also!

"And like strong winds will we live above them, neighbours to the eagles, companions of the snow, and playmates of the sun: thus do strong winds live.

"And like a wind shall I one day blow amidst them, and take away their soul's breath with my spirit: thus my future willeth it.

"Verily, a strong wind is Zarathustra to all low lands; and this is his counsel to his foes and to all those who spit and spew: 'Beware of spitting against the wind!'"

[1] The right which every Polish deputy, whether a great or an inferior nobleman, possessed of forbidding the passing of any measure by the Diet, was called in Poland the liberum veto (in Polish nie pozwalam), and brought all legislation to a standstill.—TR.

[2] Eugen Dübring is a philosopher and political economist whose general doctrine might be characterised as a sort of abstract Materialism with an optimistic colouring.—TR.

[3] This, of course, is a reference to Wagner's Parsifal. See my note on p. 96 of The Will to Power vol. i.—TR.

WHY I AM SO CLEVER
1

Why do I know more things than other people? Why, in fact, am I so clever? I have never pondered over questions that are not questions. I have never squandered my strength. Of actual religious difficulties, for instance, I have no experience. I have never known what it is to feel "sinful." In the same way I completely lack any reliable criterion for ascertaining what constitutes a prick of conscience: from all accounts a prick of conscience does not seem to be a very estimable thing.... Once it was done I should hate to leave an action of mine in the lurch; I should prefer completely to omit the evil outcome, the consequences, from the problem concerning the value of an action. In the face of evil consequences one is too ready to lose the proper standpoint from which one's deed ought to be considered. A prick of conscience strikes me as a sort of "evil eye." Something that has failed should be honoured all the more jealously, precisely because it has failed—this is much more in keeping with my morality.—"God," "the immortality of the soul," "salvation," a "beyond"—to all these notions, even as a child, I never paid any attention whatsoever, nor did I waste any time upon them,—maybe I was never naif enough for that?—I am quite unacquainted with atheism as a result, and still less[Pg 29] as an event in my life: in me it is inborn, instinctive. I am too inquisitive, too incredulous, too high spirited, to be satisfied with such a palpably clumsy solution of things. God is a too palpably clumsy solution of things; a solution which shows a lack of delicacy towards us thinkers—at bottom He is really no more than a coarse and rude prohibition of us: ye shall not think!... I am much more interested in another question,—a question upon which the "salvation of humanity" depends to a far greater degree than it does upon any piece of theological curiosity: I refer to nutrition. For ordinary purposes, it may be formulated as follows: "How precisely must thou feed thyself in order to attain to thy maximum of power, or virtù in the Renaissance style,—of virtue free from moralic acid?" My experiences in regard to this matter have been as bad as they possibly could be; I am surprised that I set myself this question so late in life, and that it took me so long to draw "rational" conclusions from my experiences. Only the absolute worth-1 lessness of German culture—its "idealism"—can to some extent explain how it was that precisely in this matter I was so backward that my ignorance was almost saintly. This "culture," which from first to last teaches one to lose sight of actual things and to hunt after thoroughly problematic and so-called ideal aims, as, for instance, "classical culture"—as if it were not hopeless from the start to try to unite "classical" and "German" in one concept. It is even a little comical—try and imagine a "classically cultured" citizen of Leipzig!—Indeed, I can say, that up to a very mature age, my food was[Pg 30] entirely bad—expressed morally, it was "impersonal," "selfless," "altruistic," to the glory of cooks and all other fellow-Christians. It was through the cooking in vogue at Leipzig, for instance, together with my first study of Schopenhauer (1865), that I earnestly renounced my "Will to Live." To spoil one's stomach by absorbing insufficient nourishment—this problem seemed to my mind solved with admirable felicity by the above-mentioned cookery. (It is said that in the year 1866 changes were introduced into this department.) But as to German cookery in general—what has it not got on its conscience! Soup before the meal (still called alla tedesca in the Venetian cookery books of the sixteenth century); meat boiled to shreds, vegetables cooked with fat and flour; the degeneration of pastries into paper-weights! And, if you add thereto the absolutely bestial post-prandial drinking habits of the ancients, and not alone of the ancient Germans, you will understand where German intellect took its origin—that is to say, in sadly disordered intestines.... German intellect is indigestion; it can assimilate nothing. But even English diet, which in comparison with German, and indeed with French alimentation, seems to me to constitute a "return to Nature,"—that is to say, to cannibalism,—is profoundly opposed to my own instincts. It seems to me to give the intellect heavy feet, in fact, Englishwomen's feet.... The best cooking is that of Piedmont. Alcoholic drinks do not agree with me; a single glass of wine or beer a day is amply sufficient to turn life into a valley of tears[Pg 31] for me;—in Munich live my antipodes. Although I admit that this knowledge came to me somewhat late, it already formed part of my experience even as a child. As a boy I believed that the drinking of wine and the smoking of tobacco were at first but the vanities of youths, and later merely bad habits. Maybe the poor wine of Naumburg was partly responsible for this poor opinion of wine in general. In order to believe that wine was exhilarating, I should have had to be a Christian—in other words, I should have had to believe in what, to my mind, is an absurdity. Strange to say, whereas small quantities of alcohol, taken with plenty of water, succeed in making me feel out of sorts, large quantities turn me almost into a rollicking tar. Even as a boy I showed my bravado in this respect. To compose a long Latin essay in one night, to revise and recopy it, to aspire with my pen to emulating the exactitude and the terseness of my model, Sallust, and to pour a few very strong grogs over it all—this mode of procedure, while I was a pupil at the venerable old school of Pforta, was not in the least out of keeping with my physiology, nor perhaps with that of Sallust, however much it may have been alien to dignified Pforta. Later on, towards the middle of my life, I grew more and more opposed to alcoholic drinks: I, an opponent of vegetarianism, who have experienced what vegetarianism is,—just as Wagner, who converted me back to meat, experienced it,—cannot with sufficient earnestness advise all more spiritual natures to abstain absolutely from alcohol. Water answers the purpose.... I have a predilection in favour of[Pg 32] those places where in all directions one has opportunities of drinking from running brooks (Nice, Turin, Sils). In vino Veritas: it seems that here once more I am at variance with the rest of the world about the concept "Truth"—with me spirit moves on the face of the waters.... Here are a few more indications as to my morality. A heavy meal is digested more easily than an inadequate one. The first principle of a good digestion is that the stomach should become active as a whole. A man ought, therefore, to know the size of his stomach. For the same reasons all those interminable meals, which I call interrupted sacrificial feasts, and which are to be had at any table d'hôte, are strongly to be deprecated. Nothing should be eaten between meals, coffee should be given up—coffee makes one gloomy. Tea is beneficial only in the morning. It should be taken in small quantities, but very strong. It may be very harmful, and indispose you for the whole day, if it be taken the least bit too weak. Everybody has his own standard in this matter, often between the narrowest and most delicate limits. In an enervating climate tea is not a good beverage with which to start the day: an hour before taking it an excellent thing is to drink a cup of thick cocoa, feed from oil. Remain seated as little as possible, put no trust in any thought that is not born in the open, to the accompaniment of free bodily motion—nor in one in which even the muscles do not celebrate a feast. All prejudices take their origin in the intestines. A sedentary life, as I have already said elsewhere, is the real sin against the Holy Spirit.

2.

To the question of nutrition, that of locality and climate is next of kin. Nobody is so constituted as to be able to live everywhere and anywhere; and he who has great duties to perform, which lay claim to all his strength, has, in this respect, a very limited choice. The influence of climate upon the bodily functions, affecting their acceleration or retardation, extends so far, that a blunder in the choice of locality and climate is able not only to alienate a man from his actual duty, but also to withhold it from him altogether, so that he never even comes face to face with it. Animal vigour never acquires enough strength in him in order to reach that pitch of artistic freedom which makes his own soul whisper to him: I, alone, can do that.... Ever so slight a tendency to laziness in the intestines, once it has become a habit, is quite sufficient to make something mediocre, something "German" out of a genius; the climate of Germany, alone, is enough to discourage the strongest and most heroically disposed intestines. The tempo of the body's functions is closely bound up with the agility or the clumsiness of the spirit's feet; spirit itself is indeed only a form of these organic functions. Let anybody make a list of the places in which men of great intellect have been found, and are still found; where wit, subtlety, and malice constitute happiness; where genius is almost necessarily at home: all of them rejoice in exceptionally dry air. Paris, Provence, Florence, Jerusalem, Athens—these names prove something, namely:[Pg 34] that genius is conditioned by dry air, by a pure sky—that is to say, by rapid organic functions, by the constant and ever-present possibility of procuring for one's self great and even enormous quantities of strength. I have a certain case in mind in which a man of remarkable intellect and independent spirit became a narrow, craven specialist and a grumpy old crank, simply owing to a lack of subtlety in his instinct for climate. And I myself might have been an example of the same thing, if illness had not compelled me to reason, and to reflect upon reason realistically. Now that I have learnt through long practice to read the effects of climatic and meteorological influences, from my own body, as though from a very delicate and reliable instrument, and that I am able to calculate the change in degrees of atmospheric moisture by means of physiological observations upon myself, even on so short a journey as that from Turin to Milan; I think with horror of the ghastly fact that my whole life, until the last ten years,—the most perilous years,—has always been spent in the wrong, and what to me ought to have been the most forbidden, places. Naumburg, Pforta, Thuringia in general, Leipzig, Bâle, Venice—so many ill-starred places for a constitution like mine. If I cannot recall one single happy reminiscence of my childhood and youth, it is nonsense to suppose that so-called "moral" causes could account for this—as, for instance, the incontestable fact that I lacked companions that could have satisfied me; for this fact is the same to-day as it ever was, and it does not prevent me from being cheerful and brave. But it was ignorance[Pg 35] in physiological matters—that confounded "Idealism"—that was the real curse of my life. This was the superfluous and foolish element in my existence; something from which nothing could spring, and for which there can be no settlement and no compensation. As the outcome of this "Idealism" I regard all the blunders, the great aberrations of instinct, and the "modest specialisations" which drew me aside from the task of my life; as, for instance, the fact that I became a philologist—why not at least a medical man or anything else which might have opened my eyes? My days at Bâle, the whole of my intellectual routine, including my daily time-table, was an absolutely senseless abuse of extraordinary powers, without the slightest compensation for the strength that I spent, without even a thought of what I was squandering and how its place might be filled. I lacked all subtlety in egoism, all the fostering care of an imperative instinct; I was in a state in which one is ready to regard one's self as anybody's equal, a state of "disinterestedness," a forgetting of one's distance from others—something, in short, for which I can never forgive myself. When I had well-nigh reached the end of my tether, simply because I had almost reached my end, I began to reflect upon the fundamental absurdity of my life—"Idealism." It was illness that first brought me to reason.

3

After the choice of nutrition, the choice of climate and locality, the third matter concerning which one[Pg 36] must not on any account make a blunder, is the choice of the manner in which one recuperates one's strength. Here, again, according to the extent to which a spirit is sui generis, the limits of that which he can allow himself—in other words, the limits of that which is beneficial to him—become more and more confined. As far as I in particular am concerned, reading in general belongs to my means of recuperation; consequently it belongs to that which rids me of myself, to that which enables me to wander in strange sciences and strange souls—to that, in fact, about which I am no longer in earnest. Indeed, it is while reading that I recover from my earnestness. During the time that I am deeply absorbed in my work, no books are found within my reach; it would never occur to me to allow any one to speak or even to think in my presence. For that is what reading would mean.... Has any one ever actually noticed, that, during the period of profound tension to which the state of pregnancy condemns not only the mind, but also, at bottom, the whole organism, accident and every kind of external stimulus acts too acutely and strikes too deep? Accident and external stimuli must, as far as possible, be avoided: a sort of walling-of-one's-self-in is one of the primary instinctive precautions of spiritual pregnancy. Shall I allow a strange thought to steal secretly over the wall? For that is what reading would mean.... The periods of work and fruit-fulness are followed by periods of recuperation: come hither, ye delightful, intellectual, intelligent books! Shall I read

German books?... I must go back six months to catch myself with a book in[Pg 37] my hand. What was it? An excellent study by Victor Brochard upon the Greek sceptics, in which my Laertiana[1] was used to advantage. The sceptics!—the only honourable types among that double-faced and sometimes quintuple-faced throng, the philosophers!.... Otherwise I almost always take refuge in the same books: altogether their number is small; they are books which are precisely my proper fare. It is not perhaps in my nature to read much, and of all sorts: a library makes me ill. Neither is it my nature to love much or many kinds of things. Suspicion or even hostility towards new books is much more akin to my instinctive feeling than "toleration," largeur de cœur, and other forms of "neighbour-love." ... It is to a small number of old French authors, that I always return again and again; I believe only in French culture, and regard everything else in Europe which calls itself "culture" as a misunderstanding. I do not even take the German kind into consideration.... The few instances of higher culture with which I have[Pg 38] met in Germany were all French in their origin. The most striking example of this was Madame Cosima Wagner, by far the most decisive voice in matters of taste that I have ever heard. If I do not read, but literally love Pascal? as the most instinctive sacrifice to Christianity, killing himself inch by inch, first bodily, then spiritually, according to the terrible consistency of this most appalling form of inhuman cruelty; if I have something of Montaigne's mischievousness in my soul, and—who knows?—perhaps also in my body; if my artist's taste endeavours to defend the names of Molière, Corneille, and Racine, and not without bitterness, against such a wild genius as Shakespeare—all this does not prevent me from regarding even the latter-day Frenchmen also as charming companions. I can think of absolutely no century in history, in which a netful of more inquisitive and at the same time more subtle psychologists could be drawn up together than in the Paris of the present day. Let me mention a few at random—for their number is by no means small—Paul Bourget, Pierre Loti, Gyp, Meilhac, Anatole France, Jules Lemaitre; or, to point to one of strong race, a genuine Latin, of whom I am particularly fond, Guy de Maupassant. Between ourselves, I prefer this generation even to its masters, all of whom were corrupted by German philosophy (Taine, for instance, by Hegel, whom he has to thank for his misunderstanding of great men and great periods). Wherever Germany extends her sway, she ruins culture. It was the war which first saved the spirit of France.... Stendhal is one of the happiest accidents of my life—for everything[Pg 39] that marks an epoch in it has been brought to me by accident and never by means of a recommendation. He is quite priceless, with his psychologist's eye, quick at forestalling and anticipating; with his grasp of facts, which is reminiscent of the same art in the greatest of all masters of facts (ex ungue Napoleonem); and, last but not least, as an honest atheist—a specimen which is both rare and difficult to discover in France—all honour to Prosper Mérimée!... Maybe that I am even envious of Stendhal? He robbed me of the best atheistic joke, which I of all people could have perpetrated: "God's only excuse is that He does not exist" ... I myself have said somewhere—What has been the greatest objection to Life hitherto?—God....

4

It was Heinrich Heine who gave me the most perfect idea of what a lyrical poet could be. In vain do I search through all the kingdoms of antiquity or of modern times for anything to resemble his sweet and passionate music. He possessed that divine wickedness, without which perfection itself becomes unthinkable to me,—I estimate the value of men, of races, according to the extent to which they are unable to conceive of a god who has not a dash of the satyr in him. And with what mastery he wields his native tongue! One day it will be said of Heine and me that we were by far the greatest artists of the German language that have ever existed, and that we left all the efforts that mere Germans made in this language an incalculable distance[Pg 40] behind us. I must be profoundly related to Byron's Manfred: of all the dark abysses in this work I found the counterparts in my own soul—at the age of thirteen I was ripe for this book. Words fail me, I have only a look, for those who dare to utter the name of Faust in the presence of Manfred. The Germans are incapable of conceiving anything sublime: for a proof of this, look at Schumann! Out of anger for this mawkish Saxon, I once deliberately composed a counter-overture to Manfred, of which Hans von Bülow declared he had never seen the like before on paper: such compositions amounted to a violation of Euterpe. When I cast about me for my highest formula of Shakespeare, I find invariably but this one: that he conceived the type of Cæsar. Such things a man cannot guess—he either is the thing, or he is not. The great poet draws his creations only from out of his own reality. This is so to such an extent, that often after a lapse of time he can no longer endure his own work.... After casting a glance between the pages of my Zarathustra, I pace my room to and fro for half an hour at a time, unable to overcome an insufferable fit of tears. I know of no more heartrending reading than Shakespeare: how a man must have suffered to be so much in need of playing the clown! Is Hamlet understood? It is not doubt, but certitude that drives one mad.... But in order to feel this, one must be profound, one must be an abyss, a philosopher.... We all fear the truth.... And, to make a confession; I feel instinctively certain and convinced that Lord Bacon is the originator, the self-torturer, of this most sinister kind of literature:[Pg 41] what do I care about the miserable gabble of American muddlers and blockheads? But the power for the greatest realism in vision is not only compatible with the greatest realism in deeds, with the monstrous in deeds, with crime—it actually presupposes the latter. ... We do not know half enough about Lord Bacon—the first realist in all the highest acceptation of this word—to be sure of everything he did, everything he willed, and everything he experienced in his inmost soul.... Let the critics go to hell! Suppose I had christened my Zarathustra with a name not my own,—let us say with Richard Wagner's name,—the acumen of two thousand years would not have sufficed to guess that the author of Human, all-too-Human was the visionary of Zarathustra.

5

As I am speaking here of the recreations of my life, I feel I must express a word or two of gratitude for that which has refreshed me by far the most heartily and most profoundly. This, without the slightest doubt, was my intimate relationship with Richard

Wagner. All my other relationships with men I treat quite lightly; but I would not have the days I spent at Tribschen—those days of confidence, of cheerfulness, of sublime flashes, and of profound moments—blotted from my life at any price. I know not what Wagner may have been for others; but no cloud ever darkened our sky. And this brings me back again to France,—I have no arguments against Wagnerites, and hoc genus omne who believe that they do honour to Wagner[Pg 42] by believing him to be like themselves; for such people I have only a contemptuous curl of my lip. With a nature like mine, which is so strange to everything Teutonic, that even the presence of a German retards my digestion, my first meeting with Wagner was the first moment in my life in which I breathed freely: I felt him, I honoured him, as a foreigner, as the opposite and the incarnate contradiction of all "German virtues." We who as children breathed the marshy atmosphere of the fifties, are necessarily pessimists in regard to the concept "German"; we cannot be anything else than revolutionaries—we can assent to no state of affairs which allows the canting bigot to be at the top. I care not a jot whether this canting bigot acts in different colours to-day, whether he dresses in scarlet or dons the uniform of a hussar.[2] Very well, then! Wagner was a revolutionary—he fled from the Germans.... As an artist, a man has no home in Europe save in Paris; that subtlety of all the five senses which Wagner's art presupposes, those fingers that can detect slight gradations, psychological morbidity—all these things can be found only in Paris. Nowhere else can you meet with this passion for questions of form, this earnestness in matters of mise-en-scène, which is the Parisian earnestness par excellence. In Germany no one has any idea of the tremendous ambition that fills the heart of a Parisian artist. The German is a good fellow. Wagner was by no means a good fellow.... But I have already said quite[Pg 43] enough on the subject of Wagner's real nature (see Beyond Good and Evil, Aphorism 269), and about those to whom he is most closely related. He is one of the late French romanticists, that high-soaring and heaven-aspiring band of artists, like Delacroix and Berlioz, who in their inmost nacres are sick and incurable, and who are all fanatics of expression, and virtuosos through and through.... Who, in sooth, was the first intelligent follower of Wagner? Charles

Baudelaire, the very man who first understood Delacroix—that typical decadent, in whom a whole generation of artists saw their reflection; he was perhaps the last of them too.... What is it that I have never forgiven Wagner? The fact that he condescended to the Germans—that he became a German Imperialist.... Wherever Germany spreads, she ruins culture.

6

Taking everything into consideration, I could never have survived my youth without Wagnerian music. For I was condemned to the society of Germans. If a man wish to get rid of a feeling of insufferable oppression, he has to take to hashish. Well, I had to take to Wagner. Wagner is the counter-poison to everything essentially German—the fact that he is a poison too, I do not deny. From the moment that Tristan was arranged for the piano—all honour to you, Herr von Bülow!—I was a Wagnerite. Wagner's previous works seemed beneath me—they were too commonplace, too "German." ... But to this day I am still seeking for a work which would be a match to Tristan in[Pg 44] dangerous fascination, and possess the same gruesome and dulcet quality of infinity; I seek among all the arts in vain. All the quaint features of Leonardo da Vinci's work lose their charm at the sound of the first bar in Tristan. This work is without question Wagner's non plus ultra; after its creation, the composition of the Mastersingers and of the Ring was a relaxation to him. To become more healthy—this in a nature like Wagner's amounts to going backwards. The curiosity of the psychologist is so great in me, that I regard it as quite a special privilege to have lived at the right time, and to have lived precisely among Germans, in order to be ripe for this work. The world must indeed be empty for him who has never been unhealthy enough for this "infernal voluptuousness": it is allowable, it is even imperative, to employ a mystic formula for this purpose. I suppose I know better than any one the prodigious feats of which Wagner was capable, the fifty worlds of strange ecstasies to which no one else had wings to soar; and as I am alive to-day and strong enough to turn even the most suspicious and most dangerous things to my own advantage, and thus to grow stronger, I declare Wagner to have been the greatest benefactor of my life. The bond which unites us is the fact that we have suffered greater agony, even at each other's hands, than most men are able to bear nowadays, and this will always keep our names associated in the minds of men. For, just as Wagner is merely a misunderstanding among Germans, so, in truth, am I, and ever will be. Ye lack two centuries of psychological and artistic discipline, my[Pg 45] dear countrymen!... But ye can never recover the time lost.

7

To the most exceptional of my readers I should like to say just one word about what I really exact from music. It must be cheerful and yet profound, like an October afternoon. It must be original, exuberant, and tender, and like a dainty, soft woman in roguishness and grace ... I shall never admit that a German can understand what music is. Those musicians who are called German, the greatest and most famous foremost, are all foreigners, either Slavs, Croats, Italians, Dutchmen—or Jews; or else, like Heinrich Schütz, Bach, and Händel, they are Germans of a strong race which is now extinct. For my own part, I have still enough of the Pole left in me to let all other music go, if only I can keep Chopin. For three reasons I would except Wagner's Siegfried Idyll, and perhaps also one or two things of Liszt, who excelled all other musicians in the noble tone of his orchestration; and finally everything that has been produced beyond the Alps—this side of the Alps.[3] I could not possibly dispense with Rossini, and still less with my Southern soul in music, the work of my Venetian maestro, Pietro Gasti. And when I say beyond the Alps, all I really mean is Venice. If I try to find a new word for music, I can never find any other than Venice. I know not how to draw any distinction[Pg 46] between tears and music. I do not know how to think either of joy, or of the south, without a shudder of fear.

On the bridge I stood
Lately, in gloomy night.
Came a distant song:
In golden drops it rolled

Over the glittering rim away.
Music, gondolas, lights—
Drunk, swam far forth in the gloom....

A stringed instrument, my soul,
Sang, imperceptibly moved,
A gondola song by stealth,
Gleaming for gaudy blessedness.
—Hearkened any thereto?

8

In all these things—in the choice of food, place, climate, and recreation—the instinct of self-preservation is dominant, and this instinct manifests itself with least ambiguity when it acts as an instinct of defence. To close one's eyes to much, to seal one's ears to much, to keep certain things at a distance—this is the first principle of prudence, the first proof of the fact that a man is not an accident but a necessity. The popular word for this instinct of defence is taste. A man's imperative command is not only to say "no" in cases where "yes" would be a sign of "disinterestedness," but also to say "no" as seldom as possible. One must part with all that which compels one to repeat "no," with ever greater frequency. The rationale of this principle is that all discharges of[Pg 47] defensive forces, however slight they may be, involve enormous and absolutely superfluous losses when they become regular and habitual. Our greatest expenditure of strength is made up of those small and most frequent discharges of it. The act of keeping things off, of holding them at a distance, amounts to a discharge of strength,—do not deceive yourselves on this point!—and an expenditure of energy directed at purely negative ends. Simply by being compelled to keep constantly on his guard, a man may grow so weak as to be unable any longer to defend himself. Suppose I were to step out of my house, and, instead of the quiet and aristocratic city of Turin, I were to find a German provincial town, my instinct would have to brace itself together in order to repel all that which would pour in upon it from this crushed-down and cowardly world. Or suppose I were to find a large German city—that structure of vice in which nothing grows, but where every single thing, whether good or bad, is squeezed in from outside. In such circumstances should I not be compelled to become a hedgehog? But to have prickles amounts to a squandering of strength; they even constitute a twofold luxury, when, if we only chose to do so, we could dispense with them and open our hands instead....

Another form of prudence and self-defence consists in trying to react as seldom as possible, and to keep one's self aloof from those circumstances and conditions wherein one would be condemned, as it were, to suspend one's "liberty" and one's initiative, and become a mere reacting medium.[Pg 48] As an example of this I point to the intercourse with books. The scholar who, in sooth, does little else than handle books—with the philologist of average attainments their number may amount to two hundred a day—ultimately forgets entirely and completely the capacity of thinking for himself. When he has not a book between his fingers he cannot think. When he thinks, he responds to a stimulus (a thought he has read),—finally all he does is to react. The scholar exhausts his whole strength in saying either "yes" or "no" to matter which has already been thought out, or in criticising it—he is no longer capable of thought on his own account.... In him the instinct of self-defence has decayed, otherwise he would defend himself against books. The scholar is a decadent. With my own eyes I have seen gifted, richly endowed, and free-spirited natures already "read to ruins" at thirty, and mere wax vestas that have to be rubbed before they can give off any sparks—or "thoughts." To set to early in the morning, at the break of day, in all the fulness and dawn of one's strength, and to read a book—this I call positively vicious!

9

At this point I can no longer evade a direct answer to the question, how one becomes what one is. And in giving it, I shall have to touch upon that masterpiece in the art of self-preservation, which is selfishness. ... Granting that one's life-task—the determination and the fate of one's life-task—greatly exceeds the average measure of[Pg 49] such things, nothing more dangerous could be conceived than to come face to face with one's self by the side of this life-task. The fact that one becomes what one is, presupposes that one has not the remotest suspicion of what one is. From this standpoint even the blunders of one's life have their own meaning and value, the temporary deviations and aberrations, the moments of hesitation and of modesty, the earnestness wasted upon duties which lie outside the actual life-task. In these matters great wisdom, perhaps even the highest wisdom, comes into activity: in these circumstances, in which nosce teipsum would be the sure road to ruin, forgetting one's self, misunderstanding one's self, belittling one's self, narrowing one's self, and making one's self mediocre, amount to reason itself. Expressed morally, to love one's neighbour and to live for others and for other things may be the means of protection employed to maintain the hardest kind of egoism. This is the exceptional case in which I, contrary to my principle and conviction, take the side of the altruistic instincts; for here they are concerned in subserving selfishness and self-discipline. The whole surface of consciousness—for consciousness is a surface—must be kept free from any one of the great imperatives. Beware even of every striking word, of every striking attitude! They are all so many risks which the instinct runs of "understanding itself" too soon. Meanwhile the organising "idea," which is destined to become master, grows and continues to grow into the depths,—it begins to command, it leads you slowly back from your[Pg 50] deviations and aberrations, it prepares individual qualities and capacities, which one day will make themselves felt as indispensable to the whole of your task,—step by step it cultivates all the serviceable faculties, before it ever whispers a word concerning the dominant task, the "goal," the "object," and the "meaning" of it all. Looked at from this standpoint my life is simply amazing. For the task of transvaluing values, more capacities were needful perhaps than could well be found side by side in one individual; and above all, antagonistic capacities which had to be free from the mutual strife and destruction which they involve. An order of rank among capacities; distance; the art of separating without creating hostility; to refrain from confounding things; to keep from reconciling things; to possess enormous multifariousness and yet to be the reverse of chaos—all this was the first condition, the long secret work, and the artistic mastery of my instinct. Its superior guardianship manifested itself with such exceeding strength, that not once did I ever dream of what was growing within me—until suddenly all my capacities were ripe, and one day burst forth in all the perfection of their highest bloom. I cannot remember ever having exerted myself, I can point to no trace of struggle in my life; I am the reverse of a heroic nature. To "will" something, to "strive" after something, to have an "aim" or a "desire" in my mind—I know none of these things from experience. Even at this moment I look out upon my future—a broad future!—as upon a calm sea: no sigh of longing[Pg 51] makes a ripple on its surface. I have not the slightest wish that anything should be otherwise than it is: I myself would not be otherwise.... But in this matter I have always been the same. I have never had a desire. A man who, after his four-and-fortieth year, can say that he has never bothered himself about honours, women, or money!—not that they did not come his way.... It was thus that I became one day a University Professor—I had never had the remotest idea of such a thing; for I was scarcely four-and-twenty years of age. In the same way, two years previously, I had one day become a philologist, in the sense that my first philological work, my start in every way, was expressly obtained by my master Ritschl for publication in his Rheinisches Museum.[4] (Ritschl—and I say it in all reverence—was the only genial scholar that I have ever met. He possessed that pleasant kind of depravity which distinguishes us Thuringians, and which makes even a German sympathetic—even in the pursuit of truth we prefer to avail ourselves of roundabout ways. In saying this I do not mean to underestimate in any way my Thuringian brother, the intelligent Leopold von Ranke....)

10

You may be wondering why I should actually have related all these trivial and, according to traditional accounts, insignificant details to you; such action can but tell against me, more particularly if[Pg 52] I am fated to figure in great causes. To this I reply that these trivial matters—diet, locality, climate, and one's mode of recreation, the whole casuistry of; self-love—are inconceivably more important than, all that which has hitherto been held in high esteem! It is precisely in this quarter that we must begin to learn afresh. All those things which mankind has valued with such earnestness heretofore are not even real; they are mere creations of fancy, or, more strictly speaking, lies born of the evil instincts of diseased and, in the deepest sense, noxious natures—all the concepts, "God," "soul," "virtue," "sin," "Beyond," "truth," "eternal life." ... But the greatness of human nature, its "divinity," was sought for in them.... All questions of politics, of social order, of education, have been falsified, root and branch, owing to the fact that the most noxious men have been taken for great men, and that people were taught to despise the small things, or rather the fundamental things, of life. If I now choose to compare myself with those creatures who have hitherto been honoured as the first among men, the difference becomes obvious. I do not reckon the so-called "first" men even as human beings—for me they are the excrements of mankind, the products of disease and of the instinct of revenge: they are so many monsters laden with rottenness, so many hopeless incurables, who avenge themselves on life.... I wish to be the opposite of these people: it is my privilege to have the very sharpest discernment for every sign of healthy instincts. There is no such thing as a morbid trait in me; even in times of serious illness I have never[Pg 53] grown morbid, and you might seek in vain for a trace of fanaticism in my nature. No one can point to any moment of my life in which I have assumed either an arrogant or a pathetic attitude. Pathetic attitudes are not in keeping with greatness; he who needs attitudes is false.... Beware of all picturesque men! Life was easy—in fact easiest—to me, in those periods when it exacted the heaviest duties from me. Whoever could have seen me during the seventy days of this autumn, when, without interruption, I did a host of things of the highest rank—things that no man can do nowadays—with a sense of responsibility for all the ages yet to come, would have noticed no sign of tension in my condition, but rather a state of overflowing freshness and good cheer. Never have I eaten with more pleasant sensations, never has my sleep been better. I know of no other manner of dealing with great tasks, than as play: this, as a sign of greatness, is an essential prerequisite. The slightest constraint, a sombre mien, any hard accent in the voice—all these things are objections to a man, but how much more to his work!... One must not have nerves.... Even to suffer from solitude is an objection—the only thing I have always suffered from is "multitude."[5][Pg 54] At an absurdly tender age, in fact when I was seven years old, I already knew that no human speech would ever reach me: did any one ever see me sad on that account? At present I still possess the same affability towards everybody, I am even full of consideration for the lowest: in all this there is not an atom of haughtiness or of secret contempt. He whom I despise soon guesses that he is despised by me: the very fact of my existence is enough to rouse indignation in all those who have polluted blood in their veins. My formula for greatness in man is! amor fati: the fact that a man wishes nothing to be different, either in front of him or behind him, or for all eternity. Not only must the necessary be borne, and on no account concealed,—all idealism is falsehood in the face of necessity,—but it must also be loved....

[1]Nietzsche, as is well known, devoted much time when a student at Leipzig to the study of three Greek philosophers, Theognis, Diogenes Laertius, and Democritus. This study first bore fruit in the case of a paper, Zur Geschichte der Theognideischen Spruchsammlung, which was subsequently published by the most influential journal of classical philology in Germany. Later, however, it enabled Nietzsche to enter for the prize offered by the University of Leipzig for an essay, De fontibus Diogenis Laertii. He was successful in gaining the prize, and the treatise was afterwards published in the Rheinisches Museum, and is still quoted as an authority. It is to this essay, written when he was twenty-three years of age, that he here refers.—TR.

[2]The favourite uniform of the German Emperor, William II.—TR.

[3]In the latter years of his life, Nietzsche practically made Italy his home.—TR.

[5]The German words are, Einsamkeit and Vielsamkeit. The latter was coined by Nietzsche. The English word "multitude" should, therefore, be understood as signifying multifarious instincts and gifts, which in Nietzsche strove for ascendancy and caused him more suffering than any solitude. Complexity of this sort, held in check by a dominant instinct, as in Nietzsche's case, is of course the only possible basis of an artistic nature.—TR.

WHY I WRITE SUCH EXCELLENT BOOKS

1

I am one thing, my creations are another. Here, before I speak of the books themselves, I shall touch upon the question of the understanding and misunderstanding with which they have met. I shall proceed to do this in as perfunctory a manner as the occasion demands; for the time has by no means come for this question. My time has not yet come either; some are born posthumously. One s day institutions will be needed in which men will live and teach, as I understand living and teaching; maybe, also, that by that time, chairs will be founded and endowed for the interpretation of Zarathustra. But I should regard it as a complete contradiction of myself, if I expected to find ears and eyes for my truths to-day: the fact that no one listens to me, that no one knows how to receive at my hands to-day, is not only comprehensible, it seems to me quite the proper thing. I do not wish to be mistaken for another—and to this end I must not mistake myself. To repeat what I have already said, I can point to but few instances of ill-will in my life: and as for literary ill-will, I could mention scarcely a single example of it. On the other hand, I have met with far too much pure foolery!... It seems to me that to take up one[Pg 56] of my books is one of the rarest honours that a man can pay himself—even supposing that he put his shoes from off his feet beforehand, not to mention boots.... When on one occasion Dr. Heinrich von Stein honestly complained that he could not understand a word of my Zarathustra, I said to him that this was just as it should be: to have understood six sentences in that book—that is to say, to have lived them—raises a man to a higher level among mortals than "modern" men can attain. With this feeling of distance how could I even wish to be read by the "moderns" whom I know! My triumph is just the opposite of what Schopenhauer's was—I say "Non legor, non legar."—Not that I should like to underestimate the pleasure I have derived from the innocence with which my works have frequently been contradicted. As late as last summer, at a time when I was attempting, perhaps by means of my weighty, all-too-weighty literature, to throw the rest of literature off its balance, a certain professor of Berlin University kindly gave me to understand that I ought really to make use of a different form: no one could read such stuff as I wrote.—Finally, it was not Germany, but Switzerland that presented me with the two most extreme cases. An essay on Beyond Good and Evil, by Dr. V. Widmann in the paper called the Bund, under the heading "Nietzsche's Dangerous Book," and a general account of all my works, from the pen of Herr Karl Spitteler, also in the Bund, constitute a maximum in my life—I shall not say of what.... The latter treated my Zarathustra, for instance as "advanced exercises in style," and expressed[Pg 57] the wish that later on I might try and attend to the question of substance as well; Dr. Widmann assured me of his respect for the courage I showed in endeavouring to abolish all decent feeling. Thanks to a little trick of destiny, every sentence in these criticisms seemed, with a consistency that I could but admire, to be an inverted truth. In fact it was most remarkable that all one had to do was to "transvalue all values," in order to hit the nail on the head with regard to me, instead of striking my head with the nail.... I am more particularly anxious therefore to discover an explanation. After all, no one can draw more out of things, books included, than he already knows. A man has no ears for that to which experience has given him no access. To take an extreme case, suppose a book contains simply incidents which lie quite outside the range of general or even rare experience—suppose it to be the first language to express a whole series of experiences. In this case nothing it contains will really be heard at all, and, thanks to an acoustic delusion, people will believe that where nothing is heard there is nothing to hear.... This, at least, has been my usual experience, and proves, if you will, the originality of my experience. He who thought he had understood something in my work, had as a rule adjusted something in it to his own image— not infrequently the very opposite of myself, an "idealist," for instance. He who understood nothing in my work, would deny that I was worth considering at all.—The word "Superman," which designates a type of man that would be one of nature's rarest and luckiest strokes,[Pg 58] as opposed to "modern" men, to "good" men, to Christians and other Nihilists,—a word which in the mouth of Zarathustra, the annihilator of morality, acquires a very profound meaning,—is understood almost everywhere, and with perfect innocence, in the light of those values to which a flat contradiction was made manifest in the figure of Zarathustra—that is to say, as an "ideal" type, a higher kind of man, half "saint" and half "genius." ... Other learned cattle have suspected me of Darwinism on account of this word: even the "hero cult" of that great unconscious and involuntary swindler, Carlyle,—a cult which I repudiated with such roguish malice,—was recognised in my doctrine. Once, when I whispered to a man that he would do better I to seek for the Superman in a Cæsar Borgia than in a Parsifal, he could not believe his ears. The fact that I am quite free from curiosity in regard to criticisms of my books, more particularly when they appear in newspapers, will have to be forgiven me. My friends and my publishers know this, and never speak to me of such things. In one particular case, I once saw all the sins that had been committed against a single book—it was Beyond Good and Evil; I could tell you a nice story about it. Is it possible that the National-Zeitung—a Prussian paper (this comment is for the sake of my foreign readers—for my own part, I beg to state, I read only Le Journal des Débats)—really and seriously regarded the book as a "sign of the times," or a genuine and typical example of Tory philosophy,[1][Pg 59] for which the Kreuz-Zeitung had not sufficient courage?...

2

This was said for the benefit of Germans: for everywhere else I have my readers—all of them exceptionally intelligent men, characters that have won their spurs and that have been reared in high offices and superior duties; I have even real geniuses among my readers. In Vienna, in St Petersburg, in Stockholm, in Copenhagen, in Paris, and New York—I have been discovered everywhere: I have not yet been discovered in Europe's flatland—Germany.... And, to make a confession, I rejoice much more heartily over those who do not read me, over those who have neither heard of my name nor of the word philosophy. But whithersoever I go, here in Turin, for instance, every face brightens and softens at the sight of me.

A thing that has flattered me more than anything else hitherto, is the fact that old market-women cannot rest until they have picked out the sweetest of their grapes for me. To this extent must a man be a philosopher.... It is not in vain that the Poles are considered as the French among the Slavs. A charming Russian lady will not be mistaken for a single moment concerning my origin. I am not successful at being pompous, the most I can do is to appear embarrassed.... I can think in German, I can feel in German—I can do most things; but this is beyond my powers.... My old master Ritschl[Pg 60] went so far as to declare that I planned even my philological treatises after the manner of a Parisian novelist—that I made them absurdly thrilling. In Paris itself people are surprised at "toutes mes audaces et finesses";—the words are Monsieur Taine's;—I fear that even in the highest forms of the dithyramb, that salt will be found pervading my work which never becomes insipid, which never becomes "German"—and that is, wit.... I can do nought else. God help me! Amen.—We all know, some of us even from experience, what a "long-ears" is. Well then, I venture to assert that I have the smallest ears that have ever been seen. This fact is not without interest to women—it seems to me they feel that I understand them better!... I am essentially the anti-ass, and on this account alone a monster in the world's history—in Greek, and not only in Greek, I am the Antichrist.

3

I am to a great extent aware of my privileges as a writer: in one or two cases it has even been brought home to me how very much the habitual > reading of my works "spoils" a man's taste. Other books simply cannot be endured after mine, and least of all philosophical ones. It is an incomparable distinction to cross the threshold of this noble and subtle world—in order to do so one must certainly not be a German; it is, in short, a distinction which one must have deserved. He, however, who is related to me through loftiness of will, experiences genuine raptures of understanding in[Pg 61] my books: for I swoop down from heights into which no bird has ever soared; I know abysses into which no foot has ever slipped. People have told me that it is impossible to lay down a book of mine—

that I disturb even the night's rest.... There is no prouder or at the same time more subtle kind of books: they sometimes attain to the highest pinnacle of earthly endeavour, cynicism; to capture their thoughts a man must have the tenderest fingers as well as the most intrepid fists. Any kind of spiritual decrepitude utterly excludes all intercourse with them—even any kind of dyspepsia: a man must have no nerves, but he must have a cheerful belly. Not only the poverty of a man's soul and its stuffy air excludes all intercourse with them, but also, and to a much greater degree, cowardice, uncleanliness, and secret intestinal revengefulness; a word from my lips suffices to make the colour of all evil instincts rush into a face. Among my acquaintances I have a number of experimental subjects, in whom I see depicted all the different, and instructively different, reactions which follow upon a perusal of my works. Those who will have nothing to do with the contents of my books, as for instance my so-called friends, assume an "impersonal" tone concerning them: they wish me luck, and congratulate me for having produced another work; they also declare that my writings show progress, because they exhale a more cheerful spirit.... The thoroughly vicious people, the "beautiful souls," the false from top to toe, do not know in the least what to do with my books—consequently, with the beautiful consistency of all[Pg 62] beautiful souls, they regard my work as beneath them. The cattle among my acquaintances, the mere Germans, leave me to understand, if you please, that they are not always of my opinion, though here and there they agree with me.... I have heard this said even about Zarathustra. "Feminism," whether in mankind or in man, is likewise a barrier to my writings; with it, no one could ever enter into this labyrinth of fearless knowledge. To this end, a man must never have spared himself, he must have been hard in his habits, in order to be good-humoured and merry among a host of inexorable truths. When I try to picture the character of a perfect reader, I always imagine a monster of courage and curiosity, as well as of suppleness, cunning, and prudence—in short, a born adventurer and explorer. After all, I could not describe better than Zarathustra has done unto whom I really address myself: unto whom alone would he reveal his riddle?

"Unto you, daring explorers and experimenters, and unto all who have ever embarked beneath cunning sails upon terrible seas;

"Unto you who revel in riddles and in twilight, whose souls are lured by flutes unto every treacherous abyss:

"For ye care not to grope your way along a thread with craven fingers; and where ye are able to guess, ye hate to argue?"

4

I will now pass just one or two general remarks about my art of style. To communicate a state[Pg 63] an inner tension of pathos by means of signs, including the tempo of these signs,—that is the meaning of every style; and in view of the fact that the multiplicity of inner states in me is enormous, I am capable of many kinds of style—in short, the most multifarious art of style that any man has ever had at his disposal. Any style is good which genuinely communicates an inner condition, which does not blunder over the signs, over the tempo of the signs, or over moods—all the laws of phrasing are the outcome of representing moods artistically. Good style, in itself, is a piece of sheer foolery, mere idealism, like "beauty in itself," for instance, or "goodness in itself," or "the thing-in-itself." All this takes for granted, of course, that there exist ears that can hear, and such men as are capable and worthy of a like pathos, that those are not wanting unto whom one may communicate one's self. Meanwhile my Zarathustra, for instance, is still in quest of such people—alas! he will have to seek a long while yet! A man must be worthy of listening to him.... And, until that time, there will be no one who will understand the art that has been squandered in this book. No one has ever existed who has had more novel, more strange, and purposely created art forms to fling to the winds. The fact that such things were possible in the German language still awaited proof; formerly, I myself would have denied most emphatically that it was possible. Before my time people did not know what could be done with the German language—what could be done with language in general. The art of grand rhythm, of grand[Pg 64] style in periods, for expressing the tremendous fluctuations of sublime and superhuman passion, was first discovered by me: with the dithyramb entitled "The Seven Seals," which constitutes the last discourse of the third part of Zarathustra, I soared miles above all that which heretofore has been called poetry.

5

The fact that the voice which speaks in my works is that of a psychologist who has not his peer, is perhaps the first conclusion at which a good reader will arrive—a reader such as I deserve, and one who reads me just as the good old philologists used to read their Horace. Those propositions about which all the world is fundamentally agreed—not to speak of fashionable philosophy, of moralists and other empty-headed and cabbage-brained people—are to me but ingenuous blunders: for instance, the belief that "altruistic" and "egoistic"; are opposites, while all the time the "ego" itself is merely a "supreme swindle," an "ideal." ... There are no such things as egoistic or altruistic actions: both concepts are psychological nonsense. Or the proposition that "man pursues happiness"; or the proposition that "happiness is the reward of virtue." ... Or the proposition that "pleasure and pain are opposites." ... Morality, the Circe of mankind, has falsified everything psychological, root and branch—it has demoralised everything, even to the terribly nonsensical point of calling love "unselfish." A man must first be firmly poised, he must stand securely on his two legs, otherwise he cannot love at all.[Pg 65] This indeed the girls know only too well: they don't care two pins about unselfish and merely objective men.... May I venture to suggest, incidentally, that I know women? This knowledge is part of my Dionysian patrimony. Who knows? maybe I am the first psychologist of the eternally feminine. Women all like me.... But that's an old story: save, of course, the abortions among them, the emancipated ones, those who lack the where-withal to have children. Thank goodness I am not willing to let myself be torn to pieces! the perfect woman tears you to pieces when she loves you: I know these amiable Mænads.... Oh! what a dangerous, creeping, subterranean little beast of prey she is! And so agreeable withal!

... A little woman, pursuing her vengeance, would force open even the iron gates of Fate itself. Woman is incalculably more wicked than man, she is also cleverer. Goodness in a woman is already a sign of degeneration. All cases of "beautiful souls" in women may be traced to a faulty physiological condition—but I go no further, lest I should become medicynical. The struggle for equal rights is even a symptom of disease; every doctor knows this. The more womanly a woman is, the more she fights tooth and nail against rights in general: the natural order of things, the eternal war between the sexes, assigns to her by far the foremost rank. Have people had ears to hear my definition of love? It is the only definition worthy of a philosopher. Love, in its means, is war; in its foundation, it is the mortal hatred of the sexes. Have you heard my reply to the question how a woman can be cured, "saved"[Pg 66] in fact?—Give her a child! A woman needs children, man is always only a means, thus spake Zarathustra. "The emancipation of women,"—this is the instinctive hatred of physiologically botched—that is to say, barren—women for those of their sisters who are well constituted: the fight against "man" is always only a means, a pretext, a piece of strategy. By trying to rise to "Woman per se," to "Higher Woman," to the "Ideal Woman," all they wish to do is to lower the general level of women's rank: and there are no more certain means to this end than university education, trousers, and the rights of voting cattle. Truth to tell, the emancipated are the anarchists in the "eternally feminine" world, the physiological mishaps, the most deep-rooted instinct of whom is revenge. A whole species of the most malicious "idealism"—which, by the bye, also manifests itself in men, in Henrik Ibsen for instance, that typical old maid—whose object is to poison the clean conscience, the natural spirit, of sexual love.... And in order to leave no doubt in your minds in regard to my opinion, which, on this matter, is as honest as it is severe, I will reveal to you one more clause out of my moral code against vice—with the word "vice" I combat every kind of! opposition to Nature, or, if you prefer fine words, idealism. The clause reads: "Preaching of chastity is a public incitement to unnatural practices. All depreciation of the sexual life, all the sullying of it by means of the concept 'impure,' is the essential crime against Life—is the essential crime against the

Holy Spirit of Life."

In order to give you some idea of myself as a psychologist, let me take this curious piece of psychological analysis out of the book Beyond Good and Evil, in which it appears. I forbid, by the bye, any guessing as to whom I am describing in this passage. "The genius of the heart, as that great anchorite possesses it, the divine tempter and born Pied Piper of consciences, whose voice knows how to sink into the inmost depths of every soul, who neither utters a word nor casts a glance, in which some seductive motive or trick does not lie: a part of whose masterliness is that he understands the art of seeming—not what he is, but that which will place a fresh constraint upon his followers to press ever more closely upon him, to follow him ever more enthusiastically and whole-heartedly.... The genius of the heart, which makes all loud and self-conceited things hold their tongues and lend their ears, which polishes all rough souls and makes them taste a new longing—to lie placid as a mirror, that the deep heavens may be reflected in them.... The genius of the heart which teaches the clumsy and too hasty hand to hesitate and grasp more tenderly; which scents the hidden and forgotten treasure, the pearl of goodness and sweet spirituality, beneath thick black ice, and is a divining rod for every grain of gold, long buried and imprisoned in heaps of mud and sand.... The genius of the heart, from contact with which every man goes away richer, not 'blessed' and overcome, not as though favoured and crushed by the good things of others;[Pg 68] but richer in himself, fresher to himself than before, opened up, breathed upon and sounded by a thawing wind; more uncertain, perhaps, more delicate, more fragile, more bruised; but full of hopes which as yet lack names, full of a new will and striving, full of a new unwillingness and counter-striving." ...

[1]Junker-Philosophie. The landed proprietors constitute the dominating class in Prussia, and it is from this class that all officers and higher officials are drawn. The Kreuz-Zeitung is the organ of the Junker party.—TR.

"THE BIRTH Of TRAGEDY"

1

In order to be fair to the Birth of Tragedy (1872) it is necessary to forget a few things. It created a sensation and even fascinated by means of its mistakes—by means of its application to Wagnerism, as if the latter were the sign of an ascending tendency. On that account alone, this treatise was an event in Wagner's life: thenceforward great hopes surrounded the name of Wagner. Even to this day, people remind me, sometimes in the middle of Parsifal, that it rests on my conscience if the opinion, that this movement is of great value to culture, at length became prevalent I have often seen the book quoted as "The Second Birth of Tragedy from the Spirit of Music": people had ears only for new formulæ for Wagner's art, his object and his mission—and in this way the real hidden value of the book was overlooked. "Hellenism and Pessimism"—this would have been a less equivocal title, seeing that the book contains the first attempt at showing how the Greeks succeeded in disposing: of pessimism—in what manner they overcame it.[Pg 69] ... Tragedy itself is the proof of the fact that the Greeks were not pessimists: Schopenhauer blundered here as he blundered in everything else.—Regarded impartially, The Birth of Tragedy is a book quite strange to its age: no one would dream that it was begun in the thunder of the battle of Wörth. I thought out these problems on cold September nights beneath the walls of Metz, in the midst of my duties as nurse to the wounded; it would be easier to think that it was written fifty years earlier. Its attitude towards politics is one of indifference,—"un-German,"[1] as people would say to-day,—it smells offensively of Hegel; only in one or two formulæ is it infected with the bitter odour of corpses which is peculiar to Schopenhauer. An idea—the antagonism of the two concepts Dionysian and Apollonian—is translated into metaphysics; history itself is depicted as the development of this idea; in tragedy this antithesis has become unity; from this standpoint things which theretofore had never been face to face are suddenly confronted, and understood and illuminated by each other.... Opera and revolution, for instance.... The two decisive innovations in the book are, first, the comprehension of the Dionysian phenomenon among the Greeks—it provides the first psychological analysis of this phenomenon, and sees in it the single root of all Greek art; and, secondly, the comprehension of [Pg 70] Socraticism—Socrates being presented for the first time as the instrument of Greek dissolution, as a typical decadent. "Reason" versus Instinct. "Reason" at any cost, as a dangerous, life-undermining force. The whole book is profoundly and politely silent concerning Christianity: the latter is neither Apollonian nor Dionysian; it denies all æsthetic values, which are the only values that The Birth of Tragedy recognises. Christianity is most profoundly nihilistic, whereas in the Dionysian symbol, the most extreme limits of a yea-saying attitude to life are attained. In one part of the book the Christian priesthood is referred to as a "perfidious order of goblins," as "subterraneans."

2

This start of mine was remarkable beyond measure. As a confirmation of my inmost personal experience I had discovered the only example of this fact that history possesses,—with this I was the first to understand the amazing Dionysian phenomenon. At the same time, by recognising Socrates as a decadent, I proved most conclusively that the certainty of my psychological grasp of things ran very little risk at the hands of any sort of moral idiosyncrasy: to regard morality itself as a symptom of degeneration is an innovation, a unique event of the first order in the history of knowledge. How high I had soared above the pitifully foolish gabble about Optimism and Pessimism with my two new doctrines! I was the first to see the actual contrast: the degenerate instinct which turns upon life with a subterranean lust of vengeance (Christianity, [Pg 71] Schopenhauer's philosophy, and in some respects too even Plato's philosophy—in short, the whole of idealism in its typical forms), as opposed to a formula of the highest yea-saying to life, born of an abundance and a superabundance of life—a I yea-saying free from all reserve, applying even to suffering, and guilt, and all that is questionable and strange in existence.... This last, most joyous, most exuberant and exultant yea to life, is not only the highest, but also the profoundest conception, and one which is most strictly confirmed and supported by truth and science. Nothing that exists must be suppressed, nothing can be dispensed with. Those aspects of life which Christians and other Nihilists reject, belong to an incalculably higher order in the hierarchy of values, than that which the instinct of degeneration calls good, and may call good. In order to understand this, a certain courage is necessary, and, as a prerequisite of this, a certain superfluity of strength: for a man can approach only as near to truth as he has the courage to advance—that is to say, everything depends strictly upon the measure of his strength. Knowledge, and the affirmation of reality, are just as necessary to the strong man as cowardice, the flight from reality—in fact, the "ideal"—are necessary to the weak inspired by weakness.... These people are not at liberty to "know,"—decadents stand in need of lies,—it is one of their self-preservative measures. He who not only understands the word "Dionysian," but understands himself in that term, does not require any refutation of Plato, or of Christianity, or of Schopenhauer—for his nose scents decomposition.

3

The extent to which I had by means of these doctrines discovered the idea of "tragedy," the ultimate explanation of what the psychology of tragedy is, I discussed finally in The Twilight of the Idols (Aph. 5, part 10).... "The saying of yea to life, and even to its weirdest and most difficult problems: the will to life rejoicing at its own infinite vitality in the sacrifice of its highest types—that is what I called Dionysian, that is what I meant as the bridge to the psychology of the tragic poet. Not to cast out terror and pity, or to purge one's self of dangerous passion by discharging it with vehemence,—this was Aristotle's[2] misunderstanding of it,—but to be far beyond terror and pity and to be the eternal lust of Becoming itself—that lust which also involves the joy of destruction." ... In this sense I have the right to regard myself as the first tragic philosopher—that is to say, the most extreme antithesis and antipodes of a pessimistic philosopher. Before my time no such thing existed as this translation of the Dionysian phenomenon into philosophic emotion: tragic wisdom was lacking; in vain have I sought for signs of it even among the great Greeks in philosophy— those belonging to the two centuries before Socrates. I still remained a little doubtful about Heraclitus, in whose presence, alone, I felt warmer and more at ease than anywhere else. The yea-saying to the impermanence and annihilation of things, which is the decisive feature of a Dionysian[Pg 73] philosophy; the yea-saying to contradiction and war, the postulation of Becoming, together with the radical rejection even of the concept Being— in all these things, at all events, I must recognise him who has come nearest to me in thought hither to. The doctrine of the "Eternal Recurrence"—that is to say, of the absolute and eternal repetition of all things in periodical cycles—this doctrine of Zarathustra's might, it is true, have been taught before. In any case, the Stoics, who derived nearly all their fundamental ideas from Heraclitus, show traces of it.

A tremendous hope finds expression in this work. After all, I have absolutely no reason to renounce the hope for a Dionysian future of music. Let us look a century ahead, and let us suppose that my attempt to destroy two millenniums of hostility to Nature and of the violation of humanity be crowned with success That new party of life-advocates, which will undertake the greatest of all tasks, the elevation and perfection of mankind, as well as the relentless destruction of all degenerate and parasitical elements, will make that superabundance of life on earth once more possible, out of which the Dionysian state will perforce arise again. I promise the advent of a tragic age: the highest art in the saying of yea to life, "tragedy," will be born again when mankind has the knowledge of the hardest, but most necessary of wars, behind it, without, however, suffering from that knowledge.... A psychologist might add that what I heard in Wagnerian[Pg 74] music in my youth and early manhood had nothing whatsoever to do with Wagner; that when I described Dionysian music, I described merely what I personally had heard—that I was compelled instinctively to translate and transfigure everything into the new spirit which filled my breast. A proof of this, and as strong a proof as you could have, is my essay, Wagner in Bayreuth: in all its decisive psychological passages I am the only person concerned—without any hesitation you may read my name or the word "Zarathustra" wherever the text contains the name of Wagner. The whole panorama of the dithyrambic artist is the representation of the already existing author of Zarathustra, and it is drawn with an abysmal depth which does not even once come into contact with the real Wagner. Wagner himself had a notion of the truth; he did not recognise himself in the essay.—In this way, "the idea of Bayreuth" was changed into something which to those who are acquainted with my Zarathustra will be no riddle—that is to say, into the Great Noon when the highest of the elect will consecrate themselves for the greatest of all duties—who knows? the vision of a feast which I may live to see.... The pathos of the first few pages is universal history; the look which is discussed on page 105[3] of the book, is the actual look of Zarathustra; Wagner, Bayreuth, the whole of this petty German wretchedness, is a cloud upon which an infinite Fata Morgana of the future is reflected. Even from the[Pg 75] psychological standpoint, all the decisive traits in my character are introduced into Wagner's nature—the juxtaposition of the most brilliant and most fatal forces, a Will to Power such as no man has ever possessed—inexorable bravery in matters spiritual, an unlimited power of learning unaccompanied by depressed powers for action. Everything in this essay is a prophecy: the proximity of the resurrection of the Greek spirit, the need of men who will be counter-Alexanders, who will once more tie the Gordian knot of Greek culture, after it has been cut. Listen to the world-historic accent with which the concept "sense for the tragic" is introduced on page 180: there are little else but world-historic accents in this essay. This is the strangest kind of "objectivity" that ever existed: my absolute certainty in regard to what I am, projected itself into any chance reality—truth about myself was voiced from out appalling depths. On pages 174 and 175 the style of Zarathustra is described and foretold with incisive certainty, and no more magnificent expression will ever be found than that on pages 144-147 for the event for which Zarathustra stands—that prodigious act of the purification and consecration of mankind.

"THOUGHTS OUT OF SEASON"

1

The four essays composing the Thoughts out of Season are thoroughly warlike in tone. They prove that I was no mere dreamer, that I delight[Pg 76] in drawing the sword—and perhaps, also, that my wrist is dangerously supple. The first onslaught (1873) was directed against German culture, upon which I looked down even at that time with unmitigated contempt Without either sense, substance, or goal, it was simply "public opinion." There could be no more dangerous misunderstanding than to suppose that Germany's success at arms proved anything in favour of German culture—and still less the triumph of this culture; over that of France. The second essay (1874) brings to light that which is dangerous, that which corrodes and poisons life in our manner of pursuing scientific study: Life is diseased, thanks to this dehumanised piece of clockwork and mechanism, thanks to the "impersonality" of the workman, 1 and the false economy of the "division of labour." The object, which is culture, is lost sight of: modern scientific activity as a means thereto simply produces barbarism. In this treatise, the "historical sense," of which this century is so proud, is for the first time recognised as sickness, as a typical symptom of decay. In the third and fourth essays, a sign-post is set up pointing to a higher concept of culture, to a re-establishment of the notion "culture"; and two pictures of the hardest self-love and self-discipline are presented, two essentially un-modern types, full of the most sovereign contempt for all that which lay around them and was called "Empire," "Culture," "Christianity," "Bismarck," and "Success,"—these two types were Schopenhauer and Wagner, or, in a word, Nietzsche....

2

Of these four attacks, the first met with extraordinary success. The stir which it created was in every way gorgeous. I had put my finger on the vulnerable spot of a triumphant nation—I had told it that its victory was not a red-letter day for culture, but, perhaps, something very different. The reply rang out from all sides, and certainly not only from old friends of David Strauss, whom I had made ridiculous as the type of a German Philistine of Culture and a man of smug self-content—in short, as the author of that suburban gospel of his, called The Old and the New Faith (the term "Philistine of Culture" passed into the current language of Germany after the appearance of my book). These old friends, whose vanity as Würtembergians and Swabians I had deeply wounded in regarding their unique animal, their bird of Paradise, as a trifle comic, replied to me as ingenuously and as grossly as I could have wished. The Prussian replies were smarter; they contained more "Prussian blue." The most disreputable attitude was assumed by a Leipzig paper, the egregious Grentzboten; and it cost me some pains to prevent my indignant friends in Bâle from taking action against it. Only a few old gentlemen decided in my favour, and for very diverse and sometimes unaccountable reasons. Among them was one, Ewald of Göttingen, who made it clear that my attack on Strauss had been deadly. There was also the Hegelian, Bruno Bauer, who from that time became one of my most attentive readers. In his later years he liked to refer to[Pg 78] me, when, for instance, he wanted to give Herr von Treitschke, the Prussian Historiographer, a hint as to where he could obtain information about the notion "Culture," of which he (Herr von T.) had completely lost sight. The weightiest and longest notice of my book and its author appeared in Würzburg, and was written by Professor Hoffmann, an old pupil of the philosopher von Baader. The essays made him foresee a great future for me, namely, that of bringing about a sort of crisis and decisive turning-point in the problem of atheism, of which he recognised in me the most instinctive and most radical advocate. It was atheism that had drawn me to Schopenhauer. The review which received by far the most attention, and which excited the most bitterness, was an extraordinarily powerful and plucky appreciation of my work by Carl Hillebrand, a man who was usually so mild, and the last humane German who knew how to wield a pen. The article appeared in the Augsburg Gazette, and it can be read to-day, couched in rather more cautious language, among his collected essays. In it my work was referred to as an event, as a decisive turning-point, as the first sign of an awakening, as an excellent symptom, and as an actual revival of German earnestness and of German passion in things spiritual. Hillebrand could speak only in the terms of the highest respect, of the form of my book, of its consummate taste, of its perfect tact in discriminating between persons and causes: he characterised it as the best polemical work in the German language,—the best performance in the art of polemics, which for[Pg 79] Germans is so dangerous and so strongly to be deprecated. Besides confirming my standpoint, he laid even greater stress upon what I had dared to say about the deterioration of language in Germany (nowadays writers assume the airs of Purists[1] and can no longer even construct a sentence); sharing my contempt for the literary stars of this nation, he concluded by expressing his admiration for my courage—that "greatest courage of all which places the very favourites of the people in the dock." ... The after-effects of this essay of mine proved invaluable to me in my life. No one has ever tried to meddle with me since. People are silent. In Germany I am treated with gloomy caution: for years I have rejoiced in the privilege of such absolute freedom of speech, as no one nowadays, least of all in the "Empire," has enough liberty to claim. My paradise is "in the shadow of my sword." At bottom all I had done was to put one of Stendhal's maxims into practice: he advises one to make one's entrance into society by means of a duel. And how well I had chosen my opponent!—the foremost free-thinker of Germany. As a matter of fact, quite a novel kind of free[Pg 80] thought found its expression in this way: up to the present nothing has been more strange and more foreign to my blood than the whole of that European and American species known as litres penseurs. Incorrigible blockheads and clowns of "modern ideas" that they are, I feel much more profoundly at variance with them than with any one of their adversaries. They also wish to "improve" mankind, after their own fashion—that is to say, in their own image; against that which I stand for and desire, they would wage an implacable war, if only they understood it; the whole gang of them still believe in an "ideal." ... I am the first Immoralist.

3

I should not like to say that the last two essays in the Thoughts out of Season, associated with the names of Schopenhauer and Wagner respectively, serve any special purpose in throwing light upon these two cases, or in formulating their psychological problems. This of course does not apply to a few details. Thus, for instance, in the second of the two essays, with a profound certainty of instinct I already characterised the elementary factor in Wagner's nature as a theatrical talent which in all his means and inspirations only draws its final conclusions. At bottom, my desire in this essay was to do something very different from writing psychology: an unprecedented educational problem, a new understanding of self-discipline and self-defence carried to the point of hardness, a road to greatness and to world-historic duties, yearned[Pg 81] to find expression. Roughly speaking, I seized two famous and, theretofore, completely undefined types by the forelock, after the manner in which one seizes opportunities, simply in order to speak my mind on certain questions, in order to have a few more formulas, signs, and means of expression at my disposal. Indeed I actually suggest this, with most unearthly sagacity, on page 183 of Schopenhauer as Educator. Plato made use of Socrates in the same way—that is to say, as a cipher for Plato. Now that, from some distance, I can look back upon the conditions of which these essays are the testimony, I would be loth to deny that they refer simply to me. The essay Wagner in Bayreuth is a vision of my own future; on the other hand, my most secret history, my development, is written down in Schopenhauer as Educator. But, above all, the vow I made I What I am to-day, the place I now hold—at a height from which I speak no longer with words but with thunderbolts!—oh, how far I was from all this in those days! But I saw the land—I did not deceive myself for one moment as to the way, the sea, the danger—and success! The great calm in promising, this happy prospect of a future which must not remain only a promise!—In this book every word has been lived, profoundly and intimately; the most painful things are not lacking in it; it contains words which are positively running with blood. But a wind of great freedom blows over the whole; even its wounds do not constitute an objection. As to what I understand by being a philosopher,—that is to say, a terrible explosive in the presence of[Pg 82] which everything is in danger; as to how I sever my idea of the philosopher by miles from that other idea of him which includes even a Kant, not to speak of the academic "ruminators" and other professors of philosophy,—concerning all these things this essay provides invaluable information, even granting that at bottom, it is not "Schopenhauer as Educator" but "Nietzsche as Educator," who speaks his sentiments in it. Considering that, in those days, my trade was that of a scholar, and perhaps, also, that I understood my trade, the piece of austere scholar psychology which suddenly makes its appearance in this essay is not without importance: it expresses the feeling of distance, and my profound certainty regarding what was my real life-task, and what were merely means, intervals, and accessory work to me. My wisdom consists in my having been many things, and in many places, in order to become one thing—in order to be able to attain to one thing. It was part of my fate to be a scholar for a while.

[1]The Purists constitute a definite body in Germany, which is called the Deutscher Sprach-Verein. Their object is to banish every foreign word from the language, and they carry this process of ostracism even into the domain of the menu, where their efforts at rendering the meaning of French dishes are extremely comical. Strange to say, their principal organ, and their other publications, are by no means free either from solecisms or faults of style, and it is doubtless to this curious anomaly that Nietzsche here refers.—TR.

"HUMAN, ALL-TOO-HUMAN"
1

Human all-too-Human, with its two sequels, is the memorial of a crisis. It is called a book for free spirits: almost every sentence in it is the expression of a triumph—by means of it I purged myself of everything in me which was foreign to my nature. Idealism is foreign to me: the title of the[Pg 83] book means: "Where ye see ideal things I see—human, alas! all-too-human things!" ... I know men better. The word "free spirit" in this book must not be understood as anything else than a spirit that has become free, that has once more taken possession of itself. My tone, the pitch of my voice, has completely changed; the book will be thought clever, cool, and at times both hard and scornful. A certain spirituality, of noble taste, seems to be ever struggling to dominate a passionate torrent at its feet. In this respect there is some sense in the fact that it was the hundredth anniversary of Voltaire's death that served, so to speak, as an excuse for the publication of the book as early as 1878. For Voltaire, as the opposite of every one who wrote after him, was above all a grandee of the intellect; precisely what I am also. The name of Voltaire on one of my writings—that was verily a step forward—in my direction.... Looking into this book a little more closely, you perceive a pitiless spirit who knows all the secret hiding-places in which ideals are wont to skulk—where they find their dungeons, and, as it were, their last refuge. With a torch in my hand, the light of which is not by any means a flickering one, I illuminate this nether world with beams that cut like blades. It is war, but war without powder and smoke, without warlike attitudes, without pathos and contorted limbs—all these things would still be "idealism." One error after the other is quietly laid upon ice; the ideal is not refuted,—it freezes. Here, for instance, "genius" freezes; round the corner the "saint" freezes; under a thick icicle the "hero" freezes; and in the end "faith"[Pg 84] itself freezes. So-called "conviction" and also "pity" are considerably cooled—and almost everywhere the "thing in itself" is freezing to death.

2

This book was begun during the first musical festival at Bayreuth; a feeling of profound strangeness towards everything that surrounded me there, is one of its first conditions. He who has any notion of the visions which even at that time had flitted across my path, will be able to guess what I felt when one day I came to my senses in Bayreuth. It was just as if I had been dreaming. Where on earth was I? I recognised nothing that I saw; I scarcely recognised Wagner. It was in vain that I called up reminiscences. Tribschen—remote island of bliss: not the shadow of a resemblance! The incomparable days devoted to the laying of the first stone, the small group of the initiated who celebrated them, and who were far from lacking fingers for the handling of delicate things: not the shadow of a resemblance! What had happened?—Wagner had been translated into German! The Wagnerite had become master of Wagner!—German art! the German master! German beer!... We who know only too well the kind of refined artists and cosmopolitanism in taste, to which alone Wagner's art can appeal, were beside ourselves at the sight of Wagner bedecked with German virtues. I think I know the Wagnerite, I have experienced three generations of them, from Brendel of blessed memory, who confounded[Pg 85] Wagner with Hegel, to the "idealists" of the Bayreuth Gazette, who confound Wagner with themselves,—I have been the recipient of every kind of confession about Wagner, from "beautiful souls." My kingdom for just one intelligent word I—In very truth, a blood-curdling company! Nohl, Pohl, and Kohl[1] and others of their kidney to infinity! There was not a single abortion that was lacking among them—no, not even the anti-Semite.—Poor Wagner! Into whose hands had he fallen? If only he had gone into a herd of swine! But among Germans! Some day, for the edification of posterity, one ought really to have a genuine Bayreuthian stuffed, or, better still, preserved in spirit,—for it is precisely spirit that is lacking in this quarter,—with this inscription at the foot of the jar: "A sample of the spirit whereon the 'German Empire' was founded." ... But enough! In the middle of the festivities I suddenly packed my trunk and left the place for a few weeks, despite the fact that a charming Parisian lady sought to comfort me; I excused myself to Wagner simply by means of a fatalistic telegram. In a little spot called Klingenbrunn, deeply buried in the recesses of the Bohmerwald, I carried my melancholy and my contempt of Germans about with me like an illness—and, from time to time, under the general title of "The Plough-share," I wrote a sentence or two down in my note-book, nothing but severe psychological stuff, which[Pg 86] it is possible may have found its way into Human, all-too-Human.

3

That which had taken place in me, then, was not only a breach with Wagner—I was suffering from a general aberration of my instincts, of which a mere isolated blunder, whether it were Wagner or my professorship at Bâle, was nothing more than a symptom. I was seized with a fit of impatience with myself; I saw that it was high time that I should turn my thoughts upon my own lot. In a trice I realised, with appalling clearness, how much time had already been squandered—how futile and how senseless my whole existence as a philologist appeared by the side of my life-task. I was ashamed of this false modesty.... Ten years were behind me, during which, to tell the truth, the nourishment of my spirit had been at a standstill, during which I had added not a single useful fragment to my knowledge, and had forgotten countless things in the pursuit of a hotch-potch of dry-as-dust scholarship. To crawl with meticulous care and short-sighted eyes through old Greek metricians—that is what I had come to!... Moved to pity I saw myself quite thin, quite emaciated: realities were only too plainly absent from my stock of knowledge, and what the "idealities" were worth the devil alone knew! A positively burning thirst overcame me: and from that time forward I have done literally nothing else than study physiology, medicine, and natural science—I even returned to the actual study of history only when my life-task compelled me to. It was at that time, too, that I first divined the relation[Pg 87] between an instinctively repulsive occupation, a so-called vocation, which is the last thing to which one is "called" and that need of lulling a feeling of emptiness and hunger, by means of an art which is a narcotic—by means of Wagner's art, for instance. After looking carefully about me,

I have discovered that a large number of young men are all in the same state of distress: one kind of unnatural practice perforce leads to another. In Germany, or rather, to avoid all ambiguity, in the Empire,[2] only too many are condemned to determine their choice too soon, and then to pine away beneath a burden that they can no longer throw off.... Such creatures crave for Wagner as for an opiate,—they are thus able to forget themselves, to be rid of themselves for a moment.... What am I saying!—for five or six hours.

4

At this time my instincts turned resolutely against any further yielding or following on my part, and any further misunderstanding of myself. Every kind of life, the most unfavourable circumstances, illness, poverty—anything seemed to me preferable to that undignified "selfishness" into which I had fallen; in the first place, thanks to my ignorance and youth, and in which I had afterwards remained owing to laziness—the so-called "sense of duty." At this juncture there came to my help, in a way[Pg 88] that I cannot sufficiently admire, and precisely at the right time, that evil heritage which I derive from my father's side of the family, and which, at bottom, is no more than a predisposition to die young. Illness slowly liberated me from the toils, it spared me any sort of sudden breach, any sort of violent and offensive step. At that time I lost not a particle of the good will of others, but rather added to my store. Illness likewise gave me the right completely to reverse my mode of life; it not only allowed, it actually commanded, me to forget; it bestowed upon me the necessity of lying still, of having leisure, of waiting, and of exercising patience.... But all this means thinking!... The state of my eyes alone put an end to all book-wormishness, or, in plain English—philology: I was thus delivered from books; for years I ceased from reading, and this was the greatest boon I ever conferred upon myself! That nethermost self, which was, as it were, entombed, and which had grown dumb because it had been forced to listen perpetually to other selves (for that is what reading means!), slowly awakened; at first it was shy and doubtful, but at last it spoke again Never have I rejoiced more over my condition than during the sickest and most painful moments of my life. You have only to examine The Dawn of Day, or, perhaps, The Wanderer and his Shadow,[3] in order to understand what this "return to myself" actually meant: in itself it was the highest kind of recovery!... My cure was simply the result of it.

5

Human, all-too-Human, this monument of a course of vigorous self-discipline, by means of which I put an abrupt end to all the "Superior Bunkum," "Idealism," "Beautiful Feelings," and other effeminacies that had percolated into my being, was written principally in Sorrento; it was finished and given definite shape during a winter at Bâle, under conditions far less favourable than those in Sorrento. Truth to tell, it was Peter Gast, at that time a student at the University of Bâle, and a devoted friend of mine, who was responsible for the book. With my head wrapped in bandages, and extremely painful, I dictated while he wrote and corrected as he went along—to be accurate, he was the real composer, whereas I was only the author. When the completed book ultimately reached me,—to the great surprise of the serious invalid I then was,—I sent, among others, two copies to Bayreuth. Thanks to a miraculous flash of intelligence on the part of chance, there reached me precisely at the same time a splendid copy of the Parsifal text, with the following inscription from Wagner's pen: "To his dear friend Friedrich Nietzsche, from Richard Wagner, Ecclesiastical Councillor." At this crossing of the two books I seemed to hear an ominous note. Did it not sound as if two swords had crossed? At all events we both felt this was so, for each of us remained silent. At about this time the first Bayreuth Pamphlets appeared: and I then understood the move on my part for which[Pg 90] it was high time. Incredible! Wagner had become pious.

6

My attitude to myself at that time (1876), and the unearthly certitude with which I grasped my life-task and all its world-historic consequences, is well revealed throughout the book, but more particularly in one very significant passage, despite the fact that, with my instinctive cunning, I once more circumvented the use of the little word "I,"—not however, this time, in order to shed world-historic glory on the names of Schopenhauer and Wagner, but on that of another of my friends, the excellent Dr. Paul Rée— fortunately much too acute a creature to be deceived—others were less subtle. Among my readers I have a number of hopeless people, the typical German professor for instance, who can always be recognised from the fact that, judging from the passage in question, he feels compelled to regard the whole book as a sort of superior Realism. As a matter of fact it contradicts five or six of my friend's utterances: only read the introduction to The Genealogy of Morals on this question.—The passage above referred to reads: "What, after all, is the principal axiom to which the boldest and coldest thinker, the author of the book "On the Origin of Moral Sensations" (read Nietzsche, the first Immoralist), "has attained by means of his incisive and decisive analysis of human actions? 'The moral man,' he says is no nearer to the intelligible (metaphysical) world than is the physical man, for there is no intelligible[Pg 91] world.' This theory, hardened and sharpened under the hammer-blow of historical knowledge" (read The Transvaluation of all Values), "may some time or other, perhaps in some future period,—1890!—serve as the axe which is applied to the root of the 'metaphysical need' of man,—whether more as a blessing than a curse to the general welfare it is not easy to say; but in any case as a theory with the most important consequences, at once fruitful and terrible, and looking into the world with that Janus-face which all great knowledge possesses."[4]

"THE DAWN OF DAY:

THOUGHTS ABOUT MORALITY AS A PREJUDICE"
1

With this book I open my campaign against morality. Not that it is at all redolent of powder—you will find quite other and much nicer smells in it, provided that you have any keenness in your nostrils. There is nothing either of light or of heavy artillery in its composition, and if its general end be a negative one, its means are not so—means out of which the end follows like a logical conclusion, not like a cannon-shot. And if the reader takes leave of this book with a feeling of timid caution in regard to everything which has hitherto been honoured and even worshipped under the name of morality, it does not alter the fact that there is not one negative[Pg 92] word, not one attack, and not one single piece of malice in the whole work—on the contrary, it lies in the sunshine, smooth and happy, like a marine animal, basking in the sun between two rocks. For, after all, I was this marine animal: almost every sentence in the book was thought out, or rather caught, among that medley of rocks in the neighbourhood of Genoa, where I lived quite alone, and exchanged secrets with the ocean. Even to this day, when by chance I happen to turn over the leaves of this book, almost every sentence seems to me like a hook by means of which I draw something incomparable out of the depths; its whole skin quivers with delicate shudders of recollection. This book is conspicuous for no little art in gently catching things which whisk rapidly and silently away, moments which I call godlike lizards—not with the cruelty of that young Greek god who simply transfixed the poor little beast; but nevertheless with something pointed—with a pen. "There are so many dawns which have not yet shed their light"—this Indian maxim is written over the doorway of this book. Where does its author seek that new morning, that delicate red, as yet undiscovered, with which another day—ah! a whole series of days, a whole world of new days!—will begin? In the Transvaluation of all Values, in an emancipation from all moral values, in a saying of yea, and in an attitude of trust, to all that which hitherto has been forbidden, despised, and damned. This yea-saying book projects its light, its love, its tenderness, over all evil things, it restores to them their soul, their clear conscience, and their superior right and privilege to exist on earth.[Pg 93] Morality is not assailed, it simply ceases to be considered. This book closes with the word "or?"—it is the only book which closes with an "or?".

2

My life-task is to prepare for humanity one supreme moment in which it can come to its senses, a Great Noon in which it will turn its gaze backwards and forwards, in which it will step from under the yoke of accident and of priests, and for the first time set the question of the Why and Wherefore of humanity as a whole—this life-task naturally follows out of the conviction that mankind does not get on the right road of its own accord, that it is by no means divinely ruled, but rather that it is precisely under the cover of its most holy valuations that the instinct of negation, of corruption, and of degeneration has held such a seductive sway. The question concerning the origin of moral valuations is therefore a matter of the highest importance to me because it determines the future of mankind. The demand made upon us to believe that everything is really in the best hands, that a certain book, the Bible, gives us the definite and comforting assurance that there is a Providence that wisely rules the fate of man,—when translated back into reality amounts simply to this, namely, the will to stifle the truth which maintains the reverse of all this, which is that hitherto man has been in the worst possible hands, and that he has been governed by the physiologically botched, the men of cunning and burning revengefulness, and the so-called "saints[Pg 94]"—those slanderers of the world and traducers of humanity. The definite proof of the fact that the priest (including the priest in disguise, the philosopher) has become master, not only within a certain limited religious community, but everywhere, and that the morality of decadence, the will to nonentity, has become morality per se, is to be found in this: that altruism is now an absolute value, and egoism is regarded with hostility everywhere. He who disagrees with me on this point, I regard as infected. But all the world disagrees with me. To a physiologist a like antagonism between values admits of no doubt. If the most insignificant organ within the body neglects, however slightly, to assert with absolute certainty its self-preservative powers, its recuperative claims, and its egoism, the whole system degenerates. The physiologist insists upon the removal of degenerated parts, he denies all fellow-feeling for such parts, and has not the smallest feeling of pity for them. But the desire of the priest is precisely the degeneration of the whole of mankind; hence his preservation of that which is degenerate—this is what his dominion costs humanity. What meaning have those lying concepts, those handmaids of morality, "Soul," "Spirit," "Free will," "God," if their aim is not the physiological ruin of mankind? When earnestness is diverted from the instincts that aim at self-preservation and an increase of bodily energy, i.e. at an increase of life; when anæmia is raised to an ideal and the contempt of the body is construed as "the salvation of the soul," what is all this if it is not a recipe for decadence? Loss of ballast, resistance[Pg 95] offered to natural instincts, selflessness, in fact—this is what has hitherto been known as morality. With The Dawn of Day I first engaged in a struggle against the morality of self-renunciation.

"JOYFUL WISDOM: LA GAYA SCIENZA"
1

Dawn of Day is a yea-saying book, profound, but clear and kindly. The same applies once more and in the highest degree to La Gaya Scienza: in almost every sentence of this book, profundity and playfulness go gently hand in hand. A verse which expresses my gratitude for the most wonderful month of January which I have ever lived—the whole book is a gift—sufficiently reveals the abysmal depths from which "wisdom" has here become joyful.

"Thou who with cleaving fiery lances
The stream of my soul from its ice dost free,
Till with a rush and a roar it advances
To enter with glorious hoping the sea:
Brighter to see and purer ever,
Free in the bonds of thy sweet constraint,—
So it praises thy wondrous endeavour,
January, thou beauteous saint!"[1]

Who can be in any doubt as to what "glorious hoping" means here, when he has realised the[Pg 96] diamond beauty of the first of Zarathustra's words as they appear in a glow of light at the close of the fourth book? Or when he reads the granite sentences at the end of the third book, wherein a fate for all times is first given a formula? The songs of Prince Free-as-a-Bird, which, for the most part, were written in Sicily, remind me quite forcibly of that Provencal notion of "Gaya Scienza," of that union of singer, knight, and free spirit, which distinguishes that wonderfully early culture of the Provencals from all ambiguous cultures. The last poem of all, "To the Mistral,"—an exuberant dance song in which, if you please, the new spirit dances freely upon the corpse of morality,—is a perfect Provençalism.

[1]Translated for Joyful Wisdom by Paul V. Cohn.—TR.

"THUS SPAKE ZARATHUSTRA: A BOOK FOR ALL AND NONE"

1

I now wish to relate the history of Zarathustra. The fundamental idea of the work, the Eternal Recurrence, the highest formula of a Yea-saying to life that can ever be attained, was first conceived in the month of August 1881. I made a note of the idea on a sheet of paper, with the postscript: "Six thousand feet beyond man and time." That day I happened to be wandering through the woods alongside of the Lake of Silvaplana, and I halted not far from Surlei, beside a huge rock that towered aloft like a pyramid. It was then that[Pg 97] the thought struck me. Looking back now, I find that exactly two months before this inspiration I had an omen of its coming in the form of a sudden and decisive change in my tastes—more particularly in music. The whole of Zarathustra might perhaps be classified under the rubric music. At all events, the essential condition of its production was a second birth within me of the art of hearing. In Recoaro, a small mountain resort near Vicenza, where I spent the spring of 1881, I and my friend and maestro, Peter Gast—who was also one who had been born again, discovered that the phœnix music hovered over us, in lighter and brighter plumage than it had ever worn before. If, therefore, I now calculate from that day forward the sudden production of the book, under the most unlikely circumstances, in February 1883,—the last part, out of which I quoted a few lines in my preface, was written precisely in the hallowed hour when Richard Wagner gave up the ghost in Venice,—I come to the conclusion that the period of gestation covered eighteen months. This period of exactly eighteen months, might suggest, at least to Buddhists, that I am in reality a female elephant The interval was devoted to the Gaya Scienza, which contains hundreds of indications of the proximity of something unparalleled; for, after all, it shows the beginning of Zarathustra, since it presents Zarathustra's fundamental thought in the last aphorism but one of the fourth book. To this interval also belongs that Hymn to Life (for a mixed choir and orchestra), the score of which was published in[Pg 98] Leipzig two years ago by

E. W. Fritsch, and which gave perhaps no slight indication of my spiritual state during this year, in which the essentially yea-saying pathos, which I call the tragic pathos, completely filled me heart and limb. One day people will sing it to my memory. The text, let it be well understood, as there is some misunderstanding abroad on this point, is not by me; it was the astounding inspiration of a young Russian lady, Miss Lou von Salome, with whom I was then on friendly terms. He who is in any way able to make some sense of the last words of the poem, will divine why I preferred and admired it: there is greatness in them. Pain is not regarded as an objection to existence: "And if thou hast no bliss now left to crown me—Lead on! Thou hast thy Sorrow still."

Maybe that my music is also great in this passage. (The last note of the oboe, by the bye, is C sharp, not C. The latter is a misprint.) During the following winter, I was living on that charmingly peaceful Gulf of Rapallo, not far from Genoa, which cuts inland between Chiavari and Cape Porto Fino. My health was not very good; the winter was cold and exceptionally rainy; and the small albergo in which I lived was so close to the water that at night my sleep was disturbed if the sea was rough. These circumstances were surely the very reverse of favourable; and yet, in spite of it all, and as if in proof of my belief that everything decisive comes to life in defiance of every obstacle, it was precisely during this winter and in the midst of these unfavourable[Pg 99] circumstances that my Zarathustra originated. In the morning I used to start out in a southerly direction up the glorious road to Zoagli, which rises up through a forest of pines and gives one a view far out to sea. In the afternoon, or as often as my health allowed, I walked round the whole bay from Santa Margherita to beyond Porto Fino. This spot affected me all the more deeply because it was so dearly loved by the Emperor Frederick III. In the autumn of 1886 I chanced to be there again when he was revisiting this small forgotten world of happiness for the last time. It was on these two roads that all Zarathustra came to me, above all, Zarathustra himself as a type—I ought rather to say that it was on these walks that he waylaid me.

2

In order to understand this type, you must first be quite clear concerning its fundamental physiological condition: this condition is what I call great healthiness. In regard to this idea I cannot make my meaning more plain or more personal than I have done already in one of the last aphorisms (No. 382) of the fifth book of the Gaya Scienza: "We new, nameless, and unfathomable creatures," so reads the passage, "we firstlings of a future still unproved—we who have a new end in view also require new means to that end, that is to say, a new healthiness, a stronger, keener, tougher, bolder, and merrier healthiness than any that has existed heretofore. He who longs to[Pg 100] feel in his own soul the whole range of values and aims that have prevailed on earth until his day, and to sail round all the coasts of this ideal 'Mediterranean Sea'; who, from the adventures of his own inmost experience, would fain know how it feels to be a conqueror and discoverer of the ideal;—as also how it is with the artist, the saint, the legislator, the sage, the scholar, the man of piety and the godlike anchorite of yore;—such a man requires one thing above all for his purpose, and that is, great healthiness—such healthiness as he not only possesses, but also constantly acquires and must acquire, because he is continually sacrificing it again, and is compelled to sacrifice it! And now, therefore, after having been long on the way, we Argonauts of the ideal, whose pluck is greater than prudence would allow, and who are often shipwrecked and bruised, but, as I have said, healthier than people would like to admit, dangerously healthy, and for ever recovering our health—it would seem as if we had before us, as a reward for all our toils, a country still undiscovered, the horizon of which no one has yet seen, a beyond to every country and every refuge of the ideal that man has ever known, a world so overflowing with beauty, strangeness, doubt, terror, and divinity, that both our curiosity and our lust of possession are frantic with eagerness. Alas! how in the face of such vistas, and with such burning desire in our conscience and consciousness, could we still be content with the man of the present day? This is bad indeed; but, that we should regard his worthiest aims and hopes with ill-concealed amusement,[Pg 101] or perhaps give them no thought at all, is inevitable. Another ideal now leads us on, a wonderful, seductive ideal, full of danger, the pursuit of which we should be loath to urge upon any one, because we are not so ready to acknowledge any one's right to it: the ideal of a spirit who plays ingenuously (that is to say, involuntarily, and as the outcome of superabundant energy and power) with everything that, hitherto, has been called holy, good, inviolable, and divine; to whom even the loftiest thing that the people have with reason made their measure of value would be no better than a danger, a decay, and an abasement, or at least a relaxation and temporary forgetfulness of self: the ideal of a humanly superhuman well-being and goodwill, which often enough will seem inhuman—as when, for instance, it stands beside all past earnestness on earth, and all past solemnities in hearing, speech, tone, look, morality, and duty, as their most lifelike and unconscious parody—but with which, nevertheless, great earnestness perhaps alone begins, the first note of interrogation is affixed, the fate of the soul changes, the hour hand moves, and tragedy begins."

3

Has any one at the end of the nineteenth century any distinct notion of what poets of a stronger age understood by the word inspiration? If not, I will describe it. If one had the smallest vestige of superstition left in one, it would hardly be possible completely to set aside the idea that one is the mere[Pg 102] incarnation, mouthpiece, or medium of an almighty power. The idea of revelation, in the sense that something which profoundly convulses and upsets one becomes suddenly visible and audible with indescribable certainty and accuracy—describes the simple fact. One hears—one does not seek; one takes—one does not ask who gives: a thought suddenly flashes up like lightning, it comes with necessity, without faltering—I have never had any choice in the matter. There is an ecstasy so great that the immense strain of it is sometimes relaxed by a flood of tears, during which one's steps now involuntarily rush and anon involuntarily lag. There is the feeling that one is utterly out of hand, with the very distinct consciousness of an endless number of fine thrills and titillations descending to one's very toes;—there is a depth of happiness in which the most painful and gloomy parts do not act as antitheses to the rest, but are produced and required as necessary shades of colour in such an overflow of light. There is an instinct for rhythmic relations which embraces a whole world of forms (length, the need of a wide-embracing rhythm, is almost the measure of the force of an inspiration, a sort of counterpart to its pressure and tension). Everything happens quite involuntarily, as if in a tempestuous outburst of freedom, of absoluteness, of power and divinity. The involuntary nature of the figures and similes is the most remarkable thing; one loses all perception of what is imagery and metaphor; everything seems to present itself as the readiest, the truest, and simplest means of expression. It actually seems, to use one of Zarathustra's[Pg 103] own phrases, as if all things came to one, and offered themselves as similes. ("Here do all things come caressingly to thy discourse and flatter thee, for they would fain ride upon thy back. On every simile thou ridest here unto every truth. Here fly open unto thee all the speech and word shrines of the world, here would all existence become speech, here would all Becoming learn of thee how to speak.") This is my experience of inspiration. I do not doubt but that I should have to go back thousands of years before I could find another who could say to me: "It is mine also!"

4

For a few weeks afterwards I lay an invalid in Genoa. Then followed a melancholy spring in Rome, where I only just managed to live—and this was no easy matter. This city, which is absolutely unsuited to the poet-author of Zarathustra, and for the choice of which I was not responsible, made me inordinately miserable. I tried to leave it. I wanted to go to Aquila—the opposite of Rome in every respect, and actually founded in a spirit of hostility towards that city, just as I also shall found a city some day, as a memento of an atheist and genuine enemy of the Church, a person very closely related to me, the great Hohenstaufen, the Emperor Frederick II. But Fate lay behind it all: I had to return again to Rome. In the end I was obliged to be satisfied with the Piazza Barberini, after I had exerted myself in vain to find an anti-Christian quarter. I fear that on one occasion, to avoid bad[Pg 104] smells as much as possible, I actually inquired at the Palazzo del Quirinale whether they could not provide a quiet room for a philosopher. In a chamber high above the Piazza just mentioned, from which one obtained a general view of Rome, and could hear the fountains plashing far below, the loneliest of all songs was composed—"The Night-Song." About this time I was obsessed by an unspeakably sad melody, the refrain of which I recognised in the affords, "dead through immortality," ... In the summer, finding myself once more in the sacred place where the first thought of Zarathustra flashed like a light across my mind, I conceived the second part. Ten days sufficed. Neither for the second, the first, nor the third part, have I required a day longer. In the ensuing winter, beneath the halcyon sky of Nice, which then for the first time poured its light into my life, I found the third Zarathustra—and came to the end of my task: the whole having occupied me scarcely a year. Many hidden corners and heights in the country round about Nice are hallowed for me by moments that I can never forget. That decisive chapter, entitled "Old and New Tables," was composed during the arduous ascent from the station to Eza—that wonderful Moorish village in the rocks. During those moments when my creative energy flowed most plentifully, my muscular activity was always greatest. The body is inspired: let us waive the question of "soul." I might often have been seen dancing in those days, and I could then walk for seven or eight hours on end over the hills without a suggestion of fatigue. I slept well and[Pg 105] laughed a good deal—I was perfectly robust and patient.

5

With the exception of these periods of industry lasting ten days, the years I spent during the production of Zarathustra, and thereafter, were for me years of unparalleled distress. A man pays dearly for being immortal: to this end he must die many times over during his life. There is such a thing as what I call the rancour of greatness: everything great, whether a work or a deed, once it is completed, turns immediately against its author. The very fact that he is its author makes him weak at this time. He can no longer endure his deed. He can no longer look it full in the face. To have something at one's back which one could never have willed, something to which the knot of human destiny is attached—and to be forced thenceforward to bear it on one's shoulders! Why, it almost crushes one! The rancour of greatness! A somewhat different experience is the uncanny silence that reigns about one. Solitude has seven skins which nothing can penetrate. One goes among men; one greets friends: but these things are only new deserts, the looks of those one meets no longer bear a greeting. At the best one encounters a sort of revolt. This feeling of revolt, I suffered, in varying degrees of intensity, at the hands of almost every one who came near me; it would seem that nothing inflicts a deeper wound than suddenly to make one's distance felt. Those noble natures are scarce who[Pg 106] know not how to live unless they can revere. A third thing is the absurd susceptibility of the skin to small pin-pricks, a kind of helplessness in the presence of all small things. This seems to me a necessary outcome of the appalling expenditure of all defensive forces, which is the first condition of every creative act, of every act which proceeds from the most intimate, most secret, and most concealed recesses of a man's being. The small defensive forces are thus, as it were, suspended, and no fresh energy reaches them. I even think it probable that one does not digest so well, that one is less willing to move, and that one is much too open to sensations of coldness and suspicion; for, in a large number of cases, suspicion is merely a blunder in etiology. On one occasion when I felt like this I became conscious of the proximity of a herd of cows, some time before I could possibly have seen it with my eyes, simply owing to a return in me of milder and more humane sentiments: they communicated warmth to me....

6

This work stands alone. Do not let us mention the poets in the same breath; nothing perhaps has ever been produced out of such a superabundance of strength. My concept "Dionysian" here became the highest deed; compared with it everything that other men have done seems poor and limited. The fact that a Goethe or a Shakespeare would not for an instant have known how to take breath in this atmosphere of passion and of the heights; the[Pg 107] fact that by the side of Zarathustra, Dante is no more than a believer, and not one who first creates the truth—that is to say, not a world-ruling spirit, a Fate; the fact that the poets of the Veda were priests and not even fit to unfasten Zarathustra's sandal—all this is the least of things, and gives no idea of the distance, of the azure solitude, in which this work dwells. Zarathustra has an eternal right to say: "I draw around me circles and holy boundaries. Ever fewer are they that mount with me to ever loftier heights. I build me a mountain range of ever holier mountains." If all the spirit and goodness of every great soul were collected together, the whole could not create a single one of Zarathustra's discourses. The ladder upon which he rises and descends is of boundless length; he has seen further, he has willed further, and gone further than any other man. There is contradiction in every word that he utters, this most yea-saying of all spirits. Through him all contradictions are bound up into a new unity. The loftiest and the basest powers of human nature, the sweetest, the lightest, and the most terrible, rush forth from out one spring with everlasting certainty. Until his coming no one knew what was height, or depth, and still less what was truth. There is not a single passage in this revelation of truth which had already been anticipated and divined by even the greatest among men. Before Zarathustra there was no wisdom, no probing of the soul, no art of speech: in his book, the most familiar and most vulgar thing utters unheard-of words. The sentence quivers with passion. Eloquence has become music. Forks of[Pg 108] lightning are hurled towards futures of which no one has ever dreamed before. The most powerful use of parables that has yet existed is poor beside it, and mere child's-play compared with this return of language to the nature of imagery. See how Zarathustra goes down from the mountain and speaks the kindest words to every one! See with what delicate fingers he touches his very adversaries, the priests, and how he suffers with them from themselves! Here, at every moment, man is overcome, and the concept "Superman" becomes the greatest reality,—out of sight, almost far away beneath him, lies all that which heretofore has been called great in man. The halcyonic brightness, the light feet, the presence of wickedness and exuberance throughout, and all that is the essence of the type Zarathustra, was never dreamt of before as a prerequisite of greatness. In precisely these limits of space and in this accessibility to opposites Zarathustra feels himself the highest of all living things: and when you hear how he defines this highest, you will give up trying to find his equal.

"The soul which hath the longest ladder and can step down deepest,

"The vastest soul that can run and stray and rove furthest in its own domain,

"The most necessary soul, that out of desire flingeth itself to chance,

"The stable soul that plungeth into Becoming, the possessing soul that must needs taste of willing and longing,

"The soul that flyeth from itself, and over-taketh itself in the widest circle,

"The wisest soul that folly exhorteth most sweetly,

"The most self-loving soul, in whom all things have their rise, their ebb and flow."

But this is the very idea of Dionysus. Another consideration leads to this idea. The psychological problem presented by the type of Zarathustra is, how can he, who in an unprecedented manner says no, and acts no, in regard to all that which has been affirmed hitherto, remain nevertheless a yea-saying spirit? how can he who bears the heaviest destiny on his shoulders and whose very life-task is a fatality, yet be the brightest and the most transcendental of spirits—for Zarathustra is a dancer? how can he who has the hardest and most terrible grasp of reality, and who has thought the most "abysmal thoughts," nevertheless avoid conceiving these things as objections to existence, or even as objections to the eternal recurrence of existence?—how is it that on the contrary he finds reasons for being himself the eternal affirmation of all things, "the tremendous and unlimited saying of Yea and Amen"?... "Into every abyss do I bear the benediction of my yea to Life." ... But this, once more, is precisely the idea of Dionysus.

7

What language will such a spirit speak, when he speaks unto his soul? The language of the dithyramb. I am the inventor of the dithyramb. Hearken unto the manner in which Zarathustra speaks to his soul Before Sunrise (iii. 48). Before[Pg 110] my time such emerald joys and divine tenderness had found no tongue. Even the profoundest melancholy of such a Dionysus takes shape as a dithyramb. As an example of this I take "The Night-Song,"—the immortal plaint of one who, thanks to his superabundance of light and power, thanks to the sun within him, is condemned never to love.

"It is night: now do all gushing springs raise their voices. And my soul too is a gushing spring.

"It is night: now only do all lovers burst into song. And my soul too is the song of a lover.

"Something unquenched and unquenchable is within me, that would raise its voice. A craving for love is within me, which itself speaketh the language of love.

"Light am I: would that I were night! But this is my loneliness, that I am begirt with light.

"Alas, why am I not dark and like unto the night! How joyfully would I then suck at the breasts of light!

"And even you would I bless, ye twinkling starlets and glow-worms on high! and be blessed in the gifts of your light.

"But in mine own light do I live, ever back into myself do I drink the flames I send forth.

"I know not the happiness of the hand stretched forth to grasp; and oft have I dreamt that stealing must be more blessed than taking.

"Wretched am I that my hand may never rest from giving: an envious fate is mine that I see expectant eyes and nights made bright with longing.

"Oh, the wretchedness of all them that give! Oh, the clouds that cover the face of my sun! That craving for desire! that burning hunger at the end of the feast!

"They take what I give them; but do I touch their soul? A gulf is there 'twixt giving and taking; and the smallest gulf is the last to be bridged.

"An appetite is born from out my beauty: would that I might do harm to them that I fill with light; would that I might rob them of the gifts I have given:—thus do I thirst for wickedness.

"To withdraw my hand when their hand is ready stretched forth like the waterfall that wavers, wavers even in its fall:—thus do I thirst for wickedness.

"For such vengeance doth my fulness yearn: to such tricks doth my loneliness give birth.

"My joy in giving died with the deed. By its very fulness did my virtue grow weary of itself.

"He who giveth risketh to lose his shame; he that is ever distributing groweth callous in hand and heart therefrom.

"Mine eyes no longer melt into tears at the sight of the suppliant's shame; my hand hath become too hard to feel the quivering of laden hands.

"Whither have ye fled, the tears of mine eyes and the bloom of my heart? Oh, the solitude of all givers! Oh, the silence of all beacons!

"Many are the suns that circle in barren space; to all that is dark do they speak with their light—to me alone are they silent.

"Alas, this is the hatred of light for that which shineth: pitiless it runneth its course.

"Unfair in its inmost heart to that which shineth; cold toward suns,—thus doth every sun go its way.

"Like a tempest do the suns fly over their course: for such is their way. Their own unswerving will do they follow: that is their coldness.

"Alas, it is ye alone, ye creatures of gloom, ye spirits of the night, that take your warmth from that which shineth. Ye alone suck your milk and comfort from the udders of light.

"Alas, about me there is ice, my hand burneth itself against ice!

"Alas, within me is a thirst that thirsteth for your thirst!

"It is night: woe is me, that I must needs be light! And thirst after darkness! And loneliness!

"It is night: now doth my longing burst forth like a spring,—for speech do I long.

"It is night: now do all gushing springs raise their voices. And my soul too is a gushing spring.

"It is night: now only do all lovers burst into song. And my soul too is the song of a lover."

8

Such things have never been written, never been felt, never been suffered: only a God, only Dionysus suffers in this way. The reply to such a dithyramb on the sun's solitude in light would be Ariadne. ... Who knows, but I, who Ariadne is! To all such riddles no one heretofore had ever found an answer; I doubt even whether any one had ever seen a riddle here. One day Zarathustra severely[Pg 113] determines his life-task—and it is also mine. Let no one misunderstand its meaning. It's a yea-saying to the point of justifying, to the point of redeeming even all that is past.

"I walk among men as among fragments of the future: of that future which I see.

"And all my creativeness and effort is but this, that I may be able to think and recast all these fragments and riddles and dismal accidents into one piece.

"And how could I bear to be a man, if man were not also a poet, a riddle reader, and a redeemer of chance!

"To redeem all the past, and to transform every 'it was' into 'thus would I have it'—that alone would be my salvation!"

In another passage he defines as strictly as possible what to him alone "man" can be,—not a subject for love nor yet for pity—Zarathustra became master even of his loathing of man: man is to him a thing unshaped, raw material, an ugly stone that needs the sculptor's chisel.

"No longer to will, no longer to value, no longer to create! Oh, that this great weariness may never be mine!

"Even in the lust of knowledge, I feel only the joy of my will to beget and to grow; and if there be innocence in my knowledge, it is because my procreative will is in it.

"Away from God and gods did this will lure me: what would there be to create if there were gods?

"But to man doth it ever drive me anew, my burning, creative will. Thus driveth it the hammer to the stone.

"Alas, ye men, within the stone there sleepeth an image for me, the image of all my dreams! Alas, that it should have to sleep in the hardest and ugliest stone!

"Now rageth my hammer ruthlessly against its prison. From the stone the fragments fly: what's that to me?

"I will finish it: for a shadow came unto me—the stillest and lightest thing on earth once came unto me!

"The beauty of the Superman came unto me as a shadow. Alas, my brethren! What are the—gods to me now?"

Let me call attention to one last point of view. The line in italics is my pretext for this remark. A Dionysian life-task needs the hardness of the hammer, and one of its first essentials is without doubt the joy even of destruction. The command, "Harden yourselves!" and the deep conviction that all creators are hard, is the really distinctive sign of a Dionysian nature.

BEYOND GOOD AND EVIL:

"THE PRELUDE TO A PHILOSOPHY OF THE FUTURE"

1

My work for the years that followed was prescribed as distinctly as possible. Now that the yea-saying part of my life-task was accomplished,[Pg 115] there came the turn of the negative portion, both in word and deed: the transvaluation of all values that had existed hitherto, the great war,—the conjuring-up of the day when the fatal outcome of the struggle would be decided. Meanwhile, I had slowly to look about me for my peers, for those who, out of strength, would proffer me a helping hand in my work of destruction. From that time onward, all my writings are so much bait: maybe I understand as much about fishing as most people? If nothing was caught, it was not I who was at fault There were no fish to come and bite.

2

In all its essential points, this book (1886) is a criticism of modernity, embracing the modern sciences, arts, even politics, together with certain indications as to a type which would be the reverse of modern man, or as little like him as possible, a noble and yea-saying type. In this last respect the book is a school for gentlemen—the term gentleman being understood here in a much more spiritual and radical sense than it has implied hitherto. All those things of which the age is proud,—as, for instance, far-famed "objectivity," "sympathy with all that suffers," "the historical sense," with its subjection to foreign tastes, with its lying-in-the-dust before petits faits, and the rage for science,—are shown to be the contradiction of the type recommended, and are regarded as almost ill-bred. If you remember that this book follows upon Zarathustra, you may possibly guess to what system of diet it owes its life. The eye which,[Pg 116] owing to tremendous constraint, has become accustomed to see at a great distance,—Zarathustra is even more far-sighted than the Tsar,—is here forced to focus sharply that which is close at hand, the present time, the things that lie about him. In all the aphorisms and more particularly in the form of this book, the reader will find the same voluntary turning away from those instincts which made a Zarathustra a possible feat. Refinement in form, in aspiration, and in the art of keeping silent, are its more or less obvious qualities; psychology is handled with deliberate hardness and cruelty,—the whole book does not contain one single good-natured word.... All this sort of thing refreshes a man. Who can guess the kind of recreation that is necessary after such an expenditure of goodness as is to be found in Zarathustra? From a theological standpoint—now pay ye heed; for it is but on rare occasions that I speak as a theologian—it was God Himself who, at the end of His great work, coiled Himself up in the form of a serpent at the foot of the tree of knowledge. It was thus that He recovered from being a God.... He had made everything too beautiful.... The devil is simply God's moment of idleness, on that seventh day.

"THE GENEALOGY OF MORALS: A POLEMIC"

The three essays which constitute this genealogy are, as regards expression, aspiration, and the art[Pg 117] of the unexpected, perhaps the most curious things that have ever been written. Dionysus, as you know, is also the god of darkness. In each case the beginning is calculated to mystify; it is cool, scientific, even ironical, intentionally thrust to the fore, intentionally reticent. Gradually less calmness prevails; here and there a flash of lightning defines the horizon; exceedingly unpleasant truths break upon your ears from out remote distances with a dull, rumbling sound,—until very soon a fierce tempo is attained in which everything presses forward at a terrible degree of tension. At the end, in each case, amid fearful thunderclaps, a new truth shines out between thick clouds. The truth of the first essays the psychology of Christianity: the birth of Christianity out of the spirit of resentment, not, as is supposed, out of the "Spirit,"—in all its essentials, a counter-movement, the great insurrection against the dominion of noble values. The second essay contains the psychology of conscience: this is not, as you may believe, "the voice of God in man"; it is the instinct of cruelty, which turns inwards once it is unable to discharge itself outwardly. Cruelty is here exposed, for the first time, as one of the oldest and most indispensable elements in the foundation of culture. The third essay replies to the question as to the origin of the formidable power of the ascetic ideal, of the priest ideal, despite the fact that this ideal is essentially detrimental, that it is a will to nonentity and to decadence. Reply: it flourished not because God was active behind the priests, as is generally believed, but because it was[Pg 118] a faute de mieux—from the fact that hitherto it has been the only ideal and has had no competitors. "For man prefers to aspire to nonentity than not to aspire at all." But above all, until the time of Zarathustra there was no such thing as a counter-ideal. You have understood my meaning. Three decisive overtures on the part of a psychologist to a Transvaluation of all Values.—This book contains the first psychology of the priest.

"THE TWILIGHT OF THE IDOLS:

HOW TO PHILOSOPHISE WITH THE HAMMER"
1

This work—which covers scarcely one hundred and fifty pages, with its cheerful and fateful tone, like a laughing demon, and the production of which occupied so few days that I hesitate to give their number—is altogether an exception among books: there is no work more rich in substance, more independent, more upsetting—more wicked. If any one should desire to obtain a rapid sketch of how everything, before my time, was standing on its head, he should begin reading me in this book. That which is called "Idols" on the title page is simply the old truth that has been believed in hitherto. In plain English, The Twilight of the Idols means that the old truth is on its last legs.

2

There is no reality, no "ideality," which has not been touched in this book (touched! what a cautious euphemism!). Not only the eternal idols, but also the youngest—that is to say, the most senile: modern ideas, for instance. A strong wind blows between the trees and in all directions fall the fruit—the truths. There is the waste of an all-too-rich autumn in this book: you trip over truths. You even crush some to death, there are too many of them. Those things that you can grasp, however, are quite unquestionable; they are irrevocable decrees. I alone have the criterion of "truths" in my possession. I alone can decide. It would seem as if a second consciousness had grown up in me, as if the "life-will" in me had thrown a light upon the downward path along which it has been running throughout the ages. The downward path—hitherto this had been called the road to "Truth." All obscure impulse—"darkness and dismay"—is at an end, the "good man" was precisely he who was least aware of the proper way.[1] And, speaking in all earnestness, no one before me knew the proper way, the way upwards: only after my time could men once more find hope, life-tasks, and roads mapped out[Pg 120] that lead to culture—I am the joyful harbinger of this culture. ... On this account alone I am also a fatality.

3

Immediately after the completion of the above-named work, and without letting even one day go by, I tackled the formidable task of the Transvaluation with a supreme feeling of pride which nothing could equal; and, certain at each moment of my immortality, I cut sign after sign upon tablets of brass with the sureness of Fate. The Preface came into being on 3rd September 1888. When, after having written it down, I went out into the open that morning, I was greeted by the most beautiful day I had ever seen in the Upper Engadine—clear, glowing with colour, and presenting all the contrasts and all the intermediary gradations between ice and the south. I left Sils-Maria only on the 20th of September. I had been forced to delay my departure owing to floods, and I was very soon, and for some days, the only visitor in this wonderful spot, on which my gratitude bestows the gift of an immortal name. After a journey that was full of incidents, and not without danger to life,—as for instance at Como, which was flooded when I reached it in the dead of night,—I got to Turin on the afternoon of the 21 st. Turin is the only suitable place for me, and it shall be my home henceforward. I took the same lodgings as I had occupied in the spring, 6111 Via Carlo Alberto, opposite the mighty Palazzo Carignano, in which Vittorio Emanuele was born; and I had a view of the Piazza Carlo Alberto and[Pg 121] above it across to the hills. Without hesitating, or allowing myself to be disturbed for a single moment, I returned to my work, only the last quarter of which had still to be written. On the 30th September, tremendous triumph; the seventh day; the leisure of a god on the banks of the Po.[2] On the same day, I wrote the Preface to The Twilight of the Idols, the correction of the proofs of which provided me with recreation during the month of September. Never in my life have I experienced such an autumn; nor had I ever imagined that such things were possible on earth—a Claude Lorrain extended to infinity, each day equal to the last in its wild perfection.

"THE CASE OF WAGNER: A MUSICIAN'S PROBLEM"

1

In order to do justice to this essay a man ought to suffer from the fate of music as from an open wound.—From what do I suffer when I suffer from the fate of music? From the fact that music has lost its world-transfiguring, yea-saying character—that it is decadent music and no longer the flute of Dionysus. Supposing, however, that the fate of music be as dear to man as his own life, because joy and suffering are alike bound up with it; then he will find this pamphlet comparatively mild and[Pg 122] full of consideration. To be cheerful in such circumstances, and laugh good-naturedly with others at one's self,—ridendodicere severum[1] when the verum dicere would justify every sort of hardness,—is humanity itself. Who doubts that I, old artilleryman that I am, would be able if I liked to point my heavy guns at Wagner?—Everything decisive in this question I kept to myself—I have loved Wagner.—After all, an attack upon a more than usually subtle "unknown person" whom another would not have divined so easily, lies in the meaning and path of my life-task. Oh, I have still quite a number of other "unknown persons" to unmask besides a Cagliostro of Music! Above all, I have to direct an attack against the German people, who, in matters of the spirit, grow every day more indolent, poorer in instincts, and more honest who, with an appetite for which they are to be envied, continue to diet themselves on contradictions, and gulp down "Faith" in company with science, Christian love together with anti-Semitism, and the will to power (to the "Empire"), dished up with the gospel of the humble, without showing the slightest signs of indigestion. Fancy this absence of party-feeling in the presence of opposites! Fancy this gastric neutrality and "disinterestedness"! Behold this sense of justice in the German palate, which can grant equal rights to all,—which finds everything tasteful! Without a shadow of a doubt the Germans are idealists. When I was last in

Germany, I found German taste striving to grant[Pg 123] Wagner and the Trumpeter of Sakkingen[2] equal rights; while I myself witnessed the attempts of the people of Leipzig to do honour to one of the most genuine and most German of musicians,—using German here in the old sense of the word,—a man who was no mere German of the Empire, the master Heinrich Schütz, by founding a Liszt Society, the object of which was to cultivate and spread artful (listige[3]) Church music. Without a shadow of doubt the Germans are idealists.

2

But here nothing shall stop me from being rude, and from telling the Germans one or two unpleasant home truths: who else would do it if I did not? I refer to their laxity in matters historical. Not only have the Germans entirely lost the breadth of vision which enables one to grasp the course of culture and the values of culture; not only are they one and all political (or Church) puppets; but they have also actually put a ban upon this very breadth of vision. A man must first and foremost be "German," he must belong to "the race"; then only can he pass judgment upon all values and lack of values in history—then only can he establish them.... To be German is in itself an argument, "Germany, Germany above all,"[4] is a principle; the Germans[Pg 124] stand for the "moral order of the universe" in history; compared with the Roman Empire, they are the up-holders of freedom; compared with the eighteenth century, they are the restorers of morality, of the "Categorical Imperative." There is such a thing as the writing of history according to the lights of Imperial Germany; there is, I fear, anti-Semitic history— there is also history written with an eye to the Court, and Herr von Treitschke is not ashamed of himself. Quite recently an idiotic opinion in historicis, an observation of Vischer the Swabian æsthete, since happily deceased, made the round of the German newspapers as a "truth" to which every German must assent The observation was this: "The Renaissance and the Reformation only together constitute a whole—the æsthetic rebirth, and the moral rebirth." When I listen to such things, I lose all patience, and I feel inclined, I even feel it my duty, to tell the Germans, for once in a way, all that they have on their conscience. Every great crime against culture for the last four centuries lies on their conscience.... And always for the same reason, always owing to their bottomless cowardice in the face of reality, which is also cowardice in the face of truth; always owing to the love of falsehood which has become almost instinctive in them—in short, "idealism." It was the Germans who caused Europe to lose the fruits, the whole meaning of her last period of greatness—the period of the Renaissance. At a moment when a higher order of values, values that were noble, that said yea to life, and that guaranteed a future, had succeeded in triumphing over the opposite values,[Pg 125] the values of degeneration, in the very seat of Christianity itself,—and even in the hearts of those sitting there,—Luther, that cursed monk, not only restored the Church, but, what was a thousand times worse, restored Christianity, and at a time too when it lay defeated. Christianity, the Denial of the Will to Live, exalted to a religion! Luther was an impossible monk who, thanks to his own "impossibility," attacked the Church, and in so doing restored it! Catholics would be perfectly justified in celebrating feasts in honour of Luther, and in producing festival plays[5] in his honour. Luther and the "rebirth of morality"! May all psychology go to the devil! Without a shadow of a doubt the Germans are idealists. On two occasions when, at the cost of enormous courage and self-control, an upright, unequivocal, and perfectly scientific attitude of mind had been attained, the Germans were able to discover back stairs leading down to the old "ideal" again, compromises between truth and the "ideal," and, in short, formulæ for the right to reject science and to perpetrate falsehoods. Leibniz and Kant—these two great breaks upon the intellectual honesty of Europe! Finally, at a moment when there appeared on the bridge that spanned two centuries of decadence, a superior force of genius and will which was strong enough to consolidate Europe and to convert it into a political and economic unit, with the object of ruling the world, the Germans, with their Wars of Independence, robbed Europe[Pg 126] of the significance—the marvellous significance, of Napoleon's life. And in so doing they laid on their conscience everything that followed, everything that exists to-day,—this sickliness and want of reason which is most opposed to culture, and which is called Nationalism,—this névrose nationale from which Europe is suffering acutely; this eternal subdivision of Europe into petty states, with politics on a municipal scale: they have robbed Europe itself of its significance, of its reason,—and have stuffed it into a cul-de-sac. Is there any one except me who knows the way out of this cul-de-sac? Does anyone except me know of an aspiration which would be great enough to bind the people of Europe once more together?

3

And after all, why should I not express my suspicions? In my case, too, the Germans will attempt to make a great fate give birth merely to a mouse. Up to the present they have compromised themselves with me; I doubt whether the future will improve them. Alas! how happy I should be to prove a false prophet in this matter! My natural readers and listeners are already Russians, Scandinavians, and Frenchmen—will they always be the same? In the history of knowledge, Germans are represented only by doubtful names, they have been able to produce only "unconscious" swindlers (this word applies to Fichte, Schelling, Schopenhauer, Hegel, and Schleiermacher, just as well as to Kant or Leibniz; they were all mere[Pg 127] Schleiermachers).[6] The Germans must not have the honour of seeing the first upright intellect in their history of intellects, that intellect in which truth ultimately got the better of the fraud of four thousand years, reckoned as one with the German intellect. "German intellect" is my foul air: I breathe with difficulty in the neighbourhood of this psychological uncleanliness that has now become instinctive—an uncleanliness which in every word and expression betrays a German. They have never undergone a seventeenth century of hard self-examination, as the French have,—a La Rochefoucauld, a Descartes, are a thousand times more upright than the very first among Germans,—the latter have not yet had any psychologists. But psychology is almost the standard of measurement for the cleanliness or uncleanliness of a race.... For if a man is not even clean, how can he be deep? The Germans are like women, you can scarcely ever I fathom their depths—they haven't any, and that's the end of it. Thus they cannot even be called shallow. That which is called "deep" in Germany, is precisely this instinctive uncleanliness towards one's self, of which I have just spoken: people refuse to be clear in regard to their own natures. Might I be allowed, perhaps, to suggest the word "German" as an international epithet denoting this psychological depravity?—At the moment of writing, for instance, the German Emperor is declaring it to be his Christian duty to liberate the slaves in Africa;[Pg 128] among us Europeans, then, this would be called simply "German." ... Have the Germans ever produced even a book that had depth? They are lacking in the mere idea of what constitutes a book. I have known scholars who thought that Kant was deep. At the Court of Prussia I fear that Herr von Treitschke is regarded as deep. And when I happen to praise Stendhal as a deep psychologist, I have often been compelled, in the company of German University Professors, to spell his name aloud.

4

And why should I not proceed to the end? I am fond of clearing the air. It is even part of my ambition to be considered as essentially a despiser of Germans. I expressed my suspicions of the German character even at the age of six-and-twenty (see Thoughts out of Season, vol. ii. pp. 164, 165),—to my mind the Germans are impossible. When I try to think of the kind of man who is opposed to me in all my instincts, my mental image takes the form of a German. The first thing I ask myself when I begin analysing a man, is, whether he has a feeling for distance in him; whether he sees rank, gradation, and order everywhere between man and man; whether he makes distinctions; for this is what constitutes a gentleman. Otherwise he belongs hopelessly to that open-hearted, open-minded—alas! and always very good-natured species, la canaille! But the Germans are canaille—alas! they are so good-natured! A man lowers himself by frequenting the society of Germans: the German places every one on an equal footing. With the[Pg 129] exception of my intercourse with one or two artists, and above all with Richard Wagner, I cannot say that I have spent one pleasant hour with Germans. Suppose, for one moment, that the profoundest spirit of all ages were to appear among Germans, then one of the saviours of the Capitol would be sure to arise and declare that his own ugly soul was just as great. I can no longer abide this race with which a man is always in bad company, which; has no idea of nuances—woe to me! I am a nuance—and which has not esprit in its feet, and cannot even walk withal! In short, the Germans have no feet at all, they simply have legs. The Germans have not the faintest idea of how vulgar they are—but this in itself is the acme of vulgarity,—they are not even ashamed of being merely Germans. They will have their say in everything, they regard themselves as fit to decide all questions; I even fear that they have decided about me. My whole life is essentially a proof of this remark. In vain have I sought among them for a sign of tact and delicacy towards myself. Among Jews I did indeed find it, but not among Germans. I am so constituted as to be gentle and kindly to every one,—I have the right not to draw distinctions,—but this does not prevent my eyes from being open. I except no one, and least of all my friends,—I only trust that this has not prejudiced my reputation for humanity among them? There are five or six things which I have always made points of honour. Albeit, the truth remains that for many years I have considered almost every letter that has reached me as a piece of cynicism. There is more cynicism in an attitude[Pg 130] of goodwill towards me than in any sort of hatred. I tell every friend to his face that he has never thought it worth his while to study any one of my writings: from the slightest hints I gather that they do not even know what lies hidden in my books. And with regard even to my Zarathustra, which of my friends would have seen more in it than a piece of unwarrantable, though fortunately harmless, arrogance? Ten years have elapsed, and no one has yet felt it a duty to his conscience to defend my name against the absurd silence beneath which it has been entombed. It was a foreigner, a Dane, who first showed sufficient keenness of instinct and of courage to do this, and who protested indignantly against my so-called friends. At what German University to-day would such lectures on my philosophy be possible, as those which Dr. Brandes delivered last spring in Copenhagen, thus proving once more his right to the title psychologist? For my part, these things have never caused me any pain; that which is necessary does not offend me. Amor fati is the core of my nature. This, however, does not alter the fact that I love irony and even world-historic irony. And thus, about two years before hurling the destructive thunderbolt of the Transvaluation, which will send the whole of civilisation into convulsions, I sent my Case of Wagner out into the world. The Germans were given the chance of blundering and immortalising their stupidity once more on my account, and they still have just enough time to do it in. And have they fallen in with my plans? Admirably! my dear Germans. Allow me to congratulate you.

[1] The motto of The Case of Wagner.—TR.

[2] An opera by Nessler which was all the rage in Germany twenty years ago.—TR.

[3] Unfortunately it is impossible to render this play on the words in English.—TR.

[4] The German National Song (Deutschland, Deutschland über alles).—TR.

[5] Ever since the year 1617 such plays have been produced by the Protestants of Germany.—TR.

[6] Schleiermacher literally means a weaver or maker of veils.—TR.

WHY I AM A FATALITY

1

I know my destiny. There will come a day $ when my name will recall the memory of something formidable—a crisis the like of which has never been known on earth, the memory of the most profound clash of consciences, and the passing of a sentence upon all that which theretofore had been believed, exacted, and hallowed. I am not a man, I am dynamite. And with it all there is nought of the founder of a religion in me. Religions are matters for the mob; after coming in contact with a religious man, I always feel that I must wash my hands.... I require no "believers," it is my opinion that I am too full of malice to believe even in myself; I never address myself to masses. I am horribly frightened that one day I shall be pronounced "holy." You will understand why I publish this book beforehand—it is to prevent people from wronging me. I refuse to be a saint; I would rather be a clown. Maybe I am a clown. And I am notwithstanding, or rather not notwithstanding, the mouthpiece of truth; for nothing more blown-out with falsehood has ever existed, than a saint. But my truth is terrible: for hitherto lies have been called truth. The Transvaluation of all Values, this is my formula for mankind's greatest step towards coming to its[Pg 132] senses—a step which in me became flesh and genius. My destiny ordained that I should be the first decent human being, and that I should feel myself opposed to the falsehood of millenniums. I was the first to discover truth, and for the simple reason that I was the first who became conscious of falsehood as falsehood—that is to say, I smelt it as such. My genius resides in my nostrils. I contradict as no one has contradicted hitherto, and am nevertheless the reverse of a negative spirit. I am the harbinger of joy, the like of which has never existed before; I have discovered tasks of such lofty greatness that, until my time, no one had any idea of such things. Mankind can begin to have fresh hopes, only now that I have lived. Thus, I am necessarily a man of Fate. For when Truth enters the lists against the falsehood of ages, shocks are bound to ensue, and a spell of earthquakes, followed by the transposition of hills and valleys, such as the world has never yet imagined even in its dreams. The concept "politics" then becomes elevated entirely to the sphere of spiritual warfare. All the mighty realms of the ancient order of society are blown into space—for they are all based on falsehood: there will be wars, the like of which have never been seen on earth before. Only from my time and after me will politics on a large scale exist on earth.

2

If you should require a formula for a destiny of this kind that has taken human form, you will find it in my Zarathustra.

"And he who would be a creator in good and evil—verily, he must first be a destroyer, and break values into pieces.

"Thus the greatest evil belongeth unto the greatest good: but this is the creative good."

I am by far the most terrible man that has ever existed; but this does not alter the fact that I shall become the most beneficent. I know the joy of annihilation to a degree which is commensurate with my power to annihilate. In both cases I obey my Dionysian nature, which knows not how to separate the negative deed from the saying of yea. I am the first immoralist, and in this sense I am essentially the annihilator.

3

People have never asked me as they should have done, what the name of Zarathustra precisely meant in my mouth, in the mouth of the first immoralist; for that which distinguishes this Persian from all others in the past is the very fact that he was the exact reverse of an immoralist. Zarathustra was the first to see in the struggle between good and evil the essential wheel in the working of things. The translation of morality into the realm of metaphysics, as force, cause, end-in-itself, is his work. But the very question suggests its own answer. Zarathustra created this most portentous of all errors,—morality; therefore he must be the first to expose it. Not only because he has had longer and greater experience of the subject than any other thinker,—all history is indeed the experimental[Pg 134] refutation of the theory of the so-called moral order of things,—but because of the more important fact that Zarathustra was the most truthful of thinkers. In his teaching alone is truthfulness upheld as the highest virtue—that is to say, as the reverse of the cowardice of the "idealist" who takes to his heels at the sight of reality. Zarathustra has more pluck in his body than all other thinkers put together. To tell the truth and to aim straight: that is the first Persian virtue. Have I made myself clear? ... The overcoming of morality by itself, through truthfulness, the moralist's overcoming of himself in his opposite—in me—that is what the name Zarathustra means in my mouth.

4

In reality two negations are involved in my title Immoralist. I first of all deny the type of man that has hitherto been regarded as the highest—the good, the kind, and the charitable; and I also deny that kind of morality which has become recognised and paramount as morality-in-itself—I speak of the morality of decadence, or, to use a still cruder term, Christian morality. I would agree to the second of the two negations being regarded as the more decisive, for, reckoned as a whole, the overestimation of goodness and kindness seems to me already a consequence of decadence, a symptom of weakness, and incompatible with any ascending and yea-saying life. Negation and annihilation are inseparable from a yea-saying attitude towards life. Let me halt for a moment at the question of the[Pg 135] psychology of the good man. In order to appraise the value of a certain type of man, the cost of his maintenance must be calculated,—and the conditions of his existence must be known. The condition of the existence of the good is falsehood: or, otherwise expressed, the refusal at any price to see how reality is actually constituted. The refusal to see that this reality is not so constituted as always to be stimulating beneficent instincts, and still less, so as to suffer at all moments the intrusion of ignorant and good-natured hands. To consider distress of all kinds as an objection, as something which must be done away with, is the greatest nonsense on earth; generally speaking, it is nonsense of the most disastrous sort, fatal in its stupidity—almost as mad as the will to abolish bad weather, out of pity for the poor, so to speak. In the great economy of the whole universe, the terrors of reality (in the passions, in the desires, in the will to power) are incalculably more necessary than that form of petty happiness which is called "goodness"; it is even needful to practise leniency in order so much as to allow the latter a place at all, seeing that it is based upon a falsification of the instincts. I shall have an excellent opportunity of showing the incalculably calamitous consequences to the whole of history, of the credo of optimism, this monstrous offspring of the homines optimi. Zarathustra,[1] the first who recognised that the optimist is just as degenerate as the pessimist, though perhaps more[Pg 136] detrimental, says: "Good men never speak the truth. False shores and false harbours were ye taught by the good. In the lies of the good were ye born and bred. Through the good everything hath become false and crooked from the roots." Fortunately the world is not built merely upon those instincts which would secure to the good-natured herd animal his paltry happiness. To desire everybody to become a "good man," "a gregarious animal," "a blue-eyed, benevolent, beautiful soul," or—as Herbert Spencer wished—a creature of altruism, would mean robbing existence of its greatest character, castrating man, and reducing humanity to a sort of wretched Chinadom. And this some have tried to do! It is precisely this that men called morality. In this sense Zarathustra calls "the good," now "the last men," and anon "the beginning of the end"; and above all, he considers them as the most detrimental kind of men, because they secure their existence at the cost of Truth and at the cost of the Future.

"The good—they cannot create; they are ever the beginning of the end.

"They crucify him who writeth new values on new tables; they sacrifice unto themselves the future; they crucify the whole future of humanity!

"The good—they are ever the beginning of the end.

"And whatever harm the slanderers of the world may do, the harm of the good is the most calamitous of all harm."

5

Zarathustra, as the first psychologist of the good man, is perforce the friend of the evil man. When a degenerate kind of man has succeeded to the highest rank among the human species, his position must have been gained at the cost of the reverse type—at the cost of the strong man who is certain of life. When the gregarious animal stands in the glorious rays of the purest virtue, the exceptional man must be degraded to the rank of the evil. If falsehood insists at all costs on claiming the word "truth" for its own particular standpoint, the really truthful man must be sought out among the despised. Zarathustra allows of no doubt here; he says that it was precisely the knowledge of the good, of the "best," which inspired his absolute horror of men. And it was out of this feeling of repulsion that he grew the wings which allowed him to soar into remote futures. He does not conceal the fact that his type of man is one which is relatively superhuman—especially as opposed to the "good" man, and that the good and the just would regard his superman as the devil.

"Ye higher men, on whom my gaze now falls, this is the doubt that ye wake in my breast, and this is my secret laughter: methinks ye would call my Superman—the devil! So strange are ye in your souls to all that is great, that the Superman would be terrible in your eyes for his goodness."

It is from this passage, and from no other, that you must set out to understand the goal to which Zarathustra aspires—the kind of man that he[Pg 138] conceives sees reality as it is; he is strong enough for this—he is not estranged or far removed from it, he is that reality himself, in his own nature can be found all the terrible and questionable character of reality: only thus can man have greatness.

6

But I have chosen the title of Immoral is t as a surname and as a badge of honour in yet another sense; I am very proud to possess this name which distinguishes me from all the rest of mankind. No one hitherto has felt Christian morality beneath him; to that end there were needed height, a remoteness of vision, and an abysmal psychological depth, not believed to be possible hitherto. Up to the present Christian morality has been the Circe of all thinkers—they stood at her service. What man, before my time, had descended into the underground caverns from out of which the poisonous fumes of this ideal—of this slandering of the world—burst forth? What man had even dared to suppose that they were underground caverns? Was a single one of the philosophers who preceded me a psychologist at all, and not the very reverse of a psychologist—that is to say, a "superior swindler," an "Idealist"? Before my time there was no psychology. To be the first in this new realm may amount to a curse; at all events, it is a fatality: for one is also the first to despise. My danger is the loathing of mankind.

7

Have you understood me? That which defines me, that which makes me stand apart from the whole of the rest of humanity, is the fact that I unmasked Christian morality. For this reason I was in need of a word which conveyed the idea of a challenge to everybody. Not to have awakened to these discoveries before, struck me as being the sign of the greatest uncleanliness that mankind has on its conscience, as self-deception become instinctive, as the fundamental will to be blind to every phenomenon, all causality and all reality; in fact, as an almost criminal fraud in psychologicis. Blindness in regard to Christianity is the essence of criminality—for it is the crime against life. Ages and peoples, the first as well as the last, philosophers and old women, with the exception of five or six moments in history (and of myself, the seventh), are all alike in this. Hitherto the Christian has been the "moral being," a peerless oddity, and, as "a moral being," he was more absurd, more vain, more thoughtless, and a greater disadvantage to himself, than the greatest despiser of humanity could have deemed possible. Christian morality is the most malignant form of all false too the actual Circe of humanity: that which has corrupted mankind. It is not error as error which infuriates me at the sight of this spectacle; it is not the millenniums of absence of "goodwill," of discipline, of decency, and of bravery in spiritual things, which betrays itself in the triumph of Christianity; it is rather the absence of nature, it is the perfectly[Pg 140] ghastly fact that anti-nature itself received the highest honours as morality and as law, and remained suspended over man as the Categorical Imperative. Fancy blundering in this way, not as an individual, not as a people, but as a whole species! as humanity! To teach the contempt of all the principal instincts of life; to posit falsely the existence of a "soul," of a "spirit," in order to be able to defy the body; to spread the feeling that there is something impure in the very first prerequisite of life—in sex; to seek the principle of evil in the profound need of growth and expansion—that is to say, in severe self-love (the term itself is slanderous); and conversely to see a higher moral value—but what am I talking about?—I mean the moral value per se, in the typical signs of decline, in the antagonism of the instincts, in "selflessness," in the loss of ballast, in "the suppression of the personal element," and in "love of one's neighbour" (neighbouritis!). What! is humanity itself in a state of degeneration? Has it always been in this state? One thing is certain, that ye are taught only the values of decadence as the highest values. The morality of self-renunciation is essentially the morality of degeneration; the fact, "I am going to the dogs," is translated into the imperative," Ye shall all go to the dogs"—and not only into the imperative. This morality of self-renunciation, which is the only kind of morality that has been taught hitherto, betrays the will to nonentity—it denies life to the very roots. There still remains the possibility that it is not mankind that is in a state of degeneration, but only that parasitical kind of man—the priest,[Pg 141] who, by means of morality and lies, has climbed up to his position of determinator of values, who divined in Christian morality his road to power. And, to tell the truth, this is my opinion. The teachers and I leaders of mankind—including the theologians—have been, every one of them, decadents: hence their) transvaluation of all values into a hostility towards; life; hence morality. The definition of morality; Morality is the idiosyncrasy of decadents, actuated by a desire to avenge themselves with success upon life. I attach great value to this definition.

8

Have you understood me? I have not uttered a single word which I had not already said five years ago through my mouthpiece Zarathustra. The unmasking of Christian morality is an event which unequalled in history, it is a real catastrophe. The man who throws light upon it is a force majeure, a fatality; he breaks the history of man into two. Time is reckoned up before him and after him. The lightning flash of truth struck precisely that which theretofore had stood highest: he who understands what was destroyed by that flash should look to see whether he still holds anything in his hands. Everything which until then was called truth, has been revealed as the most detrimental, most spiteful, and most subterranean form of life; the holy pretext, which was the "improvement" of man, has been recognised as a ruse for draining life of its energy and of its blood. Morality conceived as Vampirism.... The man who[Pg 142] unmasks morality has also unmasked the worthlessness of the values in which men either believe or have believed; he no longer sees anything to be revered in the most venerable man— even in the types of men that have been pronounced holy; all he can see in them is the most fatal kind of abortions, fatal, because they fascinate. The concept "God" was invented as the opposite of the concept life—everything detrimental, poisonous, and slanderous, and all deadly hostility to life, wad bound together in one horrible unit in Him. The concepts "beyond" and "true world" were invented in order to depreciate the only world that exists—in order that no goal or aim, no sense or task, might be left to earthly reality. The concepts "soul," "spirit," and last of all the concept "immortal soul," were invented in order to throw contempt on the body, in order to make it sick and "holy," in order to cultivate an attitude of appalling levity towards all things in life which deserve to be treated seriously, i.e. the questions of nutrition and habitation, of intellectual diet, the treatment of the sick, cleanliness, and weather. Instead of health, we find the "salvation of the soul"—that is to say, a folie circulate fluctuating between convulsions and penitence and the hysteria of redemption. The concept "sin," together with the torture instrument appertaining to it, which is the concept "free will," was invented in order to confuse and muddle our instincts, and to render the mistrust of them man's second nature! In the concepts "disinterestedness" and "self-denial," the actual signs of decadence are to be found. The allurement of that[Pg 143] which is detrimental, the inability to discover one's own advantage and self-destruction, are made into absolute qualities, into the "duty," the "holiness," and the "divinity" of man. Finally—to keep the worst to the last—by the notion of the good man, all that is favoured which is weak, ill, botched, and sick-in-itself, which ought to be wiped out. The law of selection is thwarted, an ideal is made out of opposition to the proud, well-constituted man, to him who says yea to life, to him who is certain of the future, and who guarantees the future—this man is henceforth called the evil one. And all this was believed in as morality!—Ecrasez l'infâme!

9

Have you understood me? Dionysus versus Christ.

[1]Needless to say this is Nietzsche, and no longer the Persian.—TR.

EDITORIAL NOTE TO POETRY

The editor begs to state that, contrary to his announcement in the Editorial Note to The Joyful Wisdom, in which he declared his intention of publishing all of Nietzsche's poetry, he has nevertheless withheld certain less important verses from publication. This alteration in his plans is due to his belief that it is an injustice and an indiscretion on the part of posterity to surprise an author, as it were, in his négligé, or, in plain English, "in his shirt-sleeves." Authors generally are very sensitive on this point, and rightly so: a visit behind the scenes is not precisely to the advantage of the theatre, and even finished pictures not yet framed are not readily shown by the careful artist. As the German edition, however, contains nearly all that Nietzsche left behind, either in small notebooks or on scraps of paper, the editor could not well suppress everything that was not prepared for publication by Nietzsche himself, more particularly as some of the verses are really very remarkable. He has, therefore, made a very plentiful selection from the Songs and Epigrams, nearly all of which are to be found translated here, and from the Fragments of the Dionysus Dithyrambs, of which over half have been given. All the complete Dionysus Dithyrambs[Pg 146] appear in this volume, save those which are duplicates of verses already translated in the Fourth Part of Zarathustra. These Dionysus Dithyrambs were prepared ready for press by Nietzsche himself. He wrote the final manuscript during the summer of 1888 in Sils Maria; their actual composition, however, belongs to an earlier date.

All the verses, unless otherwise stated, have been translated by Mr. Paul Victor Cohn.

SONGS, EPIGRAMS, ETC.
SONGS
TO MELANCHOLY[1]

O Melancholy, be not wroth with me
That I this pen should point to praise thee only,
And in thy praise, with head bowed to the knee,
Squat like a hermit on a tree-stump lonely.
Thus oft thou saw'st me,—yesterday, at least,—
Full in the morning sun and its hot beaming,
While, visioning the carrion of his feast,
The hungry vulture valleyward flew screaming.

Yet didst thou err, foul bird, albeit I,
So like a mummy 'gainst my log lay leaning!
Thou couldst not see these eyes whose ecstasy
Rolled hither, thither, proud and overweening.
What though they did not soar unto thine height,
or reached those far-off, cloud-reared precipices,
For that they sank the deeper so they might
Within themselves light Destiny's abysses.

Thus oft in sullenness perverse and free,
Bent hideous like a savage at his altar,
There, Melancholy, held I thought of thee,
[Pg 150]A penitent, though youthful, with his psalter.

So crouched did I enjoy the vulture's span,
The thunder of the avalanche's paces,
Thou spakest to me—nor wast false like man,
Thou spakest, but with stern and dreadful faces.

Harsh goddess thou of Nature wild and stark,
Mistress, that com'st with threats to daunt and quell me,
To point me out the vulture's airy are
And laughing avalanches, to repel me.

Around us gnashing pants the lust to kill,
The torment to win life in all its changes;
Alluring on some cliff, abrupt and chill,
Some flower craves the butterfly that ranges.

All this am I—shuddering I feel it all—
O butterfly beguiled, O lonely flower,
The vulture and the ice-pent waterfall,
The moaning storm—all symbols of thy power,—
Thou goddess grim before whom deeply bowed,
With head on knee, my lips with pæans bursting,
I lift a dreadful song and cry aloud
For Life, for Life, for Life—forever thirsting!

O vengeful goddess, be not wroth, I ask,
That I to mesh thee in my rhymes have striven.
He trembles who beholds thine awful mask;
He quails to whom thy dread right hand is given.
Song upon trembling song by starts and fits
I chant, in rhythm all my thought unfolding,
The black ink flows, the pointed goose-quill spits,
O goddess, goddess—leave me to my scolding!
[Pg 151]

AFTER A NIGHT STORM[2]

To-day in misty veils thou hangest dimly,
Gloomy goddess, o'er my window-pane.
Grimly whirl the pallid snow-flakes, grimly
Roars the swollen brook unto the plain.

Ah, by light of haggard levins glaring,
'Neath the untamed thunder's roar and roll,
'Midst the valley's murk wast thou preparing—
Sorceress! thy dank and poisoned bowl.

Shuddering, I heard through midnight breaking

Raptures of thy voice—and howls of pain.
Saw thy bright orbs gleam, thy right hand shaking
With the mace of thunder hurled amain.

Near my dreary couch I heard the crashes
Of thine armoured steps, heard weapons slam,
Heard thy brazen chain strike 'gainst the sashes,
And thy voice: "Come! hearken who I am!

The immortal Amazon they call me;
All things weak and womanish I shun;
Manly scorn and hate in war enthral me;
Victress I and tigress all in one!

Where I tread there corpses fall before me;
From mine eyes the furious torches fly,
And my brain thinks poisons. Bend, adore me!
Worm of Earth and Will o' Wisp—or die!"

HYMNS TO FRIENDSHIP

(Two Fragments)

1

Goddess Friendship, deign to hear the song
That we sing in friendship's honour!
Where the eye of friendship glances,
Filled with all the joy of friendship
Come thou nigh to aid me,
Rosy dawn in thy gaze and
In holy hand the faithful pledge of youth eternal.

2

Morning's past: the sun of noonday
Scorches with hot ray our heads.
Let us sit beneath the arbour

Singing songs in praise of friendship.
Friendship was our life's red dawning,
And its sunset red shall be.

THE WANDERER[3]

All through the night a wanderer walks
Sturdy of stride,
With winding vale and sloping height
E'er at his side.
Fair is the night:
On, on he strides, nor slackens speed,
[Pg 153]And knows not where his path will lead.

A bird's song in the night is heard,
"Ah me, what hast thou done, O bird,
How dost thou grip my sense and feet
And pourest heart-vexation sweet
Into mine ear—I must remain,
To hearken fain:
Why lure me with inviting strain?"

The good bird speaks, staying his song:
"I lure not thee,—no, thou art wrong—
With these my trills
I lure my mate from off the hills—
Nor heed thy plight.
To me alone the night's not fair.
What's that to thee? Forth must thou fare,
On, onward ever, resting ne'er.

Why stand'st thou now?
What has my piping done to thee,
Thou roaming wight?"
The good bird pondered, silent quite,
"Why doth my piping change his plight?
Why stands he now,

That luckless, luckless, roaming wight?"

TO THE GLACIER

At noontide hour, when first,
Into the mountains Summer treads,
Summer, the boy with eyes so hot and weary,
Then too he speaks,
[Pg 154]Yet we can only see his speech.

His breath is panting, like the sick man's breath
On fevered couch.
The glacier and the fir tree and the spring
Answer his call
—Yet we their answer only see.
For faster from the rock leaps down
The torrent stream, as though to greet,
And stands, like a white column trembling,
All yearning there.
And darker yet and truer looks the fir-tree
Than e'er before.
And 'twixt the ice-mass and the cold grey stone
A sudden light breaks forth—
Such light I once beheld, and marked the sign.

Even the dead man's eye
Surely once more grows light,
When, sorrowful, his child
Gives him embrace and kiss:
Surely once more the flame of light
Wells out, and glowing into life
The dead eye speaks: "My child!
Ah child, you know I love you true!"

So all things glow and speak—the glacier speaks,
The brook, the fir,

Speak with their glance the selfsame words:
We love you true,
[Pg 155]Ah, child, you know we love you, love you true!

And he,
Summer, the boy with eyes so hot and weary,
Woe-worn, gives kisses
More ardent ever,
And will not go:
But like to veils he blows his words
From out his lips,
His cruel words:
"My greeting's parting,
My coming going,
In youth I die."

All round they hearken
And scarcely breathe
(No songster sings),
And shuddering run
Like gleaming ray
Over the mountain;
All round they ponder,—
Nor speak—

Twas at the noon,
At noontide hour, when first
Into the mountains Summer treads,
Summer, the boy with eyes so hot and weary.

AUTUMN[4]

'Tis Autumn:—Autumn yet shall break thy heart!
Fly away! fly away!—
The sun creeps 'gainst the hill
And climbs and climbs
[Pg 156]And rests at every step.

How faded grew the world!
On weary, slackened strings the wind
Playeth his tune.
Fair Hope fled far—
He waileth after.

'Tis Autumn:—Autumn yet shall break thy heart!
Fly away! fly away!
O fruit of the tree,
Thou tremblest, fallest?
What secret whispered unto thee
The Night,
That icy shudders deck thy cheek,
Thy cheek of purple hue?

Silent art thou, nor dost reply—
Who speaketh still?—

'Tis Autumn:—Autumn yet shall break thy heart!
Fly away! fly away!—
"I am not fair,"—
So speaks the lone star-flower,—
"Yet men I love
And comfort men—
Many flowers shall they behold,
And stoop to me,
And break me, ah!—
So that within their eyes shall gleam
Remembrance swift,
Remembrance of far fairer things than I:—
I see it—see it—and I perish so."

'Tis Autumn:—Autumn yet shall break thy heart!
Fly away! fly away!

CAMPO SANTO DI STAGLIENO[5]

Maiden, in gentle wise
You stroke your lamb's soft fleece,
Yet flashing from your eyes
Both light and flame ne'er cease.
Creature of merry jest
And favourite near and far,
Pious with kindness blest,
Amorosissima!

What broke so soon the chain,
What does your heart deplore?
And who, pray, would not fain,
If you loved him, adore?—
You're mute, but from your eye,
The tear-drop is not far,
You're mute: you'll yearn and die,
Amorosissima?

THE LITTLE BRIG NAMED "LITTLE ANGEL"[6]

"Little Angel" call they me!—
Now a ship, but once a girl,
Ah, and still too much a girl!
My steering-wheel, so bright to see,
[Pg 158]But for sake of love doth whirl.

"Little Angel" call they me,
With hundred flags to ornament,
A captain smart, on glory bent,
Steers me, puffed with vanity
(He himself's an ornament).

"Little Angel" call they me,
And where'er a little flame
Gleams for me, I, like a lamb,
Go my journey eagerly
(I was always such a lamb!).

"Little Angel" call they me—
Think you I can bark and whine
Like a dog, this mouth of mine
Throwing smoke and flame full free?
Ah, a devil's mouth is mine.

"Little Angel" call they me—
Once I spoke a bitter word,
That my lover, when he heard,
Fast and far away did flee:
Yes, I killed him with that word!

"Little Angel" call they me:
Hardly heard, I sprang so glib
From the cliff and broke a rib:
From my frame my soul went free,
Yes, escaped me through that rib.

"Little Angel" call they me—
Then my soul, like cat in flight
Straight did on this ship alight
Swiftly bounding—one, two, three!
Yes, its claws are swift to smite.

"Little Angel" call they me!—
Now a ship, but once a girl,
Ah, and still too much a girl!
My steering-wheel, so bright to see,
For sake of love alone doth whirl.

MAIDEN'S SONG

Yesterday with seventeen years
Wisdom reached I, a maiden fair,
I am grey-haired, it appears,
Now in all things—save my hair.

Yesterday, I had a thought,
Was't a thought?—you laugh and scorn!
Did you ever have a thought?
Rather was a feeling born.

Dare a woman think? This screed
Wisdom long ago begot:
"Follow woman must, not lead;
If she thinks, she follows not."

Wisdom speaks—I credit naught:
Rather hops and stings like flea:
"Woman seldom harbours thought;
If she thinks, no good is she!"

To this wisdom, old, renowned,
Bow I in deep reverence:
Now my wisdom I'll expound
[Pg 160]In its very quintessence.

A voice spoke in me yesterday
As ever—listen if you can:
"Woman is more beauteous aye,
But more interesting—man!"

"PIA, CARITATEVOLE, AMOROSISSIMA"[7]

Cave where the dead ones rest,
O marble falsehood, thee
I love: for easy jest
My soul thou settest free.

To-day, to-day alone,
My soul to tears is stirred,
At thee, the pictured stone,
At thee, the graven word.

This picture (none need wis)
I kissed the other day.
When there's so much to kiss
Why did I kiss the—clay?

Who knows the reason why?
"A tombstone fool!" you laugh:
I kissed—I'll not deny—
E'en the long epitaph.

TO FRIENDSHIP

Hail to thee, Friendship!
My hope consummate,
My first red daybreak!
[Pg 161]Alas, so endless
Oft path and night seemed,
And life's long road
Aimless and hateful!
Now life I'd double
In thine eyes seeing
Dawn-glory, triumph,
Most gracious goddess!

PINE TREE AND LIGHTNING

O'er man and beast I grew so high,
And speak—but none will give reply.

Too lone and tall my crest did soar:
I wait: what am I waiting for?

The clouds are grown too nigh of late,
'Tis the first lightning I await.

TREE IN AUTUMN

Why did ye, blockheads, me awaken
While I in blissful blindness stood?
Ne'er I by fear more fell was shaken—
Vanished my golden dreaming mood.

Bear-elephants, with trunks all greedy,
Knock first! Where have your manners fled?
I threw—and fear has made me speedy—
Dishes of ripe fruit—at your head.

AMONG FOES (OR AGAINST CRITICS)

(After a Gipsy Proverb)

Here the gallows, there the cord,
And the hangman's ruddy beard.
Round, the venom-glancing horde:—
Nothing new to me's appeared.
Many times I've seen the sight,
Now laughing in your face I cry,
"Hanging me is useless quite:
Die? Nay, nay, I cannot die!"

Beggars all! Ye envy me
Winning what ye never won!
True, I suffer agony,
But for you—your life is done.
Many times I've faced death's plight,
Yet steam and light and breath am I.
Hanging me is useless quite:
Die? Nay, nay, I cannot die!

THE NEW COLUMBUS[8]

"Dearest," said Columbus, "never
Trust a Genoese again.
At the blue he gazes ever,
Distance doth his soul enchain.

Strangeness is to me too dear—
Genoa has sunk and passed—
Heart, be cool! Hand, firmly steer!
[Pg 163]Sea before me: land—at last?

Firmly let us plant our feet,
Ne'er can we give up this game—
From the distance what doth greet?
One death, one happiness, one fame.

IN LONESOMENESS[9]

The cawing crows
Townwards on whirring pinions roam;
Soon come the snows—
Thrice happy now who hath a home!

Fast-rooted there,
Thou gazest backwards—oh, how long!
Thou fool, why dare

Ere winter come, this world of wrong?

This world—a gate
To myriad deserts dumb and hoar!
Who lost through fate
What thou hast lost, shall rest no more.

Now stand'st thou pale,
A frozen pilgrimage thy doom,
Like smoke whose trail
Cold and still colder skies consume.

Fly, bird, and screech,
Like desert-fowl, thy song apart!
Hide out of reach,
Fool! in grim ice thy bleeding heart.

Firmly let us plant our feet,
Ne'er can we give up this game—
From the distance what doth greet?
One death, one happiness, one fame.

The cawing crows
Townwards on whirring pinions roam:
Soon come the snows—
Woe unto him who hath no home!

My Answer

The man presumes—
Good Lord!—to think that I'd return
To those warm rooms
Where snug the German ovens burn

My friend, you see
'Tis but thy folly drives me far,—
Pity for thee
And all that German blockheads are!

FRIEDRICH NIETZSCHE

VENICE

ON the bridge I stood,
Mellow was the night,
Music came from far—
Drops of gold outpoured
On the shimmering waves.
Song, gondolas, light,
Floated a-twinkling out into the dusk.

The chords of my soul, moved
By unseen impulse, throbbed
Secretly into a gondola song,
With thrills of bright-hued ecstasy.
Had I a listener there?[Pg 165]

[1] Translated by Herman Scheffauer.

[2] Translated by Herman Scheffauer.

[3] This poem was written on the betrothal of one of Nietzsche's Bâle friends.—TR.

[4] Translated by Herman Scheffauer.

[5] Campo Santo di Staglieno is the cemetery of Staglieno, near Genoa. The poem was inspired by the sight of a girl with a lamb on the tombstone, with the words underneath— "Pia, caritatevole, amorosissima."

[6] Published by Nietzsche himself. The poem was inspired by a ship that was christened Angiolina, in memory of a love-sick girl who leapt into the sea.—TR.

[7] See above, p. 157. Both poems were inspired by the same tombstone.—TR.

[8] The Genoese is Nietzsche himself, who lived a great part of his life at Genoa.—TR.

EPIGRAMS
CAUTION: POISON![1]

He who cannot laugh at this had better not start reading;

For if he read and do not laugh, physic he'll be needing!

HOW TO FIND ONE'S COMPANY

With jesters it is good to jest:
Who likes to tickle, is tickled best.

THE WORD

I dearly love the living word,
That flies to you like a merry bird,
Ready with pleasant nod to greet,
E'en in misfortune welcome, sweet,
Yet it has blood, can pant you deep:
Then to the dove's ear it will creep:
And curl itself, or start for flight—
Whate'er it does, it brings delight.

Yet tender doth the word remain,
[Pg 166]Soon it is ill, soon well again:
So if its little life you'd spare,
O grasp it lightly and with care,
Nor heavy hand upon it lay,
For e'en a cruel glance would slay!
There it would lie, unsouled, poor thing!
All stark, all formless, and all cold,
Its little body changed and battered,
By death and dying rudely shattered.

A dead word is a hateful thing,
A barren, rattling, ting-ting-ting.
A curse on ugly trades I cry
That doom all little words to die!

THE WANDERER AND HIS SHADOW
A Book

You'll ne'er go on nor yet go back?
Is e'en for chamois here no track?

So here I wait and firmly clasp
What eye and hand will let me grasp!

Five-foot-broad ledge, red morning's breath,
And under me—world, man, and death!

JOYFUL WISDOM

This is no book—for such, who looks?
Coffins and shrouds, naught else, are books!
What's dead and gone they make their prey,
[Pg 167]Yet in my book lives fresh To-day.

This is no book—for such, who looks?
Who cares for coffins, shrouds, and spooks?
This is a promise, an act of will,
A last bridge-breaking, for good or ill;
A wind from sea, an anchor light,
A whirr of wheels, a steering right.
The cannon roars, white smokes its flame,
The sea—the monster—laughs and scents its game.

DEDICATION[2]

He who has much to tell, keeps much
Silent and unavowed.
He who with lightning-flash would touch
Must long remain a cloud!

THE NEW TESTAMENT[3]

Is this your Book of Sacred Lore,
For blessing, cursing, and such uses?—
Come, come now: at the very door
God some one else's wife seduces?

THE "TRUE GERMAN"

"O Peuple des meillures Tartuffes,
To you I'm true, I wis."
He spoke, but in the swiftest skiff
[Pg 168]Went to Cosmopolis.

TO THE DARWINIANS[4]

A fool this honest Britisher
Was not ... But a Philosopher!
As that you really rate him?
Set Darwin up by Goethe's side?
But majesty you thus deride—
Genii majestatem!

To HAFIZ

(Toast Question of a Water-Drinker)

What you have builded, yonder inn,

O'ertops all houses high:
The posset you have brewed therein
The world will ne'er drink dry.
The bird that once appeared on earth
As phœnix, is your, guest.
The mouse that gave a mountain birth
Is you yourself confessed!
You're all and naught, you're inn and wine,
You're phœnix, mountain, mouse.
Back to yourself to come you pine
Or fly from out your house.
Downward from every height you've sunk,
And in the depths still shine:
The drunkenness of all the drunk,
Why do you ask for—wine?

TO SPINOZA

Of "All in One" a fervent devotee
Amore Dei, of reasoned piety,
Doff shoes! A land thrice holy this must be!—
Yet underneath this love there sate
A torch of vengeance, burning secretly
The Hebrew God was gnawed by Hebrew hate.
Hermit! Do I aright interpret thee?

ARTHUR SCHOPENHAUER

That which he taught, has had its day,
That which he lived, shall live for aye:
Look at the man! No bondsman he!
Nor e'er to mortal bowed his knee!

TO RICHARD WAGNER

O You who chafe at every fetter's link,
A restless spirit, never free:
Who, though victorious aye, in bonds still cowered,
Disgusted more and more, and flayed and scoured,
Till from each cup of balm you poison drink,
Alas! and by the Cross all helpless sink,
You too, you too, among the overpowered!

For long I watched this play so weirdly shaped,
Breathing an air of prison, vault, and dread,
With churchly fragrance, clouds of incense spread,
And yet I found all strange/in terror gaped.
But now I throw my fool's cap o'er my head,
[Pg 170]For I escaped!

MUSIC OF THE SOUTH[5]

All that my eagle e'er saw clear,
I see and feel in heart to-day
(Although my hope was wan and gray)
Thy song like arrow pierced mine ear,
A balm to touch, a balm to hear,
As down from heaven it winged its way.

So now for lands of southern fire
To happy isles where Grecian nymphs hold sport!
Thither now turn the ship's desire—
No ship e'er sped to fairer port.

A RIDDLE

A riddle here—can you the answer scent?
"When man discovers, woman must invent."——

[1010] FRIEDRICH NIETZSCHE

TO FALSE FRIENDS

You stole, your eye's not clear to-day.
You only stole a thought, sir? nay,
Why be so rudely modest, pray?
Here, take another handful—stay,
Take all I have, you swine—you may
Eat till your filth is purged away.

FRIEND YORICK

Be of good cheer,
Friend Yorick! If this thought gives pain,
[Pg 171]As now it does, I fear,
Is it not "God"? And though in error lain,
'Tis but your own dear child,
Your flesh and blood,
That tortures you and gives you pain,
Your little rogue and do-no-good,
See if the rod will change its mood!

In brief, friend Yorick, leave that drear
Philosophy—and let me now
Whisper one word as medicine,
My own prescription, in your ear,
My remedy against such spleen—
"Who loves his God, chastises him, I ween,"

RESOLUTION

I should be wise to suit my mood,
Not at the beck of other men:
God made as stupid as he could
The world—well, let me praise him then.

And if I make not straight my track,
But, far as may be, wind and bend,

That's how the sage begins his tack,
And that is how the fool will—end.

The world stands never still,
Night loves the glowing day—
Sweet sounds to ear "I will!"
[Pg 172]And sweeter still "I may!"

THE HALCYONIAN[6]

Addressing me most bashfully,
A woman to-day said this:
"What would you be like in ecstasy,
If sober you feel such bliss?"

FINALE[6]

Laughter is a serious art.
I would do it better daily.
Did I well to-day or no?
Came the spark right from the heart?
Little use though head wag gaily,
If the heart contain no glow.

[1]Translated by Francis Bickley.

[2]On the title-page of a copy of Joyful Wisdom, dedicated to Herr August Bungal.—TR.

[3]Translated by Francis Bickley.

[4]Translated by Francis Bickley.

[5]Probably written for Peter Gast, Nietzsche's faithful friend, and a musician whose "Southern" music Nietzsche admired.—TR.

[6]Translated by Francis Bickley.

[Pg 173]
DIONYSUS-DITHYRAMBS
(1888)
These are the songs of Zarathustra which he sang to himself so as to endure his last solitude.

OF THE POVERTY OF THE RICHEST

Ten years passed by—
Not a drop reached me,
No rain-fraught wind, no dew of love
—A rainless land....
Now entreat I my wisdom
Not to become stingy in this drought;
Overflow thyself, trickle thy dew,
Be thyself the rain of the parched wilderness!

I once bade the clouds
Depart from my mountains;
Once I said to them,
"More light, ye dark ones!"
To-day I entice them to come:
Make me dark with your udders:
—I would milk you,
Ye cows of the heights!
Milk-warm wisdom, sweet dew of love
I pour over the land.

Away, away, ye truths
That look so gloomy!
I will not have on my mountains
[Pg 176]Bitter, impatient truths.
May truth approach me to-day
Gilded by smiles,
Sweetened by the sun, browned by love,—
A ripe truth I would fain break off from the tree.

To-day I stretch my hands
Toward the tresses of chance,
Wise enough to lead,
To outwit chance like a child.
To-day I will be hospitable
'Gainst the unwelcome,
'Gainst destiny itself I will not be prickly....
—Zarathustra is no hedgehog.

My soul,
Insatiable with its tongue,
Has already tasted of all things good and evil,
And has dived into all depths.
But ever, like the cork,
It swims to the surface again,
And floats like oil upon brown seas:
Because of this soul men call me fortunate.

Who are my father and mother?
Is not my father Prince Plenty?
And my mother Silent Laughter?
Did not the union of these two
Beget me, the enigmatic beast—
Me, the monster of light—
Me, Zarathustra, the squanderer of all wisdom?

Sick to-day from tenderness,
[Pg 177]A dewy wind,
Zarathustra sits waiting, waiting on his mountains—
Sweet and stewing
In his own juice,
Beneath his own summit,
Beneath his ice,
Weary and happy,
A Creator on his seventh day.

—Silence!

A truth passes over me
Like a cloud,—
With invisible lightnings it strikes me,
On broad, slow stairs,
Its happiness climbs to me:
Come, come, beloved truth!

—Silence!
'Tis my truth!
From timid eyes,
From velvet shudders,
Her glance meets mine,
Sweet and wicked, a maiden's glance.
She has guessed the reason of my happiness,
She has guessed me—ha! what is she thinking?
A purple dragon
Lurks in the abyss of her maiden's glance.

—Silence! My truth is speaking!—

"Woe to thee, Zarathustra!
Thou lookest like one
That hath swallowed gold:
[Pg 178]They will slit up thy belly yet!

Thou art too rich,
Thou corrupter of many!
Thou makest too many jealous,
Too many poor....
Even on me thy light casts a shadow—
I feel chill: go away, thou rich one
Go away, Zarathustra, from the path of thy sun

BETWEEN BIRDS OF PREY

Who would here descend,
How soon
Is he swallowed up by the depths!

But thou, Zarathustra,
Still lovest the abysses,
Lovest them as doth the fir tree!

The fir flings its roots
Where the rock itself gazes
Shuddering at the depths,—
The fir pauses before the abysses
Where all around
Would fain descend:
Amid the impatience
Of wild, rolling, leaping torrents
It waits so patient, stern and silent,
Lonely....

Lonely!
Who would venture
Here to be guest—
[Pg 179]To be thy guest?

A bird of prey, perchance
Joyous at others' misfortune,
Will cling persistent
To the hair of the steadfast watcher,
With frenzied laughter,
A vulture's laughter....

Wherefore so steadfast?
—Mocks he so cruel:
He must have wings, who loves the abyss,
He must not stay on the cliff,
As thou who hangest there!—

O Zarathustra,
Cruellest Nimrod!
Of late still a hunter of God,
A spider's web to capture virtue,
An arrow of evil!

Now
Hunted by thyself,
Thine own prey
Caught in the grip of thine own soul.

Now
Lonely to me and thee,
Twofold in thine own knowledge,
Mid a hundred mirrors
False to thyself,
Mid a hundred memories
Uncertain,
Weary at every wound,
Shivering at every frost,
Throttled in thine own noose,
Self-knower!
Self-hangman!

Why didst bind thyself
With the noose of thy wisdom?
Why luredst thyself
Into the old serpent's paradise?
Why stolest into
Thyself, thyself?...

A sick man now,
Sick of serpent's poison,
A captive now
Who hast drawn the hardest lot:
In thine own shaft
Bowed as thou workest,
In thine own cavern
Digging at thyself,
Helpless quite,
Stiff,
A cold corse
Overwhelmed with a hundred burdens,
Overburdened by thyself,

A knower!
A self-knower!
The wise Zarathustra!...

Thou soughtest the heaviest burden,
So foundest thou thyself,
And canst not shake thyself off....

Watching,
Chewing,
One that stands upright no more!
Thou wilt grow deformed even in thy grave,
[Pg 181]Deformed spirit!

And of late still so proud
On all the stilts of thy pride!
Of late still the godless hermit,
The hermit with one comrade—the devil,
The scarlet prince of every devilment!...

Now—
Between two nothings
Huddled up,
A question-mark,
A weary riddle,
A riddle for vultures....
They will "solve" thee,
They hunger already for thy "solution,"
They flutter already about their "riddle,"
About thee, the doomed one!
O Zarathustra,
Self-knower!
[Pg 182]Self-hangman!

THE SUN SINKS

I

Not much longer thirstest thou,
O burnt-up heart!
Promise is in the air,
From unknown mouths I feel a breath,
—The great coolness comes....
My sun stood hot above me at noonday:
A greeting to you that are coming,
Ye sudden winds,
Ye cool spirits of afternoon!

The air is strange and pure.
See how the night
Leers at me with eyes askance,
Like a seducer!...
Be strong, my brave heart,
And ask not "Why?"

2

The day of my life!
The sun sinks,
And the calm flood
Already is gilded.
Warm breathes the rock:
Did happiness at noonday
Take its siesta well upon it?
In green light
[Pg 183]Happiness still glimmers up from the brown abyss

Day of my life!
Eventide's nigh,
Thy eye already
Glows half-broken,

Thy dew already
Pours out its tear-drops,
Already over the white seas
Walks the purple of thy love,
Thy last hesitating holiness....

3

Golden gaiety, come!
Thou, the sweetest foretaste—
Foretaste of death!
—Went I my way too swiftly?
Now that the foot grows weary,
Thine eye still catches me,
Thy happiness still catches me.

Around but waves and play.
Whatever was hard
—Sank into blue oblivion.
My boat now stands idle.
Storm and motion—how did it forget them!
Desire and Hope are drowned,
Sea and soul are becalmed.

Seventh Solitude!
Never felt!
Sweet certainty nearer,
Or warmer the sun's ray.
—Glows not the ice of my summit yet?
Silvery, light, a fish
Now my vessel swims out....

THE LAST DESIRE[1]

So would I die
As then I saw him die,
The friend, who like a god
Into my darkling youth
Threw lightning's light and fire:

Buoyant yet deep was he,
Yea, in the battle's strife
With the gay dancer's heart.

Amid the warriors
His was the lightest heart,
Amid the conquerors
His brow was dark with thought—
He was a fate poised on his destiny:
Unbending, casting thought into the past
And future, such was he.

Fearful beneath the weight of victory,
Yet chanting, as both victory and death
Came hand and hand to him.

Commanding even as he lay in death,
And his command that man annihilate.

So would I die
As then I saw him die,
[Pg 185]Victorious and destroying.

THE BEACON

Here, where the island grew amid the seas,
A sacrificial rock high-towering,
Here under darkling heavens,
Zarathustra lights his mountain-fires,
A beacon for ships that have strayed,
A beacon for them that have an answer!...

These flames with grey-white belly,
In cold distances sparkle their desire,
Stretches its neck towards ever purer heights—
A snake upreared in impatience:
This signal I set up there before me.
This flame is mine own soul,

Insatiable for new distances,
Speeding upward, upward its silent heat.

Why flew Zarathustra from beasts and men?
Why fled he swift from all continents?
Six solitudes he knows already—
But even the sea was not lonely enough for him,
On the island he could climb, on the mount he became flame,
At the seventh solitude
He casts a fishing-rod far o'er his head.

Storm-tossed seamen! Wreckage of ancient stars
Ye seas of the future! Uncompassed heavens!
At all lonely ones I now throw my fishing-rod.
Give answer to the flame's impatience,
Let me, the fisher on high mountains,
Catch my seventh, last solitude!——

FAME AND ETERNITY[2]

I

Speak, tell me, how long wilt thou brood
Upon this adverse fate of thine?
Beware, lest from thy doleful mood
A countenance 90 dark is brewed
That men in seeing thee divine
A hate more bitter than the brine.

* * * *

Speak, why does Zarathustra roam
Upon the towering mountain-height?
Distrustful, cankered, dour, his home
Is shut so long from human sight?

* * * *

See, suddenly flames forth a lightning-flash,
The pit profound with thunderous challenge fights
Against the heavens, midst clamorous crack and crash
Of the great mountain! Cradled in the heights,

Born as the fruit of hate and lightning's love,
The wrath of Zarathustra dwells above
And looms with menace of a thundercloud.
* * * *

Ye, who have roofs, go quickly, creep and hide!
To bed, ye tenderlings! For thunders loud
Upon the blasts of storm triumphant ride,
[Pg 187]And bastions and ramparts sway and rock,

The lightning sears the dusky face of night,
And eerie truths like gleams of Hades mock
The sense familiar. So in storm breaks forth
The flaming curse of Zarathustra's wrath.

2

This fame, which all the wide world loves,
I touch with gloves,
And scorning beat
Beneath my feet.
* * * *

Who hanker after the pay of it?
Who cast themselves in the way of it?
These prostitutes to gold,
These merchant folk. They fold
Their unctuous palms over the jingling fame,
Whose ringing chink wins all the world's acclaim.
* * * *

Hast thou the lust to buy? It needs no skill.
They are all venal. Let thy purse be deep,
And let their greedy paws unhindered creep
Into its depths. So let them take their fill,
For if thou dost not offer them enough,
Their "virtue" they'll parade, to hide their huff.
* * * *

They are all virtuous, yea every one.
Virtue and fame are ever in accord
[Pg 188]So long as time doth run,

The tongues that prate of virtue as reward
Earn fame. For virtue is fame's clever bawd.
* * * *

Amongst these virtuous, I prefer to be
One guilty of all vile and horrid sin!
And when I see fame's importunity
So advertise her shameless harlotry,
Ambition turns to gall. Amidst such kin
One place alone, the lowest, would I win.
* * * *

This fame, which all the wide world loves,
I touch with gloves,
And scorning beat
Beneath my feet.

3

Hush! I see vastness!—and of vasty things
Shall man be dumb, unless he can enshrine
Them with his words? Then take the might which brings
The heart upon thy tongue, charmed wisdom mine!
* * * *

I look above, there rolls the star-strown sea.
O night, mute silence, voiceless cry of stars!
And lo! A sign! The heaven its verge unbars—
[Pg 189]A shining constellation falls towards me.

4

O loftiest, star-clustered crown of Being!
O carved tablets of Eternity!
And dost thou truly bend thy way to me?
Thy loveliness, to all—obscurity,
What? Fear'st not to unveil before my seeing?
* * * *

O shield of Destiny!
O carven tablets of Eternity!
Yea, verily, thou knowest—what mankind doth hate,

What I alone do love: thou art inviolate
To strokes of change and time, of fates the fate!
'Tis only thou, O dire Necessity,
Canst kindle everlasting love in me!
* * * *

O loftiest crown of Life! O shield of Fate!
That no desire can reach to invocate,
That ne'er defiled or sullied is by Nay,
Eternal Yea of life, for e'er am I thy Yea:
For I love thee, Eternity!
[1]Translated by Dr. G. T. Wrench.

[2]Translated by Dr. G. T. Wrench.

FRAGMENTS OF DIONYSUS-DITHYRAMBS

SPEECHES, PARABLES, AND SIMILES

3

My home's in the highlands,
For the highlands I yearn not,
I raise not mine eyes aloft:
I am one that looks downward,
One that must bless,—All
blessers look downward.

11

Thus I began,
I unlearned all self-pity!

13

Not in shattering idols,
But in shattering the idol-worshipper in thee,
Consisted thy valour.

14

See, there stand
Those heavy cats of granite,
Those old, old Values.
Woe is me! How overthrow them?
* * * *

Scratching cats,
With paws that are fettered,
There they sit
[Pg 194]And their glance is poison.

17

A lightning-flash became my wisdom:
With sword of adamant it clove me every darkness!

19

A thought that still
Flows hot, like lava:
But all streams of lava
Build a fortress around them,
And every thought finally
Oppresses itself with laws.

20

Such is my will:
And since 'tis my will,
All goes as I wish—
That was my final wisdom:
I willed what I must,
And thus I forced every "must,"—
Since then has been for me no "must."

23

Deceit
Is war's whole art
The fox's skin
Is my secret shirt of mail

25

We of the new underworld
Grub for new treasures.
Godless it seemed to the ancients
To disturb the earth's bowels for treasures
And once more this godlessness revives,
Hear ye not earth's bowels thunder?

28

Looking for love and finding masks,
Finding accursed masks and having to break them!

29

Do I love you?
Yes, as the rider loves his steed,
That carryeth him to his goal.

30

His pity is cruel,
His loving hand-clasp bruises,
Give not a giant your hand!

31

Ye fear me?
Ye fear the taut-strung bow?
Ye fear a man might set his arrow to the bow?

33

I am naught but a word-maker.
What matter words?
What matter I?

34

Ah, my friends,
Whither has flown all that is called "good"?
Whither all good people?
Whither the innocence of all these falsehoods?
I call all good,
[Pg 196]Leaves and grass, happiness, blessing, and rain.

35

Not through his sins and greatest follies.
Through his perfection I suffered,
As I suffered most from men.[1]

36

"Man is evil."
So spake the wisest
For my consolement.

37

And only when I to myself am a burden
Do ye fall heavy upon me!

38

Too soon, already
I laugh again:
For a foe 'tis easy
To make me amends.

39

Gentle am I towards man and chance;

Gentle with all men, and even with grasses:
A spot of sunshine on winter curtains,
Moist with tenderness,
A thawing wind to snow-bound souls:
*   *   *   *
Proud-minded towards trifling
Gains, where I see the huckster's long finger,
'Tis aye my pleasure
To be bamboozled:
[Pg 197]Such is the bidding of my fastidious taste.

40

A strange breath breathes and spits at me,
Am I a mirror, that straightway is clouded?

41

Little people,
Confiding, open-hearted,
But low-built portals,
Where only the low of stature can enter.
*   *   *   *
How can I get through the city-gate
Who had forgotten to live among dwarfs?

42

My wisdom was like to the sun,
I longed to give them light,
But I only deceived them.
The sun of my wisdom
Blinded the eyes
Of these poor bats....

43

Blacker and eviller things didst thou see than ever

a seer did:
Through the revels of Hell no sage had ever journeyed.

44

Back! on my heels too closely ye follow!
Back! lest my wisdom should tread on you, crush you!

45

"He goes to hell who goes thy ways!"
So be it I to my hell
[Pg 198]I'll pave the way myself with well-made maxims.

46

Your God, you tell me,
Is a God of love?
The sting of conscience
A sting from God?
A sting of love?

48

They chew gravel,
They lie on their bellies
Before little round things,
They adore all that falleth not down—
These last servants of God
Believers (in reality)!

50

They made their God out of nothing,
What wonder if now he is naught?

51

Ye loftier men! There have once been
More thoughtful times, more reflective,
Than is our to-day and to-morrow.

52

Our time is like a sick woman—
Let her but shriek, rave, scold,
And break the tables and dishes!

54

Ye mount?
Is it true that ye mount,
Ye loftier men?

Are ye not, pray,
Like to a ball
Sped to the heights
By the lowest that's in you?
Do ye not flee from yourselves, O ye climbers?

55

All that you thought
You had to despise,
Where you only renounced!

56

All men repeat the refrain!
No, no, and thrice say No!
What's all this yap-yap talk of heaven?
We would not enter the kingdom of heaven,
The kingdom of earth shall be ours?

57

The will redeemeth,
He that has nothing to do
In a Nothing finds food for trouble.

58

You cannot endure it more,
Your tyrannous destiny,
Love it—you're given no choice!

59

These alone free us from woes
(Choose now I)
Sudden death
[Pg 200]Or long-drawn-out love.

60

Of death we are sure,
So why not be merry?

61

The worst of pleas
I have hidden from you—that life grew tedious!
Throw it away, that ye find it again to your taste!

62

Lonely days,
Ye must walk on valorous feet!

63

Loneliness

Plants naught, it ripens....
And even then you must have the sun for your friend.

64

Once more must ye plunge in the throng—In
the throng ye grow hard and smooth.
Solitude withers
And lastly destroys.—

65

When on the hermit comes the great fear;
When he runs and runs
And knows not whither;
When the storms roar behind
And the lightning bears witness against him,
And his cavern breeds spectres
And fills him with dread.

67

Throw thy pain in the depths,
Man, forget! Man, forget!
Divine is the art of forgetting!
Wouldst fly?
Wouldst feel at home in the heights?
Throw thy heaviest load in the sea!
Here is the sea, hurl thyself in the sea!
Divine is the art of forgetting!

69

Look forward, never look back!
We sink to the depths
If we peer ever into the depths.

70

Beware, beware
Of warning the reckless!
Thy warning will drive them
To leap into every abyss!

71

Why hurled he himself from the heights?
What led him astray?
His pity for all that is lowly led him astray,
And now he lies there, broken, useless, and cold.

72

Whither went he? Who knows?
We only know that he sank.
A star went out in the desolate void,
[Pg 202]And lone was the void.

73

What we have not
But need,
We must take.
And so a good conscience I took.

74

Who is there that could bestow right upon thee?
So take thy right!

75

O ye waves,
Wondrous waves, are ye wroth with me?

Do ye raise me your crests in wrath?
With my rudder I smite
Your folly full square.
This bark ye yourselves
To immortal life will carry along.

77

When no new voice was heard,
Ye made from old words
A law:
When life grows stark, there shoots up the law.

78

What none can refute
Ye say must be true?
Oh, ye innocents!

79

Art thou strong?
Strong as an ass? Strong as God?
Art thou proud?
So proud as to flaunt
[Pg 203]Unashamed thy conceit?

80

Beware,
And ne'er beat the drum
Of thy destiny I
Go out of the way
From all pom-pom of fame!
* * * *
Be not known too soon!
Be one that has hoarded renown!

81

Wilt thou grasp at the thorns?
Thy fingers must pay.
Grasp at a poniard.

85

Be a tablet of gold,
They will grave upon thee
In golden script.

86

Upright he stands
With more sense of "justice"
In his outermost toe
Than I have in all my head.
A virtue-monster
Mantled in white.

87

Already he mimics himself,
Already weary he grows,
Already he seeks the paths he has trod—
[Pg 204]Who of late still loved all tracks untrodden!

Secretly burnt—
Not for his faith,
Rather because he had lost the heart
To find new faith.

88

Too long he sat in the cage,
That runaway!

Too long he dreaded
A gaoler!

Timorous now he goeth his ways,
All things make him to stumble—
The shadow e'en of a stick makes him to stumble.

89

Ye chambers smoky and musty,
Ye cages and narrow hearts,
How could your spirit be free?

90

Narrow souls!
Huckster-souls!
When money leaps into the box
The soul leaps into it too![2]

92

Are ye women,
That ye wish to suffer
[Pg 205]From that which ye love?

99

They are cold, these men of learning!
Would that a lightning-flash might strike their food,
And their mouths could learn to eat fire!

101

Your false love
For the past,
A love for the graves of the dead,
Is a theft from life

That steals all the future.

* * * *

An antiquary
Is a craftsman of dead things,
Who lives among coffins and skeletons.

103

Only the poet who can lie
Wilfully, skilfully,
Can tell the truth.

104

Our chase after truth,
Is't a chase after happiness?

105

Truth
Is a woman, no better,
Cunning in her shame:
Of what she likes best
She will know naught,
And covers her face....
[Pg 206]To what doth she yield
But to violence?
Violence she needs.
Be hard, ye sages!
Ye must compel her,
That shamefaced Truth....
For her happiness
She needs constraint—She
is a woman, no better.

106

We thought evil of each other?

We were too distant,
But now in this tiny hut,
Pinned to one destiny,
How could we still be foes?
We must needs love those
Whom we cannot escape.

107

Love thy foe,
Let the robber rob thee:
The woman hears and—does it.

110

A proud eye
With silken curtains,
Seldom clear,
Honours him that may see it unveiled.

111

Sluggard eyes
That seldom love—
But when they love, the levin flashes
As from shafts of gold
[Pg 207]Where a dagger keeps guard at the treasure of love.

117

They are crabs, for whom I have no fellow-feeling.
Grasp them, they pinch you;
Leave them alone, and they walk backward.

119

Crooked go great rivers and men,
Crooked, but turned to their goal;

That is their highest courage,
They dreaded not crooked paths.

121

Wouldst catch them?
Then speak to them
As to stray sheep:
"Your path, your path
You have lost!"
They follow all
That flatter them so:
"What? had we a path?"
Each whispers the other:
"It really seems that we have a path."